HANDBOOK OF FINANCIAL MARKETS AND INSTITUTIONS

EDITORIAL CONSULTING BOARD

The editor received valuable advice on the contents of this volume from a distinguished group of editorial consultants including:

HANDBOOK OF FINANCIAL MARKETS AND INSTITUTIONS

Sixth Edition

Edited by

EDWARD I. ALTMAN

Professor of Finance
Chairman, MBA Program
Graduate School of Business Administration
New York University

Associate Editor

MARY JANE McKINNEY

WILEY PROFESSIONAL BANKING AND FINANCE SERIES

EDWARD I. ALTMAN, Editor

JOHN WILEY & SONS

New York • Chichester • Brisbane • Toronto • Singapore

This publication is designed to provide accurate and authoritative information in regard to the subject matter covered. It is sold with the understanding that the publisher is not engaged in rendering legal, accounting, or other professional service. If legal advice or other expert assistance is required, the services of a competent professional person should be sought. *From a Declaration of Principles jointly adopted by a Committee of the American Bar Association and a Committee of Publishers.*

Library of Congress Cataloging in Publication Data:

Handbook of financial markets and institutions.

(Wiley professional banking and finance series)
Rev. ed. of: Financial handbook. 5th ed. © 1981.
Bibliography: p.
Includes index.
1. Finance—Handbooks, manuals, etc. 2. Finance—United States—Handbooks, manuals, etc. 3. Corporations—Finance—Handbooks, manuals, etc. 4. International finance—Handbooks, manuals, etc. I. Altman, Edward I., 1941- . II. McKinney, Mary Jane. III. Title: Financial handbook. IV. Series.

HG173.H33 1986 658.1′5 86–11125
ISBN 0-471-81954-9

Printed in the United States of America

10 9 8 7 6 5 4 3 2 1

To my wife, Elaine, and son, Gregory

Whose love and understanding continue
to make a difference

PREFACE

The last revision of the *Financial Handbook* was published in 1981 as the fifth edition of that venerable and respected reference book. I was privileged then to be nominated by the Ronald Press of John Wiley & Sons to follow the earlier works of Dr. Jules I. Bogen, who edited the third and fourth editions (the original edition was vintage 1925). The fifth edition came out fourteen years after its most immediate predecessor and although we all agreed that the field of finance had evolved enormously in that time span, it still was a relatively long period between editions. Nobody, however, predicted that the finance and related areas would virtually explode, in the early and mid-1980s, in terms of innovation and sophistication, requiring a rapid assessment of the need to revise again. As early as 1984, just three years after its publication, those of us involved with the *Financial Handbook, Fifth Edition,* decided that it was time to map out the next revision. The result is this book and its companion volume, *The Handbook of Corporate Finance.*

When we were planning for the sixth edition of *The Financial Handbook,* it became apparent that a number of new sections were needed, especially related to financial markets and institutions. The fifth edition was already quite "heavy" with over 1,400 book pages. Since we also wanted to make the typeface larger in size to facilitate readability, we knew very quickly that a single volume could not encompass our four major designated areas related to finance—domestic financial markets and institutions, international markets and institutions, investment theory and practice, and corporate finance. We decided to concentrate on markets, institutions, and investments for the sixth edition and change its title to that of the book that you are reading. The result is that both *The Handbook of Financial Markets and Institutions* and *The Handbook of Corporate Finance* are hefty compendiums since our primary objective is to be broadly eclectic in our coverage as well as comprehensive within a specific area.

We have assembled a group of distinguished and respected experts in the fields chosen for discussion. These experts represent business executives, financial economists from the academic and business worlds, government authorities—some of whom have now moved from the public to the private sector, and financial consultants. They have synthesized the latest literature and developments in their fields in order to present fairly concise yet comprehensive studies of current principles and practice. My suggestions were as before: Write about what you know best and present the material in a modern financial analytic structure. Since our audience, for the most part, consists of practitioners of the art of finance, or those who aspire to that status in the future, a premium is put on communication of essential concepts and a summary of practices.

In the fifth edition's Preface, I stated that one of my objectives was "that the bulk of material presented not soon be out of date." Although it is true that the field of financial markets and institutions have developed and intensified in just a few short years, at the same time much of what was written before is still relevant. Indeed, 15 of 23 authors who wrote sections in the fifth edition return again to discuss their field in this volume and 14 of 15 in the corporation finance volume have been retained. What is also true, however, is that a great deal more is also worthy of its share of discussion.

We have added new sections on investment banking, microcomputer and investments, the bond rating process, option and insurance strategies for fixed income portfolios, high yield bonds, asset pricing models, and small business financing. Certain topics such as real estate financing, especially mortgage back securities, options and futures markets, commercial banking, and debt and equity markets have required substantial updating. Finally, expanded appendices on the mathematics of finance and sources of investment information are supplied.

Once again I have been assisted by several extraordinarily talented persons. My primary debt of gratitude goes to my associate editor, Mary Jane McKinney. Mary Jane and I might be considered veterans by now but we really did learn a great deal more about editing, especially in our efforts to put together two volumes at the same time. We were aided by a distinguished group of Editorial Consulting Board members from business and academia. The credit for the exceptional quality of the book, in the final analysis, must rest with the contributing authors and we are fortunate to have such a distinguished group accept the challenge. Not everyone realizes the difficulty of summarizing a field into a concise manuscript that is both comprehensive and easily read and understood in a relatively short time. Our authors have succeeded in this challenge.

My staff at New York University worked very hard and diligently in assisting in the massive logistical editing process. I would like to thank Diana Coryat, Nayan Kisnadwala, Brenda Lane, Susan Meah, Teresa Santamaria, Karen Sosnick, and Eva Wan for their tremendous contributions. Several talented individuals at John Wiley & Sons were involved in various stages of the projects and were very helpful. Reflecting back on the process, I feel *The Handbook of Financial Markets and Institutions* is indeed a team effort.

Finally, I owe a great deal to my wife, Elaine, and son, Gregory, for their encouragement and support.

EDWARD I. ALTMAN

New York, New York
October 1986

CONTENTS

CONTRIBUTORS

EDWARD I. ALTMAN is professor of finance and chairman of the MBA program at NYU. He has been visiting professor at the Hautes Etudes Commerciales and Université de Paris-Dauphine in France, at the Pontifica Catolica Universidade in Rio de Janeiro, Brazil, and the Australian Graduate School of Management. Altman has an international reputation as an expert on corporate bankruptcy and credit analysis. He was named *Laureate 1984* by the Hautes Etudes Commerciales Foundation from Paris for his accumulated works on bankruptcy prediction models and procedures for financial rehabilitation. Altman is editor of the international publication, the *Journal of Banking and Finance* and two publisher series, *Wiley Professional Banking and Finance Series* (Wiley) and *Contemporary Studies in Economics and Finance* (JAI Press). Altman has published several books and over 60 articles in scholarly finance, accounting, and economics journals. He is the current editor of the *Financial Handbook* and the author of two recently published books, *Corporate Financial Distress* and *Recent Trends in Corporate Finance.* His work has appeared in several languages including Portuguese, Japanese, German, and French. Altman's primary areas of research include bankruptcy analysis and prediction, credit and lending policies, corporate finance, and capital markets. He has been a consultant to several government agencies, major financial and accounting institutions, and industrial companies, has lectured to executives in North America, South America, Europe, and Asia, has testified before the U.S. Congress on several occasions, and is on the Scientific and Technical Committee of Italy's Centrale dei Bilanci.

STEVEN J. APPEL is managing director, Small Business/General Practice of the international accounting firm Arthur Andersen & Co. He has spent his entire 21-year career providing accounting, audit, financial, and tax consulting services to owner-managed, emerging small businesses. Under Appel's direction, Arthur Andersen has developed various programs dealing with small business personal and business taxes, cash planning, management reporting requirements, and other issues related to growth, diversification, and profitability. Previously, Appel managed the Small Business Practice of Arthur Andersen's Milwaukee office. He has also served on the firm's Chairman's Advisory Council, Audit Advisory Council, Marketing Implementation Group, Financial Consulting Services Steering Committee, and Audit Research and Development Advisory Committee. Appel is a founding Board member of the Independent Business Association of Wisconsin and participated in the 1980 White House Conference on Small Business. Appel is a member of the AICPA and has a BBA degree from the University of Wisconsin.

JOSEPH BENCH is vice president of Greenwich Capital Markets Inc. He has also served as vice president and economist of First Pennsylvania Corp., where he analyzed money market events and prospects; his other work experience includes director of financial analysis at Lionel D. Edie, an investment advisory subsidiary of Merrill Lynch, and economist at Chase Manhattan Bank. Bench has served as an adjunct professor of finance at numerous institutions, including Seton Hall University and Fairleigh Dickinson University. He received BA, MA, and PhD degrees in economics from Case Western Reserve University, Cleveland.

JAMES L. BURTLE is professor of economics at Iona College, New Rochelle, New York. Before joining Iona in 1982, he was managing editor of the *International Country Risk Guide.* Between 1958 and 1980, he was vice president in the economics department of W. R. Grace and Company responsible for advising on foreign exchange policy and forecasting foreign exchange rates. He was also a member of the economics staff of the International Labour Office. He has served as president of the Metropolitan Economic Association (1968–1969) and with the late Sidney Rolfe is coauthor of *The Great Wheel* (1973), a book on the international monetary system. He received BA and MA degrees from the University of Chicago.

JAMES W. CHRISTIAN is senior vice president and chief economist of the U.S. League of Savings Institutions, Chicago, a trade association representing more than 3,500 savings institutions nationwide. Christian's experience spans 20 years as an economist in international as well as domestic fields and includes serving as senior vice president and chief economist for the National Savings and Loan League, director of the International Division of the Federal Home Loan Bank Board, and professor of economics at Iowa State University. He is an internationally recognized expert on the establishment of housing finance systems in developing countries and has advised central banks and ministries of finance in a number of countries. Christian is the author of numerous journal articles and monographs and frequently addresses national professional organizations on general economic trends, housing finance, and related topics. He received his BA, MA and PhD in economics from the University of Texas, Austin.

LOUIS H. EDERINGTON is senior research scholar at the School of Business and Public Administration, Washington University, St. Louis, Missouri and associate director of the Institute of Banking and Financial Markets at Washington University. His research on bond and futures markets has been published in the *Journal of Finance, Journal of Business, Journal of Financial Economics,* and other journals. He is currently an associate editor for the *Journal of Financial and Quantitative Analysis* and the *Journal of Financial Research.* Ederington received a BA degree from Hendrix College, Conway, Arkansas and MA and PhD degrees from Washington University.

EDWIN J. ELTON is professor of finance at the Graduate School of Business, New York University. He is the author or coauthor of five books and over 45 articles. These articles have appeared in such journals as *The Journal of Finance, Review of Economics and Statistics, Management Science, Journal of Financial Economics, Journal of Business,* and *Journal of Financial and Quantitative Analysis.* He is coeditor of the *Journal of Finance.* He has been a member of the board of directors of the American Finance Association and associate editor of *Management Science.* Elton has served as a consultant for many major financial institutions.

JAMES L. FARRELL, JR. is chairman of MPT Associates, a New York-based investment counseling firm. He is also chairman of the Institute for Quantitative Research in Finance, New York, and is a member of the finance faculty at the Graduate School of Business Administration, New York University. He has over 15 years of experience in security analysis, portfolio management, and quantitative research at CNA Financial, College Retirement Equities, and at Citibank, where he was most recently a vice president of applied financial research. He has published several articles in professional investment journals and is author of *Guide to Portfolio Management* (McGraw-Hill, 1983). Farrell has a BS degree from the University of Notre Dame, an MBA degree from the Wharton School of Finance, and a PhD degree from New York University.

KATHERINE M. FINN has been a portfolio manager in the Options Portfolio Service at Kidder, Peabody & Co. since 1978. She is a chartered financial analyst. Finn received a BA from Ohio Northern University.

RONALD W. FORBES is associate professor of finance in the School of Business at the State University of New York, Albany. He is also the director of the Municipal Finance Study Group at SUNY-Albany, which conducts research on public finance for state and local governments and the investment banking industry. Forbes is also an independent trustee of several Merrill Lynch money funds—CMA, CBA, and CMA Tax-Exempt Fund. He serves as an independent director of other Merrill Lynch funds—Fund for Tomorrow, Municipal Bond Fund, and the Corporate Bond Fund. Forbes has published on the tax-exempt securities market and has served as an advisor or research consultant for the Council on State Priorities of the Governor of New York; the State of Alaska; the State of Oregon; the Public Securities Association; the First Boston

Corporation; and Lehman Brothers Kuhn Loeb. Forbes received his AB from Dartmouth College and earned his PhD in finance at the State University of New York, Buffalo.

GARY L. GASTINEAU is manager of the Options Portfolio Service at Kidder, Peabody & Co., New York, where he manages individual and institutional accounts using options and their underlying securities. He is the author of *The Stock Options Manual* (2nd ed., 1979). Gastineau spent several years in the long-term planning department of a major oil company, came to Wall Street as a security analyst in 1966, and has been a portfolio manager since 1969. He is a frequent speaker before business and professional groups on the subjects of option evaluation and the use of options in portfolio management. Gastineau received an AB degree in economics from Harvard College and an MBA from the Harvard Business School.

IAN H. GIDDY is an associate professor at New York University and has previously held teaching appointments at four other universities. He has served in the U.S. government at the Comptroller of the Currency and at the Board of Governors of the Federal Reserve System. Giddy has taught in numerous management development programs in the United States as well as abroad and has served as consultant to multinational corporations, banks, and the U.S. Congress. His research and teaching experience reflect his interest in international finance, financial markets, and financial management. He has participated in studies for the U.S. Treasury and is the author of many articles on international banking, Eurocurrency and foreign exchange markets, and corporate international finance. He is coauthor of both *The International Money Market* (Prentice-Hall, 1978) and the two-volume *International Finance Handbook* (Wiley, 1983).

MARTIN J. GRUBER is professor of finance at the Graduate School of Business, New York University. He has published seven books and over 40 journal articles in such journals as *The Journal of Finance, Review of Economics and Statistics, Journal of Financial Economics, Journal of Business, Management Science, Journal of Financial and Quantitative Analysis, Operations Research,* and *The Journal of Portfolio Management.* He is coeditor of the *Journal of Finance* and is presently a director of the American Finance Association. He has been a director of both the Computer Applications Committee and Investment Technology Symposium of the New York Society of Security Analysts. He was formerly department editor for finance of management science. Gruber has consulted in the areas of investment analysis and portfolio management with many major financial institutions.

JAMES P. HOLMES is senior vice president and a portfolio manager at Dreman & Embry Inc. His past experience in security analysis was at The Ford Foundation Equitable Life, ValueQuest, and Dean Witter. In addition he worked in corporate strategy at CBS Inc. He received his undergraduate degree at Marquette University and an MBA from Northwestern University.

C. DOUGLAS HOWARD works in the Bond Portfolio Analysis Group of Salomon Brothers. His current work relates to the efficient use of debt call options and sinking fund provisions, as well as other aspects of liability management. Howard received his BS in mathematics from the Massachusetts Institute of Technology and his MBA in finance from Columbia University.

ANDREW J. KALOTAY is a vice president in the Bond Portfolio Analysis Group of Salomon Brothers, where he is involved with a wide range of problems related to the management of fixed-income securities. He has particular expertise in financial and regulatory issues relating to the retirement of debt. Kalotay received his BS and MS in mathematics from Queen's University and his PhD in statistics from the University of Toronto. His numerous papers have been published in the *Journal of Finance, Financial Management,* and *Management Science,* among others.

W. MICHAEL KEENAN is associate professor of finance at the School of Business Administration, New York University. After teaching for three years at the University of California, Berkeley, he joined the faculty at NYU, where his primary teaching areas have been corporation finance and investments. Keenan's current research interests include the economic structure of the securities industry, expert systems models of equity valuation, and the growth of the service sector type of economy. His published work includes several papers on the evolving changes in the New York-based securities industry. Keenan is currently serving as the executive secretary and treasurer of the American Finance Association. He received his BS degree from Case Western Reserve University and his MS and PhD degrees from Carnegie-Mellon University.

WARREN LAW is the Edmund Coggswell Converse Professor of Banking and Finance at the Graduate School of Business Administration, Harvard University, where he has been a faculty member since 1958. Previously he taught at Southern Methodist University and was associate economist for the First National Bank of Dallas. At Harvard he has been chairman of the International Business Area and of the Program for Management Development. He received a BBA degree from Southern Methodist and MBA and PhD degrees from Harvard.

MARTIN L. LEIBOWITZ is a managing director of Salomon Brothers, where he is in charge of the Bond Portfolio Analysis Group. He joined the firm in 1969 and was admitted as a general partner in 1977. He is the coauthor of *Inside the Yield Book* (Prentice-Hall and New York Institute of Finance). His recent work includes a series of studies relating to the subject of bond immunization and several studies developing a new approach to the analysis of financial futures. In another work, he introduced the concept of a new structured approach to active bond portfolio management in a paper entitled "Contingent Immunization." Leibowitz and his group have been particularly active in the development and application of techniques for the construction of dedicated bond portfolios to support specified liability schedules.

RICHARD M. LEVICH is associate professor of finance and international business and chairman of the International Business Program at New York University. He is also a research associate with the National Bureau of Economic Research in Cambridge, Massachusetts. Levich has lectured in international economic issues at many institutions in the United States and overseas. His research on international financial markets has appeared in the *Journal of Political Economy,* the *Columbia Journal of World Business,* and other scholarly publications. He is the author and editor (as well as coeditor) of many texts on international financial management. Levich received his PhD from the University of Chicago.

NORMAN E. MAINS is director of research, Institutional Financial Futures division, and first vice president, Drexel Burnham Lambert. Prior to joining DBL, he was senior economist Government Finance Section, Division of Research and Statistics, Board of Governors of the Federal Reserve System. Mains also was an economist in the Capital Markets Section at the Board. He previously was the associate economist of the national trade association of mutual funds, the Investment Company Institute, in Washington, D.C. Mains is a member of the Index and Option Market division of the Chicago Mercantile Exchange and the Toronto Futures Exchange. He received a PhD in economics from the University of Warwick, Warwickshire, England. Prior to this Mains was awarded BA and MA degrees from the University of Colorado.

NEIL B. MURPHY is currently professor of finance and director, Center for Research and Development in Financial Services, University of Connecticut. He has completed assignments in the Federal bank regulatory agencies, the private sector, and the academic community. His academic assignments include service on the faculties of the Universities of Maine and Oklahoma and visiting professorships at Dartmouth and Tel Aviv University. He has published extensively in professional journals and the trade press. Murphy has been on the editorial boards of the *Journal of Finance,* the *Journal of Bank Research,* and the *Journal of Retail Banking.* He has a BS and MS from Bucknell University and a PhD in economics from the University of Illinois.

SCOTT A. NAMMACHER currently works for the Treasury Department at PepsiCo, in the mergers and acquisition area. Prior to joining PepsiCo, he was a research consultant for the investment banking firm of Morgan Stanley. During that time he and coauthor Edward Altman wrote and published three studies on the high yield bond marketplace. These studies will be published in book form by John Wiley & Sons in 1986. Their study on default rates also appeared in the *Financial Analyst's Journal.* Prior to receiving his MBA in finance from New York University, Nammacher was involved in the publishing industry where he cofounded the trade magazine *Recreation, Sports and Leisure.*

CHRISTOPHER NOWAKOWSKI is president and founder of InterSec Research Corp., a registered investment advisory group. Nowakowski has a broad international background in the investment business, both educationally and professionally. After completing undergraduate studies in Canada, he worked on the Paris Bourse and received a Master of Commerce in International Economics and Politics from the Hautes Etudes Commerciales. Nowakowski subsequently spent 12 years with Wood Gundy, Ltd., a leading Canadian investment bank. Since founding InterSec in 1975, he has become a recognized author and spokesperson on the rapid internationalization of the investment business which is taking place simultaneously in all the money management capitals around the world.

ROBERT B. PLATT is managing director, Fixed Income Research for Morgan Stanley. He is officer in charge of the Fixed Income Research Department, which includes analytical portfolio related research, credit research, and a systems group providing analytical support to bond trading and sales. He has a PhD in economics from New York University and has lectured in economics and finance for NYU's Graduate School of Business Administration. Platt has extensive experience covering a wide range of fixed income and related financial activities. This includes managing a fixed income portfolio department of a major institution, fixed income portfolio management, financial consulting, and economic forecasting. He and his group have published widely in the financial area. A book covering various aspects of their research activities, *Controlling Interest Rate Risk,* was published in 1986 by John Wiley & Sons.

RICHARD T. PRATT is chairman of Merrill Lynch Mortgage Capital, a new subsidiary incorporated within Merrill Lynch Capital Markets to meet the rapidly expanding demand for mortgage-related products and associated investment services. Pratt has overall responsibility for Merrill Lynch's activities in mortgage-backed securities' trading, relationships with Federal agencies, investment banking, and mortgage investment and home builders. Prior to joining Merrill Lynch, Pratt served as chairman of the Federal Home Loan Bank Board. Until he became chairman, he served as president of Richard T. Pratt Associates, a financial consulting firm. Pratt has also taught finance at the University of Utah. He holds an MBA and BA from the University of Utah and a PhD from Indiana University.

PHILIP RALLI is with Hentsch et Cie., private bankers in Geneva, which he joined as a trainee in 1975. His experience has been in accounting, fixed interest analysis, and six years as a generalist member of a team managing internationally diversified portfolios. He was on Secondment in summer 1985 in Chicago to study options and futures in preparation for the opening of a Swiss market, and with InterSec Research Corp. in Stamford, Connecticut to study issues in international performance measurement. He studied at Oxford University.

RONALD C. ROGERS is currently visiting scholar, Office of Policy and Economic Research, Federal Home Loan Bank Board. He is on leave from the Department of Finance, School of Business Administration, University of Connecticut. He has published in the major finance and real estate professional journals since receiving his PhD from Ohio State University. His predoctoral experience includes service as a leasing officer for Security Pacific Leasing Corp. and as a management consultant in finance for Ernst and Whinney.

ARNOLD W. SAMETZ is professor of finance and Sidney Homer and Charles Simon Director of the Salomon Brothers Center for the Study of Financial Institutions of the Graduate School of Business Administration, New York University. His professional and research interests include financial markets, financial innovation in a volatile financial environment, and regulation of financial markets and institutions. His most recent publications include *The Emerging Financial Industry* (1984) and "Strategic Responses to Turbulent Financial Markets," *Journal of Business Strategy* (Summer 1981). Earlier works include *Financial Management* (1967), *Financial Development and Economic Growth in Underdeveloped Capital Markets* (1972), *Prospects for Capital Formation and Capital Markets* (1978), and *Securities Activities of Commercial Banks* (1981). Sametz has served as an expert witness on rate of return in utility cases for both companies and state commissions, and in stock valuation cases including tenders, recapitalizations, and pension funds. He is an adviser to various securities exchanges in several countries, a director of the American Savings Bank, and is associate editor of the *Journal of Banking and Finance.* Sametz received an AB degree from the City University of New York and a PhD degree from Princeton University.

RICHARD L. SANDOR is manager, Institutional Financial Futures division, and senior vice president, Drexel Burnham Lambert. Prior to this he was director of ContiFinancial, a division of ContiCommodity. Previously vice president and chief economist of the Chicago Board of Trade, he is regarded widely as the "principal architect" of the interest rate futures market. He began his professional career as a faculty member of the School of Business Administration, University of California, Berkeley, and has been a visiting scholar and professor at Northwestern University. Sandor served on the Board of Directors of the Chicago Board of Trade and also chaired its Financial Instruments Committee and Options Committee. He is presently serving as an industry governor at the Chicago Mercantile Exchange. Sandor is a member of the Chicago Board of Trade, Chicago Mercantile Exchange, Toronto Futures Exchange, and the London International Financial Futures Exchange. He is a graduate of the City University of New York, Brooklyn College, and received his PhD in economics from the University of Minnesota.

JOHN A. SCOWCROFT is vice president and manager of the Mortgage-Backed Securities Research Department at Merrill Lynch Mortgage Capital where he has specific responsibilities for developing risk management strategies, computer analytics for mortgage assets, and asset/liability management models for financial institutions. Prior to joining Merrill Lynch in 1984, Scowcroft worked as a financial consultant to domestic and international corporations, banks, and government agencies. He holds an MBA from the University of Chicago and is a chartered financial analyst.

KEITH V. SMITH is professor of management, Krannert School of Management, Purdue University. He has taught courses in capital management and budgeting as well as accounting and other finance-related fields. Smith is the author of *Guide to Working Capital Management* (McGraw-Hill, 1979), *Portfolio Management* (Holt, Rinehart & Winston, 1971), and the editor of *Readings on the Management of Working Capital* (West Publishing, 2nd ed., 1974). He is the coauthor of *Essentials of Investing* (Irwin, 1974). He has also published many articles in journals dealing with diverse topics from performance evaluation to international diversification. As well as serving as a corporate director, Smith has been a consultant to several companies and financial institutions on problems of finance and investment. He is also a faculty associate of Management Analysis Center. He received a BS in engineering physics and an MBA from Ohio State University. He completed his PhD in finance at Purdue.

A. CHARLENE SULLIVAN is an associate professor of management, Krannert Graduate School of Management and associate director, Credit Research Center, Purdue University, where she is engaged in research in consumer credit, studying factors associated with consumer choice of adjustable- versus fixed-rate loans and time series models of loan delinquency. Sullivan has written numerous articles dealing with consumer bankruptcy and the effects of restrictive loan rate ceilings on consumer credit markets. Sullivan received MSM and PhD degrees in management from Purdue University.

MARTI G. SUBRAHMANYAM is a professor of finance and chairman of the finance area at the Graduate School of Business Administration, New York University. He has taught finance and economics at the Massachusetts Institute of Technology, Cambridge, the Indian Institute of Management, Ahmedabad, and at Ecole Superieur de Science Economics et Commerce (France). Subrahmanyam has published in several leading journals in finance and economics. His research interests are in the areas of capital market theory, corporation finance, and international finance. He is coauthor of *Capital Market Equilibrium and Corporate Financial Decisions* and *Financial Analysis of Corporate Assets.* He serves as an associate editor of *Management Science,* the *Journal of Banking and Finance,* and the *Journal of Finance.* Subrahmanyam received a BA from the Indian Institute of Technology, an MBA degree from the Indian Institute of Management, and a PhD in finance and economics from the Massachusetts Institute of Technology.

JORGE L. URRUTIA, assistant professor of finance at Loyola University of Chicago, has a bachelor's degree in chemical engineering from the University of Concepcion, Chile; a Master's degree in economics from the University of Chile; an MBA from the Institute of Higher Studies in Administration, IESA, Caracas, Venezuela; and a PhD from the University of Texas, Austin. He worked as an engineer for the State Railroads and the Copper Corporation, Santiago, Chile. He taught at IESA and the Institute of Technology, Caracas, Venezuela. He was assistant instructor at the University of Texas, Austin. His specialties include investments, corporate finance, and risk management and insurance economics. His work has been published in several scholarly journals, such as the *Journal of Risk and Insurance, The Geneva Papers,* and the *CPCU.*

J. PETER WILLIAMSON is professor of business administration at the Amos Tuck Graduate School of Business Administration, Dartmouth College. He was formerly on the faculties of the Harvard Business School and the University of Toronto Law School, and was a visiting professor at the Colgate Darden Business School, University of Virginia. Williamson is a consultant to a number of business and nonprofit organizations, provides expert testimony before public utility commissions, and is a trustee of the New Hampshire Savings Bank and of the Common Fund. He has written several books on legal and financial subjects and is the author of a variety of articles on law, taxation, finance, and investments. Williamson has written several articles on performance evaluation, most recently for *Journal of Portfolio Management.* He received MBA and DBA degrees from the Harvard Business School and LLB from Harvard Law School, Cambridge, Massachusetts.

ROBERT C. WITT is chairman of the finance department and the Joseph H. Blades Centennial Memorial Professor, at the University of Texas, Austin. He specializes in risk management and actuarial science. He has published numerous feature articles in the *Journal of Risk and Insurance, Journal of Insurance: Issues and Practices, CPCU Journal, Best's Review, Geneva Papers on Risk and Insurance,* and *Risk Management.* Witt received an MA and PhD in business and economics, and has also received an MS in actuarial science, BA in mathematics, and a BS in business administration. Witt has served as an advisor to the Texas Legislature, the Texas Medical Malpractice Study Commission, and the Texas Catastrophe Pool. He has acted as advisor to the Illinois Insurance Laws Study Commission, was elected to the board of directors of the American Risk and Insurance Association, and serves as educational advisor to the Insurance Information Institute.

JESS B. YAWITZ is currently managing director of fixed income research at Goldman Sachs. He was the John E. Simon Professor of Finance and director of the Institute of Banking and Financial Markets at Washington University

(St. Louis). His research interests include the management of financial institutions, money and capital markets, and financial valuation. He is coauthor of *Macroeconomics* (Prentice-Hall, 1984) and has been published in such journals as *Journal of Finance, The American Economic Review,* and *The Journal of Portfolio Management.*

HANDBOOK OF FINANCIAL MARKETS AND INSTITUTIONS

1

THE "NEW" FINANCIAL ENVIRONMENT OF THE UNITED STATES

CONTENTS

1

THE "NEW" FINANCIAL ENVIRONMENT OF THE UNITED STATES

Arnold W. Sametz

Recent developments in the money and capital markets have been extensive enough to warrant characterizing the changes in financial instruments and services as a revolution. The restructuring of financial institutions over the last two decades—the expanded use of the bank holding company device, the spread of the merger movement to finance, and the rapid growth of the giant financial conglomerate—has fundamentally altered the financial landscape. Moreover, since 1974 the objectives as well as the implementation techniques of the Federal Reserve Board's monetary controls have been significantly altered.

The revolution is evident in marketplace performance as well as structure. For example, both physical volume and price volatility in securities markets have increased radically. The markets have become more risky as well as more competitive and efficient. And that risk is mirrored, for example, in unprecedented levels of real interest rates. And to come full circle, to cope with that greater risk, additional new instruments have developed—namely, the great and increasing variety of financial futures contracts.

MAJOR SHIFTS IN THE FINANCIAL ENVIRONMENT

THE PRIMARY SHIFTS—1965–1980. Before cataloging this astonishing record of financial change and its implications for the financial industry, it is important to review the causes of this financial upheaval. For if this series of major changes is appropriately to be called a revolution, its basic causes must be considered as fundamentally irreversible even if further change proceeds at a more modest pace. And, of course, we want to be sure that this is not just a financial bubble or short-run turbulence that will run its course and be absorbed and forgotten.

It is hard to believe that the securities industry was primarily a simple corporate stock and bond business as recently as the 1960s and the early 1970s. The principal causes of the radical restructuring of financial industries were:

- The sharp rise in both the level of **inflation** and the volatility of the rate of price change.
- Parallel **volatility in the securities markets and interest rates.**
- A lagged but cumulative and cascading series of **deregulations** of financial markets and institutions, plus the accompanying widespread rise in competition in financial activities.
- As a consequences of unprecedented and unpredictable inflation and the explosive growth of new, alternative, competitive financial activities, higher levels of both business (default) risk and financial (interest rate) **risk** were built into the system.
- Rapid adaptation to the changed financial environment was greatly facilitated by the underlying revolution in electronic (e.g., computer) ***technology,*** and then this high technical capacity itself independently engendered further changes in financial activities.

VOLATILE INFLATION. To illustrate cause and effect, consider the impact of the changed annual inflation rate from the 2 to 3% of 1950–1965 and the average 7% of 1965–1973, to the 9 to 10% of 1974–1981 with a widened variability spread of 6 to 16% per year. These higher, more **volatile rates of inflation** required the lifting of interest rate ceiling regulations that prevailed in banking and mortgage markets; it also led to major change in national monetary policy which had failed to hold down inflation, and this shift to control via quantitative limits on the money further increased interest rate volatility.

VOLATILITY IN THE SECURITIES MARKETS. Interest rates rose roughly to parallel price rises as lenders required a stable "real" return on loans. This had four major financial impacts—two unfavorable and two offsetting:

1. Holders of outstanding bonds experienced large capital losses, whereas issuers of such debt had to lock themselves into historically high long-term rates to raise fresh funds. **Both** borrowers and lenders at long term thus experienced increased risk and uncertainty in this financial market. Indeed, there was talk of the impending demise of the **bond market.** However, the bulk of federal debt is short term—both outstanding and new issues. Federal debt's relative stature improved during this turbulent period.
2. Although it was not surprising that lenders were hurt by inflation, equities too turned out to be a poor inflation hedge from 1965 to 1980. Indeed, new bonds could be issued so long as they carried the new higher interest rates; new stock was difficult to issue and "real" stock prices fell even as consumer prices were rising. The probable cause of the decline

in equity prices was the lower realized and expected *real return on investment* for U.S. companies.

It turns out that during an unanticipated, rapid, and erratic period of inflation, business is unable to adjust its prices to its costs fast enough to avoid profit erosion. Thus even given price/earning (P/E) ratios, stock prices lag, and the yield competition in the capital market which requires dividends yields to rise (though absolute dividends lag) requires that stock prices *fall.* And in addition, P/E ratios fall as unpredictable inflation increased business risk. But as business learns to adjust to prices more rapidly, and as the inflation stabilizes even at higher rates, stock prices can revive. Indeed there was a revival of sorts in equity prices in the first half of 1980. But for much of the period 1965–1980, total returns from stock included little or no capital gains; dividend yields rose to parallel bond interest rates, with capital losses to those who had to liquidate shares.

3. The only market that provided *inflation offsetting yields* and no capital losses was the *short-term debt* (*deposit*) *market.* And those rates, as has been true for over 50 years, yielded a return that just matched the rate of inflation; that is, the real return was effectively zero. But that was a better return than the **negative** return on stocks and bonds over the 15-year period of inflation.
4. Positive real returns over this period were earned only on **nonfinancial assets.** The oldest law of how to live in inflationary times did indeed hold true from 1965 to 1980: flee to commodities or real assets, such as real estate, gold or diamonds, or fine art. This implies not only paucity of returns in financial markets, but increased **financial risk** to participants on both the supply and demand side. Our **traditional financial markets** failed to perform appropriately under inflationary conditions. The investing public deserts such markets unless inflation stabilizes or innovations in financial markets offset inflationary impacts.

INCREASED FINANCIAL BUSINESS RISK. In addition to the obvious increase in risk implied by the performance of the bond and stock markets as they adjusted to new higher average rates of inflation, there is the additional risk of fluctuations of returns even as average expected rates become stable. Investors in the capital markets now require higher returns for term investment because **financial risk** of security price volatility has increased. Financial risks to issuers and users of funds have also risen. This is the result of the rise in **business risk** during inflationary periods (owing to increased swings in sales and costs) and the rise in **financial risk** implied in rising **debt-equity ratios,** rising ratios of short-term to long-term debt, and especially the fall in the **earnings coverage ratios** that are typical of inflationary eras.

DEREGULATION AT HOME AND ABROAD. Just as increased price/interest rate volatility and uncertainty meant increased financial risk levels, customers sought alternative financial instruments to achieve positive real returns or risk reduction. Competing financial institutions and markets developed rapidly in the freed-up financial environment to meet those demands. For example, regulations prescribing interest rate ceilings on deposits (**Regulation Q**) and on mortgage loans (usury rates) were lifted progressively; in 1986 they will have virtually disappeared. Considering only individual transactions needs, from CDs and NOW accounts to money market accounts was the path the banks followed. Security firms got into this business via money market mutual fund and cash management accounts. New financial markets also developed, including financial futures and forward markets to hedge interest rate risk, among other things.

INCREASED INTERNATIONALIZATION. Increased internationalization is the fruit of a variety of deregulatory and regulatory trends. Financial deregulation has been extensive, as exemplified by more **flexible exchange rates** and freer movement of portfolio investment (and even direct investment) and access to **overseas capital markets.**

Increased and freer international financial flows, like domestic freer flows, result not only in more efficient financial markets—that is, lower **transactions costs** and greater information, and greater allocational efficiency—but also in more rapid and fuller **spread of inflation** and more volatile security price and interest rate fluctuations internationally. The **financial world** is more efficient but also more risky. And it is in reponse to these new conditions in the financial world that adjustments and innovations in financial instruments and activities have developed.

All five of these casual factors interacted in several sectors to magnify and sustain the amount of change in financial practice. For example, although the current rate of inflation is no longer the engine for change that it was in 1968 to 1981, the pace of technology is even faster and has more pervasive effects. And, although the pace of deregulation in the securities industry and banking may have peaked, it is still rising in the insurance/pension fund areas and is spreading overseas, especially in the United Kingdom and Japan. Finally, although risk levels are higher, risk premiums in the form of higher real interest rates spread freely throughout the financial system.

NEW AND SHIFTING CURRENTS IN THE FINANCIAL REVOLUTION—1981–1986. By 1981 when the first Altman edition (5th) of the *Financial Handbook* was published, high and volatile inflation, the driving force of the financial revolution of the 1970s, was receding. But the revolution continued. Although the rate of inflation fell to a fairly steady 3 to 4%, inflation expectations were slow to fall in line. More important, technology became the locomotive of the financial revolution. Indeed, the revolution seemed to speed up.

From filling the role of facilitating agent in the innovation process, **technology** assumed a more central role. By making the securities markets so efficient in handling transactions and in processing and disseminating information, technology shifted the balance of financial leadership away from the financial institution to the financial market—from financial intermediation to trading in securities and contingent claims to these securities. And the development of new **financial instruments**—especially tradable instruments—increased at an even faster pace. Typical of this current wave were inventions of custom-made but tradable stocks, bonds, notes, novel repackaging of old securities; swaps, and the like.

Thus, it is not surprising that in this second wave of the revolution, the commercial banks seek to get into the securities business, just as in the first wave the thrift institutions entered the commercial banking business. So change continues in the activities of financial institutions although the pace of deregulation as well as inflation has diminished. Just as technology now assumes a larger causal role, so too has internationalization. Indeed the latter may be viewed as the area where U.S. regulation does not apply and thus constrict activities. And, of course, international transactions have been made comparable to the domestic via technological advances in handling information and transactions and their rapid transmission.

These continuing developments, despite the subsidence of inflation, assure continuing change. Besides, the process is not reversible; once learned and installed, new techniques and procedures and markets are not discarded, although they will be subjected to varying use depending on customers' needs. Further, the fears and probabilities of renewed inflation are greater for this generation.

Just as a futures market, once developed, will not disappear, so the evolution of the multipurpose financial institution will not be rolled back, even if its further expansion is constrained. Major securities firms will continue to do some banking business and insurance services; banks will continue to enter the securities business and perform other financial services for fees. The fact that some banks and securities firms stick to a restricted and specialized business (boutique) only adds to the variety of financial institutions offering services to the public.

In the early 1930s, radical national financial regulation of banks and securities and insurance firms was introduced as the financial system failed to perform in a depressed economy; this set the structure and the tone of finance for 40 years. So today we should expect that the current deregulation mode, originally designed to cope with the failure of our system to stop inflation and its ruinous effects on our financial system, is setting the structure and tone of finance for the next generation as well as this one.

CATALOG OF NEWLY ESTABLISHED INNOVATIONS IN MONEY AND CAPITAL MARKETS

Exhibit 1 summarizes the significant and durable financial innovations of the last decade plus. What started with CDs and Ginny Maes ends today with CATS and TIGRS joining the old bulls and bears.

EXHIBIT 1 NEWLY ESTABLISHED FINANCIAL INSTRUMENTS, MARKETS, AND INSTITUTIONS

1. Cash Management and Money Market Services
   NOW accounts, Money Market Mutual Funds and Certificates of deposit
   Cash management or sweep accounts
   Floating rate loans and notes
2. New Security Contracts
   Zero discount and coupon stripped bonds
   Municipal bond funds and unit trusts
   Variable rate mortgages, pass-through mortgage packages, and open-ended second mortgages (equity access accounts)
   Variable and universal life insurance
   IRA and Keogh pension funds and direct participation tax shelters
3. New Financial Markets
   Financial futures: interest rate, foreign currency, and stock index futures
   Options: Exchange traded options and options on futures
   Fully electronic trading—e.g., Cincinnati Stock Exchange, OTC-NASDAQ (over-the-counter National Association of Securities Dealers Automated Quotations) and the Exchanges' Interlinked (National) Trading System
   New corporate issues via shelf or continuous registration (SEC, Reg. 415)
4. New Financial Institutions and Structures
   Discount brokerage
   Conglomerate financial firms:
      Merrill Lynch (Banking, mortgaging, insurance . . .)
   Financial mergers:
      Bache/Prudential
      Citibank & savings and loans
   Conglomerate financial and industrial firms:
      Dean Witter/Sears/All State Insurance
      American Can/S&L/Insurance and so forth

Standard stocks and bonds continue to be the major financial instruments and markets, but the ways to enter those markets have ramified widely, and supplementary and alternative investment maturities, techniques, and packages abound. Although this may seem to restrict the standard security salesperson's role, it is only true in the narrowest sense. Indeed, transactions expenditures (i.e., commissions, fees, and spreads) incurred by the average investor (and national totals) have increased sharply. To maintain the same return in volatile financial markets requires more—not less—expert financial advice and services. There is both more speculative activity and more hedging activity by investors. Many of these new instruments involve either financial institutions laying off their risk on borrowers (e.g., variable rate mortgages) or investors laying off their risks in one market by participating in another market (e.g., stock index options). These innovations add to financial transactions and turnover.

In addition to innovations in market procedures and in financial instruments, there have been **innovations in financial institutions.** Two polar developments in the structure and function of financial institutions have taken shape. First, there has been a shift toward large, multipurpose department stores of finance, in a move away from specialized institutions separated from one another by law. For example, commercial banks entered into the investment banking business. Second, and quite counter to the first trend, new highly specialized financial boutiques developed. For example, new or revamped securities firms restricted their activities to discount brokerage with little or no research or advisory activities, or offered research services and consulting only.

The trend toward one big financial institution with many functions falling between regulatory stools is largely a reaction of the large institutions to rapidly changing financial needs and practices, and especially to increasing financial and business risks. The all-purpose business is, by definition, widely diversified and thus cushioned against risk, and well equipped to move in any direction the financial wind blows. But it also may be insulated against high returns if the conglomerate proves difficult to manage.

The boutique approach is to specialize in particular financial functions that the business is uniquely qualified to deliver at profitable fee schedules. Specialists in discount brokerage, options, reinsurance, and second mortgages have proliferated. Their response to the increased pace of change and risk is not to diversify but to strip down to a lean, adaptable size and to specialize flexibly, while avoiding interest rate or default risk. In effect, such activity involves unbundling the traditional packages of financial services and laying off much of the money lending and capital needs to others, while offering selective profitable services at scheduled fees. Profitable? Probably. Powerful and adaptable? Probably not.

CAUSES AND CONSEQUENCES OF THE "SECONDWAVE" OF CHANGE IN THE FINANCIAL ENVIRONMENT—1981–1986

Although the pace of change in the financial environment seems as breathtaking in the mid-1980s as it was in the 1970s, the triggering factors are no longer the same; and the nature of the changes in financial instruments, markets, and institutions currently in process are quite different.

The driving forces today are **technology** and **internationalization** where the rate of change is even faster than in the 1970s, whereas both inflation and deregulation have lost their propulsive force in the financial world. As a consequence the key changes are:

1. **The rise of the financial markets**—trading—relative to the financial institutions—intermediation—as the focus of the financing process.
   a. The increased direct participation of the fund-**raiser** (e.g., the corporate borrower) in the financial marketplace.
   b. The simultaneous decline of the banking system as the passthrough for funds from depositor to final user, and the banks' rise as a **broker** of funds for a fee.

   c. The key word to describe this process is **"securitization":** Business increasingly raises funds via issues of commercial paper, floating rate notes, and bonds rather than via negotiated bank loans. And changes over time are arranged by **"swaps"** directly with other borrowers rather than by renegotiation of bank loans.

2. **Increased financial market volatility.** Much of the urge for borrowers to finance directly and of lenders to avoid the commitments of intermediated finance stems from the unrelenting high level and volatility of financial risks.
   a. Although stable inflation levels averaging 3 to 4% since 1981 have been comforting, both real and nominal interest rates have not yet fallen proportionately as the inflationary era passes.
   b. Security market prices are more volatile and play a more important role than previously; thus interest rate risk is high. And credit risks are naturally high in new, deregulated, impersonal financial markets.
   c. The prototype financial "instrument" for this new world is the **"swap"**—an exchange of cash flows (typically of fixed and variable rate streams) between borrowers to adjust to their evolving needs and fears.

Volatility of interest rates (and security prices) is as great as ever although the **level** of rates has dropped in the wake of dis-inflation. As a consequence, the use of new financially flexible instruments continues to soar, especially that for options, financial futures, and a variety of innovative "floating" or hedging clauses in bond indentures or contracts. Indeed, bonds may be considered and analyzed as a set of option contracts—"contingent claim analysis."

On the other hand, **commodity** futures market trading is inhibited by the low, stable rate of commodity price inflation, whereas the **financial** futures market continues to expand.

In any case, **financial** market volatility continues unabated. It will continue to do so because: Financial innovations increase risks as well as net revenues; monetary policy is the main national macro-policy tool and is conducted regardless of interest rate impacts; and **international** flows of funds are increasingly freed up, resulting in large and quick shifts in those flows.

3. **Technological advances** in information processing and back-office transactions work has made possible both the "securitization" process and facilitated risk adjustment transactions in such markets.
   a. The instantaneous or real time reporting of transactions and their transmission provide both information and rapid price flexibility in all financial marketplaces.
   b. Arbitrage activities keep prices in all related markets moving in close correspondence (e.g., stock prices and option prices) thus providing for risk transfer operations at low cost.

4. **Financial technology** is still proceeding at an accelerating pace, serving not just as a facilitating factor but as a **new driving force.**
   a. **Computer technology,** which is still increasing in speed and accuracy while unit costs continue to fall, is causing concentration of back-office clearing and collection activities. On the other hand, it also permits economic unbundling of activities so that specialists in financial research, customer contact, discount brokerage, and money market funds are setting up shop everywhere. In other words, technology is **altering the basic structure of the financial industry.** Indeed, the huge financial conglomerates are unthinkable without efficient mass back-office operations and coordinated operations of their varied financial specialties. However, the specialized financial institutions based on fixed, distinguishing features, such as deposit-taking or mortgage-making, are in relative decline.
   b. **International arbitrage,** which is the basis for the rapidly developing **internationalization** of world financial markets, is fundamentally a product of computer capacity for almost instantaneous calculation and transmission. This is where the most significant innovative activity is about to proliferate. Here, technology (not inflation) is the principal cause of overseas financial deregulation.
5. **Slowing pace of domestic deregulation and the increasing pressures for selective reregulation.**
   a. Concern is shifting to regulate rather than deregulate, especially with respect to the **trading activities** of market-makers and financial institutions and even nonfinancial business participants. There are public and congressional calls for **new** regulation of dealers in government securities markets (repos) and for the FDIC to impose risk-adjusted deposit insurance premia on banks. Regulation here follows cases of bankruptcy or other distress, whether due to fraud or mismanagement. But this urge to regulate or reregulate is restricted to specific operations rather than by institution per se.

   b. Indeed, deregulation of institutional-based restrictions continues in the insurance industry and in interstate aspects of banking. And the SEC continues to allow the self-regulatory authorities in the securities industry to take the lead in regulatory matters.

CATALOG OF THE NEW AND EVOLVING FINANCIAL INSTRUMENTS OF THE 1980s

By contrast to those of 1965–1980, this list of instruments consists predominantly of extensions or new combinations of the last decade's innovations. The never instruments tend to be custom-made for specific needs to meet particular problems of financial risk or fund raising. And, the viability of the new consumer and business finance instruments probably depends on the development of secondary markets for providing liquidity and diversification.

Here the process of **securitization** is extended toward replacing the financial negotiation of the specialized financial institution, such as the commercial bank.* In this case, the innovative instruments themselves may well induce radical financial institutional change.

Risks to holders of financial claims can be controlled by the use of futures and options. Clearly, increased risk of interest rate changes (with associated possibilities of capital loss and reinvestment loss) has been matched by the development of these new instruments.

FINANCIAL FUTURES CONTRACTS. With respect to **U.S. Government Securities'** interest rates there are now four well established futures contracts: U.S. Treasury bonds, Treasury notes, Treasury bills, and GNMAs (mortgage).

On **deposits** there are financial futures (interest rate) contracts for domestic CDs and Eurodollar time deposits.

On **equities** futures contracts are available on the following stock market indices: S&P 500, S&P 100, New York Exchange Composite, and Value Line.

Foreign Currencies: six European (British, West German, Dutch, French, Italian, and Swiss) plus Japanese and Mexican.

Monetary Metals: Gold and silver.

OPTIONS CONTRACTS ON FINANCIAL INSTRUMENTS. As with futures, there are options on government debt instruments, foreign currencies, and on individual equities and stock market indices. In addition, there are options on futures contracts for treasury bonds, S&P 500, N.Y. Stock Exchange Composite, deutsche marks, and gold.

Issuers have avoided the increased interest rates required by investors to offset interest rate risk by designing debt instruments with adjustable rates and optional maturities. Risk to issuers of securities (and their reinvestment risk) can be controlled by adding specifications to the traditional debt contract to include bank letters of credit or security bonding by insurance companies.

FIXED INCOME CORPORATE INSTRUMENTS VERSUS INTEREST RATE RISK

Floating Rate Extendable Notes. Rates tied to the Treasury bill rate with options to extend maturity by lender.

Ajustable Rate Preferred Stock (ARP). The dividend is not fixed but tied to an index such as the highest of the Treasury bill rate and the 20-year bond rate.

* This factor explains the renewed pressure from the banks to enter the security business so as to follow their customers, who now increasingly prefer to buy and sell open market instruments rather than to negotiate CDs and loans at the bank. Full bank response in this fashion will require repeal of the Glass-Steagall Act of 1933.

FIXED INCOME CORPORATE INSTRUMENTS VERSUS DEFAULT RISK

Controlled commercial paper. These first lower-quality short-term loans were successfully issued because they were distributed via an **independent** company that used the proceeds to buy the real issuers' receivables. The issue was further backed by a line of bank credit and an insurance policy.

"JUNK" BONDS. High yield, high risk bonds are called "junk" bonds because they are rated low quality or below investment grade. These are not new instruments, but they are currently newly issued in great quantity because business takeovers and buy-outs are heavily financed by high leverage (i.e., with large amounts of low quality debt). And the public has entered this security market as it has all security markets, in this case attracted by the high yields. Moreover, the default risk can be diversified away in part in "high yield" (junk bond) **Mutual Funds.**

NEW EQUITY AND EQUITYLIKE INSTRUMENTS (VERSUS INTEREST RATE AND DEFAULT RISK)

- **Convertible Adjustable Rate Preferred Notes** (i.e., convertible into common stock)
- **Subordinated capital notes** issued by banks must be paid off with equity capital
- **Convertible exchangeable preferred**—Can be turned in for common stock or subordinated debentures. (Even Corporate Zero Coupon convertible bonds are in process.)

New equity issues with restricted votes or dividends are becoming common, although the stock exchanges have had to alter their rules to accommodate these "dual" issues. They usually arise in mergers and takeovers as parts of the custom-made package of paying for the assets required.

SYNTHETIC NOTES, BONDS, AND STOCKS. All the preceding special new issues can be created by a combination of puts or financial futures or swaps; and variable rates of return can be attached to standard securities to create hybrid forms. Financing the business corporation is becoming increasingly free-form.

SWAPS: THE NEWEST "SYNTHETIC" SECURITY. Swaps are contracts between two parties to exchange cash flows of fixed and variable interest payments. Typically the exchange is made because, since first issuance, the cash inflows and/or interest rates have changed and call for financial restructuring, for example, to better match cash inflows and outflows. Swaps are a relatively low-cost way to do this for although they are custom-made they do not involve a new issue. Principals are not exchanged and thus the underlying security itself is unaltered.

Swaps as substitutes for renegotiating a term loan are another example of how financial markets are replacing financial institutions in supplying funds.

PASS-THROUGHS AND REARRANGEMENTS—PURE "SECURITIZING." Most current "innovative instruments" involve turning nonmarketable or less-marketable paper into fully marketable securities. Almost all government sponsored residential mortgages have already been "securitized" by sale of pass-through mortgage-portfolio securities and mortgage backed bonds. New are CMOs—collateralized mortgage obligations; with this instrument, unique loans, such as commercial mortgages have been turned into attractive marketable packages by combining them into funds of various maturity classes. Sellers, like insurance companies, can alter their portfolios quickly, whereas purchasers can match maturities or horizons to avoid both reinvestment and interest rate risk.

Similarly, zero discount bonds are now being created as new issues by the Treasury itself in competition with Merrill Lynch and Salomon Brothers, who stripped coupons from regular bonds to create such zeros.

The newest of all is Salomon Brothers **"CARs"** (Certificates of Automobile Receivables)—automobile loans repackaged for leading car financing companies and banks as collateral for large issues of "collateralized automobile receivables." Marine Midland Bank made the original loans but ended up in a fee business, because its funding was replaced by that of the investors in CARs. Salomon Brothers will sell CARs securities backed by the receivables in $25,000 pieces. Banks too have issued collateralized commercial paper, mortgage-backed bonds, and adjustable rate preferred stock.

REGULATORY ASPECTS OF CURRENT AND IMPENDING CHANGES IN FINANCIAL MARKETS

The set of new instruments that emerged in mid-1985 is based on well-established outstanding liabilities, such as loans to finance consumer durables (e.g., houses, cars, and business loans). By packaging such mortgages and receivables, investment banking houses and banks create marketable packages of collateralized securities. This process of "securitization" substitutes direct funding for intermediated funding. The original lenders' income flows from fees for originating and servicing the loans, not from earning interest on funds loaned. And in June 1985, after Salomon Brothers developed and sold $20 billion of **CARs**, it began to create a secondary market in these certificates.

These most recent innovations are based on earlier innovations—primarily technology driven—that made financial marketplace transactions (e.g., exchange transactions) more efficient and less expensive. The huge and growing volume of trading also developed owing to the volatility of security prices and resulting need to restructure portfolios continuously and to make hedging transactions, as well as because of the increasing array of new securities.

Liquidity needs are increasingly being met through market instruments rather than via deposits. Depository intermediaries are winding down both their deposits as sources of funds and loans as uses of funds. This broad development may lead the unsophisticated individual to invest/save in complex debt instruments or hybrid equities of greater price volatility than may be recognized. Extension of SEC and Exchange regulation to protect the public against misinformation, market manipulation, and fraud in these new instruments and markets is developing.

For example, new separate regulation bodies for new securities markets, such as financial futures and options, have been set up. And this in turn calls for intermarket regulatory structures, because certain problems, such as cross-market trading, cannot be handled by one agency; for example, how can options trading be fully supervised when the underlying securities are traded in different markets and overseas under different authorities?

Furthermore, as default risk increases in significance both absolutely and relative to interest rate risk, and failures increase for both security (e.g., bond) firms and commercial and savings banking institutions, pressure grows to expand both self-regulation and public regulation. The most likely sector for regulatory change and likely increased regulatory oversight is in banking, especially thrifts, owing to the increased awareness that deposit insurance subsidizes banks and leads banks, especially distressed banks, to "go for broke." Risk adjustable premia on deposits as a solution to the problem will require more rules and more oversight.

Current deregulation developments have also slowed, because so many of the constraints on financial institutions have already been removed. Banks, for example, continue to widen their activities by going "off-balance sheet" or off-shore.

RESPONSES OF REAL SECTORS AND THE FINANCIAL STRUCTURE TO THE CHANGING FINANCIAL ENVIRONMENT

THE REAL SECTORS

1. ***Households,*** although remaining the prime surplus or savings sector in the economy, increased their borrowing, especially long-term mortgage debt (and that, largely floating rate), relative to their lending. Household lending continued to be short term, though increasingly in money market investments rather than traditional savings accounts. Households fought price inflation via short-term interest rate instruments and sheltered their income against tax "inflation" via tax-deductible mortgage interest and real estate taxes, even at the expense of curtailing net personal savings. The predominant "hedge"motivations of investors was also evidenced in the rise of "options" and "futures" and the

revival of intermediation via mutual funds of money market instruments, municipal bonds, and corporate bonds.

2. ***The business sector,*** like household investors, increased its debt ratio, even though it is always a net "deficit" sector. Although business borrowed heavily in the short area for much of the period, it is always seeking to lengthen the debt and to find new ways to issue equity. Up to 1983 business did not choose to sell new equity shares when profits and stock prices were relatively low; and when interest rates are at historic highs, borrowers are reluctant to lock themselves into such rates via new issues of long-term corporate bonds. As a result nonfinancial business financial policy included new ways to economize on needs for short-term funds and means to raise such funds with new instruments.

Corporate finance departments developed new financial forecasting techniques to reduce liquidity needs and to minimize inventories, both of goods and receivables; long-term requirements or capital budgets were reduced by implementing strict cost of capital hurdles for fixed investments, based on high interest rates plus increased equity risk premiums. Furthermore, it was often found that outstanding fixed assets were available via merger or acquisition at bargain (stock) prices financed by private debt or through leveraged leasing. The 1983–1984 expansion was not an investment boom but a consumer/government boom.

Until recently, when business had to raise debt funds, it did so largely through the banks and short-term markets. In recent years there has been a remarkable shift to direct financing in innovative securities markets as against traditional intermediated finance. Although banks developed term loans, business developed extensive use of commercial paper sold directly to other business and to financial institutions, including banks themselves. Business also developed new forms of intermediate-term (five–seven year) bonds and expanded its use of custom-made, longer-term debt directly negotiated with insurance companies and pension funds. By the early 1980s, whereas half of all bank term loans were indexed, over half of all corporate bonds were privately placed. In the 1980s, business is showing new interest in convertible bonds and is generally less reluctant to offer a share in equity to major lenders under certain conditions. Innovations in financing business over the long term are developing rapidly, with particular attention to attracting foreign sources of funding. During the expansion of 1983–1984, new equity issues surged but new bond issues were constrained by sustained high long-term interest rates. The year 1985 was the time of new forms of long-term debt contracts.

Until the defense expenditure expansion and the tax cuts of 1981–1984, the government sectors had not been under borrowing pressure because their "incomes"—tax revenues—had been the best inflation-indexed streams in the economy. Consequently government debt had expanded less than private debt. Government finance in this sense had not been under pressure to innovate. Innovation in the governmental sector, however, has occurred in regulatory areas and in methods of executing monetary and fiscal policies. Currently, owing to record deficits and new government issues, innovations are beginning—zero rate bonds, foreign sales, and such.

THE FINANCIAL SECTORS. The potential to provide detail in this area is so great that only typical examples of major classes of adjustments of the last 15 years can be considered.

1. ***The Decline in Financial Intermediation.*** The decline of "term" intermediation by depository institutions—borrowing short and lending long—is a major adjustment to inflation (and inflationary expectations) and was a major shift in the financial structure of the United States. The parallel rise of money market certificates and variable rate mortgages to displace passbook savings accounts and 30-year fixed rate mortgages is typical. Institutions, such as savings and loan associations, were freed to issue savings shares indexed to open market Treasury bill rates and then were forced by competition to issue money market certificates. They then sought to hedge their high-cost, variable interest obligations by lending the funds out at high variable rates rather than assuming the risk of high, fixed rate loan assets. The term risk in effect has been shifted from the intermediary to the household.

Term risk is the risk of persistently rising interest rates when fixed rate, long-term outstanding loans have been financed via short-term deposits or instruments; profits will be eroded as the short-term sources of funds have to be refinanced at increasingly higher rates of interest, even though the income from the mortgages, for example, is fixed. Term intermediation under alternately rising and falling interest rates rather than constantly rising interest rates is another matter. The sharp rise in futures and options is attributable in large part to the lack of intermediary financial institutions willing to assume term risk; that is, households and businesses used direct market instruments (e.g., futures) to offset term risks.

Similarly, commercial banks via floating (variable) term loans have diminished the "term" aspect of such loans with respect to interest cost if not to maturity. And even long maturity is not assured in the five-year rollover mortgage, which is subject to periodic renegotiation of all terms. This marks a reversion to the financial practices of the 1920s, when term risk could not easily be intermediated. But interest rate futures markets and commodity option markets have developed in their place.

The increase in instrument intermediation, or hedging, to cope with "default" risk further reduces the financial institutions' role. As we will see, financial institutions are increasingly serving on a "service-for-a-fee" basis rather than serving a risk absorption function. Some financial institutions (e.g., insurance companies) are curtailing their risks via reinsurance contracts. If, and as, inflation stabilizes at lower levels, the resumption of financial institutions' term intermediation may, in part, resume.

2. ***The Rise of Financial Markets.*** Across the board, **financial markets** have become more competitive, as well as more important compared with depository institutions. The listed stock brokers' fixed commission schedules were

scrapped and negotiated rates mandated by the Securities and Exchange Commission in 1975; currently under discussion is the lifting of price maintenance of new issues while in distribution.

The **SECs'** approval of **Rule 415,** which permits investment bankers to "shelve" large issues and then to distribute them freely as financial market conditions allow, increases the influence of issuers on investment banking and increases "shopping around" by issuers. Increased competition among underwriters has also evolved via commercial bank entry into the private placement of corporate securities, both stocks and bonds. Furthermore, bank lease financing can substitute for new debt issues.

In the wings is automation of securities trading to the point when execution of trades takes place via computer rather than exchange floors. The mechanization of price determination in standardized securities markets is not far off. Trading-off-the-exchanges is increasing rapidly with the automation of trading "over-the-counter"; one of the advantages of "listing" on exchanges is thus diminishing and the volume of total trading volume (not value) off-board will soon equal that of the New York Stock Exchange.

Not only have financial assets, such as CDs and open market commercial paper (CPs) become highly negotiable, instruments such as mortgages that are not directly negotiable owing to their uniqueness have in effect become so through secondary market and pass-through packaging of the nonnegotiable instruments. Many of these innovative markets and instruments were developed under government subsidy and protection; but today most are flourishing under private, nonsubsidized auspices.

3. ***Financial Instruments.*** And of course options and futures markets are a substitute for buying the stocks or bonds themselves. So, too, the opening up of markets and expansion of information for foreign securities, especially equities and Eurodollar deposits and loans, provides competition for U.S. securities markets.

Innovations in the supply of futures contracts on financial instruments as well as commodities and other hedged contracts are directly responsive to the demand for instruments as shelters against the increased volatility of interest rates and the associated rise in both business and financial risk. Competition for ordinary savers' funds among money market certificates, Treasury bills, and money market funds is intense. Of these instruments only Treasury bills existed before 1975, and even then they were not as well known or available as they are today.

A final example of adaptation to the new financial environment is the awakening of the mutual fund industry, not only via selective index stock funds but through debt funds. In addition to money market funds there are municipal funds and corporate bond funds and government funds. Each type is offered in funds of varying maturities and varying quality, in denominations that appeal even to modest personal investors. The new **"zero"** coupon or "stripped" **bond** issues have spread from government bonds to municipal bonds. The basic purpose of stripping is to evade reinvestment risk in volatile interest rate markets, especially for those with specific investment horizons.

As the financial markets have expanded in new directions, they have replaced in part the intermediation of savers' funds through depositories and even insurance-pension contractual funds. We have come a long way since the early 1960s when CDs were first introduced. Today CDs are available to all savers, not just large depositors at large banks; CD futures markets exist. A parallel development starting in the 1970s was the expansion of CP as a substitute investment for large CDs. Commercial paper rapidly became a substitute on the borrower side for commercial bank loans; today they are substituting for term loans as well.

4. ***Financial Institutions.*** Two polar developments in the structure of financial institutions are rapidly taking shape. First, we are on the upside of the long historical cycle toward large, *multipurpose department stores* of finance and away from specialized institutions. For example, commercial banks are entering the investment banking business. Second, and counter to the first trend, we are also developing highly specialized *financial boutiques,* which permit previously specialized financial businesses such as securities firms to restrict their activities to discount brokerage with little or no researching or advisory activities or the converse.

Both developments are common to American history, rising and falling depending on economic-financial events and governmental policy. For example, during the 1930s, the last period of radical change in the financial environment—a period of deflation, depression, then controls and planned recovery—financial institutions were segregated by law, and their specialized activities were subject to meticulous regulation. During the 1960s and 1970s, a period of inflation and competition and financial euphoria, financial institutions pushed out in all directions, and financial practices became highly flexible as financial deregulation proliferated. Efficiency, competition, and flexibility typify this period, as contrasted with the concerns for safety, regulation, and measured change of the 1930s and 1950s. Currently the bias is toward allowing financial structure to evolve as financial entrepreneurs choose. Historically, such periods have ended when private financial overreaching, errors or misbehavior, and inadequate or misconceived public policy led to financial crises and then a period of restrictive financial regulation and supervision. Recent failures of commercial banks and thrift institutions, and the rescue of Continental-Illinois and Financial Corporation of America suggest that the peak of deregulatory activity may be passed.

But since the early 1960s we have seen a remarkable liberalization of financial activity. Consider the recent evolution of the large commercial banks toward continental style department stores of finance. In 1961 Citibank introduced the CD as the beginning of its effort to become a "thrift" institution, taking savings deposits and making long-term loans to all, as well as a traditional commercial bank, taking demand deposits and making short-term loans to business. By 1970 the larger banks, having grown far faster than the thrift institutions and having changed the practices in the industry, had shifted their attention to several other financial institution fields. For example, commercial banks, largely via the use of the bank holding company device, entered various financial service businesses, such as leasing, data processing, and financial consulting. Commercial banks also began to enter the investment banking or securities business (which presumably had been proscribed by the Glass-Steagall Banking Act of 1933), such as private placement of corporate securities, underwriting of municipal revenue bonds, and offerings of commingled trust funds (mutual funds of securities) to the public.

On the other side, large securities firms, such as Merrill Lynch, were opening "deposit" accounts for customers, entering the real estate and insurance businesses, and within the securities business proper, starting to compete with the New York Stock Exchange for market-making in listed securities. Some of the large thrift institutions are acquiring commercial bank functions: negotiated order of withdrawal (NOW) accounts, commercial savings deposits and loans, real estate management, and so on. Insurance companies, with their expanded term lending to business, annuity packages, real estate, equity positions and property management are also becoming all-purpose institutions.

This trend toward "one big financial institution," with many functions falling between regulatory stools, is largely a reaction of the large institutions to rapidly changing financial needs and practices, and especially to increasing financial and business risks. The all-purpose business is one that is, by definition, widely diversified; thus it is cushioned against risk and well equipped to move in any direction the financial wind blows.

However, reaction to the very same events by less than giant financial institutions can and does result in different financial business developments. The "boutique" approach (by contrast to the department store or, in this case, a variety store approach) is to specialize in particular financial functions that the business has unique capacity to deliver, for which a demand has been or can be developed, and for which profitable fee schedules can be arranged. For example, securities firms are specializing in pure brokerage transactions at discount, others are strictly research shops, selling expert opinions for a fee. Some thrift institutions are becoming mortgage servicing rather than mortgage holding businesses; that is, they pass through the loan to other lenders. Specialists in options, reinsurance, second mortgages, and so on, are proliferating. Here the response to increased pace of change and risk is not to diversify but to strip down to lean, adaptable size and to specialize flexibly. In effect such activity involves unbundling the traditional packages of financial services, and leaving many of the money lending and capital functions to others, while offering services profitably at scheduled fees.

In addition to innovation in market procedures and in financial instruments, there have thus been innovations in financial institutions. To cope with inflation and increasing risk, the banks developed money market certificates; and then securities firms responded with money market funds and then short-term municipal funds; and the insurance-pension fund industries developed variable annuities. To cope with expanding volume of trade in less regulated financial security markets, the securities industries developed automated trading practices, competitive brokerage fees, and the beginning of a national securities market; then the banks moved into the securities business; brokerage firms shifted to option trading, and so on. Thus have the various financial institutions been responding to the changing environment by shifting their structure and functions in free-form fashion.

IMPACTS ON THE STRUCTURE OF THE SECURITIES INDUSTRY—A BRIEF CASE STUDY. Considering the changes in the underlying financial environment, innovations in financial instruments, services and markets, and the development of new financial analysis, it is not surprising that the securities industry of 1985 hardly resembled that of 1970.

These are some major changes that have revolutionized the industry:

- Trading volume in the securities markets has more than tripled.
- Although the number of firms in the industry has halved, the number of nonsecurity firms in the business has increased; that is, both concentration and competition have increased.
- Mass electronic access to and manipulation of information is commonplace.
- The number of security industry employees has increased far less than proportionally to business activity.
- Because of economies of scale and competition, transaction costs have risen far less than the overall rate of inflation.
- Profits in the industry have been excellent, owing to the volume of activity. But as volume slows, because of heavy fixed (automation) costs, profits can and do fluctuate sharply.
- The choice of securities has deepened and widened by a process called **"securitization"** of claims, which previously were not dealt with in security markets, such as mortgages; these are now packaged for open market sale. The variety of debt securities is enormous, with all kinds of rate flexibility, maturity, collateralization, and tax aspects.
- Although new equity issues have proliferated and trading in outstanding equities has ballooned, proxies for equity have also grown—stock options, index futures, options on indexes for cash settlement, and so on—and they should compete to some degree with trading in the underlying securities.

Overall, it is increasingly clear that the **securities industry**—the least regulated financial industry, the fastest changing technologically, the greatest beneficiary of lowered rates of inflation, the easiest to internationalize, and the most adaptable to changing levels of risk—is the financial sector most likely to prosper in the current financial environment. And this is likely both on the brokerage side of the business and on the investment banking or new issue side of the business. But heavy capital investment is required to engage in the business today, because trading is both risky and automated, and is required to accompany the explosion of new securities.

PARALLEL DEVELOPMENTS IN FINANCIAL ANALYSIS OVER THE LAST DECADE

While price and interest rate and tax volatility became a dominant feature in the economy in the 1970s and new financial tools were developed to allow the investing public to deal with the higher risks, the academic world was also busy developing so-called modern portfolio theory (MPT)—financial analysis aimed at understanding how financial markets perform when they are uninhibited by regulatory controls, public or private.

It was not coincidental that studies of perfectly competitive or "efficient" financial markets proliferated in the 1970s. In reality, markets were becoming "perfect," the need for fresh apparatus to apply to risk analysis was pressing, and computer technology was available for gathering financial data to test the models. The result was a revolution in analysis of security pricing and in risk management of security portfolios. Accompanying these developments were a vast increase in financial data and an expansion in the availability of such information. And it was no coincidence that new instruments, especially options and financial futures, developed simultaneously. The new analysis, with its emphasis on risk analysis, could be seen as reinterpreting security valuation as a particular form or application of general "contingent claims analysis."

What effect does this have on the role of the financial planner? He or she must be knowledgeable about all forms of financial instruments and markets, from zero discount municipal bonds to Treasury bills, to options on stock indices. And in this diverse financial universe, the planner must be able, given the company's or household's risk profile and horizon, to develop or to maintain a financial portfolio suited to that unit.

The new principles of portfolio analysis include ideal use of risk-free instruments, understanding of stock Betas (that measure instrument risk vis-à-vis the whole market), immunization of bond portfolios against interest rate risk, and the like.

Greater rate risk was accompanied by heightened technological risk, regulatory risk, and tax risk as well. For example, important changes in tax laws have been occurring annually: Even as average personal income tax rates have been reduced, specific business deferrals and shelters have developed to encourage industrial investments. These major and rapid tax law changes led to the creation of new financial instruments, markets, and activities. The municipal or tax-exempt bond market in particular has been strongly affected by the tax changes which, in effect, introduced many powerful, competing, tax-avoidance instruments.

Current portfolio analysis emphasizes the role of diversification in reducing the risk unique to the particular security (or company) at hand. Indirectly, it also emphasizes the inevitability of overall financial market risk except insofar as different financial markets (instruments) experience different patterns of risk, allowing diversification via balancing different types of risky securities. And, of course, diversification or insurance versus all risks can be "manufactured" via use of hedging instruments.

In a financial environment where everything is subject to rapid and unpredictable change, opportunities abound but so do risks. Today's financial planner must be a knowledgeable risk manager and portfolio developer, and also be well-informed about the numerous new securities, claims to securities, varied financial markets, and sources of financial information. Fortunately, analytical frameworks for putting and holding all this together in a manageable package have been developing at the same time that the financial marketplace has been expanding at a rapid pace.

FINANCIAL EVENTS OF 1984—A CHRONOLOGY*

Jan 1 Ceiling rate on savings deposits at commercial banks rises from 5.25 to 5.5%, same as thrifts.

Jan 6 Dow Jones industrial stock average *closes at 1287,* high for year. (See July 23.)

Jan 20 Citicorp acquires First Federal S&L, Chicago.

April 9 Federal Reserve discount rate rises from 8.5 to 9%.

April 11 Shearson-American Express plans to buy Lehman Bros., Kuhn Loeb.

April 30 Manufacturers Hanover purchases CIT Financial from RCA for $1.5 billion.

May 17 FDIC, Federal Reserve Board, and Comptroller of Currency announce comprehensive financial assistance program for Continental Illinois Bank. FDIC guarantees all of Continental's deposits.

May 30 Yield on 20-year Treasury bonds (constant maturity index) rises to 13.92%, high for year. (See Nov. 23.)

June 25 Prime rate rises to 13%, high for year. (See Dec. 20.)

July 23 Dow Jones industrial stock average closes at 1087, low for year. (See Jan. 6 = 0% higher.)

July 26 FDIC, Federal Reserve Board, and Comptroller of Currency announce permanent assistance for Continental Bank, including FDIC agreement to buy up to $4.5 billion of problem loans. (See May 17.)

Aug 3 Trading on New York Stock Exchange hits record 237 million shares.

* *Adapted from:* Economic Perspectives, *Federal Reserve Bank of Chicago, (Spring 1985), pp. 18–19.*

Aug 15 Financial Corp. of American restates earnings to show loss. Subsidiary American S&L, nation's largest, faces liquidity problem.

Aug 27 Three-month Treasury bills yield 11.12% (coupon equivalent) in market, high for year. (Equaled Sept. 4.) (See Dec. 26.)

Oct 1 Cost-of-living raise for federal employees held to 3.5%.

Oct 15 Comptroller of Currency ends moratorium on processing of "nonbank bank" applications.

Oct 19 VA mortgage rate falls to 13%.

Oct 29 Prime rate declines to 12%.

Nov 1 OPEC agrees on oil output cuts to halt price slide.

Nov. 21 Federal Reserve cuts discount rate from 9 to 8.5%,

Nov. 23 Yield on 20-year Treasury bonds fails to 11.41%, low for year. (See May 30 13.9 or 20% higher.)

Dec. 20 Prime rate declines to 10.75%, low for year. (See June 25.)

Dec. 22 Illinois Commissioner of Banks closes bank in Sandwich, 79th U.S. bank failure in 1984, most since FDIC created in 1933.

Dec. 24 Federal Reserve discount rate falls from 8.5 to 8%, lowest since Oct. 1978.

Dec. 26 Three-month Treasury bills yield 7.89% (coupon equivalent) in market, low for the year (see Aug. 27) versus 11.1 or 40% higher.

Dec. 27 U.S. dollar reaches all-time high against several major foreign currencies.

ONE DAY'S EVENTS OF 1985: HEADLINES FROM *THE WALL STREET JOURNAL* OF MAY 16, 1985

PAGE 1 "WHAT'S NEWS—"

* * *

Maryland's governor said a member of his cabinet has met with representatives of out-of-state financial institutions, including Citicorp and Chase Manhattan, to discuss acquiring some of the state's thrifts.

* * *

The prime rate was cut by Bankers Trust to 10% from 10½%, the lowest level in more than six and a half years. Other banks are likely to follow, analysts said. Treasury bill rates fell sharply, but bond prices slumped after a brief rally.

* * *

Oil prices could weaken further due to fresh discounting and flouting of production restrictions by some OPEC members. Traders say that Iran, starved for revenue by its long war with Iraq, is offering discounts as high as $5 a barrel.

* * *

Industrial output fell 0.2% in April, confirming other signs that manufacturers have experienced practically no growth since last summer. Separately, the government said business inventories eased 0.1% in March after rising 0.5% in February.

*   *   *

The tax-overhaul plan unveiling will be delayed another week, until May 28, the White House said. The delay could hurt prospects for passage, and officials said some final decisions remain to be made to keep the plan from losing revenue.

*   *   *

The House Budget Committee went into an unusual closed session last night, in an attempt to end partisan wrangling that threatened to delay House action on the fiscal 1986 budget until next month.

*   *   *

Inside Pages

Three Universities Join Conrail Bid, Aming to Boost Endowment Income	*p. 16*
Bevill Bresler President Is Cooperating In Investigation of Company's Collapse	*p. 10*
New Limited-Service Bank Is Approved By Comptroller Despite a Court Order	*p. 33*
Bill on Money Laundering Is Expected	*p. 17*
Securities Backed by Auto Loans Offered by 2 Firms	*p. 40*

BIBLIOGRAPHY

Altman, E. I., and Sametz, A.W., *Financial Crises,* Wiley, New York, 1977.

Atchison, M. D., Deong, R., and King, J., *New Financial Instruments—A Descriptive Guide,* Charlottesville, Va., Financial Analysts Research Foundation, 1985.

Federal Reserve *Bulletin,* various issues: "Recent Developments in Corporate Finance" and "Household Finance," Washington, D.C.

Friedman, B., "Postwar Changes in American Financial Markets," in M. Feldstein (Ed.), *American Economy in Transition,* University of Chicago Press, 1981.

Kane, E. J., "Technological and Regulatory Forces in the Developing Fusion of Financial Services Competition," Working Paper 1320, National Bureau of Economic Research, April 1984.

Kaufman, Henry, "Financial Institutions and the Fragile, Volatile Financial Markets," pp. 21–29 in Sametz, *Financial Industry.*

Polakoff, M. E., Durkin, T. A., *Financial Institutions and Markets,* 2d ed., Boston, Houghton Mifflin, 1981.

Sametz, A. W., *The Emerging Financial Industry,* Lexington, MA., D.C. Heath, 1984.

———, Keenan, M., Bloch, E., Goldberg, L. "Securities Activities of Commercial Banks," *Journal of Comparative Law and Securities Regulation,* No. 2, 1979, pp. 155–193.

Silber, W. L., "Recent Structural Change in the Capital Markets—The Process of Financial Innovation," *American Economic Review,* May 1983, pp. 89–95.

2

MONEY AND CAPITAL MARKETS: INSTITUTIONAL FRAMEWORK AND FEDERAL RESERVE CONTROL

CONTENTS

2

MONEY AND CAPITAL MARKETS: INSTITUTIONAL FRAMEWORK AND FEDERAL RESERVE CONTROL

Joseph Bench

The financial officer of a corporation operates within a framework of institutions such as commercial banks, thrift institutions, life insurance companies, and pension funds. This section examines the roles these institutions play in determining interest rates. It also provides a brief introduction to the mechanics of monetary policy exercised by the Federal Reserve Bank. A better understanding of the Federal Reserve's operations—specifically its growth targets for monetary aggregates and its response when money and credit growth either falls short of or exceeds Fed objectives—will help the financial manager to cope with the constantly changing interest rate environment.

THE INSTITUTIONAL FRAMEWORK: SAVINGS SURPLUS AND SAVINGS DEFICIT SECTORS

In the traditional three-sector (households, businesses, and government) economy, there are **savings surplus** and **savings deficit** sectors. In the **savings surplus** sectors consumption is less than current income. In the **savings deficit** sectors current expenditures exceed current income and funds must be raised from external sources to make up the difference. Typically, the **household sector** is a net supplier of funds, since it is a savings surplus unit, whereas businesses are generally savings deficit units and therefore are seeking funds from the household sector. This does not mean to imply that every household has more income than it consumes. While there are many savings deficit units within the household sector, the sector collectively saves more than it borrows. In the business sector, there are both savings deficit units (the norm) and savings surplus units, firms that have extra money to invest. Collectively, however, businesses are viewed as savings deficit units attempting to make up the difference between spending on plant and equipment or inventories and income from operations.

Government has always been a deficit sector. The role of state and local governments and federal agencies as savings deficit units, however, is generally limited to periods of depressed economic activity when rising unemployment and welfare benefits, coupled with a slowdown in tax receipts, lead to a deterioration in municipal finances. As recently as 1984, state and local governments showed a net financial investment of $4.1 billion, acquiring $37.1 billion of credit market instruments, while borrowing $33.0 billion. Total receipts on a national income accounts (NIA) basis exceeded expenditures by an impressive $52.8 billion that year.

RISK AVERSION AND THE DEVELOPMENT OF THE FINANCIAL INTERMEDIARY

The description of the savings surplus and savings deficit units suggests a natural flow of funds from saver to borrower. To smooth the flow of funds between surplus and deficit units, there has developed a variety of middlemen or **financial intermediaries.** These intermediaries, which include commercial banks, savings and loan companies, mutual savings, banks, and credit unions, provide a vehicle for diversifying the risks associated with investing in projects and at the same time provide investors with **liquidity,** should they need to use the funds (or wish to redeploy them in another investment offering a higher rate of return) before the project is complete.

The financial intermediary enables investors to diversify their portfolios by making them infinitesimally small shareholders of a wide variety of projects. The "law of large numbers" suggests only a small probability that any project will go bust, which allows investors to keep their capital intact. Moreover, the financial intermediary stands ready to redeem (refund) the capital plus accumulated interest on short notice, further assuring investors of the liquidity they desire. [Meanwhile, the financial intermediary recognizes the small likelihood that all investments of reasonably long maturities will go bad and therefore is willing to make long-term investments; even though its liabilities (deposits) are generally short-term.]

HOUSEHOLD DIRECT INVESTMENT AND DISINTERMEDIATION

The household sector does not always invest through financial intermediaries. Individuals do make direct purchases of corporate securities (including both equity and debt offerings), and in many cases will purchase tax-exempt securities to insulate themselves from the tax burden on the income derived from these investments. And when interest rates get high enough, individuals reverse the normal flow of savings through intermediaries, withdrawing funds to reinvest their capital in higher yielding, fixed income investments, such as U.S. Treasury obligations. This process is called **disintermediation.** Financial intermediaries generally react to this phenomenon by sharply cutting back their new investments in real and financial assets, which serves to dampen economic activity in areas deprived of new cash.

FLOW OF FUNDS

Exhibit 1 shows the supply and demand for funds in credit markets for 1978 and 1984. On the demand side, the chart is divided into five major groupings: government, corporate securities, mortgages, consumer credit, and short-term business demands. On the supply side are eight groupings: commercial banks, contractual savings institutions (insurance companies and pension funds), thrift institutions, foreign sources, monetary authorities (the Fed), nonbank fi-

EXHIBIT 1 FLOW OF FUNDS IN PRIVATE CREDIT MARKETS ($ BILLIONS)

	1978	1984
DEMAND FOR FUNDS		
Government	109	306
Federal	55	199
Agencies	23	30
State and local	17	33
Mortgage pool securities	14	44
Corporate Securities	30	(19)
Equity	2	(68)
Bonds and notes	24	46
Foreign bonds	4	3
Mortgages	119	158
Home	112	129
Multifamily	9	14
Commercial	22	57
Farm	7	2
(less agency holdings, mortgage pool securities, and state and local government sponsorship)	(31)	(44)
Consumer Credit	49	101
Policy loans	3	1
Short-Term Business	93	111
Bank loans N.E.C.	59	66
Open market paper	26	45
Finance company loans	8	NA
Total	400	657

EXHIBIT 1 (*CONTINUED*)

	1978	1984
SUPPLY OF FUNDS		
Commercial Banks and affiliates	126	182
Contractual savings	105	133
Life insurance	36	61
Private pension funds	29	22
State and local retirement funds	20	35
Fire and casualty	20	15
Thrift institutions		
Savings and loans	64	156
Mutual savings banks	10	12
Credit unions	7	13
Foreign	38	46
Monetary authrities	7	8
Nonbank financee companies	24	33
Nonfinancial corporate business	11	5
Net trade credit	7	10
Other[a]	1	59
Total	400	657

[a]Includes bond and money market funds, real estate investment trusts, individual investors, and other investors.

Source: Federal Reserve Board.

nance companies, nonfinancial corporate business (corporations), and other (including individuals and mutual funds) investors.

DISTRIBUTION OF ASSETS AMONG FINANCIAL INTERMEDIARIES. The largest asset in commercial bank balance sheets is **bank loans.** These constitute more than one-third of the total, mortgages about one-fifth, consumer credit nearly one-sixth, U.S. Treasury and state and local government obligations each about one-tenth of their investment portfolio. Agency issues account for only 5% of commercial bank assets. The remaining 4% is invested in a variety of financial assets including open market paper, security credit, and corporate bonds. A detailed breakdown of the size and proportion of each of these is presented in Exhibit 2.

Savings Institutions. **Savings institutions** include savings and loan associations, mutual savings banks, and credit unions. Their primary investment is in mortgages, which constitute nearly two-thirds of their assets. Home mortgages

EXHIBIT 2 COMMERCIAL BANK ASSETS AT YEAR-END 1983 ($ BILLIONS)

Assets	Outstanding	As Portion of Total (%)
Credit market instruments		
U.S. Treasury issues	$179.1	11
Agency issues	78.9	5
State and local obligations	162.6	10
Corporate bonds	13.1	1
Mortgages	330.4	21
Other credit		
Consumer credit	213.2	13
Bank loans	573.5	36
Open market paper	16.7	1
Security credit	26.6	2
	$1596.1	100

Source: Federal Reserve Board, *Flow of Funds Outstanding,* September 1984.

account for 49% of their investments; commercial mortgages and multifamily mortgages account for 8% and 6% of their investment totals, respectively. Consumer credit and Treasury issues each account for 8% of the investments of savings institutions. Agency issues account for 13% of savings institution assets. The remaining 7% of their financial assets is invested in an assortment of long-term corporate paper and some state and local debt. A breakdown of these holdings is shown in Exhibit 3.

EXHIBIT 3 ASSETS OF SAVINGS INSTITUTIONS: MUTUAL SAVINGS BANKS, CREDIT UNIONS, YEAR-END 1983 ($ BILLIONS)

Assets	Outstanding	As Portion of Total (%)
Credit market instruments		
U.S. Treasury issues	$ 85.6	8
Agency	128.0	13
State and local obligations	3.1	1
Corporate and foreign bonds	22.0	2
Corporate equities	3.6	1
Other credit		
Home mortgages	495.5	49
Multifamily	55.6	6
Commercial	80.2	8
Consumer installment credit	77.4	8
Consumer noninstallment credit	10.3	1
Fed funds and security RP	26.1	3
Open market paper	20.3	2
	$1,007.7	100

Source: Federal Reserve Board, *Flow of Funds Outstanding,* September 1984.

Life Insurance Companies. These institutions also invest a large share of their assets in mortgages. Mortgage investments account for 26% of total assets. The largest holding is corporate bonds, accounting for 38% of the total. Corporate equities are a distant third, accounting for about 10% of life insurance company assets. Policy loans also account for a considerable share (one-tenth) of total holdings, with these totals gyrating over the interest rate cycle. Borrowing against cash values of policies becomes more attractive as interest rates rise and alternative sources of funds dry up. Policy loan volume rises dramatically during high rate periods, making life insurance companies subject to disintermediation because of factors similar to those in the environment that trigger savings outflows at thrift institutions. Exhibit 4 gives a detailed breakdown of the distribution of life insurance company assets.

Fire and Casualty Insurance Companies. Largely because of their higher marginal tax liability, which encourages them to invest in tax-exempt securities during profitable periods, these companies behave far differently from life insurance companies. However, when profits drop sharply (usually a consequence of high inflation rates forcing payouts of claims in excess of premium income), purchases of municipals drop off as well. Municipals constitute more than 40% of fire and casualty company portfolios. Corporate equities have taken the lead from corporate bonds, whereas equities account for one-fifth of fire and casualty company assets and one-ninth share for corporate bonds. The remaining 26% is invested in trade credit (4%) and U.S. Treasury and agency securities (9% and 6%, respectively). Exhibit 5 outlines cumulative holdings of this group of investors.

State and Local Government Retirement Funds. Nearly 40% of the assets of these institutions is invested in corporate bonds. Corporate equities constitute little more than one-fourth of such assets, with the remainder divided among U.S. Treasury (16%) and agency securities (13%), mortgages, and some

EXHIBIT 4 LIFE INSURANCE COMPANY FINANCIAL ASSETS AT YEAR-END 1983 ($ BILLIONS)

Assets	Outstanding	As Portion of Total (%)
Credit market instruments		
U.S Treasury issues	$ 28.6	5
Agency issues	25.8	5
State and local obligations	9.9	2
Corporate bonds	219.0	38
Mortgages	151.5	26
Open market paper	25.1	4
Policy loans	54.1	10
Corporate equities	60.2	10
	$574.2	100

Source: Federal Reserve Board, *Flow of Funds Outstanding*, September 1984.

state and local government obligations. A detailed breakdown appears in Exhibit 6.

Private Pension Funds. A greater preference for corporate equities over corporate bonds is seen in private pension funds. These assets constitute 60% of pension fund holdings. Corporate bonds equal about 20% of pension fund assets. Treasury and agency obligations account for another 14% and 5%, respectively, whereas mortgages account for only 1%. A breakdown of these holdings appears in Exhibit 7.

EXHIBIT 5 FIRE AND CASUALTY INSURANCE COMPANY FINANCIAL ASSETS AT YEAR-END 1983 ($ BILLIONS)

Assets	Outstanding	As Portion of Total (%)
U.S Treasury issues	$ 18.3	9
Agency issues	11.7	6
State and local obligations	86.7	42
Corporate bonds	21.6	11
Corporate equities	41.7	20
Trade credit	22.2	11
Mortgages	2.3	1
	$204.5	100

Source: Federal Reserve Board, *Flow of Funds Outstanding,* September 1984.

EXHIBIT 6 STATE AND LOCAL GOVERNMENT EMPLOYEE RETIREMENT FINANCIAL ASSETS AT YEAR END 1983 ($ BILLIONS)

Assets	Outstanding	As Portion of Total (%)
U.S Treasury issues	$ 48.3	16
Agency issues	38.0	13
State and local obligations	2.1	1
Corporate bonds	114.8	38
Equities	81.8	27
Mortgages	14.8	5
	$299.8	100

Source: Federal Reserve Board, *Flow of Funds Outstanding,* September 1984.

EXHIBIT 7 PRIVATE PENSION FUNDS ASSETS AT YEAR-END 1983 ($ BILLIONS)

Assets	Outstanding	As Portion of Total (%)
U.S Treasury issues	$ 49.1	14
Agency issues	20.0	5
Corporate bonds	70.9	20
Mortgages	5.2	1
Corporate equities	215.7	60
	$360.9	100

Source: Federal Reserve Board, *Flow of Funds Outstanding,* September 1984.

INTEREST RATES: THE BALANCING MECHANISM

Our analysis of the supply and demand for funds leads us to the determination of financial flows via some price mechanism. That price mechanism is the level of interest rates. If we assume that both issuers and investors are averse to risk, we can better understand the method by which equilibrium is determined.

CAPITAL CERTAINTY VERSUS INCOME CERTAINTY. The investor faces two types of uncertainty in any investment.

> **Risk of Loss of Capital.** An investor who tries to liquidate a portfolio acquired at lower interest rate levels will incur some loss of capital in doing so.
>
> **Risk of Loss of Income.** In periods of high interest rates the investor has an opportunity to "lock in" high rates of return for long periods of time. Should the maturity of the asset be too short, the investor will find no vehicle available that offers the same high rate of return as that available on the original investment; thus he or she risks a loss of income.

A company that issues a security faces the same risks. Loss of income may result if, in a period of rising interest rates, the company issues a security with a maturity that is too short. The firm will then have to pay too high a rate of return at the time when it wants to issue (roll-over) another debt obligation at maturity. Loss of capital is a risk in an environment of high interest rates, when a company sells an obligation whose maturity is too long, locking the firm into a high-cost obligation, and not permitting it to roll over its debt at lower rates some time down the road. In fact, the only way for the company to take advantage of the low interest rate environment after having issued high-cost debt is to refund that debt (buy back the outstanding obligations) at a considerable premium to the face value. A significant loss of capital would be incurred by a firm that took such action.

THE EQUILIBRATING PROCESS. Having demonstrated that investors and issuers (borrowers) are likely to be at odds, especially because maximizing returns to one group implies maximizing costs to the other, interest rates that will equilibrate these opposing forces will be a function of supply and demand and **interest rate expectations.** If interest rates are generally expected to rise, lenders will wish to keep their funds invested in reasonably short-term securities so that they may be able to reinvest at even higher rates later on. Issuers, by contrast, will want to issue longer-dated securities to insulate themselves from the rising cost of funds. On the other hand, if interest rates were widely expected to fall, the opposite would be true. Investors would seek to lock in high, long-term rates of return, while issuers (borrowers) would prefer to pay even higher rates for short-term funds in anticipation of being able to refund these obligations at lower interest rates when they mature.

There does not seem to be any mechanism that will bring about equilibrium and get the investor and issuer to agree on maturity and price (yield level). Flow of funds analysis suggests that disequilibrium results from either of the following:

1. A change in portfolio preference on the part of investors
2. A change in liability preference on the part of issuers
3. A change in relative wealth

All these imply some imbalance between supply and demand. Equilibrium is achieved when the marginal investor (who has no particular preference) responds to exceptional values (purchases undervalued securities or sells overvalued securities) resulting from the imbalance. For this process to occur, efficient markets must exist that have (1) easy access to information about investor or issuer preferences, (2) well-functioning secondary markets, and (3) reasonably low transactions costs. The broker and dealer community meets these requirements, since both are only transient investors, buying securities with a view to trading them at a profit.

THE FEDERAL RESERVE SYSTEM

In 1908, following the Panic of 1907, Congress created a National Monetary Commission to investigate thoroughly the whole field of banking and currency and to recommend legislation. The fruit of its work was the Federal Reserve Act of 1913, a significant landmark in banking legislation.

The Federal Reserve is the central bank of the United States. It influences the availability of money through a complex system of operations that ultimately determine the level of interest rates.

A current interpretation of the **Federal Reserve Act,** including later amendments, would state the objectives broadly as (1) the establishment of an elastic currency and credit system, (2) the inauguration of a nationwide check collection system, (3) improved bank supervision, (4) aid in government financing, and (5) national credit management to achieve a high level of employment, avoidance of inflation, and economic stability with a sustainable rate of economic growth.

The Federal Reserve System consists of the Board of Governors, 12 Federal Reserve banks with 25 branches, the Federal Open Market Committee, the Federal Advisory Council, and member banks.

1. **The Board of Governors** is composed of seven members appointed by the President and confirmed by the Senate. It is the directing agency of the system. Members are appointed for 14 years, and a term expires every 2 years. One of the seven governors is appointed as chairman. The **Chairman of the Federal Reserve** testifies before the House and Senate Banking Committees at least once a quarter, alternating between the

House and Senate each 3-month period. At these hearings, the Chairman identifies **Fed targets** for annual money and credit growth and gives a brief outline of the Fed's views on the economic outlook.

2. **The Federal Reserve banks,** one located in each of the 12 Federal Reserve Districts (Exhibit 8), supervise the member banks in each district. Each bank has its own board of directors and officers headed by a president, but its policies are largely determined by the Board of Governors.
3. **The Federal Open Market Committee:** Most of the Federal Reserve's policies regarding the availability of credit, money supply expansion, and interest rate targets are set by the Federal Reserve's **Open Market Committee** (FOMC), which meets on the third Tuesday of every month. This committee consists of eight permanent members, the Board of Governors and representative of the New York district, and four rotating members from the other districts, serving 2-year terms. House Resolution 133, passed in 1975, requires the Fed to publish up-to-date information on the discussions of its meetings. Minutes of the prior month's meeting are generally made available on the Friday following the FOMC meeting.
4. **The Federal Advisory Council** is composed of 12 members, usually commercial bankers, one elected by the directors of each of the Reserve banks. Its function is purely advisory.
5. **Member banks,** numbering over 5,000, include all national banks and those state banks that apply and are accepted for membership.

The Federal Reserve Act provided 12 regional banks rather than one central bank. This plan reflected the traditional American distrust of centralized financial control and was intended better to serve the diverse regional requirements of the nation. Such decentralization was, however, found to involve serious disadvantages, and the tendency since 1933 has been to increase greatly the authority of the Board of Governors in Washington.

A look at the currency in your pocket will indicate (1) that the currency is an obligation of the Federal Reserve and therefore is called a Federal Reserve note, and (2) the district bank that issued the money is denoted by the letters A through L appearing in the circle on the left of the bill, representing Boston, New York, Philadelphia, Cleveland, Richmond, Atlanta, Chicago, St. Louis, Minneapolis, Kansas City, Dallas, and San Francisco respectively.

THE FED IN OPERATION

The Board of Governors. The chief powers of the Board of Governors of the Federal Reserve System include (1) reviewing discount rates of the Federal Reserve banks, (2) reviewing the decisions of the Federal Open Market Committee, whose membership is numerically dominated by the board in any event: (3) raising or lowering reserve requirements for member banks within a

EXHIBIT 8 BOUNDARIES OF FEDERAL RESERVE DISTRICTS

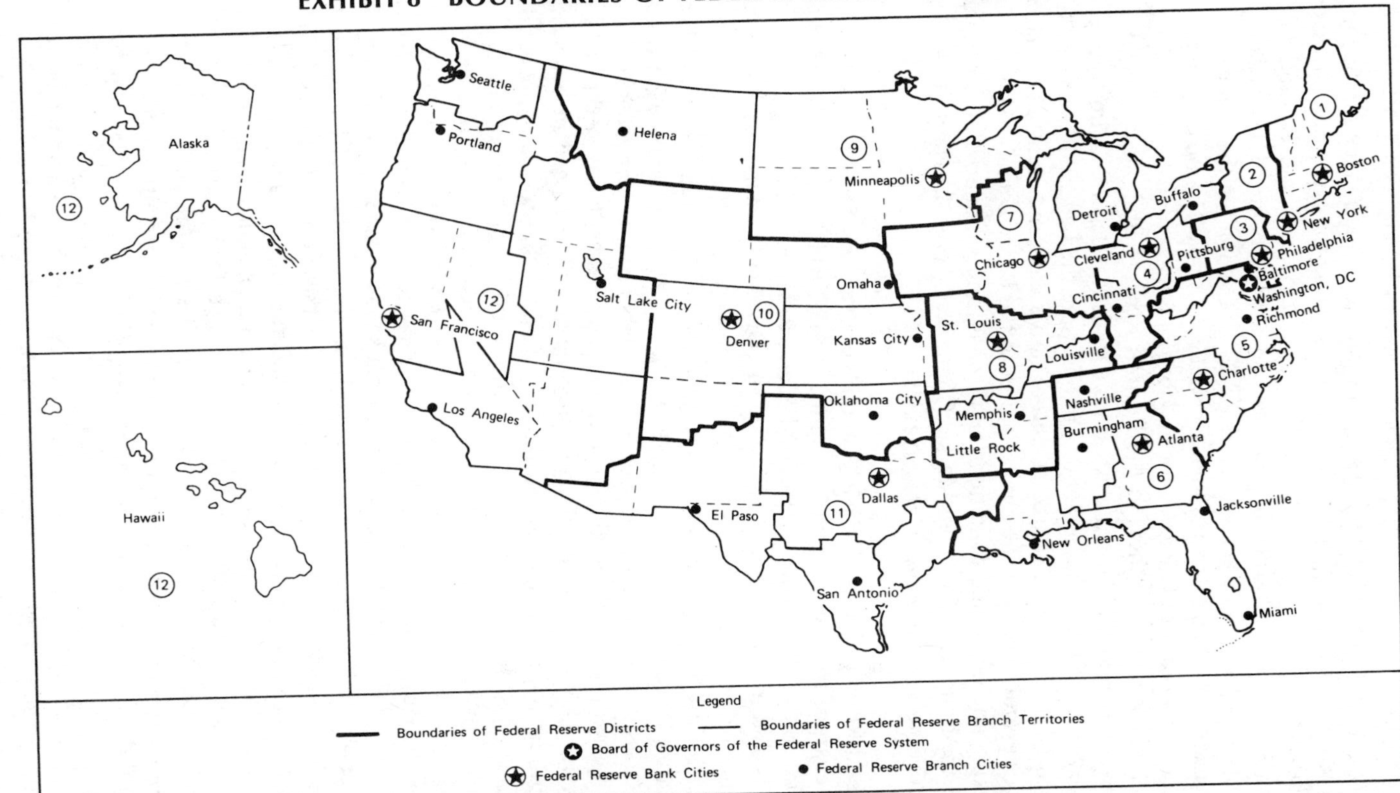

Source: Board of Governors, Federal Reserve Systems, *The Federal Reserve System, Purposes and Functions.*

specified range; (4) setting margin requirements on loans made for the purpose of buying or carrying listed securities; (5) defining the types of securities that member banks may purchase; and (6) fixing maximum interest rates payable by banks on time deposits. In addition, the Board has broad discretionary authority that has been used as a basis for "direct action" in the shape of advice and instruction to banks to influence credit conditions. The Board also presents recommendations to Congress for new banking legislation.

The board has its offices at the Federal Reserve Building in Washington, where it maintains a permanent research, statistical, legal, administrative, and supervisory staff. It issues a monthly publication, the **Federal Reserve Bulletin,** which is an invaluable source of authoritative data and statistics on money, banking, and business. The annual report of the Board contains an analysis of banking and economic conditions and trends, and summarizes the actions of both the Board and the Open Market Committee (**Annual Report of the Board of Governors of the Federal Reserve System**).

Federal Reserve Banks. Each Federal Reserve bank functions under a federal charter. Its stock is held by member banks, which must subscribe 6% of capital and surplus to the stock of its Federal Reserve bank, of which sum only 50% is paid in, the rest being subject to call. Dividends are limited to 6% on the amount paid in.

Each Reserve bank has nine **directors,** three of whom are known as Class A directors, three as Class B, and three as Class C. Member banks elect Class A and Class B directors, one director in each class being chosen by small banks, one by medium-sized banks, and one by large banks. Class A directors are bankers, whereas Class B directors must be actively engaged in business or agriculture but not connected with a bank. Class C directors are appointed by the Federal Reserve Board and may be from within or outside the banking profession. One of the Class C directors is designated as **Federal Reserve Agent,** whose special duty is to provide close liaison with the Board.

The Federal Reserve banks are primarily bankers' banks, and their deposits consist chiefly of the reserves of member banks, maintained as required by law and set by the Fed. They also hold deposits of the Treasury, of foreign central banks, and of nonmember banks whose checks they collect, but none for individuals or business concerns. Operations include note issuance, investment in government securities, lending to member banks, examination and supervision of member banks, collection of checks, and the performance of a variety of essential services for commercial banks and for the government.

Aside from representation on the **Open Market Committee,** the individual Federal Reserve banks have no major responsibility with respect to the formulation of credit policy. At times, nevertheless, their views have been very influential in shaping decisions of the Board of Governors. This primary task is the implementation of credit policies formulated by the Board.

One of the functions of the Federal Reserve banks is to make temporary loans and advances to members banks. Federal Reserve credit is designed to accommodate banks for a short period only, that is, to help them cope with sudden withdrawals of deposits or seasonal requirements beyond those that can reasonably be met from the bank's own resources. To borrow from a Federal Reserve bank, a member bank may either rediscount eligible paper (such as short-term notes obtained by the member bank from commercial, industrial, agricultural, or other business borrowers) or it may issue its own promissory notes secured by eligible paper or government securities. The latter type of member bank borrowings is called advances, as distinguished from discounting. In practice, member bank borrowings are mainly secured by U.S. Treasury securities. The interest charge on either method of borrowing is called the **discount rate.**

The principal means used by the Federal Reserve System to influence the volume of bank reserves is the purchase and sale of U.S. government securities in the open market. By paying for purchases with a credit to member bank reserves, the Fed acts to expand the nation's credit base. Sales by the Federal Reserve, on the other hand, lead to a contraction in member bank reserve accounts as these are charged in payment for the securities sold. In addition, the System makes credit available on occasion to dealers in U.S. government securities through **repurchase agreements.** These agreements represent a pledge by the dealer to repurchase the securities within 15 days or less. To affect credit conditions, the Federal Reserve also buys bankers' acceptances.

During World War II, the Federal Reserve banks made large-scale purchases of U.S. government securities. This led to a tremendous **expansion** of member bank reserves and a vast wartime expansion of bank credit and currency in circulation. The banks' **principal liabilities** consist of Federal Reserve notes in circulation and the reserve balances of commercial banks.

Collection of Checks and Other Services. A very important service performed for the entire commercial banking system by the Federal Reserve banks in the collection of checks drawn on banks throughout the country, deposited in banks located elsewhere than the towns in which the paying banks are located. The volume of checks handled by the Federal Reserve has grown rapidly over the years. All checks collected and cleared through the Federal Reserve must be paid at par—that is, in full without deduction of any exchange charge by the paying bank. This check-clearing service is provided without charge not only for member banks but also for all banks that agree to remit at par. It is fairly certain that the Fed will change its no-fee policy causing banks to incur greater costs, which will probably lead to bank strategies to limit their exposure.

Other services of the Federal Reserve banks include the collection of coupons and other items for member banks, transfers of funds between members, the safekeeping of securities for banks, supplying currency to banks, receiving and sorting currency returned from circulation, and the performance of certain tasks for foreign central bank correspondents.

A substantial part of the **personnel** of the Federal Reserve banks is engaged in providing fiscal agency, custodianship, and depositary services for the Treasury and other government departments and agencies. Most of this work is connected with the issuance, exchange, and redemption of government securities and the payment of government checks and coupons.

Issuance of Policy Directives. The FOMC **policy directives** quoted in the following paragraphs was approved by a vote of 9 to 3 at the Committee's meeting of October 2, 1984. It was issued to the Federal Reserve Bank of New York.

> The information reviewed at this meeting suggests that the expansion in economic activity slowed appreciably in the third quarter from a strong pace earlier in the year. In August, industrial production rose only slightly and gains in nonfarm payroll employment moderated further; retail sales and housing starts declined for the second month in a row. The civilian unemployment rate was unchanged in August at 7.5 percent. Information on outlays and spending plans suggests slower expansion in business fixed investment, following exceptionally rapid growth in recent quarters. Since the beginning of the year, average prices and the index of average hourly earnings have risen more slowly than in 1983.
>
> In August the monetary aggregates expanded at relatively slow rates, but data available for September suggested some strengthening. From the fourth quarter of 1983 through September, M1 apparently grew at a rate close to the midpoint of the Committee's range for 1984, M2 at a rate somewhat below the midpoint of its longer-run range, and M3 at a rate near the upper limit of its range. Growth in total domestic nonfinancial debt appears to be continuing at a pace above the Committee's monitoring range for the year, reflecting large government borrowing along with relatively strong private credit growth. Interest rates generally have fallen somewhat further since the August meeting of the Committee.
>
> Over the past month, the foreign exchange value of the dollar against a trade-weighted average of major foreign currencies has fluctuated widely under often volatile market conditions, reaching a new high in the latter part of September; since then the dollar has declined somewhat. The merchandise trade deficit rose sharply to a record high rate in the July–August period.
>
> The Federal Open Market Committee seeks to foster monetary and financial conditions that will help to reduce inflation further, promote growth in output on a sustainable basis, and contribute to an improved pattern of international transactions. In furtherance of these objectives the Committee agreed at the July meeting to reaffirm the ranges for monetary growth that it had established in January: 4 to 8 percent for M1 and 6 to 9 percent for both M2 and M3 for the period from the fourth quarter of 1983 to the fourth quarter of 1984. The associated range for total domestic nonfinancial debt was also reaffirmed at 8 to 11 percent for the year 1984. It was anticipated that M3 and nonfinancial debt might increase at rates somewhat above the upper limits of their 1984 ranges, given developments in the first half of the year, but the Committee felt that higher target ranges would provide inappropriate benchmarks for evaluating longer-term trends in M3 and credit growth. For 1985 the Committee agreed on tentative ranges of monetary growth, measured from the fourth quarter of 1984 to the fourth quarter of 1985, of 4 to 7 percent for M1, 6 to 8½ percent for M2, and 6 to 9 percent for M3. The associated range for nonfinancial debt was set at 8 to 11 percent.
>
> The Committee understood that policy implementation would require contin-

uing appraisal of the relationships not only among the various measures of money and credit but also between those aggregates and nominal GNP, including evaluation of conditions in domestic credit and foreign exchange markets.

In the implementation of policy in the short run, the Committee seeks to maintain the lesser degree of restraint on reserve positions sought in recent weeks. This action is expected to be consistent with growth in M1, M2, and M3 at annual rates of around 6, 7½, and 9 percent, respectively, during the period from September to December. A somewhat further lessening of restraint on reserve positions would be acceptable in the event of significantly slower growth in the monetary aggregates, evaluated in relation to the strength of business expansion and inflationary pressures, domestic and international financial market conditions, and the rate of credit growth. Conversely, greater restraint might be acceptable in the event of substantially more rapid monetary growth and indications of significant strengthening of economic activity and inflationary pressures. The Chairman may call for Committee consultation if it appears to the Manager for Domestic Operations that pursuit of the monetary objectives and related reserve paths during the period before the next meeting is likely to be associated with a federal funds rate persistently outside a range of 8 to 12 percent.

Votes for this action: Messrs. Volcker, Solomon, Boehne, Boykin, Corrigan, Gramley, Mrs. Horn, Messrs. Partee, and Wallich. Votes against this action: Messrs. Martin, Rice, and Ms. Seger.

Messrs. Martin, Rice, and Ms. Seger dissented from this action because they preferred a directive calling for a somewhat lesser degree of reserve restraint and marginally faster monetary growth in the fourth quarter. In their view some additional easing of reserve positions would be appropriate given the reduction in monetary growth over the third quarter and indications of further slowing in the rate of economic expansion. Somewhat lesser restraint would not incur a significant risk of stimulating inflation and would also be desirable in light of current conditions in domestic and international financial markets. Martin in particular expressed concern about strains now being experienced by some financial institutions.

TOOLS OF THE FED. The most frequently used Federal Reserve tool is the purchase and sale of government securities in the open market to affect the overnight cost of money to the banking system (federal funds rate) by expanding or contracting the availability of bank reserves. A sale of securities to the dealer community serves to absorb reserves and puts upward pressure on borrowing costs. A purchase of securities tends to expand the availability of reserves and puts downward pressure on interest rates. This almost daily procedure of buying and selling securities in the market to influence reserves and the cost of funds is called open market operations.

To influence reserve availability on a longer run basis, the Fed may decide to change the **reserve requirement** ratio, lifting the ratio of reserves that banks are required to hold against deposits to curb credit growth, and lowering reserve requiremens to stimulate credit expansion. Since these are more permanent changes, the Fed is likely to make them much less frequently. On average, reserve requirement changes are made about once in 4 years.

Another tool available to the monetary authorities is a change in the **discount rate,** defined earlier as the rate at which banks may borrow reserves from the Fed. These changes are made as often as necessary to keep the rate in line with the banking system's overnight cost of funds. In the period 1976–1985, the Fed changed the discount rate about four or five times a year, on average.

It is important to remember that rates on government securities often determine prevailing **money market rates,** and as such, Federal Reserve actions materially affect the cost of short-term funds for corporations. Whether these funds are raised in the domestic commercial paper market, in the bankers' acceptance market, or even through bank loans, the government funds rate will usually set the floor on other domestic money costs to the corporation.

THE MONEY MARKET AND FEDERAL RESERVE CONTROL

The term **money market** refers to the marketplace where borrowers and lenders exchange short-term funds. Thus, "the" money market does not exist in one unique location. Instead, it is a complex of thousands of locations across the world where purchases and sales of short-term funds take place.

As the most important buyer and seller of short-term money the Federal Reserve influences daily money market conditions through the purchases and sales of securities defined earlier as **open market operations.**

The **New York Fed** is the dominant player of the 12-bank Fed system, conducting open market operations with some three dozen recognized **U.S. Government Securities Dealers.** Thus the New York Fed carries out the FOMC policy directive targeting reserve availability, money growth, and interest rates on Federal funds, which ultimately affect other interest rates.

While the New York Fed very significantly influences money market conditions via **open market operations,** other member banks also play a role in policing the use of member bank borrowings at their discount windows. Indeed, this is one of the few privileges allowed for Fed member banks. They can borrow funds temporarily from the Fed instead of selling money market securities to meet reserve deficiencies.

MONEY MARKET INSTRUMENTS

Federal Funds. The monies that banks buy and sell among themselves to meet reserve requirements against deposits are called federal funds. Fed funds are usually bought and sold overnight, but **term funds** may be purchased for as long as a week. Fed funds are viewed as the most liquid, interest-bearing, near-cash asset.

Repurchase Agreements (RPs). These are effectively collaterlized deposits of corporations. Such corporations cannot buy and sell Fed funds, they have found a way to invest excess short-term funds in interest-bearing assets by temporarily purchasing Treasury securities from an owner (a bank) that agrees to buy these back (repurchase) at a higher price. The difference between the purchase and sale price effectively becomes the interest return earned on these securities. Since these short-term investments are collateralized, they represent the safest interest-bearing, near-cash asset. They often yield a little less than Fed funds. **Term RPs** can be arranged for as long as 3 months and sometimes even longer, though banks are often reluctant to show RPs on the books over quarterly statement periods.

Treasury Bills. The next most liquid short-term investment is in Treasury bills, primarily because there is an active primary market for newly issued bills auctioned each week, as well as an active secondary market for older bill issues. Treasury bills are U.S. government obligations maturing within 12 months. Weekly bill maturities enable sophisticated corporate treasurers to synchronize their bill maturities with expected cash outflows. And in the event of an unexpected need for cash, bills can be liquidated readily with little or no loss of capital.

Bankers' Acceptances (BAs). Orders to pay special amounts at a given time are called bankers' acceptances. These orders are usually liabilities of a firm engaged in international trade, acknowledging an obligation to pay for goods in transit. Banks often finance these instruments, on behalf of their customers under a **letter of credit agreement,** making both the customer and the bank obligated to honor the liability. Thus there is a sense of double protection for the holder of the BA. If either the bank or the customer fails to pay, the paper is backed by the assets of the other.

The Federal Reserve Bank of Richmond (*Instruments of the Money Market*, 1977) provides an excellent description of the underlying BA transaction and acceptance financing:

> A domestic concern wishing to import goods from abroad may request its bank to issue a **letter of credit** on its behalf of the foreign seller. If the bank finds the customer's credit standing satisfactory, it will issue such a letter, authorizing the foreign seller to draw a draft upon it in payment for the goods. Equipped with this authorization, the foreign exporter, on shipping the goods, can discount the draft with his bank, thereby receiving payment immediately. The foreign bank, in turn, forwards the draft together with appropriate shipping documents to its correspondent bank in this country with instructions respecting its disposition. Generally the U.S. correspondent bank will present the draft for acceptance at the drawee bank, which then forwards the shipping documents to the importer, who now may claim the shipment. The correspondent bank may be instructed to hold the acceptance until maturity as an investment for the foreign bank. Or it may be instructed to offer the acceptance for sale in the market and credit the deposit account of the foreign bank. In any event, the ultimate holder of the acceptance is the party actually financing the transaction.
>
> The **accepting bank** may, of course, buy the acceptance which it originated. In such a case, it earns the difference between the purchase price and the face amount which must be reimbursed by the customer on whose behalf the acceptance credit was opened. It also earns the commission charged for the letter of

credit. When the bank follows such a course it is actually financing the transaction, and its position is much the same as when it extends a loan directly to the customer. On the other hand, if some other party buys and holds the acceptance, the originating bank has tied up no funds. It has merely lent the prestige of its name and assumed a contingent liability, for which it collects a small fee.

Commercial Paper. This is another short-term investment vehicle, representing unsecured promissory notes of corporations whose credit rating is so high that their I.O.U.'s are immediately accepted for trading in the money market. Two major categories of commercial paper are available: those issued directly by a corporation (directly placed) and those issued through an underwriter, typically a private insurance company (dealer placed). These are further subdivided into financial and nonfinancial companies. Within the financial category the distinction is made between bank-related and nonbank paper. Since the failure of Penn Central in 1970 left holders of commercial paper with illiquid assets, commercial paper issues now follow an unwritten rule, namely, they maintain bank credit lines as a backup, in case the commercial paper issuer runs into difficulty.

Negotiable Certificates of Deposit (CDs). Uncollateralized bank deposit liabilities of $100,000 or more are negotiable CDs. Banks started issuing CDs in 1961 but these were subject to **Regulation Q** interest rate ceilings imposed by the Securities and Exchange Commission until June 1970. At that time rate ceilings were lifted for shorter dated CDs (under 90 days), and 3 years later rate ceilings on CDs were lifted altogether. Domestic CD volume dropped sharply as market rates ran through the rate ceilings banks were allowed to pay in 1969–1970. Banks substituted **Eurodollar CD** borrowings during this period. Once rate ceilings were lifted, domestic CD volume expanded at the expense of Eurodollar borrowings.

CDs are the least liquid of all the short-term assets, largely because there is no active secondary market in any but the top-name, large-bank CD liabilities. Also, during periods of intense interest rate pressure and robust loan growth, a **tiering** often develops in the marketplace such that smaller banks must pay a rate premium on CD liabilities over and above those paid by the largest, best known banks.

THE CORPORATION AND THE COST OF CAPITAL: SHORT-TERM FUNDING

Financial managers work within the institutional framework outlined earlier and, as such, have little influence on the cost of money. They generally look at two types of funding for their firm's assets: short-term and long-term. **Short-term funds** are available through one of the following sources: (1) **trade credit,** (2) **bank loans,** (3) **commercial paper,** (4) **bankers' acceptances,** and (5) **accounts receivable financing.** Exhibit 9 shows the relative importance of these sources of short-term credit.

EXHIBIT 9 SHORT-TERM LIABILITIES OF NONFINANCIAL CORPORATIONS OUTSTANDING YEAR-END 1983 ($ BILLIONS)

Type	Outstanding	As Portion of Total (%)
Bank loans	$401.9	61
Commercial paper	37.7	6
Bankers' acceptances	9.4	1
Finance company loans	100.5	15
Net trade credit	106.1	16
Profit tax payable	8.2	1
	$663.8	100

Source: Federal Reserve Board, *Flow of Funds Outstanding,* September 1984.

TRADE CREDIT. Trade credit is an asset of the vendor, who ships merchandise or provides services without immediate payment. Trade debt is a liability of the noncash customer buying goods or services on credit. The trade credit figure in Exhibit 9 is a net figure, indicating the difference between trade credit and trade debt. The net figure indicates that trade credit is not as widely used as a short-term funding method compared with the much larger 61% share for bank loans. Companies that extend trade credit rarely use it as a source of funds. Many businesses, however, fund their short-term assets (especially inventories) through the use of trade debt. When the use of gross trade debt rather than net trade credit is compared with that of the other short-term methods, the proportions change markedly, as shown in Exhibit 10.

Although trade debt is the largest source of short-term business credit under this second configuration, it is also the most expensive. Most finance books point out that the annual cost of foregoing trade discounts 2/10 net 30 is 36% + because the corporation really has the use of these funds for 20 days at a rate of 2% for that period.

Nevertheless, cash discounts are widely used first, because by paying later than net 30 days, a company is effectively reducing its annual borrowing cost. For example, if a firm pays in 60 days instead of 30, it has the use of money for 50 days and pays 2% interest for it. On an annualized basis, this is little more than 15%, probably less than the company can expect to pay for finance com-

EXHIBIT 10 SHORT-TERM LIABILITIES OF NONFINANCIAL CORPORATIONS ADJUSTED FOR TRADE DEBT OUTSTANDING AT YEAR-END 1983 ($ BILLIONS)

Bank Loans	Outstanding	As Portion of Total (%)
Bank loans	$401.9	41
Commercial paper	37.7	4
Bankers' acceptances	9.4	1
Finance company loans	100.5	10
Trade debt	427.5	43
Profit tax payable	8.2	1
	$985.2	100

Source: Federal Reserve Board, *Flow of Funds Outstanding,* September 1984.

pany loans and less than the bank prime rate, during much of 1979–1982, a period of historically high interest rates. During tight money periods, small firms are likely to have little choice but to make extensive use of trade credit because money is not available elsewhere at any price. If a business is to continue to function, it must pay the high rates to get the merchandise it needs so that production may continue uninterrupted.

BANK LOANS. Bank loans also play an important role in determining the availability of short-term financing for the corporation. Bank loans are generally tied to the prime lending rate, the rate banks charge their most favored borrowers. The amount in excess of the prime rate that is charged to less favored borrowers depends on the interest rate climate. When interest rates are generally low, banks allow almost all borrowers to borrow at the prime rate. Sometimes banks are so anxious to lend that they make loans below prime, that is, below the officially posted price for money. Another approach banks use to stimulate demand for funds when interest rates are low is to make **fixed rate loans** lasting 5 to 7 years, at something over prime, allowing companies to protect themselves from an anticipated rise in interest rates before maturity. Another approach is to offer corporations **floating rate loans** with a ceiling on interest rates. These loans are often called **"cap loans,"** referring to the interest rate lid. A third approach that became popular in 1983–1984 is the use of interest rate swaps.

To qualify for bank credit, not only does a company have to pass certain credit checks, but it usually has to pay a fee for a standby line of credit the bank makes available to it. In addition, when the firm borrows the bank funds, it must keep some percentage of these borrowings on deposit with the bank as a compensating balance. Compensating balance arrangements require either a minimum level of funds kept in the account at all times, or some average balance of funds kept on hand over the period. The latter approach is certainly more lenient, allowing the corporate borrowers to let their bank balance go through much wider swings than would be permitted if an absolute minimum balance were required. The prime rate is usually set by adding on to the commercial paper rate. At Citibank, New York's largest commercial bank, the prime formula calls for 1½% over the 3-week average of the bank's 90-day CD rate.

COMMERCIAL PAPER. Commercial paper is an unsecured promissory note of a corporation, generally used to fund self-liquidating short-term assets, such as inventory. Most commercial paper is issued by financial corporations, such as finance companies, with the proceeds being used to fund short-term and intermediate-term assets such as consumer loans. In the second quarter of 1985 the volume of commercial paper outstanding was $252 billion, of which only $74 billion was issued by nonfinancial corporations.

Because it is unsecured, commercial paper is generally issued only by the largest corporations, such as General Motors, Ford Motor Co., General Electric, and Sears Roebuck. In addition, commercial paper issuers often have **bank**

lines to **"back up"** these obligations, to be used to pay the holder of the commercial paper if for some reason the issuer cannot meet the outstanding obligations.

BANKERS' ACCEPTANCES. Bankers' acceptances (BAs) are generally used to finance international trade. As such, they constitute little more than bank loans for international transactions, with the underlying merchandise serving as collateral. Many banks count BAs into their commercial and industrial loan totals, but others break out this category to show international lending explicitly.

FINANCE COMPANY LOANS. This source of funds is important in the funding of business equipment. As the third largest source of corporate short-term funds, finance companies serve an important function. Most of the loans made by this group are usually to corporations that have limited ability to borrow at banks and no access at all to the commercial paper market. The same companies that rely on this source of financing are also likely to use trade credit heavily. As pointed out earlier, finance company loans and trade credit are the most expensive sources of short-term funds available to a corporation.

PROFIT TAX PAYABLE. Although often overlooked, this can be an important source of funds to businesses, especially in periods of rising profits. Companies have the option of paying taxes on profits as they are earned or paying them at the same rate as last year, making up the shortfall the following March 15th or June 15th. Thus if a company experiences an improving profit situation, it can decide to pay taxes at quarterly estimates equal to those of its lower payment schedule a year earlier.

THE CORPORATION'S LONG-TERM COST OF CAPITAL

Financial managers often attempt to match the maturity of their company's liabilities with those of its assets. They are reluctant to fund long-term assets with short-term funds for more than a temporary period. Although it is not unusual for a new plant to be funded with a construction loan (a short-term bank loan), some form of long-tgerm financing is usually sought.

Long-term financing generally falls into one of three categories. A popular source of long-term financing is corporate bonds. Three out of every five dollars of long-term corporate debt obligations are in corporate bonds, totaling $421.7 billion at the end of 1983.

Corporate bonds are classified according to **risk** categories primarily by two popular rating services, Moody's and Standard & Poor's. The ratings appear in Exhibit 11. The top four ratings are generally considered to be "investment grade" securities, those that are eligible for investment by institutional investors such as insurance companies, pension funds, and state and local govern-

EXHIBIT 11 BOND RATINGS FOR CORPORATE DEBT SECURITIES

Moody's	Standard & Poor's
Aaa	AAA
A	AA
A	A
Baa	BBB
Ba	BB
B	B
C	CCC
	CC
D	C

Source: Moody's Manual and Standard & Poor's Corp., both New York City.

ment retirement funds. Securities rated below investment grade are deemed to be too risky for investment by institutional investors with a fiduciary responsibility to their clients. Exhibit 12 shows the breakdown of long-term corporate debt financing as of December 1983.

In fact, commercial mortgages provided 5% of corporate long-term debt requirements at year-end 1983. When multifamily and single-family mortgages are added to the totals, mortgage-related debt provide 13% of the corporation's long-term source of borrowed funds.

With the passage of so much environmental legislation, a new source of funds was made available to the corporation, **pollution control revenue bonds.** These bonds are issued by state and local governments on behalf of a company to finance pollution control projects. Interest and principal are secured by the corporation, with the corporation getting a break on the cost of funds, since tax-exempt funds can generally be borrowed at a lower rate than taxable funds for similar risk and maturity. Tax-exempt bonds represented some 15% of long-term corporate debt at the end of 1983.

EXHIBIT 12 LONG-TERM LIABILITIES OUTSTANDING FOR NONFINANCIAL CORPORATIONS AT YEAR-END 1983 ($ BILLIONS)

Type	Outstanding	As Portion of Total (%)
Corporate bonds	$421.7	72
Mortgages		
Home mortgages	7.2	1
Multifamily	41.6	7
Commercial	30.9	5
Tax-Exempt Bonds	83.9	15
	$585.3	100

Source: Federal Reserve Bond, *Flow of Funds Outstanding,* September 1984.

THE CYCLICAL PATTERN OF INTEREST RATES

Interest rates, or the price of money, are determined by the same factors that influence prices of other commodities, namely, the supply and demand for funds. In turn, supply and demand are a function of the borrowing and lending (investing) needs of money and capital market participants. These needs are volatile, fluctuating with the ups and downs of business activity. To some extent interest rates lag behind the economic cycle, peaking after the peak in business activity and bottoming out after the economy has turned upward (see Exhibits 13 and 14). Interest rates are therefore viewed as a lagging economic indicator. For example, note in Exhibit 14 that the Federal funds rate, the Treasury bill rate, the corporate bond rate, and municipal bond yields all

EXHIBIT 13 CYCLICAL INDICATORS BY ECONOMIC PROCESS: MONEY AND CREDIT

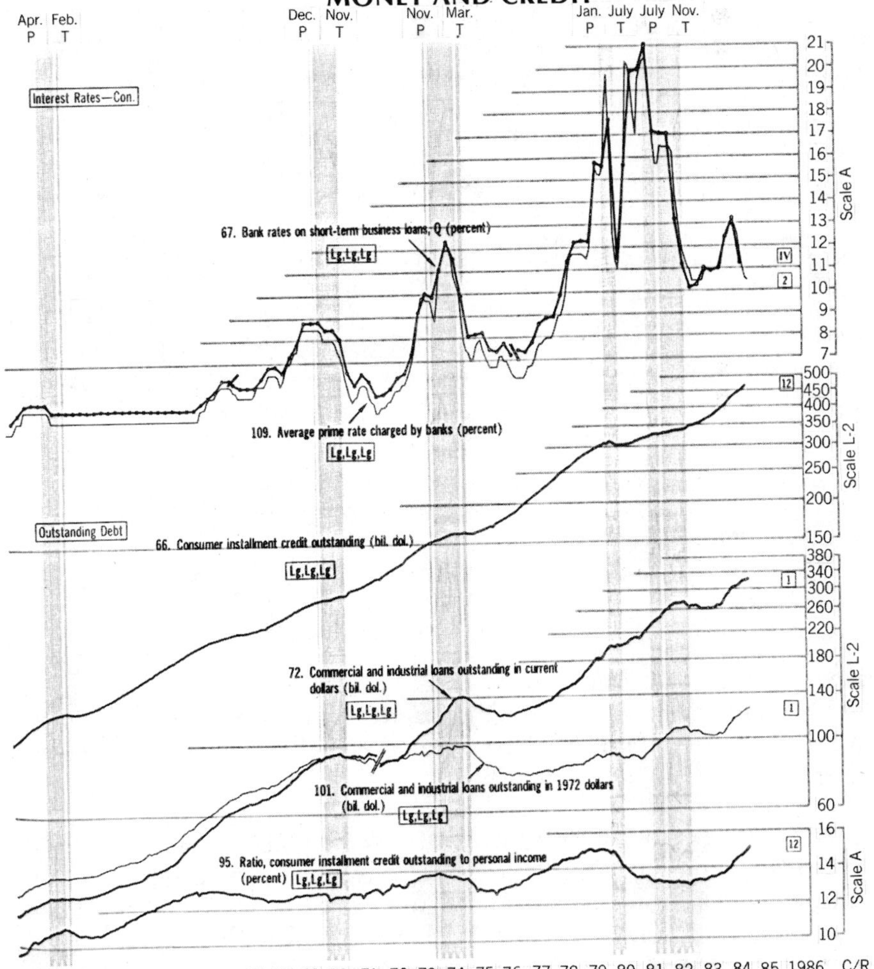

EXHIBIT 14 YIELDS ON VARIOUS OUTSTANDING DEBT OBLIGATIONS

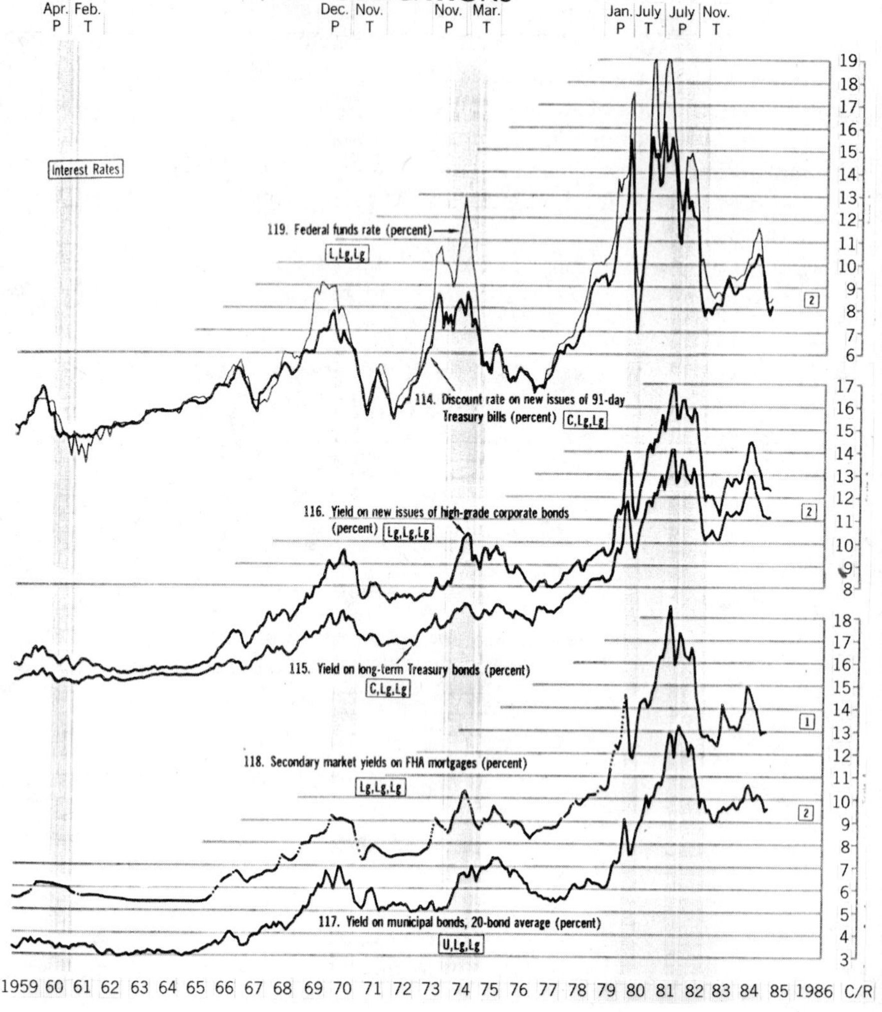

peaked several months after the business cycle turned into a recession in 1970–1971 and again in 1973–1974. The interest rate-economic cycle relationship continued in this fashion during the brief 1979–1980 recession, as well as in the prolonged 1981–1983 contraction.

THE YIELD CURVE: RELATIONSHIPS BETWEEN YIELDS AND TERM TO MATURITY. Over the interest rate cycle, the relationship between yield and term to maturity changes. Early in the interest rate cycle, short-term credit demands are generally sluggish, whereas long-term credit demands that had gone unsatisfied during the preceding interest rate period linger on. These relative pressures result from a desire on the part of borrowers to extend maturities of their liabilities, using the proceeds of long-term debt to repay short-term borrowings. One consequence of the corporation's repayment of bank loans is to put downward pressure on short-term interest rates, while the robust volume of long-term debt offerings keeps long-term interest rates from dropping. The resulting shape of the yield curve is an upward sloping line (March 15, 1977 in Exhibit 15).

As business activity picks up, accompanied by rising demands for short-term credit (as more money needs to be invested in working capital), short-term rates experience upward pressure. Long-term rates during this phase of the cycle also move higher but not nearly as much as short-term rates do. The resulting yield curve assumes a flat shape (November 15, 1977, Exhibit 15).

During the latter stages of the interest rate cycle, upward pressure on short-term rates increases. Both long- and short-term rates rise rapidly, with the upward movement short-term far outstripping the rise in long-term rates. This leaves the yield curve with a downward sloping shape, indicating borrowers' reluctance to lock in high-cost, long-term liabilities and their desire to fund long-term projects with short-term funds. Other borrowers may be locked out of the long-term market altogether, as the threat of economic slowdown or re-

EXHIBIT 15 YIELDS ON U.S. GOVERNMENT SECURITIES

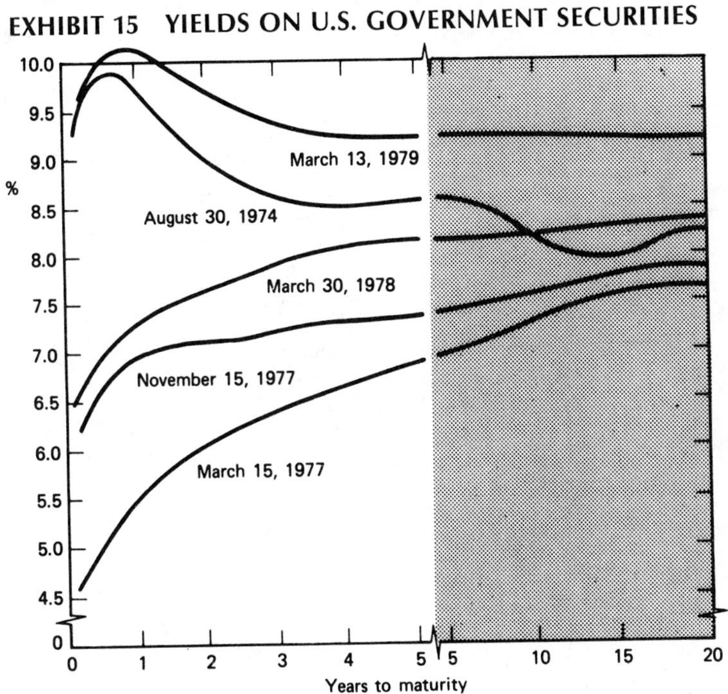

Source: Federal Reserve Bank of St. Louis.

cession makes lenders increasingly **quality conscious.** Only after the economy has peaked, and inventories begin to be worked off do short-term interest rates begin to fall.

QUALITY CONSIDERATIONS. Interest rate movement over the business cycle differs according to quality and maturity. Bond yields on low quality securities tend to increase more than yields on high quality securities, as the growing prospects of recession and business failure make investors increasingly quality conscious. The move to quality may work to shut out some would-be borrowers from the market altogether, even those who are willing to pay high rates for long-term funds. Consequently, yield spreads between low-quality bonds and U.S. Treasury and agency securities are typically at their widest at interest rate cycle peaks and at their narrowest at interest rate cycle troughs.

INFLATION AND REAL RATES OF INTEREST. Nominal bond yields move up and down with **inflationary expectations.** Real (inflation-adjusted) bond yields move up and down with expectations of business activities. That is, real rates of return are highest when business prospects are brightest and fall as the business outlook gets gloomier.

Exhibits 16 and 17 illustrate these relationships. Exhibit 16 shows bond

EXHIBIT 16 NOMINAL BOND YIELDS (20 YEAR TREASURIES) AND AN 18 MONTH MOVING AVERAGE OF INFLATION (CPI)

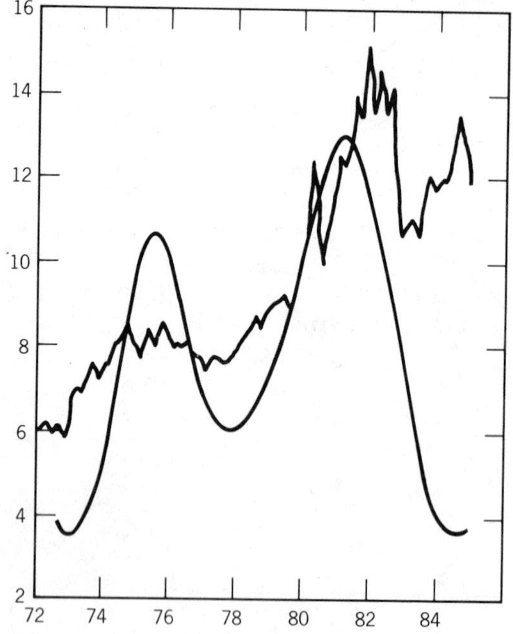

Source: Bureau of Labor Statistics data on inflation and Federal Reserve data on nominal bond yields.

EXHIBIT 17 REAL INTEREST RATES

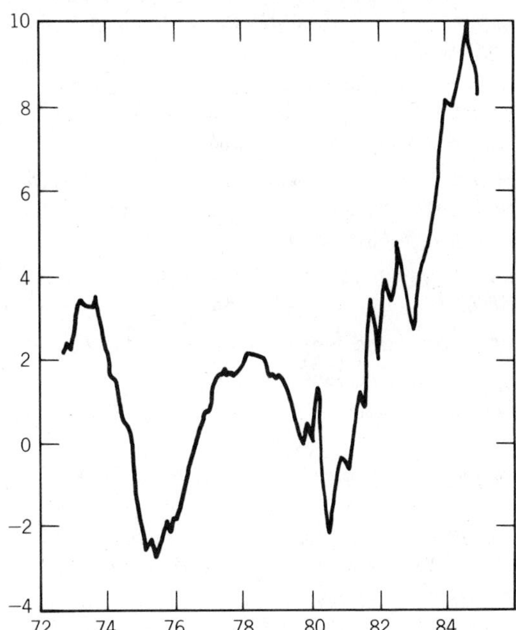

Source: Bureau of Labor Statistics data on inflation and Federal Reserve data on nominal bond yields.

yields fluctuating with inflation. To estimate inflationary expectations, we use an 18-month moving average of consumer prices, because a year-and-a-half time horizon typically determines an executive's expectations. Late in 1978, for example, business executives estimated future inflation at about 8%. A year later, after having experienced double-digit rates of inflation for most of that period, they raised the moving average to 10½%. Consequently, forecasts for future inflation were raised 2 to 3 percentage points.

Meanwhile, the business outlook progressively worsened over 1979, in part because of the accelerating rates of inflation. Consequently, real rates of return (Exhibit 17) fell sharply throughout the year. This is similar to 1973–1974 experience, when real rates of return fell 7 percentage points, from +4% to −3%. Thus the real cost is so low that long-term money is not as unattractive as high nominal rates of interest alone would indicate. In this environment, corporate treasurers are more concerned with the availability of money than with its price (yield).

BIBLIOGRAPHY

Anderson, Carl G., Jr., "Farm Debt: A Problem for Some," *Federal Reserve Bank of Dallas Review,* June 1977, pp. 10–14.

Bench, Joseph, *Money Markets,* a First Pennsylvania Report, selected issues 1975–1980.

Bench, Joseph, *Interest Rate Futures,* a Shearson/American Express weekly report, selected issues 1981–1985.

Bowsher, Norman N., "Repurchase Agreements," *Federal Reserve Bank of St. Louis Review,* September 1979.

Budget of the U.S. Government, Fiscal Year 1980, 1981, 1985.

Burns, Arthur F., *Reflections of an Economic Policymaker: Speeches and Congressional Statements: 1969–1978,* American Enterprise Institute, Washington, D.C., 1978.

Business Conditions Digest, February 1985.

Controlling Monetary Aggregates, Federal Reserve Bank of Boston (June 1979).

Economic Report of the President, January 1979.

Economic Report of the President, January 1980.

Economic Report of the President, January 1985.

Federal Reserve Chart Book, Board of Governors of the Federal Reserve System, February 1984.

Federal Reserve Readings on Inflation, Federal Reserve Bank of New York, February 1979.

Flow of Funds Accounts, Assets and Liabilities Outstanding, 1960–83, Board of Governors of the Federal Reserve System, September 1984.

Flow of Funds Accounts, IV Q 1984 and Annual Revisions, Board of Governors of the Federal Reserve System, March 1985.

Instruments of the Money Market, Federal Reserve Bank of Richmond, 1977.

Lombra, Raymond E., "Reflections on Burns's Reflections," *Journal of Money Credit & Banking,* February 1980, pp. 94–105.

Van Horne, James C., *Function and Analysis of Capital Market Rates,* Prentice-Hall, Englewood Cliffs, NJ, 1970.

3

U.S. GOVERNMENT DEBT OBLIGATIONS: FINANCIAL DEREGULATION AND THE PROLIFERATION OF INTEREST RATE HEDGE PRODUCTS

CONTENTS

3

U.S. GOVERNMENT DEBT OBLIGATIONS: FINANCIAL DEREGULATION AND THE PROLIFERATION OF INTEREST RATE HEDGE PRODUCTS

Joseph Bench

THE NATIONAL DEBT

EVOLUTION OF THE DEBT. Except for a few years during the years during the early 1830s, the United States has never been out of debt. War and slumps in economic activity breed public debt. In 1791 the national debt was about $75 million. The War of 1812 raised the debt to $109 million, and the Civil War left a legacy of $2,776 million (including greenbacks) of indebtedness. By 1913 the debt had been reduced to less than $1 billion, but during World War I it soared above $26 billion. By 1929, the debt had been whittled down to $16 billion (Exhibit 1). During the ensuing decade the debt increased substantially for the first time without a war because of large Treasury expenditures for recovery and relief. Then came the tremendous debt expansion of World War II, from $48 billion at the time of the fall of France in 1940 to $279 billion early in 1946. By the end of 1948 the debt had been reduced to $253 billion, which was also the low point in the post-World War II period. The growth in the public national debt to $257 billion by the end of 1962 was largely due to the Korean War, Treasury deficits during several recessions, and large military and foreign aid commitments. Gross federal debt grew 20% from 1962 to the end of 1969. Of the $367 billion outstanding, $280 billion was publicly held. Gross federal debt expanded even more rapidly in the 1970s. The combination of the Vietnam War and the worst recession since the depression left the debt at $650 billion by

EXHIBIT 1 PUBLIC AND PRIVATE DEBT

	1929	1945	1962	1979	1983
National debt	$16	$253	$257	$664	$1178
State and local government debt	13	14	72	322	485
Long-term corporate debt	47	38	156	339	421
Short-term corporate debt	42	47	175	370	564
Urban real estate mortgages	31	27	211	1242	1710
Farm mortgages	12	7	29	83	110
All other private debt	29	20	101	584	787
Net debt, public and private	$190	$406	$1001	$3604	$5255

Source: Board of Governors of the Federal Reserve System, *Flow of Funds Accounts, Assets and Liabilities Outstanding,* 1960–1983.

the end of the decade. The total public debt, including national, state, and local, approached $1 trillion in 1979. The Treasury debt was projected to rise to $2 trillion, less than a decade later.

INTEREST ON THE DEBT. A large government debt requires the levy of taxes to cover the interest payment on it, thus placing a burden on future generations. Interest on publicly held federal debt jumped sharply in 1979, approaching nearly four times 1969 outlays (see Exhibit 2). In part, this can be

EXHIBIT 2 COMPARISON OF TRENDS IN INTEREST ON FEDERAL DEBT ($ BILLIONS)

			The Public			Interest on Debt Held by Public as % of:	
Fiscal Year	Total	Federal Government Accounts	Total	Federal Reserve System	Other	GNP	Budget Outlays
1969	17.6	3.5	14.1	2.9	11.2	1.56	7.66
1970	20.0	4.4	15.6	3.5	12.2	1.63	7.95
1971	21.6	5.3	16.3	3.7	12.6	1.60	7.73
1972	22.5	5.8	16.6	3.7	12.9	1.50	7.16
1973	24.8	6.3	18.5	4.3	14.2	1.50	7.49
1974	30.0	7.7	22.4	5.5	16.9	1.64	8.29
1975	33.5	8.8	24.7	6.1	18.6	1.69	5.56
1976	37.7	9.0	28.7	6.3	22.5	1.77	7.84
TQ[a]	8.3	.6	7.6	NA	NA	1.78	8.07
1977	42.6	9.6	33.0	6.8	26.2	1.80	8.20
1978	49.3	10.2	39.2	7.3	31.8	1.92	8.68
1979	60.3	12.1	48.3	9.6	38.6	2.05	9.59
1986[b]	155.0	30.5	124.5	16.5	108.0	3.22	12.98

[a]Transition quarter: budget year moved from July 1 to October 1.
[b]Estimated.

Source: Office of Management and Budget, Special Analysis of the Budget of the U.S. Government, Fiscal Year 1986, pp. E-12.

attributed to the rise in interest rates that accompanied the sharp uptrend in consumer prices during the decade. Interest on the debt continued to rise rapidly in the 1980s. By the middle of that decade, interest expense was approaching $155 billion annually, representing about 13% of the federal budget (see Exhibit 2). By the end of the 1984 fiscal year, the Treasury debt was already bumping up against its $1.573 trillion debt ceiling.

TYPES OF OBLIGATIONS. Roughly 20% of the public debt consists of special obligations held by trust account and state and local governments. Foreigners own nearly 17%, whereas savings bonds account for 4%. Almost all the remainder, about 60% of the total, is represented by marketable securities. A tabulation of the debt by types of obligation is published in the *Monthly Statement of the Public Debt of the United States,* and in the *Treasury Bulletin* (Superintendent of Documents, Government Printing Office).

Exhibit 3 shows the privately held interest-bearing public debt as of June 30, 1984. Exhibit 4 gives the breakdown by maturity. Nearly 60% of the debt matures in 2 years.

LENGTH OF DEBT MATURITY. In recent years the Treasury has intensified its efforts to lengthen the maturity of the debt, which had declined substantially in the post-World War II period. In 1946 the average maturity of the marketable debt was 9 years and 1 month. It fell to as low as 2 years and 5 months in January 1976 (Exhibit 5).

One reason for the sharp rise in interest expense is the Treasury's effort to

EXHIBIT 3 PRIVATE HOLDINGS OF TREASURY MARKETABLE DEBT BY MATURITY

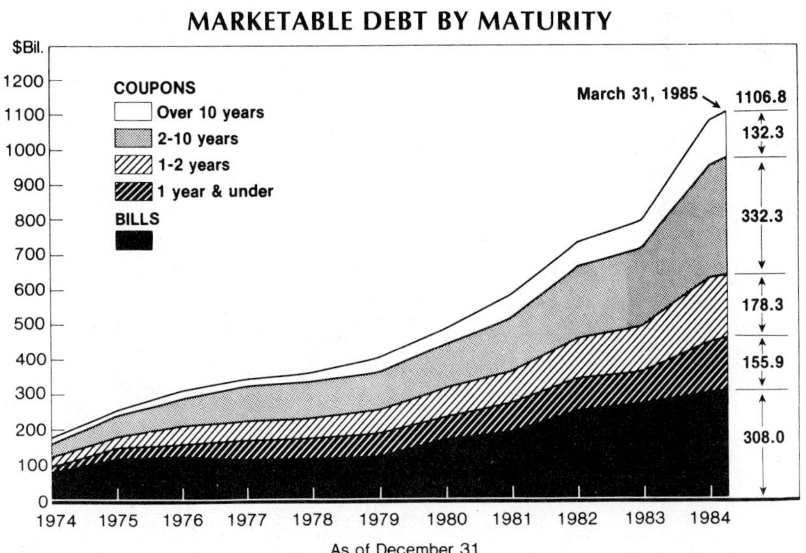

Source: Office of the Secretary of the Treasury, Office of Government Finance & Market Analysis, April 29, 1985.

EXHIBIT 4 PRIVATE HOLDINGS OF TREASURY MARKETABLE DEBT BY MATURITY

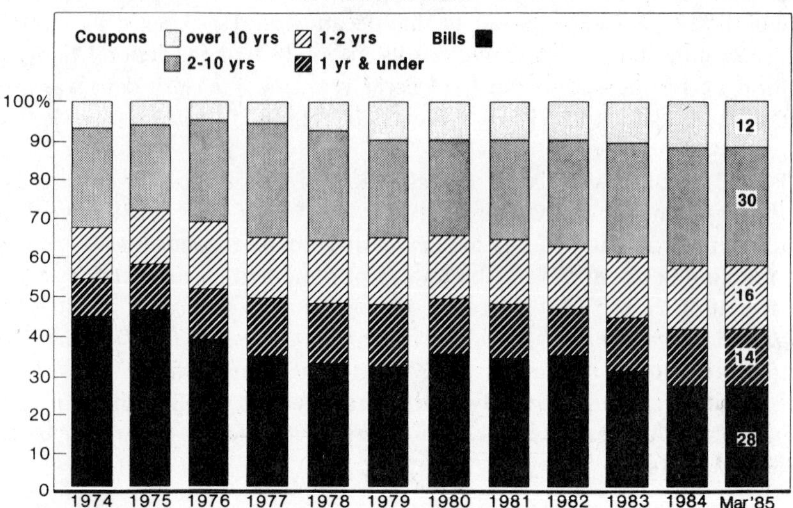

Source: Office of the Secretary of the Treasury, Office of Government Finance & Market Analysis April 29, 1985.

EXHIBIT 5 AVERAGE LENGTH OF THE MARKETABLE DEBT (PRIVATELY HELD)

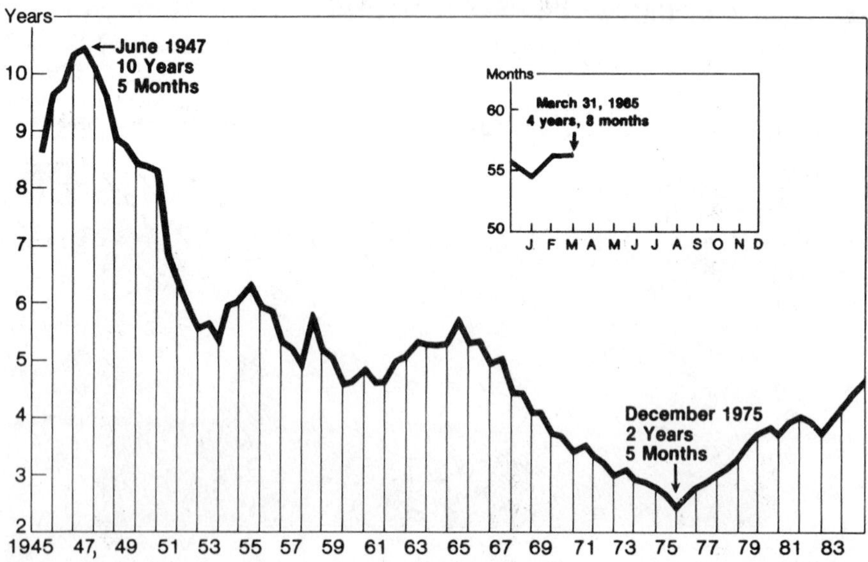

Source: Office of the Secretary of the Treasury and Office of Government Finance and Market Analysis, April 29, 1985.

lengthen the average maturity of its debt. This lengthening was accomplished by increasing the maximum maturity of Treasury notes not subject to interest rate ceilings, from 5 to 7 years (1967) and then from 7 to 10 years (1976). Another avenue of debt extension involved relaxing the $10 billion limit for bonds issued at rates about 4½%, which enabled the government to float debt more easily when interest rates rose so rapidly in the late 1970s.

Exhibit 6 shows the rise in Treasury borrowing in recent years, whereas Exhibit 7 shows the accompanying rise in size and frequency of Treasury debt offerings.

THE BORROWING CYCLE. Another by-product of the relaxation of restrictions on interest, volume, and maturity cited above is the **regularization** of Treasury debt offerings. The maturity, **frequency** of issuance, and size are illustrated in Exhibit 7.

OWNERSHIP OF THE DEBT. A growing share of the Treasury debt is held by nonbank financial institutions (see Exhibit 8). During the 1970s, increasd reliance and emphasis on purchased funds' liabilities enabled financial institutions to add both loans and investments near interest rate peaks. This is in sharp contrast with the earlier practice of liquidating investment assets to make room for loans.

EXHIBIT 6 TREASURY NET MARKET BORROWING[a]

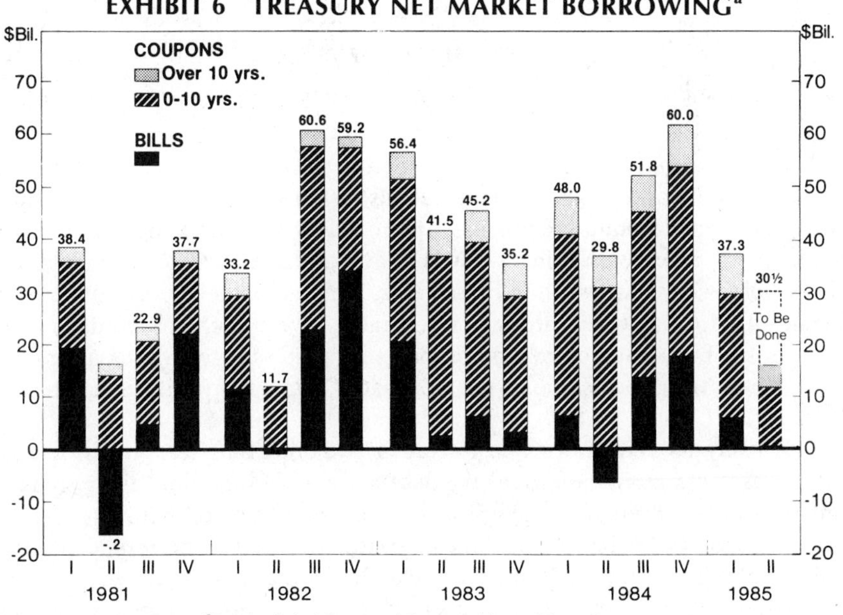

Source: Office of the Secretary of the Treasury, Office of Government Finance & Market Analysis, April 29, 1985.

EXHIBIT 7 TREASURY DEBT OFFERINGS

Type and Maturity	Approximate Size ($ Billions)	Approximate Frequency of Offering
3-Month bills	7.0	Weekly
6-Month bills	7.0	Weekly
1-Year bills	9.0	Every 4 weeks
2-Year notes	9.75	Monthly
3-Year notes	9.0	Quarterly—at midquarter refunding
4-Year notes	7.0	Quarterly—at end of quarter
5-Year notes	7.5	Quarterly—beginning last month of quarter
7-Year notes	6.75	Quarterly—at end of quarter
10-Year notes	9.0	Quarterly—at midquarter refunding
30-Year bonds	9.0	Quarterly—at midquarter refunding

Source: Department of Treasury, *Quarterly Refunding Announcements.*

EXHIBIT 8 DISTRIBUTION (%) OF OWNERSHIP OF MARKETABLE TREASURY SECURITIES

Owner	1969	1973	1978	1983
Households	21%	13%	14%	18%
State and local governments	10	9	7	8
Commercial banks	26	22	18	16
Nonbank financial	14	9	14	27
Nonfinancial business	3	2	2	2
Foreign	5	20	26	15
Other	21	25	19	14
Total	$215BLN	$270BLN	$532BLN	$1099BLN

Source: Federal Board of Governors, *Flow of Funds Outstanding.*

Two sectors that have consistently added to their share of Treasury holdings are households and **nonbank financial institutions.** Municipalities that have benefited from revenue growth have periodically increased their holdings of Treasury issues, especially in 1977 and 1978. State and local governments were heavy borrowers as rates fell in those years. Many took the opportunity to issue **advanced refunding bonds** at low interest rates, investing the proceeds in Treasury issues. They often earned more than they paid out, generating an interest arbitrage in the process. Congress eliminated this opportunity in September 1978.

Life insurance companies, pension funds, and other long-term investors have been aggressive buyers of Treasury debt since 1974, doubling their share of Treasury debt ownership in the process. This increased commitment to Treasury instruments can be traced to the **regularity of** federal **long-term debt offerings** during these years, including 10-year, 20-year, and 30-year bonds offered at least once each quarter. It may also reflect the increased emphasis on **high-quality debt** securities that is an outgrowth of laws passed in 1974 and 1975 to protect citizens' retirement incomes (e.g., the **Employee Retirement Income Se-**

curity Act (ERISA) of 1974). Finally, it shows the growing reliance being placed by long-term investors on fixed income markets rather than equities.

CERTAINTY OF PAYMENT. Despite the sharp rise in public and private debt since the 1930s, the obligations of the U.S. government continue to enjoy the highest confidence of investors. With the ownership of the public debt so widely distributed, throughout all segments of the population, **default** would be **inconceivable.** Ever since the credit of the United States was established on a solid foundation under the leadership of Alexander Hamilton, the determination of the American people to honor their obligations has rarely been questioned.

DEBT IN FOREIGN CURRENCIES. The debt is almost entirely internal (i.e., payable in American dollars rather than in gold or foreign currencies). The government never lacks dollars with which to pay. At the end of 1977 only $5.5 billion of the Treasury debt was payable in foreign currencies. The government can obtain funds through a virtually unlimited taxing power, it can borrow funds as needed by virtue of a control over the Federal Reserve System; or, should it so desire, it can print money in any denominations and amounts.

As part of the dollar defense operations announced on November 1, 1978, the Treasury began a program of issuing deutsche mark-, Swiss franc-, and yen-denominated intermediate notes. These have been nicknamed **"Carter bonds"** by the financial community. Only $6 billion worth of "Carter bonds" has been issued. Most of these were deutsche mark-denominated foreign holdings of Treasury securities and could be purchased only by foreign official institutions.

With the elimination of a 30% withholding tax on foreign interest income in the Tax Act of 1984, the Treasury once again embarked on a program to sell its debt directly to foreigners. Foreign holdings of Treasury securities denominated in dollars have nearly tripled over the past decade (see Exhibit 9). Yet, most of these securities are held by foreign official institutions. And while the total has increased, foreign holdings' share, as a percent of total debt, has dropped sharply since 1978.

In actual practice, the Treasury meets most maturing obligations by **reborrowing.** The banking system provides a flexible mechanism for supplying the Treasury with any amount that cannot be borrowed on satisfactory terms from other investors. The lending poower of the banks can be replenished almost indefinitely by means of reserves provided them through **open market operations** by the Federal Reserve banks. If commercial banks should fail to provide all funds required, the Federal Reserve banks would doubtless provide them. The **Treasury** is authorized at present to **borrow directly from the Reserve banks** but only to a limited extent. This has been done as a very temporary expedient, to prevent unsettlement of the money market. Direct borrowing of substantial amounts by a government from its **central bank** is regarded as a long step toward monetary inflation, and it is mentioned here to illustrate the ability of the

EXHIBIT 9 FOREIGN HOLDINGS OF TREASURY SECURITIES

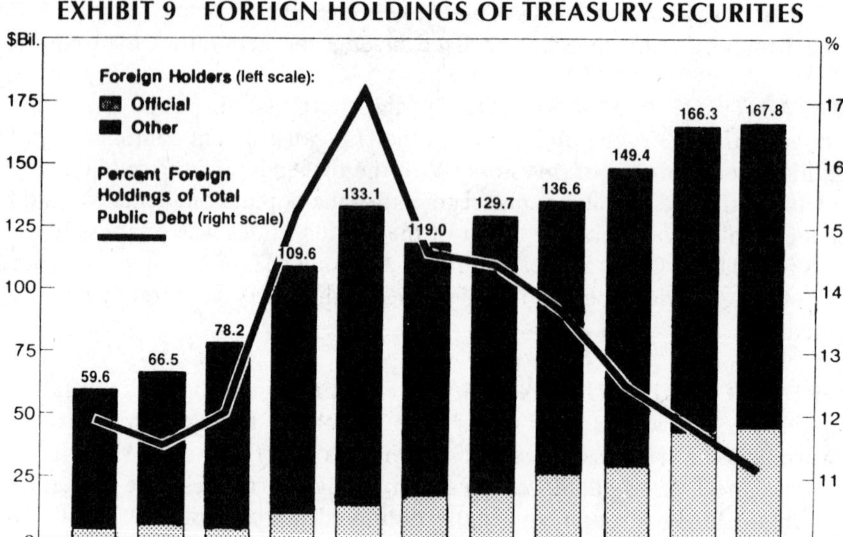

Source: Office of the Secretary of the Treasury, Office of Government Finance & Market Analysis, July 31, 1984.

Treasury under all circumstances to secure funds with which to meet its obligations.

There is no question that all obligations of the U.S. government will be paid promptly and in full as they fall due. This does not mean that the national debt will be paid off; the government can continue indefinitely to meet part of its maturing obligations by reborrowing. In fact, there are those who recommend that the Treasury refund some of its debt by issuing **perpetual obligations** bearing no maturity date, as the British Treasury has done with its "consols."

ZERO COUPON BONDS. In 1982 securities dealers introduced the zero coupon bond. These were created by separating the coupon from the corpus of a bond and trading it on a discounted cash flow basis. "Zeros" are available in all maturity ranges. They pay no current interest, in sharp contrast with coupon bearing securities. However, their interest is imputed by the difference between the discount they sell at today, and the par amount received at maturity. The size of the discount will depend on market yield and term to maturity. That is, the higher the interest rate levels in the bond market, the greater the discount on a zero coupon bond. Also, the longer the term to maturity, the greater the discount. Consequently, when market yields fall, prices of zero coupon bonds are likely to move up more than prices of coupon bearing securities. Should market yields rise, prices of zero coupon bonds would move down more than prices of coupon bearing securities. For example, let's consider two alternative investments in 30-year securities as interest rates move between 12 and 11% over one year (Exhibit 10).

EXHIBIT 10 ALTERNATIVE RETURNS ON $1,000 INVESTMENT[a]

Market Rate	$1,000 Par amount Try 12% 8/15/13	$30,000 Par amount Zero coupon @ 12%	
12%	$1,000.00	30 × $33.38	$1,001.40
@ 11%	$1,086.25	30 × $43.68[b]	$1,310.40
Capital gain (2)-(1)	$ 86.25	Interest rate effect	$ 309.00
Coupon income for one year	$ 120.00	Shorter maturity effect 30 × (48.49[b] 43.68[c])	$ 144.30
	$ 206.25		$ 453.30
Total Return	20.625%		45.27%

[a]A 100 basis point drop in rates increases the value of 12% bonds by 8 5/8 points, whereas zeros increase by 30.9 points *for comparable dollar investments.* Consequently, zeros have about 3 1/2 times the volatility that current coupon long bonds have for *comparable dollar investments.* However, on an absolute basis, a 1% drop in rates will produce about an 8 5/8 point change in the price of 12% Treasuries but only a 1 1/16 point change in the price of a zero. That is, a 1 point rise in the price of 12% Treasury bonds should raise the price of zeros by about 1/8 point.

[b]$48.49 = Present Value of $1,000 @ 11% for 29 Years

[c]$43.68 = Present Value of $1,000 @ 11% for 30 Years

This example illustrates both the strengths and shortcomings of zero coupon investments. Price volatility of zero coupon securities is significantly greater than for current coupon securities; that is, a bonus when rates move down, but a real penalty when rates move up. The bonus stems from the fact that the zero coupon security is priced to reflect discounted cash flows at the current coupon rate. Put in simple terms, a zero automatically reinvests itself at 12% during its entire life. When rates move down, the coupon clipper no longer has 12% available for reinvestment of his or her coupon proceeds, whereas the zero coupon holder has that return already locked in. That is why the zero coupon bond appreciates more, to reflect that higher locked-in return.

When rates move up, however, the zero coupon bond holder cannot take advantage of the higher interest rates available for reinvestment of coupon cash flow (because the coupon is zero). In that case, the "locked-in" effect of zero coupon works against this person.

The strong demand for zeros on the part of pension funds, IRAs, and Keoghs, indicates their preference for locking in a reinvestment rate near 12%, rather than betting on higher rates being available in the future. Alternatively, one can argue that this strategy is a way to maximize short-term gains from any near-term drop in interest rates. However, there is a corresponding greater risk if rates were to move up.

DEALERS IN GOVERNMENT SECURITIES. The great bulk of transactions in government securities is affected by 36 dealers, most of whom have their headquarters in New York City. Larger firms maintain branch offices in principal cities throughout the country.

As the volume of trading in government securities increased after 1932, more and more dealers entered the field. Some represent old firms that formerly engaged in general investment banking or dealt in acceptances; others are new concerns organized primarily to deal in government securities. There are also **"dealer banks,"** commercial banks maintaining special departments to handle government securities business.

The dealer acts as intermediary between those who wish to sell and those who wish to buy securities. The ultimate market for government securities is composed of the several classes of investors described above and dealers who provide the essential mechanism for buying and selling orders from these investors for their own account.

WHAT IS A REPO?

Securities dealers and banks often hold inventories of Treasury bills, notes, and bonds well in excess of their capital. This requires them to borrow to **finance securities inventories.** By using their **securities as collateral,** they attract short-term (often overnight) funds from investors who have a temporary surplus of cash.

Such financing involves the temporary sale of securities by the bank or dealer, with the agreement to buy the securities back at some future date—often the next day, and settled in immediately available federal funds. This buy-back agreement is referred to as RP, or **repo,** referring to the repurchase transaction. The investor is usually willing to earn a return below the federal funds rate, since this overnight funds market is restricted to banks lending to one another. Thus the RP can be viewed as a collateralized deposit on which investors earn interest that otherwise would not be available to them.

Reverse repurchase agreements are the flip side of the RP transaction, or an RP viewed from the lender's perspective. The lender buys the security with the intent to resell it at maturity.

There are many advantages to RP transactions. Not only can corporations and other holders of excess cash earn a market rate of return on a secured basis, but banks have a source of nonreservable short-term deposits, flexible maturities, and no interest rate ceiling. That is in sharp contrast with bank Certificates

EXHIBIT 11 OUTSTANDING RP

Year-End	Amount ($ Billions)
1969	4.3
1973	5.3
1978	36.0
1983	38.1

Source: Federal Reserve Board of Governors, Flow of Funds Accounts Assets and Liabilities Outstanding, 1984.

of Deposit on which banks much maintain reserves, maturities must be at least 30 days, and interest rate ceilings exist for denominations of less than $100,000.

Exhibit 11 documents the growth in the RP market over the past 15 years. Two factors influencing growth in this market are increased attention to cash management on the part of corporate treasurers and the growing volume of Treasury and agency securities in bank portfolios that need to be financed via purchased funds liabilities.

GOVERNMENT SECURITIES

PRICING GOVERNMENT SECURITIES. Government bonds and notes are quoted on a **percentage-of-parity basis.** Fractions are quoted usually in 32nds, sometimes in 64ths. A 32nd is $312.50 per million par amount. Thus a quotation of 100.16 would mean a price of $1,015 for a bond with a par value of $1,000, or $1,015,000 per million of face value.

Treasury bills, by contrast, are quoted on a **discounted basis.** The size of the discount is directly proportional to **yield to maturity.** Thus, a 1-year bill at 12% costs the investor $878,000 per $1,000,000 of maturity. The **coupon equivalent yield** is 13.44%, which is what the investor would earn if he or she were paid the $122,000 interest income on a semiannual basis. The actual return is even greater, namely, 13.9%.

TRANSACTIONS IN GOVERNMENT SECURITIES. Almost always such transactions are at **net prices.** There is no tax involved and dealers rarely charge commissions as such. They obtain compensation for their services in the form of the spread between bid and asked quotations; that is, they buy at the bid price and sell at the asked price, the differential usually amounting to 2/32 of a point, sometimes less. Treasury bills are quoted in yield, with the higher yield bid (implying a greater discount and a lower price) and a lower yield offered. The **value of each 0.01** or **basis point** differs according to term to maturity. A 0.01 for a 3-month bill represents $25/million, on a 6-month bill $50/million, and on a 1-year bill $100/million.

Bonds and notes bear **semiannual interest coupons.** Quotations do not, of course, take into account the amount of interest accrued on the current coupons attached to the securities. This sum must be computed and added to the bill of the buyer. **Accrued interest** on government securities is computed on the basis of the actual number of days in the interest period, not on a uniform 30-day-month basis.

DELIVERY AND PAYMENT OF GOVERNMENT SECURITIES. **Delivery** of securities and **payment** by check are normally made on the first business day following the transaction, Friday transactions being cleared on Monday. Agreement can usually be made with the dealer for **delayed delivery** if the security cannot be delivered on the **"regular delivery"** date. Also, if the seller of securities wishes to be paid in **"federal funds,"** by a check drawn on a Federal

Reserve bank, on the regular delivery date or even on the day of the transaction, this can be arranged with the dealer at the time of the sale.

GOVERNMENT OBLIGATIONS: AGENCY ISSUES

Federal agency obligations generally fall into one of two major categories: borrowing by **government-sponsored** entities and **government-guaranteed** borrowing. Obligations of the first type are now entirely privately owned and are not subject to the federal budget review process, and their debt is not part of gross federal debt.

Exhibits 12 and 13 summarize borrowing by government-sponsored agen-

EXHIBIT 12 BORROWING BY GOVERNMENT-SPONSORED ENTERPRISES ($ MILLIONS)

	Borrowing or Repayment (−)				Debt Outstanding
Description	1983 Actual	1984 Actual	1985 Estimate	1986 Estimate	End 1986 Estimate
Education: Student Loan Marketing Association	1,332	1,774	1,211	1,377	12,586
Housing and Urban Development: Federal National Mortgage Association	19,105	17,934	20,566	20,967	154,544
Farm Credit Administration:[a]					
Banks for cooperatives	316	263	1,147	1,150	10,726
Federal intermediate credit banks	−1,908	−761	455	938	19,588
Federal land banks	451	733	1,232	1,827	50,684
Federal Home Loan Bank Board:					
Federal home loan banks	−9,071	15,633	8,594	6,000	82,000
Federal Home Loan Mortgage Corporation	20,192	13,269	10,291	11,848	96,373
Total	30,416	48,845	43,496	44,107	426,501
Less increase in holdings of debt issued by government-sponsored enterprises	−755	−845	−600	−240	1,241
Total, borrowing by government-sponsored enterprises	31,171	49,690	44,096	44,347	425,260

[a]The debt represented by consolidated notes and bonds is attributed to the respective Farm Credit banks.

EXHIBIT 13 NET NEW MONEY IN AGENCY FINANCE, QUARTERLY

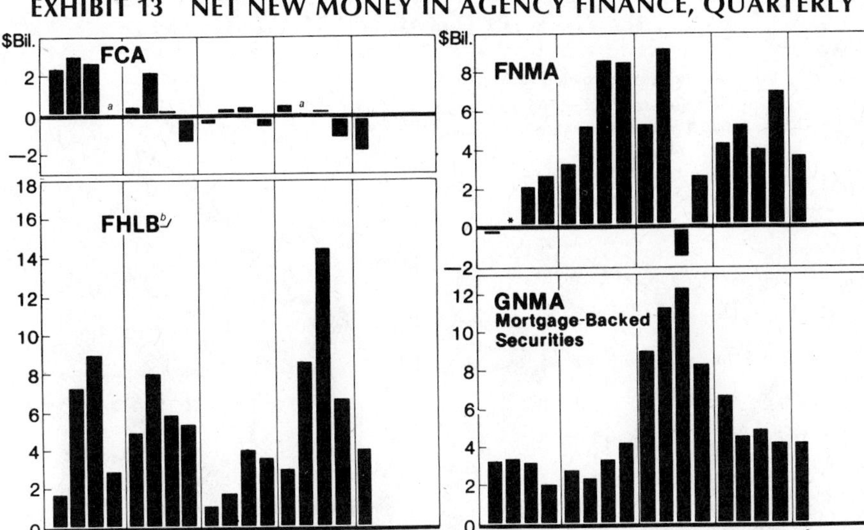

[a]Less than $50 million.
[b]Includes FHLB discount notes, bonds, and FHLMC discount notes, debentures, certificates, mortgage-backed bonds, and mortgage participation certificates.
[c]Partly estimated.
Source: Office of the Secretary of the Treasury, Office of Government Finance & Market Analysis, April 29, 1985.

cies, and Exhibit 12 gives an estimate of debt outstanding at the end of fiscal 1985.

Fluctuations in government-sponsored agency borrowing are largely due to housing-related activity. The **Federal Home Loan Bank** increased **advances** by $12 billion in 1978 and by another $8 billion in 1979 to help savings and loan institutions cope with the slowdown in savings inflows due to high interest rates. The **Federal National Mortgage Association ("Fannie Mae")** and **Federal Home Loan Mortgage Corporation ("Freddy Mac")** increased their purchases of mortgages over that time as well. In 1983, however, the FHLB found savings and loans paying down more than $9 billion in advances.

In summary, federal and federally assisted borrowing has jumped sharply over the past decade (Exhibit 14). During that time, the proportion of government-related credit demands has grown relative to the total. In some periods (such as 1976 and 1983) these public sector capital requirements have effectively "crowded out" some private sector borrowers. Federal debt usually jumps sharply in recession periods, as it did in 1975–1976, and again in 1982–1983. One result is a rise in privately held federal debt in relation to total credit market debt in both periods. At the end of 1983, this ratio had increased to 21.5%, the highest percentage since 1968. Similarly, federal debt as a percent of GNP dropped markedly from 108.4% at the end of World War II, to a low of 25.1% by the end of 1974. A decade later it jumped to 37.2%.

EXHIBIT 14 FEDERAL AND FEDERALLY ASSISTED BORROWING RELATIVE TO TOTAL BORROWING

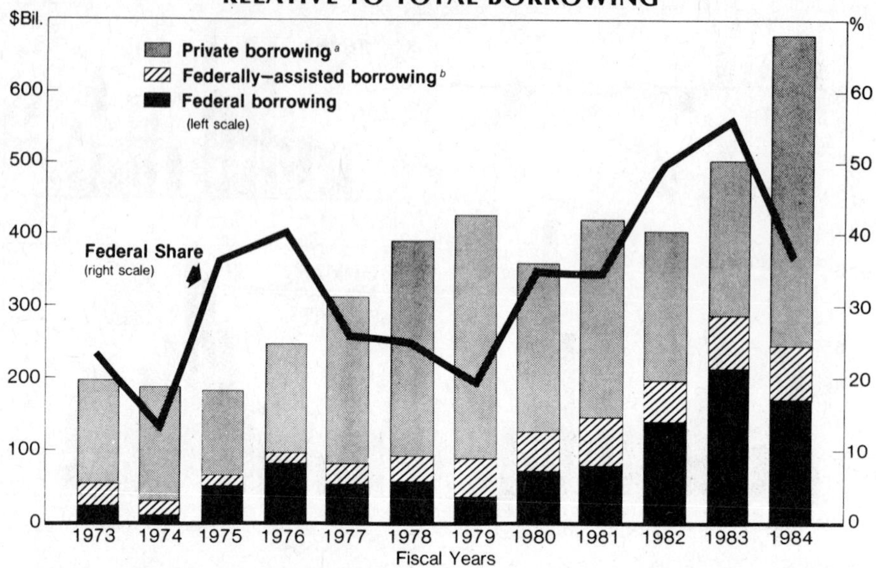

[a]Funds raised by private nonfinancial sectors.
[b]Net sponsored agency and guaranteed borrowing.
Source: Office of the Secretary of the Treasury, Office of Government Finance & Market Analysis, April 29, 1985.

INTEREST RATE FUTURES: THEIR RELATIONSHIP TO CASH MARKETS

GOVERNMENT NATIONAL MORTGAGE ASSOCIATION. In October 1975, **Government National Mortgage Association (GNMA)** interest rate **futures contracts** (also known as Ginnie Maes) were introduced on the **Chicago Board of Trade.** Since then, interest rate futures contracts have proliferated. Expanding markets for interest rate futures instruments now offer some of the best money management opportunities available to the investor or hedger. While some money managers, corporate treasurers and other cash market participants are reluctant to operate in the interest rate futures arena, much of this hesitancy will be overcome once cash market participants simply understand the relationship of the cash money market to the futures market.

Movements in the cash market tend to be less volatile than price changes for corresponding futures markets instruments. The direction of change in futures markets, however, is usually determined by factors directly influencing cash markets. Two of these factors are financing costs and the available supply of securities.

This is especially true for **Treasury bills**—relatively short-maturity instruments whose yields are influenced by their availability and the cost of financing them, namely, repurchase or RP rates. Bill yields rise and fall with RP rates, which, in turn, are influenced by the general availability of eligible collateral (Treasury bills, notes, and bonds) that needs to be financed.

CASH PUSHES FUTURES. Treasury bill futures prices move inversely to yields. Cash prices usually determine futures prices. For example, the nearest contract month (December 1986) will be influenced by the three-month bill; the second contract (March 1987) will be influenced by the six-month bill, whereas the third contract month (June 1987) will be affected by one-year bill, and so on.

When financing costs or RP rates exceed yield levels in the cash Treasury bill market, holders of cash Treasury bills, who must finance them, incur a negative yield (carrying cost). One option they have is to avoid the cash market and buy the futures contract for delivery at a time when financing costs are expected to be lower than Treasury bill yields. Normally, the futures market has already incorporated this negative interest carrying cost into its price by offering futures contracts at a premium to cash. That premium disappears as the contract month nears. The opposite (futures will trade at a discount to cash) holds true when RP rates are below cash market yields. This process is called **convergence** of futures to cash.

Many arbitragers take advantage of these premium and discount anomalies by buying futures and selling cash, or vice versa, as the situation warrants.

Arbitrage strategies between cash and futures have merit only in a stable trend environment, that is, as long as interest rates are clearly moving in one direction. The danger arises when there is a changing perception of where interest rates are heading. Strategy must change as volatility increases.

FUTURES CAN PUSH CASH. At interest rate **turning points,** the **futures market** tends to become the **dominant** market and influences the ultimate course of cash markets as well. The changing leadership role could prove to be a trap for the arbitrager who expects short-run aberrations to correct themselves when they may, in fact, go to even greater extremes. This is especially true for distant contracts that tend to overdramatize anticipated changes in future cash market interest rates.

Cash versus futures market relationships are not limited to Treasury bills. Treasury notes, bonds, and GNMAs are also repurchasable securities.

When RP rates are higher than current yields available on longer term fixed income securities, Treasury bond **futures** generally **trade at a premium** price to cash. When RP rates are below bond yields, **futures contracts trade at a discount** to cash, since the cash holder is earning income that the futures owner is not.

Thus the size of the discount or premium of futures to cash is a function of the positive or interest carrying cost incurred by the cash security holder. The greater the negative carrying cost, the bigger the premium of futures to cash. The greater the positive carrying cost, the bigger the discount.

INTRAMARKET SPREAD TRADES. Because financing cost is known today but only anticipated for the future, the positive or negative carrying cost implied in the current array of interest rate futures prices may be well off the mark, because it is an extrapolation of current market conditions.

Opportunities exist for doing intramarket spread trades if it is assumed that financing costs will change. For example, in fall 1980, the December 1980 nearby Treasury bonds futures contracts were trading at the same prices as those of June 1981 contracts. Yet, financing costs were higher than yields available on Treasury bonds and were not expected to fall anytime soon. This inverted yield curve configuration, with short-term rates above long-term rates, suggests that the June 1981 contract should have been priced at a premium relative to the December 1980 contract. Negative carrying cost resulting from high financing costs for cash market holders dictates the June 1981 contract should trade at a premium to cash. Because financing costs remained high, the sale of the December 1980 contract and simultaneous purchase of the June 1981 contract proved to be a moneymaker.

In September 1981, nearby **GNMA contracts** were trading at a 4-point discount to those one year out. By purchasing GNMAs in the cash market and selling futures a year out, annual returns of 22% could be earned.

TRADING THE YIELD CURVE. One can also develop strategies in anticipation of the changing shape of the Treasury yield curve over the interest rate cycle. Historically, the Treasury yield curve begins the rate cycle with a significant upward sloping shape when short-term rates are well below long-term yields. Then the yield curve flattens and ultimately assumes a downward slope.

As the shape of the yield curve changes while interest rates move up, Treasury bill and note futures can be sold against Treasury bond futures on a ratio basis that provides maximum return and minimum risk. Conversely, one can implement strategies that incorporate the normal maturity extension that takes place as interest rates move down.

INTERMARKET TRADES. Just as opportunities exist for anticipating changes in the Treasury futures market, opportunities also exist between markets. One example is the changing relationship between GNMA futures and Treasury bond futures.

As interest rates move up, GNMAs are a more desirable security than Treasuries. This is because the underlying mortgage-backed security pays principal and interest monthly, thus enabling its owner to reinvest the proceeds at higher yields.

Also, the supply of mortgage-backed securities shrinks as high interest rates make mortgage money scarce. Consequently, the price spread between Treasury bond futures and GNMA futures can be expected to narrow as rates rise. As rates fall, however, GNMAs become less desirable as the reinvestment rate drops and price spreads between GNMA futures and Treasury bond futures widen.

HEDGING AGAINST RISING MMC COSTS. Since their introduction in June 1978, six-month **money market certificates (MMCs)** have taken a growing share of savings deposits at banks and thrift institutions, including savings and loan associations and mutual savings banks. At the end of October 1984, MMCs outstanding equaled $223 billion. In January 1982, **money market deposit accounts (MMDAs)** were introduced. By late 1984, they totaled $387 billion, with more than a third of these deposits at thrift institutions and the remainder at commercial banks.

HEDGING WITH INTEREST RATE FUTURES AND OPTIONS

Interest rates are now a major factor in determining the cost of doing business and the returns on investments. Individuals as well as insititutions are more vulnerable than ever before to high interest rates and high debt service costs. Since interest rate "decontrol" in 1979 we have witnessed the widest interest rate swings, the greatest volatility and escalating federal budget deficits, and the most difficult planning environment since World War II. Rate volatility has been most exaggerated since 1979, as can be seen in Exhibit 15.

MARKET RISK VERSUS BASIS RISK. Using financial futures markets involves distinct risks and costs that should be weighed against the markets' ben-

EXHIBIT 15 THREE MONTH T-BILL AND THREE MONTH CD SPREAD

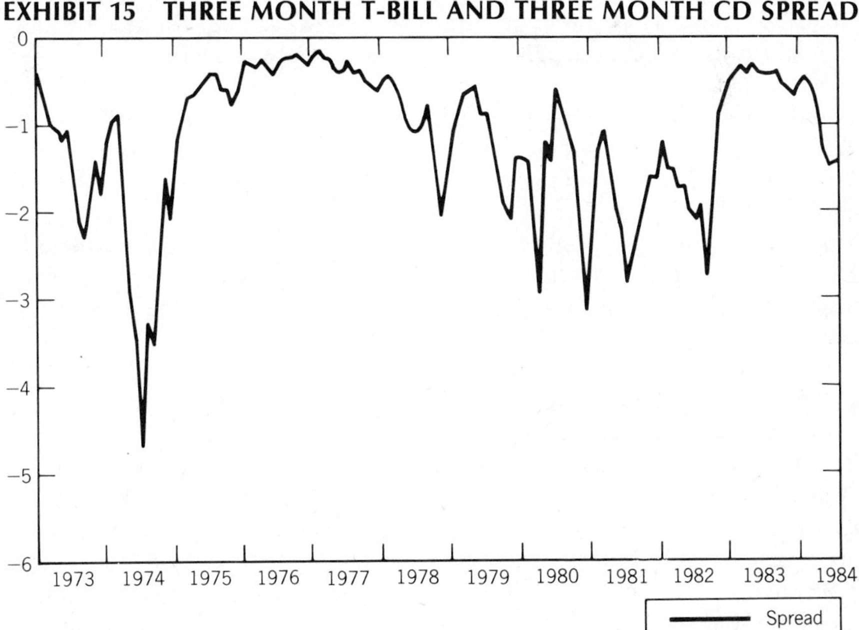

efits. Yet, that exposure is often significantly less than the outright interest rate exposure of an unhedged position, particularly given the degree of rate volatility we've experienced in recent years.

Nonfinancial corporations such as builders and developers use financial futures to hedge against a rise in their borrowing costs. Financial institutions, including banks, thrift institutions, and insurance companies find financial futures can be instrumental in preventing the deterioration of their profit margins.

Numerous financial futures trade on U.S. Exchanges. The most viable and liquid hedging tools are: Treasury Bonds, GNMAs, Treasury Notes, Treasury Bills, Certificates of Deposit (CDs) and Eurodollar time deposits. Eurodollar time deposits and bonds trade on the London International Financial Futures Exchange, as well.

The following section explains how interest rate futures and debt options markets are used to hedge against a rise in borrowing costs, to protect against a deterioration in bond holdings, or to generate incremental income via the judicious use of futures and options markets in asset management activities.

Accessibility. Actively traded, liquid markets allow for speed and ease in implementing market decisions. Large market positions can be achieved at reasonable cost, with initial margin requirements only 1 or 2% of underlying value.

Price protection. Hedging opportunities in futures and options allow fixed-income portfolios to be protected against adverse market fluctuations. Additionally, the purchasing power of future cash inflows can be protected by locking in a specific price, although this long hedge is rare in everyday use.

Speculation. The liquidity, leverage, and volatility of the markets offer the speculator potential for large gains. It is the ongoing speculative activity that allows for broad and liquid markets.

Competitive pricing. Well-integrated futures and options markets provide a centralized source of price information. The "best" price can be attained because contract prices in these markets quickly converge to the competitive level.

LIABILITY HEDGING. The extent of a firm's interest rate exposure will depend on the maturity of its liabilities. Shorter-term liabilities are reset more often and the issuer is consequently exposed at each reset date. Commercial paper issuers typically have more frequent resets, as maturities of the underlying paper tend to be quite short. CDs may be reset once every 30 days or only once a year. MMCs (Money Market Certificates) are reset every 6 months and prime rate loans are reset as often as the prime rate changes. Thus, the term to maturity of the liability being hedged influences the choice of hedging instrument and the hedging method to be applied.

Hedging Short-Term Liabilities. There are three financial contracts suitable for hedging short-term liabilities. These include CDs, Eurodollars, and T-Bills. In selecting the appropriate instrument, the hedger should compare how well each of these contracts correlates with the liability being hedged. Accordingly, the futures contract that correlates best to the cash liability could be sold in order to hedge against rising interest rate costs.

Hedging Medium- and Long-Term Liabilities. Short-term liabilities can be hedged with short-term instruments, such as CD, Eurodollar, and T-Bill futures contracts. Intermediate and long-term liabilities can be hedged simply by stringing together a sequence of short-term hedging programs that will cover the longer time to maturity. One technique is called "strip" hedging, as the hedger sells a "strip" of futures contracts. Another technique is "stack" hedging, where the hedger concentrates his or her sales in either the nearby (front-loaded stack) or deferred (back-loaded stack) contract months. Alternatively, medium-term liabilities can be hedged using T-note, T-bond, or GNMA futures.

Dollar Value of a Basis Point

In determining how to hedge medium-term liabilities with instruments of differing maturity (from 3-month CD futures to 10-year Treasury note and 30-year Treasury bond futures), it is important to first determine the dollar value of a basis point for the liability being hedged, and compare that to the dollar value response of the contract to hedge it. The dollar value of a basis point varies directly with the maturity of the liability being hedged. Consequently, the number of futures contracts used will also depend upon the basis point value relationship between the liability being hedged and the contract used to hedge it.

Dollar value of a basis point for various maturities (11¾% Coupon)

Maturity	Approximate dollar Value of a basis point (1/100 of 1%) change in yield
3 months	25.00
6 months	50.00
1 year	100.00
2 years	173.77
3 years	246.87
4 years	312.09
5 years	370.28
7 years	468.51
10 years	579.60
12 years	635.00
15 years	698.00
20 years	765.00
30 years	824.00

DETERMINING THE NUMBER OF CONTRACTS FOR SHORT-TERM HEDGES. The number of futures contracts needed to hedge a short-term liability can be calculated using the following equation:

$$C = \frac{L}{U} \cdot \frac{M}{91} \cdot F$$

where C = number of contracts
L = dollar value of the liability being hedged
U = value of cash instrument underlying the futures contract.
M = maturity of the liability, in days (hedge horizon)
F = conversion factor, used to compensate for a different dollar value of a basis point on the futures contracts versus the cash liability

Let's say a builder is worried that interest rates might go up on his $10 million CD or prime based loan. He wants to hedge his construction loan for one year. How many contracts should the builder use?

L = $10,000,000 size of his loan
U = $ 1,000,000 value of the CD contract
M = 1 year or 365 days
F = 1, because the value of a basis point in futures is the same in cash
Solving for the number of contracts, C:

$$C = \frac{\$10{,}000{,}000}{\$\ 1{,}000{,}000} \times \frac{365}{91} \times 1 = 40$$

That is, the builder will have to sell 40 contracts to guard against a rise in interest rates over the next year.

DETERMINING THE BEST BASIS. There is a risk that changes in the cash market and the futures contract used to hedge it do not correspond exactly. This so-called basis risk can greatly reduce the effectiveness of a hedge. Consequently, it is vital to select a hedging instrument with the most stable basis and the highest correlation to the asset or liability being hedged. For example, until the summer of 1981, a corporation hedging a short-term liability tied to the prime rate might have sold T-bill futures. However, T-bill rates did not move up as much as the prime rate did, leaving much of the damage from higher interest rates unhedged. Had Eurodollar and CD futures been available during this period, they would have provided better hedging vehicles than T-bill futures did for hedging against a rise in the prime. That's because Euro and CD rates more closely mirror movements in the prime rate than do changes in the

T-bill futures contract: that is, they have a better correlation to the liability being hedged. At times, T-bill futures are appropriate to hedge MMCs and other bill-based liabilities.

Another consideration when determining the appropriateness of a hedging vehicle is the quality of the underlying financial instrument. Should the credit markets undergo a flight-to-quality, perhaps in response to a domestic bank failure or a developing country defaulting on a loan to international banks, the market would experience a sudden and unexpected increase in the preference for government issue debt obligations (T-Bills) versus private debt issues (CDs, commercial paper, and Eurodollars). In this case, T-bill futures would appreciate relative to say, CDs. Exhibit 15 illustrates the volatility of the T-bill CD yield spread. A short hedge in T-bills would then leave the hedger with a large loss not necessarily offset by a drop in costs on his or her cash liabilities, whereas a short hedge in CDs might insulate a hedger from the risks of a flight to quality.

ASSET HEDGING. On the asset side of the balance sheet, financial futures can be used to hedge against the price erosion of already existing, longer-dated assets when interest rates are expected to rise. Alternatively, these tools can be used to preserve yield levels by buying contracts in anticipation of a future cash flow that will need to be invested when interest rates are expected to fall.

Designing the Hedge. The procedure in hedging an asset parallels the approach taken when hedging a long-term liability. In both instances the choice of hedging instrument is vital to the success of the hedge. Consequently, assessing the correlation between the asset being hedged and the futures contract used to hedge it, provides the greatest challenge in designing the hedge. This is particularly important when the underlying asset does not qualify for delivery against the futures contract used as a hedge (i.e., corporate or municipal bonds).

Quality Considerations. In addition, the quality of the underlying instrument must also be considered. A corporate or municipal bond will track the price fluctuations in T-note and T-bond futures contracts better if it is of highest quality. By contrast, lower quality issues do not track futures well, and we urge caution in using futures in hedging against asset erosion or in preserving current yield of low-grade bonds. Alternatively, the hedger may want to purchase put options to hedge against asset price erosion. This would limit his or her risk to the cost of the option premium.

The best correlation is between bond futures and underlying Treasury bonds. However, lower-quality corporate bonds show great cylical yield spread variation with Treasury bonds. During low interest rate periods, the yield spread from Treasuries is relatively narrow, as low as 75 basis points. When interest rates rise, however, the jump in Baa bond yields relative to Treasury yields can open up the spread to as much as 300 basis points. (See Exhibit 16).

EXHIBIT 16 LONG MARKET RATES (MONTHLY AVERAGES)

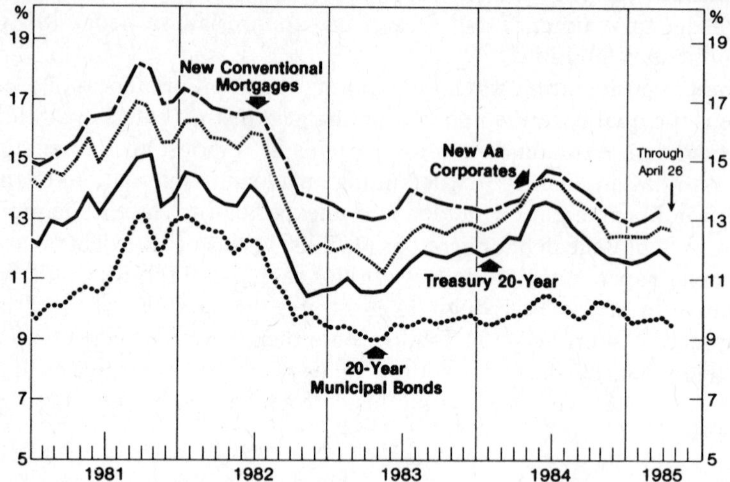

Source: Office of the Secretary of the Treasury, Office of Government Finance & Market Analysis, April 29, 1985.

This suggests that in an environment where quality considerations are paramount, investor preferences can distort the yield spread between lower quality and high quality corporate and tax-exempt securities and certainly magnify the yield spread between corporates and governments. This being the case, using high quality (Treasury) bond futures as a hedging tool to guard against a rise in corporate rates can be very imperfect and consequently, very costly.

PRICING AND DELIVERY OF TREASURY BOND FUTURES CONTRACTS. There are also special considerations in the U.S. Treasury bond futures market. Only T-bonds with a remaining time to maturity or call date (if callable) of at least 15 years are deliverable against futures. The Chicago Board of Trade contract specifies the delivery of $100,000 of 8% T-bonds or their equivalent using conversion factors.

To determine the cash equivalent of a futures contract, multiply the futures price by the appropriate factor. For example, the March 1985 factor for the 13¼% bond due May 15, 2014 is 1.5564. That is, the dollar amount that a holder of a short position will invoice to a long position when he or she delivers these securities is 1.5564, times the price of a March 1985 futures contract, plus the accrued interest.

Cheapest to Deliver. This T-bond pricing mechanism implies that there is usually one "cheapest-to-deliver" bond. As a result, investors looking to hedge their cash portfolios with futures, should be aware of which coupon is cheapest to deliver and what spread they can expect their cash positions to converge to.

The actual placement of a hedge on an asset follows the same procedural and strategic guidelines used in hedging a liability. When dealing with assets, however, the hedger should take particular care to examine correlations closely. The price behavior of various financial instruments are determined by complex relationships that must be carefully evaluated and anticipated by the hedger before implementation of a hedging program. Furthermore, these relationships can change suddenly. Accordingly, the hedger should maintain a close watch on financial markets to get the most protection from his or her hedge.

Determining the Number of Contracts for Long-Term Hedges. Consider the example of an investor that is looking to hedge against an increase in rates on \$100 million of assets. A Treasury bond futures contract represents an 8% coupon, \$100,000 par value but is selling at 67 cents on the dollar. Therefore, the investor shorts (sells) nearly 1.50 contracts to hedge each \$100,000 worth of assets, as 1.5 × .67 × \$100,000 = \$100,500. Because this investor is hedging \$100,000,000, nearly 1500 contracts must be used to hedge:

$$\frac{\text{\$ amount hedged}}{\text{\$100,000 value of contract}} \times \frac{1}{\text{price index in decimal form}} = \text{number of contracts needed}$$

$$\frac{\$100{,}000{,}000}{\$100{,}000} \times \frac{1}{.67} = 1{,}493 \text{ contracts}$$

This formula for long-term hedges is different from that for short-term hedges presented in the liability hedging section. That's because the short-term futures contracts, namely T-bills, CDs and Euros, trade in \$1,000,000 units, zero coupons, and constant, 91-day maturities. Their price is simply the inverse of the annualized yield (1 − yield) = price. Long-term contracts, however, trade in \$100,000 units, with 8% constant coupons, but different maturities.

HEDGING WITH OPTIONS. The introduction of **options on Treasury bond futures** in 1982 adds a new dimension to hedging interest rate risks. Options are similar to futures in some ways and different in others. One similarity is the underlying trading unit, namely, a \$100,000 8% coupon Treasury bond with 15 years or more to call. The deliverable instrument is the Treasury bond contract trading on the **Chicago Board of Trade.** Another strong similarity is that the four calendar months in which the option trades correspond to the December, March, June, and September futures contract cycle.

A major difference between buying puts and calls versus selling or buying futures contracts is that there is no variation margin on the buy side of options (there is on the sell side). If your opinion on interest rate direction turns out to be wrong, your loss would be limited to the premium (plus commission) paid to purchase the put or call option. In futures, however, your position is subject to daily variation margin and there is unlimited capital risk. If you are selling short futures contracts, and the market moves up in price, you must meet any variation between today's higher price and your sale price to maintain that futures contract short position. In options, being long a put simply means you are short the market at the strike price less the put premium but you would have no margin calls if the market moved up, contrary to your expectations. Another difference between futures and options is that the latter is traded in 1/64 increments, whereas future prices are quoted in 1/32nds. Thus the dollar equivalent change for a price tick in options is only half the $31.25 in futures, or $15.625. Another difference is that there are two ways to go long or go short. These differences are summarized in Exhibit 17.

Options on financial instruments and futures provide an additional tool for hedging assets and liabilities. Options now exist on bills, notes and long-term bonds futures contracts, liability hedging applications are no longer limited to issuance of long-term debts. Nevertheless, much of our discussion of options focuses on the asset side of the balance sheet. Options on Eurodollar futures were introduced in March 1985, and on bill futures, a year later.

Options can serve many purposes, depending on how much, and in which

EXHIBIT 17 INTEREST RATE FUTURES VERSUS OPTIONS ON INTEREST RATE FUTURES

		Strategy			
		Futures		Options	
Opinion	Interest Rate Direction	Conservative	Aggressive	Conservative	Aggressive
Bullish	Interest rates expected to move down	Buy bull spreads:	Buy bond contracts	Buy calls	Sell puts
		Long nearby and short distant contracts	(Subject to variation margin)	(Premium equals maximum loss)	(Subject to variation margin)
		(Subject to variation margin)			
Bearish	Interest rates expected to move up	Sell bear spreads:	Sell bond contracts	Buy puts	Sell calls
		Short nearby and long distant contracts	(Subject to variation margin)	(Premium equals maximum loss)	(Subject to variation margin)
		(Subject to variation margin)			

direction, a hedger expects interest rates to move. In a rising rate environment, a hedger might buy put options to hedge against the price erosion of his or her portfolio, or against a rise in long-term financing costs. Conversely, if rates were expected to fall, a hedger might use call options to lock in a target yield on his or her portfolio while at the same time keeping uninvested funds in a liquid form.

STRATEGIES FOR A RISING RATE ENVIRONMENT. A hedger interested in attaining downside protection when *interest rates* are *rising* has two alternative strategies available: buying puts (as mentioned previously) or selling calls. *Buyers of a put* will choose a strike price that stops out their losses at a level they can tolerate. Then, if the market price of their assets falls below the strike price, they can exercise the put options, thereby maintaining a minimum value on their portfolios. Alternatively, *sellers of a call* earn the premium on the option, as opposed to paying for the put option protection. If the value of their assets decline, as anticipated, the call option would not be exercised, whereas the premium helps to partially offset the loss in portfolio value. Consequently, selling calls is most appropriate when call premiums are large, and market prices are expected to be relatively stable. Were a sharp price drop expected, the purchase of put options would be preferable.

STRATEGIES FOR A FALLING RATE ENVIRONMENT. In a *falling rate environment,* hedgers interested in participating in market appreciation or in earning an incremental yield on their portfolios can choose from two strategies: *buying calls* or *selling puts.* The *buyer of a call* typically pays a low premium for an out-of-the-money call, being convinced that prices are going to rise. Then, assuming that bond prices rise (interest rates fall) as much as expected, they can exercise the option at the strike price and earn a profit if the market price is higher. Consequently, buying calls provides an anticipatory hedge, preserving a strike price as an alternative to a market purchase. The call buyer can lose no more than the cost of the option plus commission, whereas the outright cash market buyer has an indeterminate downside risk. The seller of a put approaches the situation from a different angle. This person is so confident that (rates will fall) prices will rise, he or she sells an in-the-money put for a sizable premium. Then, assuming that prices rise as he or she predicted and the option expires worthless, the put option seller earns the premium. If prices fall, contrary to his or her expectations, however, the put option seller is subject to unlimited downside risk.

LIMITED RISK VERSUS LIMITED GAIN. Diverse strategies can be applied to a firm's hedging needs, each involving specific costs and risks. In general though, the strategies with limited risk are those on the buy side of the options market. Regardless of whether a hedger buys a put or a call, potential losses are limited to the premium paid for the option. Should the market move against the option buyer (prices rise after purchasing puts or prices fall after purchasing calls), the option buyer can sell his or her option prior to expiration and might recoup some of the premium paid, or can wait for the market direction to change and simply allow the option to expire worthless. If it doesn't, were the market to move in the buyer's favor (prices drop after purchasing puts or price rise after purchasing calls), potential gains on his or her position are unlimited, ranging from recouping some or all of the premium costs to recognizing large profits.

The seller of a **call** or a **put option** is limited to gains equal to the premium received, whereas potential losses are unlimited. If the market moves in favor of the option seller (against the buyer), the option will typically be allowed to expire worthless, enabling the option seller to earn a profit equal to the premium received. If the market moves against the seller of the option, however, the option could be exercised and the option seller might consider liquidating his or her **short position.** The put option seller could suffer a loss equal to the difference between the **option strike price less** the put premium received and current prices; whereas the call option is subject to loss equal to the difference between the current higher market price and the lower strike price plus the call premium received. That is, if he or she sold a put with a strike price of 60 and received two points, the put seller is subject to net losses for any market price below 58 (strike price minus put option premium received). Consequently, a seller of options is subject to **margin calls,** an additional cost not accrued to a buyer of options.

BIBLIOGRAPHY

Bench, Joseph, "Ways to Trade an Interest Rate Outlook," *Commodities Magazine,* Fall 1979, pp. 14–16.

———, "Bond Market Still Vulnerable," *Bankers Monthly Magazine,* December 15, 1979, pp. 12–14.

———, "Credit Demands to Shrink Further in 1980," *Money Markets: A First Pennsylvania Report,* December 21, 1979.

———, "Stage Set for Credit Crunch," *Money Manager,* March 10, 1980.

———, *Asset Hedging Strategies,* Shearson/Am Express, Summer 1981.

———, *Liability Hedging Strategies,* Shearson/Am Express, Summer 1981.

———, "Zero Coupon vs. Conventional Bonds," *Bankers Monthly,* September 15, 1984.

Bench, Joseph, and Mazer, David, "The Case for Buying Zero Coupon Bonds," *Bankers Monthly,* February 15, 1985.

Bench, Joseph, and Mendel, W. *Asset Allocation and Strategy,* Shearson/Am Express, selected issues, 1982–1984.

Bench, Joseph, Mendel, W., and McAdams, L., *Portfolio Management Using Options and Futures,* Shearson/Am Express, May 1984.

Burger, A. E., Lang, R. W., and Trasche, R. H., "The Treasury Bill Futures Market and Market Expectations of Interest Rates," *Federal Reserve Bank of St. Louis Review,* June 1977, pp. 2–9.

Jianakoplos, Nancy A., "The Growing Link Between the Federal Government and State and Local Government Financing," *Federal Reserve Bank of St. Louis Review,* May 1977, pp. 13–20.

Stevens, Neil A., "Government Debt Financing—Its Effect in View of Tax Discounting," *Federal Reserve Bank of St. Louis Review,* July 1979, pp. 11–19.

Treasury Bulletin, U.S. Treasury Department, selected issues 1979–1980.

4

THE MARKET FOR TAX-EXEMPT SECURITIES

CONTENTS

4

THE MARKET FOR TAX-EXEMPT SECURITIES

Ronald W. Forbes

A distinctive characteristic of the debt securities issued by state and local governments and their agencies is the exemption of interest payments on such debt from federal income taxation. The basis for this exemption is in part statutory and the relevant definitions of **tax-exempt securities** are contained in section 103 of the Internal Revenue Code of 1954. State and local governments also assert that the issuance of tax-exempt securities is further protected under the Constitution, based on the decision of the Supreme Court in *Pollack* v. *Farmers' Loan & Trust Co.* (157 U.S. 429, 1895), where the Court stated:

> It is obvious that taxation on the interest would operate on the power to borrow before it is exercised, and would have a sensible influence on the contract, and that the tax in question is a tax on the power of the States and their instrumentalities to borrow money, and consequently repugnant to the Constitution.

Most states also exempt from state taxation the interest income from securities issued by governmental units located within state boundaries. Because of the exemption from federal taxation, these state and local government securities and the markets they trade in have become known as the tax-exempt market. The tax-exempt feature permits states, local governments, and the beneficiaries of projects financed through their agencies to borrow at interest rates lower than those available to borrowers, such as the federal government, from markets where interest payments represent taxable income for investors. Moreover, tax exemption has its principal appeal to investors who are in high marginal income tax brackets. Traditionally, this has defined a special market of investors consisting primarily of commercial banks, property and casualty insurance companies, and high-income individuals.

As will be apparent later in this section, the lure of low interest rates relative to alternative sources of financing has resulted in a rapid growth of "nontraditional" purposes for tax-exempt borrowing. At the same time, recent changes in federal tax provisions have caused major changes in the aggregate demand and supply of tax-exempt securities. At the present time (1986), proposed *tax reform* legislation would cause, if enacted, highly dramatic changes in the present market structure.

RECENT TRENDS IN VOLUME

One of the notable features of the tax-exempt market has been the significant growth in the volume of new debt issues. As noted in Exhibit 1 the dollar volume of new debt issues has expanded from $17.3 billion in 1966 to $138.3 billion in 1984; this represents a compound annual growth rate of 12.2%.

Market convention generally distinguishes between *short-term tax-exempt securities, or notes* which carry a final maturity of 13 months or less, and long-term debt issues with final maturities beyond 13 months. Following this convention, the data in Exhibit 1 indicate that the volume of new short-term issues generally increases during periods of high or rapidly rising interest rates (e.g., 1981–1982) and declines during periods of low or falling interest rates (e.g., 1984).

Long-term issues have recorded a persistent upward trend since 1966, with some declines evidenced during periods of high and rapidly rising interest rates, such as in 1981. In 1984, 6,955 new issues were sold raising $107.2 billion in funds. The $107 billion in bond sales in 1984 is more than double the volume

EXHIBIT 1 NEW ISSUES OF TAX—EXEMPT SECURITIES 1966–1984 ($ MILLIONS)

	Total New Issues		Long-Term Issues		Short-Term Issues	
Year	Number	Dollar Volume	Number	Dollar Volume	Number	Dollar Volume
1984	8746	$138,286	6955	$107,218	1791	$31,068
1983	9462	123,388	6545	85,093	2917	38,295
1982	9340	122,008	6164	77,295	3236	44,713
1981	7821	85,156	4734	47,724	3087	37,432
1980	7933	76,087	5589	48,368	2344	27,720
1979	7468	65,050	5391	43,335	2077	21,715
1978	8031	69,574	5695	48,190	2336	21,384
1977	8333	71,457	5358	46,706	2975	24,751
1976	7533	57,321	4920	35,416	2613	21,905
1975	8072	59,632	4689	30,659	3383	28,973
1974	7628	52,626	4214	23,585	3414	29,041
1973	8061	48,488	4655	23,821	3406	24,667
1972	8131	48,914	4814	23,692	3317	25,222
1971	8493	51,210	5143	24,929	3350	26,281
1970	7238	35,963	4335	18,083	2903	17,880
1969	6617	23,485	3824	11,702	2343	11,783
1968	7660	24,979	5487	16,320	2173	8,659
1967	7552	22,430	5417	14,405	2135	8,025
1966	6800	17,333	4964	11,079	1836	6,254

Source: Public Securities Association.

just 3 years earlier—in 1981—and nearly 10 times the volume in 1966. The record of the past decade points out that new issues of tax-exempt bonds have doubled approximately every 4 to 5 years; between 1966 and 1984 the average annual compound growth rate in bond sales was 13.3%.

It should be pointed out, however, that the tradition of classifying as long-term debt any issues that have a nominal maturity beyond 13 months does not fully capture the innovations that have been taking place, including the use of *put options* that permit investors to demand payment in periods as short as one day. These innovations will be discussed later in this chapter.

The data in Exhibits 1 and 2 highlight another important characteristic of the tax-exempt market, which is the very large number of individual new issues sold each year. In every year since 1966, there have been more than 6,800 individual debt issues sold, including more than 9,000 in 1982 and 1983. As the data in Exhibit 2 indicate, nearly 60% of the new bond issues sold in 1984 were less than $5 million in par value; but these issues accounted for only 6.4% of the total dollar volume of funds raised. The large number of individually small debt issues imposes significant information costs on the tax-exempt market as investors are confronted with a sometimes bewildering array of securities, each with its somewhat unique features. One result has been the growth of new intermediaries that seek to lower information and monitoring costs to investors. These intermediaries often offer their credit strengths (and ratings) to investors as a substitute for the credit of the borrower. The role of credit enhancements will be discussed shortly.

Some additional perspective on the tax-exempt new issue market is provided by the data in Exhibit 3, which compares tax-exempts with corporate security sales. Total public offerings of tax-exempts nearly matched total private and public corporate issues (equity and long-term debt) in 1966 and 1970. The volume of tax-exempt bonds was approximately the same as corporate bonds publicly sold in 1974. In 1978 and 1984, both total offerings and long-term bond sales in the tax-exempt market eclipsed the volume of corporate new issues. As these comparisons demonstrate, the tax-exempt market of recent years is now larger than the (taxable) market for corporate long-term securities.

EXHIBIT 2 SIZE DISTRIBUTION OF TAX-EXEMPT BOND ISSUES 1966 AND 1984

	1966		1984	
Issue size ($ millions)	Dollar Volume (%)	Number of Issues	Dollar Volume (%)	Number of Issues
<1.0	10.5	3331	.6	1258
1.0–5.0	25.4	1271	6.3	2682
5.0–25.0	29.9	302	20.8	2046
25.0–100.0	21.7	52	31.9	727
>100.0	12.4	8	40.5	242
	100.0	4964	100.0	6955

Source: Public Securities Association.

EXHIBIT 3 NEW OFFERINGS OF TAX-EXEMPT SECURITIES AND TAXABLE CORPORATE SECURITIES FOR SELECTED YEARS, 1966–1984 ($ MILLIONS)

	Tax-Exempt[a]		Corporate[b]	
	Total	Long-Term Bonds	Total[c]	Publicly Offered Bonds
1984	$138,286	$107,218	$95,986	$73,357
1978	69,574	48,190	47,230	19,815
1974	52,626	23,585	37,837	25,337
1970	35,963	18,083	38,945	25,384
1966	17,333	11,079	18,074	8,018

[a] Data from Exhibit 1.
[b] Data from Board of Governors of the Federal Reserve System, *Federal Reserve Bulletin,* various issues.
[c] Includes public offerings and private placements of debt and equity securities.

MARKETING TAX-EXEMPT SECURITIES

Exhibit 4 provides some measures of the stock of outstanding tax-exempt debt over the 1966–1983 period. Tax-exempt debt outstanding climbed from $106 billion in 1966 to $484 billion in 1983, which is equivalent to an annual compound growth rate of 9.4%. The fact that the stock of outstanding debt has increased at a much slower pace than the flow of new issues is largely attributable to the type of maturity structures commonly used in the tax-exempt bond market. Short-term issues are usually retired during the fiscal year. Moreover, only a small proportion of new bonds is sold as term bonds with a single, long-term maturity. Instead, most tax-exempts are sold with **serial maturities**; that is, a portion of the total principal borrowed is scheduled to mature on an annual basis over the life of the issue. In effect, a bond issue with a final maturity of 25

EXHIBIT 4 MATURITY COMPOSITION OF TAX-EXEMPT DEBT OUTSTANDING, SELECTED YEARS 1966–1983

Year	Tax-Exempt Debt Outstanding ($ billions)	Short-Term Debt	Outstanding Long-Term Debt
1983	$484.6	4.2%	95.8%
1980	351.9	5.2	94.8
1978	291.4	4.3	95.7
1976	239.5	6.1	93.9
1974	207.7	9.1	90.9
1972	176.5	9.0	91.0
1970	144.4	9.2	90.8
1968	123.2	6.6	93.4
1966	106.0	5.8	94.2

Source: Board of Governors of the Federal Reserve System, *Flow of Funds,* various dates.

years actually consists of a number of smaller issues, each with its own maturity, amount and, generally, yield.

Exhibit 5 demonstrates a common form of serial bond maturity structure for a $11.5 million bond issue from the city of Baltimore. In this common financing structure, serial bonds and term bonds with sinking fund redemptions are combined to produce level annual debt service payments over the period of indebtedness.

Most tax-exempt bonds outstanding are *bearer bonds,* where ownership is determined by possession. Holders of bearer bonds are not recorded on the issuer's books. Payment of principal and interest is effected on presentation of coupons or bonds to the issuer's paying agent. The bearer bond form permits tax-exempts to be exchanged among investors while owners remain anonymous to the issuer.

As part of the *Tax Equity and Fiscal Responsibility Tax Act of 1982* (*TEFRA*), the federal government has required virtually all new issues of long-term tax-exempts sold after June 30, 1983 to be registered both as to principal and interest. The registration requirement was enacted to promote more effective compliance with federal tax laws, based on concerns that the bearer bond form was increasingly used to shelter nonreported incomes. Severe penalties for investors and issuers for failure to adhere to the registration require-

EXHIBIT 5 DEBT MATURITY STRUCTURE $11.5 MILLION WASTEWATER PROJECTS REVENUE BONDS MAYOR AND CITY COUNCIL OF BALTIMORE ISSUED FEBRUARY 10, 1983

Maturity Date	Principal ($000s)	Interest Rate (%)	Total Debt Service ($000s)
1984	$ 255	5.00%	$1,314
1985	265	5.75	1,311
1986	280	6.25	1,311
1987	300	6.75	1,313
1988	320	7.25	1,313
1989	345	7.75	1,314
1990	370	8.25	1,313
1991	400	8.50	1,313
1992	435	8.70	1,314
1993	470	8.90	1,311
1994	515	9.10	1,314
1995	560	9.30	1,312
1996	615	9.50	1,315
1997	670	9.75	1,312
1998	735	10.00	1,311
1999	810[a]	10.125	1,313
2000	895[a]	10.125	1,316
2001	985[a]	10.125	1,315
2002	1,085[a]	10.125	1,315
2003	1,190[a]	10.125	1,310

[a] Mandatory sinking fund installments for term bonds due July 1, 2003.

ment were also instituted by TEFRA. (It must be emphasized that registration refers solely to the recording of ownership; it does not refer to the registration of new issues under the Securities Acts with the Securities and Exchange Commission. Tax-exempt securities are not now subject to new issue registration.) The TEFRA registration requirement is now the subject of what may be a landmark Supreme Court case on the tax-exempt market. In this case, *South Carolina* v. *Regan,* the state of South Carolina is asking the Court to rule that TEFRA violates the constitutional protections accorded state and local governments under the doctrine of intergovernmental tax immunity.

Most new issues of tax-exempt securities are sold to *underwriting syndicates.* In recent years, the state of Massachusetts and a small number of municipalities have sold small amounts of bonds directly to investors. Private placements with institutional investors are generally used in the sale of *small-issue industrial development revenue bonds,* which are generally purchased by local commercial banks.

Underwriters may be commercial banks or investment banking firms, and syndicates may range in size from a single firm to as many as 100 firms. Exhibit 6 lists the top 20 underwriters in 1984. Under the Banking Act of 1933 (the *Glass-Steagall Act*), commercial banks are prohibited from underwriting most revenue bond issues. Underwriters serve as important intermediaries between the governmental units that issue securities and the investors who purchase them. The syndicate purchases the entire issue from the borrower and then at-

EXHIBIT 6 LEADING UNDERWRITERS OF TAX-EXEMPT BOND ISSUES 1984 ($ MILLIONS)

Rank	Underwriter	Volume Underwritten	Number of Issues
1	Merrill Lynch Capital Markets	$8305	1030
2	E F Hutton & Co.	6054	708
3	Salomon Brothers	5962	329
4	Shearson Lehman	5363	632
5	Smith Barney, Harris Upham	5320	401
6	Goldman Sachs & Co.	4604	351
7	Kidder Peabody & Co.	4459	538
8	Paine Webber	4290	630
9	Prudential-Bache Securities	3605	690
10	First Boston Corp.	3104	188
11	Dean Witter Reynolds	2715	495
12	Bear, Stearns & Co.	2002	230
13	Bankers Trust Co.	1786	214
14	Morgan Stanley & Co.	1587	99
15	Drexel Burnham Lambert Inc.	1536	215
16	Morgan Guaranty Trust Co.	1511	122
17	Citibank	1507	139
18	LF Rothschild, Unterberg, Towbin	1360	154
19	Miller & Schroeder Municipals	1130	130
20	Rauscher Pierce Refsnes Inc.	983	162

Source: Public Securities Association.

tempts to resell the bonds to investors. Issuers can select underwriters in two ways: (1) by competitive bidding or (2) through negotiation. As noted in Exhibit 7, most general obligation bonds are sold by competitive bid and most revenue bonds are sold through negotiation. As discussed later in this section, general obligations are secured by the full faith and credit and the taxing powers of a governmental unit, whereas revenue bonds are limited obligations secured by special user charges or loan repayments, and not by general taxing power.

Under the competitive bidding method, issuers solicit bids from competing underwriters and award the bonds to the syndicate with the lowest interest cost bid. In a negotiated sale, an underwriting syndicate is selected well in advance of the sale date and the final terms of the bond issue are negotiated between the issuer and the syndicate.

Although there are common services performed by underwriters regardless of which method of sale is used, there are important differences in the level of services provided in competitive and negotiated sales. These differences can be discussed under the three primary functions performed by underwriters: origination services, risk-bearing, and distribution.

Origination services generally refer to the range of presale activities necessary to prepare a bond issue for the market. Under competitive bidding, the issuer carries out most of these activities, often with the assistance of an outside financial adviser. In a competitive sale, the issuing governmental unit determines the number of serial bond maturities and the final maturity for the bond issue; the par amounts of principal for each maturity; call features; and other structural characteristics of the bond issue. The issuer takes the responsibility of securing a credit rating from one of the bond rating agencies; the issuer also prepares an official statement (or prospectus) of information necessary for underwriters and investors to gauge the investment merits of the bonds. In a competitive sale, the official notice of sale provides prospective underwriters with the necessary information on the date and time of bond sale and other terms on which the bids will be evaluated. Underwriters then submit bids detailing the coupon rates and yields necessary to market the bonds and the total dollar amount to be paid the issuer for the bond issue. In a negotiated sale, the underwriter works closely with the issuer in carrying out many of these presale

EXHIBIT 7 NEW TAX-EXEMPT BOND SALES BY TYPE OF OFFERING, 1984 ($ MILLIONS)

Type of	General Obligation		Revenue	
Offering	Number	Amount	Number	Amount
Competitive	2,489	$15,636	596	$ 6,717
Negotiated	772	10,305	2,749	70,771
Private placement	32	588	317	3,202
	3,293	$26,529	3,662	$80,690

Source: Public Securities Association, Statistical Yearbook, 1985.

activities; the cost of these services is then incorporated in the compensation paid to the managing underwriters.

Underwriters also provide *risk-bearing services,* which are needed because once the issue has been purchased at a fixed price from the issuer, the underwriting syndicate faces uncertainty over the price at which these securities can be marketed to investors. This is basically an inventory risk and underwriters expect compensation for incurring this risk. For negotiated issues, however, this risk may be lower than for competitive issues. The negotiated method of sale involves the underwriter in the early stages of a bond issue and enables the underwriter to engage in substantial *presale marketing* efforts. These efforts enable the underwriter to gauge demand for the issue and can lead to a more marketable combination of bond issue features (e.g., maturities). Although presale activities can and do take place in a competitive sale, there is often little that can be done to provide a more "salable" package of debt features.

Distribution services include the activities and costs involved in selling and delivering bonds to investors; these transaction services are largely independent of the method of sale, whether competitive or negotiated.

The compensation received by underwriters is termed the **underwriting spread,** and it is the difference between the aggregate price at which bonds are sold to investors and the aggregate price received by the issuer. This underwriting spread typically ranges between .5 and 3% of the total par value of the issue. For negotiated issues this total or gross spread is usually divided among four categories: (1) expenses incurred by underwriters for legal fees, advertising, travel expenses, and computer costs are deducted from the spread; (2) the managing underwriters receive a **management fee** as compensation for organizing and structuring the actual syndicate operations; (3) generally the largest component of the spread is the **concession,** which is paid to underwriters and dealers for actual selling effort; and (4) the **underwriting fee** is distributed among the syndicate members in proportion to the underwriting commitments of each firm. Exhibit 8 provides summary data on the gross spread and its components for a sample of new negotiated tax-exempt bonds issued in 1984.

Underwriting spreads vary on different bond issues depending on market conditions and issue and issuer characteristics. Generally, spreads per $1000

EXHIBIT 8 SUMMARY STATISTICS ON GROSS UNDERWRITING SPREADS, NEGOTIATED NEW ISSUES OF TAX-EXEMPT BONDS (SEPTEMBER–DECEMBER 1984)

Gross underwriting spread	$25.90
Management fee	4.61
Underwriting fee	1.61
Expenses	3.29
Takedown	15.56

Source: Public Securities Association.

par value of bonds are higher (1) the more volatile the market conditions at the time of sale; (2) the greater the credit risk associated with the issue or issuer; and (3) the smaller the total bond size. Spreads are also higher on bond issues than short-term notes because most notes are marketed in large blocks to institutional investors. Underwriting spreads are often higher on negotiated sales, reflecting in part the added services provided.

In negotiated sales, the underwriting spread is generally taken in the form of a discount from the total par value of the bond issue. In competitive sales, coupons on the bond maturities are typically set to result in the overall bond issue having a market value above the par value. The underwriter's spread is deducted from this premium, and the issuer typically receives a total dollar value equal to or slightly above par value.

Most competitive sales are awarded to the underwriting syndicate that specifies the lowest **net interest cost (NIC)**. The NIC method of awarding bonds:

> Is primarily a measure of the scheduled total dollar coupon interest payments over the life of the serial bond issue. It simply is the sum of the coupon payments that have to be made in each year, plus or minus the dollar amount by which the proposed purchase price from the underwriter exceeds or falls short of, respectively, the aggregate par value of the issue. (Hopewell and Kaufman, 1977, p. 13).

Under the NIC method, the interest payments are equally weighted in calculating the overall interest cost of the bond issue; that is, a dollar of interest paid in 1 year is given the same weight as a dollar of interest paid in 40 years. In this sense, the NIC method ignores the time value (or present value) of interest payments. One result of this practice is that some bond issues carry high coupons on short-term maturities and lower coupons on longer maturities. Exhibit 9

EXHIBIT 9 COUPON-YIELD STRUCTURE ON $175 MILLION STATE OF NEW YORK SERIAL BOND ISSUE DATED NOVEMBER 17, 1982 (AMOUNTS IN $ MILLIONS)

Amounts, Maturities, Rates, and Yields							
Amount	Due	Coupon	Yield	Amount	Due	Coupon	Yield
$7,955	1983	10.5%	5.75%	$5,840	1998	10.0%	10.05%
7,955	1984	10.5	6.50	5,840	1999	10.10	10.10
7,955	1985	10.5	7.00	5,840	2000	10.10	10.15
7,955	1986	10.5	7.50	5,840	2001	10.20	10.20
7,955	1987	10.5	7.90	5,840	2002	10.25	10.25
7,955	1988	10.5	8.20	3,605	2003	10.30	10.30
7,955	1989	10.5	8.50	3,605	2004	10.30	10.35
7,955	1990	10.5	8.70	3,605	2005	10.40	10.40
7,955	1991	10.5	8.90	3,605	2006	10.40	10.45
7,955	1992	10.5	9.20	3,605	2007	9.00	10.50
6,040	1993	9.7	9.40	3,605	2008	9.00	10.50
6,040	1994	9.6	9.60	3,605	2009	9.00	10.50
6,040	1995	9.8	9.80	3,605	2010	9.00	10.50
6,040	1996	9.9	9.90	3,605	2011	9.00	10.50
6,040	1997	10.0	10.00	3,605	2012	9.00	10.50

provides an example of these *coupon strategies* for a $175 million bond issue of New York State. For this issue, higher coupons (e.g., 10.5%) are placed on short-term maturities, whereas lower coupons (e.g., 9%) are placed on the longest maturities. Yields to investors, on the other hand, increase with maturity, ranging from 5.75% in 1983 to 10.5% in 2012. As a result of the coupon-yield relationship, short-term maturities are priced at premiums above par, whereas long-term maturities are priced at discounts below par. This practice has been criticized as inefficient because it "front loads" the total interest payments and thereby raises the present value cost of borrowing.

THE SECONDARY MARKET FOR TAX-EXEMPT SECURITIES

After new issues have been sold, trades are conducted in the secondary market, which is an "over-the-counter" market. Although borrowers are most concerned with achieving the lowest borrowing costs possible at the date bonds are sold, efficient secondary markets are necessary to achieve low costs in the new issue market.

To investors, the ability to convert bonds into cash prior to final maturity is important for portfolio flexibility. To underwriters, the breadth of the secondary market for an issue is one determinant of the risk in pricing and distributing a new issue; this risk is reflected in the underwriting spread and the interest cost to borrowers. For governmental units that borrow, a secondary market that provides investors with liquidity throughout the maturity range facilitates the sale of securities with longer final maturities than would otherwise be feasible; this permits borrowers to hedge against future changes in interest rates by matching debt maturities to the useful life of capital assets.

The secondary market for tax-exempts depends on characteristics of investors and their transactions. Large institutional investors—commercial banks, mutual funds, or insurance companies—tend to place large orders of $250,000 or $1 million or more and these institutions transact with well-known dealer firms. Individual investors, however, place small orders of $25,000, or even $5,000, and these orders are generally placed with brokers. Because many small orders may also involve "seasoned" issues that have infrequent sales, an extensive regional network of brokers has developed to meet the needs of small investors. Two sources that facilitate broker search activities are *The Blue List* and the *Kenny Wire.*

The most comprehensive source of information on volume and activity in the secondary tax-exempt market is the *Blue List of Current Municipal Offerings,* a daily financial publication that carries a listing of bonds offered for sale. Approximately 700 dealer and brokerage firms participate in the secondary market, ranging from large investment banking firms to small local securities dealers. In 1984 the daily volume of tax-exempts listed for sale in the *Blue List* ranged between $900 million and $2 billion. Although the *Blue List* can provide indications of the securities available, orders cannot be executed by it; executions (e.g., purchases or sales) must be conducted by direct contact between buyers and sellers (or more appropriately, their brokers). By contrast, the *Kenny Wire,* established by the firm of JJ Kenny and Company, does provide for executions. The *Kenny Wire* is a form of "electronic auction" market, whereby members (brokers or dealers) can place "bids wanted" orders on the "wire." These orders are transmitted to a national network of firms which may then submit bids; the bids are tallied and ranked by Kenny and submitted to the original broker, who may then decide whether to execute.

THE MUNICIPAL SECURITIES RULE-MAKING BOARD

For the most part, the tax-exempt market has remained free from the widespread regulation that encompasses the corporate securities market. Although transactions in tax-exempt securities have historically fallen under the umbrella of the general antifraud provisions of federal securities laws, there never has been specific authority to regulate or otherwise control the reporting of information by issuers of tax-exempt securities.

In 1975, however, the Securities Acts Amendments passed by Congress established an independent self-regulatory organization, the *Municipal Securities Rulemaking Board.* This agency was created as a response to the growing evidence of improper and unethical practices in the secondary market trading and selling of tax-exempts. Under the Securities Acts Amendments, the Board is required to adopt rules of conduct for market professionals, including standards for professional qualification, rules of fair practice and record keeping, compliance examinations, quotations on municipal securities, and underwriting practices. Although the Board is an independent organization, its rules are subject to approval by the Securities and Exchange Commission and they carry the force of law.

SECURITY FEATURES OF SHORT-TERM TAX-EXEMPT SECURITIES

Although market convention attempts to encapsulate the wide variety of tax-exempt securities into the broad categories of general obligations and revenue bonds, there are important distinctions recognized by informed market participants. Exhibit 10 provides a breakdown of short-term tax-exempt notes into five categories.

LOCAL HOUSING AND URBAN RENEWAL PROJECT NOTES. These short-term issues traditionally accounted for most tax-exempt notes, reaching a peak volume of $26.7 billion in 1982. Project notes are obligations of local housing authorities or urban renewal agencies, the proceeds of which have been used for low income housing or urban redevelopment projects. The un-

EXHIBIT 10 NEW ISSUES OF SHORT-TERM TAX-EXEMPT DEBT BY TYPE, 1984

Type	Amount Issued ($ millions)
Project notes	$11,574
Tax and revenue anticipation notes	16,774
Bond anticipation notes	3,729
Tax-exempt commercial paper	6,800

Source: Public Securities Association. The volume of tax-exempt commercial paper is based on authorized program amounts as estimated by Shearson/American Express.

derlying security behind these notes, however, has been an agreement between the local issuers and the Department of Housing and Urban Development (HUD) whereby the federal government, through HUD, unconditionally agreed to lend the agencies funds sufficient to pay principal and interest on maturing notes.

As a result of provisions in the *Deficit Reduction Act of 1984* (DRA) passed by Congress, new issues of these notes were indefinitely suspended late in 1984. The DRA imposed new and more restrictive constraints on the ability of tax-exempt issuers to earn arbitrage profits from borrowing at tax-exempt rates and investing at higher taxable rates. The suspension of new project notes resulted from the inability of HUD and the IRS to determine whether local authorities complied with these arbitrage restrictions.

TAX ANTICIPATION NOTES (TANs) AND REVENUE ANTICIPATION NOTES (RANs). Basically analogous to working capital loans, these obligations provide a cash flow bridge between nonsynchronous revenues and expenditures. In a number of governmental units, revenues tend to be realized during one or two concentrated periods of the fiscal year. Property taxes, for example, are often payable once a year; aid payments from other governmental units are payable perhaps quarterly. Expenditures, on the other hand, tend to be more evenly spaced over the fiscal year. Thus, notes payable from anticipated taxes (TANs) or other revenues such as state aid (RANs) have become accepted means of financing periodic cash shortages over the fiscal year. Perhaps the most notable example of recurring borrowings for these purposes is the annual spring borrowing of New York State. At approximately $4 billion in recent years, this state note sale is the largest debt issue by a single entity outside the federal government, and it is required to offset the uneven patterns of revenue collections and expenditures that have characterized New York fiscal policies for many years.

Standard & Poor's Corporation, in its rating criteria for TANs and RANs, noted that:

> Cash flow protection is especially important for ratings on TANs and RANs, since these are generally paid from tax or other revenue . . . Investment-grade

> ratings are generally warranted for RANs and TANs only if the issuer's revenues have historically provided coverage on a cash basis sufficient for worst-case declines in net pledged revenues. (Standard & Poor Corporation, *Creditweek,* May 27, 1985.)

BOND ANTICIPATION NOTES (BANs). Where legally permitted, these instruments are used to finance periodic construction work-in-progress payments. The use of BANs can provide short-term funds for interim contract expenditures until projects are completed and final costs are estimated. Normally, BANs are retired through the issuance of long-term bonds. Thus, BANs—by contrast with TANs and RANs—depend on access to long-term bond markets for repayment. As summarized by one analyst:

> Market access is determined by two factors. One is the inherent quality of the loan in terms of ordinary debt structure criteria; this is a debtor characteristic controlled by the legal security, financial condition, and so on, of the borrower. . . . The other determinant of market access is the condition of the market and its ability and willingness to meet the particular demand. (Smith, 1979, p. 102.)

TAX-EXEMPT COMMERCIAL PAPER (TECP). A relatively new form of short-term tax-exempt security, TECP is derived from its counterpart in the corporate market. TECP is a short-term unsecured promissory note with maturities on issuance ranging from as short as 7 days to 270 days. Governmental units have issued TECP in lieu of traditional notes for working capital and for long-term capital projects. Although initial maturities are short, the "life" of a TECP program may be indefinite. Most TECP is expected to be rolled over or refinanced at maturity with new issues. To ensure adequate liquidity for maturing TECP, most issuers have been required to establish letters of credit or other liquidity support agreements with commercial banks.

SECURITY FEATURES ON LONG-TERM BONDS

GENERAL OBLIGATIONS. As defined by one analyst, the term *general obligation bond* should be reserved for bond issues with the following attributes:

> First, it is the obligation of a governmental unit with the power to levy and collect taxes and is repayable, initially or ultimately, from the general revenues provided from such taxes as well as from other available revenues; and second, it is backed by a pledge of the full faith and credit of the issuer. (Smith, 1979, p. 140)

In most instances, general obligations of local governmental units are backed by the requirement that the governmental unit levy **ad valorem taxes** on all taxable real property without limit, if necessary. These bonds are more completely described as **full faith and credit**, **unlimited-tax general obligations**.

Other tax-supported bonds can be described as limited-tax general obligations. In some instances, the tax limit may be a general limit on the amount of tax levy for any governmental purpose. California, in 1978, and Massachusetts, in 1980, approved constitutional changes that imposed such limits on local governments in those states. In other cases, the tax limit may apply specifically to levies for debt service payments. If, however, the debt also carries a pledge of the full faith and credit of the governmental issuer, revenues other than taxes may be used to meet debt service payments and these debts would appropriately be labeled **full faith and credit, limited-tax general obligations**.

SPECIAL ASSESSMENT BONDS. In some jurisdictions, street paving and lighting, sewage lines, and other "neighborhood" improvements are constructed by the municipality but paid for by the residents in the form of special assessments. The improvements involve a substantial cost and carry useful benefits over future periods; however, financing them with a lump-sum outlay could create unexpected hardships on many residents. Therefore the municipality may issue bonds to finance construction and pledge the special assessments as the source of funds for repayment. In effect, the municipality is issuing debt on behalf of the residents who benefit. When such bonds are secured solely by the assessments levied against specific properties, the bonds are called **special assessment limited liability bonds**.

At times, the security features of both general obligations and revenue bonds are combined in one bond issue, creating what is often referred to as a **double-barreled obligation**. In this type of financing, bond repayment is typically designed to be met first from specific user charges or fees levied on the direct beneficiaries of the facilities. However, to enhance the credit quality of the security, the bonds also carry a general obligation pledge of the governmental issuer. In this type of financing, the general revenues of the governmental unit serve as supplemental resources to be called on in the event that shortfalls occur from the primary revenue stream.

REVENUE BONDS. The distinguishing characteristic of the broad class of bonds commonly referred to as revenue bonds is that such bonds are payable solely from revenue received from the users or beneficiaries of the projects financed. Here, the liability of the governmental issuer is limited and neither the full faith and credit nor the general taxing power of the government is pledged as security.

Historically, one of the common uses of the revenue bond security has been to finance capital outlays of municipally owned utility systems, that provide water, sewer, or electric services. These **utility revenue bonds** are repaid from charges to customers of the utility systems. Revenue bonds are also used to finance other enterprise-type projects owned or operated by governmental units. Examples include regional sewage and solid waste disposal facilities, parking garages, bridges, tunnels, ports and airports, state university dormitories, and municipally owned hospitals. **Fee and user charges** for services provided generate the primary revenues available for meeting bond debt service requirements.

In other cases, projects are financed by special purpose authorities organized solely for the delivery of a specific service or function to other governmental units. These authorities issue revenue bonds for capital projects and receive revenues under long-term service contracts with other governments. Although the issuing authority itself may not have general taxing power and may pledge only revenues derived from service contracts, the contracts are often general obligations of the participating governmental units. These arrangements appropriately define an **indirect general obligation bond**.

Also classified under the heading of revenue bonds are securities paid from the collection of special taxes. One relatively common application of the *limited-liability special tax bond* is used to finance highway construction. State highway bonds are frequently designed to be repaid solely from the proceeds of motor fuel taxes or motor vehicle taxes collected by the state. Other examples of special taxes that have been pledged as revenues to secure bond issues include general sales taxes, excise taxes, and severance taxes.

Among the fastest growing types of bond security are **lease rental bonds**. Under the lease rental approach, public borrowing entities issue tax-exempt bonds and use the proceeds to construct facilities that are then leased to other governmental units, to nonprofit corporations, or to private enterprises. Under the lease agreements, lease rental payments are pledged to fully cover the issuer's debt service requirements.

Another rapidly growing form of **conduit financing** in the tax-exempt market is the **cash flow bond**. These bonds have been widely used by state and local agencies to raise funds from the tax-exempt market for the purpose of acquiring portfolios of single-family or multifamily mortgage loans, loans to college students, or loans to local governments. The repayment of the tax-exempt bonds is dependent on the cash flows from the loan portfolios acquired by the issuing agencies. In many instances, these cash flows are uncertain; therefore special bond features have been designed to match loan repayments appropriately with bond retirements.

As Exhibit 11 indicates, lessee revenue and "cash flow" bonds are now the major types of securities issued in the tax-exempt market, accounting for 50%

EXHIBIT 11 NEW TAX-EXEMPT BOND SALES, BY TYPE OF SECURITY, 1984

Security	Par Value of New Issues ($ millions)
Lessee-revenue and "cash flow" bonds	$53,671
Full faith and credit GO, unlimited tax	19,722
User charge revenue	11,380
Utility revenue	8,930
Full faith and credit, limited tax	1,747
Special tax revenue	753
Other	10,731

Source: Public Securities Association.

of new issues in 1984. Full faith and credit general obligations follow, with 18.4% of new issues, and revenue bonds backed by user charges (10.6%) and utility revenues (8.3%) also account for significant market shares.

RECENT TRENDS IN TAX-EXEMPT BOND SECURITY FEATURES AND USES. Over the last decade or more, some important changes have taken place in the tax-exempt market; the persistence of these trends has fashioned a tax-exempt market different from its traditional role as the "municipal" bond market. The important characteristics of the recent past include:

1. The pronounced decline of the general obligation bond and the concomitant rise of the revenue bond
2. The substitution of nongovernmental or "private purpose" borrowing for governmentally owned facilities

In the 1960s over 60% of all new tax-exempt issues were tax-supported obligations of general units of government (e.g., states, cities). By 1984, however, GOs had declined to less than 25% of new bond issues. As Exhibit 12 illustrates, governmental units have turned increasingly to the revenue bond, where debt repayments are linked to specific user charges, special taxes, or other nongovernmental revenues. Revenue bonds now account for more than 75% of all new issues and amounted to more than $80 billion in 1984.

EXHIBIT 12 NEW ISSUES OF GENERAL OBLIGATION AND REVENUE BONDS, 1966–1984

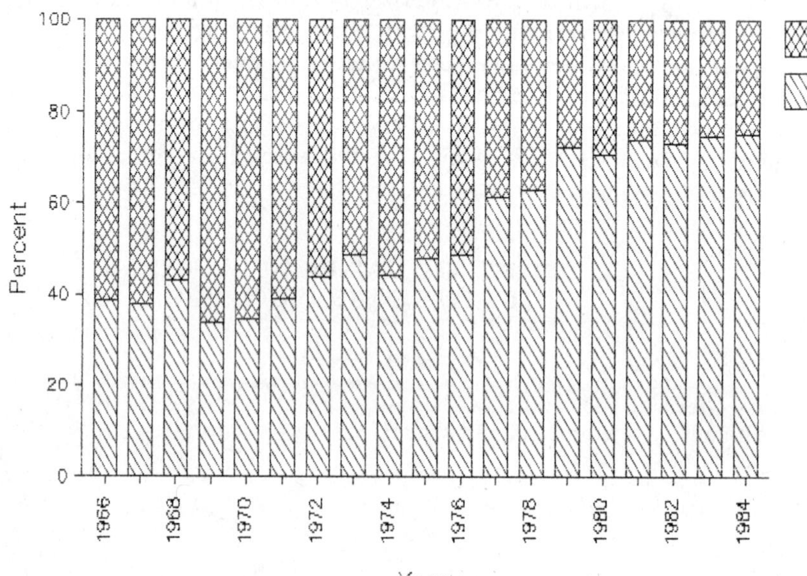

At the same time, the purposes for tax-exempt debt have also undergone dramatic change. In earlier years, tax-exempt borrowing was used to provide funds for governmentally owned capital facilities; Exhibit 13 indicates that governmental purposes accounted for 71% of new bonds sold in 1975. By 1984, as demonstrated in Exhibit 13, government projects accounted for only 37% of new borrowing. Increasingly in recent years, the tax-exempt market has been used to raise funds for nongovernmental purposes, including not-for-profit hospitals, loans for owner-occupied housing, privately owned rental housing, student loans, pollution control facilities of corporations, and a variety of other facilities such as fast-food franchises, shopping centers, hotels, professional office buildings, and commercial bank branch offices.

Tax-exempt financing of government capital facilities is a derived demand that is shaped largely by underlying demographic factors. Thus the decline of the GO bond is partly explained by recent slowdowns in population growth, and the completion of the basic "infrastructure" needed to accommodate this growth. Coinciding with this slowdown, however, has been a shift in public priorities away from "concrete and steel" to human services and programs. Capital outlays by state and local governments in nominal dollars have continued to rise over the last two decades, but real outlays have declined substantially. As shown in Exhibit 14, "real" capital outlays by state and local governments peaked in the late 1960s and early 1970s; by the 1978–1982 period, real outlays had declined more than 25% from the levels of a decade earlier.

A further restraint on the growth of capital investment by state and local governments that emerged in the late 1970s and has continued since then is increased taxpayer resistance. This new force exploded on the scene with the passage of *Proposition 13,* amending the California Constitution in 1978. Proposition 13 limited the maximum tax on real property from all taxing units to no more than 1% of the full cash value (as assessed in 1975–1976). With some exceptions, notably for taxes to repay debts issued in prior years, this taxpayer initiative removed the basic underpinnings of the GO security for governmental units in California. Tax initiatives followed suit in other states—most notably **Proposition 2 1/2** in Massachusetts—requiring government officials to seek alternative methods for capital finance. The growth of the revenue bond has been one response.

Perhaps the most important driving forces in the shift to nongovernmental purposes have been the significant interest cost savings available in the tax-exempt market and federal tax policy as embodied in section 103 of the Internal Revenue Code. As Exhibit 15 points out, interest rates generally have followed an irregular but pronounced upward trend since the mid-1960s. Accompanying this secular upward drift in rates has been a widening of the interest rate differential between taxable and tax-exempt debt. Using yields on AAA-rated bonds as indicators of the relative costs of borrowing, the data in Exhibit 15 indicate that the yield differential has widened from 1.46% in 1966 to more than 3.0% in the last several years.

EXHIBIT 13 USE OF PROCEEDS, NEW ISSUES OF TAX EXEMPT BONDS: (*a*) 1975 AND (*b*) 1984

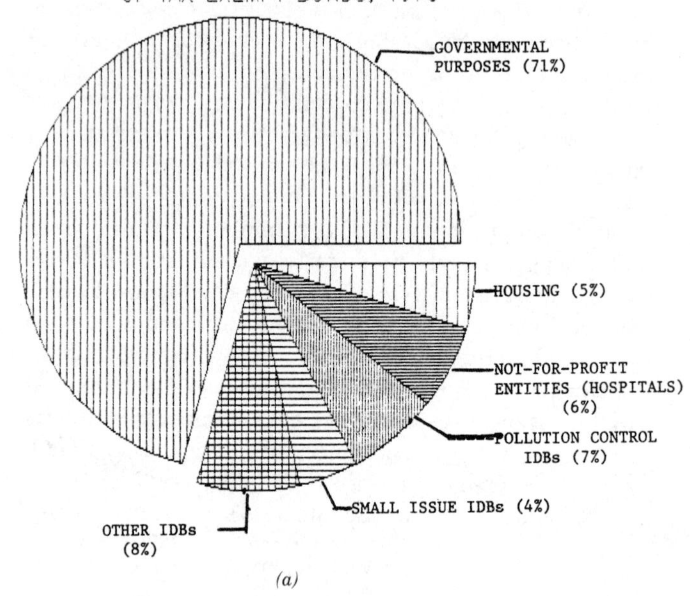

(*a*)

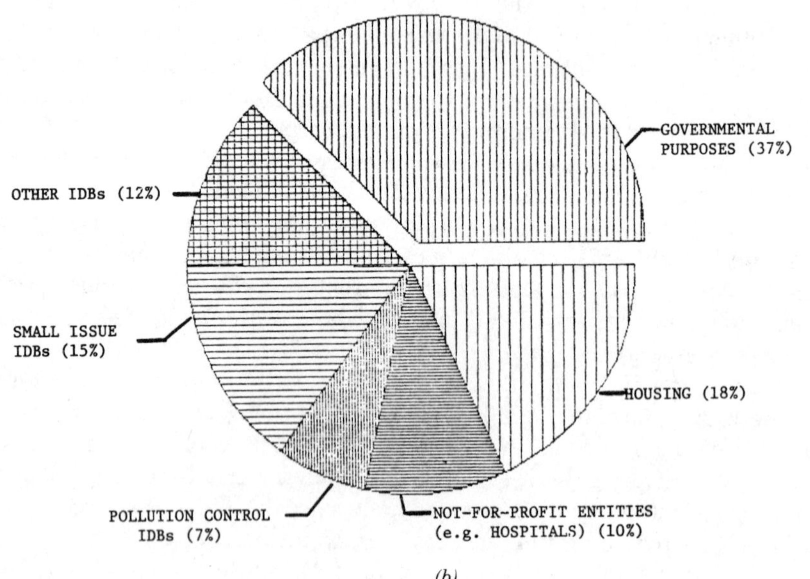

(*b*)

EXHIBIT 14 CAPITAL SPENDING BY STATE AND LOCAL GOVERNMENTS

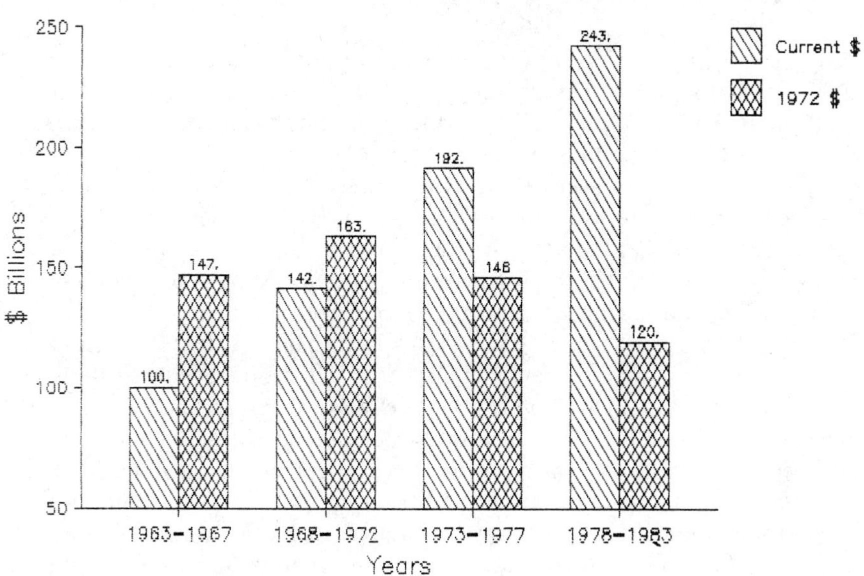

EXHIBIT 15 YIELDS ON AAA-RATED TAXABLE AND TAX-EXEMPT BONDS, 1966–1984

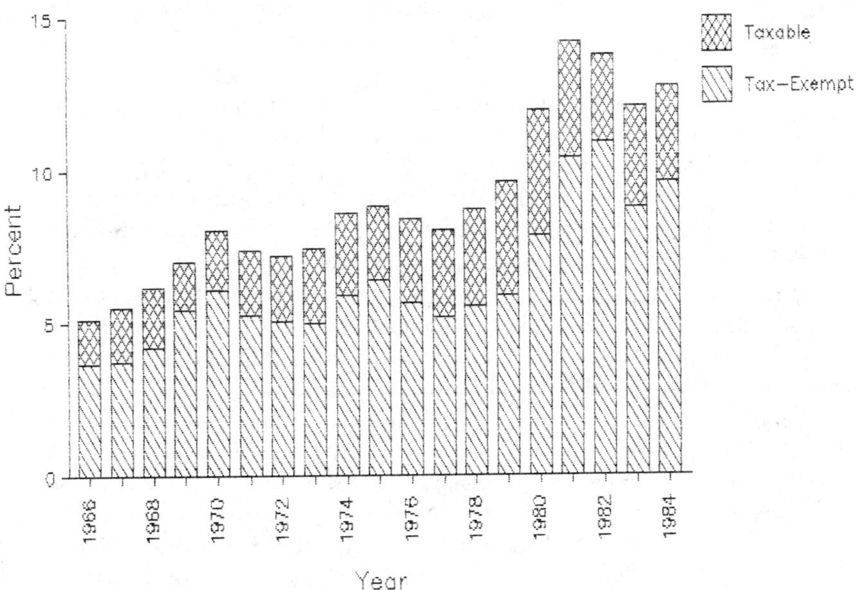

SECTION 103 AND FEDERAL TAX POLICY

The rising cost of borrowing from traditional (taxable) loan markets and the potential for substantial interest savings provided a strong economic incentive for eligible borrowers to seek access to the tax-exempt market. This access, since 1968, has been controlled by the federal government through legislative and regulatory changes in **section 103 of the Internal Revenue Code**. Section 103 has become a major instrument of federal tax policy, shaping the supply of tax-exempt securities and the activities they finance.

Prior to 1968, section 103 defined tax-exempt securities by reference to the issuers (e.g., state and local governments) and not by reference to the users of bond proceeds. As a result, many states began issuing large volumes of tax-exempts to provide low-interest loans for industrial expansion. Alarmed by the growth in these **industrial development bonds (IDBs)**, Congress in 1968 passed the **Revenue and Expenditure Control Act**, which amended section 103 to prohibit or curtail tax-exempt financing for nonexempt persons or purposes. However, the prohibitions were not all-encompassing. Tax-exempt financing was permitted for a long list of "exempt activities," including owner-occupied housing, rental housing, sports facilities, convention centers, airports and ports, mass commuting, sewage or solid waste facilities, water and pollution control, industrial parks, and so-called small issue IDBs ($10 million or less) for virtually any depreciable real property owned by private enterprises. Other sections detailed a range of constraints governing these financings, including limitations on arbitrage or the investment of low cost tax-exempt bond proceeds in higher-yielding "taxable" investments. Since the 1968 legislation, the umbrella provided to so-called exempt activities has encouraged an ever-expanding volume of nongovernmental financing and the burgeoning growth of these bonds has focused new attention on the federal subsidy embodied in tax-exempt finance.

Under the **Congressional Budget Act of 1974**, the federal budget is required to list **tax expenditures**. The concept of a tax expenditure is based on the premise that not taxing certain income is equivalent to a decision by legislators to spend the same amount. Under the 1974 Act, tax expenditures are defined as "revenue losses attributable to provisions of the federal tax laws which allow a special exclusion, exemption, or deduction from gross income. . . ," a definition that includes tax-exempt finance. Although the measurement of these revenue losses is imprecise and subject to intense debate, the Congressional Joint Committee on Taxation has estimated that revenue losses from tax-exempt financing will amount to $29.4 billion in fiscal year 1986.

One important construct in the methodology for estimating these revenue losses is the "break-even marginal tax rate" of investors in tax-exempts. Although this rate cannot be measured directly, it is often inferred by reference to the ratio of tax-exempt and taxable yields. The implied break-even marginal tax rate at which after-tax yields on taxable bonds equal the tax-exempt bond rate is traced in Exhibit 16. This "break-even" tax rate is the lowest marginal

EXHIBIT 16 THE RATIO OF TAX-EXEMPT TO TAXABLE YIELDS

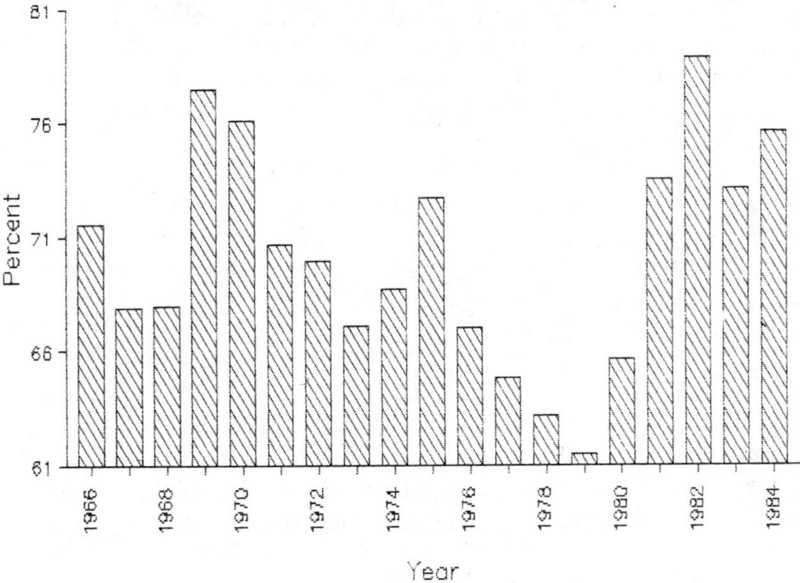

tax rate at which investors would be indifferent, on the basis of yield alone, in the choice between tax-exempt and taxable securities. Expressed another way, investors who pay taxes at a marginal rate *higher* than this break-even rate would earn higher yields from tax-exempt securities. The equation that relates tax-exempt yields to after-tax equivalent yields on taxable securities is:

$$MTR = 1 - (RTE/RTX),$$

where

MTR = marginal tax rate
RTE = tax-exempt yield
RTX = taxable yield

To demonstrate, if the taxable rate (RTX) is 12% and the tax-exempt rate (RTE) is 9%, the break-even marginal tax rate is 25%; investors in a marginal tax bracket above this could earn higher returns from tax-exempts. For example, an investor in the 40% marginal tax bracket would earn 7.2% after taxes on a taxable yield of 12%, versus a 9% yield on tax-exempts. This concept of the break-even marginal tax rate has played an important role in national policy debates over the efficiency and equity of tax exemption. Because the stock of outstanding tax-exempt debt is held by investors who, on average, pay taxes at a marginal rate **in excess** of the break-even rate, these investors are perceived to earn windfall gains at the expense of the federal treasury. This debate generally takes on impetus when the ratio of tax-exempt yields to taxable yields rises above 70%. Alarmed by the rapid growth in nongovernmental financing and the rising ratio of yields (and the declining break-even tax rate), Congress passed the Deficit Reduction Act of 1984 which placed limits on the volume of many private purpose tax-exempt bonds. This cap includes IDBs and student loan bonds and limits the volume to the greater of $200 million per state or $150 per capita ($100 per capita after 1986). In 1985, mounting concerns over an exploding federal deficit renewed interest at the federal level in reducing the revenue losses associated with tax-exemption. Current proposals again are focusing on section 103 and on far more restrictive limitations on the aggregate volume of nongovernmental bonds eligible under this section of the Internal Revenue Code.

EVALUATING CREDIT RISK AND CREDIT QUALITY

Although the value of tax-exempt income weighs most heavily in investors' decisions, other factors are important in determining which securities will be purchased or sold and what interest rate will be required. Important among these factors is an assessment of the relative risks on different securities. The risk arises because investors are purchasing claims on the future revenues of issuers of tax-exempt debts, and these future revenues cannot be known with certainty. Until 1975, this risk was of generally small import to investors; defaults were few, small in size, and most often the result of somewhat speculative ventures uniquely susceptible to competitive forces or changes in demand.

In 1975, however, a major public authority of New York State, the Urban Development Corporation, temporarily defaulted on maturing bond anticipation notes. Shortly thereafter, New York City was denied market access when underwriters and investors were unable to obtain adequate financial information. Faced with billions in maturing notes, the city declared a "moratorium" on certain of these notes, creating in effect a "de facto" default. Cleveland, in 1978, also defaulted on note issues. In 1982, the Washington Public Power Supply System (or "Whoops") terminated construction on two large nuclear power generating projects for which $2.25 billion in tax-exempt bonds had been sold. In 1983 the Washington State Supreme Court ruled that the contracts of participants (so-called take or pay contracts) to repay the outstanding debt were not legal. As a result, the bonds were declared in default, representing the largest municipal default in history. One consequence of these dramatic and recurring credit crises has been a widening of the yield spread between bonds of different quality. Exhibit 17 points out that the yield spread between AAA and Baa—rated tax-exempts jumped sharply after 1975, from about 65 basis points in prior years to more than 120 basis points, on average, since then.

The events of 1975 and thereafter also focused attention on the adequacy of financial information and reporting practices. Historically, states and their local governments had developed a bewildering variety of formats for

EXHIBIT 17 YIELD SPREAD AAA-RATED VERSUS BAA-RATED GO BONDS

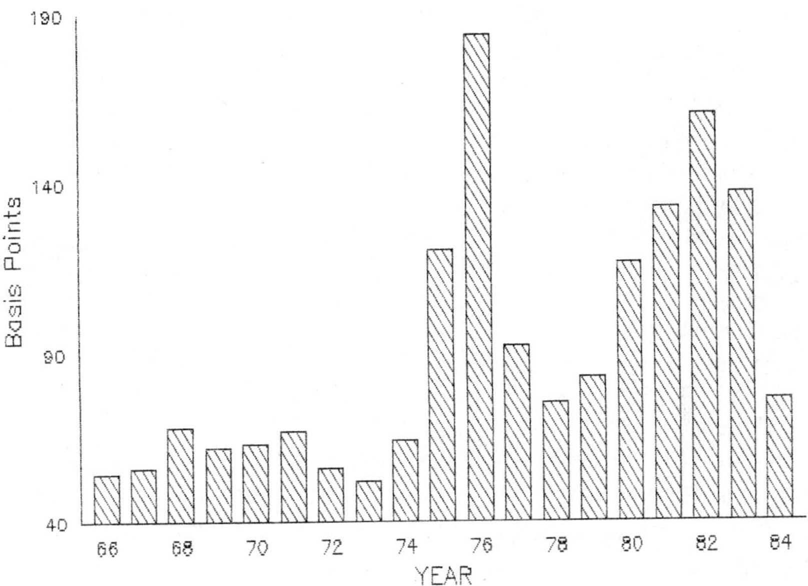

recording the collection of revenues and the disbursements of expenditures. These financial reporting practices generally were not geared toward uniformity and their purpose was not oriented toward the investor. Often, financial information was designed as an adjunct to trace funds in compliance with programmatic requirements, and too often methods of accounting were the captives of political expediency. The credit markets since 1975 have demanded reform in these practices, and governmental units have increasingly responded, developing in the process a voluntary set of national standards that define GAAP or generally accepted accounting practices. The importance of adequate financial reporting has been emphasized by one of the major bond rating agencies—Standard & Poor's Corporation—which has issued a policy statement that says in part:

> S&P can and must take into account in its rating process the type and quality of reporting and accounting standards being used . . .
> All financial statements submitted to S&P . . . are expected to be prepared in accordance with Generally Accepted Accounting Principles (GAAP) . . .
> These statements should be independently audited, either by a certified public accounting firm or by a qualified independent State or local agency, on a timely basis, i.e, no later than six months after the fiscal year-end. (Standard & Poor's Corporation, *Municipal Credit Overview,* November, 1983, p. 11.)

The lack of audited financial statements on a timely basis is now an important signal to investors to proceed with caution. Other factors used to gauge credit quality include trends in the economic base of the borrower—such indicators as the level and growth of incomes, the employment mix, unemployment rates, and the level and growth of taxable property. Administrative factors reviewed by analysts relate principally to the tax assessment and collection system, budgeting practices, and the contingent costs of possible litigation.

The most meaningful measures of debt for credit analysis of general obligation bonds are *net debt* and *overall debt.* Net debt refers to the total long- and short-term debt supported by the general revenues of the government. Overall debt includes the outstanding debt of all other governmental units that tap the same tax base for revenues to repay debt. Typically both debt measures are stated in ratio form relative to taxable property or income as standard measures of community wealth.

Although many of the same factors are reviewed in developing a risk profile of revenue bonds, the growth of "enterprise-type" activities has required a somewhat special focus on industry trends with an associated review of supply and demand conditions relevant to the "product" or business financed with tax-exempt debt. The risks here are familiar to the commercial loan analyst and include:

1. Competition from new or improved products or services
2. Obsolescence or problems of maintenance and capital replacement
3. Shifts in demand due to changing economic or social factors
4. Risks of poor management
5. Construction period risks that the project may not be completed on time and/or may vastly exceed budget.

Analyzing the bonds of public financial intermediaries, which hold asset portfolios of other debt instruments such as mortgage loans, requires information on the credit quality of the loan portfolio, including some measure of the "systematic" risks. These systematic risks—factors common to each of the loans in the portfolio—determine the likelihood that a decline in creditworthiness for one loan will be followed by similar deterioration in other components of the portfolio.

BOND RATINGS AND CREDIT ENHANCEMENTS

The multiplicity of issuers of tax-exempts and the remarkably varied security features of their debts have given rise to intermediaries that specialize in the collection and dissemination of credit information. Foremost among these intermediaries are the bond rating agencies and two agencies—*Moody's Investors Service* and *Standard & Poor's Corporation*—have become the dominant information brokers in the tax-exempt market. Exhibit 18 summarizes the symbols used by Moody's in assigning ratings to bond issues and Exhibit 19 summarizes data on the volume of new bond issues by rating for 1983. As these data indi-

EXHIBIT 18 KEY TO MOODY'S MUNICIPAL RATINGS

Aaa

Bonds which are rated Aaa are judged to be of the best quality. They carry the smallest degree of investment risk and are generally referred to as "gilt edge." Interest payments are protected by a large or by an exceptionally stable margin and principal is secure. While the various protective elements are likely to change, such changes as can be visualized are most unlikely to impair the fundamentally strong position of such issues.

Aa

Bonds which are rated Aa are judged to be of high quality by all standards. Together with the Aaa group they comprise what are generally known as high grade bonds. They are rated lower than the best bonds because margins of protection may not be as large as in Aaa securities or fluctuation of protective elements may be of greater amplitude or there may be other elements present which make the long-term risks appear somewhat larger than in Aaa securities.

A

Bonds which are rated A possess many favorable investment attributes and are to be considered as upper medium grade obligations. Factors giving security to principal and interest are considered adequate, but elements may be present which suggest a susceptibility to impairment sometime in the future.

Baa

Bonds which are rated Baa are considered as medium grade obligations; i.e., they are neither highly protected nor poorly secured. Interest payments and principal security appear adequate for the present but certain protective elements may be lacking or may be characteristically unreliable over any great length of time. Such bonds lack outstanding investment characteristics and in fact have speculative characteristics as well.

Ba

Bonds which are rated Ba are judged to have speculative elements; their future cannot be considered as well-assured. Often the protection of interest and principal payments may be very moderate, and thereby not well safeguarded during both good and bad times over the future. Uncertainty of position characterizes bonds in this class.

B

Bonds which are rated B generally lack characteristics of the desirable investment. Assurance of interest and principal payments or of maintenance of other terms of the contract over any long period of time may be small.

Caa

Bonds which are rated Caa are of poor standing. Such issues may be in default or there may be present elements of danger with respect to principal or interest.

Ca

Bonds which are rated Ca represent obligations which are speculative in a high degree. Such issues are often in default or have other marked shortcomings.

C

Bonds which are rated C are the lowest rated class of bonds, and issues so rated can be regarded as having extremely poor prospects of ever attaining any real investment standing.

Con. (. . .)

Bonds for which the security depends upon the completion of some act or the fulfillment of some condition are rated conditionally. These are bonds secured by (*a*) earnings of projects under construction, (*b*) earnings of projects unseasoned in operation experience, (*c*) rentals which begin when facilities are completed, or (*d*) payments to which some other limiting condition attaches. Parenthetical rating denotes probable credit stature upon completion of construction or elimination of basis of condition.

Note: Those bonds in the Aa, A, Baa, Ba and B groups which Moody's believes possess the strongest investment attributes are designated by the symbols Aa 1, A 1, Baa 1, Ba 1 and B 1.

Source: Moody's Investors Service, *Moody's Bond Record,* January 1980.

EXHIBIT 19 NEW TAX-EXEMPT BOND SALES BY MOODY'S RATING GRADE, 1983 ($ MILLIONS)

Moody's Rating	General Obligation	Revenue
AAA	$2,578	$ 3,309
AA	5,465	11,427
A	6,235	24,503
BAA	1,848	2,962
Below BAA	620	40
Not rated by Moody's	4,665	20,252

Source: Public Securities Association.

cate, virtually all new issues that carry ratings have investment grade ratings in the top four letter grades.

The growing complexity of new tax-exempts has also spawned a new "growth" industry, and that is the business of supplying *credit enhancements.* Exhibit 20 points out that the par volume of bonds with full or partial credit enhancement issued in 1984 amounted to $36.5 billion or 34% of all bonds sold. Exhibit 20 also points out that a variety of credit enhancements now exist, including bond "insurance," irrevocable letters of credit from domestic and foreign commercial banks and thrift institutions, surety bonds from other financial intermediaries, and state guarantees of local government debts.

Credit enhancements have two purposes—to reduce borrowing costs to issuers, and to reduce information costs and risks to investors. Those that supply enhancements (e.g., banks or insurance companies) indicate their willingness, for a fee, to substitute their credit standing and resources for those of the borrower. Although the mechanisms differ in important ways, the credit enhancements listed in Exhibit 20 provide that investors can look to the supplier of the enhancement rather than the issuer of the bonds for ultimate debt repayment. In most cases the superior credit standing of the supplier results in a higher bond rating, thereby improving market access and lowering interest costs to borrowers. Credit enhancements can also be viewed as a form of **put option**

EXHIBIT 20 VOLUME OF NEW TAX-EXEMPT BONDS WITH CREDIT ENHANCEMENTS, 1984

Type of Credit Enhancement		Par Value of Bonds ($ billions)
Private bond insurance		$18.174
Letters of Credit—Total		17.260
Domestic commercial banks	$10.716	
Foreign commercial banks	5.956	
Thrift institutions	.588	
Surety bonds		.537
State guarantees		.446

Source: Public Securities Association. Amounts include par value of all bond issues fully or partially insured.

available to investors. In the future event that the borrower would otherwise default on a promised payment, investors are permitted to "put" the bonds to the supplier for repayment. For many investors, the availability of this type of "put" option from a widely recognized financial institution is a valuable asset. Among other factors, this option reduces the costs to investors of monitoring and analyzing ongoing credit performance over the life of a bond.

The standard bond insurance contract runs for the life of the outstanding bonds. It provides that in the case of an issuer who fails to make principal and/or interest payments in full and on time, the insurer will do so. The payments are made according to the original maturity/coupon schedule on the bonds. Insurance premiums, paid directly or indirectly by borrowers, are scaled to risk and they range from .5 to 2% of the combined principal and interest payments over the life of the debt. Most often these premiums are payable in full at the time of original issuance of the bonds. Irrevocable letters of credit from banks and other financial institutions constitute direct guarantees of the borrower's obligation by the bank. By contrast with bond insurance, however, the term of the LOC is generally shorter than the life of the bonds. Terms run from 5 to 15 years, with provisions included for future renewals at the bank's option. In the event of a nonrenewal, substitute enhancements can be supplied or the bonds may be subject to mandatory redemption prior to the expiration date of the original LOC. Thus, although investors receive a "put option" similar to that provided by bond insurance, the duration of this option is uncertain.

In its simplest form, a state guarantee is an explicit promise by the state to an investor in its local governments' bonds that any shortfall in local resources will be automatically replenished by the state. In its strongest form, a state guarantee places the full faith and credit of the state behind the contingent call on state funds. States have devised other forms of **credit assistance** for local governments, and a particularly effective approach is **state financial intermediation** on behalf of localities. State financial intermediaries issue tax-exempt bonds and use the proceeds to make loans to local governments. One major purpose of the intermediary is to achieve economies in the sale of bonds by pooling numerous small local debt issues into a larger bond designed to reach a national market. The best known example is the **bond bank** concept, which has been implemented in several states. The bonds of the bond bank are secured in the first instance by the loan repayments from local governments, with added pledges of state assistance in the event of shortfalls.

The rapid growth of credit enhancements has improved the market access for many types of tax-exempt borrowers. However, it is appropriate for investors to remember that the underlying risks have not been erased—they have merely been shifted to other parties, who *may* have special talents or resources that can better bear these risks. Investors in bonds with credit enhancements have substituted the underlying risk of the supplier for that of the issuer. As the recent spate of downgradings in commercial bank ratings indicates, the value of credit enhancement can deteriorate.

THE DEMAND FOR TAX-EXEMPT SECURITIES

The exemption of interest income from federal taxes is of greatest appeal to institutions or individuals in high marginal income tax brackets. Exhibit 21 points out that three investor sectors—commercial banks, households and their surrogates, mutual funds, and property/casualty insurance companies—account for most purchases of tax-exempts. These data also indicate that there is a considerable degree of volatility in the purchases of tax-exempts by these investor segments.

Bank demand for tax-exempts since 1966 has been characterized by periods of strong demand (1966–1971), and 1977–1980) followed by periods of relatively weak demand (1972–1976 and 1980–1984). Property and casualty company demand began a strong upward trend in 1969, culminating in 1977–1978, when casualty companies absorbed nearly 50% of the net new supply in tax-exempts. Since then, casualty companies have progressively withdrawn from the market. The behavior of demand from these two groups of financial intermediaries is determined primarily by profitability, and only secondarily by the relative attractiveness of tax-exempt interest rates. As summarized by one econometric study:

> When these investors have large profits to shield from taxes, they invest heavily in tax-exempts. When profits are small, these investors reduce their purchases of

EXHIBIT 21 CHANGE IN TAX-EXEMPT SECURITIES HELD BY INVESTOR SECTORS AS A PERCENT OF NET CHANGE IN OUTSTANDING TAX-EXEMPTS

Year	Commercial Banks	Households	Mutual Funds	Property/ Casualty Insurance
1966	42.9%	71.4%		12.5%
1967	116.7	−29.5		19.2
1968	90.5	−5.3		9.5
1969	6.1	93.9		11.1
1970	94.7	−8.0		13.3
1971	72.4	.6		20.1
1972	49.0	15.7		29.3
1973	38.8	36.1		25.2
1974	32.7	49.7		13.3
1975	11.2	38.5		16.2
1976	19.1	12.7	3.2%	34.4
1977	42.0	−6.9	7.3	48.9
1978	33.8	14.4	1.8	47.5
1979	31.7	34.3	4.6	32.7
1980	44.9	23.1	6.6	25.4
1981	22.0	45.4	12.8	17.6
1982	8.7	60.8	20.3	5.6
1983	6.9	72.8	18.3	−.5
1984	21.2	55.5	22.8	.9

Source: Board of Governors of the Federal Reserve System, *Flow of Funds* (1979).

tax-exempts even if tax-exempt interest rates rise, because exemption is valuable only if there exist profits to be shielded from taxation at the full corporate rate. (Hendershott and Koch, 1977, p. 11.)

Commercial bank demand is also subject to regional variations based on "pledging" requirements for state and local government deposits. These requirements, which vary among states, mandate that banks hold in-state tax-exempts as collateral for public deposits. Until recently banks have also been able to engage in a unique form of tax arbitrage and this has increased aggregate bank demand for tax-exempts. Unique among all investor segments, banks have been able to deduct from their taxable income, the interest expenses on debt (e.g., time deposits) incurred to purchase tax-exempts. Thus, for banks that at least "break-even" on their taxable asset portfolio, there are strong incentives to borrow and buy tax-exempts as long as the after-tax cost of debt is less than the tax-exempt rate. In 1982, TEFRA removed a portion of this interest deductibility for tax-exempts purchased after 1982. The *Deficit Reduction Act of 1984* removed more of this deductibility for tax-exempts purchased after 1984; thus some of the increased market share for banks in 1984 can be attributed to the "stocking-up" of portfolios prior to the loss of this deductibility. Present proposals for tax reform would remove all of this deductibility; if enacted, banks would then require tax-exempt yields at least equal to the *before tax* cost of funds.

When banks and casualty companies do purchase tax-exempts, they exhibit distinct preferences for securities with specific attributes. Bank demand has for many years been concentrated in shorter-term, higher-rated securities, and tax-exempts with maturities of 10 years or less are commonly referred to as "bank range" securities. Casualty companies, on the other hand, have traditionally purchased long-term maturities with lower ratings and higher yields—these institutions have been especially important as investors in long-term revenue bonds.

Given the supply of new tax-exempts and the demand for them by banks and insurance companies, any remaining net supply must be absorbed by the household sector. With the exception of individuals in the very highest income classes, most individuals will face marginal tax rates below the full corporate rate paid by institutions. Therefore as the share of new tax-exempts that must be absorbed by individuals increases, more tax-exempts will need to be marketed to individuals in progressively lower tax brackets. As noted by a comparison of the data in Exhibit 21 with the data in Exhibits 15 and 16, the recent years of increased market share by households correspond to a rising ratio of tax-exempt rates relative to taxable rates and a declining "break-even" marginal tax rate in the market. Added pressure on the tax-exempt rate also resulted from the sharp reductions in all marginal tax rates from the 1981 **Economic Recovery Tax Act**.

The need to market increasing shares of new tax-exempts to investors in lower tax brackets has other implications. Individuals in lower tax brackets may have substantial incomes, but they are less likely to have accumulated significant financial wealth. As a result it is difficult for these individuals to achieve diversified portfolios of tax-exempts in conventional denominations (e.g., $5,000). Mutual funds can provide this diversification in the small denominations preferred by investors; it is not surprising therefore that the share of tax-exempts purchased by funds has increased dramatically in recent years to nearly 23% of net new issues in 1984. Among funds the most dramatic growth has been achieved by tax-exempt money market funds, which held net assets of $23 billion at 1984 year-end.

THE MATURITY STRUCTURE OF TAX-EXEMPT YIELDS

Exhibit 22 graphs yields on AAA-rated tax-exempt bonds by maturity for October 1981, the most recent cyclical peak in long-term interest rates, and October 1985, when rates descended to the lowest levels since 1981. Also presented for comparison are yields by maturity for U.S. Treasury bonds. The most interesting feature of these data is that yields typically increase with a lengthening of maturity for tax-exempts, even in periods such as 1981 when the yield-maturity relationship for Treasury bonds was negative (i.e., short-term yields were higher than long-term yields). In 1981, for example, the yield spread between 20-year and 1-year tax-exempts was 300 basis points (e.g., 12.20% − 9.20% = 300 bp) whereas the 20-year, 1-year spread in the Treasury market was a negative 99 basis points. In October 1985 the Treasury yield curve was positively

EXHIBIT 22 YIELD CURVES ON U.S. TREASURIES AND AAA-RATED TAX-EXEMPTS

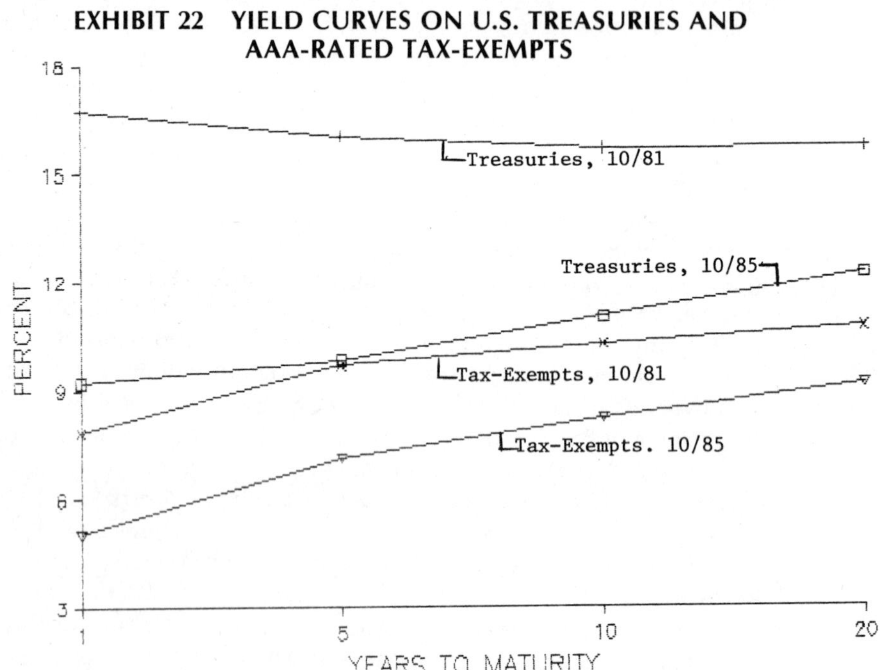

sloped with a spread of 288 basis points, but the tax-exempt yield curve was even more steeply sloped, with a 415 basis point differential between 20-year and 1-year yields. For the past two decades, the tax-exempt yield curve has been upward sloping, through many periods such as 1981, when the yield curve in the taxable market was downward-sloping.

The strong correlation between yields and maturities in the tax-exempt market is generally believed to be the consequence of unique factors at work in this market. One important factor is the character of demand. Commercial banks, with high marginal tax rates and the possibility of "tax arbitrage," have dominated the short-term market, whereas individuals, who face lower marginal taxes, have been relatively more important in the long-term market. This type of "tax bracket" segmentation casts an upward bias to the tax-exempt yield curve. Moreover, uncertainty over future marginal tax rates can foster uncertainty over the future value of tax-exempt income, and higher yields on long-term bonds may be necessary to compensate for this uncertainty. On the supply side, many borrowers in taxable loan markets shift from long-term to short-term debt when interest rates begin approaching cyclical peaks, and these shifts tend to reinforce the well-known correlation between high levels of interest rates and downward-sloping yield curves in the taxable market. Many governmental units, however, are constrained by state laws or other factors to carry out their capital financing plans with long-term debt. There is, therefore, a less pronounced shift to short-term borrowing during cyclical periods of high and rising interest rates.

The general trend toward higher long-term interest rates over the last two decades has been accompanied, since 1979, by a dramatic increase in the volatility of rates. Exhibit 23 records the month-to-month changes in the Bond Buyer 20-Bond Index since 1977. The Bond Buyer Index is an average of yields on 20-year maturities of 20 GO bonds with an average rating of A+/AA−. Prior to 1979 the absolute value of monthly changes in the Bond Buyer Index averaged less than 20 basis points. Since 1979 the absolute value of monthly changes has exceeded, on average, 50 basis points, and changes above 100 basis points have not been uncommon.

CREATIVE FINANCING: VARIABLE RATE BONDS. The high level of long-term rates, the increased volatilityof these rates, and the steep positive slope of the yield curve have stimulated the development of a variety of new and complex financing techniques. Among them, the use of variable rate bonds has been prominent; in 1984 more than $25 billion in variable rate tax-exempt bonds were issued. These bonds have a long-term final maturity date but an interest rate that is "reset" at scheduled intervals. Variable rate bonds may have provisions for daily, weekly, monthly, semiannual, or annual interest rate reset intervals.

Original versions of the variable rate bond tied the tax-exempt rate to easily available market rates such as U.S. Treasury bill or bond yields. These bonds were often called "floaters" because the interest rate would automatically follow the market. These early versions of variable rate bond encountered prob-

EXHIBIT 23 MONTH-TO-MONTH CHANGES; THE BOND BUYER 20-BOND INDEX

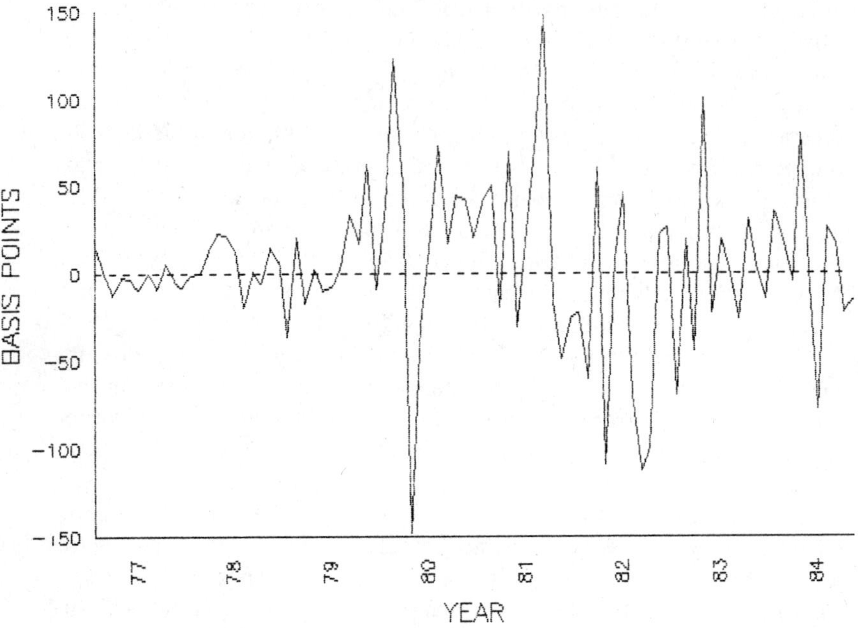

lems, however, because the tax-exempt/taxable yield ratio pegged in the interest reset formula often did not reflect actual market conditions. These difficulties prompted the current-day versions of the variable rate demand bond which possess four distinctive features:

1. A demand feature, which permits investors to redeem their bonds at par on the next interest rate reset interval
2. An interest rate index pegged solely to the tax-exempt market
3. A remarketing provision which is designed to avoid the need for continuous issuer approvals of new debt sales
4. A standby credit agreement with a commercial bank, which provides additional liquidity in the event that bonds cannot be remarketed

The demand feature is an example of a **put** option or a **bondholders' tender option** and it is an important and necessary component of the variable rate bond. The **put** option allows investors the choice of holding or redeeming at par their investments at specified future intervals. Depending on the frequency of the put option interval, investors may convert otherwise long-term bonds to investments with effecive maturities as short as one week. As a result, yields on these bonds follow closely the yield on fixed maturity notes with maturities corresponding to the put option interval. Exhibit 24 summarizes these features for a weekly tender bond.

EXHIBIT 24 EXAMPLE OF VARIABLE RATE DEMAND BOND PROVISIONS $50,000,000 TEXAS HEALTH FACILITIES DEVELOPMENT CORPORATION ADJUSTABLE RATE HOSPITAL REVENUE BONDS SERIES 1984A ISSUED MAY 22, 1984 SELECTED BOND PROVISIONS

Remarketing and indexing agent:	The First Boston Corporation
Tender agent	Bankers Trust Company
Adjustable interest rate:	Bondholders tender or "put" options:
Prior to a conversation to a fixed interest rate, interest on the bond will be paid at an adjustable interest rate on the first business day of each month. The adjustable rate index will be calculated weekly by the indexing agent and shall equal the average thirty (30) day or less yield evaluation at part of at least five comparable tax-exempt issues. Interest on the bonds will be calculated on a 365 or 366 day year and will not exceed 15% per annum.	Prior to a conversion to a fixed interest rate, each bondholder shall have the right to demand the purchase of that holder's bonds on any business day which is at least seven days after such demand (the "purchase date") , upon presentation of a bondholder election notice to the tender agent (or in the case of a bondholder which is a registered investment company, to the trustee with a copy to the tender agent) at the time of demand.

The variable feature of the variable rate demand bond refers to the interval between interest rate changes and the process by which new rates are set. In Exhibit 24 the interest rate reset interval is one week. Pegging the interest rate to yields on tax-exempt instruments avoids the problems of shifting relationships between tax-exempt and taxable markets. The remarketing agreement "backstops" the demand feature and provides for the continuous marketing of tendered bonds to new investors. In the event that some or all investors choose to tender bonds, the tender agent exchanges bonds for cash. Rather than turning to the issuer or to a bank credit facility for funds, the tender agent first notifies the remarketing agent, who then attempts to resell tendered bonds at the new interest rate. Exhibit 25 outlines the numerous parties involved in a variable rate demand bond program and it illustrates the complex mechanics required to make it work. Most of the current generation of variable rate bonds also have **conversion options** that permit issuers to convert the bond issue from a variable rate to a long-term fixed rate bond after notice to investors.

BONDS WITHOUT COUPONS: ZERO COUPON BONDS. Some investors have as an investment objective the accumulation of maximum future wealth. For such investors, the stream of semiannual coupon payments on a conventional bond subjects them to reinvestment rate risk, because future wealth depends on the interest earned from the reinvestment of interim coupon payments. This reinvestment rate is in general unknown, and the heightened volatility of rates in recent years has increased this uncertainty.

Long-term **zero coupon bonds** provide an investment alternative that re-

EXHIBIT 25 AGENTS IN VARIABLE RATE DEMAND BOND TRANSACTIONS

Agent	Function	Cost of Service
Underwriter	Negotiates original sale of bonds; also may serve as remarketing, tender agent	Gross spread ranges between $6 and $15 per $1,000 par value
Remarketing agent	Remarkets tendered bonds; generally, senior underwriting manager is appointed	⅛ to ½ of par amount tendered.
Tender agent	Receives and holds tendered bonds until remarketed; usually marketing fees. Performed by senior manager	Included with remarketing agent.
Indexing agent	Prepare and publishes interest rate index; may be outside service (e.g., JJ Kenny) or remarketing agent	Fee ranges from zero when remarketing agent is used to $25,000 per year
Paying agent	Performs record-keeping functions and records principal and interest payments to bondholders	$5,000 to $10,000 initial fee; $5,000 to $15,000 per year depending on number of transactions
Trustee	Monitors all parties to transactions to ensure compliance with indenture. Normally serves as paying agent also.	Same as paying agent
Commercial bank liquidity agreement	Provides funds for tendered bonds not immediately remarketed	¼ to ½% of par amount of bonds outstanding
Commercial banks bond insurance company: Credit support	Provides credit enhancement for bonds to insure payment of principal and interest to bondholder	½ to 1½% of principal (banks) or of principal and interest (insurance)

duces the risks of uncertain future reinvestment rates. These bonds are sold at a substantial discount from their value at maturity, and they provide a "locked-in" compound rate of return that may be especially valuable to investors who anticipate that future reinvestment rates may be lower than present coupon rates. Exhibit 26 provides an example of a **serial bond issue** sold by Tampa, Florida, in April 1982. This issue combined traditional coupon-bearing serial bonds maturing from 1984 to 1988 with serial zero-coupon bonds maturing from 1989 through 2015. According to statements at the time, the zero coupon bonds carried yields that were as much as 250 basis points below the estimated coupon rates that would have been required to sell conventional debt. The lower yields reflected the strong demand from investors to avoid reinvestment risk.

THE MUNICIPAL BOND INDEX FUTURES CONTRACT. The heightened volatility of interest rates in recent years has increased the risks faced by underwriters and issuers as well as investors. Concerns for methods of transferring

EXHIBIT 26 EXAMPLE OF ZERO COUPON BONDS $129,115,000 CITY OF TAMPA, FLORIDA WATER AND SEWER SYSTEMS REVENUE BONDS (SERIES 1982)

Dated: May 1, 1982
Due: October 1, as shown below
$15,850,000 Serial Bonds

Due October 1	Amount	Coupon Rate	Price	Due October 1	Amount	Coupon Rate	Price
1984	$2,620,000	9.00%	100%	1987	$3,445,000	10.25%	100%
1985	2,860,000	9.50	100	1988	3,795,000	10.50	100
1986	3,130,000	10.00	100				

$54,535,000 Zero % Serial Discount Bonds

Due October 1	Amount	Offering Price	Due October 1	Amount	Offering Price
1989	$4,195,000	47.0%	1996	$4,195,000	20.0%
1990	4,195,000	42.0	1997	4,195,000	18.5
1991	4,195,000	37.0	1998	4,195,000	16.5
1992	4,195,000	33.0	1999	4,195,000	14.5
1993	4,195,000	29.0	2000	4,195,000	13.0
1994	4,195,000	25.0	2001	4,195,000	11.5
1995	4,195,000	22.5			

$16,780,000 Zero % Term Discount Bonds Due October 1, 2005 Offering Price 10.0%
$20,975,000 Zero % Term Discount Bonds Due October 1, 2010 Offering Price 6.0%
$20,975,000 Zero % Term Discount Bonds Due October 1, 2015 Offering Price 4.0%
(Plus accrued interest, if any)

these risks has led to the development of a **Municipal Bond Index Futures Contract**. This contract, which began trading on the Chicago Board of Trade on June 11, 1985, differs from futures contracts on other commodities or debt instruments in several ways. First, the Municipal Bond Index contract is based on an index of prices for a "market basket" of 40 different bonds. Moreover, the market basket may change semimonthly, when less-actively traded bonds can be replaced with new issues. The bonds in the market basket used to construct the index are priced based on an average of dealer quotes, not on actual transactions prices. All bond prices are converted to a price equivalent to an 8% bond yield. Finally, the contract is settled in cash at maturity; there are no provisions for delivery of actual securities.

Although this contract is new and based on a complex and "synthetic" index, the availability of a tax-exempt futures contract may provide bond dealers, underwriters, portfolio managers, and issuers with an important vehicle to hedge against the effects of unanticipated interest rate changes on existing positions in the tax-exempt market.

As these examples of creative financing indicate, the tax-exempt market has proved its ability to adapt to rapid and sometimes wrenching changes in market conditions.

REFERENCES

Hendershott, P.H., and Koch, T., "An Empirical Analysis of the Market for Tax-Exempt Securities: Estimates and Forecasts" Monograph Series in Finance and Economics, New York University, Graduate School of Business Administration, 1977

Hopewell, M., and Kaufman, G., *Improving Bidding Rules to Reduce Interest Costs in the Competitive Sale of Municipal Bonds: A Handbook for Municipal Finance Officers,* Center for Capital Market Research, Eugene: University of Oregon, 1977

Kaufman, G. (Ed.), *Efficiency in the Municipal Bond Market,* Greenwich, Conn.: JAI Press, 1981

Kaufman, G., and Rosen, K. (Eds.), *The Property Tax Revolt: The Case of Proposition 13,* Cambridge, Mass.: Ballinger, 1981

Petersen, J., and Hough, W., *Creative Capital Financing for State and Local Governments,* Government Finance Research Center, Chicago: Government Finance Officers Association, 1983

Smith, W., The Appraisal of Municipal Credit Risk, *Moody's Investors Service,* New York, 1979, p. 102

Standard & Poor's Corporation, *Creditweek* (May 27, 1985), p. 4.

Standard & Poor's Corporation, *Municipal Credit Overview,* New York, 1983.

U.S. Advisory Commission on Intergovernmental Relations, *Financing Public Physical Infrastructure,* Washington, D.C. (June 1984).

5

LONG-TERM DEBT AND EQUITY MARKETS AND INSTRUMENTS

CONTENTS

5

LONG-TERM DEBT AND EQUITY MARKETS AND INSTRUMENTS

C. Douglas Howard
Andrew J. Kalotay

The primary sources of permanent capital for U.S. corporations are the long-term debt, preferred stock, and the common stock markets. The funds from these sources of capital are referred to as a firm's capital structure. One of the objectives of the firm is to combine these funds in such a way as to minimize its overall cost of capital. Although the issue of whether an optimal capital structure can be determined is still a question of debate among financial theorists, an understanding of the various sources of funds and the market in which they operate is important to the financial manager. For a discussion on the financial management issues and the cost of capital, see Section 12, Long-Term Sources of Funds and the Cost of Capital, Altman, *Handbook of Corporate Finance*, Wiley, 1986.

This section describes and analyzes the various markets and instruments for corporate capital. It highlights the public markets for debt and preferred and common stock and also refers to the private or negotiated market for debt and equity instruments.

LONG-TERM DEBT SECURITIES

There are numerous types of long-term debt security, as well as various debt equivalents, that are alternative fixed income sources for corporations. The primary debt equivalent, leases, is discussed in depth in a separate section of this text. Short-term debt instruments and sources are also discussed elsewhere.

BOND TYPES

Mortgage Bonds. These are long-term obligations that are secured by specific property. In addition, mortgage bonds are unsecured claims on the general assets of the firm. In the event of default, holders of mortgage bonds receive ownership of the mortgaged property.

Collateral Trust Bonds. Backed by other securities, usually held by a trustee, collateral trust bonds are frequently used by a parent firm when it pledges the securities of a wholly owned subsidiary as collateral.

Equipment Trust Certificates. Instruments backed by specific pieces of equipment or machinery frequently are used by airlines, railroads, and shipping companies. These certificates may be issued by a trustee who holds the equipment, issues obligations, and leases the equipment to the corporation that uses it. Cash received from the corporation is used to pay the interest and principal on the equipment trust certificates. Eventually the firm will take title to the equipment.

Debenture Bonds. These general obligations of the issuing firm are unsecured credit. They are claims only on the general assets of the corporation and are protected by their indenture restrictions. The four most common types of indenture provision are (1) provisions against the issuance of more debt, (2) restrictions that limit dividend payments, (3) provisions restricting merger activity, and (4) restrictions on the disposition of the firm's assets.

Subordinated Debentures. These debentures are junior debt. In the event of bankruptcy their claims against the firm will be met only after the claims of senior debtholders have been fully satisfied.

Income Bonds. Such bonds pay interest only when the corporation's net income is above a prespecified level. Occasionally they are called adjustment bonds because they may be issued to readjust fixed interest debt by corporations undergoing reorganization. Unfortunately, if the issue bears too many of the characteristics of equity, the Internal Revenue Service may view the interest payments as "essentially equivalent to a dividend" and taxable as such. In this event the interest payments are no longer deductible as an expense before taxes.

Guaranteed Bonds. These instruments are guaranteed by the assets of a corporation other than the issuing firm. Usually the guaranteeing corporation is a parent firm.

Participating Bonds. These provide fixed interest payments and, in addition, a portion of surplus earnings accruing over the life of the bond if earnings are above the fixed interest.

Joint Bonds. Obligations jointly issued by two or more corporations (usually railroads) are sometimes called pooled or joint bonds because they provide joint collateral.

Voting Bonds. Usually issued in connection with reorganizations, voting bonds give holders the right to vote for directors if interest payments are not paid for a certain length of time.

Serial Bonds. These bonds have different portions of the issue maturing at different dates. A default on any portion coming due constitutes default on the entire issue.

Medium-Term Notes. A significant development in the capital markets has been the unprecedented activity, on the part of both borrowers and investors, in the intermediate maturity sector. The growth of medium-term note programs (MTNs) reflects this trend.

A medium-term note program is a financing vehicle that allows for the issuance of either secured or unsecured promissory notes on a continuous basis. Generally MTNs are offered in small amounts over a range of established maturities. The issuer typically offers notes over the entire range of maturities but offers the highest spreads (over Treasury securities) in the maturity ranges that it most desires to raise capital. By continuously varying the spread over Treasuries the company can achieve both its volume and maturity objectives.

Mechanically, MTNs are very similar to other corporate bonds. The only major difference is that they have a fixed semiannual interest payment cycle that disregards issue and maturity dates. Interest is paid on cycle dates and at maturity. For example, company X might have an MTN program with all notes paying interest on April 1 and October 1, regardless of the date of issuance or maturity. This methodology may result in a short first and last coupon payment period.

Convertible Bonds. The bond's indenture may give bondholders the privilege of converting their bonds into another security of the issuing company at a specified price, within a given time, and under stated terms and conditions. Bonds that carry this privilege are most often debenture issues, and the securities into which they are convertible are almost always junior issues, usually preferred or common stock, or units consisting of both. There have been instances among public utilities and railroads of short-term notes that were convertible into long-term mortgage bonds which were deposited as collateral to secure the notes. There are instances also in which bonds are made convertible into the securities of another company. The typical convertible bond is one exchangeable for common stock of the same issuer at the option of the holder.

Adjustable Rate Bonds. The interest rates on adjustable rate bonds are usually tied to the rates on specified Treasury securities or some other "index," such as the London Interbank Offered Rate (LIBOR). Investors usually charge a spread above the index, although there is no single formula used by all. Rates can also be expressed as a percentage (e.g., 110%) of the index. Rates are adjusted periodically—a typical issue will have rate changes every year or perhaps every 2 years.

Prior to 1980 these adjustable rate securities were primarily restricted to private placements where the institutional lender could negotiate the type of inflation hedge or protection that suited its desires. The attractiveness of these securities spread to the public market in late 1980 (see "The Wave of Adjustable Rate Debt," *BusinessWeek,* December 1, 1980 pp. 100–101). Although financial companies have floated these securities most frequently, the wave of new adjustable debt has spread to industrial and public utility companies as well.

Borrowers in the adjustable rate market are essentially choosing a floating-rate, which may come down, over a fixed-rate, which firms could be forced to fund for up to 30 years. Adjustable rate debt is a more popular means of financing for firms when interest rate levels are historically high. The uncertainty about future rates, however, is what makes this market attractive to buyers and sellers.

Original Issue Discount Bonds and Zero Coupon Debt. An original issue discount bond (OID) is one whose original discount (face amount less issue price) equals or exceeds .25% multiplied by the number of years to maturity. For example, a 10-year bond is an OID if its original price is at or below 97.5% of par. Such a substantial discount results when a bond's coupon payment (as a percent of par) falls short of the market yield to maturity. For example, a 10-year bond bearing a 10% coupon would be priced at 88.53% of par in a 12% market yield environment.

Zero coupon debt is the extreme example of an OID. Because "zeros" pay their face value at maturity with no coupon payments during the term, they sell at a large discount. For example, a 10-year zero issued to yield 12% would sell at 31.18% of face value. This discount of 68.82% far exceeds the 2.5% discount (.25% multiplied by 10 years) required for OID characterization. At a given yield, a zero will sell at a greater discount the longer the maturity. Also, given a fixed maturity, higher market yields will result in larger discounts.

In the early 1980s OIDs became popular when interest rates were reaching record high levels. Favorable tax treatment allowed the issuer to amortize the original discount on a straight-line basis over the life of the issue. This tax impact substantially reduced the after-tax effective cost as compared with a full coupon or par bond. The OIDs issued subsequent to July 1982 are subject to the less favorable tax treatment of the Tax Equity and Fiscal Responsibility Act of 1982. The original discount for these issues must be amortized over the term of the bond using the "scientific" or "constant yield" method. This generates lower tax deductions in the early years and greater tax deductions in the later years as compared with straight-line amortization. To illustrate the impact

EXHIBIT 1 INTEREST EXPENSE TAX DEDUCTIONS FOR ZERO COUPON DEBT

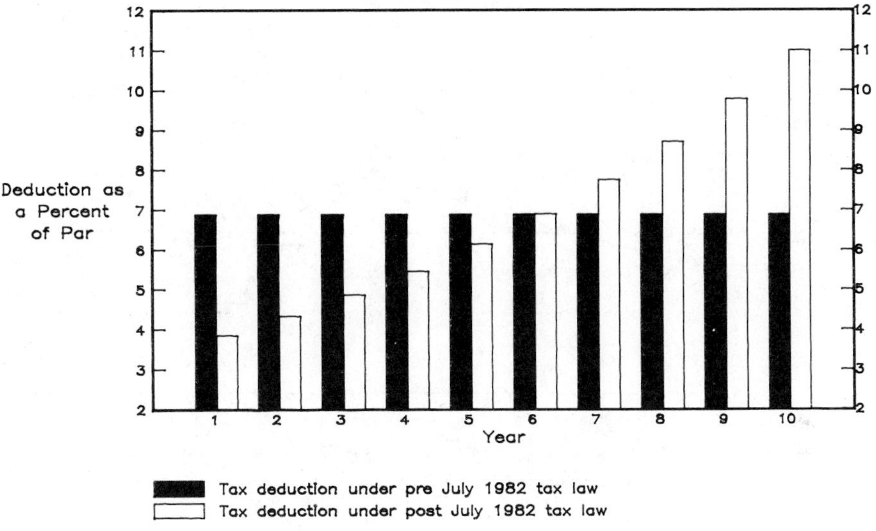

on the issuer of the tax treatment, consider the above-mentioned 10-year zero priced to yield 12%. Under the current tax law, the effective cost (pretax equivalent) to the issuer is 12%. Under the pre-July 1982 tax law, however, the effective cost would have been only 11.39%.

Exhibit 1 illustrates the tax treatment of **zero coupon debt** (from the issuer's standpoint) under the pre- and post-July 1982 tax laws. The top graph shows the annual interest expense deduction for the 10-year zero priced at 31.18% of par to yield 12% (or a 12.36% effective yield). Under the old straight-line tax treatment the deduction is the same amount in each year. Because the total interest actually paid on zero coupon debt over the life of the issue is exactly equal to the original discount, this annual deduction is equal to (100%–31.18%)/(10 years), or 6.88% of par per year. Under current tax law, in contrast, the constant yield method generates a tax deduction in the first year equal to the accrued liability, then 31.18%, multiplied by the effective yield of 12.36%. This gives an initial tax deduction of only 3.85% of par. The deduction subsequently grows exponentially by 12.36% each year. As under the old tax treatment, the sum of the 10 annual deductions exactly equals the original discount. Clearly, after the time value of money is considered, the deductions generated by the old tax law were more favorable. Although the total tax deduction over 10 years remains unchanged, the old tax treatment produced deductions that were relatively "front loaded."

Exhibit 2 illustrates the progression of a zero coupon bond's tax basis under both tax treatments. For zero coupon debt, the tax basis at any given time is

EXHIBIT 2 TAX BASIS OF ZERO COUPON DEBT

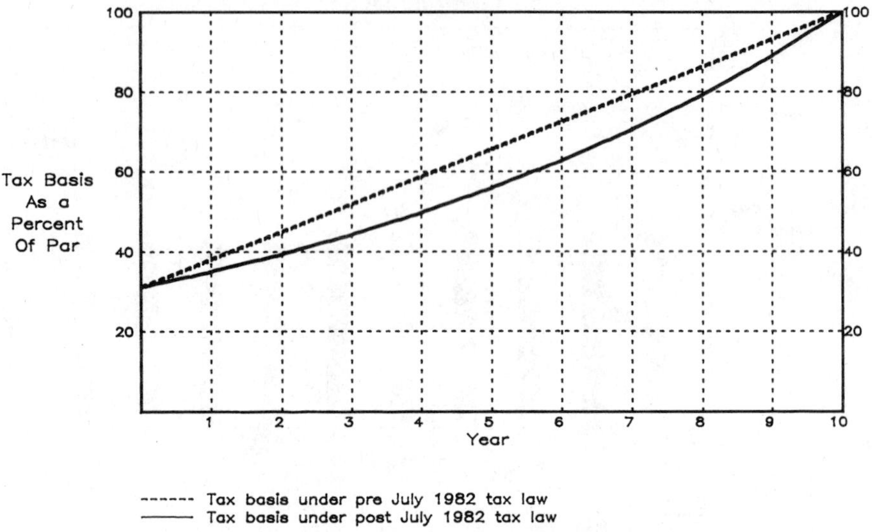

equal to the original proceeds plus cumulative interest deductions. Under the pre-July 1982 law, the tax basis increases more rapidly from the date of issuance; this reflects the larger interest deductions in the early years. With post-July 1982 tax treatment, the tax basis initially increases gradually and then more rapidly as maturity approaches. This reflects the relatively modest tax deductions early on and the larger deductions in later years. This effect becomes more exaggereated the longer the term of the bond.

The tax basis represents the carrying value of the zero for tax purposes. For purposes of financial statement reporting, the "book" value has always been reported based on the constant yield method. Issuers of zeros prior to the tax law change therefore have "deferred tax" accounts reflecting the differential between tax and book carrying values. This is not the case for zeros issued after the tax law change.

The **Dual Series Zero Coupon Debenture** is a security designed to look like a conventional full coupon bond from the standpoint of the issuer. From the standpoint of the investor, however, the cash flows are segregated and sold in separate markets. The coupon payments for the first 5 years are all sold separately as zero coupon bonds. The remaining coupon payments and the principal repayment at maturity are sold as a unit. The issue must be nonrefundable for at least 5 years to protect the holders of the coupon payments. By tapping the different markets that value these components most highly, the issuer is able to achieve a lower effective cost.

Bonds with "Put" Options. A **"put" option** on a bond entitles the bondholder to sell, or put, the bond to the issuer at a predetermined time or period of time during the bond's life. If the option is exercised, the issuer must repurchase the bond from the holder at a price agreed upon when the bond is first issued. The put price may be par value or at a premium to par. The terms of put options are far less standardized than those associated with call options. A putable bond is often issued in conjunction with an issuer call option.

A put option offers the holder protection against an increase in interest rates. The bondholder can lock in a long-term rate while hedging against the possibility of a further increase in rates. As a concession for this hedge, the bondholder settles for slightly less yield than is available on comparable nonputable securities.

Extendible Notes. An extendible note is a putable bond with additional provisions allowing the issuer to adjust the coupon rate periodically. The coupon, for example, might be adjustable at the issuer's discretion in 3-year intervals. Typically, the issuer has substantial flexibility in setting the new coupon rate. If dissatisfied with the rate, the holder has the option of selling the bond back to the issuer at par value.

In contrast to the putable bond, the extendible issuer has control over the likelihood of the put option being exercised. Resetting the coupon to a rate below market will induce a substantial portion of bondholders to exercise the put option, whereas a more competitive rate will induce bondholders to retain their bonds. The issuer of an extendible bond essentially has short- or medium-term debt outstanding without incurring the periodic costs of reissuance.

Sinking Fund Bonds. A sinking fund is usually included with public industrial and pipeline issues, although it is notably absent from the issues of telephone and finance companies. Electrical utilities are sometimes subject to a "blanket" sinking fund requirement, according to which the utility must spend a specified amount of cash annually for retiring bonds from any of several issues. Another form of the sinking fund provision is the "mainenance and replacement" provision, which can be satisfied either by retirement of debt or by capital expenditures. Many preferred and preference equity issues also carry sinking fund provisions.

The standard sinking fund provision requires the firm to retire a portion of an issue each year. In the case of a publicly held issue, this can be accomplished by one of two means. The issuer may make a cash payment, in the face amount of the bonds to be retired, to the trustee, who in turn calls the bonds by lot. The second option available to the issuer is the actual delivery of the bonds to the trustee. If the bonds are selling at a discount (below par value), it is cheaper to make an open market purchase than to call at or close to par. In this case, the delivery of the bonds is the obvious option for the issuer.

An open market purchase can be made in advance of the required sinking fund redemption for later delivery to the trustee. This would occur if the issuer believes that market conditions are such that purchase now is more advantageous than a purchase on the required sinking fund payment date. (This is explored further later in this section.) It is noteworthy that in certain instances the bond indentures do not allow for open market purchase; that is, they specify that the bonds be called by lot. Because privately placed sinking fund bonds have no market trading price, their indentures specify a sinking fund repurchase price of par value. The open market sinking fund purchase at prices below par value is therefore not an option with a private bond.

Callable Bonds. Call provisions give the firm the right to redeem a bond prior to maturity. Sometimes the call option specifies that the issue cannot be redeemed with cash generated by the issuance of additional lower cost debt. In contrast, the "refunding" call provision allows for the issuance of additional debt. Throughout this discussion attention is confined to such "refunding" provisions. Refunding provisions provide an increased degree of flexibility, because debt can be reduced, its maturity altered via refunding, and most important, expensive debt with high interest rates may be replaced with cheaper debt if rates decline. Usually the call price is established above par value. Nevertheless, from the investor's point of view the call provision establishes an upper limit on the amount of capital gain that can be obtained if interest rates fall. For this reason the investor will require a higher yield to maturity on callable bonds than on straight debt of equal risk and maturity.

In effect, a callable bond is equivalent to an ordinary bond with an option giving the issuer the right to call in the debt early at some predetermined price. On the date of issue the bondholder equates the market price B_0 of the callable bond with the present value of the cash payments from the bond less the cost C_0 of the call option. Mathematically, this may be expressed as follows:

$$B_0 = \sum_{t=1}^{T} \frac{\text{Coupon}}{(1+R)^t} + \frac{\text{Face value}}{(1+R)^T} - C_0$$

where B_0 = present value of callable bond
Coupon = coupon payment in period t
Face value = face value if bond is refunded at maturity
R = cost of issuing noncallable debt of similar maturity
C_0 = present value of call feature

Investors are usually given some call protection. During the first few years an issue may not be callable. In addition, a premium may be paid when a bond is called. Often this amount becomes smaller, the closer the bond is to its scheduled maturity date. Sometimes an entire issue is called and other times only specific bonds, drawn by lot by a trustee, will be called. In either case, a notice of redemption will appear in advance in the financial press.

A **call option** reduces the value of a bond to the bondholder. In the preceding expression this reduction in value is denoted by C_0. In exchange for this reduction in value, the issuer must offer the bondholder sufficient additional coupon to achieve parity with alternative investments. From the issuer's perspective, the call feature is an item of some value V_0. It can be shown that, because of the differing tax situations of the typical issuer and typical investor, V_0 exceeds C_0, that is, the value to the issuer is greater than the cost to the bondholder. It is precisely because of this condition that a coupon rate exists (above the coupon rate of a noncallable bond) which simultaneously satisfies the bondholder, while not proving onerous to the issuer.

Although V_0 exceeds C_0, both quantities depend on the same factors. In particular, assuming the bond was issued and purchased at par, the value (and cost) of the call option depends on the term of the bond, the number of years of call protection, the schedule of call prices, and the volatility of interest rates. All other factors being equal, the value to the issuer (and cost to the holder) of the call option is greater the longer the term of the bond, the shorter the period of call protection, the lower the call prices, and the greater the volatility of interest rates.

THE MANAGEMENT OF LIABILITIES

MANAGEMENT OF A SINKING FUND. A sinking fund can provide the active liability manager with interesting opportunities. Assume, for example, that long-term rates are high. If an issue's maturity date is in the distant future and the prevailing long-term rate is much higher than the coupon rate, the bonds normally will trade substantially below par value. Superficial examination of the situation may suggest that the firm should retire the bonds in advance rather than wait until the sinking fund date and pay a significantly higher price.

In fact, the problem is complicated once the following considerations have been taken into account. First, interest rates manifest themselves not only in low bond prices, but also in high borrowing or opportunity cost, or equivalently, in a high discount rate. Second, the future price of the bonds is uncertain. It is entirely possible that even though the bonds are presently selling at a low price, an even more advantageous situation will arise in the future.

As an illustration, assume that the bonds can be purchased either at the present or at the sinking fund date, but not at intermediate points in time. In this case the problem can be approached in the following manner. Given an assumed price at the sinking fund date, we can determine the present value of savings due to a current purchase rather than purchase at the sinking fund date. This savings is equal to the sum of (1) the present value of the after-tax coupon payments which would not have to be paid from the present through the sinking fund date, and (2) the present value of the avoided after-tax cost of retirement at the sinking fund date. The cost of retirement is based on an assumed future price at the sinking fund date, which, in the case of a public issue, can be below par. We then compare this present value savings with the after-tax cost of current repurchase. This procedure can be repeated over a range of assumed prices at the sinking fund date. The higher that price, the more would

EXHIBIT 3 COMPUTATION OF THE AFTER-TAX PRESENT VALUE SAVINGS OF CURRENT REPURCHASE

	Pretax Cash Flows		After-tax Cash Flows		Total After-tax	Present Value of
Period	Interest	Principal	Interest[a]	Principal[b]	Cash Flow	Cash Flow
1	3.5%	0%	1.89%	0%	1.89%	1.84%
2	3.5	0	1.89	0	1.89	1.78
3	3.5	0	1.89	0	1.89	1.73
4	3.5	76.14	1.89	87.12	89.01	79.17
						84.52%

Computation of the After-tax Cost of Current Repurchase

Pretax cost of current purchase:	71.33%
Taxable gain of repurchase:	28.67%
Tax liability:	13.19%
After-tax cost of current purchase:	84.52%

[a] After-tax interest equals pretax interest multiplied by 1 minus the tax rate. The tax rate is assumed to be 46%.

[b] After-tax principal equals pretax principal plus the tax impact of the discount. The tax impact of the discount equals the discount multiplied by the tax rate.

be saved by making a purchase at the present time. The assumed price at the sinking fund date that equates the present value savings and the cost of a current repurchase is the breakeven price.

Consider the Series X debentures, with a coupon rate of 7% and 10 years left to maturity. The next open sinking fund date is 2 years from now and the current price is 71.33% of par for a yield to maturity of 12%. The issuer's marginal tax rate is 46%, taxes on the gain are paid immediately, and the 2-year borrowing rate is 11%. In this example the breakeven price is 76.14% of par. Exhibit 3 illustrates the computation of the present value savings as defined above when the future repurchase price is the breakeven price. Notice that the savings of 84.53% is exactly equal to the after-tax cost of a current repurchase at a price of 71.33%. Exhibit 4 shows graphically the net present value savings (the excess of the present value savings over the after-tax cost or repurchase) under a range of future repurchase prices.

The maximum future price facing the issuer is the sinking fund call price, which is usually at par. Purchase should never be made in advance if the breakeven price exceeds the sinking fund price. A common mistake among financial analysts, however, is to assume that the only alternative to current open market purchase is to retire the bonds at par on the sinking fund date. That assumption normally indicates that the issuer should make his or her purchase at the present. Having to pay par is the worst possible future outcome, not the expected outcome under reasonable assumptions.

TAX TREATMENT OF THE DISCHARGE OF DEBT AT A DISCOUNT. In the preceding sinking fund early repurchase analysis, the discount on repurchased debt was treated as taxable income in the year of repurchase. For Series

EXHIBIT 4 SENSITIVITY OF NET PRESENT VALUE SAVINGS TO FUTURE PRICE

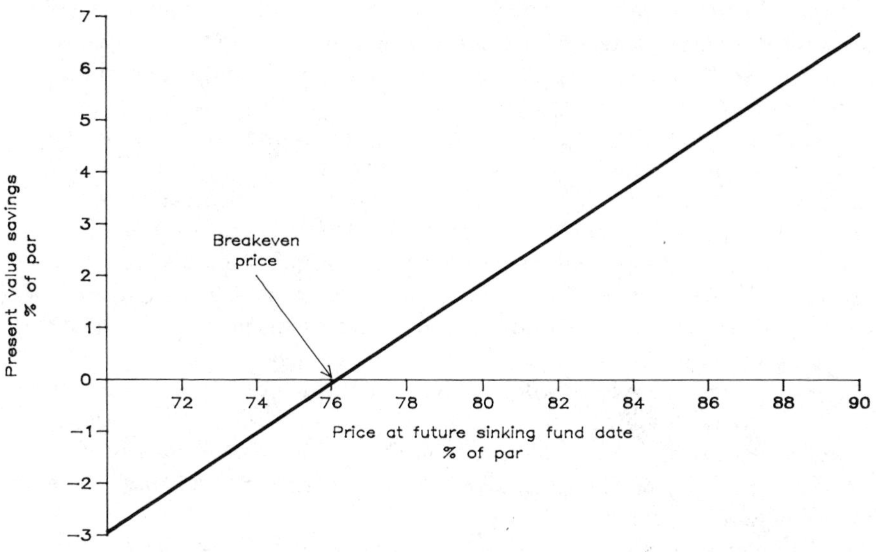

X, the taxable gain on repurchase was 100% – 71.33%, or 28.67% of par. Under current tax law, however, this gain is not necessarily recognized all in one year. Rather, the gain can sometimes be used to "write down" or reduce the basis of a depreciable asset. In this fashion it generates taxable income over that asset's depreciable life, which in aggregate is equal to the amount of the discount. This pushing forward of taxable income is more favorable than recognizing the income immediately. This tax treatment is spelled out in the **Bankruptcy Tax Act of 1980.**

Until recently, corporations often raised funds to retire discounted debt by issuing equity. Until 1983, if properly executed, such "equity for debt swaps" were deemed tax exempt; that is, when equity was issued to retire debt, the discount was not treated as taxable income. This, of course, is extremely favorable tax treatment and such equity for debt swaps were very common. However, the **Deficit Reduction Act of 1984** eliminated the tax-exempt status of these swaps except for companies that either (1) are undergoing reorganization pursuant to Chapter 11, (2) are insolvent (as explicitly defined), or (3) do the swap as part of a qualified workout program. This has effectively put an end to these swaps.

MANAGEMENT OF CALLABLE BONDS. As discussed previously the call option on a long bond is an item of value to the issuer. In the previous discussion the value of the call option on the date of issuance was denoted by V_0. At any point in the life of the bond, say t years from issuance, the option will have some value V_t. As mentioned earlier V_t depends in a very complex way on several factors, including the remaining time (if any) until expiration of call protection and the current level of long-term refunding rates.

Once the bond becomes callable, the issuer is in a position to recognize some or all of the value V_t through the exercise of the call option. If the call option is exercised and the bond is refunded at a lower interest rate, the present value savings generated by the call and subsequent refunding (together called the refinancing) can be calculated in a manner similar to that of the preceding sinking fund analysis.

Specifically, let S be the present value of the resulting reduction in interest expense (after-tax) less the after-tax call premium paid on calling. Then S will be a positive number only if refunding rates fall far enough below the current coupon to compensate for the call premium. The refunding rate at which this occurs is called the breakeven refunding rate. A refinancing at this rate will generate neither a gain nor loss in present value terms. The computation of S above assumes that the refunding issue remains outstanding until maturity. This assumption is equivalent to refunding with a noncallable bond. Typically, however, a refunding issue will itself be issued with a call option. Therefore in addition to the "hard cash flow" savings S generated by a refinancing, the refunding issue's call option will have some theoretical value V_n on the refunding date. The aggregate savings generated by exercising the call option and refunding at a lower rate is $S + V_n$.

Exhibit 5 illustrates this analysis for a hypothetical 35-year bond issued in 1980, paying a coupon of 14½%. The bond becomes callable in 1985 at a price of 110% of par. Notice that the call option on the 14½ of 2015 has substantially greater value (V_t) in low interest rate environments.

To determine the advisability of exercising the **call option**, the aggregate

EXHIBIT 5 THEORETICAL VALUATION OF THE CALL OPTION

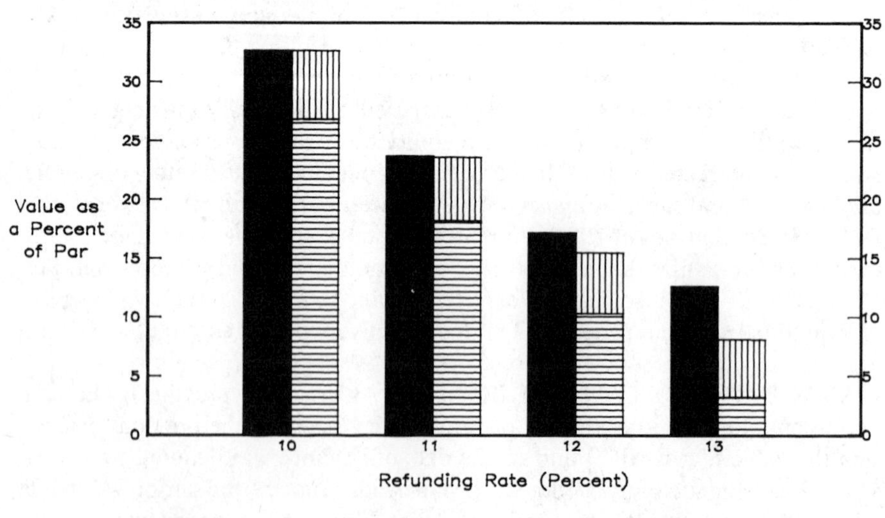

EXHIBIT 6 EFFICIENCY OF REFINANCING ON FIRST CALL DATE

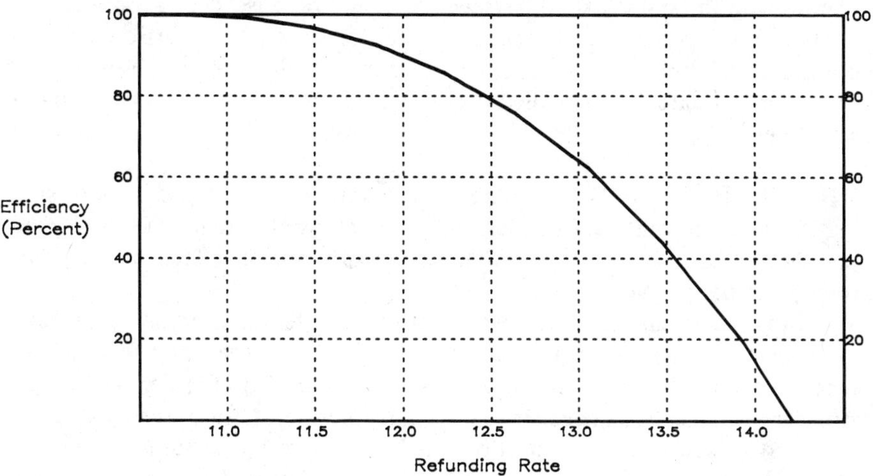

savings $S + V_n$ must be compared with the current theoretical value V_t of the call option. Clearly $S + V_n$ represents the portion of the theoretical value of the call option that would be recognized by exercising it. The ratio $(S + V_n)/V_t$ is known as the "efficiency" of calling. The efficiency of a call is greater the lower the refunding rate (see Exhibit 6). The issuer of a callable bond may wish to exercise the call option only if rates decline to the point where a "trigger" efficiency is reached. For example, an issuer may elect to exercise a call option only if doing so will capture 90% of its theoretical value. For the 14 ½s this gives a trigger refunding rate of approximately 12%.

It should be noted that the more efficiency the issuer insists on, the longer it must wait to exercise the call. Waiting longer increases the risk that refunding rates will rise again and available savings will disappear. Therefore the "high efficiency" call option management strategy is also the high-risk strategy.

CALLABLE BONDS WITH SINKING FUND PROVISIONS. When deciding whether or not to call a bond that also has a sinking fund provision, the interaction of the two redemption provisions has an interesting effect. Depending on interest rates, the optimal strategy may be to call only part of the issue at a premium and to sink the rest at par. The amount called at a premium depends on the call premium and the level of interet rates relative to the coupon rate. More of the issue will be called at lower market rates.

The motivation behind the partial call can be understood by conceptually treating the sinking fund issue as if it were a portfolio of bullet bonds with different maturities. The call analysis can be performed separately for each maturity (i.e., each sinking fund payment) to produce a target rate corresponding to each individual maturity. The target rate will be lower as the sinking fund payment date approaches. This happens because the closer the sinking fund payment date, the less time is available to offset the call premium through the lower coupon payments generated by refunding. Because the target rate increases with the sinking fund payment date, and because a call is optimal only if the refunding rate is below the target rate, a situation can arise where it is optimal to call only the portion of the bond that would be sunk subsequent to a certain cutoff date. The uncalled portion of the issue should be sunk at par as scheduled.

INTEREST RATE SWAPS. Interest rate swaps have emerged rapidly since 1982 as an important liability management tool. Swaps are usually used to adjust the average maturity of a debt portfolio, or lower the effective cost of borrowing, or both.

Swap agreements in recent years have achieved substantial complexity, often involving foreign capital markets, foreign currencies, and forward currency exchange contracts. In this section we confine our attention to the basic structure, often called the generic swap. The interest rate swap is a contract between two issuers of debt. In effect, each firm agrees to assume the interest payments on a specified portion of the other firm's debt. There is no exchange of principal involved and the debtholders continue to have recourse to the initial issuer for debt service payments. The debtholders are not parties to, nor typically aware of, the swap agreement.

The **swap contract** usually involves a floating-rate debt issuer and a fixed-rate debt issuer (see Exhibit 7). Under the swap contract the floating-rate issuer will make periodic fixed-rate payments set at a negotiated spread above a Treasury security whose maturity corresponds to the term of the agreement. These payments are made to the fixed-rate issuer who in turn uses them to satisfy its fixed-rate debt obligation. Additionally, the fixed-rate issuer will make

EXHIBIT 7 CASH FLOWS OF THE GENERIC INTEREST RATE SWAP AGREEMENT

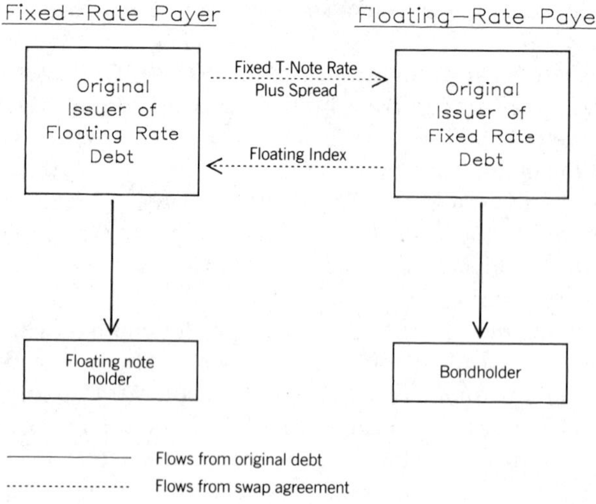

periodic floating-rate payments to the floating-rate issuer. The floating-rate payment is determined with reference to an agreed on index such as LIBOR, commercial paper, Treasury bills, or the prime rate. These payments are used by the floating-rate issuer to satisfy its floating-rate obligation.

Because the floating-rate issuer ultimately pays a net fixed amount, it is referred to as the "fixed-rate payer." Similarly, the fixed-rate issuer pays a floating-rate by virtue of the swap and is called the "floating-rate payer."

The net affect of the swap agreement is as follows. The fixed-rate payer (who initially issued floating-rate debt) has now locked in a fixed interest rate for the term of the swap. The floating-rate payer (who originally issued fixed-rate debt) is paying interest based on a current short-term rate.

The obvious question is "why bother with this elaborate construct?" Why doesn't the fixed-rate payer simply issue fixed-rate debt and the floating-rate payer issue floating-rate debt? One answer is that the fixed-rate payer has access to cheaper funds in the short-term markets than does the floating-rate payer. Often, for example, the fixed-rate payer is a thrift or savings and loan institution. These institutions hold long-term assets in the form of mortgages. Their least costly access to funds, however, is through short-term deposits bearing floating interest rates. For thrifts, then, the swap arrangement serves two functions. First, it helps to structure liabilities more compatible with the maturity or duration of their assets. Second, because each party to the swap is accessing the market in which it has a relative cost advantage, the total cost of financing is lowered. When the swap agreement is reached, this savings can be shared by both parties.

SEC RULE 415. Effective March 1982, the SEC promulgated "Rule 415." After a trial period and with some modification, Rule 415 was made permanent in December 1983. The purpose of Rule 415 is to offer certain qualified issuers more flexibility in the timing of their financings. The Rule allows these issuers to file "shelf registrations," which set forth in fairly vague terms financing plans for a period of up to 2 years. Because domestic shelf registrations are filed on Form S-3 (the "short form") and full SEC reviews are unusual, the registration usually becomes effective in 48 hours. The securities registered in the filing may be issued without further SEC approval at any time during the period for which the plan was filed. The pricing and even certain terms (e.g., coupon and maturity) are not determined until just prior to issuance. On issuance, a prospectus supplement containing the final pricing and terms is delivered to the SEC and investors. The disclosure documents of the Exchange Act (such as the 10-K report) are incorporated in the shelf registration and prospectus supplement by reference only and need not be explicitly included.

Rule 415 affords the issuer potential savings in several ways. Most important, after a shelf registration the issuer is poised to issue the registered securities at virtually a moment's notice at any time for a period of up to 2 years. The issuer can therefore take advantage of "market windows" (periods of low interest rates or a high common stock price) to issue the securities. In this fashion the overall cost of capital can theoretically be reduced. Second, as noted previously, the Rule permits last-minute changes in the structure and terms of the securities. This allows issuers to meet the prevailing appetite of the marketplace. Finally, the simplification of the registration process is a cost saver because only a single registration statement is filed for a series of offerings.

Domestic issuers are eligible for shelf registration under Rule 415 if they are eligible to file using the "short form" S-3. Basically, the issuer must have been subject to the reporting requirements of the Securities Exchange Act of 1934 for at least 3 years (and current in all filings for the most recent year), and must not have defaulted on any debt or preferred stock obligations since the end of the previous fiscal year. Also, the issuer must have common voting stock outstanding with aggregate market value of at least $150 million ($100 million if the annual trading volume of the stock exceeds 3 million shares). However, this "float test" need not be satisfied if the issuer is filing investment grade nonconvertible debt or preferred stock.

These complex eligibility requirements are designed to ensure that the issuer have a high profile in the marketplace. In theory, at the time of an actual issuance under shelf registration, sufficient information has already been disseminated to the marketplace via the ongoing Exchange Act reporting for investors to make an informed decision.

DEBT RATINGS

Corporate debt securities, as well as other securities such as municipal bonds and preferred equity, often receive a rating from one or more rating agencies. In the case of debt securities this rating represents that agency's judgment of the creditworthiness of the issuer (and possibly third-party guarantors or insurers) with respect to the rated security issue. Although rating systems vary from one agency to the next, securities are usually placed in one of two broad categories. Securities in the higher category are referred to as **investment grade securities** and possess a relatively low amount of default risk. The lower-rated securities are referred to as **speculative grade**. For these securities, the opinion of the rater is that the company's outlook is sufficiently uncertain as to place significant risk of default on its fixed indebtedness.

The two most often quoted rating agencies are **Moody's Investors Service, Inc. (Moody's)** and **Standard & Poor's (S&P)**. The rating categories used by these two organizations are listed in Exhibit 8. Securities rated in one of the top four ratings in each system are regarded as investment grade. For a detailed discussion of the rating process, refer to Section 20.

PREFERRED STOCK

Preferred stock represents a curious combination of various features of debt and equity. It is like common stock in that the instrument is called stock and is included in the equity section of the balance sheet; payments are considered

EXHIBIT 8 BOND RATINGS AND DEFINITIONS

Moody's		Standard and Poor's	
Rating	Definition	Rating	Definition
Aaa	Judged to be of the best quality.	AAA	Highest rating. Capacity to pay extremely strong.
Aa	Judged to be of high quality	AA	Very strong capacity to pay.
A	Possesses many favorable attributes. Upper-medium grade obligations.	A	Strong capacity to pay. Somewhat more susceptible to adverse circumstances.
Baa	Medium-grade obligations. Neither highly projected nor poorly secured.	BBB	Adequate capacity to pay interest and principal.
Ba	Judged to have speculative elements.	BB	Speculative; lowest degree of speculation.
B	Generally lacks characteristics of a desirable investment.	B	Speculative.
Caa	Poor standing. May be in default.	CCC	Speculative.
Ca	Speculative in a high degree. Often in default.	CC	Speculative; highest degree of speculation.
C	Lowest rated class of bonds. Extremely poor prospects.	C	No interest is being paid.
		D	In default. Payment of interest and/or principal is in arrears.

dividends and are not deductible for tax purposes; the payment of dividends is not legally required; and the issue usually has no fixed maturity. Preferred stock is also similar to debt in that the **dividends** have a fixed maximum rate; investors in preferreds generally have no vote (unless a specified number—often four to six quarters—of dividends are not paid, in which case they may elect a minority of the board); holders are entitled to no more than the amount paid in to the firm in case of liquidation; and preferred stock may contain the same call, sinking fund, or conversion feature as bonds. In the event of liquidation, preferred stockholders are treated as creditors of the corporation. Their claims on assets are ahead of common stock but behind all bonds.

If a corporation has a poor year, it can forgo distributing dividends to holders of preferred stock without the danger of bankruptcy. Unlike bonds, failure to meet a stipulated dividend does not constitute default, and thus the legal ramifications resulting from such action are avoided. Preferred investors can protect themselves from this situation if their issue contains a provision for what are known as cumulative dividends. This provision specifies that all past preferred stock dividends must be paid in full before any dividends to common stock can be distributed. Companies that issue preferred stock with **cumulative dividends** can find themselves in the unenviable position of disbursing large amounts of money to preferred stockholders to pay off dividend arrearages before they can distribute to their common shareholders. Companies in such a position try to strike a compromise with the holders of the preferreds. Exchange of the preferred stock for debt or common stock has been the most popular solution to the problem at hand. Generally, no interest accrues on dividends in arrears; therefore, preferred holders may be more inclined to an exchange offer than continuing to hold the preferred issue.

TYPES OF PREFERRED STOCK

Sinking Fund Preferreds. Preferred stock with sinking funds has become a popular financial instrument. The popularity has been stimulated primarily by a 1978 ruling by the National Association of Insurance Commissioners (NAIC), allowing insurance companies holding preferred stock with a sinking fund provision to carry these preferreds at cost rather than market value for statement purposes. Because of this ruling, changes in the market value no longer have an impact on the insurance companies' inventory of preferred issues with sinking funds. To take advantage of the ruling, the preferred stock must have a sinking fund that meets the following requirements: (1) 100% of the issue will be retired at a rate of not less than 2.5% per year, and (2) the sinking fund must begin within 10 years of the issuing date.

With the advent of the new NAIC ruling, preferred stocks with sinking funds have become an attractive investment alternative for insurance companies. Since the new ruling went into effect, the yield spread between preferreds with sinking funds and bonds has increased, with the preferred requiring a relatively lower yield. Furthermore, preferreds with sinking funds typically yield slightly less than perpetual preferreds of comparable quality.

Convertible Preferreds. Preferred stocks that are convertible into common stock have also become a popular security. Most companies use the convertible feature as a "sweetener." This provision is a technique used to make the preferred issue more attractive to investors and less costly for the issuer. Some investors are willing to accept a lower yield in exchange for a chance to participate in the potential appreciation of a firm's stock. Convertible preferred stock offers the investor such an opportunity.

Convertible preferred stocks can also be used to finance a merger. Convertible preferreds offer the shareholders of the target company equity in potential higher earnings as well as in assets. If the combination proves to be successful, they can convert and reap the benefits of higher earnings. If, however, the potential increase in earnings does not materialize, they can keep their preferred stock and enjoy whatever protection and dividends it may produce. Preferreds with the convertible feature offer the stockholders of the target company a tax-free exchange. In contrast, a stockholder receiving bonds or cash in exchange for stock will have to pay capital gains tax on the amount received in excess of their cost. Mergers financed with convertible preferred stock are also beneficial to the shareholders of the acquiring firm. An exchange of convertible preferred for common will not immediately cause dilution of the earnings per share.

With a convertible, preferred dilution will be gradual and could be absorbed by the growth in earnings.

Convertible Exchangeable Preferred Stock. This version of convertible preferred stock has an option allowing the issuer to exchange convertible subordinated debentures for the outstanding preferred stock. The exchange is at a rate of $1.00 face value of debenture for $1.00 par value of stock. The exchanged debenture is typically convertible into common stock at the same conversion rate as the underlying preferred stock.

This financing vehicle is attractive to companies that are not currently paying taxes (because of current tax losses or an operating loss carry forward) yet expect to return to taxability. When the company is not taxable, the nondeductibility of the preferred dividend is irrelevant and preferred stock is less costly than debt. When the company becomes taxable, however, the tax-deductible debt becomes less costly on an after-tax basis and the company's option to exchange is valuable.

Adjustable Rate Preferred Stock. As a long-term fixed-rate instrument, preferred stock is subject to substantial price fluctuations induced by the movement of long-term interest rates. Adjustable Rate Preferred Stock (ARPS) was an early attempt to structure a preferred stock security whose price is relatively insensitive to rate movements. It is issued as perpetual preferred stock, typically redeemable at the issuer's option after 5 years. The dividend rate is reset periodically (usually every 3 months) to reflect current market conditions. The dividend rate is typically a predetermined spread below the greater of selected short-, medium-, and long-term Treasury securities. The reduced price fluctuation was intended to broaden the preferred market and lower the cost of issuing preferred stock. Purchasers of ARPS settle for lower dividends in favor of greater capital protection.

Convertible Adjustable Rate Preferred Stock. Convertible Adjustable Rate Preferred Stock (CARPS) is a modified version of ARPS designed to further reduce price fluctuation. As with ARPS, the dividend is periodically reset to reflect current market conditions. The CARPS holder, however, has the option to exchange his or her preferred stock for common stock equal in market value to the preferred's par value. This virtually ensures that CARPS will trade at or above par value. To help keep the security trading near par, the CARPS issuer is afforded considerably more flexibility in setting the dividend rate as compared with the ARPS strict formula format. Investors have found the additional price stability attractive enough that CARPS dividends are generally priced substantially below a comparable ARPS.

Dutch Auction Rate Preferred Stock. In August 1984 another form of preferred stock designed to trade at par was introduced to the marketplace. Dutch Auction Rate Preferred Stock is a perpetual preferred stock whose dividend rate is reset every 7 weeks. Unlike ARPS, however, the dividend is not reset via formula with reference to selected market securities, but rather by the market itself. Every 7 weeks the auction rate preferred holders and any prospective purchasers submit bids to the agent handling the auction. A bid consists of the amount of stock desired to be purchased and an "acceptable" dividend rate. The dividend rate is then set by the agent so that the total amount of stock desired to be purchased at rates equal to or below the selected rate just equals the issue size. In this fashion a dividend rate is selected that just clears the market for transfers at par value. The dividend rate is allowed to float through the auction mechanism in a range typically set to be between 59 and 110% of the current AA 2-month commercial paper rate. This range comfortably accommodates issuers of high credit standing. Issuers whose preferred stock is rated below "aa"/AA are usually advised to provide additional credit enhancement either in the form of a standby puchaser (at par) of the shares or through collateral or letters of credit support.

Auction rate preferred provides the holder principal protection equivalent to the CARPS format and far greater than the ARPS format. The issuer typically pays a dividend that would be somewhere below an ARPS dividend and above a CARPS dividend. The auction rate preferred issuer, however, does not have the risk of earnings dilution through conversion that a CARPS issuer faces.

Participating Preferreds. Some preferred stockholders participate with common stockholders in sharing the firm's earnings. This feature is rare, but in some cases this "sweetener" is used to sell preferred issues. Participating preferred stock generally works as follows: (1) the stated preferred dividend is paid; (2) dividends, up to an amount equal to the preferred dividends, are distributed to common stockholders; and (3) any remaining income is shared equally among common and preferred stockholders.

Preference Stocks. Subordinated issues of preferred stock are also found in the market. These are known as preference stocks and can have all the same features of preferred issues. However, the claims of holders of these preference stocks are subordinated to the claims of preferred stockholders. They tend to be more risky, and therefore will pay a higher dividend rate than a similar preferred issue.

PAR AND LIQUIDATION VALUES. The preferred stock's par value serves two important functions. First, it establishes the amount due to the holder of the preferred issues in the event of the firm's liquidation. Second, the dividend of the preferred stock is frequently stated as percentage of the par value. Dividend rates can also be stated in dollar values. Generally, the par value of a preferred stock is $100. Recently, preferreds with par values of $10, $25, and $50 have been issued to attract small investors.

PREFERRED STOCK RATINGS. Preferred stock, like debt, is rated by Moody's and Standard & Poor's. Factors considered in arriving at a preferred

EXHIBIT 9 PREFERRED STOCK RATINGS AND DEFINITIONS

Moody's		Standard & Poor's	
Rating	Definition	Rating	Definition
"aaa"	Top-quality preferred stock.	AAA	Highest rating.
"aa"	High-grade preferred stock.	AA	High-quality fixed income security.
"a"	Upper-medium grade preferred stock.	A	Sound capacity to pay preferred stock obligations.
"baa"	Medium-grade preferred stock.	BBB	Adequate capacity to pay preferred stock obligations.
"ba"	Considered to have speculative elements.	BB	Speculative. Lowest degree of speculation.
"b"	Lacks characteristics of a desirable investment.	B	Speculative, medium degree.
"caa"	Likely to be in arrears on dividend payments.	CCC	Speculative. Highest degree of speculation.
"ca"	Speculative in high degree with little likelihood of eventual payment.	CC	In arrears on dividends but currently paying.
"c"	Lowest rated class of preferred stock.	C	Nonpaying issue.
		D	Nonpaying issue with issuer in default on debt instruments.

stock rating are essentially the same as those reviewed in the case of a corporate bond. The most important are provisions of articles of incorporation, asset protection, financial resources, future earnings protection, and management.

Preferred stock will generally have a lower rating than bonds issued by the same corporation. This is true because preferred stockholders are ranked behind bondholders in the event of a firm's liquidation.

Preferred stock ratings represent a considered judgment of the relative security of dividends and the implied prospective yield stability of the stock. Exhibit 9 provides a list of the various preferred stock ratings and a paraphrase of their definitions as set forth by Moody and Standard & Poor. For a further discussion of preferred stock ratings, see Section 20.

PREFERRED STOCK ISSUERS. The primary issuers of preferred stock are utility companies. This is because preferred stock dividends are treated as fixed costs and can be passed along to the customers. Corporations with a low marginal tax rate may find preferred stocks, rather than debt, a more attractive means of raising capital. Firms in this tax situation will not benefit by writing off their interest expense. Therefore, given the favorable tax treatment of dividends on preferred stock held by corporations, the yield on a preferred stock may be less than the yield on a bond. If a corporation's stock is depressed and it has a high debt-to-equity ratio, preferred stocks may offer a viable source of capital. A company can effectively lower its debt-to-equity ratio by selling preferred stock instead of the more costly common stock.

Preferred stocks offer a number of advantages and opportunities for companies seeking to raise capital. First, a new source of funds is available to issuers of preferreds. Investors have various investment strategies and by offering a number of financial instruments (bond, preferreds, or equity) a company can tap a larger supply of capital. Second, a firm can increase its equity base by issuing preferred stock and therefore improve the borrowing base for future debt financing. Third, the control of existing shareholders is not diminished when nonconvertible preferred stock is issued. When convertible preferred stock is issued, the control of existing shareholders is threatened. As mentioned before, however, this process tends to be gradual and could be absorbed by future growth in earnings. Also because the conversion price is generally above the current market price, issuers of convertible preferreds are said to sell equity "ahead of the market."

PREFERRED STOCK PURCHASERS. Corporations, especially life insurance companies, tend to be the primary holders of preferreds. This is because of preferential tax treatment of preferred dividends paid to corporate holders of preferreds: 85% of the dividend received by corporations in their preferred investment is not taxable. Yields on preferred stock tend to follow yields on other fixed income securities rather closely. Because of the 85% exclusions of preferred dividends, however, the after-tax yield on preferreds tends to be higher than a bond issued by the same corporation. Holders of preferred stocks receive other benefits from their investment. Preferreds provide reasonably steady income, and preferred stockholders have a preference over common stockholders in the event of liquidation.

COMMON STOCK

Common stock or, for unincorporated firms, the proprietors' or partners' interest constitutes the ownership of the firm. The laws of the state in which the company is chartered and the terms of the charter granted by the state define the rights of the holders of common stock. The rights and responsibilities attached to equity consist of positive considerations (income potential and control of the firm) and negative considerations (loss potential, legal responsibility, and personal liability).

COMMON STOCKHOLDERS' RIGHTS. A number of common stockholders' rights are usually found in most corporate charters. Holders of common stock are usually given certain collective rights. Some of the more important rights allow stockholders (1) to amend the charter with the approval of the appropriate officials in the state of incorporation, (2) to adapt and amend bylaws, (3) to elect directors of the corporation, (4) to authorize the sale of fixed assets, (5) to enter into mergers, (6) to change the amount of authorized common stock, and (7) to issue preferred stock, debentures, bonds, and other securities.

Stockholders also have specific rights as individual owners:

1. They have the right to vote in the manner prescribed by the corporate charter.
2. They may sell their stock certificates, their evidence of ownership, and in this way transfer their ownership interest to other persons.
3. They have the right to inspect the corporate books. This does not extend to an examination of the books of account or minutes of directors' meetings except under special circumstances.
4. They have the right to share residual assets of the corporation on dissolution; but the holders of common stock are last among the claimants to the assets of the corporation.

Stockholders, through their right to vote, have legal control of the corporation. In practice, however, holders of common stock do not run the corporation. Common stockholders elect a board of directors to oversee the running of the corporation.

The board of directors names the management team which will direct the everyday business operations of the corporation. In effect, in a corporation, ownership and control are separate, but the goal of decisions made by management should always be to maximize the wealth of the shareholders. Also, it must be remembered that common stockholders have the right to vote on any matter that will have a significant impact on the firm's operation. In most cases the shareholders temporarily transfer their voting rights. The instrument that transfers the voting rights is known as a proxy. The proxy is typically limited in duration, generally for a specific occasion, such as the annual meeting of stockholders.

There are primarily two methods of voting employed in the **election of directors**. The first method, which assigns one vote to one share of stock, is called the **majority voting system**. Thus, a person who owns 100 shares has the right to cast 100 votes for each opening on the board of directors. The second method is known as **cumulative voting**. This method allows a shareholder to accumulate all his or her votes and cast them for one director. For example, if a person owns 100 shares of stock and there are three openings on the board of directors, the shareholder has 300 votes overall. When cumulative voting is permitted, the stockholder can cast all 300 votes for one director. Cumulative voting is designed to enable a minority group of stockholders to obtain some voice in the control of the company by electing at least one director to the board.

Shareholders are usually given the first option to purchase additional issues of common stock. This is known as the preemptive right. This right protects the current position of the present stockholders in terms of control and dilution. The latter is usually more important because it provides for old shareholders to retain their respective proportion of outstanding shares. The former prevents management from issuing new shares to "friendly" persons to ensure management's continued control of the firm.

COMMON STOCK CHARACTERISTICS. Common stock is a perpetual security with no fixed payment schedule. Unlike debt securities, where failure to meet interest payments entails default and bankruptcy proceedings, a corporation is under no such pressure to pay out dividends to its stockholders. However, most large corporations pride themselves on their history of paying out dividends with no interruption regardless of economic conditions. Dividends on common equity cannot be deducted for tax purposes; therefore they are paid directly out of the after-tax profits of the firm.

Corporations can be classified by their dividend payment policies and the potential price appreciation of their stock. The shares of firms that do not generate large returns on their investment in assets, but that pay out in such dividends most of what they do earn, are called **income shares**. These stocks sell almost entirely on a pure dividend yield basis, because appreciation from retained earnings is limited. **Income stocks** may be above-average risk securities issued by declining firms that have exhausted their most profitable investment opportunities (e.g., railroad, fire and casualty, undiversified tobacco companies). On the other hand, income stocks may also be lower than average risk securities issued by firms that have their return on investment regulated by the government. These equities, which are usually stable and relatively safe even during periods of recession, may retain earnings and show capital appreciation. Nevertheless, their growth rates are constrained by the regulated rate of return that they are allowed to earn on plant and equipment. The best examples of **low-risk income stocks** are the shares of most American public utilities.

An equity whose average return is much better than the average increase in sales and earnings of all corporations for a consistent period of time is called a **growth stock**. These shares outperform the economy and most other equities in their respective industries. Growth companies typically pay negligible dividends because they can do better for their shareholders by retaining earnings and reinvesting in plant and equipment. They are aggressive in their search for new profitable opportunities, and they typically spend a great deal on research and development. The returns on their stocks are derived primarily from their price appreciation.

COMMON STOCK RISK. In the event of a firm's liquidation, common stockholders are the last group to be compensated. The claims of creditors must be satisfied before assets can be distributed to equity holders. Because of its low priority in liquidation situations, common stock has the greatest risk of any security in the corporate structure. The required rate of return on equity (price appreciation plus dividends) must be high enough to compensate the holders of equity for the risk they are assuming. Therefore the rate of return on equity should be higher than the return on any other security in the same corporation or corporations with similar risk structures. If this were not the case, a corporation would be hard pressed to find any investors interested in holding its common stock.

ISSUING COMMON STOCK. Usually a firm employs an investment banker when it decides to float a stock issue to raise capital. If the firm's stockholders have preemptive rights, the new stock must be offered to existing stockholders. Otherwise, the firm, in consultation with its bankers, must decide whether to offer the stock to existing stockholders. There are a number of issues that affect this decision. Among them are (1) flotation costs, (2) effects on price stock, (3) potential dilution of earnings per share for current stockholders, and (4) the distribution of shares held by the public.

Advantages of Issuing Common Stock. From the viewpoint of the issuer, raising capital with common stock has a number of advantages. One major advantage is that common stock, unlike debt, entails no fixed charges. Second, common stock increases the creditworthiness of the corporation because it provides a cushion against losses for creditors. Usually, equity increases in value when the value of real assets rises during a period of inflation. Investors can benefit from holding common stock because, under current tax law, the capital gain resulting from price appreciation is taxed at a lower rate than an investor's ordinary income.

Disadvantages of Issuing Common Stock. Sale of new common stock, except in the case of preemptive rights offering, reduces the control existing stockholders have over the company. As noted earlier, rights offerings provide for existing stockholders to purchase new shares so that their proportional ownership of the company is not diluted. Also, a sale of common stock may dilute earnings for existing stockholders. Dilution of earnings is a reduction in the earnings per share of stock. In this case, dilution may occur because the number of outstanding shares of common stock was increased. This can be prevented, however, if the capital raised from the stock sale generates increased earnings. Underwriting costs tend to be higher for common stock than for debt or preferred issues. Also, if there is more equity than is called for in the optimum capital structure, the average cost of capital will be higher than necessary.

Registration with the SEC. A registration statement must be filed with the SEC unless the stock being issued is already included in a Rule 415 shelf registration. If the issuer is able to file on the short S-3 form, the registration usually becomes effective in 48 hours. The SEC may, however, decide to perform a full review. In this case the SEC may file exceptions to the registration statement or may ask for additional information from the issuing company of the underwriters during the examination period. During this period investment bankers are not permitted to offer the securities for sale, although they may print preliminary prospectuses with all the customary information except the offering price.

Determining Flotation Costs. The firm and its investment banker must agree on the banker's compensation or the flotation cost involved in issuing the stock. Flotation costs to the firm consist of two elements—compensation to the investment banker, plus legal, accounting, printing, and other out-of-pocket costs borne by the issuer. The investment banker's compensation consists of the spread between the price the company is paid for the stock and the price at which the stock is sold to the public, called the offering price. The company, of course, wants to receive the highest possible price for its stock from the investment banker, so it bargains with the banker over both the offering price and the spread. The higher the offering price and the lower the spread, the more the company receives per share of the stock sold; and the more it receives per share, the fewer number of shares required to raise a given amount of money. On the other hand, the lower the offering price, the easier it is for the investment banker to market the new shares. If, however, the investors can be persuaded that the funds raised from the new stock can be used to enhance the future earnings potential of the company, the offering price of the stock need not be below the preoffering market price.

Secondary Market. The secondary market plays an important role in the issuance of new securities. The secondary market facilitates the buying and selling of seasoned securities. A security that is actively traded in the secondary market tends to be liquid; that is, a holder of a liquid security can sell his or her security with little difficulty. Also, a security that is actively traded tends not to fluctuate greatly in price. Therefore the holder of an actively traded security does not face as great a risk of capital loss as does the holder of an illiquid issue.

It will be to the benefit of the holder, the issuer, and the investment banker if the banker is able to "make a market" for the issuer's securities. An investment banking firm will create an active secondary market for its clients if it expects to have referral business and keep its own brokerage customers happy.

COMMON STOCK WARRANTS. Both preferred stock and debt instruments are sometimes issued in conjunction with common stock warrants. A warrant is a security affording the holder the right to purchase the issuer's common stock directly from the issuer at a fixed price (the strike price) for a specified period of time. Typically, the strike price of a warrant is set substantially above the current market value of the common stock. For example, the strike price might be $60 per share when the stock is currently trading at $40 per share. In this case, the warrant will ultimately have value for the holder only if the company's stock rises by more than $20 before the warrant expires. Although very similar in concept to a stock option, a warrant is different in two significant ways. First, the term of a warrant, or its time to expiration, is generally much longer than that of a stock option. Warrants, for example, are often issued with a 5-year period to expiration. Stock options, on the other hand, have terms of 9 months or less. Second, when a warrant is exercised, additional common stock is issued by the company to satisfy the warrant obligation.

When an option is exercised, stock purchased in the marketplace is used to satisfy the contract. Stock warrants may usually be detached from the accompanying debt or preferred stock issue after a period of time to trade separately.

An issuer of debt or preferred stock may prefer to attach stock warrants instead of offering a more conventional convertible issue in order to limit the potential increase in its common stock account. An issuer of a large convertible issue is subject to a sizable increase in its common stock account. Under the more flexible warrant format, the issuer can adjust the potential future stock issuance to any desired level simply by setting appropriate warrant terms.

The **valuation of stock warrants and options**, pioneered by Black and Scholes is a topic that is extensively covered in economic literature. Virtually all models of warrant valuation consider the following factors: current stock price, strike price, stock price volatility, stock dividend payments, and time to expiration. A change in these factors in any of the following ways will increase the value of the warrant: an increase in the stock price, a decrease in the strike price, an increase in stock price volatility, a decrease in stock dividends, and an increase in time to expiration.

Decreasing the spread between the strike price and the stock's current price will increase the chances of the price ultimately rising above the strike price. Similarly, larger price fluctuations (price volatility) and a longer time to expiration increase the likelihood of a price movement above the strike price. A lower dividend can reflect greater corporate growth which theoretically should appear as appreciating stock price. In general, anything that increases the likelihood of a price movement above the strike price before the expiration date will increase the value of a warrant.

PRIVATE PLACEMENT MARKET

The private placement market is an important source of capital for U.S. corporations. During 1984, 39% of corporate financing was accomplished privately. Despite the size and importance of this segment of the capital markets, there is very little available information on individual financings sold or the private placement market as a whole. This is in contrast to the public market, where detailed descriptions of individual issues are available in prospectuses, and aggregate data on volume and interest rate levels are widely published.

The Securities Act of 1933, which was designed to secure full and fair disclosure on the part of companies proposing a public sale of securities, is the fountainhead of today's private placements. Section 4(2) of the law exempts offerings made to knowledgeable purchasers from the normal registration process that the SEC enforces on public security offerings. Rule 146, issued by the SEC in 1974, provides detailed guidelines that issuers may elect to follow in arranging private placements. Basically the rule restricts qualified transactions to those marketed through contacts with purchasers who are directly solicited, well grounded in investment matters, informed about a financing (or at least able to become so), limited in number, and investment rather than resale oriented.

A **private placement** (also known as a **direct placement**) is a direct sale of securities to a limited number (at times only one) of sophisticated investors such as insurance companies, banks, or pension funds. Like the public market for new issues, the private placement market is a system designed to permit the sale of securities. However, it differs from the primary public market in two important respects: method of distribution and degree of liquidity.

Customarily, when a company makes a public offering of securities, the issue is underwritten by an investment banking firm. For a fee the underwriter assumes the risk of reselling them to the public. No such interim step occurs in a private placement; the issue is sold directly by the company to a limited group of investors.

When purchasers of public issues wish to dispose of their holdings, they normally encounter little difficulty because stock exchanges and brokerage houses facilitate such transactions. The market in direct placement is far less liquid, however: formal trading centers do not exist, and there is usually a paucity of holders of any given issue. Moreover, the SEC qualifications (proscribing indiscriminate sale) imposed on purchasers of private placements inhibit turnover. Despite these obstacles, trades of issues directly placed do occur.

During the early 1980s the private placement market continued to show tremendous growth in dollar volume. The primary market in private placements demonstrated a 21% average annual growth rate in dollar volume between 1975 and 1984. During the same period the private share of the total corporate financing market varied from a low of 22% in 1975 and 1980 to a high of 39% in 1984. (See Exhibit 10.)

Even though preferred stocks and equity instruments can be found in the private placement market, debt offerings dominate. For example, debt made up

EXHIBIT 10 THE PRIVATE PLACEMENT MARKET

Year	Volume ($ billions)	Share of total financing market (%)
1975	13,515	22
1976	21,240	33
1977	25,748	41
1978	32,456	43
1979	22,545	38
1980	15,728	22
1981	18,430	25
1982	24,268	28
1983	35,580	27
1984	53,140	39

Source: IDD Information Services, Inc.

approximately 82% of the newly issued private placements in 1984; preferred stock accounted for 5%; and the remainder consisted of common stock and equity in other financing arrangements.

ADVANTAGES AND DISADVANTAGES. Raising capital in the private placement market frequently offers corporations many advantages not available in the public market. Among these advantages are speed, ability to complete complex financings, reduced fees, and opportunity to sell issues in a variety of sizes.

For many issuers, funds can be raised more quickly in the private markets than in the public marketplace. For large investment grade corporations, shelf registration under Rule 415 and the S-3 short registration form have dramatically reduced the delays inherent in the SEC registration process. However, some issuers are not able to use these procedural shortcuts. By using the private market, these issuers are not confronted with the delays encountered with the SEC registration process. This advantage can be particularly important during periods of volatility in the securities markets, when attractive financing opportunities can suddenly appear and just as suddenly disappear.

Because the investors who participate in the private placement market are highly sophisticated and a limited number of investors are contacted, it is often possible to complete financings which for many reasons may not be sold in public offerings. Complexity of financing, size, nature of credit, or a combination of all these factors may make it extremely difficult to sell unless a sophisticated investor is involved. However, even sophisticated investors can be confused by a multitude of complex terms. Therefore, it may be necessary for the issuer to give the investor a detailed explantion of the terms of the financing. This is almost inconceivable when issues are publicly offered.

Project financing, with many attendant complexities (e.g., large amounts of funds often required and frequent need for a series of repayments over time) is a type of financing usually best suited to the private market. A further discussion of project financing follows.

Fees and other expenses on direct placements tend to be lower than those of publicly offered issues of similar size. A simple and inexpensive offering circular, which is used to disseminate information about the new issue, is usually prepared by a corporation issuing a private placement. In contrast, a costly and elaborate prospectus must be prepared by the issuers (or investment banker) when they are going into the public sector for financing. When selling issues in the public markets, an underwriter is retained. The underwriter temporarily assumes the ownership risks of the new offering and must be compensated for assuming such risks. Corporations that issue private placements, however, are not burdened with these underwriting fees. Advisers, usually investment bankers or corporate finance departments of commercial banks, are often retained by corporations to aid in structuring the private placement agreement. These advisers assume no ownership risks; therefore their fees tend to be much lower than the fees of underwriters.

The private market used to be regarded as appropriate for small- or medium-size deals. In recent years the direct placement market has demonstrated that it can handle large deals. For example, huge privately placed project financings in excess of $500 million are no longer uncommon. In 1984, 39% of the dollar volume of private placements resulted from transactions in excess of $100 million.

The private placement market has always been able to handle small issues. This, however, is not true for the public markets, because secondary markets in small issues tend to be illiquid and investors interested in reaping trading profits tend to shy away from small issues. Small issues are therefore not well received by investors in the primary public markets.

The **public market** does, however, have the advantage of flexibility. Private placement agreements are generally held to be more restrictive. They often include provisions that impose tighter controls on additional debt issues, for example, than do covenants governing public security issues. This drawback, however, is offset to some degree by the comparative ease with which private placement provisions can be amended or waived.

The use of a private placement also reduces the flexibility of issuers in meeting sinking fund requirements. Because of the repayment provisions that are attached to issues privately placed and because of the minor trading that takes place in them, scheduled retirement payments are usually made pro rata to original owners in cash in stipulated amounts. These conditions normally prevent private issuers from repurchasing their obligations at substantial discounts—a real possibility for public market issuers during periods when interest rates are sharply above those prevailing at the time of the issue's origination.

MARKET PARTICIPANTS. Industrials have always been the major issuers in the private market. Apart from conventional debt and equity issues, privately placed leveraged lease financing is a vehicle commonly used by industrials. Companies chronically in the position of generating tax losses can obtain relatively low cost financing of plant and equipment through the leveraged leasing market. (Refer to Section 11: "Leasing.") The high yield or "junk bond" issues that are often used in connection with leveraged buyouts or acquisitions in the public market are also becoming common in the private marketplace.

Banks and finance companies have grown rapidly in recent years as issuers in the private market. Banks are common issuers of privately negotiated certificates of deposit. The growth of mortgage-backed securities and pass-throughs in the public market has a private counterpart. Mortgage companies, thrifts, and other finance companies are issuers of these instruments.

Public utilities have been a declining force as issuers in the private market. A growing aversion by investors to exposure to nuclear energy is certainly a factor. Also, public utilities have historically been substantial issuers of preferred stock in the private market. However, the Deficit Reduction Act of 1984 places restrictions on the 85% dividend exclusion (for tax purposes) as applied to preferred stock purchased with borrowed money. This has had an adverse impact on the issuance of preferred stock.

The scope of institutional purchasers of private placements has broadened in recent years. Insurance companies and pension funds have historically played dominant roles. These sophisticated investors are attracted by slightly higher yields and the ability to structure transactions to meet specific needs. Commercial banks and thrift institutions have become major investors in the private marketplace. Commercial banks are very active in the areas of project financing, construction loans, leveraged buyout loans, and leveraged lease financing. As previously mentioned a large portion of the mortgage-backed securities business is conducted in the private market. Thrifts, in addition to being major issuers of mortgage-backed securities, also are large purchasers of these instruments.

DUAL MARKET. Traditionally, yields on higher quality issues placed privately have been slightly higher than their comparable public counterparts. Although the spread varies rapidly (and is sometimes negative), it is usually somewhere between 10 and 30 basis points. This yield differential is primarily a result of the lesser liquidity of directly placed issues. The average spread of lesser quality paper (e.g., Baa/BBB) has been virtually zero since 1982; that is, public and private issues of this quality tend to offer virtually identical yields.

Caution must be taken when analyzing yield spreads. In this situation, even though credit ratings were held constant, the average maturities of the various market segments were probably not similar. Publicly issued securities tend to have longer maturities than do similar securities issued in the private sector.

Also it has been suggested that the private market lags the public market by a period of 4 to 6 weeks. This "lag" between the private and public markets is a direct result of the time difference between the agreement to terms and the distribution of funds in the private sector. In the private market, borrowers and lenders usually agree to terms several weeks before the funds are actually transferred to the borrower. In the public market, on the other hand, the issuer generally takes possession of the funds once an agreement has been reached.

RESALE OF PRIVATE PLACEMENTS. Sales of direct placements by investors tend to be inhibited by the illiquidity of the securities. A secondary market in private placements does exist, however. The resale of these securities can be completed only when certain legal requirements have been fulfilled. The issuer of the private placement must register the securities with the SEC, and a prospectus must be prepared for prospective investors. There are, however, certain exceptions to the rule. SEC Rule 144 describes requirements which, if met, exempt the directly placed issue from the registration process when it is sold in the secondary market. These requirements are:

1. The seller must have owned the securities for at least 2 years.
2. The amount sold in any 3-month period must not exceed 1% of the total

number of securities outstanding or, if the securities are listed on an exchange, the greater of 1% or the average weekly volume of all the exchanges in which the security is listed during the 4 weeks prior to the sale. Holders of private placements not affiliated with the issuer for a period of 3 months prior to the sale can disregard this requirement if the securities are listed on an exchange and held for 3 years. If the securities are not listed on an exchange, the securities must be held for 4 years.)

3. The sale must occur as a normal broker's transactions.
4. Form 144 must be filed with the SEC at the time of the sale to provide the public with the necessary information about the issuer.

PROJECT FINANCING

Project financing is not a specific financing vehicle such as a bond or preferred stock, rather it is a package of financing that is associated with a particular industrial project. Projects financed in this manner typically have attributes that make them too risky to finance through the traditional corporate source of funds. Sometimes unproven or vanguard technology is involved. Cogeneration facilities and waste recovery facilities are examples. Sometimes the potential rewards are great, but the cost of failure exceeds the threshold of any one corporation. Oil and gas exploration can be an example of this. Occasionally economies of scale make feasible a project whose size is beyond the means or needs of a single firm. Several corporations then form a joint venture and share the project's output. This often occurs, for example, with electric power generating facilities or port facilities.

MAJOR PARTIES INVOLVED. The more traditional sources of corporate capital involve two major parties: the issuer and the purchaser of the security involved. Project financing, in contrast, involves a host of players. A project financing usually includes the following roles: a project developer, a contractor, short- and long-term lenders, equity participants, and a facility operator. To make matters more complicated, sometimes two or more of these roles are filled by one firm.

It is the developer that first perceives the need for the project and starts the ball rolling by planning and arranging for its construction. As mentioned earlier the developer can consist of just one corporation or several corporations that have formed a joint venture. The developer's profit consists of the excess of project revenues over contractual obligations such as debt service and rental payments (as described later) and other ongoing project expenses.

In addition to their role as builder of the facility and equipment, the contractors and/or manufacturers often provide or use their own credit rating to arrange short-term financing during the project's construction phase. Furthermore, they often contractually warrant that the product will perform as promised. Sometimes the contractor also agrees to operate the facility on behalf of the developer on a long-term basis. If the operator is a hired third party, the contractor might promise to step in and operate the facility under certain adverse circumstances.

The long-term lenders are also important players in a project financing. Often the construction is substantially completed before long-term lenders have been lined up. As the project's in-service date approaches, the project manager's financial advisers put together an offering memorandum for the private market or a prospectus for the public market. The long-term debt is then used to pay down the short-term interim financing. Typically, the lenders are accepting substantial project risk. Although the lenders are superior to the equity participants (discussed in later paragraphs) in payment priority, they usually cannot look beyond the project for repayment of debt. The long-term debt is usually collateralized by one or more of the following: the project revenues, the equipment or facility, project insurance proceeds, and an assignment of other contractual rights such as the manufacturer's performance warranty. In the event of default, the lenders can rely on this collateral for repayment.

Frequently the project developer is also its legal owner and has a substantial financial investment in the project. Sometimes, however, additional parties called the equity participants assume the ownership role. Although the equity participants usually provide only 20 to 50% of the financing funds, they are the legal owners of the equipment or facility. If equity participants are distinct from the developer, they enter into a lease agreement with the developer. The lease agreement entitles the developer to use the facility for a substantial portion of its useful economic life. In return the developer agrees to make periodic rental payments.

The equity participants earn their return on investment from three sources: the rental payments, tax benefits of property and equipment ownership, and the residual value of the facility realized at the end of the lease. The equity participants are subject to substantial risk on all three fronts. The rental payments are often payable only out of project revenues (without recourse to the developer or other parties) and are paid only after the lenders have received their scheduled payments. Under the tax law effective at the time of this writing, the owners of the equipment for tax purposes (the equity participants) are entitled to an Investment Tax Credit usually equal to 10% of equipment cost and a rapid depreciation write-off under the Accelerated Cost Recovery System. Recently, the tax benefits of ownership (and therefore the economic return on investment) have been subject to legislative modification. Furthermore, if the transaction is not properly structured, there is a risk that the IRS will rule that the equity participants are not actually the owners for tax purposes. In this event they would be denied the preceding tax benefits. Finally, the residual value of the facility at the end of a lengthy lease term is impossible to ascertain with any degree of certainty. Often the deal is structured giving the equity participants an acceptable yield based on a conservative residual value assumption. Any excess residual value actually realized can then be viewed as a windfall. In light of the substantial risk inherent in the equity position, the equity participants usually negotiate a substantial yield.

OTHER PARTIES. In addition to these major participants in a project financing, the following parties are usually involved contractually to some degree: facility and equipment liability and property damage insurers, suppliers of project raw materials or inputs, and purchasers of project outputs. Sometimes the project developer is also the major user of the project's output. If not, long-term output purchase contracts are often negotiated in advance as part of the financing. Additionally, long-term raw material supply contracts can be part of the package. These contracts have the effect of fixing, to some extent, project revenues and costs over a period of time. This can substantially lessen the risk to the equity and debt investors, thus reducing the overall cost of financing.

REFERENCES

Altman, Edward I., "Computerized Bond Rating Replication: Worthwhile or Futile?" *Basis Point,* Equitable Life Assurance Society of America, Fall 1979, pp. 8–11.

Auster, Rolf, "Bond Investments: How to Use the Tax Rules to Maximize Benefits," *Journal of Taxation of Investments,* Vol. 3, No. 1, Autumn 1985, pp. 3–30.

Bowlin, O. D., "The Refunding Decision: Another Special Case in Capital Budgeting," *Journal of Finance,* Vol. 20, No. 1, March 1966, pp. 55–68.

Boyce, W. M., and Kalotay, A. J., "Optimum Bond Calling and Refunding," *Interfaces,* November 1979, pp. 36–49.

Boyce, W. M., and Kalotay, A. J., "Tax Differentials and Callable Bonds," *The Journal of Finance,* Vol. 34, No. 4, September 1979, pp. 825–838.

Brigham, Eugene F., *Financial Management: Theory and Practice,* 2d ed., Dryden Press, Hinsdale, IL, 1979.

Callahan, J. R., and McCallum, J. S., "The Sinking Fund Decision: Buy Forward or Wait?" *Cost and Management,* January–February 1978, pp. 36–39.

Castle, G., "Project Financing—Guidelines for the Commercial Banker," *Journal of Commercial Bank Lending,* April 1975, pp. 14–30.

Davey, Patrick J., "Private Placements: Practices and Prospects," *Conference Board,* No. 52, New York, January 1979.

Dyl, E. A., and Joehnk, M. D., "Sinking Funds and the Cost of Corporate Debt," *Journal of Finance,* Vol. 34, No. 4, September 1979, pp. 887–893.

Federal Register, Vol. 48, No. 277, Wednesday, November 1983, Rules and Regulations, pp. 52889–52897.

Freed, Felicia, and Brown, Gregory A., "An Introduction to Medium-Term Notes," Salomon Brothers Inc., January 1986.

Johnson, R., and Klein, R., "Corporate Motives in Repurchase of Discounted Bonds," *Financial Management,* Autumn 1974, pp. 44–49.

Kalotay, Andrew J., and McIntyre, Patrick, "Sinking Fund Issues: A Challenge for the Active Manager," Salomon Brothers Inc., November 1984.

Kalotay, A. J., "On the Advance Refunding of Discounted Debt," *Financial Management,* Summer 1978, pp. 14–18.

Kalotay, A. J., "On the Management of Sinking Funds," *Financial Management,* Summer 1981.

Kintner, Earl, *Primer on the Law of Mergers,* Macmillan, New York, 1973.

Lipton, Richard M., "Are Debt/Equity Swaps Dead?" *Investment Dealers Digest,* January 15, 1985, pp. 14–16.

McDaniel, William R., "Sinking Fund Preferred Stock," *Financial Management,* Vol. 13, No. 1, Spring 1984, pp. 45–52.

Morton, T. Gregory, "A Comparative Analysis of Moody's and S & P's Municipal Bond Ratings," *Review of Business & Economic Research,* Winter 1975, pp. 74–81.

Private Placements Market Review 1984, Kidder Peabody & Co. Inc. 1985.

Project Financing 1985 Power Generation, Waste Recovery, and other Facilities, Robert Thorton Smith, Chairman, 1985 Practising Law Institute

Roderick, Pamela H., "Salomon is the #1 for Half-Year," *Investment Dealers' Digest,* August 1985, pp. 11–13.

Van Horne, J. C., *Financial Management and Policy,* 4th ed. Prentice-Hall, Englewood Cliffs, NJ, 1977.

Weston, J. F., and Brigham, E. F., *Managerial Finance,* 6th ed., Dryden Press, Hinsdale, IL, 1978.

William, Edward E., and Findlay, M. Chapman, *Investment Analyses,* Prentice-Hall, Englewood Cliffs, NJ 1974.

Zwick, Burton, "Yields on Privately Placed Corporate Bonds," *Journal of Finance,* Vol. 35, No. 1, March, 1980, pp. 23–29.

6

THE HIGH YIELD DEBT MARKET

CONTENTS

6

THE HIGH YIELD DEBT MARKET

Edward I. Altman
Scott A. Nammacher

INTRODUCTION

Rising interest rates and rapid expansion of the high yield corporate debt market since the late 1970s have led a wide variety of financial institutions to explore the relative attractions of lower-rated securities. In addition to the promised superior yields and realized impressive returns, the high yield (or **"junk bond"**) sector now offers considerable liquidity and diversification potential. It has been estimated that total outstanding debt in this area was over $90 billion by late 1985. The segment analyzed in this section, *all low-rated, public, nonconvertible debt,* grew from under $10 billion in 1978 to almost $42 billion in 1984 and was almost $60 billion by the end of 1985. Estimates from individuals dealing in these markets indicate that an additional 15–20% of the $60 billion rated debt can be found in nonrated, high yield securities. By 1985, the low-rated segment represented almost 15.0% of the total corporate, straight debt market, versus just 3.8% in 1978. In 1984 and again in 1985, nearly $15 billion in new straight, high yield financing was issued. Given the market's size, growth rate, yield, and capital-raising potential, it has become an increasingly important area for investors and the **investment banking community**.

In this section we present a comprehensive documentation and analysis of the publicly traded, straight (nonconvertible), **high yield bond market**. The findings of this report are based on this specific segment of the overall high yield marketplace. The report does not encompass convertible debt or companies not rated by either *S&P* or *Moody's,* except where specifically noted. This will include a discussion of the anatomy of the market, its history, issuers, investors, and underwriters as well as an introduction to risks and returns. The

---

This section is reprinted with permission from Morgan Stanley & Co., Incorporated and is based on a report prepared by the authors for Morgan Stanley & Co., Incorporated, "The Anatomy of the High Yield Debt Market," September 1985.

anatomy also includes a summary of the analysis of recent **default experience of high yield debt** and a profile analysis of new issuers in 1983 and 1984.

MARKET ANATOMY

SIZE, GROWTH, AND RETURNS. The 1978–1985 period was an exceptionally volatile period for interest rates and corporate profitability. Interest rates on 3-month T-bills and on 10-year government bonds rose from 7.4% and 8.4% yield levels respectively in early 1978, to record heights, peaking in mid-1981 at 17.2% and 15.3% respectively. By the fourth quarter of 1982, T-bills had dropped to 8%, whereas 10-year governments were near the 10.5% level (see Exhibit 1). At the same time, corporate profits plummeted in the 1981–1982 recession and bankruptcies reached record post-Depression levels. Despite the overall economy's expansion in 1983–1985, the number of **business failures** and **corporate distress** situations has remained at historically high levels.

This volatility caused large variations in bond returns and yields over the period. Investment managers holding a portfolio equivalent to the *Shearson Lehman Long-Term Government Bond Index* would have experienced losses or marginally positive returns for all but two (1982 and 1984) years of the 7-year period from 1978 through 1984 (see Exhibit 2). In effect, rising **interest rates** caused substantial reductions in the market value of their holdings, more than offsetting the coupon income these bonds generated. The decline in rates in

EXHIBIT 1 GOVERNMENT YIELDS (MONTHLY AVERAGE)

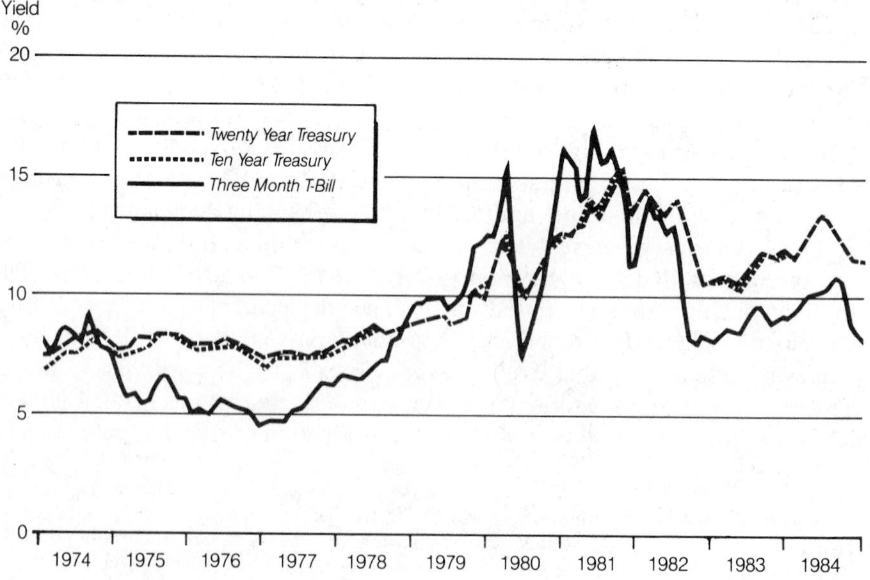

EXHIBIT 2 ANNUAL RETURNS, YIELDS, AND SPREADS ON LONG-TERM (LT) GOVERNMENT BONDS AND HIGH YIELD (HY) BONDS (CALENDAR YEARS)

	Return			Promised Yield[c]		
Year	HY[a] Return	LT Govt[b] Return	HY Return Spread	HY	LT Govt	Spread
1978	7.57%	−1.11%	8.68%	10.92%	8.11%	2.81%
1979	3.69	−0.86	4.55	12.07	9.13	2.94
1980	−1.00	−2.96	1.96	13.46	10.23	3.23
1981	7.56	0.48	7.08	15.97	12.08	3.89
1982	32.45	42.08	−9.63	17.84	13.86	3.98
1983	21.80	2.23	19.57	15.74	10.70	5.04
1984	8.50[d]	14.82	−6.32	14.97	11.87	3.10
Arithmetic Average:						
1978–1983	12.01	6.64	5.37	14.32	10.68	3.64
1978–1984	11.51	7.81	3.70	14.42	10.85	3.57
Compounded Average:						
1978–1983	11.45	5.62	5.83			
1978–1984	11.02	6.89	3.30			

[a] Morgan Stanley composite generated from over 440 high yield issues. Actual portfolios ranged in size from 153 in 1978 to 339 issues in 1983. This database goes through 3/31/84.
[b] *Shearson Lehman Long-Term Government Bond Index.*
[c] Promised yield as of beginning of year. It represents the internal rate of return based on the security's current price and scheduled payments of interest and principal.
[d] *Drexel Burnham Lambert Index,* from *High Yield Newsletter* (February 1985). Note this index does not include reinvested coupon payments and differs somewhat from the 1978–1983 measures.

1982 and 1984 saved investors in long-term government bonds from having a negative return over the entire period.

With high quality bond returns fluctuating at or below zero returns from 1978 through 1981, portfolio managers began looking for new opportunities to boost their returns. High yield bonds from 1978 to 1981 returned an average of 4.4% on investment, whereas long-term government bonds returned an average of −1.1% The high yield bond marketplace became an increasingly attractive option.

Based on data from the **Morgan Stanley database**, we found that portfolio managers investing in high yield bonds from December 31, 1977 to December 31, 1983 would have realized a compounded return of 11.45% versus 5.62% for long-term government bonds, a 583 basis point difference annually! Returns are very sensitive to the time period examined. For example, the return spread for the period March 31, 1978 to March 31, 1984 was 490 basis points. A 3-month shift caused a 93 basis point change in returns. That differential narrowed to 330 basis points by the end of 1984. The arithmetic average annual return spread was 3.70% or 370 basis points at the end of 1984 versus 5.37% or 537 basis points at the end of 1983. The average yield spread between high yield bonds and long-term governments over the same time frame (measured annually at the beginning of each year) was 364 basis points through 1983 and 357 basis points through 1984. Selected annual returns and yields are displayed in Exhibit 3. Thus the average yield spread (ex-ante) and average return spread (ex-post) from 1978–1985 were actually quite similar (3.57% versus 3.70%) but there is very little similarity for each specific year.

Exhibit 4 indicates the fixed income *mutual bond fund performance* of a

EXHIBIT 3
(A) CALENDAR YEAR YIELDS AT THE BEGINNING OF EACH YEAR
(B) CALENDAR YEAR RETURNS 1978 THROUGH 1984

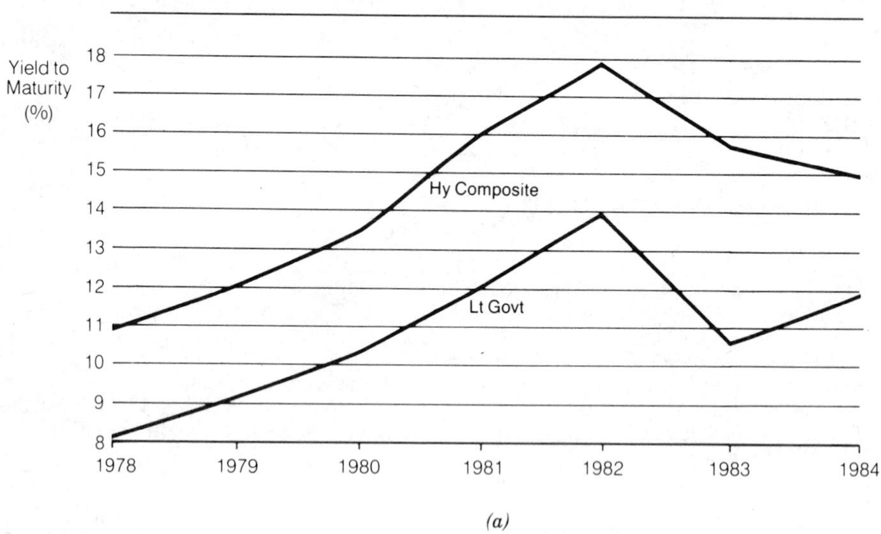

(a)

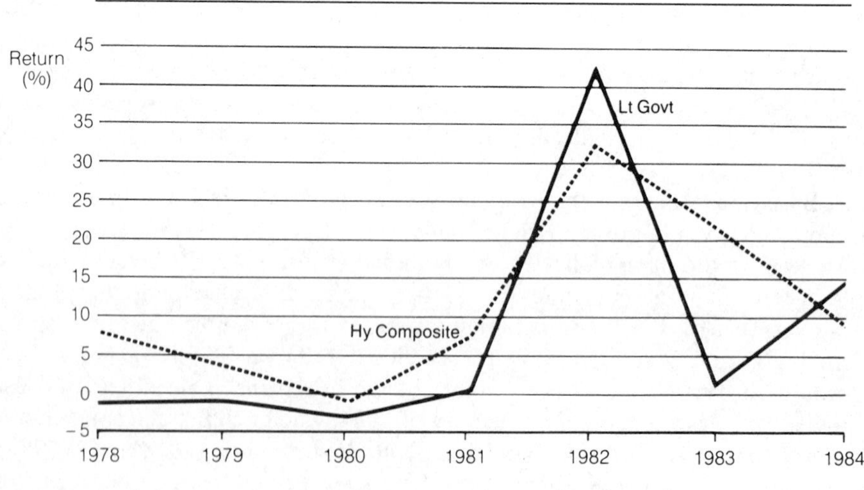

(b)

EXHIBIT 4 SELECTED GROUPS OF LONG-TERM TAXABLE BOND FUNDS TOTAL REINVESTED RETURN FOR SELECTED TIME PERIODS (A) 10 YEARS (1975–1984), (B) 1 YEAR (1984), AND (C) 6 MONTHS (JANUARY–JUNE 1985).

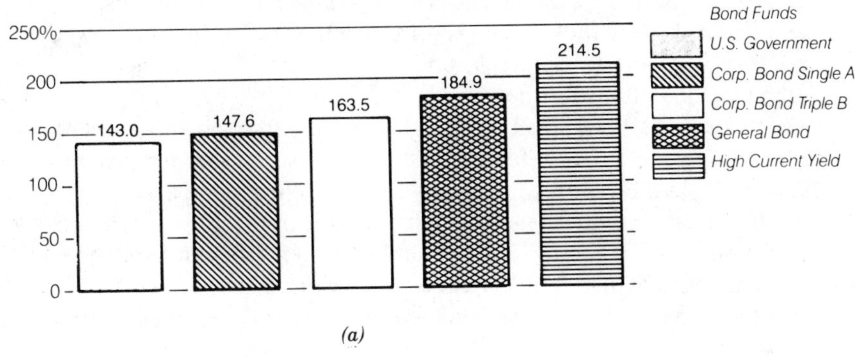

(a)

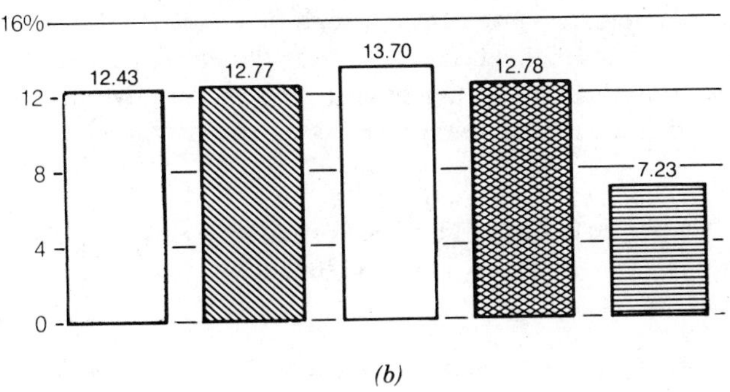

(b)

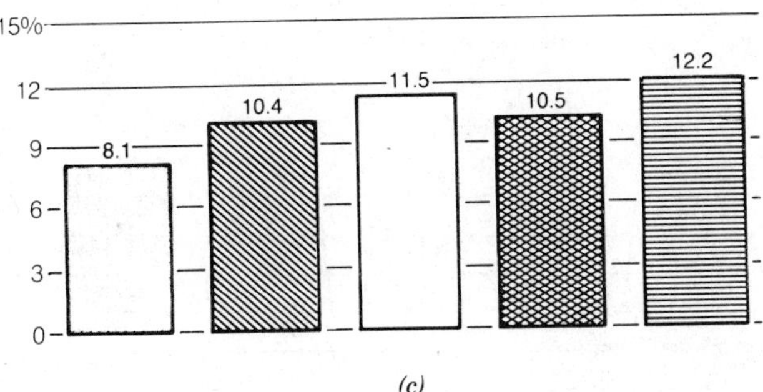

(c)

Source: Lipper Analytical Services, Inc.

number of strategies over the period 1975–1984, for 1984 alone, and for the first 6 months of 1985 These statistics were compiled by *Lipper Analytical Services, Inc.* and represent the average reinvested return performance of a number of funds investing in each category. Note that the return performance for the 10-year period is consistent with perceived risk attributes. The highest yielding funds were those of the High Current Yield category followed by General Bonds, Triple-B, Single-A, and U.S. Governments categories. Our own database calculations for the period April 1978–April 1984 show the same relative rankings as the Lipper rankings. This relative performance record also holds true approximately for the first 6 months of 1985, but not for 1984. In 1984, high yield bonds recorded only a 7.23% return compared to over 12% for all other fixed income categories. Whether or not the 1984 results are a 1-year aberration in the expected return spreads between different fixed income strategies, only time will tell. We believe, however, that the risk-reward tradeoff among different quality issues will in all likelihood be reflected in actual returns over the long run.

Exhibit 5 presents the monthly index of returns for our composite of high yield bonds. Monthly returns varied from a high of 13.13% in April 1980 to a low of −7.61% in October 1979. The average over the entire period March 31, 1978 to March 31, 1984 was 0.92% per month. Long-term government bonds had their highs and lows in the same months as the high yield bonds and

EXHIBIT 5 MONTHLY RETURNS FOR HY COMPOSITES (3/31/78 TO 3/31/84)

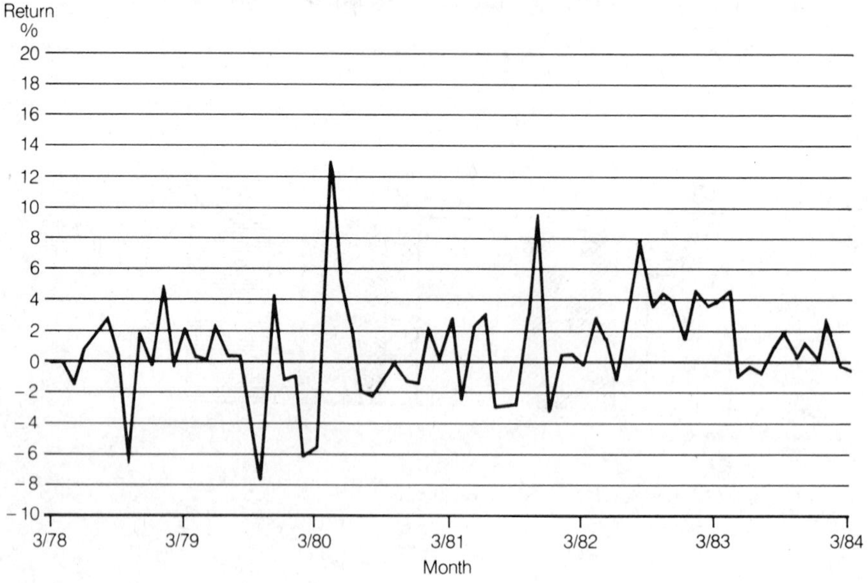

averaged 0.52% per month over the same period. Premiums like these are a major reason that demand in the high yield market expanded so rapidly. We compared our monthly return results to those of Blume and Keim, "Risk and Return Characteristics of Lower Grade Bonds," Working Paper, Rodney White Center for Financial Research, The Wharton School, Phila. Pa. (1984) and Drexel Burnham Lambert's (DBL 100 index) and found all three highly correlated (R = 0.92 or higher).

Exhibit 6 shows how quickly the market has changed. In 1978 the par value of public, low-rated straight debt outstanding represented 3.8% of the total public straight debt outstanding. By 1984 low-rated debt had grown to over 11% and to almost 15% in 1985. Total public, straight debt outstanding grew 61% from 1978 to 1985. High yield, rated public debt grew by over sixfold, from $9.4 billion to over $59 billion. At the same time, the amount of debt per company and per issue grew substantially. The debt per company moved from $50 million to $98 million and the average outstanding per issue grew from $30 million to nearly $60 million in just seven years.

EXHIBIT 6 PUBLIC STRAIGHT DEBT OUTSTANDING 1970–1984 ($MM)

		Low-Rated Debt[b]			
Year	Par Value Public Straight Debt Outstanding Over Year[a]	Straight Public Debt	% of Public St. Debt	Amount Outstanding Per Issuer	Amount Outstanding Per Issue
1985	$395,500 (Est.)	$59,078	14.9%	$ 98	$61
1984	363,300	41,700	11.5	125	49
1983	339,850	28,223	8.3	93	39
1982	320,850	18,536	5.8	69	33
1981	303,800	17,362	5.7	62	32
1980	282,000	15,125	5.4	59	31
1979	260,600	10,675	4.1	47	30
1978	245,000	9,401	3.8	49	30
1977	228,500	8,479	3.7	46	27
1976	209,900	8,015	3.8	41	27
1975	187,900	7,720	4.1	41	27
1974	167,000[c]	11,101[d]	6.6	59	35
1973	154,800	8,082	5.2	45	29
1972	145,700	7,106	4.9	45	29
1971	132,500	6,643	5.0	45	29
1970	116,200	6,996	6.0	48	32

[a] Average of beginning and ending years' figures (1975–1984).
[b] *Source: Standard & Poor's Bond Guide* and *Moody's Bond Record,* July issues of each year. Defaulted railroads excluded. Also includes non-rated debt equivalent to rated debt for low-rated firms.
[c] Estimates for 1973 and earlier based on linear regression of this column vs. the Federal Reserve's Corporate Bonds Outstanding figures (*Federal Reserve Bulletin*).
[d] Includes $2.7 billion in Con Edison debt.
(Est.) = Estimate

EXHIBIT 7 NEW NONCONVERTIBLE DOMESTIC DEBT ISSUES: 1978–1984 ($MM)

	Total New Issues-Public Straight Debt		High Yield Debt					
			Total New High Yield Debt Issues[a]		% New Issue Dollars	Issued with Warrants or Stock	Variable Rate Debt	
Year	Amount	No.	Amount	No.			Amount	No.
1985	$101,098	1,212	$14,670	188	14.5%	18	$2,543	12
1984	99,416	721	14,952	124	15.0	18	3,927	27
1983	46,903	511	7,417	86	15.8	35	—	—
1982	47,798	513	2,798	48	5.9	10	40	1
1981	41,651	357	1,648	32	4.0	6	104	2
1980	37,272	398	1,442	43	3.9	8	137	4
1979	25,678	277	1,307	45	5.0	14	—	—
1978	22,416	287	1,493	52	6.7	15	—	—
Total:	$423,536	4,284	$45,757	618	10.8%	124	$6,751	46

[a]Not including exchange offers, secondary issues, tax-exempts, convertibles or government agencies.
Source: Morgan Stanley & Co. Incorporated.

NEW ISSUES. The new issue public, straight debt marketplace (see Exhibit 7) has grown phenomenally, moving from the $1.5 billion level in 1978 to just under $15 billion in 1984 and again in 1985 (with a 100% increase between 1983 and 1984). The high yield marketplace represented 15% of 1984's new, straight corporate debt issues and 14.5% in 1985. New issue business in 1984 alone accounted for over 48% of the new issue business in the high yield marketplace since 1978 with a record number of issues with $200 million (par value) or more. Exhibit 8 lists these issues (20), up from only six the year before. The number of deals $100 million or larger rose from 2 in 1978, to 23 in 1983 and finally to 58 in 1984 (representing over 46% of the issues done in 1984, up from 27% in 1983). These figures do not include "best efforts" offerings. Since 1978 there have been 21 CCC rated, 256 B rated, 96 BB rated and 13 BBB/Ba rated new issues. The B and CCC rated issues accounted for over 62% of the high yield debt issues and 53% of the new, high yield issue dollars in 1984.

The average issue size has changed over the years, from $28 million in 1978 to over $120 million in 1984 (see Exhibit 9). The median issue in 1984 was $77 million. This year saw both record size issues (i.e., Metromedia—$1.3 billion raised using a complex combination of four types of securities) and a record number of offerings (124, up by 44% over the prior year).

The average "years to maturity" of new issues dropped as interest rates increased. In 1978, the average life was 19 years (ignoring sinking funds). By 1984 it had fallen to 12 years. The average **duration** of bonds in our high yield

EXHIBIT 8 NEW STRAIGHT DEBT ISSUES OF $200 MILLION OR MORE (PAR VALUE)[a] ($MM)

Issuer	Coupon	Maturity	Par Value	Rating[b]
Occidental Petroleum	9.65s	1994	$1,200	BB−
Occidental Petroleum	8.95s	1994	700	BBB/Ba3
Coastal Corp., Houston	VRN	1994	600	BB−
Rapid American	Os	1984–2007	506	CCC
Mesa Petroleum	VRN	1994	500	BB−
ACF Industries	15.25s	1996	400	BBB/Ba3
Metromedia Broadcasting	Adj. Rate	2002	400	B−
Occidental Petroleum	VRN	1994	350	BBB/Ba3
Metromedia Broadcasting	VRN	1996	335	B+
Middle South Energy	16.0s	2000	300	BB−
Chrysler Financial	VRN	1992	300	B
Metromedia Broadcasting	15.625s	1999	225	B−
Chrysler Financial	13.5s	1991	200	B
Chrysler Financial	VRN	1994	200	B
Chrysler Financial	12.75s	1999	200	BB−
Chrysler Financial	13.25s	1999	200	BB−
I.C.H. Corp.	16.5s	1994	200	BB−
Rapid American	14.5s	1994	200	CCC
Resorts International	16.25s	2004	200	B+
Turner Broadcasting	12.875s	1994	200	B−

[a] Not including best effort offerings.
Note: two large issues (Metromedia 0's 1998 and Harte-Hanks Comm. 0's 2004) were not listed because their final issue amounts could not be verified.
[b] Moody's rating indicated when its rating differed from S&P's investment grade.
Source: Morgan Stanley & Co. Incorporated.

universe was 6.45 years in 1983, down from 7.87 years in 1978, and has averaged 6.64 years over the 6-year period. By contrast, the average duration of Shearson Lehman's Long-Term Government Bond Index over the same period was 8.53 years. See Exhibit 10 for **yield and duration** attributes of various portfolios. In 1984 and 1985, despite interest rates moving in a downward trend, issuers continued to shorten the years to maturity and duration on their debt.

The S&P rating distribution of new issues in recent years has been skewed toward single-B. In 1984 the number of single-B rated issues exceeded double-B rated issues by threefold.

In addition to the change in status of companies listed earlier, there have been, on occasion, several types of **"bailouts"** of firms that otherwise would likely have **defaulted** on outstanding debt. The most dramatic one was the government's guarantee of Chrysler's debt. More recently, Muse Air, Castle & Cooke, and Sharon Steel are striving to avoid default through a restructuring of their finances. There are numerous other examples of **debt restructurings**. The actual number and amount of exchange debt issues increased to 27 and

EXHIBIT 9 PUBLIC HIGH YIELD NEW ISSUE STATISTICS

Year	S&P Rating[a]	Total Amount Issued ($M)	Number of Issues	Years to Maturity	Average Issue Amount ($M)
1984	BBB/Ba	$ 1,290,000	5	9	$258,000
	BB	4,698,000	23	13	204,260
	B	6,484,500	68	11	95,360
	CCC	1,476,000	9	12	164,000
	No Rating	1,003,469	19	13	52,814
Total:		14,951,969	124	12	120,580
1983	BBB/Ba	—	—	—	—
	BB	2,893,738	24	17	120,572
	B	3,713,451	46	14	80,727
	CCC	285,000	5	17	57,000
	No Rating	525,000	11	11	47,727
Total:		7,417,189	86	15	86,246
1982	BBB/Ba	60,000	2	11	30,000
	BB	1,378,000	16	12	86,125
	B	1,122,292	24	14	46,762
	CCC	145,050	2	13	72,525
	No Rating	92,311	4	23	23,078
Total:		2,797,653	48	14	58,284
1981	BBB/Ba	290,000	4	11	72,500
	BB	290,000	6	19	48,333
	B	893,667	15	18	59,578
	CCC	—	—	—	—
	No Rating	174,500	7	11	24,929
Total:		1,648,167	32	16	51,505
1980	BBB/Ba	50,000	1	7	50,000
	BB	418,000	9	18	46,444
	B	878,625	28	19	31,379
	CCC	25,000	1	15	25,000
	No Rating	70,000	4	14	17,500
Total:		1,441,625	43	18	33,526
1979	BBB/Ba	—	—	—	—
	BB	359,000	8	18	44,875
	B	852,600	33	18	25,836
	CCC	91,400	3	15	30,467
	No Rating	4,000	1	15	4,000
Total:		1,307,000	45	18	29,044
1978	BBB/Ba	40,000	1	20	40,000
	BB	407,875	10	19	40,787
	B	1,029,025	39	19	26,385
	CCC	12,000	1	15	12,000
	No Rating	4,000	1	15	4,000
Total:		1,492,900	52	19	28,710
Totals 1978–1984:		$31,056,503	430	15	$ 72,224

Does not include convertibles, exchange or best efforts offerings.
[a] BBB included if Moody's ranked below investment grade.
Source: Morgan Stanley & Co. Incorporated.

EXHIBIT 10 YIELD AND DURATION COMPARISON ON FIXED INCOME PORTFOLIOS[a]

Portfolio	1978	1979	1980	1981	1982	1983	Average
High Yield Composite							
Yield %:	10.71	11.52	16.16	15.90	18.62	13.77	14.45
Duration yrs:	7.87	7.52	6.25	6.12	5.63	6.45	6.64
No. of bonds:	153	203	243	280	286	339	
Shearson Lehman Long Term Govt Bond Index							
Yield %:	8.38	9.13	12.48	12.77	13.70	10.85	11.22
Duration yrs:	9.90	9.55	8.04	7.84	7.44	8.44	8.53
Portfolio by S&P Rating							
BB Rated Portfolio							
Yield %:	9.80	10.85	14.99	15.12	17.21	13.07	13.51
Duration yrs:	8.70	7.77	6.57	6.62	5.87	6.39	6.99
No. of bonds:	34	51	61	49	55	70	
B Rated Portfolio							
Yield %:	10.83	11.79	16.73	15.96	18.50	14.20	14.67
Duration yrs:	7.84	7.67	6.23	6.17	5.57	6.27	6.63
No. of bonds:	60	93	114	137	143	150	
CCC Rated Portfolio							
Yield %:	12.86	13.38	17.89	17.91	22.70	15.60	16.72
Duration yrs:	7.16	6.87	5.83	5.63	4.80	5.82	6.02
No. of bonds:	17	14	16	33	21	35	

[a] Yields and duration are from 3/31 of each year and are weighted by the amounts outstanding.
Source: Morgan Stanley & Co. Incorporated.

almost $3.4 billion in 1985, respectively. The number of restructurings is indicated in Exhibit 11. These artificial outside influences and debt exchanges serve to reduce the default rate on bonds and do, in many cases, preserve investor capital. On the other hand, they may merely delay the bankruptcy of the company with all or partial loss of principal resulting.

EXHIBIT 11 HIGH YIELD EXCHANGE DEBT ISSUES, 1978–1985

Year	Number of Issues	Dollar Amount ($MM)	Average Amount ($MM)
1978	12	$662.0	$ 55.2
1979	6	227.1	37.9
1980	5	645.7	129.1
1981	2	323.0	161.5
1982	5	529.0	105.8
1983	16	486.0	30.4
1984	10	702.0	70.2
1985	27	3399.0	147.4

EXHIBIT 12 NEW HIGH YIELD PUBLIC DEBT ISSUES:

Underwriter	1985 Amount	1985 No.	1984 Amount	1984 No.	1983 Amount	1983 No.	1982 Amount	1982 No.
Drexel Burnham	$ 7,238,515	83	$10,358,000	67	$4,346,151	46	$1,543,800	28
Salomon Brothers	1,464,311	13	865,000	9	422,538	4	—	—
Morgan Stanley	1,050,000	13	319,000	5	80,000	1	—	—
Lehman/Loeb	707,653	8	718,000	8	230,000	1	25,000	1
Merrill Lynch	665,776	9	530,000	4	427,000	5	699,000	7
First Boston	640,000	9	390,000	5	325,000	3	—	—
Goldman Sachs	615,000	5	100,000	1	125,000	1	—	—
Bear, Stearns	456,100	7	360,000	4	380,000	5	35,000	1
Prudential-Bache	435,000	8	950,000	13	275,000	6	40,000	1
E.F. Hutton	280,000	2	145,000	3	190,000	2	82,542	2
Blyth/Paine W.	206,044	2	65,000	1	235,000	3	225,000	1
Others	804,025	29	151,969	4	381,500	9	147,311	7
Total	$14,670,424	188	$14,951,969	124	$7,417,189	86	$2,797,653	48

[a] Bonds rated BB, Ba or lower, and high yield non-rated bonds.
Includes utilities *excludes* convertibles and exchange offers.
[b] In cases of consolidation, credit goes to surviving firm.
Source: Securities Data Company, Inc. Giving full credit to the lead manager.

MARKET PARTICIPANTS

Underwriters. Drexel Burnham Lambert Inc. has been the largest underwriter in the high yield market. The firm has been responsible for 287 issues and about 60% of all new issue dollars since 1978. Drexel, once a relatively small firm in its field, became the second largest underwriter in the industry in 1984 (U.S. securities), behind Salomon Brothers, because of its specialization in this new area. Prudential-Bache and Salomon Brothers followed at a distant level, in the high yield area, with under $1 billion each (see Exhibit 12). Exhibit 13 provides detail on new issue ratings by underwriter.

Investors. The relatively high yields and annual returns in this market offer substantial benefits to investing institutions. One reason investors are drawn to this market is the power of compounding interest over time. Exhibit 14 shows the effects of a 300 and 500 basis point difference in current yields between two bonds. After 10 years, a $100 million portfolio, invested (and compounded semi-annually) at 10, 13 and 15%, would have resulted in final total holdings before taxes and charges of $265, $352 and $424 million respectively. A difference of 300 basis points means a 33% difference in value at the end of 10 years and a 500 basis point yield differential results in a 60% increase in wealth. The longer the holding period, the greater the level of ending wealth, due to the impact of compounding. At the end of 20 years, the 300 basis point advantage would have resulted in a 74% difference in the ending value ($1.2 billion versus $688 million). **Compounding** over time helps to lock in superior returns even after defaults and price fluctuations take their toll.

Another way of looking at the impact of high coupons and the **compounding effect** is to compare a **high yield bond** to an **investment grade bond** in a break-

1978–1985[a] FULL CREDIT TO LEAD MANAGER[b] ($000)

1981		1980		1979		1978	
Amount	No.	Amount	No.	Amount	No.	Amount	No.
$ 935,667	19	$ 498,000	15	$ 408,000	14	$ 464,500	15
60,000	1	115,000	2	—	—	—	
—	—	40,000	1	—	—	—	—
225,000	2	222,500	5	75,000	2	75,000	2
240,000	4	50,000	1	75,000	1	157,875	3
—	—	—	—	171,000	1	68,750	3
—	—	—	—	—	—	—	—
30,000	1	105,000	4	235,000	7	120,775	6
—	—	—	—	30,000	2	20,000	1
25,000	1	89,125	2	68,000	4	90,000	3
—	—	52,000	1	173,000	4	155,000	3
132,500	4	270,000	12	72,000	10	341,000	16
$1,648,167	32	$1,441,625	43	$1,307,000	45	$1,492,900	52

even analysis. The figures below compare a 12.5% high yield bond with a 10.0% investment grade issue (assumed to be called at 100% of par in the indicated year).

Year	Percentage of High Yield Principal Required to Maintain Equivalent Return
1	97.44
2	94.63
3	91.55
4	88.17
5	84.46
6	80.39
7	75.92
8	71.02
9	65.64
10	59.74
11	53.27
12	46.16
13	38.37
14	29.82
15	20.43

Assumption

- Bonds have 15-year term and no sinking fund.
- Interest income reinvested at prevailing intermediate government (IG) interest rate, 9.5%.
- Market interest rates remain constant such that the IG security trades at 100% of par.

EXHIBIT 13 NEW ISSUES—UNDERWRITER BY S&P RATING LARGEST HIGH YIELD BOND UNDERWRITERS 1978–1984

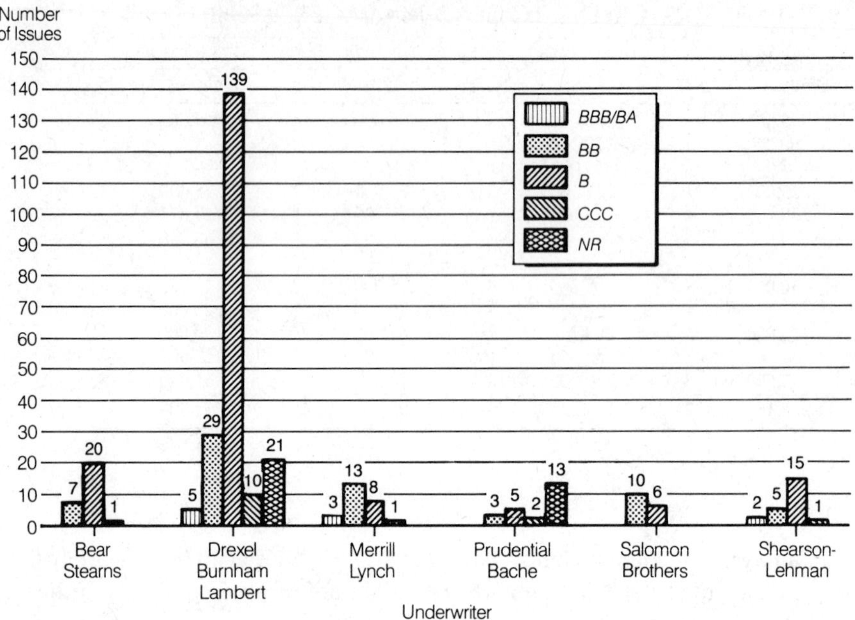

EXHIBIT 14 EFFECTS OF COMPOUNDING OVER TIME $100 MILLION STARTING VALUE

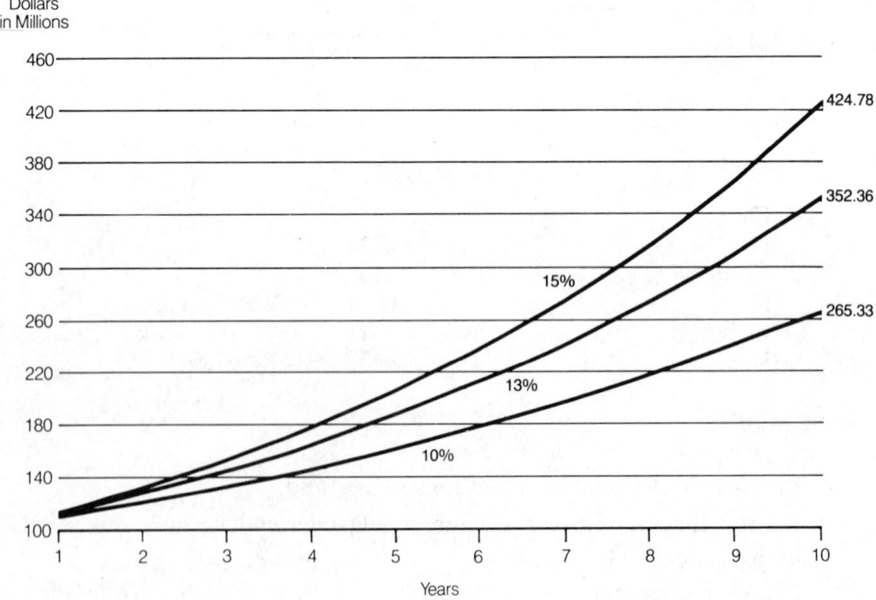

After 13 years, an investor in the high yield bond would have had to retain only 38.4% of the bond's principal to have equaled the returns of an investment grade bond called at 100% of par in the same year. Interestingly, the 38.4% level is actually slightly below what we found to be the average market value of bonds just after default (41%). This means that if a high yield portfolio experienced defaults of this magnitude at the end of the 13th year, then, on average, the portfolio would have performed as well as if funds had been invested in an investment grade portfolio. If the reinvestment rate was 11.5%, the breakeven year would change from 13 to 11.

The high returns and the power of compounding have helped attract several types of major buy side participants. These include **Mutual Funds**, **Savings and Loans**, **Pension Funds** and **Insurance Companies**.

In 1985, there were 24 major funds that invested primarily in the high yield marketplace. A $10,000 investment split equally over each of these funds and invested for 7 years from January, 1978 to December, 1984, assuming reinvestment of all dividend and capital gain payouts, would have resulted in a final portfolio worth $19,228. On an annual basis, this represents a bond equivalent return of 9.6%. (Returns calculated using data from *Wiesenberger Investment Company Service.*) Exhibit 15 summarizes the returns by fund from 1978 through 1985. In 1985, *Lipper Analytical Services* counted 40 funds holding some level of high yield debt. The 40 funds held total net assets of over $10 billion.

Lipper Analytical Services reported that when compared with various types of investment funds (U.S. Govt., Corp. A Rated Bond, Corp. BBB Rated/Trading and General Bond), the High Current Yield Bond Funds outperformed the others, in terms of returns, in 6 out of the last 10 years (see Exhibits 4 and 16). Only in 1984 were the high yield funds the worst performers. Lipper suggests the reason for the poor record in 1984 was the mutual funds portfolios, on average, have shorter durations and therefore underperform in a period of declining interest rates.

As of March 31, 1986, the 40 funds that Lipper classified as High Current Yield Funds had $16.6 billion in net assets, more than any other type of mutual fund followed. (U.S. Government Bond mutual funds were second.) With respect to the diversification of holdings, most large funds appear to have over 100 issues ranging between 30 and 300 issues. The average unweighted asset turnover rate for the 24 major funds in 1983 was 106%, with a range of 19% (Federated High Incomes) to 325% (Putnam High Yield Trust).

Although it is difficult to estimate **savings and loan associations'** potential impact on the investing side of the high yield marketplace, it is important to note that the larger institutions are either already involved or beginning to look more seriously at high yield bonds as a viable investment opportunity. Savings and Loans have been saddled with large portfolios in low interest mortgage loans. These loans, until recently, locked in the returns on their assets at levels below what new money was costing them. High yield bonds have offered them a way to increase the returns on their assets and so, cut losses. There is, how-

EXHIBIT 15 HIGH YIELD FUND ANNUAL RETURNS (%)[a]

Mutual Fund Name	1978	1979	1980	1981	1982	1983	1984	1985
American Capital High Yield	—	2.2	1.4	5.8	30.2	16.4	8.7	25.1
American Investors Income Fund	3.0	15.1	18.4	−4.9	13.0	26.9	−8.4	22.7
CIGNA High Yield Fund	—	3.3	0.0	5.9	31.7	17.5	9.8	23.5
Colonial High Yield Securities	4.6	7.7	0.3	6.4	24.6	20.4	10.5	21.8
Dean Witter High Yield Sec.	—	—	1.8	6.5	36.1	14.7	5.7	23.0
Delchester Bond Fund	2.2	1.7	0.7	0.9	37.5	12.9	8.7	21.2
Eaton Vance High Yield Fund	0.4	−0.4	1.3	1.5	33.6	11.4	15.0	22.0
Federated High Income	1.0	6.6	2.7	3.9	32.5	14.5	10.8	21.7
Fidelity High Income fund	3.8	4.6	4.4	6.9	35.8	18.5	10.5	25.5
First Inv. Bond Appreciation	—	10.8	16.6	11.8	17.3	12.0	1.3	20.0
High Yield Securities	0.3	4.5	2.4	7.3	30.5	19.4	5.5	17.9
Kemper High Yield Fund	−4.9	2.4	−1.0	8.7	39.5	17.7	10.2	23.1
Keystone (B-4) Bond Fund	4.2	1.6	8.3	10.0	31.5	15.4	4.9	20.5
Lord Abbett Bond Deb. Fund	2.9	7.0	8.9	5.3	27.5	16.6	5.0	21.0
Mass. Finl. High Income Trust	—	6.8	5.3	7.3	35.8	26.7	6.4	23.1
Merrill Lynch Corp. Bond Fund	—	2.4	3.1	6.5	23.1	18.4	8.6	21.6
Oppenheimer High Yield Fund	—	4.2	1.2	−6.3	28.8	14.7	3.5	18.8
Phoenix High Yield Fund Series	—	—	—	8.0	28.5	13.4	7.9	21.0
Pru-Bache High Yield Fund	—	—	4.9	4.0	28.1	15.7	10.2	20.6
Putnam High Yield Trust	—	2.8	7.0	5.2	38.9	15.6	7.0	19.9
Shearson High Yield Fund	—	—	—	5.1	32.2	14.8	9.8	18.8
United High Income Fund	—	—	7.8	5.3	32.7	13.9	9.6	23.3
Vanguard Fixed Inc. Securities	—	5.6	3.4	9.4	27.5	15.1	7.9	22.0
Venture Income (+) Plus	—	—	—	9.0	30.3	18.8	6.6	25.5
Average	1.8	4.9	4.7	5.4	30.3	16.7	7.3	21.8

[a]Return: Change in value of initial $10,000 investment over 1-year period, reinvesting all income.

Source: Wiesenberger Investment Company Service, a division of Warren, Gorham & Lamont, Boston, MA.

ever, growing political momentum to limit the level of high yield bond investments that Savings and Loans can make on the basis of the market's risky profile. This could affect the growth potential in this market.

Pension funds are another large source of investment funds. Over 150 pension funds (state and corporate) have assets in excess of $1 billion. The top 200 pension funds represented over $605 billion in assets at the end of 1983. The returns on high yield bonds are also helping to draw investment funds from this pool. Higher returns and yields mean lower annual funding requirements from the parent corporation or organization.

According to A. M. Best Inc., there were 78 insurance companies that have

EXHIBIT 16 SELECTED GROUPS OF LONG TERM TAXABLE BOND FUNDS TOTAL REINVESTED RETURN AVERAGES ANNUAL RESULTS 1975–1984

	U.S. Government	Corp. Bond A Rated	Corp. Bond BBB/Trading	General Bond	High Current Yield Bond
1975	16.07%	15.91%[b]	18.03%	19.93%	23.94%[a]
1976	18.30	16.56[b]	21.39	24.27	29.82[a]
1977	0.31[b]	4.20	4.50	5.54	5.58[a]
1978	1.95	1.71	1.38	1.13[b]	2.21[a]
1979	4.39	1.40	−0.69[b]	0.11	5.57[a]
1980	5.72[a]	1.83	0.79	0.75[b]	4.68
1981	6.35[a]	4.59	4.31[b]	4.65	6.15
1982	23.59[b]	32.39	33.67[a]	33.28	29.40
1983	5.85[b]	7.97	9.08	10.06	16.77[a]
1984	12.43	12.77	13.70[a]	12.78	7.12[b]
Ratio Best/Worst	2/3	0/2	2/2	0/2	6/1

[a] Best compared to the other four strategies in a specific year.
[b] Worst compared to the other four strategies in a specific year.
Source: Lipper-Fixed Income Fund Performance Analysis, Lipper Analytical Services, Inc. December 31, 1984.

bond holdings of over $1 billion in 1984, with Metropolitan Life and Prudential holding $31.3 billion and $23.6 billion, respectively. Here again, higher returns help to boost profitability and protect against unforeseen contingencies, and pressure is being put on a number of insurance companies to participate in the high yield market as a substitute for reduced activity in private placements.

The investors listed earlier are not the only participants on the buy side. Other buyers include money managers, individuals, commercial banks, investment managers, corporations, and investment banks themselves. As the risks and returns become more quantifiable, the number and scope of investing participants will probably decrease.

DEFAULT EXPERIENCE ON HIGH YIELD DEBT. High yield bond investors in the past have experienced healthy return premiums over investment grade securities, but they have also experienced substantial defaults. This section summarizes an earlier study by the authors, "The Default Rate Experience on High Yield Corporate Debt," Morgan Stanley & Co. Incorporated, March 1985, and the *Financial Analysts Journal,* July–August 1985. Without a reliable measure of past losses from defaults, investors cannot intelligently estimate the net returns over time on high yield bonds.

Default rates can be measured using several different base levels or denominators (i.e., total public debt, total straight debt, low-rated debt, etc.). The default rates discussed here were derived by dividing the par value of defaulting debt by the total low-rated, straight debt outstanding. We found that the default rate on high yield bonds from 1974 to 1984 averaged 1.60% (or 160 basis points annually). Exhibit 17 illustrates the annual default rates from 1970–1984. The default rate was 1.52% if Johns Manville's debt, the only issues rated investment grade just prior to default, is excluded. Year-to-year variations in this rate were substantial. This default level is significantly higher than rates generated using total straight debt outstanding as the base, that is, .08 of 1% for the same period. We feel the higher rate is much more relevant to investors with portfolios in the high yield area because virtually all defaults occur in the low-rated segment of the corporate debt market. The default rate in 1985 was 1.679% (see "The Anatomy of the High Yield Debt Market, 1985 Update").

The actual losses from default, however, are somewhat lower than these rates would imply. Defaulted bonds, far from becoming valueless, traded, on

EXHIBIT 17 HISTORICAL DEFAULT RATES—LOW-RATED,[a] STRAIGHT DEBT ONLY ($MM)

Year	Par Value Outstanding with Utilities[b]	Par Value Defaulted	Default Rate	Par Value Public Outstanding Less Utilities[b]	Default Rate
1985	$59,078	$992.10	**1.679%**[e]	45,356	2.187%
1984	41,700	344.16	**0.825**	32,120	1.071
1983	28,233	301.08	**1.066**	22,167	1.358
1982	18,536	752.34	**4.059**[c]	16,111	4.670
1981	17,362	27.00	**0.155**	15,010	.180
1980	15,126	244.11	**1.482**	12,807	1.750
1979	10,675	20.00	**0.187**	10,031	.199
1978	9,401	118.90	**1.265**	8,995	1.322
1977	8,479	380.57	**4.488**	7,548	5.042
1976	8,015	29.51	**0.368**	7,024	.420
1975	7,720	204.10	**2.644**	6,971	2,928
1974	11,101[d]	122.82	**1.106**	7,445	1.650
1973	8,082	49.07	**0.607**	7,195	.682
1972	7,106	193.25	**2.719**	6,245	3.094
1971	6,643	82.00	**1.234**	5,935	1.382
1970	6,996	796.71	**11.338**	6,448	12.356
Average default rate—1970 to 1984:			2.240%		2.430%
Average default rate—1974 to 1984:			**1.604%**[c]		**1.773%**
Average default rate—1978 to 1984:			1.291%		1.791%
Average default rate—1978 to 1985[e]			1.199%		1.415%

[a] Issues rated below Baa3 by Moody's or BBB–by Standard & Poor's. Includes nonrated debt of issuers with the equivalently rated issues and exchange debt in 1985.
[b] Source: *Standard & Poor*'s *Bond Guide* and *Moody*'s *Bond Record,* July issues of each year.
[c] Excluding Johns Manville, the default rate for 1982 was 3.115% and it was 1.518% for the 1974–1984 period.
[d] Includes almost $2.7 billion of Consolidated Edison Co. debt.
[e] The default rate also includes those issues whose bond rating fell to D ($564.5 billion in 1985) due to a missed interest payment but did not legally default and go bankrupt. In 1985 there were 11 companies that missed the interest payment but did not default due to a restructuring. The 1985 default rate without these issues was 0.688%.

average, at 41% of par shortly after default. After accounting for the bonds' retained value and the loss of interest, the average reduction in returns to the investor would have been approximately 100 basis points annually, assuming purchase at par. As noted earlier, the (1978–1983) net returns on high yield debt have been very impressive.

We also looked at industry segments that may be especially prone to default. Railroads and real estate investment trusts were particularly vulnerable in the past, but are unlikely to represent a large portion of future defaults. Retailer, electronic/computer, airline, and oil and gas defaults have become more common in recent years.

CREDIT QUALITY OF HIGH YIELD DEBT

MEASURING A FIRM'S OPERATING AND FINANCIAL RISK. In our prior discussion on the anatomy of the high yield market, we documented the impressive increase in the number and size of new issues from 1978–1984. A lurking question related to this increase concerns the credit quality of these new issues and the impact that increased competition among underwriters has had on the profile of new, high yield issuers. This section examines the overall trends of issuer credit quality in the market and looks at **credit techniques** to be used to identify and avoid credit deterioration. Although the most "sensational" questions revolve around leveraged buyouts, hostile takeovers, and defensive strategies used by firms issuing debt securities, our study does not address these new phenomena directly.

Traditional **financial statement analysis** is basically a univariate approach whereby individual measures of firm performance, primarily ratios, are compared with other firms in the same sector or perhaps within a specific bond rating and also examined over time to assess trends in such performance categories as liquidity, profitability, cash flow, leverage and solvency, and asset turnover. Although a pervasive tool among credit practitioners, **traditional ratio analysis** suffers from potential problems in ambiguity, subjectivity, and misleading numbers. Essentially, there is no "bottom line" as to firm performance and risk attributes. Hence, the final determination is a subjective product of the individual observing the ratios. Because our goal is to assess the credit quality of hundreds of firms in the high yield market and to compare aggregate measures with investment grade securities over time, we need an objective approach which is capable of summarizing a number of disparate operating and financial characteristics into a single, unambiguous measure. We have chosen **Zeta**™ credit evaluation scores, to assess credit quality in our high yield firm universe. Zeta was developed by Altman, Haldeman, and Narayanan (*Journal of Banking and Finance,* June 1977) to identify the bankruptcy risk of industrial corporations. Building upon earlier bankruptcy classification works, Zeta combines traditional financial measures with a multivariate technique known as discriminant analysis so as to lead to an overall **"credit-score"** for each of the firms being examined. This model is of the form:

$$\text{Zeta} = a_0 + a_1X_1 + a_2X_2 + a_3X_3 \ldots a_nX_n$$

where Zeta = Overall credit score
$X_1 - X_n$ = Explanatory variables (ratios and market measures)
$a_1 - a_n$ = Weightings or coefficients

The explanatory variables include measures of a firm's profitability, stability of earnings, debt service capability, cumulative profitability, liquidity, capitalization, and size. The lower the firm's Zeta score,the more "in-distress" the model reports for the firm. Negative Zetas do not indicate default or bankruptcy with certainty but the lower the score, the greater the similarity between that particular firm and those that have gone bankrupt in the past. The average Zeta score for past bankrupts was about −4.0 in the original sample and −5.0 for those filing subsequent to the model's construction.

CREDIT QUALITY OF INDIVIDUAL ISSUERS. We have investigated the **credit quality** and risk identification questions from several dimensions. The primary assessment tool used is the Zeta credit risk model. We also examined the trends of numerous traditional ratio measures of performance but found it difficult to summarize credit quality from a large number of sometimes disparate results. Hence, the unambiguous, composite statistic of Zeta was utilized to assess:

- The trend in Zeta of new issuer, high yield straight debt securities over time and relative to the absolute levels and trends of existing bonds in the different bond rating categories.
- The default predictive qualities of Zeta with particular emphasis on the securities in the Morgan Stanley database.

NEW ISSUER CREDIT QUALITY. Through 1984, new issue, high yield securities appear to have experienced an upward (better quality) trend over the last half-dozen years (with the exception of 1983). Exhibit 18 lists the median and average Zeta scores of new issuer firms. In 1978, the central tendency of new issuer scores was roughly equivalent to or slightly above the average S&P single-B rated debt. Note that the high yield new issuer's score increased from a −1.05 median in 1978 to −0.65 in 1980. But we observed that the trend was also favorable for all single-B rated debt in that 3-year period. Indeed, the median or average high yield new issuer score was just about the same (−0.65) as all S&P single-B rated debt (−0.52) in 1980.

The divergence between the trend in new issuer, high yield debt and the entire debt market started to take place in 1981 and continued to 1984. Exhibits 19 and 20 clearly illustrate these differences. The Zeta trend in **new issuer** debt

EXHIBIT 18 HIGH YIELD NEW ISSUER ZETA SCORES 1978–1984 (STRAIGHT DEBT ONLY)[a]

Year	Number of New Issues	Number of Companies With Zeta Scores	Median Zeta	Average Zeta
1978	52	27	−1.05	−0.96
1979	45	33	−0.84	−0.54
1980	43	24	−0.65	−0.40
1981	32	15	−0.03	−0.52
1982	48	20	0.30	0.29
1983	86	46	−0.15	−0.30
1984	124	53	0.35	0.31
1985	188	46	−0.24	−0.86

[a] Does not include convertible or exchange offers.

rated BB/B continued to improve in the 1981–1984 period (except 1983), especially the median score, whereas the overall BB/B market deteriorated in the face of the recession. This deterioration has continued in the most recent expansionary years. No doubt, a number of deteriorating higher grade securities, the so-called "**fallen angels**," helped to contribute to this decline. The trend in investment grade debt rated BBB and A was only slightly negative over this most recent period and was essentially unchanged from 1978–1984. In 1985, however, the trend in new issue Zeta scores deteriorated again probably due to an increasing number of small issuers.

EXHIBIT 19 ZETA SCORES: NEW VERSUS EXISTING ISSUERS RATED BB/B BY S&P

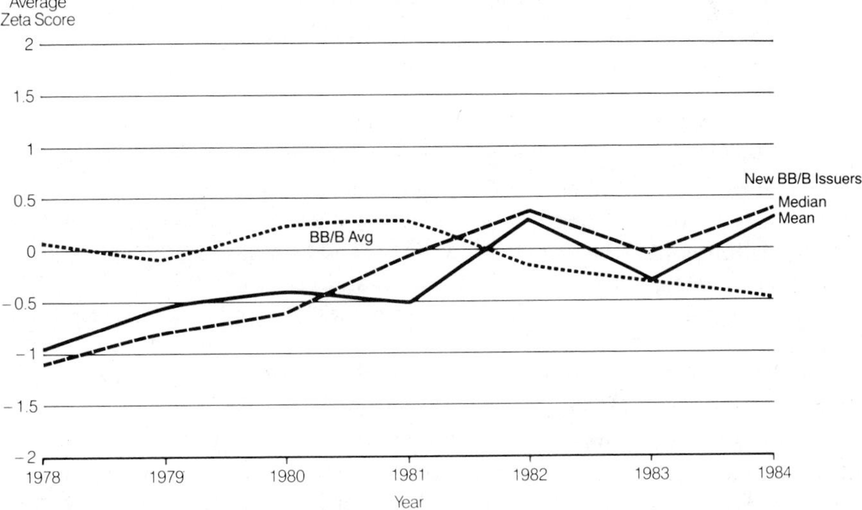

Source: Zeta Services, Inc., Hoboken, NJ.

EXHIBIT 20 ZETA SCORES: NEW VERSUS EXISTING ISSUERS BY S&P RATING

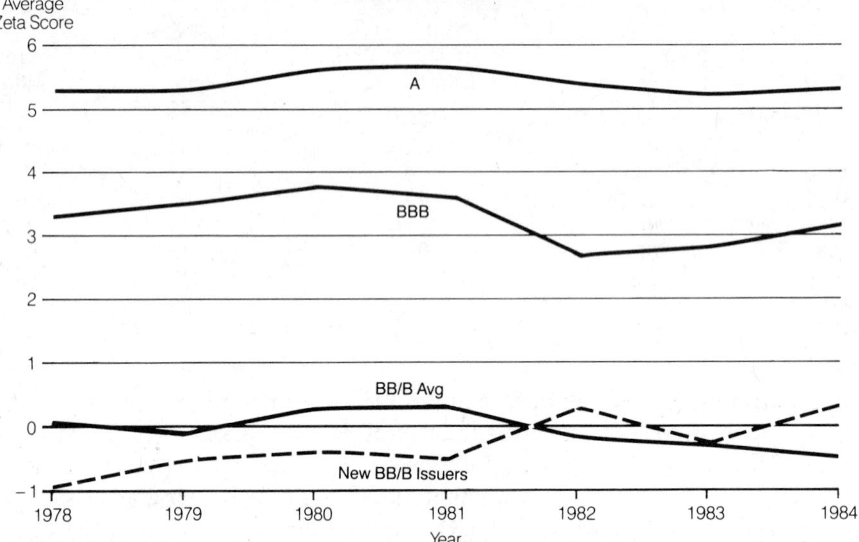

Source: Zeta Services, Inc., Hoboken, NJ.

Although the overall credit profile of new issuer, high yield debt is still in the risky zone, around a Zeta of zero, we have observed an overall improvement in this group both in absolute and relative terms. This does not mean that the credit analyst or risk arbitrageur can relax, because the distribution of scores is wide with several new issues fairly deep in the negative Zeta zone (7 of 46 (15%) had Zetas −3.0 or below in 1983 and 7 of 53 (13%) in 1984). Still, if one had to assess the average quality of the new issue, high yield marketplace, the conclusion would be a slight improvement over the 1978–1984 period.

DEFAULT RISK ASSESSMENT. Zeta scores correctly identified **Chapter X and XI** (now **Chapter 11) bankruptcies** 95% of the time based on data from one statement prior, over the postmodel development period 1977–1982. The accuracy rate is probably lower if we include the most recent data, because firms like Johns Manville, Revere Copper & Brass, and Storage Technology were not identified correctly. A more relevant examination for this study is to assess the ability of Zeta to "red-flag" defaulting companies with publicly traded, straight debt securities.

The Morgan Stanley high yield data base contained 20 issuer defaults involving 30 different straight debt issues. These firms are listed in Exhibit 21 with their Zeta scores one and two statements prior to default. The results indicate that all but two of the defaults could have been avoided with a strategy of not including (or selling) a firm's debt when its Zeta score was below zero. The number drops to just one firm (Storage Technology) using a strategy of

EXHIBIT 21 HIGH YIELD DEFAULTS AND PRIOR ZETA SCORES (DATA BASE FIRMS ONLY)[a]

Company	Default Date	Zeta One Statement Prior to Default	Zeta Two Statements Prior to Default
AM International	4/82	−4.60	−0.18
Altec Corp.	9/83	−9.28	−7.88
Amarex Corp.	12/82	−1.61	−1.25
Anglo Company	11/83	−0.15	1.20
Braniff (4 Issues)	5/82	−5.37	−3.40
Charter Co. (2 Issues)	4/84	0.77	1.40
Emons Industries	4/84	−4.30	−4.99
Food Fair (2 Issues)	10/78	−0.61	−0.68
Gamble Skogmo	4/82	−3.20	−1.58
Grolier (2 Issues)	7/77	−8.95	−1.73
Hardwicke Corp.	7/83	−10.10	−4.61
Lionel Corp.	2/82	−1.61	−1.91
MGF Oil	5/83	−4.19	−2.42
Mego Int'l	3/82	−7.46	−0.36
Morton Shoes	1/82	−5.05	−2.72
Storage Technology	11/84	1.63	3.13
Telcom Corp.	12/82	−4.72	−2.75
Texas Int'l Air	9/83	−4.11	−4.26
United M&M	7/77	−0.38	0.24
Wickes Co. (5 Issues)	4/82	−3.85	−1.17
Average Zeta Score		−3.85	−1.79

[a]Morgan Stanley database.

holding only issues with Zeta scores greater than 1.0. And, if an investment grade triple-B equivalent Zeta score (approximately 2.5) is adhered to, every default would have been avoided. There were just four firms with positive Zetas two financial statements prior, and just three with Zeta scores above 1.0. In 1985, Zeta identified every default prior to the default date.

In summary, a fundamental credit approach like **Zeta** can probably eliminate most of the **default risk** in a dynamic, actively managed portfolio. It can certainly be argued that other credit evaluation tools can also successfully reduce default risk. The earlier the credit system detects impending defaults, the smaller the realized credit deterioration and principal loss will be for the portfolio. The average price deterioration on defaulting issues, from one year prior to default, was about 26%, based on a study of 70 defaulting issues.

THE TYPICAL NEW ISSUER IN 1983 AND 1984

AGE, SIZE, AND RATING. In 1984, the "typical" new, straight debt issuer in the high yield market was a 26-year-old firm with $735 million in assets earning

EXHIBIT 22 PROFILE OF NEW ISSUES HIGH YIELD STRAIGHT DEBT MARKET (1983 AND 1984)

ISSUE CHARACTERISTICS

	Average				Median				Standard Deviation			
	1978	1979	1983	1984	1978	1979	1983	1984	1978	1979	1983	1984
Size of issue ($ Millions)	28.7	29.0	86.2	120.6	25.0	20.0	60.0	77.5	19.6	21.3	123.7	150.6
Coupon rate (%)	—	12.3	12.0	13.3	—	12.3	11.8	14.5	1.0	1.1	1.8	3.9
Yield to maturity (%)	—	12.6	14.0	15.2	—	12.6	13.8	15.4	1.1	1.2	1.3	1.4
S&P rating	B/B+	B/B+	B/B+	B/B+	B	B	B	B	—	—	—	—
Number of issues	52	41	86	124								

FIRM CHARACTERISTICS

	Average				Median				Standard Deviation			
	1978	1979	1983	1984	1978	1979	1983	1984	1978	1979	1983	1984
Age of firm (Years)	22.8	26.0	28.2	31.1	18.0	20.0	20.1	26.0	14.7	19.6	22.4	23.1
Asset size ($ Million)	176	285	1,074	1,588	107	127	322	735	187	487	1,776	2,435
Return on assets (%)	—	—	1.5	1.9	—	—	2.7	2.7	—	—	7.8	8.2
Zeta score (Issues)	−0.89	−0.76	−0.16	0.74	−1.15	−0.84	−0.30	0.78	1.7	1.3	3.4	3.3
			(52)	(65)								
Zeta score (Firms)	−0.96	−0.54	−0.30	0.31	−1.05	−0.84	−0.03	0.35	1.5	1.2	3.0	3.1
	(28)	(31)	(46)	(53)								
Number of firms	50	40	68	99								

2.7% after taxes on those assets. The new issue was for $77 million, yielding 15.4% and paying a 14.5% coupon; the issue received a single-B rating from *Standard & Poor's.* The firm's credit rating was relatively good compared with other single-B rated issues with a median Zeta score of 0.35 versus −2.06 for single-B's.

In 1983 our "typical" issuer was a 20-year-old firm with $322 million in assets and the same 2.7% return on assets. The new issue was $60 million in size, yielding 14%, with a coupon of 12% and received a single-B rating from *Standard & Poor's.* The median Zeta credit rating was lower at −0.03 but still above the average single-B rated company.

These are the results of an in-depth profile analysis of new issues in 1984 and 1985. The generalized profile is based on median issue and issuer characteristics summarized in Exhibit 22. These data are based on 124 new issues (99 issuers) in 1984 compared with 86 issues and 68 firms in 1983. We also report the mean results for the aforementioned categories and note a fairly large standard deviation for most of them. Hence, it will be instructive to observe frequency distributions of the variables in Exhibits 23–25. From the frequency distributions, one can note the following:

- In 1984, 26% of the firms were relatively young (less than 15 years in business). A rather large proportion, over 50%, however, were seasoned firms, in business over 25 years. This compares with 43% for 1978–1979 new issuers. This might be the result of more aggressive underwriting efforts and buyouts, as well as the robustness of the market. Surprisingly, the median age of new issuers in 1983–1984 is only slightly above the 1978–1979 median (23 versus 19).

EXHIBIT 23 HIGH YIELD, STRAIGHT DEBT, NEW ISSUERS AGE OF FIRM DISTRIBUTION (1983 AND 1984 ISSUERS)

Age of Issuer (Years)	Number of Firms		Percent of Firms	
	1983	1984	1983	1984
0–4	8	11	10.4%	10.2%
5–14	23	17	29.9	15.7
15–24	15	24	19.4	22.2
25–34	5	21	6.5	19.4
35–44	4	5	5.2	4.6
45–54	5	4	6.5	3.7
55–64	11	14	14.3	13.0
65–74	5	8	6.5	7.4
>75	1[a]	4	1.3	3.7
Total	77[a]	108[a]	100.0%	100.0%
Average	28	31	—	—
Median	20	26	—	—

[a] Includes exchange debt issuers.

EXHIBIT 24 HIGH YIELD NEW ISSUE SIZE DISTRIBUTION (1983 AND 1984 ISSUERS)

Size of Issue ($ Million)	Number of Issues 1983	Number of Issues 1984	Percent of Total Issues 1983	Percent of Total Issues 1984
$ 0–20	7	6	8.1%	4.8%
21–40	25	27	29.1	21.8
41–60	12	18	13.9	14.5
61–80	15	13	17.4	10.6
81–100	10	19	11.6	15.3
101–150	10	15	11.6	12.1
151–200	1	14	1.2	11.3
201–300	4	3	4.7	2.4
301–500	1	5	1.2	4.0
501–1000		3	0.0	2.4
>1001	1	1	1.2	0.8
	86	124	100.0%	100.0%
Average size	86.2	120.6	—	—
Median size	60.0	77.5	—	—

EXHIBIT 25 HIGH YIELD, STRAIGHT DEBT, NEW ISSUER SIZE OF FIRM (TOTAL ASSETS) DISTRIBUTION (1983 AND 1984 ISSUERS)

Size of Firm's Assets ($ Million)	Number of Firms 1983	Number of Firms 1984	Percent of Firms 1983	Percent of Firms 1984
$ 0–100	14	12	20.3%	14.6%
101–200	14	12	20.3	14.6
201–300	7	10	10.2	12.2
301–400	7	9	10.2	11.0
401–500	4	3	5.8	3.7
501–600	2	0	2.9	0.0
601–700	0	2	0.0	2.4
701–800	2	2	2.9	2.4
801–900	2	2	2.9	2.4
901–1000	2	1	2.9	1.2
1001–2000	5	12	7.2	14.6
2001–3000	6	6	8.7	7.3
3001–4000	0	1	0.0	1.2
4001–5000	1	4	1.4	4.9
5001–10000	3	5	4.3	6.2
>10001	0	1	0.0	1.2
	69	82	100.0%	100.0%
Average size	1,075	1,588	—	—
Median size	322	735	—	—

Firm size was impressive with over 26% of the firms having assets over $1 billion compared with 21% in 1983. Median total assets of new issuers in 1983–1984 ($322 and $735 million) is, as expected, considerably higher than the earlier 1978–1979 medians ($107 and $127 million). No longer is the new issue market the primary province of the small, unseasoned company.

CONCLUSION

This section has concentrated on presenting a generalized description of the high yield debt market. We have specifically not included analysis of individual firms and have laid the foundations, we hope, for a more in-depth analysis of specific investments and portfolio strategies by investment professionals. Those and other aspects of the high yield debt market can be found in Altman and Nammacher, *Investing in Junk Bonds: Inside the High Yield Bond Market,* Wiley, 1986.

REFERENCES AND BIBLIOGRAPHY

Altman, E.I., *Corporate Financial Distress,* New York: Wiley, 1983.

Altman, E.I., Haldeman, R., and Narayanan, P., "Zeta™ Analysis, A New Model to Identify Bankruptcy Risk of Corporations," *Journal of Banking & Finance* (June 1977).

Altman, E.I., and Nammacher, S.A., The Default Rate Experience On High Yield Debt, Morgan Stanley & Co., Incorporated, March 1985 and *Financial Analysts Journal* (July–August 1985).

———, "The Anatomy of the High Yield Debt Market," Morgan Stanley & Co., Incorporated (September 1985) and "Update 1985" (June 1986).

———, *Investing in Junk Bonds: Inside the High Yield Debt Market,* New York: Wiley, 1986.

Atkinson, T.R., "Trends in Corporate Bond Quality," *National Bureau of Economic Research,* 1967.

Blume, M.E., and Keim, D.B., "Risk and Return Characteristics of Lower-Grade Bonds," Working Paper, *Rodney White Center for Financial Research,* Philadelphia, PA: The Wharton School, 1984.

Bookstaber, R., and Jacob, D., "The Composite Hedge: Controlling the Credit Risk of High Yield Bonds," Morgan Stanley & Co., Incorporated (March 1985), and forthcoming *Financial Analysts Journal.*

———, "Risk Management for High Yield Bond Portfolios," forthcoming, Morgan Stanley.

Bookstaber, R., and Clark, R., "Problems in Evaluating the Performance of Portfolios with Options," *Financial Analysts Journal* (January–February 1985).

Drexel, Burnham Lambert, *High Yield Newsletter,* Los Angeles, CA, Bimonthly.

———, *The Case For High Yield Bonds,* Los Angeles, CA, 1985, 1986.

Fitzpatrick, J.D., and Severiens, J.T., "Hickman Revisited: The Case for Junk Bonds," *The Journal of Portfolio Management,* Vol. 4, No. 4 (Summer 1978).

Hickman, W.B., *Corporate Bond Quality And Investor Experience,* Princeton University Press and the National Bureau of Economic Research, 1958.

Hill, J.H., and Post, L.A., "The 1977–78 Lower-Rated Debt Market: Selectivity, High Yields, Opportunity," *Smith Barney Harris Upham & Co.* (December 1978).

Macauley, F., "Some Theoretical Problems Suggested by the Movements of Interest Rates, Bond Yields and Stock Prices in the U.S. Since 1856," NBER, 1938.

Soldofsky, R., "Risk and Return for Long Term Securities: 1971–1982," *The Journal of Portfolio Management* (Fall 1984).

Standard & Poor's, "Corporate Debt Default Risk," *Credit Comment* (February 20, 1984).

Standard & Poor's Credit Week, "Corporate Debt Default Risks," February 20, 1984.

ADDITIONAL PROFESSIONAL INVESTMENT ARTICLES

Bianco, Anthony, "The Growing Respectability of the Junk Heap," *BusinessWeek,* April 22, 1985.

Bleakley, Fred R., "Junk Bond Market Growing," *New York Times,* June 28, 1984.

———, "The Power and the Perils of Junk Bonds," *New York Times,* April 14, 1985.

Curran, John J., "Fewer Jitters about Junk Bonds," *Fortune,* April 29, 1985.

"Junk Debunked," *Grant's Interest Rate Observer,* September 24, 1985.

Horowitz, Janice, "Junk Picking," *Personal Investor,* July 1985.

Joseph, Frederick H., "High-Yield Bonds Aren't Junk," *Wall Street Journal,* May 31, 1985.

McGough, Robert, "Research for Field," *Forbes,* September 16, 1985.

Metz, Robert, "Junk Bonds High on Defaults," *Daily News,* March 8, 1985.

Quinn, Jane Bryant, "Are High Yielding Junk Bonds Worth the Risks of Default?" *Newsweek,* June 18, 1985.

———, "Scouting the Junk Shop," *Newsweek,* July 22, 1985.

Rohatyn, Felix G., "Junk Bonds and Other Securities Swill," *Wall Street Journal,* April 18, 1985.

Sivey, Michael, "Separating Junk from Toxic Waste," *Money,* June 1985.

Sloan, Allan, and Rudnitsky, Howard, "Taking In Each Other's Laundry," *Forbes,* November 19, 1984.

Solomon, Mark B., and Airozo, David J., "Transportation Research Forum Looking Beyond Deregulation," *Traffic World,* November 5, 1984.

Wheeler, George, "Junk Bonds: Ammo for Raiders," *Newsday,* April 21, 1985.

Yacik, George, "Roses in the Junkyard," *Credit Markets,* April 8, 1985.

7

OPTIONS MARKETS AND INSTRUMENTS

CONTENTS

7

OPTIONS MARKETS AND INSTRUMENTS

Gary L. Gastineau
Katherine M. Finn

INVESTMENT CHARACTERISTICS OF BASIC OPTION CONTRACTS

DEFINITIONS. Before we examine the investment characteristics of puts and calls, it will be helpful to define a few terms:

Option. A negotiable contract in which the writer, for a certain sum of money called the option premium, gives the buyer the right to demand, within a specified time, the purchase or sale by the writer of a specified number of shares of stock at a fixed price called the striking price. Unless otherwise stated, options are written for units of 100 shares. They are ordinarily issued for periods of less than 1 year.

Call Option. An option to buy stock from the writer.

Put Option. An option to sell stock to the writer.

Combination Option. An option consisting of at least one put and one call. The individual option contracts that make up the combination are originally sold as a unit, but they may be exercised or resold separately.

Straddle. A combination option consisting of one put and one call with a common striking price and a common expiration date.

Striking Price or Exercise Price. The price at which an option is exercisable, that is, the price per share that the buyer of a call option must pay the writer for the stock or the price that the writer must pay the holder of a put option.

Option Premium. The price of an option contract. In this section the convention of stating the option premium in terms of dollars per share under option is adopted. If the total premium for a 100-share option is $1,000, the option premium is given as $10.

Expiration Date. The date after which an option is void.

Option Buyer. The individual or institutional investor who buys options.

Option Writer. The individual or institutional investor who sells or writes options.

Spread. (1) For listed options: the purchase of one option and the sale of another option on the same stock; the investor setting up the spread hopes to profit from a change in the difference between the prices of the two options. (2) In the conventional option market: a straddle in which the put side and the call side are written at different striking prices; typically, the put striking price is below, and the call striking price is above, the market price of the stock at the time the spread is established. In the listed option market this position is usually called a **spraddle.** (3) The put and call dealer's margin between the option premium paid by the buyer and the premium paid to the writer is also called a **spread.**

RISK MODIFICATION. No matter how intricate an option investment strategy the investor may adopt, **the principal result of any option purchase or sale is to modify the risk characteristics of an investor's position.** This feature of options can have an important impact on portfolio structure and on the investor's overall risk exposure.

Stock options provide the investor with a unique way to modify exposure to market risk. In particular, listed options traded on securities exchanges around the world are extremely versatile instruments for the modification of risk. This statement appears to be at odds with the popular view of call options as speculative tools that permit the small investor to obtain superior leverage on a small amount of capital. Options can fulfill much more important functions in an investment portfolio than this popular view suggests. Options can be of substantial aid to investors, large or small, who wish to modify the exposure of their portfolios to market fluctuations and improve their risk-adjusted return on investment.

RISK-REWARD CHARACTERISTICS OF PUT AND CALL CONTRACTS. Exhibit 1 illustrates the basic investment characteristics of a call option from the respective viewpoints of the buyer and the writer. As most investors who have any familiarity with options are aware, an option buyer can never lose more than the premium paid for the option contract. On the other hand, if the price of the stock rises substantially over the life of the call option, the buyer's potential reward is theoretically unlimited. This position is illustrated by the line that begins in the lower left-hand corner of Exhibit 1.

The uncovered or "naked" call writer's position is, in many respects, the exact opposite of the call buyer's position. As the line that begins in the upper left-hand corner of Exhibit 1 illustrates, the call writer keeps the entire premium unless the stock price rises above the exercise price at the time the option expires or is exercised. In return for the option premium received, the writer of the call agrees to sell the stock at the striking price, no matter how high the stock may go. If the writer does not own the shares covered by the option, the writer's position deteriorates by $1 per share for every point by which the price of the stock exceeds the exercise price.

The essence of the uncovered call writer's position is that he or she can earn no more than the amount of the option premium and can lose a large amount if the price of the underlying stock runs up. In contrast to the call buyer who is fixing the risk at the amount of the premium and accepting the possibility of a

EXHIBIT 1 PROFIT AND LOSS POSITIONS OF THE BUYER AND WRITER OF A CALL

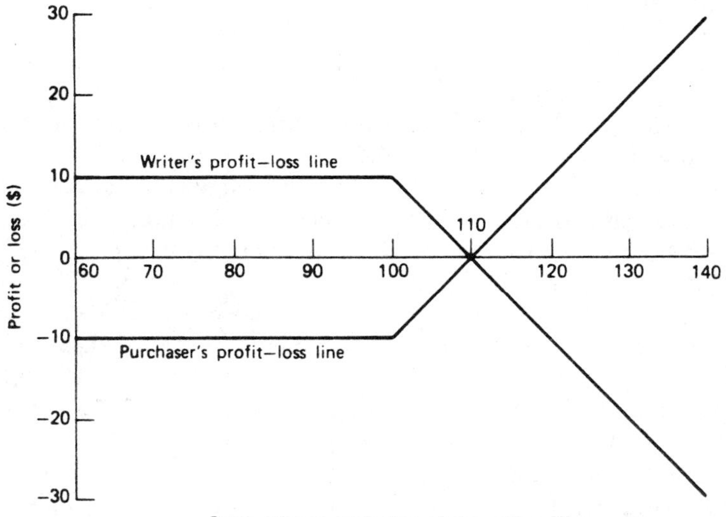

EXHIBIT 2 PROFIT AND LOSS POSITIONS OF THE BUYER AND WRITER OF A PUT

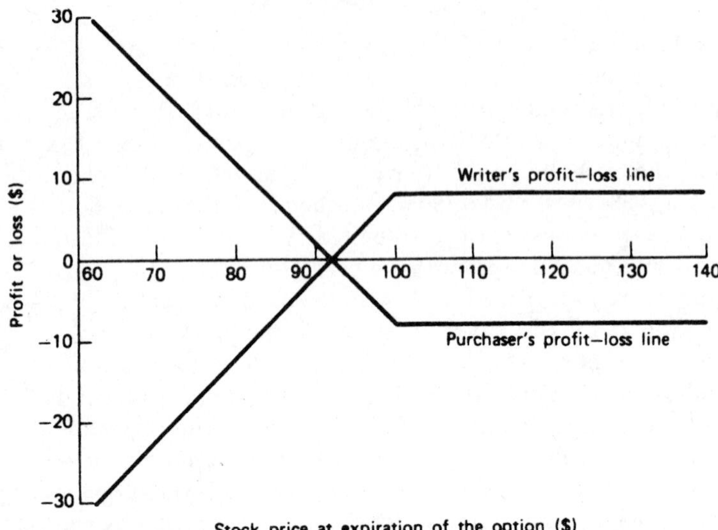

widely varying reward, the uncovered writer is fixing the reward at the amount of the premium and accepting a highly variable risk. Exhibit 2 illustrates the profit and loss positions of the buyer and writer of an uncovered put. In return for a fixed premium, the buyer of a put obtains the right to receive a reward that increases as the price of the underlying stock declines. As in the case of the call, both the buyer and the writer of a put option fix one side of the risk-reward equation and permit the other side to vary.

The offsetting risk-reward features of the buying and writing positions are clarified by Exhibits 1 and 2. Any profit to the option buyer is exactly offset by a loss to the writer, and vice versa. Neglecting transaction costs, **the net effect of an option transaction is simply a reallocation of risk and reward between buyer and writer.**

It is no accident that the word **"premium"** is used in both the insurance business and the option business. Option contracts, like insurance policies, are used to protect the investor, whether writer or buyer, from unacceptable risk. In Exhibits 1 and 2, the option buyer appears to be in a position analogous to that of the owner of an insurance policy. The option writer is like the insurance underwriter who accepts risk in return for premium income. When options are incorporated in an overall portfolio plan, however, the risks and rewards are changed remarkably. For example, the call writer who has a position in the underlying stock will actually be **reducing** the overall volatility or market risk of his portfolio by writing the option because the premium he receives protects his assets in the event of a price decline, while his writer's obligation limits his gain on the up side. Although options do not increase or decrease the total level of risk in the financial system, **both parties to a particular option transaction can reduce their portfolio risk simultaneously through a combination of stock, option, and short-term debt positions.**

SIGNIFICANCE OF EXCHANGE-LISTED OPTIONS

Although options in one form or another have been around since the days of ancient Greece (some would argue since the days of the Old Testament), both modern theory and the widespread use of option contacts awaited development of the **listed option,** initiated by the **Chicago Board Options Exchange (CBOE)** in 1973.

IMPORTANT CHANGES INITIATED BY CBOE. Before 1973 the market in options on securities was one of the less significant segments of the securities business. In that year the Chicago Board Options Exchange, a division of the Chicago Board of Trade, introduced standardized listed option contracts. Neither the stock market nor the option market will ever be the same. Innovations introduced by the CBOE have been adopted by virtually every other securities options market in the world.

Standardization of Terms. The importance of standardized option terms in the development of a secondary market in option contracts cannot be overemphasized. Standardization facilitates secondary trading because the number of distinct contracts a buyer or seller must evaluate is reduced. In contrast to the conventional option market, where it is possible to buy or write an option with practically any striking price or expiration date, the terms of contracts available on the exchanges are more limited. The striking price of a listed option always ends in $5, $2.50, or $0 unless a stock dividend or other capital change occurs after trading in the option begins. If General Motors is selling at $61 a share at the time options for a new expiration month are being listed for trading, the new GM option will have a striking price of $60 per share. If the stock price closes above $62.50, the exchange will add $65 contracts for each expiration date beyond 60 days. Barring stock dividends, splits, or other capital changes, it will be impossible to buy or write a GM option on the exchange with a striking price between $60 and $65 per share.

In addition to standardization of striking prices, the exchanges have standardized expiration dates. The expiration date is the Saturday after the third Friday in the month. Options trade on three cycles throughout the year: January, April, July, and October; February, May, August, and November; March, June, September, and December.

Fungibility. Fungibility, or interchangeability, is a second important characteristic of listed options necessary for the development of an active secondary market. Fungibility means substitutability or equivalence. Each listed option with a common expiration date and striking price is interchangeable with any similiar listed option.

Either party to a listed option can usually, without undue sacrifice, close out a position that no longer meets his needs. The buyer and writer in a listed option transaction have no direct connection. Each has a contract only with the **Options Clearing Corp.,** which is the issuer of listed options. The option buyer relies on the Clearing Corporation to make good on the contract. The writer's obligation is an obligation to the Clearing Corporation, not to the buyer his broker happens to meet on the exchange floor. Either the option buyer or the writer can close out his position by simply reversing the initial transaction. For a more complete explanation of the relationship between the Clearing Corporation and the other parties to an option contract, the reader should examine the relevant sections of the **Options Clearing Corp. Prospectus.**

Lower Transaction Costs. A third important characteristic of listed options is their relatively low transaction cost. The total transaction cost of any listed option trade is substantially lower than the transaction cost of a similar conventional option trade. Lower transaction costs have an important effect on trading volume and market liquidity. As the spread between the premium paid by the buyer and the premium received by the writer grows smaller, the number of transactions will tend to grow larger. If the option premium paid by the buyer is $500 and the amount received by the writer, net of transaction costs, is only $400, a writer who was willing to accept a net premium of $425 and a buyer who was willing to pay a premium of $475 would be excluded from the market. On the other hand, if the spread were narrower, both the buyer and the writer could be accommodated and the total volume of option transactions would increase. Relatively low transaction costs have been an important factor in the high trading volume of listed options.

Organized Secondary Market. In contrast to the conventional options market, where both buyer and writer are literally locked into a transaction until the expiration date unless they can reach agreement for an earlier liquidation of their positions, depth of the market in listed options often exceeds the depth and liquidity of the market in the underlying stock.

Because both writer and buyer can close out positions relatively quickly, trading and investment strategies that require the use of options for only a short period of time are feasible. Strategies that depend on an investor's ability to buy or sell additional options as time passes are facilitated by a secondary market.

Published Transaction Prices. The prices at which listed option transactions actually take place are published daily. Published prices and known commission rates assure both buyer and writer of a fair market. In spite of the apparent absence of any widespread abuse of the relative obscurity of conventional option dealer spreads, the mere fact that daily trading summaries are published in the newspapers removes some of the mystery and, quite frankly, some of the suspicion from the option market.

Certificateless Clearing. In some respects, one of the most important innovations pioneered by the CBOE is the introduction of certificateless clearing. Except in unusual cases when an option trader insists on evidence of the transaction in addition to a brokerage firm confirmation slip, the Options Clearing Corp. does not issue an actual option contract or certificate. This feature of listed option trading reduces the amount of paperwork and eliminates the physical movement of securities, in this case option contracts, between brokerage firms. The Options Clearing Corp. has sharply reduced the time required to clear a transaction and, as the brokerage community gains additional experience with certificateless trading, the cost of clearing a transaction should decline. The CBOE was a pilot project not only for organized trading of option contracts but also for the introduction of certificateless trading to the securities markets. On the basis of results to date, both features of the pilot project can be called unqualified successes.

COMPARISON OF CONVENTIONAL AND LISTED OPTIONS AND MARKETS. Exhibit 3 compares conventional and listed options and markets.

COMPARISON OF TRANSACTION COSTS. Probably the single most significant contribution of **listed option trading** to the expansion of the option market is that it sharply reduces the cost of a transaction. Both the writer and the buyer of a call can fare better on an exchange than with a conventional call. If commission and other transaction costs are too large, they act as a deterrent

EXHIBIT 3 COMPARISON OF CONVENTIONAL AND LISTED OPTIONS AND MARKETS

	Conventional	Listed
Type of options traded	Calls, puts, combination options	Calls, puts, combination orders permitted
Striking price	Any price buyer and writer negotiate	Standardized price ending in \$5, \$2.50, or \$0
Expiration date	Any date buyer and writer negotiate	Saturday after the third Friday in the designated expiration month
Expiration time	3:15 P.M. eastern time	5 P.M. eastern time
Last date and time option can be sold	Same as expiration date and time	3 P.M. central time 4 P.M. eastern time on the business day immediately prior to the expiration date
Adjustment for cash dividend	Striking price reduced on ex-dividend date	No change in striking price
Adjustment for stock dividends, stock splits, and reverse splits	Both striking price and number of shares covered by options are adjusted to reflect the capital change	

EXHIBIT 3 (*CONTINUED*)

	Conventional	Listed
Adjustment for rights or warrants issued to common shareholders	Striking price reduced by the value of the rights or warrants	
Limitation on purchase or sale of options on one stock	None, but limits have been proposed	3000, 5000 or 8000 contracts on the same side of the market (e.g., long calls **and** short puts); limit applies to all expiration dates
Unit of trading	One contract is an option on 100 shares of the underlying stock before any adjustments	
Method of option price determination	Buyer and writer negotiate through put and call broker	Central auction market
Secondary market	Limited; special options advertised in newspaper	Very active secondary market
Buyer's recourse to obtain performance on option contract	Primary responsibility for performance belongs to the endorsing broker who may be any member of the NYSE	The Options Clearing Corp. is the primary obligor guaranteeing the writer's performance
Evidence of ownership	Bearer certificate	Broker's confirmation slip
Method of closing out transaction when stock sells above striking price	Option may be exercised by buyer or sold to put and call broker who exercises the option and sells the stock	Exercise is rare; contract is usually closed out in a closing purchase-sale transaction
Transaction costs	High	Moderate
Commission structure	Basic charge is negotiated by put and call broker as a spread between premium paid by buyer and premium paid to writer	Negotiated commission rates since May 1, 1975
Stocks on which options are available	Almost any stock	Over 400 selected stocks in the United States and a growing list of stocks elsewhere in the world
Pricing information	Brokers publish indicated premiums to buyers or writers	Actual transaction prices published daily
Procedure for exercise	Buyer exercises by notifying endorsing broker	Buyer's broker notifies the Options Clearing Corp. which selects writers essentially at random
Extensions	Available if writer agrees	Not available
Tax treatment	Identical	
Margin Requirement		
Call buyer	100% of the option premium	
Covered writer	No margin required beyond that needed to carry stock position	
Uncovered writer	Minimum requirement is related to price of stock with adjustment for amount of premium received and amount by which option is in or out of the money. Margin requirements should be checked in detail with each brokerage firm.	

to trading. Commissions on the exchange are low enough to permit the buyer to consider purchasing options for a relatively small expected move in the stock. The writer has reasonable assurance that the commission cost to close out the transaction will not consume most of the premium. The lower transaction cost leads to more active trading and, consequently, to more liquid markets. The example chosen for Exhibit 4 illustrates a typical difference between transaction costs for a listed option and those for a conventional option. The actual difference in a particular case always depends on what happens to the price of the stock and what the parties do to close out their respective sides of the contract.

Nonetheless, examination of Exhibit 4 reveals that the costs of the conventional option transaction are, in this case, more than 2.5 times as high as for the comparable listed option transaction. In fact, commissions and other charges paid by the two parties to the conventional option trade are equal to about two-thirds of the total option premium paid by the buyer. If one assumed that the transaction involved **one** call rather than 10, the costs would consume an amount nearly equal to the entire premium. With transaction costs of this magnitude, neither buyer nor writer can realistically expect superior performance unless premiums are grossly out of line with any measure of fair value.

ROLE OF OPTIONS IN INTELLIGENT PORTFOLIO MANAGEMENT

BACKGROUND. One reason options are avoided by many investors is that the successful use of options requires more attention and analysis than most people devote to their portfolios. Much of the aura of complexity that surrounds options is due to a tendency to view them as unique or unusual investments. It is far more useful to relate the **risk-reward characteristics** of **options** to those of stocks and bonds than to emphasize the differences between options and other investment vehicles. The idea that "highly leveraged" options fit into the same risk-reward hierarchy as corporate bonds or common stocks can be difficult for many investors, including some experienced option traders, to accept at first. Nonetheless, most investors find options easier to understand when they examine them in terms of their impact on total portfolio risk.

This subsection demonstrates that the intelligent use of options requires evaluation of option contracts combined with measurement and control of portfolio risk. This discussion is directed at the investor who attempts to analyze investment positions in terms of **risk** and **reward.** Such an investor is sensitive to the tradeoff between opportunities to obtain high rates of return and the increased risk of loss which usually comes with such opportunities. Those who view investments in this framework can improve their decision-making process, and perhaps their results, by understanding the **risk-reward characteristics** of stock **options.**

EXHIBIT 4 COMPARISON OF TRANSACTION COSTS: CONVENTIONAL VERSUS LISTED OPTION MARKETS[a]

Assumptions

Buyer buys 10 calls at $500 each with a $50 striking price. Stock rises to $60 where buyer sells or exercises calls, receiving $1,000 per contract before costs. Writer initially buys 500 shares of stock or enough to cover one-half of his obligation. All figures are expressed on a per contract basis with commissions calculated on the assumption that the transaction consists of 10 contracts.

	Conventional	Listed
Buyer's Position		
Premium paid by buyer	$ 500.00	$ 500.00
Commission to buyer's broker	12.50	12.70
Cost to buyer to establish position	$ 512.50	$ 512.70
Gross proceeds from selling call		
($60–$50) × 100 shares	$1,000.00	$1,000.00
Listed option commission		(17.20)
Round-trip stock commission on sale of options	(107.06)	
Transfer taxes	(5.00)	
Subtract: Cost to establish position	(512.50)	(512.70)
Net profit to buyer	$ 375.44	$ 470.10
Writer's Position		
Premium paid by buyer	$ 500.00	$ 500.00
Option commission paid by writer to his broker	(12.50)	(12.50)
Put and call broker's spread (est.)	(75.00)	
Net premium to writer	412.50	$ 487.30
Cost of repurchasing call from buyer	$1,000.00	$1,000.00
Add: Listed option commission		17.20
Purchase commissions initial stock position	30.13	30.13
Sale commission initial stock position		33.58
Purchase commission additional stock called	33.58	
Sale commission on stock called	50.83	
Transfer taxes	5.00	2.50
Subtract: Net premium received	(412.50)	(487.30)
Profit on stock owned	(500.00)	(500.00)
Net loss to writer	$ 207.04	$ 96.11
Net profit to buyer	$ 375.44	$ 470.10
Subtract: Net loss to writer	(207.04)	$ (96.11)
Net profit to investors	$ 168.40	$ 373.99
Total transaction costs	$ 331.60	$ 126.01
Less:	(126.01)	
Difference in transaction costs: Conventional vs. listed calls	$ 205.59	per contract

[a]Note the following: (1) If the writer had written conventional straddles instead of two calls against each round lot owned, he would have fared better but the **total** transaction cost would have been even higher. (2) If the stock declines, total transaction costs may drop slightly faster for the conventional option but they are always substantially higher than listed option costs. (3) Transfer taxes are based on New York residence. (4) Commissions are calculated on the basis of an initial position of 10 calls and a stock position of 500 shares bought by the writer. Stock and option commission rates are those in effect prior to May 1, 1975, on the NYSE and CBOE, respectively. These commission charges are then stated on a per call basis. The total charges are 10 times the figures listed.

RISK-REWARD CHARACTERISTICS OF OPTIONS To illustrate the risk-reward characteristics of options, let us analyze the covered writing of a call option. In Exhibit 5 the ownership of shares of common stock is designated by the solid (*A-A′*). The ownership of common stock, combined with the sale of a call option on that underlying stock, is designated by the broken line (*B-B′*). The vertical axis represents the profit or loss from each of these positions at a particular stock price on the day the option expires. The horizontal axis represents the price of the stock on that day. In this example the stock is purchased at $95 per share. The shareholder who does not sell the call option participates point for point in every increase or decrease in the price of the stock. His profit is theoretically unlimited on the upside, and his loss is limited only by a stock price of zero on the downside.

The alternative strategy of **covered call writing,** illustrated by the broken line, is based on the sale of a call option against the stock position. The hypothetical call option used in Exhibit 5 has a $100 striking price and a life of about 6 months from the time it is sold. The writer obtains a $10 per share premium. Any loss on the long stock position will be reduced by the $10 per share obtained from the option.

The covered call writer's position does have some disadvantages. If the price of the stock rises above $110 per share (the striking price plus the call premium), the investor would have been better off not selling the call. In return for

EXHIBIT 5 COMPARISON OF PROFIT AND LOSS: LONG STOCK POSITION VERSUS COVERED WRITER POSITION

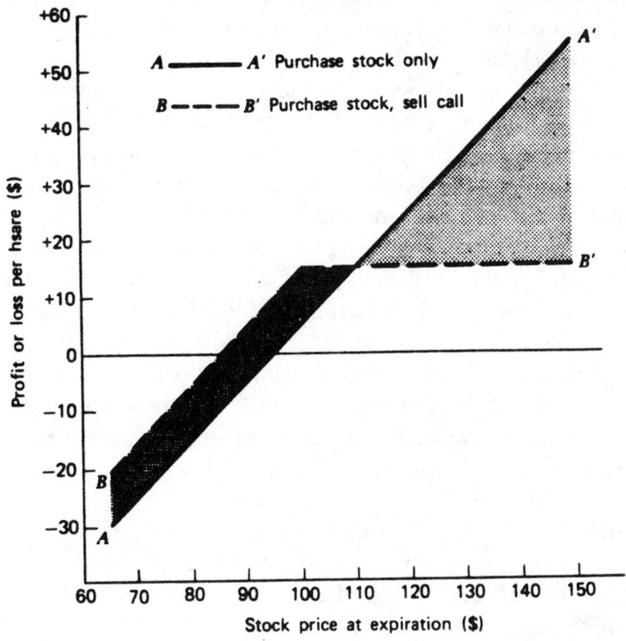

a degree of downside protection, he has given up the opportunity to participate in any rise in the price of the underlying stock above $110 per share.

The downside protection provided by the option premium received is designated by the cross-hatched trapezoidal area to the left of the intersection of the two profit-loss lines in Exhibit 5. The upside opportunity given up by the covered call writer is represented by the shaded triangular area to the right of the intersection of the two lines.

COVERED CALL WRITING. Exhibit 5 highlights several features of covered call writing. Note that the seller of the covered call option **reduces the variability of his return on investment.** If the stock rises sharply, the return on the stock position will be reduced by the amount of any loss on repurchase of the option. If the stock is called away at a price of $100 per share when the market price at the time of exercise is much higher, the investor may experience a sizable opportunity loss. If the stock declines, the loss will be reduced by the amount of the premium collected. Regardless of the direction in which the stock price moves or how far it moves, **covered call option writing reduces the variability of the return from a portfolio of equity securities.** The importance of this point is hard to overemphasize.

If the value of the premium received is too small relative to the value of the opportunity for appreciation given up, the covered writer will obtain a substandard return on investment over a period of time. When the value of the premium received equals the value of the opportunity forgone, after adjustment for risk, the option is said to be **fairly priced.** When the value of the protection is inadequate, the option is **underpriced.** When the premium is more than adequate to compensate for the capital appreciation opportunity given up, the option is **overpriced.**

To appreciate the importance of the size of the **option premiums** in determining investment results, compare Exhibits 5 and 6. In Exhibit 6 the option premium received by the covered call writer is only $1, not the $10 assumed in Exhibit 5. With this very low premium for a 6-month option, the cross-hatched area representing the downside protection afforded by the premium is much smaller, and the shaded area depicting the downside protection afforded by the premium is much smaller, and the shaded area depicting the upside opportunity loss is considerably larger. A change in the size of the option premium affects the size of **both** areas, with obvious implications for investment results. Exhibit 6 provides an excellent demonstration that covered call writing is not a simple technique that almost magically adds to the income of a portfolio. Actually, as we will see momentarily, **covered call writing is more likely to reduce portfolio returns than it is to increase them.**

RISK-RETURN TRADEOFF. Perhaps the significance of overpriced and underpriced options and their effect on investment results can be brought into perspective best by an examination of Exhibit 7, which represents the expected risk-return tradeoff characteristics of a variety of investment opportunities. The

EXHIBIT 6 COMPARISON OF PROFIT AND LOSS: LONG STOCK POSITION VERSUS COVERED WRITER POSITION WITH LOW OPTION PREMIUM

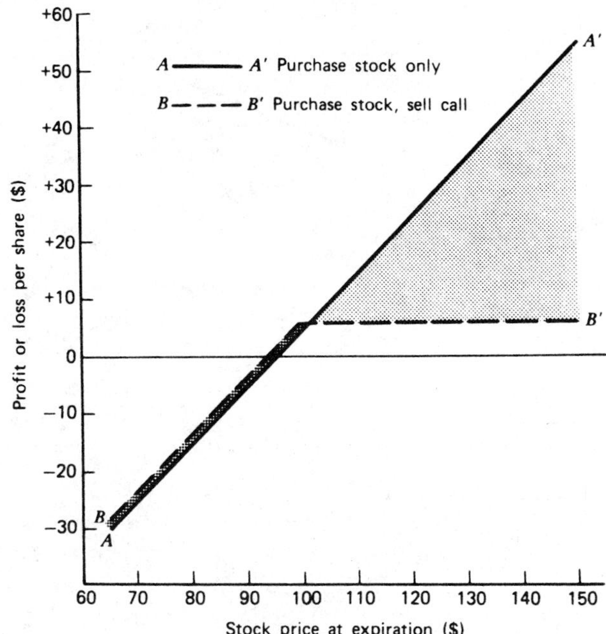

vertical axis (Y) measures the investor's expected annual return on investment for different investment opportunities. The horizontal axis (X) measures the degree of risk associated with a particular investment. Risk is expressed as the **standard deviation** (or variability) of the rate of return.

Treasury bills show essentially no variability of return relative to the yield anticipated at the time the bills are purchased. Though the interest rate structure as a whole can move up or down, the Treasury bill rate is fixed for the life of each bill at the level the investor accepts when he buys the bill. If an investor wishes to increase his expected return, he can purchase long-term **corporate bonds.** Because of changes in the market value of bonds due to interest rate fluctuations and the risk of default by some borrowers, the return from an investment in bonds for a particular time period may be greater or less than the risk-free rate of return on Treasury bills. Most investors will not be willing to hold long-term bonds unless they have the **expectation** of a higher rate of return than they would be able to obtain from Treasury bills. The same argument holds for any other investment. Investors who buy **common stocks** generally require a higher expected total rate of return than they would be willing to accept from long-term bonds or Treasury bills. To compensate for the risk to principal and the consequent variability in the return on investment, investors in **venture capital** projects require an even higher expected rate of return.

EXHIBIT 7 THE RISK-RETURN TRADEOFF

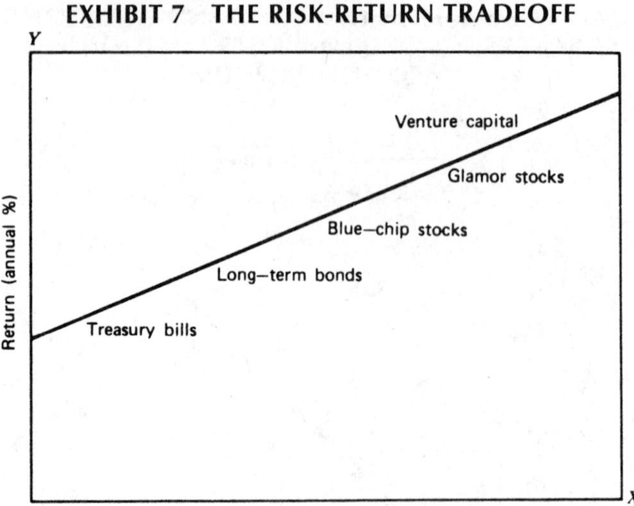

COVERED CALLS AND MODERN PORTFOLIO THEORY. Like any other investment vehicle, options fit into this risk-reward structure. As we saw in Exhibit 5, selling a call option against a stock position reduces the variability of the rate of return on investment. Thus selling a call will have the effect of reducing portfolio risk levels. If the call option an investor sells is neither overpriced nor underpriced, sale of the option will also have the effect of **reducing the expected return on investment** because the overall risk of the portfolio will be reduced. By definition, **sale of a fairly priced option will simply move the risk-return position of a portfolio downward and to the left along the risk-return tradeoff line** of Exhibit 7. On the other hand, purchase of an option will increase the variability of the expected return from a portfolio. An investor who buys a fairly priced call option demonstrates willingness to accept greater variability of return in exchange for the expectation of a higher average rate of return.

The prospective option investor should keep in mind that selling call options will tend to move the expected risk-reward position of a portfolio down and to the left along the risk-reward tradeoff line of Exhibit 7, whereas the purchase of call options will tend to move the expected return up and to the right. Theoretically, it is possible to reduce the risk level of a portfolio of glamour stocks to the risk level of a portfolio of Treasury bills through the sale of an appropriate number of call options. In practice, commissions and other trading costs make it difficult to maintain such a low risk level with options. Within reasonable limits, however, it is possible to use options to adjust the risk posture of a portfolio rather closely to an individual's risk preferences.

IMPROVING RISK-ADJUSTED RETURNS. The opportunities for risk modification that options provide are extremely important, but they are not the principal reason for using options. It is possible, if option premiums are too high or too low relative to their fair value, to structure a portfolio that provides a **higher expected return per unit of risk** than any portfolio of conventional securities lying along the risk-return tradeoff line. If a call option is **overpriced** and an investor sells that option, the risk-reward structure of the portfolio will move not only to the left along the risk-return line but also **above** the line. If the investor starts with Treasury bills or other short-term debt instruments and **buys underpriced** call options with a portion of his assets, it is possible to achieve an expected rate of return **above** the line while obtaining a degree of risk equivalent to the risk associated with owning a portfolio of long-term bonds or common stocks.

In contrast to the seller of overpriced call options, the investor selling underpriced calls will be reducing his return **more than proportionately to the reduction in risk.** This investor would generally be better off reducing the risk exposure of a portfolio by selling a portion of the stock and investing the proceeds in bonds or some other lower risk investment rather than accepting inadequate option premiums. The risk-return position of a portfolio will fall below the risk-reward tradeoff line in Exhibit 7, if underpriced options are sold against stock positions or if overpriced options are bought.

Selling a call option in a diversified equity portfolio will **always** reduce risk, as measured by the variability of the expected total return on the portfolio. Selling the option will **not** always (or even usually) enhance the overall rate of return. **By consistently selling overpriced options and/or buying underpriced options as part of a program of risk management, an investor can break away from the risk-reward tradeoff line.** Few serious investors will use options for any reason other than to enhance the rate of return per unit of risk.

VARIATIONS IN OPTION PREMIUM LEVELS. Exhibit 8 shows a monthly **index of listed option premium levels** since shortly after the beginning of listed option trading on the Chicago Board Options Exchange. The index roughly approximates the degree of price variation in a "typical" option contract with the striking price and market price equal. The index indicates that a typical premium was just under 1.0 on the index, or the approximate equivalent of $4 for a 6-month option on an "average" $40 stock at the end of April 1974. The index rose to about 1.75, or the rough equivalent of about a $7 premium for the same option in November 1974. In early 1978 the index was consistently below 0.70 or the equivalent of less than $3 for the "typical" 6-month option on a $40 stock.

The index is based on premium levels of options on 14 of the first stocks listed on the CBOE. The fluctuations in option premium levels for individual stocks or the fluctuations for the most overpriced or most underpriced options on a specific stock show even more dramatic changes. It is not at all unusual for premium levels on some stocks to vary by a factor of 2 or 3 over the course of a year. Given the magnitude of these premium fluctuations, opportunities for

EXHIBIT 8 AN INDEX OF LISTED OPTION LEVELS: BASE PERIOD STOCK PRICE VOLATILITY, OCTOBER 1973-JULY 1985 = 1.0

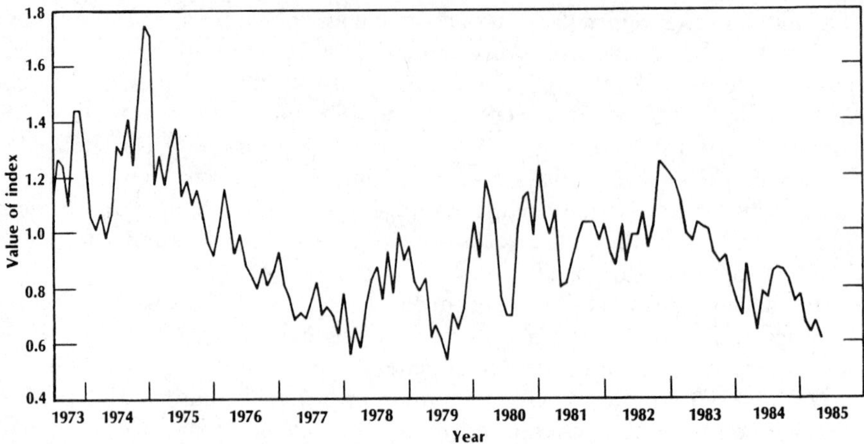

Source: Gastineau, *The Stock Options Manual,* 2d ed., McGraw-Hill, New York, 1979. Recent data courtesy of Kidder, Peabody, & Co., Inc.

portfolio risk adjustment and return enhancement through the purchase and sale of options are obviously extensive.

OPTION EVALUATION AND PORTFOLIO MANAGEMENT. Most individuals and portfolio managers who use options take one of two approaches to the use of options. Some investors focus strictly on the fundamental or technical outlook for the underlying common stock and, on the basis of their fundamental or technical analysis, construct either a bullish or a bearish investment position using options or stock and options. Investors accustomed to conventional analytical and portfolio management approaches frequently pay little heed to computerized evaluation of option contracts.

In marked contrast to those who focus strictly on their investment attitude toward the underlying common stock, there is a sizable group of investors who focus strictly on **computerized option evaluation.** This group believes that no analytic technique can forecast stock price direction but that an investor can consistently make money selling overpriced and buying underpriced options. Overpricing and underpricing will be consistently determined by complicated computer programs.

Who is correct? Both. And neither. I agree with the conventional investor who says it is ridiculous to sell an overpriced naked call option on IBM if there are sound reasons for believing that IBM's stock will rise in price over the life of the option. I also agree with the computer evaluation advocate who argues that one should not buy that option. Fortunately, the approaches are not as contradictory as they may seem.

A portfolio manager or an individual investor can integrate conventional stock selection techniques with computerized option evaluation. The resulting portfolio would be carefully designed to reflect a desired degree of risk exposure. Each position in the portfolio would reflect the best analysis of the outlook for the particular stock in question and would integrate that analysis with evaluation of the option contract. For example, a covered writing position in IBM would be appropriate if the option was overpriced and the investor felt the stock was going up. Because selling the option reduces the risk associated with a long position in IBM, the investor should **buy more IBM stock** as a covered writer than as an owner who was not using options.

Fundamental analysis should also have an impact on the computerized evaluation of the option contract. Nearly all the more sophisticated option evaluation models base their calculation of the fair **value of an option** on five factors:

1. Time remaining until expiration.
2. Money market interest rates.
3. The size and pattern of dividend payments on the underlying stock.
4. The relationship between the current stock price and the striking price of the option (sometimes divided to make six factors).
5. The expected volatility (range of price movement) of the underlying stock.

All these factors except future stock price volatility can be easily observed and appropriate values supplied to the computer. Most users of computerized option evaluation models derive a stock price volatility estimate from the past volatility pattern of the underlying stock. While historic stock price volatility data are important, intelligent portfolio managers and individual investors temper their use of historic data with judgments based on fundamental analysis of the stock.

No option strategy is inherently superior to any other. At times option premiums on particular stocks are so high that it makes no sense to purchase these options. At other times premiums are so low that it is impossible to justify a covered writing position on any rational basis. If an investor is flexible in his choice of option strategies, there will almost always be attractive investment opportunities based on the use of options.

ANALYSIS OF RISK. While evaluation of the expected profit from buying or selling a particular option can be complex, analysis of the risk impact of an option position on a portfolio is straightforward. To appraise the risk position quantitatively, the investor must translate each option into a risk-equivalent position in the underlying stock. If the option contract used in the example in Exhibit 5 moves up or down in price by one-half point for each one-point change in the price of the underlying stock, that option contract is the risk equivalent of 50 shares of the stock. The dollar gain or loss from a long or short position in that option will be approximately one-half the gain or loss from movement in a corresponding long or short position in a round lot of the underlying stock. If an investor wants to establish a position that is the risk equivalent of owning 100 shares of this stock, he can do so in any one of three ways:

1. Buy 100 shares of stock.
2. Buy 2 options (50 shares equivalent × 2 contracts = 100 shares).
3. Buy 200 shares of stock and sell 2 options [200 shares − (50 shares equivalent × 2 contracts) = 100 shares].

The fraction of a point by which an option price is expected to change when the underlying stock price changes by a full point is called the **neutral hedge ratio.** The concept of the neutral hedge ratio and the notion of options as stock equivalents are basic to the informed use of options.

Any option or option and stock position, no matter how complicated, can be readily translated into the risk equivalent of a specific number of shares or a dollar investment in the underlying stock. If this analysis is undertaken for the entire portfolio, it is a surprisingly simple matter to convert all positions into stock equivalents. Once this has been done, the portfolio can be analyzed using the techniques of conventional portfolio management to appraise diversification and market risk exposure. Obviously, the fraction of a point that an option price will change for each one-point move in the stock will vary as the option nears expiration and as the relationship between the option striking price and the stock price changes. Consequently, the investor must analyze the risk structure of a portfolio frequently to be certain that the risk exposure to a particular underlying stock has not changed beyond acceptable limits. In turbulent markets the risk exposure to a particular stock may change significantly in a short period of time. The alert and flexible investor can usually maintain adequate diversification and appropriate overall market risk exposure, even when the market is unsettled.

INVESTMENT SIGNIFICANCE OF LISTED PUT OPTIONS

BACKGROUND. Most of the previous examples have been based on **call option strategies.** This focus on calls reflects the interest of most option users and the fact that an option to buy seems to be easier to comprehend than an option to sell. While many investors will never use puts, an investor will never fully understand calls without some knowledge of the relationship between calls and puts.

BASIC RISK-REWARD CHARACTERISTICS OF PUT CONTRACTS. Examining a possible transaction with the aid of a pair of diagrams should help clarify the risk-reward features of the put contract. Someone who **buys** an option to **sell** (a put) will not exercise that option unless the actual market price falls below the striking price. Consequently, the buyer of a put who holds the option until the expiration date will lose the entire premium paid for the put option unless the stock falls below the striking price. As the stock drops further below the striking price, the put buyer will begin to recover the premium paid and eventually earn a profit. The **writer** of a put will not be required to buy stock unless the market price of the stock falls below the striking price. The writer retains the entire premium if the stock price remains above the striking price.

Exhibit 9 shows the risk-reward positions for investors on both sides of a put contract with a $40 striking price and a $4 option premium. In Exhibit 9*a* the put buyer's profit-loss position is shown as of the date of exercise or expiration. The buyer loses the entire $4 premium if the stock price stays above $40 per share because the right to sell at $40 is worthless if a higher price is available on the stock exchange. The put buyer begins to recover premium as the stock drops below $40 and fully recovers the premium at the break-even price of $36 per share.

If the put buyer can buy stock on the market at $36 and deliver it to the writer of the put contract at a price of $40, the difference of $4 exactly equals the put premium before commissions. Below $36, the put buyer profits point for point as the stock continues to decline because the stock can be purchased at the lower price and sold to the writer of the put at $40. The put buyer's profit per share is equal to the $40 striking price less the sum of the $4 premium and the price at which the stock is ultimately purchased.

Exhibit 9*b*, the put writer's profit-loss line, contrasts with Exhibit 9*a*. The put writer's profit is the put buyer's loss, and vice versa. If the stock sells above $40, the put writer keeps the entire premium. As the stock drops, the put writer will still be required to buy stock at $40. The put writer's loss per share, like the put buyer's profit, is equal to the $40 striking price less the sum of the $4 premium and the price at which the stock can be sold after the put is exercised.

Comparison of Exhibits 5 and 9*b* reveals in both cases the same general shape that characterizes the covered call option writer's profit-loss position. The covered call writer, like the put writer, has a fixed profit if the stock is

EXHIBIT 9 COMPARISON OF PROFIT AND LOSS: BUYER OF PUT (*a*) VERSUS WRITER OF PUT (*b*)

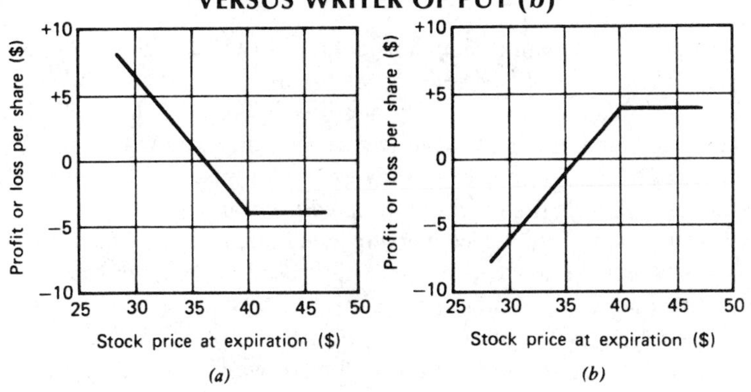

above the striking price on the date the option expires. The covered call writer also has a measure of downside protection, represented by the option premium. The profit-loss diagrams for the put writer and the covered call writer look the same because, **in most important respects, they are the same.**

CONVERSION: KEY TO ANALYZING PUTS. A thorough understanding of puts requires an understanding of the **conversion** process. Through conversion, calls can be transformed into puts, and puts transformed into calls. Most of the confusion surrounding puts will be eliminated if the investor keeps in mind that the sale of a put option, margined by a Treasury bill or similar short-term debt instrument, should be the approximate risk-reward equivalent of a covered call writing position using the corresponding listed call option (i.e., the call with the same striking price and expiration date as the put).

The **conversion formula** expressed in terms of the present value of a put is:

$$P_p = P_c - P_s + D + \frac{S}{1 + nr}$$

where P_p = price of put
P_c = price of a corresponding call with identical striking price and expiration date
S = striking price of options
P_s = price of underlying stock
n = life of options expressed as fraction of a year
r = interest rate on Treasury bills or high-grade commercial paper
D = present value of all dividents expected to be paid before expiration of options

For some investors the appropriate rate r may be the interest rate a broker charges on debit balances. Learned papers can be written (and undoubtedly will be) on the selection of an appropriate interest rate. Note that the **present value** of the anticipated dividends will be slightly less than the actual dividend payment.

Apart from tax and commission considerations (which will occasionally lead to material differences) and neglecting for the moment the possibility of early exercise of the put, the investor who deposits interest-earning collateral and sells a put at conversion parity with the corresponding call will have an identical profit-loss position to that of the investor who buys 100 shares of the underlying stock and sells the corresponding call option.

This formula is called the **conversion equation** because some investment firms, popularly known as **"converters,"** have used it to convert puts into calls and calls into puts when writers prefer to sell one type of option and buyers want the other type. With listed puts trading on all option stocks, the equation is used primarily to determine the most efficient way to take a position.

Because the risk characteristics of the covered call writer's position are nearly identical to those of the put writer's position, an investor's return may be improved by taking one of these positions in preference to the other and earning a small arbitrage profit if the prices of the two options differ from the appropriate relationship. **Arbitrage** opportunities based on conversion relationships between puts and calls may be consistently available to certain investors, but understanding these possible arbitrage opportunities will be easier if the reader is able to calculate **stock risk equivalents** for simple stock and option positions.

CONVERSION AND CALCULATION OF RISK EQUIVALENTS. Earlier I introduced the idea that it is possible to translate any listed call option position into a risk equivalent position in the underlying stock by calculating the fraction of a point by which the price of the option will change if a one-point move occurs in the underlying stock (the **neutral hedge ratio**). Specifically, if the price of an option changes by one-half point when the price of the underlying stock changes by a full point, then that option, over a reasonable period of time and a range of stock prices, will behave in essentially the same manner as 50 shares of the underlying stock. If a call changes in price by one-quarter point for each one-point move in the stock, the option will behave like 25 shares of stock.

The same concept holds for translating put options into stock equivalents. Because the put writer's position is the risk equivalent of covered call writing, the number of equivalent shares represented by a put is equal to 100 minus the number of equivalent shares represented by the corresponding call. If a call behaves like the equivalent of 25 shares of the stock, by moving one-quarter point for each one-point move in the stock, then a position in the analogous put contract will be the equivalent of 75 shares (100 shares minus 25 shares). The buyer of the put is "buying" the risk equivalent of a 75-share short position in the stock because, through the conversion mechanism, buying a put is the risk equivalent of buying the analogous call (plus 25 shares) and selling the underlying stock short (minus 100 shares).

Complex option positions are usually less attractive than relatively simple ones because transaction costs rise as the complexity of the position increases. The **risk-reward characteristics** of complex positions can also be difficult to evaluate. An investor may find that a position he meant to be bearish was, in fact, bullish. A position that is bullish at current stock prices may become bearish if the stock advances sharply. The best way to keep track of a complex position is to translate each component into its common stock equivalent and total these equivalents to get the stock equivalent risk exposure of the entire position.

Exhibit 10 shows the **risk equivalents** of a number of simple and complex stock and option positions. The security or combination described in the left-hand column is usually the most common way to establish a position. The other securities or combinations in the same row are risk equivalents of the

EXHIBIT 10 RISK COMPARABILITY OF INVESTMENT POSITIONS[a]

1. Buy 100 shares	Buy a call Sell a put	
2. Buy a call	Buy 100 shares Buy a put	
3. Buy 200 shares Sell two calls	Sell two puts	Buy 100 shares Sell a put Sell a call
4. Sell a call	Sell 100 shares short* Sell a put	
5. Buy a put	Sell 100 shares short* Buy a call	
6. Sell a put Sell a call	Buy 100 shares Sell two calls	Sell 100 shares short* Sell two puts
7. Buy a put Sell a call	Sell 100 shares short*	
8. Buy a put Buy a call	Sell 100 shares short* Buy two calls	

[a]The security or combination in the left-hand column is usually the most common of several possible ways of establishing an investment position. If all puts and calls are assumed to have the same striking price and expiration date, the positions in each row have equivalent risk characteristics. Positions marked with an asterisk involve a short sale of the underlying common stock and are unattractive for most investors.

left-hand column. Unusual combinations may be the most efficient way to establish a position if they can provide the expectation of an arbitrage-type profit. The opportunity for arbitrage will arise if the market mechanism does not force put and call prices into conversion parity adjusted for the possibility of early exercise of the put.

EARLY EXERCISE OF PUTS. Sellers of calls are familiar, sometimes distressingly so, with the phenomenon of early exercise. Though other factors occasionally lead to early exercise of calls, the most common cause is the call buyer's desire to obtain a dividend paid on the underlying stock. Consequently, early exercise is most common when the call is in the money and there is a relatively short time period between an ex-dividend date and expiration of the option.

Sellers of puts must be prepared for early exercise under a different set of circumstances. Specifically, the seller of a put that is in the money (i.e., the stock is selling significantly **below** the striking price) will frequently experience early exercise **after** the stock goes ex-dividend if the option has a relatively short remaining life. Whereas sellers of calls find early exercise a problem when the dividend is sizable and the call is in the money. sellers of puts will find early exercise a problem when future dividends will be small or nonexistent and the put is in the money. Early exercise of in-the-money puts will be a particular problem in less volatile stocks. A moment's reflection will suggest that early exercise of puts may become quite common in bear markets and during any period when interest rates are high.

The reasons behind the early exercise of a put are related to the economics of short selling. The total investment return to the holder of **any** security consists of the algebraic sum of any periodic dividend or interest payment and any capital gain or loss. Frequently, there will be no divided due on the underlying stock during the remaining life of a put. Consequently, the holder of a deep-in-the-money put will not benefit from a stock price reduction on an ex-dividend date. The holder of this put will be carrying the equivalent of a short position in the stock. Only if the put is bought **below** intrinsic value will the buyer of the put get credit for the proceeds of the implicit short sale. On the other hand, if the put is selling below its intrinsic value, an **arbitrageur** can profit by exercising it and reinvesting the cash received in a security with a higher expected total return. A deep-in-the-money put is an unstable position.

Call writers have learned that the buyer of a call has absolute control over who will receive a particular dividend on the underlying stock. The call buyer may exercise this control to deprive a call writer of the dividend. The owner of a put exercises similar control over who will receive a dividend. Ordinarily, the holder of a put will choose to "receive" dividends or get "credit" for them in the form of a probable decline in the stock price on the ex-dividend date. If there will be no dividends during the remaining life of an in-the-money put option, it can sell at or slightly below intrinsic value. There will probably be a greater tendency to exercise in-the-money puts than in-the-money calls because, in effect, **the carrying cost of a long position can be eliminated by exercising the put.** The effect of early exercise on the value of a put can be significant. Because of the potential for early exercise, the value of a put will always be greater than the value given by the conversion equation.

TAX TREATMENT OF OPTION TRANSACTIONS

TAX TABLES. Exhibit 11 summarizes the tax treatment of a variety of option positions. Options and stock positions are considered separately and, where appropriate, as they relate to one another. These tables assume that the user of options is an individual or other entity that treats options as a capital asset. Broker dealers, certain corporations, and other entities are subject to special tax considerations not covered in these tables. The tables are based on what we believe are realistic assumptions about regulations that had not been issued by the Internal Revenue Service when this chapter went to press. Before relying on the tables, the reader should consult a professional tax adviser or, at least, an up-to-date tax booklet obtained from a broker doing an active option business.

EXHIBIT 11 TAX TREATMENT OF OPTION TRANSACTIONS

Type of Position	Closing Transaction	Holding Period of Option	Nature of Gain or Loss	Timing of Recognition of Gain or Loss	Effect on Common Stock Holding (if any)	Comments
Buy call (do not own related stock during life of call)	1. Sell call	Short term	Short-term gain or loss	Date of sale of option		
		Long term	Long-term gain or loss	Date of sale of option		
	2. Let call expire	Short term	Short-term loss	Date of expiration		
		Long term	Long-term loss	Date of expiration		
Buy put (do not own related stock during life of put)	1. Sell put	Short term	Short-term gain or loss	Date of sale of option		
		Long term	Long-term gain or loss	Date of sale of option		
	2. Let put expire	Short term	Short-term loss	Date of expiration		
		Long term	Long-term loss	Date of expiration		
Buy put Buy stock same day (Identity put as intended to be used with this stock position)	1. Sell put	Short term	Short-term gain or loss	Date of sale of option/(gain); stock (loss)	If stock is sold for a gain, holding period starts on day option is sold. If stock is sold at loss, holding period starts on day stock was purchased.	Commonly referred to as a married put. There is a chance the IRS may try to eliminate the married put by regulation.
		Long term	Long-term gain or loss	Date of sale of option/(gain); stock (loss)		

	2. Exercise put	Short term (stock)	Short-term loss	Date of exercise	Cost of put is added to basis of stock.	
		Long term (stock)	Long-term loss	Date of exercise		
	3. Let put expire	N/A	N/A	Date of sale of stock	Cost of put is added to basis of stock.	Holding period of stock starts on day stock and put are purchased. Note recognition of put loss is deferred until stock is sold.
Buy put Buy stock (not on same day)	1. Sell put	Short term	Short-term gain or loss (See Comments)	Date of sale of option/(gain); stock (loss)	Unless stock was already long term when put purchased, holding period of stock is eliminated for purposes of long-term gain by purchase of put. Any gain on stock is long term 6 months and 1 day after put is sold. Any loss on stock is long term 6 months and 1 day after stock was purchased.	Under the loss deferral rule, a long-term gain may not be realized on the sale of the put if the stock has previously been sold at a loss. Under straddle rule any loss on put cannot be realized until stock is sold.
		Long term	Long-term gain or loss (See Comments)	Date of sale of option/(gain); stock (loss)		

EXHIBIT 11 (*CONTINUED*)

Type of Position	Closing Transaction	Holding Period of Option	Nature of Gain or Loss	Timing of Recognition of Gain or Loss	Effect on Common Stock Holding (if any)	Comments
	2. Exercise put	Immaterial	Any gain on common stock is short term unless the stock was held for 6 months and 1 day before put was purchased. Any loss will be long term if the date of exercise is more than 6 months and 1 day after purchase of the stock	Date of exercise	Cost of put is deducted from the proceeds of sale of stock	
	3. Let put expire	Short term	Short-term loss	Date of expiration or date of sale of stock, whichever comes later	Unless stock was already long term when put purchased, holding period of stock for purposes of determining long-term gain begins on date of expiration of put. For purposes of determining loss, holding period begins on day stock was purchased.	
		Long term	Long-term loss			

Write or Sell Call (no stock position)	1. Call expires	Immaterial	Short-term gain	Date of expiration	N/A	Straddle rule loss deferral may apply to related option position.
	2. Call exercised	Immaterial	Call premium is subtracted from cost basis	Date of covering purchase of stock	N/A	
	3. Call repurchased	Immaterial	Short-term gain or loss	Date of repurchase		
Write call (Long stock qualified)	1. Call expires	Immaterial	Short-term gain	Date of expiration	No effect if shareholder is an individual	
	2. Call exercised	Immaterial	Call premium subtracted from cost basis of stock; character of gain or loss on stock determines nature of total gain	Date of exercise if stock delivered long Date of covering purchase if stock delivered short	No effect except on lot of stock delivered against exercise	Holding period of stock extends from purchase date to exercise date if stock long term or call not in-the-money when sold. Holding period stops if call in-the-money.
	3. Repurchase call (stock held for 6 months or less at time option sold)	Immaterial	Short-term capital gain or loss	Date of repurchase	If the option was in-the-money at the time call was written, holding period is suspended while call is outstanding.	

EXHIBIT 11 (*CONTINUED*)

Type of Position	Closing Transaction	Holding Period of Option	Nature of Gain or Loss	Timing of Recognition of Gain or Loss	Effect on Common Stock Holding (if any)	Comments
	4. Repurchase call (stock held for more than 6 months and 1 day at time option sold)	Immaterial	Short-term capital gain. If the option was in-the-money at the time written, long-term capital loss. Otherwise short-term capital loss.	Date of repurchase	If option closed at loss in 1 year, loss deferral rule applies if stock not held unoptioned for 30 days before sale at gain in next year	Note interest and carrying charges on position must be capitalized.
Write call (long stock not qualified)	1. Call expires	Immaterial	Short-term gain	Date of expiration	Any loss on stock deferred until option gain realized	Holding period of stock not relevant to tax treatment of option gain except for effect of loss deferral rule.
	2. Repurchase call					
	a. Stock not long term when call sold	Immaterial	Short-term gain or loss	Gain: date of repurchase	Straddle rule loss deferral	
				Loss: Later of date of repurchase or date of sale of stock held at gain when option sold		
	b. Stock long term when call sold	Immaterial	Short-term gain	Date of exercise	Straddle rule loss deferral	
			Short or long term loss	Date of exercise		

	3. Call exercised a. Stock not long term when call sold	Immaterial	Short-term gain or short or long-term loss	Gain: date of repurchase	Pertinent holding period is that of stock	Holding period for gain ends when call is sold.
				Loss: later of date of repurchase or date of sale of stock held at gain when option is sold		Holding period for loss extends to exercise date.
	b. Stock long term when call sold	Immaterial	Long-term gain or loss	Date of exercise	Pertinent holding period is that of stock	
Write put (no stock position)	1. Put expires	Immaterial	Short-term gain	Date of expiration	N/A	
	2. Put assigned	Immaterial	Proceeds from sale of put reduce basis of stock purchased	Date stock acquired through assignment is sold	Reduces basis	Holding period of stock starts on day put is exercised. Note that tax recognition is deferred until stock is sold.
	3. Put repurchased	Immaterial	Short-term gain or loss	Date of repurchase	N/A	
Multiple Option Positions a. On same side of market			Treat separately as if isolated positions	In general, losses are deferred until comparable amount of gain (if any) is realized on related transactions		The tax treatment of these positions has become highly unattractive for most taxpayers. See text.
b. Characterized by risk offset			Straddle rule loss deferral applies			

RECENT TAX CHANGES

HOLDING PERIOD. The holding period for purposes of achieving long-term gains was shortened from a year and a day to six months and a day until January 1, 1988. It is generally expected that the shorter holding period will be retained after that date.

60/40 SPLIT ON NONEQUITY OPTIONS. Nonequity options such as those on indexes and debt securities have been accorded 60/40 status to make this tax treatment symmetrical with that of futures contracts and their related options; 60% of any gain or loss incurred on these contracts is considered to be a long-term capital gain or loss and 40% is a short-term capital gain or loss. This makes the effective maximum tax rate for an individual taxpayer 32%.

THE STRADDLE RULE. Straddles as defined in the Internal Revenue Code are risk-offsetting positions in personal property. The risk of economic loss from holding one position in a straddle is substantially diminished by a related offsetting position. Commodity transactions have been subject to the straddle rule for some time, but with the 1984 tax act, certain stock options and related positions came under the straddle rule. The straddle rule is basically an extension of the wash sale and short sale rules designed to prevent the acceleration of short-term losses combined with deferral of gains. A related change in 1984 requires the capitalization of interest and carrying costs on certain straddle positions to prevent acceleration of deductions.

QUALIFIED COVERED CALLS. To avoid unnecessarily complicated tax reporting for all investors, qualified covered call transactions were exempted from the straddle rule. The rules for "qualifying" a covered call are summarized in Exhibit 12. These rules are complicated by recharacterization of option losses as long-term and suspension of the holding period if an in-the-money call which is otherwise "qualified" is sold before the underlying stock position is held for the long-term holding period.

SPECIAL TAX PROBLEMS AND OPPORTUNITIES. Prior to passage of the 1984 tax act, discussions of special tax problems and opportunities were very extensive. Today, tax treatment of multiple option positions has become extremely complex and many of the former opportunities have disappeared. However, most investors who are not deliberately trying to complicate their positions will find enough favorable developments in the new tax structure to make some attention to the tax characteristics of options worthwhile. The shorter holding period alone makes the other changes tolerable for most individuals. In addition, special tax opportunities are available to investors with loss carry forwards, high bracket individuals and nonresident aliens.

Using Capital Loss Carry Forwards. Options can be used in conjunction with low-yielding conventional securities to get a larger fraction of the portfolio

EXHIBIT 12 REQUIREMENTS FOR QUALIFIED COVERED CALLS

Stock price	Expiration Date of Call Options: Call Options with More than 30 Days and Not More than 90 Days to Run at the Time Written	Call Option with More than 90 Days to Run at the Time Written
$25 or less	One strike price in-the-money but no more than 15% in-the-money	One strike price in-the-money but no more than 15% in-the-money
$25 to not more than $60	One strike price in-the-money	One strike price in-the-money
More than $60 but not more than $150	One strike price in-the-money	Two strike prices in-the-money but no more than $10
More than $150	One strike price in-the-money	Two strike prices in-the-money

Source: Chicago Board Options Exchange.

return as capital gain and a smaller fraction as dividend income. If the pretax return is identical, the after-tax return to the investor with capital loss carry forwards will be higher in the low-dividend portfolio.

High Tax Bracket Individuals. The tax opportunities for high bracket individuals can sometimes be integrated with the use of small loss carry forwards through appropriate timing of the realization of short- and long-term capital gains and losses. Use of options in a long-term investment strategy can lead to larger long-term capital gains than can be attained using conventional securities alone. The keys to this result are the timing of short- and long-term gains and losses and the purchase of options with a life of more than 6 months and a day.

Nonresident Aliens. Nonresident aliens are generally subject to a 15 to 30% withholding tax on some interest and nearly all dividends from sources in the United States.

Investors subject to nonresident withholding should be aware of the principal exemptions from this tax. The recently broadened interest exemption opens up the domestic bond market to foreign investors. Obviously, care must be taken that any bond purchased was issued after July 18, 1984. Capital gains on securities transactions will not be taxed unless a foreign citizen is resident in the United States more than half of the year in which the gain is realized. Gains from an option trade fall under the capital gains exemption. Interest on Eurodollar bonds, Treasury bills, and bank deposits was not subject to withholding before the 1984 interest liberalization.

After analyzing option premium levels and the relative yields on exempt bonds, Treasury bills, and bank CDs, an astute investor can construct a portfolio designed to imitate a U.S. stock or bond portfolio without the penalty of a withholding tax. To understand how, the investor should focus on the key investment characteristic of an option contract: The price of a put or call option rises or falls in conjunction with changes in the price of underlying stock. Because exchange-listed option prices change predictably in response to stock price changes, an option contract can be translated into the risk equivalent of shares in the underlying stock.

EVALUATION OF AN OPTION CONTRACT

Evaluation of an option relative to the **risk-reward characteristics** of the underlying stock is the single most important step an investor must take to achieve superior investment performance using options.

SIGNIFICANCE OF OPTION EVALUATION. Many option services and option users stress calculations based on (1) the leverage inherent in a particular option contract, (2) the option premium as a percentage of the stock price or the striking price, or (3) the stock price parameters within which an option writing strategy is profitable. While it is helpful to know the leverage potential of an option relative to a possible price change in the underlying stock, the option premium as a percentage of the stock price, or the range of prices over which a given strategy will be profitable, a far more useful approach is to try to arrive at a single figure for the **fair value of an option.** Not only will that figure tell the investor whether, other things being equal, he should buy or write that option, but on the basis of that single figure, he also can make any other appropriate calculations easily.

Whether the fair value of an option is expressed in dollars and cents or the desirability of the option to a buyer or writer is appraised by calculating the ratio of the market price of the option to the fair value of the contract, the important thing is to arrive at a single figure that provides meaningful guidance to the use of that option in a possible investment strategy.

Exhibit 13 illustrates the process of determining the value of an option from the viewpoint of the buyer. Evaluation of the writer's position is essentially similar. This discussion deliberately omits several points that have an important bearing on any practical application of this approach or on any advanced discussion of the theoretical value of an option. The most important of these points is the notion of risk adjustment illustrated by Exhibit 7 and described in the accompanying discussion. Any option evaluation must be adjusted to reflect the effect of the purchase or sale of that option on the **risk-reward characteristics** of the portfolio. While this simplified discussion omits this risk adjustment, any working option evaluation model must take it into account.

The buyer's profit-loss line begins in the lower left-hand corner of Exhibit 13, runs parallel to the horizontal axis until it reaches the striking price (in this case, $100 per share), and rises toward the upper right-hand corner. The approximately bell-shaped curve superimposed on the graph is a hypothetical

EXHIBIT 13 CALL BUYER'S PROFIT-LOSS LINE AND STOCK PRICE PROBABILITY DISTRIBUTION

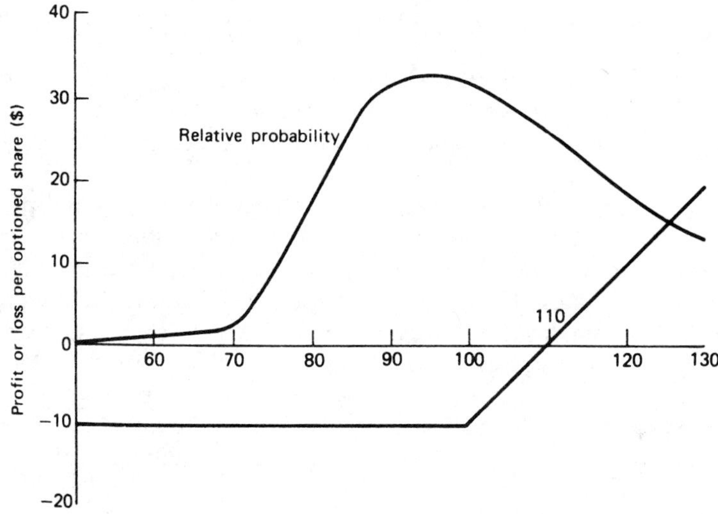

probability distribution of the stock price on the day the option expires. The shape and the location of the stock price distribution curve are a function of the price of the stock at the time the option is purchased, interest rates, the volatility of stock price changes, and the time remaining before the option expires. In the present instance, the price of the stock is assumed to be $95 on the day the buyer purchases the 6-month call at an option price of $10. The interest rate is the intermediate-term, low-risk interest rate. For simplicity, the volatility of the stock is assumed to be the average volatility over some past period.

While it is not possible to determine the exact price of the stock on the date 6 months in the future when the option will expire, it is possible to estimate the **probability** that it will sell at any particular price. This probability estimate is based largely on the way common stock prices have behaved in the past. The probability estimate should not be confused with technical analysis of stock price behavior. Derivation of the probability curve neither requires nor provides a forecast of the **direction** of any change in the stock price. It is concerned only with the likely **magnitude** of stock price changes.

Certain characteristics of this probability distribution are intuitively obvious. For example, most observers, whether they are avid chart readers or exponents of the random walk hypothesis, would agree that the price of a typical stock is more likely to be close to the present price 6 months from today than it is to be selling for either twice or half the present price. As the time period is extended from 6 months to, say, 2 years, the probability distribution will tend to spread out. Over the longer period, doubling or halving the stock price will become more likely events.

Some stocks are more likely to double or collapse than others. Both Atlantic

Richfield and Honeywell were selling near $60 per share in early 1985. Regardless of their opinions on the merits of the two issues, most market participants would expect Honeywell stock to trade over a broader price range than Atlantic Richfield over the next several years. Beyond these areas of agreement, there is considerable controversy about the exact shape of the probability distribution of future stock prices. The curve shown in Exhibit 13 is for illustrative purposes only, though it does approximate the shape of observed probability distributions.

Once the difficult task of estimating the characteristics of the probability distribution has been completed and both shape and location of the probability curve have been determined, it is a relatively simple matter to calculate profitability of a call option. Using the example in Exhibit 13, we divide the probability curve into small segments. The area under the curve in each segment, say in the stock price range between $70 and $71 per share, is divided by the total area under the curve. The resulting fraction is multiplied by the profit or loss to the buyer ($10 loss) if the stock sells in the range of $70 to $71 per share on the day the option expires. When the results of these calculations over the range of all possible stock prices are added up, the total is the profit or loss the buyer of that call can expect.

This explanation of the calculation of the expected profit or loss from buying a call will seem quite straightforward once the reader understands the basic principle of multiplying the fraction of the total area under the probability curve times the profit or loss associated with the price range under that part of the curve. In practice, the calculation is very time-consuming unless the probability distribution curve is similar to one of a family of curves that can be defined by a simple equation. The complexities of option evaluation can be appreciated by noting that calculation of the expected profit or loss occurs only after an analyst has carefully estimated the shape and location of the probability distribution and has made numerous adjustments to the probability distribution and/or the profit-loss line for the effect of commissions, dividends, and interest rates.

Before we can compare an **option evaluation method** with this theoretical model, we must convert the expected profit or loss figure into an estimate of the **value of the call.** This is simply a matter of adding the buyer's expected profit *to* or subtracting his expected loss **from** the market price of the call and subtracting an additional amount as an adjustment for risk.

The importance of the **fair value of an option contract** is hard to overestimate. Once this value has been determined, it can serve as the foundation for any further work the investor might wish to do. It can also serve as part of a simple decision rule such as:

> A call option is never written unless the premium received by the writer exceeds the fair value of the call, and a call option is never purchased unless the premium falls below the fair value of the option.

The fair value of a call or the ratio of the call price to fair value can serve as the basis of a whole series of calculations that permit the investor to structure the risk and return parameters of his investment position in virtually any desired way.

If we use an expected value calculation, such as the fair value of a call, as the sole criterion for a decision, we implicitly assume that the investor is neutral toward risk. Stated another way, relying solely on the expected value of an option implies that an individual is indifferent to the choice between, say, a 100% chance of gaining $1 and a 10% chance of gaining $10, combined with a 90% chance of no gain. While there is considerable evidence that this assumption is not valid when the amounts of money involved are quite large, the calculation of expected value provides a useful starting point. An individual's risk preferences can be reflected in the development of an investment strategy once the expected value has been calculated.

PROBABILITY MODELS. At one time or another a number of leading economists have written articles on option or **warrant pricing.** Most of this work has used options or warrants as a tool to study some other phenomenon that interested the author. To the reader who appreciates the nuances of academic literature, few of the option value models developed by these economists are exactly identical. To the reader less concerned with nuances, the similarities among these models are either comforting or boring, depending on one's mood.

Sprenkle and Samuelson-Merton. One of the more important probability models was derived by **Case M. Sprenkle** in his doctoral dissertation at Yale University in 1960. Sprenkle's work was published in *Yale Economic Essays,* and reprinted in *The Random Character of Stock Market Prices,* edited by **Paul Cootner.** The Sprenkle model is similar in most respects to other classical option and warrant models based on the probability approach. Apart from a few practical considerations that limit its usefulness, Sprenkle's model describes fairly well the relationship between the probability distribution of stock price changes and option or warrant values. The Sprenkle model approximates the description of the probability approach already given and soon to be developed further.

A second important model was developed by **Paul Samuelson** and **Robert Merton** of MIT and described in an article in the Winter 1969 issue of *Industrial Management Review.* The unique feature of this model is that it is based on what the authors call a "util-prob" or combined utility and probability distribution. Though most observers would argue that some of the complexities of the Samuelson-Merton model are rendered obsolete by the work of **Fischer Black** and **Myron Scholes,** this model in its most general form is one of the most flexible approaches to warrant and option evaluation.

Black-Scholes Model. Almost as if it were timed to coincide with the opening of the **Chicago Board Options Exchange,** a theoretical valuation formula for options, derived by **Fischer Black** and **Myron Scholes,** was published in *The Journal of Political Economy* for May–June 1973. The principal difference between the Black-Scholes formulation and the techniques proposed by other economists over the years is that Black and Scholes focus on the **neutral option**

hedge as the key to the determination of option value. The Black-Scholes formula and its major assumptions are outlined in Exhibit 14.

While the mathematical derivation of the formula is an important feature of the Black-Scholes article, the focus here is on the principle behind the Black-Scholes approach and its usefulness as a practical method of evaluating options.

EXHIBIT 14 THE BLACK-SCHOLES MODEL

$$P_o = P_s\,N(d_1) - \frac{E}{e^{rt}}N(d_2)$$

where $d_1 = \dfrac{\ln(P_s/E) + (r = \frac{1}{2}\sigma^2)t}{\sigma\sqrt{t}}$

$d_2 = \dfrac{\ln(P_s/E) + (r - \frac{1}{2}\sigma^2)t}{\sigma\sqrt{t}}$

where P_o = current value of option
P_s = current price of stock
E = exercise price of option
e = 2.71828
t = time remaining before expiration (years)
r = continuously compounded riskless rate of interest
σ = standard deviation of continuously compounded annual rate of return on the stock
$\ln(P_s/E)$ = natural logarithm of (P_s/E)
$N(d)$ = probability that a deviation less than d will occur in a normal distribution with a mean of 0 and a standard deviation of 1

The key assumptions of the **Black-Scholes model** are:

1. The short-term interest rate is known and is constant through time.
2. The stock price follows a random walk in continuous time with a variance rate proportional to the square of the stock price.
3. The distribution of possible stock prices at the end of any finite interval is log normal.
4. The variance rate of return on the stock is constant.
5. The stock pays no dividends and makes no other distributions.
6. The option can be exercised only at maturity.
7. There are no commissions or other transaction costs in buying or selling the stock or the option.
8. It is possible to borrow any fraction of the price of a security to buy it or to hold it, at the short-term interest rate.
9. A seller who does not own a security (a short seller) will simply accept the price of the security from the buyer and will agree to settle with the buyer on some future date by paying him an amount equal to the price of the security on that date. While this short sale is outstanding, the short seller will have the use of, or interest on, the proceeds of the sale.
10. The tax rate, if any, is identical for all transactions and all market participants.

Source: Chicago board Options Exchange.

The Black-Scholes model is based on the fact that it is possible, subject to a number of assumptions, to set up a **perfectly hedged position** consisting of a long position in an underlying stock and a short position in options on that stock, or a long position in the options and a short position in the stock. "Perfectly hedged" means that over a stock price interval close to the current price, any profit resulting from an instantaneous increase in the price of the stock would be exactly offset by a loss on the option position, or vice versa. The Black-Scholes formula, then, is developed from the principle that **options can completely eliminate market risk from a stock portfolio.** Black and Scholes postulate that the ratio of options to stock in this hedged position is constantly modified at no commission cost to offset gains or losses on the stock by losses or gains on the options. Because the position is theoretically riskless, the option premium at which the hedge yields a pretax return equal to the risk-free short-term interest rate is the fair value of the option. If the price of the option is greater or less than fair value, the return from a risk-free hedged position could be different from the risk-free interest rate.

Readers familiar with **modern capital market theory** should recognize that the Black-Scholes evaluation of options with a **neutral hedge** and the risk-reward analysis that accompanied the discussion of options in portfolio management is an extension of modern capital market theory. Establishing the relationship of options to other securities was one of the more important contributions of the Black-Scholes papers (Black and Scholes, "The Valuation of Option Contracts and a Test of Market Efficiency," *Journal of Finance,* May 1972, pp. 399–417, and "The Pricing of Options and Corporate Liabilities," *Journal of Political Economy,* May–June 1973, pp. 637–654). The Black-Scholes articles are an appropriate starting point for anyone wishing to explore option theory in greater depth.

Probably the most important **shortcoming of the Black-Scholes model** is that it relies heavily on the assumption that the probability distribution of future stock prices is a **log normal distribution.** Unfortunately for the usefulness of the Black-Scholes model, virtually every significant empirical study ever made of the distribution of stock price changes indicates that the actual probability distribution of stock prices deviates materially from the log normal curve.

While economists are satisfied that the log normal distribution provides a better approximation to the actual probability distribution of stock prices than the standard normal distribution, the log normal distribution does not fit observed data on stock prices well enough to permit its use for all purposes. Empirical studies have shown that the probability distribution of stock prices differ from the log normal approximation in several ways. First, there is a slight tendency for future stock prices to cluster more around the current stock price than might be expected on the basis of the log normal distribution. Second, and even more significant when options are involved, there is a pronounced tendency for stock prices to be more concentrated in the tails of the distribution than predicted by the log normal curve.

Exhibit 15 illustrates for comparative purposes the difference between the

EXHIBIT 15 COMPARISON OF EMPIRICAL DISTRIBUTION OF STOCK PRICES WITH LOG NORMAL DISTRIBUTION

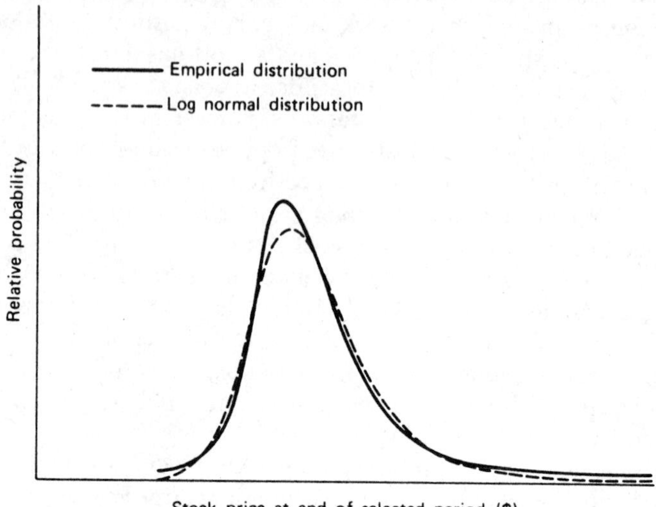

log normal distribution (dashed line) and the observed distribution with its higher peak and fatter tails.

Option evaluation techniques based on the log normal distribution give reasonably satisfactory results as long as the market price and the exercise price are identical. When these prices differ materially, however, an option evaluation based on a log normal distribution of expected stock prices is subject to substantial error. For example, a call option selling well out of the money might appear, from the log normal distribution, to have little value. The "skinny" tails of the log normal distribution suggest a low probability of a large price advance. Using the **empirical distribution,** with its fatter tails, the value of the out-of-the-money call would be much higher.

Recent Attempts to Deal with Probability Distribution Problem. Even before the Black-Scholes articles were published, a number of writers focused on the analytical complexities caused by the fact that the actual distribution of stock price changes is not log normal. The work of **Mandelbrot, Fama,** and **Press** preceded the Black-Scholes articles and focused primarily on finding a standard function that fit the observed data better than the log normal curve. More recent articles have explored the **whys** of non-log normality with the analytical tools provided by Black and Scholes. Although the authors referred to in subsequent paragraphs have much more to say, we focus on their analysis of why the distribution of stock price changes is not log normal.

Robert Merton has probably done as much to extend and improve the realism of the theoretical framework developed by Black and Scholes as any one. Though their work differs in some respects from Merton's, John Cox and Stephen Ross have also attempted to reconcile the Black-Scholes model with empirical data. A major contribution of Merton, Cox, and Ross has been to develop models that combine the log normal Black-Scholes equations with a **"jump" process.** Their explanation for non-log-normality is that the log normal movement of stock prices in the absence of new developments is combined with jumps caused by major events that significantly change the mean value around which log normally distributed fluctuations take place. In essence, they argue that the observed stock price distribution is really a combination of several interacting distributions. Merton points out that this **dual distribution** approach helps explain not only the observed stock price distribution but also the tendency for certain options to sell for relatively more or less than the Black-Scholes model predicts.

Robert Geske has proposed another explanation for the observed distribution of stock price changes that is consistent with the work of Merton and of Cox and Ross. His approach also helps tie option theory more closely to capital market theory, a process initiated by Black and Scholes. Geske argues that a call option is really an option on an option if the firm's capitalization consists of debt as well as common stock. Because common shareholders cannot be assessed if a firm is bankrupt and because they have an "option" to purchase the balance of a firm's assets and cash flows from bondholders by redeeming the bonds, **common stock can be evaluated as an option to purchase the entire firm.** A call option on common stock is therefore best analyzed as an option on an option. Like the Merton-Cox-Ross dual distribution analysis, Geske's **compound option approach** improves on some of the empirical weaknesses of the simple Black-Scholes model. In addition to explaining the Black-Scholes undervaluation of deep-out-of-the-money options, Geske's model explains the tendency of stock price volatility to increase as the stock price declines. An extension of the Geske model permits very precise dividend adjustments.

The problem with these extensions of the Black-Scholes model is that the user of these complex models is called on to deal with more unknowns than the average human mind can handle. It is almost certain that several probability distributions do interact to determine the observed pattern of stock price changes. Likewise, the leverage characteristics of the firm do affect the volatility of the stock and the shape of the stock price distribution. These models may be intuitively more satisfying, but they require a user to deal with too many variables. Whereas the Black-Scholes model has five variables, four of which are known, Geske's model has seven variables, and four of them require complex estimation techniques. The practitioner needs a model that is as easy to use as the Black-Scholes formulations but gives results closer to the more sophisticated extensions that attempt to deal with the non-log-normality of the distribution of stock prices.

Cox, Ross, and Rubinstein. Most of the alternative derivations of the Black-Scholes evaluation model have been of value primarily in explaining the mechanism behind the model from different perspectives. One of these derivations, by Cox, Ross, and Mark Rubinstein was published as Working Paper 79 of the Institute of Business and Economic Research at the University of California at Berkeley and has appreciably extended the usefulness of the Black-Scholes model. Specifically, the use of the **binomial approximation** to the log normal distribution permits a more accurate adjustment for dividends. Good dividend adjustments had been a major problem with the traditional Black-Scholes formulation. The binomial approach is also of value in dealing with the early exercise problem in put evaluation. Although a binomial model requires more computer memory and operating time than the traditional Black-Scholes model, the improvement in accuracy may be worth the cost.

Gastineau-Madansky Model. The development of the **Gastineau-Madansky model,** described in Gastineau (*The Stock Options Manual*), has drawn heavily on the work of the authors whose formulations were discussed above. In general form, the Gastineau-Madansky model is a probability model. By modifying an assumption here and dropping an equation there, it is possible to reduce the Gastineau-Madansky formulation to the format of any of the probability models, including the Black-Scholes model.

The fair value of an option determined by the Gastineau-Madansky model can be adjusted for dividends, interest rates, and option commission charges. The model can also be adjusted for tax rates. One feature, but by no means the only unique feature, of the Gastineau-Madansky model is that it does not use a simple mathematical function to represent the stock price probability distribution. The complex **empirical probability distribution** gives more useful results than the commonly used log normal distribution.

USING AN OPTION EVALUATION MODEL. Exhibit 16 lists some of the data generated by the Gastineau-Madansky computerized option model for listed options on **McDonald's Corp.** and **Polaroid.** Even a casual examination of these data suggests, under the assumptions incorporated in the model, that the McDonald's option was slightly underpriced and that the Polaroid option was substantially overpriced. At the risk of repeating a point, it should be emphasized that the terms "overpriced" and "underpriced" do not imply **anything** about the likely direction of stock price movement; they suggest **only** how an option should be used.

If an investor is bearish on McDonald's, he might not be interested in buying a call just because it is cheap. Instead, an underpriced call might be reversed to create a put, or the call might be purchased to hedge a short sale. Likewise, a bull on Polaroid might want to write uncovered puts, write straddles against a long position, or set up a bullish spread. The option evaluation model is a tool to help the investor choose a strategy that is appropriate to his attitude on the stock, the value of the option contract, and his personal risk preferences.

A careful examination of Exhibit 16 will indicate that some of the calculations are based on the fair value of a call option. Others, such as the probability

EXHIBIT 16 PARTIAL LISTING OF THE OUTPUT OF THE GASTINEAU-MADANSKY COMPUTERIZED OPTION MODEL: DATE OF ANALYSIS, AUGUST 12, 1974[a]

	Stock	
	McDonald's	Polaroid
Symbol	MCD	PRD
Expiration month	January	January
Striking price	$50.00	$30.00
Stock price	$41.125	$26.375
Call price	$ 2.75	$ 3.75
Stock price variance assumption	0.8	1.0
Gastineau-Madansky fair value	$ 3.00	$ 2.79
Call price-fair value	0.92	1.34
Black-Scholes fair value full adjusted	$ 2.82	$ 2.72
Neutral hedge ratio (pretax)	0.37	0.47
Net margin required for uncover writer (30% rate) per share	$ 0.71	$ 0.53
Probability option will be exercised	31%	39%
Probability uncovered writer will lose money or buyer will make money	25%	26%
Probability writer of pretax neutral hedge will lose money	36%	24%
Profit parameters pretax neutral hedge	$33.72–$59.62	$18.47–$40.40
Expected annualized return on equity from a neutral hedge	5.8%	34.9%
Implied stock price variance	0.7	1.6

[a]Note the following:

1. Stock and option prices are closing prices for the previous Friday.
2. Margin requirements are based on an assumed 30% margin rate for uncovered writers and expressed net of any credit for the premium received by the writer.
3. The profit parameters are simply the prices that bracket the stock price range over which a neutral hedge is profitable.
4. The expected annualized return on equity from a neutral hedge is annualized probability weighted profit or loss from a neutral hedge divided by the net equity of the investor in the hedge after option premiums received are credited.
5. Implied stock price variance is the level of stock price volatility that is consistent with the market price of the option.

that an option will be exercised or the probability that an uncovered writer will lose money, require direct reference to the probability curve of the stock price distribution. Still others, such as the required margin calculation, are easy enough to obtain without reference to a particular model and are included on the computer run for convenience.

While the amount of data that a computerized model generates can be truly staggering (most of the computations that can be furnished by the computer are not listed in Exhibit 16), very few data need be understood or evaluated to reach an intelligent decision on a **particular** option strategy. In fact, the most important lessons that a **portfolio manager** who uses options must learn are to analyze assumptions about the underlying stock carefully and to organize the computer output in a format that is relevant to a decision. Usually, organizing the output means disregarding all but a few pertinent numbers.

PROFITABILITY OF OPTION TRADING

Many people believe that determining the "inherent" profitability of an option strategy should be easy. It is not. In many respects the issue of option profitability is the most controversial of all option topics.

STUDIES OF OPTION PROFITABILITY. The academic community was fascinated with the issue of option profitability even when the high transaction costs of conventional options made it difficult to believe that either option buyers or option writers could enjoy consistently superior results in the absence of brilliant investment decisions to overcome the cost disadvantage of dealing in options. Most of the **early studies of option profitability** reached the conclusion that the option writer enjoyed a modest advantage over the option buyer. However, none of these early surveys of option profitability covered a long enough period to assure representative market behavior.

Kassouf. The leading apologist of the "covered writing is best" school is probably **Sheen Kassouf.** His documented simulation of option profitability appeared in an article entitled "Options Pricing: Theory and Practice." The principal weakness of this simulation is that it systematically used option premiums that were too high.

Merton, Scholes, and Gladstein. Perhaps, in spite of themselves, Merton, Scholes, and Mathew Gladstein are usually considered to be advocates of option buying. Their study appeared in the *Journal of Business* (April 1978). This simulation combined option premiums that were systematically too low with failure to maintain a consistent degree of stock equivalent risk exposure within and between simulation periods. Exhibit 17 compares the Merton, Scholes, and Gladstein results with those of Kassouf.

Common Flaws in Simulations. Gastineau and Madansky (1979) carefully analyzed the weaknesses of the Kassouf and Merton-Scholes-Gladstein simulations and developed a list of common flaws inherent in the use of simulation techniques to evaluate option strategies. By far the most important criticism of **all** option simulations is that they fail to maintain a consistent degree of stock equivalent risk exposure between the simulated option portfolio and the market indexes with which the option portfolio is compared. In other words, a portfolio that starts out with approximately the same risk exposure as the **Standard & Poor's 500 stock index** will have a great deal more or a great deal less risk exposure by the end of the simulation period.

Although inconsistent changes in stock equivalent risk exposure are the pri-

EXHIBIT 17 OPTION STRATEGY SIMULATIONS: KASSOUF VS. MERTON, SCHOLES, AND GLADSTEIN

Period Covered by Study	Kassouf (Quarterly Returns): February 1, 1950–January 31, 1975	Merton, Scholes, and Gladstein (Semiannual Returns): July 1, 1963–December 31, 1975
Return from Dow Jones unoptioned stock portfolio	2.74%	4.1%
Standard deviation	6.74	13.7
Return from at-the-money covered call writing	4.20	2.9
Standard deviation	3.63	6.2
Return from 90% money market instruments, 10% at-the-money call purchase strategy	−1.60	5.1
Standard deviation	5.71	10.1

mary cause of misleading results in option strategy simulations, other factors can lead to misleading results as well. Factors mentioned in the Gastineau-Madansky article include various techniques by which option premiums are systematically over- or underestimated. Among the reasons for misestimation are failure to adjust properly for risk, use of an inappropriate risk-free interest rate, and use of an inappropriate option evaluation model. Option premiums can be incorrectly estimated as a result of secular changes in the volatility of the underlying stocks. In addition, decision rules for constructing simulation portfolios may overweight or underweight various sectors of the market.

HISTORIC PROFITABILITY RECORD. The only meaningful study of historic profitability in the listed options market was provided in the Gastineau-Madansky article. This study is brought up to 1982 in Exhibit 18. It compares option premium levels with fair values as measured by subsequent stock price volatility: when the solid line was above the dashed line, options were overpriced and the risk-adjusted advantage lay with the seller of options; when the solid line was below the dashed line, the advantage lay with the buyer of options because options were underpriced. Over the entire period covered in the original article there was a modest advantage accruing to option sellers. In the subsequent period there are indications that this advantage has reversed. Since the inauguration of listed option trading in 1973, there has been no material net advantage to the option buyer versus the option seller, or vice versa.

OPTIONS AND THE CORPORATE TREASURER

Until recently, the only stock options that concerned most corporate financial officers were the **qualified** or nonqualified **stock options** corporations issued to

EXHIBIT 18 COMPARISON OF OPTION PREMIUM LEVELS WITH FAIR VALUES AS MEASURED BY SUBSEQUENT STOCK PRICE VOLATILITY

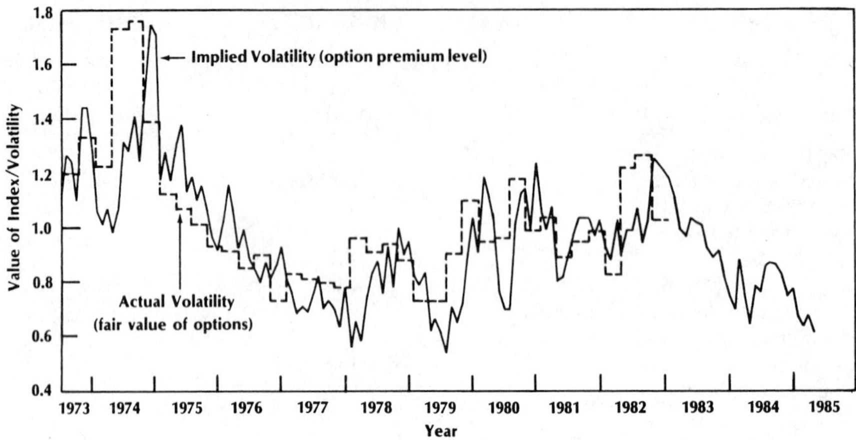

executives and other key employees. Trading in listed stock options promises to have a broader impact on the corporation than executive stock options ever had. The theoretical framework that has developed as a result of the introduction of listed option trading has important implications for the everyday activities of corporate treasurers.

EVALUATING CORPORATE SECURITIES. Black and Scholes and, more recently, **Jonathan Ingersoll** of the University of Chicago, have done extensive work on the use of option theory in the evaluation of corporate securities. While the role of option theory in evaluating a convertible bond or warrant may seem obvious, option analysis can be used in such diverse areas as planning corporate strategy, maximizing the value of the firm for equity shareholders, and evaluating the impact on corporate strategy of the Employee Retirement Income Security Act (**ERISA**) of 1974. The latter topic has been covered extensively by Treynor, Regan, and Priest in *The Financial Reality of Pension Funding Under ERISA*.

PUT AND CALL PROVISIONS ON CORPORATE SECURITIES. The use of **call provisions on debt securities** is common. Some bond and note issues in recent years have received considerable publicity because buyers have the right to "put" bonds to the issuing corporation at par prior to maturity. These put provisions have helped companies sell their debt at a lower net interest rate.

Few corporate treasurers realize that the absence of a call provision on a bond can reduce the interest cost of debt financing by even more than the presence of a put provision. An article by Jonathan Ingersoll (1977) analyzes the effect of call provisions on convertible securities. One of the key implications of

Ingersoll's work is the probability that a corporation that does not plan to call a convertible issue at 110% or 120% of parity will be able to pay a materially lower interest rate if a higher call price is used. In other words, it makes no sense to demand a call provision that the corporation has no intention of using.

PENSION AND PROFIT SHARING INVESTMENTS. The option-related implications of **ERISA** for corporate strategy and ERISA's impact on the value of corporate securities were described earlier. In addition to these strategic considerations, an increasing number of corporate pension and profit sharing plans are embarking on the use of options in their portfolios.

Most such option investment programs are based on the invalid premise that there is something inherently attractive about covered writing of call options. Fortunately, a regulation issued by the **Department of Labor** in 1979 has encouraged the use of additional options strategies. If used properly, options can materially improve the performance results of corporate pension and profit-sharing plans.

MANAGEMENT OF CORPORATE FUNDS. A number of corporations use options in the management of corporate funds. The most common corporate options strategy is to purchase high-yield common or convertible preferred stocks and to sell call options. This strategy can limit exposure to stock price fluctuations while the corporation takes advantage of the 85% intercorporate dividend deduction. This strategy has been restricted somewhat by the Tax Reform Act of 1984.

A more sophisticated corporate option strategy uses put and call options on interest-sensitive common stocks to hedge the interest rate risk of a preferred stock or municipal bond portfolio. Because most preferred stock dividends qualify for the 85% intercorporate dividend deduction and because municipal bond interest is totally tax exempt, a hedged portfolio of this nature should provide an **aftertax** yield advantage over commercial paper or certificates of deposit. The basis of this technique is the use of options to remove a substantial element of risk from an investment vehicle that has unique tax advantages for the corporate investor. A similar effect can be achieved through the use of interest rate futures contracts or bond options that hedge a preferred or utility common stock portfolio.

OPTIONS ON FIXED INCOME SECURITIES. Bond options, like interest rate futures contracts, can modify interest rate risks and help match the maturities of assets and liabilities.

MERITS OF OPTION LISTING. A few corporations have taken steps to discourage the listing of their stocks for option trading. A greater number of corporate managements have launched campaigns to interest the listing committees of the options exchanges in their stocks. Although the evidence is not definitive, an active option market appears to reduce the tendency for the underlying stock price to fluctuate. This stock price volatility reduction results from the **risk transfer characteristics of options.** A brokerage firm asked to bid on a block of stock or an institutional investor offered part of the block can offset some of the risk of the stock position in the option market. Because volume in the option market is a proxy for volume in the underlying stock, each option trade increases the depth and the liquidity of the market in the stock, with a consequent reduction in stock price fluctuations.

The significance of lower stock price volatility to the financial officer is that lower volatility helps reduce the corporation's cost of capital. Other things being equal, a less volatile stock is a more desirable investment. Lower volatility means lower risk. Investors will accept a lower return on a lower risk investment. A lower future risk expectation means a higher current stock price and a lower cost of equity capital. Even a slight reduction in stock price volatility should tend to improve the average price-earnings multiple or reduce the dividend yield that investors will demand from a common stock.

In addition to the generally favorable effect of an option listing on liquidity and stock price volatility, an option listing can reduce the **corporation's cost of capital** in another way. A growing number of individual investors and institutional portfolio managers work extensively or even exclusively with options and their related stocks. For these investors it is frequently a case of "no options, no interest." A growing number of advisory services and brokerage firm research departments are influenced by the combined trading volume in stocks and options when they select stocks for statistical and analytical coverage. Obviously, if a corporation has problems, more attention is not always desirable. After weighing positive and negative factors, however, managements of most large corporations have concluded that they want increased interest from the investment community.

A corporation can do relatively little to encourage one or more of the option exchanges to list its stock. While an investment banker can help with a presentation to the exchange's listing committee, these committees are usually controlled by floor members. Consequently, listing decisions are based on the floor members' expectations for option trading volume. With few exceptions (e.g., Bally Manufacturing) most companies listed for option trading after 1975 have experienced only modest option trading volume. If a company has not already been selected for option trading, management should not expect too much from an option listing.

It is a relatively simple matter for a corporation to **discourage** an option listing if the preceding paragraphs have not been persuasive. Because option terms must be modified in the event of a noncash dividend or a stock split, any corporation that declares small quarterly stock dividends will soon have an unmanageable number of option series with irregular striking prices and unusual numbers of shares underlying each option. Traders will shy away from the issue, volume will dry up, and the option exchange will rue the day the stock was admitted to trading.

BIBLIOGRAPHY

Black, Fischer, "Fact and Fantasy in the Use of Options," *Financial Analysts Journal,* July–August 1975, pp. 36–72.

———, and Cox, John C., "Valuing Corporate Securities: Some Effects of Bond Indenture Provisions," *Journal of Finance,* May 1976, pp. 351–367.

———, and Scholes, Myron, "The Valuation of Option Contracts and a Test of Market Efficiency," *Journal of Finance,* May 1972, pp. 399–417.

———, and ———, "The Pricing of Options and Corporate Liabilities," *Journal of Political Economy,* May–June 1973, pp. 637–654.

Brennan, Michael J., and Schwartz, Eduardo S., "Convertible Bonds: Valuation and Optimal Strategies for Call and Conversion," Working Paper No. 336, University of British Columbia, Vancouver, July 1976.

Cootner, Paul, Ed., *The Random Character of Stock Market Prices,* MIT Press, Cambridge, MA, 1964.

Cox, John C., and Ross, Stephen A., "The Valuation of Options for Alternative Stochastic Processes," *Journal of Financial Economics,* January–March 1976, pp. 145–166.

———, ———, and Rubinstein, Mark, "Option Pricing: A Simplified Approach," Working Paper No. 79, Institute of Business and Economic Research, University of California, Berkeley, September 1979.

———, ———, and ———, *Option Markets,* Prentice-Hall, Englewood Cliffs, NJ, 1985.

Gastineau, Gary L., *The Stock Options Manual,* 2d ed., McGraw-Hill, New York, 1979.

———, and Madansky, Albert, "Why Simulations Are an Unreliable Test of Option Strategies," *Financial Analysts Journal,* September–October 1979, pp. 61–76.

———, and Madansky, Albert, "Some Comments on the Chicago Board Options Exchange Call Option Index," *Financial Analysts Journal,* July–August 1984, pp. 58–67.

Geske, Robert, "The Valuation of Compound Options," unpublished working paper, University of California, Berkeley, December 1976.

Ingersoll, Jonathan E., Jr., "A Contingent Claim Valuation of Convertible Securities," *Journal of Financial Economics,* May 1977.

———, "An Examination of Corporate Call Policies on Convertible Securities," *Journal of Finance,* May 1977, pp. 463–478.

Kassouf, Sheen T., "Option Pricing: Theory and Practice," Columbia University Graduate School of Business, Institute for Quantitative Research and Finance, Spring 1977 Seminar.

Merton, Robert C., "Theory of Rational Option Pricing," *Bell Journal of Economics and Management Science,* Spring 1973, pp. 141–183.

———, "Option Pricing when Underlying Stock Returns Are Discontinuous," *Journal of Financial Economics,* January–March 1976, pp. 125–144.

———, Scholes, Myron S., and Gladstein, Mathew L., "A Simulation of the Returns and Risk of Alternative Option Portfolio Investment Strategies," *Journal of Business,* April 1978, pp. 183–242.

Parkinson, Michael, "Option Pricing: The American Put," *Journal of Business,* January 1977, pp. 21–36.

Ross, Stephen, "Options and Efficiency," *Quarterly Journal of Economics,* February 1976, pp. 75–89.

Samuelson, Paul, and Merton, Robert C., "A Complete Model of Warrant Pricing that Maximizes Utility," *Industrial Management Review,* Winter 1969, pp. 17–46.

Treynor, J. L., Regan, P. J., and Priest, W. W., Jr., *The Financial Reality of Pension Funding Under ERISA,* Dow Jones-Irwin, Homewood, IL: 1976.

8

FUTURES MARKETS

CONTENTS

8

FUTURES MARKETS

Richard L. Sandor
Norman E. Mains

DEVELOPMENT OF FUTURES TRADING

GROWTH AND COMPOSITION OF FUTURES TRADING. **Futures trading** in the United States has soared over the last 2½ decades from a level of 3.9 million contracts in 1960 to 158.7 million contracts in 1985 (Exhibit 1). Annual volume increases amounted to 13.3% during the 1960s and represented mainly expanded trading in **agricultural commodities.** More recently, volume accelerated to an average annual increase of 17.8% as further growth in the trading of traditional agricultural and metal futures contracts was supplemented by the spectacular growth of **financial futures.** A nascent market in **foreign currency futures** began in 1972. This was followed by the introduction of **interest rate futures** in the middle 1970s and **stock index futures** in early 1982. As a group, trading activity in financial futures accounted for nearly three-fifths of total futures trading in 1985 (Exhibit 2).

ORIGIN OF FUTURES MARKETS. The origin of futures markets can be traced to the needs of individual and commercial enterprises that produced, merchandised, and processed commodities. The history of **commodity exchanges** reveals that commercial participants entered into **forward contracts** (the purchase or sale of a specific quantity and quality of a commodity for delivery at some specific time and place in the future) to prevent losses that might

Richard L. Sandor is senior vice president, Institutional Financial Futures division, Drexel Burnham Lambert.
Norman E. Mains is first vice president, Institutional Financial Futures division, Drexel Burnham Lambert.

EXHIBIT 1 TRADING ACTIVITY IN FINANCIAL AND COMMODITY FUTURES MARKETS (MILLIONS OF CONTRACTS)

Year	Contracts Traded	Financial Futures as a Percent of Total[a]
1960	3.9	—
1965	8.4	—
1970	13.6	—
1975	32.2	0.7
1980	92.1	15.0
1981	98.5	25.7
1982	112.5	34.9
1983	139.9	38.7
1984	149.4	49.3
1985	158.7	59.6

[a] Financial futures include interest rate, foreign currency, and stock index contracts.

Source: Futures Industry Association.

arise from interim price changes. These forward contracts were eventually traded by individuals or firms that desired either to be hedged against price changes or to profit from fluctuations in market prices.

Organized futures markets evolved from **spot** or **cash markets** (markets for immmediate delivery) in many commodities where forward contracting (markets for deferred delivery) became prevalent. The oldest of the U.S. exchanges,

EXHIBIT 2 FUTURES CONTRACTS TRADED IN 1984 AND 1985 BY COMMODITY GROUP

Group	Trading Volume (thousands of contracts)		Percent of Total	
	1984	1985	1984	1985
Financial—total	73,664	94,534	49.3	59.6
Interest rate	41,221	55,125	27.6	34.7
Stock index	18,442	22,243	12.3	14.0
Foreign currency	14,001	17,166	9.4	10.8
Nonfinancial—total	75,708	64,163	50.7	40.4
Agricultural	49,618	39,332	33.2	24.8
Metals—precious	18,880	14,720	12.6	9.3
Petroleum products	4,620	7,002	3.1	4.4
Metals—nonprecious	2,590	3,109	1.7	2.0
Total	149,372	158,697	100.0	

Source: Futures Industry Association.

the **Chicago Board of Trade,** came into existence in 1848 by offering the opportunity for trading for immediate and deferred delivery. **Trading in futures contracts** for **grain** evolved on the Chicago Board of Trade during the 1860s. The grain futures contracts differed from forward contracts in several important ways: The futures contracts were not tailored to the needs of a specific buyer or seller but instead had **standardized specifications** allowing for homogeneity in grade, time, and point of delivery with terms established by the exchange and prices determined in a **competitive auction** market. In addition, only a small proportion of futures contract holders stand for **delivery,** whereas delivery is almost always contemplated in forward contracts.

Most open futures contracts are closed out by taking an **offsetting position** in the same contract prior to the delivery period. All U.S. futures contracts are traded on a central exchange that is now federally regulated by the **Commodity Futures Trading Commission** (CFTC). As of the end of 1985, there were 11 exchanges registered with the CFTC (Exhibit 3).

CONTRACT ATTRIBUTES. Futures contracts are **delayed delivery contracts** for a specific quantity and quality of either a commodity, specified property, or index of the same at prices that are determined currently. Both contracting parties (the **"long"** commits to take delivery and the **"short"** commits to make delivery) are obligated to perform in accordance with the **specifications of the contract** established by the listing exchange. A large and diverse group of financial and nonfinancial futures contracts exist currently in the United States (Exhibit 4). The Chicago Board of Trade corn futures contract specifies, for example, 5,000 bushels of USDA No. 2 Yellow Corn as the **contract grade,** although other grades can be delivered at premiums or discounts to the quoted

EXHIBIT 3 TRADING ACTIVITY BY COMMODITY EXCHANGE

1984 Rank	Exchange	Symbol	Trading Volume (thousands of contracts) 1985	1980
1	Chicago Board of Trade	CBOT	70,554	45,282
2	Chicago Mercantile Exchange	CME	52,115	22,261
3	Commodity Exchange	CMX	15,116	11,009
4	New York Mercantile Exchange	NYM	7,832	1,155
5	Coffee Sugar & Cocoa Exchange	CEX	4,583	4,886
6	New York Futures Exchange	NYFE	2,834	184
7	MidAmerica Commodity Exchange	MA	2,485	2,994
8	Kansas City Board of Trade	KCBT	1,959	1,298
9	New York Cotton Exchange	CTN	916	2,654
10	Minneapolis Grain Exchange	MPLS	301	361
11	Chicago Rice & Cotton Exchange	CRCE	2	—
	Total		158,697	92,096

Source: Futures Industry Association.

EXHIBIT 4 FINANCIAL AND NONFINANCIAL FUTURES CONTRACTS TRADED ON THE U.S. FUTURES EXCHANGES (DECEMBER 31, 1985)

Type	Principal Contract		Traded on
	Size	Exchange	Other Exchange[a]
Financial:			
Interest rate:			
Certificates of Deposit (3-mo.)	$1,000,000	CME	—
Eurodollar Time Deposits (3-mo.)	$1,000,000	CME	—
GNMA-CDR	$ 100,000	CBOT	—
GNMA-II	$ 100,000	CBOT	—
Muni Bond Index	$ 100,000	CBOT	—
U.S. Treasury bills	$1,000,000	CME	MA
U.S. Treasury bonds	$ 100,000	CBOT	MA
U.S. Treasury notes	$ 100,000	CBOT	—
Stock Index:			
KC Value Line	$500 × Index	KCBT	—
KC Mini Value Line	$100 × Index	KCBT	—
Major Market Index	$100 × Index	CBOT	—
NASDAQ 100	$250 × Index	CBOT	—
NYSE Composite	$500 × Index	NYFE	—
S&P 100	$500 × Index	CME	—
S&P 500	$500 × Index	CME	—
S&P OTC 250	$500 × Index	CME	—
Foreign Currency:			
British pound	25,000 BP	CME	MA
Canadian dollar	100,000 CD	CME	MA
Deutsche mark	125,000 DM	CME	MA
French franc	250,000 FF	CME	—
Japanese yen	12,500,000 JY	CME	MA
Mexican peso	1,000,000 MP	CME	—
Swiss franc	125,000 SF	CME	MA
Nonfinancial:			
Agricultural:			
Cocoa	10 metric tons	CEX	—
Coffee	37,500 lb	CEX	—
Corn	5,000 bu.	CBOT	MA
Cotton	50,000 lb	CTN	—
Feeder cattle	44,000 lb	CME	—
Live cattle	40,000 lb	CME	MA
Live hogs	30,000 lb	CME	MA
Lumber	130,500 bd ft	CME	—
Oats	5,000 bu	CBOT	MA
Orange juice	15,000 lb	CTN	—
Pork bellies	38,000 lb	CME	—
Potatoes	50,000 lb	NYME	—
Rice	200,000 lb	CRCE	—
Soybeans	5,000 bu.	CBOT	MA
Soybean meal	100 tons	CBOT	—
Soybean oil	60,000 lb	CBOT	—
Sugar	112,000 lb	CEX	—
Wheat	5,000 bu.	CBOT	KCBT,MGE,MA

EXHIBIT 4 (*CONTINUED*)

Type	Principal Contract Size	Principal Contract Exchange	Traded on Other Exchange[a]
Metals—Precious:			
Gold	100 troy oz	CMX	CME,CBOT,MA
Platinum	50 troy oz	NYME	—
Silver	5,000 troy oz	CMX	CBOT
Metals—Nonprecious:			
Aluminum	40,000 lb	CMX	—
Copper	25,000 lb	CMX	—
Palladium	100 troy oz	NYME	—
Petroleum Products:			
Crude oil	42,000 gal	NYME	—
Heating oil	42,000 gal	NYME	—
Leaded gas	42,000 gal	NYME	—
Propane	42,000 gal	CTN	—
Unleaded gas	42,000 gal	NYME	—

[a] Contract specifications may differ.

Source: Institutional Financial Futures Division, Drexel Burnham Lambert Incorporated.

prices. The corn contract is traded in units of quarter-cents per bushel (or $12.50 per tic) with maximum price fluctuations during the trading day of up or down 10 cents per bushel ($500 per contract) from the previous day's close. Some futures contracts do not have daily price fluctuation limits, however. **Contract months** for corn are March, May, July, September, and December. Trading in the corn contract is usually concentrated in the months closest to delivery, although some trading takes place as much as 1 year or more ahead (some futures contracts, such as U.S. Treasury bonds, trade as much as 2½ years into the future). Grain contracts in general, and corn in particular, are traded from 9:30 A.M. to 1:15 P.M. central time.

THE DELIVERY PROCESS. Delivery in the corn contract can occur at any time during the delivery month at warehouses approved by the exchange (currently in Chicago at par and in Toledo and St. Louis at a 4-cent per bushel discount). Although successful futures contracts do not favor either the long or the short market participant, the delivery process of many contract specifications allows the seller to initiate the delivery process. In the corn contract, for example, the seller decides both the specific day of the month when delivery occurs, the location of the delivery, and the contract grade. Delivery of corn is accomplished by exchanging a **warehouse receipt** issued by an approved grain elevator and registered by the exchange for a check drawn on an approved bank or a cashier's check.

The contract specifications for the delivery process of certain future contracts are precise with regard to the specific deliverable instrument, time, and the method of payment. For example, the **Chicago Mercantile Exchange's** contract specifications for its 3-month (13-week) **U.S. Treasury bill futures** call for delivery to be made on three successive business days, beginning with the first day of the spot month on which a 13-week Treasury bill is issued and a previously issued 1-year Treasury bill has 13 weeks remaining to maturity. These specifications also allow the previously issued 6-month bill (which has 13 weeks remaining maturity) to augment the deliverable supply. A somewhat broader **delivery "window"** is used in the CBOTs **long-term U.S. Treasury bond** futures contract. The contract specifications allow for the delivery of any U.S. Treasury bond having at least 15 years to maturity or 15 years to its first call date. The contract grade is $100,000 par amount of a hypothetical 20-year bond bearing an 8% coupon. The par amount is adjusted by a predetermined factor (based on coupon and maturity) to determine the value of the contract for any qualifying bond that is delivered by the short contract holder to the long contract holder.

An innovational development in the delivery process in the last few years has been cash settlement futures contracts based on indexes rather than delivery of some commodity or instrument. The Chicago Mercantile Exchange initiated this development with its 3-month Eurodollars futures contract that had the first cash settlement in the first quarter of 1982. The specifications of the contract are based on a **Eurodollar Time Deposit** having a principal value of $1 million with a 3-month maturity. Bids and offers are quoted in terms of the **International Monetary Market's (IMM) index** (100 minus the yield on an annual basis for a 360-day year). The final settlement price is determined on the last day of trading by the **London Interbank Offered Rate (LIBOR)** for 3-month Eurodollar Time Deposit funds.

The use of cash settlement on the final trading day rather than the physical transfer of a commodity, instrument, or warehouse receipt of the same paved the way for other index-based futures contracts, the most notable of which were **stock index futures contracts.** The **Kansas City Board of Trade** inaugurated stock index futures in the spring of 1982 with its futures contract based on the **Value Line Index,** an equal-weighted index of 1,700 companies. The CME and the **New York Futures Exchange** began trading stock index futures contracts shortly thereafter based on the value-weighted **S&P 500** and **NYSE Composite** indexes, respectively. More recently the CBOT introduced a stock index futures contract in the summer of 1984 based on the American Stock Exchange's **Major Market Index,** an equal weighted index of 20 large industrial issues. The various stock index futures contracts have been very well received by market participants, and the value of the aggregated trading of these contracts regularly exceeds the value of trading of all issues listed on the New York Stock Exchange (Exhibit 5). This activity is not spread equally among the various stock index contracts, however, because the S&P 500 stock index futures account for approximately two-thirds of such activity. It was the second most actively traded futures contract in 1985 (Exhibit 6).

EXHIBIT 5 VALUE OF TRADING IN STOCK INDEX FUTURES AND ON THE NYSE

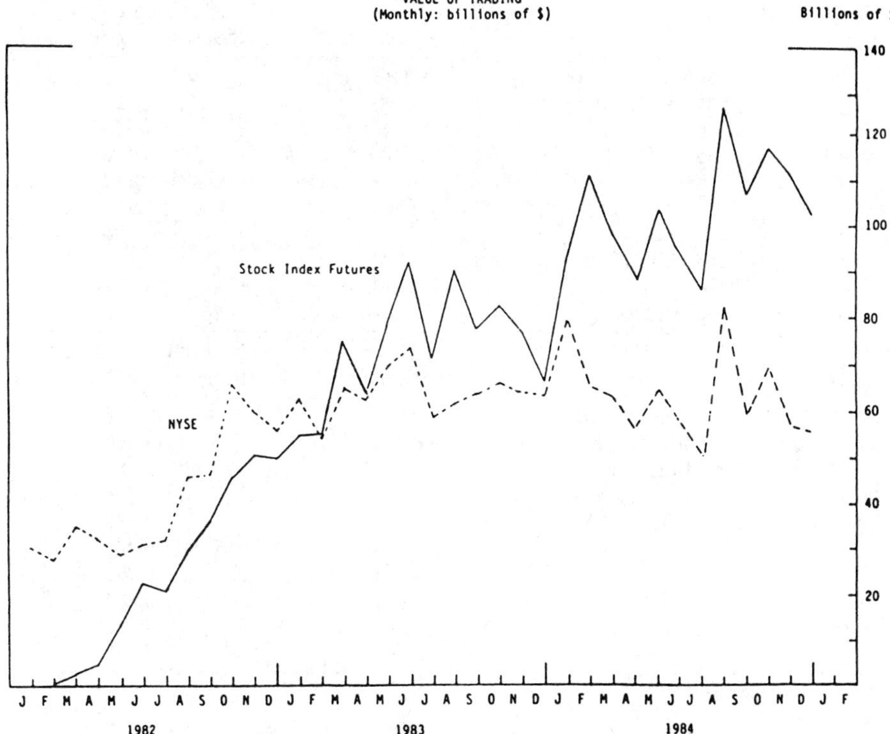

NECESSARY CONDITIONS FOR A VIABLE CONTRACT. The wide and diverse group of financial and nonfinancial futures contracts has a number of significant elements in common. All of the futures contracts are based, for example, on commodities, financial instruments, or indexes that are characterized by significant price volatility in a market environment where prices are competitively determined. The commodities or financial instruments are typically homogeneous in that there are close price movements among different grades or instruments. There is also the common characteristic of an active **spot, or cash market,** and the breadth of the underlying market must be large enough that participants are convinced that the market for the underlying instrument, commodity, or index cannot be manipulated or cornered. This is an especially important feature of the cash settlement or index contracts. Finally, the contract design must be appropriate to attract both professional **speculators** and other market participants on the floor of the exchange for the contract to be viable.

OPTIONS ON FUTURES CONTRACTS. An important development in the financial and commodity futures market in recent years has been the introduc-

EXHIBIT 6 FUTURES CONTRACTS TRADED IN 1984 AND 1985 BY CONTRACT

1984 Rank	Contract	Exchange	Trading volume (thousands of contracts)
1	U.S. Treasury bonds	CBT	29,963
2	S&P 500 Index	CME	12,364
3	Soybeans	CBT	11,363
4	Gold (100 oz)	CMX	9,116
5	Corn	CBT	9,109
6	Silver (5000 oz)	CMX	6,743
7	Deutsche mark	CME	5,508
8	Eurodollar (3-mo.)	CME	4,193
9	Swiss franc	CME	4,130
10	Soybean Oil	CBT	4,010
1985 Rank	**Contract**	**Exchange**	**Trading volume (thousands of contracts)**
1	U.S. Treasury bonds	CBT	40,448
2	S&P 500 Index	CME	15,056
3	Eurodollar (3-mo.)	CME	8,901
4	Gold (100 oz.)	CMX	7,774
5	Soybeans	CBT	7,392
6	Deutsche Mark	CME	6,449
7	Corn	CBT	6,393
8	Silver (5000 oz.)	CMX	4,821
9	Swiss Franc	CME	4,758
10	Live Cattle	CME	4,437

Source: Futures Industry Association.

tion of **options on futures contracts.** Exchange-traded options were initiated by the **Chicago Board Options Exchange (CBOE),** then a division of CBOT, in 1973, but exchange-listed options on futures contracts did not appear until several years later. Such trading began on a date designated by the CFTC in its 3-year pilot program. The CFTCs program has resulted in a phased introduction of exchange-traded commodity options, with the initial rules permitting one option on a futures contract (other than on a domestic agricultural commodity) to be traded on each exchange. Subsequently, the CFTC adopted rules permitting the trading of one option on a physical (but nonagricultural) commodity per exchange and, following this, the pilot program was expanded to allow two options per exchange.

Options on futures contracts began trading on October 1, 1982, with **options on Treasury Bond** and **Sugar futures contracts** on the CBOT and NYSCE, respectively, and **options on the CMXs Gold futures** contract shortly thereafter. The Treasury bond and Gold option contracts were very well received by market participants and both contracts immediately recorded active daily trading activity and increasing open interest (Exhibit 7). Augmenting the overall activity in options on futures was the introduction of **option contracts on stock**

EXHIBIT 7 OPTIONS ON FUTURES CONTRACTS TRADING VOLUME AND OPEN INTEREST (MONTHLY AVERAGE; NUMBER OF CONTRACTS)

Period	Trading Volume	Open Interest[a]
1982-Q4	59,094	24,224
1983-Q1	144,713	49,098
Q2	188,605	84,077
Q3	231,451	99,992
Q4	316,006	414,313
1984-Q1	597,419	288,141
Q2	867,220	411,312
Q3	843,287	326,130
Q4	973,891	424,424
1985-Q1	1,368,834	584,076
Q2	1,607,622	681,896
Q3	1,687,337	783,200
Q4	2,017,788	898,945

[a] End of period.

Source: Institutional Financial Futures, Drexel Burnham Lambert Incorporated.

index futures at the CME and NYFE in early 1983, and approximately 1 year later the CME instituted an option on its **Deutsche mark futures contract.**

The CFTC further modified its pilot program for nonagricultural options by boosting the number of contracts from two to five per exchange in August 1984 and, at the same time, instituted a separate 3-year pilot program for options on agricultural commodities. The latter program initially allowed two option contracts per exchange. In response to these regulatory developments several additional options on futures contracts were approved in the latter half of 1984, thereby further boosting the overall totals for such contracts. The Treasury bond and Deutsche Mark options on futures contracts constituted the greatest proportion of 1985 activity (Exhibit 8), and activity in several other contracts was growing rapidly by year-end. Moreover, most futures exchanges introduced additional options on futures contracts in 1985 for both financial and nonfinancial futures contracts.

The extraordinary growth of options on futures over their brief period of existence has occurred against a background of enhanced activity in exchange-listed options on physicals as well as **over-the-counter options.** Options have enjoyed this growth in part due to their unique reward/risk profiles. The purchase of either a **call** or **put** allows the option holder to participate in a price change for the outlay of a certain **premium** that limits one's exposure to this amount. Option prices are competitively determined, of course, and a large amount of literature exists on their theoretical foundations (the subject of op-

EXHIBIT 8 OPTIONS ON FUTURES CONTRACTS IN 1984 AND 1985 BY CONTRACT

1984 Rank	Contract	Exchange	Trading Volume	Open Interest[a]
1	U.S. Treasury bonds	CBT	6,636,209	214,518
2	Gold (100 oz)	CMX	1,432,514	92,546
3	Deutsche marks	CME	727,634	35,543
4	S&P 500	CME	672,884	20,399
5	NYSE composite	NYFE	246,359	3,568
6	Silver	CMX	99,843	30,023
7	Soybeans	CBT	72,969	12,267
8	Live cattle	CME	20,772	8,670
1985 Rank	**Contract**	**Exchange**	**Trading Volume**	**Open Interest[a]**
1	U.S. Treasury bonds	CBT	11,901,116	407,947
2	Deutsche marks	CME	1,562,438	56,606
3	Gold (100 oz)	CMX	1,395,896	70,366
4	S&P 500	CME	1,090,068	37,176
5	Soybeans	CBT	840,786	41,696
6	Eurodollars (3-mo.)	CME	743,080	43,077
7	Silver (1000 oz)	CMX	531,315	35,207
8	Corn	CBT	363,549	48,123

[a] As of December 31, 1984, and 1985.
Source: Futures Industry Association.

tions is discussed in more detail in Section 7 of this Handbook). The contract specifications of options on futures contracts allow for the delivery of the underlying futures contract upon **exercise** (a long position on the exercise of a call option and a short position on the exercise of a put). The trading location (or pit) of such contracts is usually in close proximity to the underlying futures contract, and this juxtaposition contributes to enhanced liquidity for both vehicles.

PARTICIPANTS IN FUTURES CONTRACT TRADING

HEDGING. One of the two broad categories of participants in futures markets is hedgers. **Hedging** is defined as a temporary substitute for a transaction in the spot market to protect against adverse price movements. An example of a hedger would be a dealer in U.S. government notes and bonds that establishes a short position in the Treasury bond futures contract in order to hedge some or all of the price risk of the firm's position. Similarly, a multinational grain company that receives an order from a foreign government for corn may be unable to locate quickly a sufficient number of farmers or grain elevator operators willing to sell the spot commodity for deferred delivery. In this case the company will purchase futures contracts as a substitute for spot purchases to fix the price of grain. An individual or firm that has a position in the cash market which is fully hedged in the futures market is theoretically price neutral, that is, a change in spot prices is fully offset by a change in the futures price such that the individual or firm is neither better nor worse off. Commercial enterprises use the futures market to hedge their risks for several reasons:

1. Futures markets result in a broader and deeper market in the underlying commodity, instrument, or index that allows transactions to be executed quickly with minimal price impact.
2. Futures markets allow for price discovery.
3. Futures markets provide for the redistribution of risk by allowing hedgers the ability to fix the price of commodities, obligations, or indexes that are used in their commercial or financial activities. This price insurance function is the critical element in the markets.
4. Futures markets usually offer an enhanced ability to sell short.
5. Futures markets allow participants to conduct their activities with a greater degree of anonymity.
6. Futures markets can result in price or cost effectiveness.

SPECULATING. The second broad category of participants in futures markets is speculators. **Speculation** is the use of a futures market to profit from a movement in prices and is usually not related to the principal business activity of the participant. It is important, however, to distinguish between speculation and gambling. In the former, **uncertainty** exists in the system, but it remains to be decided just who will bear its cost more efficiently. **Gambling risk** is, on the other hand, created and generally is assumed for the purpose of leisure.

FUNCTIONS OF THE FUTURES EXCHANGE. The **functions of commodity exchanges** can be summarized by quoting directly from the Rules and Regulations of the Chicago Board of Trade:

> The objects of the Association are: To maintain a Commercial Exchange; to promote uniformity in the customs and usages of merchants; to inculcate principles of justice and equity in trade; to facilitate the speedy adjustment of business disputes; to acquire and disseminate valuable commercial and economic information; and, generally to secure to its members the benefits of co-operation in the furtherance of their legitimate pursuits.

This preamble was adopted more than 100 years ago but its scope remains valid. In promoting "uniformity in the customs and usages of merchants," an exchange standardizes the contracts as discussed previously. An exchange establishes the physical environment, or the technological means, where transactions occur. In all cases, a price competitive market environment must exist in which transactors are assured of the highest bids and lowest offers available at any time. In those cases where a delivery process is present, the exchange's contract specifications must indicate the grade and quality delivered, as well as specify the conditions under which different commodities or instruments can be delivered and the physical instrument of delivery. As noted earlier, warehouse receipts are utilized in the various grain futures contracts. Delivery of other commodities occurs through a **shipping certificate** (a promissory note that a processor or shipper will deliver a certain commodity within a certain period of time). Only exchange-approved warehouses and shippers can issue instruments that can be used in the delivery process. The approval of warehouses and shippers is accomplished through inspection procedures outlined by the exchange. The process is simplified for most financial futures contracts, because most of these contracts allow for either the financial instruments to be delivered directly or cash settlement for those contracts that are based on indexes.

FUNCTION OF THE CLEARINGHOUSE. Financial integrity is established by the existence of the **clearinghouse** (or clearing corporation, when it is a separate firm) that mediates between buyers and sellers. When a buyer transacts with a seller, the clearinghouse serves on the opposite side of the contract for both parties. In this triad, the clearinghouse interposes itself as buyer from the seller and as seller to the buyer. Trading can be done only by members of the exchange, and only those designated as **clearing members** can assume the financial responsibilities associated with initiating a position in the futures market.

EXCHANGE OPERATIONS. The administration and management of an exchange are executed jointly by a professional staff and committees of members. Most exchanges are operated as if they were nonprofit membership associations, and membership implies privileges in addition to equity. These include permission to act as **futures commission merchants** (brokers), **clearing members, floor brokers** (individuals executing orders on the exchange floor), as well as to trade from the floor. **Floor traders (professional speculators,** or **locals,** located on the exchange floor) often speculate in more than one commodity and may behave as market makers or specialists, although they are not charged with this function. Some exchanges have issued conditional membership in recent years, which limits the scope of commodities in which the seat holder may participate.

MECHANICS OF FUTURES TRADING

POSITION TAKING. Initiating a position in the futures market is accomplished by placing an order with a firm that is designated as a **futures commission merchant (FCM).** The purchase of a futures contract is commonly called taking a long position in the market, whereas the sale of a contract is taking a short position. When either buying or selling a contract, the exchanges require an initial margin deposit. These deposits differ from stock market margin requirements (which are considered to be extensions of credit), because futures contract margins are actually **performance bonds.** They typically vary between 2 and 10% of the full value of the contract with the exact level established by the individual exchanges for each commodity. Once a position is established, each position is marked-to-market on a daily basis. If the equity in a market participant's account falls below a predetermined level, termed **maintenance margin,** then additional money must be posted; this is known as **variation margin.**

MARGIN MECHANICS. A speculator may choose, for example, to go "long" the CBOTs Treasury bond futures contract in the June delivery cycle at a price of 80-00 (a yield of 10.39%). The speculator would be required to post **initial margin** of, say, $2,000 with his or her futures commission merchant and be faced with a maintenance margin of $1,500. Because a one-half point move in the market is worth $500 (16/32nds times $31.25), then a price decline (using settlement or closing prices) of more than this amount would result in a breaching of the **maintenance margin** level of $1,500. This, in turn, would require the market participant to post an amount of money that would restore the $2,000 margin. Conversely, if prices in the June contract rose to 80-16/32nds, the speculator would be credited with $500. Although this $500 is unrealized profit, the amount of the credit can be withdrawn from the account or used as margin for the purchase of additional contracts by the market participant. In addition, initial margins can be satisfied with U.S. government securities, or, on some exchanges, with letters of credit from major banks.

POSITION LIQUIDATION. Positions in the futures market can be liquidated by either offset or by making or taking delivery. In delivery, as noted earlier, the long and short contract holders exchange the specific commodity at the last price at which trading occurred when the buyer received notice from the seller that delivery will be made. Nevertheless, less than 1% of all future contracts are settled by the delivery process. The more common alternative is to liquidate either long or short positions before delivery by establishing an equal and opposite position in the market. This is known as the **offset provision** of a futures contract. A market participant with a long position, for example, would sell an equal amount of the same contract and similarly a "short" would buy an equal amount of the same contract. To illustrate this point, suppose that a "long" established a position in the June delivery cycle of the CBOTs Treasury bond futures contract at a price of 80-00 on April 1 and sold the contract on May 1 at a price of 81-00. On April 1, the market participant established an initial margin deposit of $2,000. Ignoring the day-to-day movements, on May 1 the contract holder would have received the initial margin of $2,000 plus $1,000 in profit less commissions. **Commissions** on futures contracts are generally quoted on a round turn basis (including both the purchase and sale) and are levied at the time that the position is liquidated. The number of transactions that take place in the market during any given day is termed the **volume.** The number of positions remaining outstanding at the end of a day that have not been offset is termed the **open interest** (the outstanding purchases or sales).

TYPES OF ORDERS. Futures markets allow a wide variety of orders to be entered. Nevertheless, orders fall into three broad categories: market orders, limit orders, and contingent orders. A **market order** is an order to buy or sell at the best possible price available in the market. A **limit order** is an order to buy or sell at a predetermined price. To illustrate this with the previous example, assume that the market participant had ordered his or her futures commission merchant to enter an order on April 1 to buy the June Treasury bond futures contract with a limit of 80-00 or better. (A limit order can always be satisfied at a lower price if it is a purchase or a higher price if it is a sale.) **Contingent orders** may refer to actions that must be taken if certain prior conditions are satisfied. The most widely used contingent orders are **stop limits** and orders that have time contingencies. A stop limit order specifies that a contract should be bought or sold only if a particular price is reached. An illustration of such an order would be a market participant that sold the June Treasury bond futures contract at 80-00 on April 1, placing an order to buy one June contract at 82-00 stop. If the price of the June contract reaches 82-00, then this order is transformed into an order to buy one June T-bond contract at the market. This mechanism is frequently used by participants to limit potential losses. Another type of contingent order refers to the time of day an order is to be executed. A market participant electing to purchase June T-bond futures might, for example, enter an order to buy at the close as **market on close (MOC).** Limit or contingent orders may be entered for a single day or perhaps for a longer period of time such as a month. The latter case is referred to as an **open order.**

FLOW OF ORDERS. Orders to buy or sell can reach the trading floor in several distinct ways. An order may be entered through an account executive or a **Registered Commodity Representative (RCR)** at the branch office of a futures commission merchant. The order might then be telexed to a central order desk which then wires the order to the floor. Next, the order is transmitted by a **"runner"** (who carries the order to the trading pit or ring) where it is executed by a **floor broker**—a member licensed by the exchange and by the Commodity Futures Trading Commission to perform this function. All orders are made by **open outcry,** often supplemented by **hand signals.** The **trading pit** is divided in such a manner that different delivery months are executed in different portions of the pit or ring. Once the order has been executed, the process takes place in reverse, and the market participant is notified of this action by the RCR. A confirmation of the action is then sent by mail on the following day. Orders might reach the exchange floor by telephone directly from the RCR or from an order desk. To facilitate the quickest possible execution, large market participants often call the trading floor directly and place an order with a member of the exchange. In many instances large participants have direct lines to the trading floor.

FLOOR TRADING. The trading pit, or ring, contains floor brokers and speculators. This latter category fulfills several different functions. It includes **market makers,** also referred to as **scalpers,** that simply may agree to make a market to buy or sell in a particular delivery month. **Day traders** will buy and sell throughout the day but normally do not hold positions overnight. Nevertheless both types of participants provide liquidity and bridge the gap between orders from buyers to sellers who trade from outside the exchange floor. Another type of pit trader is the **spreader,** who buys and sells different contract months of the same commodity, instrument, or index. It is the spreader's function to maintain the appropriate equilibrium price relationship between different delivery months. Floor traders also may be professional speculators, who establish positions in a market for extended periods of time. Many of these individuals may initiate and liquidate positions based on fundamental macro or micro relationships or on the basis of previous price relationships or technical analysis. Their actions also provide greater liquidity for hedgers.

THE LINK BETWEEN CASH AND FUTURES MARKETS: THE BASIS

The **basis** is the price difference between the cash market commodity and the corresponding futures contract at a particular time. Factors that influence the basis include:

1. Specific futures contract month
2. Interest rate levels and risk differentials
3. Yield curve configuration
4. Price relationships between deliverable grades of the cash commodity or instrument
5. Carrying costs including financing, storage, and insurance
6. Seasonal supply and demand factors
7. Transportation costs
8. Costs of making or taking delivery
9. Changing supply and demand conditions or variations in quality over time and/or location

Several of these factors play roles in the basis relationships of agricultural and metal futures contracts, but the first few items are the most important for most financial futures contracts. Exhibit 9 displays the cash and futures markets discount interest rates for 3-month Treasury bills, respectively, as well as their **basis relationship.** (The data are displayed as interest rates rather than prices; prices are determined by the IMM index equal to 100.00 minus the discount interest rates.) The CMEs T-bill **contract specifications** call for the delivery of a T-bill with a face value of maturity of $1 million and maturing exactly 90

EXHIBIT 9 TREASURY BILL FUTURES BASIS (3-MONTH DISCOUNT INTEREST RATE)

Date	Spot Market	IMM T-bill Futures (June 1984)[a]	Basis
May 1	9.71	10.05	−.34
2	9.71	10.10	−.39
3	9.70	10.13	−.43
4	9.92	10.30	−.38
7	9.95	10.39	−.44
8	10.05	10.36	−.31
9	9.99	10.42	−.43
10	9.87	10.38	−.51
11	10.02	10.49	−.47
14	9.98	10.46	−.48
15	10.00	10.42	−.42
16	9.80	10.27	−.47
17	9.83	10.41	−.58
18	9.80	10.31	−.51
21	9.74	10.28	−.54
22	10.06	10.38	−.32
23	9.97	10.27	−.30
24	9.67	9.96	−.29
25	9.62	9.82	−.20
29	9.64	9.86	−.22
30	9.73	9.82	−.09
31	9.75	9.82	−.07
June 1	9.82	9.87	−.05
4	9.85	9.83	.02
5	9.75	9.73	.02
6 (10.00 A.M.)	9.73	9.72	.01

[a] Discount rate basis at market close.

days from the first of three delivery days. The first delivery day is the first day of the cycle month on which a 13-week T-bill is issued and a previously issued 1-year T-bill has 13 weeks remaining to maturity. Because there is very little variation with respect to quality, quantity, and delivery date in the contract, the basis relationship diminishes as the **cash and futures markets converge on delivery.** The day-to-day changes in the basis were also much more muted than were the day-to-day price changes in both the cash and futures markets. The convergence over time of the prices in the T-bill cash and futures markets is heavily dependent on the shape of money market yield curve over the period as well as the fact that the two instruments are functionally identical upon delivery. As a result, **cash/futures arbitrage** (buying the cash instrument and selling the futures contract, or vice versa) typically produces a relatively tight basis relationship. Most of the convergence shown in Exhibit 9 represents, for example, a change in the T-bill futures caused by a movement down the money market yield curve from 4 to 3 months because the yield curve profile was upward sloping over this period.

A more problematic basis relationship exists when the contract specifications allow for the delivery of more than one class or grade of commodity or instrument or when cash/futures arbitrage opportunities are limited for any number of reasons (institutional rigidities, government regulations, etc.). For example, the CBOTs Treasury bond futures contract specifications allow the "short" to deliver to the "long" any U.S. Treasury bond that has at least 15 years until maturity from the delivery day if not callable or, if callable, 15 years until the call date. The T-bond contract is based on a 15-year, $100,000 face value bond carrying an 8% coupon, but coupons other than 8% and with longer maturities can be delivered by an invoicing process employing factor adjustments. This process allows market participants to determine which of the various qualifying bonds is "cheapest-to-deliver" by comparing each issue's invoice amount with its market price. Market participants holding long positions can usually expect to receive the cheapest-to-deliver issue (or issues) assuming that other factors, such as an adequate supply, do not interfere. The delivery period for the Treasury bond contract is from the beginning business day to the last business day of the delivery month. Deliveries are typically concentrated in the last few days when the yield curve is upward sloping. The prices of two deliverable Treasury bonds are displayed in Exhibit 10 together with the settlement prices of the December 1984 T-bond futures contract. Also displayed are the respective bases for each issue after prices have been factor-adjusted, and the data demonstrate that the 7⅝s issue was cheaper to deliver than the 11¾s throughout the period.

The **S&P 500 Stock Price Index futures contract** is based on the broadly

EXHIBIT 10 TREASURY BOND FUTURES BASIS (PRICES IN POINTS AND 32NDS)

	Cash Market		DEC	Cash/Futures Basis (32nds)	
Date	7⅝s of '07	11¾s of '14	T-Bond Futures	7⅝s	11¾s
Nov. 29	70–07	102–19	72–14	−9	−35
30	69–11	101–09	71–20	−6	−29
Dec. 3	69–15	101–17	71–25	−5	−30
4	69–23	101–30	72–02	−4	−31
5	69–22	101–25	71–31	−6	−30
6	69–12	101–09	71–19	−8	−31
7	68–23	100–11	70–30	−7	−30
10	69–04	100–27	71–13	−6	−25
11	69–16	101–11	71–26	−5	−23
12	69–24	101–18	72–01	−6	−20
13	68–30	100–21	71–09	−4	−25
14	69–24	101–19	72–03	−4	−18
17	70–00	102–03	72–15	−1	−18
18	71–06	103–16	73–22	−1	−8
19 (noon)	70–24	102–28	73–08	−1	−8

[a] The factors for the 7⅝s and 11¾s were 0.9655 and 1.4012, respectively.

based index of common stocks. The pricing of a stock index futures contract relative to its underlying spot index is similar to other financial futures contracts. However, the cash/futures bases of these contracts has been somewhat more volatile than for most interest rates or foreign currency futures contracts, reflecting both the relatively short period of their existence and the relative difficulty of cash/futures arbitrage activity, even by institutional investors. Most of the stock index futures contracts are based on indexes that contain a large number of issues. This feature makes such arbitrage activities difficult because of both transaction costs and the need for simultaneous transactions. The cash/futures basis displayed in Exhibit 11 demonstrates, for example, wide basis swings over a relatively short period of time, although the convergence of the index and futures contract occurred on the final settlement day.

RELATIONSHIP BETWEEN CONTRACT MONTHS. In addition to the cash/futures basis relationship, the prices of the various **contract months** will display a profile that also reflects such factors as carrying costs and interest rate differentials. For agricultural and other nonfinancial futures contracts, a normal or carrying change market is reflected in futures contract prices that increase with maturity. In these instances, the **contract spreads** (or differences between successive contracts) are negative, because contract month-to-contract month differences often reflect and are generally only limited on the upside by carrying costs such as storage, financing, and insurance. The opposite condition, an **inverted market,** is present when succeeding contract prices decrease with maturity. Prospects of a shortage in the delivery process, strong expectations of lower prices, or interest rate differentials may lead to such a condition.

Most financial futures contracts are based, on the other hand, on instruments or indexes that yield a return to the holder in the form of interest payments or dividends. Because this is the case, the time profile of futures contracts will usually depend on the cash-and-carry relationship of purchasing the deliverable instrument in the cash market and simultaneously being short a future contract against it. If the cash market vehicle yields more than it costs to finance it until delivery **(positive carry),** then successive contracts will typically sell at prices below the spot market price. Similarly, when the yield curve is **inverted (negative carry),** then the prices of financial futures contracts typically rise as maturity increases. Finally, a hybrid V or inverted-V shape sometimes can result from a combination of two basic types of markets.

HEDGING

REQUIREMENTS OF A HEDGE. As noted previously, hedging is broadly defined as a temporary substitute for a spot market transaction with an objective of protection against adverse price movements. Effective hedging is predicated on two assumptions: (1) a high correlation between cash and futures prices, and (2) convergence between these prices as the delivery and/or final

EXHIBIT 11 S&P 500 INDEX FUTURES BASIS (POINTS)

Date	Spot Index	DEC S&P Futures	Cash/Futures Basis
Oct. 15	165.77	168.80	−3.03
16	164.78	167.95	−3.17
17	164.14	167.65	−3.51
18	168.10	172.75	−4.65
19	167.95	171.75	−3.80
22	167.36	171.45	−4.09
23	167.09	171.55	−4.46
24	167.20	171.25	−4.05
25	166.31	168.95	−2.64
29	164.78	167.60	−2.82
30	166.84	169.50	−2.66
31	166.09	168.60	−2.51
Nov. 1	167.49	170.40	−2.91
2	167.41	170.05	−2.64
5	168.58	170.70	−2.12
7	169.17	170.05	−0.88
8	168.68	170.15	−1.47
9	167.60	168.55	−0.95
13	165.97	167.25	−1.28
14	165.99	167.40	−1.41
15	165.89	167.60	−1.71
16	164.10	165.85	−1.75
19	163.09	164.75	−1.66
20	164.18	165.90	−1.72
21	164.52	166.55	−2.03
23	166.92	168.00	−1.08
26	165.55	166.80	−1.25
27	166.29	168.20	−1.91
28	165.01	166.00	−0.99
29	163.91	164.85	−0.94
30	163.58	164.55	−0.97
Dec. 3	162.81	164.15	−1.34
4	163.38	164.30	−0.92
5	162.10	162.65	−0.55
6	162.76	163.20	−0.44
7	162.26	162.45	−0.19
10	162.82	163.75	−0.93
11	163.07	163.95	−0.88
12	162.62	163.30	−0.68
13	161.81	161.70	0.11
14	162.69	163.05	−0.36
17	163.61	164.10	−0.49
18	168.11	168.35	−0.24
19	167.16	167.60	−0.44
20	166.38	166.40	−0.02

settlement period approaches. Both the cash and futures markets prices generally should move in the same direction, because both markets share a common set of factors. Moreover, the difference between the cash and futures market prices should narrow over time as the futures contract becomes functionally equivalent to the cash commodity or instrument while approaching its expiration date. As long as certain basis relationships between futures and cash markets do not change, a price movement in the cash commodity or instrument can be mostly offset by an equal and opposite price movement in a futures position.

It is probably accurate to state that designing and implementing a hedge is more of an art than a science, although most risk managers are increasingly applying modern statistical and financial techniques to structure hedging programs. A futures market hedging program effectively takes most of the price risk associated with a position (long or short) in a commodity, instrument, or index and transforms it into basis risk. A well-designed hedge should result in a level of **basis risk** that is substantially smaller than the price risk of the unhedged position. Thus the objective of a hedging program should be to minimize basis risk and to maximize basis profits. Hedging programs must begin by first identifying the price risk to be hedged, and next this price risk must be measured. Once identified and measured, the price risk can be hedged in futures markets if the overall price risk of the position can be reduced by adding the futures position to the portfolio. Several methods with various degrees of complexity can be utilized to determine the appropriate number of futures contracts (the **hedge ratio**) to employ. Broadly speaking, these ratios can be determined by relying on either historical relationships and/or the theoretical relationship between the prices of the cash and futures market instruments. In most instances, however, the price correlations between the cash and futures markets will be less than perfect due to maturity and instrument mismatches, so that some amount of basis risk is inescapable.

TYPES OF HEDGES. A **short hedge** is appropriate when one owns or expects to own the cash commodity or instrument and accordingly sells futures contracts to be protected against declines in price. If the price movements in the cash and the futures markets positions are approximately equal, then the overall position is considered a **total hedge;** if the futures positions are less than the cash position, then it is a **partial hedge.** Hedges are typically unwound or lifted (i.e., the short futures market position is eclipsed by buying back the contract) when the cash market position is liquidated.

The success of a hedge is gauged by its downside risk protection and on fluctuations in the basis. The short hedge benefits by a narrowing of the basis if the price of the futures contract is executed above the cash market price and a widening of the basis if the futures position is sold under the cash. As noted previously, most fixed income financial futures contracts are based on an asset yielding an interest return such that the futures prices are below their spot market counterparts. In those instances, a widening in the basis will typically enhance the overall results of a hedge, whereas a narrowing of the basis will detract somewhat from the overall results. It should be clear that basis movements can either contribute or detract from the overall results.

Short Hedge Example One: Price Change Hedge. A mutual fund portfolio manager manages a broadly diversified portfolio, and the manager is concerned that a recent run up in stock prices is vulnerable to a short-run retracement, although the longer-run outlook is favorable. Therefore the portfolio manager needs to sell stock index futures contracts to protect the value of the portfolio from a decline in stock prices. Using statistical techniques, the manager determines that the portfolio has been only 90% as volatile as the S&P 500 stock price index and a high correlation exists between the two. The value of the manager's portfolio on January 3, 1984 is $16.5 million. Because the portfolio has a **beta coefficient** of 0.9, the manager should sell 180 March 1984 S&P 500 stock index futures contracts in order to be fully hedged. The following represents a breakdown of a short hedge using closing settlement prices and assuming that the hedge is lifted on February 15:

Date	Spot Market Position	Futures Market Position	Basis
January 3	Portfolio value is $16,600,000	Sell 180 MAR contracts at 165.80 for a short position of $14,922,000	Spot market S&P 500 index of 164.04 results in a basis of −1.76
February 15	Portfolio value declines by 4.1% to $15,923,300	Buy 180 MAR contracts at 156.90, or a value of $14,121,000	Spot market S&P 500 index of 156.25 results in a basis of −0.65
Results:	Portfolio value declined by $676,700	Futures position gained by $801,000	Basis narrowed by 1.11

As can be seen, the stock portfolio declined by 4.1% percent over the 6-week period, resulting in a decline in value of $676,700. At the same time the futures position gained $801,000 so that the total value of the portfolio increased by $124,300. This improvement was more than accounted for by the narrowing of the MAR basis from −1.76 to 0.65. (Recall that a narrowing of the basis impacts favorably on a short hedge when the price of the futures contract is initiated above the cash market price).

Short Hedge Example Two: Interest Rate Change Hedge. The treasurer of a highly rated U.S. corporation expected in January 1984 to issue $50 million of 20-year bonds in May to finance the company's capital spending program. However, the treasurer was concerned that longer-term interest rates would increase substantially over the period, thereby increasing the project's **cost of capital.** Because a sizable increase in the level of interest rates would jeopardize the profitability of the project, the treasurer elected to determine the cost of the long-term debt issue using the U.S. Treasury Bond futures market. On January 9, 1984, the JUN Treasury bond futures contract was as 69 24/32nds, which is a yield of 12.03% for a 20-year bond with an 8% coupon. Moreover, the treasurer's investment banker determined that the corporation could issue 20-year bonds at a spread of 75 basis points over U.S. Treasury bonds, such as the 9 1/8s of '09 which were selling at 79-00 to yield 11.73% on that day. The treasurer elected to sell 618 JUN T-bond futures contracts (a **hedge ratio** determined by historical data) at 69 24/32nds on January 9 and to repurchase the position on May 15 with the following results:

Date	Spot Market Position	Futures Market Position	Basis[a]
January 9	Proxy: U.S Treasury 9 1/8s of '09 priced at 79–00 to yield 11.73%. Firm's estimated borrowing cost equals 12.48%.	Sell 618 JUN T-bond futures at 69 24/32nds (yield of 12.03%)	1 17/32nds
May 15	U.S. Treasury 9 1/8s of '09 priced at 69 6/32nds to yield 13.43%.	Buy 618 JUN T-bond futures at 61 27/32nds (yield of 13.43%)	16/32nds
Results:	Cost of borrowing by firm rose 0.95%, or an opportunity loss of $4,403,950 (the present value of the increased interest expense discounted over 20 years).	Futures position gained $4,886,063	Basis narrowed by 1 1/32nds or $637,313

[a] Factor adjusted.

The treasurer's decision to accept the prevailing cost of borrowing by using the Treasury bond futures market was timely; the previous example demonstrates that longer-term interest rates increased sharply between January and May. As a result the short futures position of 618 JUN T-bond gained more than $4.8 million over the period. At the same time the borrowing cost available to the corporation increased by 0.95%, which translates into a discounted present value interest expense of more than $4.0 million over the 20-year span. (The overall results were also augmented by narrowing in the basis of approximately $637,000 because of the convergence of the cash and futures markets.) The treasurer did not actually have a cash market position over the period, but because the corporation anticipated that it would issue bond in May, the transaction qualifies as an anticipatory hedge transaction.

LONG HEDGE. A long, or buy, hedge utilizes a long position in the futures market and is appropriate when one has sold or expects to sell the cash commodity or instrument and therefore buys futures contracts to be protected against increases in price. In a long hedge the hedger benefits from a narrowing of the basis if the price of the futures positions is bought below the price of the spot market poition and a widening in the basis if the futures price is bought above the spot market price.

Long Hedge Example One: Exchange Rate Change Hedge. The treasurer of a multinational corporation contracts with a British manufacturer in early January 1984 to buy £1 million worth of equipment payable in 60 days. The treasurer wants to defer the payment until the end of the payment period, but is concerned that an increase in the foreign exchange value of the British pound may encroach on the profitability of the transaction. Accordingly, the treasurer elects to hedge the transaction by buying 40 March British pound futures contracts on January 6 and then selling the futures position on March 6. The transaction produced the following results:

Date	Spot Market Position	Futures Market Position	Basis
January 6	Future commitment to deliver £1 million; exchange rate at $1.4040/British pound	Buy 40 MAR BP futures at 1.4070	−.0030
March 6	Delivery of £1,000,000 at $1.4835/British pound	Sell 40 MAR BP futures at $1.4860	−.0025
Results:	The cost of delivery £1 million rose, thereby resulting in an opportunity loss of $79,500	Futures position gained $79,000 (.0790 ÷ .0005) × 40 × $12.50)	Basis narrowed by .0005, or $500

The foreign exchange value of the British Pound rose by 5.6% over the 2-month period, so the treasurer benefitted by the decision to hedge the exposure. The previous results show that an unhedged exposure would have been $79,500 less profitable for the company. The futures position gained, on the other hand, $79,000, and therefore the basis narrowed slightly.

Long Hedge Example Two: Interest Rate Change Hedge. The portfolio manager of an insurance company committed $100 million to an issue of floating rate notes (FRNs) in the second quarter of 1984. The FRN issue bears interest at a rate per annum calculated for each quarterly period equal to 3-month LIBOR plus 100 basis points. The portfolio manager became concerned in early September that 3-month Eurodollar rates would decline over the final quarter of the year. Because a decline in such interest rates would reduce the interest income on the FRNs, the manager decided to hedge the interest rate risk with a 3-month Eurodollar futures contracts. This had the effect of temporarily transforming the FRNs into a **synthetic fixed-rate instrument.** In order to protect against a decline in 3-month Eurodollar rates over the final quarter of the year, the manager purchased 100 Eurodollar futures contracts in the December cycle on September 14, then liquidated the position in December 14 with the following results:

Date	Spot Market Position	Futures Market Position	Basis
September 14	Three-month LIBOR at 11.75% (equivalent to 88.25)	Buy 100 DEC ED futures contracts at 88.24 (11.76%)	0.01
December 14	Three-month LIBOR at 9.00% (equivalent to 91.00)	Sell 100 DEC ED futures contracts at 90.96 (9.04%)	0.04
Results:	Three-month LIBOR declined by 2.75%, thereby reducing the FRNs interest payments by $687,500	Futures position gained 2.72% or $680,000	Basis widened

The portfolio manager was correct in being concerned about the prospects for the FRNs based on 3-month LIBOR. Assuming that the pricing formula for the FRNs was such that the issue reset on or about the days of the futures market transactions, LIBOR declined by 275 basis points which translates into reduced interest income of $687,500 over a 3-month period. At the same time the futures position gained $680,000 with the difference, $7,500, being attributed to a shift in the basis.

ACCOUNTING FOR HEDGES. The rapid growth of financial futures and options on futures in recent years resulted in uncertainties arising in the accounting treatment of hedges. In December 1980 the **Accounting Standards Executive Committee of the American Institute of Certified Public Accountants (AICPA)** approved an issues paper, "Accounting for Forward Placement and Standby Commitments and Interest Rate Futures Contracts," that was used as input for the **Financial Accounting Standard Board's (FASB)** project on accounting for interest rate futures. The FASB released **Statement of Financial Accounting Standards No. 80,** "Accounting for Futures Contracts," in August 1984. Statement No. 80 applies to all exchange-traded futures contracts, except foreign currency futures contracts. The accounting and reporting of foreign currency transactions, including futures and forward contracts, are governed by the **FASB Statement No. 52.**

FEDERAL REGULATION

EARLY REGULATION. The federal government's interest in commodity futures dates back to the 1830s. Since 1900 an average of more than two regulatory bills per year have been introduced in Congress. In 1922 Congress enacted the **Grain Futures Act,** replacing the **Futures Trading Act,** which had been declared unconstitutional. Revamped in 1936 as the **Commodities Exchange Act,** this legislation established a ruling agency under the auspices of the **Department of Agriculture** entitled the **Commodity Exchange Authority (CEA).**

THE COMMODITY FUTURES TRADING COMMISSION. The 1936 Act was amended intermittently until Congress established the **Commodity Futures Trading Commission (CFTC)** in a complete legislative overhaul in 1974. The scope of the CFTC Act includes two broad mandates: (1) to protect and strengthen the functional aspects of the futures markets, and (2) to protect the participants themselves. Specifically, the following areas and practices are regulated or prohibited:

1. Market manipulation
2. Dissemination of false information
3. Unfair trading practices
4. Market emergencies
5. Customer moneys
6. Registration of appropriate firms and individuals
7. Record keeping
8. Mandatory reporting requirements

Although jurisdiction as specified by the CFTC includes all commodities traded in organized contract markets, various agencies and governmental units provide input to the commission.

In civil regulatory matters, the CFTC retains jurisdiction over the exchanges and registered participants, but cedes to individual states the enforcement capability against those dealing with the public.

REQUIRED REPORTING. Besides requiring certain information to be filed for individuals, the CFTC requires financial statements, certain minimum financial standards, thorough record keeping, and reporting by futures commission merchants. The CFTC also acts as a watchdog and sets guidelines for commodity trading advisers, pool operators, and floor brokers to protect customers. To curb excessive speculation the CFTC sets position limits on certain futures contracts and establishes minimum reporting levels. In addition to its regulatory capacity, the CFTC regularly publishes pertinent information regarding participant composition and deliverable supply status.

THE NATIONAL FUTURES ASSOCIATION. The **National Futures Association (NFA)** formally applied to the CFTC for recognition in late 1981. The NFA is an organization aimed at providing a self-regulatory program for futures markets participants similar to the **National Association of Securities Dealers.** The NFA establishes, among other things, industrywide ethical codes and a forum for the arbitration of certain customer-broker disputes. The NFA does not enact, however, any rules affecting the specifications of any futures contracts or the execution of transactions. Membership in the NFA is open to futures market participants (including financial and nonfinancial firms) and to futures industry professionals.

It is important to stress that the NFA, CFTC, and the organized exchanges provide the framework in which the economic and social benefits of futures markets can be realized. Increased volatility in markets as well as innovation in new areas should provide an environment for futures markets to prosper and serve the hedging and trading needs of a wide variety of users.

BIBLIOGRAPHY

Annual Databook, Commodities Futures Trading Commission.

Arthur Andersen & Co., "Interest Rate Futures Contracts: Accounting and Control Techniques for Banks," Chicago, IL, 1978.

———, "Federal Income Tax Implications," Chicago, IL, 1979.

———, "Accounting for Interest Rate Futures: An Explanation of FASB Statement No. 80," Chicago, IL, 1984.

Chicago Board of Trade, "Financial Instruments Markets: Cash-Futures Relationships," Chicago, IL.

———, "A Guide To Financial Futures at the Chicago Board of Trade," Chicago, IL.

Commodity Futures Trading Commission, "Annual Report," Government Printing Office, Washington, DC.

Commodity Trading Manual, Chicago Board of Trade, Chicago, IL, 1982.

Commodity Year Book, Commodity Research Bureau, New York, NY (annual).

The Dow Jones Commodities Handbook, A Guide to Major Futures Markets, Princeton, NJ: Dow Jones Books (annual).

Hieranymous, Thomas, *Economics of Futures Trading for Commercial and Personal Profit,* New York: Commodity Research Bureau, 1977.

Hill, Joanne and Schneeweis, Thomas, "The Economic Role of Financial Futures Markets," American Enterprise Institute, Washington, DC, 1983.

Irwin, Scott and Peck, Anne E. "Margins on Futures Markets: Contract Security and Pricing Performance," American Enterprise Institute, 1984.

Jones, Oliver H., *Financial Futures Markets—An Operations Guide,* Chicago, IL: U.S. League of Savings Institutions, 1983.

Kaufman, Perry J. (ed.), *Handbook of Futures Markets,* New York: Wiley, 1984.

Labuszewski, John W. and Sinquefield, Jeanne Cairns, *Inside the Commodity Options Markets,* New York: Wiley, 1984.

Loosigian, Allan, *Interest Rate Futures,* Princeton, NJ: Dow Jones, 1980.

McMillian, Larry, *Options as a Strategic Investment,* New York: Institute of Finance, 1980.

Mains, Norman E., and Sandor, Richard L., "Financial Futures and Mortgage-Backed Securities," in *The Handbook of Mortgage-Backed Securities,* Frank J. Fabozzi (ed.), Chicago, IL: Probus Publishing, 1984.

Paul, Allen B., "The Role of Cash Settlement in Futures Contract Specification," American Enterprise Institute, Washington, DC, 1980.

Powers, Mark J. and Vogel, David J., *Inside the Financial Futures Markets,* New York: Wiley, 1981.

Rebell, Arthur, and Gordon, G., *Financial Futures and Investment Strategy,* Homewood, IL: Dow Jones-Irwin, 1984.

Rothstein, Nancy H. (ed.), *The Handbook of Financial Futures,* New York: McGraw-Hill, 1984.

Rules and Regulations, various exchanges.

Schwager, Jack D., *A Complete Guide to the Futures Markets,* New York: Wiley, 1984.

Schwartz, Edward, *How To Use Interest Rate Futures,* Homewood, IL: Dow Jones-Irwin, 1979.

Statistical Annuals and Yearbooks, various exchanges.

Stein, Jerome L., "Futures Markets and Capital Formation," American Enterprise Institute Occasional Paper on the Economics and Regulation of Futures Markets, Washington, DC, 1984.

Stigum, Marcia, *The Money Market,* rev. ed., Homewood, IL: Dow Jones-Irwin, 1983.

Study of the Effects of the Economy of Trading in Futures and Options, Board of Governors of the Federal Reserve System, CFTC, and SEC, U.S. Government Printing Office, Washington, DC.

Tomek, William G., "Margins on Futures Contracts: Their Economic Roles and Regulation," American Enterprise Institute, Washington, DC, 1981.

Van Horne, James C., *Financial Markets Rates and Flows,* 2d ed., Englewood Cliffs, NJ: Prentice-Hall, 1984.

9

THE SECURITIES INDUSTRY: SECURITIES TRADING AND INVESTMENT BANKING

CONTENTS

9

THE SECURITIES INDUSTRY: SECURITIES TRADING AND INVESTMENT BANKING

W. Michael Keenan

WHAT IS THE SECURITIES INDUSTRY?

A SMALL INDUSTRY. Most people have some idea of what constitutes the securities industry in this country; it is the brokerage firms with whom they do business and the securities exchanges on which the common stocks of larger firms are traded. And indeed, it is the securities brokerage firms and exchanges, plus related commodity broker groups, that constitute most of the industry as defined by the Standard Industrial Classification codes of the federal government. By this definition there are about 350,000 people employed in the securities industry throughout the United States. This is small compared with the more than 380,000 people employed by the Ford Motor Company alone.

SCOPE OF THE INDUSTRY. This complex industry is broader than the preceding narrow definition suggests. The economic impact of the industry is far greater than the impact of any single firm of 350,000 employees. The securities industry includes: (1) the suppliers of securities—the industry's clients; (2) the buyers of securities—the industry's customers; (3) the inner industry—brokerage firms, exchanges, associations; (4) industry regulators—self-regulatory groups, the Securities and Exchange Commission, and others; (5) direct supporting services—transfer of certificates, custodial services, special communications networks; and (6) other supporting services—legal, accounting, educational, outside computer support, office space, and indirect service requirements. Many of these groups are not counted as part of the securities industry, but they are essential to its operation.

SUPPLIERS OF SECURITIES. The suppliers can be divided into four categories: (1) the federal government and its agencies, (2) state and local governments, (3) private business firms, and (4) individuals. The problems in properly defining the scope of the securities industry are immediately apparent on listing the suppliers of securities. For example, should trading and distribution of short-maturity securities be counted as part of the securities industry? In the case of short-term government debt and commercial paper, the primary intermediaries—banks and finance companies—are not counted as part of the securities industry. On the other hand, trading and promotion of some short-maturity equity-type instruments such as options, commodity contracts, even commodity contracts in short-term government debt, are considered to be functions of the securities industry.

BUYERS OF SECURITIES. The buyers are usually divided into two groups: individuals and institutions. It is sometimes said that the former are nonprofessionals or amateurs in the investment process, whereas the latter are "professionals" in securities transactions. There is no systematic difference between the two groups in investment returns earned over the long run, but there are differences between the two groups. Pension fund managers, insurance companies, mutual funds, and other institutional buyers tend to transact larger amounts and with greater frequency than individuals. The typical institutional portfolio will be more diversified than the individual's portfolio, having a larger number of securities whose returns are not highly correlated than the typical individual's portfolio. And institutions are more likely to support their transactions' decisions with formal research or background data for the issuer of the security being bought or sold. Institutions hold most of the debt instruments outstanding in the United States, including 80% of the corporate debt. Institutions are responsible for two-thirds of the public volume on the New York Stock Exchange, but individuals still own directly about 70% of the value of stock outstanding in this country.

SUPPORTING SERVICES. These include direct supporting services—facilities necessary for the day-to-day conduct of the business, and other supporting services that are necessary chiefly because this industry exists with people to be fed and housed, rather than because of the particular nature of brokerage firm activities. Direct supporting services relate to the registration, transfer, custodial care, and physical transportation of securities. Providing such services has traditionally been a complex activity. Because more than one brokerage firm is involved, and because the valuable nature of the instruments requires considerable security, usually a third party participates. Commercial banks have long assumed major responsibility for registration and transfer activities and have been significant in providing custodial arrangements. Other firms have also specialized in such activities and in providing the bonded messenger services necessary to move securities. As long as physical delivery of securities was the customary mode of business, these services had to be in close proximity to the brokerage firms and major customer groups—and that meant the Wall Street area.

With the advent of computer balancing of securities transactions, with changes in perceived legal requirements by major customer groups (particularly pension and mutual funds) so that direct physical possession of all securities is not always required, and with the increased volume of trading, the whole back-office procedure is changing rapidly. Now regional consortia associated with the various exchanges handle many of the clearing and custodial functions. Equity securities are increasingly immobilized (i.e., not subjected to actual physical transfer). This is the most significant technological change to occur in the securities industry this century. Although the same sort of progress has not been made for debt securities, it is likely to develop over the next decade. By the end of the century the "direct supporting services" as they existed at mid-century will be gone. Perhaps 50,000 jobs in close proximity to the financial community will be replaced by fewer than 5000 jobs associated with a national clearing and depository service. That national center need not be located in close proximity to the financial community.

The other direct supporting service is the telecommunications network. The securities industry requires a higher level of rapid communication than do most industries. A significant portion of the hardware is not directly owned within the industry, however, but is equipment rented or leased from outside suppliers.

Other supporting services may be divided into those that provide services to the firms in the securities industry and those that provide services to the employees in the industry. The following are included in the first group: (1) real estate owners and brokers—most of the physical facilities in the securities industry are not owned by firms in the industry; (2) legal and accounting services, particularly for investment banking functions; (3) specialized printing firms—to produce securities, registration forms, industry reports, specialized newspapers, and so on; (4) external computer support groups; and (5) specialized educational units and libraries.

The second group includes: luncheon clubs, bars and sandwich shops, transportation services, small retail stores, and all the variety of indirect services supplied simply because a community of people exists—incremental police, fire, and hospital protection, grocery stores, and the rest.

FUNCTIONS OF THE SECURITIES INDUSTRY

There are at least four distinguishing **functions** performed by the securities industry. One is to make more orderly the buying and selling of existing securities. Another is to promote the raising of certain types of new capital for public and private groups. A third function is to analyze financial and economic information, to make the capital markets more efficient by relating such information to security value or the proper utilization of new investment flows. A fourth function is to use such analysis and other tools in managing pools of investment capital.

ORDERLY MARKETS. The primary function of a securities market is to provide a "meeting place" for buyers and sellers to effect transactions. Historically, early security marketplaces (in France and England in the late seventeenth century, in the United States at the end of the eighteenth century) were literally designated taverns or lanes where buyers and sellers could meet to transact. Eventually these places of convenience became organized into "exchanges." The markets were made orderly by promoting rules and standards for such matters as (1) the hours of operation, (2) the mode of payment for transactions, (3) the process for transferring securities, (4) the description of ethical behavior and the characterization of fraudulent practices, (5) the training required for those providing specialized services or acting as agents in the marketplace, and (6) the fees to be charged for various services provided.

Modern markets for the exchange of securities can be put together in numerous diverse ways. Exhibit 1 suggests three organizing elements: type of buyer representation, type of seller representation, and the market process for effecting transactions. There are 12 combinations of the buyer-seller-market process elements.

The buyer-seller representation can be either an **agency transaction** (acting on behalf of another) or a **principal transaction** (acting on behalf of oneself). The prices of the security may be posted, as is true for most retail goods markets. Or the pricing may be determined by direct negotiation between buyer and seller, as it usually is in a used car market. The price may be determined by some type of auction system, where buyers display their "bid" prices and sellers display their "offer" prices and there is a mechanism for insuring that transactions occur according to an agreed upon set of rules. There are many types of **auction markets,** from the continuous auction market with specialist intervention of the New York Stock Exchange, to the periodic auction markets with round-robin calls once a day of some European exchanges.

Some examples may make the alternative structures clearer. Suppose that you want to buy a U.S. Savings Bond. This is likely to be a case of a buyer principal (you), buying from a selling agent (your bank), in a posted pricing

EXHIBIT 1 ORGANIZING ELEMENTS IN A SECURITIES MARKETPLACE

Function	Element
Buyer representation	Agent Principal
Seller representation	Agent Principal
Market process	Posted pricing Negotiated pricing Auction pricing

market. If you ask your broker to buy an insurance stock not listed on any exchange, it could be buyer-agent seller-principal negotiated-market pricing, meaning that your broker is buying for you a stock directly from the owner (who may be another broker holding it in his or her own inventory, or an individual or institution owning the stock), after at least a little negotiation. If you buy a stock on a major stock exchange, it is probably a buyer-agent (your brokerage firm) seller-agent (seller's brokerage firm) auction-pricing transaction. Whatever the elements of a particular market structure, if that market is to persist successfully, there must be rules to give it order.

RAISING NEW CAPITAL. An important part of the investment banking function of the securities industry is the **raising of new capital.** In the United States the securities industry is only one of the groups helping to raise new capital for public and private groups. Commercial banks, insurance companies, other financial institutions, and industrial corporations are all involved in this process. This competitive effort to provide funds for long-term investment has made the U.S. markets for new capital the largest and most efficient in the world.

The magnitude of capital raised is indicated by the benchmark figures in Exhibit 2, which show that less than 10% of the total credit market funds raised in a year consists of the long-term corporate capital usually associated with the

EXHIBIT 2 NET CREDIT MARKET FUNDS RAISED IN 1984 (BILLIONS OF DOLLARS)

Mortgages	$220
U.S. government securities	280
State and local obligations	70
Bank loans	70
Open market paper	50
Other loans	50
Consumer credit	100
Corporate bonds	60
Corporate stocks	(30)
External Funds Raised	$870

INTERNAL FUNDS FROM NONFINANCIAL CORPORATE BUSINESSES

Net income	$120
− dividends	−80
= Earnings retained	40
+ Depreciation and adjustments	280
= Internal Fund Sources	$320

Source: Federal Reserve, "Flow of Funds Summary Statistics," September 18, 1985.

investment banking function of the securities industry. But the securities industry also plays a role in helping to raise government debt capital (particularly state and local obligations), and increasingly has a role in making the mortgage market liquid.

It is important to note that for existing corporations most long-term funds are from internally generated sources—earnings retained in the business and noncash depreciation charges that provide funds if the firm is generating offsetting revenues. In 1984 these internal sources amounted to about $320 billion, whereas the new external capital sources from bonds and stocks amounted to less than $40 billion. The securities industry helped raise most of the net of $30 billion in new outside capital but did not play a direct role in the corporate decisions about inside sources—how much earnings to retain. Securities markets do play an important secondary role in this process, however. The earnings retained by the firms are generally "capitalized" by the marketplace over time; that is, stock prices increase in the expectation that these retained earnings will be reinvested by firms to generate even higher future earnings and dividends. If the capital markets were not reasonably efficient, this whole process could break down. Stockholders would not be as willing to invest in firms that retained earnings, more capital would have to be raised by directly selling new issues (at higher cost), and a smaller fraction of individuals' savings might be held directly in corporate securities.

ANALYZING FINANCIAL AND ECONOMIC INFORMATION. To ascertain whether the earnings retained by firms are usefully invested (to generate even higher future earnings), someone must be prepared to analyze current financial information and future plans of these firms. To a degree, everyone who buys or sells a security must be a bit of a security analyst. But because it takes time and experience to perform this function, an area of professional expertise has developed. The securities industry supports several thousand professional security analysts, and additional thousands are found among the banks, insurance companies, pension fund advisers, and other groups responsible for the investment of significant pools of capital.

A security analyst has the task of analyzing all currently available information to evaluate and project the economic status of the firms, the industry, and the economy. These evaluations and projections are combined into an estimate of the true value of a security (or, more likely, a reasonable range for such value), hence a recommendation to buy or sell the security based on its current market price. Truly superior security analysis thus requires some combination of (1) better information than others have, (2) a superior way to screen out "noise" and locate the essential information, (3) a superior way to make future projections, and (4) more complete or better refined valuation frameworks than others are using. To the extent competitive conditions force professional security analysts to do the best possible job, and the information on how they do that job is quickly disseminated, there may be only a few relatively superior analysts at any one time. See the sections "Modern Portfolio Theory and Management" and "Performance Measurement" for a more extensive discussion of these issues.

The information professional security analysts utilize is supposed to be publicly available. Although an analyst may talk to officers or managers of a firm, they are legally bound not to reveal any new information likely to have a significant impact on the firm's security prices if the information is not also made generally available to the public.

For U.S. corporations with more than a few hundred shareholders, somewhat detailed financial income and balance sheet statements must be released at least yearly. These are distributed to shareholders, creditors, and other interested parties, and copies are filed with the Securities and Exchange Commission. For large, exchange-listed firms more abbreviated reports are distributed quarterly. A significant change in the structure or financial condition of any firm is supposed to be quickly reported to the SEC and announced.

In addition to a firm's own reports, analysts can draw on a great deal of other data. Examples include: (1) government reports and studies; (2) industry trade association reports and magazines; (3) business news publications such as the *Wall Street Journal, BusinessWeek, Forbes,* and *Fortune;* and (4) academic journals and special studies. This wealth of information is a development of the past 100 years in the United States. In some countries today corporations are still required to issue only very abbreviated financial statements. As an adjunct to security analysis, there is the industrial detective agency specializing in ferreting out private financial information. But it is clear that this approach makes value determination more uncertain, and the capital markets less efficient, than is the case when information is more readily available.

MANAGING INVESTMENT CAPITAL. Different sectors of the industry are organized to provide investment capital management services for major capital pools such as mutual funds and pension funds, and for individual brokerage firm clients. Professional investment management is one of the most rapidly growing services offered by the securities industry. This growth results from a need by clients for greater expertise than has traditionally been required.

There are two factors contributing to the expanded specialization of investment capital management. One is the growth in the applications of modern portfolio theory to investment decisions. This requires specialists who have an understanding of the benefits and limitations of such theory, and who have access to the computers, data banks, and security analysts needed to implement the theory. (The theory itself is described in the section "Modern Portfolio Theory and Management.") A second factor is the broadened line of services many brokerage houses have begun to offer individual clients. In addition to advice on traditional stocks and bonds, clients are now being counseled about investment opportunities in real estate and tax shelters, and gold, silver, diamonds, and a variety of other collectibles that may be considered as investment vehicles. To provide such services the brokerage houses have created new subsidiaries, acquired existing firms, or hired special consultants. In addition, some of the larger brokerage firms have extended the scope of their services to include credit management and insurance agency activities, thus offering an almost complete package of financial services.

STRUCTURE OF THE INDUSTRY

A LITTLE BIT OF HISTORY. To better understand the national structure of the securities industry and some currently evolving trends, it is useful to take a selective look at a little bit of history. Some securities trading began in this country with its first settlement. Many of the original colonies represented charter grants from the various crowns of Europe (primarily Spanish, English, and French) to groups that financed initial expeditions by issuing financial instruments to European capitalists. In the case of the land companies some of the deeds and other financial instruments, and some of the capitalists themselves, soon found their way to America. It was natural that some of these instruments would change hands—because of death or gifts, or because of a desire to move or a changed perception of the wealth potential of this new land. Most of these transitions were either private arrangements between the buyer and seller or were carried out in London or another European money center. There was scarcely even an embryonic securities industry in what would become the United States.

The Revolutionary War provided the real impetus for the formation of the securities industry. During the war the Continental Congress, some states, and the Continental Army all issued various notes and forms of scrip. Washington's periodic pleas for more scrip for his army are well known, and the amount forthcoming and its subsequent market value (purchasing power) depended in part on perceptions of how the war was going. After the war the Congress of the newly formed United States funded part of the debt incurred by various states and the debt incurred by the Confederation. This funding of $80 million in federal debt provided the basis on which the securities industry was organized in this country.

As early as May 1792 a group of 24 brokers met in New York City to sign an agreement as to the minimum commission they would charge the public and the terms and conditions for trading among themselves. New York City was then the largest city in the nation (35,000), the state capital of New York, and a principal gateway to Europe. The rates and conditions for consummating trades within the group of brokers were of course more favorable than rates or conditions for brokers not a party to the agreement or for the public at large. This cartel of New York brokers was the precursor of today's **New York Stock Exchange.** In 1817 the brokers adopted a formal constitution and selected the name New York Stock and Exchange Board. This name was shortened in 1863 to New York Stock Exchange (NYSE). Thus the original purpose of the 1792 group was to regulate prices for brokerage services to ensure minimum levels of profitability and to create a systematic procedure for transferring ownership of securities. These remained the principal objectives of the NYSE throughout the first 180 years of its history.

It should be noted that at the outset the NYSE was organized to deal in bonds—the $80 million in federal debt authorized by Congress in accepting most of the Secretary of the Treasury Alexander Hamilton's report; other securities included small amounts of state paper and regionally backed transportation issues. Bonds remained the principal instrument of broker activity for a number of years. The federal government debt rapidly expanded for a period as a result of the War of 1812. After that war various types of transportation issues began to find their way to market. Initially demand for funds came from local turnpike authorities and canal charters, but by 1840 the age of railroads was beginning.

With the substantial reduction in federal government debt in the 1820s, the nature of the Exchange market began to change. Federal bonds became less important. Trading in the transportation bond-type securities became more important, and stocks as an instrument of trading were gaining rapidly in popularity. Whereas most available domestic equities had been the stocks of banks or insurance companies, now some common stock of nonfinancial corporations began to appear. There were two other basic changes in the securities industry in the 1830s and 1840s. First, domestic investment banking houses largely replaced their European predecessors. Although large amounts of capital continued to flow into the United States from European sources, it was now domestic investment bankers who arranged the terms of new securities issues and solicited domestic and foreign buyers.

A second change occurred about the time **gold was discovered in California.** The prospect of potential wealth from underground proved irresistible to many. Mines, mining claims, mining services—some real, some only imagined in the back room of a bar—were all incorporated to sell shares of their stocks to an eager public. It did not seem to matter that many of the mines proved unproductive, or that many of the mining claims were fraudulent or nonexistent. People were willing to gamble on the rumor of a strike, or on the small probability that at the mine they had bought shares in, there would be a strike large enough to make all the owners rich. This sometimes happened, but for many investors the fact that gold was involved was incentive enough. The interesting points about this development from the securities industry viewpoint are that (1) this is probably the first instance of large-scale public participation in the equity markets in the United States, and (2) the securities were promoted and sold not in New York City or other eastern markets, but in the West. Exchanges were organized throughout the West, bringing brokers together to deal in mining stocks and local securities. In most cases these exchanges were short-lived, lasting only so long as the local mines were productive. In some cases not only did the mines peter out, the cities disappeared.

In cumulative numbers there seem to have been more than a hundred such exchanges in the United States. Only a few survived into the twentieth century, shifting focus from gold speculations to silver to oil or uranium as the type of prospecting activity shifted. Why did most of the mining exchanges die? They died because the brokers who organized them could not make enough money. It was not simply that the mines or the stocks listed failed or were worthless claims to begin with. Often the local exchanges were organized at a time of speculative excitement in each area. Much of the activity of the brokers consisted of issuing and promoting the sale of new stock. In the years before the creation of the Securities and Exchange Commission (SEC) this could be done virtually at any time, in any amount, by anyone. The real money opportunities for brokers lay in this promotion of new stock. Although a few brokers might sustain themselves by acting purely as brokerage agents, these were exceptions. And only a few exchanges had enough activity to maintain any sort of existence once the initial new deals, the speculative phase, had passed. The exchanges that did survive were usually in already established cities such as San Francisco, Denver, and Salt Lake City.

The **modern structure of the securities industry** did not appear until 1934, with the enactment of the Securities Exchange Act. The legislation passed in 1933 and 1934 was a direct outgrowth of the collapse of the securities markets in the period 1929–1932. Stock volume and prices had advanced spectacularly in the late 1920s, financed by a very large amount of bank credit. As speculative fever rose and new issues all seemed to climb sharply after their initial distribution, the public crowded into the market. Throughout history, whenever the public (i.e., those who were not part of the wealthiest classes in society) has entered a financial market in significant numbers, it has been a sign of excessive speculation. This was true of the "tulipomania bubble" of the 1630s, when Dutchmen paid fortunes for tulip bulbs. It was true of the "Mississippi Scheme" of the early 1720s, when the frenzied speculative excesses of Frenchmen in the shares of the Mississippi Company virtually bankrupted them and their entire country. We have already noted that in the United States one of the first great waves of public participation in the equity markets was in the short period of mining stock promotions. The game of chance being played toward the end of the 1920s ended in 1929 with the great market crash on Wall Street.

Three points can be made from this brief historical digression. First, New York City became the financial center of the nation because of its close proximity to the suppliers of securities (the federal capital was in New York until 1790), because of the relative proximity to the suppliers of funds (primarily European investment banking groups in the beginning), and because the city had strong prospects of replacing Philadelphia as the commercial center of the nation. Second, for better or worse, the public at large has historically been active in security markets only when speculative instruments were available to be traded. Third, it is not economically feasible to maintain many stock exchanges in a country. Like several other countries, the United States at one time had many local exchanges (more than 100). Now there are fewer than a dozen left. Most countries end up with one or two.

LEGAL ENVIRONMENT. With the collapse of the financial markets in the early 1930s a series of laws was passed to separate commercial banking from investment banking in the United States and to impose stricter federal regulatory oversight on the securities industry. Major laws include the Securities Act (1933); the Securities Exchange Act (1934); acts related to trustee responsibilities—the Trust Indenture Act (1939), the Investment Company Act (1940), and the Investment Advisors Act (1940); and laws passed in the early 1970s—the Securities Investor Protection Corporation Act (1970), the Employee Retirement Income Security Act (1974), and the National Exchange Market System (NEMS) Act (1975).

The primary thrusts of the 1930s acts were to inhibit fraud and deceit in the issuance and trading of securities, and to provide a regulatory framework for federal oversight of the securities industry. The **Securities Act (1933)** focused on new issues. New security issues must be registered with the SEC. Before the securities are offered for sale, audited financial statements, statements about the issuer's business, other securities outstanding, major contracts, salaries and other payments to officers and directors, and other matters must be filed. Much of this is summarized in a **prospectus,** a booklet that must be sent to every customer who purchases part of the new issues. Before the securities are issued, the SEC has a limited period to review the prospectus for completeness of disclosure. The SEC does not, however, pass judgment on the value of the security as an investment—that is the responsibility first of the selling investment banker and ultimately of the buying customer. Small issues, private offerings to a small group of knowledgeable investors, and secondary offerings of already outstanding securities were exempt from registration under the 1933 Act.

The **Securities Exchange Act (1934)** focused on providing information disclosure for already outstanding securities, and on the formal establishment of the SEC as the agency responsible for regulating nongovernmental securities markets. Under this law securities listed for trading must file registration statements and annual reports similar to those filed for new securities. Organized exchanges must register with the SEC, must abide by whatever rules the SEC promulgates, and must put forth bylaws of rules of their own to ensure the orderly operation of the exchanges and the ethical behavior of representatives of member firms. The 1934 Act also provides explicit rules for proxy solicitation (requests to shareholders for their votes), insider trading activities (e.g., officers, directors, and others inside the firm may not earn "speculative trading profits" by buying or selling stock before an important piece of information is made public), and price manipulation schemes. Finally, the Act and associated Federal Reserve regulations enabled a mechanism for controlling credit extended to brokerage firms and their customers in securities transactions.

The acts in the early 1940s primarily involved fiduciary responsibility and related institutional structures. The **Trust Indenture Act (1939)** promulgated rules to avoid some of the conflicts of interest between a firm and the bank or other institution that is trustee for some debt security of the firm. The **Investment Advisors Act (1940)** requires individuals who offer investment advice or analysis for money to register with the SEC, and permits rules to be specified placing limitations on the forms of compensation received and the forms of advertising for new clients. A third piece of legislation was the **Investment**

Company Act (1940), which specified the structural form of operation for mutual funds and closed-end investment companies, as well as the responsibilities of officers, advisers, and others associated with such funds.

In a series of acts passed in the early 1970s, Congress significantly changed the protection accorded individual investors, and recommended procedural steps that will eventually change the structure of the exchange market in this country. The **Securities Investor Protection Act (SIPC) (1970)** provides insurance to small investors for their securities and cash left on deposit with a brokerage firm if that brokerage firm goes bankrupt. Currently the total claims limit is $100,000 per customer, but many firms have private insurance that increases this protection. The **Employee Retirement Income Security At (ERISA) (1974)** and related pieces of legislation significantly changed the protection accorded individuals who participate in pension funds. For company-sponsored pension plans the law requires full vesting of an employee's share within a few years of work, and requires all underfunded plans to become fully funded within the next three decades. For all employees not covered by firm pension plans, and all individuals who are self-employed, there are tax-advantage opportunities to set up their own pension fund account plans. The securities industry has been one of the leaders in providing this service for millions of customers.

A third series of bills, including the **Securities Amendments Act (1975)** (the National Exchange Market System Act), provided some structural direction for future developments in the securities industry. Congress set up a Commodity Futures Trading Commission (CFTC) to provide oversight regulation for the commodities markets and has encouraged some regulation of the markets for state and local government securities, an area outside the jurisdiction of the SEC. In the 1975 Act and during the associated hearings, Congress made clear its preference for more competitive commission rates and related conditions, and encouraged the development of a technologically efficient National Exchange Market System within a reasonable period of time. Details were left to the industry, with the SEC having authority (and responsibility) to step in when necessary. Finally, a proposed new **Federal Securities Code** has been reviewed by the SEC and interested groups inside and outside the industry. Congress has held some hearings on this legislation to determine whether the numerous rule changes in securities transaction codes should become law, but it appears that revisions will be a piecemeal process rather than a broad new piece of legislation.

TYPES OF BROKERAGE FIRMS. In the mid-1970s there were more than 4000 firms in the securities industry, almost 2000 in the New York region alone. By the beginning of the 1980s the nationwide total had declined by 10% or so because of increased competitive conditions within the industry. As part of their reaction to new competitive conditions, many brokerage firms have been making fundamental changes in their organizational structure.

Traditionally brokerage firms were organized as small private partnerships.

Even today that is the primary form of legal organization. The "typical" firm has about 15 employees; two or three partners, perhaps five other professionals, and a small support staff. The firm operates out of one office and has its own equity capital of less than $100,000 invested in the business. Since 1953 the NYSE has permitted its member brokerage firms to incorporate, but at first only as private corporations with restrictions. It was not until 1970 that public ownership of brokerage firm corporations was approved by the NYSE Board of Governors. Even in 1980 more than 200 of the member organizations of the NYSE remained partnerships. Of the more than 300 of these larger brokerage firms that have incorporated, about 15 have public shareholders.

These legal changes are not merely technical changes in the structure and report-filing formats for the firms. Often accompanying the legal change are possible fundamental changes (1) in the administrative structure of the firm (lines of responsibility are more clearly defined); (2) in firm goals (at least in public firms, profits and trends in profits become more important); and (3) in sources of capital for the firms (partnership-subordinated capital is replaced by debt and equity funds raised in the capital markets). Finally, many of the larger brokerage firms have not stopped at incorporation, but have gone on to set up holding company corporate structures. The traditional brokerage firm business thus becomes one subsidiary of a parent company that may seek to diversify into other business opportunities.

Exhibit 3 indicates the variety of brokerage firms by reporting results of a 1979 study of the part of the securities industry that is based in New York. The "principal product line" designation is just a rough guess of the principal type of business, as revealed by directory listings. Only about 10 of the more than 1300 firms represented are public firms that release standard financial reports; the rest of the firms do not. In this sense brokerage firms remain more like partnerships of physicians than like banks or other regulated financial institutions.

Most firms in the New York area are, as expected, small firms operating either in some market-making role or specializing in a few lines of business. Omitted are probably hundreds of "investment counseling" organizations for which almost no information can be obtained. The district is headquarters for about two-thirds of the large brokerage firms in the country. Thus in the same area the firms competing for business range in size from fewer than 10 employees to more than 10,000 employees.

ORGANIZED EXCHANGE MARKETPLACE. The existing securities exchanges plus the National Association of Securities Dealers (NASD) are the primary vehicles for regulation within the industry. Those groups are also the primary organizational structure for trading in already issued equity shares. That there is a potential conflict of interest in this setup is self-evident. Historically, much of the "self-regulation" was aimed at protecting the economic interest of current members by forming price-setting cartels, curtailing entry and exit from the groups, and controlling competition for business in a variety of other ways. For a number of reasons this type of behavior began to break down

EXHIBIT 3 NEW YORK DISTRICT FIRMS ENGAGED IN THE SECURITIES BUSINESS IN 1979[a]

	Number of firms[b]		
Principal Product Line	Small	Medium	Large
Multiple-line products	265	135	55
State and local bonds	90	40	0
Over-the-counter shares	125	15	0
Mutual funds	175	20	5
Floor traders	120	0	0
Specialists	30	30	0
Options dealers	35	5	0
Others	55	15	0
Bank dealers	65	30	30
Foreign firms	10	10	5
Totals = 1365	970	300	95

Regional Breakdown	
New Jersey	180
New York City	985
Other New York State	200
Total	1365

[a] The number of NASD member firms in the district was aproximately 900 in 1979.

[b] Firm size based on the estimated number of employees: small, 0–25; medium, 26–250; large, 251–up.

Source: Goldberg and Keenan, *The New York Based Securities Industry: 1979 Survey,* Occasional Papers in Metropolitan Business and Finance (1980, No. 2), New York University, Graduate School of Business, New York, NY.

rapidly in the 1970s. Now the focus is much more on providing brokerage exchange services and on auditing the behavior of member firms.

Exhibit 4 lists **securities exchanges** that were operating in the 1980s. In addition there are more than 10 active commodity exchanges in the United States. The most rapidly growing segments of exchange business at the beginning of the 1980s were the options and financial futures lines of business. Most exchanges have set up subsidiaries to compete for some part of this business, but the results are not always successful. The American Stock Exchange Commodities Exchange in effect went out of business in 1980, with the pieces absorbed by the New York Stock Exchange Futures Exchange.

The **New York Stock Exchange** is the largest stock exchange in the United States. Like many brokerage firms, the exchange was reorganized in the early 1970s to a structure that closely parallels that of a private holding company corporation. Now governed by a board of directors, NYSE is made up of about 10 public representatives, 10 representatives of exchange member groups, and a full-time paid chairman. He is assisted in operating management and policy planning by a number of executive officers. At present the NYSE has the following operating divisions: (1) market operations, to handle trading and facili-

EXHIBIT 4 SELF-REGULATING ORGANIZATIONS

American Stock Exchange
Boston Stock Exchange
Chicago Board Options Exchange
Chicago Board of Trade
Chicago Mercantile Exchange

Cincinnati Stock Exchange
Detroit Stock Exchange[a]
Intermountain Stock Exchange[a]
Midwest Stock Exchange
National Association of Securities Dealers (NASD)

New York Futures Exchange
New York Stock Exchange
Pacific Stock Exchange
Pittsburgh-Baltimore-Washington Stock Exchange[a]
Philadelphia Stock Exchange

Public Securities Association
Spokane Stock Exchange[a]

[a] Exchange is virtually inactive.

ties management; (2) member firm regulation and surveillance, to provide the regulatory oversight required of the exchange; (3) finance and office services management; (4) product development and planning; and (5) marketing services and customer relations. In addition there are specialized staff groups to handle legal problems and government relations, economic research, personnel relations, and similar activities. Some of the specialized functions in the operation of the NYSE have been transferred to subsidiary corporations, only partly controlled by the NYSE itself.

Important service-related corporations only partly controlled by the NYSE include the following three firms, each with its own officers and board of directors. The **National Securities Clearing Corporation (NSCC),** organized in 1977 and one-third owned by the NYSE, was formed by the merger of similar subsidiaries at the NYSE and American Stock Exchange with the National Clearing Corporation. The NSCC is essentially a channel through which the books of brokerage firms, exchanges, and other clearing corporations are brought into balance. The **Depository Trust Company,** organized in 1973 and about 40% owned by the exchange, is a central certificate depository organized by the NYSE, American Stock Exchange, banks, and others to immobilize the physical transfer of securities. The third organization, the **Securities Industry Automation Corporation (SIAC),** was organized in 1972 and is two-thirds owned by the NYSE and one-third owned by the American Stock Exchange. Much of the communications and computer facilities and systems now necessary to operate the exchange are provided by SIAC.

At present the NYSE has a total voting membership of 1366. Only individuals may be members of the NYSE, although in most cases the individual is acting as a representative of a firm. There are about 630 brokerage firms represented on the NYSE. Almost 400 of these are firms dealing in some way with the public; the other 230 are specialists and others who do not deal directly with the public. One of the issues in the early 1970s was whether banks, insurance companies, or others who were major customers of exchange member brokers, should be allowed to become exchange members. In general the answer was no (although there were exceptions, particularly if the institution did no trading for its own account or was foreign based), and the issue died once negotiated commission rates became possible. At the beginning of the 1980s the issues were how to expand voting membership without decreasing the value of existing seats, and whether voting power should be shifted more toward the firms that provide much of the exchange's revenues than is currently the case. These issues are still not resolved.

Typically the largest public corporations are listed for trading on the NYSE and they are handled by brokerage firms large enough to be members of the exchange. But there are thousands of traded securities not listed on any exchange, and thousands of individuals and firms in the brokerage industry that are not exchange members. Regulatory oversight for these usually smaller brokerage firms, and for the trading done in private securities away from an exchange floor, is provided by (NASD). The traditional role or NASD has been to help provide a structure for the training and registering of individuals and firms not part of an exchange, and to provide regulatory oversight for the trading and clearance of nonexchange-listed securities (called over-the-counter securities, hence OTC markets). In the past decade, however, NASD and private computer firms have been developing a computerized communications network that permits member dealers to display price information and do some computer-linked trading for the more active OTC stocks. Moreover, SEC rule changes permit the trading of some exchange-listed securities on this system. Thus NASD is in the process of creating a new nationwide exchange with characteristics quite different from the other existing exchanges.

GOVERNMENT REGULATORY GROUPS. The principal government regulator for the securities industry since the 1930s has been the **Securities and Exchange Commission.** The SEC is charged with regulating the issuance of securities, specifying the information to be provided periodically to owners, and regulating the exchanges and brokerage firms that are at the core of the distribution-trading process. In addition to SEC regulations, the Federal Reserve Board has jurisdiction over the amount of credit that can be extended to customers and brokers for the securities they buy. The Department of the Treasury plays a minor role when international transactions are involved—particularly for foreign governments or agencies selling bonds in the United States, but also for private foreign purchases and sales.

Two new federal agencies were created in the 1970s to provide regulatory oversight. The **Securities Investor Protection Corporation (1970)** provides insurance to small investors for the cash and securities left on deposit with a broker. The SIPC has authority to liquidate bankrupt brokerage firms and is seeking authority to merge or dissolve "troubled" firms before they become insolvent. The **Commodity Futures Trading Commission (1975)** was created to provide regulatory oversight for the rapidly developing commodities markets in the United States. Because both the exchanges and the products offered in this are relatively new or rapidly changing, there is considerable flux in the regulatory process. In addition to the federal agencies, a number of **offices of state attorneys general** became more active in securities regulation in the 1970s. In particular a number of states passed legislation to slow down tenders for the acquisition of firms with significant resources or employment in their state by a "foreign" corporation, whether that corporation was from another state or overseas. Because in many cases these laws directly conflict with SEC rules or practices, they are slowly being struck down in federal courts.

Despite this governmental regulation, the securities industry is still considered to be basically a **self-regulated industry.** The SEC establishes broad principles and some guidelines, but most of the day-to-day implementation of the regulations is left to industry groups—the NASD or the exchanges. The SEC then audits the rules and performance of these groups. In most of the business report filings, the SEC has traditionally been most directly concerned about timeliness and format. Responsibility for content and accuracy falls mostly on the firm, its auditors, or the investment banking firms that help to prepare the document. Also a number of industry trade associations take part in the process. Although the associations, such as the **Securities Industry Association** or the **Public Securities Association** are not directly charged with regulation, they do promulgate standards of business ethics as professional practice. The associations also are active in representing member interests in any hearings on rule changes by the regulators.

INSTABILITY OF EXISTING STRUCTURE. The structure of the securities industry as described in this section is much like the structure that might have been described one decade, or even three decades ago. Because of strong tradition, the complex interrelationships in the trading process, and an egalitarian approach to making changes in the industry, structural changes have come slowly.

There are two areas in which the structure of the securities industry may be unstable. First, there are few industries in this country where more than 4000 firms, let alone 100 large firms, compete for the same type of business. Once the principle of competitive commission rates became established in 1975, economic pressure of "cost efficiency" began to be more important in traditional brokerage business. These cost pressures and related competitive developments have already forced a number of brokerge firms out of business (usually through merger with another firm, or through dissolution of the firm): more attrition is likely over the next two stock market cycles. Although firms providing traditional brokerage services may decline, the ease of entry into this industry may lead to an increase in the number of small firms offering investment counseling or other specialty services.

The second area of obvious instability is in the number and relative sizes of the existing exchanges in this country. It is unlikely, for political reasons, that the number of exchange floors will drop much in the 1980s (although a severe market recession could well lead to the disappearance of the Boston Stock Exchange, the PBW Exchange, and a merger of the American Stock Exchange with another group). The economics of tied-together communications-computer systems for solving rapid transaction clearing and reporting problems is so overwhelmingly favorable that such a system will evolve. It is more likely to creep in as an expansion of "jointly owned" subsidiaries of exchanges to handle specific tasks than as an overt monopolization of trading by one exchange. But in fact, the subsidiaries will eventually dominate their respective parent exchanges in services provided.

SECURITIES TRADING

CUSTOMER CLASSES. The traditional role of the securities industry is to facilitate and promote the trading of securities. The efficiencies of having a "marketplace" for doing this have led brokers to form associations to set common rules for transacting and stock exchanges to formalize marketplace administrative procedures. The customers attracted to this marketplace are sometimes divided into two different categories when discussing rationales for securities trading: individual versus institutional customers, and investors verses speculators. **Institutional** customers include such groups as private pension funds, mutual funds, life insurance companies, and property and liability insurance firms. Institutions hold about one-third the value of stock outstanding but account for more than half the trading on the NYSE. This is because institutions concentrate their stock holdings in the larger corporations listed on that exchange, and because they tend to turn over their portfolios more frequently than do individuals. **Individuals** (including personal trust accounts and other categories lumped into the "household" sector) still hold about two-thirds of the value of stock outstanding. Individuals own most of the stock, and do most of the trading, in the thousands of over-the-counter stock transactions and trades of the stocks listed on exchanges other than the NYSE.

Investors are generally regarded as customers who are buying or selling securities with the longer term in mind, and who undertake "fundamental analysis" of the economic performance of a firm whose shares they may be buying to try to estimate the true worth of the security. Most institutional buying is "professional," hence investor-oriented transacting. **Speculators** are often defined as customers who are buying or selling securities with the expectation of short-term gain, who base buying decisions more on price fluctuations or other technical factors than on any fundamental analysis of underlying economic conditions. Speculation tends to be seen in pejorative terms as an activity that mostly benefits the speculator and may lead to unnecessary market excesses if speculators all decide to buy or sell a security at about the same time. Indeed, over the years the government and the NYSE have worked actively to reduce speculation. Actions taken include (1) closing down mining-type exchanges and inhibiting the trading of securities selling for less than $5 per share; (2) increasing the holding period for capital gains treatment from 6 months to a year; (3) increasing brokerage transactions cost to the point where "day trading" (buying and selling a stock the same day, or within a few business days) is no longer attractive to many investors; (4) inhibiting the activities of independent floor traders on the exchange; and (5) slowing down the expansion of options and futures markets (e.g., postponing several proposals for futures instruments that are calls on stock price indexes such as the Dow Jones Industrial Average).

Despite such attitudes, some speculative activity is regarded as beneficial because it (1) increases the liquidity of a market for a security; (2) attracts to the securities industry capital that would otherwise go elsewhere, and some of this capital seems to end up helping to finance new high-risk enterprises; and (3) provides additional revenues for brokerage firms, thus helping to maintain the distribution network necessary to sell new securities to others. In **modern portfolio theory,** what constitutes investing and what is speculating becomes very blurred. It is no longer possible to designate as "probably speculative" the buying of a stock option or financial future, the buying and selling of a bond within a week, or similar activities. Taken together with other decisions, such activities may lead to portfolios that are far less risky than if such "speculations" had not been undertaken (for a discussion of these issues, see Sections 7 and 8).

TYPES OF ORDER. Customers may specify a variety of terms relating to the execution of an order placed with a brokerage firm. **Market orders** are orders to buy or sell at the market price prevailing when the order reaches the specialist's post on the floor of the exchange. Under normal circumstances this should take less than an hour for an order placed with a brokerage firm in the United States (but it may take longer for the confirmation of transaction to reach a given broker). **Limit orders** are orders by the customer to place limits on the price at which the order can be executed. For example, a limit order to buy IBM at 120 must be executed (if possible) at a price of 120 or less. Usually, some time limit is placed on limit orders. "Day orders" are automatically canceled at the end of the day given if not executed. "Good till canceled" orders remain on the books until executed or canceled by the customer.

Limit orders that cannot be executed as soon as they reach the Exchange are left with the specialist in the stock, who notes the order in his or her book, showing amount, broker leaving the order, and time placed. Thus 10 different brokers may place limit orders to buy IBM at 120. When this price is reached on a decline, the amount of stock available for sale at 120 may be only a fraction of the total of the buying orders. Specialists' books for most securities are "thin," containing orders to buy or sell only a few hundred shares away from the current market.

Stop-loss orders are orders that can be used to help limit losses on existing positions. An order to sell "on stop" 100 shares of IBM at 110 is a type of limit order. When the market price of IBM reaches 110 or less, the customer's 100 shares are offered "at market." Thus if market conditions are unsettled, with many sell orders, the customer may get less than 110. Similarly, short sellers may seek to limit their losses by placing buy "on stop" orders. An order to buy IBM at 130 stop would trigger a market order to buy the required number of shares when the price reached 130 or more.

Short selling consists of selling securities that are not owned by the seller. Customers engaged in short selling do so in the expectation that they will be able to buy the stock later (or elsewhere) at a lower price, thus making a profit. Permitting short selling can have several advantages for a securities market: (1) the liquidity of the market will be increased; (2) to the extent that short sellers have contrary expectations, the sharpness of price fluctuations may be reduced as these customers sell as prices increase or buy back securities as prices drop; and (3) specialists and other market makers can better stabilize their markets without having large inventories, and can better arbitrage across markets selling the same security. The disadvantage of short selling is that under certain market conditions short selling focused on particular securities may temporarily accentuate price trends—for example, driving the prices too high as short sellers scramble to buy to cover their position.

From the customer's viewpoint, short selling is simple. Suppose she tells a broker to sell 100 shares of IBM short as a market order, and the price turns out to be 120. The customer's broker arranges to "borrow" the stock from her own or another broker's inventory (or from the inventories of stock held in margin accounts at brokerage firms) for delivery to the buying customer's broker. To provide security for the loan of the stock, the borrowing broker deposits with the lender broker a sum of money equal to the market price of the borrowed shares ($12,000 here). Stock is usually loaned flat; that is, no interest is paid on the money put up as collateral, and a premium is not usually collected by the lender of the stock. The lender broker is compensated, however, for she can earn a return on the $12,000 as long as it is held. In addition, the short customer must turn over to the lender any dividends paid on the stock while it is loaned. The short customer's broker subtracts the amount from the short's account, transfers it to the lending broker, who adds it to the account of the customer from whom the stock was "borrowed." Short customers do not know from whom stock is borrowed, and lending customers do not know that "their" stock has been loaned. It is all a broker-to-broker arrangement. The Securities Exchange Act does require that customers of brokerage houses give permission to have their stock loaned; this permission is a standard part of the agreement signed by a customer opening a general account.

A general account is a customer account; the purchase of securities may be for cash or **on margin** (i.e., the customer pays down only a portion of the price of the security). Margin requirements are set by the Federal Reserve, with additional terms or conditions imposed by the stock exchanges and customer's brokerage firm. In a margin purchase the customer is required to deposit with the broker, either in cash or in acceptable securities, a fraction of the purchase price (currently 50%). The balance is loaned to the customer by the brokerage house, which usually obtains the funds by pledging the purchased securities with a bank for a collateral loan.

Only listed securities, and the securities of certain larger over-the-counter firms may be carried in margin accounts. Stocks selling for less than $5 may not be purchased on margin. The NYSE requires that customers maintain margin of at least 25% of the market value of all securities long or short in their accounts. Some brokerage firms set higher maintenance margins (usually 30%). When the margin in an account becomes inadequate, a "margin call" is sent to the customer requesting payment of any deficiency. If payment is not forthcoming immediately, the broker may sell the margined stock at market and close out that transaction.

Suppose a customer bought 100 shares of IBM at 120 on margin. He or she would send a check to the broker for $6,000 (50% margin), and the broker would lend the customer $6,000. If the price of IBM suddenly dropped to 70, the customer's "equity" position would be only $1,000 ($7,000 value of stock minus $6,000 borrowed). The customer would receive a margin call to put up at least another $750 (for the maintenance margin requirement of $1,750). The interest that must be paid on the borrowed funds and the need to put up additional capital in declining markets are indications of the disadvantages of buying on margin. The advantages are those usually associated with financial leverage. If the price of the stock goes up enough (or dividends are higher than the customer's after-tax interest expenses), the customer will earn more money on the $6,000 equity investment than if he or she had bought 50 shares for cash.

On exchanges in the United States, orders for fewer than 100 shares are generally regarded as **odd lots;** that is, the standard unit of trading is 100 shares or a multiple, and fractions of the standard unit are handled slightly differently than the regular order. Traditionally, odd-lot transactions were handled by a number of individuals and firms on the floor of, say, the NYSE which specialized in providing this service. The dealer stood ready to buy or sell the odd lot at the next price at which a round lot (a standard order) transaction took place plus a service charge of 12.5 cents (lower-priced stocks) or 25 cents (higher-priced stocks). Gradually, competition reduced the number of dealers to two, then to one. In the late 1970s exchanges began experimenting with letting computers automatically process odd-lot orders and even small round-lot orders. The NYSE has not been entirely successful in this endeavor, so some major firms have begun processing odd-lot orders "in house" much as they might have been processed on the exchange. This competition, and the decision to let exchange specialists handle odd-lot business if they desire, forced the last major odd-lot firm out of business.

EXCHANGE EXECUTION: OLD PROCESSES AND NEW. The large exchanges in the United States have, for a number of decades, operated under what is known as the "continuous auction" process; that is, specialists and others try to complete transactions any time orders arrive during the 6 hours the market may be open. Exchanges in other countries may follow other customs, such as having a round-robin call in a stock once a day at which time an attempt is made to match accumulated buy and sell orders.

In continuous auction markets the **specialists** and related market makers play an important role. At any given hour, orders arriving at the "trading post" for a particular stock may not be in balance. Specialists must decide, on the basis of long training and experience, how much to adjust the quote on a stock to bring the market closer to balance. The quote is in terms of a **bid** price (offer to buy) and an **ask** price (offer to sell). For actively traded stocks the bid-ask spread may be only one-eighth of a point (the standard price jump on U.S. exchanges) or sometimes a quarter-point. For small imbalances, specialists may buy and sell from their own inventories, in the expectation of rebalancing their positions by a transaction on the other side of the market later.

The trading post is likely to be a large circular counter (there are about 20 at the NYSE), with specialists standing around the edge and clerks inside. Each stock listed on an exchange is assigned to a specialist and post. Once two dealers, or a dealer and specialist, agree on a transaction, it is recorded on a machine-readable card. The card is fed into a computer system that quickly flashes the quotation on the ticker service and records the order for the exchange's back-office clearing operation. Computer tapes with time-date records of every transaction are kept for a period in case of errors and to provide audit measures of the adequacy of specialist performance.

The **costs of transaction** from a customer's viewpoint are the brokerage charges for buying or selling a stock. Until the early 1970s these rates were fixed by mutual agreement of the members of the NYSE and were effectively the minimum rates charged throughout the industry. Exhibit 5 reports the last rate structure before competitive commission rates became effective in 1975. At that time the cost to buy or sell 100 shaes of a $40 stock would have been almost $65, or 65 cents per share. Since then, despite rising inflation, those costs have remained stable or gone up slowly at major brokerage firms. For a small institutional-sized order of, say, 1000 shares of a $40 stock, the 1975 basic cost might have been about $365 or 35 cents a share (even then some firms were offering discounts). Since then, competition has forced rates down as low as 5 cents per share, although the current institutional rate is probably more than 10 cents per share. For individuals, small "discount brokers" have gone into business to compete for individuals' orders by offering 30 to 50% discounts from the 1975 rates for no-frills brokerage service. In addition to these brokerage fees, there are small New York State and SEC transfer taxes, which aggregate to less than 3 cents per share.

Once a transaction is completed, the information is routed through the exchange's computers and also messages go to the booths of the brokerage firms involved so that they may begin their own back-office processing. On some of

EXHIBIT 5 BASIC COMMISSION RATES FINAL COMMON SCHEDULE, 1975

Money Involved			Basic Rate	Plus
On orders for 100 shares[a]				
under	$2,000		as mutually agreed	
above	$2,000 but under	$2,500	1.3%	$ 12
	$2,500 and above		0.9%	$ 22
On multiple round-lot orders				
under	$2,000		as mutually agreed	
above	$2,000 but under	$2,500	1.3%	$ 12
above	$2,500 but under	$20,000	0.9%	$ 22
above	$20,000 but under	$30,000	0.6%	$ 82
above	$30,000 but under	$300,000	0.4%	$142
	$300,000 and above		negotiated	
Plus for each round lot of 100 shares:				
	First to tenth round lot		$6 per round lot	
	Eleventh round lot and above		$4 per round lot	

[a] The "minimum" commission on any order for 100 shares could not exceed $65.00.
Source: New York Stock Exchange Fact Book, 1980.

the smaller exchanges, for some of the smaller regional brokerage firms, this may be done automatically, for a fee, by the exchange's computer service corporation. If a broker is not too busy, he or she may call the customer the same day with the results of the transaction. By late that night or early the following morning, the brokerage firm will have in the mail a **confirmation slip,** specifying the **transaction date** (when the order was executed on the exchange), the terms, the charges, and the **settlement date** (when the account of the customer will be debited or credited, as the case may be, for any cash or securites due). The settlement date was once as short as the end of the third working day after the transaction, but in recent years back-office processing complications for some brokerage firms and delays in postal deliveries have increased the time before cash or securities are due in the broker's office to five working days.

As institutional trading on the NYSE has grown to the point where it constitutes the majority of public transactions on that exchange, special methods have had to be devised to handle **large block trades,** generally tabulated as trades of 10,000 shares or more. An indication of the vitality and liquidity of the American securities markets is that many such trades are handled every day on the floor of the exchange in a regular way. For very large offers, or when there simply is no customer on the other side, the exchange has a group of special methods to handle these trades away from the auction market at the specialist's post. Although these "special method distributions" may sometimes take place after regular trading hours, every attempt is made not to close out the public's opportunity to participate—particularly if there are limit orders on the specialist's book at the block distribution price.

Large block trades constitute more than 25% of the volume of trades listed on the NYSE. This has become one of the most competitive aspects of the brokerage industry. In addition to trades that occur on the NYSE, institutional block trades in NYSE-listed securities occur on some of the regional exchanges (where some institutions were permitted to buy memberships in the early 1970s). Trades also occur in the "third market" (the over-the-counter market in exchange-listed securities), and in the "fourth market" (a market directly between institutions, perhaps facilitated by arrangements such as "Instinet," which provides direct computer terminal links among institutions so they can display tentative volume interest and bid-ask quotes to others linked to Instinet). The third and fourth market arrangements have captured about 10% of the block trading business and the regional exchanges, smaller amounts.

IMPACT OF COMPUTERS. Because the brokerage part of the securities industry is mostly a process of transferring orders from one point to another, then processing the paperwork that develops out of the transactions process, it should be the ideal industry for computerization. The cost savings and other benefits could be enormous. Such a changeover has not occurred, however, for at least three reasons.

1. With its thousands of small firms, many with partnerships passed down from father to son, tradition in the securities industry is very important—and is perceived as "efficient," because new ways do not have to be learned.
2. There is no incentive for the firms and exchanges to set up a particular system. It does only limited good for one firm to set up a computer system if the exchange and broker on the opposite side of the transaction are utilizing normal systems or different computer systems.
3. Hundreds of millions of dollars of capital would be required to develop a sophisticated industrywide system. Although the industry has been enormously successful in raising capital for others, brokerage firms and exchanges have not always been able to raise capital for their own needs.

Despite these factors slowing down industrywide computerization, the pressures to convert are great. Pressures include rising volume that simply cannot be handled manually in the short run because of the limited supply of trained industry personnel, rising labor costs, and falling profit margins as commission rates became competitive. Recognizing these factors, industry leaders began in the 1970s to establish a framework in which their own firms and the exchanges could be modernized. The 1970s may be remembered as the decade that computers came to Wall Street. The 1980s will be the decade when they began to be fully utilized.

ITS CLOB, BLOB, and CUSIP to you DOTty NASAQ—which is to say, there are a great many acronyms being bandied today on Wall Street as names for the different computer systems under development. Because new systems are evolving almost monthly, we restrict this discussion to the thrust of these new systems. Development focus seems to be concentrated in three areas: electronic telecommunications, back-office paper processing after an order is completed, and the market transactions process. Systems cannot always be placed in one of these areas, for the objective of the ultimate system is to integrate all parts of the process.

Communications systems have been the most rapidly developing systems on Wall Street. Ticker tape and the associated tickers that printed out each transaction are now mostly sold as antiques. High-speed transmission facilities that can transmit thousands of characters a minute send transactions data around the world, whereupon information may be displayed on large electronic screens, fed to cable companies, or other vendors to send to home TV screens or minicomputers, or sent directly to clients' computers for subsequent analysis and use. To transmit this information, brokerage firms and exchanges are using land lines, microwave, and even satellite facilities.

Most of the larger brokerage firms have direct lines to their exchange floor booths and, at least in the bond areas, direct lines to other brokers and even major customers. A firm's trader on the floor may carry an electronic beeper so that he or she can be called back to the booth; in addition, all exchanges have message board systems to signal traders when they are wanted. In 1980 the NYSE started an experiment to permit a few traders to carry around miniature radio telephones, which could be used to call the booth without leaving the trading floor. There have been some problems with this new technology. Specialists complained about traders "standing in the crowd" all day and blocking opportunities for brokers who came and went, to and from the post. More important, brokers could easily call "upstairs" (headquarters management) or make direct long-distance calls to major customers. Because those off the floor of the exchange are not supposed to have information on floor activity until it is equally available to all via the transactions tape, the exchange has had to rethink this experiment.

Back-office paper processing is in a sense the most difficult part of the securities transaction process to automate fully, because it depends on the other systems being in place. Still, cost pressures have forced virtually all firms to partially automate these activities. There has been considerable success insofar as the number of employees in this area has remained virtually constant in recent years (about 100,000 individuals), even though share volume and number of transactions for most firms have more than doubled.

Three factors have contributed significantly to progress. First, after more than a decade of effort, most of the actively traded securities now have an identifying code (called CUSIP numbers), used in describing securities when certificates are exchanged. Not all firms use these codes in their internal inventory systems, however, and code identification has lagged for governmental-type securities and special instruments. Second, the physical transfer of certificates is slowly being curtailed as depository corporations become the resting places for the actual certificates. This has been a very slow process requiring changes in federal and state law, negotiated agreements with banks and others, and an educational program on the adquacy of a transactions slip and periodic statement of position as substitutes for the actual certificate. It will take at least another decade to achieve anything approaching full participation. The third factor contributing to back-office computerization has been the ability of computer software companies to develop generic systems that can be installed in particular firms with only modest changes. Thus many smaller firms can afford to buy these systems, or to get their processing done by one of the computer service bureaus (both private ones and exchange-affiliated bureaus have developed) at reasonable fees.

Because customer identification has not been standardized, and because computer systems for larger firms tend to be self-designed with features unique to each firm, when brokerage firms merge there may be serious problems in putting the "books" of the two firms together. Indeed, in several cases in recent years the problems have been serious enough to impose a significant drain on the acquiring firm's capital base. The lack of standardization across firms has also caused external audit systems to lag the changes being made in back-office processing. Thus it remains a lengthy procedure to trace actual trading by source in a specific security, or to test a firm's net capital position independently.

Computer systems related to the **market transactions process** have been the most controversial in development. These systems have been the slowest to develop, and probably the most expensive to put in place. In the hearings for the 1975 Securities Act, Congress seemed to indicate an interest in a **"National Exchange Market System" (NEMS)** which would be, among other things, a truly national system that was highly automated, but preserved the regional exchanges, an exchange that maintained continuous auction markets but had competing specialists or market makers, and an exchange that had uniform standards for professionals' participation, although perhaps with different "levels" of standards participation. These goals are not precisely required by the Act. Development supervision was turned over to the SEC, which has delegated actual development to industry committees.

At the beginning of the 1980s a number of partial systems began to be developed. None are likely to evolve into a full-fledged NEMS, and some will eventually have to be abandoned. The reasons for this rather strange and collectively expensive type of evolution are both economic and political. It is reasonably clear that it is technically feasible to develop a highly automated transactions system, but at a cost of hundreds of millions of dollars. How will such development costs be funded? Once developed, the exchange would probably put out of business the regional exchanges as they currently exist. The new Exchange would also change the nature of business for many on the "floor." Because many transactions would be semiautomated, there would be less revenues from floor brokerage and relatively more to be derived from the higher risk market-making activities where inventory positions must be taken.

There are three types of partial system under development. One type attempts to upgrade communications links between market makers to broaden the marketplace. An early version is found at the **Pacific Stock Exchange,** which was organized as a merger of the San Francisco and Los Angeles exchanges. Separate trading floors are maintained in each city, but the floors (and each specialist's post) are continuously linked, while the exchange is in operation. A second example of this type of linkage is the NYSEs **Intermarket Trading System (ITS).** This is a video-computer display system that links a specialist's post at the exchange with specialists on the regional exchanges who are selling the same securities. The bid-ask quotes are displayed and are "firm" (good) for at least 100 shares, or more where indicated. By having a card marked, a broker standing in the crowd at the NYSE viewing the ITS screen may direct his or her order to another exchange if the quote there seems better. A third example of this type of system is the work the **National Association of Security Dealers** has done to develop its NASDAQ (automated quotation) system. Dealers (i.e, brokerage firms taking positions in over-the-counter securities, but not required to be "specialists" making continuous markets) are linked in a nationwide computer system with video display units. Dealers interested in making a market in a particular security enter bid-ask quotes, good for at least 100 shares. Any dealer with a basic level screen may put on the screen the stock of interest and, if the price seems attractive, call the dealer to try to arrange a transaction at the desired volume. At higher levels, the system may be used to execute transactions for the volume displayed and to interface with other brokerage firms and exchange computer systems.

Another type of partial system automatically directs orders from a brokerage firm's computers to the specialist's post on an exchange. This step alone may save several minutes. The specialist presents the order to the crowd for execution at the best price available, and the completed order is routed back through the exchange and brokerage firm computers. The NYSE Designated Order Turnaround (DOT) system handles market orders for up to 299 shares and day limit orders up to 500 shares. Some regional exchanges, which developed such systems earlier, have even more sophisticated features permitting "automatic" execution at the current quote unless the specialist intervenes, or screening of ITS and other market makers for best quote.

A third type of system that was under development is known as the "Cincinnati experiment" because it was conducted under the nominal jurisdiction of the Cincinnati Stock Exchange. Actually, the computer systems involved and most of the participating brokers and their computers were based in New York and New Jersey. This experiment at the beginning of the 1980s was a small prototype with some of the features (but not all) that may be desirable in a NEMS. In the automated **"National Securities Trading System" (NSTS)** package being used in the Cincinnati experiment, brokerage firm computers entered orders in the NSTS computer, which matched orders there (or on limit books) and to the extent possible cleared the orders back through the brokerage firms' computers. Small imbalances were taken by the Cincinnati specialist or other market makers or laid off on one of the larger exchanges. The NSTS needed a direct link to ITS to do this automatically, but the opposition of the rest of the exchange community to this experiment was so strong that it was not possible. This experiment failed because of lack of order support from the brokerage houses, the fierce opposition of other exchanges, and the huge amounts of capital that would have been required to make it cost competitive to existing systems.

As long as partial systems such as this and the exchanges' computerized order execution systems continue, there is no national "central limit order book" (CLOB) to ensure that all limit orders left with the system receive the priority that time dating would suggest is due to them. Of course, there never has been such a system. Whether this desirable feature of a national market system is promoted or hindered by the currently evolving partial systems is a matter of much debate.

INTERNATIONALIZATION OF SECURITIES MARKETS. Securities trading systems are not only becoming more national in scope, they are becoming more international. Already the trading desks of some major brokerage firms and banks are open 24 hours a day. Information passes back and forth from home-based computers to foreign branches at all hours. Activity is greater for credit and commodity instruments, but multinational equity trading is increasing.

The shares of several large American corporations are listed on foreign exchanges, and a number of foreign firms have shares or their equivalents listed on U.S. exchanges. Transactions by foreigners with Americans in both U.S. and foreign stocks reached records by the beginning of the 1980s. The total, more than $50 billion, seems to increase yearly. Of the more than 1500 corporations with stock listed on the NYSE, only about 40 are foreign firms, but the number is slowly increasing.

More than 100 foreign institutions have trading desks in the United States. The American subsidiary may be organized as a special bank or brokerage firm, but the foreign parent is likely to be a financial institution with a commercial bank as its main subsidiary. In the United States the law makes it very difficult for this country's commercial banks to have brokerage firm subsidiaries, so there may be some unevenness in regulatory burden applied. Of course, American financial institutions can usually operate in foreign countries according to the laws of the host country. With the rapidity with which funds are being switched from one country to another, and the increasing numbers of U.S. and foreign institutions doing non-home–country trading, regulators are losing control over transaction audit trails and the real ownership and balance sheet position of some firms. In essence, the SEC itself and other regulatory groups have not kept pace with technology.

SECURITIES INDUSTRY TRENDS: SOME SIGNIFICANT CHANGES

The securities industry continues to evolve more rapidly than most other industries, although the frenetic pace of the 1970s has slowed somewhat. In the decade of the 1970s the securities industry was an industry in transition, subject to tremendous structural strains. These pressures included deregulation of pricing for its major product lines (brokerage commission rate deregulation), major new product areas and associated regulatory groups (options, commodities, financial futures, mortgage certificates), a new computer technology that is forcing changes in decades-old processing procedures, and a new level of competition within the industry and outside it. Most of these pressures were still present at the beginning of the 1980s.

Given these pressures and the difficulty some securities firms have in raising their own firm capital, it would not be surprising to see further mergers within the industry—particularly if there is a significant economic downturn in industry profitability. Over the past 5 years there have been at least 200 mergers involving securities firms with other securities firms or, less frequently, with firms outside the industry. But the industry still has a relatively low concentration ratio, so further consolidation can be expected if it follows a pattern similar to the development of most other industries. Such consolidations, and the increased competition from other financial institutions, will continue to make investment banking a particularly competitive activity.

The operating leverage of most securities firms is still very high. Thus periods of high brokerage transactions are associated with very good profits, and periods of relatively lower volume can result in substantial losses. The trend has been for the volume break-even point to increase steadily at most brokerage firms as "permanent employees," leased communications and computer facilities, and other fixed costs replace the traditional hiring and firing processes in the securities industry. Although many brokerage firms are trying to diversify into other industries to offset part of this operating risk, their success has not been tested by a decline in market volume. The risk exposure of exchanges may be even greater, because their overhead is increasing even more rapidly and they cannot diversify away from their brokerage functions. It is likely that in a significant market volume decline, one or more of the existing exchanges would be forced out of business.

The decade of the 1980s has added a new layer of problems onto the structural changes that have occurred in the industry. These new problems include (1) additional problems created by technology, (2) a dramatic increase in the types of product available, (3) serious managerial problems, and (4) a decline in ethical standards within the industry.

NEW PROBLEMS WITH TECHNOLOGY. Recent **advances in technology** have created opportunities for new markets within the securities industry, but have also posed significant threats by increasing competition and regulatory problems. The technological advances have come primarily on three fronts: (1) improvements in the computerized trading procedures at the exchanges, (2) improved communications networks, and (3) improved computer and complex computer program facilities that are available to the buyers and sellers of securities.

The improvements in computerized exchange trading have been the most modest development in recent years. The major exchange still strongly resists the mandated notion of a national market system. But the facilities for trading over-the-counter securities have been significantly upgraded and thus the number of active stocks on the NASDAQ system increased. This has been one of the factors that has permitted institutions to take into their portfolios the stocks of smaller companies they find so attractive.

Some of the newer options exchanges have also been structured around computer systems, although the process of tying trades into the system at each point has not yet been accomplished. But these exchange computer systems do provide expanded "back-office" clearing procedures for the options and futures markets.

Congress has not been entirely satisfied with the pace or evolving structure of the national market system. Because this is an area requiring considerable professional expertise not possessed by Congress, it is unlikely that anything will be done about the problem directly. But the SEC is likely to find it increasingly difficult to get support for budget increases unless NEMS begins to make more rapid progress. It now appears that 1995 is the earliest date for a functioning national market system, and it is more likely to be longer than one decade before there is a fully integrated marketplace. Thus the late 1980s may subject the securities industry to at least as much stress as the early 1980s.

The divestiture of the **American Telephone and Telegraph** operating companies in 1984 has created another set of technical problems within the industry. As costs are shifted to local telephone companies, there are increasing incentives for the largest brokerage houses to create their own multinational telephone networks. Using laser light cable technology, satellite transmission and receiving facilities, and digital switching computers, some firms have already begun to do this—either on their own or in combination with nontraditional telephone companies. This large investment in fixed capital creates significant operating risks for these firms, but may also give them significant cost and marketing advantages in good markets.

Personal computers have begun to impact on the securities markets. So far the computers are not being used for direct trading purposes to any extent. But they are used to analyze portfolios and the valuation of complex instruments. The results of such analysis are then turned into trades through regular brokerage channels. Because many are using the same software programs to analyze options or financial futures, buy and sell decisions may be triggered at almost the same time for a large number of traders. Large numbers trying to take action on the same side of the market will accentuate the fluctuations in that market or the underlying stock market. There is some evidence this has happened. And smaller private groups in the United States and Britain are now tying these portfolio programs into actual trading by transmitting the data directly to the floor trader for a seat they own on an exchange.

TOO MANY PRODUCTS. Some are beginning to believe that the last half of the 1980s will be known in the securities industry as the period when professionals lost track of what they were trying to sell. There have been literally thousands of new instruments created in recent years from the basic spectrum of stocks-bonds-insurance features-options-futures-indexes. No one knows how many instruments are being traded; no one agency has supervisory control of all these instruments; no one knows the return-risk characteristics of many of these instruments; no one has studied the portfolio interrelationships of them all; no one has studied how many of these derivative instruments should be valued relative to the base instrument, or how it might be affecting the base instrument. (Example: How would an option on a futures guaranteed mortgage package relate to the writing of current mortgages?)

There is another problem. Most of these new instruments carry higher incentives to brokers (commissions, bonuses, etc.) than the selling of stocks and bonds (which has become almost a commodity-type business). But brokers are not well trained in the analysis or portfolio implications of most of these instruments. Thus they are reduced to reading prepared speeches to clients or to pretending a mystic knowledge that doesn't exist.

Finally, because brokerage firms are "market makers" for most of these instruments and not simply brokers, the brokerage firms must assume risk positions. The required capital base for most of these instruments has not been defined or even studied, so as a brokerage firm changes its product mix it may not know how it is changing its risk exposure. Nor may the regulatory agency know how risk has changed.

MANAGERIAL PROBLEMS. Managerial problems are probably no more serious in the securities industry than they are in a number of other industries undergoing dynamic secular changes. But the consequences of mismanagement in the securities industry can be much more serious because of the high financial leverage of individual firms and the interrelated nature of the trading. A failure of one small bond house can indeed have serious consequences for the profitability of a number of major firms.

We have already indicated one type of management problem—the inability to control the product portfolio for the firm, and hence the inability to train the firm's marketing force properly on the characteristics of the product. This also leads to an inability to train the internal auditing force on how to detect unethical or illegal activities. As firms have struggled to educate their own personnel, they have also struggled to find ways to keep their customers informed and educated about the new types of products as they are brought to market.

Another management problem relates to the **growth of technology** as it is used by the firm. Traditionally, back-office operations have been a weak area for many firms. But large-scale computer and communications systems demand strong leadership; unfortunately, there has not yet been time to develop such leadership. Some firms have invested millions of dollars in "hardware and software" development that will be obsolete by the time it is operational.

Mergers and acquisitions have contributed to some of the managerial problems faced by firms in the industry. In many cases key personnel in acquired brokerage firms have been bidden away by competing firms. The value of a brokerage firm is mostly in its key personnel, so their departure is a serious setback to realizing any benefits from the merger. In other cases there have been major problems when brokerage firms were acquired by banks or insurance companies outside the industry. These larger firms do not seem to understand the risks or the compensation schemes of the securities industry. In almost every case where a brokerage firm has been made a subsidiary of an outside firm, that brokerage firm has had a serious deterioration in the quality of its leadership, and in most cases a relative decline in the profitability and market share position of the brokerage firm within the industry.

ETHICAL STANDARDS. What some view as the most serious long-run problem for the industry is a noticeable decline in the **ethical standards** of many of the firms and individuals in this industry. Sharp dealing and illegal activities seem to be replacing the handshake honesty that had developed in this industry since the 1930s. Some believe that it is happening because of the increased competitive pressures from inside and outside the industry. Some believe it is because a whole generation of senior partners who started in the 1930s are retiring and being replaced by people who do not know each other on a face-to-face basis. Some believe that the rapid growth in the size of the industry and the number of products being sold has created situations where "the right path" is just not clear to many. Whatever the root causes, there is a growing apprehension that the next several years will see an increase in the importance of professional conduct issues compared with recent decades.

The types of misbehavior comes in a variety of forms, and of course ultimately must depend on the greed and culpability of the customers. At the firm level we see a large number of investment banking firms promoting mergers and acquisitions, not because there are any real benefits here for the acquiring firms in most cases, but because this has become a very important profit center for the investment banker. We see tax shelters of very doubtful liquidity or legality created. We see mutual funds calling themselves "no load" funds that have cumulative "marketing fees" hidden in their costs that may ultimately be higher than the load fees of load funds. We see brokerage firms engaged in illegal cash laundering activities or sharp cash management practices. We see exchanges modifying rules designed to protect the public when brokerage firms do not meet stated capital requirements, or when listed firms insist on multiple classes of securities to protect management from takeover threats. We see outright fraud when individuals or firms walk away from trades without paying if the market suddenly against them.

Since the 1930s the securities industry has prided itself on being a self-regulated industry that could, and for the most part did, develop the highest ethical and professional standards. That regulatory machinery worked so long as (1) entry into the industry was controlled by limited access to the NYSE, (2) industry employees were carefully screened, and (3) the products being sold were well-understood and did not change very often. These conditions have now disappeared. Hundreds of new firms have entered the industry in the past 5 years; access to the NYSE can be easily gained indirectly if not directly, and it is not so important now because the NYSE has played a very limited role in most new products. Screening of personnel has deteriorated as lawyers have forbidden firms to write honest negative appraisals of individuals employed in the industry, and technology has permitted dishonest people to operate from any state or country.

The regulatory framework simply has not been able to keep up with or comprehend all the new products or the implications of portfolio strategies involving a mixture of these new products. Each exchange monitors activity in its own products and that part of brokerage firm activity related to its products. Meanwhile the brokerage firm holding company and the industry's customers are dealing with products that cross multiple exchanges or multiple federal and state regulatory agencies. Because of the failure to create a national market system for trading, even tracing trades may take weeks or months when fraud can be committed multiple times in hours.

Another serious complication in regulating today's markets is the degree to which the markets have become international markets. Trading hours are expanding in the United States, and in some cases brokerage firms are staying open 24 hours a day to participate in the open markets around the world. Individuals and firms can place orders from other countries that are even more difficult to trace than orders placed within the United States. Cooperation between the securities industry and the IRS is minimal. Indeed, there has been some indication that investment banking holding companies themselves are using overseas subsidiaries to manipulate profits for tax reasons for themselves and clients. In some cases it may have become more serious as some in the industry use overseas accounts to take advantage of "insider trading" information (illegal in the United States) or manipulate markets directly.

AN OVERRIDING POSITIVE FACT. Despite the number of serious problems that must be faced by the securities industry in the coming decade, there is one overriding fact that should be remembered. The securities industry in the United States is, and has been for some time, the most dynamic, the most vital, the most liquid financial market in the world. If anything, this position is strengthening at this time. The tremendous inflow of overseas capital to this country is partly responsible for today's problems in the industry, as well as the macroeconomic consequences for our country's balance-of-payments problems.

The great danger is that today's market structure has never been tested by the fire of a serious recession within the securities industry. That downturn, when it comes, will bankrupt a number of firms and exchanges in the industry and create the temporary temptation for even greater sharp practices and unethical dealings. If the securities industry can come through that period without the trauma of a 1930s-type setback and reorganization, we will reach the new millennium in the year 2000 with an industry so different from the industry of

1950 that it must be counted as another prize example of the power of private capitalism.

BIBLIOGRAPHY

Block, Ernest, and Schwartz, Robert A. (eds.), *Impending Changes for Securities Markets: What Role for the Exchanges?,* Greenwich, CT: JAI Press, 1979.

Bogen, Jules I. (ed.), *Financial Handbook,* 4th edition New York: Ronald Press, 1964; particularly Sections 9 and 10 by David Saperstein, Loring C. Farwell, and Paul L. Howell.

Cox, Charles C., and Kohn, Bruce A., "Regulatory Implications of Computerized Communications in Securities Markets," paper from the Salomon Brothers Center Conference on Technology and the Regulation of Financial Markets, New York University Graduate School of Business, May 1985.

Goldberg, Lawrence G., and White, Lawrence J. (eds.), *The Deregulation of the Banking and Securities Industries,* Lexington, MA: Lexington Books, 1979.

Goldberg, Lawrence G., and Keenan, Michael, *The New York Based Securities Industry: 1979 Survey,* Occasional Papers in Metropolitan Business and Finance (1980, No. 2), New York University Graduate School of Business.

Keenan, Michael, *Profile of the New York Based Securities Industry,* New York University Monograph Series in Finance and Economics, New York University Graduate School of Business, 1977.

New York Stock Exchange, *Fact Book,* NYSE, New York, annually.

Securities and Exchange Commission, *Staff Report on the Securities Industry in 1978,* SEC Directorate of Economic and Policy Research, SEC, Washington, DC, July 1979.

Securities Industry Association, *SIA Trends Reports*, economic research staff of the SIA, New York, 1970s to date.

Stoll, Hans R., *Regulation of Securities Markets: An Examination of the Effects of Increased Competition,* New York University Monograph Series in Finance and Economics, New York University Graduate School of Business, 1979. (This monograph also contains a more extensive bibliography of some of the academic research on the securities industry.)

Young, Allan "The New York Securities Industry: Its Contribution to New York State and City," Study Paper for the New York District of the Securities Industry Association, June 1985.

Zarb, Frank G., and Gabriel T. Kerekes, *The Stock Market Handbook,* Homewood, IL: Dow-Jones Irwin, 1970.

10

REAL ESTATE FINANCE

CONTENTS

10

REAL ESTATE FINANCE

Richard T. Pratt
John A. Scowcroft

This section looks at sources of mortgage financing, the terms of mortgage loans, and the evaluation of mortgages for investment purposes.

SOURCES OF REAL ESTATE FINANCING

FINANCIAL INSTITUTIONS. At the end of 1984 **mortgage debt** outstanding exceeded $2 trillion. Of this, the major financial institutions held over $1.2 billion, with federal and related mortgage credit agencies issuing $158 billion directly and guaranteeing $331 billion of **mortgage pools** and **trusts.** Individuals and others held approximately $295 billion or 15%. Exhibit 1 shows these totals and subtotals by type of property. One- to four-family (mostly single-family) housing dominates mortgage debt with $1.3 billion of the total.

Savings and Loan Associations. As of 1984, the largest single type of financial institution providing home mortgage loans is **savings and loan associations (S&Ls),** with $431 billion of mortgages on one- to four-family dwellings. The portfolio concentration of S&Ls is also shown in Exhibit 1. Of S&Ls $55 billion total mortgage portfolio, mortgages on one- to four-family loans make up 78%, multifamily loans, 9%, and commercial loans, 13%.

A S&L institution may be a federal institution chartered under the Homeowners Loan Act of 1933 or a state-chartered institution. All "federals" are regulated directly by the three-member **Federal Home Loan Bank Board (FHLBB)** in Washington, D.C. This Board also has certain regulatory powers over state-chartered institutions, as the FHLBB members also constitute the Board of the **Federal Savings and Loan Insurance Corp.,** the entity that insures to $100,000 each deposit in almost all S&Ls. Because most state regulators give state-chartered institutions at least as much lending and operating power as the FHLBB grants to "federal," the operations of federally chartered and state-

EXHIBIT 1 MORTGAGE DEBT OUTSTANDING, 1984 (MILLIONS OF DOLLARS, END OF PERIOD)

Holder	Amount
All holders	$2,030,930
1- to 4-family	1,349,951
Multifamily	163,977
Commercial	406,139
Farm	110,863
Major financial institutions	1,247,106
Commercial banks[a]	374,186
1- to 4-family	197,944
Multifamily	21,142
Commercial	144,623
Farm	10,477
Mutual savings banks	160,761
1- to 4-family	114,364
Multifamily	20,190
Commercial	26,176
Farm	31
Savings and loan associations	554,868
1- to 4-family	431,132
Multifamily	48,274
Commercial	75,462
Life insurance companies	157,291
1- to 4-family	14,218
Multifamily	18,881
Commercial	111,692
Farm	12,500
Federal and related agencies	157,826
Government National Mortgage Association	2,500
1- to 4-family	597
Multifamily	1,903
Farmers Home Administration	1,800
1- to 4-family	449
Multifamily	124
Commercial	652
Farm	575
Federal Housing and Veterans Administration	4,782
1- to 4-family	2,007
Multifamily	2,775
Federal National Mortgage Association	87,940
1- to 4-family	82,175
Multifamily	5,765

EXHIBIT 1 (CONTINUED)

Holder	Amount
Federal Land Banks	50,679
1- to 4-family	2,948
Farm	47,731
Federal Home Loan Mortgage Corporation	10,125
1- to 4-family	9,425
Multifamily	700
Mortgage pools or trusts[b]	331,019
Government National Mortgage Association	179,873
1- to 4-family	175,089
Multifamily	4,784
Federal Home Loan Mortgage Corporation	70,417
1- to 4-family	69,817
Multifamily	600
Federal National Mortgage Association[c]	36,215
1- to 4-family	35,965
Multifamily	250
Farmers Home Administration	44,514
1- to 4-family	21,578
Multifamily	5,835
Commercial	7,403
Farm	9,698
Individual and others[d]	294,979
1- to 4-family[e]	192,243
Multifamily	32,754
Commercial	40,131
Farm	29,851

[a] Includes loans held by nondeposit trust companies but not bank trust departments.

[b] Outstanding principal balances of mortgages backing securities insured or guaranteed by the agency indicated.

[c] Outstanding balances on FNMA's issues of securities backed by pools of conventional mortgages held in trust. Implemented by FNMA in October 1981.

[d] Other holders include mortgage companies, real estate investment trusts, state and local credit agencies, state and local retirement funds, noninsured pension funds, credit unions, and U.S. agencies for which amounts are small or for which separate data are not readily available.

[e] Includes estimate of residential mortgage credit provided by individuals.

NOTE. Based on data from various institutional and governmental sources, with some quarters estimated in part by the Federal Reserve in conjunction with the Federal Home Loan Bank Board and the Department of Commerce. Separation of nonfarm mortgage debt by type of property, if not reported directly, and interpolations and extrapolations when required, are estimated mainly by the Federal Reserve. Multifamily debt refer to loans on structures of five or more units.

Source: Federal Reserve.

chartered S&Ls are similar. Both state and federal regulations require that S&Ls maintain a majority of their portfolio in home mortgages with limited but increasing percentages permitted in other real estate loans. A small percentage of S&Ls portfolio comes from direct ownership of real estate. The investment powers of S&Ls are slowly being broadened, but with a continuing emphasis on residential real estate lending.

Commercial Banks. Commercial banks have a greater concentration of their real estate loan portfolio in commercial loans and construction loans than do S&Ls. Exhibit 1 shows that of the $374 billion of mortgage debt outstanding at commercial banks, 53% is in one- to four-family loans, 6% in multifamily loans, 38% in commercial loans, and 3% in farm real estate loans. Often, a second institutional investor such as a **life insurance company** will issue a commitment to make the long-term loan on property while a local commercial bank services and supervises both the **construction loan** to the builder and the drawing down of funds by the borrower as construction progresses. In addition to direct mortgage lending, commercial banks loan to real estate-related institutions. Many commercial banks have mortgage companies that originate, sell, and service loans for other mortgage investors.

Commerical bank participation in mortgage investments has been sensitive to economic and interest rate cycles. Generally, banks have avoided making long-term, fixed-rate loans during periods of high rates and tight money but have shown renewed interest in the long-term mortgage sector.

Life Insurance Companies. Exhibit 1 shows that life insurance companies as an industry hold approximately 40% as much mortgage debt as commercial banks and 30% as much as S&Ls. Of $157 billion outstanding, 9% was in one- to four-family debt, 12% in multifamily loans, 71% in commercial loans, and 8% in farm real estate loans.

Mutual Savings Banks. Mutual savings banks, chartered in only a few states, notably Washington, New York, and the New England states, had $161 billion in mortgages, $3.5 billion more than the much larger life insurance industry. Of this, 71% was in one- to four-family loans, 13% in multifamily, and 16% in commercial loans.

MORTGAGE COMPANIES. A **mortgage company,** sometimes called a **mortgage banker** or **mortgage bank,** is not actually a bank but a company whose principal activity is originating mortgage loans, selling them to others, and retaining the servicing of the monthly payments. They also cure defaults and process foreclosure for the investor when necessary. Mortgage companies earn **origination** and **servicing fees,** profits on resale of loans, and a profit or loss from the spread between mortgage yields and the cost of their borrowings (usually from commercial banks under credit liens), during the short time that a given mortgage is held or "warehoused" before sale. To protect against negative spreads and to assure the presence of a subsequent buyer for mortgages originated, mortgage companies secure commitments to purchase the loans from institutional lenders or from the **Federal Home Loan Mortgage Corporation,** the **Federal National Mortgage Association,** or the **Government National Mortgage Association.** Thus mortgage companies play an important part in maintaining the flow of mortgage funds, but are not significant investors in outstanding mortgages.

FEDERAL AND QUASI-FEDERAL MORTGAGE CREDIT AGENCIES. Federally sponsored agencies have been the dominant presence in the growing **secondary market for mortgages.** The **Federal Housing Administration (FHA),** the grandfather of such agencies, was created in response to the Depression of 1929–1933 in order to insure lenders against loss on home mortgages. It also standardized construction and housing tract layouts with its underwriting standards for insurance eligibility. The Veterans Administration (VA) loan guarantee program was established in 1944. Together the VA and FHA programs encouraged lenders to increase the **loan-to-value price ratio** on owner-occupied homes. The Farmers Home Administration (FmHA), created in 1946, provides similar insurance for loans in rural areas and smaller communities.

The **Federal National Mortgage Association (FNMA),** nicknamed **"Fannie Mae,"** was created in 1933 to provide liquidity to mortgage lending institutions through the purchase of FHA and VA mortgages. Historically, the controlling stockholder of FNMA was the federal government, whereas sellers to FNMA were required to buy its stock. The Housing and Urban Development Act of 1968 made FNMA a government-sponsored corporation owned solely by private investors. The Act gave the subsidized mortgage purchase programs part of FNMA to a new government corporation within the Department of Housing and Urban Development, the **Government National Mortgage Association (GNMA),** nicknamed **"Ginnie Mae."**

The Emergency Home Finance Act of 1970 empowered FNMA to deal in conventional mortgages (those not FHA-insured). Currently, FNMA purchases conventional mortgages and seasoned (outstanding more than 1 year) FHA and VA mortgages.

The Federal Home Loan Mortgage Corporation (FHLMC), nicknamed "Freddie Mac," was created by the Emergency Home Finance Act of 1970. It is owned by the 12 District Federal Home Loan Banks and is governed by the Federal Home Loan Bank Board. Although empowered to deal in FHA and VA mortgages, FHLMC concentrates on conventional mortgages sold to it by S&Ls, commercial banks, and mortgage bankers.

Both FNMA and FHLMC purchase mortgages which are packaged into "mortgage-backed securities" and traded in the secondary market. Whereas FNMA guarantees the timely payment of both interest and principal on the securities it issues, FHLMC guarantees the timely payment of interest and the ultimate payment of principal. The GNMA does not purchase mortgages. Rather, it acts solely as a guarantor of the timely payment of both interest and principal on those mortgage-backed securities that are collateralized by either FHA or VA mortgages and which are issued by FHA approved lenders.

In recent years there has been a dramatic rise in **mortgage-backed bonds, pass-through securities,** and **mortgage participation interests** issued by FNMA, FHLMC, savings and loan associations, commercial banks and mortgages companies, and which in turn are purchased by thrift institutions in areas of capital surplus. These mortgage-backed securities are also attractive to diversified financial institutions such as life insurance companies, pension funds, and even foreign buyers who want to avoid the bother of dealing with individual mortgage payments and risks, but want a safe, negotiable security with bondlike terms and mortgagelike yields. (A further discussion of mortgage-backed securities can be found in the section entitled "Mortgage-Backed Securities."

REAL ESTATE INVESTMENT TRUSTS (REITS). The **Real Estate Investment Trust Act** of 1960 sanctioned firms known as REITs. A REIT is a real estate company that distributes to its shareholders 90% of ordinary income and meets other qualifications in order to be nontaxable. REITs have the same tax status as that of mutual funds. REITs became popular in the 1960s and early 1970s. Some REITs chose to specialize in equity investment, whereas others made mortgage loans. Mortgage REITs concentrated on riskier lending for land acquisition, development, and construction, and on short-term first and second mortgages on completed projects that were not yet eligible for long-term financing. Unfortunately growth was rapid and little attention was paid to real estate project quality. Also, much of the heavy debt structure was borrowed from commercial banks and insurance companies at rates tied to the prime rate. As the **prime rate** moved to 12%, and as tight money and recession caused projects to slow down and fail, a large portion of the mortgage REIT industry was forced to default on loans. This segment of the REIT industry is still working out "asset swaps" and other debt compromises to its creditors. In the mid-1980s there has been a resurgence of REITs. Older REITs began to perform well and many new REITs were started

FINANCIAL ASPECTS OF THE MORTGAGE INSTRUMENT

This section describes the basic level payment mortgage instrument and its variations. All mortgages that appear on the market today are variations of three fundamental types: the level payment mortgage, the graduated payment mortgage (GPM), and the adjustable rate mortgage (ARM).

THE MORTGAGE AS A DEBT INSTRUMENT. A mortgage is a pledge of property by a mortgagor (property owner) to secure the payment of a loan from a mortgagee (lender). Mortgage loans involve a specific amount of money to be paid back with interest over a set term. The main distinction between a mortgage loan and other loans is that the mortgage loan is collateralized by real property. If the mortgagor defaults on interest or principal payments, the mortgagee can foreclose by taking ownership of the property, and then sell the collateral to cover the remaining loan balance.

MORTGAGE PAYMENTS. The most common mortgage has a monthly, level payment that is a mixture of monthly interest on the outstanding loan balance and an increasing paydown of the principal. Exhibit 2 shows the breakdown of principal and interest in the mortgage payment over the 30-year mortgage term. Each month outstanding principal on the mortgage is reduced, leading to a reduction in the next interest payment. The reduced interest payment allows a larger percentage of the level payments to go toward principal.

Early payments in the amortization of the loan are almost entirely interest. The principal component of the level payment increases each period by $1 + r$ times the previous principal payment, where r is the contract interest rate. Thus if a level payment mortgage bears an interest rate of 12%, each monthly principal payment will be 1% larger than the principal payment in the previous month.

A loan's interest rate (coupon) and maturity (term) together determine the monthly payment required to pay off a loan of a given size. The loan's maturity is the term of the mortgage contract, the maximum time that the mortgage can remain outstanding without being renegotiated. The interest rate on a fixed-

EXHIBIT 2 COMPOSITION OF MORTGAGE PAYMENTS

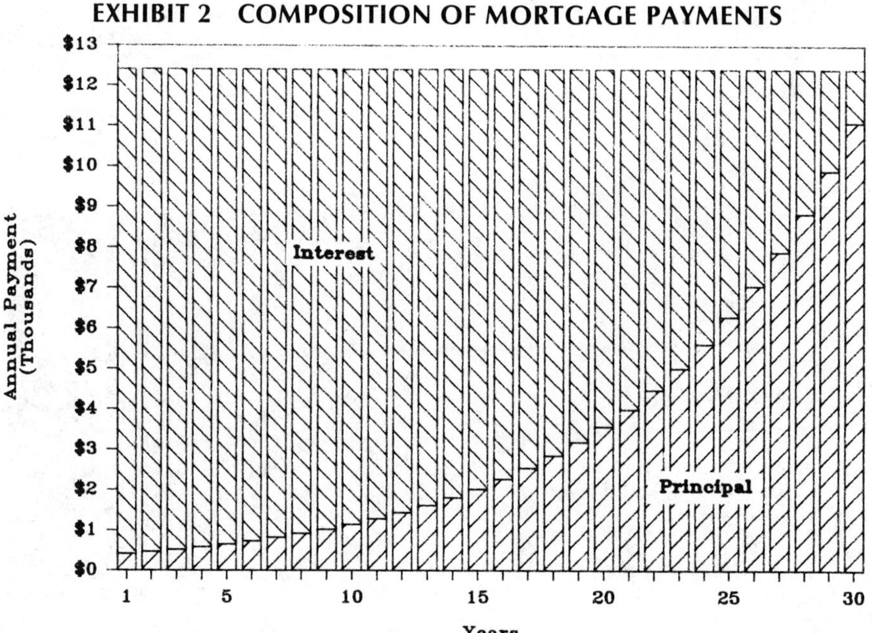

rate mortgage depends on the market interest rates at the time the loan was originated. Market rates are determined primarily by economic factors.

The effects of changing the coupon and the term of a mortgage contract can be summarized as follows:

- Monthly payments increase (decrease) as the coupon increases (decreases)—**the coupon effect**
- The coupon effect increases (decreases) as the coupon increases (decreases)—**coupon convexity**
- Monthly payments increases (decrease) as the term decreases (increases)—**term effect**
- The term effect increases (decreases) as the term decreases (increases)—**term convexity.**

Given a mortgage amount and an interest rate level, the longer the mortgage maturity, the lower the monthly payment (Exhibit 3). Reducing the term on a 12% mortgage from 20 to 10 years increases the monthly payment by 30%. Extending the loan term on a high interest rate loan decreases monthly payments less than extending the loan term by the same amount on a lower interest loan. Further, the payment decreases less for a term extension from 20 to 40 years than for a term extension from 10 to 20 years (Exhibit 4).

Given a mortgage amount and a maturity, the higher the contract interest

EXHIBIT 3 MONTHLY MORTGAGE PAYMENTS AND TERM

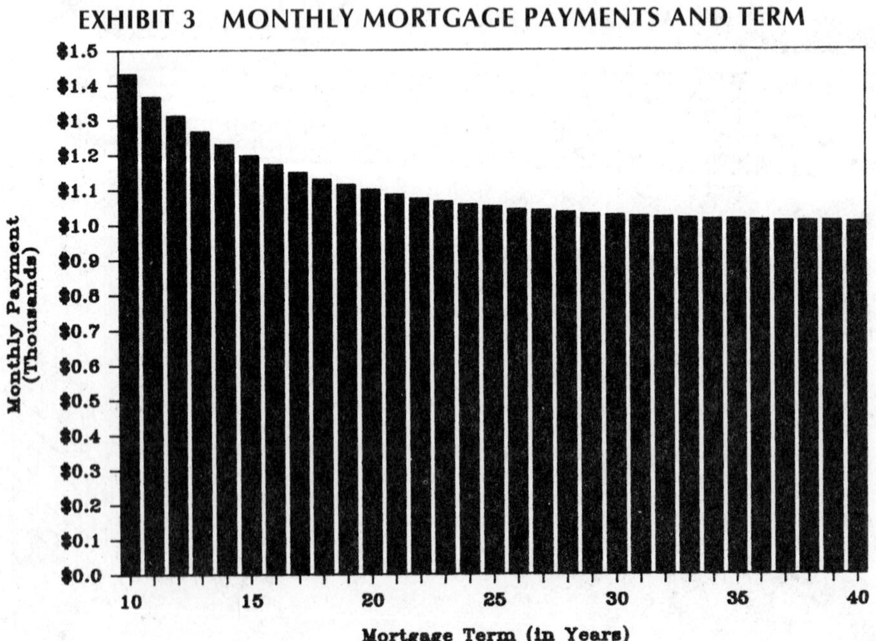

EXHIBIT 4 MONTHLY MORTGAGE PAYMENTS AND COUPON

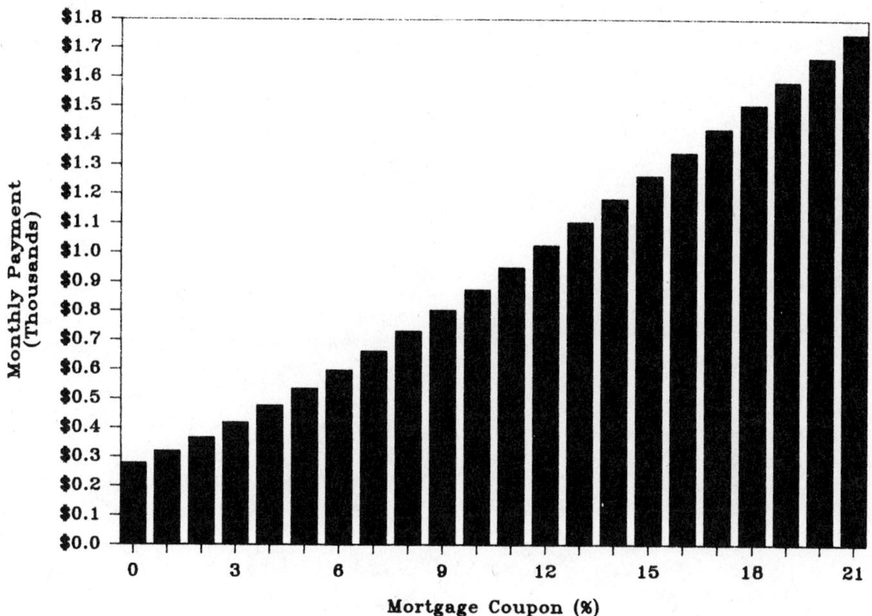

rate, the higher the monthly payment (Exhibit 4). At a mortgage interest rate of 12%, the monthly payment on a $100,000, self-amortizing, 30-year loan is $1,028.61, whereas the monthly payment on an 8%, 30-year loan of the same amount is $733.76, or approximately 30% lower.

MORTGAGE PRINCIPAL BALANCE. By paying off ever-increasing amounts of principal in each monthly payment, the outstanding balance on the loan is paid down, or is **amortized,** slowly at first and then more rapidly, until it is fully paid by the end of the loan term. Exhibit 5 shows amortization schedules of the mortgage balances for both an 8% and a 12% mortgage. Loans such as these, which pay off the entire principal balance over the required term, in equal monthly payments of principal and interest, are called **self-amortizing loans.**

Different Amortization Plans. **Straight term loans** require no principal payments during the mortgage term. They usually involve periodic interest payments with the full principal amount due at the end of the loan term. Generally, loan amounts are 50 to 60% of the property value and maturities are relatively short, seldom exceeding 5 years. Straight term loans, also known as interest only or balloon loans, are used primarily for interim financings.

A **partially amortizing loan** is a loan that requires refinancing of the unamortized portion of the mortgage before the full term of the loan. Level

EXHIBIT 5 MORTGAGE LOAN BALANCES

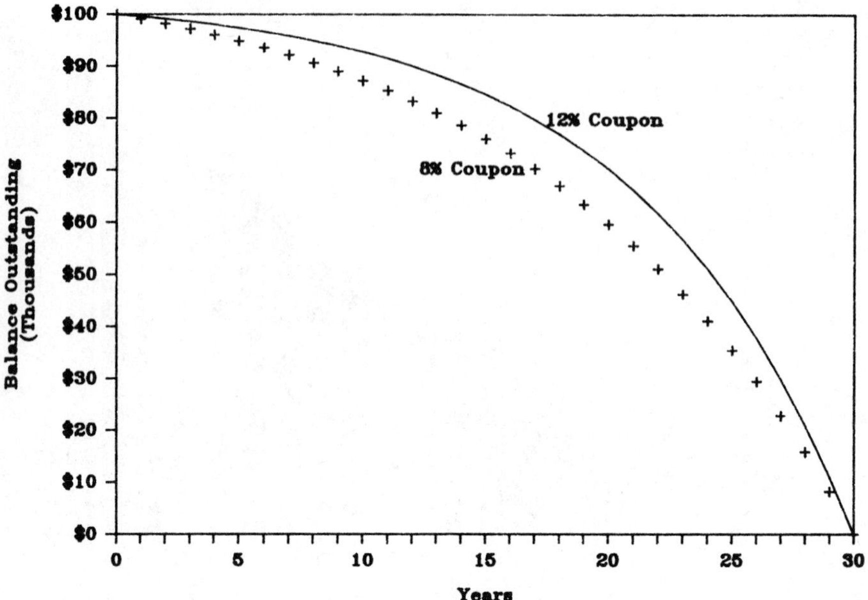

monthly payments on the original debt are made according to a long-term amortization schedule. Because the principal paydown is so low in initial years, payments for short-term loans are similar to the interest-only loan payments. At the loan term, a lump sum, or balloon payment, covering the outstanding principal balance on the loan discharges the debt. Instead of making a cash payment, the borrower often refinances with a new loan.

Another alternative to the level payment mortgage calls for **equal principal payments** to be made each period, with interest paid on the outstanding balance. The principal payment is constant each period during the life of the loan, and the interest payment declines by a constant amount per period as the remaining principal is paid off. Consequently, the total payment declines as interest payments decrease. The equal principal payment approach will ordinarily place a greater initial cash flow burden on the purchaser than amortizing under a different plan, because early payments are larger than later payments. This approach is even more burdensome on an after-tax basis. Because interest is deductible, a greater proportion of the early payments must be made with after-tax funds.

PREPAYMENTS. If the homeowner makes a monthly payment greater than the amount due, the excess payment is applied toward paying off the outstanding loan balance. This can occur when a homeowner wishes to accelerate the payment of his or her mortgage or when the homeowner terminates the mortgage by moving. The prepayment option is comparable to the call privilege of corporate or government security issuers but is generally less restrictive.

Mortgage loans may incorporate a penalty for unscheduled prepayment principal. This fee discourages prepayment, protecting lenders against borrower refinancings that reduce the yield on the portfolio of lending institutions. Either by policy or by state law, some prepayments may be exempted from the penalty provision. Prepayment charges are often patterned after Federal Home Loan Bank Board regulations.

Financing constraints for industrial or commercial properties usually incorporate a prohibition against prepayment for a certain period, a balloon payment requiring prepayment at a later date, and a penalty for prepayment between those two dates. For example, a loan on an office building may have a 30-year amortization schedule with a balloon payment required after 15 years. Prepayment may be prohibited for the first 5 years and a sliding scale of prepayment charges may be set for the fifth through the tenth or fifteenth years of the loan.

VARIATIONS ON THE LEVEL PAYMENT RESIDENTIAL MORTGAGE. Prior to the 1970s the traditional mortgage payment with its constant coupon rate and fixed monthly payments was attractive to both borrowers and lenders. Since the early 1970s, increased rate volatility has made lenders less willing to lend money for 30 years at a fixed interest rate. Borrowers have become less willing or able to meet the higher mortgage payments that resulted from higher interest rates. This new economic environment has motivated lenders to create new types of mortgages and has generated a renewed interest in some old approaches. Most important among these new products are graduated payment and adjustable rate mortgages.

Graduated Payment Mortgages. Graduated payment mortgages (GPM) allow borrowers to make low initial mortgage payments that rise through time. Generally, for the first 5 to 10 years, monthly payments start at a significant percentage (commonly 9 to 24%) below level mortgage payments for a mortgage with the same interest rate and rise by a fixed percentage (2½ to 7½% is common) per year until the graduated payment period (5 to 10 years) has expired. At this point the mortgage's payment schedule becomes identical to a level payment mortgage for the remainder of the loan term (Exhibit 6).

Initial GPM payments may be lower than the interest due on the loan amount. The shortfall in interest is deferred and added to the outstanding balance. This is called **negative amortization.** The negative amortization causes the outstanding loan balance to rise (1 to 5% is common) over the initial years of the mortgage loan. As Exhibit 7 shows, the outstanding balance on a negative amortizing GPM loan will always be slightly larger than the balance on an equal coupon level payment mortgage and remain above the initial mortgage balance for several years. If the value of the property collateralizing the loan increases sufficiently with inflation, the loan-to-value ratio of mortgage may

EXHIBIT 6 BREAKDOWN OF GPM PAYMENT

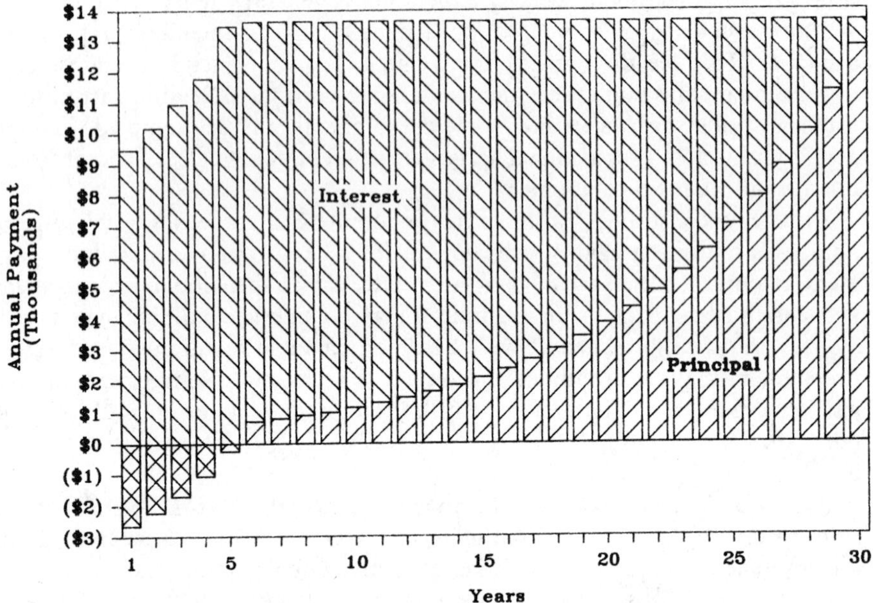

even remain constant. If the property value or homeowner's income fail to keep pace with the loan's increasing outstanding balance and monthly payments, credit risk on the loan may rise over the graduated payment period. To protect against such credit risk, most negative amortization loans are originated with insurance that adjusts to the outstanding loan balance.

The essential characterisatics of graduated payment mortgages are:

- Lower initial payments that rise periodically until the graduated payment period expires
- Negative amortization (deferred interest is added to the principal outstanding
- More credit considerations than level payment mortgages
- Higher payments than on a level payment, fixed-rate mortgage once the graduated payment period is ended.

Adjustable Rate Mortgages. An **adjustable rate mortgage** (ARM) is a mortgage whose contract interest rate changes periodically over time based on a specific interest rate index. The interest rate charged on the loan is equal to the index plus a fixed margin. The advantage to lenders is that if interest rates rise over the term of the loan, lenders are able to charge higher interest rates on the remaining balance of the loans. Also, because many mortgage lenders (such

EXHIBIT 7 GPM LOAN BALANCES

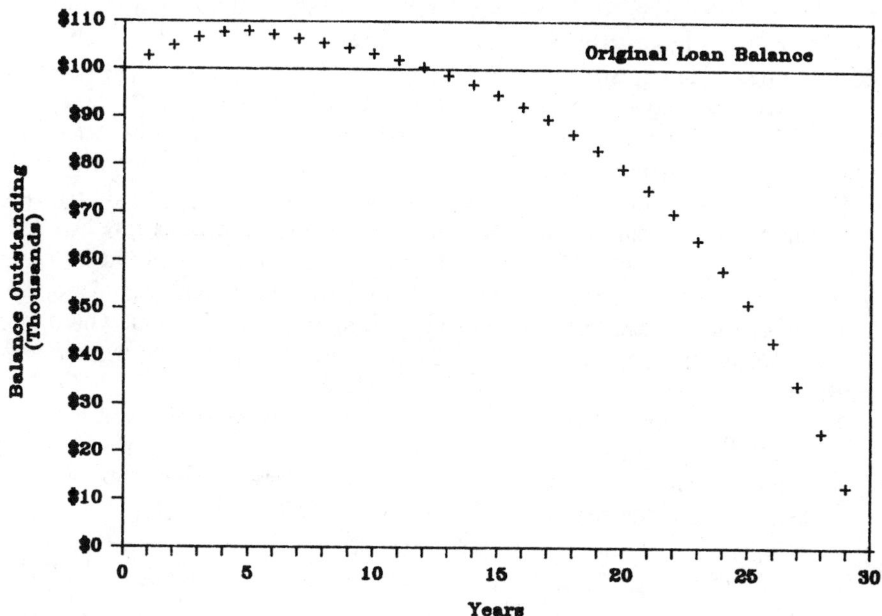

as savings and loans) finance mortgages with short-term funds, ARMs allow them to maintain a better asset/liability spread match. The lower interest rate risk from the lender's point of view results in lower initial rates in a positive yield curve environment, and borrowers can qualify for larger loans.

Sometimes, initial rates, known as **"teaser rates,"** lower than the index plus the margin are charged for the first few months of the loan to attract and qualify more borrowers. Teaser rates are good for only a short period of time (usually 1 year or less), after which the coupon adjusts to reflect current market interest rates.

Adjustable rate mortgages shift interest rate risk inherent in long-term financing from the lender to the borrower. Some early forms of ARMs tried to shift all the interest rate risk to the home buyer, substituting credit risk for interest rate risk. Lenders were increasing the likelihood of defaults on their loan portfolios because many homeowners simply were unable to grasp the potential impact of unlimited interest rate increases. In recognition of this interest-rate risk trade-off, most of today's ARMs have **payment** and/or **interest rate caps** to protect borrowers from wide swings in interest rates. These caps limit the interest rate responsiveness of ARMs, but they also reduce the probability of default on the loans; the lender is now shifting only some of the interest rate risk to the borrower in exchange for reduced credit risk.

Interest rate caps limit the actual accrual rate that may be charged on a loan. For example, consider an ARM with a 2% interest rate cap per adjustment, and a current contract interest rate of 12% based on an interest rate index of 9.5%. If the interest index used for adjustments moves to 13%, and the loan should adjust to 250 basis points (the margin) over this index (to 15.5%), the caps would limit the new rate adjustment to 14%. Any interest above this level is lost.

Payment caps have a different effect on ARM rates. A payment cap limits the actual dollar increase in monthly payments for an ARM, rather than the underlying accrual rate of the loan. Payment caps minimize "payment shock" to the homeowner when interest rates are rising rapidly. To continue the previous example, if the loan had a 7.5% payment cap, and no interest rate cap, the new rate at adjustment would be 15.5%, but the new payment would be 7.5% greater than the previous payment. In this case, the payment would not be large enough to cover interest on the outstanding balance. The loan would experience negative amortization for a period at least up to the next payment adjustment.

The essential characteristics of adjustable rate mortgages are:

- Responsiveness to changes in market interest rates. Hence, borrowers bear interest rate risk.
- Rates tied to short-term interest rates. In a positive yield curve environment, initial ARM rates and payments will be lower than those for level payment mortgages with fixed rates.
- Teaser rates lower initial monthly payments but may introduce default risk because of payment shock.
- Caps limit the borrower's exposure to interest rate changes, thereby reducing the credit risk to the lender.
- Payment-capped ARMs may result in negtive amortization that reduces the homeowner's equity in the loan.

HOW A MORTGAGE IS ORIGINATED

THE APPLICATION PROCESS. The **mortgage application process** requires a period of time for the lender to determine the creditworthiness of the borrower and the value of the property. Generally, the origination of a loan includes the follow steps:

- The borrower must have firm agreement to purchase a house.
- The borrower must sign a loan application that includes a personal balance sheet and monthly income statement.
- The lender orders a credit report and obtains third-party verification of the borrower's employment and deposits.
- The lender applies for private mortgage insurance or FHA/VA insurance, if necessary.
- If the borrower is approved, the lender orders an appraisal and title report.

- If the property is acceptable, the lender issues a commitment to originate a mortgage for a limited time period. The interest rate is usually committed to at this time.
- Just prior to closing, the lender prepares the loan documents.
- On proof that the borrower has obtained hazard insurance, closing occurs and the lender disperses the cash.
- The homeowner begins monthly payments.

CREDIT CONSIDERATIONS. To obtain a mortgage to purchase a home, most prospective buyers are required to make cash down payments of at least 5% of the value of the home. Down payments typically range between 5 and 20% of the lower of either the purchase price or the appraised value of the home. In most cases the size of the down payment relative to the value of the home determines a key ratio that mortgage lenders use when evaluating loans. The ratio of the loan balance to the value of the property is called the **loan-to-value ratio (LTV).** A smaller LTV gives the lender a greater chance of recovering its loan value after the expense of a default or foreclosure. Hence it is more likely that the lender will originate a mortgage if the LTV is small. Lenders may require mortgage insurance to insure a portion of the loan balance if the LTV is too large.

Lenders limit the monthly payments to a stated percent of the monthly disposable income of the potential borrower. Disposable income is defined as gross income less other debt obligations and sometimes less other household expenses, such as taxes, insurance, utilities, and maintenance. Rules of thumb usually dictate that the mortgage payment be no more than 25 to 33% of disposable income, depending on the income definition. These rules vary with the net worth of the borrower, the quality of the underlying property, and the desire of the lender to maintain mortgage origination volume.

Lenders often require a monthly payment, in addition to the mortgage payment, that goes into an escrow account to be used for property taxes and insurance to insure that the homeowner budgets these items. The homeowner may or may not receive interest on the escrow account.

ORIGINATION AND CLOSING FEES. Borrowers are charged **closing costs** associated with mortgage originations. **Origination fees,** usually 1 to 2% of the loan balance, are partially used to cover lender loan origination expenses. **Discount points** are usually charged when originating FHA/VA loans to bring lender yields to the market rate. **Miscellaneous charges** include mortgage insurance, title search, credit reports, appraisals, and other items for which the borrower must reimburse the lender.

Closing costs are either paid directly by the borrower or are withheld from the loan proceeds at closing. Whenever fees are greater than expenses, the mortgage yield to the lender will exceed the nominal contract rate. Federal truth-in-lending laws, as generally implemented in **Regulation Z,** require disclosure of the effective interest rate on noncommercial loans. The effective interest rate includes the contract interest rate, initial discounts, and certain charges, treated as if they were interest.

Monthly installments that become overdue incur late charges. Generally the mortgage lender provides a grace period before the fee is imposed. Late charges are usually some portion of the late payment. Regulations in some states prohibit basing late payment charges on the loan balance outstanding or adding unpaid late charges to the unpaid balance of the loan, a practice known as **pyramiding.**

MORTGAGE INSURANCE. Mortgage insurance is used widely throughout the housing finance industry to reduce the credit risk borne by the originator and the ultimate investor. Without mortgage insurance, investors in conventional loans would bear all the risk of loss associated with the loans. Mortgage insurors became widely used with the development of the secondary market providing third-party credit assurance to investors unfamiliar with individual borrowers or loan sellers.

FHA-VA Insurance. The Federal Housing Administration's and the Veterans Administration's insurance are government-insured loan programs that set standards for loan terms and eligible properties, and insure lending institutions producing qualifying loans against loan losses. The FHA program insures each eligible loan 100%, whereas the VA guarantees a percentage of the loan.

Private Mortgage Insurance. A lending institution or mortgage banker can insure loans that are not eligible for FHA-VA insurance with private insurance companies. These companies insure loans with LTVs as high as 95%. However, they ordinarily insure only the first 20 to 25% of the mortgage balance. Fees for basic coverage on a 99% loan typically consist of an initial premium of 0.5% of the loan amount, with annual renewal premiums of 0.25% of the outstanding loan balance. These fees are either paid directly by the borrower or are built into the contract and paid by the lender.

MORTGAGE LIENS. Most mortgages are first mortgages, which carry a first claim against the real estate pledged as security. There are many situations in which second and third mortgages are also used.

With a **second mortgage,** the lender's claim to the property is subordinated to the first mortgage. Maturities are usually shorter than those of the first mortgage loan. Second mortgages often make economic sense when a low interest rate, assumable first mortgage exists.

SPECIAL TYPES OF MORTGAGES

The preceding sections illustrate the fundamental types of mortgages. In practice there are many variations on these basic themes which are combined to meet particular situations. This section highlights some of these products.

CONSTRUCTION LOANS. Most construction is financed with construction loans that typically are notes or a series of short-term notes drawn at intervals during the building period. Disbursement schedules are designed to meet the specific cash flow requirements of particular projects being financed. Most commercial construction loans are made by commercial banks, whereas residential loans are often drawn on thrifts. Construction loans for individual houses sometimes convert into mortgages on completion of the house. Otherwise, interim financing is repaid with the proceeds from the permanent mortgage loan once the project is completed.

Construction loans adapt to the situation for which the financing is required. Disbursement schedules can be determined in several ways. For some loans, disbursements are made after completion of certain phases of the construction project. For example, 25% of the loan may be paid out when the foundation is completed; 25% when the roof, rough plumbing, and wiring are installed; 35% when the structure is completed and ready for occupancy; and 15% after the period of filing mechanics' liens has passed. Another disbursement schedule is the voucher system, which requires the builder to submit bills to the lender for payment as the building progresses, or permits the borrower to draw loan funds in amounts equal to a certain percentage of the cost of the work completed for which payment has already been made.

Construction loans carry origination fees and are usually issued at rates pegged to the prime lending rate. The effective yields on construction loans are relatively high because of the short maturity periods, partial disbursement of funds, and high closing costs. The high yields are justified by the high risk and high administrative costs of the loans.

DEPOSIT COLLATERAL MORTGAGES. The desposit collateral mortgage is secured by real estate and a specified deposit account and is used when a borrower requires a loan with a high LTV. Usually, a third party agrees to pledge an account at a financial institution as collateral for the loan. The pledged account is gradually released to the third party as the mortgage is paid off and the collateral is no longer needed. The third party collects interest on the unreleased balance in the pledged account.

ESCROW DEPOSIT INTEREST REDUCTION MORTGAGES. The escrow desposit interest reduction mortgage is a level payment, fixed-rate, fully-amortizing mortgage where the interest from tax and insurance escrow accounts is applied monthly toward principal payment of the mortgage. Monthly payments remain at the initial contract level, shortening the mortgage term.

LAND DEVELOPMENT FINANCINGS. Subdivision developers typically require financing to install costly capital facilities. The cost of converting a farm into residential subdivision lots, for example, can far exceed the investment in the raw land.

The **blanket mortgage** note is used often in land development financing of subdivisions. The mortgage attaches to each lot in the subdivision. As the project is completed and the lots are ready for sale, an individual lot may be removed (partial release) as security for the loan upon the payment of a specified sum. The release payments usually are set at such levels that the entire loan will be repaid before all the pledged lots have been released.

LEASEHOLD MORTGAGES. Leasehold mortgages are used to finance large-scale developments such as office buildings, shopping centers, and some industrial properties. They can be used in combination with other types of financing to subdivide property interests in a single unit of real estate. In a leasehold mortgage, one party leases a piece of property from another to develop the buildings to be leased to other tenants. A mortgage is obtained to develop the property secured by the borrower's rights as a lessee and by future rents due under tenant lease contracts. The security for the mortgage is essentially the right to access future rents from the improvements.

OPEN-END MORTGAGES. An open-end mortgage includes provisions for future advances from the lender to the borrower, secured by the original mortgage. The advance is generally repayable over the unexpired term of the original mortgage. If additional advances are optional, the lender can use discretion to decide whether to lend additional funds. Open-end mortgages are used primarily to finance improvements, expansion, or remodeling of residential property financed by the original mortgage.

PACKAGE MORTGAGES. A package mortgage is a standard first mortgage that involves personal property as well as real estate. The pledged personal items are treated as a separate loan secured by a **chattel** (lien against personal property). Payments for the real estate and personal property are consolidated in one note with one payment, eliminating the need to negotiate separate installment loans on each item.

PLEDGED ACCOUNT AND BUYDOWN MORTGAGES. Pledged account and buydown mortgage loans are variations on the graduated payment mortgage. Both of these loans require an amount of cash in an interest-bearing savings account to be used to cover the negative amortization. Pledged account mortgages require the home purchaser to fund the savings account; buydown loans require the home seller, usually a homebuilder, to fund the account.

PURCHASE MONEY MORTGAGES. The purchase money mortgage is used when a buyer acquires property partially on credit from the seller and pledges as security the property being bought. This mortgage is used often in land acquisition and subdivision development projects. The seller usually agrees that the lien will be subordinated to a claim of another lender supplying either land development or construction funds. The seller is secured only by the value of the pledged property.

REVERSE ANNUITY MORTGAGES. The reverse annuity mortgage converts the equity in a home to an income stream from the lender to the borrower of equal monthly payments. The balance on this loan increases constantly over time. Homeowners effectively borrow each month against the value of their property. This loan is primarily originated for the elderly to supplement their retirement income.

ROLLOVER MORTGAGES. The rollover mortgage is a type of adjustable rate mortgage that has been popular in Canada for many years. Simply defined it is a fixed-rate mortgage whose interest rate is renegotiated every 3 to 5 years. The homeowner may or may not stay with the same mortgage lender, thus retaining some bargaining power in contract renegotiations.

SHARED APPRECIATION MORTGAGES. The shared appreciation mortgage is another contact designed to reduce monthly payments in times of inflation. It allows the borrower to pay a reduced contract interest rate in return for sharing a specified percentage of the increase in the value of the mortgaged property with the lender. The lender receives compensation either when the property is sold or at a specified future time such as the loan maturity date.

WRAPAROUND MORTGAGES. If a property is subject to an existing, assumable mortgage at less than current mortgage interest rates and if the new homeowner wishes additional funds, a wraparound mortgage can be issued that includes both the amount of the existing mortgage and an additional amount loaned under the new wraparound mortgage. The homeowner than amortizes the wraparound mortgage as if it were the first mortgage.

Typically in today's environment, the wraparound mortgage has a higher interest rate than the existing mortgage rate, has a longer term, and requires payments in excess of those required for the existing loan. The lender of the wraparound mortgage receives payments on the new loan and makes payments on the old mortgage, retaining any difference between the two payments. The resulting yield may provide an attractive return to the lender originating the wraparound. Some lenders issue wraparound mortgages with lower payments than the first mortgage payments. These loans have a longer term than the existing mortgage and involve negative amortization.

LEASING

LONG-TERM LEASES. A **long-term lease** is often used instead of mortgage financing by firms wishing to conserve working capital or even to free working capital invested in real estate. In some instances the deductibility of lease payments as an expense for income tax purposes makes leasing more economical for business firms than buying real property on a mortgage, because lease payments are deductible as a business expense whereas principal repayments are not. Long-term real estate leases are of two types: (1) net leases, under which the tenant maintains the property; and (2) gross leases, under which the tenant pays a given rental to the owner, who assumes all maintenance expenses.

Net Leases. There are three standard forms of the **net lease:** the long-term lease (often 99-year lease to a developer), the 21-year lease and the lease to a user-tenant of improved space. To the owner of the real estate the 99-year lease is likely to appear as a sale on an annuity basis. This type of lease is usually made on large pieces of valuable land and is typically regarded as well-secured, long-term investment on a net basis. Frequently it results from the owner's inability to sell the property because of complications with an estate, a desire to avoid reinvestment of proceeds of the sale, or a deferred payment of a capital gains tax.

Ninety-nine-year leases are often used on prime commercial or office building sites. The lessee may agree to purchase for cash any buildings on the site and then replace them with a new building or buildings. The lessor receives a net rental (i.e., in addition to the rent, the tenant pays the taxes, water rates, insurance, and operating expenses of the building). Typically, 99-year leases made after 1945 include provisions for rental adjustments to combat inflation.

The **21-year lease,** characteristic of New York real estate, is basically a ground lease. It differs from the 99-year lease mainly in that under the ground lease, if the land is improved, the tenant purchases the improvements, but is not obligated to erect a new building. If there are no improvements, or if the improvements are obsolete, the tenant may, at his or her option, erect a new structure. The 21-year lease usually gives the tenant one to three options to renew for additional terms of 21 years each. The rent paid is also net, the tenant paying all maintenance. There may or may not be step-up provisions for the rentals. The renewal options provide that 1 or 2 years prior to the expiration of the original term, the tenant must signify his or her intention to exercise the renewal privilege. The renewal options may specify that the rent be set at a percentage of the market value at the time of renewal or at a predetermined figure but, in any event, the rental in the renewal period is seldom set at a figure below the amount paid in the preceding term.

Early **sale-leaseback transactions,** dating from the 1940s and 1950s, set the initial rental at a figure sufficient to amortize completely the initial investment with interest on the outstanding balances during the first-term lease. The renewal options then called for sharply reduced rentals for the succeeding term. Sale-leaseback transactions are more like financial arrangements between insurance companies and substantial tenants than they are like real estate transactions. The credit rating of the tenants, the former owners, is at least as important as the value of the property as security for the lease. Early sale-leaseback transactions were generous to the tenant, because the owners gave up the opportunity for value appreciation.

In the **long-term net lease,** the lessee is typically the property user, who will occupy all or the greater portion of the building. The term of the lease is usually 20 years or less and is written on a net rental basis. Ordinarily it is on improved property, and the lessee is not expected to erect a structure or provide improvements to it.

Long-term net leases usually have the following provisions:

1. The landlord provides no maintenance; the tenant pays all operating charges. The landlord receives the monthly or quarterly rental and pays interest and amortization on the mortgage, if there is one.
2. The landlord is not obligated to make repairs. In the event of fire or other casualty causing damage or destruction of the building, the tenant is obligated to repair or rebuild; and if the insurance proceeds are insufficient, the tenant makes up the deficiency. Rent does not cease for any reason.

Gross Leases. Gross leases represent the most common type of lease contract and are typical of rental situations involving short-term tenancy. Normally they contain no provision for periodic rent adjustments, and there are no standard arrangements regarding renewals.

The tenant pays a given rental to the owner, who has the burden of management. The leases sometimes require the lessee to pay the real estate taxes in excess of a certain stipulated amount. Tenants may also be assessed for operating expenses of certain types, such as snow removal, and institutional advertising and grounds care in the case of shopping centers. As operating costs have risen, landlords have become less willing to write gross leases.

The rent on commercial properties is frequently based on gross revenues of the tenant, with a stipulated minimum rent. (A summary of percentage lease rates on selected types of properties is given in "Percentage Leases," National Institute of Real Estate Brokers.)

TYPICAL PROVISIONS OF LEASES. The essential parts of the real estate lease are the names of the parties; the extent and boundaries of the properties; the term of the lease; the amount of the rent; and the time of payment and execution by the parties.

VARIABLE RENT LEASES. The longer a lease's term, the greater the possibility that the real flow of rent to the lessor will be diminished by inflation, rising taxes, or changes in the production capacity of the property. Several devices have been used to alter lease payments to meet changed conditions. Among such variable leases are the expense-participating lease, the step-up or step-down lease, the reappraisal lease, the percentage lease, and leases based on a cost-of-living index. Leases calling for reappraisals are likely to be burdensome to one or the other of the parties and difficult to administer because the rent to be paid during certain periods of the term of the lease will be determined by strangers to the contract. The uncertainty about rent levels is a mental hazard to both the landlord and the tenant and a hindrance to the sale of the building as well as to the sale of the tenant's business.

In addition to objecting to the uncertainty attending appraisals, the parties often object to the inconvenience and expense incident to the process. It appears that if the appraisal accomplishes its purpose, the inconvenience and expense are amply justified by the result.

Leases adjusted according to changes in some price index, such as the Consumer Price Index (CPI) may frustrate as well as protect lease parties. To guard against too frequent readjustment, the leases usually prohibit an adjustment more frequently than once a year, and then only if the CPI has changed by not less than a stipulated percentage.

The **percentage lease** is the most common of all the variable leases. Because rent payments are expressed as a percentage of gross sales, leases automatically take into account inflation, changes in the attractiveness of the site, and variable performance by the tenant. Current operating data provide the basis for rent determination without the necessity for special calculations or reviews. The disadvantages are (1) underreporting of sales by tenants and (2) failure of weak tenants to produce enough sales.

SALE-LEASEBACK FINANCING. A sale and leaseback arrangement is created when the owner of real estate, usually a well-established business corporation, sells property to an investor and then leases the property from the purchaser for a stipulated period. Office buildings, retail outlets, and industrial properties are types of real estate commonly covered by this type of financing, which is also referred to as a **"purchase and leaseback"** or a **"liquidating lease."**

Terms of sales and leasebacks typically range from 20 to 40 years. Provisions for renewal or repurchase may be included in the contract. The lessor receives a net rental; that is, the lessee pays maintenance and repair costs, taxes and assessments, utility charges, insurance, and so on. The net rent is fixed so that the lessor's original investment will be repaid by the end of the first term of the lease and a return comparable with rates currently available on government bonds will be yielded by the rent payments. The rate of return may be graduated, rather than level, over the life of the lease, with higher rates during the early years of the lease. This enables the lessor to recover his or her investment more rapidly.

The price at which the property is sold to an institutional investor is not necessarily the same as the current market price. The purchaser might be willing to pay a premium price that would be reflected in the higher rents received under the lease. The selling corporation, in turn, would have a gain taxable at capital gains rates, whereas the higher rents would be tax-deductible as operating expenses.

The **main advantages** to the seller initiating a **sale-leaseback** are (1) the seller retains possession of real estate with no capital investment, (2) the seller may deduct rent as an operating expense, and (3) the proceeds of the sale provide capital for business purposes. Advantages to the purchaser-lessor include the following points: (1) a relatively higher rate of return is obtained after amortization of the principal of the investment; (2) the lessor maintains more control over real estate it leases than over that on which it holds a mortgage; (3)

the sale and leaseback arrangement is a long-term investment involving no early prepayments, with the burden of taxes, maintenance, repairs, and insurance expenses borne by the lessee; (4) the sum of money invested is usually quite large, thus involving relatively low investment management costs; and (5) the purchaser is in a position to realize any capital gains from appreciation after the lease term.

The disadvantage to the purchaser-lessor is the long-term, relatively fixed nature of the lease.

OPTIONS, ESCROWS, AND LAND TRUSTS

REAL ESTATE OPTIONS. An **option** is a contact that gives the buyer the right to complete a real estate transaction in accordance with predetermined terms within a given time period in return for a consideration. If the option is exercised in compliance with all terms of the agreement, the consideration (i.e., option price) ordinarily becomes part of the purchase price of the real estate. If, however, the holder of the option fails to act before the expiration of the option, consideration is forfeited and he or she loses any further rights in the property.

An option contract may prove extremely valuable to its holder in that the option holder, with no commitment to buy, has secured property at a known price and on known sale terms. This enables the buyer to negotiate for other property, obtain zoning amendments, secure financing, process a subdivision plot, or abandon his or her original plan and let the option expire if other factors make completion of the project infeasible.

REAL ESTATE ESCROWS. An **escrow** is an arrangement wherein a disinterested third party serves to protect the interests of two or more contracting parties while a title transfer is being effected or after a default has occurred. An escrow agent performs many functions that the parties to the contract would normally undertake themselves in completing the transaction. According to the instructions of the escrow agreement, the escrow agent may collect all the papers, releases, and money necesssary to the transaction and effect the exchanges with full protection to all parties. The escrow holder coordinates the activities of the interested parties, making certain that all legal and contractual obligations have been fulfilled before a title is transferred. For example, it is not unusual in real estate transactions for the seller to be unable to satisfy the mortgage until he or she receives the proceeds from the buyer. The buyer, in turn, or the mortgagee, will be unwilling to pay the full purchase price to the seller until the mortgage claim against the seller's property has been satisfied. The escrow arrangement allows the impasse to be overcome.

The escrow period may be a relatively short time, to allow for the completion of a title search or the arrangement of financing. It may, however, extend for months or years, during which a long-term contract for the purchase of land is fulfilled.

LAND TRUSTS. A **land trust** is created by a deed in trust under which the grantor conveys to a trustee, usually a corporate trustee, a title to property to be held for a specified beneficiary. The warranty deed conveying the title of the property must be recorded in the public records, but the trust agreement need not be recorded and, accordingly, the identity of the beneficiary need not become public information. The beneficiary may be the creator of the trust.

The land trust is used both for the holding of single properties and for the assembling of parcels of land. It permits privacy of ownership, limited liability for beneficiaries, and multiple ownership without the legal complexities of joint tenancies or tenancies in common. Interests in trusts may be conveyed by assignment of the beneficial interest.

MORTGAGE SECONDARY MARKETS

In addition to the primary real estate lending market when buyers and sellers deal directly, substantial **secondary markets** exist that deal both in spot loans and in future and forward contracts. In secondary markets dealing in spot loans, mortgages can be bought or sold for immediate delivery. A typical selling institution for the secondary market would be a **mortgage banker,** which is in the business of originating mortgage loans, selling them to investors, and servicing the loans for the investors.

Secondary mortgage markets range from being highly organized to very informal. The major formal secondary markets in the United States consist of the **Federal National Mortgage Association (FNMA),** which now primarily purchases conventional loans but which has historically been the primary purchaser of FHA and VA loans; the **Government National Mortgage Association (GNMA),** which serves as a guarantor for modified mortgage pass-through securities issued by lenders and backed by FHA or VA loans and the **Federal Home Loan Mortgage Corporation (FHLMC),** which serves as a secondary mortgage market for conventional loans. Secondary markets are important to real estate finance transactions because they move real estate funds from areas of capital surplus to areas of deficit. They also standardize many real estate finance instruments so that a mortgage originated in one part of the country will closely resemble a similar mortgage originated in another part of the country. Both the Federal National Mortgage Association and the Federal Home Loan Mortgage Corporation require that mortgages be originated on approved forms before these loans can be purchased.

MORTGAGE-BACKED SECURITIES. A **mortgage-backed security (MBS)** is formed when a group of similar mortgages is pooled together in a security to be sold and traded. For a mortgage pool to be traded actively, information costs and transaction costs must be low. This section describes the complex requirements for efficient trading of **mortgage pools,** as well as the securities and industry trading standards that have evolved to meet these requirements.

Securitizing Mortgages. Historically, residential mortgages were funded regionally. Beginning in the 1930s, FHA-insured loans were sold in pools among large institutions. Since the early 1970s the trading of mortgage debt has accelerated. The sheer size of the mortgage market and the increasingly volatile and dynamic economy created the need for liquidity and trading. The advent of modern data processing allowed the complicated transactions to become manageable.

Pooling mortgages into MBSs brings new considerations into the analysis of the cash flows. Payment delays, fees for mortgage servicing, and prepayment patterns make the cash flows to investors different from the cash flows of a single mortgage.

To convert a group of mortgage loans into a security that can be actively traded in the secondary market, many details need to be worked out to reduce information and transaction costs. The potential investor would want to know several things before investing in a pool of mortgages, such as:

1. How will the bookkeeping and loan servicing be managed?
2. What are the security risks?
3. What analytical information is available to evaluate the security?

Exhibit 8 details some of these investor concerns. Mortgage-backed securities must be designed so that the answers to these questions are known and will not hamper efficient trading.

Loan originators sellers and servicers also are interested in knowing:

1. What method of pool securitization and sale yields the highest revenues?
2. What are the limitations on pooling and loan qualification?
3. What are the residual administrative responsibilities?

Exhibit 9 details some of these seller/servicer concerns. These concerns must be resolved efficiently through effective MBS design so that new pools can be securitized easily and the market can grow.

Institutions such as GNMA, FNMA, and FHLMC have evolved to solve these problems by facilitating the standardization of documentation and un-

EXHIBIT 8 MBS INVESTOR CONCERNS

Recordkeeping:	Competence of servicers, consolidation of checks, accounting information on pools
Guarantee:	Comprehensiveness of guarantee and financial strength of guarantor
Marketability:	Liquidity, ease of registration
Standardization:	Pool size and geographic distribution uniformity of underlying security

EXHIBIT 9 MBS ISSUER CONCERNS

Administrative costs:	Security holder record maintenance and tax withholding and reporting, Pool processing, accounting, balance reporting
Funds management:	Ease of making timely payments, float
Pool formation:	Range of interest rates, mortgagee qualifications
Market risk:	Exposure in pipeline, liquidity, length of forward commitment

derwriting practices, and the securitization of mortgages into large homogeneous pools. They also create the appropriate incentives to monitor the credit aspects of the loans. Mortgage originators pay a fee to these institutions in return for:

1. Guaranteeing to the investors that the documents are held by a trustee
2. Approving qualified and competent servicers to collect mortgage payments
3. Providing some form of interest and principal insurance (some institutions guarantee timely payments of both interest and principal)

Each institution performs these functions and designs its securities in different ways. Exhibit 10 lists the categories of MBS features that differ among the securities.

The largest participants in the MBS secondary market are the government-sponsored agencies: the Government National Mortgage Association (GNMA), the Federal Home Loan Mortgage Corporation (FHLMC), and the Federal National Mortgage Association (FNMA). Their roles are to enhance

EXHIBIT 10 DIFFERENCES AMONG MBSs

Origination
Packager
Issuer
Servicer

Loan Type
Collateral requirements
Maturty
Contract interest rate
Amortization and payment plans

Risk
Guarantor
Guarantee
Pool insurance
Pool size and geographical distribution
Credit standards for underlying loans

Liquidity
Number of pools outstanding
Dollar amount outstanding

Market Information
Yields

the flow of funds from the capital markets to the housing market via the purchase of mortgages and the sale of guaranteed mortgage-backed securities.

Other large financial institutions have issued mortgage-backed securities. These have come to be known as **private pass-throughs,** conventional mortgages, or **Connie Macs.**

Large pools of nonsecuritized mortgages or **whole loans** are often sold in the secondary market. These transactions involve the sale of an entire pool of loans, or the sale of a "participation" interest in the underlying pool.

FORWARD AND FUTURES MARKETS. In addition to the spot secondary markets, formal markets exist for both forward and future trading.

Forward contracts are agreements to buy for a set price, a security to be delivered at a specified date in the future. The forward delivery price is set so that the contract itself has no value at the date the contract is originated. No cash changes hands until the contract is delivered.

A **futures contract** is like a forward contract, but it is marked to market every day. The parties have margin accounts from which they "settle up" daily. For example, if party A contacts to buy an asset for $100 from party B in 60 days and the price of that asset rises, party A's account will receive compensation from party B. The Chicago Board of Trade has an active market in 30-year Treasury Bond Futures.

An asset forward price is not necessarily equal to its current "cash" price or "spot" price. The price may differ if expectations are that the asset will have a different value on the delivery date. Also, a forward price is often lower than its cash price to compensate the forward purchaser for bearing the risk of price fluctuations over the contract term. The difference between the forward and cash price is known as the basis drop, or carry.

Forward Trading. Forward trading is maintained by FHLMC, FNMA, and GNMA **underwriters.** Primary lending institutions may sell for forward delivery a package of mortgages using a number of possible vehicles. The sale for forward delivery allows the mortgage lender to quote a certain rate to large builders, developers, and individual customers who may be seeking real estate loans.

Because the trading of mortgage-backed securities is so complex, most routine secondary market trades are done on a forward basis. The delivery dates are standard for the industry for each security and coupon traded. By having set delivery dates, the delivery process is simplified.

MBS forward contracts are called TBAs (To Be Announced). The actual pools traded are unknown when the forward contract is made and pools must be announced by the delivery date.

Future Trading. Organized futures trading is carried on by the Chicago Board of Trade and the American Commodities Exchange in **GNMA modified**

pass-through securities. The mortgage futures market operates similarly to the futures market in grain or other commodities. It allows mortgage lending institutions to hedge portfolio positions and remove interest rate risk, and serves functions similar to those served by the forward delivery market, except that mortgages are generally not actually traded in the futures market, because futures positions are normally closed out prior to the delivery date.

PUT AND CALL OPTIONS. An option contract is a contingent agreement to make or take delivery of a specific asset at a specified "exercise" or "strike" price by a specified "expiration" or "notice" date.

The owner of a **call option** has the right, but not the obligation to buy an asset at a specified price by a certain date. The owner of a **put option** has the right, but not the obligation, to sell an asset at a specified price by a certain date.

The seller of the call is subject to having an asset called away and is sold at the exercise price. Put sellers are subject to having an asset put to them, in which case they must buy the asset at the exercise price.

Assume that a call option, priced at $1, grants the owner of the option the right to buy an asset worth $100 from the option seller, at any time over the next month. The owner of the call will profit if the value of the asset exceeds the exercise price by at least the purchase price of the call. For example, if the asset value rises to $102, then the asset can be purchased at the exercise price of $100 and immediately sold for $102. The profit covers the $1 of the call, for a net profit on the transaction of $1.

If the value of the asset is $100 or less at the end of the month, the option expires worthless. The option seller profits if the asset value stays below $101 and gives up any price increase above $101 to the call owner. From the example, it is clear that the call owner is long the asset and the call seller is short the asset.

Consider a $1 put option with an exercise price of $100 expiring in 1 month, with the value of the underlying asset at $100. If the asset value is at or above $100, the put is worthless. The put seller profits if the market rises and put expires unexercised, and loses if the market falls and he or she must buy the asset above market. Thus the put owner is short the asset and the put seller is long the asset.

With the growth of the secondary MBS cash and forward (TBA) markets, MBS option trading has become very active and many conventions have developed. Options are typically sold on current coupon MBS TBAs. Most options are sold "at-the-money," or with the exercise price equal to the price of the TBA at the time of the option's origination. The notice date is normally 2 weeks before the industry delivery date.Thus a typical December call option might have a notice date of December 5 and strike price equal to today's December TBA price. The call would grant the owner the option to go long a December TBA at any time between now and December 5, at today's price.

INVESTMENT FEATURES OF REAL ESTATE

Real estate features of major interest to both lenders and equity investors are value stability, investment safety, investment yield (in terms of certainty and stability), marketability or investment liquidity, capital appreciation, protection from inflation, and tax minimization opportunities. Real estate, however, cannot be rated as a homogeneous investment asset. Different types of real estate have different investment attributes.

RISK CHARACTERISTICS. The risks inherent in any real estate investment arise from the following factors: (1) environmental and physical characteristics of the real estate, (2) type of property, (3) market trends, (4) financing arrangements of the investor, (5) governmental influence, and (6) taxes.

Environmental and Physical Characteristics. The physical characteristics of real estate obviously determine its capacity to produce useful service. One of the most significant criteria is the **functional character of the design,** which may influence the profitability of operations of a business using the structure, maintenance costs and, of course, the rents that can be obtained from the property. Other important physical attributes are construction quality, convertibility, architectural style, and adaptation of the structure to the site.

Construction quality is measured by whether the building will be capable of performing its functions satisfactorily during the entire economic life of the structure without requiring unusually heavy maintenance expense.

The **architectural style** and the adaptation of the structure to the site each may influence the uses to which the building may be put as well as the efficiency with which the property can be used. To a great extent, the value characteristics of real estate are determined by the attributes of the neighborhood, the district, or the immediate environment of the property.

Type of Property Is a Key Indicator of Risk. Properties such as shopping centers provide cubes of space for various retail and office tenants. If the tenant does poorly or sells a fad item that drops from favor, the tenant can terminate the lease replaced with another shop. If the property type is a racquetball club, however, and the sport decreases in popularity or the market area becomes oversaturated with facilities, the next-best use for the property (such as warehousing) may produce less rent and incur high conversion costs. In contemplating a specific use for improving land, one must consider carefully the current and future market demand for the property type and its alternative future uses.

Market Trend and Lease Terms. Real estate improvements are long-lived assets, whose present value is based primarily on long-term net operating income streams. Analyzing present market conditions at the time of conception of the development is not sufficient. Projections about future population, employment, incomes, space needs, buying power, consumer preferences, and inflation rates also must be made. The investor can insulate himself or herself, to some degree, against unexpected trends by preleasing, and by the use of long-term net leases. By doing so, however, he or she often sacrifices the opportunity for future value appreciation. Over the last 40 years greater real estate value probably has been lost by charging too little rent for too long than has been lost by overcharging or by ill-considered projects.

Financing Arrangements for Investor. The investment character of a fee interest in improved property is directly related to the financial obligations involved. A leaseholder's interest may have risk comparable with those of a fee holder, depending on the position of the leasehold and whether the leaseholder is an investor in improvements. The greater the number of mortgage commitments and subleases a leaseholder has, the greater the risks of the leasehold position.

The amount of leverage involved in either a fee or a leasehold situation is a factor in determining whether a particular program represents an investment or a speculation. For many years the **loan-to-value ratio** was the principal measure of financing risk. A 75% first mortgage, at a fixed interest rate lower than the ratio of net operating income to cost, would give the 25% equity holder positive leverage. If the property produced a 10% return on cost and 75% of cost could be borrowed at 8% interest, then the investor was left with 4% for this 25% of cost or a 16% rate of return:

75% LTV	% of Cost
Operating income	10
Interest 75% × 8%	6
Residual to owner	4
−Owner's investment	25
Owner's rate of return	16

The preceding example ignores both required amortization of the mortgage and changes in operating income over time, however. As interest rates have risen to double digits, the **income-to-debt service ratio** test is being utilized to analyze whether the adequacy of fluctuating operating income will cover required mortgage payments for interest and amortization, yet still leave the owner a cushion for repairs, vacancies, dips in rent, and any unexpected costs. The income-to-debt service ratio looks more to the property's income performance to service the debt and less at how much the lender thought the borrower had invested in the property as the principal risk factor. This shift in emphasis is part of the trend for lenders (1) to remain interested in the future profitability of projects; (2) to accept shorter leases with more frequent opportunities to increase rents and pass on increases in operating costs; (3) to require equity participation in loans; (4) to be more willing to finance all the cost if the income justifies it; and (5) to become direct equity investors.

Governmental Influence. It is increasingly necessary to consider the role of local, state, and federal government in assessing the risks of real estate investment. Local planning and zoning processes can delay projects, change project design, access, density and pricing, and impose large percentage costs of fees, site work, payment for schools, inclusion of low-income housing units, and so on. State laws can impose energy regulations and air and water quality requirements. Federal laws can change the expensing versus capitalizing tax status of development costs and alter other tax aspects such as depreciation and interest. All levels of government can condemn the property or change its environment for better or worse from an investment standpoint.

Income taxes play a major role in real estate finance because of the industry's tendency to finance a high portion of cost through long-term debt, and because of the depreciation deduction for structures, fixtures, and personal property. The **real estate tax "shelter"** has become emphasized—often overemphasized. Shelter is the ability of real estate investments to show a negative taxable income, which not only frees the owner's property income from tax but reduces the tax he or she would otherwise have to pay on other income. It is wisely said that tax shelter cannot make a bad real estate investment good, but it can certainly make a good one better. Consider the following example:

Investment Returns

Operating income, first year	$10.00
Less: Interest, 75% loan at 12%	9.00
Amortization	0.30
Residual to owner	$ 0.70
−Owner's investment	25.00
Owner's rate of return, pretax	2.8%

The owner's return of 2.8% looks inadequate; however, he or she is allowed to deduct depreciation. Let us assume that 75% of cost is depreciable and that the owner uses **component depreciation.** (The structure, carpets, roof, paving, etc., are depreciated over their separate useful lives.) Assume that this compound depreciation averages 30 years. On a straight-line basis, depreciation expense would be 2.5% of cost per year (75% × costs × 3.33%). The owner's taxable income for the first year would be:

Operating income	$10.00
Less: Interest	9.00
Depreciation	2.50
Taxable income	$ (1.5)%
× Tax rate of 50%	$(0.75)
− Owner's investment	$25.00
Owner's return from tax loss	3%

The investor has **tax-free cash flow** in the first year equal to 2.8% of his or her cash investment. The tax saving from otherwise taxable income equals 3% of his or her cash investment. The total is 5.8%. This is equivalent to a fully taxable return on investment of (10.6% at the 50% tax bracket). Additionally, if operating income goes up over time 30% from 10% of cost to 12% of cost, and all other factors remained constant (and ignoring the slight increase in amortization), the results would be as follows:

Operating income	$12.00
Less: Interest	9.00
Depreciation	2.50
Taxable income	$ 0.50
× Tax rate of 50%	$ 0.25

Cash Flow to Investor

Operating income	$12.00
Less: Interest	9.00
Amortization	0.30
Income tax	0.25
Cash flow after tax	$ 2.45
– Owner's investment	$25.00
Owner's rate of return after tax	9.80%

This return equals 19.5% pretax to an investor in the 50% bracket. A 20% increase in operating income caused the owner's single-year after-tax return to increase 69%, from 5.8 to 9.8%. The increase in operating income could come from percentage higher rents. Note, however, that a decrease in operating income of only 7% (from 10% of cost to 9.3% of cost) would eliminate the investor's pretax cash flow from the property, because 9.3% operating income less 9% of cost for interest and 0.3% for amortization uses all the property cash flow. Decreases in operating income increase the value of the tax shelter. In fact, it would take a 39% decrease in operating income, from 10% of cost to 7.1% of cost, to make the 50% tax bracket investor have zero total return as follows:

Operating income	$7.10
Less: Interest	9.00
Depreciation	2.50
Taxable income	(4.40)
× Tax rate of 50%	(2.20)

After-tax Cash Flow to Investor

Operating income	$7.10
Less: Interest	9.00
Amortization	0.30
Plus: Tax savings	2.20
	0.00

The preceding examples show the combined effects of leverage and income tax. The last example shows that tax benefits cushion the return impact of a decrease in operating results. A property that has turned bad and shows substantially lower operating income cannot be "made good" simply by its tax benefits, however. The computations in this section are simplified, single-period analyses and are no subtitle for multiperiod analysis of **internal rate of return** and **net present value.** (These techniques are discussed in the companion *Handbook of Corporate Finance,* Section 9.)

Real Estate Valuation. **Appraisals** for mortgage lenders differ little from analyses for equity investors. Mortgage lenders are concerned with the probability that the debt will be satisfied on schedule and that, in the event of default, the property value will be large enough to cover any outstanding loan balance. The equity investor seeks essentially the same information, because the probable rate of return on his or her equity is closely related to the value of the property. This investor is also interested in depreciation allowances, in a property's value stability, and especially in the prospects for capital gains.

Three standard approaches to **value analysis** are in use (1) market comparison, (2) income capitalization, and (3) cost of replacement. Data rarely are available to permit the satisfactory use of all three methods in a single value analysis.

Market Comparison Approach. Whenever a property is of a type actually traded in the real estate markets, the appraiser or analyst will determine what has been paid for similar properties to arrive at the consensus of the market about the present worth of the property. The market comparison method examines property sales under market conditions comparable with those at the given time. The comparisons units should be properties with physical, legal, environmental, and financing characteristics similar to those of the property being evaluated. Truly comparable situations are difficult to find. This method, however, is used in the valuation of all kinds of property and is employed whenever possible, even when other appraisal methods are used in the valuation analysis.

Income Capitalization Analysis. The capitalization of income approach is used whenever it is possible to estimate the net operating income stream of the property. The value analysis of investment property almost always involves income capitalization appraising. The basic objective is to estimate reasonable net operating income stream for the economic life of the property and to translate this into a present worth estimate, often through the use of annuity factors. This requires that the remaining economic life of the property be estimated, together with the gross income potential, and probable operating expenses.

Market comparison techniques also come into play in the income capitalization analysis, because the process involves the application of appropriate capitalization rates to projected income. The discount rates selected must be close to those being earned by investors in properties of comparable risks.

Replacement Cost Approach. Certain kinds of real property are not readily traded in the market and produce no measurable money income. These special purpose or amenity producing properties are valued or analyzed on a replacement cost basis.

The analysis technique is divided into two parts: (1) estimation of the cost to replace the subject structure with new facilities that would render comparable services, and (2) measurement of any differences in productivity between the subject property and the hypothetical replacement that might occur because of technological advances in the new property. The differential is called depreciation or penalty, so that the method of valuation is called either the "replacement cost less depreciation" method or the "penalized cost of replacement" approach.

The market comparison and replacement cost methods can be combined to compare a proposed new development with the price of existing properties of the same type in the area. If a new shopping center costs $100 per square foot of leasable space, whereas existing centers are available for $70, the investor and the lender must be able to show why the new center can produce sufficiently higher operating income to justify the development.

INVESTMENT CHARACTERISTICS BY PROPERTY TYPE. Although there are often major differences among properties of the same type in different geographic markets, some general statements can be made.

Office Buildings. Many of the major office buildings in urban centers are built for a specific corporate user who may own the building or **net lease** the entire space. This type of user may hire a management and leasing firm to rent out space not currently needed. Corporations have sold their buildings to institutional investors and leased them back so that the corporation can keep its operating capital in its own business. Rising utility and other operating costs and increased emphasis on rising operating income and value have caused office building landlords to seek shorter leases and to pass on cost increases to tenants. With the movement of the population to suburbia and the rise of small, entrepreneurial companies, suburban office parks have grown in popularity. "Incubator offices," with small spaces available on very short leases—even month to month, sometimes—with central secretarial and computer services, exercise rooms, and luncheon facilities, also are being built in increasing numbers.

Shopping Centers. Ownership of the downtown retail hubs in many of the cities generally is spread among many owners. It is not unusual for a family that bought property and started a business downtown to retire and become landlords to the successor occupants. Since the 1940s, major suburban regional shopping centers have boomed. These centers with major department stores as "anchors" and between 50–150 other stores succeeded so well that they sometimes became almost new downtowns, from a retail and weekend social standpoint. Retail revitalization projects have developed in many downtowns, within both town shopping centers and mixed use projects (retail, office, and housing all in one complex). Some feel that the high cost of suburban housing and the costs of commuting to work and to shop will slow this rapid growth. Neighborhood shopping centers continue as strong as the communities they serve, provided owners and managers perform good maintenance, refurbish the appearance regularly, and pay attention to securing a strong tenant mix. In shopping centers, tenants typically pay for all increases in operating costs. They pay utilities and common area charges for the mall, parking area, and open space maintenance.

Apartments. Apartment building ownership has long been a popular type of investment for individuals. Smaller buildings often are owner-occupied and managed. Owner-managers, however, frequently find it difficult to raise rents, evict tenants, and enforce rules. Many foreigners coming to the United States have purchased apartment buildings as an inflation and currency hedge. In some markets these buyers have pushed prices to the point where there is little or no cash flow for the equity investor. Concern about the ability to raise rents to match rising operating costs, as well as concern about rent control, are causing some investors to evaluate this investment type very carefully. Similarly, lenders are questioning income-to-debt service ratios, particularly for new properties. Yet, vacancies are low. This is certainly not an equilibrium situation, and risk is high, but there also exists the possibility for higher capital appreciation returns. Some investors are converting rental apartments to condominium ownership units.

Single-Family Houses. An area of increasing importance is investment in single-family homes. A large share of personal wealth is represented by the ownership of one's own home for personal residence. Some individual investors buy homes to rent to others. Often, the cash flow to the investor is negative. The investors are looking to leverage and price appreciation of the home to offset negative cash flows.

In areas of the country where demographic growth is high, the economy strong, and utility costs not too high, house prices can appreciate rapidly. If the price of a home goes up 10% in a year and the investor's down payment is 20% of cost, then the appreciation on his equity is 50%. This can more than offset any negative cash flow.

Some lenders are beginning to look at equity returns on houses and other investment real estate compared with the cost of long-term fixed rates on mortgages. Investing in real estate is usually a long-term investment, and its liquidity is limited compared with stocks and bonds. It requires careful analysis of the economic, physical, financial, and tax aspects of each transaction.

BIBLIOGRAPHY

Denz, R. E., "Lease Provisions Designed to Meet Changing Economic Conditions," *University of Illinois Law Forum* (Fall 1952).

Kahn, Sanders, *Real Estate Appraisal and Investment,* New York: Ronald Press, 1977.

Leider, Arnold, "How to Wrap Around a Mortgage," *Real Estate Review* (Winter 1975): 29–34.

Levinson, D., "Basic Principles of Real Estate Leases," *University of Illinois Law Forum* (Fall 1952).

Plant, Kenneth, M., "Playing the Futures Market Game," *Federal Home Loan Bank Board Journal* (November 1975): 15–21.

Smith, David L., "Reforming the Mortgage Instrument," *Federal Home Loan Bank Board Journal* (May 1976): 2–9.

11

CONSUMER FINANCE

CONTENTS

11

CONSUMER FINANCE

A. Charlene Sullivan

PRINCIPLES AND FORMS OF CONSUMER CREDIT

DEFINITION OF CONSUMER CREDIT. Families and individuals use credit to provide for short- and intermediate-term financing and as a payment system to increase convenience of making transactions. As defined by the Federal Reserve Board, consumer credit includes short- and intermediate-term credit that is extended through regular business channels to finance the purchase of commodities and services for personal consumption, or to refinance debts incurred for such purposes. Thirty-day charge credit held by retailers, oil and gas companies, and travel and entertainment companies is not included in the consumer credit statistics published by the Federal Reserve Board. Loans against the cash value of insurance policies are not included. Home mortgage credit for financing the purchase of single-family or multifamily homes, which is long term and reported separately, is not included. However, personal loans secured by amortized second mortgages are included in the statistics.

Consumer credit is subdivided for reporting purposes by the Federal Reserve Board into installment and noninstallment credit. **Installment credit** includes all consumer credit scheduled to be repaid in two or more payments; **noninstallment credit** includes credit scheduled to be repaid as a single, lump sum.

GROWTH OF CONSUMER CREDIT OUTSTANDING. Total consumer credit outstanding has grown rapidly in the past two decades, from a level of $44 billion in 1960 to $447.5 billion in September 1984. In 1970 consumer credit comprised 7.97% of the total public and private debt. Exhibit 1 shows the amount of consumer credit outstanding, together with all net public and private debt outstanding for year-end 1978, 1980, and 1982. In 1978, 8.97% of total debt was consumer credit. From the 1978 high, that percentage fell to 7.34 in 1982.

EXHIBIT 1 NET PUBLIC AND PRIVATE DEBT, SELECTED YEARS 1978–1982 ($ BILLIONS)

Credit Market Debt Owed By	1978	1980	1982
Public	1,099.2	1,373.6	1,808.0
U.S. government and agencies	626.2	742.8	991.4
U.S. government sponsored credit agencies and mortgage pools	181.7	273.9	379.6
State and local	291.3	356.9	437.0
Private financial and nonfinancial	1,571.3	1,962.9	2,382.6
Corporate and foreign bonds	432.5	507.9	567.7
Mortgages	413.7	493.6	617.0
Other debt	725.1	961.4	1,197.9
Consumer	1,079.8	1,366.7	1,637.7
Home mortgages	759.9	978.5	1,209.8
Consumer credit	337.9	388.2	427.9
Total	3,768.3	4,703.2	5,828.3

Source: Federal Reserve Board Flow of Funds Series.

Total consumer borrowing including **mortgage credit,** as a percentage of total private and public debt outstanding, grew from 26.4% in 1970 to 28.1% in 1982. Mortgages outstanding on one- to four-family homes rose by approximately $231.2 billion or 24% between 1980 and 1982. Consumer installment credit grew by approximately $40 billion or 10% during the same period.

VARIABILITY OF CONSUMER CREDIT OUTSTANDING. Consumers' demand for credit is derived from their demand for consumption durables. As a consequence, changes in consumer credit outstanding have been used to predict turns in the business cycle. Exhibit 2, a chart of changes in consumer credit outstanding over time, reveals that consumer credit outstanding as well as mortgage credit outstanding fell sharply before and during the recessionary periods in 1969–1970, in 1973–1975, and again during the recessionary periods in 1980–1982.

The ratio of changes in consumer installment credit outstanding to disposable personal income (Exhibit 3), the "credit change ratio" typically turns down about eight months before the peak in a business cycle and turns up slightly in advance of a business cycle trough.

TYPES OF INSTALLMENT CREDIT. The four types of installment credit are automobile, revolving, mobile home, and other loans. **Automobile credit** includes loans originated directly by the lending institution (direct paper) plus loans originated by a dealer and purchased by a creditor (indirect paper) for the purpose of financing a private automobile. The automobile generally serves as security for the loan. **Revolving credit** includes credit on credit cards at retailer establishments, gasoline companies, and commercial banks, and check credit at commercial banks. Revolving credit is credit obtained under an ar-

EXHIBIT 2 NET CHANGES IN CONSUMER AND MORTGAGE CREDIT OUTSTANDING

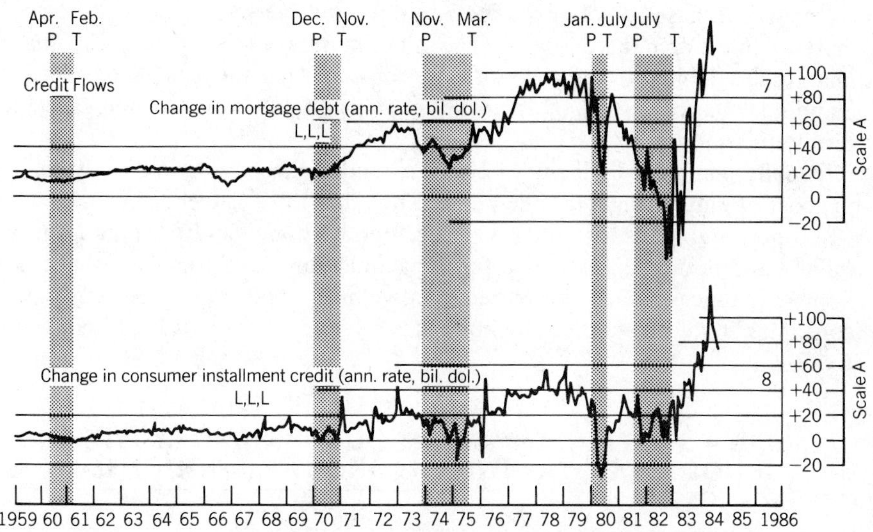

Source: U.S. Department of Commerce, *Business Conditions Digest,* October 1984, p. 2.

EXHIBIT 3 CREDIT CHANGE RATIO (CHANGE IN CONSUMER INSTALLMENT CREDIT TO DISPOSABLE PERSONAL INCOME)

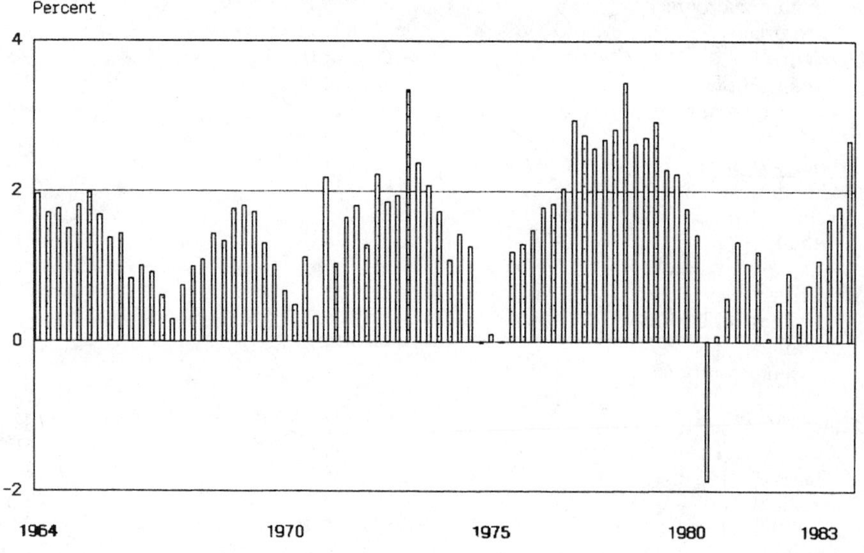

rangement whereby the consumer has an approved line of credit and is allowed to make purchases or obtain a loan against the line by presenting the credit card to the merchant or bank. The amount financed and periodic finance charges are debited to the account. The consumer has the right to pay the outstanding balance in full or in installment payments equal to a prespecified minimum amount.

Mobile home credit includes credit extended directly or indirectly for the purpose of purchasing a mobile home. The other loans category includes unsecured personal loans, personal loans secured by home equity, home improvement loans, and credit extended for the acquisition of such consumer goods as home appliances, boats, and recreational vehicles. The amount of each type of consumer credit outstanding by holders at year-end 1979 and 1983 is shown in Exhibit 4.

EXHIBIT 4 INSTALLMENT CREDIT OUTSTANDING BY TYPE AND HOLDER AT YEAR-END 1979 AND 1983 ($ BILLIONS)

	1979	1983
Total Installment Credit	311.3	381.5
Commercial banks	194.8	174.7
Finance companies	68.3	97.2
Credit unions	48.2	53.2
Retailers	27.9	30.1
Others[a]	17.1	26.3
Automobile	115.0	146.1
Commercial banks	65.2	71.8
Indirect	37.2	
Direct	28.0	
Credit unions	23.0	25.4
Finance companies	26.8	48.8
Mobile Home	17.4	20.4
Commercial banks	10.0	9.7
Finance companies	3.4	5.0
Others	4.0	5.7
Revolving	55.5	72.4
Commercial banks	29.2	41.7
Retailers	22.1	26.4
Gasoline companies	4.3	4.3
Other	123.4	142.7
Commercial banks	45.4	51.4
Finance companies	38.2	43.4
Credit unions	24.6	27.2
Retailers	5.9	3.7
Others[a]	9.3	17.0

Source: Federal Reserve Bulletin, "Consumer Installment Credit," Board of Governors of the Federal Reserve, Washington, D.C., January 1980 and 1984.

[a]Includes savings and loan, gasoline companies, and mutual savings banks.

EXHIBIT 5 TYPES OF CONSUMER INSTALLMENT CREDIT (AS A PERCENT OF TOTAL INSTALLMENT CREDIT)

	Auto	Revolving	Mobile Home	Other
1970	.344	.049	.023	.584
1975	.333	.087	.084	.496
1976	.350	.089	.075	.486
1977	.359	.170	.065	.405
1978	.371	.177	.057	.396
1979	.373	.182	.054	.391
1980	.377	.177	.056	.390
1981	.380	.183	.054	.384
1982	.372	.188	.063	.377
1983	.365	.194	.060	.380
September 1984	.363	.201	.058	.379

The type of installment credit that has experienced the greatest growth since 1970 is revolving credit (see Exhibit 5). Twenty percent of total consumer credit outstanding in September 1984 was revolving credit compared with about 5% in 1970. As this third-party credit has grown, the volume of unsecured personal loans and outstandings on credit cards issued by retailers have declined as a percentage of total installment credit outstanding.

Installment credit contracts are also subclassified as open end or closed end. **Closed-end** contracts are those under which the consumer borrows a specified amount and repays the loan with a fixed number of equal periodic payments over a specific period of time. **Open-end** contracts or revolving credit allow the consumer to borrow up to the limit of a preapproved credit line and repay principal plus interest over an unspecified period of time; however, the periodic payment must be at least as large as a specified minimum.

SECOND MORTGAGES. The second mortgage, which was once perceived as the "court of last resort" for people who could not obtain less expensive credit, has become a preferred vehicle for obtaining consumer credit. As the market for such credit has developed, banks, brokerage firms, thrift institutions, and finance companies have brought more innovative products to the market.

Consumers who are homeowners have the ability to use mortgage credit to finance commodities and services for personal consumption instead of consumer credit. For example, a consumer buying a home is typically buying appliances, carpets, drapes, and such. Consequently, some percentage of mortgage credit could technically be classified as consumer credit.

In the last two decades, inflationary forces have caused equity in the primary residence to be the single largest asset owned by households. Recent estimates show that between 1947 and 1978 the share of residential housing in the U.S. wealth portfolio grew from 27% to 39%. Since 1975 second mortgage credit outstanding has grown rapidly. An important factor that contributed to the growth of second mortgage credit for consumption purposes was lower available rates for secured loans versus unsecured loans. In addition, second mortgages grew in popularity among lenders after the Bankruptcy Reform Act of 1978.

In 1977 second mortgage loans represented 5.6% of total consumer receivables held by finance companies. In 1982, that percentage had grown to 18%. The greatest growth spurt in second mortgage loans held by finance companies came in 1978 and 1979 when second mortgage loans grew by 78% and 83%, respectively. The level of second mortgage activity subsided between 1980 and 1982 but began to grow again in 1983 as market interest rates for nonmortgage credit increased. In 1983, 8% of personal loans made by finance companies were second mortgage loans, whereas 40% of the dollar volume of total personal loans made by finance companies was secured by home equity.

Loans for consumption purposes that are secured by home equity can take the form of a standard second mortgage contract through which the consumer borrows an amount equal to a percent (up to 70–75%) of the equity (market value less outstanding mortgage claims on property) and repays the loan (principal plus interest) in a series of fixed monthly payments. The alternative is a revolving line of credit secured by the home equity. The consumer may access the line with a credit card or a check and use any amount up to the stated limit of the line. The credit line is usually priced with an initial application fee and a finance rate that floats with the prime lending rate.

Many brokerage firms and investment conglomerates are offering a plan similar to a second mortgage except the equity used as collateral may be that held in a securities portfolio. The assets must be worth at least half the line of credit requested and there is a minimum line offered. The arrangement is priced with a variable rate that is indexed to the prime rate; there is an application fee based on the size of the line; and there may be closing costs.

Under the various programs described here, monthly payments may include only interest on the amount of credit used with a balloon payment of the principal at maturity; or the monthly payment may include interest and principal.

TYPE OF NONINSTALLMENT CREDIT. The components of noninstallment credit are single-payment loans, nonrevolving charge accounts, and service credit. Most single-payment loans are extended by commercial banks. The nonrevolving segment includes traditional 30-day charge accounts of retailers, home heating oil accounts, and other credit card accounts. The most important component of service credit is debt to doctors and hospitals. A smaller portion is owed to public utilities and other service establishments. The Federal Reserve Board reports noninstallment credit outstanding as a single figure. Therefore it is impossible to analyze the various classes of noninstallment consumer credit. Less than 20% of consumer debt is in the form of noninstallment debt.

HOLDERS OF CONSUMER CREDIT. The Federal Reserve Board classifies the amount of consumer credit by holder rather than by originator. A large portion of automobile paper is originated by an auto dealer and sold to a bank or finance company. Thus the bank or finance company, the ultimate supplier of the credit, is classified as the holder of the paper.

The holders of consumer credit include banks, credit unions, retailers, gas and oil companies, savings and loan associations and mutual savings banks, and all the corporations, partnerships, and proprietorships that comprise the **consumer finance industry.** Originally the primary purpose of the entities in the consumer finance business was to finance the consumer. The institutions specializing in financing the consumer were classified as consumer finance companies (small loan), sales finance companies, industrial banks, and industrial loan companies. The distinctions were made because the various types of lenders had unique attributes. In the last decade, however, finance companies have diversified their activities between commercial and consumer markets. And the various types of businesses classified as consumer finance companies have diversified both their assets and liabilities.

Commercial banks are the primary holders of consumer credit contracts, followed by finance companies, credit unions, retailers, and others, including savings and loan associations, gasoline companies, and mutual savings banks (Exhibit 6). Commercial banks' share of consumer credit outstanding declined from 1980 through 1983, reflecting the effects of high market interest rates and restrictive loan rate ceilings. During this period, the share held by finance companies increased as financial affiliates of auto manufacturers offered below market rates on auto loans to facilitate consumers' purchases of automobiles. When loan rate ceilings were removed and the market level of interest rates subsided after 1982, however, banks won back some of the share lost to the financial affiliates.

THE DEVELOPMENT OF THE CONSUMER CREDIT INDUSTRY. The consumer credit industry as it exists today developed from the first consumer credit law, conceived in 1916 to remedy the "loan shark" evil by creating a strictly regulated, legal consumer money-lending business. This remedial law was called the **Uniform Small Loan Law.** The small loan law contained only one permission—the right to charge an economically practicable rate—but it promulgated many stringent regulations designed to prevent abuse of bor-

EXHIBIT 6 MARKET SHARE—TOTAL OUTSTANDING CREDIT

	Commercial Banks	Finance Companies	Credit Unions	Retailers	Savings and Loans	Gasoline Companies	Mutual Savings
December 70	.46	.26	.12	.13	.01		.01
75	.48	.21	.15	.11	.03	.02	.01
80	.47	.25	.14	.08	.03	.01	.01
81	.44	.27	.14	.09	.04	.01	.01
82	.43	.28	.13	.09	.05	.01	.01
83	.43	.26	.14	.08	.06	.01	.02
September 84	.45	.24	.14	.08	.06	.01	.02

rowers and to deter people from borrowing except after careful consideration of their responsibilities. Consumer credit in the United States, at the time the Uniform Small Loan Law was passed, was limited to the charge accounts of wealthy customers, Morris Plan banks that made small loans secured by the borrowers' deposits, a few scattered credit unions, and a few installment sales systems administered by manufacturers of durable goods, such as the Singer Sewing Machine Co.

Consumer Finance Companies. After the passage of the small loan law, consumer finance companies provided the bulk of small personal loans, often on an unsecured or signature basis. When security was required, it usually took the form of a chattel mortgage on an automobile or on household goods.

Traditionally, consumer finance companies positioned themselves as the lender of last resort for people who could not obtain cash credit elsewhere. Recently, many consumer finance companies have adopted policies designed to attract better credit risks and larger loans. In addition, the traditional lines that distinguished consumer finance, sales finance, and commercial finance companies have blurred. In 1983, the 10 largest consumer finance companies included four financial affiliates of manufacturers or retailers, one finance company owned by a bank holding company, one financial affiliate of a company issuing a travel and entertainment card, and three independent consumer finance companies. Finally, the Bank Holding Company Act amendments of 1970 provided the legal basis for bank holding companies to acquire finance companies. Eight of the 50 largest finance companies in 1983 were owned by domestic commercial banking firms.

Until the 1970s the major loan product of consumer finance companies was the small unsecured loan (under $500). With the rapid inflation of the 1970s, however, the need for a $500 loan decreased. And, with increasing labor costs and operating expenses, the $500 loan was not profitable, even in states with very high rate ceilings. In 1970, according to data collected from its members by the American Financial Services Association, 33% of the total number of loans made and 11.3% of all dollars loaned by finance companies reporting such data were in loans under $500. In 1983 only 4.7% of the total number of loans made and 0.9% of all dollars loaned were in loans under $500.

Today, the second most important holder, in terms of dollars of installment credit outstanding, is the consumer finance industry. The financing is done through direct cash loans or through the purchase of installment sales contracts from dealers or retailers, which are created when consumers buy automobiles and other consumer durables on time. Personal loans secured by second mortgages have become a major vehicle for financing and, to a limited extent, finance companies offer revolving credit. At year-end 1981, about 15% of total consumer receivables held by finance companies were unsecured personal loans. Almost 69% of the dollar value of loans extended were secured by automobiles, household goods, and other chattels. Loans secured by real estate made up 18% of total consumer receivables.

In 1982, 36% of the dollar value of consumer loans held by consumer finance companies were classified as personal loans, whereas 52% were auto loans, 5% were mobile home loans, and 7% were other types of loans. According to the American Financial Services Association, about half the dollar volume of personal loans were secured by second mortgages. The average size of the second mortgage loans was $14,675, whereas the average amount borrowed for the rest of the personal loans was $1,433.

To meet the varying credit needs of consumers in the United States, several other types of lenders serve the market. These include commercial banks, credit unions, retailers, savings and loan associations, and mutual savings banks. Each differs from the others in terms of origin, background, method of operation, and objectives.

Commercial Banks. Commercial banks entered the field of consumer installment lending in the late 1920s. The opening of a personal loan department in 1928 by the National City Bank of New York, then the largest commercial bank in the country, was widely publicized. A year after the National City Bank department was established, about 200 personal loan departments had been established in other banks, but many were discontinued during and shortly after the Great Depression. Bankers considered consumer installment lending to be outside their field of activity. After the Depression, however, the favorable experience of sales finance companies, consumer finance companies, and industrial banks showed commercial bankers that consumer installment lending could be safe and profitable.

Although consumer installment lending is not the predominant type of lending for most commercial banks, it has steadily increased in importance both in proportion of total loans and in number of banks participating in the business. In December 1982, nonmortgage loans to individuals accounted for about 10.3% of total assets for all insured banks in the United States; 41% of installment credit outstanding at commercial banks was in the form of auto loans, 27% in the form of revolving credit, 13% in mobile home loans, and 28% in other loans.

Automobile credit held by commercial banks is classified as either direct or indirect credit. Indirect auto credit contracts are created when sales credit contracts are written by an auto dealer, with the vehicle as security, and the contract is sold to the bank. Direct auto credit contracts are created when the consumer negotiates directly with the bank to acquire a personal loan to be used to purchase an automobile.

Revolving credit from commercial banks includes that which is extended through bank credit cards and bank check credit plans. Revolving credit extended by commercial banks more than doubled between year-end 1979 and September 1984, from $29.2 billion to $53.9 billion. There are two major bank credit cards, MasterCard and Visa, which are singly or jointly issued by commercial banks extending revolving credit. The process of extending revolving bank credit involves the issuance of the card(s) to the customer, servicing the local merchants who accept the card, approving and processing transactions and billing to customer accounts, and financing the outstanding balances.

Many banks only issue the cards and/or service the merchants. These are referred to as **agent banks.** Banks that carry the receivables are called **principal banks.** International information networks connecting institutions involved in the business of revolving bank card credit allow customers to use their cards at thousands of locations throughout the world.

The technology of the **credit card** has provided commercial banks with the means to serve a national market for consumer credit. However, a national card issuer was restricted by the panoply of state laws governing maximum credit rates. The Marquette National Bank case of 1980 provided card-issuing banks with the legal basis to avoid restrictive loan rate ceilings by issuing cards from banks domiciled in a state with no legal limit on the rate of the finance charge. In 1981 Citibank moved its credit card operations facility to South Dakota, which had eliminated rate ceilings for revolving credit. By issuing the card from South Dakota, the finance rate charged on the credit card was not subject to the rate ceilings of the state in which the card holder resided. In 1983, 10% of consumers with income above $15,000 held a bank card issued by a bank domiciled in a state other than the one in which the consumer resided.

The emergence of banks serving a national market for credit cards was accompanied by a significant consolidation in the business which was motivated by the presence of significant economics of scale in the credit card business. From 1979 to 1982, only the largest card issuers earned a profit, after cost of money, on their credit card divisions.

Check credit plans account for a small percentage of revolving credit held by commercial banks. A check credit plan basically allows the customer to convert an overdraft on a checking account into an unsecured loan. The customer has a preapproved overdraft line of credit from the bank and pays for the use of the line either on a charge per check basis or through a finance charge.

Credit Unions. Congress passed the Federal Credit Union Act in June 1934, enabling federally chartered credit unions to operate in every state with immunity from general usury laws. Credit unions developed rapidly after the passage of the Act. However, after a fairly rapid increase in share of consumer credit outstandings held by credit unions between 1960–1970, the share held by credit unions has been stable at about 14% since 1970 (Exhibit 6). At year-end 1983, 48% of installment credit outstanding at credit unions was auto credit, 1% was mobile home credit, and 51% was classified as other credit.

Retailers. Retailers have historically originated much of the installment credit extended to consumers for the purchase of goods. Most retailers do not hold the contracts until they are paid off. Rather, they sell all or part of the contracts to a financial institution. Some of the large retailers, such as Sears and J.C. Penney, do not sell their receivables but hold them through a captive finance company.

Retailers who sell on credit can choose from many different alternatives of open- or closed-end credit plans. Some retailers have their own credit plans, administered and financed in-house. Frequently cited advantages to having an in-house credit plan are increased patronage, higher sales to customers who use the credit plan, ease of transaction and merchandise returns, and higher impulse buying. The disadvantage is the high cost of financing. Retailers can also choose to accept third-party revolving credit systems, such as bank cards and travel and entertainment cards. The advantages are larger customer base, lower default losses, and lower financing needs. The disadvantages are high cost (merchant discounts) and the absence of a credit avenue for developing customer loyalty. A popular plan being provided by financial institutions to retailers is the private label financing plan, where retailers have revolving or closed-end credit, but the credit operation is administered and financed by a financial institution or a finance company.

A recent analysis of volume of transactions at retailers accepting various types of payment systems showed that percentage of total sales on a proprietary card ranged between 39 and 58% for various classifications of stores by size. About 40% of total sales transactions involved checks or cash. The balance of total sales (8–12%) were made to a customer offering a third-party card for payment.

Others. The most notable other consumer lenders are the **industrial banks,** savings and loan associations, and mutual savings banks. The idea of industrial banking was developed by Arthur J. Morris, who maintained that he could profitably lend money on a comaker basis in sums as small as $50, to be repaid through monthly savings required for the purpose of liquidating the loan. The first industrial bank was established in 1910. After World War I, industrial banks performed many of the functions of commercial banks. In addition to making consumer loans, industrial banks, where permitted, were accepting time deposits and checking accounts.

Savings and loan associations and mutual savings banks have sought and won permission to provide consumer loans in an attempt to diversify their loan portfolios. Provisions of the Depository Institutions Deregulation and Monetary Control Act of 1980 permitted savings and loan associations to issue credit cards and to invest up to 20% of their assets in consumer and commercial loans. The Depository Institutions Act of 1982 raised to 30% the portion of total assets of savings and loan associations which could be allocated in consumer and commercial loans. Since year-end 1980, the average annual growth rate of consumer credit held by savings and loan associations was 29%. Annual growth rates for the period ranged between 17 and 44%.

PRINCIPLES OF ADMINISTRATION AND CONTROL

COST FACTORS IN DETERMINING RATES FOR FIXED-RATE CONTRACTS.

In a perfect market setting with positive transactions costs, the equilibrium rate charged on any fixed-rate credit contract of given maturity is a function of three variables: the market-determined risk-free rate offered by securities with zero default risk with similar maturity; a risk premium to reward the lender for accepting the default risk inherent in the contract; and the administrative costs of originating and enforcing the contract over the life of that contract.

Risk-Free Rate. The risk-free rate considered in pricing fixed-rate consumer credit contracts is the rate of return attainable to the party investing in a security that has zero default risk and a maturity equivalent to that of the credit contract being priced; for example, yields to maturity on a Treasury security with equivalent maturity.

Default Risk Premium. Consumer credit contracts normally have a short maturity (five years or less) which minimizes the impact of interest rate risk on the pricing of the contract. Therefore the most important source of risk incurred by the lender is default risk. Default risk of a contract is evaluated in terms of the borrower's creditworthiness. Methods commonly used to evaluate the creditworthiness of an individual are discussed later.

In an unrestricted market, the cost of credit or rate of charge will increase as the risk of default increases, holding everything else constant. However, the rates of charge allowed for various types of consumer loan have been highly regulated. Given the creditworthiness of the individual, default risk of the credit contract can be reduced by adjustment of other terms of the contract. Holding all other things constant, default risk decreases as the size of the loan decreases, as maturity decreases, and as collateral requirements relative to the size of the loan increase. Types of collateral commonly used for security in consumer credit contracts are the durables being purchased with proceeds of the loan, bank balances, household goods, wages, or the promise of a cosigner to pay the indebtedness.

Because of the high cost of determining default risk for small contracts, the consumer credit marketplace was historically segregated by risk in that some lenders served high-risk consumers (consumer finance companies) and some served low-risk consumers (commercial banks). This specialization was reinforced by loan rate ceilings that were differentiated by type of lender.

With the trend toward loan rate deregulation, there is less evidence of risk segmentation in the marketplace. In fact, there has been a rather dramatic shift into secured lending activities by consumer finance companies, especially since the passage of the Bankruptcy Reform Act of 1978.

Administrative Expenses. Given the short maturity and small average size of consumer loans relative to other types of debt, the administrative costs of issuing consumer credit are high relative to the average amount outstanding. As a result, many sizes and maturities of consumer loans cannot be offered profitably unless rate ceilings allow explicit charges to be made to cover administrative expenses.

Exhibit 7 shows a simulation of expected net rate of return (before default losses) for loans of various sizes and maturities as origination costs and monthly collection costs vary. These net returns are calculated for loans bearing a 12% annual finance charge (annual percentage rate). It is clear that varia-

EXHIBIT 7 NET RATES OF RETURN (BEFORE LOSSES) ON 12% CONSUMER LOANS, CONTRACT RATE = 12.00

	Size of Consumer Loan					
	$1000			$2500		
Contract Maturity (months):	12	24	36	12	24	36
Payment collection cost						
Origination cost = $50						
$3.75	−5.574	−1.560	0.012	4.540	6.353	7.063
2.50	−3.006	1.181	2.790	5.660	7.505	8.206
1.00	0.131	4.499	6.121	7.013	8.892	9.578
0.50	1.190	5.612	7.232	7.467	9.355	10.036
Origination cost = $25						
$3.75	−1.302	0.741	1.594	6.475	7.386	7.774
2.50	1.401	3.567	4.438	7.619	8.552	8.929
1.00	4.703	6.990	7.850	9.001	9.957	10.315
0.50	5.818	8.138	8.988	9.464	10.427	10.777
Origination cost = $10						
$3.75	1.422	2.183	2.580	7.665	8.017	8.208
2.50	4.211	5.064	5.466	8.824	9.192	9.369
1.00	7.619	8.552	8.929	10.224	10.608	10.764
0.50	8.770	9.723	10.084	10.693	11.082	11.229

tions in the administrative expenses have a sharp impact on the net rate of return for consumer loans and on the sizes and maturities of loans the credit grantor will be willing to offer. As administrative expenses increase, creditors are forced to increase the size and maturity of the loan, given fixed rate ceilings, to earn their economically justified rate of return.

ADJUSTABLE RATE CONSUMER LOANS. The deregulation of rates paid for savings, which followed the enactment of the Depository Institutions Deregulation and Monetary Control Act in 1980, and the increased volatility of interest rates from about 1975 significantly increased the problem of managing interest rate risk for consumer credit lenders. As a result, there has been a rather dramatic shift in both consumer and mortgage credit markets to adjustable-rate contracts. Adjustable-rate loans allow lenders to adjust the rate of finance charge on outstanding credit to reflect market conditions.

The adjustable-rate contracts usually fall into three categories. The first is the "balloon" loan where the monthly payment and term stay the same and changes in the rate are reflected in the size of the last "balloon" payment. The second type is one with a monthly payment that adjusts to reflect changes in the interest rate. The final type is one for which the monthly payment is constant and the term of the loan is extended to reflect changes in the interest rate of charge.

In some states, a minimum and maximum range is specified within which the rate may fluctuate or a limit on how many percentage points the rate can change during the life of the contract is specified. The index used to price the adjustable-rate loan is typically a money market rate such as the six-month Treasury bill rate or the 180-day bank CD rate.

TRENDS IN CONSUMER LOAN RATES. In 1983 automobile and revolving credit made up 56% of total consumer installment credit outstanding, and commercial banks were the holders of the bulk of those two types of credit. Consequently, an analysis of trends in rates charged by commercial banks for auto and revolving credit provides a credible analysis of trends in rates charged for consumer loans.

Between 1972 and 1983 (the period shown in Exhibit 8) the most likely rate charged by commercial banks for direct auto loans with maturity of 36 months

EXHIBIT 8 RATES CHARGED ON FIXED-RATE AUTO LOANS[a]

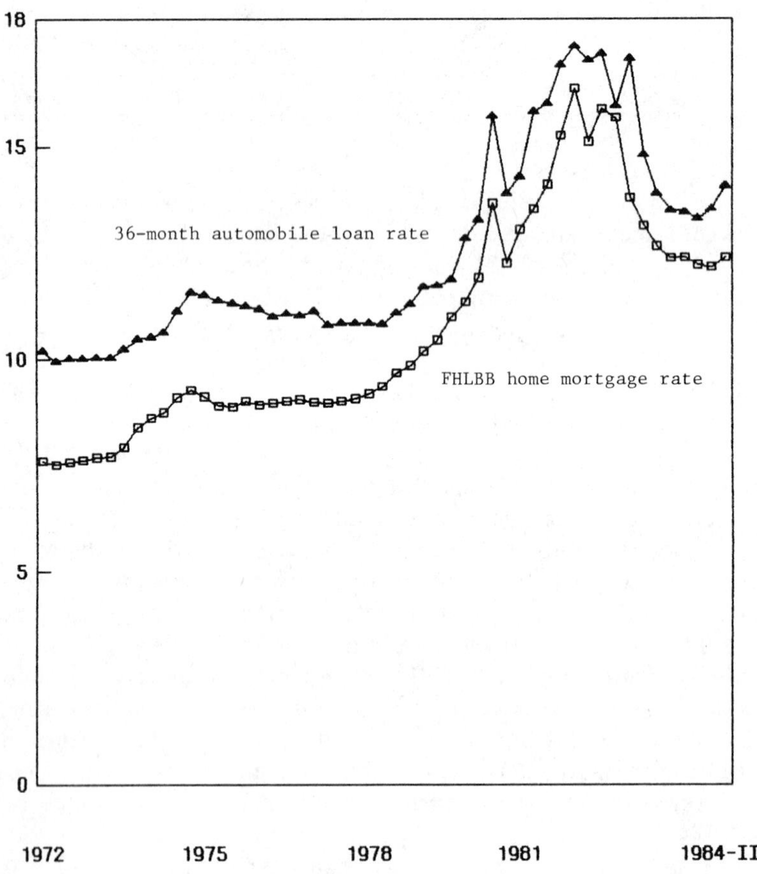

[a] Rates charged on fixed-rate loans.

followed market rates as specified by the three-year constant maturity Treasury bond rate and the average rate for home mortgages with maturity of 10 years. There was no evidence that rates for intermediate-term consumer credit contracts followed trends in the prime rate or other money market rates.

The rate charged for revolving retail lines of credit did not follow trends in market interest rates and, in fact, the rate charged was rather inflexible (see Exhibit 9). The rationale for this apparent disassociation between rates charged on revolving lines and other market rates is that the retail revolving line has no term. Rather, the consumer has an approved line of credit with a fixed finance charge for an indefinite period of time and uses it for credit purposes or for simple transactions by choice. In 1983, almost 50% of the active accounts with commercial banks did not use their cards for credit but simply used the card for transactions purposes, paying no interest charge. (See Exhibit 10.)

To reflect the realities of consumers' card use patterns, credit card issuers began assessing an annual fee to cardholders in 1980. In 1982, about 80% of card-issuing banks charged an annual fee. Some banks use other pricing innovations such as charging from date of purchase (no free period) and charging a transactions fee.

REVENUES FROM CONSUMER CREDIT. The main sources of revenue to an issuer of consumer credit are the finance or interest charge, origination fees, credit insurance fees, and interchange fees and merchant discounts in the case of revolving credit, which are obtained by the use of internationally accepted credit cards.

Finance Charges. Finance charges may be limited by state law and vary considerably from state to state. Since 1980, 32 states have significantly raised or totally removed consumer loan rate ceilings.

EXHIBIT 9 CREDIT CARD RATES AND PRIME RATE

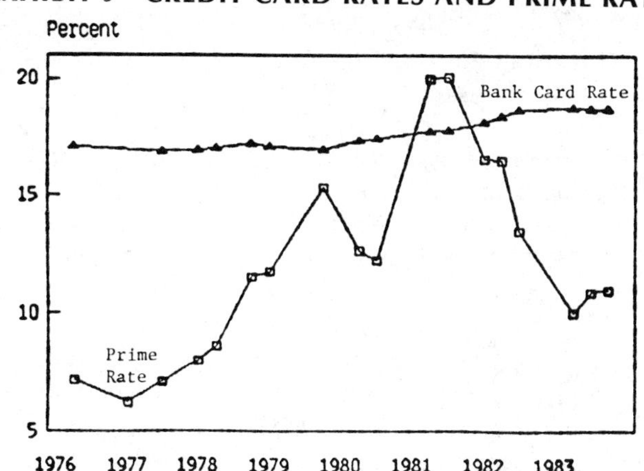

EXHIBIT 10 INTEREST PAID TO MONTH OF PREPAYMENT: RULE OF 78 VERSUS ACTUARIAL METHOD

Interest paid under the Rule of 78 is always more than under the declining balance—

but how much more depends on:

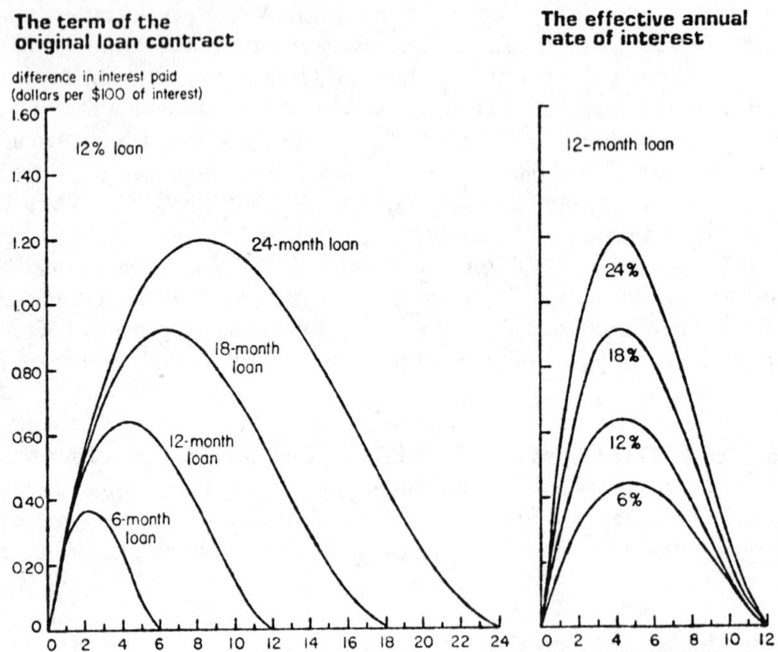

Source: Federal Reserve Bank of Chicago, *Business Conditions,* September 1973, p. 8.

Origination Fees. Origination fees are allowable charges to cover administrative costs of originating a loan. Origination fees are also limited by state law in terms of their size and the frequency with which they can be assessed. If paying the fee is a requirement for getting a loan, the fee must be included in the calculation of the annual percentage rate.

Credit Insurance Fees. Credit insurance fees are the insurance premiums on credit life, or accident and health insurance policies that are sometimes sold in conjuction with consumer credit. When insurance is required as a condition of obtaining credit, however, the premiums must be included in the quotation of the finance charge.

Annual Fees. Annual fees are allowable fixed charges to credit cardholders. They typically fall in the range of $10 to $30 per year per card.

An innovation in the consumer credit market in recent years is the premium credit card which is marketed to upper-income, high-credit quality customers.

The product is a revolving line of credit, but the annual fee is considerably higher than that for a regular bank card. In return, the cardholder has a larger line of credit and is entitled to a portfolio of services such as flight insurance, and so on.

Interchange Fees and Merchant Discount. Interchange fees are paid among credit card issuers to facilitate the cardholder's use of the credit card universally at all merchant locations that accept the card, regardless of who issued the card. The merchant discount is a fee paid by the merchant who accepts a third-party revolving payment system to the financial institution for processing the resulting invoices. Both types of fees are expressed as a percentage of the face value of the invoice.

METHODS OF SPECIFYING FINANCE CHARGES. The interest rate of charge for various types and sizes of consumer loans is limited by state law rather than federal law. The state statutes use a multitude of different methods to specify the permissible rates. This patchwork of rates, together with differences across institutions in terms of methods of quoting rates, motivated the passage of the Federal Truth in Lending Act, effective July 1, 1969, which specifies that rates on consumer loans must be expressed as an annual percentage rate.

Annual Percentage Rate. The truth-in-lending legislation established a common standard measure of rate, which is called an "annual percentage rate" (APR). Thus, every consumer credit transaction carries an annual percentage rate and may be directly compared with every other such transaction. Financial institution managers are responsible for providing consumer borrowers with information on the total dollar finance charge and the APR of interest. The credit grantor may use loan terms of its choosing, but must compute and provide the individual borrower with the annual percentage rate equivalents.

Nonrevolving installment credit contracts specify that a series of equal payments at equal time intervals, usually a month apart, be made to retire the indebtedness. The APR charged on a consumer loan is the internal rate of return for the contract cash flows or the percentage discount rate that equates the scheduled periodic payments with the original principal amount of the loan extended. This concept is exemplified by the following equation:

$$\mathrm{P} = \sum_{t=1}^{T} \frac{M_t}{(1+r)^t}$$

where M = original principal balance
M = periodic monthly payment
r = periodic discount rate
T = number of regularly scheduled payments

The total dollar finance charge on an amount financed is equal to the difference between the sum of the scheduled periodic payments and the original principal balance of the loan.

Many of the relevant state laws specifying maximum rates predate the Truth-in-Lending Act. Thus maximum legal rates are not consistently stated as annual percentage rates but are sometimes specified as add-on or discount rates.

The Add-on Rate. The maximum allowable rate of charge on consumer loans is specified in many states as an add-on rate, which must be converted to the annual percentage rate for disclosure purposes. The annual percentage rate is roughly double the "add-on" rate. To convert an "add-on" rate to an annual percentage rate the following procedure is used:

1. To determine the total amount to be repaid, multiply the stated add-on rate by the original principal balance of the loan. Multiply the product times the number of years the loan is outstanding. For example, a $1,000 loan with a 1 year to maturity at 10% add-on yields a total amount to be repaid of $1,100 ($1,000 × 0.10 × 1 year = $1,100).
2. To determine the size of monthly payments, divide the total amount to be repaid by the number of scheduled monthly payments. For example, $1,100 : 12 = $91.67.
3. To calculate the equivalent monthly percentage rate, find the monthly internal rate of return for a $1000 loan to be repaid in 12 monthly payments of $91.67 each (equation 1), r = 1.49%.
4. Multiply the monthly rate by 12 to get the annual percentage rate: APR = 17.88%.

The Discount Rate. A maximum discount per year rate is quoted in many state statutes. Under this method, the lender deducts the total interest charge from the principal amount of the loan and actually lends the borrower the difference. Thus for a $1000 one-year loan at a $10 discount per year rate, the lender actually lends only $900.

The relationship between the discount rate and the annual percentage rate is a function of the number of payments specified in the contract and the maturity of the loan. For loans with long maturity, it is possible under a discount method for the amount of the discount to equal the total principal amount of the loan. Under these circumstances, the borrower gets nothing and the interest return to the lender approaches infinity, which is why most state statutes specify discount rates for loans with short maximum terms.

To convert a discount per year rate into an annual percentage rate, the amount actually loaned to the borrower is set equal to the discounted value of the scheduled monthly payments as is shown in the preceding equation. The size of monthly payments is determined by the amount loaned plus the discount, divided by the number of scheduled periodic payments. The annual percentage rate is higher than the discount rate. The difference between the two rates increases as the term of the loan increases.

Simple Interest. Accrual of interest begins at the first day of a simple interest loan and is calculated throughout the life of the loan. The simple interest method generates less interest income in the first third of the term of the loan but yields more interest for the remainder of the loan than the add-on method.

NOMINAL RATES VERSUS YIELDS ON REVOLVING CREDIT. For revolving credit, the nominal monthly rate on the unpaid balance is frequently fixed by law, but the actual yield to the lender is a function of the methods used by lenders to assess finance charges. In their discussion of yields under various assessment methods, McAlister and DeSpain (1978) stated that the yield is affected by the method of assessment as well as the timing of consumers' purchases and payments and the period of time over which the yield is calculated. The most common of the various methods of assessing finance charges on revolving credit accounts are previous balance method, adjusted balance method, and ending balance method.

Previous Balance. In this approach, also known as the "beginning balance" method, the finance charges are calculated on any beginning unpaid balance shown on the current month's statement before deducting payments or credits received during the billing period and before adding purchases made during the billing period. If the previous balance is paid in full, no finance charge is assessed. If no payment is made, the unpaid finance charge may become part of the principal balance owed.

Adjusted Balance. Finance charges are calculated on the basis of any beginning unpaid balance shown on the current month's billing statement less payments and credit received during the current billing period, but before adding the current month's purchases. The date of payment on an account is irrelevant to the calculation.

Ending Balance. Finance charges are based on the balance owed at the end of each billing period, including purchases, payments, and credits occurring during the current month. Under this method, no "free period" is given to a customer who pays the account in full unless there is no outstanding balance at the end of the month.

In simulations of gross yields under the various billing methods, McAlister and DeSpain found that the adjusted ending balance, on average, provided 98.4% of the nominal annual rate followed by 86.6% of the nominal annual rate under the previous balance method. Finally, the adjusted balance method yielded 76.7% of the nominal annual yield.

RISK EVALUATION. The rate that a creditor quotes on a loan is a function of the default risk assumed by the creditor when the loan is granted. The default risk for a particular individual is a function of the willingness and ability of the borrower to repay the loan according to the terms specified by the credit contract. Willingness and ability of an individual are evaluated on the basis of type and duration of employment, stability of residence, level and stability of income, past and current credit usage, financial assets, and personal characteristics. The Equal Credit Opportunity Act severely limits the personal characteristics of an individual that may be used in evaluating creditworthiness. The characteristics limited by the Equal Credit Opportunity Act are discussed later in this section. To evaluate the default risk of an individual, given the necessary information, the credit grantor may use a judgmental system or a credit scoring system.

Judgmental System. In a judgmental risk evaluation system, each credit application and the information contained therein are evaluated individually by an employee of the creditor. The success of a judgmental system depends on the experience and common sense of the credit evaluator.

Credit Scoring System. Some creditors have used their historical experience with debtors to derive a quantitative model for the segregation of acceptable and unacceptable credit applications. With a credit scoring system, a credit application is processed mechanically and all credit decisions are made consistently. The scoring system is based on the addition or subtraction of a statistically derived number of points to the applicant credit score on the basis of responses given to a set of predictor variables, such as time on job or number of credit sources used. Given a statistically derived cutoff credit score, a creditor can segregate the acceptable from the unacceptable credit applicants.

Credit scoring has been criticized because statistical problems with the data used to derive the model frequently violate the assumptions of the statistical technique used to derive the points (multiple discriminant analysis). It is also pointed out that some of the variables used in a credit scoring system may have the effect of discrimination, although the variable may appear to be neutral. For example, using zip code in a scoring system may have the effect of discriminating against members of minority groups. Finally, the credit scoring model is derived by analysis of the characteristics of customers who were once granted credit by the creditor for whom the system is derived. The characteristics of the part of the population to which the credit grantor has not granted credit are not directly considered. Thus the scoring system may provide biased results when it is applied to new credit applicants. For a discussion of credit scoring systems, see Altman, Avery, Eisenbeis, and Sinkey (1981).

Credit Reporting Agencies. A credit reporting agency is a clearinghouse of credit information about consumers. To assist the creditor in the process of risk evaluation, the credit reporting agency or credit bureau assimilates information on the credit history of an individual. The credit report is coded in a common language that refers to the types of accounts a customer has with various creditors, the terms of the accounts, and the customer's usual method of payment.

The credit reporting agency does not assign a credit rating to an individual but rather provides the creditor (for a fee) with information about the applicant for purposes of evaluating creditworthiness. The type, condition, and distribution of information maintained by credit reporting agencies on consumers are restricted by the **Fair Credit Reporting Act.**

OTHER CONTRACT TERMS

Creditors' Remedies. Creditors' remedies are actions specified in the credit contract that the creditor may take in the event of delinquency or default to recover the accrued interest and outstanding balance of a loan or to reduce default losses. Creditors' remedies play the same role in consumer credit contracts that indenture provisions play in a commercial loan contract.

The methods that a creditor may use to collect past due accounts have become increasingly more restricted by state and federal law. Laws have been written and adopted which are meant to restrict or abolish creditors' remedies or collection practices that are likely to place undue hardship on the defaulting consumer. Feldman and Reiley (1977, pp. 540–573) have described the set of creditors' remedies available in most states.

The extent to which each of these remedies can be used is specified by state law and varies widely from state to state. These remedies are briefly summarized as follows:

Late Payment Charges. Legally allowed penalty charges to debtors for late payment—for example, \$5 or 5% of the delinquent monthly payment.

Attorney's Fee Charges. Legal charges against a defaulting debtor for the creditor's costs of using attorneys to collect the debt. Such a charge is usually expressed as a percentage of the amount in default irrespective of the actual amount of attorney's fees incurred by the creditor.

Repossession. Legal seizure, initiated by a creditor, of property securing a debt. The role of the security in a debt contract is to secure payment or performance of an obligation. When the debtor defaults, the creditor has the right to take possession of the property specified as security without judicial process if this can be done without breach of the peace. In the event of repossession, the debtor must pay repossession costs, storing and selling costs, and attorney's fees.

Delinquency Judgment. A judgment or decree against a debtor for any part of a debt not recovered by sale of the collateral. Given depreciation and the obligation of the debtor to pay the cost of repossession, the total amount of the outstanding obligation may be significantly higher than the net resale value of the security.

Blanket Security. A lien taken by a creditor on household goods of a debtor beyond those for which the creditor is extending credit. This is also called cross-collateral.

Waiver of Statutory Exemption. A clause in a note waiving the laws shielding the consumer's home or other necessities from a creditor's claims. The effect of the waiver is that state laws are replaced by common law of absolute liability of the debtor, and any or all personal property can be seized to satisfy the obligation of the debtor to the creditor.

Garnishment. A legal procedure whereby some of the debtor's wages or other assets held by an employer or other third party may be assigned to the creditor. As it applies to wages and salaries, the process of garnishment requires an employer to withhold part of an employee's compensation upon order of the court and pay it directly to, or for the account of, the employee's creditor. The maximum amount that may be withheld from a debtor's paycheck is specified by federal law as the lesser of a percentage of the check or some multiple of the federal minimum wage.

Wage Assignment. A voluntary assignment of wages made by the debtor to the creditor at the time a loan is made, which becomes effective in case of default. The function of the wage assignment is to provide the creditor with a speedy method of collection without the time and expense of a hearing on the underlying claim. It is usually an instruction to the employer to pay the creditor a portion of the debtor's wage.

Acceleration upon Default. A clause permitting the creditor to claim the entire balance due in the event of default on a credit agreement. In its most common form, the clause permits the creditor to accelerate when the debtor defaults. The credit contract specifies those actions that constitute default. In some cases, the acceleration clause allows the creditor to accelerate at will when he or she believes the loan to be insecure. Under common law the creditor has the burden of justifying the acceleration and proving good faith.

Reaffirmation of Debts after Bankruptcy. An agreement made by a debtor who has declared bankruptcy, to repay a debt even though he or she is freed of the debt by the bankruptcy proceedings.

Cosignor Agreement. An agreement whereby parties other than the principal debtor agree to pay a debt if the debtor defaults.

Contacting Third Parties. A creditor's right to contact employers, relatives, or others in an effort to locate a delinquent debtor or to encourage payment of a delinquent balance.

Foreclosure. Legal seizure of property to liquidate a defaulted debt secured by a mortgage on the property.

In 1984 the Federal Trade Commission adopted a set of trade regulation rules that would prohibit creditors from using certain of the remedies listed above. (The rules went into effect in 1985.) The rule states that a creditor could not enter into a credit contract with a consumer, either directly or indirectly, which contained any of the following:

1. A confession of judgment clause
2. A waiver of exemption
3. Wage assignment
4. Blanket security

The rules also prohibit misrepresentation of a cosigner's liability and require that a creditor give a cosigner a notice informing the cosigner of the nature of the obligation and potential liability.

Collection Practices. The collection practices of a credit grantor are the activities engaged in to obtain payment from a delinquent debtor, exclusive of creditor's remedies. Normal collection practices include letters, phone calls, and personal visits to the home or office of the debtor. Within the last few years, unfair collection practices have been defined and restricted by state law and the **Federal Fair Debt Collection Practices Act.**

The activities or practices that are considered to be harassment, and hence unlawful, are:

1. The use of threats of violence, force, or criminal prosecution against the consumer in an attempt to enforce collection of a debt.
2. Communicating with the debtor or the debtor's family members frequently and at unusual hours to harass them concerning payment of the debt.
3. The use of communications, such as letters or telegrams, that simulate legal process or court suit papers.
4. Threatening or causing damages to a debtor's credit rating, knowing that the information is false or is being actively contested by the debtor.
5. Threatening legal action, directly or by implication, against a delinquent debtor unless such action can and will in fact be instituted as represented if the debtor fails to make payment or otherwise settle the account.
6. Communicating with the debtor's employer before securing a final judgment on the debt, challenging the debtor's creditworthiness except as permitted by statute for the purpose of determining the employment status of the debtor.

PREPAYMENT PROVISIONS. Most consumer credit contracts are written such that a schedule of periodic payments is specified over the life of the contract. The periodic payments are allocated between principal and the total interest that will be paid over the life of the contract. Because consumer loan contracts typically specify a fixed periodic payment, the interest is not paid at the same rate that it accrues. Therefore in the event that a debtor prepays a loan, he or she may have paid a greater amount of interest than was justifiable, given the actual period over which the loan was outstanding. In the event of prepayment, the consumer is entitled to a rebate of the unearned finance charges that may have been paid. The amount of the rebate owed to the consumer is determined by one of two methods: the rule of 78 or the actuarial method.

Rule of 78. When an installment debt was prepaid in full, the unearned portion of the finance charge was determined by the Rule of 78. This can be illustrated simply. Assume that you hire some workers to dig a hole that narrows as it becomes deeper. The first day you will use four workers, each at $1 per day. The next day you have three workers, the next two, and finally, one. Your total wage bill is $10 ($4 + $3 + $2 + $1). At the end of the second day, the workers quit. What do you owe them? Even though they have worked half the days, they have earned more than half the total wage bill. The unearned portion of the total wage bill is three-tenths; that is $3, the sum of the remaining days' wages, divided by $10, the total wage bill. This might be called the "rule of 10," because the sum of the digits—1, 2, 3, 4—is 10.

Because many installment contracts in the early 1900s were for 12 months, and because the sum of the digits 1 through 12 is 78, the refund rule became known as the "rule of 78," or the "sum-of-the-digits" method. To calculate the amount of unearned interest that should be refunded by the creditor, determine the proportion of the term of the contract that has expired before prepayment and multiply that by the total dollar finance charge. This determines the amount of the total finance charge that should be retained by the creditor. The difference between that amount and what the debtor actually paid is the amount to be refunded.

Actuarial Method. An alternative method is to apply the annual percentage rate on a monthly basis to the declining balance on the loan. The monthly payment is thus allocated between principal and interest payments. On prepayment, the amount owed by the consumer is the sum of the remaining payment less the unearned finance charges by the actuarial method. For example, assume a 12-month loan for $1200 at an 8% add-on, giving a finance charge of $96, total amount owed $1296, and monthly payment of $108. Assume that the loan is prepaid at the end of the sixth month, with six payments outstanding. Those six payments total $648, but a portion is unearned finance charge that should be deducted. What portion? (1 + 2 + . . . = 60 /78 or 21 /78 × 96 =

$25.85. Thus the borrower must pay $648 − $25.85 = $622.15. If the refund were calculated under the actuarial method, the unearned finance charge would be $26.47, and the total payment owed would be $648 − $26.47 = $621.53—a difference of $0.62.

The rule of 78 has been questioned for two main reasons. First, for longer contract maturities, the difference between the refund paid the consumer under the rule of 78 and under the actual method increases. As shown in Exhibit 10, when a loan is prepaid, the finance charges paid are always greater under the rule of 78 than under the actuarial method of determining the refund. The maximum differential increases, the longer the term of the original installment contract.

Second, the rule of 78 has been challenged because computers are now available to calculate the unearned finance charge on the basis of the actuarial method. Presently, firms having computers can compute the refund almost instantaneously under either the rule of 78 or the actuarial method, whichever is required by the applicable state law. Small credit grantors without computers will still find calculation of refunds under the actuarial method laborious.

CREDIT INSURANCE. Credit insurance is usually life or accident and health insurance that is sold in conjunction with a credit contract. Credit life insurance insures the creditor against loss if the debtor dies. Accident and health insurance insures the creditor against loss if the debtor becomes sick or disabled. Rates on credit insurance are normally regulated by state law and stated as an amount per $100 of the original outstanding balance of the loan.

LAWS REGULATING CONSUMER CREDIT

FEDERAL LAWS. The activities involved in the extension of consumer credit are highly regulated because of the extreme difference in the information and market power of the creditor compared with those of the individual consumer. A multitude of state and federal laws apply to the extension of consumer credit, although most are state laws. The following is a brief description of the major federal laws that apply to the activities of consumer credit issuers.

Truth-in-Lending Act (1969). The Truth-in-Lending Act, part of the **Consumer Credit Protection Act,** is essentially designed to assure meaningful disclosure of credit terms to facilitate credit shopping and comparison of credit terms. The Act requires that the two key terms in a credit contract, the total dollar finance charge and the annual percentage rate, be disclosed conspicuously and in a uniform manner.

The finance charge is determined as the sum of all charges payable by the consumer and imposed by the creditor as an incident of or condition of the extension of credit. Included in the total dollar value of finance charges are interest, service, transaction, activity or carrying charges, loan fees, points, finder's fees, and charges for premiums for credit life and accident insurance if such is required as a condition for obtaining the amount advanced by the lender.

The Consumer Credit Protection Act Prohibits the issuance of unsolicited credit cards and limits the liability of the cardholder to $50 for unauthorized use of a credit card.

Fair Credit Reporting Act (1971). The basic purpose of this law is to protect consumers from inaccurate or obsolete information in a report that serves as a factor in evaluating an individual's eligibility for credit, insurance, or employment. It does not limit the type of information that can be gathered or the relevance of the information; nor does it give Consumers the right to physically possess or receive copies of the information files. The major rights created by the law for consumers are:

1. *Disclosures by Users to Consumers.* Consumers have the right to be told by the user the name and address of the consumer reporting agency if adverse action is taken.
2. *Access to Information in a Credit File.* Consumers have the right of access to their information files to learn the contents of such files. All information in credit files is available to consumers except medical information and the sources of investigative information.
3. *Sources and Recipients of Information.* Consumers have the right to be told the sources of information in their respective files and to have a list of recipients of the file for the previous six months.
4. *Confidentiality.* Consumers have the right to have information in their files kept confidential and reported only for credit or business purposes.
5. *Reinvestigation of Disputed Entries.* Consumer reporting agencies must reinvestigate disputed items and correct inaccuracies within a reasonable period of time.
6. *Care and Accuracy.* Consumer reporting agencies are required to provide reports only when these are requested for legitimate business purposes. They are also required to exercise care and accuracy in releasing the reports and in verifying that the reported information is not obsolete.
7. *Elimination of Obsolete Data.* Credit reporting agencies must notify individual consumers when adverse information is being reported and must verify the current status of public information items.
8. *Obtaining Information in a File by False Pretenses.* The law provides criminal penalties for obtaining information under false pretenses or for providing loan information to unauthorized persons.

Fair Credit Billing Act (1969). This law specifies a billing dispute settlement procedure that allows customers to challenge perceived billing errors in their periodic statements. The act applies only to open-end credit plans, which include credit cards and overdraft checking plans.

Equal Credit Opportunity Act (1975). This act prohibits discrimination by creditors on the basis of sex, marital status, race, color, religion, national origin, age (provided the applicant has the capacity to enter into a contract), because all or part of the applicant's income comes from public assistance programs, or because the applicant has in good faith exercised any right under the Consumer Credit Protection Act.

Fair Debt Collection Practices Act (1977). The purpose of this law is to protect debtors from harassment, deception, and other abuse in collection practices, while recognizing the legitimate need to collect consumer debts. The main thrust of the legislation is directed toward independent (third-party) professional debt collectors and collection agencies. The federal law regulates the following practices: (1) the acquisition of location information concerning the debtor, (2) communication to the debtor or third parties, (3) harassment or abuse, (4) false or misleading representations, and (5) unfair practices.

STATE LAWS. The state laws relating to the extention of consumer credit are many and varied across states; they apply to all facets of the extension of consumer credit.

Usury Laws. The usury or interest statutes set out the basic guidelines for permissible interest rates charged for the use of money. Some states have adopted the **Uniform Consumer Credit Code,** which specifies a uniform set of rates that apply to specified sales and loan transactions.

Small Loan Laws. This category of lending was started to provide unsecured personal loans to blue-collar workers who were unable to qualify for bank loans. Small loans are defined by the individual statutes. Small loan laws restrict the maximum term, maximum amount, and interest rate that can be charged by financial institutions making small loans, primarily consumer finance companies. Small loan laws sometimes specify a graduated rate ceiling such that a higher rate may be charged on small loans and lower rates charged on larger loans. The maximum interest rates are generally higher for "small loans" than for other types of loans.

DEREGULATION OF CONSUMER LOAN RATES. In 1979 and 1980, the prime rate for most banks was about 20%. However, state laws limited rates charged for various types of consumer loans to levels well below the prime rate. To accommodate consumer lenders, many states raised the legal ceiling rates for consumer loans or totally eliminated rate ceilings. This trend toward deregulation of consumer loans markets has had a positive effect on the supply of credit and innovations in price and nonprice credit terms. In 1984, 17 states had no ceiling on allowable rates for consumer loans.

CONSUMERS WHO USE INSTALLMENT CREDIT

The demand for consumer credit is a derived demand, based on consumers' consumption decisions, given each individual's level of income and wealth. The results of a national survey of consumers, cosponsored by the Federal Reserve Board of Governors, the Comptroller of the Currency, and the Federal Deposit Insurance Corporation, and performed in 1983 by the Survey Research Center at the University of Michigan, provide information about consumer installment credit and who uses it. About 38% of families in the United States had no consumer installment (including revolving) credit outstanding during the summer of 1982. The median dollar value of consumer debt outstanding per household using installment credit was $2382 (Exhibit 11).

A comparison of the families that had installment debt outstanding and those that did not use installment debt revealed that the probability of installment debt usage and the amount of debt outstanding increased as income increased and as liquid assets decreased. Installment debt usage was also related to the age of the family head. Families with heads between the ages of 25 and 44 had the highest probability of having installment debt outstanding. Married couples with children with a family head younger than 45 had an 83% probability of using installment credit. An examination of other characteristics of

EXHIBIT 11 DISTRIBUTION OF CONSUMER DEBT OUTSTANDING, SELECTED YEARS (PERCENTAGE DISTRIBUTION OF FAMILIES WITH SUCH DEBT EXCEPT AS NOTED)

Amount of Consumer Credit Outstanding ($)[a]	Current Dollars		
	1970	1977	1983
None	46	37	38
1–499	20	15	13
500–999	9	10	6
1,000–1,999	12	11	9
2,000–2,999	6	8	6
3,000–4,999	5	11	9
5,000–7,400	2	5	7
7,500 and more	1	4	12
Total	100	100	100
Memo (dollars)[b]			
Mean	1,438	2,713	5,400
Median	858	1,599	2,382

Source: Survey of Consumer Finances, 1983: *Federal Reserve Bulletin.*

[a]Consists of credit card and other open-end debt, installment debt, and noninstallment consumer debt from all sources (except 1970, which does not include noninstallment consumer debt).

[b]Mean and median values are for families with outstanding consumer debt.

credit users indicates that homeowners are more likely to use credit than renters.

TRENDS IN CONSUMER DEBT USAGE. Although the percentage of households using some kind of consumer credit has been relatively stable at about 40% since 1977, the amount of consumer debt outstanding relative to disposable income is not stable. Between 1975 and 1984, that measure of the "burden" of consumer credit outstanding fluctuated between 14.75% and almost 18% (Exhibit 12). Inflation, changing social attitudes toward the use of consumer debt, and alterations in the demographic characteristics of the general population can account for much of the growth in consumer installment credit outstanding relative to disposable income.

Inflation and expectations of higher inflation affects demand for credit in ways other than its effect on prices paid for consumer durables bought on credit. First, expectations of increased future rates of inflation may cause consumers to "buy now to avoid higher prices later." Much of the inflation experienced in 1978–1980 was attributed to this "buy now" psychology. Second, expectations of higher inflation make the increased use of credit a rational consumer choice, especially when the credit can be acquired at a fixed interest rate. The prospect of borrowing today and repaying with cheaper future dollars results in a transfer of real wealth from the creditor to the debtor.

Installment Debt and Changes in Demographic Characteristics. Changing demographic characteristics of the population in general have been associated with some of the increase in outstanding consumer installment debt relative to income since 1964. Families in the family formation years, with fam-

EXHIBIT 12 CONSUMER CREDIT OUTSTANDING TO DISPOSABLE PERSONAL INCOME

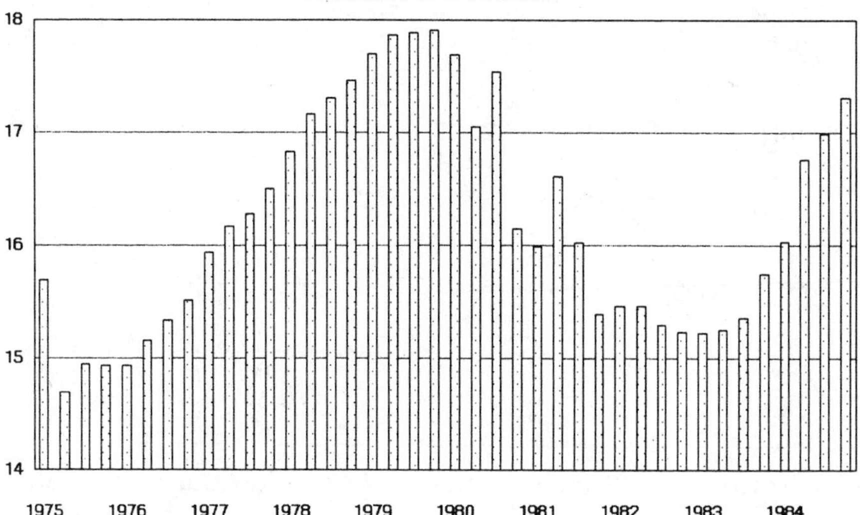

EXHIBIT 13 AGE STRUCTURE OF THE U.S. POPULATION (MILLIONS)

Age	1977	1985	1990	2000
18–24	28.6	28.7	25.8	24.6
25–44	56.7	73.8	81.4	80.1
45–64	43.8	44.7	46.5	60.9
65+	23.5	28.7	31.8	35.0

Source: U.S. Department of Commerce, *Statistical Abstract of the United States,* Washington, D.C., 1984.

ily heads in the age bracket group of 25 to 44 years, are most likely to use debt. Statistics on the age structure of the population (Exhibit 13) indicate that there will have been a net increase of 17.1 million people in that age bracket between 1977 and 1985, but that the increase will only be an increase of 7.6 million people in that age bracket between 1985 and 1990. After 1990, the number in that age category is expected to decline. These projections suggest that consumer credit outstanding will continue to grow relative to income through 1990 but will level off, holding other things constant.

DELINQUENCY OF CONSUMER CREDIT CONTRACTS. Generally, the incidence of delinquency is low on consumer credit contracts but varies over the business cycle. Delinquency statistics for consumer finance companies that historically have extended loans to high-risk borrowers indicate that normally only about 2% of the dollar value of loans outstanding is classified as delinquent. During the recession period of 1974–1975 delinquencies reached as high as 4% for some firms in the industry. National statistics of installment credit delinquencies over time (Exhibit 14) suggest that during the 1974–1975 recession, delinquencies of 30 days and over rose to 3.0% from an average level of about 1.8%.

The main cause of delinquency, as indicated by a survey of creditors performed for the National Commission on Consumer Finance (1972, p. 23), are

EXHIBIT 14 DELINQUENCY RATE, 30 DAYS AND OVER CONSUMER INSTALLMENT LOAN

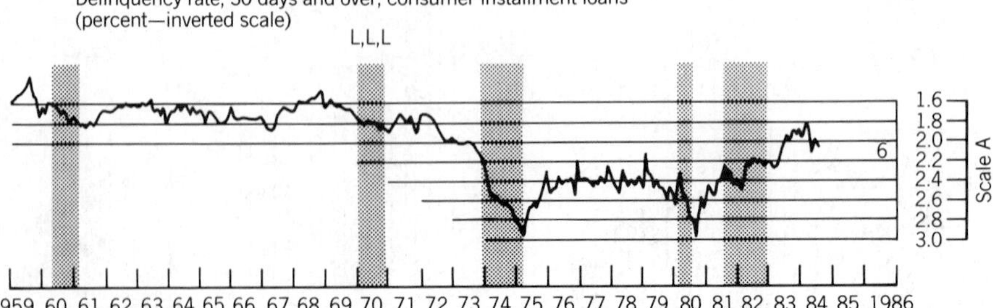

Source: U.S. Department of Commerce, *Business Conditions Digest,* October 1984, p. 33.

unemployment, sickness, and overuse of debt. Most creditors did not believe that consumers who became delinquent were "deadbeats" who never intended to repay their debts.

PERSONAL BANKRUPTCY

The bankruptcy law in the United States generally provides for a procedure for a consumer to work out debt problems under the protection of the court. Since 1898, a consumer seeking bankruptcy could voluntarily file and did not have to be delinquent on loan payments, insolvent, or have no ability to repay debts out of income. And, the consumer could choose one of two avenues to bankruptcy—chapter 7 or chapter 13. Under chapter 7, the nonexempt assets of the debtor are liquidated and the proceeds are used to satisfy the claims of unsecured creditors. Under chapter 13, the debtor proposes a plan for repaying debts out of future income.

Until 1979, the rate of personal bankruptcy per 100,000 population fluctuated to reflect higher bankruptcy rates during recessionary periods and lower rates during recovery periods. In 1979 the Bankruptcy Reform Act of 1978 was enacted and was followed by a dramatic increase in the rate of personal bankruptcy. Although there were two short economic slumps between 1979 and 1981, which may have contributed to the high rate of bankruptcy during that period, the rate did not fall substantially with the economic recovery in 1982 (Exhibit 15).

EXHIBIT 15
RATE OF PERSONAL BANKRUPTCY
1970–1984
(per 100,000 population)

Year	Personal Bankruptcy Rate
1970	86.98
1971	88.02
1972	78.88
1973	74.00
1974	79.64
1975	105.05
1976	98.23
1977	84.01
1978	78.83
1979	89.30
1980	141.32
1981	199.80
1982	193.90
1983	187.78
1984	170

The effect of the Bankruptcy Reform Act of 1978 was to decrease sharply the costs of taking bankruptcy. Some of the major provisions of the bill were:

1. A federal override of state personal property exemptions laws
2. An automatic stay of all collection activities once a bankruptcy petition is filed
3. A reduction in the availability of reaffirmation of debts after bankruptcy
4. A liberalization of qualifications for chapter 13

The sharp and apparently permanent increase in the rate of personal bankruptcy motivated lobbying efforts by the consumer credit industry for reform of the Bankruptcy Act. The Bankruptcy Reform Act of 1984 went into effect in October of that year. Highlights of the bill that may have a dampening effect on the rate of personal bankruptcy are:

1. A debtor's petition for bankruptcy may be dismissed if the judge determines that the debtor could, over a period of several years, repay all or a substantial part of debt under a court-approved repayment plan.
2. A debtor is required to receive debt counseling from the clerk or other court designee prior to the commencement of the case.
3. A debtor is required to be informed of the differences between chapter 7 and chapter 13 prior to the commencement of bankruptcy proceedings.
4. Debts will not be discharged if they were incurred to obtain luxury goods costing more than $500 in aggregate, within 40 days of the filing of the bankruptcy petition.
5. Court approval is not required for all Reaffirmation.
6. Exemptions for household goods are limited to $4000.

REFERENCES

Altman, Edward, Avery, Robert, Eisenbeis, Robert, and Sinkey, Joseph, *Application of Classification Techniques in Business, Banking, and Finance,* JAI Press, Greenwich, CT, 1981.

Booth, S. Lees, *NCFA 1983 Finance Facts Yearbook,* National Consumer Finance Association, Washington, D.C., 1983.

Durkin, Thomas A., and Elliehausen, Gregory E., *1977 Consumer Credit Survey,* Board of Governors of the Federal Reserve, 1978.

Feldman, Sheldon, and Reiley, Kimberly A., "A Compilation of Federal and State Laws Regulating Consumer Financial Services," Monograph No. 8, Vols. 1 and 2, Credit Research Center, Purdue University, Lafayette, IN, 1977.

Kane, Edward, "Accelerating Inflation and the Distribution of Household Savings Incentives," Working Paper No. 30, Credit Research Center, Purdue University, Lafayette, IN, 1979.

McAlister, Ray, and DeSpain, Edward, "Bank and Retail Credit Card Yields Under Alternative Assessment Methods," Working Paper No. 21, Credit Research Center, Purdue University, Lafayette, IN, 1978.

National Commission on Consumer Finance, *Consumer Credit in the United States,* NCCF, Washington, D.C., December 1972.

Sullivan, A.C., and Fain, J.R., "The Behavior of Consumer Loan Rates Charged by Commercial Banks," Working paper No. 50, Credit Research Center, Purdue University, Lafayette, IN, 1984.

Survey of Consumer Finances, 1983: A Second Report, *Federal Reserve Bulletin,* December 1984, pp. 857–868.

BIBLIOGRAPHY

Cole, R.H., *Consumer and Commercial Credit Management,* 5th ed., Irwin, Homewood, IL, 1977.

Eisenbeis, Robert A., "Problems on Applying Discriminant Analysis in Credit Scoring Models," *Journal of Banking and Finance,* Vol. 12, No. 3, October 1978.

Financial Publishing Co., *The Cost of Personal Borrowing in the United States,* Financial Publishing Co., Boston, 1979.

Hsia, David C., "Credit Scoring and the Equal Credit Opportunity Act," *Hasting Law Journal,* November 1978.

Redding, H.T., and Knight, G.H., *The Dun and Bradstreet Handbook of Credit and Collections,* Harper & Row, New York, 1974.

Sexton, Donald E., Jr., "Determining Good and Bad Credit Risks Among High- and Low-Income Families," *Journal of Business,* Vol. 50, No. 2, April 1977.

12

SMALL BUSINESS FINANCIAL PLANNING

CONTENTS

12

SMALL BUSINESS FINANCIAL PLANNING

Steven J. Appel

Most entrepreneurs initially approach finance with one main objective in mind: obtaining adequate funds for current and expected business needs. This primary objective requires planning. From the outset, potential lenders and investors require assurances—in the form of financial information integrated within an overall business plan—that a business will efficiently use capital. As a business grows, its needs for capital often increase geometrically, both in size and in complexity. To attain adequate financing entrepreneurs have come to depend on increasingly sophisticated planning techniques. Financial planning is not, however, limited in use to raising capital; it is also the means whereby ever more broadly defined financial goals can best be met.

Financial planning encompasses a host of complex considerations, varied approaches, and sophisticated (often computer-based) techniques. This section provides an overview of these multifaceted aspects. The section is divided into four main parts: the general considerations associated with financial planning, the stages of financial planning, the role of annual financial planning, and specialized applications of financial planning. The information presented here is drawn from many years' experience in working closely with entrepreneurs and their key employees in all types and sizes of small businesses. Although these planning concepts are broadly applicable to small businesses, each entrepreneur needs to develop specific approaches—incorporating both business and personal goals—to business planning in general, and to financial planning in particular.

FINANCIAL PLANNING AND THE PLANNING PROCESS

THE PROCESS IS THE PRODUCT. Although financial planning is an umbrella term that encompasses many activities, it should always be a means to achieve certain objectives, never an end in itself. Several different types of financial plans are developed during the planning process. These plans serve to help organize and focus the financial management function. The effectiveness of planning is ultimately measured by the growth and profitability of a business. Financial planning and bottom-line performance go hand in hand. An important and often misunderstood aspect of planning is that the *process* of planning is the most valued *product* of the process.

PLANS VERSUS PROJECTIONS. Financial planning employs various types of projections. Plans and projections differ in scope: planning is a broadly based process; projection is usually a narrow function, a technique applicable to virtually all aspects of planning. They also differ markedly in nature: planning is primarily concerned with shaping the future course of events to the extent possible; projection is limited to predicting likely results or action, in light of specified assumptions. A budget, for example, is a planning document. In contrast, the various "what if" spreadsheet computer programs produce projections or forecasts, not plans.

INTEGRATED IN THE BUSINESS CYCLE. Planning, operations, and control are the three main components of the **business cycle,** a continuous process as illustrated in Exhibit 1.

The role of each of these cycle functions can be summarized as follows:

Planning. The decision-making process prior to taking action, through which specific targets for business operations are set.

Operations. The profit-making activities of the business, through which business objectives are met.

Control. The performance-measuring process, through which results are interpreted; it provides, in turn, the information needed for further planning and future operations.

EXHIBIT 1 THE BUSINESS CYCLE

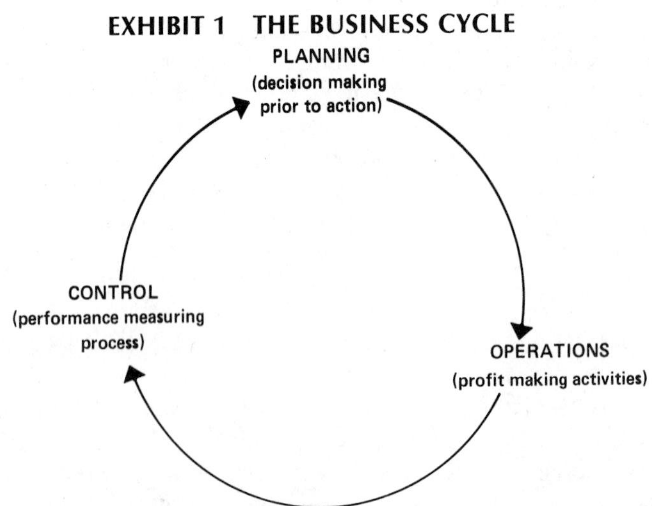

ROLE OF FINANCIAL PLANNING

Controlling Growth. Business growth can have a positive or negative financial result depending on whether growth is properly controlled. By taking steps to control growth, entrepreneurs ensure that they shape the powerful forces of growth. Financial planning serves as a means to control growth. The result is improved company performance.

Attracting Financing. Because few lenders or investors can readily examine how a business' financial planning function operates on a day-to-day basis, a convenient indicator of quality is commonly used: the plans submitted in support of formal applications for financing. Entrepreneurs' assumptions, preferences, rationales, and similar factors must be taken into account. Formal plans, therefore, need to incorporate much more than "the numbers"; they need to describe key reference-points in the planning process, the why's and wherefore's of decision making. Success in securing financing is related, in part, to how clearly the plans themselves communicate the bases of decision making. As a general rule, the clearer the plan, the greater the opportunity for obtaining financing. In view of this fact, it is easy to understand why business advisers frequently emphasize the need for careful preparation of the financial portion of a business plan.

Fostering Discipline. In addition to helping control growth and attract financing, the added discipline of the financial planning process benefits small business in many other respects. Purchasing, personnel, and marketing, for instance, are more finely focused in their action by the bottom-line emphasis that planning fosters. Perhaps more important, entrepreneurs' leadership in financial planning often has a ripple effect throughout the business, encouraging middle managers and employees to apply the precepts of sound planning in day-to-day operations. In this fashion, emphasis on financial planning can lead to significant, sustained increases in efficiency, productivity, and morale.

CHALLENGES FOR SMALL BUSINESSES

Choosing to Plan Adequately. All planning entails making choices. The first step is to choose to plan adequately, to refocus time and energy on a perspective wider than merely managing day-to-day operations. In order to take this initial step, many entrepreneurs must first overcome a common obstacle: an unwillingness to delegate responsibility. Much that is most admired about small business—such as creativity, high energy, and the ability to react quickly—can be traced, in part, to the concentration of power in the hands of a few decision makers, generally the founders. It is therefore hardly surprising that entrepreneurs initially approach the delegation of key responsibilities with caution. However, all successful entrepreneurs ultimately reach much the same conclusion: Adequate financial planning may not come easily, but neither can a growing business afford to do without it.

Avoiding Extremes. Overly optimistic approaches result in wasted opportunities. Such "wishful planning" can seriously damage the process itself, leading managers and employees alike to doubt the usefulness of planning. Similarly, overly cautious approaches are equally wasteful. The restrictive focus of "self-fulfilling" financial plans can significantly impair long-term profitability and growth. To develop good financial plans, entrepreneurs must set their sights on target, neither too high nor too low.

Accepting Imperfections. Although financial planning can provide valuable benefits, its inherent shortcomings must also be taken into account. The planning process relies extensively on mathematical models and statistical approximations, on expectations and projections, and on evaluations and choices. The limitations of these tools and approaches can ultimately be traced to a basic fact: The future cannot be known with certainty. The best laid plans still do go astray. Even so, the benefits of financial planning far outstrip its imperfections. Entrepreneurs need to focus on the benefits without ignoring the shortcomings.

Adopting the Process. A sound, overall approach to planning is a prerequisite for developing good financial plans. Although each entrepreneur *adapts* planning to meet specific business and personal goals, entrepreneurs must also wholeheartedly *adopt* the planning process. Like any tool, planning requires proper maintenance as well as proper use. For example, the planning process demands continuing refinement and modification, which in turn requires commitments of time and resources. And, like most highly sophisticated tools, sound planning simply will not work with half-measures or shortcuts. Consequently, entrepreneurs must fully commit themselves—and their organizations—to the planning process in order to gain the advantages of financial planning.

Involving all Appropriate Personnel. Supervisory and managerial personnel, almost without exception, need to be involved in various aspects of financial planning. However, involvement in the planning process is not necessarily limited to supervisors and managers. The success of small businesses' plans relies heavily on the significant contributions of trusted, highly trained employees. Just who is to be involved in planning—and to what extent—depends on the particular circumstances of each business. Entrepreneurs need to ensure that all who participate in financial planning clearly understand how their specific roles relate to the general purpose and goals of the planning process.

Communicating Overall Objectives. Entrepreneurs' interest in planning must also extend to facilitating communication and education. Certain basic information about planning needs to be shared by all participants in the planning process. Although the definition of "need to know" fundamentals varies from business to business, the overall objectives of planning offer a useful starting point. Summing up the key features noted previously, the overall objectives of the planning process are:

- Structuring a disciplined yet flexible approach
- Integrating analysis and decision making
- Encouraging creativity
- Building management and employee support
- Involving all appropriate personnel
- Fostering the establishment of acceptable performance standards
- Communicating aspects of plans throughout the organization
- Reviewing goals and refining planning approaches on a regular basis

INITIAL STAGES OF FINANCIAL PLANNING

To develop effective financial plans, entrepreneurs must adequately prepare themselves and their businesses to use financial planning techniques. A well-defined planning process in which financial planning is carefully integrated needs to be thoughtfully implemented. The business' form of organization and its general financing requirements must be taken into account. Also, various organizational concerns and aspects of accounting and bookkeeping need to be considered. As noted previously, the financial plan must be integrated with the overall business plan which is often utilized to attract initial capital investments from outsiders. The business plan is, then, a key document in the initial stages of growth. This planning document and other early alternatives are discussed later in the section.

INTEGRATION WITH THE BUSINESS PLAN. Financial planning is but one aspect of the planning process; it must be integrated within the overall business plan. The main purposes of an effective business plan include:

- Helping to crystallize and focus entrepreneurs' ideas
- Charting a path for management to follow in the early years of a business
- Setting benchmarks—by identifying and quantifying specific business objectives—against which entrepreneurs and the management team can measure progress
- Serving as a persuasive vehicle for attracting additional financing

Financial planning is closely related to each of these basic goals.

Format of the Plan. Business plans are as varied—in organization, length, and content—as the businesses they mirror. There is no single best approach. The following planning format has been used to advantage by many small businesses; it is also comparatively easy to develop.

Executive Summary. A several-page synopsis of the key elements of the plan; intended primarily to capture the attention of lenders and investors.

Business History. An in-depth overview of the business' background, including its founding and progress to date, the founders' relevant experience and roles in the business, the form of organization (S corporation, regular corporation, partnership, etc.), details of capitalization (stock or partnership shares), summary of outside financing and financial commitments (loans, investments, stock options or warrants, royalty arrangements, leases, etc.), and an overview of the performance of the business' products and services. This section is also intended mainly for lenders and investors.

Products and Services. A detailed, nontechnical description of the business' products and services, including existing and planned products and services, competitive advantages (such as lower cost or longer life), applicable legal protections (patents, trademarks, copyrights, etc.), and applicable regulatory approvals and clearances. Appendixes frequently include lengthy or detailed diagrams, technical documents, descriptions, or other specific data that can help provide a comprehensive understanding of the business' products and services; however, such details may be omitted from the business plan or provided as supplementary data to individuals who require this information, especially if the information is proprietary.

Markets. A comprehensive description of the business' present and projected markets, organized by relating market segments to such factors as historic (last five years) and forecasted (next five years) rates of growth, location of markets, sales approaches, level at which purchasing decision is made, purchasing methods (such as bids, contracts, or unit purchases), critical product/service characteristics, and any special characteristics of markets (seasonal, cyclical, and other factors).

Competitors. An overview of the present and prospective competitive environment, serving to identify competitors and to indicate the special strengths, weaknesses, and market share of each; also includes forecasts (three to five years) of—and accompanying rationale for—the market share expected to be captured and a review of the principal product/service characteristics.

Marketing. Usually a detailed summary of the marketing plan, describing key aspects of overall strategy, channels of distribution, the sales compensation plan, pricing strategy, promotional concepts, the distribution plan, market research and analysis, including provisions for periodic market monitoring and plans to conduct any necessary product/service evaluations, pricing comparisons, or market-share analyses.

Manufacturing and Operations. An overview of the nature, quality, and extent of the business' manufacturing and research facilities, including production strengths and limitations (and corrective measures), location of existing and planned facilities, use and selection of subcontractors, supply and price considerations for any critical materials or components, expansion plans (detailing such factors as timing, cost, extent, and importance), and related financing issues and tax implications.

Management. A discussion of the business' overall management structure as well as the experience and competence of all key members of the management team, including organizational structure and reporting relationships (typically outlines in chart form), detailed job descriptions, minimum qualifications and level of compensation for each unfilled slot, and current compensation and background of management personnel (including experience, education, patents or copyrights, awards, equity interest, etc.).

Financial Projections. A detailed, summary-type presentation of the business' financial plans (generally using three- to five-year projections), including past financial statements (balance sheets, profit and loss statements, and statements of source and application of funds) for up to three years, current financial statements, projected balance sheet information on an accrual basis for the next three to five years, profit and loss projections and cash flow projections (preferably on a monthly or quarterly basis for the first two years; annually, for the three subsequent years); also provides descriptive information about accounting principles, sales and market share assumptions, and such related financial assumptions as the anticipated number of days' sales in accounts receivable, bad debts, interest expense, R&D costs, facility costs, warranty costs, payroll expense, costs of materials and components, and federal and state taxes.

Note that the modular design of this suggested format provides great flexibility. The configuration discussed pertains to business plans intended mainly for external use, such as for lenders' and investors' review. For internal use, a simpler format may be preferable. For example, the first two sections (executive summary and business history) may be omitted, the amount of descriptive and explanatory materials used throughout can be sharply curtailed.

Financial Data as Foundation. Financial information is provided in every section of the business plan, not just in the section reserved for financial projections. Because of the importance of "good numbers," entrepreneurs typically rely on their accountants to help integrate the financial aspects of the business plan with all the other components. Serving as the business' chief financial advisers, the accountants' role frequently includes:

- Assisting entrepreneurs and key managers in developing a realistic business plan.
- Developing or reviewing financial projections to provide truly meaningful data for the business plan.
- Assisting both in selecting the best accounting methods for the business and in establishing appropriate accounting policies.
- Advising on establishment of suitable financial/recordkeeping and cost controls.

- Reviewing data-gathering and control systems to determine their adequacy for meeting current and future needs.
- Examining and evaluating the tax consequences arising from key business decisions, such as the form of organization, capital structure, and accounting policies.

Such a team approach—emphasizing cooperation among entrepreneurs, their accountants, and other business advisers—helps ensure that financial data are suitably presented within the overall context of the business plan.

GENERAL FINANCING CONSIDERATIONS

Matching Terms of Assets and Liabilities. In finance, the uses and types of funds are broadly categorized within a three-part structure: short term (less than a year), intermediate term (from one to five years), and long term (more than five years). The most efficient use of available financing broadly entails closely matching the terms of assets and liabilities. For example, short-term uses of funds, such as for accounts receivable or inventory, are ordinarily matched with short-term financing, such as factoring or secured loans. Lenders and investors generally prefer, if not require, this integration of terms because it helps to minimize risk.

Financial planning seeks, in part, to optimize the benefits of available capital by unifying the many term-oriented considerations—those specifically related to short-, intermediate-, and long-term financing—into an overall approach to meeting profitability and growth objectives.

Choosing among Sources of Funds. Although many entrepreneurs find that capital is difficult to obtain, there is certainly no dearth of potential sources among which to choose. The most common sources for financing a small business include: founders' equity (personal contributions and loans from family and friends), banks, finance companies and factors, leasing companies, suppliers, customer deposits, venture capitalists, stockholders (public sales of stock), insurance companies, savings institutions, and government assistance at the federal, state, and local level. In addition, entrepreneurs can realize significant financial benefits from various related planning activities, such as planning for tax minimization, compensation, and business continuation.

The process of selection is influenced by a variety of factors including interest rates, collateral required, and repayment terms. Such so-called external factors are, in fact, directly related to a business' current and anticipated performance, as assessed by the financial community. Entrepreneurs know the general rule that the better a business performs—in terms of both profitability and growth—the more readily lenders and investors will agree to provide financing, at increasingly favorable rates and terms. What is not so widely understood is that good financial planning also helps entrepreneurs in choosing among sources of funds by encouraging the development of ongoing, cooperative financial relationships.

Building Financial Relationships. Although entrepreneurs and the financial community need to cooperate, such cooperation is frequently lacking. Each often comes to perceive the other as uninformed about, uninterested in, and generally suspicious of differences in approaches and objectives. Such misunderstandings can lead to counterproductive, adversarial relationships. By using financial plans—in concert with the overall business plan—to focus discussions, entrepreneurs and their business advisers can easily move relationships with lenders to a "partnership basis." Lenders are thus perceived as investors who have an important stake in the business' success. Financial plans serve as vehicles for communicating well-defined needs for funds; this, in turn, assists lenders in their decision making. Moreover, the cooperation evident among entrepreneurs and their business advisers serves to foster cooperation with lenders.

When profits and growth advance according to plan, sound financial relationships help entrepreneurs to secure better borrowing rates and terms. When unexpected difficulties arise, the trust that has been built during these relationships encourages entrepreneurs and lenders alike to work even more closely, emphasizing long-term strengths instead of short-term weaknesses.

PLANNING FOR THE FORM OF ORGANIZATION. The legal form a business takes—regular corporation, S corporation, partnership, or sole proprietorship—needs to be determined in relation to each entrepreneur's short- and long-term objectives. Each of the four main forms is useful in its proper context, as summarized in the following paragraphs.

Regular Corporation. A corporation is a legal entity; that is, it is viewed as separate and distinct from its owners in the eyes of the law. By virtue of this status, a corporation can acquire, hold, sell, or transfer property; sue and be sued; and generally act in its own name. These rights are derived from state statutes and from the articles of incorporation and bylaws. A corporation's liabilities are generally limited to its own resources; thus creditors' claims pertain only to the corporation's assets, not to its owners' assets.

S Corporation. This is a hybrid—a cross between a corporation and a partnership. Encompassing virtually all the features of a corporation (such as limited liability), the S corporation acts as a partnership in one key respect: profits and losses generally flow directly to the shareholders, who are responsible for reporting such gains or losses on their individual tax returns. This avoids the tax problem inherent in a regular corporation—taxation of profits in the corporation and again at the shareholder level when distributed in the form of dividends.

Partnership. A partnership is usually defined as an association of two or more persons who, as co-owners, carry on a business for profit. It can be created by formal agreement or oral understanding, or be implied by the conduct and acts of the co-owners. A partnership is frequently referred to as a *conduit* because, although the co-owners have associated themselves in pursuit of profits, a partnership is not considered a separate legal entity. As a conduit, therefore, a partnership cannot sue or be sued solely in its own name; each partner may be held personally liable (known as **joint and several liability**) for any portion—even all—of the claims against the partnership. There are two main types of partnerships. In a **general partnership,** each partner participates in all profits and losses either on an equal basis or according to some predetermined ratio. Ordinarily, a general partner has unlimited personal liability. In a **limited partnership,** each limited partner's liability is limited to the amount of capital contributed. A limited partnership must have at least one general partner who manages the business and has unlimited liability.

Sole Proprietorship. This is a business entirely and directly owned by one person. As sole owner of all the assets, a sole proprietor is entitled to all the profits and must bear personal liability for all losses and claims. The sole proprietorship is not considered a separate legal entity; no legal formalities are required to establish a business in this form. The major sources of financing for a sole proprietorship are generally limited to cash flow from operations and borrowings. Some of the major business and tax considerations pertaining to each of the four forms of organization are compared in Exhibit 2.

EXHIBIT 2 BUSINESS AND TAX CONSIDERATIONS FOR COMPARISON OF CORPORATIONS, S CORPORATIONS, PARTNERSHIPS, AND SOLE PROPRIETORSHIPS

Factor	Corporation (Regular Corporation)	S Corporation (Small Business Corporation)	Partnership	Sole Proprietorship
Life	Unlimited or perpetual, unless limited by state law or terms of its charter.	Same as regular corporation. Election may be revoked or terminated without affecting continuity of life.	Generally set up for a specific, agreed term, usually will be terminated by death, withdrawal, insolvency or legal disability of a general partner.	At death, business assets pass with proprietor's estate.
Entity	Completely separate from owners and recognized as such.	Same as regular corporation.	Generally recognized separate by the business community, but not for all purposes.	Generally recognized as separate by the business community, but not for all purposes.
Liability of owners	Limited. Stockholders are generally sheltered from any liabilities of the corporation.	Same as regular corporation.	Each general partner is fully liable as an individual for all debts. A limited partner's liability is usually limited to the amount of his or her capital contribution.	Owner has unlimited risk. Creditors can attach all personal assets for business debts.
Ease and effect of transfer of ownership interest	Generally, stock is easily and readily transferable, and transfer has no effect on the corporate entity.	Same as regular corporation. Consideration must be given to the effect of the transfer on the election to be sure it does not result in an unintended termination of S Corporation status.	Transfer may require approval of all other partners and may cause termination of old partnership and creation of a new one.	Transfer terminates entity and creates new firm.
Availability of outside capital or financing	May sell stock or bonds to the public.	Limited in that there can be only one class of stock outstanding. The corporation can have "straight debt," which will not be treated as a second class of stock. Also, different voting rights are applicable.	Limited to borrowing from partners or outsiders, or to admitting new partners who contribute additional capital.	Limited to owner's personal assets and outside credit.

EXHIBIT 2 (*CONTINUED*)

Factor	Corporation (Regular Corporation)	S Corporation (Small Business Corporation)	Partnership	Sole Proprietorship
Management of business operation	Much flexibility. Control can be exercised by a small number of officers without having to consult owners, regardless of the total number of shareholders.	About the same as a regular corporation, except that more active participation by all owners can usually be expected since the total number of shareholders cannot exceed 35.	Usually, all gereral partners will be active participants in management. However, other partners may grant management control to one or more partners by agreement.	Owner has complete control.
Who is the taxpayer?	The corporation is taxed on its taxable income, whether or not it is distributed to the shareholders.	The shareholders are taxed on the taxable income of the corporation, whether or not it is distributed to them.	The partners are taxed on the taxable income of the partnership, whether or not it is distributed to them.	The owner is taxed on the taxable income whether or not it is drawn by owner.
Distribution of earnings	Taxable to shareholders as ordinary dividends to the extent of earnings and profits.	No tax effect to the shareholders unless the distribution exceeds the Accumulated Adjustments Account and/or tax basis of stock. A distribution in excess of current and cumulative S Corporation earnings will be a dividend if the corporation has accumulated earnings and profits.	No tax effect on partners, unless distribution exceeds partner's basis. Excess taxed as capital gain to partner.	No tax effect to proprietor.
Net Operating Loss	Deductible only by the corporation within prescribed carryback and carryover period.	Deductible by shareholders subject to adequate basis to cover losses.	Deductible by partners, subject to adequate basis to cover losses.	Deductible by owner, subject to adequate income to cover losses.
Salaries paid to owners	When owners are employees, salaries are taxable to them and deductible by the corporation. Salaries must be reasonable in amount in relation to services rendered.	Same as regular corporation. The question of unreasonably large salaries is not so important unless salaries are used as a device for shifting income among stockholders within a family group.	Generally, amounts paid are considered partial distributions of income. If the distribution is a guaranteed payment of salary, it will be deductible by the parthership and ordinary income to the partner.	Sole proprietor is not an employee. Amount paid is considered a partial distribution of income.
Liquidation of the business	Amount received in excess of basis in stock is taxable as capital gain, unless the corporation is collapsible.	Same as regular corporation.	Normally no tax unless cash or equivalent exceeds basis in partnership interest. Excess is taxed as a capital gain, unless the partnership is collapsible.	No gain or loss until business or assets are sold to a third party.
Pension or profit-sharing plan	Owners are employees and can be included in a regular, qualified plan.	Owners who are employees can be included in a regular qualified plan.	Partners may participate only in a self-employed qualified plan.	Same as partnership.
Capital gains and losses	Taxed to the corporation at a maximum rate of 28%. No capital loss deduction is allowable.	Generally, taxed to the shareholders as such, but may be taxed to the corporation in certain cases.	Taxed to the partners as such.	Same as partnership.
Tax on transfer of assets to business	Generally none if the transferors retain control of at least 80% of the corporation after the transfer (unless liabilities assumed by the corporation exceed transferor's basis).	Same as regular corporation.	None, unless liabilities assumed reduce transferor's basis in the partnership below zero.	None.
Allocation of net income or loss or different types of income and deductions among owners by agreement	Not possible.	Not possible.	Can be done, so long as there is substantial economic substance to the agreement.	Not applicable.
Effect of death or sale of interest on basis of assets in business	None.	None.	Election may be filed to adjust basis of partnership assets applicable to transferor partner's interest.	Upon death, basis adjusts to fair market value for heirs. Upon sale, basis adjustment not applicable.
Earnings accumulation	May be subject to penalty tax if accumulation is unreasonable.	No limit since all income is taxed to the shareholders whether distributed or not.	No limit since all income is taxed to partners whether distributed or not.	Same as partnership.
Passive investment income	May create a personal holding company taxed at penalty rates.	In limited cases, may disqualify the S corporation and cause termination ot the election.	No effect.	No effect.

EXHIBIT 2 (*CONTINUED*)

Factor	Corporation (Regular Corporation)	S Corporation (Small Business Corporation)	Partnership	Sole Proprietorship
Selection of taxable year	No restriction.	Calendar year, unless justified business purpose and consent of the Commissioner to use fiscal year.	Must conform to that of the principal partners unless consent of the Commissioner is obtained; Rev. Proc. 72-51 generally grants permission for 9/30 (or later) for calendar-year partners.	Same as that of the owner
Sale of ownership interest	All capital gain unless corporation is collapsible, then ordinary income.	Same as regular corporation.	May be part capital gain and part ordinary income.	Same as partnership
Charitable contributions	Deductible by the corporation limited to 10% of taxable income. Excess may be carried over.	Same as partnership.	Not deductible by the partnership on its return, but may be deducted by the partners on their individual returns subject to the limitations applicable to individuals.	Not deductible by the proprietorship, but may be deducted by the owner on the individual return subject to the limitations applicable to individuals.
Minimum tax on preferences	Tax preference items are subject to minimum tax at the corporate level.	Tax preferences pass through to the shareholders except for certain capital gains subject to tax under Sec. 1374.	Tax preferences pass through to the partners.	Same as partnership.

PLANNING FOR ORGANIZATIONAL EFFICIENCY. Because a business organizational structure is the framework for translating plans into action, a well-structured organization is a prerequisite for successfully implementing financial plans. The design of a business organization generally corresponds in size and complexity to the scope and nature of operations. Exact requirements are determined in the context of each business' objectives and stage of development. However, certain overall design objectives are shared by all businesses.

Structural Design Objectives. A business' structural design helps management coordinate organizational activities by clarifying the interrelationships among communication channels, reporting relationships, levels of authority, line and staff distinctions, and similar considerations. In essence, a well-designed organization strikes an appropriate balance between centralization and decentralization. This balance is achieved through a variety of organization-wide objectives, including:

- Efficient use of personnel and physical resources
- Appropriate division of functions and activities into organizational units
- Suitable coordination of functions and activities among organizational units
- Meaningful definition of assigned duties and responsibilities
- Adequate integration of job specialization with career development

Entrepreneurs and their key managers must also be concerned with their special role in structuring the business, focusing on such issues as:

- Delegation of authority and broadening of reporting relationships
- Division of management time and resources, especially as related to balancing operational concerns with planning and other strategic considerations
- Development of managerial talent, especially among middle managers and supervisors
- Modification of the organizational structure, particularly related to maintaining flexibility, fostering simplicity, and facilitating growth.

Patterns of Organization. There are many different approaches to structuring a business. The four general patterns summarized in the following paragraphs are the most widely used by entrepreneurs.

Functional Organization. Uses a business' various functions (manufacturing, marketing, personnel, etc.) as the basis for organizing related activities into departments. Thus the marketing department encompasses all functions related specifically to marketing, such as sales, promotion, market research, and customer service. This approach encourages specialization and efficiency by enabling employees who share related expertise and interests to work together. Although departments are interdependent, employees tend to perceive their roles—and attach their loyalties—along departmental lines. Such "departmentalism," left unchecked, can foster a sort of tunnel vision through which specific, functional goals are pursued, whereas overall business objectives are largely ignored. Because it is well suited to a business with few products or services, a functional structure is commonly employed by many small businesses in their earliest stages of growth. Rapidly growing businesses, however, may outgrow this structure; functional departments are an impractical means of organizing diversified, multiproduct or multiservice operations.

Product/Service Organization. Uses a business' products or services as the means for structuring all related activities; thus each product or service unit is self-sufficient in functional terms. This approach encourages an independent, "market driven" orientation in which entrepreneurship can be successfully integrated with product management techniques. However, specialization is not encouraged; marketing experts, for example, are assigned to each product or service unit, not to a centralized, functional department. The product/service structure can be especially useful in fostering growth and profitability—on a product- or service-line basis—for rapidly expanding businesses.

Location-Based Organization. Uses geographical location as the basis for structuring a business; thus all operations within an area are organized into a territorial unit. This approach can often best serve the market needs of large, typically multistate, areas.

Customer-Targeted Organization. Uses categories of customers or clients as the basis for structuring the top echelons of each department; thus sales and marketing may be organized into retail, wholesale, original equipment manufacturer (OEM) parts, and government sales units.

Note that each of the preceding structures may be used with the others in various aspects of a business. For example, a manufacturing company's operations may be organized along product lines, within which location-based and customer-targeted structures are employed; the same company's administrative and "corporate" activities (personnel, finance, planning, etc.) may be organized into functional departments. All of these approaches are valuable in their own right. Ultimately, their utility is measured in terms of their impact on bottom-line performance.

PLANNING TO PROVIDE ACCURATE FINANCIAL INFORMATION. Accurate financial information is essential for making informed management decisions in general, and for implementing effective financial planning in particular. Each business' accounting and information requirements must be reviewed to determine the most suitable financial recordkeeping system. A well-designed recordkeeping system will, at a minimum, provide:

- Detailed operating statements
- Comparison of current results to budgets and prior periods (where available)
- Financial statements suitable for use by management and creditors
- Information required for tax returns and reports to regulatory agencies
- Sufficient control for safeguarding assets and detecting errors

Various specific recordkeeping capabilities—related to size, complexity, and type of business—may also be required. The types of books and records generally required by most small businesses are summarized in the following paragraphs.

Chart of Accounts. A chart of accounts serves to index the general ledger accounts, indentifying each such account by number and by ledger. This chart offers a convenient means of summarizing and categorizing transactions.

General Ledger. Posted to the general ledger—which contains all of the business' accounts—are all the monthly totals, previously accumulated by summarizing the individual transaction records of various journals (described in subsequent paragraphs). After all postings have been made, a trial balance from the general ledger is usually prepared (an adding machine tape ordinarily suffices) to check the accuracy of the posting process. Information in the general ledger is used to prepare all financial statements.

Sales and Cash Receipts Journal. All incoming cash is recorded in a sales and cash receipts journal. The debit amount (cash received) is generally entered item by item using the "remittance advice" or receipt (stub showing type of monies deposited) as the source for these figures. The credit amount is entered against the appropriate account (accounts receivable, income, etc.). This journal is totaled and posted to the corresponding general ledger accounts on a monthly basis. An accounts receivable aged trial balance (showing receivables outstanding by due date, by customer) is also prepared monthly. Accounts receivable entries are also posted to receivable cards (showing initial sale amounts, payments received, and balance owing) maintained for each customer.

Cash Disbursements Journal. Used to record all checks written, the cash disbursements journal shows—typically in check-number order—the check number, date, payee, and amount. The debit amount is entered against the proper account (accounts payable, office supplies, etc.). This journal is totaled and posted to the corresponding general ledger accounts on a monthly basis.

Purchase Journal. Used to record all vendor invoices that are not paid at the time goods are received or services are performed, the purchase journal shows the invoice date, vendor, amount, and account classification for each invoice or group of invoices. The total amount of each vendor invoice is posted to detail cards (showing initial purchase amounts, payments made, and balance due) maintained for each vendor's payables. This journal is totaled and posted to the corresponding general ledger accounts on a monthly basis. An accounts payable listing is also usually kept, showing the payables on an end-of-month basis.

Payroll Journal. Used to summarize payroll information, this journal is totaled and posted to the correspondingly general ledger accounts (payroll expense, as well as related payables and cash disbursements), on a monthly or more frequent basis. Supporting documents for payroll preparation (deduction authorizations, withholding status, properly approved pay rate forms, etc.) are maintained on a current basis in personnel files.

General Journal. Used to record transactions that cannot logically be entered in the sales and cash receipts, purchase or cash disbursement journals, the general journal's entries are classified in two categories: recurring and nonrecurring. Recurring entries are those that are made monthly (depreciation expense, accrued liabilities, and adjustments to prepaid expense balances); a standard journal entry is ordinarily used to record these items. Nonrecurring entries are those made to record unusual transactions, such as the correction of errors in general ledger accounts.

Fixed Assets Ledger. Used to summarize details for all real and personal property—thus ensuring ready availability of reliable information on these assets—a fixed assets ledger is usually prepared and updated on a monthly basis. A depreciation lapsing schedule (showing each item recorded in the fixed asset accounts of the general ledger) may be used as the detailed fixed asset record. The lapsing schedule, updated for acquisition and disposition of assets, includes all pertinent details for each listed asset (complete description, date acquired and purchaser's name, estimated useful life, etc.). Total depreciation expense (summarized monthly) generally serves as a basis for the monthly standard journal entry for depreciation. A capitalization policy is used to determine the minimum cost of assets to be capitalized; lesser amounts are charged to expense.

Inventory Stock Record Control. Containing a card on every major stock item in inventory, the stock record control shows both additions to and removals from inventory, including corresponding dates and prices. The clerical accuracy of this file needs to be regularly verified by comparing its records with accurate counts of physical inventory. Any necessary adjustments—for discrepancies between the records and physical inventory—are recorded in the general journal.

Monthly Financial Statements. For financial management and planning purposes, monthly financial statements are prepared and retained on file to provide a record of the business' growth and details of changes in its financial position.

ANNUAL FINANCIAL PLANNING—THE BUDGET

The overall financial planning process is generally described in terms of ongoing short-range (annual) and long-range (strategic) planning. The annual profit plan—**the budget**—explored in this section is a central feature of short-range planning. Although the budgeting process also plays a significant role in long-range planning, the intricacies of strategic budgeting and forecasting are beyond the scope of this section.

ROLE OF THE BUDGETING PROCESS. Budgeting is a planning tool. Like planning itself, budgeting is a process. It is a means of managing business operations that combines planning and control activities. Because planning incorporates both budgeting and forecasting, it is useful to clarify the distinctions between budgets and forecasts. The two differ along many of the same general lines as was noted for plans and projections.

Budgets. A budget is a management tool for planning and control, generally covering a one-year period. It expresses financial guidelines, predominantly in monetary terms (units of sales or production may be included), within which managers are expected to operate, and against which management performance is periodically measured. Budgets require formal review and approval; once approved, budgets may be changed only as specifically provided by top management. Actual expenses are regularly compared with budgeted levels; variances are reviewed and explained.

Forecasts. In contrast, a forecast or projection is an estimating tool for any chosen time period, used widely throughout the planning process. It expresses anticipated results or actions, not necessarily in monetary terms, based on stated assumptions or "what if" questions. As estimates, forecasts entail no management commitment; forecasters are not responsible for achieving the projected results. Updates or revisions are generally made on an as-needed basis; they are not subject to formats or periodic analysis by management.

Budgeting and Forecasting. All budgets make use of various applications of financial forecasting. Forecasts of cash flow, sales projections, and estimates of maintenance costs are all routinely used in preparing budgets. Although financial forecasting is employed throughout the planning process, it is also used *within* the budgeting process as a tool.

Planning and Control. A budget is a hybrid document, combining planning and control functions. In its final form, the budget serves to define and focus key objectives of the financial planning process. The budget charts the course that managers need to take so that the business can attain targeted levels of profitability and growth. Budgetary control requires that managers operate within the limits imposed by budgeted amounts. In this respect, the budget also serves as an important measurement of management performance, providing a basis for comparing actual results with expectations.

As a general rule, the responsibility for changing budgets is borne solely by top management. Changes are made only as warranted by specific, generally unforeseen, circumstances.

Bottom-Up Process. In contrast to such "top-down" management activities as setting company policies—which originate at the highest levels of management and are passed down through the lower levels of the organization—budgeting is a "bottom-up" process. Following the planning process' general approach to information gathering, the basic facts and figures required for budgeting are collected by managers and their subordinates and passed upward to top management. In most budgeting processes, managers also have the responsibility for preparing proposed budgets for superiors' review and approval. This approach is especially useful because it ensures direct participation in budget decision making by those who are responsible for meeting budgeted goals. The direct involvement of managers and supervisors fosters the sharing of information and encourages the development of more realistic budget proposals. Thus the final budget emerges as a more accurate planning tool. Note that managers' and supervisors' participation is focused on *devel-*

oping proposed budgets. The responsibility for making the key decisions—for reviewing the approving budgets in final form—always rests with top management.

BUDGETING PROCESSES: THE BASIC TYPES OF BUDGETS. Budgets may be categorized in a variety of ways, each incorporating several types of budgets. For simplicity's sake, this variety can be reduced to three basic types: fixed budgets, flexible budgets, and zero-based budgets. However, only the first two types are widely applicable to small business' needs. Zero-based budgeting—so named because budgeting begins from a zero basis, requiring justification of each proposed item of expense—is too complex and time-consuming to be of any practical value for most small businesses.

Fixed Budgets. Fixed budgets, also known as fixed-forecast budgets, are used primarily as planning tools. They are fixed in a variety of respects, including the use of:

- Specified time periods (usually a year, divided into months)
- Set monetary amounts for all budgeted items
- Forecast sales volumes and production levels

Fixed budgets are developed by applying estimated or standard unit costs to activity levels derived from forecasts. Each budgeted amount therefore corresponds with projected sales volumes and/or production levels. Thus the budget assumes the role of a profit plan, specifying how each item contributes to profits for the period. Exhibit 3 shows one of the fixed budgets used by a hypothetical manufacturing company.

Limitations of Fixed Budgeting. Although fixed budgets provide a clear plan for attaining profit goals, their usefulness in controlling expenses and measuring managers' performance chiefly depends on the accuracy of the incorporated forecasts. For example, when monthly sales activity differs from projections, all related budgeted amounts are no longer appropriate for the month. Because variations in actual performance—owing either to faulty assumptions or to unforeseen circumstances—can be expected, fixed budgeting routinely calls for regular "rebudgeting." Such revisions are often cumbersome, requiring additional management time and effort to ensure that budget variances continue to be compared with the original budget, whereas actual results are compared with the revised budget. For this reason, fixed budgeting best serves as a planning tool. The overall budgeting needs of most small businesses call for a different approach—the use of flexible budgeting.

Flexible Budgets. Flexible budgets, also known as variable budgets, are especially useful for expense control and evaluation of managers' performance. Other names sometimes used for flexible budgets include expense formula budgets, expense control budgets, step budgets, and sliding-scale budgets. They

EXHIBIT 3 FLEXIBLE BUDGETS

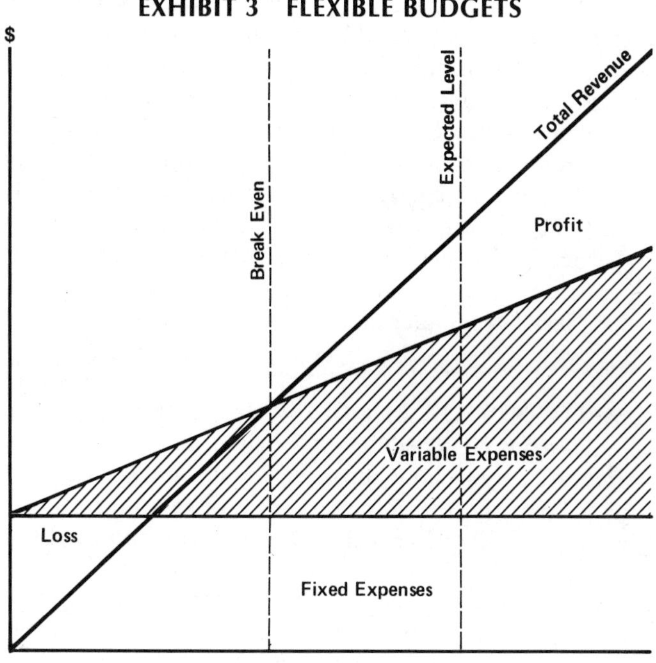

are flexible in that their design—including designation of expense items among fixed, semivariable, and variable categories—readily allows comparison of budgeted and actual expenses for the same level of activity. Flexible budgets require the use of specially developed budget formulas for each of the listed expense items. These formulas help determine expense projections based on the sales volume or production level actually attained. Thus the flexible budget combines a profit plan with an expense control system.

Requirements of Flexible Budgeting. The preparation of flexible budgets demands detailed consideration of such challenging issues as the classification of expenses as fixed or variable (expense behavior), the selection of appropriate measures of activity levels (units produced, dollar amount of sales, etc.), and the adjustment of historical expense figures to exclude bookkeeping errors and extraordinary conditions. Commitments of management time and resources are clearly required. However, because the usefulness of these and similar analyses extends far beyond the budgeting process, entrepreneurs typically discover that the "effective cost" of preparing either flexible or fixed budgets is roughly comparable.

Advantages of Flexible Budgeting. For small businesses, flexible budgets often provide the most effective approach to budgeting. These budgets work so well because their specially designed flexibility assists entrepreneurs in *manag-*

ing change. And significant change is a pervasive, dynamic force in small business. Because entrepreneurs tend to be concerned primarily with whether expenses are more or less than what they should be for the actual level of sales or production attained, why actual results differ from expectations (a self-evident issue in some circumstances) may well be of secondary importance. Flexible budgets help entrepreneurs and their managers address these two issues—the efficiency of both expense control and planning—by incorporating mechanisms for making needed comparisons. The objective is a cycle of progress: Developing a keener understanding of the interrelationships among items of income and expense leads to a more thorough consideration of operating approaches, which leads to sounder decision making, resulting in increased profitability and growth.

MAIN COMPONENTS OF BUDGETS. In addition to various budget breakdowns and required schedules of revenue and expense, budgeting includes preparation of projections for three key documents: the profit and loss statement, the balance sheet, and the statement of cash flow. How each relates to the budgeting process is described in the following paragraphs.

Profit and Loss Statement. The profit and loss (P&L) statement, also known as the income statement, summarizes the main items of income (generally sales) and expense related to a particular product or unit of the company. To facilitate comparison and review, the P&L statement commonly used in the budgeting process is a hybrid document. It generally shows actual and budgeted P&L figures, both as dollar amounts and as percentages of sales; budget variances also may be included. Exhibit 4 is a P&L statement used in budgeting by a hypothetical manufacturing company.

Analyzing P&L Figures. Comparison of actual and budgeted P&L figures may call for more detailed examination to determine the relative significance of budget variances. Among the basic analyses widely used are various types of:

Sales Analysis. Detailing sales activity by product, customer, territory, sales representative, or similar factors

Gross Margin Analysis. Establishing the cost of goods sold for each of the categories in the sales analysis, and showing how each contributes to the business' gross profit margin

Net Income Analysis. Reducing each of the sales categories by the appropriate amount of related expenses (allocated sales and administrative expenses), and showing how each contributes to the business' return on investment

These analyses can help entrepreneurs gain added insight into business operations, while suggesting avenues of corrective or supportive action. For example, it is often valuable to review the performance of individual sales representa-

EXHIBIT 4 ACE MANUFACTURING COMPANY, 1986 INCOME STATEMENT

	1986												TOTAL
PROFIT AND LOSS	1	2	3	4	5	6	7	8	9	10	11	12	1986
SALES	300000	303000	306000	309000	312000	315000	318000	321000	324000	327000	330000	333000	3798000
COST OF SALES	−120000	−121000	−122000	−124000	−125000	−126000	−127000	−128000	−130000	−131000	−132000	−133000	−1519000
GROSS PROFIT	180000	182000	184000	185000	187000	189000	191000	193000	194000	196000	198000	200000	2279000
SELLING EXPENSES & BAD DEBTS	−55000	−55000	−56000	−56000	−57000	−57000	−58000	−58000	−59000	−59000	−60000	−60000	−690000
GENERAL & ADMINISTRATIVE	−100000	−100000	−100000	−100000	−100000	−100000	−100000	−100000	−100000	−100000	−100000	−100000	−1200000
OTHER EXPENSES	−5000	−5000	−5000	−5000	−5000	−5000	−5000	−5000	−5000	−5000	−5000	−5000	−60000
RESEARCH & DEVELOPMENT	−25000	−25000	−25000	−25000	−25000	−25000	−25000	−25000	−25000	−25000	−25000	−25000	−300000
L/T INTEREST EXPENSE	−13000	−13000	−13000	−13000	−12000	−12000	−12000	−12000	−12000	−12000	−12000	−12000	−148000
OTHER INCOME	1000	1000	1000	1000	1000	1000	1000	1000	1000	1000	1000	1000	12000
INT INCOME CASH MANAGEMENT	1000	5000	4000	4000	9000	14000	14000	14000	14000	15000	1000	0	95000
INT EXPENSE CASH MANAGEMENT	0	0	0	0	0	0	0	0	0	0	0	−3000	−3000
GAIN/LOSS ON SALE OF P & E	5000	0	5000	−20000	24000	15000	0	5000	0	0	0	−50000	−16000
GAIN/LOSS ON SALE OF LAND	0	0	0	250000	0	0	0	0	150000	0	0	0	400000
TOTAL	−191000	−192000	−189000	36000	−165000	−169000	−185000	−180000	−36000	−185000	−200000	−254000	−1910000
NET INCOME BEFORE TAXES	−11000	−10000	−5000	221000	22000	20000	6000	13000	158000	11000	−2000	−54000	369000
DEFERRED TAXES	−8000	−8000	−8000	−8000	−8000	−8000	−8000	−8000	−8000	−8000	−8000	−12000	−100000
CURRENT TAXES	1000	1000	1000	−29000	−3000	−3000	−1000	−2000	−21000	−1000	0	9000	−48000
TOTAL INCOME TAXES	−7000	−7000	−7000	−37000	−11000	−11000	−9000	−10000	−29000	−9000	−8000	−3000	−148000
NET INCOME	−18000	−17000	−12000	184000	11000	9000	−3000	3000	129000	2000	−10000	−57000	221000

tives, how well the business is serving certain market segments, how sales territories compare in various measures of performance, or how each product or product line is performing in relation to the business as a whole. The nature and scope of analysis needed depend on a variety of factors, related to a business' size and stage of development.

Balance Sheet. The budgeting of balance sheet items is a relatively straightforward process in most respects. Much like P&L statements, comparative balance sheets are frequently used to facilitate comparison and review of end-of-period results. Exhibit 5 is a comparative balance sheet used by a hypothetical manufacturing company.

Analyzing Balance Sheet Figures. Various applications of financial ratio analysis are widely used to review balance sheet performance. Among the basic analyses useful to small businesses are the following ratios.

Current Ratio. A measure of financial soundness and effective use of assets, expressed as:

$$\frac{\textit{Current assets}}{\text{Current liabilities}}$$

A current ratio of at least 2 to 1 is usually desirable.

Quick Ratio. Also known as the liquidity ratio or acid test, it qualitatively considers assets and liabilities in terms of the business' most liquid assets (such as cash and marketable securites), expressed as:

$$\frac{\textit{Quick assets}}{\text{Current liabilities}}$$

A quick ratio of at least 1 to 1 is generally desirable.

Days' Sales Outstanding. A measure of efficient use of funds, showing the quality of receivables and the effectiveness of credit policies, generally expressed as:

$$\frac{\textit{Accounts receivable}}{\text{Net sales}} \times 360 \text{ days}$$

Inventory Turnover. A measure of the efficient use of working capital, variously expressed; when used in the preparing budgets, generally expressed as:

$$\frac{\textit{Cost of sales}}{\text{Average inventory}}$$

The method used for calculating inventory turnover depends on the nature and scope of inventory analysis undertaken.

EXHIBIT 5 ACE MANUFACTURING COMPANY, 1986 BALANCE SHEET

BALANCE SHEET	LAST YEAR LAST MNTH	1986: 1	2	3	4	5	6	7	8	9	10	11	12	TOTAL 1986
CASH	90000	100000	9000	9000	100000	100000	53000	28000	100000	100000	9000	9000	48000	48000
CASH MGT INVESTMENT	100000	467000	410000	350000	936000	1363000	1363000	1363000	1367000	1522000	61000	0	0	0
ACCOUNTS RECEIVABLE (NET)	800000	216000	233000	205000	225000	214000	212000	224000	227000	255000	242000	224000	265000	265000
INVENTORY	500000	506000	511000	517000	523000	530000	536000	538000	540000	542000	544000	544000	544000	544000
PREPAID EXPENSES	10000	9000	8000	12000	11000	10000	9000	8000	7000	6000	10000	9000	8000	8000
OTHER CURRENT ASSETS	1000	1000	1000	1000	1000	1000	1000	1000	−1000	−1000	−1000	−1000	−1000	−1000
TOTAL CURRENT ASSETS	1501000	1299000	1172000	1094000	1796000	2218000	2174000	2162000	2240000	2424000	865000	785000	864000	864000
LAND	530000	630000	730000	828000	378000	428000	478000	528000	528000	578000	578000	728000	728000	728000
PLANT & EQUIPMENT	2410000	2376000	2332000	2303000	2244000	2738000	2688000	2588000	2524000	2524000	4024000	4224000	3724000	3724000
ACCUM. DEPRECIATION (−)	−500000	−502000	−498000	−504000	−505000	−515000	−494000	−437000	−420000	−438000	−456000	−475000	−144000	−144000
NET FIXED ASSETS	2440000	2504000	2564000	2627000	2117000	2651000	2672000	2679000	2632000	2664000	4146000	4477000	4308000	4308000
OTHER L/T ASSETS (NET)	7500	8000	8000	8000	8000	8000	8000	8000	−7000	−7000	58000	58000	58000	58000
TOTAL NONCURRENT ASSETS	2447000	2512000	2572000	2635000	2125000	2659000	2680000	2687000	2625000	2657000	4204000	4535000	4366000	4366000
TOTAL ASSETS	3948500	3811000	3744000	3729000	3921000	4877000	4854000	4849000	4865000	5081000	5069000	5320000	5230000	5230000
LIABILITIES														
ACCOUNTS PAYABLE	200000	124000	120000	137000	141000	128000	123000	135000	141000	132000	132000	158000	133000	133000
WAGES PAYABLE (MANUFACTURING)	36000	8000	8000	9000	9000	9000	9000	9000	9000	9000	9000	9000	9000	9000
ACCRUED LIABILITIES	40000	40000	40000	40000	40000	40000	40000	40000	40000	40000	40000	40000	40000	40000
CASH MANAGEMENT DEBT	0	0	0	0	0	0	0	0	0	0	0	230000	230000	230000
INCOME TAXES PAYABLE – LAST YEAR	50000	50000	50000	25000	25000	25000	0	0	0	0	0	0	0	0
INCOME TAXES PAYABLE – THIS YEAR		−1000	−2000	−3000	16000	19000	12000	13000	15000	26000	27000	27000	10000	10000
L/T DEBT – CURRENT PORTION	10000	59000	58000	57000	56000	55000	102000	151000	52000	51000	50000	49000	48000	48000
OTHER CURRENT LIABILITIES	2000	2000	2000	2000	2000	2000	2000	2000	2000	2000	2000	2000	2000	2000
TOTAL CURRENT LIABILITIES	338000	282000	276000	267000	289000	278000	288000	350000	259000	260000	260000	515000	472000	472000
LONG TERM DEBT	1000000	948000	946000	944000	942000	940000	890000	838000	934000	932000	930000	928000	926000	926000
DEFERRED TAXES	10000	18000	26000	34000	42000	50000	58000	66000	74000	82000	90000	98000	110000	110000
OTHER L/T LIABILITIES	2000	2000	2000	2000	2000	2000	2000	2000	2000	2000	2000	2000	2000	2000
TOTAL LIABILITIES	1350000	1250000	1250000	1247000	1275000	1270000	1238000	1256000	1269000	1276000	1282000	1543000	1510000	1510000
NET WORTH														
CAPITAL STOCK	800000	800000	800000	800000	800000	1600000	1600000	1600000	1600000	1600000	1600000	1600000	1680000	1680000
ADDITIONAL PAID IN CAPITAL	100000	100000	100000	100000	100000	300000	300000	300000	300000	310000	310000	310000	330000	330000
CURRENT YEAR PROFIT/LOSS		−18000	−35000	−47000	137000	148000	157000	154000	157000	286000	288000	278000	221000	221000
RETAINED EARNINGS	1748500	1729000	1729000	1729000	1709000	1709000	1709000	1689000	1689000	1689000	1669000	1669000	1669000	1669000
TREASURY STOCK	−50000	−50000	−100000	−100000	−100000	−150000	−150000	−150000	−150000	−80000	−80000	−80000	−180000	−180000
TOTAL NET WORTH	2598500	2561000	2494000	2482000	2646000	3607000	3616000	3593000	3596000	3805000	3787000	3777000	3720000	3720000
TOTAL LIAB & NET WORTH	3948500	3811000	3744000	3729000	3921000	4877000	4854000	4849000	4865000	5081000	5069000	5320000	5230000	5230000

Fixed Assets Turnover. A measure of the efficiency of investment, expressed as:

$$\frac{\textit{Net sales}}{\text{Average fixed assets}}$$

Total Assets Turnover. Another measure of asset utilization, expressed as:

$$\frac{\textit{Sales}}{\text{Average total assets}}$$

When this turnover figure is multiplied by net income—expressed as a percentage of sales—the result is the percentage return on investment in total assets.

Debt-to-Assets Ratio. A general measure of solvency, expressed as:

$$\frac{\textit{Total liabilities}}{\text{Total assets}}$$

Note that this ratio does not tell the whole story; it excludes consideration of the *quality* of assets.

In addition to these ratios, many small businesses routinely employ a variety of other tools of financial analysis, including capitalization ratios and per-share valuations. Although various financial ratios are used in the budgeting process and its associated review/refinement functions, ratio analysis forms an important aspect of many other financial planning activities.

Statement of Cash Flow. The statement of cash flow, also known as the flow of funds statement or statement of changes in financial position, is prepared to aid both in the review and analysis of balance-sheet changes and in the projection of cash flow throughout the budgeting process. In most small businesses' budgeting, the statement of cash flow used in the handier form of various cash-flow summaries. Exhibit 6 is a cash-flow summary used in budgeting by a hypothetical manufacturing company.

Effective planning and control of cash flow are critical to the success of any business—especially so for small businesses in the earliest stages of development—therefore the preparation and use of cash-flow schedules are central aspects of budgeting. The purpose of these documents is to translate the items of income and expense considered in the P&L statement and the balance sheet into an integrated overview of the business' cash requirements.

Preparing Cash-Flow Summaries. A number of approaches are widely used in preparing cash-flow summaries. All are drawn from the following transactional model:

- Start with total cash available at the beginning of period.
- Add cash sources including cash from sales, issuance of debt instruments, and sales of equity interests to determine total cash received.

EXHIBIT 6 ACE MANUFACTURING COMPANY, 1986 CASH FLOW STATEMENT

CASH FLOW	1986												TOTAL
	1	2	3	4	5	6	7	8	9	10	11	12	1986
BEGINNING CASH	90000	100000	9000	9000	100000	100000	53000	28000	100000	100000	9000	9000	90000
A/R COLLECTED	875000	277000	325000	280000	314000	308000	297000	309000	287000	331000	339000	283000	4225000
A/P PAID	−325000	−254000	−235000	−250000	−270000	−258000	−241000	−248000	−265000	−257000	−230000	−282000	−3115000
MANUFACTURING WAGES PAID	−62000	−34000	−34000	−35000	−36000	−36000	−35000	−35000	−36000	−36000	−35000	−36000	−451000
S/T INTEREST INC/EXP	1000	5000	4000	4000	9000	14000	14000	14000	14000	15000	1000	−3000	92000
L/T INTEREST EXPENSE	−13000	−13000	−13000	−13000	−12000	−12000	−12000	−12000	−12000	−12000	−12000	−12000	−148000
SALE OF PLANT & EQUIPMENT	25000	25000	25000	25000	25000	25000	25000	35000	0	0	0	100000	310000
SALE OF LAND	0	0	2000	800000	0	0	0	0	300000	0	0	0	1102000
PURCHASE OF PLANT & EQUIP	−1000	−1000	−1000	−1000	−500000	0	0	−1000	0	−1500000	−200000	0	−2205000
PURCHASE OF LAND	−100000	−100000	−100000	−100000	−50000	−50000	−50000	0	−200000	0	−150000	0	−900000
IC/DC(−) OTHER CURR ASSETS	0	0	0	0	0	0	0	2000	0	0	0	0	2000
IC/DC(−) OTHER L/T ASSETS	0	0	0	0	0	0	0	15000	0	−65000	0	0	−50000
IC/DC(−) OTHER CURR LIABS	0	0	0	0	0	0	0	0	0	0	0	0	0
IC/DC(−) OTHER L/T LIABS	0	0	0	0	0	0	0	0	0	0	0	0	0
PREPAYMENTS	0	0	−5000	0	0	0	0	0	0	−5000	0	0	−10000
ACCRUALS PAID	0	0	0	0	0	0	0	0	0	0	0	0	0
LONG TERM DEBT PAYMENTS	−5000	−5000	−5000	−5000	−5000	−5000	−5000	−5000	−5000	−5000	−5000	−5000	−60000
LONG TERM DEBT INCREASE	2000	2000	2000	2000	2000	2000	2000	2000	2000	2000	2000	2000	24000
INCOME TAXES PAID													
PRIOR YEAR TAXES	0	0	−25000	0	0	−25000	0	0	0	0	0	0	−50000
CURRENT YEAR TAXES				−10000		−10000			−10000			−8000	−38000
SALE OF CAPITAL STOCK	0	0	0	0	1000000	0	0	0	0	0	0	100000	1100000
SALE OF TREASURY STOCK	0	0	0	0	0	0	0	0	80000	0	0	0	80000
PURCHASE OF TREASURY STOCK	0	−50000	0	0	−50000	0	0	0	0	0	0	−100000	−200000
PAYMENT OF CASH DIVIDENDS	−20000	0	0	−20000	0	0	−20000	0	0	−20000	0	0	−80000
CASH FLOW BEFORE CASH MANAGEMENT	377000	−148000	−60000	677000	427000	−47000	−25000	76000	155000	−1552000	−291000	39000	−372000
CASH BEFORE CASH MANAGEMENT	467000	−48000	−51000	686000	527000	53000	28000	104000	255000	−1452000	−282000	48000	−282000
CASH MANAGEMENT LOAN	0	57000	60000	0	0	0	0	0	0	1461000	291000	0	1869000
CASH MANAGEMENT INVESTMENT	−367000	0	0	−586000	−427000	0	0	−4000	−155000	0	0	0	−1539000
ENDING CASH	100000	9000	9000	100000	100000	53000	28000	100000	100000	9000	9000	48000	48000

- Subtract total expenses cash uses including operating expenses, investment in assets, and repayments of debts from total cash received.
- The result is total cash available at the end of the period.

Depending on a business' particular needs, projected cash flows may be prepared for each product or product line, each plant or other operating location, each sales territory, or each division or other unit. Quarterly cash flows are most widely used; monthly or weekly cash flows are used by certain businesses, in the start-up mode when cash flow is extremely important. Like other tools used in the budgeting process, cash-flow projections are employed in many other aspects of planning, including the specialized applications of financial planning that are explored in the following paragraphs.

SPECIALIZED APPLICATIONS OF FINANCIAL PLANNING

There are many specialized, interrelated applications of financial planning. The most common of these applications—various types of tax planning, compensation planning, information planning, and business continuation planning—are briefly described in the following paragraphs (see also Exhibit 2 for a comparison of selected aspects). Although each of these specialties is often treated as a "type" of planning in its own right (and each entails a host of technical considerations), all serve well-defined functions within both the financial planning and the overall business planning processes.

BUSINESS TAX PLANNING. Because federal and state income taxes are among the most significant costs borne by a business, effective tax planning is important for the efficient use of available capital. All techniques of tax planning share two overall objectives: minimizing tax liabilities and maximizing deferral of taxes. Various elections, deductions, and credits can be used to reduce a business' tax bill. Deferred taxes amount to an "interest-free" loan from the government—a source of short-term financing. A sampling of general considerations commonly taken into account in business tax planning is presented in the following paragraphs.

Form of Organization. As noted earlier, each main form of business organization—regular corporation, S corporation, partnership, and sole proprietorship—has different tax attributes. Consequently, each form of business relies on different tax planning techniques. A business can adopt several forms—growing from one to another, or organizing various units as S corporations, partnerships, and so on—and thereby increase the flexibility of its tax planning.

Accounting Period. Selection of the annual accounting period or **"taxable year"** can be important both for general business considerations and for tax deferral opportunities. For example, a calendar year is not suitable for most retailers; the busiest sales period, from November through January, should not be allowed to conflict with the year-end closing process. The choice of accounting period is also governed by the form of organization. Regular corporations, for instance, can select any year-end; whereas S corporations are generally limited to a calendar year-end with exceptions allowed for valid business reasons.

Accounting Methods. The methods used by a business to account for its income and expenses have a profound effect on tax liabilities. The two overall accounting methods are:

Cash Method. Which recognizes income and expense at the time that cash is received or disbursed; not generally used if sizable inventories need to be maintained by a business.

Accrual Method. Which recognizes income at the time it is earned, and recognizes expense at the time an obligation to pay a debt is incurred; provides a better matching of revenue and expenditures, and is typically required for financial reporting purposes.

Once either the cash or the accrual method is adopted, Internal Revenue Service permission is required for any change. Permission is usually granted for requests to change from the cash to the accrual method; it is routinely denied for changes from the accrual to the cash method. The need for IRS permission for certain changes in methods can prove an important tax-related aspect of financial planning. Other, more specialized accounting methods in wide use include:

Installment Sales. Which recognizes income in each year as equal to the amount of installment payments received during the year, divided by the total purchase price, and then multiplied by the expected gross profit; a useful method for deferring income for tax purposes while currently recognizing payments received.

Inventory Methods. Among the most commonly used methods of accounting for inventory are average cost, FIFO (first-in, first-out) and LIFO (last-in, first-out). The **average cost method** values inventory based on the average cost of all similar goods available during the period; adopted mainly for its simplicity and ease of use. The **FIFO method** assumes that inventory is used in the same order as goods are purchased or produced; it also enables a business to "write off" excess inventory costs (on a "lower of FIFO cost or market" basis) to account for a decline in the goods' market value. The **LIFO method** reverses the FIFO assumption, treating the most recently purchased or produced goods as used first; it can provide significant tax-deferral savings during times of inflation, but does not permit the market write-downs allowed by FIFO. For manufacturing operations, *overhead costs* of production need to be related to inventory costs, typically by allocating a "pool" on the basis of a standard unit (such as labor dollars or hours).

Long-Term Contract Accounting Methods. Mainly useful for construction businesses, such approaches as the percentage-of-completion method, completed-contract method, accrual acceptance method, and advance payment elections can provide significant opportunities for tax deferral. Under the completed contract method of accounting, profit is not reported until completion of the contract. For a contract performed over several years, taxes on the profit are deferred until the end of the contract regardless of the cash received in the interim.

R&D Accounting Methods. Enable a business to treat **research and development (R&D) expenditures** either as current expenses (deductible in the year they are paid or incurred) or as amortizable expenses (deductible over a 60-month period); this option provides greater flexibility for tax planning. An **R&D tax credit** (dollar-for-dollar reduction in the amount of tax payable) may also be available; tax savings realized from this credit can, in effect, help a business finance its R&D activities. Additional advantages can be provided by **R&D syndications,** which combine tax benefits with alternative sources of financing.

Accounting for Bad Debts. Entails a choice between expensing bad debts (deducting the full amount when each becomes uncollectible) and "reserving" bad debts (charging an expected amount against the year-end accounts receivable balance); generally, the reserve method is preferable because a tax benefit is allowed for a "noncash expense."

Accounting for Depreciation. Various depreciation methods, including straight-line depreciation and "cost recovery" allowances under the Accelerated Cost Recovery System (ACRS), can provide valuable flexibility in planning the timing and amount of depreciation deductions. An election to expense certain capital assets costs (up to an annual dollar-amount limitation) is also available. *Investment tax credits,* a dollar for dollar reduction of tax, are available for investment in certain business assets.

Other Specialized Methods. Include various techniques of accounting for field support and demonstration equipment, vacation pay, organizational expenses, and start-up expenses; generally, these provide opportunities for deferring taxes, though tax savings may also be obtained.

Although these considerations pertain generally to planning for federal tax liabilities, these must also be evaluated in terms of applicable state and local tax rules.

INDIVIDUAL TAX PLANNING. Because most **entrepreneurs'** personal finances—in terms of both income and wealth—are linked closely with the business' performance, individual and business tax planning are often in effect, two sides of the same coin. Entrepreneurs generally need to explore the interrelated tax aspects of such issues as:

Compensation. Determining how best to divide annual compensation among salary, dividends, benefit and retirement plans, and stock; also, the extent to which rules governing "excess compensation" and "excess retained earnings" apply.

Family Income Shifting. Considering various techniques (including hiring family members) for distributing income and tax-free benefits among those in lower tax brackets, resulting in overall tax savings for the family.

Gift and Estate Planning. Integrating related aspects in terms of business valuation, gifts of cash and stock, and use of trusts and other wealth-transfer techniques (including asset value freezes), and successor ownership and management.

State tax considerations (especially those that govern aspects of estate planning) also need to be taken into account.

COMPENSATION PLANNING. The magnitude of wages and benefits as items of expense clearly emphasizes the importance of savings realized through compensation planning. Such savings, however, are secondary in their importance. The main purpose of compensation planning is to attract, retain, and motivate employees at all levels.

Often, a small business' ability to offer significant opportunities for equity participation, for example, can prove decisive in attracting and retaining management talent. And the many long-term benefits of maintaining a stable, highly motivated workforce are difficult to overestimate. In the following pages some of the basic types of compensation plans in widespread use are outlined.

Cash-Oriented Incentive Compensation Plans. Based on the premise that "cash motivates," these plans generally seek to match individual performance with various measures of company performance. Cash-oriented plans include:

Bonuses. Traditionally designed to be paid currently, as a supplement to base salary, for meeting predetermined objectives; in recent years, "front-end" bonuses have frequently been used for attracting talented personnel.

Deferred Compensation Plans. By enabling current payment for services to be deferred to a subsequent year, these plans serve both to better match performance with multiyear objectives and to assist entrepreneurs and managers in deferring income for individual tax planning.

Equity-Oriented Plans. By permitting employees to share in ownership of the business, these plans foster cooperation and help extend the entrepreneurial spirit throughout the organization. Equity-oriented plans generally must meet complicated tax requirements; the main types of plans are:

Incentive Stock Options (ISOs). Enable employees to participate in the appreciation in value of the company's stock, based on the stock's fair market value as of the date of the option; employees' gains on ISOs can qualify for favorable capital gain treatment.

Nonqualified Stock Options. Offering greater flexibility than ISOs, nonqualified options can be granted at any exercise price and can be exercised at any time, subject to the requirements of the employer's plan; however, employees' gains on these options are taxed as ordinary income.

Restricted Stock Plans. Permit employees to purchase stock that does not carry full rights (such as voting rights) until some later date; in addition to providing favorable capital gain treatment, these plans also allow flexibility in timing of income recognition.

Because equity-oriented plans are individually designed to meet each company's requirements, a number of specialized arrangements—variations on the types noted previously—have evolved; these include stock appreciation rights (SARs), formula plans, performance-share arrangements, and junior stock plans.

Fringe Benefit Programs. Because fringe benefits are generally tax free to employees and generally fully deductible by the employer, these are often doubly valuable supplements to cash and equity-oriented compensation plans. Additionally, group participation in many fringe benefits (such as insurance plans) provides individuals with benefits that might otherwise be unaffordable. Fringe benefits commonly include:

- Life and disability insurance
- Health insurance (medical, dental, family coverage, etc.)
- Vacation pay
- Training and tuition assistance
- Employee discounts
- Company food services (coffee service, cafeteria, etc.)

Many entrepreneurs and their key managers receive such additional benefits as use of company-owned automobiles, expense accounts, relocation allowances, company loans, and individual financial planning services.

Retirement Programs. The goal of maintaining a skilled, stable workforce often operates hand in hand with offering suitable retirement programs to employees. Among small businesses, the vast majority of these programs are defined as *qualified plans,* which allow employers' contributions to be deducted currently and permit employees' income recognition to be deferred until benefits are paid out. The most common qualified plans include various types of:

- Defined-benefit pension plans
- Profit-sharing plans
- Money purchase plans
- Stock bonus plans

- Employee stock ownership plans (ESOPs)
- Tax credit ESOPs
- Thrift and savings plans
- Simplified employee pension plans (SEPs, which are employer-sponsored individual retirement accounts)
- Keogh plans (for sole proprietors, partners, and individuals with self-employment income; also known as H.R. 10 plans).

Several different types of plans may simultaneously be offered to employees; however, all must be nondiscriminatory (as defined by law) in their coverage and operation.

INFORMATION PLANNING FOR FINANCIAL DATA. Sound financial planning requires that accurate and timely data be supplied by **information systems** to meet current and anticipated needs. In recent years the need for information planning has grown with advances in computer technology; now, many sophisticated computerized processes—for accounting, financial analysis, and strategic planning purposes—are well within most entrepreneurs' reach. Clearly, the ability to file, retrieve, and analyze information can significantly affect short- and long-term business performance.

Developing a Systems Foundation. Although information planning necessarily entails an in-depth review of computer hardware and software requirements (both current and anticipated), such technical considerations are secondary to this planning process. First, entrepreneurs and their key managers need to clarify their priorities in order to develop a systems foundation, as suggested in Exhibit 7. In light of the need both to meet business' changing infor-

EXHIBIT 7 MANAGEMENT PRIORITIES/SYSTEMS FOUNDATION

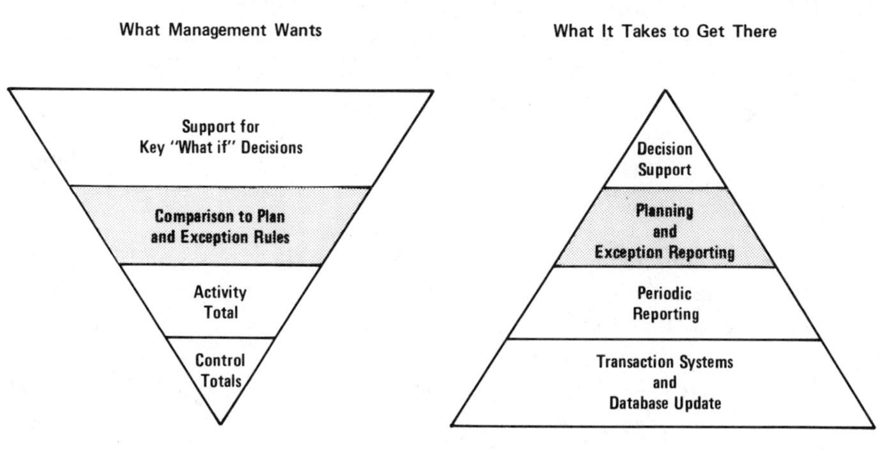

mation requirements and to integrate various information systems into a unified resource for decision making, this planning process has recently come to be known as systems-migration planning.

Developing a Systems Migration Plan. A systems-migration plan serves as a framework for identifying and satisfying a business' information requirements. The plan usually includes the following sections:

> **Systems Implications of Business Objectives.** Outlining the particular information systems implications of short- and long-term plans for growth and of other aspects of the overall business plan.
>
> **Information Requirements.** Identifying the business' current and anticipated needs for information.
>
> **Status of Current Systems.** Reviewing the strengths and weaknesses of current information systems, including an estimate of the capability for handling increasing transaction volumes and more sophisticated analyses.
>
> **Recommendations.** Detailing the level of hardware best suited to the business' future plans, including a number of hardware/software alternatives.
>
> **Action Plan.** Identifying and prioritizing the applications required for the information systems, including schedules for the process of hardware/software selection and installation of system modules.

Note that such related issues as the use of paper-based information systems, the need for manual inputting and bookkeeping, and the criteria for records retention also need to be reviewed in the overall context of systems-migration planning.

BUSINESS CONTINUATION PLANNING. Entrepreneurs are almost invariably prompted, at some point in their careers, to plan for the business' continuation in other hands. In general, business continuation planning entails coordination with many aspects of business tax, compensation, and financial planning. For closely held businesses, this planning must also be integrated with entrepreneurs' gift and estate plans to ensure appropriate matching of family needs with business considerations.

Key Issues. The business continuation issues that face most entrepreneurs usually include:

- Whether any member of the family has both the interest and the ability to lead the company in future years. If so, how best to pass control of the business to that individual while ensuring equitable treatment for all other family members.
- How to attract, motivate, and retain a nonfamily management team either to manage the family's interests in the business or to acquire the business at the owner's retirement or death.

- How to ensure sufficient estate liquidity for unimpeded continuation of family ownership of the business.
- How best to structure personal compensation and investment programs in order to avoid subsequent financial problems, such as those arising from a lack of diversification.
- How to minimize the impact of inflation on both business and personal planning as regards taxes and overall financial/investment goals.

Entrepreneurs also need to consider many related aspects of these issues, such as the need for business valuation and the appropriate use of recapitalization and asset value freeze techniques, buy/sell agreements, trusts, and formally structured giving programs. Again, these considerations cannot be separated from entrepreneurs' personal tax and financial planning.

SUMMARY

Small business financial planning is an ongoing process that employs the full spectrum of management tools to identify, quantify, and focus financial decision making. The overall goal is to help optimize profitability and to control growth. The financial planning function, however, is an integral part of the overall business plan and the business cycle. Each company's particular need for financial planning changes in relation to its stage of development, general financing considerations, form of organization, type and structure of management, and nature and scope of accounting and bookkeeping systems. Clearly, financial planning requires teamwork—on the part of entrepreneurs, their key managers, and business advisers—so that all its many components can be effectively harnessed to further profitability and to control growth.

BIBLIOGRAPHY

Arthur Andersen & Co., *An Entrepreneur's Guide to Starting a Business,* Chicago, IL, 1983.

Arthur Andersen & Co., *How to Develop Systems-Migration Strategies for High-Technology Companies,* Chicago, IL, 1984.

Arthur Andersen & Co., *How to Develop a High Technology Business Plan,* Chicago, IL, 1983.

13

COMMERCIAL BANKING

CONTENTS

13

COMMERCIAL BANKING

Neil B. Murphy
Ronald C. Rogers

OVERVIEW OF CHANGES IN THE COMMERCIAL BANKING INDUSTRY

The commercial banking industry is in the process of adapting to an economic and technological environment that is both volatile and rapidly changing. This process has resulted in vast changes in services, delivery systems, organizational structure, and the type of regulation faced by banks. Indeed, the 1980 and 1982 changes in federal legislation substantially removed distinctions among depository financial institutions (see subsections "Depository Institutions Deregulation and Monetary Control Act of 1980" and "The Garn-St Germain Act of 1982.")

To comprehend the current banking industry situation and make reasonable judgments about its future directions, it is necessary to review the changes that have occurred during the past 15 years or so. This period may be characterized in the following manner:

- Rapid innovation in liability products and management, beginning with money market and wholesale products and culminating in retail products
- Rapid changes in the organizational form of banking, with the bank holding company becoming the dominant organizational form
- Substantial product and geographical diversification, largely through the bank holding company organization
- A substantial change in lending practices, with a volatile interest rate environment moving lenders toward floating rate pricing
- A changing delivery system resulting from increasingly automated internal operations plus a growing number and dollar volume of electronic transactions

- A growth in the number of type of nonbank competitors, including securities firms, thrift institutions, large retailers and, recently, money market mutual funds
- An increase in the international activities of U.S. banks
- A regulatory framework that has responded, with a lag, to the external environment, in some cases creating opportunities for nonbank competitors
- A continuing debate over the age-old question of branching within states and branching across state lines

WHAT IS COMMERCIAL BANKING AND WHAT IS A COMMERCIAL BANK?

Before discussing the changes just noted, it would be helpful to define commercial banking and to indicate how one recognizes such a bank. These questions are neither easy nor trivial. The answers suggest the degree and amount of competition facing the banking industry.

The easiest, most precise, most accurate answer is probably also the least helpful. A commercial bank is one that is recognized as such and is called a "commercial bank" by governmental regulatory agencies. It is not clear, however, that any set of products and services is so unique to commercial banking that one such institution would be instantly recognizable. For example, a major product of commercial banks is the demand deposit, or checking account. However, for more than 10 years, the credit union industry has offered its members (customers?) the share draft.

Notwithstanding legal technicalities, the share draft account is one on which the member may write drafts and transfer funds to a third party. In essence, it is a checking account. Similarly, mutual savings banks and certain savings and loan associations in New England have offered negotiable order of withdrawal (NOW) accounts since the early 1970s. These accounts are checking accounts that pay interest. Consider also the cash management account pioneered by Merrill Lynch. A number of nonbank firms have successfully offered an account in which credit balances are placed in a mutual fund and may be transferred by check or credit card. The list could continue, but these examples show that through legislation, regulatory action, and technology, financial institutions other than banks have come to offer products traditionally thought to be the province of commercial banks.

Some examples in the lending area might also be instructive. For the past 20 or more years, banks have been active in issuing bank credit cards that may be used nationally even though issued by a local bank. That is, an international interchange system is operative, permitting a customer with bank card issued in Maine to use the same piece of plastic in California. However, several major retailers issue credit cards that are also valid in their stores nationwide. Indeed, Sears Roebuck has a consumer receivables portfolio exceeding that of any bank. Similarly American Express, Diners Club, and Carte Blanche issue travel and entertainment cards that have many of the same features as bank cards. In the area of business lending, a highly developed market now competes with banks. In this market, which is known as the commercial paper market, large, well-known corporations issue unsecured, short-term debt directly to investors. Thus corporate treasurers for large, creditworthy companies have the alternative of borrowing from a bank or placing debt directly in the **commercial paper market.** Commercial paper interest rates are competitively determined in the open market. Banks that lend to such corporations must consider commercial paper rates in setting loan terms.

Similarly, banks have moved into areas traditionally restricted to other financial service providers. One example of this is the provision of stock brokerage services. Several years ago banks began acquiring or establishing brokerage activities. These have been "discount" brokers not offering a full range of services. Although the securities industry has challenged these new services in court, the banking industry has prevailed and these services are being offered directly by a bank or through a brokerage subsidiary of a bank holding company.

Returning to our original question, the answer must be that commercial banking is what commercial banks do, and banks do what they are allowed to do by law and regulation. In addition, other firms, including but not limited to financial institutions, compete with banks in a variety of product and service markets.

Who gives any individual commercial bank the power to be in the commercial banking business, and who establishes the laws and regulations that determine what commercial banks may do? As mentioned earlier, the answer is less straightforward than it may seem. Basically, except for a small number of private banks, a commercial bank is granted a **charter** by either the federal government or a state government. Under existing law, such a bank may establish branches in only one state, whether federally or state chartered. The process of granting a bank charter is by no means simple, but once a bank has successfully cleared the applicable regulatory hurdles, what can it do? In very basic terms, it gathers funds from customers by issuing liabilities on itself. The liabilities are generally known as **deposits** and have a wide variety of price and nonprice terms. The funds so acquired are then used to purchase the liabilities of other organizations and/or individuals. The types of liabilities issued by the other organizations are **loans and investments,** depending on their characteristics and terms. Both the issuing of liabilities to acquire funds and the use of funds by commercial banks are subject to a high degree of regulation.

COMMERCIAL BANK REGULATORS

Having indicated the arbitrariness in defining "commercial banking" and the regulated nature of the banking business in a general way, let us look at the asset/liability structure of the system and the particular regulators and major kinds of constraint on any commercial bank. The major regulators and their duties are summarized briefly as follows:

Office of the **Comptroller of the Currency (OC).** The Comptroller of the Currency is an official of the U.S. Department of the Treasury who has the primary responsibility for chartering and supervising national banks. All such banks must be members of the Federal Reserve System. The Comptroller of the Currency is bound by state laws in deciding on applications by national banks to establish branch offices. Only the Comptroller of the Currency may declare a national bank insolvent.

The **Federal Reserve System.** This quasi-governmental agency has primary responsibility for the conduct of monetary policy. However, the implementation of the policy directly affects the use of funds by banks through the system's reserve requirements. In addition, the Federal Reserve handles all regulatory matters concerning bank holding companies as well as operating a substantial part of the check clearing system. Also, Congress gave the Federal Reserve the responsibility for writing regulations in the consumer credit protection area.

Federal Deposit Insurance Corporation (FDIC). This agency insures deposits of insured banks up to $100,000 per account. The FDIC examines state-chartered banks not members of the Federal Reserve System. Although it does not grant charters, the FDIC can refuse to grant deposit insurance; thus it is an effective partner to states in granting charters. The FDIC acts as receiver in all national bank insolvencies and must act in this capacity in state-chartered bank insolvencies if asked to do so by state authorities. In addition, it administers most federal regulatory matters that apply to state-chartered banks which are not members of the Federal Reserve.

State Banking Departments. Each state has an official and/or board (with various titles) that charters and examines banks under state law. It is important to note that state law determines the conditions and criteria (if any) under which banks may establish branch offices. State-chartered banks may join the Federal Reserve System voluntarily. Until the passage of the Depository Institutions Deregulation and Monetary Decontrol Act of 1980, a state-chartered bank generally would have had lower reserve requirements by not being a Federal Reserve member bank. However, this law puts all banks under the reserve requirements of the Federal Reserve. In addition state banks may join the FDIC voluntarily. As a practical matter the vast majority do so, because deposit insurance is a virtual necessity for being in the banking business.

The number of regulators seems excessive, or at least confusing, to many observers of banking. If one agrees that commercial banks are indistinguishable from their thrift institution brethren, then the number of regulators dealing with essentially similar institutions is even larger. This apparent confusion and overlap has spawned numerous reports and recommendations for consolidation. The most recent such report, appearing in July 1984, is entitled *Blueprint for Reform: The Report of the Task Group on Regulation of Financial Services,* commonly referred to as the "Bush Commission Report" after the chairperson, Vice President George Bush. That report recommended that the FDIC be removed from all regulatory responsibilities except those dealing with the administration of the deposit insurance system. The remaining regulatory responsibilities would be shared by a new agency, the Federal Banking Agency, an upgraded OCC, and the Federal Reserve. The history of recommended consolidation and lack of follow-up in the post–World War II era must raise some doubts about the likelihood of any major substantive changes in the regulatory structure.

BANKING PRODUCTS AND SERVICES AS SHOWN IN ASSET ACCOUNTS OF COMMERCIAL BANKS

The asset and liability structure of banks serves as an indication of their activities. Total assets represent the use of funds acquired by banks and indicate some of the types of products and services they provide. Assets for all U.S. banks are shown in Exhibit 1: It is important to note that this exhibit is for all banks and that the composition of assets for any one bank may vary greatly for many reasons, including size, management preferences, and market conditions.

CASH ACCOUNT. The first asset account to be examined is the cash account. Exhibit 1 shows that almost 15% of all bank assets are held in the form of cash. It is perhaps more instructive, however, to look at the breakdown of the cash account to learn the role of banks in the clearing and processing of the payments mechanism in this nation. For example, the largest component of the cash account is called cash items in the process of collection. This highlights the role of banks in managing the payments mechanism.

Check Clearing. If a business, individual, or government agency receives payment by check, that check is deposited in the payee's checking account. Once the check is deposited, the individual customer knows little of what goes on and usually doesn't care. However, a number of steps are necessary to integrate the individual bank into the entire payments and clearing system. First, a simple internal transaction takes place if the account on which the check is drawn is in the depositor's bank. But if the check is drawn on another bank, the receiving bank must collect that check. This can occur in various ways. To process local checks, for example, banks often use a local clearinghouse; that is, all banks in the local area meet once a day and exchange checks drawn on each other. This makes it possible to record the net difference on clearinghouse books without a large number of accounting transactions among individual banks.

EXHIBIT 1 ASSETS OF ALL COMMERCIAL BANKS IN THE UNITED STATES, DECEMBER 31, 1983 ($ MILLIONS)

Cash and due from depository institutions		$ 341,849.6
U.S. Treasury securities		168,095.3
Obligations of other U.S. government agencies		76,525.7
Obligations of state and local political subdivisions		158,384.9
Federal Reserve funds sold and securities held under repurchase agreements		93,484.0
All other securities		38,341.6
Net loans		1,284,243.7
Real estate loans	$327,430.1	
Loans to financial institutions	109,212.1	
Loans for purchase of securities	19,216.5	
Loans to finance agriculture production	39,892.6	
Commercial and industrial loans	524,748.1	
Loans to individuals	218,081.6	
All other loans	64,419.3	
Less: Unearned income and allowance for losses	(34,584.2)	
Direct lease financing		17,064.5
Bank premises, furniture, fixtures		36,604.4
Real estate other than bank premises		5,174.6
All other assets		122,331.9
Total assets		$2,342,100.2

Source: Federal Deposit Insurance Corp., "Bank Operating Statistics, 1983," FDIC, Washington, D.C., 1984.

There are two major alternatives available to the bank that receives a nonlocal check. First, it can go to another bank. In the United States many small banks have accounts with larger banks, called correspondent banks. The correspondent banks provide clearing services for small banks that are not members of the Federal Reserve System. The check is deposited, and the correspondent bank then collects it from the bank on which it is drawn. That correspondent bank may go to a local clearinghouse or, as is more likely, it will deposit the check in its own account at the local Federal Reserve office. The local Federal Reserve office will then clear the check itself or through another Federal Reserve bank. Thus the banking system is responsible, in conjunction with the Federal Reserve, for clearing checks, and that particular activity is shown on the books of the banking system as cash items in the process of collection. Banks have a tremendous incentive to collect those funds as quickly as possible, because while in the process of collection the funds cannot be used for loans or investments, which are the banks' primary source of revenue.

Due-From Accounts. The next important category in the cash account is demand balance with banks in the United States, known as "due-from" accounts. This amounts to almost 11% of the total cash account. These accounts are held by respondent banks with their correspondent banks. This cash account also indicates the role of the banks in the process of collecting checks. When checks are collected (as discussed earlier), a cash account immediately turns into demand balances with U.S. banks. Now, in addition to the checks that are collected and increase in the balance, respondent banks also have customers writing checks on their accounts for deposit in yet other banks. These other banks go through the same process of collecting the check, and in many cases collect through the correspondent bank. Thus when a check comes in for collection, the respondent bank must have funds in its account against which the check may be drawn.

In addition to the role in the check collection process, there are other ordinary transactions for which the respondent banks use these balances. For example, bank transactions in the federal funds market (banks borrowing from other banks) are normally conducted through their correspondents, and those correspondent banks make the appropriate adjustment through the respondent bank's checking account. Until recently, in many states, banks that were not members of the Federal Reserve System were allowed to count correspondent balances as reserves. However, the Monetary Control Act of 1980 (discussed in detail later) makes all financial institutions that offer transactions accounts subject to Federal Reserve requirements.

Currency and Coin Account. The next interesting account indicating the activities of banks is the currency and coin account. This is an asset on which there is no return. Banks are involved in the process of supplying currency and coin as needed to the economy. The entire banking system is in partnership with the Federal Reserve System in providing this service. Essentially anyone who has a checking account, or a savings account of most types, may withdraw currency and coin at any time. The needs of the public for currency and coin are served by the banking system, and its currency and coin account reflects this. All currency and coin comes initially from the Federal Reserve System and is shipped to individual banks, which then make distribution as needed. Banks maintain an inventory of currency and coin to meet the needs of the customers.

Reserves with the Federal Reserve System. The next account of interest is the reserves held with the local Federal Reserve bank. Those balances, together with coin and currency, are counted as reserves to meet reserve requirements under Federal Reserve regulations. In addition those accounts serve as clearing accounts against which incoming checks are debited and outgoing checks are credited. In essence the Federal Reserve Bank acts not only as an institution establishing reserve requirements against deposit accounts, but it also serves as the ultimate correspondent bank for the entire system and handles much of the clearing of checks between different regions of the country. That is, even if a local bank never deposits its checks in the local Federal Reserve Bank, choosing instead to use its correspondent, many checks clearing out of the area come through the local Federal Reserve bank. The level of reserve requirements and the extension of reserve requirements to banks not members of the Federal Reserve System had been a matter of substantial controversy in the banking industry for many years. However, that controversy has ended. It has ended in favor of the position long held by the Federal Reserve itself; that is, all banks offering transaction accounts are subject to Federal Reserve requirements. It must also be noted that these accounts may also be accessed electronically through a number of wire transfer systems managed by the Federal Reserve and the banking system.

Role of Cash Accounts. The cash accounts of all banks in the United States serve to show their role in the process of clearing checks and in assisting the monetary authorities in achieving their objectives. It is ironic that one usually views liquidity as the capability to realize cash from an asset and to be able to use that cash. Interestingly enough, many of the items in the cash account of the banking system are actually not at all liquid. First, cash items in the process of collection have no value in terms of either earning a return or being used for any other purposes. Those balances with correspondent banks are used for clearing, meeting transactions needs, and also compensating those banks for services provided. Currency and coin also must be kept to meet the day-to-day needs of customers, and the reserves with the Federal Reserve bank are established by regulation rather than by transactions needs and hence cannot be utilized to meet any liquidity drains on the bank. Thus we must look elsewhere on the balance sheet to determine how banks meet their liquidity needs.

INVESTMENT SECURITIES. A major source of both liquidity and earnings in the banking system is investment securities. In December 1983 the banking system held about $535 billion worth of securities broken down into several different categories.

U.S. Treasury Securities. The first category we might look at is the securities issued by the U.S. Treasury. These are Treasury bills, Treasury bonds, and Treasury notes, and in December 1983 banks held over $168 billion worth of such securities. Basically, those securities are sold by the Treasury on open market to all buyers. Banks have special interest in buying Treasury securities because the risk of default is nonexistent and because of the very high liquidity of many of the securities. However, there is usually a relationship between yield and maturity that makes relatively short-term securities less attractive for earnings purposes or more attractive for liquidity purposes. Longer-term securities tend to have higher yields but greater risk of price fluctuations. Thus in seeking liquidity, banks typically stay in the short end of the maturity structure.

U.S. Government Agency Securities. Many other agencies in the federal government are permitted to issue securities, either directly by the agency or guaranteed by the U.S. Treasury. Over $76 billion worth of such securities was held by banks in December 1983. These securities are held mainly for earnings purposes because there is not an active secondary market for them. Hence the yields are somewhat higher, and most banks do not like to sell such securities before maturity.

State and Local Securities. The obligations of state and local political subdivisions include those of state governments, local governments, and various other state and local governmental agencies, such as school districts, water districts, and turnpike authorities. In December 1983 that category constituted the second largest use of funds in the investments area, and over $158 billion worth of such securities was held by banks. These securities are especially attractive for banks because they are exempt from federal income tax. Hence the market for such securities is generally known as the "tax-exempt market." Pension funds and mutual funds do not pay any taxes directly; thus state and local securities are of little interest to their managers. Those securities, however, can provide very high after-tax yields to banks, which are subject to federal income tax. In addition to the yield characteristics, many banks have deposit relationships with their state and local governments; that is, local governments must maintain their checking accounts somewhere, and to compete for such business banks bid on the obligations of these agencies. This is an additional attractive feature of the obligations of many state and local political subdivisions. In addition to supporting the activities of various governmental organizations, the U.S. Treasury, federal agencies, and state and local political subdivisions, the banking system, by acting as a securities dealer, is actively involved in providing liquidity to the government securities market. Other organizations are securities dealers, but in 1983 banks held trading account securities worth approximately $17 billion, spread out among a relatively small number of banks that are actively involved in trading. By providing such services, banks add a substantial amount of liquidity to the government securities market.

A bank involved in trading establishes prices at which it will buy and sell a list of government securities. Those securities are quoted on a bid-and-asked basis. The spread between the price to be paid for such a security and the price at which it is sold provides the income for trading account activity. This activity entails risk, however, because government security prices change from day to day. Hence the value of the inventory of dollars is subject to change. Thus the spread is compensation to the bank for maintaining the activity and taking the risk. Because the banks provide this service, a substantially more liquid government securities market exists.

Federal Funds and Repurchase Agreements. The final investment account to be examined consists of federal funds sold and securities purchased under repurchase agreements, or **"repos."** Banks held $93 billion worth of such securities in December 1983. Those securities, which represent a use of funds for extremely short periods of time, are perhaps among the more liquid assets held by any bank. When securities are purchased under repurchase agreements, the bank is essentially lending money for a day or two. Rather than actually making a loan, investigating the credit, and taking the risk, it simply takes title to securities for a few days; then, in accordance with the repo agreement, the securities are resold. The difference in the buying price and the selling price of the securities represents a return to the bank for that short period of time. If the securities are not repurchased, the bank of course holds the collateral.

"Federal funds" is shorthand for the balances on the books of Federal Reserve banks. Banks that have excess reserves lend those reserves for a very short period—usually overnight—to other banks with deficiencies in their reserve positions. This represents an alternative and more productive use of any funds that banks may have idle for a very short period of time.

Hence these two categories—federal funds sold and securities purchased under repurchase agreement—represent a very short-term use of funds and may be viewed as a highly liquid asset turning into cash that may be used for other purposes very quickly.

COMMERCIAL LOANS. By far the most important use of assets by banks is in the lending area. Almost 55% of all assets ($1284 billion in 1983) were loans. Banks make a variety of loans to many types of customers. Data discussed here relate to the entire banking industry in the United States. However, individual banks in specific markets have very different patterns.

Real Estate Loans. First, banks had over $327 billion worth of real estate loans outstanding in December 1983 (Exhibit 1). This was the second most important loan category, next to commercial and industrial loans. By far the most important categories are: loans for construction and land development, conventional single-family mortgage loans, and loans secured by nonfarm, nonresidential properties. Thus the banking industry contributes on several different levels to the construction and housing needs of both business and households. First, construction and land development loans support the very important domestic construction and building trade industries. This contributes both to the total stock of housing and building used by business, providing jobs and production for the entire economy. Most construction loans and land development loans are of relatively short duration and are maintained on the books while the project is under construction or development. At that time the builder usually seeks more permanent financing for the useful life of the project. In the case of housing, the individual buyers usually seek to have longer-term mortgages that can be used to pay for the property and house. The builder then pays down the construction and land development loans. Most of the real estate loans made by commercial banks are in the conventional area; that is, they are not insured or guaranteed by either the **Federal Housing Authority (FHA)** or the **Veterans Administration (VA).** In addition, most of the loans to business for nonfarm, nonresidential properties are underwritten and funded by banks. Thus banks play a major role in the financing of construction and real estate in the United States.

Loans to Financial Institutions. In addition, banks make loans to other banks and other financial institutions, both domestically and in foreign countries. These institutions may be **real estate investment trusts (REITs)** and **mortgage companies,** which provide a further link between the banking industry and the real estate and construction business. These loans can also be made to **finance companies,** which essentially means that banks participate indirectly in the financing of the projects of individuals. Loans are often made to other depository financial institutions or to insurance companies.

In addition to making loans directly to financial institutions, banks make a number of loans to facilitate the functioning of securities markets. They make loans to brokers and dealers to purchase and hold securities and to individuals for purchasing securities. Thus banks participate in the financing of the activities of securities markets that are essential to the allocation of resources and the raising of capital for the economy.

Agricultural Loans. Banks are major lenders to farmers. In the aggregate, banks had almost $40 billion worth of loans to farmers on their books in 1983. This represents 1.7% of total assets of the banking industry. At first glance this may appear to be a relatively low figure. These data represent all activities of all banks, however, and it is instructive to examine the commitment to farm lending of banks in the rural areas of an agricultural state. The results for Nebraska, which is primarily an agricultural state, are interesting. For all banks in the state, 38% of all loans are made to finance agricultural production. This is clearly a different picture from that suggested by the national figures.

Commitment to agriculture is probably even greater than indicated previously, because many of the commercial and industrial loans in rural regions are undoubtedly made to seed companies and suppliers and other providers of services to the agricultural industry. Hence, the commitment of the banking industry to any particular segment of the economy is related to the market in which it functions. Thus although the aggregate loans to farmers make up a small part of total bank loans, that proportion is very much higher in agricultural regions. Similarly, small banks in suburban areas show a commitment to lending to households and individuals that probably is much higher than that of downtown metropolitan banks primarily engaged in business lending.

Commercial and Industrial Loans. In the aggregate, the most important component of total loans consists of commercial and industrial loans. In December 1983 that figure exceeded $524 billion. Banks are the prime lenders to most business firms. A relatively small number of very large business firms have access to the **commercial paper market,** in which corporate treasurers can issue unsecured IOUs on the open market and have them purchased by institutional investors. These corporations have very high **credit ratings** and their securities are generally rated very high by agencies involved in evaluating the risk of lending to such institutions. Most businesses are not in that fortunate situation, however, and have a relatively small number of alternatives for seeking funds. Hence the term *commercial banking*, which indicates the long-term substantial commitment of the industry to financing the needs of business.

The historic role of commercial banks looms very large in the development of individual firms. Indeed, commercial banks supply most of the funds and almost all the financial advice to most medium-sized and small business firms. Commercial lending is done on a variety of terms with a variety of contractual agreements between lender and borrower. Many years ago banks provided primarily short-term loans that were liquidated according to the seasonal cycles of the particular business. In recent years, however, banks have provided a very large number of **"term loans"**; that is, loans that have maturity exceeding one year. These loans have many different characteristics; they vary greatly from business to business and are tailored to needs of the individual business. This flexibility is unique to the commercial banking industry. For example, the maturity may vary from relatively short seasonal loans to longer-term loans, 10 years perhaps, to finance the purchase of equipment. The rate or price charged to the borrower may vary also: It may be fixed, or it may fluctuate with other interest rates in the economy. Indeed, in recent years the trend has been toward greater **floating of interest rates** that move as interest rates in the economy move.

Other loans may be collateralized by business assets, such as receivables or inventory, or by other assets, such as government securities that are pledged as security. The collateral becomes the property of the bank if the loan results in a default. Most loans to business firms are made on the basis of an overall, long-term relationship between the bank and the firm. Typically, business firms make arrangements for needed funds, perhaps annually, under a **line of credit.** That is, at any time during the period of the agreement, the firm may **draw down** its line of credit and utilize those funds for business purposes. Typically the lines must be cleared up (i.e., have a zero balance) from time to time, and they are renegotiated, usually once a year. Thus the firm can have continuous and flexible access to funds to meet its needs.

Individual Loans. Loans made to individuals, or **consumer loans,** are another major use of funds in the banking industry. These loans may be made with collateral or they may be made unsecured, and they may have varying maturities. Loans to individuals are primarily a phenomenon of the past 50 years, with most of the growth coming in the post–World War II era. Before 1945, most banks did not make such loans, hence truly deserved the title "commercial banks." All banks in the economy in December 1983 had loaned over $218 billion to consumers, and this component was, in the aggregate, the next largest compared with commercial and industrial loans. These loans are made to purchase private automobiles and other types of consumer goods, to repair and modernize residential property, and in single payment loans; most recently there has been substantial growth in loans connected with **credit card** and **retail charge account plans.**

BANKING PRODUCTS AND SERVICES AS SHOWN IN LIABILITY AND CAPITAL ACCOUNTS OF COMMERCIAL BANKS

The liability accounts of commercial banks are the major sources of funds necessary to make loan and investment services and products available. It is in this area that banks have seen the greatest changes in the past decade. These changes are due to a combination of volatile and relatively high interest rates, the persistent in)lation of the decade, the inroads of nonbank competitors, and the movement and direction of technology. Exhibit 2 shows the liability accounts of all commercial banks in the United States as of December 31, 1983.

DEMAND DEPOSITS. The first item of interest—namely, demand deposits of individuals, partnerships, corporations (IPC), and the public sector—exceeded $389.5 billion. Over $316 billion represent the checking accounts of the private sector of the economy. The demand deposit is the most prevalent form of "third-party transaction service," although other products have been developed by banks and others to compete with demand deposits. The checking account has several important features:

EXHIBIT 2 LIABILITIES AND CAPITAL OF ALL COMMERCIAL BANKS IN THE UNITED STATES, DECEMBER 31, 1983 ($ MILLIONS)

Total demand deposits	$ 389,526.9
Total savings deposits	462,567.6
Total time deposits	682,009.5
Deposits in foreign offices	308,398.5
Federal funds purchased and securities sold under repurchase agreements	178,533.7
Interest-bearing demand notes and other borrowing	55,038.4
Mortgage indebtedness	2,798.1
All other liabilities	115,588.5
Total liabilities	$2,194,461.2
Subordinated notes and debentures	7,092.8
Preferred stock, par value	663.8
Common stock, par value	25,723.3
Surplus	47,903.7
Undivided profits and capital reserves	66,255.3
Subordinated notes and debentures plus equal capital	$140,546.1
Total liabilities and capital	$2,342,100.1

Source: Federal Deposit Insurance Corp., "Bank Operating Statistics, 1983," FDIC, Washington, D.C., 1984.

- The owner may exchange his or her account balance for cash and currency on demand.
- The owner may use a highly efficient, well-developed system to transfer balances to another party.
- The owner may transfer funds by paper or electronically; the paper medium (checks) dominates such transactions, however.
- Banks have not paid interest on balances in checking accounts since 1933, but inroads by similar, competitive products have resulted in changes in the laws effective December 31, 1980 and October 6, 1982.

Although demand deposits are a major source of funds to banks and an essential component of any modern, diversified economy, they also are a major component of the nation's **money supply.** Although the definition of the monetary aggregates has undergone substantial change, at least in part because of innovations designed to compete with demand deposits, the major component of the narrow definition of money (M1) is the demand deposits of banks. For a discussion of the various definitions of the money supply see Section 2, "Money and Capital Markets." Thus the commercial banking industry is an important component of the process by which the **Federal Reserve** attempts to control monetary aggregates to accomplish its macroeconomic goals.

For the past 30 years, demand deposits have grown less rapidly than other forms of bank deposits. For example, at year-end 1954, demand deposits were almost 74% of the sum of demand and time deposits. By year-end 1983, demand deposits represented only 25% of total deposits. The primary reason for this was the tendency of business firms and individuals to economize on the balances held in checking accounts. Because banks could not then pay interest on such balances, there was an incentive for business firms and individuals to place those balances where they could earn a return. With interest rates reaching record highs in the 1970s, these funds were viewed with great envy by other institutions, which devised new products to attract them out of demand deposits. Banks responded by offering services that may increase interest expense but nonetheless keep the deposits in house.

A very large proportion of the dollar volume and number of transactions in the economic system moves through bank demand deposit accounts. Some of the transactions move directly by check from one account to another, either inside a single bank or from one bank to another. Another method of moving funds is through wire transfers. Wire systems for moving funds are offered both by the Federal Reserve and by a private company, Bank Wire Corp., owned by a group of banks. Interestingly enough, these wire systems handle a relatively small number of transactions, but the average value exceeds $2 million. Of course, these transfers are made from demand accounts to demand accounts. Often the transactions are between accounts of the same business firm to consolidate cash at one bank to invest in the money markets for periods as short as one day.

Major innovations in this area have occurred on three levels, all making the demand deposit account a more viable, but more costly product. Those three items are as follows:

- The use of technology to assist corporations in the aggressive management of cash to minimize idle funds (see Stone, 1986).
- The development of substitutes for retail accounts by nonbank competitors.
- The adaptation of banks by competing effectively with new products, culminating in the authority to offer **NOW accounts** nationwide after December 31, 1980 and **SuperNOWs** in 1983.

CASH MANAGEMENT SYSTEMS. These are varied in nature and degree of sophistication, but they work as follows. For incoming payments, a series of banks is selected based on location to minimize the time a check is in the mail from the customer to the corporation. Usually, the corporation instructs its customers to remit it to a post office box. The chosen bank manages the box, known as a "lockbox," and several times daily will remove all materials, send the checks for collection, and send all other materials plus a record of checks in process to the corporation. Those checks are available faster because of the strategic location of the bank. A corporation that has many retail outlets, for example, will have the local manager deposit funds daily. In both cases, the information may be relayed daily to a data center, which records the information from many sources and makes it available on a data terminal in the corporate treasurer's office. Armed with that information and knowing the cash needed to honor outstanding checks, the corporate treasurer will wire funds to a single, lead bank for disbursement and investment.

The number of wire transfers, undoubtedly reflecting the use of these techniques, has grown rapidly, as has the corporate use of repurchase agreements, a popular way of investing funds for very short periods of time.

NOW Accounts. The number of payment system innovations on the retail level has been substantial. In 1972 the NOW account was born in Massachusetts. "NOW" means negotiable order of withdrawal, and such an instrument is functionally equivalent to a check. The major innovation was the payment of interest on the balance in the NOW account. The NOW was pioneered by mutual savings banks, a thrift institution competitor, in Massachusetts and New Hampshire. After legislative, regulatory, and court skirmishes, Congress extended NOW account powers to all depository financial institutions in Massachusetts and New Hampshire in 1974. In March 1976 the NOW was extended to the rest of New England. In November 1978 NOW was extended to New York, and in December 1979 to New Jersey. Thus the entire Northeast, including two major financial centers, New York and Boston, was an experimental ground from 1974 to 1980. Congress extended the NOW to all financial institutions beginning in 1981. In 1983 Congress authorized a "SuperNOW" account with no ceilings on rates which the bank can pay to attract funds. For an extended discussion see Murphy and Mandell (1980).

Share Drafts. While the NOW account was being introduced, a major competitor appeared with a new product. In 1974 credit unions started to market their "share draft" account. This was again functionally equivalent to a check with two differences: interest was paid on the balance, and the draft (check) was "truncated," or not returned to the customer.

The development of **NOWs, SuperNOWs,** and share drafts has resulted in a category of transaction accounts on which interest is paid. This category is known as "other checkable deposits." As one would expect, these accounts are attractive to consumers. This may be seen by reviewing the relative growth of traditional demand deposits and "other checkable deposits." These figures include the deposits of all depository financial institutions. At year-end 1980, demand deposits were $266.5 billion, whereas other checkable deposits were $27.6 billion. By April 1985, demand deposits had fallen to $252.5 billion, whereas other checkable deposits had grown to $155.3 billion. Thus banks can no longer rely on the availability of deposit funds for which no interest is paid. The removal of the prohibition of interest payments on demand deposits is the final remaining step in the process of deposit interest deregulation and is likely inevitable.

Current Status of Demand Deposits. Although demand deposits of individuals, partnerships, and corporations (IPC) are $316.5 billion, total demand deposits are $389.5 billion. Who has the rest? Other banks maintain correspondent balances and are referred to as **"due to" accounts.** Also, all levels of government maintain demand deposit accounts. These accounts have one unique feature: Securities must be pledged by banks to equal or exceed those balances of public funds. Thus the securities portfolio is less liquid if pledgings are anywhere near the total investment portfolio.

In summary, demand deposits are an important source of funds to banks and a product over which the industry once had a virtual monopoly. As interest rates have risen, all sectors of the economy, especially the corporate sector, have economized on the holdings of noninterest-yielding assets. Nonbank competitors have innovated interest-yielding transactions accounts in various ways. Consequently the trends noted previously will continue until all balances pay some kind of return.

TIME AND SAVINGS DEPOSITS. A major source of funds for commercial banking consists of time and savings deposits. These deposits have grown more rapidly than demand deposits and have substantially changed in offering terms in the past 25 years. The trend in economizing on cash balances had already begun in the decade of the 1950s, although it was limited to major corporate entities. That banking system had no deposit products to compete with **money market instruments** for the short-term use of idle corporate funds. During the

1946–1960 period, total commercial bank liabilities grew at an annual rate of only 3.7%, compared with a 10.5% growth rate for deposits at thrift institutions (savings and loan associations, mutual savings banks, and credit unions). As a result, commercial bank shares of total financial intermediation fell to a low of approximately 26% in 1960 (see Beebe, 1977).

Certificates of Deposit. To counter the trend to economize on cash balances, commercial banks in New York City announced (in the early 1960s) that they would issue large-denomination negotiable **certificates of deposit (CDs)** and that a major securities dealer had agreed to "make a market" in them. The new instrument would be priced to compete with **U.S. Treasury bills.** Whereas previously the major deposit product at commercial banks had been the demand deposit, as a result of the introduction of CDs and other new market instruments, banks embraced a new management philosophy known as **"liabilities management."** Although banks used nonprice-competitive techniques such as opening conveniently located branches, staying open longer hours, mounting aggressive advertising campaigns, and other devices, the amount of funds available was not directly under their control. Thus the asset portfolio was viewed as a major source of liquidity. With the advent of new markets and products, banks gained more control over deposit sources of funds, and the amount of money available to fund asset growth was a matter of bank discretion. The success of this strategy depended on the banks' ability to price the CDs attractively; that is, Federal Reserve regulatory ceilings—in this case the maximum interest rates payable to customers **(Regulation Q)**—had to respond to the movements in market rates. Such changes occurred in June 1970 and again in June 1973 when ceilings on CDs were lifted to enable banks to raise capital. (A discussion of the situation prior to 1970 appears later in this section.)

The new financial instrument was an immediate success, growing rapidly to $18.6 billion in August 1966. At that time, money market rates rose rapidly and exceeded the ceilings set in place by **Regulation Q** of the Federal Reserve System. The result was a predictable "runoff" of CDs at commercial banks as corporate treasurers found better return-risk opportunities in other money market instruments. As rates fell in 1967, CDs renewed their growth and reached a high of $24.3 billion at year-end 1968. Shortly after this interest rates rose once again, and the Regulation Q ceiling was not increased. A spectacular runoff ensued and, at year-end 1969, only $10.9 billion worth of CDs was outstanding.

Commercial Paper Market. If banks could not offer competitive rates to attract funds through CDs, they would be hard pressed to meet loan requests. With corporate treasurers seeking funds but not finding them at banks, and placing funds but not purchasing bank CDs, some other market was needed to handle these requirements. A market that grew rapidly in this environment was the commercial paper market. Corporate treasurers issued these instruments that had no ceiling rates, and other corporate treasurers purchased them. Indeed, banks even began issuing commercial paper through holding company subsidiaries to avoid the effects of **Regulation Q.** Two major problems are associated with reliance on the commercial paper market to provide the services normally performed by financial intermediaries.

- Many business firms do not have the size or credit rating necessary to be able to issue commercial paper.
- No loan reserves, no capital cushion, and no deposit insurance exist to absorb losses in case of a default.

In June 1970 the **Penn Central Railroad** defaulted on its commercial paper obligations. As a result, the financial markets were severely disrupted, and the Federal Reserve moved quickly to suspend all ceilings on large CDs with maturities less than 90 days. This permitted the commercial banking system to provide a product with a competitive price to attract funds, and an alternative to commercial paper to meet corporate borrowing needs. In a series of moves over the next several years, all ceilings on all maturities of large CDs were removed and the Federal Reserve System abandoned its attempt to regulate credit expansion through restrictive deposit interest ceilings.

Money Market Deposit Account (MMDA). It became clear during the late 1960s and 1970s that deposit interest ceilings were ineffective in protecting the soundness of financial institutions. As a result a number of new savings instruments have appeared in response to competition. Most of these occurred as legislators and regulators recognized competitive reality.

A major change occurred in October 1982 with the passage of the Garn-St Germain Act. Although Congress had earlier instructed the bank regulatory agencies to remove deposit interest ceilings, progress was slow. Congress reacted by passing specific legislation to create a major new savings product, the **money market deposit account (MMDA).** This is an account with a minimum balance of $2500 (soon lowered to $1000), and the rate an institution could offer was totally unregulated. The result was a shift in deposit funds that was truly explosive.

For example, from a base of zero in late 1982, these accounts grew to $375.9 billion in December 1983 with $230.0 billion in commercial banks and $145.9 billion in thrift institutions. After the initial explosive growth, the balances have leveled off and in April 1985 totaled $460.3 billion. The spectacular success of this is explained by the attractive returns, the convenience of dealing with banks that have well-developed delivery systems and, very important, deposit insurance. After this major initiative, all remaining deposit interest ceilings are relatively unimportant and removing them is actually just tidying up.

Money Market Certificates. The success of the money market deposit account should not have been surprising. In June 1978, Federal bank regulators created a new deposit account known at that time as a **"money market certificate."** That account had a minimum balance of $10,000, a maturity of 6 months, and a rate tied to the U.S. Treasury bill yield. Despite the large denomination and relative lack of liquidity, the certificate was a success, growing to $103.2 billion at year-end 1979. Evidently the combination of a reasonable return and deposit insurance was attractive. As a result the regulators have removed all ceilings and lowered the minimum balance on all certificates. In April 1985, small time deposits at depository institutions were $879.7 billion.

Passbook Savings Accounts. The remaining consumer account is the time-tested regular, or **"passbook" savings account.** Once the staple of retail financial institutions, this has diminished in importance because of the developments noted previously. It is not surprising that savings deposits have eroded; what is surprising is that there are any left at all. In April 1985, there was $290.2 billion in savings accounts, down both absolutely and in relation to total deposits. However, the staying power of the product is impressive. Convenience, ease of understanding and use, liquidity, inertia, and deposit insurance combine to overcome the low ceiling that existed on these accounts. This remaining regulatory ceiling will be eliminated on January 1, 1986.

In summary, the products of the banking industry as shown on its balance sheet have changed dramatically. The process has resulted in a less regulated environment. Most of the changes occurred on the liability side and resulted in higher interest costs to the industry.

MAJOR CHANGES IN REGULATORY ENVIRONMENT

Despite the apparent or actual geographic limits placed on commercial banks by state laws, a number of changes in the regulatory environment have had the effect of removing the restriction on where banks can operate. In addition, there has been a major change in the kinds of regulation and restriction on bank product lines and prices. These developments portend a substantial and yet unknown change in the structure and operations of commercial banks. These developments are as follows:

- The Bank Holding Company Act of 1970 and subsequent interpretations and decisions
- The International Banking Act of 1978
- The Depository Institutions Deregulation and Monetary Control Act of 1980
- The Garn-St Germain Depository Institution Act of 1982

BANK HOLDING COMPANY ACT OF 1970. This Act was an important milestone in the adaptation of the banking system to a changing financial environment. Prior to 1970, bank holding companies owning or controlling more than one bank were regulated by the Board of Governors of the Federal Reserve System. For our purposes several important factors are noteworthy. First, bank holding companies were not permitted to own banks outside their state of incorporation unless both that state and the other state or states had enacted statutes permitting out-of-state entry. This prohibition is the subject of the **Douglas Amendment.** Second, for practical purposes, the bank holding company was confined to owning banks and firms with very narrowly restricted activities. Third, a holding company owning or controlling only one bank was exempt from regulation. For a complete discussion see *The Bank Holding Company Movement of 1978: A Compedium* and Jesse and Seelig (1977).

For a number of reasons, Congress enacted legislation in late 1970 to end all distinctions between one-bank and multibank holding companies and to regulate them. A major facet of the law involved permission to own nonbank subsidiaries engaged in activities so closely related to banking or managing or controlling banks as to be a proper transaction. Congress conveniently left that determination to the Board of Governors of the Federal Reserve System. It is important to note here, however, that although the banks are subject to geographic constraints inside the United States, this is not so for nonbank subsidiaries. Thus a 36-month automobile loan made by a finance company subsidiary of a bank can be made from offices anywhere in the country, whereas a bank is limited to making such a loan from an office within a prescribed area.

The Federal Reserve Board has interpreted this legislation to include activities that essentially remove geographical restrictions from the asset products of commercial bank balance sheets. These include finance companies (consumer and commercial), mortgage banking, and leasing. These are credit activities that are similar to the lending done by banks themselves, and banks have penetrated—indeed dominated—those parts of the industry. For example, 6 of the top 10 mortgage banking firms are owned by bank holding companies. The holding company device has permitted bank holding companies to circumvent the constraints placed on their banks in locating their lending activities. In addition, bank holding companies have major positions in finance company, factoring, and leasing industries. Although there are no comprehensive data available for the geographical distribution of these lending offices of nonbank subsidiaries, it is generally accepted that the large holding companies have located them in most of the major growing areas of the nation.

INTERNATIONAL BANKING ACT OF 1978. Another major step that is changing the regulatory environment was the passage of the International Banking Act (IBA) of 1978. In a strange anomaly of the laws regulating banks prior to 1978, branches of foreign banks were permitted to locate anywhere in the United States, but, of course, the branching capabilities of U.S. banks are constrained. The IBA solution was to allow previously established foreign branches to remain intact but to restrict all new foreign branches in the same way that American banks are.

For our purposes, a most interesting development was the relaxation of the restrictions on **Edge Act corporations** and their activities.

An Edge Act corporation is a subsidiary of a bank established to provide financial services to business firms engaged in foreign trade. A bank could establish such a subsidiary in a location outside its home state. However, each office was a separate corporation. In addition, the Edge Act corporation could finance only activities related to the export of goods or services. The IBA permitted the consolidation of all Edge Act corporations of a bank into a single, multibranch, interstate subsidiary. Also, under IBA, Edge Act corporations may finance activities related to the production of goods for export. Thus IBA substantially increased the scope and flexibility of Edge Act corporations by giving them essentially interstate branching powers and broadening their lending powers. After all, almost all major U.S. corporations are engaged in some production for foreign trade, expanding the potential target market substantially.

DEPOSITORY INSTITUTIONS DEREGULATION AND MONETARY CONTROL ACT OF 1980

A major change in the regulatory environment occurred on March 31, 1980, with the passage of the Depository Institutions Deregulation and Monetary Control Act (DIDMCA). (See Federal Reserve Bank of Chicago, 1983.) This Act contains a number of major provisions that have altered the nature of the banking industry. The various pressures and developments discussed previously led to a consensus that the protection afforded by such regulatory props as Regulation Q was not appropriate, equitable, or effective. In 1971 the President's Commission on Financial Structure and Regulation (**Hunt Commission**) made a broad set of recommendations to alter the powers of and regulations applying to depository financial institutions. Those recommendations have been substantially incorporated into the DIDMCA. (See the Report of the President's Commission on Financial Structure and Regulation.)

There are a number of important provisions in the DIDMCA:

- Any depository financial institution offering transactions accounts is subject to universal reserve requirements set by the Board of Governors of the Federal Reserve System regardless of the Federal Reserve membership status of the financial institution.
- Any financial institution with deposit-withdrawal transaction accounts or nonpersonal time accounts is entitled to the same discount and borrowing privileges as member banks.
- The Federal Reserve must charge for Federal Reserve bank services such as check clearing, wire transfer, automated clearinghouse, and providing currency and coin. Services will be available to members and nonmembers on an equal basis.
- Interest ceilings on deposits (**Regulation Q**) are being eliminated.
- All depository financial institutions are permitted to offer **NOW accounts** effective December 31, 1980.

- Thrift institution asset portfolio powers are broadened to lend up to 20% of assets in consumer loans, commercial paper, and corporate debt securities.
- State usury ceilings are nonapplicable for 3 years.

THE GARN-ST GERMAIN ACT OF 1982. The DIDMCA was extended in 1982. The process of dismantling interest rate ceilings was not moving fast enough to suit Congress. Nonbank competitors were making continuous inroads and increasing their market share. This was especially true for money market mutual funds. The major product developments of this Act were the money market deposit accounts and the SuperNOW accounts discussed earlier. The rapid response of the marketplace has already been noted, and this Act is best viewed as one of the last efforts to dismantle the interest ceilings on deposit accounts effectively and continue the process of granting more flexibility to thrift institutions in acquiring assets.

In summary, the past two decades saw unprecedented changes in the commercial banking industry in response to volatile movements in prices, interest rates, and fund flows. Many new competitors entered the market with products that were close substitutes for traditional banking products. Through all this, banks have adapted fairly well, and the regulatory environment has changed, albeit with a lag, to meet the challenge.

MAJOR UNRESOLVED ISSUES

BRANCH BANKING. "Perhaps the most important question of domestic banking policy before the country is that of branch banking." Charles Wallace Collins made that statement almost 60 years ago, but the question is still of major concern today. The branching status of banking may be changed in one of two ways. First, individual states may change their laws. In recent years there has been a trend in the direction of more permissive branching laws, with New York, New Jersey, Virginia, Florida, and Illinois among states with large populations that have removed restrictions on bank expansion. Second, the federal government could change its laws (primarily the **McFadden Act** and the **Douglas Amendment** to the Bank Holding Company Act of 1970) to permit wider branching. Although the federal government has not changed its laws, a number of developments have transpired that have affected branch banking and geographical expansion. In 1981 an important policy document was published by the U.S. Treasury. (See U.S. Department of the Treasury, 1981). The major recommendations of that document are as follows:

1. Phased relaxation of current geographic constraints
2. Deployment of electronic funds transfer terminals with less onerous restrictions than those placed on brick and mortar branches
3. Removal of interstate restrictions on acquisitions in the face of failing banks

Pros and Cons of Branching. Before discussing the current state of branching, some of the issues that have been raised with regard to branching are discussed. See the *Journal of Bank Research* (1980) for a detailed discussion of these issues. They are as follows:

1. Branching allows banks to grow sufficiently large to achieve scale economies necessary to produce financial services at low costs.
2. Branching results in an undue concentration of resources in a small number of financial institutions.
3. Prohibition of branching protects local monopolies by not allowing banks outside a market to enter.
4. Branching achieves diversification of lending and investing necessary to promote safety and soundness of the banking system.
5. Branching allows funds to flow from areas where supply is strong to areas where demand is strong.
6. Branching results in funds leaving rural areas for the financial centers.
7. Branching restrictions are an unwarranted government intrusion on the ability of private firms to decide where to conduct business.
8. Any change in federal laws will result in an unwarranted intrusion on the rights of the individual states.

Obviously, these issues are not mutually compatible. Branching cannot simultaneously increase and decrease competition. The issues are to a certain extent questions of fact, and a number of studies have addressed them. The results are briefly summarized in the following sections. Unfortunately, they are not clear cut.

Economies of Scale. The existence of economies of scale has been studied by numerous researchers. Differences in approach, methodology, and data have characterized a wide variety of studies. Major questions have centered on the appropriate definition of bank output, recognizing several unique characteristics of banking activities. First, banks lend and acquire dollars, but costs are related to number of transactions rather than number of dollars acquired or loaned. Second, the multiproduct nature of banking makes it difficult to disentangle joint costs and to determine the effect of changing any single output on costs. Keeping these difficulties in mind, a consensus of results across these studies may be summarized as follows:

1. Although economies of scale exist in many bank activities, they are not sufficient to indicate that small and medium-sized banks are at a substantial cost disadvantage in competing.
2. The method of expansion affects the extent of scale economies. If expansion takes place by increasing the number of branches, the benefits of scale economies are largely offset.

The policy conclusion is that there appear to be no compelling social reasons to encourage large financial institutions; on the other hand, small- and medium-sized banks do not have any inherent disadvantages that require special protection if they are to coexist with large banks.

Concentration and Competition. The question of concentration, competition, and branching has been studied in two ways. First, the differences in concentration in different types of branching environments have been analyzed. Second, the effect of changing branching laws has been studied; that is, **concentration ratios** before the change in the law are compared with those following the change. The results suggest the following:

1. States with statewide branching tend to have fewer banks, higher concentration ratios, and more offices than limited or unit banking states.
2. States with statewide branching tend to have more offices and competitors in individual retail banking markets. Concentration ratios in branch banking metropolitan areas were reduced between 1966 and 1975.

Problem Banks. The results of analyses of the effect of branching on safety and soundness are inconclusive; that is, branching does not seem to affect the probability of a bank's being on the problem list or being closed. Clearly, other factors dominate the movement of a bank from financial viability to problem status.

CURRENT DEVELOPMENTS IN BRANCHING ACTIVITY. Although there have been some recommendations for changing the federal statutes, only minor changes have occurred. Nonetheless, change has been rapid within the existing constraints. The major change has been the aggressive use of the **Douglas Amendment,** which has spurred interstate banking in a piecemeal fashion. In addition the interstate banking restrictions have been lifted in the case of failing banks, and banks have set up **automatic teller machine (ATM) networks** to allow some interstate presence for all banks.

When a bank fails, the FDIC seeks to deal with the situation in a way that minimizes the cost to the deposit insurance fund. In most cases this means that an assisted merger, known as a "P&A," or purchase and assumption, is arranged. In general, the FDIC seeks potential bidders to take over the failed bank and selects the bid that minimizes its cost. Prior to the passage of the **Garn-St Germain** bill, the potential bidders were limited to the state in which the failure occurred. This posed no particular problem as long as the bank that failed was a relatively small bank. As a number of relatively large banks experienced financial difficulties in the 1970s, however, it became apparent that the number of potential bidders would be severely limited if banks inside the state were the only candidates. That is, because most states have a few relatively large banks together with many small- and medium-sized banks, the failure of one of the large banks leaves few viable candidates to acquire it. This was dealt with in the Garn-St Germain bill, which specified a procedure that allows out-of-state banks to bid on failed banks. This gives the FDIC more flexibility in dealing with such situations.

Automated Teller Systems. The development of the **automatic teller machine (ATM)** as the most popular retail electronic funds transfer device has provided opportunities for some interstate presence for banks even though no change in the legislative environment has occurred. As banks deployed ATMs, the incentive to allow shared use by a number of banks became apparent. The use of a single ATM shows substantial economies of scale. Hence, banks would wish to avoid the deployment of a large number of machines that would show a small volume of transactions. One way to increase the number of transactions is to open the machine to use by customers of other banks. As the number of banks involved in such reciprocal arrangements increases, it becomes necessary to have a central "switch" that clears transactions on the various machines from bank to bank. If a customer from bank A withdraws funds from the machine of bank B, an interbank transfer must be arranged. Obviously, if customers of banks A, C, D, and E all withdraw funds from the machine of bank B, the number of interbank transfers increase. Hence, there evolved a number of networks of ATMs with the switch being operated by either an organization owned by the member banks, a large correspondent bank, or a private vendor. The first such networks were local or statewide.

The advance of technology has proceeded to the point where it is possible to link large numbers of banks and ATMs under a single network and switch. Several such networks have arisen. As a result, at year-end 1984, there were over 55,000 ATMs deployed and 45% of those are shared. The sharing of ATMs, representing a networking arrangement, has grown from 30% of all ATMs in 1982 to the present 45%. There are many regional and statewide networks that have evolved in different parts of the nation. In addition there are several national networks, the largest of which are the "Plus" system and the "Cirrus" system. Both of these national systems operate in more than 46 states and have several thousand members.

It should be noted that some banks may participate in a number of networks, including both a local and national system. This seems to have implemented the intent of the Treasury study cited earlier. That is, the recommendation indicated that banks should be less constrained in deploying ATMs than in establishing the traditional brick and mortar branch. The report advocated changing the federal law, but it appears that technology has outpaced the regulations, and banks can have some minimal interstate presence through these networks. (See Felgran, 1984 and 1985.)

Interstate Banking. The most important change in the interstate banking area has occurred as a result of state action rather than federal law or regulation. The **Douglas Amendment** to the Bank Holding Company Act contains some provision for interstate banking in the event that states enact legislation allowing banks in other states to establish operations. The method for entry would have to be through a subsidiary bank rather than a branch. Hence, if the legislatures of both states permitted such reciprocal entry, a bank could enter another state by establishing a de novo subsidiary or acquiring an existing bank. Implementation of this type of interstate activity has occurred in two ways. First, some states have aggressively used this power to attract new business into the state from outside. Two such states are South Dakota and Delaware. Second, states have entered into regional compacts that are designed to allow expansion of large banks inside the region to the exclusion of all other states. One state, New York, will allow any other state to enter, but it has few takers on the other side of the transaction; that is, most regional compacts specifically exclude New York. New York banks have argued that this is unconstitutional.

The most advanced set of state laws evolved in New England, especially in the southern New England states of Connecticut, Massachusetts, and Rhode Island. These states are close to New York State, and several banks wished to establish an interstate organization spanning New York and Connecticut. In doing so, the banks were violating the Connecticut statute which they immediately challenged in court as unconstitutional. The issue was whether a state could enact interstate banking legislation that excluded banks from some states. This was alleged to be a violation of the Equal Protection, Commerce, and Compact clauses of the Constitution. In March 1984, the Board of Governors of the Federal Reserve System approved two interstate acquisitions under the laws of Connecticut and Massachusetts, finding no violation. The decisions were appealed by Citicorp, a New York bank holding company, and Northeast Bancorp, a Connecticut bank holding company. On June 10, 1985, the U.S. Supreme Court ruled 8–0 that regional compacts are not unconstitutional, clearing the way for a number of states that were considering such agreements but were holding back due to the constitutional uncertainty.

At present the law of the land permits interstate banking on a regional basis. The New England region was farthest along at the time of the Supreme Court decision. That decision essentially ratified several mergers that had been approved pending the resolution of legal uncertainties. The result has been a number of mergers among banks in the southern tier of the region. In the northern tier, Maine had already passed an interstate law that allowed banks from any state to acquire Maine banks. As a result most of the relatively large Maine banks have been acquired by New York banks, interestingly not New York City based, or other New England banks. The other region that has moved quickly is the Southeast, with interstate mergers among banks in North and South Carolina, Georgia, and Florida.

Interstate banking is now a reality in that banks have a number of devices available to locate their operations wherever their business interests are best served. However, it is not complete. The devices of nonbank subsidiaries, Edge Act subsidiaries, electronic networks, and regional compacts give banks much greater freedom, but the nation does not yet have complete interstate banking.

Because instituting complete interstate banking requires Congressional action, it is necessary to examine the conditions under which Congress takes action. Congress tends to respond either to emergencies or situations in which a regulatory environment appears to be clearly unrealistic. It is likely that interstate banking will evolve under the current set of constraints with aggressive banks finding loopholes that allow them to expand. Hence, within the next five years or so, interstate banking will be sufficiently well advanced that no further action will be necessary to achieve it. Any change in legislation will merely ratify what market forces and technology have already achieved.

Bank Failure and Deposit Insurance Reform. During the past few years, the wave of deregulation of financial institutions has been impressive. In the last major such legislation, the Garn-St Germain Bill, it was recognized that the structure of the deposit insurance system should be reviewed to determine whether the current arrangements make sense in a new environment. To that end, each of the federal deposit insurance organizations—the Federal Deposit Insurance Corporation (FDIC), the Federal Savings and Loan Insurance Corporation (FSLIC), and the National Credit Union Administration (NCUA)—were required to prepare a study that addressed the issue of the appropriate structure of deposit insurance arrangements in a deregulated environment. Since the passage of Garn-St Germain, the rate of bank failure has increased rapidly, totaling 79 in 1984. In addition to the increase in the numbers of bank failures, the size of bank failing has increased also, culminating in the failure of the $40 billion asset Continental Illinois National Bank in 1984. The entire topic, which was effectively dormant for many years, has generated a great deal of discussion and controversy in the past few years. A consensus appears to have arisen regarding the need for deposit insurance reform without total agreement on exactly how to proceed.

Before proceeding with the discussion of reform, it is useful to sketch the outline of the current system. The main features of the current system are as follows:

1. Each account of an insured institution is insured for $100,000, although the effective coverage may be 100%, depending on how the insuring agency handles the failure.
2. The premium paid by the bank is based on its total deposits, not its insured deposits.
3. The premium paid per dollar of deposits by the bank is invariant with regard to the risk exposure represented by the bank's activities.
4. The insuring agency chooses the least cost method of dealing with a failed bank.
5. The method of managing a failure affects the treatment of uninsured depositors, that is, those whose deposit balance exceeds $100,000 at the time of the failure.

Every national bank and state chartered member of the Federal Reserve System is automatically insured by the FDIC. Banks chartered by states and not members of the Federal Reserve System usually join the FDIC voluntarily. In some states the granting of a charter is contingent upon qualifying for FDIC insurance.

Once a bank is in the deposit insurance system, it must pay premiums to the FDIC which then invests the funds in its portfolio of U.S. government securities. The insurance premium is set by statute at one-twelfth of 1% of all deposits. If the FDIC has a year in which the failures do not cause its portfolio to be depleted, a rebate of as much as 60% of the premium occurs in the ensuing year. (In recent years there have not been too many rebates.) Banks pay the premium based on both insured and uninsured deposits. For banks whose primary customers are large corporations, other banks, and domestic and foreign governments, the deposit insurance is not worth as much because all of their customers have deposits that far exceed the $100,000 maximum. It is scant comfort for the depositor with a $2 million deposit to know that it is insured up to $100,000.

Perhaps the most controversial feature of the deposit insurance system is the lack of a relationship between the risk incurred by the bank and its insurance premium. There is then little incentive effect from the pricing of the deposit insurance to discourage risk taking. This becomes more important in a deregulated environment in which banks are much freer and able to take risks. Assume that a bank knows that it is likely to face extreme financial difficulties and possible insolvency in the next year. Assume also that a very risky project with a chance of yielding an enormous return is brought before the bank. With the advent of modern technology, it is possible for the bank to pay an above-market return and inform deposit brokers, who will package deposits from many investors into chunks that are under the insurance limits for each depositor but add up to a large single infusion of funds, totally insured. Hence, our distressed bank is using the deposit insurance system to underwrite a risky venture. It is both logical and prudent for the bank, given our assumption of it being under stress anyway. It's a "heads we win, tails the FDIC loses" proposition. The harmful effects of this are as follows:

- Banks will undertake more risk than is beneficial to society as a whole.
- Those banks that play by the rules and do not undertake excessively risky activities initially pay for the excesses of those that do because FDIC losses initially show up as reduced rebates.
- The public is ultimately at risk because it is understood that the full faith and credit of the U.S. government is behind the deposit insurance funds. Excessive risk taking is paid for by the public as both taxpayers and as bearers of the cost of the disruption caused by any ensuing instability.

Reform of the system to avoid excessive risk taking in a deregulated environment is a goal that most participants agree is worthwhile. However, the precise form of that reform is still controversial. The general thrust of the proposals is as follows:

1. A move to risk-based deposit insurance premia that would penalize those banks that engage in excessive risk taking.
2. Requiring banks to disclose more detailed information on their potential loan losses to allow uninsured creditors to exercise a market discipline on risk taking.
3. Lowering the maximum size of an insured deposit from $100,000 to raise the cost of gathering brokered deposits.
4. Arranging that uninsured creditors are at risk no matter how a failed bank case is handled.
5. Raising capital requirements to higher ratios of total assets, implying that growth must be accompanied by the scrutiny of the capital markets.
6. Improving the process of bank supervision and examination to solve problems before they become unmanageable.

The Congress is presently holding hearings on the process of deposit reform, and the agencies are moving ahead with those steps that do not require Congressional action. It is difficult to determine at this time exactly how the new structure will look, but it is reasonably certain that change will occur. The change will be in the direction of reducing incentives to take excessive risks.

SMALL BANK OUTLOOK

Given the economic, financial, technological, regulatory, and legislative developments of recent years, forecasts of the demise of the small bank have become familiar. For a number of reasons, however, it is not all clear that the small bank should be written off as a dinosaur now or in the foreseeable future. Before discussing those reasons, a few facts are in order.

First, the United States has many more banks than any other developed country. There were 14,808 commercial banks in the United States at year-end 1983. Only 53 of those banks had more than $5 billion in assets, and they were located in 17 states, with California and New York having 18 of them. Thus there is a very small number of large commercial banks in this country. If up to $50 million in assets for a bank is considered "small," then 12,521 banks are small banks. The demise of these small banks must be predicated on the basis of their inability to compete in a new environment. Ability to compete may be measured by a number of criteria, but the most important are related to earnings performance. As will be indicated later, the numbers do not seem to support the contention that smaller banks lack earnings capability.

One widely followed performance measure is the ratio of net income to assets, or return on assets (ROA). For all insured commercial banks operating in the United States throughout 1983, ROA followed the pattern shown in Exhibit 3. No size class has a lower ROA than that of the giant banks and, for the

EXHIBIT 3 RETURNS ON ASSETS AND EQUITY, EQUITY TO ASSETS, AND BANK SIZE CLASS, DECEMBER 31, 1983

Size Class, Assets ($ millions)	ROA	ROE	Equity Assets
5.0–9.9	.50	4.30	11.59
10.0–24.9	.79	8.31	9.49
25.0–49.9	.91	10.72	8.50
50.0–99.9	.92	11.51	7.97
100.0–299.9	.83	11.43	7.30
300.0–499.9	.79	11.61	6.77
500.0–999.9	.71	10.72	6.65
1000.0–4999.9	.69	11.94	5.78
5000.0 and above	.46	9.84	4.65

Source: Federal Deposit Insurance Corp., "Bank Operating Statistics, 1983," FDIC, Washington, D.C., 1984.

very small banks, ROA increases until the group having $50 to $99.9 million in assets is reached, followed by a steady decline to banks with assets exceeding $5 billion. Another measure is the ratio of net income to equity (ROE), indicating the return to the stockholders and the potential for capital retention in the bank. Exhibit 3 shows a flatter pattern in ROE versus ROA without as much consistent variation by size. However, this implies that large banks, with lower earnings per dollar of assets, must have fewer dollars of equity per dollar of assets to generate this type of return on equity pattern. The ratio of equity to assets in Exhibit 3 shows that smaller banks have proportionally more equity than large banks. Thus the record shows that smaller banks have higher earnings and are more highly capitalized than large banks, hardly a scenario for doom.

Studies have shown that entry by new banks into small towns has not resulted in any systematic, substantial reduction of profitability of small banks already located in these towns. It is also interesting to note that in California, where some of the largest banks in the nation are located, there were 400 banks out of 426 with assets less than $500 million in 1983. Thus 94% of the banks are relatively small in the state most widely identified with statewide branching and giant financial institutions. Although banks of all sizes must adapt to a new environment, the process has been continuous for at least a decade, and the banking system has remained a vigorous and essential part of the nation's economy.

SUMMARY AND CONCLUSION

This review of the structure, services, and functions of commercial banking has emphasized the rather dramatic recent changes in the industry's financial, legislative, regulatory, and technological environments. It was shown that an inflationary environment with attendant rising and volatile interest rates changes the attractiveness of product lines, encourages new product lines, and creates opportunity for nonbank competitors. In addition, the regulatory structure becomes unrealistic in the new total environment but, with a lag, it adapts to the altered situation.

It is important, however, to note that these changes have been occurring for more than a decade. A brief list will suffice to demonstrate the point:

June 1970	Interest rate ceilings removed from large CDs with maturity less than 90 days
June 1972	Mutual savings banks in Massachusetts begin issuing NOW accounts
July 1973	All interest rate ceilings on large CDs removed
Early 1974	Beginning of money market mutual fund growth
August 1974	Credit unions permitted to offer share drafts
March 1976	All financial institutions in New England permitted to issue NOW accounts
June 1978	Six-month money market certificate implemented
November 1978	NOW accounts spread to New York; automatic transfer service authorized nationally
January 1979	Explosive growth in money market mutual funds
January 1980	Implementation of DIDMCA
January 1983	Implementation of Garn-St Germain

Thus the industry has weathered a number of storms and changes. Although banking has been viewed as a conservative, staid industry for many years, it is clear that increased competition and dramatic change have altered that situation for the foreseeable future.

REFERENCES

Beebe, Jack W., "A Perspective on Bank Liability Management and Bank Risk," *Economic Review,* Federal Reserve Bank of San Francisco, Winter 1977.

Blueprint for Reform: The Report of the Task Group on Regulation of Financial Services, The Task Group, Washington, D.C., 1983.

Board of Governors of the Federal Reserve System, *The Bank Holding Company Movement to 1978: A Compendium,* The Board, Washington, D.C., 1978.

Dunham, Constance, and Syron, Richard F., "Interstate Banking: The Drive to Consolidate," *New England Economic Review,* May/June 1984.

Federal Deposit Insurance Corporation, *Bank Operating Statistics, 1983,* Federal Deposit Insurance Corporation, Washington, D.C., 1984.

Federal Reserve Bank of Chicago, *Leveling the Playing Field: A Review of the DIDMCA of 1980 and the Garn-St Germain Act of 1982,* Federal Reserve Bank of Chicago, 1983.

Federal Reserve Bank of Kansas City, "Recent Developments in Interstate Banking," *Financial Newsletter,* Federal Reserve Bank of Kansas City, June 1985.

Felgran, Stephen D., "Shared ATM Networks," *New England Economic Review,* January/February 1984.

———"From ATM to POS Networks: Branching, Access, Pricing," *New England Economic Review,* May/June 1985.

Jesse, Michael A., and Seelig, Stephen A., *Bank Holding Companies and the Public Interest,* Heath-Lexington, MA, 1977.

Journal of Bank Research, Special Issue, Summer 1980.

Kane, Edward J., *Gathering Crisis in Federal Deposit Insurance,* MIT Press, Cambridge, MA, 1985.

Murphy, Neil B., and Mandell, Lewis, *The NOW Account Decision: Profitability, Pricing, and Strategies,* Bank Administration Institute, Rolling Meadows, IL, 1980.

President's Commission on Financial Structure and Regulation, *Report,* President's Commission on Financial Structure and Regulation, Washington, D.C., 1971.

Summers, Bruce J., "Negotiable Certificate of Deposit," in *Instruments of the Money Market,* Federal Reserve Bank of Richmond, 1981.

Stone, Bernell K., "Cash Management," in E.J. Altman, Ed., Handbook of Corporate Finance, Wiley, New York, 1986.

Syron, Richard F., "Interstate Banking in New England," *New England Economic Review,* March/April 1984.

U.S. Department of the Treasury, *Geographical Restrictions on Commercial Banking in the United States,* U.S. Department of the Treasury, Washington, D.C., 1981.

14

INVESTMENT BANKING

CONTENTS

14

INVESTMENT BANKING

Warren Law

THE INDUSTRY

In 1949 Judge Harold R. Medina dismissed the U.S. government's antitrust case against 17 leading investment banking firms. The description of the investment banking "industry" revealed in the lengthy investigation surrounding that case still fits, in broad outline, but recent dramatic changes suggest that eventually the industry will be far different, although there is considerable debate about its long-run characteristics. (See, for example, I. Walter, *Deregulating Wall Street,* Wiley, 1985.)

Traditionally the **investment banker** has advised companies and governments on when and how to raise capital, and has assisted them in doing so. The industry is dominated by a relatively small number of firms. Although there are about 3,000 members of the **National Association of Securities Dealers,** only about 400 are members of the **New York Stock Exchange** and, of these, perhaps two dozen account for the lion's share of traditional capital raising. In 1977, for example, four firms were lead manager or co-manager of more than half the total negotiated corporate equity and debt public offerings, and the top eight firms managed 74% of those offerings.

Although there has been some shuffling of rank, and some mergers, the same firms consistently appear high in the underwriting "sweepstakes." Exhibit 1 shows the **lead managers** of U.S. bond and equity **underwritings** in 1984, together with their Eurobond total.

It is generally accepted that underwriting is less profitable than it once was, for reasons noted later, but investment firms are still anxious to rank high in this list because it is believed that providing underwriting services to a major corporation indicates a significant "client relationship," and the prestige of an investment bank is closely linked with the nature of its client list.

EXHIBIT 1 LEAD MANAGERS OF UNDERWRITINGS, UNITED STATES AND EUROBOND, 1984

	United States		Eurobond	
	Value ($ billion)	Number of Issues	Value ($ billion)	Number of Issues
Salomon Brothers	21.22	186	4.98	31
Drexel Burnham Lambert	10.48	102	—	—
First Boston	9.92	128	12.24[a]	78
Merrill Lynch	8.62	125	4.17	26
Goldman Sachs	7.91	97	2.49	24
Shearson/American Express	6.69	94	1.29	11
Morgan Stanley	4.90	58	5.47	47

[a] First Boston/Credit Suisse First Boston.

Sources: Investment Dealers Digest; International Financing Review.

THE UNDERWRITING PROCESS

Until 1982 the **underwriting process** had not changed much in this century. In that year the SEC introduced **Rule 415** (discussed later) which changed the system for many large issuers, but the traditional capital raising process is still more the rule than the exception. It may be divided into several steps.

ORIGINATION. A firm contemplating raising money selects an investment banker to act as an adviser early in the formulation of its financing plans (often having been first solicited by one or more bankers). The adviser conducts an exhaustive study of the client's firm and industry, in order both to give good advice and to meet the "due diligence" requirements of regulators. These regulators will hold the investment bank responsible for adequate and truthful disclosure in the prospectus describing the issue (and issuer) which must eventually be approved by the SEC. The prospectus must, for example, spell out any unusual "risk factors" associated with the security being issued.

The originating investment banker, who will usually "manage" or "co-manage" the eventual underwriting, brings at this stage not only a general knowledge of corporate or municipal finance but also a "feel" for the capital markets, including the ease or difficulty of selling a specific type of security at a given time, its probable behavior during given types of business and market conditions, the need for restrictive covenants, redemption features, and such. Having agreed on the security to be issued, a lengthy process of documentation begins, usually requiring several weeks and involving preparation of registration statements, a preliminary prospectus ("red herring"), "blue sky" memoranda, and so on.

SYNDICATION. The predominance of the syndicate method of underwriting and distribution, whereby a group of bankers joins together in a temporary partnership for the purpose of selling a particular issue of securities, has been attributed to the large size of many issues compared with the capital of most investment banks. A banker reduces the overall riskiness of his or her portfolio of projects by accepting small participations in a number of underwritings rather than employing all the capital in one or several large deals. Moreover, it may be desirable or necessary to have many salespeople selling a given issue. The syndicate method combines the resources of many firms under the leadership of the managing underwriter.

The management of syndicates has tended to become the specialty of a relatively small number of investment banking houses, and other firms which may have "originated" the deal frequently bring it to one of these specialists, often accepting a **"co-managership"** which involves publicity (and fees) but little participation in actual management. Perhaps the most important task of the manager is to decide which firms should be invited to join the purchase group and what proportion of the issue is to be offered to each participant. Over the longer run, membership and participations in a syndicate are based on (1) the financial strength and market image of a firm, (2) its strength in selling ("placing") securities, (3) its ability to work effectively with, and provide reciprocal business for, the manager, and (4) special requests of the issuer—firms located in the same area as the issuer, firms that have "followed the stock" in the past, and so on. In the shorter run, as a matter of practice, the manager usually consults the membership list of his or her recent syndicate for issues of similar size and character and invites the same firms to join the new syndicate.

Each member is assigned a **"participation"** or share of the issue, and "underwrites" it—that is, is legally obligated to purchase that share from the issuer if the security is not successfully placed with a buyer. Custom requires that the manager establish several blocks of firms, so-called **"brackets,"** with each firm in a bracket having the same participation as other firms in the same bracket. There is usually a pyramidal structure to a syndicate, with a few leading Wall Street firms in a "special bracket" with the largest participations, and increasing numbers of firms in each successively lower bracket (and participations per firm smaller as the bracket is lower.)

The specific bracket in which a syndicate member falls is one of the most visible symbols of its standing in the industry, and there is considerable professional jealousy over the ranking, which has wide public visibility through the familiar **"tombstone" ad** that announces the offering in financial publications and lists syndicate members. A firm's place in a bracket is vested with a good deal of tradition, and may lag its actual stature as an underwriter by several years. A syndicate manager will think very seriously before promoting (or demoting) a firm to another bracket.

It is not unusual for firms to accept a larger participation than they expect to sell and to put the difference in the "pot," a portion of the offering reserved for the manager to sell on behalf of the syndicate. Only the manager knows the size of each firm's actual "retention." The manager may also take part of a firm's retention away from it when the firm is having difficulty placing the issue, and give the securities to another syndicate member to sell. The allocation of securities or awarding of a pot liability is subject to the manager's discretion, so "running the books" on a deal is a source of political and financial power, in addition to the added fee for managing a syndicate.

As long as the issue is **"in syndicate"** each member can sell the security only at the price specified in the **"Agreement Among Underwriters."** This agreement usually sets the date for disbanding the syndicate, although the manager usually has the authority to change it. The agreement also gives managers the authority to "stabilize the market" during the syndication period. Market stabilization may require the manager to buy any part of the issue that reappears on the market while the syndicate exists, or even to buy shares or bonds not part of the underwriting, in order to support the price of those being offered. Any ultimate losses in this process are allocated to syndicate members according to their participation.

The effect of market stabilizing agreements in bond underwriting has been reduced by the accepted practice of allowing **"exchanges" of bonds.** An underwriter may offer to exchange bonds in the new issue for other bonds already held by institutional investors. In so doing they may accept old bonds with a market value below the offering price of the new issue, thus effectively "selling" the new issue at a discount without violating the letter of the underwriting agreement.

DISTRIBUTION. The ability to place securities—both retail and institutional—is a significant factor in achieving major-bracket status for an investment bank. Indeed, some "wire houses" (large retail brokers) have often succeeded in persuading originating firms to accept them as co-manager of a deal which may require their ability to unleash thousands of salespeople to place a large issue.

If a manager anticipates difficulty in placing an issue, he or she may form a "selling group," composed of selected security dealers who are not syndicate members and not subject to the liability that binds underwriters, but who receive a commission if they place any of the securities. The Agreement Among Underwriters usually permits the manager to create a "short position," that is, to allocate among the syndicate an aggregate number of shares which exceeds the total offering. This allows a margin for misjudgment about the number of shares that would actually be sold by individual firms and for stabilization. To enable the manager to cover this short position, or to provide for market demand if the issue is very successful, the issuing corporation may agree in advance to give the manager a **"Green Shoe" option** (named after the shoe company that first used it) under which the corporation will increase the size of the offering (up to a specified amount) at the request of the manager.

PRICING AND PROFIT. Setting the terms of a new issue theoretically confronts the investment banker with a dilemma. The issuing corporation wants a high price for a security, whereas the purchaser wants a low price, and both are his or her clients. The banker "solves" this problem by "letting the market set the price" that is, he or she tries to find similar securities already outstanding and bases the prices of the new issue on existing prices of the old securities.

From this "public offering price" is deducted the "spread," that is, the total compensation expected by investment bankers, and the result is the price paid to the issuer. The underwriting **spread** comprises: (1) the fee to the manager, (2) an underwriting fee (allocated among the syndicate according to each member's participation), and (3) a selling concession (allocated according to the actual placement of the issue). For decades the spread for long-term investment grade corporate debt has been seven-eights of 1% of the public offering price ($8.75 per $1,000 bond), and the industry has retained this spread despite changes in the environment—the advent of computers, telephone sales, simplified SEC, registration procedures, economies of scale, and so on. These economies, however, may have been offset by greater underwriting risk as interest rate volatility has increased. Spreads on low-grade bonds and on equity offerings tend to be higher, and on some smaller, riskier equity offerings may exceed 10%.

Actually earning the spread is the goal of the manager, but if the issue is "sticky" (i.e., difficult to sell), the manager may cut the offering price, thus reducing the spread, or eventually disband the syndicate, leaving firms free to sell at any price. A successful issue is usually placed in a short time (often in a few hours) and any issue still in syndicate after several days is usually regarded as unsuccessful; thus syndicate members place pressure on the manager to dissolve the syndicate so they can take their losses and move on to the next deal. The great majority of issues is successful, but losses in a few unsuccessful syndicates may offset the fees earned on a much larger number of successful ones.

RULE 415

Since April 1982 the SEC has allowed large firms (those with more than $150 million in stock held by outside investors—about 1400 firms) to streamline the process just described by filing a "shelf registration" outlining its intent to sell, within an extended period (up to 2 years) a certain maximum amount of securities. The issuer may then sell all or part of these securities "off the shelf," without further disclosure, when it feels market conditions are most favorable—in the parlance, when "the window is open." The issuer invites bids from investment banks to buy the issue, or may be approached by a bank with a bid for a specific security. The investment banker may buy the entire issue or parcel it out to a small group of other banks. In either case the deal is done swiftly, often in a matter of minutes, without forming the traditional syndicate and without conventional "preselling" (calling on potential investors to determine their interest in a proposed deal).

Although **Rule 415** is still supposedly "experimental," the industry accepts it, or a variant, as almost certainly permanent. The rule has passionate defenders and opponents. Critics say (1) the rule makes a mockery of the concept of due diligence and will inevitably result in a fraudulent issue scandal; (2) underwriters are forced to take bigger risks, which gives an edge to firms with substantial capital, and will eventually drive smaller and regional firms out of business; (3) the necessity for speed results in placing issues with a few large institutional investors, which may not be desirable for the issuer; (4) a rush of issues to take advantage of a "window" may make the market even more volatile. Defendants argue that (1) market volatility in recent years makes spur-of-the moment issuing capability almost mandatory; (2) the rule increases competition by potentially allowing any investment bank to take business from an issuer's traditional banker; and (3) it promotes creativity among bankers hoping to capture a deal by offering a new idea to an issuer who has previously been another banker's client.

One undeniable fact is that Rule 415 requires the investment banker to move quickly, putting a premium on the "trading" ability of an investment bank, the constant dealing in different markets which makes the banker confident of successfully placing an issue on which he or she has bid. In turn, large-scale trading requires a firm to have substantial capital to support its security positions, again giving an edge to firms with substantial capital, as suggested by Exhibit 2 which shows the shares of corporate debt issues underwritten in the 16-month periods before and after Rule 415.

There is some evidence that the spread on Rule 415 deals has been lower than on traditional syndicated deals. This is counterbalanced by the larger size of the successful bidders' share of an underwriting.

MUNICIPAL UNDERWRITING

The process of underwriting debt issues of state and local governmental entities (usually called "municipals") is similar to that of corporates, but there are some substantial differences. Probably most important is that commercial banks are permitted to underwrite **General Obligation bonds ("GOs"),** backed by the "full faith and credit" and tax-raising ability of the issuer, but are prohibited by the Glass-Steagall Act from underwriting other municipals. Because municipal

EXHIBIT 2 MARKET SHARE BEFORE AND AFTER RULE 415

	1984 Capital ($ millions)	Share Before (%)	Share After (%)
Salomon Brothers	1,269	4.9	15.8
Goldman Sachs	712	3.9	8.7
Merrill Lynch	2,024	5.6	7.1
Shearson Lehman	1,724	2.7	4.5
Morgan Stanley	355	4.0	3.9

Sources: SIA, Salomon Brothers.

"Revenue" bonds (backed by the income producing activity of a turnpike, water authority, etc.) and "Industrial Revenue Bonds" (issued by municipalities to provide funds for local private firms) constitute the largest part of the market, commercial bankers have lobbied for many years to change this law, without result to date (1985).

Another difference is that municipals are generally issued as "serials"; that is, each issue contains bonds of several maturities, due over a period of many years. Although for the issuer the required payments are similar to those of corporate debt with a sinking fund requirement, serial issues meet the requirements of diverse buyers seeking different degrees of futurity. Because most municipals are sold by competitive bid, a bidding syndicate is confronted with a complex problem of selecting the coupon (or "reoffering yield") for each different maturity. Oddly, many issuers award the bonds to the bidder submitting the lowest "net interest cost," a method under which coupon payments in later years are weighted as heavily as those in earlier years (i.e., which does not assign any time value to money and sometimes leads to odd bids). The problem lends itself to linear programming and many syndicate managers use such programs in submitting bids.

Finally, the tax-exempt feature of municipals has more appeal to individuals than institutions, who either pay no taxes or have other methods of reducing taxes. Thus, retail brokers play a more significant role in selling municipals than corporates. E. F. Hutton, for example, ranked second in underwriting municipals in 1984, compared with fifteenth in corporate underwriting.

EUROMARKET UNDERWRITING

The rise of the **Eurobond market** is traceable to the imposition by the United States of the **Interest Equalization Tax** (1963) and controls on foreign investment of American firms (1968). These regulations drove both foreign and American corporations to raise funds outside the United States. The larger American investment banks followed their clients and today most have offices in London, the center of the Eurobond market. The underwriting system is similar to the traditional American system, but syndicates may include commercial banks and other financial institutions not solely devoted to securities, and the number of co-managers may be very large in order to gather local support for the issue in several countries. (As a result the management group typically accounts for a larger part of the amount underwritten and sold than in the United States.)

The market is largely unregulated. Because registration of an offering is not required by the SEC, an underwriting can be done rapidly. An offering circular describing the issue is distributed to develop investor interest, and receives a cursory review by the stock exchange on which the issue is to be listed, if any.

Strictly speaking, Eurobond issues are not public issues at all. During a "selling period" the syndicate manager invites indications of potential sales, which are not made until the issue is offered to the syndicate for immediate acceptance on terms finally agreed to with the issuer. Individual investors then go to their banks or other dealers to buy the bonds. Similarly, issues are not "underwritten" in the American sense. If an issue fails the syndicate may raise the coupon, cut the size, or even cancel the issue. Because spreads tend to be larger than in the American market, there is also more room to cut price before the syndicate loses money. Instead of forming a syndicate, one or a small number of firms will often bid competitively to buy the bonds. This is known as the "bought deal" and is the forerunner of Rule 415 in the United States.

It has been estimated that as much as 80% of new Eurobond issues end up in Switzerland, which partly explains why Credit Suisse–First Boston has led the list of Eurobond underwriters for several years. This joint venture benefits from First Boston's ability to place securities in New York, but its real strength is the placing ability of the Swiss commercial bank, Credit Suisse, which manages billions of dollars for individual investors worldwide.

After the U.S. Interest Equalization Tax was removed in 1974, some observers predicted the demise of the Eurobond market. Instead, its size and liquidity have increased steadily, and in 1984 the value of dollar denominated bonds issued in the Eurobond market exceeded the value of bonds issued in the United States.

PRIVATE PLACEMENTS

The Securities Act of 1933 provided exemption from registration procedures for new issues of securities which are "transactions by an issuer not involving a public offering." SEC Rule 146 limits such transactions to those in which (1) there are no more than 35 "offerees" (purchasers), (2) the offerees have sufficient knowledge and experience to be capable of evaluating the merits and risks of the investment, and (3) the purchaser must plan to hold the security for investment with no present intention of resale (generally construed to require a 2-year holding period).

Private placements meeting these criteria have become an important part of the investment banker's capital raising arsenal. (See Exhibit 3.) The proportion of private placements to total financings averaged 32% over 1973–1984.

The "other equity" placed privately consisted of limited partnerships in real estate, research and development programs, and other forms of tax shelters (sold primarily to individual investors), and venture capital and leveraged buyout funds (sold primarily to institutions). Traditionally the major market for private placements has been insurance companies, but in 1984 thrift institutions and banks accounted for almost a third of institutional private placements, including a wide range of project loans, leveraged lease transactions, leveraged buyout loans, and so on.

In general, private placements are complex financial instruments (partly because the issuer is usually a smaller firm with uncertain credit rating). The in-

EXHIBIT 3 PUBLIC AND PRIVATE NEW CORPORATE FINANCINGS—1984

	Public ($ billions)	Private ($billions)
Bonds	69.2	43.8
Preferred stock	3.9	2.7
Common stock	8.9	0.8
Other equity	—	5.8
	82.1	53.1

Source: IDD Information Services, Inc.

vestment banker plays a vital role in preparing an offering memorandum, negotiating with offerees, arranging details of the closing, and such. The banker's real skill is knowing what kinds of deals are "doable" under existing market conditions, and knowing potential investors. By dealing with a limited number of investors, a private placement specialist (most large investment banks have such departments) can negotiate a loan directly tailored to an issuer's needs, including schedules for drawing the funds down over time. Such complexities make public offerings difficult. (It is also much easier to obtain waivers and exceptions later in a private offering.) Without the restrictions imposed by regulators in public financings, the specialist can provide detailed earnings projections, proposed solutions to problems of the issuer, and so on. The private placement also has obvious advantages of speed and confidentiality.

Because he or she is acting as **agent/negotiator** and not assuming an underwriting risk, the fee received by the investment banker is lower. Other expenses—printing, legal, and such—are also reduced, so total cost to the issuer is substantially less, if, in fact, a public placement could have been done at all.

MERCHANT BANKING

Traditionally investment banks were partnerships, and partners often put their individual capital into a broad array of long-term investments. In recent years, despite the trend toward incorporation and outside shareholders, many investment firms have begun supplementing their traditional role of intermediary by actively becoming a "principal," a longer-term owner and investor in projects that they helped finance (and in some cases originated). By so doing they perform a role familiar to British **merchant banks** and French **banques d'affaires.**

Opponents of this trend argue that it creates a conflict of interest, both in competing with clients for investments and in later offering to the public shares in a company of which the investment bank is a major owner. Defenders argue that the willingness of an investment firm to risk its own funds may speed up a deal and persuade other investors to become participants. Moreover, it helps publicly held firms compete with partnerships, by helping employees amass their own capital. (In this case the firm invests, *pari passu,* on behalf of both employees and stockholders.) Finally, venture capital investments offer a chance to create new clients for future investment banking business.

LEVERAGED BUYOUTS. Perhaps the most common merchant banking investments to date have been in **leveraged buyouts (LBOs),** which constitute one of the remarkable financial trends of recent years. In 1983 the value of LBOs of publicly traded companies was $7.1 billion, up from $636 million in 1979, and LBOs accounted for about 19% of all takeovers of public firms.

Put simply, a LBO involves the heavy use of borrowed money to purchase a company or a division of a company, which is then converted into a privately held concern. Typically, candidates for a LBO are firms with substantial liquid assets, unexciting growth prospects, and assets with replacement costs far above book value. By reducing the liquidity, and benefiting from the added depreciation tax shield made possible by writing up the assets, the new owner hopes to service the very heavy debt charges resulting from unusually high leverage. Because little growth is anticipated, cash flow need not be used to finance more assets, but is available to repay debt. Usually the new owner hopes to liquidate his or her investment in 5 to 7 years (after enough debt has been retired to make the balance sheet less frightening) either by a public stock offering or a private sale. The new owners usually include several members of senior management of the public firm.

Early players of the game tended to be small firms specializing in LBOs, but their remarkable returns, averaging over 50% of equity, soon attracted investment banks. Financing tends to be complex in a LBO, including several layers of debt. Subordinated lenders, in view of the risk in high leverage, usually receive an equity "kicker," in stock or warrants to buy stock. A level of subordinated debt, often called "mezzanine financing," is crucial to most LBOs. The investment banker, who may have invented and structured the deal, and arranged financing, usually receives equity and often a continuing annual cash fee for overseeing it.

TRADING

In recent years the trading activities of investment banks have become so important as to overshadow traditional underwriting. (Trading does not include "brokerage," in which the firm acts only as agent, but instead requires a firm to put its own capital to risk by carrying an inventory of securities in a "trading account.") Exhibit 4 shows gross profits of securities firms in the two activities (before direct expenses and overhead), in millions of dollars.

Apart from potential profits in trading, firms have believed that the volatile markets of the early 1980s required that an underwriter have an active trading floor in order to be "on top of the market" and thus price an offering success-

EXHIBIT 4 PROFITS FROM UNDERWRITING AND TRADING 1979–1983

	1979	1981	1983
Underwriting			
Equity	177	428	754
Debt	594	1,145	2,783
Trading			
OTC equities	440	609	1,381
Debt securities	1,161	3,083	4,418
Other securities	557	551	1,045
Total	2,929	5,816	10,381

Source: Securities Industry Trends (Securities Industry Association).

fully. This volatility, particularly in debt instruments, is shown in the variations of month-to-month growth rates around trend (measured in percentage points):

	1975–1979	1980–1984
S&P 500 Stock Index	3.4	3.9
Treasury bills	5.1	9.9
20-year government bonds	1.9	4.6

Source: Data Resources Inc.

Market volatility has of course increased the risk in trading, which fortunately has been mitigated by the proliferation of an array of vehicles for hedging that risk: interest rate futures, options and futures on the Standard and Poor's 500, the NYSE index, and indexes on specific stock groups (e.g., oils). In turn, the complexity of available hedging techniques, compounded by a dramatic increase in computerized information, has led firms to recruit traders with advanced university degrees and to employ Ph.D. mathematicians to refine techniques of "basis" or "relationship" trading. This enables bond traders to hedge away market risk (caused by interest rate fluctuations) and lock in profits by arbitraging momentary disparities among various fixed-income securities.

Nevertheless, trading remains a risky occupation and trading losses were reportedly responsible for the sale of two major firms in 1984—Becker Paribas and Lehman Brothers Kuhn Loeb. Again the competitive advantage of a large capital base is obvious.

BLOCK TRADING. The two decades after World War II saw a striking growth in the size of institutional investors, particularly mutual funds and pension funds, and the rise of "performance-oriented" fund managers, who traded stocks actively and in large volume. By 1963 over 25% of NYSE volume was accounted for by institutional investors and concentration was much higher in those stocks that were mutual fund favorites. Fixed commissions made these institutional "block trades" very profitable. Most large investment firms established block trading desks, and a few small "boutique" firms were devoted exclusively to trading for institutions. The large commissions compensated for the risk in "positioning" a large block, that is, owning it while searching for a buyer.

Beginning May 1, 1975 ("Mayday") the SEC ordered the end of fixed commissions and institutions exerted their power to force commissions down, until most block traders were losing money and many firms closed. After the stock market revival of 1982, however, block trading again flourished, as low commissions (as low as 5¢ per share) were offset by extremely large volume. By 1984 blocks (trades of 10,000 shares or more) represented half of NYSE activity, and 100,000 shares trades were commonplace. Institutions have increased the turnover of their portfolios, reaching 61% in 1984, up from 23% in 1977.

The risks in trading large blocks of stock are obvious and most firms do not expect to make a trading profit, aiming only at holding trading losses below commissions. In addition, Rule 415 has meant that block trading has partly replaced the syndication role in equity underwritings.

RISK ARBITRAGE. A more specialized form of trading is **"risk arbitrage,"** but for those Wall Street firms that engage in it (approximately a dozen) the profits therefrom have been substantial. The **arbitrageurs**—commonly called "arbs"—have flourished in step with the merger wave of recent years, and particularly with the emergence of hostile takeovers and bidding contests. An arb usually commits his or her firm's capital to a "deal," and the risk is that the deal will not be consummated. For example, in a tender offer of $40 in stock of Company X for $30 of stock in Company Y, the arb might buy Y while simultaneously selling X short, hoping to lock in a $10 profit. If the tender for any reason does not succeed, he or she must unwind both positions and, because other arbs are behaving similarly, the potential for loss on both the long and short positions is great. (Cancellation of Gulf Oil's bid for Cities Service in 1982 produced huge losses for arbs.)

Thus, the basic question is whether the deal will go through and if so, how long it will take. To answer this question, arbs develop wide sources of information and maintain legal consultants to aid in deciding whether litigation to stall a takeover is likely to succeed.

After a tender offer has been announced arbs are likely to account for most of the trading in the target firm's stock. Often more than half of the stock eventually tendered comes from arbs, and in a bidding war they usually hold the balance of power in deciding which bidder will win.

As the number and size of takeovers have increased, a few firms have raised pools of money from outside investors to employ in arbitrage. And at least one firm publishes research for its institutional customers, evaluating the potential of 15 or 20 arbitrage situations monthly.

FINANCIAL INNOVATION

As noted previously, the traditional long-standing relationship between an investment banker and a client has eroded, and been replaced by "transactional finance," a world in which bankers chase each others' clients, primarily by aggressive marketing of new financing ideas. It is generally accepted that, if the firm being approached likes the idea, the investment banker proposing it gets the deal, no matter what previous relationship existed with another investment bank. As a result, most large investment firms maintain groups devoted to inventing new financing ideas. A monopoly of any such idea, if successful, will have a very short half-life, because other investment firms will quickly copy it, or offer an improved variation.

One example illustrates the point. In March 1981, Goldman Sachs persuaded Martin Marietta Corp. to issue the first **"deep discount"** bond of a high rated corporation. (Such bonds have coupon payments below the market rate of return and therefore must be sold at a substantial discount from par.) Following this successful issue, other investment banks pushed the idea. By the end of July there had been 21 similar issues and in November discount bonds accounted for almost one-quarter of the total funds raised publicly in the domestic bond market. Soon Merrill Lynch created **"zero-coupon"** U.S. Treasury bonds by buying conventional long-term Treasuries, "stripping" the coupon payments, and then offering the coupons to the public, thus creating a series of certificates maturing at 6-month intervals but paying no interest. This idea was so successful that other firms copied it, and over $6 billion of these coupons were sold in a few months, with the Treasury eventually changing the call feature of long bonds to make them more attractive for stripping. Similarly, zero-coupon corporate bonds spread to the Eurobond market in January 1982, and within five weeks 25 similar issues were floated there.

Many other innovations, however, have been less successful. The **"drop lock" bond,** for example, failed to gain market acceptance. (This was a floating rate security carrying a very high minimum coupon, with automatic conversion to a fixed rate security at the minimum coupon rate should interest rates fall below that for a predetermined period.) A few issues of commodity-linked bonds, with the principal being convertible at the buyer's option into a fixed quantity of some commodity, also failed to attract imitators. But a few innovations have been so highly successful as to transform the nature of corporate finance. Among them are the following.

ASSET-BACKED OBLIGATIONS. Investment bankers have arranged for corporations with large portfolios of financial assets to "securitize" these assets by placing them without recourse in a trust and selling "pass-through" certificates, which represent interests in the pool of assets. Commercial banks, for example, have sold automobile loans in this way, and other firms have sold leases and receivables. All collections of principal and interest on these assets are passed through to the certificate holder. There are many potential advantages to the seller. The quality of the assets often enables the certificate to obtain a higher rating, and thus lower interest costs, than straight debt of the issuer. Interest rate and maturity risks are removed from the issuing firm, whereas it may still receive fee income from servicing the assets and may retain depreciation and investment tax credit benefits.

By far the most important example of the genre is the **"mortgate backed security,"** first developed in 1970 by the Government National Mortgage Association. The original **"Ginnie Mae pass-throughs"** have spawned so many variations that issues of mortgage backed securities, which totaled only $2.8 billion in 1970, reached $85 billion by 1983, more than twice the volume of debt issued by U.S. corporations that year. It has been predicted that, by the late 1980s, two-thirds of all newly issued mortgages will be packaged and traded as securities. One result has been the emergence of a truly national mortgage market, with uniform rates replacing the regional differences common until recently.

The growth of mortgage backed securities is significantly attributable to the development of an active trading market in them, thus providing liquidity for an instrument (residential mortgages) formerly illiquid. Almost every major Wall Street firm has expanded its trading activity in these securities dramatically. Salomon Brothers, for example, tripled its staff in this area between 1980 and 1984, and it is estimated that mortgage-related activity provided 40% of the firm's roughly $500 million in net income in 1983. As one would predict, trading spreads on these securities have narrowed and it is now agreed that future profits will depend partly on an investment bank's ability to locate and package a continuing and reliable stream of new mortgages. With this goal, firms have been establishing ties with major originators such as savings institutions and developers.

JUNK BONDS. In the mid-1970s the market for original issues of debt of B and BB rated companies was almost nonexistent. The market for so-called junk bonds (more politely **"high yield bonds"**) was primarily a secondary one, concentrated on issues whose originally higher ratings had slipped after the firm fell on hard times. In 1984, however, approximately $15 billion of junk bonds were issued. The creation of this market is due largely to one firm—Drexel Burnham Lambert Inc.—which underwrote over two-thirds of these issues in 1984, and thus ranked second in total underwriting. This firm's overall underwriting ranking dropped to fifth in 1985 (behind Salomon Brothers, First Boston, Goldman Sachs, and Merrill Lynch Capital) but it still dominated the high yield market.

Drexel accomplished this by demonstrating empirically to institutional investors that the long-term returns to holders of junk bonds had over time surpassed that of higher grade bonds, even after defaults, and by creating a reputation for providing secondary market liquidity for these bonds via a very active trading floor. This market has been very profitable and has attracted other, larger firms. For a description of this market, see Section 6. One side effect of this market has been the rise of the **"junk bond takeover,"** in which small firms have been able to finance tender offers for much larger ones by arranging this type of financing.

SWAPS. Since 1982, when interest rate swaps totaled an estimated $100 million, the market has burgeoned phenomenally, reaching an estimated $85 billion in early 1985. (All estimates in this area are extremely rough, because there is no commonly accepted way of reporting or measuring a swap.) It is believed that in early 1985, 70 to 80% of all Eurobond offerings eventually resulted in some sort of swap.

Put simply, an interest rate swap is a transaction in which two companies with equal but opposite needs (the "counterparties") exchange their respective positions. If Company A, for example, has a floating rate 5-year debt and wishes to fix its interest costs, an investment banker may persuade Company B to issue a 5-year fixed-rate bond of similar size and then "swap" the interest obligation with Company A; that is, each agrees to pay the other's interest costs. (In practice the payments are usually netted, so at each settlement date only the difference between the two is paid.) Similarly, a cross-currency swap involves two counterparties with debts expressed in different currencies, who assume each other's obligation. A single deal may involve swaps both of interest rates and currencies.

The number of financial institutions arranging **swap transactions** has grown almost as rapidly as the market. Commercial banks originated the market and still have the largest share, but several investment banks are very active in the area. Originally investment banks acted merely as brokers, bringing the two parties together for a fee. As competition increased, however, they have increasingly acted as "intermediaries" or "principals." If the bank acts as an intermediary, it stands between the two parties, guaranteeing the cash payments of each. In early 1985 it was estimated that Salomon Brothers had as much as $15 billion of swaps on its books in which it was an intermediary, assuming the credit risk. Because an interest rate swap does not require an exchange of principal, but only of the difference between two rates, this risk is limited.

If necessary to arrange a swap, an investment bank may even act as principal, playing the role and assuming the obligation of one of the counterparties. Normally the banker would hope to find some party willing to take over this obligation within a short time, but if one is not found within a few weeks, the task becomes difficult because interest rates may have changed enough since the swap was first booked that any new party might have to pay a substantial "up front" fee to participate. Recently, however, a small number of firms have started "making a market" in swaps, that is, quoting two-way prices in certain types of long-dated swap transactions, and a market is developing for **option contracts on swaps.** Thus, deals are now available on demand, and firms can guarantee the future availability of a swap at a known price.

At one time an investment bank's fees for arranging and participating in swaps were quite lucrative. The fixed-rate payer usually paid 0.5% of the principal for arranging a swap and preparing documentation. An intermediary might get 0.15%, whereas spreads on Eurobond underwriting approximated 1.87%. By early 1985, however, fees ran much lower, and competition often made it necessary to forgo any fee, in order to facilitate the **Eurodollar underwriting** associated with it. (Conversely, some investment firms were apparently willing to lose money on an underwriting, hoping to make it upon the subsequent swap.)

The basic characteristic of swaps is that they arbitrage market imperfections. Swiss firms, for example, may be able to borrow fixed-rate Swiss francs at a lower rate than outsiders, whereas an American firm might sell commercial paper in New York more easily than Swiss firms. Thus, a swap opportunity is created. The inevitable result has been a "globalization" of money markets, and borrowers have at least indirect access to the cheapest sources of money worldwide. Similarly, the successful investment banks in this area are those with a large client base and representation in the major world money markets, so deals can be made quickly, and a large capital base so the firm can act as principal if necessary.

BALANCE SHEET RESTRUCTURING. Many American corporations have found that balance sheets which seemed ideal in the 1960s do not fit the volatile economic conditions of the 1980s. Investment bankers have responded by devising means for restructuring clients' balance sheets in a very short time. Indeed, perhaps both the left and right sides of the balance sheet may be regarded as flexible and subject to rapid change. As already noted swaps produce great flexibility in managing liabilities, but they also enable firms to diversify their existing investment portfolio and change their exposure to foreign exchange risk. Similarly, creation of asset-backed securities enables firms to remove financial assets from their balance sheets almost at will.

More fundamental restructuring occurs when equity is replaced with debt, and vice versa. Firms have repurchased their stock with borrowed funds for decades, thus creating instant leverage, but recently some firms have reversed the process, in order both to reduce balance sheet risk and to gain a bookkeeping profit. In a stock-for-debt swap of this type an investment bank may purchase outstanding bonds from institutional investors at a discount from par and trade these bonds to the corporation that issued them, in exchange for common stock that the bank then immediately resells (having previously registered the issue with the SEC). The corporate issuer may report an immediate profit from repurchasing bonds at a discount.

Or a firm may "defease" a debt issue. **Defeasance** allows a borrower to be released from the obligation by placing with a trustee sufficient government securities to generate a cash flow adequate to pay all interest and principal on the defeased issue, which then is removed from the borrower's balance sheet. A noncallable debt issue can thus be effectively "retired," for example. More important, the borrower reports a gain in income if the cost of the treasuries is less than the book value of the debt being defeased, which is likely if interest rates have risen since the debt was issued, and defeasance is a nontaxable event. Moreover, defeasance doesn't involve negotiating with bondholders and allows the debt to be extinguished without driving up the price of the bonds, as would be likely in a cash buyback. Defeasance may be applied to almost any form of debt with a specified payment schedule, including capitalized leases and mortgages, and produces great flexibility in managing the right side of the balance sheet.

The search for new ideas in capital raising has led investment bankers to generate some esoteric deals. In 1983, for example, Prudential Insurance issued Eurodollar debt with warrants attached entitling the holder to purchase AT&T stock. (Prudential had previously purchased the stock and placed it in escrow, and the after-tax dividends on the stock more than covered debt service.) More recently, **zero coupon bonds** which are convertible into common stock and "putable" (sellable) back to the issuing company at various dates in the future have been successfully issued.

MERGERS AND ACQUISITIONS

For a few investment banks, undoubtedly the most profitable activity in recent years has been so-called M&A—the business of advising firms engaged in mergers and acquisitions (or firms trying to avoid being merged or acquired). One of the leaders in this field, First Boston, probably earned $75 million in M&A fees in 1984, in contrast to a total firm pretax income of $2 million in 1978, before the recent merger mania began. Because First Boston's M&A department includes only 70 people, the attraction of such work is obvious. Investment banking fees in large M&A deals are remarkable, even by Wall Street standards. In Chevron's takeover of Gulf Oil, for example, three investment banks representing both parties earned total fees approximating $64 million. In another widely publicized deal, one firm earned $10.8 million for 79 hours of work. Moreover, because the investment bank's capital is not at stake, little risk is involved and there is no theoretical limit to how many deals a firm can be involved in at one time. Fees in **hostile takeovers involvin**g high yield bonds have been phenomonal in 1985, for example, the Pantry Pride-Revlon deal.

What an investment bank does to earn these fees varies widely from deal to deal. In a **friendly merger** negotiated by the firms involved without outside help, the bank may only be asked to write a **"fairness opinion,"** a short statement that the terms of the merger, in the view of the bank, are equitable. The fee for such a letter may be several hundred thousand dollars, because the investment banker may be called on to justify the opinion in any subsequent litigation.

In most cases the investment bank is much more deeply involved. For an acquisition-minded client it may prepare a list of logical "targets" (using a computerized data base that is the foundation of most M&A departments), suggest an offering price (including combinations of cash and securities), help to raise funds for the offer, and even negotiate the deal. In a **contested takeover** the firm will be actively involved in suggesting tactics to increase the chance of success. Because investment banking fees are usually much higher in successful takeovers than failed attempts, some critics contend this produces a "win at any cost" attitude and causes the banker to pursue takeovers that may not, in fact, be advisable for the client in the long run.

For the banker advising the target firm, the task is complex. Acquirers have become so sophisticated and aggressive that it is generally conceded that once a target is "in play" (i.e., has received an unfriendly offer) the odds are high that it will eventually be acquired by *some* firm. To avoid this, investment bankers suggest that a firm hoping to remain independent should retain the services of a skilled M&A department *before* receiving an unsolicited tender offer. In this case the banker can analyze the vulnerability of the company to a potential raid, and suggest ways to discourage one. These may range from changing the firm's charter or by-laws (e.g., to adopt staggered terms for the board of directors or a "super majority clause," requiring a vote of holders of a minimum of 80% of the outstanding shares to approve a merger) to more draconian devices, such as sale of a particularly attractive division. Meanwhile the banker may identify attractive alternative acquirers (so-called **White Knights**) and prepare information about the client to present to them on short notice in the event of a **hostile offer.**

The level of hostility in both takeover and defensive tactics rose dramatically in 1984, leading to Congressional investigations into the need to make takeovers more difficult. Opposition by the administration to any legislation, however, coupled with the lack of any consensus on what form such legislation should take, has led many observers to predict that M&A will continue to represent a major source of income to the small number of firms which have established a reputation for expertise in the area. In early 1986, the Federal Reserve passed a rule (by a 3 to 2 vote) that certain types of hostile takeovers could not be financed 100% by debt and would need to adhere to the 50% margin requirement.

RESEARCH

Most Wall Street firms of size maintain a **research department,** staffed by "analysts" and economists who study and prepare reports on industries, specific firms, and market conditions in general. Those departments may be large (e.g., the research staff at Salomon Brothers exceeds 100 people). The research output may be used to help the firm in its own trading, but the primary goal is to provide it to individual and institutional investors, sometimes for a fee but usually in hope of being compensated with brokerage commissions.

Reports provided "retail" clients (i.e., smaller individual investors) tend to be short, usually including the firm's judgment on the direction of the market and of specific securities. As the market has come to be dominated by institutional investors, investment firms have developed more sophisticated, in-depth reports for their use, often exceeding 50 pages, and the analyst may supplement these reports with personal discussions with institutions (which may maintain their own research staff, called "buy side" analysts). Institutional analysts tend to specialize in one or a few industries, and *Institutional Investor* magazine publishes an annual "all-America research team" of those analysts regarded by their peers as the best in covering each industry.

A highly regarded analyst is well rewarded, often earning several hundred thousand dollars annually. Such salaries, of course, can only be supported by attracting large institutional commissions. Before 1975, when commissions were fixed, several small research-oriented firms (often called **"boutiques"**) were established to cater to institutional investors. Commissions from these investors were so large and profitable that the institution was often able to direct the broker to "give up" some of the commission to another firm, to reward it for services to the institution (such as selling shares of a mutual fund). **Give-ups** were outlawed by the SEC in 1968, but institutions were still able to receive almost anything from brokers, from free office space to computer services and magazine subscriptions, in return for "soft dollars" (brokerage commissions).

When **fully negotiated commissions** were introduced in 1975, institutions felt legally obligated to pay the lowest possible rates, and many research boutiques foundered. (Today institutional commissions average less than one-third the pre-Mayday level.) As institutional trading has grown, however, some boutiques have revived and new ones established. Recently there has been a boom in **"third-party research"** in which investment banks buy research for cash and provide it to institutions for commissions. An extreme case is Autranet (a subsidiary of Donaldson, Lufkin and Jenrette, one of the early boutiques), which buys research from 225 research "originators" and trades for some 500 institutions.

Some academic critics maintain that much of this effort is wasted, pointing to numerous studies showing that the average investment performance of institutions has been no better than that from an unmanaged portfolio with equivalent risk characteristics, and others demonstrating that both short- and long-run earnings forecasts of individual firms provided by analysts have been woefully inaccurate.

INVESTMENT MANAGEMENT

A surprisingly small share of investment banking income is derived from fees for managing investment portfolios for clients. In fact, some firms do not engage in this business at all. One reason is that so many of their important clients—mutual funds, insurance companies, and commercial banks—are already active in the area, and there are other potential conflicts. Investment firms might, for example, trade for their own firm accounts at the expense of clients' accounts, or might solve the problem of a sticky underwriting by placing the security in managed accounts. (Pension law prohibits a money management firm from purchasing securities for a pension fund if the firm has underwritten those securities.) Or a firm might "churn" the portfolio being managed in order to generate brokerage fees. Finally, a corporate client might object if a banker dumped a block of his or her stock from other clients' managed accounts, or vice versa. Recognizing these problems, those investment banks that do manage money attempt to maintain a **"Chinese wall"** between this activity and other parts of the firm.

All major wire houses sponsor and manage **money market funds,** where retail customers' funds can be parked between trades, and have developed a plethora of specialized mutual funds investing in tax-exempt securities, Treasuries, and such to offer diversification to small clients desiring to invest in those instruments. A few offer more exotic funds, ranging from real estate portfolios to investments in motion pictures.

One variation of money management is **pension fund consulting.** A number of investment firms have departments offering plan design and actuarial services, or may advise on choice of a manager for the fund. Again there is possibility for abuse, in that the consultant may recommend a manager who channels brokerage to the investment firm.

THE FUTURE

In recent years the American securities industry has been very profitable. Although the fortunes of retail-oriented wirehouses have fluctuated with the stock market, large investment banks in general averaged after-tax returns on equity capital of more than 26% over the 1979–1983 period, and a few leading **"wholesale" firms** have been remarkably profitable, earning pretax returns of 80% or better. Literally hundreds of individuals on Wall Street earn more than $1 million annually. In a competitive economy such profits are usually in danger, and some observers have predicted that increasing competition will shave these rewards, as has happened to institutional brokerage commission rates and underwriting spreads.

COMPETITION. Commercial bankers hope the erosion of legal barriers will enable them to provide that competition and have lobbied vigorously for repeal of the most important barrier, the **Glass-Steagall Act of 1933,** which prohibits deposit-taking institutions from underwriting or dealing in corporate securities or any municipals other than General Obligation bonds. The Senate voted in 1984 to allow banks to underwrite commercial paper, municipal revenue bonds, and mortgage-backed securities. Since then, however, Congressional sentiment seems to have hardened in response to widely publicized commercial bank loan losses and, in some cases, failures. (Commercial bankers argue that these problems would be reduced if they were allowed to generate profits from prohibited investment banking activities.) Commercial banks have been allowed to enter the discount brokerage business, but there is little evidence to date that they have been very successful in this area.

In fact, some skeptics doubt that commercial banks pose much of a threat, noting that they have always been allowed to make private placements and engage in merger and acquisition work, without much success, and have made a weak showing in the Eurobond market, where Glass-Steagall does not apply. (Even BankAmerica used Goldman Sachs as adviser when it bought Seafirst Corporation.) These critics argue that commercial banks face fundamental barriers, including an inability to offer the salaries common in Wall Street without destroying their own salary structure. Moreover, most commercial banks refuse to become involved in unfriendly takeovers, and some corporate executives fear that commercial banks, in view of their size, have greater confidentiality problems than smaller investment firms. It is even argued that a cultural gap exists, and a slow-paced commercial bank is not a congenial environment for hard-driving investment bankers. (For a discussion of the commercial bank versus investment bank issues, see I. Walter, *Deregulating Wall Street,* Wiley, 1985.)

On the other hand, adequate capital is clearly vital in today's investment banking environment, and commercial banks have much larger capital bases. (The 25 largest commercial banks have more than five times the capital of the top 25 investment firms.) And some commercial banks have had success in trading government securities and foreign currencies, and are more active in swaps than investment banks. Moreover, the worldwide branch system of Citibank, for example, should be an asset, because capital markets are increasingly global. It is difficult to believe that competition from a few large commercial banks will not eventually reduce the profits now accruing to investment banks.

Similarly, **Japanese investment banks** seem determined to gain a share. They are large and aggressive (Nomura Securities has more capital than Merrill Lynch. It has a staff of 120 in New York, largely selling Japanese securities to Americans but also cultivating potential American corporate clients.) In 1985's first quarter, the four major Japanese firms (Nomura, Daiwa, Nikko, and Yamaichi) all ranked among the top lead underwriters of corporate Eurobond issues. All are trying to use Euroyen bond issues (yen-denominated bonds sold outside Japan) to gain entrée to U.S. clients, and have reportedly been willing to make deals at little or no profit to obtain experience and increase their visibility. At the same time, however, American investment firms have been opening and expanding branches in Tokyo, because Japan has become the world's biggest capital exporter.

Finally, investment banks face increasing competition from their own clients. The size and quality of financial staffs in large American corporations have increased in recent years, until they are able to deal with investment bankers as equals, and some have started "in-house" services to replace those previously performed by intermediaries. Several issue their own commercial paper, some have formed credit subsidiaries to generate leveraged lease opportunities, others are making direct private placements, both in the United States and Europe, and at least one has created an employee money market fund. These trends may be expected to continue.

MERGERS. Over the last decade a large number of well-known investment firms have disappeared as independent entities, as a result of mergers within the industry and acquisitions of investment banks by nonbanks. Intraindustry mergers have been motivated by a need for capital in an increasingly capital-intensive business and by a desire to go "full service," by acquiring firms with complementary product lines (thus, Becker Paribas sold to Merrill Lynch to overcome capital problems, and Merrill wanted Becker's commercial paper operation). Also, regional firms have been absorbed by larger firms wishing to achieve or increase nationwide market penetration.

The need for capital and the increasing globalization of markets have led most observers to predict an industry that will eventually resemble the accounting profession, with a small number of very large fully integrated firms, with worldwide operations but a sizable number of smaller specialist and regional firms. Capital requirements also suggest the eventual demise of the partnership form, which still exists in a few large firms. (Capital may be the weakness of British merchant banks. Nomura, for example, has more capital than the 10 largest U.K. firms.)

We have also seen the acquisition of a few **retail-oriented investment firms** by giant nonbanks—Sears, Prudential, and American Express—in an apparent attempt to dominate personal financial services in the same way a few investment banks expect to dominate corporate services. It is too early to tell whether this is a successful trend, because the prices paid and results obtained do not yet suggest a very high return on the investment.

One difficulty with all mergers is the fact that investment banking is a "people" business, in which long-run success is built not on a product or a technology but on ability to attract and hold first-class people. Job-hopping is endemic on Wall Street and firms have been able to enter new lines of business (e.g., trading mortgage-backed securities) virtually overnight by hiring experts away from rival firms. It is this flexibility, however, which suggests that investment banks will be able to cope with an uncertain future.

BIBLIOGRAPHY

Carosso, Vincent P., *Investment Banking in America: A History,* Cambridge, MA: Harvard University Press, 1970.

Friend, Irwin, *Investment Banking and The New Issues Market,* Securities Research Unit, Wharton School of Finance and Commerce, University of Pennsylvania, 1965.

Hayes, Samuel L., III, "Investment Banking: Power Structure in Flux," *Harvard Business Review* (March–April 1971): 136–152.

Hayes, Samuel L., III, "The Transformation of Investment Banking," *Harvard Business Review* (January–February 1979): 153–170.

Hayes, Samuel L., III, Spence, A. Michael, and Marks, David V.P., *Competition in The Investment Banking Industry,* Cambridge, MA: Harvard University Press, 1983.

Hoffman, Paul, *The Dealmakers,* Garden City, NY: Doubleday, 1984.

Park, Yoon S., *The Eurobond Market,* New York: Praeger, 1974.

Twentieth Century Fund, *Abuse on Wall Street,* Westport, CT: Quorum Books, 1980.

Walter, Ingo, *Deregulating Wall Street,* New York: Wiley, 1985.

Williamson, Peter, *The Investment Banking Handbook,* New York: Wiley forthcoming, 1987.

Wyser-Pratte, Guy, *Risk Arbitrage II,* Monograph Series in Finance and Economics, Graduate School of Business, New York University, 1982.

15

SAVINGS INSTITUTIONS

CONTENTS

15

SAVINGS INSTITUTIONS

James W. Christian

INTRODUCTION

Savings and loan associations, mutual savings banks, and **credit unions** are known collectively as thrift, or **savings, institutions.** Together with commercial banks, these institutions comprise the intermediaries of the U.S. financial system.

Savings institutions trace their roots to the household sector when, in the early 1800s, small groups of wage earners, craftsmen, and shopkeepers began to form mutual, self-help societies to further certain common aims of their members. In the case of savings and loan associations, that common aim was to build and finance homes for their members. For mutual savings banks, the primary object was pooling the savings of their members to secure a favorable investment return and, for credit unions, it was to provide credit to farmers and workers at reasonable costs.

Historically, these institutions were specialized by choice; the purpose for which they were founded remained the purpose for which they continued to operate. The collapse of the financial structure during the Great Depression of the 1930s, however, introduced a regulatory framework which, until recently, essentially locked financial institutions in general and savings institutions in particular into their traditional lines of activity and severely restrained their ability to follow an evolving household market. Nonregulated financial service firms were free to invade this market, significantly increasing the level of competition.

The passage of the Depository Institutions Deregulation and Monetary Control Act of 1980 and the Depository Institutions Act of 1982, together with a number of regulatory actions, granted savings institutions new asset and liability powers which, in time, can be expected to change significantly the operating characteristics of these financial institutions.

Indeed, the traditional distinctions among savings institutions are blurring rapidly today, as savings and loan associations incorporate "federal savings bank" into their names and mutual savings banks change their charters to come under the supervision of the Federal Home Loan Bank Board. More and more financial institutions also identify themselves with the "financial services industry," including not only commercial banks and savings institutions, but also investment bankers, insurance companies, mortgage bankers, finance companies, and so forth.

Yet savings institutions are deeply rooted in the household sector and will find ample opportunity for diversification without venturing far from their traditional fields. As the following exhibits suggest, the extraordinary growth in the affluence of American households since the end of World War II has contributed substantially to the development of savings institutions.

Exhibit 1 shows the **growth of assets of savings institutions** compared with commercial banks since 1950. Savings and loan associations and credit unions display extremely high average annual (compound) rates of asset growth, outstripping the commercial bank asset growth rate even in the difficult days of the early 1980s. The total assets of savings institutions are, however, only about half those of commercial banks.

EXHIBIT 1 ASSETS OF DEPOSITORY INSTITUTIONS ($ BILLIONS)

Year	Commercial Banks	Savings and Loan Associations	Mutual Savings Banks	Credit Unions
1950	$ 168.9	$ 16.9	$ 22.4	$ 1.0
1955	210.7	37.7	31.3	2.7
1960	257.6	71.5	40.6	5.7
1965	377.3	129.6	58.2	10.6
1970	576.2	176.2	79.0	18.0
1975	964.9	338.2	121.1	38.0
1980	1703.7	630.7	171.6	71.6
1981	1808.7	663.8	175.6	77.7
1982	1972.2	706.0	174.2	88.8
1983	2093.8	836.6	193.5	104.3
1984	2273.8	1001.0	203.3	117.6
Average annual growth	8.20%	13.16%	6.91%	15.54%

Sources: Federal Home Loan Bank Board, Federal Reserve Board.

Exhibit 2 shows that savings institutions have made the most of their connection to the household sector in increasing their market share of **household financial assets.**

These data show how large the pool of household financial assets has become, reaching $6.6 trillion in 1984, and how households have altered the composition of their financial asset holdings over time. Savings institutions in general, and savings and loan associations in particular, secured substantial gains in their share of the household savings market during the postwar period.

This market share was eroded in the high interest rate period of the early 1980s, when savings and loan associations and mutual savings banks suffered a severe earnings squeeze at the same time that the money market mutual funds made significant inroads into their deposit bases. These events accelerated the pace of financial deregulation and introduced a variety of new asset and liability powers for these institutions to enable them to diversify their portfolios.

With the decline of interest rates in 1982, savings institutions began to recover profitability and, by 1984, had regained some of their share of the household savings market.

Exhibits 3 and 4 show the shares of depository institutions in the markets for the two major types of household debt—home mortgages and consumer credit.

The dominance of the **home mortgage market** by savings and loan associations is evident in Exhibit 3. Together with mutual savings banks, these institutions have held in portfolio approximately half of all outstanding home mortgages through most of the postwar period. That market share fell during the thrift institution crisis of the early 1980s, but returned to near its historical level with the decline in interest rates and the resumption of deposit inflows.

Credit unions have not been a factor in the home mortgage market. They specialize in the extension of **consumer credit,** as Exhibit 4 indicates.

With the smallest asset base among the depository institutions, credit unions have nevertheless captured a significant share of the consumer credit market. Commercial banks, of course, dominate, but the market share held by savings and loan associations has been increasing sharply in recent years, reflecting their use of new consumer lending powers granted under deregulation legislation.

The **trends** depicted in this introduction may or may not continue into the future because the financial sector of the United States is in its greatest ferment in at least the last 50 years. Financial deregulation has liberated the depository institutions, particularly savings institutions, to respond to the challenges of a financial services market that is changing at an extremely rapid pace. At the same time, new technologies in the delivery of financial services to the household sector are offering opportunities to nontraditional competitors of depository institutions.

Among those new technologies are the spread of electronic financial service delivery that, for some segments of the household market, will render branch offices virtually obsolete and open the market to new financial enterprises.

EXHIBIT 2 INCOME AND FINANCIAL ASSETS OF HOUSEHOLDS ($ BILLIONS AND PERCENT)

				Time and Savings Deposits									
Year	Disposable Personal Income	Total Financial Assets	Demand Deposits and Currency	Commercial Banks	All Savings Institutions	Savings and Loan Associations	Mutual Savings Banks	Credit Unions	Money Market Mutual Funds	Mutual Funds and Equities	Bonds	Life Insurance	Pension Funds
1952	$ 237.7	$ 521.2	12.0%	7.0%	8.3%	3.7%	4.3%	0.3%	—	32.7%	16.4%	11.6%	6.3%
1953	252.2	534.7	11.9	7.3	9.1	4.3	4.5	0.3	—	30.4	16.4	11.9	7.0
1954	257.1	627.9	10.4	6.6	8.8	4.3	4.2	0.3	—	37.4	14.0	10.6	6.8
1955	275.0	707.7	9.3	6.1	8.8	4.5	4.0	0.3	—	40.4	13.3	9.8	7.1
1956	292.9	754.0	9.0	6.0	9.3	4.9	4.0	0.4	—	40.5	13.2	9.6	7.5
1957	308.6	741.5	9.0	6.8	10.3	5.6	4.2	0.5	—	36.1	13.8	10.2	8.4
1958	319.0	878.3	7.8	6.3	9.6	5.4	3.8	0.4	—	42.5	11.5	8.9	8.3
1959	338.4	946.5	7.6	6.2	9.8	5.7	3.6	0.5	—	42.5	11.8	8.7	8.7
1960	352.0	973.2	7.5	6.3	10.5	6.3	3.7	0.5	—	40.6	11.8	8.8	9.3
1961	365.8	1116.8	6.4	6.1	10.2	6.3	3.4	0.5	—	44.8	10.4	7.9	9.3
1962	386.8	1092.3	6.5	7.4	11.7	7.3	3.8	0.6	—	40.0	10.7	8.5	10.0
1963	405.9	1221.3	6.2	7.5	11.7	7.5	3.6	0.6	—	42.1	9.6	7.9	10.0
1964	440.6	1331.7	6.1	7.6	12.0	7.7	3.7	0.6	—	42.4	9.1	7.6	10.4
1965	475.8	1466.4	6.0	7.9	11.7	7.5	3.6	0.6	—	43.3	8.6	7.2	10.4
1966	513.7	1459.1	6.2	8.7	12.4	7.9	3.8	0.7	—	39.4	9.5	7.6	11.3
1967	547.9	1685.7	6.0	8.6	11.7	7.4	3.6	0.7	—	42.7	8.4	6.8	11.0
1968	593.4	1910.8	5.9	8.5	11.1	7.0	3.4	0.7	—	44.9	7.9	6.3	10.9
1969	638.9	1860.4	5.9	8.9	11.6	7.3	3.6	0.7	—	40.1	9.8	6.7	11.8

1970	695.3	1926.3	6.1	9.6	12.4	7.8	3.8	0.8	—	37.8	9.8	6.8	12.4
1971	751.8	2151.4	6.1	9.9	13.1	8.3	3.9	0.9	—	38.7	8.6	6.4	12.8
1972	810.3	2388.4	6.0	10.1	13.7	8.9	3.9	0.9	—	38.2	8.2	6.0	13.7
1973	914.5	2301.9	6.8	11.4	15.9	10.4	4.4	1.1	—	31.0	9.6	6.6	14.4
1974	998.3	2206.3	7.4	13.1	18.1	11.9	4.8	1.4	0.1%	22.9	11.6	7.2	14.7
1975	1096.1	2564.3	6.7	12.6	17.5	11.6	4.5	1.4	0.1	25.8	11.3	6.5	15.8
1976	1194.4	2905.3	6.4	12.8	17.4	11.7	4.3	1.4	0.1	26.6	10.8	6.0	16.1
1977	1314.0	3081.7	6.7	13.1	18.9	12.8	4.5	1.6	0.1	23.8	10.7	6.0	16.7
1978	1474.0	3375.9	6.8	12.8	19.4	13.3	4.4	1.7	0.3	22.2	10.7	5.9	17.6
1979	1650.2	3861.2	6.5	12.1	18.1	12.5	4.0	1.6	1.2	23.7	11.1	5.5	18.1
1980	1828.9	4540.5	5.7	11.7	16.8	11.6	3.6	1.6	1.6	26.9	10.3	4.9	18.9
1981	2041.7	4838.8	5.9	12.0	16.0	11.1	3.4	1.5	3.8	24.0	10.7	4.8	19.4
1982	2180.5	5384.4	5.7	12.5	14.8	10.3	3.0	1.5	3.8	24.6	10.6	4.6	20.9
1983	2340.1	6057.4	5.6	13.2	14.5	10.2	2.7	1.6	2.7	24.2	10.6	4.0	21.8
1984	2578.1	6608.5	5.8	13.4	14.9	11.0	2.7	1.2	3.2	22.6	10.0	3.8	21.7

Source: Federal Reserve Board, *Flow of Funds;* Department of Commerce, *National Income and Product Accounts.*

EXHIBIT 3 DEPOSITORY INSTITUTION SHARE OF HOME MORTGAGES OUTSTANDING[a] ($ BILLIONS AND PERCENT)

		Shares Held By			
Year	Home Mortgages	Savings and Loan Associations	Mutual Savings Banks	Credit Unions	Commercial Banks
1952	$ 56.1	31.3%	11.0%	0.2%	20.0%
1953	63.8	32.9	11.6	0.2	18.8
1954	72.4	34.5	12.4	0.2	18.4
1955	84.6	35.5	13.1	0.2	17.8
1956	95.8	35.5	13.6	0.2	17.0
1957	104.6	36.3	13.5	0.2	15.7
1958	113.4	37.8	13.8	0.3	15.5
1959	126.0	39.3	13.4	0.3	15.2
1960	137.4	39.4	15.0	0.3	14.0
1961	149.6	40.6	15.0	0.3	13.4
1962	163.7	41.4	15.1	0.3	13.5
1963	179.9	42.5	15.4	0.3	13.8
1964	197.4	43.0	15.6	0.3	13.8
1965	214.4	42.9	15.8	0.3	14.2
1966	228.5	42.1	15.6	0.3	14.4
1967	240.9	42.0	15.6	0.3	14.6
1968	257.7	41.8	15.3	0.3	15.1
1969	276.3	41.8	14.9	0.3	15.0
1970	290.4	42.0	14.5	0.3	14.6
1971	316.7	43.2	13.7	0.3	15.2
1972	358.0	45.7	13.1	0.3	15.9
1973	404.5	45.3	12.2	0.3	16.8
1974	442.3	45.0	11.1	0.3	16.9
1975	482.9	46.0	10.6	0.4	16.0
1976	544.3	47.4	10.0	0.5	15.8
1977	635.1	47.8	9.1	0.4	16.6
1978	746.5	46.9	8.5	0.5	17.3
1979	869.2	44.3	7.6	0.5	17.2
1980	967.5	43.2	7.1	0.5	16.6
1981	1051.0	40.5	6.6	0.5	16.2
1982	1096.9	37.2	5.8	0.5	15.8
1983	1200.1	36.1	6.2	0.5	15.1
1984	1347.0	42.2	5.5	0.5	14.7

[a] Data for savings and loan associations and mutual savings banks include mortgage-backed securities after 1972.

Source: Federal Reserve Board, *Flow of Funds.*

EXHIBIT 4 DEPOSITORY INSTITUTION SHARE OF CONSUMER CREDIT OUTSTANDING ($ BILLIONS AND PERCENT)

		Shares Held By			
Year	Consumer Credit	Savings and Loan Associations	Mutual Savings Banks	Credit Unions	Commercial Banks
1957	$ 52.2	1.9%	0.6%	4.6%	38.9%
1958	52.7	2.3	0.6	5.1	39.3
1959	60.7	2.3	0.5	5.4	39.9
1960	65.1	2.5	0.5	6.0	40.7
1961	67.6	2.7	0.7	6.4	41.1
1962	73.9	2.4	0.7	6.6	41.4
1963	82.8	2.5	0.6	6.6	41.9
1964	92.6	2.3	0.8	6.8	43.0
1965	103.2	2.2	0.8	7.1	43.8
1966	109.7	2.2	0.9	8.0	46.7
1967	115.4	2.2	0.9	7.8	44.8
1968	126.9	2.1	0.9	8.1	46.0
1969	137.7	2.4	1.0	9.5	50.0
1970	143.1	2.4	1.0	9.1	45.8
1971	157.8	2.3	1.0	9.4	47.1
1972	177.6	2.0	0.9	9.6	49.0
1973	203.7	3.2	0.9	9.6	48.9
1974	213.6	3.5	1.0	10.2	48.2
1975	223.2	3.7	1.0	11.5	47.5
1976	248.6	3.7	1.0	12.6	47.5
1977	289.1	3.7	1.1	13.0	48.5
1978	337.9	3.3	1.2	13.1	49.2
1979	383.4	3.8	1.0	12.1	48.6
1980	389.7	4.4	1.4	11.3	46.2
1981	416.4	4.3	1.3	11.0	44.2
1982	441.7	5.0	1.5	10.7	43.2
1983	493.0	6.0	1.7	10.8	43.4
1984	593.6	7.3	1.9	11.6	43.7

Source: Federal Reserve Board, *Flow of Funds.*

Other technologies broaden the number and variety of mortgage originators and investors through the secondary mortgage market.

Changes in organization through vertical and horizontal integration of previously separate and independent elements of the housing market and of the consumer market also promise to oblige all of the competitors in the financial services market to adapt, innovate, and reposition themselves in that market.

These new trends are unfolding today. Combined with an uncertain economic environment and the growing affluence and financial sophistication of

American households, the sector of the financial services market that has been dominated by savings institutions is likely to be subject to the greatest changes in structure, operating procedure, and portfolio composition.

In this section we will examine in more detail the operational characteristics of savings institutions and attempt to identify those changes in the legislative, regulatory, economic, and competitive environments that are likely to shape the future of these institutions.

SAVINGS AND LOAN ASSOCIATIONS

HISTORICAL PERSPECTIVE. **Savings and loan** associations are entering their third organizational and operational incarnation in the 1980s. Their first spanned the period from 1832, when the first building society was formed in the United States, to 1932, when the Federal Home Loan Bank System was established and savings and loan associations came under federal support and supervision. The second incarnation extended for approximately 50 years, from the 1930s to the early 1980s, and was characterized by regulated specialization. Although federal support and supervision continue today, the financial deregulation legislation of 1980 and 1982 ushered in a new era of savings and loan association operations.

During their first 100 years, savings and loan associations (often known as building and loan associations) operated primarily as mutual, self-help organizations following their British building society ancestors. Here, and in Britain, these societies were typically community-based organizations dedicated to the development and financing of homes for their members. They were, at first, self-liquidating societies that disbanded and ceased to exist as soon as the original members obtained a home. Later societies found that growing communities created the need for permanent home financing facilities.

As mutual societies, their members contributed savings capital and received dividends, rather than interest on deposits, as today's savings institution depositors do. Some societies actually contracted for the construction of homes for their members once sufficient capital had been accumulated (hence the term *building* society), but the more common practice was the provision of loans to members to build or buy the homes of their choice.

By 1920 the number of savings and loan associations operating in the United States had reached 8,633, with combined assets of $2.5 billion. (By contrast there were 23,695 commercial banks, with combined assets of $33.0 billion.) And on the eve of the Great Depression, the number of savings associations had risen to 12,342 and assets had grown to $8.7 billion.

Then came the Depression and the collapse of the financial system. During the 1930s, 1,700 savings and loan associations failed, roughly 14% of the total number in existence at the end of 1929. Losses to shareholders (depositors) of these failures during the 1930s amounted to just over $200 million, or 2.3% of total savings and loan association assets. Commercial banks suffered much more, their numbers dropping by 9,275, or 39% of the banks in business at the end of 1929.

These events inspired a variety of supportive federal responses. The Federal Home Loan Bank System was established in 1932 to provide a central credit facility, much like the Federal Reserve System, for savings and loan associations. A year later, the Home Owners Loan Corporation was set up to deal with the wave of home foreclosures that was imposing such great costs on borrowers and lenders alike. Also in 1933, Section 5 of the Home Owners Loan Act provided for federal chartering of savings and loan associations. Commercial bank depositors received the protection of the newly created Federal Deposit Insurance Corporation in 1933 and, in 1934, the Federal Savings and Loan Insurance Corporation was established to accord the same protection to savings and loan association shareholders.

Two further measures—the establishment of the Federal Housing Authority (FHA, in 1934) to ensure mortgages and the Federal National Mortgage Association (in 1938) to create a secondary market for FHA-insured mortgages—completed the federal institutional support structure around savings and loan associations and introduced a new era of supervised and regulated housing finance activity.

For the most part these actions were supportive and served to create a more sound and efficient financial system. Yet many of the regulations that accompanied them also rigidified the operational structure of savings and loan associations. For example, the Home Owners Loan Act prescribed the activities in which federally chartered savings and loan associations could engage, so that if savings associations sought to offer new products or to enter new lines of business, they were obliged to apply for the authority to do so, either from the Federal Home Loan Bank Board or through statutory amendment. Moreover, the mortgage insurance provided by the Federal Housing Authority applied only to fixed-rate, long-term, amortizing mortgages, which soon became the predominant home mortgage instrument.

Commercial banks, by contrast, found certain activities in which they had previously engaged proscribed by Depression-era legislation and regulation. Banks could no longer pay interest on demand deposits and the rates they were allowed to pay on savings deposits were limited under the Federal Reserve Board's Regulation Q. Certain securities transactions were also prohibited, but, in the main, commercial banks were allowed to engage in a wide variety of lending activities without having to seek specific statutory or regulatory authority to do so.

The asymmetry in operating authority between savings and loan associations and commercial banks posed no apparent problem for savings associations through the first 20 years of the postwar period. Although the total assets of the savings and loan business fell from $8.7 billion at the end of 1929 to $5.6 billion at the end of 1939, the prosperity of the war years revived savings association deposit inflows and, by 1945, savings association assets were back to their 1929 level of $8.7 billion. Thus as World War II came to a close, savings and loan associations were prepared to meet the wave of postwar housing demand. Because savings associations were naturally and historically specialized in housing finance, government regulation dictating that they do so had no binding effect.

The economic environment of the 1950s and 1960s was also benign. Interest rates were low and stable, long-term rates remained consistently above short-term rates, and the economy, together with personal income and employment, grew steadily, with only minor interruptions from mild recessions. Given these factors and strong demand for mortgage credit, savings and loan associations had little difficulty writing fixed-rate mortgages or in finding investment outlets for their savings capital.

Moreover, because savings and loan associations were not limited by government regulation as to the interest rates they could pay for deposits, whereas commercial banks were, savings associations consistently paid substantially higher rates for deposits through most of this period. As late in this period as 1960, savings associations paid an average of 130 basis points more for savings deposits than commercial banks.

Savings associations paid higher rates in part because, as mutual organizations, they were simply passing through earnings to their shareholders (depositors), in part because they paid little or no federal income tax until 1963 and in part because they could offer no financial services other than home financing and passbook accounts to their depositors and had to compete for deposits on price alone.

Under these circumstances, savings and loan associations grew rapidly during the 20 years spanning 1945 and 1965. From total assets of $8.7 billion in 1945, savings association assets grew to $129.6 billion in 1965, reflecting an average annual compound rate of growth of 14.5%.

Forces were set in motion in the 1960s, however, that began to change these favorable operating conditions. Higher federal income taxes were imposed on savings institutions; from an effective tax rate of less than 2% prior to 1963, savings associations paid an average effective tax rate of 15.7% between 1963 and 1970, putting them roughly on a par with commercial banks. The **Regulation Q** ceilings imposed on the rates commercial banks could pay on savings deposits were also gradually raised from a range of 1.0 to 2.5% in 1957 to a range of 4.0 to 5.5% in 1966. Higher federal taxes impaired the ability of savings associations to pay for deposits at the same time that commercial banks were allowed to pay more. These events precipitated a crisis in 1966, when savings associations suffered their first episode of deposit disintermediation of the postwar era—savings associations experienced a net outflow of deposits that brought to a close their "golden age of growth" and introduced a new "age of intervention."

To stabilize the competition for deposits between commercial banks and savings associations, Regulation Q controls were extended to savings and loan associations in 1966. Savings associations were permitted to pay a slightly higher rate—a "differential"—than commercial banks, primarily to keep funds flowing to the housing sector. That differential also recognized the fact that savings association asset and liability powers were distinctly limited relative to commercial banks and that individual depositors would require some premium to compensate for the inconvenience of maintaining at least two financial relationships. Specifically, a commercial banking relationship was necessary to obtain checking services, so that if commercial banks and savings associations paid the same rate of interest on savings deposits, there would be no compelling reason for an individual also to maintain an account with a savings and loan association.

Concurrently, evolving changes in economic policy significantly altered the savings association operating environment and made the legislative and regulatory limitations on savings and loan associations much more binding than they had been during the "golden age of growth."

From the end of World War II to the mid-1960s, federal budgets had been structured to achieve "cyclical-balance"—with budget deficits designed to appear in recessions and surpluses designed to appear in periods of excess aggregate demand and inflationary pressure. The role of monetary policy in maintaining economic growth and stability was, during this period, essentially one of maintaining orderly financial markets and assuring interest rate stability.

Although monetary policy had begun to play a more active role in stabilization efforts in the late 1950s, it was not until the late 1960s and 1970s, when federal budgets ceased to be cyclically balanced, that the burden for economic stabilization shifted strongly toward monetary policy.

The legislated linkage between the savings and loan business and housing, the most interest-sensitive sector of the economy, the Regulation Q controls on deposit interest, and the exclusive use of long-term, fixed-rate mortgages made it possible for monetary policy to bear this burden.

Under conditions of excess aggregate demand and inflationary pressure, the monetary authorities could induce a sufficient increase in open market interest rates to cause deposit disintermediation at savings and loan associations, reducing the funds available for home lending and driving up mortgage rates. Under long-term, fixed-rate mortgage lending, prospective home buyers would be reluctant to commit to "high" mortgage rates that could be expected to be lower in the future. Thus mortgage demand would fall and home building would sag, taking with it the demand for building materials, appliances, furniture and fixtures, and so on, such that aggregate demand would weaken.

Under recessionary conditions, the whole process would be reversed. The monetary authorities would drive open market rates down, savings associations would experience net deposit inflows, mortgage rates would fall, home buyers would rush to lock in "low" fixed-rate mortgage credit, home building would surge, together with the industries to which housing is so closely linked, and aggregate demand would strengthen.

This policy produced extraordinary housing cycles during the 1970s that had deleterious effects on the housing sector. In an attempt to deal with this problem, a short-term (6-month maturity) certificate of deposit was authorized for banks and savings institutions in mid-1978. This certificate, known as the **Money-Market Certificate,** was still governed by Regulation Q ceilings, but offered a rate pegged to the 6-month Treasury bill. The intent of the authorization of this new certificate was to allow savings associations to prevent disintermediation and thereby to maintain the flow of mortgage credit to housing when market interest rates rose.

Such a deposit instrument, of course, seriously undermined the ability of monetary policy to stabilize the economy by stimulating and depressing the housing sector and within 15 months of the authorization of the Money Market Certificate, the monetary policy that featured interest rate management had to be abandoned and a new policy introduced.

The timing of the authorization of the Money Market Certificate was unfortunate because it came at a time when the worst inflation experienced by the United States in the twentieth century was gaining momentum. This inflation, largely inspired by the oil price increases imposed by an international cartel of oil producers (the Organization of Petroleum Exporting Countries), sent interest rates to extremely high levels and produced expectations of future inflation that drove households in two directions—toward tangible assets such as housing and toward short-term financial assets that offered money market yields. Savings associations experienced a massive shift of lower-cost and longer-term deposits into the new Money Market Certificate, effectively raising their cost of funds. These funds were necessarily directed into a strengthening housing market, but at fixed rates that could not adjust upward as market rates were driven higher and higher by the tide of inflation. Operating spreads and profits were consequently squeezed.

Concurrently, new competition appeared on the scene in the form of **Money Market Mutual Funds.** Although these mutual funds lacked the federal insurance provided by federal agencies, they offered yields that floated with money market interest rates and immediate liquidity. Consequently, the Money Market Mutual Funds rapidly gained favor with interest-sensitive depositors of savings associations and commercial banks. Against this new, essentially unregulated competition, even the Money Market Certificate could not maintain strong deposit inflows.

These events set the stage for the passage of the Depository Institutions Deregulation and Monetary Control Act of 1980, which provided for the phase-out of Regulation Q deposit interest rate controls under the supervision of the Depository Institution Deregulation Committee, authorized nationwide checking (**Negotiated Order of Withdrawal**) accounts for savings institutions and conferrerd a few new asset powers such as consumer lending authority on savings associations. The Act also increased service corporation investment authority and preempted state usury laws, a measure that offered some relief for the earnings problems being experienced by savings associations. The Act did not, however, address the problems of fixed-rate mortgage lending or of the

Money Market Mutual Funds. Nevertheless, the Act initiated the process of financial deregulation and brought to a close the "age of intervention."

Regulatory action by the Federal Home Loan Bank Board in 1981 permitted savings associations to write adjustable rate mortgages with few restrictions, but with interest rates at extremely high levels and the housing market almost moribund, little use was made of this new authority until 1983, when interest rates at last fell and the housing market revived.

The problem of the Money Market Mutual Funds was dealt with in the Depository Institutions Act of 1982 through the authorization of a **Money Market Deposit Account** free of interest rate limitations. The account was an immediate success, returning in just 5 months the total net outflow of savings experienced by savings associations over the preceding 21 months.

The Depository Institutions Act of 1982 also provided limited commercial lending authority to savings and loan associations, authorized the issuance by savings associations of demand deposit accounts to their commercial loan customers, and allowed depository institutions to offer limited service stock brokerage services to their customers.

Savings and loan associations were thereby granted asset and liability powers that would enable them to reposition themselves in the financial services market, thus inaugurating a new, deregulated era of savings association operations.

The character of this new era is unfolding in the 1980s. The early evidence indicates that, armed with flexible mortgage and deposit powers, savings and loan associations will, where their individual markets provide profitable opportunities, remain specialized in housing finance by choice, rather than by legislative or regulatory mandate, and will use their new consumer and commercial lending authorities mainly as means to enhance and stabilize their earnings.

Savings associations have paid a very high price for this new freedom. The number of associations was reduced by more than a thousand, from 4,684 at the end of 1979 to 3,391 at the end of 1984. Moreover, the net worth of savings associations fell from 5.6% of total assets in 1979 to only 3.9% of total assets in 1984.

As mutual associations, **net worth** is built strictly through the retention of earnings. Although earnings have improved in 1983 and 1984 after the net loss years of 1981 and 1982, which so depleted net worth positions, profit margins of savings associations still burdened with fixed-rate mortgage portfolios whose yields are not yet equal to the cost of funds are increasingly converting from the mutual form to stock charter in order to obtain the necessary infusion of capital to take advantage of their new asset and liability powers. To a significant extent, therefore, the ability of savings associations to reposition themselves and keep pace with a rapidly evolving financial services market will depend upon their ability to improve their net worth positions.

The data that follow provide a more detailed picture of savings and loan association operations.

FORM OF ORGANIZATION. **Mutual ownership** is the traditional and still predominant form of organization for savings and loan associations. Yet **stock ownership** is growing rapidly, for reasons indicated earlier. In 1984, 27.7% of savings associations, representing 54.6% of the total assets of the business, were stock associations, up substantially from the 17.2% of associations and 25.3% of total assets in 1979 (Exhibit 5).

Currently and traditionally, the majority of savings and loan associations hold state charters (56.4%), rather than federal charters. But the vast majority (86.6%) are insured by the **Federal Savings and Loan Insurance Corporation.** Through this relationship and their relationship with their district Federal Home Loan Banks, savings associations are subject to federal examination and supervision. All federally chartered associations are insured by the Federal Savings and Loan Insurance Corporation (Exhibit 6).

Although the majority of associations are state-chartered, federally chartered associations have gained a growing proportion of the total assets of the savings and loan business (50.1% in 1950, 58.5% in 1984) (Exhibit 7).

ASSET SIZE DISTRIBUTION. The average size of savings associations has increased substantially over time, rising from $2.8 million in 1950 to $266.1 million in 1984. The distribution of associations by asset size has also changed significantly, with larger associations increasing their share of the total assets of the savings and loan business. To a significant extent, the recent changes in the asset size distribution among savings and loan associations have been the result of mergers and acquisitions arising from earnings difficulties during the extremely high interest rate period of 1981 and 1982.

Note particularly that associations with assets in excess of a billion dollars accounted for only 4.6% of all associations at year-end 1984, but for more than half (52.6%) of the assets of the savings and loan business (Exhibit 8).

EXHIBIT 5 MUTUAL AND STOCK ASSOCIATIONS (ASSETS IN BILLIONS OF DOLLARS)

	Total Associations		Mutual Associations		Stock Associations	
Year	Number	Assets	Number	Assets	Number	Assets
1975	4,931	$338.2	4,214	$317.3	717	$ 70.6
1976	4,821	391.9	4,085	305.1	736	86.8
1977	4,761	459.2	4,012	352.0	749	107.2
1978	4,725	523.5	3,945	398.5	780	125.0
1979	4,709	579.3	3,901	432.3	808	147.0
1980	4,613	629.8	3,752	456.5	861	173.3
1981	4,292	664.2	3,422	469.9	870	194.3
1982	3,825	707.6	2,995	487.9	830	219.7
1983	3,502	773.4	2,677	444.7	836	327.0
1984	3,391	902.5	2,451	409.7	940	492.8

Source: U.S. League of Savings Institutions.

EXHIBIT 6 NUMBER OF SAVINGS ASSOCIATIONS BY TYPE OF CHARTER

				State-Chartered	
Year	Total Associations	Federal Charter	State Charter	FSLIC Insured	Noninsured and State Insured
1950	5,992	1,526	4,466	1,344	3,132
1955	6,071	1,683	4,388	1,861	2,527
1960	6,320	1,873	4,447	2,225	2,222
1965	6,185	2,011	4,174	2,497	1,677
1970	5,669	2,067	3,602	2,298	1,304
1975	4,931	2,048	2,883	2,030	853
1976	4,821	2,019	2,802	2,025	777
1977	4,761	2,012	2,749	2,053	696
1978	4,725	2,000	2,725	2,053	672
1979	4,709	1,989	2,720	2,050	670
1980	4,613	1,985	2,628	2,017	611
1981	4,292	1,907	2,385	1,872	513
1982	3,825	1,727	2,098	1,616	482
1983	3,502	1,553	1,949	1,487	462
1984	3,391	1,478	1,913	1,460	453

Sources: Federal Home Loan Bank Board; U.S. League of Savings Institutions.

EXHIBIT 7 ASSETS OF SAVINGS ASSOCIATIONS BY TYPE OF CHARTER ($ BILLIONS)

				State-Chartered	
Year	Total Associations	Federal Charter	State Charter	FSLIC Insured	Noninsured and State Insured
1950	$ 16.9	$ 8.4	$ 8.4	$ 5.2	$ 3.2
1955	37.6	20.0	17.6	14.2	3.4
1960	71.5	38.5	33.0	28.9	4.0
1965	129.6	66.7	62.9	57.9	5.5
1970	176.2	96.2	79.9	74.4	5.5
1975	338.2	195.4	142.8	134.8	8.0
1976	391.9	225.8	166.1	157.4	8.7
1977	459.2	261.9	197.3	188.1	9.2
1978	523.5	298.2	225.3	215.1	10.2
1979	579.3	323.0	256.2	245.0	11.2
1980	629.8	348.5	281.4	270.0	11.4
1981	664.2	407.4	256.8	243.7	13.1
1982	707.6	483.9	223.7	208.8	15.0
1983	773.4	499.2	274.2	255.0	19.2
1984	902.5	528.1	374.3	351.9	22.5

Sources: Federal Home Loan Bank Board; U.S. League of Savings Institutions.

EXHIBIT 8 DISTRIBUTION OF SAVINGS ASSOCIATIONS BY ASSET SIZE

	1979				1984			
Assets ($ millions)	Number of Assns.	Percent	Assets	Percent	Number of Assns.	Percent	Assets	Percent
Under $1	234	5.0	$ 108	NA	70	2.1	$ 35	NA
$1– $5	279	5.9	790	0.1	130	3.8	370	NA
$5– $10	318	6.8	2,447	0.4	135	4.0	1,067	0.1
$10– $25	851	18.1	15,225	2.6	422	12.4	7,385	0.8
$25– $50	957	20.3	36,466	6.3	600	17.7	22,586	2.5
$50– $100	870	18.5	64,414	11.1	671	19.8	49,644	5.5
$100– $150	406	8.6	51,814	8.9	376	11.1	47,423	5.3
$150– $250	347	7.4	69,402	12.0	356	10.5	71,312	7.9
$250– $500	250	5.3	85,525	14.8	302	8.9	105,450	11.7
$500–$1,000	113	2.4	78,580	13.6	173	5.1	122,882	13.6
Over $1,000	84	1.8	174,536	30.1	156	4.6	474,295	52.6

Sources: Federal Home Loan Bank Board; U.S. League of Savings Institutions.

ASSET AND LIABILITY STRUCTURE. Major changes in the asset and liability structure of savings associations have been made since 1979. Particularly evident is the trend toward the securitization of mortgages. From a relatively small 3.5% of assets held in insured mortgages and mortgage-backed securities in 1979, these assets increased to 11.1% of assets in 1984. Concurrently, holdings of whole loans fell from 82.1% of portfolio in 1979 to 61.2% in 1984. Also significant is the increase in **consumer loans** from a mere 0.3% of assets in 1979 to 1.9% of assets in 1984 (Exhibit 9).

In recognition of the increase in economic uncertainty and interest rate volatility that has characterized the early 1980s, savings associations increased their liquidity from 6.9% of assets in 1979 to 10.2% in 1984.

Savings associations also increased their service corporation investment sharply, from 0.4% of assets in 1979 to 1.7% in 1984 in order to take advantage of the broad investment authority of these subsidiaries.

On the liability side of the portfolio, savings associations continued to rely on retail time and savings deposits as their major source of funds; more than 80% of **liabilities** in both 1979 and 1984 are shown as time and savings deposits. The balance sheet, however, conceals major changes in the composition of these deposits inspired by financial deregulation and by the need to manage assets and liabilities to match maturities (or the frequency of interest rate adjustments) more closely to reduce interest rate risk.

Savings Deposits. With the removal of interest rate controls by the Depository Institutions Deregulation Committee, depository institutions became free to fashion deposit accounts that conform, in terms of rate, maturity, and other features, to their perception of what their market desires rather than to offer only those types of accounts prescribed by regulation. Thus although savings associations have continued to rely heavily on retail deposits as their primary

EXHIBIT 9 CONDENSED STATEMENT OF CONDITION OF FSLIC-INSURED INSTITUTIONS[a] ($ MILLIONS)

	1979		1983		1984	
	Amount	Percent	Amount	Percent	Amount	Percent
Assets						
Mortgage loans outstanding	$479,797	82.1	$521,308	63.6	$599,021	61.2
Insured mortgages and mortgage-backed securities	20,507	3.5	90,902	11.1	108,219	11.1
Mobile home loans	2,190	0.4	3,857	0.5	5,284	0.5
Home improvement loans	4,484	0.8	5,490	0.7	5,583	0.6
Loans on savings accounts	6,135	1.1	3,195	0.4	3,914	0.4
Education loans	898	0.2	2,465	0.3	3,768	0.4
Other consumer loans	1,576	0.3	14,091	1.7	18,379	1.9
Cash and investments eligible for liquidity	39,825	6.9	84,958	10.4	99,924	10.2
Other investments	6,716	1.2	24,965	3.0	35,716	3.7
Investment in service corporations	2,085	0.4	8,196	1.0	16,988	1.7
Federal Home Loan Bank stock	4,900	0.8	6,100	0.7	6,200	0.6
Building and equipment	7,583	1.3	11,347	1.4	12,855	1.3
Real estate owned	1,510	0.3	6,800	0.8	10,100	1.0
All other assets	5,101	0.9	35,494	4.3	52,563	5.4
Total Assets	$579,307		$819,168		$978,514	
Liabilities and Net Worth						
Time and savings deposits	$470,171	81.2	$671,057	81.9	$784,724	80.2
Federal Home Loan Bank advances	40,441	7.0	57,253	7.0	71,719	7.3
Other borrowings	14,934	2.6	41,258	5.0	65,404	6.7
All other liabilities	21,195	3.7	16,620	2.0	18,746	1.9
Net worth	32,566	5.6	32,980	4.0	37,921	3.9
Total Liabilities and Net Worth	$579,307		$819,168		$978,514	

[a] Includes FSLIC-insured savings banks.

Sources: Federal Home Loan Bank Board; U.S. League of Savings Institutions.

source of funds, the character and composition of those deposits have changed significantly since 1979.

In the early phases of deregulation, changes in the composition of savings association deposits were the result of external forces; recently, those changes are much more the result of conscious asset-liability management decisions.

Until 1965 savings associations were authorized to offer only passbook savings. Beginning in 1965, however, regulatory authority was granted for the issuance of time **certificates of deposit, or CDs.** Although savings associations had not experienced a net outflow of deposits (disintermediation) during the postwar period, up to that time, commercial banks were successful in expanding their retail deposit base by issuing small-denomination CDs and the concern arose that these new deposit instruments might serve to channel funds away from housing. Indeed, the appeal of the commercial bank CDs is offered as a primary explanation for the disintermediation that savings associations experienced in 1966; CD authority for savings associations came too late.

Once the retail savings market had been stabilized by the extension of Regulation Q interest rate ceilings to savings associations and to the small-denomination CDs of both types of depository institutions, new certificates, generally with longer maturities, were authorized from time to time through the 1970s.

These longer-maturity certificates, bearing comparatively high interest rates, were both successful in attracting funds and in improving the match between the maturities of savings associations' assets and liabilities. A 2-year certificate was authorized in 1970, a 4-year certificate in 1973, a 6-year certificate in 1974, and an 8-year certificate in 1978, which carried an 8% ceiling rate. At year-end 1977, prior to the June 1978, authorization of the 6-month **money market certificate (MMC),** CDs accounted for 62.1% of savings association deposits, up from 11.7% in 1966.

Caught on a tide of rising interest rates, the 6-month MMC was an instant success, even though it required a $10,000 minimum deposit. Many depositors paid the early withdrawal penalties on their longer-term certificates in order to invest in the MMC. In the first 7 months of its existence, MMC balances at savings associations grew to $42.8 billion, of which roughly $17 billion (40%) represented shifts from existing passbook and certificate accounts. During the second half of 1978, the MMC, whose ceiling rate varied weekly with the auction rate on the 6-month Treasury bill, paid roughly the same rate as the 8-year certificate and by year-end 1978, was paying almost two percentage points more than the 8-year CD.

Savings associations thus suffered a shortening of the maturity structure of their liabilities at the same time that they began to experience a significant increase in their cost of funds. More bad news was also on the way.

Money market mutual funds (MMMFs) first offered in 1974 by securities dealers for their customers, began to attract the attention of nonbrokerage customers. The MMMFs offered both money market yields that changed daily and immediate liquidity through a checking privilege. Although principal balances were not insured, as the MMC was, SEC regulations did require that the funds be invested in short-term, highly liquid assets. At year-end 1978, only about $10 billion of household financial assets were invested in MMMFs, but those balances grew extremely rapidly to $45 billion in 1979, $74 billion in 1980, $182 billion in 1981 and, finally, to a peak of $206 billion at year-end 1982.

The deposit balances of savings associations were major casualties of the success of the MMMFs. With the passage of the Depository Institutions Act of 1982, which directed the Depository Institutions Deregulation Committee (DIDC) to authorize an insured account for depository institutions that would compete directly with the MMMFs, the explosive growth of the MMMFs came to an end. The new account created by the DIDC was the **money market deposit account,** which had a low minimum balance ($2,500) requirement and offered limited checking privileges. Within 5 months of the December 1982 authorization of the MMDA, savings associations had recaptured all the net savings outflows of the preceding 21 months.

In many respects, however, savings institutions faced an embarrassment of riches. By the end of 1983, $124.6 billion (17% of total deposits) had flowed into the MMDA account, significantly shortening the average maturity of association liabilities at a time when longer-term deposits might have been more welcome.

Fortunately for savings associations, regulatory changes had been made by the Federal Home Loan Bank Board in 1981 to authorize **adjustable rate mortgages (ARMs)** nationwide with very few restrictions. It was not until 1983, however, that the general level of interest rates declined sufficiently to revive mortgage demand. During 1983 and 1984, savings associations used a substantial portion of their MMDA balances to fund ARMs, thereby shortening the maturity structure (or rate adjustment frequency) of their assets to bring them into better balance with their liabilities.

During 1984 savings associations used their new freedom from deposit rate ceilings to adjust interest rates across the whole spectrum of their deposit liabilities to increase the proportion of longer-term deposits. As a consequence MMDA balances declined slightly as savings associations bid less aggressively for them. Similarly, because most associations were offering ARMs with 1-year interest rate adjustment frequencies, savings associations priced their deposits to increase the proportion of 1-year certificates, allowing 6-month certificate balances to decline relatively.

The success of these measures was evident by the end of 1984, as Exhibit 10 illustrates. Deposits with original maturity greater than 6 months increased from 36% of deposit liabilities in 1983 to almost 40% in 1984.

Mortgage Lending. Savings and loan associations remain the largest originators and holders of **home mortgages** in the United States. Savings associations have increased their market share of originations, even as their share of mortgage loans held has declined in recent years (See Exhibits 3 and 11).

Although savings associations continue to originate the lion's share of total

EXHIBIT 10 DEPOSIT STRUCTURE OF FSLIC-INSURED SAVINGS INSTITUTIONS[a] ($ BILLIONS)

						Small Denomination CDs										
Year	Total	MMDA	Super NOW	NOW and Passbook	Large Denomination CDs	Subtotal	6-Month MMCs	2½ Year SSCs	Other	7–31 Days	32–91 Days	92–182 Days	183 Days–1 Year	Over 1 Year Less than 2½ Years	2½ Years or More	Other
1970	$141.8			$ 84.2		$ 57.6			$ 57.6							
1971	169.0			92.3		76.7			76.7							
1972	201.0			101.6		99.3			99.3							
1973	220.9			103.2		117.7			117.7							
1974	236.7			104.4		132.3			132.3							
1975	278.8			119.0		159.7			159.7							
1976	328.2			132.4	$ 7.6	189.0			189.0							
1977	378.8			143.7	9.0	226.1			226.1							
1978	422.2			134.8	14.3	272.9	$ 43.9		229.0							
1979	460.7			116.5	27.4	316.8	127.8		189.0							
1980	501.2			105.1	40.0	356.1	184.2	$ 49.8	122.1							
1981	513.8			99.8	47.6	366.4	183.7	96.2	86.5							
1982	554.6	$ 33.6		94.0	55.8	371.1	161.8	134.8	74.5							
1983	724.2	124.6	$8.1	115.7	84.1	417.4				$3.8	$ 4.0	$139.6	$22.2	$44.8	$191.5	$11.4
1984	864.3	121.4	9.5	88.9	122.6	521.9				4.2	11.5	149.0	86.2	76.2	178.0	16.8

[a] Includes FSLIC-insured savings banks after 1982; distribution of savings bank deposits among accounts estimated to be the same as the distribution of savings and loan association accounts.

Source: Federal Home Loan Bank Board.

EXHIBIT 11 MORTGAGE LOAN ORIGINATIONS ($ BILLIONS)

Year	Total Loans Originated	Originated by Savings Associations	Share of Originations
1970	$ 44.4	$ 21.4	48.2%
1971	70.2	39.4	56.1
1972	91.3	51.4	56.3
1973	93.1	49.4	53.1
1974	79.8	39.0	48.9
1975	88.6	55.0	62.1
1976	125.1	78.8	63.0
1977	177.8	107.4	60.4
1978	201.4	108.3	53.8
1979	202.4	98.7	48.8
1980	146.3	71.3	48.7
1981	110.2	52.3	47.5
1982	106.2	53.4	50.3
1983	221.6	138.2	62.4
1984	225.5	165.2	73.3

Source: Federal Home Loan Bank Board, Washington, D.C., 1985.

mortgage loans, the composition of those loans has been changing. These changes reflect both changes in the composition of mortgage loan demand and the efforts of savings associations to restructure their asset portfolios (Exhibit 12).

Originations of ARMs increased dramatically in 1983 and 1984 with the return of mortgage demand following the general decline in interest rates in late 1982. In 1983, ARMs represented approximately 39% of all mortgage loans originated by savings associations. That proportion increased in 1984 to approximately 60%.

Most ARMs are held in portfolio by savings associations, although sales and purchases do occur between associations outside the formalized channels of the secondary mortgage market.

The decline in market share of loans held in portfolio is the result of several factors. First, the development of new secondary mortgage market techniques has broadened the market for nontraditional mortgage investors.

Second, some of the decline in the share of mortgage loans held by savings associations is due to accounting adjustments in the value of the mortgages held by associations. For example, in restructuring their portfolios of old, fixed-rate mortgages, many savings associations have **"swapped" mortgages,** discounted to market value, for **Federal Home Loan Mortgage Corporation Participation Certificates (PCs).** The mortgages being "swapped" leave the portfolio at face value and return to the portfolio as PCs at their discounted value, thus reducing the reported amount of loans outstanding.

Third, savings associations have sold outright a substantial volume of **fixed-**

EXHIBIT 12 COMPOSITION OF MORTGAGE LOANS CLOSED BY SAVINGS ASSOCIATIONS ($ BILLIONS)

	1978	1979	1980	1981	1982	1983	1984
Construction loans							
1–4 units	$ 19.8	$18.3	$13.3	$10.1	$ 9.0	$ 18.6	$ 19.4
5 & more units	2.3	2.0	1.4	1.3	2.6	7.9	7.4
Other	2.2	2.1	2.0	2.3	4.4	12.2	17.0
Subtotal	24.3	22.4	16.7	13.7	16.0	38.7	43.8
Purchase loans							
New 1 family	17.5	17.6	13.8	11.0	7.2	12.4	15.5
Existing 1-family	43.4	38.9	25.7	15.1	12.1	36.8	44.6
2–4 units	3.4	3.1	1.7	0.9	0.7	2.3	3.2
5 & more units	2.7	1.9	1.0	0.7	1.3	3.9	6.7
Other improved real estate	1.7	1.4	1.3	1.2	2.0	5.9	9.0
Subtotal	68.7	62.9	43.5	28.9	23.3	61.3	79.0
Refinancings	10.7	9.2	7.6	5.6	7.6	25.2	26.2
Other mortgage loans	4.5	4.1	3.6	4.1	6.3	7.4	7.8
Total loans closed	108.2	98.6	71.4	52.3	53.2	132.6	156.8

Source: Federal Home Loan Bank Board.

rate loans in the interest of portfolio restructuring. The proceeds of these loan sales were then used to originate ARMs and to diversify the associations' asset portfolios (Exhibit 13).

Broader participation in the secondary mortgage market is another way in which savings associations are increasing their portfolio flexibility. Indeed, developments in the secondary mortgage market are, in many ways, as important to the asset side of savings association operations as financial deregulation is to the liability side.

Secondary Mortgage Market. As noted earlier, the **Federal National Mortgage Association (FNMA,** also known as **Fannie Mae)** was established in 1938, in part as means of encouraging the origination of FHA-insured, long-term, fixed-rate, amortizing mortgages to replace the short-term loans commonly used for home financing prior to the Depression of the 1930s.

The FNMA was also conceived in theory as a means of improving the liquidity of home mortgages and of regionally distributing mortgage credit. For example, at times when some areas of the country might be experiencing heavy loan demand and others weak loan demand, loans could be originated and sold

EXHIBIT 13 MORTGAGE PORTFOLIO OF SAVINGS ASSOCIATIONS BY TYPE OF PROPERTY

Type of Property	1978	1979	1980	1981	1982	1983	1984
				Amount ($ Billions)			
Single-family	$325.3	$360.9	$393.9	$397.7	$375.0	$398.5	431.1
2–4 family	21.1	23.4	24.2	24.6	23.4	24.0	
Multifamily	34.9	36.4	36.9	36.5	39.3	51.0	48.3
Commercial	36.2	38.8	40.1	42.2	46.8	64.6	75.8
Other	6.1	7.0	7.5	8.3	10.1	16.4	
Total	423.5	466.5	492.7	509.4	494.6	554.6	555.2
				Percent Distribution			
Single-family	76.8%	77.4%	80.0%	78.1%	75.8%	71.9%	77.6
2–4 family	5.0	5.0	4.9	4.8	4.7	4.3	
Multifamily	8.2	7.8	7.5	7.2	8.0	9.2	8.7
Commercial	8.6	8.3	8.1	8.3	9.5	11.7	13.6
Other	1.4	1.5	1.5	1.6	2.0	3.0	

Source: Federal Home Loan Bank Board, *Combined Financial Statements of FSLIC-Insured Institutions,* 1983.

to FNMA. The FNMA would then resell those loans to investors in areas experiencing weak loan demand. Should loan demand be heavy all over the nation, FNMA would buy loans for its portfolio, financing them through the issuance of its own securities. In periods of weak national loan demand, FNMA could then stabilize the market by selling its portfolio to investors.

In practice, FNMAs portfolio has grown steadily through time. Currently, FNMA holds about $90 billion of mortgages.

Originally established as a wholly owned government enterprise, FNMA was made private in 1969. Although still classified as a government-sponsored enterprise because of its Congressional charter, FNMA is a private, shareholder-owned, taxable enterprise whose borrowing and lending activities have no on-budget or off-budget effect on federal finances. Initially limited to dealing in federally insured (FHA) and guaranteed (VA) mortgage loans, FNMA began dealing in conventional loans as well in 1980.

The **Federal Home Loan Mortgage Corporation (FHLMC,** also known as **Freddie Mac)** was chartered by Congress in 1970 to perform functions similar to those of FNMA for conventional mortgage loans. From the outset, however, the operating mode for FHLMC was different from that of FNMA, and its original capitalization was supplied indirectly by savings and loan associations, rather than by the federal government. The FHLMC was made private in 1984 by making it a taxable corporation and by devolving its stock back to savings and loan associations. Like FNMA, FHLMC continues to be classified as a government-sponsored enterprise, but its activities have no on-budget or off-budget effect on federal finances.

The FHLMC was designed primarily to improve the liquidity of savings associations' conventional mortgage loan portfolios and to improve the regional distribution of mortgage credit. The FHLMC, however, was never designed to acquire a portfolio of loans. Instead, it was designed to buy conventional mortgage loans, form them into pools, and sell direct participations in those pools, rather than issue its own securities to fund a portfolio of mortgage loans. In a number of respects, FHLMCs Participation Certificates (PCs) may be thought of as the first **Mortgage-Backed Securities (MBSs).**

Savings associations have made increasing use of the secondary mortgage market in recent years. Both whole loan purchases and sales have increased relative to their total originations, as have savings association holdings of mortgage-backed securities (Exhibit 14).

The increasing use of securitization of mortgages is, in large part, due to the development of the **Collateralized Mortgage Obligation (CMO),** first introduced in 1983. For many years institutional investors, such as life insurance companies and pension funds, were reluctant to invest in home mortgages because of their lack of call protection. Home mortgages can prepay at any time, when the homeowner sells his or her home or when the mortgage is refinanced. The investor was thus left uncertain about how long funds invested in mortgages would remain invested at the given yield. Moreover, the risk of having to reinvest those funds at yields below those carried by the original pool of mortgages was more likely than being able to reinvest at higher yields. Generally speaking, the mortgage market is much more active during periods of low in-

EXHIBIT 14 SECONDARY MORTGAGE MARKET ACTIVITY OF SAVINGS ASSOCIATIONS ($ BILLIONS)

Year	Total Originations	Purchases	Sales	Net Purchases	Net Mortgage-Backed Security Purchases
1970	$ 21.4	$ 3.7	$ 1.1	$ 2.6	
1971	39.4	7.5	2.2	5.3	
1972	51.4	10.6	3.7	6.9	
1973	49.4	7.2	3.4	3.8	$ 1.3
1974	39.0	5.9	3.5	2.4	1.7
1975	55.0	8.5	5.2	3.3	4.4
1976	78.8	12.8	8.4	4.4	4.1
1977	107.4	14.5	13.8	0.7	4.7
1978	108.3	11.0	15.5	(4.5)	5.1
1979	98.7	12.0	18.3	(6.7)	5.7
1980	71.3	13.0	15.8	(2.8)	8.9
1981	52.3	10.5	12.6	(2.1)	6.1
1982	53.4	23.3	53.4	(30.1)	29.0
1983	138.2	45.8	55.4	(9.6)	29.1
1984	165.2	63.8	63.7	0.1	17.3

Source: Federal Home Loan Bank Board.

terest rates than during periods of high interest rates. Thus more homes are sold and more loans refinanced when rates are low than when rates are high.

The CMO solves most (but not all) of these problems by constructing several maturities on the security of the cash flow of principal and interest thrown off by a pool of mortgages. In a simple case, a CMO may consist of four maturities (or tranches)—a short-term, an intermediate-term, a long-term, and a Z-bond, or long-term zero-coupon, tranche. Each tranche is priced according to the yields on the underlying mortgage pool and according to its maturity (the short-term tranche yielding less than the long-term). Interest is paid semiannually, as is customary with other types of bonds. A CMO investor, however, may begin to receive principal payments after a minimum period of call protection has been satisfied.

To meet the terms of each tranche, a trustee applies receipts of principal and interest from the mortgage pool; the call protection on a given tranche expires when the preceding, shorter-term, tranche has been satisfied. The Z-bond is the last tranche to be satisfied, receiving neither principal nor interest until the long-term tranche has been satisfied. Once this occurs, the Z-bond tranche receives both principal and interest payments from the mortgage pool until all of the mortgages in that pool have been retired.

The advent of the CMO has attracted substantial interest from institutional investors and has increased their awareness and understanding of home mortgages. As a consequence, other types of mortgage-backed securities have been issued, using less complicated constructions than the CMO.

The trend toward the securitization of home mortgages has also increased the flexibility of savings association operations in that savings associations can now rely on an even broader secondary market for the loans they originate.

COMPOSITION OF REVENUE AND EXPENSES. Interest income from **home mortgages** remains the primary source of revenue, and **interest paid on deposits** the primary expense of savings associations. Financial deregulation has, however, allowed savings associations to develop new sources of revenue in consumer loans and other investments. This is a trend that can be expected to continue for several more years as savings associations seek to enhance and stabilize their earnings (Exhibit 15).

PROFITABILITY TRENDS. The coincidence of financial deregulation and the period of extremely high interest rates during 1981 and 1982 produced overall operating losses for the savings and loan business for the first time since the Great Depression. With the subsidence of interest rates in 1983 and 1984, savings associations returned to profitability, although their profit margins remained below previous levels (Exhibit 16).

THE REGULATORY SYSTEM. The regulatory system for the vast majority of savings and loan associations was established by three legislative actions in the early 1930s. The Federal Home Loan Bank Act of 1932 established a system of

EXHIBIT 15 SELECTED INCOME AND EXPENSE ITEMS OF SAVINGS AND LOAN ASSOCIATIONS (PERCENT OF GROSS INCOME)

				Interest on	Interest Income			
Year	Operating Expense	Compen-sation	Adver-tising	Savings Deposits	Mortgage Loans	Other	Net Operating Income	Net Income
1965	19.3%	9.0%	1.9%	63.2%	86.8%	5.4%	77.2%	11.7%
1970	17.8	8.1	1.8	64.6	84.3	7.7	75.0	8.7
1971	16.7	7.8	1.5	65.3	82.6	8.8	78.6	10.4
1972	16.3	7.6	1.6	65.5	82.9	7.9	80.5	11.1
1973	16.3	7.5	1.7	64.3	83.0	8.3	78.7	10.4
1974	16.4	7.6	1.7	65.0	82.0	9.0	75.6	7.1
1975	16.7	7.7	1.5	67.5	81.1	8.5	76.6	6.1
1976	16.2	7.6	1.2	67.7	78.8	7.5	78.8	7.9
1977	15.7	7.4	1.1	66.5	79.8	6.7	79.8	9.3
1978	15.2	7.2	1.2	64.1	80.2	7.4	78.2	9.7
1979	14.6	7.0	1.2	66.1	78.3	9.0	76.6	7.4
1980	14.1	6.8	1.1	74.1	77.2	10.0	75.6	1.4
1981	13.8	6.6	1.1	83.0	74.9	11.6	72.1	7.1
1982	14.1	6.4	1.0	81.9	71.0	11.4	69.6	−6.0
1983	15.4	6.7	0.9	72.9	64.9	11.3	72.9	2.5
1984	15.2	N.A.	N.A.	71.7	60.4	11.9	84.8	1.5

Source: Federal Home Loan Bank Board.

12 regional Federal Home Loan Banks patterned after the Federal Reserve System. The principal function of these banks was and is to provide a central credit facility for member savings and loan associations. This Act also established the Federal Home Loan Bank Board, initially to supervise the activities of the regional banks and subsequently to provide regulatory supervision of federally chartered and federally insured savings associations.

The Homeowners' Loan Act of 1933 provided authority for federal charters for savings and loan associations and the National Housing Act of 1934 created the Federal Savings and Loan Insurance Corporation, under the supervision of the Federal Home Loan Bank Board, to insure the savings accounts of depositors of member savings and loan associations.

Both the Federal Home Loan Banks and the Federal Savings and Loan Insurance Corporation were originally capitalized by the federal government. Retirement of the stock held by the U.S. Treasury in the Federal Home Loan Banks was completed in 1951 and the banks have been completely member-owned since that time, although the Banks continue to be considered "government-sponsored" agencies by virtue of the source of their charter. The Federal Savings and Loan Insurance Corporation began in the early 1950s to apply 50% of its annual net income to the retirement of Treasury-held stock and

EXHIBIT 16 MEASURES OF INCOME AND PROFITABILITY OF SAVINGS AND LOAN ASSOCIATIONS ($ BILLIONS AND PERCENT)

Year	Net Worth	Net Income After Tax	Return on Average Net Worth	Effective Tax Rate	Profit Margin	Net Worth to Assets
1950	$ 1.3	$0.179	15.1%	-0-	24.9%	7.6%
1955	2.6	0.370	15.7	1.6%	21.9	6.8
1960	5.0	0.577	12.4	0.7	15.5	7.0
1965	8.7	0.821	10.0	16.1	11.6	6.8
1970	12.4	0.904	6.7	21.5	8.2	7.0
1971	13.6	1.291	9.9	28.8	9.9	6.6
1972	15.2	1.729	12.1	27.3	11.1	6.3
1973	17.1	1.950	12.1	28.5	10.4	6.3
1974	18.4	1.532	8.6	30.8	7.1	6.2
1975	19.8	1.485	7.8	29.6	6.2	5.8
1976	22.0	2.300	11.0	30.8	7.9	5.6
1977	22.3	3.198	13.8	30.6	9.3	5.5
1978	28.1	3.920	14.9	31.6	9.6	5.5
1979	31.6	3.620	12.1	30.4	7.4	5.6
1980	33.3	0.784	2.4	34.3	1.4	5.3
1981	28.4	(4.632)	−15.4	—	−7.0	4.3
1982	26.2	(4.271)	−16.1	—	−5.6	3.7
1983	30.9	2.045	7.2	25.2	2.3	4.0
1984[a]	34.8	1.592	4.8		1.5	3.9

[a] Preliminary.

Source: Federal Home Loan Bank Board.

completed this process in 1958. Although FSLIC enjoys the full faith and credit of the federal government, it has been self-sustaining since 1958.

Federal Home Loan Banks. Like the Federal Reserve System, there are 12 districts in the Federal Home Loan Bank System, with regional banks located in principal cities of each district—Boston, New York, Pittsburgh, Atlanta, Cincinnati, Indianapolis, Chicago, Des Moines, Dallas, Topeka, San Francisco, and Seattle.

The FHLB activities can generally be subsumed under two categories—service and supervision. In the supervisory area, the president of each FHLB, in addition to his or her operational responsibilities, also carries the title of principal supervisory agent. Together with the bank's board of directors, the president is responsible in this role for assuring the compliance of the member institutions in his or her district with all relevant federal statutes and Federal Home Loan Bank Board regulations. Departments within each FHLB that are counterparts to those in the Federal Home Loan Bank Board assist the FHLB president in performing these duties. The most important of these are the office of examinations and supervision, with responsibility for assuring the safety and soundness of the operations of member institutions, and the office of industry development, with responsibility for approving applications for membership, new branch offices, mergers and acquisitions, and so forth.

The service activities of the Federal Home Loan Banks consist primarily of providing banking services to member institutions. The FHLBs accept deposits from member institutions and provide extensions of credit (advances). The FLHBs also provide clearing services for NOW account transactions and safe-keeping of securities.

Although most of these same services are also provided by district Federal Reserve Banks to their commercial bank members, there is an important distinction between the types of credit extended by the two systems. The credit granted to commercial banks (and to thrift institution members) by the Federal Reserve Banks is typically very short-term and is granted at concessional (or below-market) interest rates to meet short-term liquidity needs. The credit granted to members of the Federal Home Loan Bank System can be both short-term or long-term and is placed at market rates of interest.

Traditionally, these differences arose primarily from differences between the operational characteristics of commercial banks and savings institutions. The needs of commercial banks for "lender of last resort" type credit typically arise from adverse clearing drains in the course of demand deposit transactions and in the adjustment of required reserve positions, both of which are of brief duration—a matter of a few hours or, at most, a few days. Savings institutions do not process nearly so large a volume of demand deposits and therefore are much less subject to experiencing adverse clearing drains. Savings institutions do, however, make mortgage loan commitments well in advance of loan disbursements and sometimes encounter a shortfall in anticipated net savings inflows with which to meet those commitments. Federal Home Loan Bank advances thus provide a means of meeting those commitments.

As the asset and liability powers of savings institutions have been expanded in recent years, however, the FHLB advance program has been used to serve other purposes, most notably facilitating access to longer-term liabilities to better match the maturities of savings institution assets.

Thus although commercial bank borrowing through the Federal Reserve discount window may be thought of as meeting immediate and temporary needs of the borrower, savings institution borrowing through the Federal Home Loan Bank advance window may be characterized as meeting somewhat longer-term and structural needs of the borrower.

Given these different functions, the Federal Home Loan Banks will have something on the order of $60 billion of advances outstanding to their members at any given time, whereas the Federal Reserve Banks may have only about $1 to $2 billion of discounts outstanding at any one time.

Thus the Federal Home Loan Banks have much greater need of external funding sources than the Federal Reserve Banks. About 20% of the funding for FHLB advances is covered by the demand and time deposits of member institutions. Much of the balance is obtained through the issuance of **consolidated obligations.**

Consolidated obligations are the "joint and several" obligations of the 12 Federal Home Loan Banks. Each FHLB is responsible for repayment of its own participation in the issue as well as being legally liable for the repayment of the indebtedness of the other FHLBs. Although these issues do not carry the full faith and credit of the federal government, they are nevertheless very high-quality instruments because of the terms under which they are issued.

The outstanding consolidated obligations of the Federal Home Loan Banks may not exceed 12 times the paid-in capital and reserves of the FHLBs. Additionally, the FHLBs must carry unencumbered assets of cash, federal government securities, federal agency securities, and secured advances equal to or greater than their total outstanding consolidated obligations. The paid-in capital and reserves derived from retained earnings thus constitute an important constraint on the issuance of consolidated obligations and therefore on the FHLB advance program.

All federally chartered and federally insured savings and loan associations are required to be members of the Federal Home Loan Bank system. **Membership** entails the purchase of at least $500 of FHLB stock. Additional stock ownership is encouraged by the requirement that extensions of credit (FHLB advances) to a member institution by its FHLB may not exceed 20 times the value of the institution's holdings of FHLB stock.

Federal Savings and Loan Insurance Corporation. The Federal Savings and Loan Insurance Corporation, together with the **Federal Deposit Insurance Corporation,** was established in 1934 in the wake of the virtual collapse of the financial system to reestablish and maintain public confidence in depository institutions.

Savings institutions are private enterprises subject to gains and losses from operations. Like any other private enterprise, losses are absorbed by the net worth of the institution and when that net worth is exhausted, the enterprise is technically insolvent. In the case of depository institutions, the FSLIC and FDIC have the responsibility of shielding depositors from loss, up to the limits of deposit insurance, in the event of an institution's insolvency.

The FSLIC has several ways of dealing with an insolvent institution, the most commonly practiced of which is the merger of the insolvent institution with another, healthy institution. Depending on the circumstances, the FSLIC is empowered to provide financial assistance to the acquiring institution to facilitate such mergers. In the vast majority of such cases the acquiring institution continues to operate the branch network of the acquired institution, and depositors experience little or no inconvenience. At the other extreme, the FSLIC may liquidate the institution, in which case the FSLIC itself acquires the assets of the institution and pays off the depositors, to the extent that their deposits are insured, and satisfies other creditors as the assets are liquidated.

Liquidations are unambiguous examples of insolvency, but mergers of savings institutions do not necessarily imply the insolvency of an institution. The vast majority of mergers of savings institutions over time have been for reasons other than insolvency—to secure economies of scale in providing financial services, for example. Such mergers are voluntary and do not involve the FSLIC.

Thus although the number of savings institutions declined steadily from 6,320 in 1960 to 4,613 in 1980 through voluntary and **statutory** (involuntary) mergers, the FSLIC was obliged to liquidate only six institutions during this 20-year period.

With the onset of financial deregulation in 1980 and the period of extremely high interest rates in 1981–1982, the FSLIC caseload increased dramatically. In 1981 the FSLIC effected the supervisory merger of 30 savings institutions, providing financial assistance to the acquiring institution in many of these cases. In 1982 supervisory mergers rose to 48 institutions. Although interest rates declined in 1982, supervisory merger activity continued to increase in 1983 with FSLIC resolving 53 cases.

When supervisory mergers require financial assistance and in liquidation cases in which the realized value of the assets of the insolvent institution is insufficient to pay the insured depositors, the FSLIC draws on its accumulated reserves. Although the federal government originally capitalized FSLIC, the premiums paid by FSLIC-insured institutions and the earnings on the investment of those premiums enabled FSLIC to repay the original government capitalization fully by 1958. Since that time, although FSLIC enjoys the full faith and credit of the U.S. government, investment income and the insurance premiums paid by insured institutions for the benefit of their depositors have been more than sufficient to meet these expenses.

The **FSLIC reserves** consist of regular premiums paid by insured institutions, special assessments, and earnings on the investment of the reserves funds. Reserves are deemed adequate at 1.25% of insured deposits. The FSLIC-insured institutions pay annual insurance premiums of 1/12 of 1% of their deposit liabilities to maintain FSLIC reserves at approximately this level, including earnings on FSLIC investments. The FSLIC is also empowered to impose additional annual assessments of up to 1/8 of 1% of deposit liabilities in the event that FSLIC reserves fall below 1.25% of insured deposits.

During the 1940s and 1950s, savings institution deposits grew very rapidly. As a consequence, the 1/12 of 1% regular premium, plus earnings on FSLIC investments, proved inadequate to maintain reserves at 1.25% of insured deposits. Beginning in 1962 savings institutions were required to make an annual prepayment of the regular premium equal to 2% of insured deposits outstanding during the preceding year. These prepayments were credited to the FSLIC secondary reserve. The earnings on the investment of the secondary reserve at year-end were then prorated among the institutions to reduce the amount of the prepayment for the next year.

Under this program, FSLIC reserves grew rapidly during the 1960s, reaching 2.138% of insured deposits in 1969. Further prepayments were then suspended at the end of 1969 and the regular premiums were paid from the secondary reserve. By 1972 FSLIC reserves had declined to 1.564% of insured deposits and the regular cash premium of 1/12 of 1% was reinstated.

In 1973 Congress passed legislation discontinuing prepayments to the secondary reserve and extended this legislation in the Depository Institutions Act of 1974 to phase out the secondary reserve completely over a 10-year period. The FSLICs power to assess insured institutions up to 1/8 of 1% of deposits when FSLIC reserves fall below 1.25% was, however, retained.

The FSLIC reserves fell below this level, to 1.137%, in 1982 as a result of heavy supervisory merger activity, and the FSLIC invoked its assessment powers in early 1985 in order to rebuild its reserves.

MUTUAL SAVINGS BANKS

HISTORICAL PERSPECTIVE. Like savings and loan associations, mutual savings banks were established as community-based, self-help organizations, first in Britain at the turn of the nineteenth century and shortly thereafter in the United States. The first American mutual savings banks were established in 1816.

Although mutual savings banks and savings and loan associations currently display many of the same characteristics, differences nevertheless remain, a significant number of which can be traced to differences in the motivation for their original establishment.

Historically and currently, mutual savings banks are somewhat less specialized than savings and loan associations. Whereas savings and loan associations were specifically formed to provide home finance to their members (depositors), mutual savings banks were established primarily to provide their members with a safe place to deposit their small savings and with prudent management of the investment of those funds. Consequently, although mutual savings banks have played a prominent role in home financing, their portfolios include a higher proportion of other assets such as corporate bonds then savings and loan associations.

Indeed, mutual savings banks were originally established by community leaders to encourage thrift among working class families and individuals. These initiatives were generally motivated by a desire to prevent or mitigate poverty among the working class. The encouragement of thrift, it was reasoned, would provide for the widows and orphans of workers, for the workers themselves in their old age, and contingency funds to sustain workers and their families in times of illness or other family financial crises.

Although it has been suggested that these community leaders were motivated as much by a desire to relieve themselves of the burden of taxes for poor relief as to relieve the poor of their suffering, the fact remains that the mutual savings banks performed a useful socioeconomic function that commercial banks were uninterested in performing.

Because the purpose for which these early mutual savings banks were formed was to safeguard the savings of working class families so that those funds would be available to them in time of need, the strategy for the investment of those funds was dictated by prudence and yield (or "best advantage," as the early charters termed it). Data for this early period in the history of mutual savings banks are sketchy, but to illustrate, the asset portfolio of the Savings Bank of Baltimore in 1821 consisted of state and local government obligations (45.8%), U.S. government obligations (30.2%), bank stocks (15.5%), and bank deposits (9%).

Through most of the nineteenth century the commercial and industrial activity of the United States was concentrated in the New England and Middle Atlantic states. Consequently, the largest concentration of wage earners—the principal group that the mutual savings banks sought to serve—was also found in these two regions. The rest of the country was primarily agricultural.

In the twentieth century, as industry and commerce grew relative to agriculture in the other regions of the country, mutual savings banks were unable to spread because these financial markets had been preempted by commercial banks, savings and loan associations, and credit unions. Consequently, mutual savings banks are today largely a phenomenon of the New England and Middle Atlantic regions of the country. Indeed, at the end of 1983 more than three-quarters (76.4%) of all mutual savings banks, with approximately the same proportion (74.9%) of the total assets of the business, were located in Massachusetts, New York, and Connecticut. Mutual savings banks currently operate in eight other states, only one of which (Washington) is outside the New England and Middle Atlantic regions.

Mutual savings banks came to invest heavily in **home mortgages** during the latter half of the nineteenth century, primarily because both the yield and quality of mortgages improved relative to their traditional investments—government securities and bonds. Mortgage holdings of mutual savings banks in Massachusetts reached 48% of assets as early as 1873; in New York, mortgages accounted for 47% of the assets of that state's mutual savings banks in 1906. From this time forward, mutual savings banks have been heavily involved in mortgage investment, although to a somewhat lesser extent than savings and loan associations.

During the 1920s, savings bank investment in home mortgages outpaced their deposit growth, so that at the dawn of the Depression, mutual savings banks held slightly more than 50% of their assets in real estate loans.

Mutual savings banks weathered the Depression much better than either commercial banks or savings and loan associations. Only eight out of almost 600 savings banks failed during the difficult days of 1930–1933. This fact accounts, to a large extent, for the lack of specific Depression era legislation directed toward mutual savings banks and their continuation as state-chartered and state-supervised institutions through most of their history.

Given that savings banks increased their mortgage portfolios during this period, logic might have dictated that mutual savings banks be placed under the supervisory umbrella of the Federal Home Loan Bank System and the Federal

Savings and Loan Insurance Corporation. What in fact occurred was that mutual savings banks were permitted membership in the Federal Home Loan Bank System and offered deposit insurance from the Federal Deposit Insurance Corporation, the agency charged with the responsibility for insuring the deposits of commercial banks. Furthermore, unlike savings and loan associations, mutual savings banks were not granted the opportunity for federal charter. Thus through most of the period following the Depression, mutual savings banks operated under a combined state and federal regulatory system.

Federal legislation in the late 1970s and early 1980s began to remove the anomalies inherent in FDIC (rather than FSLIC) insurance of accounts and attendant regulation of mutual savings banks. The Financial Institutions Regulatory and Interest Rate Control Act of 1978 authorized federal charters for mutual savings banks and permitted savings banks to convert from FDIC to FSLIC insurance. The Depository Institutions Act of 1982 further authorized the conversion of mutual savings banks to stock and authorized the Federal Home Loan Bank Board to charter de novo stock savings banks, as well as stock savings and loan associations.

Taken together with the granting of broader asset powers contained in the Depository Institutions Act of 1982, these legislative changes promise a further blurring of the distinctions between savings banks and savings and loan associations in the future.

These **changes in the structure of the mutual savings bank system** can be perceived in the data presented in Exhibit 17, which shows the trend toward membership in the Federal Home Loan Bank System and the beginning of the trend toward conversion to FSLIC insurance coverage. It is also worth noting that after 1982, many savings and loan associations changed their names to include the words "savings bank," even though they continued to operate under the regulations provided for savings and loan associations. Although this change must initially be regarded as cosmetic, the fact that increasing numbers of traditional mutual savings banks have become members of the Federal Home Loan Bank System and have opted for FSLIC insurance reflects the trend toward the coalescing of these two (formerly distinct) elements of the thrift sector.

Although mutual savings banks did not fully participate in the "golden age of growth" enjoyed by savings and loan associations during the period immediately following the end of World War II, both types of institutions were placed in similar circumstances by the economic policy mix and the regulatory constraints of the 1970s. Thus as the era of deregulation dawned in the 1980s, mutual savings banks and savings and loan associations were much more similar than they were different.

ASSET AND LIABILITY COMPOSITION. Many of the remaining differences in operating style between mutual savings banks and savings and loan associations can be discerned from a comparison of the asset and liability

EXHIBIT 17 NUMBER OF MUTUAL SAVINGS BANKS, ASSETS, AND INSURANCE STATUS[a]

Year	Number of Savings Banks	Total Assets ($ Billion)	Deposits Insured By			Member FHLB System
			FDIC	State	FSLIC	
1950	529	$ 22.4	194	253		29
1960	515	40.6	325	185		19
1970	494	79.0	329	172		46
1971	490	89.6	327	170		47
1972	486	100.6	326	167		47
1973	482	106.6	322	167		47
1974	480	109.6	320	167		55
1975	476	121.0	329	166		68
1976	473	134.8	331	166		76
1977	467	147.3	323	166		73
1978	465	158.2	325	163		85
1979	463	163.4	324	163		97
1980	463	171.6	323	162	3	140
1981	448	175.7	331	159	6	144
1982	424	174.2	315	155	6	130
1983	399	193.5	315	146	8	143
1984	383	206.3	291	131	11	229

[a] A number of savings banks carry both federal and state deposit insurance.
Source: National Council of Savings Institutions.

composition of the two types of institutions. The data for savings and loan associations are shown in Exhibits 9 and 10 and those for mutual savings banks are given in Exhibits 18 and 19.

Within the context of their **mortgage** investments, mutual savings banks have been involved to a greater degree than savings and loan associations in the origination and acquisition of mortgages outside their own communities or market areas. In part, this characteristic of mutual savings bank operations may be attributed to their geographic concentration and to the philosophical flexibility of their investment policy. For similar reasons, savings banks have also shown great receptivity to mortgage-backed securities, tending to reduce their portfolios of FHA and VA mortgages and replace them with mortgage-backed securities (Exhibit 20).

The long-standing tradition of mutual savings banks to invest in high-yield, high-quality capital market instruments and their geographic concentration in the mature housing markets of the Northeast make mutual savings banks relatively more active participants in the **secondary mortgage market** than savings and loan associations.

PROFITABILITY. Until 1980 mutual savings banks, taken as a group, enjoyed an unbroken chain of profitable years following the Depression of the

EXHIBIT 18 CONDENSED STATEMENT OF CONDITION OF MUTUAL SAVINGS BANKS ($ MILLIONS)

	1979		1983		1984	
Assets	Amount	Percent	Amount	Percent	Amount	Percent
Mortgage investments	$110,729	67.7	$115,552	59.7	$123,064	59.7
Mortgage loans	98,908	60.5	97,347	50.3	103,547	50.2
Mortgage-backed securities	11,820	7.2	18,205	9.4	19,517	9.5
Other loans	9,253	5.7	19,129	9.9	25,596	12.4
Education loans	1,274	0.8	2,713	1.4	2,984	1.4
Consumer installment loans	1,622	1.0	4,737	2.5	5,126	2.5
Home improvement loans	884	0.5	1,149	0.6	1,904	0.9
Federal funds	3,076	1.9	4,702	2.4	6,613	3.2
Other	2,398	1.5	5,828	3.0	8,969	4.4
Cash and due from banks	3,156	1.9	6,263	3.2	4,992	2.4
U.S. Treasury and agency securities	7,658	4.7	15,360	7.9	14,652	7.1
State and local obligations	2,930	1.8	2,177	1.1	2,075	1.0
Corporate bonds	16,922	10.4	17,708	9.2	16,789	8.1
Other bonds, notes, and debentures	3,584	2.2	4,196	2.2	3,677	1.8
Corporate stock	4,760	2.9	3,472	1.8	3,313	1.6
Other assets	4,412	2.7	9,670	5.0	12,127	5.9
Total Assets	$163,405	100.0	$193,527	100.0	$206,285	100.0
Liabilities						
Time and savings deposits	$146,006	89.4	$172,665	89.2	$182,789	88.6
Borrowings	3,653	2.2	7,128	3.7	9,476	4.6
Other liabilities	2,220	1.4	3,368	1.7	3,457	1.7
Total Liabilities	$151,879	93.0	$183,161	94.6	$195,722	94.9
Net Worth	$11,525	7.0	$10,366	5.4	10,563	5.1

Source: National Council of Savings Institutions.

1930s. Loss years were suffered in 1980, 1981, and 1982, however, as the savings banks' interest costs far outstripped their earnings on long-term, fixed-rate assets, primarily home mortgages. Although mutual savings bank losses were proportionately larger than those of savings and loan associations, mutual savings banks also entered this period with slightly higher net worth ratios, so that the failure rate among mutual savings banks was lower.

EXHIBIT 19 DEPOSIT STRUCTURE OF MUTUAL SAVINGS BANKS ($ BILLIONS)

					Time						
	Total Deposits	MMDA	Now and Super NOW	Passbook	3 Month	6 Month	More than 1.5 years	More than 2.5 years	More than $100,000	Other Time	Other
1972	$ 91,613		$ 45	$68,238						$23,162	$ 213
1973	96,496		143	65,221						31,021	254
1974	98,701		213	64,286						34,120	295
1975	109,873		386	69,653						39,838	383
1976	122,877		580	74,535						47,634	708
1977	134,017		799	78,005						54,941	1,070
1978	142,701		955	71,816						68,399	1,531
1979	146,006		1,292	61,123		$35,000				48,146	1,737
1980	153,501		1,592	53,971		50,551		$12,430		34,463	2,086
1981	155,110		2,314	49,425		53,641		21,794	$5,428	22,716	2,108
1982	155,196	$ 9,547	3,005	48,305		48,340		28,340	4,731	14,992	2,419
1983	172,665	33,004	3,448	38,554	$2,021	36,367	$14,865	17,261	5,845	18,770	2,530
1984	179,526	35,395	3,956	33,838	1,305	38,715	11,082	17,659	8,707	28,869	3,263

Source: National Council of Savings Institutions.

EXHIBIT 20 MORTGAGE INVESTMENT OF MUTUAL SAVINGS BANKS ($ BILLIONS)

Year	Total Mortgage Investment	Type of Property: 1–4 Family	Type of Property: Multifamily	Type of Loan: FHA	Type of Loan: VA	Type of Loan: Conventional	Nonresidential	Mortgage-backed securities
1970	57.9							
1971	62.0							
1972	67.6			16.0	12.6			
1973	75.2	48.8	12.3	15.5	12.9	32.7	12.1	1.9
1974	77.2	49.2	12.9	14.8	12.7	34.6	12.8	2.2
1975	80.6	50.0	13.8	14.4	12.4	37.0	13.4	3.4
1976	87.4	53.1	14.2	14.6	12.3	40.4	14.4	5.8
1977	96.4	58.0	15.0	14.2	11.9	46.9	15.1	8.3
1978	105.2	63.3	15.9	14.2	11.8	53.2	16.0	10.0
1979	110.7	66.1	16.6	13.8	11.4	57.5	16.2	11.8
1980	113.7	67.5	16.0	13.3	10.8	59.4	16.3	13.8
1981	113.9	68.2	16.0	12.8	10.5	60.9	15.8	13.9
1982	109.2	66.7	13.8	11.7	9.6	59.1	14.7	14.0
1983	115.3	69.1	13.7	10.7	8.8	63.2	14.3	18.2
1984	123.1	73.6	13.7	9.5	7.8	70.0	15.3	19.5

Source: National Council of Savings Institutions.

Both savings and loan associations and mutual savings banks returned to profitability in 1983. Although both types of institutions will remain vulnerable to another episode of interest rates of the magnitude seen in 1981–1982 for several more years, their new asset powers and the success of their portfolio restructuring efforts to date have already laid the basis for improved earnings stability in a volatile interest rate environment.

Exhibit 21 details the income and expense record of mutual savings banks over the past 20 years.

CREDIT UNIONS

HISTORICAL PERSPECTIVE. The development of credit unions owes its impetus to rather different considerations than either savings and loan associations or mutual savings banks, yet like these other institutions, their original structure was that of mutual, community-based, self-help organizations. Credit unions in America continue to be structured on these principles today, whereas savings and loan associations and mutual savings banks have evolved toward profit-making financial enterprises. Also unlike savings and loan associations and mutual savings banks, credit unions trace their roots to Continental Europe, rather than to Great Britain, and to much broader socioeconomic reform movements.

A variety of cooperative schemes developed in Europe in the early nineteenth century as general efforts to ameliorate social and economic conditions among workers, craftsmen, small shopkeepers, and farmers. The European

EXHIBIT 21 INCOME AND EXPENSES OF MUTUAL SAVINGS BANKS ($ MILLIONS)

Year	Total Operating Income	Total Operating Expenses	Interest Expense	Net Operating Income	Net Gains on Asset Transactions	Taxes	Retained Earnings
1961	$ 1,835	$ 280	$ 1,326	$ 229		$ 18	$ 211
1962	2,022	293	1,530	198	$ 6	20	184
1963	2,241	319	1,700	222	14	26	210
1964	2,485	337	1,895	253	5	29	229
1965	2,745	361	2,076	308	−18	34	256
1966	2,991	387	2,383	221	16	42	195
1967	3,302	410	2,713	179	−6	44	128
1968	3,702	450	2,967	284	26	56	255
1969	4,110	511	3,219	381	−56	70	255
1970	4,487	596	3,452	439	−143	89	208
1971	5,222	667	3,936	619	−67	144	408
1972	6,081	770	4,517	795	−15	210	570
1973	6,978	928	5,139	910	−112	237	561
1974	7,471	1,074	5,620	777	−198	201	377
1975	8,117	1,223	6,165	729	−89	199	441
1976	9,276	1,460	6,970	846	−14	255	577
1977	10,494	1,633	7,757	1,103	−12	313	779
1978	11,842	1,998	8,524	1,320	−69	357	894
1979	13,316	2,374	9,876	1,066	−33	292	741
1980	14,713	2,955	11,881	−123	−30	53	−206
1981	16,440	3,424	14,680	−1,664	90	−136	−1,438
1982	16,976	3,669	14,779	−1,492	211	−19	−1,263
1983	17,794	3,522	14,117	156	164	45	275
1984	19,764	4,292	15,367	105	93	196	2

Source: National Council of Savings Institutions.

credit union movement grew out of this general philosophical approach to socioeconomic organization. These early efforts were driven as much by philanthropic and humanitarian forces as by practical considerations, yet it was not until the practical aspects of organization were brought to bear that durable, functioning, financial institutions emerged.

Historians generally agree that the prototypes of formal credit unions were first established in Germany in the 1850s and that the two persons most instrumental in promoting the formation of credit unions were Hermann Schulze-Delitzsch and Friedrich Wilhelm Raiffeisen. Schulze-Delitzsch's credit unions, or "people's banks," were organized around craftsmen and small shopkeepers, and credit was granted only for "productive" purposes. Raiffeisen's credit unions were organized around farmers. In each case, Schulze-Delitzsch and Raiffeisen were strongly motivated by a desire to improve the economic conditions of people who lived very near the margin of existence. Also in each case, the lack of credit on reasonable terms with which to purchase equipment, raw material, seed, and livestock appeared as a critical constraint to their advancement and economic security. Inasmuch as the commercial banks catered to the large merchant and producer, small merchants and farmers were left to the mercies of local moneylenders, who charged exorbitant interest rates and were quick to foreclose.

Several aspects of these early credit unions are relevant for an understanding of modern American credit unions. First, their membership was organized around some common bond. In the beginning the common line of economic activity simplified and facilitated the development of the organization. In the United States today the common bond is a legal requirement designed to maintain credit unions' primary role within the financial sector.

Second, although these early credit unions were dedicated to the provision of credit, that credit was destined for commercial purposes rather than for consumption. They were, therefore, much more in the mold of commercial banks than consumer credit institutions, as credit unions in the United States are today.

Third, like savings and loan associations, which promoted thrift for a specific household purpose—achieving homeownership—and unlike mutual savings banks, which promoted thrift to alleviate poverty and hardship caused by unforeseen contingencies, these early European credit unions promoted thrift primarily as a means of establishing a capital base on which to lend as well as to borrow for on-lending to their members. Indeed, both the Schulze-Delitzsch and Raiffeisen credit unions employed the principle of unlimited liability of the credit union members as the basis for borrowing funds to supplement their share capital.

Credit unions did not come directly to the United States from Europe, but rather from Canada. The first North American credit union was established in Quebec in 1900 by Alphonse Desjardins and it differed from European examples in at least two important respects. First, it rejected the principle of unlimited liability in borrowing from outside sources and restricted its lending primarily to the capital raised by the contributions of its members. Second, its establishment was motivated more by the plight of wage earners forced to depend on usurious moneylenders in times of family financial need than by a desire to provide "productive" credit to small-scale entrepreneurs and farmers. The Desjardins credit union served as the model for U.S. credit unions, the first of which was legally chartered in New Hampshire in 1909.

The tap roots of the U.S. credit union movement, however, were planted in Massachusetts as a result of the efforts of Edward A. Filene, a wealthy Boston merchant, and Pierre Jay, Commissioner of Banks for Massachusetts, with the active assistance of Desjardins. From Massachusetts flowed the inspiration and the financial and technical assistance for the establishment of credit unions in other states.

The process of developing a national credit union system gathered momentum slowly, such that by 1929 there were only 974 legally chartered credit unions. In contrast with other depository institutions, however, credit union growth accelerated during the Depression of the 1930s, with the number of credit unions reaching 2,016 in 1933, 5,241 in 1936, and 7,964 in 1939 (Exhibit 22).

All credit unions were state-chartered institutions until 1934, when the Federal Credit Union Act was passed. This legislation, which authorized the federal chartering of credit unions under common bond limitations, was controversial both in the Congress and among the credit union leadership.

Inasmuch as credit unions had not experienced the large number of failures that other financial institutions had, they did not face an immediate crisis with which only the federal government could deal. Depression era legislation therefore dealt with the credit unions rather differently than it did with other elements of the financial sector. The principal Congressional sponsors of credit union legislation envisioned credit unions as a means of providing needed

EXHIBIT 22 NUMBER AND ASSETS OF CREDIT UNIONS ($ BILLIONS)

Year	Number of Credit Unions	Total Assets	Number State Chartered	Assets	Number Federally Chartered	Assets
1929	974		974			
1933	2,016		2,016			
1936	5,241	$ .083	3,490	$ .074	1,751	$ .009
1939	7,964		4,782		3,185	
1945	8,683	.435	4,923	.282	3,760	.153
1965	22,160	10.551	10,617	5.385	11,543	5.166
1970	23,768	17.949	10,701	9.089	12,977	8.861
1971	23,270		10,553		12,717	
1972	23,070		10,362		12,708	
1973	22,905		10,217		12,688	
1974	22,856		10,108		12,748	
1975	22,611	38.013	9,874	17.804	12,737	20.208
1976	22,538		9,781		12,757	
1977	22,330		9,580		12,750	
1978	22,202		9,443		12,759	
1979	22,012		9,274		12,738	
1980	21,465	73.235	9,025	33.143	12,440	40.092
1981	20,786	75,295	8,817		11,969	
1982	19,650	90,211	8,231		11,457	
1983	19,205	100,156	8,158		11,045	
1984	18,530	114,570				

Source: National Credit Union Administration; Credit Union National Association.

credit in the distressed agricultural sector, even though the credit union movement had been notably unsuccessful in establishing rural credit unions. And both the Treasury and the Federal Reserve objected to early versions of the proposed legislation which, in effect, would have given credit unions access to the Federal Reserve discount facility.

Within the credit union movement, some were fearful that federal intervention would destroy the self-help principles on which credit unionism was based, whereas others saw federal chartering as a way to accelerate the organizing process by bypassing the arduous task of working for enabling legislation on a state-by-state basis. Still others, Filene among them, saw the credit unions as a means through which the federal government might channel credit to stimulate consumption in order to aid in the economy's general recovery.

In the light of these divisions of opinion, the Federal Credit Union Act of 1934 served primarily to facilitate the organizing effort. No mechanism for channeling federal funds through the credit unions was created, no provision for federal deposit insurance was made, and no elaborate regulatory system was established. Indeed, responsibility for administration of the law and the supervision of federal credit unions was shifted from one agency to another until 1970. First vested in the Farm Credit Administration, this responsibility was given over to a branch of the Federal Deposit Insurance Corporation between 1942 and 1945. From 1945 to 1953 the Federal Security Agency oversaw federal credit unions, and from 1953 to 1970 the Bureau of Federal Credit Unions, under the Department of Health, Education and Welfare, supervised federal credit unions. Finally, in 1970, Congress deemed credit unions to be of sufficient financial importance to establish an independent regulatory agency, the National Credit Union Administration, and to provide federal deposit (or share) insurance through the National Credit Union Share Insurance Fund.

Share insurance clearly came recently relative to deposit insurance for the other elements of the financial system, in large measure because credit unions have traditionally placed great stress on mutuality. In theory and to a substantial degree in practice, loans are made only to members of the credit union, who are joined by some common bond and are considered worthy credit risks to their fellow credit union members.

Although this approach to the financial safety and soundness of credit unions in general worked reasonably well over time, the lack of share insurance must have served to limit the growth of credit unions. Regardless of the creditworthiness of individual borrowers, the common bond also limits the ability of a given credit union to diversify its lending risks and, until 1979, when the **National Credit Union Central Liquidity Fund (CLF)** was established by Congress, exposed its members to the illiquidity of their savings in the event of common hardship such as a plant closing. Prior to the establishment of the CLF, credit unions were obliged to borrow commercially against their capital and earning assets or to draw down their liquid assets to meet the needs of their members.

Since the passage of the National Credit Union Act of 1934, the number of federally chartered credit unions has grown relative to state-chartered institutions, as Exhibit 22 reveals. Credit unions have also grown in average asset size, as well as in total assets, but they remain substantially smaller than either savings and loan associations or mutual savings banks. In 1984 the average credit union had $6.2 million in assets and employed only four full-time employees (Exhibit 23).

SOURCES AND USES OF FUNDS. Regular share accounts, comparable with the passbook accounts of other depository institutions, remain the primary source of funds for credit unions and comparatively short-term consumer loans to their members constitute their primary use of funds (Exhibit 24).

Until 1978, when the 6-month Money Market Certificate was authorized, credit union shares consisted entirely of regular share accounts. Credit unions at first resisted offering certificates, but competitive pressures compelled them to do so as savings growth declined. By the end of 1983 credit unions held 26.8% of their savings capital in the form of term certificates.

Compared with savings and loan associations and mutual savings banks, however, credit unions were able to retain a substantially higher proportion of their funds in lower-cost share accounts.

Furthermore, the loan portfolios of credit unions are fully funded by their retail share accounts. At the end of 1983 credit unions had $90.4 billion in share accounts and only $58.2 billion of loans outstanding. The balance was held in investments such as government securities and deposits at commercial banks, other savings institutions, and the CLF.

In recent years almost half (44%) of credit union loans have been for automobile purchases. The balance of credit union loans is for a wide variety of personal purposes.

Although federal credit unions gained the authority to make long-term home mortgage loans in 1977, comparatively little use has been made of this authority. At the end of 1983 credit unions had outstanding slightly more than $4 billion of all types of real estate loans, including home improvement loans.

EXHIBIT 23 SIZE AND STRUCTURE OF CREDIT UNIONS 1983

Distribution by Asset Size ($ Thousand)		Distribution by Common Bond	
$ 200 or less	17.6%	Associational	17.1%
201 to 500	18.7		
501 to 1,000	15.5	Occupational (all)	77.2
1,001 to 2,000	14.5	Manufacturing	33.0
2,001 to 5,000	15.5	Wholesale and retail trade	3.6
5,001 to 10,000	7.7	Governmental	16.0
10,001 to 20,000	5.1	Educational	8.6
20,001 to 50,000	3.4	Other	16.0
50,001 or more	2.0		
		Residential	5.7

Source: Credit Union National Association, *Credit Union Report.*

EXHIBIT 24 ASSETS AND LIABILITIES OF CREDIT UNIONS ($ BILLIONS)

Year	Total Loans Outstanding	Assets: Auto Loans	Assets: Reserves	Ratio of Reserves to Assets
1975	$28.2	$12.7	$2.0	5.3%
1976	34.2	15.2	2.3	5.0
1977	41.9	18.1	2.6	4.7
1978	50.3	21.2	2.8	4.4
1979	52.3	22.2	3.0	4.4
1980	49.0	21.1	3.1	4.3
1981	50.4	22.0	3.4	4.4
1982	51.5	22.6	3.6	4.3
1983	58.2	25.6	4.3	4.3

Year	Total Shares	Liabilities: Regular Shares	Liabilities: Certificates	Share Drafts
1975	$32.8			
1976	38.6			
1977	46.0			
1978	52.7			
1979	55.9			
1980	61.7	$46.4	$12.8	$2.5
1981	64.6	43.5	17.7	3.4
1982	74.8	51.4	18.3	5.1
1983	90.4	58.8	24.3	7.3

Source: Credit Union National Association, *Credit Union Report;* National Credit Union Administration, *Annual Report.*

INCOME AND EXPENSES. The principal source of income for credit unions is interest on loans made to members and their principal expense, other than dividends on share accounts, is the compensation of employees (Exhibit 25).

Credit unions are exempt from taxation, so that net income is employed primarily to pay dividends on shares and to increase reserves and undivided earnings. The payment of dividends on share accounts is by no means assured. These accounts are analogous to the equity capital of a corporation and do not guarantee the payment of dividends. Indeed, in 1980, 6.4% of all federal credit unions paid no dividend; 6.8% of federal credit unions paid no dividend in 1981. A little more than half (52.0%) of federal credit unions, however, paid 7% or more on share accounts in 1981, substantially higher than the 5.5% allowed savings and loan associations and mutual savings banks on their comparable passbook accounts under the Regulation Q ceilings at that time.

REGULATORY SYSTEM. Like other depository institutions, credit unions may be established under either state or federal charter and are subject to the supervision of the regulatory agencies of the governmental power granting their charter. In addition, those state-chartered credit unions that also have fed-

EXHIBIT 25 INCOME AND EXPENSES OF FEDERALLY INSURED CREDIT UNIONS 1981 ($ MILLIONS)

	All Federally Insured Credit Unions	Federal Credit Unions	State-Chartered Credit Unions
Income			
Gross income	$7,546.7	$5,071.7	$2,475.0
Interest on loans	5,255.9	3,347.5	1,908.4
Income on investments	2,419.3	1,643.0	776.3
Other income	141.5	81.3	60.2
Expenses			
Total expenses	2,581.3	1,676.2	905.1
Employee compensation	1,019.1	661.8	357.3
Office operations	343.1	222.1	121.0
Office occupancy	103.6	62.4	41.2
Members insurance	244.8	163.5	81.3
Interest on borrowed funds	178.1	98.7	79.4
Education and promotion	56.7	33.5	23.2
Professional fees	160.6	112.5	48.1
Other	475.3	321.7	153.6
Net Income	4,965.4	3,395.5	1,569.9
Distribution of Net Income			
Dividends		2,997.4	
Retained earnings		233.3	
Regular reserves		152.2	
Interest refunds		20.3	

Source: National Credit Union Administration, *Annual Report.*

eral share insurance fall under the federal regulatory umbrella. At the end of 1983, 83.1% of all credit unions holding 80.9% of all credit union assets were federally insured. Moreover, 27 state credit union statutes contain tie-in provisions that confer powers and regulations on their state-chartered credit unions which are equivalent to those of federal credit unions. Thus to a very substantial degree, federal regulations promulgated by federal agencies constitute the regulatory system for credit unions.

National Credit Union Administration. The National Credit Union Administration (NCUA) was established in 1970 as an independent regulatory agency. Its functions are similar to those of the Federal Home Loan Bank Board, with several important organizational distinctions. Both agencies are responsible for chartering and supervision of compliance with regulations, but whereas the Federal Home Loan Bank Board oversees a system of regional Federal Home Loan Banks that perform a variety of financial service functions, the NCUA oversees a system of regional administrative offices and the CLF. Furthermore, the Federal Home Loan Bank Board oversees the Federal Savings and Loan Insurance Corporation, whereas the National Credit Union Share Insurance Fund is an integral part of the NCUA.

Central Liquidity Fund. The CLF was authorized by the Credit Union Modernization Act of 1978 to serve as a "lender of last resort" facility to meet the emergency liquidity needs of member credit unions. Membership in the CLF is voluntary and is obtained by subscribing to the stock of the CLF. Member credit unions must subscribe stock in the amount of one-half of 1% of their paid-in capital and surplus.

The CLF provides three types of credit to member institutions: "short-term adjustment" credit, "seasonal" credit, and "protracted adjustment" credit. These advances are secured by a general pledge of all assets of the borrowing credit union. During fiscal year 1981, the CLF made loans to member institutions of $67 million.

The CLF obtains funds for lending through the issuance of notes and debt securities through the Federal Financing Bank. Its 1981 borrowing limit was $600 million, but under emergency circumstances, the CLF may access a $500 million line of credit with the U.S. Treasury.

On occasion, the CLF and the National Credit Union Share Insurance Fund collaborate in dealing with troubled institutions. Under these arrangements the CLF grants "protracted adjustment" credit to an institution as part of the effort to salvage an essentially sound credit union, and allows it to return to viability rather than proceed to liquidation or merger under National Credit Union Share Insurance Fund procedures.

National Credit Union Share Insurance Fund. Legislation establishing the National Credit Union Share Insurance Funds was enacted in 1970. Like the FDIC and FSLIC, the National Credit Union Share Insurance Fund is funded by premiums paid by insured credit unions. The statutory maximum annual premium is 1/12 of 1% of the total amount of savings in insured accounts.

LEGISLATIVE AND REGULATORY ISSUES

The financial deregulation legislation of the early 1980s was, to a substantial degree, precipitated by the appearance of nontraditional competition in the thrift sector. The money market mutual funds were only the most visible of these new competitors. New competition in the origination and placement of mortgage loans has also emerged in the form of financial service networks among builders, realtors, and investment bankers, which threatens to weaken the link between local financial institutions and the communities that they traditionally have served. Coming concurrently with a period of high and volatile interest rates, these changes in the marketplace combined with financial deregulation to make their most profound effect on savings and loan associations and mutual savings banks. The consequence was a significant depletion of the net worth of these two types of institutions. Credit unions, because their asset portfolios were dominated by short-term loans, suffered much less relative to the other savings institutions.

Inasmuch as it appears unlikely that interest rates will regain the stability they once evinced at any time during the forseeable future, or that the new competition in the financial services industry will abate, savings and loan associations and mutual savings banks face multiple challenges in the years ahead. They must not only meet the new competition, they must also rebuild their net worth positions and restructure their asset and liability portfolios to reduce their exposure to interest rate risk.

The legislative and regulatory framework put in place during the early 1980s is permissive to the accomplishment of these tasks. Yet that framework is also permissive to the assumption of substantially more credit risk than these institutions have customarily carried.

The transition from an environment characterized by stringent regulation and a comparatively stable economic environment to an environment characterized by permissive regulation and a comparatively volatile economic environment has sorely taxed the regulatory machinery. During this period the major emphasis of the regulatory agencies appears to have been placed on liberalizing the regulatory environment. Few companion measures were taken until 1984 to reorient the regulatory machinery from one designed to assure compliance with the regulations to one featuring the preservation of safety and soundness in the operation of depository institutions. Indeed, the regulatory framework remained structured very much as it was before financial deregulation began.

The economic and technological forces working to change the structure of the financial services industry appear to be too powerful to give way to any effort to return to a highly regulated, segmented, and specialized financial sector. Consequently, the restructuring of the regulatory machinery to assure the safety and soundness of depository institutions will have to be high on the legislative and regulatory agenda of the last half of the 1980s.

This process will also have to be undertaken in the context of continuing financial deregulation. Although there are a number of proposals for further deregulation still awaiting action, perhaps the one that is most compelling is the authorization of **interstate banking.** This issue transcends economic considerations, such as broader asset powers, because it involves the relationship between the federal government and states' rights. As a result it seems likely that reciprocal regional compacts among individual states will precede action at the federal level.

What all of these emerging issues presage for savings and loan associations and mutual savings banks, but not for credit unions, is the gradual demise of mutual institutions. Because of the need for rapid net worth accumulation, capital stock institutions will become increasingly prevalent. Furthermore, although savings and loan associations and mutual savings banks can be expected to remain heavily oriented toward their traditional home mortgage lending activities, their separate institutional identity is likely to disappear.

Although credit unions are not completely immune to these processes, mutuality and the common bond of affiliation are integral parts of their organizational structure that cannot be altered without substantially transforming the institution. One public policy action could, however, set in motion the forces that would bring about such a transformation.

Savings and loan associations and mutual savings banks were not originally taxed because of their mutual status—earnings distributed to shareholders (depositors) were taxable as a part of shareholder income, but no tax was imposed on the earnings of the institution. The balance of earnings that was retained was treated as general reserves against losses, to which the shareholders (depositors) held a claim. These principles are those on which the nontaxability of credit unions are based today. Yet savings and loan associations and mutual savings banks have been fully exposed to federal taxation since 1969.

The major tax reform proposals discussed by the Congress in 1985 included the taxation of credit unions. Should credit unions become subject to federal taxation, they will experience the same diminution of ability to add to capital reserves that savings and loan associations and mutual savings banks experienced. In all likelihood, credit unions would then have to seek relief from the common bond restrictions that limit their growth; they would also be obliged to charge and pay interest rates on loans and share deposits that corresponded more closely to those of other financial institutions.

Taxation would therefore change substantially the nature of credit unions, making them much more like other financial institutions than they currently are.

The legislative and regulatory actions affecting the financial sector that have already been taken in the first half of the 1980s must be regarded as the most significant since the Great Depression. Much more remains to be done in the legislative and regulatory arenas to establish a new system of financial regulation that permits financial institutions to respond safely and soundly to evolving market forces. The highest priority will be accorded to actions that seek to achieve these ends during the years to come.

BIBLIOGRAPHY

Bodfish, H. Morton, *History of Building and Loan in the United States,* Chicago, IL: United States Building and Loan League, 1931.

Carron, Andrew S., *The Plight of the Thrift Institutions,* Washington, DC: The Brookings Institution, 1982.

Cohen, Deborah, and Robert Freier, *The Federal Home Loan Bank System,* Washington, DC: Federal Home Loan Bank Board, 1980.

Cooper, S. Kerry, and Fraser, Donald R., *Banking Deregulation and the New Competition in Financial Services,* Cambridge, MA: Ballinger, 1984.

Friend, Irwin, *Study of the Savings and Loan Industry,* Washington, DC: Federal Home Loan Bank Board, 1969.

Kendall, Leon T., *The Savings and Loan Business,* Englewood Cliffs, NJ: Prentice-Hall, 1962.

Moody, J. Carroll and Fite, Gilbert C., *The Credit Union Movement: Origins and Development,* Lincoln: University of Nebraska Press, 1968.

Ornstein, Franklin H., *Savings Banking,* Reston, Va.: Reston Publishing, 1985.

Pugh, Olin S., and Ingram, F. Jerry, *Credit Union Management,* Reston, Va.: Reston Publishing, 1984.

Salm, L. Joseph, *Study of Credit Unions,* Chicago, IL: United States League of Savings Associations, 1979.

United States League of Savings Associations, *Fact Book,* Chicago, IL: United States League of Savings Associations, various years through 1980.

United States League of Savings Institutions, *Source Book,* Chicago, IL: United States League of Savings Institutions, various years, 1981 through 1984.

Welfling, Weldon, *Mutual Savings Banks,* Cleveland, OH: The Press of Case Western Reserve University, 1968.

16

INSURANCE, REINSURANCE, AND RISK MANAGEMENT

CONTENTS

16

INSURANCE, REINSURANCE, AND RISK MANAGEMENT

Robert C. Witt
Jorge L. Urrutia

As an overview of **insurance, reinsurance** and **risk management,** we begin with an analysis of risk because a sound understanding of the concept of risk is essential for the study of the insurance mechanism. Insurance companies are financial intermediaries with some unique financial characteristics. These unique characteristics of insurers are reflected in their financial statements, which have several important differences when compared with those prepared by other business firms. The developing concept and main characteristics of risk management are presented together with the different methods of dealing with pure risk.

A general description of the entire insurance industry and its channel of distribution is also presented. As is well known, people insure their homes, automobiles, and other properties. They also buy insurance to protect themselves against the liability arising out of injuries to other persons or damages to the property of others. This is the field of **property-liability insurance.** The major insurance lines in this field are briefly analyzed. People also purchase insurance to protect themselves and their dependents against loss of income and medical expenses because of premature death, sickness, disability, or old age. The main characteristics of life and health insurance, annuities, and pension plans are also briefly discussed. Clearly, insurance is a necessary service in our society. Many times insurance is the only protection against severe losses that can threaten the financial stability of families and businesses. Insurance is a complex, expensive product, however, and some scientific search for agents and insurers is necessary in order to get the proper coverage at a reasonable price. Some tips for buying insurance are also given. This general review of the insurance business is concluded with an analysis of the regulation of the industry, the reinsurance mechanism, and the growing role of insurance companies in international business.

RISK AND RETURN

Insurance is intimately associated with the treatment of pure risk for individuals and business firms. Thus it is important to understand the meaning of risk in general prior to a detailed discussion of insurance.

CONCEPT OF RISK AND RETURN IN FINANCE. Individuals planning to invest in the stock market face the problem of estimating the future returns on securities. These estimates represent expected values. However, actual returns usually differ from expected returns. The deviation of the actual from expected returns on a financial asset is one measure of the investment risk associated with the asset.

The expected return on a security is simply the weighted average of the possible returns multiplied by the respective probabilities associated with the returns. For illustrative purposes, assume a particular security offers the following possible rates of returns during the first year: 25% with a probability of 0.40, 15% with a probability of 0.35, and 5% with a probability of 0.25. The expected return on this security is therefore 16.5%; that is, $25 \times 0.40 + 15 \times 0.35 + 5 \times 0.25 = 16.5\%$. The investment risk associated with this particular security can be measured by the standard deviation of the returns. The standard deviation is merely the square root of the weighted sum of the squared differences between the projected future returns and the expected return multiplied by the corresponding probabilities. In our example, the standard deviation is 7.9 percentage points, that is, the square root of 62.75, calculated as follows:

$$(25 - 16.5)^2 \times 0.40 + (15 - 16.5)^2 \times 0.35 + (5 - 16.5)^2 \times 0.25 = 62.75$$

In the preceding example only three future returns for the security were assumed. In the real world, however, there is an unlimited number of future returns, each of which has a given probability of occurrence. In this regard, there exists a probability distribution for the returns on an asset. If the returns are normally distributed, it is easy to conduct a hypothesis test and to develop confidence intervals for returns. The normal distribution is a bell-shaped curve that is symmetric around the mean. It is well known that a given percent of the actual values fall within a certain number of standard deviation around the mean. For instance, the actual returns will fall within plus or minus one, two, or three standard deviations of the expected return in 68.3, 95.5, and 99.7% of the cases, respectively. In the problem here, investors could be 68.3% confident that the actual returns will not deviate by more than plus or minus one standard deviation from the expected return, that is, $16.5 \pm 7.9\%$ or from 8.6 to 24.4%. These boundary values, 24.4% and 8.6%, are the upper and lower bounds of the 68.3% confidence interval. The higher the desired confidence level interval, the greater will be the range of values between the confidence-interval boundaries.

CONCEPT OF RISK IN INSURANCE. Insurance is concerned mainly with pure risk rather than speculative risk. A pure risk can only produce a loss. For example, the risk of premature death or the risk of a home being destroyed by fire are associated with contingent losses. A pure risk differs from a speculative risk, which can produce a gain or loss such as the risk involved in betting on a horse race or investing in a stock. Generally, only pure risks are insurable.

In insurance, risk is also classified as objective or subjective. Objective risk is the variation of actual losses around expected losses, a variance concept. It can be measured directly by the standard deviation associated with losses. It is similar to the concept of total risk in finance and is computed in the same way. In contrast, subjective risk is psychological in nature. It is the perception of risk that individuals have in their minds. It is not directly measurable, but it can be indirectly measured through the concept of utility and risk aversion in economics.

Insurance scholars usually divide pure risks into three categories: personal, property, and legal liability risks. **Personal risks** are those risks or contingent loss exposures that directly affect an individual, such as illness and accident. **Property risks** are those exposures that can affect the value of property already accumulated by individuals, such as the risk of automobile collision. **Legal liability risks** are those contingent loss exposures arising from legal responsibility for injuries to others or damages to the property of others under tort or negligence law such as product liability and professional liability.

PORTFOLIO THEORY APPROACH TO RISK AND RETURN. Utility theory classifies individuals into three categories based on their psychological reaction to risk: risk neutral, risk loving, and risk averse. Risk neutral individuals are those who are indifferent to risk; for example, they are indifferent to playing a lottery. Risk lovers are individuals who love risk; they derive pleasure from it. They like to play a lottery and do not buy insurance. In contrast, risk averters are individuals that dislike risk. They generally would not play a lottery except for entertainment purposes, and they would be willing to buy insurance in order to avoid the uncertainty of future losses.

Modern economic and financial theory assumes that individuals are risk averse. Because a risk averter dislikes risk, he or she must be offered some compensation to take the risk. In investment theory the concept of risk aversion implies that riskier assets must offer higher returns than less risky assets. Any risky security such as a stock must have a return higher than a risk-free security such as a Treasury bill. The difference between the return on a risky security and the return on the risk-free security is known as the risk premium in finance theory.

A portfolio is a collection of securities. The portfolio concept is important because most securities are not held in isolation. More important, a security held as part of a portfolio is less risky than one held in isolation because returns of securities are usually correlated with each other. The rate of return on a portfolio is simply a weighted average of the returns on the individual securities. This concept can be illustrated with the following example.

An investor has decided to invest \$400 in security A, \$350 in security B, and \$250 in security C. Because a total of \$1,000 is invested, the proportions invested in each security are 0.40, 0.35, and 0.25. The expected returns on the three securities are 20, 10, and 5%, respectively. The expected return on this portfolio is 12.75% ($20 \times 0.40 + 10 \times 0.35 + 5 \times 0.25 = 12.75$).

The risk associated with a portfolio of securities requires some explanation. Securities tend to be correlated with each other, so it is possible to reduce risk by combining securities into portfolios. The amount of risk in a portfolio depends on the number of securities in the portfolio and the degree of correlation among these securities. The portion of the total risk of a security that can be eliminated by diversification is referred to as unsystematic risk. The portion of the total risk that cannot be eliminated by diversification is referred to as systematic risk. In contrast, unsystematic risk is associated with factors inherent in the firm such as strikes and uninsurable risks. Systematic risk is due to factors that affect all the securities in the market such as inflation and changes in interest rates. Because unsystematic risk can be diversified away theoretically, the only portion of the total risk of a security priced by the market is the systematic risk. A measure of the systematic risk is the beta coefficient, which is the covariance of the returns on the stock and the market portfolio relative to the variance of the market portfolio. The systematic risk of a portfolio or the beta of a portfolio is the weighted average of the betas of the individual securities. In the earlier example, assume the betas of securities A, B, and C are 2.0, 0.7, and 0.4, respectively. Therefore the portfolio has a beta of 1.15 ($2.0 \times 0.40 + 0.7 \times 0.35 + 0.4 \times 0.25$).

The **Capital Asset Pricing Model (CAPM)** was an important development in modern financial theory because it suggested a way to relate returns and systematic risk. The CAPM specifies a linear relationship between the return on an asset and its systematic risk. Under the CAPM, the return on an asset is equal to the return on a risk-free security plus a risk premium. The risk premium of an asset is the risk premium of the market portfolio weighted by the beta coefficient of the asset. The risk premium of the market portfolio is the difference between the return on the market portfolio and the return on a risk-free security. Theoretically, the market portfolio contains all the assets that exist in the economy. In practice a proxy is chosen for the market portfolio, such as a portfolio composed of all the securities traded on the New York Stock Exchange. If we assume for illustrative purposes that the rate of return on Treasury bills is 8% and the return on the market portfolio is 12%, then a security having a beta of 1.5 is expected to earn a return of 14%; that is, $8 + 1.5\,(12 - 8) = 14\%$.

The impossibility of measuring the return on the true market portfolio has generated much criticism of the CAPM. In addition, the CAPM assumes that asset returns are normally distributed, individual investors have quadratic utility functions, and markets are perfect and efficient. Clearly, these assumptions are not very realistic. In fact, the normal distribution assumption implies individuals have unlimited liability, and the assumption about the quadratic utility function implies that individuals become more risk averse in an absolute sense as they accumulate more wealth. Both of these assumptions conflict with reality.

The Arbitrage Pricing Theory Model (APT) is a more recent development, which provides an alternative to the CAPM. The APT is also based on a linear return generating process, but it is built with weaker assumptions than the CAPM. Moreover, the market portfolio does not play an important role in it. Indeed, under the APT, the risk of an asset is described by its covariances with several common factors and not just by its covariance with the market portfolio. These common factors affect all the securities in the market. According to the APT, the return on an asset is the return on a risk-free security such as a Treasury bill plus a risk premium. The risk premium is a weighted average of the risk premiums associated with the several common factors.

RISK MANAGEMENT

DEFINITION AND SCOPE OF RISK MANAGEMENT. Risk management involves the decision-making function of an executive in the handling of pure risks of a business firm through insurance, self-insurance, and other transfer and retention methods.

In the past, risk management used to be a part-time job. The functions of the risk manager were essentially to buy insurance and to assume some responsibilities for safety and loss control. But recently firms have realized that scientific risk management could save a lot of money for them, and thus they started to pay more attention to the cost of pure risk. In fact, large business firms have developed separate risk management departments in recent years. As a result, risk managers have become relatively important executives who usually report to the treasurer or finance manager and have a continuous interaction with other managers of the firm, insurance companies, and insurance agents.

The scope of modern risk management is much broader than just buying insurance. It includes noninsurance methods of dealing with risks such as leasing and nontransfer risks methods, such as retention, self-insurance, and loss control. In addition, risk management has also been extended to the protection of human assets. In fact, risk management is becoming more involved with the administration of employee benefit plans, which includes pension plans, health rehabilitation, and life insurance. Moreover, the handling of risks such as the liability risks involved with a new product is also becoming a risk management function.

Clearly, **risk management** is different than **insurance management.** The insurance manager is concerned only with the insurance program of the business firm. The risk manager, on the other hand, stresses the identification and measurement of the exposures to loss of the firm and considers noninsurance methods of treating risks. Moreover, he or she administers and conducts periodical evaluation of the risk management program. Risk management is basically more complex than insurance management, and the decisions of the risk manager have greater financial impact on the firm.

Given the nature of the responsibilities of the risk manager, the **insurance agent** cannot serve as a substitute. The risk manager is an employee of the firm, has greater familiarity with the enterprise, and can coordinate the risk management program from an inside position. The insurance agent, on the other hand, is an outsider and tends to deal only in areas of his or her competence. A risk manager does not necessarily eliminate the need for an insurance agent, however, because the risk manager cannot be an expert in all the different insurance contracts and markets required by the business firm. The knowledge and expertise of an insurance agent are valuable to the risk manager, especially when one considers that a business firm usually buys insurance from many insurance companies.

RESPONSIBILITIES OF THE RISK MANAGER. The responsibilities of the risk manager can be classified as general and specific. The main objective of a risk manager is the treatment or transfer of risks and the elimination or reduction of exposure to loss as means of reducing costs and increasing efficiency of the business firm. In other words, the main responsibility of the risk manager is the protection of the assets and profits of the firm. This general responsibility of the risk manager is translated in practice into the design, administration, and evaluation of a risk management program.

A good **risk management program** must contain definitive policies for handling the pure risks of the firm. Such a program is necessary because it makes evident and tries to correct the various errors associated with buying insurance and the inadequate use of noninsurance methods. Some of the errors associated with an insurance program include the following: (1) under-insurance or the failure to buy adequate amounts of insurance, in some cases risks are not insured at all, such as the crime exposure; (2) coverage errors such as the lack of use of deductible and coinsurance clauses which result in higher insurance costs; (3) uneconomic arrangements of insurance such as insuring small exposures to loss, buying collision insurance for old cars, and under-insuring large exposure to loss such as in the product liability area; and (4) failure to adopt loss control programs, such as installing sprinklers or implementing a safety program.

Among the several specific **responsibilities** of the **risk manager** are the following.

1. *Identification* of exposures to loss, which requires that the risk manager be familiar with the operations of the business firm and keep records of the exposures to loss, insurance claims, damages to properties, accidents of employees, employee dishonesty, and so forth. A necessary task in the identification of risks is the preparation of a risk exposure inventory.

Physical inspections and the analysis of the financial statements allow for the detection of bottlenecks and the main exposures to loss.

2. *Measurement* of the exposure to loss involves the analysis of frequency and severity of losses, which must be estimated by studying the past records of the firm, consultation with other firms and insurance companies, and the constant surveillance of real estate and other properties.
3. The risk manager must also *select methods* of handling risks. He or she must decide which risk-handling technique is best suited for treating each exposure to loss. Commercial insurance, assumption or retention, self-insurance, transfer, and loss control are some of the methods of dealing with risks available to the risk manager.

DIFFERENT WAYS OF HANDLING RISKS. As indicated earlier, insurance is not the only method of handling pure risks of a business firm. Other ways of dealing with such risks are described below in the following paragraphs. They include avoidance, retention, transfer, self-insurance, and loss control.

1. **Avoidance.** The firm can avoid risk simply by eliminating the activity that can cause a loss. For instance, the firm may avoid the risk of product liability suits by discontinuing the production of certain products. The risk of damage to products during the transportation from the factory to the customer's warehouse can be avoided by not offering this service.

2. **Retention.** This can be unplanned or planned. Unplanned retention is simply ignoring the risk; for instance, ignoring inconsequential losses associated with collision for an old automobile fleet. Even though unplanned retention implies doing nothing, the very act of being aware of the risk is important because awareness of risk is a basic requirement for better risk management. Planned retention, on the other hand, is a conscious effort of the firm to retain some specific risk and implies some financial arrangement to meet future losses. Good examples are the use of deductibles and coinsurance clauses and the retention of potential losses up to certain levels and the purchase of excess-loss insurance for larger losses.

Some advantages of retaining risk are the elimination of costs associated with the transfer of risks and the encouragement of loss control. Problems associated with retention include the greater variation of costs due to the uncertainty associated with potential losses, the loss of services of the insurers, and the loss of tax benefits because reserves created to meet losses are generally not tax deductible, except for certain workers' compensation losses. The amount of retention to select is a very difficult problem faced by the risk manager. A maximum aggregate limit of retention must be determined on the basis of the overall financial position of the firm. A rough rule of thumb is to retain between 1 and 5% of the firm's net worth, depending on the financial strength of the firm.

3. **Transfer.** This is a popular method of handling risks. The most common way of transferring risk is, of course, through the use of insurance. A nonin-

surance method of transferring risk is through a lease. For instance, by leasing a fleet of cars the business firm can transfer ownership problems, insurance details, and collision expenses to the lessor. A firm can also use lease plans for buildings and other properties. Hold-harmless agreements can also be used to transfer some liability risks.

4. **Self-Insurance.** Self-insurance is basically a misnomer but can be conceived of as a scientific form of retention in that it involves formal financial planning for potential future losses. Self-insurance is different than insurance because it does not involve transfer of risk. However, a self-insurance plan should have all the characteristics required for insurable risks. A basic requirement for the implementation of a self-insurance program is a healthy financial condition of the business firm. The self-insurance program can consist of bearing all losses from a given source or bearing losses up a to certain amount and buying insurance for the losses above such a level.

There are several reasons for using self-insurance, including: (1) saving money by avoiding some of the costs included in insurance premiums; (2) dissatisfaction with the services of insurers (e.g., the firm cannot obtain a favorable rate classification or the insurer does not offer the right coverage); (3) to handle a risk not covered by commercial insurers (e.g., nuclear radiation); and (4) to handle large deductibles under current insurance contracts.

Even though self-insurance has its advantages, many business firms prefer to buy commercial insurance. Among the reasons for not using self-insurance are the following: (1) insurance premiums are predictable and more stable than loss costs in a self-insurance program; (2) avoidance of the details involved in self-insurance; (3) desire to have the services of the insurer; (4) the exposures to loss do not meet all the requirements for self-insurance; and (5) loss of tax benefits because loss reserve funds are not tax deductible, whereas premium payments are deductible.

A form of self-insurance used by big corporations is buying insurance through a captive insurance company. The captive is established to write insurance on the risks of the parent company. Captives have several advantages, including: easier direct access to reinsurance markets, substantial savings in commissions and state premium taxes, earnings from investments, and tax benefits because premiums are tax deductible (this deduction has recently been constrained by the Internal Revenue Service).

5. **Loss Control.** Loss control techniques can be divided into loss prevention and loss reduction. Loss prevention attempts to decrease the frequency or number of losses, for example, by using fire-resistant construction, tight quality control rules, or a safety program. Loss reduction, on the other hand, seeks to limit the severity or dollar amount of loss. For example, the installation of an automatic sprinkler system would reduce the severity of a fire after it had started.

Loss control is the ideal method of dealing with risk from the viewpoint of the society because it tries to minimize the real economic impact of losses by eliminating or reducing risks and costs. In regard to the other methods of risk treatment, it should be noted that transfer does not reduce risk in the aggregate, avoidance eliminates the risk and the activity, and insurance involves the economic costs of operating the insurance mechanism. Loss control, although socially desirable, is not always economically feasible. An evaluation of the trade-off between the potential gains and the costs of a loss control program is necessary. Potential gains are derived from the savings in losses and insurance premiums. Some of the costs are the required investment in loss control devices and their maintenance costs, and the costs of associated training programs.

The responsibility of loss control can be established at different management levels. The concern of the federal, state, and local governments for loss control is very important, because they have the authority to impose certain standards on business firms and individuals. The Occupational Safety and Health Act (OSHA) resulted in the development of a federal organization that requires business firms to maintain a safe working place for their employees. There are hundreds of state and local agencies that impose loss control standards such as state fire offices, water and sewer control agencies, and industrial accident commissions. Private insurers are also involved with loss control. Examples of insurer-supported loss control organizations include the National Safety Council, which collects statistics on highway accidents and conducts safety conferences, and the National Fire Protection Association, which conducts research and establishes standards for fire protection.

In spite of the several national and state organizations, the final responsibility of loss control remains with the business firm itself. Large corporations generally have loss control programs, which include safety inspections, safety training, and installation of safety equipment. These programs are intended to save costs for the firm and to provide a safer working environment for its employees.

MANAGEMENT OF THE COMMERCIAL INSURANCE PROGRAM. Insurance is a mechanism for transferring risk from an insured to an insurer. Insurance companies pool a large number of relatively homogeneous exposure units so that losses become highly predictable.

Commercial insurance has several **advantages.** First, losses are paid by the insurer, which allows the business firm to continue its operation after a major loss. Second, uncertainty is reduced because the premiums are fixed ahead of time. Third, insurers provide technical assistance in claim settlements, loss control, and other areas. Finally, tax benefits are derived because premiums are deductible for income tax purposes.

Some of the **disadvantages of insurance** are as follows. First, insurance tends to be expensive because commissions and expenses of insurers have to be added to expected losses when premiums are developed. Second, needed coverages are not always available. Third, the time and personnel required to negotiate contracts with insurers are indirect costs. Finally, selection of good insurers and agents may be difficult and time-consuming.

Commercial insurance is the most frequently used method of handling pure risk by business firms. Therefore transferring the risk to an insurance company is one of the important decisions that must be made by the risk manager. Given the complexity and the huge amounts of money involved in an insurance program, it is usually suggested the risk manager should consider insurance last; that is, alternative ways of handling risk should be considered first. Sometimes, however, the firm has no choice, because the insurance is required by law or contract or the potential losses are catastrophic.

The **management of the insurance program** involves the following steps:

1. **Classification of Coverages.** In deciding what types of coverages to buy, the risk manager can be assisted by **insurance agents** and insurers. Premiums, deductibles, and dividends must be carefully evaluated. The risk manager can divide the coverages into essential, desirable, and available categories. Essential coverages are those required by law or contract such as workers' compensation, and catastrophic losses, such as nuclear radiation. Desirable coverages would handle risks that can produce financial stress to the firm such as fire and product liability. Finally, available coverages are those offered by the insurance industry that may not cover all insurance desired by a firm.

2. **Selection of Insurance Agents and Insurers.** Important factors to be considered in choosing an agent are professionalism, years in business, quality of services, areas of competence, professional designations, and insurance companies represented. In selecting an insurance company, the financial strength is of utmost importance because future loss coverage depends on insurer solvency. Other factors to consider are the coverages offered by the insurer, insurance premiums, claim settlement practices, and other services.

3. **Negotiation for Coverage.** The business firm may have very specialized needs that are difficult to meet by coverages available in the insurance market. Negotiations with insurers may be necessary to obtain the proper coverages at reasonable prices. This task can be very complicated because negotiations usually involve several insurance companies. The cost of insurance is of primary importance to the risk manager. Accordingly, he or she must negotiate the premiums, deductibles, coinsurance, and loss control clauses in order to obtain the best insurance rates for the coverage desired.

4. **Loss Settlement.** When a loss has occurred, the risk manager must decide whether a claim should be filed, establish the amount of loss, and represent the firm in discussions with the insurer.

5. **Record Keeping.** An insurance program should be revised periodically and any errors must be corrected. The terms of the insurance contracts should be altered if circumstances have changed, and premiums should be renegotiated. In assuring the success of an insurance program, the risk manager must maintain adequate records for premiums, losses, accidents, and renewals of insurance policies.

TAX IMPLICATIONS OF RISK MANAGEMENT. Risk management decisions may have important tax implications for the business firm. Keeping complete and accurate records of losses is necessary because the IRS may require proof of loss. This is especially true for uninsured losses such as when retention and self-insurance are involved.

Insurance premiums paid by the business firm are tax deductible in the year in which they are incurred. Property insurance proceeds for losses are not taxable up to the book value of the property. If replacement cost is paid by the insurer and this amount exceeds the book value, the excess is usually taxed as ordinary income or capital gains. Uninsured property losses are usually deductible in the year they occur, but only up to their book value, and any recovery is subtracted. The reserves for **self-insurance** are generally not tax deductible.

If the losses exceed the taxable income for the year, the IRS allows the excess to be carried forward 7 years or carried back 3 years. In this way the business firm can reduce future income taxes or recover taxes paid in the past.

IMPACT OF RISK MANAGEMENT ON THE PROFITABILITY OF THE FIRM. Risk management considerations are generally ignored in **capital budgeting techniques** such as the net present value approach. However, losses associated with pure risks can have a significant impact on the cash flows generated by a project. Net present value, for instance, estimates the economic feasibility of a project by discounting at a certain interest rate the estimated net cash flows generated by the project during its useful life. If the net present value of the project is positive, the project is profitable and should be implemented. But what happens to the profitability of the project if a machine is totally or partially destroyed by fire before the estimated useful life? This question is usually not addressed by financial managers.

If the business firm decides to insure the equipment involved in the project, the payments of the insurance premiums reduce the net cash flow of the project. Retention of losses or self-insurance also have the effect of reducing the net cash flow of the project because the firm must absorb the future losses. The purchase of loss control devices increases the initial investment of the project and also reduces its net cash flows because of maintenance costs associated with the loss control equipment. The risk manager needs to make these assessments for higher level managers.

FINANCIAL ANALYSIS OF INSURANCE COMPANIES

DIFFERENCES BETWEEN FINANCIAL STATEMENTS OF INSURANCE COMPANIES AND OTHER BUSINESS FIRMS. The **balance sheet of an insurance company** differs from that prepared by other business firms in various ways. The assets of insurance companies are mainly securities, such as bonds and stocks, mortgages, and real estate. Insurance companies have few fixed assets, and they are not allowed to use debt. In fact, insurer liabilities are comprised primarily of various reserves for unearned premiums and losses or benefits. The equity of insurance firms is known as policyholders' surplus for a mutual company and capital and surplus for a stock firm.

The **income statement of an insurance company** also differs from that of other business firms but is similar in many ways. Premiums earned are comparable with net sales of other firms. Losses and expenses incurred are similar to the cost of goods sold. The income statement of an insurance company also contains the investment earnings of insurers generated by its invested assets. An insurer develops a pool of investable funds from policyholders because premiums are received before losses or benefits are paid.

DIFFERENCES BETWEEN FINANCIAL STATEMENTS OF PROPERTY-LIABILITY INSURERS AND LIFE INSURERS. The balance sheets of property-liability and life insurers differ in the nature of their components. From Exhibit 1, it can be seen that property-liability insurers invest heavily in securities such as government bonds, common stocks, and preferred stocks. They invest little in mortgages and real estate. The tendency of property-liability insurers to invest in relatively liquid securities is explained by the short-term nature of their contractual obligations. Indeed, the terms of most property-liability insurance policies cover only short periods of time such as 6 months or 1 year. Life insurance contracts, on the other hand, are generally long-term in nature. Exhibit 2 shows that life insurers invest mainly in corporate bonds and mortgages. They invest little in common stocks because of regulatory constraints.

EXHIBIT 1 BALANCE SHEET OF A PROPERTY-LIABILITY INSURER ($ THOUSANDS)

Admitted Assets	
Cash	$ 1,512
Bonds	67,676
Stocks	18,377
Mortgages	4,615
Real estate	1,801
Short-term investments	2,080
Other assets	19,302
Total admitted assets	$115,363
Liabilities	
Loss and loss adjustment expense reserves	$ 55,980
Unearned premium reserves	19,802
Other liabilities	9,831
Total liabilities	85,613
Policyholders' surplus	29,750
Total obligations	$115,363

EXHIBIT 2 BALANCE SHEET OF A LIFE INSURER ($ THOUSANDS)

Assets	
Government securities	$ 27,758
Corporate bonds	106,386
Corporate stocks	27,865
Mortgages	70,995
Real estate	10,312
Other assets	50,766
Total assets	$294,082
Liabilities	
Policy reserves	$239,680
Other obligations	31,575
Total liabilities	271,255
Policyholders' surplus	22,827
Total obligations	$294,082

It is important to note that in the balance sheet of an insurance company, bonds and mortgages are carried at amortized values and common stocks are carried at market values. This statutory accounting procedure helps to bring more stability to the book value of the assets of a life insurer than the assets of a property-liability insurer, because bonds are a much more significant portion of a life insurer's portfolio. However, the recent practice of property-liability insurance companies is to invest more in fixed-income securities and less in common stocks than in the past. According to the 1984–1985 edition of *Insurance Facts,* investments in bonds increased from 59.6% in 1973 to 71.4% of property-liability assets in 1983. In the same period, the investment in common stocks declined from 35.3% to 21.5%.

The main liabilities of a property-liability insurer are the unearned premium reserve and loss and loss adjustment expense reserves. Because insurers collect premiums in advance, they are required to set up the unearned premium reserves. These reserves represent the portion of premiums that the insureds have paid in advance for future insurance coverage. Loss reserves are created to cover unpaid claims. For life insurers, the primary liability is policy reserves, which are created from level premiums that exceed mortality costs during the early years of a life insurance policy. This excess payment builds up the savings element under a life insurance policy which the insured can partially reclaim as a cash value if the policy is surrendered before death occurs. Life insurers also establish reserves for unpaid death claims, which are equivalent to the loss reserves of property-liability insurers. Loss reserves in life insurance are relatively unimportant, however, because of the rapid payment of most death claims. Finally, the policyholders' surplus of a property-liability insurer tends to be relatively larger than the capital and surplus of a life insurer because of the greater variability associated with the losses and the invested assets of the former.

SOME UNIQUE FINANCIAL CHARACTERISTICS OF INSURANCE COMPANIES. The capital structure of an insurance company differs from that of most other business firms because long-term debt is not permitted. The major liabilities of insurers are reserves. These reserves play an important role in the capital structure of insurance companies. The largest liability for property-liability insurers is the loss and loss adjustment expense reserve. The second most important liability is the unearned premium reserve. According to the 1984 edition of *Best's Aggregates and Averages*, loss reserves have increased from 42.2% in 1974 to 49.3% of assets in 1983. This is probably due to the growing significance of liability lines in insurer portfolios, which are characterized by relatively long delays in the payment of losses. Unearned premium reserves, on the other hand, have decreased over time because of the tendency to write shorter-term policies. In fact, unearned premium reserves have decreased from 24.7% of assets in 1974 to 16.8% in 1983. Policyholders' surplus has increased from 24.6% of total assets in 1974 to 26.3% in 1983.

Policy reserves constitute by far the most important liability of life insurers, accounting for more than 80% of total assets. This percentage has been relatively constant over the time period 1974–1983. These reserves provide great financial leverage for a life insurer. Policyholders' surplus is only about 7% of the total assets of a life insurance company.

Insurance companies exhibit heavy financial leverage because of reserves. Traditional leverage ratios such as the debt-to-equity ratio, are not relevant for insurers because they cannot use debt. Insurers implicitly borrow money from their policyholders, however, and these funds are reflected by the reserves, a by-product of selling insurance. In essence, the reserves are obligations of the insurers to their policyholders and generate financial leverage for them. In this sense the ratio of reserves to policyholders' surplus can be used as a measure of financial leverage for insurers. By using data from *Best's Aggregates and Averages* (Property-Casualty) and the *1984 Life Insurance Fact Book*, it can be shown that the ratios of reserves to policyholders' surplus for property-liability and life insurance companies were 2.5 and 11.5, respectively, in 1983. Life insurers have a very high leverage ratio because of the long-term nature of their contractual obligations. In the property-liability insurance industry, financial leverage varies among insurance lines. Liability lines provide greater leverage because loss reserves are outstanding for a longer period of time than is the case for reserves in property lines of insurance.

Insurance companies are financial intermediaries because they collect premiums in advance for future performance contracts and pay claims later. The reservoir of assets accumulated is invested in the capital markets. The investment activity generates an important source of revenues for insurance companies. The 1984–1985 edition of the *Property-Casualty Fact Book* reports that investment income of property-liability insurers reached a record of $15.97 billion in 1983 on their invested assets, whereas the underwriting loss on their insurance portfolio was $13.32 billion. Property-liability insurers have a unique borrowing rate relationship because unlike other financial intermediaries such as commercial banks and savings and loan associations, they do not pay an explicit interest rate for the use of the money provided by their policyholders. In contrast, life insurers explicitly recognize the time value of money in their premium calculations. However, the interest rate used for discounting purposes is very low or conservative.

Because property-liability insurers have traditionally included a provision for underwriting profit in their insurance rates, this implies they have tried to charge their policyholders for the use of their money (a negative cost of capital approach). Recently, regulatory authorities became concerned about this unique borrowing arrangement of insurers. In fact, some states have ruled that investment income should be explicitly recognized and incorporated in the insurance pricing formula. As a result some sophisticated financial models for pricing insurance have been developed. In general, these rating formulas contain a negative term that represents the implicit interest payment an insurance company should expect to pay to the policyholders for the use of their funds. Historically, competition in most property and liability markets has prevented insurers from earning underwriting profits even though they tried to include them in rate-making formulas. Price compeitition has generally been more effective than price regulation in most insurance markets.

By observing Exhibits 1 and 2, it is easy to see that securities dominate the asset portfolio of insurers. In essence, insurers invest heavily in bonds, stocks, and mortgages. Inventories and fixed assets are absent on the left-hand side of the balance sheet of insurance companies because they are treated as nonadmitted assets in insurance accounting because of the focus on liquidation values for solvency purposes.

STATUTORY ACCOUNTING PRINCIPLES AND GENERALLY ACCEPTED ACCOUNTING PRINCIPLES. The **preparation of financial statements** for **insurance companies** is based on **statutory accounting principles (SAP).** These principles differ in several ways from the Generally Accepted Accounting Principle (GAAP) used by other business firms. The SAP involve a mix of accrual and cash accounting methods and tend to be much more conservative than GAAP.

One important difference between SAP and GAAP is in the valuation of assets. The GAAP recognize all assets, whereas the SAP only recognize so-called admitted assets (i.e., assets that are readily convertible into cash or are liquid). Other assets of an insurance firm, which are referred to as nonadmitted assets, do not appear in the balance sheet. GAAP recognize the value of investments at market or cost, whichever is lower, whereas SAP require stocks to be carried at market value and bonds and mortgages at their amortized values. Finally, unrealized capital gains and losses are recognized differently under SAP than under GAAP.

A fundamental difference between SAP and GAAP resides in the treatment of income and expenses. The GAAP use the accrual method, under which prepaid expenses are deferred and charged to operations when the corresponding income is recognized. The SAP, on the other hand, involves a mix of accrual and cash methods. Expenses are treated on a cash basis; that is, they are deducted when they are paid rather than incurred. In contrast, premiums are treated on an accrual basis. Thus they are only recognized as income as they are earned.

Because expenses are deducted when paid and premiums are recognized only when they are earned, the net effect of SAP is to understate underwriting profits of a growing insurance company and to overstate profits of a declining company. Thus SAP create a drain on the policyholders' surplus of a growing company, which constrains its ability to grow.

FINANCIAL RATIOS ANALYSIS OF INSURANCE COMPANIES. The financial performance of a business firm can be analyzed by using the traditional method based on financial ratios. Financial ratios are easy to compute, they summarize large amounts of financial data, and they allow a quick evaluation of a firm. However, they are simple numbers that are meaningful only when compared with those of the same company in the past or with those of other firms in the same industry.

Financial ratios can be classified in five categories: solvency, liquidity, efficiency, profitability, and market-value ratios. Solvency ratios are useful in determining the significance of debt in a business firm's capital structure and are important to long-term investors. Liquidity ratios help to determine whether a company has enough cash to repay its debts on a timely basis. They are relevant to credit analysts and bankers. Efficiency ratios attempt to measure how efficiently a firm is utilizing its assets; they are important to the management of the firm. Profitability ratios evaluate the combined effects of liquidity, assets management, and debt management on the operating results of a business firm. They are relevant to investors, creditors, and management. Market value ratios combine accounting and market information about the firm. They are important to the managers of a firm because they indicate how investors are evaluating the performance of the firm.

The traditional financial ratios are generally not appropriate for use in analyzing financial results of insurance companies because of their unique financial characteristics. As noted earlier, insurers do not use long-term debt, but they "borrow" money from their insureds through reserves. Moreover, insurers have little invested in inventories and fixed assets. Insurers also have two sources of revenues: investment income and underwriting profits. Nevertheless, several specific financial ratios for insurance companies have been developed and are discussed in the following paragraphs.

1. ***Capacity or Solvency Ratios.*** These are designed to evaluate the adequacy of the capitalization of an insurance firm relative to the volume of its business. Some of these ratios are presented in this section. Most of the data for the computation of the financial ratios are taken from Exhibit 1. The income statement for the hypothetical insurance company is shown in Exhibit 3.

$$\text{Kenney's fire ratio} = \frac{\text{Policyholders' surplus}}{\text{Unearned premiums reserves}}$$

$$= \frac{\$29{,}750}{\$19{,}802}$$

$$= 1.5 \text{ times}$$

The rule of thumb used by the insurance industry for Kenney's fire ratio is that it should be one or greater.

$$\text{Kenney's casualty ratio} = \frac{\text{Premiums written}}{\text{Policyholders surplus}}$$

$$= \frac{\$52{,}019}{\$29{,}750}$$

$$= 1.8 \text{ times}$$

$$\text{Cover ratio} = \frac{\text{Admitted assets}}{\text{Premiums written}}$$

$$= \frac{\$115{,}363}{\$\ 52{,}019}$$

$$= 2.2 \text{ times}$$

The rule of thumb for the cover ratio is 1.25 or greater.

2. ***Liquidity Ratios.*** The liquidity of an insurance firm can be established by comparing its invested assets with its reserves, as follows:

$$\text{Liquidity ratio} = \frac{\text{Invested assets}}{\text{Loss reserve} + \text{unearned premium reserve}}$$

$$= \frac{\$96{,}061}{\$55{,}980 + \$19{,}802}$$

$$= 1.3 \text{ times}$$

EXHIBIT 3 INCOME STATEMENT FOR A PROPERTY-LIABILITY INSURANCE COMPANY ($ THOUSANDS)

UNDERWRITING ACCOUNT

Gains		*Losses*	
Premiums written	$52,019	Losses incurred	$35,393
Premiums earned	51,035	Adjustment expenses incurred	5,313
Other revenues	1,166	Underwriting expenses incurred	14,531
Underwriting loss	4,152	Other expenses	116
Total	$55,353	Total	$55,353

INVESTMENT ACCOUNT

Gains		*Losses*	
Investment income	$7,851	Investment expenses	$ 397
Sales	286	Investment gain	9,194
Appreciation	1,454		
Total	$9,591	Total	$9,591

Invested assets are derived from the difference between total admitted assets and other assets. The rule of thumb is a liquidity ratio should be equal to or greater than one.

3. ***Profitability Ratios.*** Insurers use several profitability measures, a few of which are presented here.

$$\text{Combined ratio} = \frac{\text{Losses} + \text{loss adjustment expense incurred}}{\text{Premiums earned}} + \frac{\text{expense incurred}}{\text{Premiums written}}$$

$$= \frac{\$35{,}393 + 5{,}313}{\$51{,}035} + \frac{\$14{,}531}{\$52{,}019}$$

$$= 108\%$$

$$\begin{aligned}\text{Underwriting profit} &= 100 - \text{combined ratio}\\ &= 100 - 108\\ &= -8\%\end{aligned}$$

$$\text{Return on net worth} = \frac{\text{Net profit}}{\text{Policyholders' surplus}}$$

$$= \frac{\text{Underwriting Profit} + \text{Investment Income} + \text{Realized capital gains}}{\text{Policyholders' surplus}}$$

$$= \frac{-\$4{,}152 + \$9{,}194 + \$286}{\$29{,}750}$$

$$= 18\%$$

SCOPE AND STRUCTURE OF THE INSURANCE INDUSTRY

SCOPE OF THE INSURANCE INDUSTRY. The insurance industry has two distinct business components: property and liability insurance and life and health insurance. The following **economic statistics for the insurance industry** in the United States for 1983 have been extracted from *Property-Liability Insurance Facts*, 1984–1985 edition, and *Life Insurance Facts*, 1984 edition. These statistics provide some insight about the economic significance of insurance in the U.S. economy.

In 1983 there were more than 5,500 insurance companies based in the United States that provided about two million jobs and controlled approximately $904 billion of assets. The property-liability insurance industry wrote about $105 billion in premiums. Even though property-liability insurers suffered an underwriting loss of more than $13.3 billion, investment income of about $16.0 billion more than covered these losses and allowed property-liability insurance companies to continue their underwriting activities. Some of the major sources of loss payments under contracts were economic losses from automobile accidents that amounted to nearly $62.7 billion; robbery, burglary, larceny, and car theft accounted for about $9.3 billion; and property losses from fires reached about $5.9 billion.

In 1983, purchases of new life insurance were more than $1,026 billion, of which $753 billion corresponded to ordinary life. Total life insurance in force was about $4,966 billion. The average amount of life insurance held by American families in 1983 was about $54,200 per family. Two-thirds of Americans owned some form of life insurance. Benefit payments in life and health insurance reached a record of $51.9 billion in 1983. These payments provided $15.7 billion to beneficiaries, $22.6 billion to policyholders, and $13.6 billion to annuitants.

CLASSIFICATION OF INSURERS. The insurance industry can be categorized according to the type of ownership, type of demand, and type of coverage. The interrelations among the different classifications are illustrated in Exhibit 4.

Type of Ownership. Insurance can be public or private. Public or governmental bodies at federal, state, and local levels are involved in public or social insurance. The main purpose of public insurance is to provide protection to the members of the society against particular personal risks such as premature death, disability, medical expense, and loss of income during old age. For this reason most of the public insurance involves personal insurance. The main characteristics of public insurance include the following. First, coverage is generally compulsory rather than voluntary. Second, eligibility for benefits is not dependent on need or inadequate financial resources, but it is generally related to contributions to the program. Third, benefits are determined by law. Finally, the insurance plan is supervised by governmental agencies. Examples

EXHIBIT 4 CLASSIFICATION OF INSURERES

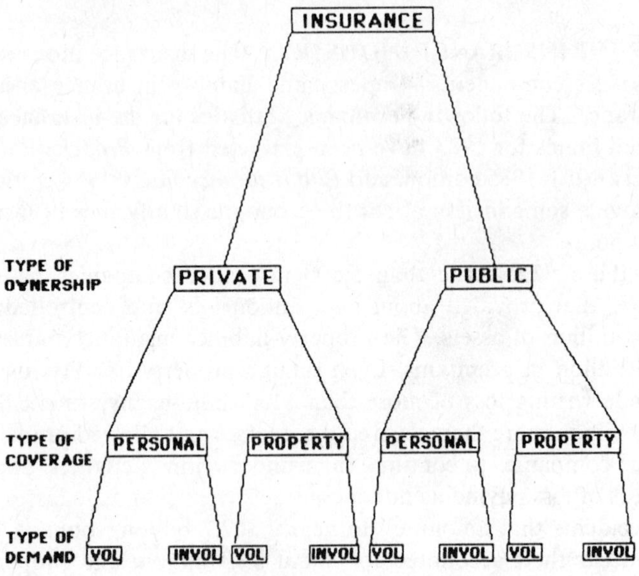

of social insurance programs are Old Age Survivor's and Disability and Health Insurance (OASDHI), unemployment compensation insurance, and workers' compensation insurance. About 47% of total premium income in 1981 was associated with public insurance.

Private insurance is coverage written by private business organizations. About the 53% of total premium income in 1981 was generated by the private sector. Private insurance is bought by individuals and business firms as a means of protecting themselves against various exposures to loss. It is usually voluntary, even though some coverages such as automobile liability insurance and workers' compensation are almost compulsory. The benefits obtained from private coverages are related to the amount of insurance purchased. Private insurers operate in the fields of personal and property-liability insurance. In 1981, 63% of the private insurance premium income corresponded to personal lines and 37% to property lines.

Type of Demand. Depending on the type of demand, insurance can be classified as either voluntary or involuntary. Most private insurance is based on voluntary demand. Public insurance, on the other hand, is mainly involuntary because it is required by law.

Type of Coverage. Two types of insurance coverages are offered in the market: personal and property. Personal coverages are those designed to provide direct protection for the individual. The losses involved in personal lines are loss of income and extra expenses. The perils against which the individuals seek protection are premature death, old age, unemployment, disability, illness, and accident. Private insurers specialize in life and health insurance, and public insurance covers primarily unemployment and old age perils. In 1981 about 79% of total premium income was for personal insurance, and only 21% was for property and liability coverages. As already noted, most of the public insurance is personal insurance. Property coverages are directed against perils that can damage property already accumulated by the individuals or businesses. The losses associated with property coverages are the direct losses of property, such as the destruction of a factory building by fire, and indirect losses such as the loss of income because of interruption of production due to the destruction of the factory by fire. Legal liability risks are covered by liability insurance. Property and liability insurance is generally offered by private insurers.

TYPES OF PRIVATE INSURERS. Private insurers can also be classified according to the types of ownership and organization: stock companies, mutual companies, Lloyd's associations, and reciprocals.

Stock Companies. A stock company is a corporation owned by stockholders. It is a profit-seeking venture where the shareholders bear the risk and reap the profits. Stockholders elect a board of directors who appoints the management. A minimum initial amount of capital is required in all states as a protection for the policyholders. Stock companies operate mainly in property-liability insurance, but the participation of stock companies in life and health insurance has grown dramatically in recent years. The usual channel of distribution for insurance sold by stock insurance companies is through independent agents rather than exclusive company agents.

Mutual Companies. A mutual insurer is also a corporation but owned by the policyholders. It is a nonprofit organization in the sense that any excess income is returned to the policyholders as dividends, used to reduce future premiums, or used to finance growth. If premiums are insufficient to meet losses and expenses, additional assessments may be allowed in small mutuals. Usually a minimum amount of "capital" is required to initiate operation. The policyholders elect a board of directors, which controls the company. The usual marketing system of mutual companies is through exclusive agents. Mutuals are very important in life insurance; however, their participation in the property-liability insurance market is growing, especially in automobile, homeowners, and workers' compensation insurance.

Reciprocals. A reciprocal is a form of cooperative insurance society. It is not a corporation because it is owned by the policyholders, and no initial minimum amount of capital is required. It is a nonprofit organization in which each member insures all other members and, in turn, is insured by them—a reciprocal relationship. The members authorize an "attorney-in-fact," generally a corporation, to manage the reciprocal. Reciprocals are usually small companies and operate mainly in automobile insurance. The United States Automobile Association is the largest example of a reciprocal in the United States.

Lloyds Associations. These associations are organizations of individuals who underwrite insurance on a cooperative basis. Each member assumes the risk personally and is liable for losses in proportion to the share of risk undertaken. These organizations operate for profit. There are two basic types of Lloyds associations: Lloyds of London and American Lloyds. Lloyd's of London is extremely important in insurance markets. In contrast, American Lloyds are not very important in the marketplace and do not enjoy the same financial reputation as Lloyd's of London.

Lloyd's of London is not an insurance company, and it does not write insurance. Rather, it is a marketplace where more than 19,000 individuals associate with each other in more than 300 syndicates and write insurance. Lloyd's of London operates all over the world and generally takes risks that the domestic insurers have rejected. Its underwriters specialize in heterogeneous risks such as losses from special events, a pianist's fingers, or an actress' extremities. It is also very important in ocean marine, aviation, and reinsurance.

INSURANCE MARKETING. **Sales** are the lifeblood of insurance companies. In addition, accurate estimation of future losses is dependent on an adequate volume of sales. Insurance coverages that are usually deemed to be sold rather than bought are life and disability. Insurance coverages that are usually deemed to be bought rather than sold are automobile, fire, homeowners, workers' compensation, and other property and liability contracts.

Insurance companies can use a direct distribution system for marketing their product, where the contact between the insured and the insurer is without intermediaries (sales by mail), or the insurance agent is an exclusive representative or employee of the insurer. Historically, this direct approach has usually been the primary distribution system used by life insurers. Insurers can also market their products through indirect distribution channels. Under such a system the consumers acquire their insurance from an independent insurance agent or intermediary who represents more than one insurance company. Property-liability insurance companies make use of both direct and indirect distribution systems.

Life Insurance Marketing. Life insurers use two channels of distribution: the general agency and branch office systems. The general agent is an individual employed to hire, train, and supervise other agents. Moreover, he or she represents only one insurer and works on a commission and/or salary, and is in charge of a specific territory. The general agent does not own the business sold, has no control over the terms of the contracts or premiums, and cannot bind coverage for the insurance company without consent.

The branch office approach corresponds to the sales branch of a business firm. The branch manager is an employee of the insurance company and earns a salary plus a bonus. This system gives the insurer more control over the insurance product and the hiring and training of its sales force.

Property-Liability Marketing. The direct distribution channel for property-liability insurance is referred to as the direct writing system. Agents working for direct-writing insurers are exclusive agents of the insurer or primarily represent only one insurer and generally work on a commission basis. The agents do not own the business they sell and cannot bind the insurance company. This channel of distribution is very popular in markets for automobile and homeowners insurance, but it is also becoming important in other property-liability lines.

Property-liability insurance is also distributed indirectly through the independent agency system. The general agent of a property-liability insurance company is different than the general agent of life insurer. In essence, the agent is an independent businessperson who works on a commission basis and owns the business sold; that is, he or she controls the renewal of contracts. The general agent can bind coverage for the insurance company, change the terms of the contract, and negotiate premiums, which cannot be done in the life insurance area.

Mass Merchandising. This mass-marketing approach initially developed slowly for selling insurance in the property-liability area. However, it has become more popular in recent years. A common method is distribution through employer payroll deduction. Underwriting is done on an individual basis, however. The premiums are generally less expensive because of scale economies and savings in commissions associated with this mass marketing approach. Because the enrollment in plans is voluntary, this kind of insurance tends to attract bad risks, which increases the adverse selection problem. Other types of mass merchandising make use of master contracts and no proof of insurability is necessary. These plans may or may not have employer contributions.

THE INSURANCE INDUSTRY AND EMERGING FINANCIAL SERVICES. Traditionally, the insurance industry has been a product-oriented business; that is, insurers have concentrated their efforts on selling insurance products instead of trying to fill the financial needs of their clientele. This philosophy has been changing in recent years. In essence, many insurance companies are becoming more customer oriented. These companies have understood that the clients do not need insurance specifically, but require a financial plan that best fulfills their financial goals within a budgetary constraint. Indeed, these changes are affecting the entire financial services community. A basic marketing revolution is taking place in the world of financial intermediaries: life insurers are extending their operations to the property-casualty sector and vice versa; insurance companies and commercial banks are buying brokerage houses; at the same time, major brokerage firms such as E.F. Hutton and Merrill Lynch, are buying insurance companies; savings and loan associations are acting as banks; retail stores such as Sears–Roebuck through Allstate, and commercial banks are selling insurance directly to their customers. In fact it may be difficult in the near future to distinguish between functions performed by the various financial intermediaries.

The tendency toward diversification and homogenization of the financial services has been facilitated by important technological, economic, social, and governmental changes. The progress in communication technology has made faster computers available to medium- and small-size firms. The high inflation levels and high interest rates of the 1970s switched the strategies of investors from long-term investments to short-term, liquid, and more flexible investments. Consumers have become more sophisticated and more demanding. Apparently, more consumers have decided to conduct most of their financial transactions at one place and like to have easy access to financial products and services. Finally, the tendency toward deregulation of the operations of commercial banks, credit unions, and savings and loan associations has brought about more flexibility and greatly increased the competition among financial intermediaries.

The insurance industry appears to be responding effectively to the new trends. Insurers have the financial resources and human expertise to compete successfully in the new financial markets. They are becoming more consumer oriented and offering a larger variety of higher-quality, lower-cost, and more flexible insurance products such as the adjustable life and universal life insurance policies. Insurers are offering different types of financial services to the public, of which financial planning guidance is one of the most important and popular. Some insurers are reducing commission costs by distributing their products through mass merchandising, stock brokerage firms, and credit-related firms.

PROPERTY-LIABILITY INSURANCE

The various types of property-liability insurance coverages are briefly discussed in this section.

AUTOMOBILE INSURANCE. Automobile insurance is the largest of the property-liability insurance lines. Statistics given by the *1984–1985 Property-Casualty Fact Book* indicate that the premium volume for automobile insurance in 1983 was $47.8 billion. This represents 43.9% of the premium written by the property-liability insurance industry. Automobile liability insurance accounted for about 60% of the automobile premium written in 1983; the remaining percentage was related to automobile physical damage insurance. Over 83% of the automobile insurance purchased in 1983 was by individuals or family groups. Commercial automobile insurance accounted for only 15.7% of the premium volume.

The automobile is an important and necessary capital investment for most individuals. Automobile driving, however, exposes one to several types of losses: liability, physical damage, and bodily injury losses. These losses can have catastrophic financial impact, especially in the case of the liability risk. The *1984–1985 Property-Casualty Fact Book* reports that in 1983 there were about 29.4 million motor vehicle accidents, which resulted in about 4.7 million nonfatal injuries and 44,600 deaths. Drivers under age 30 accounted for more than 50% of car accidents, even though they represented only 33.6% of the driving population. As a consequence of the large number of automobile accidents, insurance companies have encountered escalating costs and incurred large underwriting losses. The *Fact Book* reports that the average paid bodily injury claim increased 130.5% from $2,472 in 1974 to $5,699 in 1983. Property damage liability claim payments climbed from $397 to $1,020 or 156.9% during the same period. The automobile insurance industry suffered an underwriting loss of $3.8 billion in 1983 because loss payments and expenses exceeded premiums by this amount.

Given the high frequency and potential catastrophic nature of losses associated with automobile accidents, most individuals and businesses have realized that the most feasible way to protect against the financial consequences of these perils is through the purchase of automobile insurance. Moreover, automobile liability insurance is required in most states under financial responsibility laws. Canadian provinces have similar laws.

The most popular automobile insurance policy is the **Personal Automobile Policy (PAP).** The PAP has been designed to replace the Family Automobile Policy still used by some insurers. The insured car under the PAP is a car owned or leased by an individual or family for nonbusiness use. The insured car can be an auto, station wagon, jeep, van, pickup, trailer, or panel truck. The PAP provides automatic liability insurance protection for a replacement vehicle. To obtain coverage for physical damage, however, it is necessary to notify the insurer that a temporary substitute automobile is being used. The persons covered under the PAP are the named insured, his or her spouse, and any family member if living in the same household, or any person using the covered car with permission.

The PAP has four main components, each of which constitutes a separate policy. These four components are briefly discussed in the following paragraphs.

Liability insurance covers bodily injury and property damage liability for which the covered person is legally responsible. The limit of liability may be specified as a single limit per accident, for instance, $25,000. However, it can also be written with split limits for bodily injury and property damage if desired. For example, 25/50/10 means that the policy pays up to $25,000 per person injured subject to a $50,000 maximum for bodily injury payments in an accident, and up to $10,000 for property damage liability claims.

Medical payments coverage pays on a no-fault basis medical and funeral expenses up to 3 years after the accident. The injuries can be suffered while driving a car or as a pedestrian. The limit is $2,000 per person, but higher limits can be purchased. There is no coverage for work-related accidents when workers' compensation provides benefits. If there is other insurance available, the PAP pays on a pro rata basis.

Uninsured motorist coverage pays for bodily injuries suffered by the covered person when the other driver is at fault but has no liability insurance, does not carry enough insurance, is financially irresponsible, his or her insurance company is insolvent, or is a hit-and-run driver.

Physical damage coverage for an insured's car pays on a no-fault basis for damages to the covered automobile. It is divided into collision and comprehensive coverages. Collision insurance pays for damages suffered by the covered car because of collision with another car or object. Comprehensive insurance covers losses caused by perils other than collision, such as fire, theft, falling objects, and explosion. It is an all-risk coverage and deductibles run from $50 to $250 or even higher. Transportation expenses, towing, and labor costs are also covered.

There are other components of the PAP that relate to duties after an accident and some general provisions that are discussed in the following paragraphs.

Duties after an accident and loss. The insured is supposed to give written notice of a loss to the insurer or agent as soon as possible, cooperate with the insurer in the investigation of the accident and settlement of the claim, and submit a written proof of loss.

General Provisions. The PAP is valid in the United States, its territories or possessions, and Canada. The policy can be canceled by the insured at any time. The insurer can cancel the policy within the first 60 days. The company can also cancel the policy if the insured does not pay the premiums or if his or her driver's license is suspended. Financially irresponsible drivers or failure to prove in court the negligence of a driver at fault leave many automobile accident victims inadequately compensated or not compensated at all. The following laws have been passed attempting to solve this compensation problem.

Financial responsibility laws require that motorists involved in an automobile accident must obtain automobile liability insurance or give other proof of future financial responsibility. Because the only penalty is the suspension of the driving license, these laws do not guarantee all drivers will carry liability insurance.

Compulsory insurance laws have been enacted in more than half the states. Under these laws, automobile liability insurance is required for all registered car owners. In spite of these laws there exist a relatively high percentage of uninsured registered vehicles. In addition, the limits of liability required are too low to cover the needs of many accident victims.

Unsatisfied judgment funds are funds created by states to compensate accident victims when the driver at fault is insolvent and there is no other means of collection.

No-fault compensation exists in about half the states that have implemented some kind of no-fault law. No-fault laws require first-party coverage, which allows the injured insureds to recover from their own insurers regardless of fault. No-fault compensation developed as an alternative to the tort liability compensation system, which has been strongly criticized.

Under a tort system, accident victims must prove in court that another party responsible for an accident was negligent in order to collect. Proving negligence makes the tort system delay compensation for accident victims because of court delays. It is also expensive because of trial costs and lawyers' fees, and it leaves many innocent accident victims inadequately compensated or not compensated at all.

No-fault plans help to eliminate litigation costs and claim payment delays. In addition, no-fault systems have provided benefits to consumers of automobile insurance more efficiently by returning a higher portion of the premium dollar to policyholders in the form of loss benefits. No-fault plans have been designed to compensate all accident victims for economic losses, that is, medical expenses and loss of income. Critics of no-fault systems have argued that these systems are unconstitutional because they deny accident victims recourse to court, immoral because drivers at fault may escape the consequences of their negligent acts, provide no payment for pain and suffering, and that the efficiency of the system in reducing costs has been exaggerated. The impact of no-fault laws cannot be evaluated in isolation because a tort system is still in effect above some threshold in most of the states that have adopted some type of no-fault law. For a detailed economic evaluation of these compensation systems, see Witt and Urrutia (1983).

WORKERS' COMPENSATION. Workers' compensation laws were developed because many employees were unable to collect for work-related accidents or occupational diseases under the negligence system. Workers' compensation imposes absolute liability under which the employers are liable for job-related injuries of their employees without regard to fault. Workers' compensation insurance usually provides unlimited coverage for medical expenses, loss of income, and rehabilitation expenses. Total and partial disability and survivor benefits are also provided.

Workers' compensation is compulsory in almost all states and currently 9 of 10 workers in the United States are covered. Weekly income benefits cover about two-thirds of the workers' weekly wage. Employers generally cover the insurance premium. The costs of workers' compensation programs are relatively expensive because they consume about 2% of a firm's payroll.

Workers' compensation can be acquired from private insurers and state funds. The employer can also use self-insurance in most states. Most employers, however, prefer to buy workers' compensation insurance from commercial insurers for several reasons. Private insurers offer a comprehensive contract that covers all kinds of liability arising from work-connected injuries, provides claim service, pays dividends, and uses experience and retrospective rates that modify the premiums according to the loss record of the insured. The private insurance contract provides two coverages: coverage A that pays for all claims assessable to the employer, and coverage B that protects the employer against liability suits.

State funds are an alternative to commercial insurance; however, they are not very popular and are mandatory only in a few states. Some federal agencies also provide workers' compensation programs to their employees. Most of the states allow employers to self-insure their workers' compensation benefits. Self-insurance may reduce the cost of the program and generates additional cash inflows because of interest earned on the investment of funds held for loss reserves. However, self-insurance is seldom used because it requires substantial knowledge of the insurance mechanism and sufficient loss statistics for accurate estimation of losses.

Other disadvantages of self-insurance include the loss of tax benefits because loss reserves are generally not tax deductible, the loss of an insurer's services for claim settlements, data processing, loss control, and administration of the workers' compensation program. A combination of insurance and self-insurance is a common solution. The employer absorbs a certain portion of losses below some threshold or limit, and the insurer pays the excess. The deductible or loss retention can be specific (i.e., applied to each particular loss), or aggregated (i.e., a large overall deductible for all losses suffered in one period). In the latter case the aggregate deductible would have to be exceeded before insurance would apply.

THE LIABILITY RISK. The liability risk is one's legal obligation for damages caused to others by negligent actions. Two kinds of loss-producing events are important in legal liability: injuries to others and damages to the property of others. There are five types of losses associated with liability risks: loss of income, medical expenses, funeral expenses, disfigurement, and pain and suffering.

Legal liability results from negligent conduct as defined in tort law. Liability insurance is designed to provide protection against the financial losses caused by one type of tort known as negligence. A negligent act is the failure to exercise the care required by the circumstances. Negligence must be proven in court; in fact, in order to collect the plaintiff must prove that the defendant was negligent, there was a financial loss, and the negligent act was the proximate cause of loss.

Defenses to Negligence. Several legal defenses discussed in the following paragraphs are available to the person alleged to be at fault. First, under the defense of contributory negligence, the plaintiff cannot collect if he or she is found partially to blame for a negligent act; that is, a person cannot collect anything if he or she is found to be 10% guilty for a collision of two automobiles in an intersection. Second, under the assumption-of-risk defense, the defendant can avoid legal responsibility if the injured person places himself or herself voluntarily in a position of danger. For example, a spectator injured by a ball at a baseball game may be unable to collect anything because this risk was assumed by attending the game. Guest-host statutes can also serve as a defense. Under this type of law an injured passenger in a car cannot sue the driver unless the driver is guilty of gross negligence, such as driving at an excessive speed or being intoxicated. These statutes do not apply to paying passengers.

Absolute Liability Trend. Despite the several defenses for negligence, there has been a trend toward absolute liability with total or partial abandonment of the principle of negligence. As noted earlier, workers' compensation is based on the doctrine of absolute liability. Under workers' compensation, employees receive payments for job-related injuries regardless of fault. No-fault laws for automobile accidents ignore fault determination below some threshold because persons injured can collect from their own insurers, regardless of fault. The doctrine of comparative negligence also reduces the liability of the defendant if the plaintiff is partially at fault, but the plaintiff is still able to collect for some damages. For example, if there is a loss of $10,000 and the plaintiff is found to be 10% negligent, he or she may only be able to collect $9,000 from the defendant. Under the doctrine of contributory negligence he or she would not have been able to collect anything. The doctrine of res ipsa loquitur, or the "thing speaks for itself," allows the plaintiff to collect without proof of negligence. For example, if a dentist extracts the wrong tooth, fault is presumed. The doctrine of vicarous liability places liability on the owner of a car for the negligent acts of the driver. Under this doctrine, one is liable if his or her friend injures someone while driving his or her car. The doctrine of respondent superior imposes legal liability on employers for negligent acts of their employees. For example, the owner of a pizza parlor is liable if an employee injures a pedestrian while driving a car to deliver a pizza.

Types of Liability Exposures. The common types of liability exposures are as follows: Contractual liability is imposed by contracts; for example, liability may be assumed when property is leased or a contract to perform services or to supply goods is signed. Employer liability to employees is operative when the employee is not covered by a workers' compensation program. The property owner or tenant owes a certain degree of care to the individuals who enter his or her premises. The law recognizes three kinds of individuals: an invitee, a licensee, and a trespasser. An invitee is someone who enters the premises for the benefit of the owner-tenant, such as customers in a food store, guests in a motel, a mail carrier, or a garbage collector. The highest degree of care is owed to an invitee. A licensee is someone who is on the premises for a legitimate purpose with the permission of the owner-tenant, such as firefighters, police, or invited guests. The host must warn the licensee of any danger on the premises. A trespasser is someone who is on the premises without permission or knowledge of the owner or tenant (e.g., a thief). No special care is owed to a trespasser. If the trespasser is injured, the owner-tenant generally is not liable. Landlords, however, cannot deliberately set a trap to injure a trespasser. An important exception for trespassers is associated with the attractive nuisance doctrine under which a trespasser who happens to be a small child is considered as an invitee. Product liability law requires that manufacturers, wholesalers, and retailers have to maintain certain standards and exercise a certain degree of care in the production and distribution of goods. Legal liability of a producer or distributor arises from breach of warranty, strict tort liability, or negligence. Professional liability is based on the doctrine that professionals who provide services such as physicians, engineers, lawyers, and insurance agents are required to provide reasonable professional care in order to avoid injury or damage to their clients. The principal-agent relationship establishes that employers are responsible for negligent acts of their employees or agents. Owner-operators of an automobile who drive a car owe a reasonable degree of care to pedestrians and other drivers in order to avoid harming them. Owners of automobiles are also held liable for negligence of others operating their cars with permission.

Types of Insurance Policies. Three major types of liability policies should be discussed here. First, the **comprehensive personal liability policy** can be purchased as a separate contract or as a part of an automobile or homeowners insurance contract. The most common way of obtaining personal liability protection is through the purchase of a homeowners' policy. Automobile liability insurance is, however, almost compulsory in most states and is basically excluded under the homeowners' policy. The comprehensive personal liability coverage attached to the homeowners' 1976 policy consists of two separate coverages: personal liability (or coverage E) and medical payments to others (or coverage F). These two coverages are explained under the homeowners' policy. The liability coverage attached to an automobile insurance policy covers bodily injury and property damage. Second, an **umbrella policy** is designed to broaden the limits of the comprehensive personal liability policy and was developed especially for professionals and corporate executives who need higher limits of protection. Finally, the **comprehensive general liability policy** provides protection against business liability. It covers bodily injury and property damage resulting from adverse conditions on the premises of a firm such as injuries caused by slipping on a wet floor. It also covers the following liability losses from business operations: damage to furniture during delivery; product liability such as illness caused by spoiled food; completed operations such as water damages caused by a defective installation of a pipe; independent contractors such as damages or injuries caused by defective construction.

FIRE INSURANCE. The fire insurance contract was one of the first commercial insurance policies offered by the insurance industry. Currently, it is generally sold as part of the homeowners and multiperil policies. The 1984–1985 edition of the *Property-Casualty Fact Book* reports that fire losses in 1983 totaled $5.85 billion. Fatalities in the same year were 4,600; 82% of the victims died in residential fires. Residential fires accounted for 57% of the total dollar losses and for 74% of all building fires. The most common causes of fire in residential buildings were heating, cooking, arson (incendiary/suspicious), and smoking. In nonresidential buildings the most common causes of fire were arson (incendiary/suspicious) and electrical problems.

The standard fire policy was developed in New York in 1943. It contains 165 lines of provisions and stipulations. The standard fire policy is not a complete contract, and a declarations page and appropriate forms or endorsements must be added to it. The forms vary according to the specific needs of the insured. The 165 lines are the basis for the insurance coverage and they contain the following. The first six lines are concerned with misrepresentation of material facts and concealment and fraud. Lines 7–10 specify the excluded properties. Lines 11–24 name the perils that are excluded from coverage, for example, fires caused by war or invasion. Excluded losses are described in lines 28–37. These are losses occurring when the fire hazard is increased by any means within the control of the insured, losses occurring while the building is vacant for more than 60 days, and losses occurring because of explosion or riot. Lines 56–57 specify the terms under which the policy may be canceled by the insured or the insurer. The standard mortgage clause is outlined in lines 68–85. The pro rata clause for loss sharing is in lines 86–89. The procedures to be followed when a loss occurs and how damages are to be appraised are explained in lines 90–161. When a loss occurs, the insured must notify the insurer or agent immediately, protect the property from further damage, and give a detailed written proof of loss within 60 days of the loss. Finally, lines 162–165 state the right of the insurer to subrogation against liable third parties.

The declaration page contains the insured's name, location of the property, premiums, amount of insurance, and the insurance agreement. The insurance agreement states that the insured is entitled to recover the actual cash value or replacement cost minus depreciation of the property. To be able to collect, however, the insured must have an insurable interest in the property. The standard fire policy covers only three perils: fire, lightning, and losses resulting from removal of property from the premises. The endorsements extend the basic coverage to additional properties and additional perils.

HOMEOWNERS' INSURANCE. The homeowners' policy is the most comprehensive coverage offered to fulfill the insurance needs of owner-occupied one- or two-family residences. The homeowners' policy is only for owners; separate "homeowners' " forms can be obtained for renters and condominium owners. The homeowners is a package policy and is less expensive than the same portfolio of separate coverages.

The homeowner's form is divided in two sections. Section one contains the coverages for the dwelling, other structures, personal property, and additional living expenses. Section two contains the coverages for personal liability and medical payments to others. There are seven versions of the homeowners' policy, from HO-1 to HO-6 and HO-8. The version briefly analyzed here is the

HO-3, which covers owner-occupied one- to two-family property with a minimum coverage of $20,000.

Coverage A—Dwelling. This coverage protects the residence itself, that is, the dwelling and structures attached to it and additions such as a patio roof. Coverage A corresponds to the amount of insurance bought, that is, if the purchase of homeowners' insurance is $100,000, coverage A is for $100,000.

Coverage B—Other Structures. Coverage for structures clearly separated from the dwelling or connected to it only by a fence or utility line (a garage or a greenhouse are included here). The coverage provided is 10% of coverage A; that is, if coverage A is for $100,000, then the other structures are protected up to $10,000.

Coverage C—Unscheduled Personal Property. This covers personal property owned or used by the insured, such as furniture, kitchen appliances, clothes, television sets, and stereos. Properties of others while on the premises may also be covered. Coverage C is 50% of A. Protection for personal property at a secondary residence (e.g., a vacation home in the mountains) is also covered up to 10% of coverage A. Coverage C specifically excludes several types of properties, among them animals, automobiles, and sound equipment while in an automobile.

Coverage D—Additional Living Expenses. This covers necessary expenses incurred by the insured when the residence premises are damaged and he or she has to move to a hotel or rent another home. Other expenses such as eating out and transportation are also covered. This protection is up to 20% of coverage A.

Coverages E and F. Coverage E is for personal liability, and coverage F is for medical payments to others. A single limit applies to both coverages. Coverage E is on an occurrence basis and has a maximum limit of $25,000. Coverage F is on an accident basis and has a limit of $500 per person.

The homeowner's policy HO-3 provides coverages at replacement cost on the dwelling with a 80% coinsurance clause, and actual cash value for personal property. The HO-3 provides all-risk coverage on the dwelling and other structures and broad named-peril coverage on unscheduled personal property. The all-risk coverage, however, lists several excluded losses, such as damages caused by freezing or the weight of ice or snow on fences, pavement, or a swimming pool; and several excluded risks such as earth movement, flood, and war. The named-peril coverage lists 16 different perils such as fire, lightning, windstorm, hail, explosion, and mist.

Buying a homeowners' insurance policy is an important matter that requires a careful analysis. The proper amount of insurance on the dwelling and personal property is difficult to determine, but a general rule of thumb is to carry 80% of the replacement cost. It is advisable to add an inflation endorsement to allow for escalating replacement costs, to add an endorsement on earthquake, and to choose high deductibles to save on the premium. Moreover, it is highly advisable to shop around because prices vary widely among insurers.

BUSINESS INSURANCE. Business insurance in different forms is available to protect buildings, equipment, machinery, inventories, and other valuable contents. Some of the various commercial insurance policies are described in the following paragraphs.

General Property Form. This is a coverage generally attached to the standard fire policy. It is divided into three categories: (1) owned real property, which includes the buildings, its additions, machinery and equipment; (2) owned personal property, which includes business personal property owned by the insured; and (3) nonowned personal property, which includes the improvements made by the insured such as decorations, paneling, and personal property of others in the insured's control. The general property form has several extensions of coverage, such as newly acquired personal property at another location, and outdoor trees and plants. The policy can be written with scheduled coverage, under which the properties insured are specifically listed, or under blanket coverage, where several properties are insured under a single item. The general property form usually includes coinsurance and subrogation clauses. The basic perils insured against are fire, lightning, and removal from premises. Extended coverage for windstorm, riot, hail, smoke, vehicles, aircraft, explosion, and vandalism/malicious mischief is available. There are also various other endorsements available.

Special Multi-Peril Policy. This is a very comprehensive multi-peril policy offered by the insurance industry to business organizations. It attempts to meet the insurance needs of wholesalers, retailers, apartment complexes, hotels/motels, industrials, and service firms. It covers buildings and personal property, liability, crime, and boiler-machinery. The property coverage can be obtained on a named-peril or all-risk protection basis.

Business Owner's Program. This coverage is an insurance policy designed for small to medium-sized businesses, such as a 60-unit apartment complex or a four-story office building. Property forms are available on a named-peril or all-risk basis. Liability and medical payments are also included.

Business Interruption. This insurance indemnifies the insured for profits lost and fixed expenses incurred as a result of interruption of normal operations because of damages to the property due to fire or another insured peril. Indirect losses are sometimes more important than the direct loss of property; for example, when a fire causes a plant to shut down, the manufacturer has to continue paying salaries, taxes, insurance, interest, and energy costs.

Extra-Expense Insurance. This coverage is designed for those businesses that cannot close down following the destruction of their properties. For example, commercial banks, newspapers, and oil dealers must continue operations, otherwise they would lose their business to competitors. They may need to rent a new building, pay extra wages to employees, lease equipment, and incur additional transportation costs. All of these extra expenses are not covered by business interruption insurance because the firm continues its operation.

Profit Insurance. This insurance covers only the loss of profit that would have been derived from finished goods destroyed by an insured peril.

TRANSPORTATION INSURANCE. Transportation insurance is probably the oldest type of insurance. Currently it is even more important because of the development of industrial production and world trading. There are two major types of transportation insurance: ocean marine and inland marine.

Ocean Marine Insurance. This coverage provides protection against destruction of ocean vessels and transported goods. Four types of coverage are available.

1. The hull policy covers the vessel itself. It is extended for a given period of time and is subject to geographical limits.
2. The cargo policy covers the goods transported. It can be written for a specified voyage or on an open basis. The open basis has no termination date, and all the shipments are automatically covered.
3. The freight policy protects the interests of the vessel owner in case the expenses incurred in the transportation of goods are not paid.
4. The legal liability policy protects the ship owner against legal liability for damages to other ships. Liability coverage is also provided for bodily injury and damages to properties other than vessels.

Inland Marine Insurance. This covers domestic shipments, instrumentalities of transportation and communications, and floaters. Some of the policies offered are the following.

1. Inland transit policy, which protects manufacturers, wholesalers, and retailers who have to transport large volumes of goods. The policy covers transportation by railroad, truck, ship, and steamer. The contract is written on a named-peril basis. Typical perils covered are collision, derailment, fire, lightning, and theft. Excluded perils are illegal trade, riot, strike, and war losses.

2. The trip transit policy has been designed for those that make shipments only occasionally. The coverage is on a named-peril basis and gives protection for a particular shipment between named locations.
3. The floater policy provides coverage for property and goods that are not at a fixed location; that is, the equipment of a contractor that is being moved constantly from job to job.

LIFE AND HEALTH INSURANCE

RATIONALE FOR LIFE INSURANCE. Life insurance can be viewed as a way of creating an estate in case the head of the family dies prematurely and, in some cases, a method of saving for future income needs. Life insurance is designed to provide financial security for individuals and families. It is especially important when an individual has dependents without income. Life insurance needs vary over time. For instance, small children, teenagers, and college students usually need little, if any, life insurance. A young couple with small children, on the other hand, may have great need for life insurance.

PROTECTION VERSES SAVINGS. Life insurance can meet two kinds of needs: (1) the protection need (i.e., protection for the family in case the breadwinner dies); and (2) the savings need (i.e., accumulation of money for retirement). Life insurance contracts are designed to reflect these two needs in different proportions. For instance, a whole life insurance contract contains elements of protection and savings. The element of protection decreases over time, whereas the savings element increases over time. A term-life insurance contract is primarily designed to fulfill the protection need. An endowment contract, on the other hand, emphasizes the savings element because it pays off if an individual dies during the term of the contract or if he or she survives to the end of the term. An endowment policy is basically a term-life insurance contract plus a pure endowment based on the survivorship principle.

CONCEPTS OF LEVEL PREMIUM AND CASH SURRENDER VALUE. Life insurance is usually sold on a level premium basis under which the policyholder is charged a fixed annual premium for the whole term of the contract. During the early years the level premium exceeds mortality costs and this excess is accumulated with interest to cover higher mortality costs in later years. The overpayments are placed in a reserve required by law. Thus the savings element of the life insurance contract is referred to as a legal reserve. The cash surrender value is somewhat less than the reserve on a policy because various liquidity and surrender costs must be recognized if a contract is surrendered. The difference between the face amount of the policy and the legal reserve is the pure amount of protection or the net amount at risk. The cash surrender value belongs to the policyholder, who can borrow against it or recapture it by terminating the policy. The cash surrender value is important but it is only a by-product of the level premium, which is designed to provide lifetime protection to the insured at a fixed-level cost.

MAJOR TYPES OF LIFE INSURANCE. Life insurance is offered in three basic types of contracts: term, whole life, and endowment.

Term insurance is issued for a specified number of years, such as 5, 10, or 20 years or up to age 65. It is mainly protection and generally does not contain any significant savings element except for relatively long-term policies. The protection is temporary and the policy is paid only if the policyholder dies during the term of the policy. Most term insurance contracts are renewable and convertible to a permanent form. However, they generally cannot be renewed after age 65. This kind of contract is most useful when the maximum coverage is needed for a given sum of money. There are three types of term insurance: level term, decreasing term, and increasing term. Level terms provides a constant amount of protection during its term or contract period, and it is renewable without proof of insurability. Under decreasing term the amount of protection declines gradually each year, and under increasing term the amount of protection increases each year during the term of the contract.

Whole life insurance provides lifetime protection. There are two kinds of whole life insurance—straight life and limited-payment life. Under straight life or continuous premium life insurance, premiums are paid in installments for as long as the insured lives. Under limited-payment life, the policyholder pays a higher premium than for the same face amount of straight life, but for a shorter period of time. Common payment periods are 20 or 30 years and life paid up at age 65.

Endowment insurance is a combination of term insurance and a pure endowment, as indicated earlier. It is issued for a specified period of time. The savings element is very important because the insured can collect whether he or she lives or dies. The policy provides protection against premature death during a specified period, and the policyowner is paid the face of the policy if he or she is alive at the end of the period.

Two major policy innovations introduced recently by life insurance companies are the variable life and the universal life policies.

Variable life insurance was designed to provide protection against inflation and its adverse effects on savings. The policy is sold with a fixed-level premium, but the face amount and cash value vary with the investment performance of the portfolio of stocks, bonds, and money market securities supporting it. A minimum guarantee is usually associated with the face of the policy, but not with its cash value. The minimum death benefit is usually set equal to the initial face amount of the policy. If the value of the portfolio increases, the face of the policy is increased in accordance with a specific formula in the contract. As is well known, there is no perfect positive correlation between the consumer price index and equity dominated portfolios. Thus variable life insurance provides no guarantee that inflation will be offset by the corresponding increases in the policy face and cash value, especially in the short run.

Universal life insurance has been developed as an alternative to whole life insurance. Basically, the policy combines life insurance with savings, but these elements are distinct and separate rather than a mere by-product of the level premium method used in ordinary life insurance policies. The separation of the savings and protection elements of the contract makes this policy distinctive. Premium payments are also flexible rather than fixed and level over an insured's lifetime. A large initial premium is required to purchase the policy, but subsequent premiums vary according to how much the insured desires to save. The interest paid on the savings portion of the plan is related to money market rates. Premiums can be paid monthly or weekly. Each month the insurer credits interest and deducts mortality charges based on the policyholder's age from the savings fund or cash value. The investment income on this policy is accumulated on a tax-free basis. Universal life allows the insured to increase or decrease the amount of death protection without purchasing a new policy, subject to a policy-face minimum specified by the insurer. This contract has become one of the most popular ones in the market.

There are all kinds of other possible combinations of the basic life insurance contracts. Some common life insurance packages sold are the following.

1. The family income policy is a combination of decreasing term and whole life. It is a popular contract designed to give income protection during the dependency period.
2. The family maintenance policy is a combination of level term and whole life insurance. The term protection is for a given number of years and does not decrease over time.
3. Juvenile insurance is designed to provide life insurance for small children and to develop a savings program to cover the cost of a college education.
4. The family group policy provides life insurance coverage for each member of a family. The head of the family usually obtains a larger amount of permanent coverage than the spouse and children.

GROUP LIFE INSURANCE. Group life insurance plans are generally employer-sponsored plans that pay benefits if an employee dies. The plan covers a group of persons under a master contract with a certificate of insurance issued to each member. A medical examination is usually not required. Group life insurance plans provide protection at a lower cost than individual insurance because of savings in commissions and administrative expenses. Certain requirements must be met to constitute a group for insurance purposes such as (1) the insurance should be incidental to the group, (2) there should be a flow of younger members into the group, (3) benefits must be automatically determined by some formula, (4) a minimum percentage of the employees must participate in the plan, and (5) the employer should help fund the plan. An employee is eligible for the plan if he or she is a full-time employee, has satisfied a probationary period, and is actively at work. According to the 1984 *Life Insurance Fact Book*, group life insurance in force totaled about $2,220 billion, which represented 44.7% of the total life insurance in force in the United States during 1983. There are several group life insurance plans, which are discussed briefly in the following paragraphs.

Group term is the most popular form of group life insurance. It provides relatively low-cost protection through yearly renewable term insurance. The employee generally has the option to convert the term insurance into some permanent form of life insurance after leaving the group.

Group creditor life insurance is insurance that protects the financial rights of the creditor in case the borrower dies. It is usually issued as decreasing term life insurance, which corresponds to the amount of the loan.

Group ordinary life insurance provides permanent life insurance for employees of a firm. Under this plan an ordinary life insurance contract is separated into two components: decreasing term protection and savings (the cash value). The employer's contributions cover the cost of term insurance, and the employee's contributions are used to build up the cash value (technically, the reserve for the policy).

MAIN PROVISIONS OF LIFE INSURANCE CONTRACTS. Some of the most important provisions of life insurance contracts are discussed briefly, including nonforfeiture options, settlement options, policy loans, the incontestable clause, the suicide clause, the grace period, and dividend options.

The nonforfeiture option assures the policyholder that he or she will not lose the savings element of a life insurance contract if it is surrendered or canceled. The insured can receive the cash value as a lump-sum payment, as extended term insurance for the same face amount of the policy surrendered, or as reduced paid-up whole life insurance—that is, a smaller amount of life insurance than exists under the policy surrendered.

Settlement options provide in the event of the death of the insured that the beneficiary has several alternative ways to collect the proceeds of the life insurance policy. These options include a lump-sum payment in cash; a fixed period option, under which the insurer pays installments over a specific time period; a fixed amount option, under which the insurer pays installments of a fixed amount of dollars for a time period determined by the funds available and the interest rate assumed; an interest option, under which the principal is left with the insurer and the beneficiary receives the interest income; and a life income option, under which the beneficiary receives an annuity income for life.

The policy loan provision provides that policyholders can borrow from the savings in their life insurance policies by paying a fixed interest rate without terminating the contract.

The incontestable clause states that the insurer cannot cancel or void the contract because of fraud or misrepresentation discovered after 2 years from the inception of the contract.

The suicide clause specifies that suicide committed 2 years after the inception of the policy cannot void or cancel the contract.

The grace period and reinstatement provisions are designed to save the contract and protect the insured and beneficiary under special circumstances. The insured has a grace period of 30 days to pay premiums that he or she did not pay on time in order to prevent lapsation of the policy. A lapsed contract can also be reinstated after a period of 3 to 5 years, but evidence of insurability is required and all unpaid premiums with interest must be paid. Reinstatement may be desirable for a policyholder because acquisition costs for a new policy can be avoided and provisions under the old policy may be better than those available under a new one.

Dividend options under some insurance policies, known as participating policies, provide dividends for the policyholders that can be used to reduce premiums, buy additional insurance, accumulate with interest, help pay up a permanent policy before the normal premium payment period ends, or taken in cash.

COST OF LIFE INSURANCE. It is important to understand the way life insurance costs are determined, because life insurance can be expensive and prices vary substantially from company to company. There are two main approaches in computing the cost of life insurance, which are discussed here.

First, the traditional **net cost method** has been commonly used by life insurers and agents in the past. The total cost of life insurance in this case is determined by the total premiums paid less dividends received and the cash value available upon surrender of the policy. For example, let us assume that Maggie, age 20, wants to buy $15,000 of ordinary whole life insurance. Her agent has informed her she will have to pay annual premiums of $100. However, she will get $400 dividends over a period of 20 years. The cash surrender value at the end of 20 years will be $2,000. The cost of this life insurance policy can be shown to be negative under the traditional method. The total cost is $\$100 \times 20 - (\$400 + \$2000) = -\$400$, and the average annual cost is $-\$20$. A negative average price of $-\$20$ results here. It would appear that the insurance company is paying Maggie for buying the policy. Obviously, such a result is misleading and wrong. The problem with this method is that it ignores the time value of money and other factors.

The **interest-adjusted method** provides a better measure of life insurance costs because it takes into account the time value of money. The total interest-adjusted cost corresponds to the future value of premiums less the future value of dividends and the cash value available. The previous example, assuming a rate of interest of 5% would generate different results under this method, as shown here.

Total premiums paid for 20 years accumulated with interest at 5%	\$3742
less	
– Dividends for 20 years accumulated with interest at 5%	– 920
less	
– Cash value at the end of 20 years	–2000
equals	
Total life insurance cost for 20 years at 5%	\$552
Accumulated value of 1 per year for 20 years at 5%	34.719

$$\text{Average interest-adjusted cost per year} = \frac{\$552}{34.719} = \$16$$

LIFE INSURANCE PROGRAMMING. A **life insurance program** is a systematic method for determining the financial needs of the family in the event of premature death of the breadwinner, and how these needs can be met by buying life insurance. The method is based on a comparison of the various family needs with all possible sources of income and financial assets available at the death of the breadwinner. The difference corresponds to the life insurance needed. There are two approaches for determining the amount of life insurance to purchase: the human life value and the needs approach.

The **human life value approach** is based on the present value of the estimated annual earnings of the breadwinner over her or his productive life after deductions are made for taxes, insurance premiums, and costs of self-maintenance. This method does not consider other sources of income. It is not as popular as the needs approach in marketing life insurance.

The **needs approach** evaluates all the family needs in case the breadwinner dies and compares them with all the sources of income and financial assets available to the family. The difference then supposedly should be met by purchasing life insurance for this amount. Needs are divided into cash and income needs. Immediate cash needs are for an estate clearance fund (the money that is immediately required when the family head dies, such as burial expenses and income tax payments due), mortgage redemption funds to provide the family with a mortgage-free home, emergency funds to cover the cost of a sudden illness of a family member, and educational funds to provide a proper education for the children. The income needs include the income required during the readjustment period following the death of the family head, income during the dependency period for children, a lifetime income for the widow, which is necessary during the period when Social Security is not available and when the widow is over 60, to supplement the Social Security income available at that time.

The life insurance program should be revised periodically, because cash and income needs can change drastically over time; for example, after divorce, remarriage, or early retirement. Each of these events can affect the amount of insurance required. The technical assistance of professionals, such as life insurance agents with a Certified Life Underwriter (CLU) designation, is always advisable.

HEALTH INSURANCE COVERAGE. Health insurance protects loss of income resulting from loss of health and the expenses associated with illnesses and accidents. The 1984 edition of the *Life Insurance Fact Book* reports that life insurance companies paid out $26.9 billion in health insurance benefits in 1983; $22.8 billion of this amount was paid under group insurance contracts, and $4.1 billion was paid under individual health insurance policies; $21.6 billion of the total amount covered medical expenses; about $3.3 billion covered loss of income; and nearly $2.0 billion provided for dental care.

Types of individual health insurance coverage. Individual health insurance is provided under several types of coverages, including hospitalization, surgical, regular medical, major medical, disability income, and dental. These coverages may be offered under separate contracts or provided in some combinations under a more comprehensive single contract, as indicated in the following paragraphs.

A ***hospitalization policy*** covers necessary hospitalization expenses, including room and board, laboratory fees, operating room charges, nursing care, and medicine costs while in the hospital. The policy will usually pay a maximum daily hospital benefit for a maximum number of days.

A ***surgical contract*** provides for the payment of licensed physicians for surgical operations they perform. The insurance usually establishes a maximum dollar amount for each type of operation specified in a schedule. This coverage is usually added to the hospitalization policy.

A ***regular medical policy*** covers the cost of services of physicians for other than surgical procedures up to some maximum amount per visit. This contract is not sold separately but is usually attached to the hospitalization and surgical policies.

The ***major medical policy*** is a blanket contract designed to cover catastrophic medical bills. It provides broad coverage with few exclusions and limits from $10,000 to $100,000 and even higher. The contract has a relatively large deductible and coinsurance provision for losses in excess of the deductible. Usually the insurer only pays 80% of the cost in excess of the deductible. The major medical policy is usually written in conjunction with or on top of the basic medical coverages.

The ***disability income policy*** provides periodic payments when the insured is unable to work because of injury, disease, or illness. Payments do not start until a given waiting period has been satisfied and are usually subject to some maximum number.

Dental insurance covers such procedures as oral examinations, extractions, fillings, bridgework, cleaning, and x-rays.

Group Health Insurance. Group health insurance contracts account for about 80% of the premiums earned in the health insurance area. Private group health contracts have grown rapidly during the past three decades because they are available at a lower cost and usually provide better benefits than individual health insurance policies. Employer contributions to cover group health insurance are also deductible for federal income tax purposes. The major health and disability insurance coverages are briefly presented here.

Group basic health usually covers hospitalization expenses, surgical expenses, physicians' visits, and diagnostic x-ray and laboratory fees.

Group major medical is usually issued as a supplement to the basic plan. The plan includes deductible and coinsurance similar to individual major medical. Common maximum limits for coverage are $100,000 to $250,000.

Group disability income provides disability income benefits for short-term disability for up to 2 years and sometimes for long-term disability for periods longer than 2 years.

Group dental insurance covers all types of dental services under a comprehensive plan, or pays a flat dollar amount for each service under a schedule plan.

Group Health insurance contracts are offered by three kinds of insurers: commercial insurers, Blue Cross/Blue Shield associations, and health maintenance organizations.

Commercial insurers sell over 50% of all health insurance and cover more individuals than any of their competitors. The types of individual and group policies they sell were discussed previously.

Blue Cross/Blue Shield Associations are independent, community-oriented, nonprofit corporations that sell prepayment health plans. Blue Cross provides coverage for hospital services instead of cash benefits. Similarly, Blue Shield covers medical and surgical expenses of physicians for its subscribers.

Health Maintenance Organizations (HMO) provide comprehensive medical care to their members for a prepaid fee. HMOs own or lease private clinics and hire physicians on a salary basis with some additional financial incentives. Deductible and coinsurance are not significant because the costs of most services are fully covered on a service basis. HMOs emphasize preventive medicine with diagnosis and treatment in order to keep their members healthy.

ANNUITIES AND PENSION PLANS

ANNUITIES. Annuities are bought for retirement income purposes. The peril covered is the opposite of the one for life insurance. Life insurance protects against the peril of dying too soon, whereas annuities protect against the peril of living too long and outliving one's financial resources. An annuity is a series of equal periodic payments made for a given period or during an annuitant's life. Annuities can be classified according to the way the payments are guaranteed, the period when the payments begin, the method of premium payment, the number of lives insured, and the type of income payments.

Annuities with Guaranteed Payments. Under this category there are three types of life annuities, which are listed here.

1. A straight-life annuity, under which payments are made as long as the annuitant is alive. There is no minimum guarantee for this life annuity.
2. A period-certain life income annuity, where the payments are guaranteed for a minimum number of years and for life thereafter.
3. An installment and cash refund life annuity provides for a beneficiary to receive the income payments of the annuitant until a sum equal to premium payments is received or an equivalent lump sum when the annuitant dies before receiving total annuity payments equal to the premiums paid.

Period When the Payments Begin. In this category are the immediate life annuity under which the payments start when the annuity is bought for a lump-sum payment and the deferred life annuity under which the payments begin some time in the future, usually near the expected retirement age.

Method of Paying Premiums. There are two ways to pay premiums: The single-premium method, under which the annuitant pays only one premium in a lump sum, and the annual-premium method, under which the annuitant makes periodic premium payments until the payout period under the life annuity starts.

Number of Lives Insured. A popular life annuity in this classification is the joint and last survivor annuity, which is based on the lives of two or more annuitants, such as a husband and wife. It provides payments until the last survivor dies. Obviously, many annuities are also based on a single life, rather than multiple lives.

Fixed or Variable Payments. The life annuity can be a fixed annuity that pays a fixed amount of dollars, or it can be a variable annuity. The purpose of the variable life annuity is to provide protection against inflation by attempting to maintain the purchasing power of annuity payments. The payments vary according to the changes in value of a stock market fund associated with the annuity. It has been assumed that the long-run positive correlation between common stock returns and the cost of living would provide an inflation hedge for these annuitants.

PENSION PLANS. The 1984 edition of the *Life Insurance Fact Book* reports that about half of the full-time workers in U.S. private industry are covered by some kind of retirement plan other than Social Security. The main purpose of private pension plans is to provide future retirement income for long-term employees, which is based on age and years of service of the employee. These plans usually supplement or are integrated with Social Security. Private pension plans are also an important source of capital in financial markets. In fact, private pension plans invested assets over $650 billion in the financial markets in 1983, according to the *Life Insurance Fact Book*.

A private pension plan can be placed with an insurance company, trust company, commercial bank, or may be self-administered under certain conditions. The design of the plan is greatly influenced by regulations under the Employee Retirement Income Security Act (ERISA) of 1974. An important provision of ERISA is the vesting provision, under which an employee is entitled to some or all of the benefits attributable to the employer's contributions if he or she leaves the firm after some minimum number of years. Pension plans receive favorable tax treatment because the employer's contributions are income-tax deductible and investment earnings generated by reserve funds are allowed to accumulate tax free. Eligible workers must be full-time employees and meet minimum and maximum age requirements. A typical pension plan usually has three retirement ages: a normal retirement age, usually 65, where full pension benefits are paid; an early retirement age, usually 55, in order to allow employees to retire early with reduced benefits; and a late retirement age, usually 70, so some employees can delay retirement and receive increased benefits.

The benefits under a pension plan can be a flat dollar amount for all employees, for example, $500 a month; a flat percentage of average annual earnings, for example, 50% of the worker's average annual earnings; a flat dollar amount for each year of service, for example, $20 a month for each year of service; or a combination of these.

Some major types of private pension plans include the following:

Individual Policy Plan. This pension plan is designed for small business firms. An individual policy, usually a deferred life annuity, is purchased for each employee in units of $10 of monthly retirement income.

Group Permanent Plan. This pension plan is based on the purchase of cash-value or permanent life insurance for each qualified individual in the group. The amount of life insurance purchased is generally $1,000 for each $10 of monthly retirement benefits desired. Cash values available under the policies when employees retire are used to fund the retirement annuity.

Deferred Group Annuity. Under this plan, a single-premium deferred life annuity is purchased each year for the amount equal to the retirement income earned during the year. The benefits paid at retirement are the sum of the benefits payable under all the deferred annuities purchased for the employee.

Deposit Administration Plan. The contributions under this pension plan are deposited in an unallocated fund, and a life annuity is purchased when the employee retires. A separate account is frequently used by a life insurance company to invest these funds in stocks and bonds in order to compete with trusteed plans, which have more liberal investment constraints than those imposed on insurer investment portfolios.

Trust Fund Plan. The contributions under this popular type of pension plan are deposited with a trustee, usually a commercial bank, which invests the funds in the financial markets. The pension benefits are usually paid directly out of the fund, so life annuities are not purchased when employees retire.

Keogh Plans. These plans are designed for the self-employed. The contributions are income-tax deductible, and the investment earnings can be accumulated income tax free. The maximum annual contribution is limited to 20% of earned income or $30,000, whichever is less. The funding of a Keogh can be done through a trust plan, a nontransferable annuity from an insurer, and in various other legal ways.

GOVERNMENT INSURANCE

OVERVIEW OF GOVERNMENT INSURANCE. **Social insurance** programs are usually compulsory forms of government insurance. They have been designed to handle complex social problems and risks, to ensure perils not covered by private insurance, and to provide a minimum floor of economic security to all segments of the population. Government insurance is primarily concerned with personal and social risks of premature death, illness, disability, catastrophic medical expenses of the aged, old-age dependency, and unemployment.

Social insurance programs have several distinct characteristics that distinguish them from private insurance programs. First, they are compulsory or mandatory. All employers and employees that qualify under the law must be covered in order to avoid adverse selection problems and to solve a social problem. Second, they provide a floor of protection for income. Social insurance is intended to provide a minimum level of income that is supposed to supplement personal savings and private insurance. Third, social adequacy is emphasized over individual equity in the sense that benefits are not directly proportional to individual contributions to the cost of the program. Benefits are intended to provide a certain standard of living to all contributors. Fourth, benefits are prescribed by law and tend to vary with wages and years of work. Fifth, contributions to the program require direct or indirect contributions from the covered employer, employees, and self-employed. Finally, the programs are designed to be financially self-supporting; that is, the programs are supposed to be financed by the contributions of potential beneficiaries without support from general revenues of the government.

The **Social Security Act** passed in 1935 as a result of the Great Depression included the Old-Age, Survivors, Disability, and Health Insurance Program (OASDHI). This program is the most significant social insurance program in the United States. Other important social insurance programs are unemployment insurance, medical assistance to dependent children and the poor or Medicaid, and workers' compensation.

OLD-AGE, SURVIVORS, DISABILITY, AND HEALTH INSURANCE. The OASDHI program is administered and financed by the federal government and accounts for about 60% of the benefits provided by government insurance. To qualify for various benefits, the insured must have credit for a certain minimum amount of work in covered employment. There are three types of insured categories: (1) fully insured, (2) currently insured, and (3) disability insured. Retirement benefits require a fully insured status, disability benefits require a disability insured status, and survivor benefits require either a fully or currently insured status.

The OASDHI program has four major types of benefits: (1) retirement, (2) survivor, (3) disability, and (4) Medicare benefits.

Retirement benefits provide monthly income benefits that represent a high proportion of preretirement covered income. The monthly retirement income benefits are based on the employee's primary insurance amount (PIA), which is the monthly payment to a retired worker at age 65. The PIA is determined from a worker's average monthly earnings for several years prior to retirement. In general, the formula used in computing the monthly benefits is weighted in favor of low-income workers and workers with large families. To qualify for benefits, the extra income earned by the insured after retirement must be below certain limits. If earnings exceed this limit, income benefits are reduced.

Survivors benefits provide support for the spouse and dependents of a deceased worker. These benefits are payable only if the deceased worker was currently or fully insured. A widow receives benefits until dependent children are 16, and they start again when she is 60. Children receive benefits until they are 18. Benefits for college students are currently being phased out.

Disability benefits provide coverage for workers who become disabled between the ages of 50 and 64, and their dependents. To be eligible, the insured worker must have disability insured status, have a specified minimum work record, give medical evidence of disability; there is a 5-month waiting period before benefits begin.

Medicare benefits are provided for workers age 65 and older and for disabled workers under 65 who meet certain eligibility requirements. The program is divided into two parts: hospital insurance and supplementary medical insurance. Hospital insurance pays for inpatient hospital care, inpatient care in a nursing facility, and some home health services. The supplementary medical insurance is voluntary and covers the fees of physicians and the cost of other medical-related services.

The OASDHI program is basically financed on a pay-as-you-go basis from Social Security contributions or taxes. The program has encountered some serious financial problems in recent years that required increases in the tax base and rate. Other solutions are also currently being considered.

UNEMPLOYMENT INSURANCE. Unemployment insurance plans are federal-state programs that provide weekly income benefits to workers involuntarily unemployed. These programs developed in 1935 when the Social Security Act was passed. Each state administers its own program. These programs are financed mainly by payroll taxes paid by employers and usually cover firms with four or more employees. To be eligible for the coverage, an employee must have worked for some specific minimum period during a base year or have earned some specified minimum amount of wages or both. A waiting period of at least a week is usually required before benefits can be claimed. The amount of benefits is some proportion of the wages earned during the base year. Payments are generally made for a maximum period of about 26 weeks. To be eligible for benefits, an unemployed worker must provide proof of unemployment and that he or she is actively looking for a job and is willing and able to work.

GOVERNMENT PROPERTY-LIABILITY INSURANCE. Federal insurance is available for losses resulting from flood, crop, fire, and crime perils. At the state level there are insurance programs for injured workers under workers' compensation and for damage to state-owned property. A joint federal-state program for property insurance on buildings in hard-to-insure areas is referred to as plans for Fair Access to Insurance Requirements or FAIR plans. Some federal property-liability insurance programs will be discussed briefly in the following paragraphs.

FAIR plans provide reinsurance against excessive losses from riot and other civil disorders. These plans are actually operated by pools of private insurers who share the losses and expenses in proportion to their share of the premiums. They originated in 1968 when the federal government decided that a riot reinsurance plan was needed.

Flood insurance is offered by the federal government in conjunction with some land-use controls. Eligible properties include one- to four-family dwellings and properties occupied by small business firms. The policy is written with a deductible and covers flood and mudslide. Federal subsidies were needed in order to provide this coverage because of obvious adverse selection problems associated with the flood peril.

Crop insurance is offered by the federal government and private insurers. The private insurance covers crop damage from fire or hail. The federal coverage is an all-risk coverage that must be bought at planting time. It is only intended to indemnify a farmer for the loss associated with the cost of the crop investment.

Crime insurance covers burglary, robbery, and theft. It is offered by both private insurers and the federal government. The federal insurance is administered by the Federal Insurance Administration (FIA), but sold through private insurers who act as service agents. Crime insurance is expensive and has high deductibles.

Federal Deposit Insurance provided by the Federal Deposit Insurance Corporation (FDIC) is designed to protect the depositors of commercial banks that fail.

BUYING INSURANCE

In buying insurance, a common error involves an improper allocation of premium dollars. People usually spend too much on some high-frequency but low-loss-severity perils and too little on low-loss-frequency but high-loss-severity perils. This situation can be partially avoided by following two basic principles: insure large potential losses first and use deductibles to avoid paying premiums for high-frequency, low-severity losses.

Choosing the right insurer can be a complex matter because insurance companies differ greatly in types of coverages offered, costs, financial strength, and services provided. Even though a careful selection of insurers and agents can be time-consuming, it can be time and effort well spent because one can save a lot of money on insurance purchases.

CHOOSING AGENTS. Qualified agents can provide valuable services to insurance consumers. A good agent is familiar with the different kinds of risks faced by individuals and business firms, can find insurance policies that meet the specific needs of the potential insured at reasonable prices, handle premium collection, and help manage claim settlements. A good agent can also develop a comprehensive insurance program for his or her clients. Unfortunately, some insurance agents merely sell insurance rather than risk management services, so insurance buyers can get little assistance from them. The quality and quantity of services offered by insurance agents can vary substantially. Because the commissions earned by good and bad agents may be the same, it pays to shop around because the variation in information and services provided can make the difference between getting a good insurance program and a bad one. It is important to know the experience of the agent and professional designations he or she has earned; for example, the number of years the agent has been in business, professional designations such as CPCU and CLU, courses and seminars attended, quality of insurance companies represented, and types of coverages offered should be considered. A good strategy is to work with two insurance agents—one a specialist in life and health insurance, and the other a specialist in property and liability insurance. These two major insurance areas are quite different, so agents tend to specialize in one area or the other.

CHOOSING PROPERTY-LIABILITY INSURERS. An insurance agent may represent one or more insurance companies. Therefore when a consumer chooses an agent, he or she is usually indirectly choosing an insurer. In many cases the selection of the insurance company is left to the agent, and even though good agents can arrange satisfactory coverage, it may be advisable for the consumer to participate directly in the process of choosing an insurer. In selecting a property-liability insurance company, the following factors should be considered.

Availability of Coverage. The first thing to find out is whether the insurer offers the coverage the consumer desires. Insurance contracts are, generally, unstandardized and not all insurers offer every type of contract. In analyzing an insurance contract the consumer should look for important aspects of the coverage, such as the perils covered, persons or properties covered, claim settlement policies, and available endorsements.

Cost of Coverage. In comparing costs of insurance policies, it is necessary to make sure the contracts are basically similar; that is, they should have the same contractual provisions. If the contracts are different, any cost comparison may be misleading. The cost comparison of participating policies providing for policy dividends must be made after estimated dividends are discounted to the inception of the contract. An analysis of the efficiency of the insurer's operations may also be appropriate. More efficient insurers should be able to provide cheaper coverage in the long run. Analysis of an insurer's loss ratio, expense ratio, and combined ratio can be helpful in evaluating the efficiency of an insurance company. Sources of statistics about insurance costs are available in *Consumer Reports,* and *Best's Insurance Reports: Property-Liability Edition.* The agent, of course, can be a primary source of some insurance cost information.

Financial Strength. The financial condition of an insurer is a very important factor to consider in selecting an insurer, because insurance involves a future performance contract that is good only if the insurer is solvent. It is not a minor point even though insurance regulation is primarily concerned with the solvency of insurers, and regulators examine each insurance company at least once every 3 years. Regulation cannot guarantee that no insurance companies will fail. A financial ratio analysis of the insurer can reveal significant information about its financial health. According to the so-called Kenney rules, the ratio of policyholders' surplus to unearned premium reserves should be equal to one, and the premium-to-surplus ratio should not be greater than two. Financial ratings of insurers are published yearly in *Best's Insurance Reports.*

CHOOSING LIFE INSURERS. In selecting a life insurer, the following factors should be considered: contractual coverage, cost, and financial strength of the insurer.

Comparison of coverages is a difficult task because life insurance contracts vary widely. Whole life insurance involves a long-term future-performance contract with high commissions in the first year. Therefore choosing the wrong insurer and switching to another firm can be a very expensive mistake. To make the right decision, the insured should determine what kind of coverage he or she wants in regard to term or whole life insurance, the amount of insurance needed, participating or nonparticipating policy, and length and frequency of premium payments.

Cost of coverage is a major factor because life insurance costs vary substantially among companies for similar contracts. The participating policy is a common type of policy in life insurance, especially with mutual insurers, which provide dividends to policyholders if mortality, expense, and investment experience are better than expected. Therefore in comparing costs an adjustment is necessary if the policy pays dividends. The cost of a life insurance policy is determined by three elements: mortality, interest, and overhead expenses. Mortality is important but may not be a significant factor in comparing costs because most companies use similar mortality tables. Interest earned on investments and overhead expenses, on the other hand, vary substantially among companies and should be carefully considered.

Cost comparisons in life insurance can be misleading in some instances. Insurance agents sometimes provide cost comparisons to their customers based on the traditional net cost method. This method, as indicated earlier, ignores the time value of money and sometimes shows a negative net cost. A better way to determine the cost of life insurance is to use an interest-adjusted cost method, which allows for the time value of money. Information about costs of life insurance can be obtained from various sources, including the agent, *Consumer Reports*, and *Best's Insurance Reports* (Life-Health edition).

Financial Strength analysis can be focused primarily on the investment of funds derived from an insurer's legal reserves and surplus. Life insurers invest heavily in high-quality corporate bonds and mortgages with low default risks. Policyholders' surplus is relatively small as compared with policy reserves, because mortality experience is relatively stable and predictable. Ratings of life insurance companies according to their financial strength are reported annually by *Best's Insurance Reports*. Insurers are ranked from A+ (excellent) to C (fair). A consumer should be careful about selecting a policy from companies rated below B or not shown in the rating report.

INSURANCE REGULATION

WHY IS THE INSURANCE INDUSTRY REGULATED? Insurance involves a future performance contract that is dependent on the honesty, competence, and solvency of the insurer. Economically viable insurance markets require public confidence in an insurer's ability to honor its promise to pay for future losses of its customers. The solvency or solidity of insurers is the most important goal of insurance regulation. Historically, price regulation has also been very important because insurance rates have to be set before losses and expenses are known, and state regulators frequently have been unwilling to allow competitive market forces to determine equilibrium prices. Regulatory authorities are also concerned with the availability of insurance, especially in those cases where insurance is required by law such as automobile liability insurance. Finally, regulators try to protect consumers against abuses of unscrupulous operators in the industry.

STATE REGULATION. The insurance business is regulated at the state rather than federal level. Each state has its own insurance laws and regulates many different aspects of the insurance activities, including pricing, investments, claim settlement practices, and agent licensing. State Insurance Departments are responsible for administering their insurance regulatory laws. They have enforcement authority and the power to create and enforce new rules. The Insurance Commissioner of a state usually has the power to license insurers, revoke or suspend licenses, conduct periodical examinations of insurers, approve new policy forms, control investment policies, approve or review rates, and regulate marketing practices.

REGULATION OF PRICES AND SOLVENCY. State regulators have frequently assumed erroneously that rate (price) regulation and solvency go together. Supposedly, rates have been regulated in order to promote insurer solvency in many states. State rate regulation in property-liability insurance varies widely from state-made rates and prior approval laws to no-filing and no-rate regulatory laws. In general, rates are required to be reasonable (not too high), adequate to cover losses and expenses (not too low), and not unfairly discriminatory (equitable) among insureds. Some insurers use rates developed by rating bureaus (a form of price fixing sanctioned by many states). These bureaus are subject to supervision and examination by State Insurance Departments. Life insurance rates are regulated indirectly through regulation of expenses and minimum reserve valuation requirements. Interest and mortality rates assumed for reserve valuation purposes are closely regulated in order to assure adequate reserves for future claims.

Property-liability insurance companies must maintain both unearned premium reserves and loss reserves. Life insurers are required to maintain policy reserves that are similar to unearned premium reserves. The methods of valuation of reserves are also regulated, because undervalued reserves understate liabilities and can lead to insolvency, and overvalued reserves might result in excessive insurance rates. Insurers must admit annual financial statements to State Insurance Departments. These financial reports have been standardized by the National Association of Insurance Commissioners (NAIC). Finally, stock insurance companies and mutual insurers are required to have an initial amount of capital and/or surplus to operate, and their investment activities are closely regulated. Safety and liquidity are the main factors in investment regulation.

REGULATION OF AGENTS AND BROKERS. The activities of agents and brokers are regulated because they are usually the only contact between the insured and insurer. Insurance is a business dealing with a public interest, which offers complex products and requires competent and well-trained agents. Most states require agents to pass an examination or complete specific courses to obtain a license. For some special products such as variable life annuities, the agent must also pass an examination covering investments and security and markets. The State Insurance Department has the power to suspend or revoke the license of a dishonest or incompetent agent. In addition, all states forbid rebating of commissions and misrepresentation of policies.

REINSURANCE

REASONS FOR REINSURANCE. Reinsurance provides insurance for insurers. In essence, reinsurance involves the transfer of a portion of the insurable risk assumed by one insurance company to another. The company shifting the insured risk is referred to as the ceding company or primary company. The company accepting insurance is referred to as the reinsurer. The amount of insurance initially written that remains with the ceding company is the net retention. The net retention is determined by the retention limits set by the ceding company. The amount of insurance transferred to the reinsurer is the cession.

Reinsurance exists and is used for several purposes, including the following. First, reinsurance increases the underwriting capacity of an insurer by allowing it to write insurance in excess of its retention limits. The excess amount is placed with a reinsurer. Thus an insurance agent can place large insurance limits with one company rather than using several companies. Accordingly, reinsurance is valuable to consumers, agents, and insurers.

Second, reinsurance helps stabilize profits of a ceding company by covering unexpected large or catastrophic losses. This enables an insurer to avoid large fluctuations in its loss experience over time.

Third, reinsurance reduces the unearned premium reserves required by law. When an insurance policy is sold, the insurer must create an unearned premium reserve for the entire premium because of special statutory accounting principles imposed on insurers. However, the company must use part of this premium income to pay commissions and other expenses incurred in issuing the policy. The accounting deficit must be covered by the insurer's surplus. This drain on surplus is especially serious in new, growing companies. If the company transfers a portion of the business to a reinsurer, this action reduces the unearned premium reserve requirement in proportion to the transfer. Hence the drain on surplus is reduced and the insurer can continue to sell additional insurance and grow.

Finally, reinsurance protects against catastrophic losses such as damage caused by hurricanes, earthquakes, and other catastrophic events (e.g., liability suits associated with asbestos).

TYPES OF REINSURANCE CONTRACTS. Reinsurance contracts can be classified as facultative reinsurance and automatic treaty reinsurance.

Facultative Reinsurance. Under this type of contract, reinsurance is optional for both the insurer and reinsurer and negotiated case by case. For instance, a reinsurer might agree to cover 60% of the losses under a $1.5 million insurance policy for 60% of the premium. Under facultative reinsurance, the insurer has no obligation to cede insurance, and the reinsurer retains the right to accept or reject any reinsurance deal offered by the ceding company. Facultative reinsurance can increase the underwriting capacity of a primary company, but its availability is uncertain because the company must shop around every time such reinsurance is needed.

Automatic Treaty Reinsurance. Treaty reinsurance is based on an agreement in advance by which the primary company (the insurer) must cede insurance and the reinsurer must accept it. Treaties have the advantage of covering a wide range of perils automatically; thus time-consuming negotiations can be avoided. There are several types of automatic reinsurance treaties, including quota-share and surplus-share, which are proportional reinsurance treaties; and excess-loss and stop loss, which are nonproportional reinsurance treaties. In a proportional reinsurance contract, the insurer and reinsurer share on a pro rata basis both the premiums and the losses on some prearranged basis. Under a nonproportional contract, the share of premium and losses is established for each particular case. The various automatic reinsurance treaties are discussed in the following paragraphs.

1. **Quota-Share Treaty.** The ceding company and reinsurer agree to share losses and premiums on each insurance policy. The quota share is some predetermined proportion usually expressed as percentage. For instance, a 50% quota-share treaty implies that the reinsurer will pay 50% of the losses and will take 50% of the premiums less a ceding commission. The reinsurer pays a ceding commission to the primary insurer in order to compensate for the first-year acquisition expenses incurred in selling the policy. Quota-share agreements are useful in reducing the unearned premium reserve and drain on surplus caused by writing new business for small insurers. However, they may cede a significant share of profitable business to a reinsurer.

2. **Surplus-Share Treaty.** The reinsurer agrees to take insurance on each risk in excess of a specified net retention limit of the primary insurer up to some maximum dollar amount. The retention limit is called a line, and it is expressed in dollars. For example, a net retention of $20,000 with four lines of reinsurance implies that the reinsurer will accept the excess amount on policies over $20,000 up to a maximum of $80,000. Thus an insurer could sell a $100,000 policy and retain only $20,000 of the exposure. The reinsurer pays a ceding commission to the ceding company out of its proportional share of the premium. Surplus-share agreements increase the underwriting capacity of the ceding company.

3. **Excess-of-Loss Treaty.** Reinsurance is designed to cover catastrophic exposures. The reinsurer bears losses in excess of the retention limit of the ceding insurer up to some maximum limit. The treaty can be written on a single exposure or on all losses from a single occurrence. It is like a regular insurance contract with a large deductible; for example, the reinsurer could agree to pay any loss in excess of $15,000 on a particular risk or to pay losses in excess of $200,000 from any one occurrence.

4. **Stop-Loss Treaty.** This is used to place an upper bound on the loss ratio of the ceding company. The loss limit is the higher of a given loss ratio or a specified dollar amount. The reinsurer covers the aggregate excess loss over the

stop-loss limit up to a specified maximum. For example, the stop-loss limit can be 80% of the net earned premiums of the ceding company or $500,000, whichever is greater, and the maximum liability of the reinsurer can be 60% of the net earned premiums of the ceding company or $500,000, whichever is less.

Reinsurance in life insurance can be arranged in several ways, but only two will be discussed here: **term reinsurance** and **coinsurance**.

Under term reinsurance the ceding company buys yearly renewable term insurance equal to the net amount at risk, which is the difference between policy face amounts and reserves. This enables the ceding company to keep the assets associated with reserves.

Under coinsurance the ceding company transfers a percentage of the face amount of the policy to the reinsurer, together with the associated reserves.

INTERNATIONAL INSURANCE

INSURANCE AS AN INTERNATIONAL BUSINESS. International activities of insurance companies have grown dramatically with the development of the world economy and foreign trade. At the same time the growth of the world economy has benefited from the presence of well-established international insurance markets, which efficiently spread large risks around the world. The developed countries account for almost all the world insurance business. The United States, Canada, Japan, West Germany, United Kingdom, France, and Switzerland have the largest insurance firms in the world. The main reasons for the concentration of international insurance among developed countries are based on well-developed economies and international trade systems, fewer restrictions or barriers to trade, lower political and commercial risks, economic systems emphasizing private property, and narrower cultural differences. Despite the smaller markets, government intervention, and high political risks, the third world countries now appear to present attractive potential markets for international insurers.

Insurance companies operate internationally for several reasons, including the need to meet the insurance requirements of domestic customers operating in other countries, the desire to find opportunities for higher profits, the need for diversification and broader spreading of risks, and the desire to obtain the power and prestige associated with international firms.

INTERNATIONAL OPERATIONS OF AMERICAN INSURERS. United States insurers operate abroad as multinational insurers, international reinsurers, or as suppliers of insurance for international American firms. The major reasons for the international expansion of American insurers are based on the excess capacity sometimes existent in the U.S. domestic market, the huge amount of capital and surplus available to U.S insurers, the need for new markets that increase demand for insurance and improve U.S. balance of payments, and an attempt to escape some of the intensive price competition in the United States.

United States insurers have been relatively successful in competing in the international insurance markets because of higher levels of technical skills available to large domestic companies, together with their great financial strength. There are several ways an American insurer can gain access to international markets, including the acceptance of shares of foreign reinsurance, by being represented by a local agent in another country, by establishing a branch or subsidiary, by acquiring an existing local insurer, by forming a joint venture with a domestic insurer, by establishing a reinsurance company, and/or by operating as a nonadmitted insurer. U.S. insurers also operate abroad as pools or a part of a group of insurers, such as the American Foreign Insurance Association (AFIA).

The operations of multinational insurers involve some special problems. There are sometimes barriers to entry because of political reasons or protection of a domestic insurance industry, prohibitions on buying insurance from alien insurers, restrictions on the use of foreign exchange, requirements to place all reinsurance with some local reinsurer, and/or discriminatory tax treatment.

INSURANCE AND RISK MANAGEMENT OF MULTINATIONAL CORPORATIONS. Multinational firms are exposed to local barriers, political risks, tax discrimination, and legal differences in many countries. This is also true for insurance companies competing for business in foreign countries. Some of the special problems faced by multinational corporations in buying insurance for their operations in foreign countries include the following.

1. Insurance regulation and legal aspects of the insurance business are different for each country. Some insurance is required by law or contract; other insurance must be bought from government-owned insurance companies; and, sometimes, the purchase of insurance from alien companies is prohibited.
2. Exchange-rate risk associated with floating exchange rates can greatly increase the cost of insurance.
3. Political risk associated with expropriation and nationalization of the subsidiaries abroad can create special insurance problems.
4. Credit risk associated with the insolvency of the importers of goods and services of multinational firms can involve substantial losses.

Even though insurance is still the primary risk management method used by multinational corporations, other risk management techniques such as risk retention and risk control are becoming more important. The development of the risk management function in international firms has been slow because of the various special problems faced by multinational corporations, which were mentioned earlier. The identification of exposures to risk is usually accomplished by plant inspections, analysis of flow charts, analysis of financial statements, and analysis of past loss data. The measurement of exposures to risk is complicated by the lack of reliable data about losses, the different methods of measuring frequency and severity of losses, and the impact of inflation and foreign exchange fluctuations on loss data, especially in developing countries. Finally, data may not exist or they have been distorted for political reasons.

The task of the risk manager in a multinational corporation is complicated by the lack of qualified personnel, lack of authority, conflict with other top managers, local regulations, and lack of good technical services from insurance companies. International risk managers are usually more knowledgeable about financial techniques involving risk retention and insurance than about loss control techniques, because risk control services are usually not available in developing countries.

BIBLIOGRAPHY

Allen, E.T., Malone, J.J., and Rosenbloom, J.S., *Pension Planning*, 5th ed., Homewood, IL: Irwin, 1984.

American Council of Life Insurance, *Life Insurance Fact Book*, Washington, D.C., 1983.

Athearn, J.L., and Pritchett, S.T., *Risk and Insurance*, 5th ed., St. Paul, MN: West, 1984.

Best's Insurance Reports, Life and Health, Morristown, NJ: Alfred M. Best, 1983.

Best's Insurance Reports, Property and Casualty, Morristown, NJ: Alfred M. Best, 1983.

Bickelhaupt, D.L., *General Insurance*, 11th ed., Homewood, IL: Irwin, 1983.

Bickelhaupt, D.L., and Bar-Nir, Ran, *International Insurance*, New York: Insurance Information Institute, 1983.

Brealey, R., and Myers, S., *Principles of Corporate Finance*, 2nd ed., New York: McGraw-Hill, 1984.

Breslin, C.L., and Troxel, T.E., *Property-Liability Insurance Accounting and Finance*, American Institute for Property and Liability Underwriters, 1978.

Brigham, E.F., *Financial Management: Theory and Practice*, 3rd ed., Hinsdale, IL: Dryden Press, 1982.

Copeland, T.E., and Weston, J.F., *Financial Theory and Corporate Policy*, 3rd ed., Reading, MA: Addison-Wesley, 1980.

Doherty, N.A., *Corporate Risk Management, A Financial Exposition*, New York: McGraw-Hill, 1984.

Elton, E.J., and Gruber, M.J., *Modern Portfolio Theory and Investment Analysis*, 2nd ed., New York: Wiley, 1984.

Fireman's Fund Insurance Companies and Risk Sciences Group, Inc., *Financial Applications for Risk Management Decisions*, 1983.

Greene, M.R., and Serbein, O., *Risk Management: Text and Cases*, 2nd ed., Reston, VA: Reston, 1983.

Greene, M.R., and Trieschmann, J.S., *Risk and Insurance*, 6th ed., Cincinnati, OH: South-Western Publishing, 1984.

Gregg, D.W., and Lucas, V.B., *Life and Health Insurance Handbook*, 3rd ed., Homewood, IL: Irwin, 1973.

Insurance Information Institute, *Insurance Facts:* 1984–1985 *Property-Casualty Fact Book*, New York, 1983–1984.

Insurance Institute of America, *Readings on Risk Financing*, Malvern, PA, 1983.

Long, J.D., *Issues in Insurance, Volume II*, Malvern, PA: American Institute for Property and Liability Underwriters, 1978.

Mathur, I., *Personal Finance*, 1st ed., Cincinnati, OH: South-Western Publishing, 1984.

McGill, D.M., *Fundamentals of Private Pensions*, 5th ed., Homewood, IL: Irwin, 1984.

Mehr, R.I., *Fundamentals of Insurance*, Homewood, IL: Irwin, 1983.

Mehr, R.I., and Gustavson, S.G., *Life Insurance, Theory and Practice*, 3rd ed., Plano, TX: Business Publications, 1984.

Rejda, G.E., *Principles of Insurance*, Glenview, IL: Scott Foresman, 1982.

Vaughan, E.J., *Fundamentals of Risk and Insurance*, 3rd ed., New York: Wiley, 1982.

Weston, F., and Brigham, E., *Essentials of Managerial Finance*, 5th ed., Hinsdale, IL: Dryden Press, 1979.

Williams, C.A., and Heins, R.M., *Risk Management and Insurance*, 4th ed., New York: McGraw-Hill, 1981.

Witt, R.C., and Urrutia, J.L., "A Comparative Economic Analysis of Tort-Liability and No-Fault Compensation Systems in Automobile Insurance," *Journal of Risk and Insurance* (December 1983).

17

THE INTERNATIONAL MONETARY SYSTEM

CONTENTS

17

THE INTERNATIONAL MONETARY SYSTEM

James L. Burtle

International monetary systems arise because independent countries issue their own currencies. For trade and investment to take place between countries, part of the currency of each country is usually converted into the currency of other countries. The **international monetary system** is the set of markets, government regulations, international agreements, and business practices that provides for conversions of currencies. Here, of course, it is understood that the term **currency** is broadly defined to comprise all forms of money, including bank deposits, that can be traded internationally.

In the past there has been a wide variety of international monetary systems, ranging from the gold standard to floating rate systems—depending on government policies and on the development of financial institutions in participating countries. This section will begin with a review of the gold standard, the Bretton Woods system, and other monetary systems culminating in the present system of managed floating. Various modifications of managed floating will be reviewed. Major international institutions that impinge on the world monetary system—including the International Monetary Fund, the World Bank, and the European Monetary System—will also be considered.

HISTORY OF THE GOLD STANDARD. Since ancient times there have been **foreign exchange markets**, sometimes operating freely and in other cases under strict government control. Although much can be learned from earlier history, the gold standard, which applied from the latter part of the nineteenth century until 1914, is a convenient starting point for a survey of the development of the monetary system as it exists today. Indeed, regardless of whether the apparent success of the gold standard was a historical accident, there has been a tendency to look back on the 1880–1914 era as a period of international monetary stability that helped to generate worldwide high productivity and employment.

MONEY SUPPLIES AND PRICE LEVELS. The **gold standard** operated without direct fixing of exchange rates between currencies but, in major countries, there was a fixing of units of each currency to its so-called mint parity in ounces of gold. In addition, there was some tendency for the central bank of each country to adjust its money supply according to its holdings of gold. Thus when gold moved into a country, the money supply tended to rise and when gold moved out of a country, the money supply tended to fall.

Another requirement for a workable gold standard was flexibility in price levels such that they would tend to move both up and down with money supplies. Thus a rise in the money supply in a country would push up prices and a fall in the money supply would lower prices.

PAYMENTS BALANCES. When money supplies moved with gold supplies and prices moved with money supplies, the gold standard tended to be self-adjusting. If a country had acquired additional gold because of a balance of payments surplus, the rise in its money supply would push up prices. Because of its higher prices compared with the rest of the world, the country would sell less abroad. Moreover, since prices abroad were lower, it would import more. As a result, the trade surplus would be eliminated.

In a country with a trade deficit, the process would work in the opposite direction. The country would lose gold, and as its gold supply declined, the central bank would reduce the money supply. Prices would fall relative to those of other countries. As a result, exports would rise and imports would fall until the trade deficit was reduced.

INTEREST RATES: ROLE OF THE BANK OF ENGLAND. In actual practice the gold standard worked better with smaller gold movements and small relative price changes than might have been expected. Major reasons for the absence of disruptive gold movements and price changes were the dominance of London in the world money market and the policy of the **Bank of England** to adjust British interest rates to prevent excessive gold movements. When gold began to move out of London, the Bank of England usually raised interest rates, thus attracting money to London and improving the overall British balance of payments so that the gold outflow was reversed. Conversely, interest rates were usually lowered when gold moved into London.

TECHNICAL ADJUSTMENTS. It is also worth noting that under the gold standard the tie between gold supplies and money supplies was not as restrictive as might have been supposed. After 1890 new gold supplies were developed in South Africa and Alaska, and there were technological advances permitting the use of lower grade ores. Also the spread of checking accounts, not necessarily tied to gold holdings of central banks, increased world money supplies. Thus the gold standard did not lead to the stringency in world purchasing power that might have occurred without these favorable special circumstances.

THE GOLD EXCHANGE STANDARD

Major European countries abandoned the gold standard during World War I. Notes issued to pay for the war expanded more rapidly than gold supplies, and the convertibility of bank notes into gold was suspended because there was not enough gold for redemption. Nevertheless, most governments and central bankers looked back on the gold standard as a near-perfect system that they wanted restored. In the Genoa Conference of 1922 Britain proposed the so-called **gold exchange standard**. This system economized on gold by using as a reserve a **key currency** backed by gold. The key currency would have the same equilibrating function exercised by gold under the gold standard. Countries gaining the key currency would raise their money supplies and prices and countries losing the key currency would lower their money supplies and prices. With higher prices, balance of payments surpluses would disappear, and with lower prices, balance of payments deficits would disappear. Britain wanted sterling to be the key currency because it was anxious to return sterling and the Bank of England to their central roles in the world monetary system.

Although the gold exchange standard was proposed in 1922, Europe remained on an essentially **floating exchange rate system** until 1925, when Britain went back on the gold standard. Britain, in effect, underwrote the gold exchange standard by promising that sterling would be redeemable in gold, although it was hoped that most countries, as had been the practice before 1914, would regard sterling as good as gold, and would not ask to have sterling redeemed in gold.

BRITAIN'S RETURN TO GOLD

Britain's **"return to gold"** was not a success. Instead of adopting a lower gold value for sterling, it was decided that confidence in **sterling** could be maintained only by using the prewar rate, which turned out to be too high for Britain to compete in world markets. Moreover, there had been a structural change in the world economy: relative wages and prices no longer moved downward easily, as had been the experience before 1914. The British coal strike and general strike in 1926 demonstrated these resistances to downward wage-price flexibility.

Under the gold exchange standard most of the British dominions and many of the smaller countries used sterling as a major part of their reserves. But the use of gold instead of sterling was the rule of major countries, notably the United States, France, and Germany (after the German mark was stabilized in 1924).

Already weakened and not fully supported by major financial centers, the gold exchange standard could not withstand the onslaught of the Great Depression. In September 1931, Britain was forced off the gold standard and sterling was allowed to float. There had been, of course, previous cases of countries abandoning gold convertibility, as in the United States from 1861 to 1879 and in France from 1871 to 1878, but these experiences were considered temporary and usually were related to recovery from wartime disturbances. The 1931 **sterling depreciation** was a shock: a leading financial power had dropped convertibility, and there was little hope that it would be restored.

THE GOLD BLOC

The reaction to the 1931 sterling depreciation—particularly from central banks that suffered losses from holding sterling reserves—was a total repudiation by major continental powers of the gold exchange standard. In the **World Economic Conference of 1933** the United States refused to stabilize the dollar, which had in effect gone off the gold standard when President Roosevelt took office in March 1933. Following the failure of the World Economic Conference, France, Belgium, the Netherlands, Switzerland, Italy, and Poland agreed to remain on the gold standard.

The **gold bloc**, as this group of countries was called, had basically the same problem as Britain. Their relative prices were too high and, in spite of trade restrictions, they suffered from chronic balance of payments deficits. The gold bloc came to an end when, after lengthy discussions with Britain and the United States on a new exchange rate, France devalued its currency in September 1936.

THE TRIPARTITE AGREEMENT

In the period between 1936 and 1939 most currencies were floating or had fixed exchange rates subject to frequent change. Germany and a number of central European countries were maintaining balance of payments equilibria by means of complicated systems of **exchange controls.** There was, however, some recognition that there could be dangers in uncontrolled floating. **Stabilization accounts,** set up notably by the United States, France, and Britain, at least in principle were intended to smooth out erratic fluctuations in exchange rates. In the **Tripartite Agreement** issued in 1936 by the United States, Britain, and France simultaneously with the devaluation of the French franc, and in a subsequent statement in October 1936, it was agreed (1) not to use exchange rate changes to "obtain an unreasonable competitive advantage and thereby hamper the effort to restore more stable economic relations," (2) to maintain cooperation between exchange stabilization funds, and (3) to inform the other parties to the agreement of the exchange rate that would be maintained for the next 24 hours.

Prior to this agreement, the United States and the United Kingdom had indicated their opposition to a devaluation of the franc that would put France in an excessively competitive position in international trade. This fear of **competi-**

tive devaluation was the major reason for the emphasis on exchange rate stability in the Bretton Woods Agreement of 1944.

THE BRETTON WOODS SYSTEM

The ideas advanced in negotiating the Tripartite Agreement might have been extended, because the world in the late 1930s seemed to be tiring of floating exchange rates. Before any action could be taken, however, World War II brought about exchange controls in most of the belligerent countries except the United States. Even before the end of the war, however, demands for monetary reconstruction were pervasive enough to lead to the **Bretton Woods Conference of 1944.**

PLANS OF KEYNES AND WHITE. At Bretton Woods rival plans for world monetary reform were presented by John Maynard Keynes for Britain and by Henry Dexter White for the United States. The Keynes plan provided for a new international means of payment called the **bancor.** Member countries would agree to accept payments in bancors. A clearing process would be established among member countries with some limitations on the extent to which they could become debtors or creditors in bancors. The Keynes plan had the advantage that world trade would not be restrained by shortages of key currencies. White and the American delegation to the conference were, however, concerned that the expansion of bancor liabilities might become excessive. As an alternative to the Keynes plan, White proposed a plan that turned out to be a variant of the gold exchange standard in which dollars would be used as international reserves of central banks and dollars would be convertible into gold. The Bretton Woods Agreement emerged primarily as the White plan rather than the Keynes plan.

PAR VALUES. In addition to the use of gold-convertible dollars as reserves, the agreement as it was actually implemented provided for essentially fixed exchange rates known as **par values.** Each member country was committed to maintain its exchange rate in the **1% band**—that is, not more than 1.0% above or below the par value. A country was permitted, however, to change its par value if there was a "fundamental disequilibrum" in its balance of payments. This term was not defined explicitly, but it appears that the Bretton Woods Agreement reflected the widespread viewpoint of the late 1930s that exchange rates should ordinarily remain stable. Thus a "fundamental disequilibrum" seems to refer to an extraordinary situation in which an exchange rate change could not be avoided by any realistic fiscal-monetary policy.

FOREIGN EXCHANGE INTERVENTION AND THE IMF. Countries adhering to the Bretton Woods Agreement maintained their exchange rates within the 1% limit above or below par value by means of foreign exchange intervention. If a country's exchange rate went below the 1% lower limit, the central bank of that country would sell foreign exchange and thus buy back its own currency until the exchange rate was pushed above the lower 1% limit. On the other hand, if the currency went above the upper 1% limit, the central bank would sell its own currency, to bring its exchange rate to a point below the upper 1% limit. Under this system there was a possibility that countries might exhaust their gold and foreign exchange holdings while attempting to hold a currency above the 1.0% lower limit.

To make it easier for countries to maintain exchange rates during periods of temporary adversity, the Bretton Woods Agreement provided for the establishment of the **International Monetary Fund (IMF).** The IMF was set up to make loans (technically known as **drawings**) to countries experiencing balance of payments difficulties not severe enough to be considered "fundamental disequilibria." Thus as it was originally conceived, the IMF was intended to prop up exchange rates that were under temporary downward pressure. Loans from the IMF to member countries were provided from contributions by its members.

THE TRIFFIN DILEMMA. The Bretton Woods system in the earlier years of its operation appeared to be remarkably successful. World trade and output grew at record rates, fueled by the growth in dollar liquidity in a process roughly similar to the growth of gold supplies in the 1890–1914 period. In the 1960s, however, doubts began to arise about the basic soundness of the system. To increase world liquidity, a continuing U.S. dollar deficit was required; but as the cumulative deficit increased, it was not certain whether the value of the dollar could be maintained. This dilemma—sometimes called the **Triffin dilemma** after Professor Robert Triffin of Yale University—might have been the undoing of the Bretton Woods system.

Before there could be any test of the validity of the Triffin dilemma, however, for quite different reasons mainly related to military expenses and the overheating of the U.S. economy from the war in Vietnam, the dollar came under downward pressure in the late 1960s and early 1970s. In August 1971 President Nixon stopped conversions of the dollar into gold, thus ending the international monetary system that had been set up at Bretton Woods.

THE SMITHSONIAN AGREEMENT

Because the dollar was no longer supported by gold conversion, most exchange rates were allowed to float in world money markets from August until December 1971, when a new world monetary agreement, known as the **Smithsonian Agreement**, was adopted. In this agreement convertibility between gold and the dollar was not restored, but the theoretical gold value of the dollar was devalued 8.0%; that is, the price of gold was raised from $35 to $38 per ounce.

Most other major currencies were adjusted up against the dollar by various amounts, including revaluations of the West German mark and the British pound by 13.6 and 8.6%, respectively. To permit greater flexibility in exchange rates, fluctuations were permitted within 2.25% of parity instead of within 1% as under the Bretton Woods system.

Despite high hopes for its success, the Smithsonian Agreement lasted only about 14 months. By February 1973 it was evident that the revaluations against the dollar had been insufficient. The dollar was devalued an additional 10%, thus raising the official price of gold to $42.22 per ounce. But this devaluation also failed to stabilize the dollar, and since March 1973 most currencies of the world have been floating.

THE IMF ROLE TODAY

In January 1976, in the so-called **Jamaica Agreement**, the IMF—which under the Bretton Woods Agreement had been set up to assist countries in maintaining fixed exchange rates—changed its Articles of Agreement to provide that countries would be free to choose their own form of foreign exchange arrangements although in principle these arrangements would be under the surveillance of the IMF. This surveillance would (1) prevent countries from manipulating foreign exchange rates to gain unfair advantages, and (2) attempt to restrain actions that would produce erratic movements in foreign exchange markets. In practice, however, the IMF has ceased to be directly concerned with exchange rate movements and its theoretical surveillance function is rarely applied. Nevertheless, the IMF continues to be the most important international organization relating to the world monetary system. This is because it continues to be a major lending agency although its loans are not ordinarily used to support the value of a currency. Instead, paradoxically, a requirement for an IMF loan today may be that a country adjust its exchange rate to a realistic level.

Today IMF lending is applied to overcome balance of payments deficits and structural problems in production, trade, and prices instead of lending simply to stabilize exchange rates. However, unlike **World Bank** lending discussed later, IMF lending is not identified with any particular project in borrowing countries. (Theoretically, an IMF loan, also called a **drawing**, is made by a **purchase** by the borrowing country from the IMF of another country's currency in exchange for the borrowing country's currency. A repayment is usually made by a **repurchase** of the borrowing country's own currency with the foreign currency originally borrowed. In practice, however, IMF lending is similar to ordinary nonsecured lending, because the currencies "sold" to the IMF may not have strong international markets and may not be usable by the fund.) Ordinary fund lending, sometimes called ***credit tranche drawing***, is based on the size of a member's ***quota.*** Each country's quota in relation to other countries is determined by its gross national product, international trade data, international reserves, and other factors determining the country's relative economic importance. Member countries contribute 75% of their quota in their own currencies and 25% in other currencies acceptable to the IMF. Members may ordinarily borrow amounts up to their quota, called ***credit tranche facilities***, in order to improve international payments positions. A credit tranche line of credit, also called a ***standby***, is usually required to be repaid within 3 to 5 years. If there are more serious adjustment problems, however, a member may use the ***extended facility*** for up to 140% of its quota with a longer period of 4 to 10 years required for repayment.

Another type of IMF lending is the ***compensatory facility***. This provides that primary producing countries may borrow from the IMF to offset losses from unfavorable price fluctuations in their export earnings. ***Buffer stock financing*** is also available to pay for contributions by member countries to international buffer stock plans to stabilize major world commodity prices. Finally, under the ***enlarged access policy*** adopted in March 1981, the IMF borrows additional funds from member countries—as for example, the May 7, 1981 borrowing by the IMF from Saudi Arabia which committed more than $8 billion to the fund—and makes these funds available to countries with serious payment imbalances relative to quotas. Countries borrowing under the enlarged access policy may obtain loans up to 450% of quotas to be drawn over up to 3 years with repayment over 7 years.

Fund lending is very important today, but not just because of the size of outstanding fund lending, which was about $35 billion at year end 1984. Fund lending is significant because member countries are usually permitted to draw on IMF lines of credit only if they meet ***conditionality*** requirements of the IMF. The IMF conditionality is a specific program for the financial and economic policies that a borrowing country is required by the IMF to follow. The IMF conditionality requirements include credit policies, amounts of government borrowing, trade policies, and other policies for monetary and financial stability. Maintaining conditionality requirements of the IMF has become crucial in many cases for obtaining not only IMF loans but private credits as well. Conditionality is often critical to successful borrowing on world money and capital markets. Countries that have complied with IMF conditionality requirements usually find it easier to borrow from private international lending institutions because an agreement with the IMF becomes a kind of "seal of approval" for private lenders. On the other hand, countries that cannot get IMF loans or which cannot comply with IMF conditionality are less likely to obtain international bank credits—which in many cases are larger than IMF credits.

Since 1983, international indebtedness of many less-developed countries has become a serious problem, with widespread debt restructurings and fears of defaults. The IMF conditionality requirements are playing a key role in working out debt restructurings.

WORLD BANK LENDING

The other major international lending institution is ***The World Bank*** which together with the IMF was established by the Bretton Woods Agreement in 1944. Loans of the World Bank are usually intended to promote production and economic growth in developing countries, usually for specific projects. Loans are guaranteed by borrowing countries. Thus World Bank credits from its general lending facility called the **International Bank for Reconstruction and Development (IBRD)**, focus less than the IMF on immediate balance of payment adjustment problems and more on long-term project objectives. World Bank lending is also financed differently than IMF lending. Member quotas, in principle, finance IMF lending, whereas World Bank financing comes mainly from its issuing securities on world capital markets.

The second major affiliate of the World Bank is the **International Development Association (IDA)**, which provides loans to very poor developing countries at low rates of interest with repayment terms extending over long periods. The third affiliate of the World Bank is the **International Finance Corporation (IFC)**, which makes loans mainly to the private sector in developing countries.

Since 1980, the World Bank, in addition to loans for specific projects, has adopted a program for ***structural adjustment lending***. This promotes programs for more efficient use of resources and policy development without the borrowed funds necessarily going into specific projects.

In addition to lending by the World Bank, credits, usually for specific projects on a regional basis, are extended by the regional development banks: ***The Asian Development Bank, The African Development Bank, The Inter-American Development Bank,*** and ***The European Development Bank.***

THE BANK FOR INTERNATIONAL SETTLEMENTS

No survey of international monetary institutions would be complete without including **The Bank for International Settlements (BIS).** The BIS was set up in 1930 under a charter from the government of Switzerland with major central banks as shareholders (except for the United States where shares were subscribed by Guaranty Trust Co., the First National Bank of New York, and the First National Bank of Chicago). The original purpose of BIS was to act as an agent of central banks for financial settlements, especially payments connected with the Dawes Plan for World War I German reparations payments. The reparations settlement function is no longer significant, but the BIS continues to function as a source of credits for central banks, as an outlet for central bank deposits, for arranging currency stabilization loans between countries, for sponsoring highly regarded research on the international monetary system, and for sponsoring a regular monthly meeting among central bankers. Views of the BIS on international monetary policy are *inter alia* issued in its Annual Report, which is widely read and very influential among central bankers and treasury officials.

THE FLOATING RATE SYSTEM

BUYING IN FORWARD MARKETS. In the past many critics of floating exchange rates had questioned whether world money markets could adapt to the floating rate system. In particular, it was argued that for most major currencies there would be no forward markets. As a result, in the financing of international trade and investment, there would be inescapable risks of foreign exchange losses. It turned out, however, that for most major currencies there was a rapid development of **forward markets that enabled the hedging of exchange risks. For example, an importer who was billed in deutsche marks (DM) could reduce the foreign exchange of ris**k of higher costs from a rising mark by buying the currency forward. A **forward currency contract** is an agreement to buy or sell the stated currency at a fixed date ahead. Typically, foreign exchange contracts are available for periods of 1, 2, 3, 6, and 12 months. Thus the importer, by making forward contracts can guarantee the exchange rates at which payment will be settled.

Ordinarily, if an **exchange rate** is expected to appreciate, the seller of the foreign exchange forward contract will demand something more than the spot rate (today's price). He or she will want some compensation for the risk of having to supply marks at some date ahead, at which time he or she expects that the German currency will have revalued. The additional cost for delivery of a currency at a future date is called a **premium**. Premiums are often quoted on a percentage basis. For example, if the mark were selling at a spot exchange rate of 50¢ and the 6 months forward rate were 51¢, the nonannualized premium would be 2.0% = (0.51 − 0.50)/0.50. On an annualized basis the premium would be 4.0%. To annualize, multiply by 12/(duration of contract). For example, a nonannualized premium of 1.0% over 3 months would be multiplied by 12/3=4 to obtain an annualized premium of 4.0%.

SELLING IN FORWARD MARKETS. Likewise, an exporter is concerned that there may be a devaluation of the currency in which he or she bills his or her sales abroad. The exporter can **hedge** this risk by selling the currency forward—for example, by making an agreement that another party (usually a bank) will buy the proceeds from the export sale in lire at some period ahead. Ordinarily this kind of hedging takes place when a currency is likely to be devalued. Thus it can be expected that the buyer of the foreign exchange contract will be willing to trade dollars for the foreign currency only if the amount supplied is less than the spot rate. This negative difference between the spot rate and the forward rate is called a **discount**. For example, if the lira is 0.15¢ and it sells forward 6 months at 0.14¢, the discount on the lira would be 6.6% [(0.15 − 0.14)/0.15 = 6.6] nonannualized, or 13.2% annualized.

EURODOLLARS AND EUROCURRENCIES

External currency accounts have been another unique development in the post-World War II monetary system. These are bank deposits denominated in a currency different from the currency of the home country. Thus a bank deposit in London denominated in dollars rather than sterling is an external dollar account. External dollar accounts are commonly known as Eurodollars, though such deposits are not necessarily confined to Europe. They also exist in Asia and the Caribbean. External accounts in all currencies are commonly known as Eurocurrency accounts or, for particular currencies, as Eurosterling, Euromarks, Euro-Swiss francs, and so on. For example, a deposit of British pounds in Luxembourg would be a Eurosterling deposit.

Eurocurrency deposits are believed to have begun when, after World War II, the Soviets deposited dollars in European banks to avoid danger of confiscation by the Americans. Growth of Eurodollar deposits received its strongest push with the imposing of various U.S. exchange controls in the 1960s. This created an incentive to keep dollar deposits out of the United States. Eurodollar deposits persisted after the lifting of U.S. exchange controls in early 1974, mainly because Eurodollar deposits were free of various costs and controls that would arise from deposit banking in the United States. Eurocurrency deposits other than dollars also developed because of almost total freedom from regulation. The value of net Eurocurrency deposits in mid-1983 was estimated at about $2.2 trillion by the Morgan Guaranty Trust Co. This figure may involve some double counting, but it is nevertheless large compared with recorded outflows of dollars from the United States. It has been alleged that a multiplier process works in the Eurodollar market, with the proceeds of Eurodollar loans again becoming Eurodollar deposits. Although there are no formal **reserve requirements on Eurodollars,** there are "leakages" from this multiplier process because much Eurodollar borrowing is repatriated to the United States. Thus the extent of the Eurodollar multiplier is a matter of unsettled controversy.

Long-term lendings of Eurodollars are known as **Eurobonds**. This term is often used broadly to apply to offshore lending instruments in any currency not of the host country of the loan.

MANAGED FLOATING

It had been widely believed, especially by advocates of **floating exchange rates**, that if currencies were allowed to move freely, once they reached equilibrium positions, subsequent fluctuations would be relatively small. But, for reasons that have not been fully explained, fluctuations of exchange rates under floating have been very wide. For example, the deutsche mark in relation to the dollar (in DM per dollar) appreciated from 2.1050 at year-end 1977 to 1.7315 at end-1979 and then depreciated to 2.9886 at end-November 1984. In view of the volatility of exchange rates, very few monetary authorities were willing to let their currencies float without intervention to influence exchange rates. Thus the financial world since 1973 has been compromising between floating rates and fixed rates. The wide differences in inflation between countries have made fixed rates almost impossible. On the other hand, freely floating rates are rejected by most central banks because of the possibility that speculative forces will produce a sharp decline in a weak currency or a sharp rise in a strong currency. As a general rule, neither of these extremes is desired.

A strong currency depreciation will affect not only the price of imports but the price of all goods, imported or not, that compete with imports. To a greater extent than in the early postwar period, the proportion of a country's goods that is internationally traded—even in a somewhat self-sufficient country like the United States—is much larger than the percentage of imports. Today most U.S. consumer goods and vehicles compete with imports—a situation that certainly did not exist in the late 1940s and early 1950s.

Most monetary authorities are also afraid of sharp revaluations that raise the price of exports and thus damage export industries. Traditional economic theory states that this is a signal to move resources from export industries to domestic industries. For this shift to be politically acceptable, however, it must be gradual, and a strong currency appreciation is not likely to induce a gradual reaction.

Some countries—notably Canada, Japan, the United Kingdom, and Switzerland practice managed floating without any specific rule to guide the intervention process (where, as already discussed, a central bank sells foreign currencies to prevent its own rate from falling and sells its own currency to prevent its own rate from rising). In other countries, however, specific rules have been applied to guide the intervention process. Exhibit 1 classifies major currencies of the world in terms of how the currency is managed. Three systems of intervention are discussed in detail: tied exchange rates, minidevaluation systems, and the **European Monetary System (EMS).**

TIED EXCHANGE RATES. A currency that is "**tied**" moves parallel to some other currency or group of currencies. In spite of all its vicissitudes, the U.S. dollar remains the currency to which other currencies most frequently are tied. If the dollar rises 10%, the tied currency rises 10%; if the dollar falls 8%, the tied currency falls 8%. For example, the Trinidad and Tobago dollar was worth 41.7¢ as of end-November 1984, an exchange rate that will hold as long as the tie lasts.

Most currencies in Central America, the Caribbean area, Paraguay, and a scattering of other countries are tied to the dollar. The second most important tying currency is the French franc, which is tied to most of the African countries (except Guinea) that were formerly French colonies. After World War II a number of British colonies were tied to the British pound, but as of 1984, the only currency formally tied to sterling was that of Gambia. Other intercurrency ties are the South African rand to the currencies of Lesotho and Swaziland and the Spanish peseta to the currency of Equatorial Guinea.

Basket Currencies. Some tied currencies move in line with a group of more than one currency. Usually a group of currencies is known as a **basket.** For example, a simple basket might consist of 50¢, American, one-half a British pound, and 3 French francs. For each trading day the value of the basket is calculated and the currency of the basket country adjusted in line with the overall percentage change in the value of the basket. In a simple case, suppose the pound is a $2 and the French franc at 25¢, and the pound gains 2% whereas the French franc loses 4%. The value of the basket is calculated as follows:

	First Period	Second Period	Change (%)
U.S. dollar	$0.50	$0.50	—
0.5 British pound	1.00	1.02	2.00
3 French francs	0.75	0.72	−4.00
Basket	$2.25	$2.24	−0.40%

Thus the basket currency in the second period would be lowered about 0.4% in value in relation to the U.S. dollar.

SDR-Tied Currencies. In most cases the central bank of the "basket currency" country constructs its own basket, usually giving the most weight in the basket to the country's most important trading partners. (In some instances the actual weights in the basket are a central bank secret.) In other cases, exemplified by Kenya and Jordan, the currency is tied to the **Special Drawing Right (SDR)**, which, as will be discussed further on, is a special basket used by the IMF as a reserve asset and for the valuation of its transactions.

MINIDEVALUATION SYSTEMS. Among several Latin American countries it has become customary to make small monthly adjustments in exchange rates. These adjustments, known as **minidevaluations**, tend to reflect economic indicators, including price levels and reserve positions, but are usually less than 2% per month. In some cases, however, a series of minidevaluations may be insufficient to protect a country's reserve position; then it may become necessary to supplement the minidevaluations with a **maxidevaluation**." This was done in the case of the 30% maxidevaluation of the Brazilian cruzeiro in December 1979. Ordinarily, after a maxidevaluation, a country will return to a new series of minidevaluations.

THE EUROPEAN MONETARY SYSTEM. Of the schemes for coordinated intervention in currency markets, the **European Monetary System (EMS)** is the most important today. It now comprises the currencies of Germany, France, Belgium, Luxembourg, the Netherlands, Italy, Denmark, and Ireland. Up until March 1979 the EMS was known as the **joint float** or "**snake**" agreement and had been in operation since 1972. At various times the United King-

EXHIBIT 1 WORLD FOREIGN EXCHANGE INTERVENTION SYSTEMS, 1984[a]

Pegged To					Flexibility Limited vis-à-vis a Single Currency or Group of Currencies		More Flexible		
U.S. Dollar	French Franc	Other Currency	SDR	Other Composite	Single Currency[b]	Cooperative Arrangements	Adjusted According to a Set of Indicators	Other Managed Floating	Independently Floating
Antigua and Barbuda Bahamas[c] Barbados Belize	Benin Cameroon Central African Republic Chad Comoros	Bhutan (Indian rupee) Equatorial Guinea (Spanish peseta)	Burma Burundi Guinea[c] Iran Islamic Republic of	Algeria[c] Austria Bangladesh[c] Botswana Cape Verde China[c]	Afghanistan[c] Bahrain[d] Ghana Guyana Maldives Qatar[d]	Belgium[c] Denmark France Germany, Federal Republic of	Argentina Bolivia Brazil Chile[c] Colombia Ecuador Mexico Peru[c] Portugal Somalia[e]	Costa Rica[c] Greece	Australia Canada Japan Lebanon South Africa
Djibouti Dominica Dominican Republic[c] Egypt[c]	Congo Gabon Ivory Coast Mali Niger Senegal	The Gambia (pound sterling) Lesotho (South African rand)	Jordan Kenya[f] Rwanda São Tomé and Principe Seychelles	Cyprus Fiji Finland[f] Hungary Kuwait Madagascar	Saudi Arabia[d] Thailand United Arab Emirates[d]	Ireland Italy[g] Luxembourg[c] Netherlands		Guinea-Bissau Iceland India[h] Indonesia Israel	United Kingdom United States Uruguay
El Salvador[c] Ethiopia Grenada Guatemala Haiti	Togo Upper Volta	Swaziland (South African rand)	Vanuatu Viet Nam	Malawi Malaysia[f] Malta Mauritania Mauritius Nepal				Jamaica Korea Morocco New Zealand Nigeria	
Honduras Iraq Lao People's Democratic Republic Liberia Libyan Arab Jamahiriya				Norway Papua New Guinea Romania Singapore				Pakistan Philippines Spain Sri Lanka Turkey	

Nicaragua[c]	Solomon Islands	Uganda[c]
Oman	Sweden	Western Samoa
Panama	Tanzania	Yugoslavia
Paraguay	Tunisia	Zaire
St. Lucia	Zambia	
	Zimbabwe	
St. Vincent and the Grenadines		
Sierra Leone		
Sudan[c]		
Suriname		
Syrian Arab Republic[c]		
Trinidad and Tobago		
Venezuela[c]		
Yemen Arab Republic		
Yemen, People's Democratic Republic of		

[a] No current information is available for Democratic Kampuchea.

[b] All exchange rates have shown limited fexibility vis-à-vis the U.S. dollar.

[c] Member maintains dual exchange markets involving multiple exchange arrangements. The arrangement shown is that maintained in the major market.

[d] Exchange rates are determined on the basis of a fixed relationship to the SDR, within margins of up to ±7.25%. However, because of the maintenance of a relatively stable relationship with the U.S. dollar, these margins are not always observed.

[e] The exchange rate is maintained within overall margins of ±7.5% around the fixed shilling/SDR relationship, however, the exchange rate will be re-evaluated when indicative margins of ±2.25% are exceeded.

[f] The exchange rate is maintained within margins of ±2.25%.

[g] Margins of ±6% are maintained with respect to the currencies of other countries participating in the exchange rate mechanism of the European Monetary System.

[h] The exchange rate is maintained within margins of ±5% on either side of a weighted composite of the currencies of the main trading partners.

Source: International Monetary Fund.

dom, Sweden, and Norway have belonged to the joint float, but they are not now participating.

In March 1979 the old joint float became the European Monetary System. The main provisions of the EMS agreement were:

1. A unit of account known as the **European currency unit (ECU)**, which is a weighted average of EMS exchange rates.
2. The **parity grid system**, which places restrictions on the extent to which each EMS currency will be permitted to rise or fall in relation to every other EMS currency. This system had been applied under the joint float.
3. A **divergence indicator** system that sets limits within which each currency is permitted to vary from central rates denominated in ECUs.
4. A **European Monetary Cooperation Fund (EMCF)** for financing interventions in foreign exchange markets and for granting assistance to members in balance of payments difficulties.

The European Currency Unit (ECU). The **ECU** is the monetary unit used in the EMS. The ECU is composed of the following amounts of the currencies of each of the member states of the EMS:

Belgian francs (BF)	3.66	Italian lire (LIT)	109.00
Luxembourg francs (LF)	0.14	French francs (FF)	1.15
German marks (DM)	0.828	Danish krone (DKR)	0.217
Dutch guilders (Hfl)	0.286	Irish pounds (IL)	0.00759
UK pounds (UKL)[a]	0.0885		

The value of the ECU and the relative importance of member currencies thus fluctuates every day, depending on the values of its component currencies. In February and June 1982, proportions of member currencies in the ECU were as follows:

Currency	February 1982	June 1982
Belgian and Luxembourg francs	8.50%	8.45%
Danish krone	2.65	2.63
German mark	34.24	35.48
French franc	18.56	17.39
Irish pound	1.11	1.10
Italian lira	8.35	8.07
Dutch guilder	10.70	11.09
British pound	15.89	15.79
Total	100.00%	100.00%

[a] The UK is not a member of the EMS, but the UK pound is, nevertheless, included in the calculation of the ECU.

The ECU has two principal functions in the EMS. First, it is used as the unit of account in the EMS (i.e., quotations of exchange rates in the EMS are in ECUs). Second, it is used as the unit of account for settlements between EMS members. Moreover, the ECU is beginning to be used in private transactions. Some international banks take deposits in ECUs and some international credits and bond issues are now quoted in ECUs.

Parity Grid System. One way to understand the parity grid system is to consider the value of each EMS currency in relation to other EMS currencies. These ***bilateral ceiling and floor rates*** are shown in Exhibit 2 as ratios of each other's currency. Each currency is required to remain between the ceiling rate and the floor rate for each other currency. For example, the DM may not go higher than 15.235% above the HFl (for the Netherlands). As another example,

EXHIBIT 2 CROSS RATES IN THE EMS, NOVEMBER 6, 1984

	DM	HFL	BF	DK	FF	Li	IL
DM		115.235 112.737 110.167	2048.35 2017.64 1958.50	371.40 362.280 355.06	313.63 306.733 299.855	664.730 623.474 589.60	33.1015 35.4986 31.6455
HFL	90.770 88.702 86.760		1818.00 1789.68 1738.00	329.63 321.348 315.130	278.35 272.078 266.10	589.970 553.031 523.290	29.3820 31.4879 28.0904
BF	5.106 4.9563 4.882	5.7535 5.5876 5.5005		18.543 17.9556 17.7270	15.659 15.2026 14.9700	33.1890 30.9011 29.4380	1.6530 1.75941 1.5803
DK	28.165 27.603 26.925	31.7325 31.119 30.3375	564.10 556.93 539.30		86.365 84.668 82.565	183.050 172.097 162.360	9.11680 9.79869 8.71570
FF	33.350 32.602 31.885	37.5800 36.754 35.925	668.00 657.78 638.60	121.11 118.109 115.78		216.770 203.262 192.270	10.7964 11.5731 10.3214
Li	0.1696 0.1604 0.1504	0.1911 0.1808 0.1695	3.3970 3.2361 3.013	0.6159 0.5811 0.5463	0.52010 0.4920 0.4613		0.54901 0.05694 0.04869
IL	3.160 2.8170 3.021	3.5600 3.1758 3.4030	63.2810 56.8371 60.4965	11.4735 10.2054 10.9687	9.6885 8.6407 9.2625	2053.53 1756.33 1821.45	

Each cell shows the ceiling rate, the market rate (in the middle), and the floor.

Key: Deutsche mark DM
Holland florin (Dutch gilder) HFL
Belgian franc BF
Danish krone DK
French franc FF
Italian lira Li
Irish pound IL

the FF must not be higher than 21.11% above the DKr (for Denmark) or lower than 15.78% above the DKr. (As is customary, rates for the Irish pound are stated as multiples rather than ratios to every other EMS ccurrency.) Each of the ceiling and floor rates is taken at 2.25% above or below the ***Central Rate*** (except for Italy where the required percentage difference is 6.0%). The central rate is simply the average of the ceiling and floor rates. For example, in the case of the FF in relation to the DKr, the central rate at 84.465 is an average of the ceiling at 86.365 and the floor at 82.565. The floor rate is 2.25% below the central rate and the ceiling rate is 2.25% above the central rate.

The ceiling and floor rates remain fixed in the EMS unless there is an agreement to change a central rate, but market rates change every day. However, if market rates move above the ceiling rates or below the floor rates for any two currencies, the central banks of the two currencies will intervene in foreign exchange markets to bring the wayward exchange rates back within the required interval. The central bank of the country where the currency has moved too high will purchase the currency that is too low and will sell its own currency. On the other hand, the central bank of the currency that has moved too low will buy its own currency and sell the currency of the country with the exchange rate that has gone too high (and as discussed later, financing may be made available for these actions). For example, if the FF went above 37.58% of the Hfl, both the French and Dutch central banks would sell FF and buy Hfl. Notice that the parity grid system is based purely on relations of EMS currencies with each other. It is not affected by changes in values of EMS currencies against the dollar or any other currency outside of the system. Action in the EMS is required only when one EMS currency moves outside of its upper bilateral limit or its lower bilateral limit with respect to another EMS currency.

Divergence Indicator System. Divergence indicators are percentage differences of each EMS currency from EMS central rates as measured in ECUs. The EMS currencies are, in principle, not permitted to rise or decline below the central rate by more than a fixed percentage known as the divergence indicator. Exhibit 3 shows divergence indicators for each EMS currency. Divergence indicators are different for each country because they are adjusted from the 2 1/4% limits used for the grid (except for Italy at 6.0%). These adjustments are required in order to take into account the effect on the ECU of changes away from ECU by its component currencies. Thus divergence indicators tend to be smaller for the larger currencies where a rise in the currency value will cause the ECU as well as the currency itself to rise significantly.

For example, if the DM rises, the ECU will also become significantly larger. This effect is allowed for by setting a relatively small divergence indicator for West Germany at 1.51%. On the other hand, the Irish pound, because it has a small weight in the ECU, will have very little effect on the ECU if the IL rises or falls. So the divergence indicator for Ireland at 2.22% is close to the full 2.25% that would be required if the value of the ECU was not affected by changes in a component exchange rate. As is shown in the second column of Exhibit 3, divergence indicators show a ***maximum divergence spread*** either

EXHIBIT 3 DIVERGENCE INDICATORS IN THE EMS

Currency	Maximum Spread (%)	Divergence Threshold: 75% of Maximum Spread
BF	±2.03	±1.52
DM	±1.51	±1.13
HFl	±2.01	±1.51
DKr	±2.18	±1.64
FF	±1.80	±1.35
Li	±5.43	±4.07
IL	±2.22	±1.67

above or below the central rate. The third column of Exhibit 3 indicates ***divergence thresholds*** that are 75% of the maximum divergence spread. If a country's currency exceeds the divergence threshold, immediate action will not be required in the foreign exchange market (as is required in the case of the parity grid), but the country is required to undertake consultations with other member countries on what action should be taken to bring the currency within the divergence threshold. These policies may include intervention, changes in monetary and economic policies and, in some cases, changes in central rates when it is believed that divergences are of a more structural character that cannot be changed by adjustments in market rates.

The European Monetary Cooperation Fund (EMCF). This fund is divided into three parts: very short-term financing (VSTF), short-term monetary support (STMS), and medium-term financial assistance (MTFA). The VSTF is used to assist countries to intervene in foreign exchange markets as is required by the grid mechanism. The STMS is used to overcome temporary balance of payments deficits. The MTFA is used to overcome more serious, longer-term balance of payments difficulties.

The VSTF financing is provided by direct credits without any specific limits by member central banks to the EMCF for a duration of up to 45 days. Whereas VSTF financing must be used for intervention in foreign exchange markets, STMS financing may be used for other monetary support purposes. The STMS credits are for 9 months' duration. Funding for STMS assistance, as of July 1982, was ECU 14 billion. MTFA assistance is granted for 2 to 5 years' duration. As of July 1982, MTFA funding amounted to ECU 11 billion.

EXCHANGE CONTROLS

In addition to the various methods used by leading countries for intervention on foreign exchange markets, exchange rates are maintained or influenced by a wide variety of restrictions and controls on payments.

TARIFFS, SUBSIDIES, AND IMPORT CONTROLS. Perhaps the best known method of protecting the value of a currency is the application of **tariffs**

on imports and/or **subsidies** to exports. In many cases, when it is believed that tariffs are ineffective, **quantitative restrictions** are applied to imports. Quantitative restrictions limit amounts imported regardless of the import price. In developing countries where balance of payments equilibria are fragile, imports of nonessential consumer goods are often subject to quantitative restrictions. Import quotas are also common in developed countries, mainly to protect employment in industries threatened by foreign competition. In many cases these restrictions are worked out in ***orderly marketing agreements (OMAs)*** between countries. An example is the agreement to restrict Japanese auto imports into the United States. In some instances, notably in Latin American countries, a special ***advance deposit*** to the central bank may be required in addition to payment for permitted imports. By tying up the importer's funds until the deposit is refunded—usually within 6 months or less—the advance import deposit tends to limit outlays for imports. There are other widespread restrictions on funding available for foreign trade. In many cases a central bank will attempt to balance its payments by ***slower approvals*** of applications for foreign exchange. At the same time that governments attempt to discourage imports, they try to encourage exports by means of subsidies often in the form of tax relief and easier credit.

CONTROLS ON CAPITAL MOVEMENTS AND PROFIT REMITTANCES. Restrictions on capital movements outward and incentives on capital movements inward are also frequent. In many cases capital outflows or inflows require approval from the central bank that the movement is in the country's interest. In some Latin American countries, for example, profit remittances are not permitted to exceed a specific return on capital. Another type of capital control—employed by countries attempting to avoid an unwanted appreciation of their currencies—is a reserve requirement on capital inflows. This type of control has been applied in West Germany.

MULTIPLE EXCHANGE RATES. In some cases governments apply restrictions on both current account (trade and other noninvestment payments) and **capital account** by systems of **multiple exchange rates.** These have been used in Latin America and are currently used in Belgium. In Belgium there are two foreign exchange markets: the commercial market and the financial market. The first market includes most current account payments and receipts, whereas the second market includes most capital transactions and the collection of dividends and interest coming into Belgium. A separate foreign exchange market thus operates in each type of currency, and each day there are separate quotations for the Belgian "commercial franc" and "financial franc."

In the past, but not currently, **multiple exchange rates** were also applied in France and Italy. In Great Britain, up until 1979, a special exchange rate was required for the purchase of foreign securities by British residents. Proceeds of the sale of British securities abroad were deposited in a "dollar pool." Foreign exchange in the dollar pool, minus certain taxes, was then auctioned off to British residents wishing to buy foreign securities. In effect, a "dollar premium" was required for the purchase of foreign securities. In South Africa a similar system was applied, with the result that the "**securities rand**" and the ordinary rand had different exchange rates.

In multiple exchange rate systems the two (or more, in a few cases, as in Chile in the 1960s) exchange rates cannot be widely different; otherwise "**false invoicing**" is likely to appear, in which funds are moved out of the country at a high rate and into the country at a low rate. However, there can be a wide disparity of rates when a special rate (usually lower than the principal exchange rate) is applied to a commodity, as in the case of Colombian coffee. Here, false invoicing can be easily detected when the price of the commodity is widely known. An excessively low exchange rate (or the equivalent in a tax on export proceeds) on an export commodity can lead to widespread smuggling.

STATE TRADING, BARTER, AND OTHER EXOTIC FINANCIAL ARRANGEMENTS. As balance of payments have deteriorated in many less developed countries, special devices have been developed to conserve foreign exchange and in some cases to avoid its use altogether. In some cases all imports and exports of particular products are required to be bought or sold through a government agency that attempts to secure more advantageous terms through ***state trading***. ***Barter*** agreements often arise in state trading. Some countries also engage in ***counter-trade*** agreements requiring that a trading partner for imports will agree to purchase exports of the country of equal value. Some countertrade agreements may provide for a ***buy-back***. For example, imports of equipment for a mining project might be paid for with the output of the mine after it begins production. ***Clearing agreements*** provide that for trade in certain products, accounts will not exceed a certain percentage imbalance known as a ***swing***. In some cases in order to maintain the clearing agreement, the country with a surplus may be permitted to transfer certain of the products of the deficit country to a third country, sometimes at a discount. ***Switch traders*** act as intermediaries to facilitate these transactions.

BALANCE OF PAYMENTS

Thus far this section has considered how the international monetary system determines exchange rates and the inflows and outflows of foreign exchange to and from a country. Because inflows and outflows are not necessarily equal, however, settlements are required to balance surpluses and deficits.

As discussed, under the pre-1914 gold standard a large part of international settlements was made with gold. Today, however, settlements are much more complicated; they are made with gold, foreign exchange, **reserve positions in the International Monetary Fund, Special Drawing Rights,** and changes in official liabilities of reserve currency countries. As background for considering these means of settlement, Exhibit 4 shows the U.S. balance of payments, 1975–1983.

EXHIBIT 4 U.S. INTERNATIONAL TRANSACTIONS 1975–1983 ($ MILLIONS)

Line	(Credits +; debits −)[1]	1975	1976	1977	1978	1979	1980	1981	1982	1983	Line
1	**Exports of goods and services**[2]	**155,729**	**171,630**	**184,276**	**219,994**	**286,796**	**342,485**	**375,721**	**349,448**	**332,201**	1
2	Merchandise, adjusted, excluding military[3]	107,088	114,745	120,816	142,054	184,473	224,269	237,085	211,198	200,257	2
3	Transfers under U.S. military agency sales contracts	4,049	5,454	7,351	7,973	6,516	8,274	10,003	12,209	12,737	3
4	Travel	4,697	5,742	6,150	7,183	8,441	10,588	12,913	12,393	11,408	4
5	Passenger fares	1,039	1,229	1,366	1,603	2,156	2,591	3,111	3,174	3,037	5
6	Other transportation	5,840	6,747	7,090	8,136	9,971	11,618	12,560	12,313	12,802	6
7	Fees and royalties from affiliated foreigners	3,543	3,531	3,883	4,705	4,980	5,780	5,794	5,561	6,275	7
8	Fees and royalties from unaffiliated foreigners	757	822	1,037	1,180	1,204	1,305	1,490	1,572	1,579	8
9	Other private services	2,920	3,584	3,848	4,296	4,403	5,158	5,856	6,635	6,474	9
10	U.S. Government miscellaneous services	446	489	557	620	520	398	499	533	630	10
	Receipts of income on U.S. assets abroad:										
11	Direct investment	16,595	18,999	19,673	25,458	38,183	37,146	32,549	22,269	20,757	11
12	Other private receipts	7,644	8,955	10,881	14,944	23,654	32,798	50,182	57,474	51,414	12
13	U.S. Government receipts	1,112	1,332	1,625	1,843	2,295	2,562	3,680	4,119	4,832	13
14	**Transfers of goods and services under U.S. military grant programs, net**	**2,207**	**373**	**203**	**236**	**465**	**756**	**675**	**594**	**205**	14
15	**Imports of goods and services**	**−133,000**	**−162,425**	**−194,170**	**−230,335**	**−282,110**	**−333,510**	**−362,593**	**−350,590**	**−365,113**	15
16	Merchandise, adjusted, excluding military[3]	−98,185	−124,228	−151,907	−176,020	−212,028	−249,781	−265,086	−247,667	−261,312	16
17	Direct defense expenditures	−4,795	−4,895	−5,823	−7,352	−8,294	−10,511	−11,118	−12,014	−12,222	17
18	Travel	−6,417	−6,856	−7,451	−8,475	−9,413	−10,397	−11,479	−12,394	−13,977	18
19	Passenger fares	−2,263	−2,568	−2,748	−2,896	−3,184	−3,607	−4,487	−4,772	−5,532	19
20	Other transportation	−5,708	−6,852	−7,972	−9,124	−10,906	−11,790	−12,474	−11,722	−12,322	20
21	Fees and royalties to affiliated foreigners	−287	−293	−243	−393	−523	−428	−435	72	−170	21
22	Fees and royalties to unaffiliated foreigners	−186	−189	−262	−277	−309	−297	−289	−267	−282	22
23	Private payments for other services	−1,551	−2,006	−2,190	−2,573	−2,822	−2,909	−3,002	−3,529	−3,609	23
24	U.S. Government payments for miscellaneous services	−1,044	−1,227	−1,358	−1,545	−1,718	−1,730	−1,865	−2,238	−2,193	24
	Payments of income on foreign assets in the United States:										
25	Direct investment	−2,234	−3,110	−2,834	−4,211	−6,357	−8,658	−7,053	−4,129	−6,734	25
26	Other private payments	−5,788	−5,681	−5,841	−8,795	−15,481	−20,893	−28,553	−33,833	−29,104	26
27	U.S. Government payments	−4,542	−4,520	−5,542	−8,674	−11,076	−12,512	−16,753	−18,097	−17,657	27
28	**U.S. military grants of goods and services, net**	**−2,207**	**−373**	**−203**	**−236**	**−465**	**−756**	**−675**	**−594**	**−205**	28
29	**Unilateral transfers (excluding military grants of goods and services), net**	**−4,613**	**−4,998**	**−4,617**	**−5,106**	**−5,649**	**−7,077**	**−6,833**	**−8,058**	**−8,651**	29
30	U.S. Government grants (excluding military grants of goods and services)	−2,894	−3,146	−2,787	−3,176	−3,550	−4,731	−4,452	−5,423	−6,060	30
31	U.S. Government pensions and other transfers	−813	−934	−971	−1,086	−1,180	−1,302	−1,464	−1,473	−1,579	31
32	Private remittances and other transfers	−906	−917	−859	−844	−920	−1,044	−918	−1,162	−1,012	32

Line											Line
33	**U.S. assets abroad, net (increase/capital outflow (−))**	**−39,703**	**−51,269**	**−34,785**	**−61,130**	**−64,331**	**−86,118**	**−110,978**	**−118,898**	**−49,490**	33
34	U.S. official reserve assets, net [4]	−849	−2,558	−375	732	−1,133	−8,155	−5,175	−4,965	−1,196	34
35	Gold			−118	−65	−65		(*)			35
36	Special drawing rights	−66	−78	−121	1,249	−1,136	−16	−1,824	−1,371	−66	36
37	Reserve position in the International Monetary Fund	−466	−2,212	−294	4,231	−189	−1,667	−2,491	−2,552	−4,434	37
38	Foreign currencies	−317	−268	158	−4,683	257	−6,472	−861	−1,041	3,304	38
39	U.S. Government assets, other than official reserve assets, net	−3,474	−4,214	−3,693	−4,660	−3,746	−5,162	−5,107	−6,143	−5,013	39
40	U.S. loans and other long-term assets	−5,941	−6,943	−6,445	−7,470	−7,697	−9,860	−9,667	−10,063	−9,931	40
41	Repayments on U.S. loans [5]	2,475	2,596	2,719	2,941	3,926	4,456	4,395	4,282	4,969	41
42	U.S. foreign currency holdings and U.S. short-term assets, net	−9	133	33	−131	25	242	165	362	−52	42
43	U.S. private assets, net	−35,380	−44,498	−30,717	−57,202	−59,453	−72,802	−100,694	−107,790	−43,281	43
44	Direct investment	−14,244	−11,949	−11,890	−16,056	−25,222	−19,222	−9,624	4,756	−4,881	44
45	Foreign securities	−6,247	−8,885	−5,460	−3,626	−4,726	−3,563	−5,714	−8,102	−7,676	45
46	U.S. claims on unaffiliated foreigners reported by U.S. nonbanking concerns	−1,357	−2,296	−1,940	−3,853	−3,291	−3,174	−1,181	6,626	−5,333	46
47	U.S. claims reported by U.S. banks, not included elsewhere	−13,532	−21,368	−11,427	−33,667	−26,213	−46,838	−84,175	−111,070	−25,391	47
48	**Foreign assets in the United States, net (increase/capital inflow (+))**	**15,670**	**36,518**	**51,319**	**64,036**	**38,752**	**58,086**	**81,313**	**95,181**	**81,722**	48
49	Foreign official assets in the United States, net	7,027	17,693	36,816	33,678	−13,665	15,497	5,003	3,318	5,339	49
50	U.S. Government securities	5,563	9,892	32,538	24,221	−21,972	11,895	6,308	5,034	6,502	50
51	U.S. Treasury securities [6]	4,658	9,319	30,230	23,555	−22,435	9,708	5,019	5,728	6,989	51
52	Other [7]	905	573	2,308	666	463	2,187	1,289	−694	−487	52
53	Other U.S. Government liabilities [8]	1,517	4,627	1,400	2,476	−40	615	−300	382	199	53
54	U.S. liabilities reported by U.S. banks, not included elsewhere	−2,158	969	773	5,551	7,213	−159	−3,670	−1,747	433	54
55	Other foreign official assets [9]	2,104	2,205	2,105	1,430	1,135	3,145	2,665	−351	−1,795	55
56	Other foreign assets in the United States, net	8,643	18,826	14,503	30,358	52,416	42,589	76,310	91,863	76,383	56
57	Direct investment	2,603	4,347	3,728	7,897	11,877	16,892	23,148	14,865	11,299	57
58	U.S. Treasury securities	2,590	2,783	534	[13] 2,178	[13] 4,960	[13] 2,645	[13] 2,946	[13] 7,062	[13] 8,731	58
59	U.S. securities other than U.S. Treasury securities	2,503	1,284	2,437	2,254	1,351	5,457	7,171	6,397	8,612	59
60	U.S. liabilities to unaffiliated foreigners reported by U.S. nonbanking concerns	319	−578	986	1,889	1,621	6,852	917	−2,383	−1,318	60
61	U.S. liabilities reported by U.S. banks, not included elsewhere	628	10,990	6,719	16,141	32,607	10,743	42,128	65,922	49,059	61
62	**Allocations of special drawing rights**					**1,139**	**1,152**	**1,093**			62
63	**Statistical discrepancy (sum of above items with sign reversed)**	**5,917**	**10,544**	**−2,023**	**12,540**	**25,404**	**24,982**	**22,275**	**32,916**	**9,331**	63
	Memoranda:										
64	Balance on merchandise trade (lines 2 and 16)	8,903	−9,483	−31,091	−33,966	−27,555	−25,512	−28,001	−36,469	−61,055	64
65	Balance on goods and services (lines 1 and 15) [10]	22,729	9,205	−9,894	−10,340	4,686	8,975	13,128	−1,141	−32,912	65
66	Balance on goods, services, and remittances (lines 65, 31, and 32)	21,011	7,354	−11,724	−12,270	2,586	6,629	10,746	−3,776	−35,503	66
67	Balance on current account (lines 65 and 29) [10]	18,116	4,207	−14,511	−15,446	−964	1,898	6,294	−9,199	−41,563	67
	Transactions in U.S. official reserve assets and in foreign official assets in the United States:										
68	Increase (−) in U.S. official reserve assets, net (line 34)	−849	−2,558	−375	732	−1,133	−8,155	−5,175	−4,965	−1,196	68
69	Increase (+) in foreign official assets in the United States (line 49 less line 53)	5,509	13,066	35,416	31,202	−13,624	14,881	5,303	2,936	5,140	69

TRADE ACCOUNT. Exhibit 4 shows the main "**balances**" in the overall U.S. balance of payments (lines 64–67) and also the main settlement items (lines 68 and 69). The first important balance is the trade balance, defined as exports minus imports (line 2 minus line 16). In addition to imports and exports, there are payments and receipts for services, including travel, transportation, military, fees and royalties, and earnings on investment abroad. These are totaled in lines 1 and 15, and the overall balance on goods and services is shown in line 65. Current transactions also include **one-way** or **transfer payments** such as foreign aid, pensions, and private remittances abroad (lines 29–32). The sum of the goods and services balance and transfer payments is the current account balance (line 67).

CURRENT ACCOUNT. Because the balance of payments is based on accounting principles, the current account deficit is financed by changes in assets and liabilities. If a country's current account is in deficit, it is financed by a decrease in its assets (or an increase in its liabilities) abroad.

In Exhibit 4 the 1983 current account balance at −$41,563 million is offset by changes in U.S. assets abroad at −$49,490 million (line 33) and changes in foreign assets in the United States at $81,722 million (line 48). The net balance of these two capital account items is $32,232 million, which is less than the current account balance at $41,563 million. This difference of $9,331 million consists of unreported items (including errors in trade accounts, delays in payment for imports and exports, unreported capital transactions, and illegal transactions), and is shown in line 63 as the "statistical discrepancy."

CAPITAL ACCOUNT. As Exhibit 4 indicates, many of the capital account items in the balance of payments represent government long-term lending and private investment, including direct investment, security transactions, and bank transactions. However, other changes in assets and liabilities are undertaken by central banks in a usually conscious effort to promote balance of payments adjustments. These official asset changes are listed in lines 34–38 for U.S. official assets and in line 49 less line 53 for foreign official assets in the United States. (Line 53 is excluded from foreign official assets used in official balance of payments settlements because these assets (line 49) are short-term assets, whereas line 53 for "other U.S. liabilities" consists mainly of prepayments for military goods and services from the United States, an item that is considered a long-term asset.)

The items in the category represented by line 49 (excluding line 53) arise because the United States is a reserve currency country. This means that when foreign central banks acquire dollars, they do not necessarily sell them on foreign exchange markets as would ordinarily be done with nonreserve currencies. Instead the dollars acquired by foreign central banks are used to buy U.S. assets, mainly in the form of government securities (lines 51 and 52) and bank deposits (line 54).

SOURCES AND USES OF FOREIGN EXCHANGE. As a tool for further analysis of foreign exchange flows, it may be helpful to consider the sources and uses of each currency. This is done for the dollar by the London firm of Phillips and Drew in their monthly publication, *Currency Trends*, as shown in Exhibit 5. Actual data estimated for 1983 are shown with forecasts for 1984 and 1985, as of August 1984, assuming no change in the value of the dollar. Of special interest, the exhibit shows estimates of dollar transactions entirely outside of the United States and, therefore, not necessarily appearing in the U.S. balance of payments. These transactions include flight capital and investment income dollars that tend to move to tax havens without necessarily being recorded in the balance of payments statistics of any country.

EXHIBIT 5 SOURCES AND USES OF FOREIGN SAVINGS IN DOLLARS

Sources	$bn 1983	$bn 1984	$bn 1985	Uses	$bn 1983	$bn 1984	$bn 1985
Savings from international investment income	34	40	40	Financing non-OPEC LDC deficits	23	21	18
Savings from invisible export payments received into tax-havens	10	10	10	Financing OPEC deficits	10	2	0
Japanese purchases of dollar bonds	12	18	16	Financing OECD deficits (outside USA)	10	−8	−8
Recorded bond purchases from Europe	4	8	6	Direct investment outflows from USA	7	10	10
Flight capital from Latin America, Far East, and Europe	10	10	10	Portfolio capital outflows from USA[a]	4	4	6
Purchases of U.S. equities	6	3	3	U.S. current account deficit	40	90	90
Pure direct investment in the USA	5	5	3				
Acquisition of dollar reserves by non-Group of 10 countries	13	16	10				
Subtotal	94	110	98		94	119	116
Financing gap	0	9	18				

Source: "International Dollar Flows and Risks" in London: Phillips and Drew, (ed.), *Currency Trends*, Brendan Brown, June 1984.

[a] Excludes purchases of international dollar bonds by U.S. residents.

BALANCE OF PAYMENTS SETTLEMENTS

Aside from the buildup of assets in reserve currencies (which is mainly the U.S. dollar although sterling, German marks, Swiss francs, Japanese yen, and French francs are sometimes held as reserves), international balances are settled by transfers of reserve assets. Under the gold standard most international settlements in a country's own assets consisted of gold. Today, however, there are four assets used: foreign exchange, gold, reserve positions in the IMF, and Special Drawing Rights.

FOREIGN EXCHANGE. **Foreign exchange** is defined to include short-term assets in a currency. It thus includes bank deposits and short-term government securities such as Treasury bills. Under the IMF definition, foreign exchange included in reserves should be "readily available to support a currency" on foreign exchange markets. Thus long-term financial instruments (e.g., long-term government bonds) are excluded from the definition of foreign exchange.

Most official transactions in foreign exchange arise from intervention. As discussed, this takes place when a central bank buys its own currency to keep it from going too low or sells its own currency to keep it from going too high. Under the Bretton Woods system, intervention was required to maintain exchange rates within the 1.0% band above or below parity. Similarly, intervention is required in the EMS system to maintain currencies within the 2.25% range. In other cases there are no requirements for intervention, and in the amendment to Article 4 of the IMF agreement (adopted at Jamaica in January 1976), freely floating exchange rates are permitted if countries do not manipulate them to their own advantage. Nevertheless most central banks intervene in foreign exchange markets to prevent wide swings in the exchange rates of their currencies.

GOLD. As discussed, **gold** was the major medium of international settlement under the gold standard. With the breakdown of the gold standard, **reserve currencies**—particularly the pound and the dollar—were mainly used for international settlements. Reserve currencies under the Bretton Woods system were, however, expected to be convertible into gold.

Gold Pool. Under the gold standard central banks had maintained the value of gold at $20.67 per ounce. This value was raised to $35 in 1934 when President Roosevelt devalued the dollar. There was little upward pressure on the price of gold until October 1960, when it was temporarily pushed up to $40 on the London market. The price of an ounce of gold was brought back down to $35 by central banks selling gold. This procedure was institutionalized in the so-called **gold pool** into which leading central banks contributed gold supplies. Gold from the gold pool was sold in sufficient amounts to hold the price of gold down to $35 until March 1968, when it was decided that gold sales by central banks could no longer stabilize the gold price. A "two-tier" system was adopted in which the gold price at $35 was maintained for transactions among central banks. In private markets, however, the price of gold moved freely. Central banks agreed not to sell gold on free markets.

Two-Tier Agreements. The $35 gold price under the two-tier system lasted until August 1971 when the United States stopped free sales of gold to other central banks. In the **Smithsonian Agreement** the United States raised the theoretical gold price to $38, though this action did not have much meaning for U.S. gold because it remained inconvertible. In February 1973 the United States again raised the theoretical price of gold—this time to $42.22.

Jamaica Agreement. It became evident, however, that $42.22 was not a realistic price for gold in view of market prices, which were much higher than the official price. By August 1975 gold on free markets had gone up to $160. In January 1976, in the **Jamaica Agreement** between major IMF member countries, it was decided to **demonetize gold**. Gold holdings of major countries were not to be increased for two years. One-sixth of gold holdings of the IMF would be returned to member countries that had contributed it, and another one-sixth would be sold on free markets, with the proceeds of the sale to be used for the benefit of less developed countries.

At the beginning of 1978, in accordance with the Jamaica Agreement, gold was officially demonetized. Central banks had the right to use their gold supplies in any way that they saw fit. By 1980 gold had reached a price exceeding $600 per ounce (it had exceeded $800 per ounce briefly in 1979), and most central banks continue to maintain their holdings intact although as of January 1985 the price fell to about $300 per ounce. Very few international monetary transactions are currently in gold, but it is sometimes used as collateral for foreign exchange loans. One hint of remonetization of gold is found in the EMS agreement already discussed. Member countries in the EMS are required to exchange 20% of their gold and foreign exchange reserves into the European Monetary Cooperation Fund for ECUs. The gold in the fund is periodically revalued at market prices. This constitutes the first recognition by central banks of the actual price of gold on world markets.

RESERVE POSITIONS IN THE IMF. As already discussed, the basic financing of the IMF arises from contributions in line with the member countries' quotas. Quotas are arbitrarily determined roughly in proportion to each country's economic importance in the world: The larger countries have the larger quotas and the smaller countries smaller quotas.

IMF quotas are three-quarters in the country's own currency and one-quarter in gold or convertible currencies. The **gold** or **convertible currency contribution** of a country is also considered a reserve asset, together with dollars, gold, and SDRs. This is known as the "**reserve position in the IMF**" and is considered to be a reserve asset because a member country may borrow an equivalent amount from the IMF on a virtually "no questions asked" basis whenever it needs balance of payments financing. Additional conditions are required for further borrowing from the fund. Actually in the formal IMF language there is no borrowing or repayment with the IMF. Countries "purchase" required currencies from the fund instead of "borrowing," and currencies are "repurchased" instead of being "repaid." But these actions have long since become identified with borrowing and repayment.

SPECIAL DRAWING RIGHTS (SDRs). The most recent addition to world reserve assets are SDRs. The SDR plan, adopted in 1969, authorized the IMF to create a special asset that would be accepted among IMF members in exchange for dollars and other currencies. Thus the SDR functions similarly to gold settlements and has been dubbed **"paper gold."** Each participating country received an amount of SDRs in proportion to its IMF quota. Total outstanding SDR issues have been raised from \$3.5 billion in 1970 to \$21.4 billion in 1981, after which there have been no additional issues. Originally each SDR was valued at the equivalent of one 1969 gold dollar. Thus given the devaluation of the dollar with respect to gold in 1971 and 1973, the value of the SDR was raised to \$1.080 in 1971 and to \$1.188 in 1973. In July 1974, however, the IMF decided to fix the value of the SDR for each business day in terms of a basket of currencies, a weighted average of exchange rates of the 16 major world currencies. In the third quarter of 1980, the basket of currencies was again revised to include only the five major currencies (U.S. dollar, German mark, British pound, French franc, and Japanese yen) with the following percentage weights:

US \$	42
DM	19
L	13
Y	13
FF	13

Less developed countries have continued to press for additional SDR issues, possibly based on the needs of the LDCs, the so-called **SDR link.** But developed countries, concerned that an excessive SDR issue might be a danger to world financial stability, have resisted this proposal.

BIBLIOGRAPHY

Bank for International Settlements, *Annual Report*, BIS, Basel, Switzerland, issued each year.

———, *Recent Innovations in International Banking,* BIS, Basel, Switzerland, 1986, prepared by a study group established by The Group of Ten Countries.

Brown, Brendan, "International Dollar Flows and Risks" in *Currency Trends*, London: Phillips and Drew, June 1984.

Commission of the European Community, "Documents Relating to the European Economy," in *European Economy* (July 1979 and July 1982), Brussels.

Dam, Kenneth W., *The Rules of the Game. Reform and Evolution of the International Monetary System*, University of Chicago Press, 1982.

Hooke, A.W., *The International Monetary Fund, Its Evolution, Organization and Activities*, Washington: IMF, 1983.

International Monetary Fund, *Annual Report*, Washington.

———, *Annual Report on Exchange Arrangements and Exchange Restrictions.*

———, *IMF, An Introduction*, 1983.

———, *IMF Survey*, published each month.

———, *International Financial Statistics*, published each month.

Kindleberger, Charles P., *A Financial History of Western Europe*, London: George Allen and Unwin, 1984.

Morgan Guaranty Trust Company, *World Financial Markets*, New York, monthly.

Schloss, Henry H., *The Bank for International Settlements*, New York University Graduate School of Business Administration Institute of International Finance, Bulletin Nos. 65 and 66, September 1970.

Solomon, Robert, *The International Monetary System*, 1945–1976, New York: Harper & Row, 1977.

Verzariu, Pompiliu, *Countertrade, Barter, Offsets*, New York: McGraw-Hill, 1985.

World Bank: *Annual Report*, Washington.

———, *The World Bank and the International Finance Corporation*, Washington: World Bank, 1983.

Yeager, Leland B., *International Monetary Relations: Theory, History, and Policy*, Second Edition, New York: Harper & Row, 1976.

18

EXCHANGE RATES AND CURRENCY EXPOSURE

CONTENTS

18

EXCHANGE RATES AND CURRENCY EXPOSURE

Richard M. Levich

FUNDAMENTALS OF FOREIGN EXCHANGE

BASIC CONCEPTS, TERMINOLOGY, AND DEFINITIONS. The foreign exchange market establishes the link between financial activities in different currencies. As a simplifying assumption, it is convenient to associate each currency with a single country and to assume that only domestic currency is acceptable for domestic transactions. In an economy closed off to international trade, domestic residents need hold only domestic currency balances to carry out transactions. In the real world, which is highly open to international trade in goods and financial assets, we can sketch two separate arguments for the ***development of foreign exchange markets.***

First, ***international trade*** in goods is an important (although not sufficient) explanation for the existence of foreign exchange markets. For example, if West German residents would accept and hold U.S. dollars in exchange for Mercedes automobiles, and if U.S. residents would accept and hold German marks in exchange for Boeing aircraft, there would be no need to develop an elaborate foreign exchange market. The problem of course, is that neither the dollar nor the Deutsche mark (DM) is particularly efficient as a ***medium of exchange*** in Germany and the United States, respectively. As a consequence, Mercedes is likely to demand payment in DM whereas Boeing is likely to demand payment in dollars. This forces foreign buyers to enter the foreign exchange market to trade their domestic currency for an acceptable means of payment. Then, unless the German buyer (who wants to exchange DM for dollars) meets a U.S. buyer (who wants to exchange dollars for DM), the German buyer must convince a satisfied holder of dollars (probably a U.S. resident) to hold DM instead. Why would a U.S. resident trade his or her dollars for DM—an unacceptable medium of exchange in the United States?

The answer constitutes our second major explanation for the rise of foreign exchange markets: residents of one country may desire to hold financial assets issued in a foreign country and/or denominated in a foreign currency. For example, the common solution to the international trade transaction just described is the presence of a ***foreign exchange trader***—an agent who stands ready to buy and sell currencies out of inventory and plans to earn a fair profit for the costs and risks he or she incurs. The foreign exchange trader is an intermediary who smooths the transactions between German buyers of Boeing aircraft and American buyers of Mercedes automobiles, each of whom arrives at the market at irregular and unpredictable times.

But there are other important reasons for domestic residents to hold assets denominated in foreign currency. First, domestic currency may be subject to high and variable inflation and therefore it may provide a poor *store of value.* As a consequence, domestic residents (e.g., Brazil, Argentina, and Mexico) desire foreign currency balances (very often U.S. dollars). Second, foreign currency balances may reduce risks. Also, foreign currency assets act to ***hedge anticipated foreign currency liabilities***. In addition, a portfolio of international assets may diversify away some risks that are present in a portfolio containing only domestic currency securities. Finally, if domestic residents simply view foreign currency assets as undervalued, they may demand them for speculative or investment purposes. ***Consols*** (perpetuities) of the British government, common stock of a Japanese automobile company, or a ***Eurobond*** issued by a Swiss firm and denominated in Swiss francs may have particular characteristics (e.g., maturity, expected return and risk, or tax consequences) that are desired but unavailable in U.S. financial markets.

An excellent introduction to foreign exchange market terminology and operations has been prepared by Kubarych (1983). Much of the material that follows draws on this source.

Contracts. The ***spot foreign exchange market*** involves an exchange of ***bank drafts*** denominated in different currencies. A ***spot contract*** implies an "immediate" exchange. In the New York foreign exchange market, immediate delivery is 1 business day for exchanges between North American currencies (i.e., U.S. dollar, Canadian dollar, and Mexican peso) and 2 business days otherwise. Same-day exchange and delivery of bank drafts is possible, but generally at a premium above standard quotations given by traders and reported in newspapers. A much smaller market, which we might call the ***cash foreign exchange market,*** exists for the immediate exchange of bank notes, traveler's checks, and paper currency. This market, located in international airports, hotels, and retail sections of commercial banks, incurs higher transaction costs and offers less favorable rates than those received by larger customers in the spot market.

The ***forward exchange market*** involves contracts for exchange of currency at some date in the future. The standard maturities for which contracts are available (and trading volume is greater) are 1, 2, 3, 6, and 12 months. A forward contract for any maturity can be negotiated, but ***transaction costs*** may be slightly higher than for the standard maturities. For the major industrial currencies, quotations on maturities less than 1 year are routinely available from commercial bank traders. Quotations on maturities from 1 to 5 years and longer are available. The markets here are thinner but growing in importance.

Delivery conventions for forward contracts also require explanation. A 1-month forward contract will be delivered in 1 calendar month plus 2 days (again, 1 business day for North American currencies). For example, a 1-month forward contract executed on July 30, 1984, matured on August 30 (a Thursday). In 1984, September 1 and 2 were a weekend, so no delivery was possible, and September 3 was Labor Day (a bank holiday). Therefore delivery of clearinghouse funds would have been scheduled for September 4, *36 days* after the July 30 contract. The February 6, 1985 contract matured on March 6 (a Wednesday) for delivery of funds on March 8 (a Friday) or *30 days* after the original contract. The difference in actual horizons for seemingly similar 1-month contracts has strong implications for treasurers planning ***exposure management strategies*** or for analysts studying the forecasting and efficiency properties of forward rates.

Futures contracts, unlike forward contracts, are highly standardized. Futures contracts are always written against the ***exchange clearinghouse*** for a fixed number of foreign currency units and for delivery on a fixed date, say June 15. This high level of standardization makes a futures contract an asset that can be traded readily in a secondary market. The ***International Monetary Market*** (of the Chicago Mercantile Exchange) and the ***London International Financial Futures Exchange*** are centralized auction markets where currency futures contracts are traded. This market organization is substantially different from the interbank market that specializes in forward contracts. Large corporations generally prefer to use forward contracts from the interbank market because forward contracts offer more flexibility, i.e., any amount of any currency on any delivery date, and also because banks supply many other services and information to corporations. Corporations may have a bank line of credit that allows them to trade forward exchange contracts without explicit ***margin requirements***. It may appear that forward trading is "free" once the corporation maintains, say, $1 million in bank balances. In contrast, futures contracts require an explicit margin. However, this margin can be in U.S. Treasury bills which earn interest for the owner. Smaller investors generally confine their activities to futures contracts. ***Arbitrage*** to ensure consistent pricing between forward and futures contracts is an important activity discussed later.

The ***swap contract*** discussed by Kubarych (1983, pp. 10–11) represents a "simultaneous purchase and sale of foreign currency for two different value dates." The swap can be viewed as a simultaneous borrowing and lending operation, much like swap transactions in domestic money markets. An important point is that the swap represents a single transaction between two parties. Because the rates (for simultaneously buying and selling) are set in advance, the trader is not exposed to changes in the foreign exchange rate.

One purpose of a ***swap transaction*** is to allow a trader or corporate treasurer to invest (or protect) idle currency balances that will be needed at a later date. For example, a corporation with idle DM balances might use a "spot against forward" swap—a simultaneous sale of DM today for U.S. dollars and purchase of DM for delivery in, say, 1 month. As a strategy, this swap transaction will be profitable if the DM depreciates against the U.S. dollar and the extent of depreciation is not reflected in the price of the swap. (The price of a swap is the interest differential between the two currencies. If we expect DM to depreciate, the interest rate on DM should exceed the interest rate on U.S. dollars. In this case, the lender of DM receives more in interest than he or she pays in interest for the use of U.S. dollars for 1 month.) Another common swap is the ***"rollover*** or ***"tomorrow-next" swap.*** Here, the first sell (or buy) transaction is for delivery tomorrow (i.e., the next business day) and the simultaneous buy (or sell) transaction is for delivery on the next day.

For our purpose, swap contracts help to illustrate two important points: (1) when quotations on outright forward contracts do not exist, swap transactions can be used to ***construct a forward position***; and (2) because traders often use swap contracts to construct their outright quotations, the ***interest rate parity theorem*** (IRPT) will hold exactly within a trading room. Exhibit 1 is used to illustrate these points. A similar exhibit was used by Deardorff (1979) to illustrate the interrelationships between transaction costs and deviations from interest parity.

Assume that on January 1 a U.S. firm orders a machine from Germany and on July 1, DM 100,000 will be required to pay for it. (In Exhibit 1, DM on July 1 are noted as cell D.) Assume further that the firm wishes to conclude all financial arrangements now rather than waiting until July 1 and buying DM in the spot market at the prevailing rate. There are two ways for the firm to proceed. If a forward market exists, the firm may obtain an outright forward quotation, say, F = \$0.512195/DM. This transaction represents a "direct" exchange of dollar balances for DM balances (between cells A and D in Ex-

EXHIBIT 1 DIRECT AND INDIRECT TECHNIQUES FOR EXCHANGE OF CURRENCIES AT A FUTURE DATE.

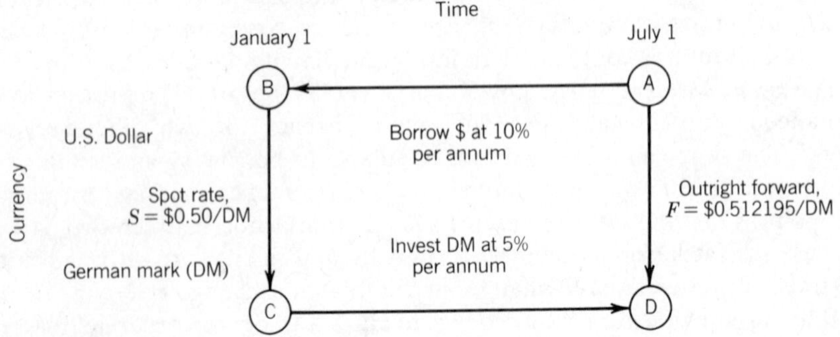

Source: Adapted from Deardoff, "One-Way Arbitrage and Its Implications for the Foreign Exchange Markets," *Journal of Political Economy,* April 1979, pp. 351–364.

hibit 1). The T-accounts show that using the forward market, the firm agrees to pay $51,219.51 for DM 100,000 (Exhibit 2).

What if a forward market does not exist and an outright forward quotation is unavailable? The firm can construct its own forward contract if domestic borrowing and lending are available. For example, if U.S. dollar and DM interest rates are 10% and 5%, respectively, the firm can complete the following transactions on January 1:

1. Borrow $48,780.49 (= $51,219.51/1.05) for 6 months at 10% per annum
2. Use the loan proceeds to buy DM 97,560.98 in the spot market at $0.50/DM
3. Buy a DM security with 6 months maturity earning 5% per annum

The T-accounts confirm that both the direct and indirect methods establish the same balance sheet positions. In this sense, and apart from transactions costs and any tax considerations, the example demonstrates that *a forward transaction is fully equivalent to a spot market transaction combined with simultaneous borrowing and lending* (a swap contract). For currencies or maturities where active forward markets do not exist, firms may construct their own forward positions for any desired purpose (i.e., risk reducing or risk taking).

Naturally, the forward rate (F) we used in Exhibit 2 was not selected at random. We selected F so that

$$F = \$0.512195 = \$0.50(1.05/1.025) = S\ (1 + i)/(1 + i^*)$$

where S = spot rate, i = U.S. interest rate *per period* and i^* = DM (foreign) interest rate *per period.*

When F is set according to the previous formula, we see that both the direct and indirect methods for establishing forward positions lead to the same re-

EXHIBIT 2 T-ACCOUNTS FOR DM 100,000 BALANCES ON JULY 1

DIRECT METHOD (FORWARD CONTRACT)

January 1		July 1	
A/R July 1 DM 100,00	A/P July 1 $51,219.51	A/R July 1 DM 100,000	A/P July 1 $51,219.51

INDIRECT METHOD (SWAP CONTRACT PLUS SPOT TRANSACTION)

January 1		July 1	
DM security DM 97,560.98	Dollar loan $48,780.49	DM security plus interest DM 100,000	Dollar loan plus interest $51,219.51

sults. Traders must set an outright forward price very near this formula for consistency; otherwise firms will choose the least expensive way to establish their desired forward position. In addition, the formula for F is the same as the equation for interest rate parity (discussed further in this section and elsewhere in the *Handbook*). ***Risk-free arbitrage*** profits are available if the trader does not quote a forward rate consistent with the prevailing spot rate and relative interest rates.

Actors. The primary actors in the New York foreign exchange market are brokers and traders. A ***broker*** is an individual who matches orders between people who want to buy foreign exchange and people who want to sell. Brokers do not hold an inventory of currencies and therefore they do not have any capital subject to foreign exchange risks. A ***trader***, on the other hand, is an individual (generally employed by a bank or other large financial institution) who actively buys and sells currencies for his or her own account, for the purpose of making a profit. Traders, by definition, have capital invested in currency holdings (if only for a few minutes at a time) and therefore they are fully exposed to the risk of foreign exchange rate changes.

Transactions in the New York foreign exchange market can be arranged through brokers or ***direct dealing***. Until September 1978, most U.S. banks, when trading among themselves, used brokers as intermediaries. Since 1978, practice has given way to greater direct dealing among banks. A few U.S. banks have always preferred to deal directly.

The ***function of a broker*** is to maintain a list of the best available prices offered by many foreign exchange traders. To accomplish this, the broker maintains direct telephone lines to as many as 150 bank traders. When a trader deals through the New York brokers' market, he or she expects to trade at the best prices represented in the market. Because the cost of obtaining up-to-the-minute quotes can be very high, brokers can provide a very valuable service. In addition, the brokers' market provides anonymity, because the names of the trading parties are revealed to each other only after the transaction, for the purpose of completing delivery. In the brokers' market, size differences between banks will matter less. On the negative side, a broker may be unable to collect meaningful quotations in certain market conditions, or the quotations themselves may be very old. With direct dealing, the trader always receives a fresh quotation. In the interbank market, a trader (A) is obliged to make a ***two-way quotation*** (i.e., both bid and offer prices) without knowing whether the calling trader (B) wishes to buy or sell. And whether trader B hits A's bid price, offer price, or refuses to trade, trader A may interpret this as evidence that one or both of his or her prices are out of line.

Activities. Several activities in the foreign exchange market are important for linking together the various prices and segments in the foreign exchange market. These trading activities are important because they contribute to the efficient operation of the market. An implication of efficiency is that at both the interbank (wholesale) and retail levels, individuals are assured of transacting at fair prices that fully reflect available information.

Arbitrage is the simultaneous, or nearly simultaneous, purchase of securities in one market for sale in another market with the expectation of profit. ***Spatial arbitrage*** suggests arbitrage between segments of the foreign exchange market that are physically separated. Because foreign exchange traders are not housed in a centralized auction market (like the New York Stock Exchange), it is unlikely that all traders will quote exactly the same prices at exactly the same instant. This ***price dispersion across traders*** very likely represents the cost of searching for favorable prices and the uncertainty that comes from knowing that expected arbitrage profits may disappear before all transactions can be completed. Spatial arbitrage between a foreign exchange futures market and the interbank forward market is another important example. Finally, spatial arbitrage to keep the DM/$ rate in Frankfurt equal to the reciprocal (i.e., the $/DM rate in New York) represents another potential profit opportunity. However, because the 1978 agreement standardizes interbank foreign exchange quotations in European terms (e.g., DM/$), this variety of spatial arbitrage may be very limited in the interbank market.

Triangular arbitrage suggests that ignoring transaction costs, the prices for any three currencies (e.g., U.S. dollars, DM, and Canadian dollars) must be consistent with the following relationship:

$$\frac{\$}{\text{DM}} = \frac{\$}{\$\text{C}} \times \frac{\$\text{C}}{\text{DM}}$$

This relationship applies to spot rates as well as to all forward rates. For example, if the U.S. dollar price of Canadian dollars is $0.75 and the Canadian dollar price of DM is $C0.50, the U.S. dollar price of DM must be $0.375/DM. Given the other two exchange rates, any price other than $0.375/DM establishes the opportunity for profits by triangular arbitrage.

In the preceding case, the $C/DM rate is called a ***cross-rate***, a term used to describe exchange rates between non-U.S. dollar currencies. In a practical sense, a market for the direct exchange of $C for DM does not exist. The $C/DM cross-rate is most often calculated from the ***direct rate*** for $/$C and $/DM quoted in these active markets. A trader with Canadian dollars who instead wants to hold DM will probably engage in two transactions: first, an exchange of $C for $ and second an exchange of $ for DM. That these two transactions are preferred to a direct exchange between $C and DM suggests that the transaction costs must be lower. The time required to complete the two transactions may also be shorter than the time required to arrange a direct trade or DM for $C, suggesting that the ***liquidity risk*** is smaller by trading through the U.S. dollar. In fact, because both transactions involve the more active U.S. dollar market, the costs of two "indirect" transactions are less than the cost of one direct exchange between Canadian dollars and DM.

A more striking example would match a Brazilian exporter and a Swedish importer. Few Brazilians (Swedes) might willingly hold krona (cruzeiros), but both would find it easier to trade their domestic currencies versus U.S. dollars. These examples illustrate that the volume of U.S. dollar transactions in the foreign exchange market may be very large relative to the U.S. share of world trade or the share of world trade denominated in U.S. dollars. In addition, the examples illustrate the role of the U.S. dollar as a ***vehicle currency***, expediting the flow of transactions between smaller countries whose currencies have more limited circulation.

Our equation for triangular arbitrage illustrates another important relationship—with three currencies ($, $C, and DM) there are only two independent prices. Similarly, with four currencies there are only three independent prices and, in general, with N currencies only $N - 1$ prices are independent. This straightforward observation describes the role of the U.S. dollar during the ***Bretton Woods*** period (see Section 17). As the Nth country, the United States passively absorbed exchange rate policies developed in the rest of the world. Under floating exchange rates, triangular arbitrage reminds us that exchange rate policies or targets must be consistent, or else periods of instability and profit opportunities will develop.

Covered interest arbitrage describes capital flows that seek risk-free profits based on differences between the forward premium and relative interest rates (see the discussion on forward contracts). Covered arbitrage transactions ensure consistent pricing of spot rates, forward rates, and interest rates on securities that are similar in all respects except currency of denomination.

All these examples reinforce the point that if exchange rate policies or targets and market prices are not internally consistent, there will be capital flows motivated by arbitrage profit opportunities.

Speculative transactions, in contrast to arbitrage, expose the individual to risk. However, speculation involves more than risk. For example, an investor who holds a widely diversified portfolio of stocks is exposed to risk, but he or she is not necessarily speculating. Holding risky stocks may simply reflect risk preferences rather than a desire to trade the portfolio actively and to exploit inside information or superior trading skills. *Speculation* implies financial transactions that develop when an individual's expectations differ from the market's expectations (see Kohlhagen, 1979). Speculators may transact in any international financial market. As a practical matter, because of low transaction costs, low margin requirements, and convenience, speculators prefer to use the forward market. It should be noted that some corporate transactions which, for accounting purposes or otherwise, might be called hedging, are actually speculation. For example, a firm may sell its product in Germany and hold DM accounts receivable. If the firm believes that the DM will appreciate (depreciate) relative to the current forward rate, the firm may maintain ("hedge") its DM receivable. Because the decision is selective (depending on expectations), the transactions are speculative.

FOREIGN EXCHANGE TRADING. The great majority of foreign exchange trading takes place in the ***interbank market*** between ***traders*** or ***market makers*** who represent large commercial banks or other financial institutions. The interbank market is worldwide with 24-hour trading. The foreign exchange market has the largest volume, the lowest cost of transacting, and perhaps the fastest pace of any financial market. However, there is no national or international agency (such as the Securities and Exchange Commission or the International Monetary Fund) that is charged with monitoring foreign exchange market practices and reporting fundamental market data. Market practices therefore depend on **self-regulation** (through the Foreign Exchange Brokers Association and the Forex Association of North America) and competitive pressures.

Other comparisons between regulated securities markets and the foreign exchange market are illuminating. Unlike U.S. securities markets, in the foreign exchange market there are no requirements for traders to divulge their "***inside information***." Accounting and reporting requirements for firms may be partially standardized, but macroeconomic data reported by countries are often difficult to compare, untimely, and inconsistent with meaningful accounting standards. If substantial uncertainties exist regarding corporate operations, the SEC may halt trading and request clarifying statements from the firm. Great uncertainty and unstable market conditions may similarly force a halt to foreign exchange trade (e.g., markets were essentially closed during the first few days of floating rates in February 1973), but it is market pressure and informal governmental pressures that eventually lead to clarifying statements and the resumption of trading. Finally, corporations intervene to repurchase their own shares and, similarly, governments intervene to buy and sell foreign exchange. Presumably corporations are always guided by the profit motive, whereas the goals for government intervention are not so clearly identified.

The failure of *Bankhaus Herstatt* and *Franklin National Bank* in the mid-1970s, both closely associated with mismanaged or uncontrolled foreign exchange trading, has raised the awareness of both bank officials and government agencies concerning the lack of foreign exchange market regulation. Individual banks seem to have reduced their willingness to hold speculative positions (no formal statistics are available to support this). However, the number of banks trading foreign exchange has risen substantially since 1973. The U.S. government response has been to ask both banks and nonbanks to report their foreign exchange positions for various currencies and maturities on a regular basis (see *U.S. Treasury Bulletin*, monthly, Department of the Treasury, Washington, DC). But no formal regulations exist for interbank foreign exchange trading in the United States.

DIMENSIONS OF THE MARKET. A paper by Giddy (1979) discusses several estimates of the size of the foreign exchange market. Giddy suggests that before the U.S. dollar devaluation of August 15, 1971, worldwide foreign exchange trading volume was less than $25 billion per day. During 1980 there was very good reason to believe that worldwide trading volume was $200 billion per day and perhaps much larger. This daily figure suggests an annual volume of more than $50 trillion!

These are enormous figures, many times larger than world GNP or the worldwide volume of foreign trade transactions. Thus a great many foreign exchange transactions cannot be motivated directly by underlying real trade transactions. For another way to view this, consider Exhibit 3, which reports that 87.7% of transactions in the U.S. segment of the foreign exchange market are interbank transactions and only 12.3% are with final or retail customers.

Do these figures suggest that interbank trading is excessive and that many transactions are "unnecessary" or even "speculative?" Perhaps not. The retail market for foreign exchange has become highly competitive. Commercial bank traders must continuously interact with the market—to have fresh quotes, to have a sense of the market, and perhaps to have a small inventory of currencies to sell to retail customers. A retail customer who wants to purchase DM 10 million will calculate the difference between a $0.5321 and $0.5326 quote as $5,000. The treasurer for a large multinational corporation might trade these amounts weekly or even daily. Therefore strong incentives exist for commercial bank traders to offer competitive quotes, and these pressures (along with a desire to exploit temporary informational advantages or trading expertise) may help explain the large percentage of interbank trading.

Exhibit 3 also illustrates the geographic breakdown of foreign exchange trading. London and the rest of Europe clearly hold a dominant position in the foreign exchange market. New York is a distant factor, with only $8 billion of an estimated $103 billion per day trading volume in 1977. The survey conducted by the Federal Reserve Bank of New York in April 1983 suggests that daily New York volume has risen sharply to $33.4 billion. Recent volume estimates for the rest of the world are not available.

Another important measure of the foreign exchange market is the currency composition of trading. Exhibit 3 indicates that a U.S. dollar is included in 99% of all transactions. (*Note*: A transaction involves *two* currencies.) This strongly confirms the ***vehicle currency role*** for the U.S. dollar. The second most actively traded currency (worldwide) is the West German mark, followed by the Swiss franc and British pound.

Finally, Exhibit 3 also reports the breakdown of U.S. foreign exchange market transactions. Roughly two-thirds of all transactions are for spot delivery and about one-half of these transactions are arranged through brokers. Outright forward contracts comprise only 3.9% of daily volume. The remaining 32.9% of daily volume represents swap contracts.

Transaction Costs. Professional interest in transaction costs has increased over the past 10 years, for several reasons. First, if markets are efficient, transaction costs may be the only "true" cost of using the foreign exchange market.

EXHIBIT 3 DIMENSIONS OF THE FOREIGN EXCHANGE MARKET

Location	Volume ($ Billions)[a]	Currency	%[b]	Transaction	Volume ($ Billion/day)[c]	Volume ($ Billion/day)[c]	%	%
London	$ 29	U.S. dollar	99.0	Spot	21.1		63.2	
Germany	24	German mark	40.0	U.S. brokers		10.7		32.0
Switzerland	18	Swiss franc	18.0	Other interbank		8.3		24.9
Amsterdam	9	British pound	15.0	Customers		2.1		6.3
New York	8	French franc	6.0	Outright forwards	1.3		3.9	
Paris	5	Canadian dollar	5.0	Swaps	11.0		32.9	
Brussels	2	Japanese yen	5.0	Short-dated[d]		5.6		16.7
Far East	3	Dutch Guilder	5.0	Long-dated		5.4		16.2
Rest of world	5	Belgian franc	2.0	Total	33.4		100.0	
	$103	Italian lira	1.0					
		Swedish Krona	1.0	Total interbank	29.3		87.7	
		Other	3.0	Total customer	4.1		12.3	
			200.0	Nonfinancial institutions		2.0		6.1
				Financial institutions		2.1		6.2

[a] Daily volume, 1977 estimate.

[b] Estimated 1977 currency compoition of worldwide foreign exchange trading. Total adds to 200% because two currencies are involved in every foreign exchange transaction. (*Source:* Ian H. Giddy, "Measuring the World Foreign Exchange Market." *Columbia Journal of World Business* (Winter 1979): 36–48.)

[c] Daily volume of transactions in the U.S. foreign exchange market, April 1983 estimate. *Source:* Federal Reserve Bank of New York, press released dated September 8, 1983.

[d] For 1 week or less.

For example, foreign exchange risk management strategies sometimes use the forward premium as the "***cost of hedging***" or the differential between the forward rate and the expected future spot rate as an "***opportunity cost***" measure. In an efficient market, alternative hedging opportunities are priced fairly so transaction costs capture all of the real resource costs involved.

Second, by almost any measure, the cost of transacting has risen sharply over the floating rate period. On days when unexpected news reaches the market and uncertainty is high, transaction costs may increase dramatically and reduce, or even completely halt, the flow of trading. Therefore transaction costs may be interpreted as a barometer for how well the ***floating exchange rate system*** is performing. Changes in transaction costs are one component of the real resource costs of operating a floating exchange rate system rather than a ***pegged rate system***.

Concepts of Transaction Costs. The ***liquidity theory*** argues that the ***bid-ask spread*** is only one component in the total cost of transacting. The spread represents the cost of making a quick exchange of a financial claim for money, that is, the cost of ***liquidity services***. The theory suggests that the spread should decline as trading volume and the number of market makers increase. Notably, the spread ignores the costs of producing financial claims, the cost of being informed, and similar costs. More important, the liquidity theory assumes that prices are set at a fair or equilibrium level, and so the trader's major costs are associated with awaiting the arrival of buyers and sellers who want liquidity services. A transactor with inside information may be able to trade at a disequilibrium price and reduce his or her positioning cost below the quoted bid-ask spread.

The ***adversary theory*** explicitly considers the impact on transaction costs that results if there are two groups of investors with different information. Adversary theory suggests that there are indeed two groups of traders. One group is "informed," trading to earn unusual profits based on their information advantage. The second group is "uninformed," expecting to trade at fair prices for liquidity purposes only. In theory, the trader or market maker will respond differently to these two groups because he or she fears losing money to informed traders and expects to earn a fair profit from uninformed traders. Adversary theory also helps us to refine the relationship between risk and transaction costs. ***Price risk*** is associated with the price volatility of the underlying asset, whereas ***liquidity risk*** refers to the uncertainty from holding assets that trade a small volume per unit time. Transaction costs are positively related to both types of risk. According to this view, the percentage spread in spot gold prices should exceed the spread in U.S. Treasury bill prices (because the price of gold is more volatile than the price of T-bills). Furthermore, we expect that the (per unit) cost of trading DM 1 million is smaller than for a DM 1,000 transaction (because of economies of scale). The (per unit) cost of trading DM 100 million may exceed the cost for DM 1 million, however, because of liquidity risks.

Empirical Measures. The bid-ask spread measures the cost of buying and then immediately selling an asset. Therefore the cost of one transaction equals 1/2 (ask price–bid price) /ask price. Estimates of transaction costs based on the bid-ask spread vary considerably across currencies and over time. During the early 1960s, spreads were extraordinarily small, roughly 0.01% for sterling, 0.02% for DM, and 0.03% for Canadian dollars. By the mid-1970s, these figures averaged 0.05% for spot contracts and 0.15% for forward contracts. But a substantial number of spreads in the 0.25–0.50% range were observed (see Levich, 1979).

Triangular arbitrage offers another approach for measuring transaction costs. When transaction costs are stationary, the upper limits of the deviations from triangular parity (e.g., \$/DM = \$/\$C × \$C/DM) should equal the cost of one currency market transaction. Estimates using the triangular arbitrage approach should be larger than the bid-ask spread, because the costs required to monitor the deviations from triangular parity are included. Using the triangular approach for a 6-month period during 1976, McCormick (1979) estimated spot transaction costs in the range 0.09–0.18%. It should be noted that these estimates of transaction costs are for major currencies during relatively tranquil periods. For less actively traded currencies or during turbulent periods, the cost of transacting can increase substantially. (See Frenkel and Levich, 1977).

MANAGING COMMERCIAL BANK TRADERS. Some banks operate to break even on foreign exchange trading, treating it as an important service to provide for customers. Other banks consider foreign exchange trading as another profit center, and traders are expected to earn profits. In either case, foreign exchange trading activities are closely monitored.

Traders can be exposed to several types of risk. ***Exchange rate risk*** arises because of unexpected spot exchange rate volatility. Exchange rate risk is controlled by limiting the open position traders are allowed to hold. Often separate daytime and overnight limits are imposed. Position limits may vary further across currencies and individual traders. ***Interest rate risk*** pertains to unexpected shifts in the structure of forward rates. Restricting open positions at different maturities controls this variety of risk.

Credit risk is related to the fact that foreign exchange contracts, especially forward contracts, are an extension of bank credit. For example, Bank A may buy DM 10 days forward from Bank B. If Bank B failed in 7 days, Bank A will not receive its DM as originally planned. As a consequence, Bank A will have a shorter DM position than planned. The results would be identical if instead Bank B were a bankrupt firm (e.g., W.T. Grant or Penn Central). A bank's decision to trade with a particular bank or firm clearly involves credit risks. Consequently, bank lending officers rather than foreign exchange traders are responsible for setting trade limits for customers. ***Country risk*** is somewhat similar. It represents the possibility of unanticipated exchange controls or taxes that might alter the expected profitability of foreign exchange trades.

Foreign exchange trading income earned by major U.S. commercial banks is

EXHIBIT 4 FOREIGN EXCHANGE TRADING INCOME OF MAJOR U.S. BANKS[a]

	1977	1978	1979	1980	1981	1982	1983	1984	1985
1. American Express International Bank	14.5	23.1	27.3	35.0	28.0	38.0	32.0	43.0	54.0
2. Bank of America	54.1	63.7	90.2	101.0	112.2	113.8	102.4	101.4	150.1
3. Bankers Trust	14.5	23.1	16.6	22.8	30.8	46.2	27.8	67.7	107.5
4. Chase Manhattan Bank	48.5	74.7	77.0	96.5	123.4	130.5	116.7	119.5	173.4
5. Chemical Bank	6.6	19.2	9.9	34.8	39.5	55.5	40.4	60.6	101.5
6. Citibank[b]	68.0	172.4	113.6	175.0	265.0	241.0	274.0	258.0	358.0
7. Continental Illinois	15.3	20.0	11.3	31.0	34.3	19.5	24.4	20.0	N.A.
8. First Chicago	8.4	13.1	11.2	21.8	28.0	27.2	35.5	25.5	N.A.
9. Irving Trust	2.9	1.9	10.0	16.9	11.6	16.1	12.6	15.9	30.4
10. Manufacturers Hanover	8.5	13.4	16.1	15.1	28.6	30.0	27.1	34.2	45.8
11. Marine Midland	4.1	6.7	11.0	20.7	32.4	27.0	18.8	17.8	26.2
12. Morgan Guaranty Trust	40.3	56.4	35.9	62.8	106.0	57.0	74.3	29.5	172.6
13. Republic New York Corp.	5.3	14.9	4.9	12.9	7.9	11.5	8.1	12.5	25.3

[a] Foreign exchange income is in millions of dollars exclusive of translation income.

[b] Includes translation gains and losses.

Source: Lynn Dominquez, "Management of Commercial Bank Foreign Exchange Trading Operations," MBA thesis, New York University, 1980, and company annual reports.

illustrated in Exhibit 4. The data suggest that for some financial institutions (e.g., American Express, Chase Manhattan, Citibank) the contribution of foreign exchange trading to total profits is substantial. Furthermore, foreign exchange income varies considerably from year to year. It is not clear whether this variability reflects changing exposure to risk or changing volatility in foreign exchange markets.

ECONOMICS OF EXCHANGE RATES

DESCRIBING EXCHANGE RATE MOVEMENTS. Tracing the value of a nation's currency is an important exercise. After we observe a time series graph of exchange rates, a number of questions demand attention. What factors determine the price of a currency? What causes currency prices to change? Are currency prices and price changes set fairly and in an orderly manner, or are foreign exchange markets inefficient and characterized by excessive price volatility? Before we explore these questions, we must define the notion of "currency value" more carefully.

Alternative Measures of a Currency's Foreign Exchange Value. The most common notion of currency value is the ***bilateral exchange rate*** that is quoted by a foreign exchange trader or reported in a newspaper. This is a ***nominal exchange rate*** because it expresses the number of units of one currency that must be offered in exchange for a unit of another currency such as 2.5 DM/$ or

\$1.50/£. The first example expresses the rate as units of foreign currency per U.S. dollar (so-called European terms), whereas the second example expresses the rate as U.S. dollars per foreign currency unit (so-called American terms). Note that in European terms, a decrease in the exchange rate from 2.5 DM/\$ to 2.0 DM/\$ corresponds to a ***nominal appreciation*** of DM and a ***nominal depreciation*** of the U.S. dollar. In American terms, however, a decrease in the exchange rate from \$1.50/£ to \$1.40/£ would have the opposite interpretation—nominal depreciation of the pound sterling and nominal appreciation of the U.S. dollar. A nominal, bilateral exchange rate is essential, obviously, for translating cash flows in one unit of account, say DM, into the U.S. dollar equivalent.

The ***real exchange rate***, however, expresses the value of a currency in terms of real purchasing power (i.e., the currency's value in purchasing real goods and services). The need for measuring a real exchange rate arises because inflation often accompanies changes in the nominal exchange rate. This is identical, of course, to the rationale for computing real income, real wages, or real interest rates in addition to their nominal counterparts. Like some of these real magnitudes, the real exchange rate is often expressed as an index.

Exhibit 5 illustrates the price of a hypothetical market basket of goods in the United States and in Germany. In 1974 we assume the market basket costs \$400 in the United States and DM 1,000 in Germany. At the prevailing nominal exchange rate (we assume 2.5 DM/\$), the real value of \$400 equals the value of DM 1,000 (i.e., one market basket). With the passage of time, both the prices of goods and the nominal exchange rate are subject to change. By 1978 assume the market basket costs \$600 in the United States. But at the prevailing exchange rate, 2.0 DM/\$, we could exchange this sum for DM 1,200 and command over 1.09 market baskets in Germany. An index of the real exchange rate is calculated by taking the ratio of the actual exchange rate to its parity value. In this illustration, we have

$$\text{Real rate} = \frac{\text{actual rate}}{\text{parity rate}} = \frac{2.0 \text{ DM/\$}}{\text{DM } 1{,}100/\$600} = 1.09$$

EXHIBIT 5 PRICES OF HYPOTHETICAL MARKET BASKET OF GOODS IN UNITED STATES AND GERMANY

	1974[a]		1978[b]	
	United States	Germany	United States	Germany
Television set	\$270	DM 625	\$325	DM 650
Two pairs of blue jeans	40	125	75	125
Dinner for two at a nice restaurant	40	90	75	125
Hotel room for one night	50	160	125	200
Total price of basket	\$400	DM 1,000	\$600	DM 1,100

[a] Nominal exchange rate \$1 = DM 2.5

[b] Nominal exchange rate \$1 = DM 2.0

Our example illustrates a case of U.S. dollar depreciation (by 20%, from 2.5 DM/$ to 2.0 DM/$) in nominal terms, but a U.S. dollar appreciation (from 1.00 to 1.09) in real terms. In our illustration, it would be incorrect to infer, for example, that the nominal exchange rate change would lead consumers to view U.S. goods as cheaper; in real terms, U.S. goods are more expensive relative to German goods in 1978 than in 1974. If we assume that economic agents make decisions based on real values, then we must utilize real exchange rates to measure the incentives facing consumers and investors.

The difficulties of calculating and using real exchange rates are suggested by Exhibit 5. The price differences between U.S. and German hotel rooms and dinners may reflect quality differences and the fact that these goods cannot be traded. Whereas blue jeans can be traded, some price difference may be the result of transportation costs and tariff barriers. The nominal exchange rate itself may reflect economy-wide factors (and as we argue shortly, expectations of these factors) that are not reflected in the posted prices for a particular market basket of goods. Notwithstanding these difficulties, the real exchange rate is an important concept, especially as it relates to future changes in trade patterns and the evaluation of long-term investment projects.

The ***effective exchange rate*** is a multilateral rate that measures the overall nominal value of currency in the foreign exchange market. It is calculated by forming a weighted average of bilateral exchange rates. For example, the effective U.S. dollar exchange rate combines many exchange rates (e.g., $/£, $/DM, $/yen, . . .) using a weighting scheme that reflects the importance of each country's trade with the United States. Several institutions (International Monetary Fund, Federal Reserve Bank, Morgan Guaranty Trust, and others) regularly calculate and report effective exchange rates. Each institution uses a slightly different weighting scheme. The effective exchange rate is a useful statistic for gauging the overall supply and demand for a currency on the foreign exchange market. By its nature, however, the effective exchange rate conceals the price behavior of individual bilateral markets.

The ***real effective exchange rate*** is a multilateral real rate, calculated by dividing the home country's nominal effective exchange rate by an index of the ratio of average foreign prices to home prices. The real effective exchange rate attempts to measure the overall competitiveness of home country goods in international markets. Although it is important to gauge international competitiveness, a summary statistic such as the real effective exchange rate should be interpreted with caution. An article on this subject by Hooper and Morton (1978, p. 787) concluded that

> Any such aggregate measure is subject to problems due to incorrect measurement of prices, incorrect weighting system, and an inability to measure sectoral shifts in productivity. In addition, real exchange-rate indexes are rough measures of price competitiveness only and do not measure important nonprice factors such as quality, dependability, and servicing which have an important influence on trade patterns but may change relatively slowly.

Recent Exchange Rate Behavior. Prior to the early 1970s, most exchange rates were pegged to the U.S. dollar, and their values were held within 1% of the central rate through official intervention. In response to a fundamental disequilibrium, the central bank would permit a discrete, step adjustment in the currency value and then resume its official support as a new central rate. Since March 1973, the value of major industrial currencies has been determined primarily by free-market forces in a ***floating exchange rate system***. (The Canadian dollar began floating in June 1970 and the British pound in June 1972.) From time to time central banks have intervened, ostensibly to smooth "disorderly" market conditions, making the term ***managed floating*** more appropriate. In either case, the volatility of exchange rates increased dramatically under the floating exchange rate system.

Exhibit 6 presents an index of selected bilateral exchange rates vis-á-vis the U.S. dollar. The graph clearly illustrates how the value of nominal exchange rates, once pegged for long stretches of time, have strayed over a wide range. From 1973 through mid-1975, several currencies (noticeably the DM) demonstrated a cyclical pattern, leading observers to propose that exchange rates may overshoot their equilibrium value. During mid-1975 through mid-1977, exchange rate movements were relatively flat. The strong appreciation of the Swiss franc, the German mark, and the Japanese yen resumed in mid-1977, to be capped by the major U.S. intervention announced on November 1, 1978. The Canadian dollar and the Italian lira generally weakened over the period. The British pound depreciated sharply until late 1976. The development of

EXHIBIT 6 SELECTED NOMINAL EXCHANGE RATES

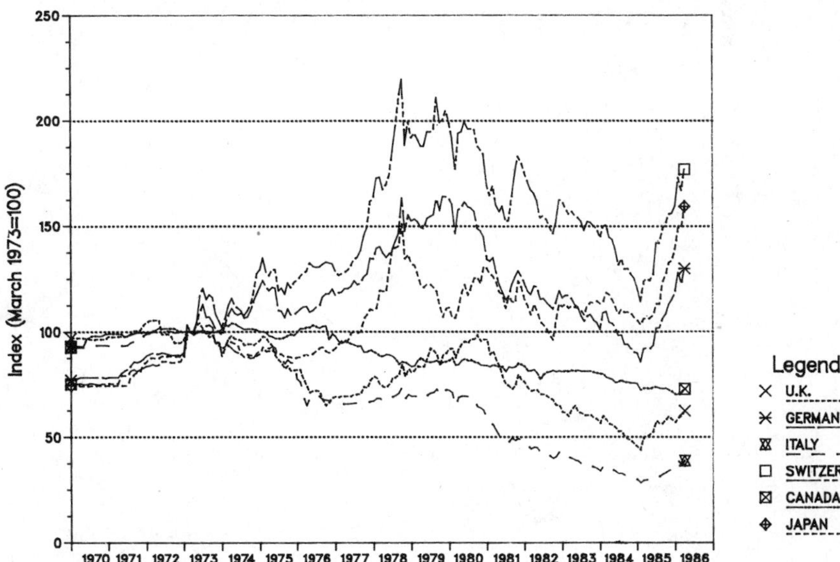

Source: International Financial Statistics.

North Sea oil coincided with the recovery of the pound until the end of 1980. Starting in 1980, the U.S. dollar appreciated steadily against all currencies, reaching post-1973 peaks against the British pound and the German mark among other currencies in early 1985. Since 1985, most nominal currency values (with the exception of the Canadian dollar) have risen sharply against the U.S. dollar.

The record of ***effective exchange rates*** is illustrated in Exhibit 7. The general appearance of Exhibit 7 differs from Exhibit 6 because we have selected the average of effective exchange rates over the period 1980–1982 to define as our 100 benchmark. (See the explanation that follows.) Nevertheless, because most countries appreciate against some of their trading partners and depreciate against others, the pattern of effective exchange rates should be smoother than for bilateral exchange rates. The Swiss franc is an exception because it appreciated vis-á-vis every currency and it appreciated considerably more against some currencies (notably the Italian lira and British pound) than it did with respect to the U.S. dollar.

Exhibit 7 also illustrates the effective value of the U.S. dollar. Even though the U.S. dollar depreciated against the Swiss franc, the German mark, and the Japanese yen, the U.S. dollar appreciated against the Canadian dollar. And because the Canadian share of U.S. trade is large (roughly 30% in 1980), the effective value of the U.S. dollar changed relatively little between 1972 and 1982. At the end of 1982 the effective U.S. dollar exchange rate stood at 109.8. Thus the average appreciation in the U.S. dollar of 6.9% since 1972 thoroughly disguises the varied performance of the dollar against individual currencies.

EXHIBIT 7 EFFECTIVE EXCHANGE RATES

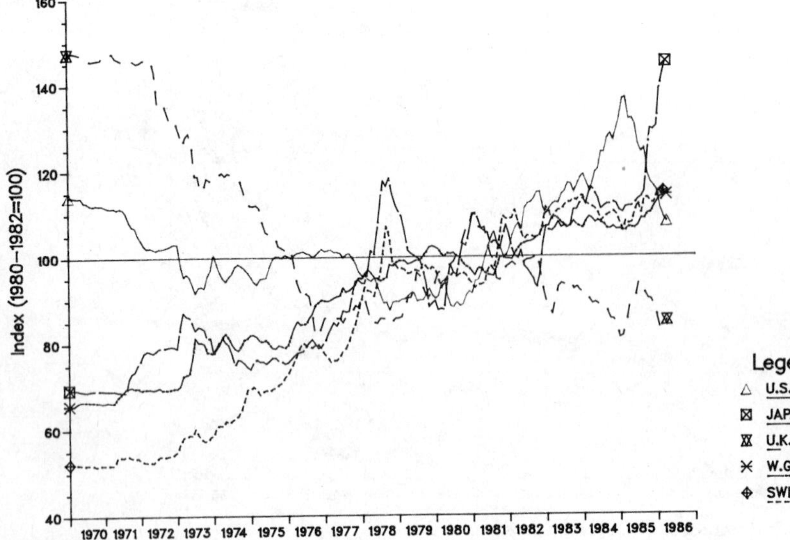

Source: Morgan Guaranty Trust.

A set of ***real effective exchange rates*** is illustrated in Exhibit 8. Note that in Exhibit 8 the average real effective exchange rate over the period 1980–1982 is defined as 100. In the calculation of these multilateral rates, Morgan Guaranty Trust (July, August 1983) utilized weights based on 1980 trade in manufactures and argued that the average experience of 1980–1982 was a "more useful reference base" for judging overvaluation or undervaluation of currencies. Previously, Morgan Guaranty Trust had used 1976 trade weights and March 1973 as a reference base for computing real effective exchange rates. Thus the values in Exhibit 8 do not represent an arbitrary scaling, but rather they rest on the assumption that if structural conditions remain the same as in the 1980–1982 period, then real effective exchange rates ought to fluctuate within a narrow band around 100. This highlights the role of judgmental factors noted by Hooper and Morton (1978). Whether any period represents a valid reference base and what constitutes reasonable fluctuation about 100 are important issues that are discussed further in Bernstein et al. (1984), Cooper (1984), and Morgan Guaranty Trust (July, August 1983).

Despite these factors, the pattern of real effective exchange rates is generally less volatile than other series because relative inflation rates often move to offset exchange rate changes. Several currencies (Japan, Germany, and Switzerland) demonstrate this clearly as the real effective exchange rate change over the 1972–1982 period is a small fraction of the nominal rate change. The United Kingdom presents an odd case. The nominal effective British pound rate depreciated by roughly 30% over the period, but the real effective rate in-

EXHIBIT 8 REAL EFFECTIVE EXCHANGE RATES

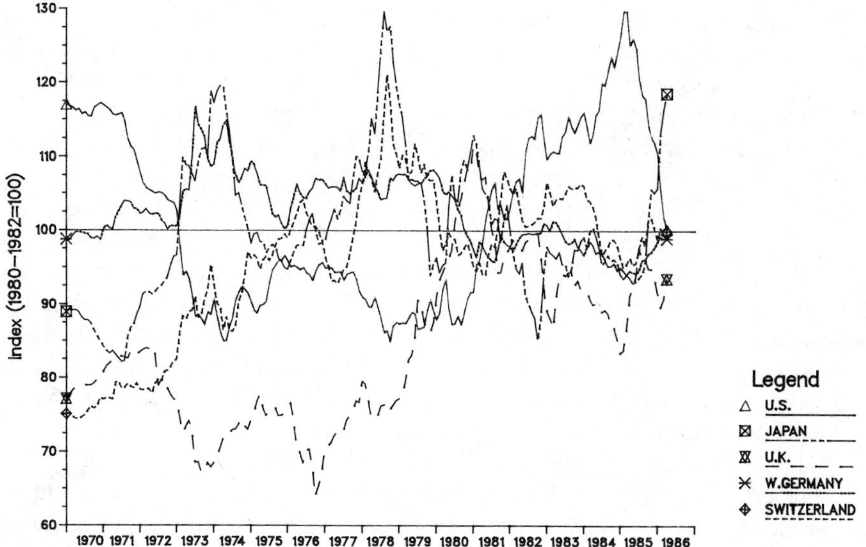

Source: Morgan Guaranty Trust.

creased more than 20%. The real effective U.S. dollar rate rose by nearly 50% over the period 1980–1985, but by April 1986, it had retreated near its 1980–1982 parity level.

EXCHANGE RATE DETERMINATION. A central question facing economists and currency forecasters is the following: What data should be collected and how should the information be combined to explain past exchange rate behavior and to predict future exchange rates? To put it another way, *what is the model by which exchange rates are determined*? This is clearly a very complicated issue for which a huge literature exists. The interested reader should refer to the articles by Dornbusch (1980) and Isard (1978) and the many studies cited therein. The goal of this subsection is to briefly outline the major themes of exchange rate models.

Purchasing Power Parity Theory. Perhaps the most popular and intuitive model for exchange rate behavior is represented by the theory of *purchasing power parity (PPP)*. The main thrust of PPP is that nominal exchange rates are set so that the real purchasing power of currencies tends to equalize. As a result, PPP suggests that in the long run, nominal bilateral exchange rate changes will tend to equal the differential in inflation rates between countries. The term *purchasing power parity* is associated with Gustav Cassel, who studied alternative approaches for selecting official exchange rates at the end of World War I and the resumption of international trade. As Frenkel (1978) has pointed out, the intellectual origins of purchasing power parity can be traced to the early nineteenth century and the writings of Wheatley and Ricardo. Economists have long debated whether the PPP doctrine applies to the short run or the long run and whether the relevant inflation rate is describing a narrow class of goods (e.g., traded goods) or a broad class of goods (e.g., all traded and nontraded goods in the consumer price index). Frenkel has argued that much of the controversy over the usefulness of the PPP doctrine results from the fact that PPP specifies a final equilibrium relationship between exchange rates and prices without specifying the precise linkages and details of the process. If in the world economy, prices and exchange rates are determined by many other variables, then PPP represents an equilibrium relationship more than a precise theory of exchange rate determination.

The many writings on purchasing power parity have been surveyed by Officer (1976). The following discussion of PPP is based on a recent book by McKinnon (1979, Chapter 6). The heart of PPP doctrine is the *law of one price*, that is, perfect *commodity market arbitrage*. For example, if the price in New York is \$18 per barrel, we expect the price in London to be £12 per barrel when the exchange rate is \$1.50/£.

Absolute purchasing power parity requires that the exchange rate equalize the price of a market basket of goods in the two countries. Because the composition of market basket and price indexes varies substantially across countries, and because many goods are nontraded or are subject to tariffs, it is unlikely that absolute PPP will hold in the real world.

Relative purchasing power parity, however, requires that the *percentage change* in the exchange rate equal the differential *percentage change* in the price of a market basket of goods in the two countries. If the factors that cause absolute PPP to fail (e.g., tariffs, some goods being nontraded) are constant over time (i.e., zero percentage change), relative PPP might hold even when the absolute version does not. (See the subsection on *real* exchange rates. It should be clear that when relative PPP holds, the *real* exchange rate is constant, and the relative competitiveness of countries in foreign markets is unchanged.)

The empirical evidence on PPP is mixed. Moreover, the evidence may be sensitive to the countries, time period, and price indexes that we select. Over long time periods and during periods of hyperinflation (when monetary factors swamp real changes), PPP offers a fairly good description of exchange rate behavior. However, over shorter time periods, say 3–12 months, it has not been uncommon to observe substantial exchange rate changes, say 10–20%, which are unrelated to commodity price changes. McKinnon (1979, p. 133) concluded that "Substantial and continually changing deviations from PPP are commonplace. For individual tradable commodities, violations in the 'law of one price' can be striking."

The last statement refers to a study by Isard (1979) that compared the movement of the dollar prices of German goods relative to their American equivalents for specific goods selected at the 2- and 3-digit levels of the Standard Industrial Trade Classification (SITC). The results implied persistent violations of the law of one price. In part, Isard (1979, p. 942) concluded that "In reality the law of one price is flagrantly and systematically violated by empirical data . . . Moreover, these relative price effects seem to persist for at least several years and cannot be shrugged off as transitory." More recent evidence by Crouhy-Veyrac et al. (1982) on goods at the 8-digit SITC level offers results more favorable to the law of one price, but the presence of transfer costs still poses serious empirical problems.

Not withstanding the previous arguments, McKinnon concluded:

> Until a more robust theory replaces it, I shall assume that purchasing power parity among tradable goods tends to hold in the long run in the absence of overt impediments to trade among countries with convertable currencies. But . . . because commodity arbitrage is so imperfect in the short run, it cannot be relied on to contain nominal exchange rate movements within the predictable and narrow limits suggested by the law of one price. (1979, p. 136)

As a consequence, economists have turned to monetary and portfolio balance models of exchange rate determination which are discussed in the following subsection.

Monetary Theory, Portfolio Theory, and Exchange Rates. It is perhaps trivial to observe that whenever a voluntary foreign exchange transaction occurs, say between U.S. dollars and DM, it represents an excess demand for one currency (say DM) and an excess supply of the other currency (in this case,

U.S. dollars). If we can identify the sources of this excess demand for DM (perhaps these sources include a transaction demand or a speculative demand for currency, or perhaps DM balances offer a more reliable store of real purchasing power), we have the basis for a ***monetary theory of exchange rates***. The basic monetary approach to exchange rate determination is a direct outgrowth of purchasing power parity theory in combination with the quantity theory of money. Although PPP concludes that the exchange rate is the relative price of goods in two countries, monetary theory suggests that the exchange rate is the relative price of two moneys. In this context, it follows that the exchange rate represents the ***relative demand*** for two moneys.

According to the monetary theory, factors that lead to an increase in the demand for domestic currency (i.e., the U.S. dollar) should lead to an increase in the price of domestic currency on the foreign exchange market. Two factors that would increase the demand for domestic currency balances are an increase in U.S. income (that increases the demand for transactions balances) and a drop in U.S. dollar interest rates (that lowers the opportunity cost of holding currency balances). Correspondingly, monetary theory predicts that these factors should cause the U.S. dollar to appreciate on the foreign exchange market. Notably, these predictions are contrary to other theories of trade and capital flows.

Trade models correctly argue that higher U.S. income will lead to greater demand for imports, and in turn an increased demand for foreign currency and a depreciation of the U.S. dollar. But capital flows would also respond to an increase in U.S. income, and monetary theory suggests that the net effect of higher U.S. income should be a U.S. dollar appreciation. Capital flow models correctly argue that high *real* U.S. interest rates should attract foreign capital which, in turn, acts to appreciate the U.S. dollar. Monetary theory, however, emphasizes that high *nominal* U.S. interest rates which incorporate a large premium for anticipated inflation actually portend a U.S. dollar depreciation to maintain purchasing power parity. Thus whether a change in observed interest rates is due to changes in real factors or anticipated inflation is critical for determining the impact on the foreign exchange rate.

The ***portfolio-balance theory*** enlarges on monetary theory, arguing that investors' excess demand is not for currency *qua* currency. Rather, investors are attempting to optimize the risk-return trade-off on their portfolios by exploiting their flexibility to choose among a variety of assets denominated in foreign currencies. In the portfolio-balance model, demand in the foreign exchange market is derived largely from demand for financial assets. Consequently, as investors receive information causing them to reassess the expected return and risk of an asset, investors will rebalance their international portfolios, leading to foreign exchange transactions. Other economic shifts such as (1) accumulation of wealth (e.g., via current account surpluses) in a country with asset preferences different than the world's average or (2) a change in spending patterns, say, away from goods priced in DM and toward goods priced in U.S. dollars, would similarly influence investor/consumers to rebalance the currency profile of their portfolios.

Both the monetary and portfolio-balance theories suggest that a relatively short list of factors determines the bulk of exchange rate movements. This list would include the expected real interest rate in each currency, the expected productivity and income changes, and other factors affecting national wealth, including the current account. Unfortunately, the numerical formula for combining these factors can only be estimated, and the results in terms of offering a complete explanation of exchange rate movements are far from satisfactory.

EXCHANGE RATE DYNAMICS. Alternative models of exchange rate determination may agree that the equilibrium price of DM increased from $0.25/DM to $0.50/DM between 1973 and 1979, yet the models may disagree considerably concerning the *path of adjustment* between $0.25/DM and $0.50/DM. The topic of ***exchange rate dynamics*** examines the movement of exchange rates between two points in time, in addition to the beginning and end-of-period values of the exchange rate. Analyzing the movement of exchange rates over shorter time intervals is important for several reasons. We want to assess more closely the performance (i.e., efficiency) of foreign exchange markets. We also want to understand better the causes of these short-run movements and to gauge whether they are excessive and/or predictable.

Causes of Exchange Rate Volatility. The most fundamental change for exchange rate modeling in the 1970s was the realization that foreign exchange is a financial asset. And as such, foreign exchange rates should exhibit characteristics common to other financial assets—namely, quick and sometimes large price changes in response to new information (which is observable) or to changes in expectations (which cannot be observed). Therefore we expect to observe that foreign exchange rates move quickly and responsively relative to commodity prices (e.g., automobiles and grocery items).

Exhibit 9 illustrates one measure of the daily volatility of exchange rate changes during the current floating rate period. We see that it is not uncommon for exchange rates to change by 0.5 to 1.0%, or even 2.0% in a single day. We are interested in determining whether this volatility is "excessive" relative to some standard.

Studies by Frenkel and Mussa (1980) offer some insights on this issue. Because exchange rates are determined by a list of variables (e.g., relative money supply growth rates, income growth rates), we would expect the volatility of exchange rates to reflect the volatility of underlying factors.

Exhibit 10 indicates that recent exchange rate volatility is considerably greater than the volatility of relative cost-of-living indexes. This suggests that other factors (e.g., volatility in relative income, government intervention, or unanticipated news events) have contributed to exchange market volatility. Exhibit 10 also indicates that recent exchange rate behavior has been less volatile than that of national stock markets. Most national stock markets are felt to be fairly efficient in the sense that price swings in these markets represent a reasonably accurate assessment of changing real economic events and changing expectations. By this standard, recent exchange rate volatility does not appear

EXHIBIT 9 DAILY EXCHANGE RATE VOLATILITY

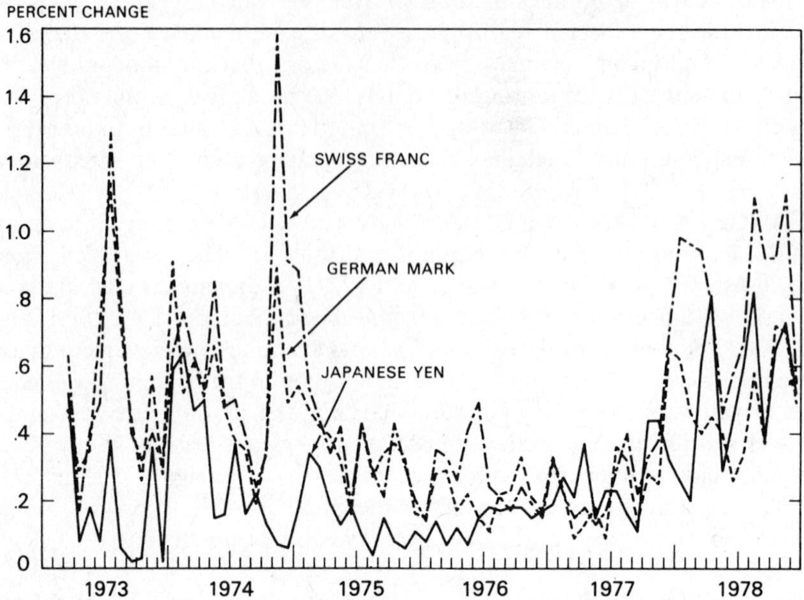

Source: Economic Report of the President, January 1979, P. 153.

to be "excessive" or "unprecedented." This does not contradict the viewpoint that world welfare and the gains from international trade in commodities and capital would very likely increase if national economic policies were set to make exchange rate changes smoother and more predictable.

Exchange Rate Overshooting. The recent period of floating exchange rates has caused some market observers to wonder whether exchange rate volatility, by some standard, is excessive. The term *overshooting* was coined to describe exchange rate changes in excess of this standard. Interest in overshooting arises from two general concerns. First, exchange rate overshooting may signal that the market is inefficient and profit opportunities exist, and/or that some sort of corrective governmental action (*not* necessarily intervention) is required. Second, if the foreign exchange market is operating efficiently, overshooting may simply suggest that investing in foreign currency assets is somewhat riskier than is suggested by more simple models. The following discussion draws heavily on the study by Levich (1980).

Three definitions of overshooting can be stated briefly as follows:

1. The current spot exchange rate S_t does not equal some long-run equilibrium rate $\bar{S}$ that may be based on purchasing power parity or another long-run model.

EXHIBIT 10 MEAN ABSOLUTE PERCENTAGE CHANGES IN PRICES AND EXCHANGE RATES, (MONTHLY DATA: JUNE 1973–FEBRUARY 1979)

	Variable[a]				
Country	WPI	COL	Stock Market	Exchange Rate Against the Dollar	$COL/COL_{U.S.}$
United States	.009	.007	.038	—	—
United Kingdom	.014	.012	.066	.020	.007
France	.011	.008	.054	.020	.003
Germany	.004	.004	.031	.024	.004

[a] WPI = wholesale-price index: COL = cost of living.

Source: Frenkel and Mussa, "The Efficiency of Foreign Exchange Markets and Measures of Turbulence," *American Economic Review,* Vol. 70, No. 2 (May 1980), p. 375.

2. The equilibrium exchange rate change that occurs in the short run ΔS_{sr} exceeds the equilibrium exchange rate change in the long run ΔS_{lr}.
3. The actual exchange rate change that occurs in the marketplace $\Delta S_t'$ exceeds the equilibrium exchange rate changes $\Delta S_t'$ that would be required if the market had full information about economic structure and disturbances.

The first definition reflects the conventional notion of overshooting as it is often reported in the press such as "The Swiss franc is currently overvalued relative to any reasonable standard." If the exchange rate model $\bar{S}$ accounts for transportation costs, lags in price adjustment, and other factors, then profit opportunities exist when we can transact at S_t rather that $\bar{S}$. In this case when $S_t \neq \bar{S}$, the market is not efficient, and we should wonder why investors do not buy foreign exchange when $S_t < \bar{S}$ or sell it when $S_t > \bar{S}$).

Demonstrating empirically that the market does not establish a fair price ($S_t \neq \bar{S}$) is extremely difficult. Most empirical tests have been unable to reject market efficiency in favor of an alternative hypothesis. However, these tests of market efficiency are actually tests of a joint hypothesis. That is, when we observe that $S_t \neq \bar{S}$, we cannot be sure whether it is because S_t is set too low (or high) and/or our estimate of $\bar{S}$ is too low (or high). Therefore this definition of overshooting is not likely to be an operational success. It is too easy to be led to the ***efficient market tautology***: A price set by a freely competitive market must be a fair price, and so overshooting or undershooting is impossible.

If we maintain the $\bar{S}$ is the true equilibrium exchange rate, then economic costs exist when the market fails to establish $S_t = \bar{S}$. However, if we can demonstrate valid reasons for the inequality of S_t and $\bar{S}$, this type of overshooting need not entail additional costs.

Interestingly, overshooting of this type could be explained by two very different stories: a ***shortage of speculative capital***, so that transactions to stabilize S_t around $\bar{S}$ are not sufficient, or an ***excess of speculative capital***, so that many speculative bandwagons push S_t far from $\bar{S}$. In either case unexploited profit opportunities exist for speculators who recognize the divergence between S and $\bar{S}$.

Both these explanations may reflect a confusion between ex ante and ex post results. Ex post, it may be clear that too little or too much speculative capital was committed to the foreign exchange market, but ex ante there would be no way to determine this. Similarly, the stock of speculative capital committed to the foreign exchange market may have been low in 1973, but if a slow and gradual buildup of capital was expected to be more efficient, then the resulting overshooting need not imply a resource misallocation once these capital adjustment costs have been considered.

The second definition of overshooting draws a distinction between short-run and long-run equilibriums, while maintaining the notion that the exchange rate is priced fairly at all times, a perfect reflection of all information. Overshooting of this type might be viewed as the result of forcing a given amount of international adjustment through a limited number of channels, because it is assumed that other potential adjustment channels operate slowly or do not exist. Dornbusch (1976) elegantly formalized a monetary model of the exchange rate in which consumer prices adjust very slowly relative to the speed of adjustment in the foreign exchange market. Within this framework, an unanticipated change in the money supply leads to exchange rate overshooting (type 2) because domestic consumer prices cannot move immediately to reflect the money supply change. A similar overshooting result can be illustrated with a portfolio-balance model. In this case, a desired accumulation of assets denominated in a foreign currency proceeds slowly through cumulative current account surpluses. As this slow process evolves, the foreign exchange rate overshoots to establish equilibrium in this market.

It seems intuitively clear that the greater the number of channels that exist and are free to operate, the less likely we are to observe overshooting behavior in exchange rates. A paper by Frenkel and Rodriguez (1982) formalizes this idea. Specifically, the authors show that if prices are free to adjust somewhat (in the Dornbusch model) or if investors elect to spend some of their wealth on nontradable domestic goods (in the portfolio balance model), overshooting behavior (of type 2) need not occur.

The third definition of overshooting rests on the idea that agents may have heterogeneous or incomplete information about the world, thus leading them to place "unfair" prices on financial assets (i.e., prices that do not reflect *all* available information). This framework posits that the actual exchange rate oscillates about the value that would be achieved if prices reflected all available information. If agents vary in terms of wealth, risk aversion, and confidence in their forecasts, or if they operate subject to constraints, it is easy to see how this type of overshooting might occur. Suppose that Widget Co. has a policy of using the forward exchange market to hedge real business transactions only. Widget Co. will transfer a DM 1 million dividend in 3 months; the 3-month forward rate is \$0.55/DM, and Widget is confident that the future spot rate will be less than \$0.50/DM. Consequently, Widget sells its DM 1 million forward (causing the forward rate to decline slightly), but Widget does not continue selling DM until the forward market fully reflects Widget's expectation about the future spot rate.

FOREIGN EXCHANGE MARKET EFFICIENCY. Tests of the efficiency of asset markets as processors of information began in the 1950s and gained increasing popularity and significance during the 1960s. With the establishment of floating exchange rates in the early 1970s (presumably dominated by free-market behavior), it was natural to begin the investigation of foreign exchange market efficiency. The evidence on foreign exchange market efficiency is important for several reasons. First, macroeconomic models typically include price variables under the assumption that prices fairly aggregate bits of information that are dispersed throughout the economy. Economic agents who make decisions on the basis of observed prices will ensure an efficient allocation of resources. Second, if the foreign exchange market is judged inefficient, some corrective actions might be required. These might include increased profit-motivated private speculation, increased distribution of accurate market information, or central bank intervention. Finally, tests of market efficiency may influence financial management strategies. In an efficient market, managers would tend to favor *passive hedging strategies* to minimize *transaction costs* and maximize *diversification gains*. If the market is not efficient, however, *selective hedging strategies* to exploit available profit opportunities may be preferred.

Definition. The classic definition of capital market efficiency was formalized by Fama (1970). We can compress a definition into one sentence: A market is efficient if market prices "fully reflect available information." The key words are in quotation marks. The expression "fully reflect" implies the existence of an equilibrium model. But one model, which concludes that $2.25 is the fair spot price of sterling, may not agree with another model, which draws a different conclusion. Similarly, one forecaster who uses only public information may conclude that $2.30 is the fair spot price of sterling, whereas another forecaster with "inside" information may disagree strongly, even though both forecasters use the same framework for predicting exchange rates.

These arguments have been refined in two important directions. First, when information itself is costly to collect, market participants, in their self-interest, will never choose to be completely informed. As a result, market prices will never reflect all information, although they still may reflect available information. Furthermore, if investors are heterogeneous in terms of their wealth, expectations, forecasting accuracy, and risk aversion, actual market prices will reflect a "mixture" of diverse opinions. However, this "mixture" will correspond to investors' "dollar votes" rather than a set of optimal weights.

In economic jargon, the preceding remarks imply that tests of market efficiency are testing a "joint hypothesis." Any investigation that rejects market efficiency might be explained in two ways: (1) profit-seeking private investors had information they could have used to earn unusual profits, but they failed to do so (i.e., in reality, the market is inefficient); or (2) our empirical tests are in error—we have used a false measure of "fair value" insofar as we assumed that the investor used information that, in fact, was not available to him or her, or we forgot to include the costs of learning about or exploiting these profit opportunities. Naturally, in a market populated with thousands of sophisticated, profit-seeking investors who can transact at low cost, the second explanation seems more reasonable. This takes us dangerously close to the efficient market tautology, namely, that any free market must be efficient. But because there is little agreement on what constitutes the "true" or "fair" value of foreign exchange, tests of market efficiency are difficult both to formulate and to interpret.

Empirical Evidence. The literature on foreign exchange market efficiency increased greatly during the 1970s. Surveys of this literature have been prepared by Kohlhagen (1978) and by Levich (1978). We briefly discuss three aspects of this evidence.

Tests of ***covered interest arbitrage*** have clearly established that the market efficiently polices risk-free profit opportunities in the Eurocurrency markets. Studies of arbitrage between traditional or onshore securities (e.g., U.S. and U.K. Treasury bills) suggest that covered differentials do appear in the market. However, it is not clear whether these differentials are the result of known costs (e.g., future controls and taxes), or an actual market failure to exploit ***risk-free arbitrage*** profits.

Tests of ***spot market efficiency*** began by analyzing the time series properties of spot rates. Several studies examined the ***random walk hypothesis***, that is, that changes in spot exchange rates are serially uncorrelated. For a number of reasons, including the fact that exchange rates are driven by economic factors, which themselves may be serially correlated, random walk exchange rate behavior (1) is not necessary for spot exchange market efficiency and (2) is not sufficient to prove spot exchange market efficiency.

Other studies of the spot foreign exchange market have analyzed the performance of investment strategies that use a filter rule as a guide for picking speculative positions. A ***filter rule*** is a mathematical rule that can be applied mechanically to produce buy signals and sell signals. For example, if the $/DM rate rises 1% above a previous low, this could be interpreted as a buy signal, under the assumption that momentum will carry the $/DM rate still higher. However, if international financial markets are efficient, Eurodeposit traders should also recognize the expected momentum in the exchange market. As a result, Eurodeposit traders would set relatively low DM interest rates and high U.S. dollar interest rates that tend to offset the anticipated exchange rate change. This summarizes the efficient market process: Eurodeposit interest rate differentials should exactly offset the expected exchange rate change, so there are no expected profits from the filter rule strategy.

The results of empirical studies of filter rules are mixed. Some academic studies have concluded that simple filter rule strategies could have been profitable, especially during periods of exchange rate volatility (See especially the studies by Dooley and Shafer, 1983, and by Sweeney, 1986.) Studies of commercial technical or momentum advisory services have also suggested that their predictions could have led to profitable results. However, none of these studies has suggested that their trading profits are risk free. On the contrary, we know that investors who seek to profit from "market timing" lose the "time diversification" associated with maintaining a steady portfolio over time. It is therefore unclear whether filter rule profits are unusually large relative to the risk involved.

Tests of ***forward market efficiency*** have focused on the relationship between the current n-period forward rate $F_{t,n}$, the *expected* future spot rate $E(S_{t+n})$ and the *actual* future spot S_{t+n}. Market efficiency requires that market agents be able to process available information and form reasonable expectations: $E(S_{t+n}) = S_{t+n}$. However, market efficiency allows for the possibility that investors may demand a risk premium on forward contracts, much the same as long-term interest rates may reflect liquidity premiums rather than simply pure interest rate expectations. Therefore market efficiency does not require that $F_{t,n} = E(S_{t+n})$. As a result, the relationship between the current forward rate $F_{t,n}$ and the actual future spot rate S_{t+n} is ambiguous, *even in an efficient market.*

Numerous empirical tests of the relationship between today's forward rate $F_{t,n}$ and the future spot rate S_{t+n} have been published over the past 5 years. Some of the econometric tests are too technical for our purposes and some of the details of the analyses might be disputed, but the general thrust of this literature is as follows:

1. In early studies, the forward rate was shown to be an unbiased predictor of the future spot rate. In more recent studies using more advanced econometric techniques, this view has been rejected. Nonetheless, there is a close association between the level of the forward rate and the level of the future spot rate. In a linear regression, variation in $F_{t,1}$ generally explains more than 90% of the variation in S_{t+1}.

2. Similarly, in early studies the forward premium $(F_t - S_t/S_t)$ was shown to be an unbiased predictor of the future exchange rate change, $(S_{t+1} - S_t)\ S_t$. Later studies reversed this view. However, all studies confirm that the forward premium is a poor predictor in the following sense: In a linear regression, variation in $(F_t - S_t)\ S_t$ generally explains less than 10% of the variation in $(S_{t+1} - S_t)/S_t$. This suggests that the bulk of the short-run exchange rate changes is dominated by unanticipated events (i.e., news) and that the forward premium sits roughly in the middle of a wide distribution of exchange rate expectations. Exhibit 11 illustrates the wide variation in exchange rate changes relative to the forward premium for the deutsche mark.

3. Empirical studies of forward rate bias report mixed evidence regarding the existence of a positive risk premium in forward contracts. This may be because (a) the premium actually is zero; (b) the premium is too small to measure in the limited history of floating; or (c) the premium changes signs and averages near zero.

4. Adding variables beyond the current forward rate might improve the

ability to fit a regression equation explaining S_{t+1}. But in postsample comparisons, the forward rate by itself has often exhibited better predictive ability.

The results of early studies suggest that the foreign exchange market is fairly efficient and that the forward rate can offer stiff competition to other forecasts. More recent studies challenge this view. They suggest that other forecasts can beat the forward rate without concluding that the forward exchange market is inefficient.

FORECASTING EXCHANGE RATES. As we have discussed already, the character of international financial markets has changed dramatically in recent years. In particular, we have noted that the volatility of foreign exchange rates has increased significantly. Correspondingly, professional and academic interest in currency forecasting has increased, and a large number of commercial foreign exchange advisory services have developed. In the current environment, firms that maintain exposure to foreign exchange risks are likely to find exchange market volatility reflected in volatility of the firm's financial statements and in changes in the firm's competitive position. The discussion in this subsection is based on two studies by Levich (1980*b*, 1980*c*), which address these issues in more detail.

For the multinational firm, exchange rate forecasts play a role in a wide variety of decisions. Obviously, any foreign borrowing or investment decision requires a forecast of future exchange rates, to permit the conversion of future foreign cash flows into units of domestic currency and the computation of a comparable domestic cost of funds or return on investment. A currency forecast is generally required for the firm to manage its currency exposure, which results from current and planned holdings of foreign currency. Currency forecasts can play a role in marketing, specifically with respect to pricing decisions. Suppose a Japanese automobile that sells for 2.0 million yen in Japan is priced at $10,000 in the United States when the exchange rate stands at 200 yen/$. If the yen appreciates to 180 yen/$, each U.S. auto sale will earn only $10,000 × 180 yen/$ = 1,800,000 yen. The Japanese firm is now in a worse position, and it is clear that the decision to raise U.S. prices will depend on many factors, including the future yen/$ exchange rate. From this example we can see that assessing subsidiary performance will also require exchange rate projections. If the real exchange rate is expected to change, the U.S. firm can maximize its dollar profits (revenues − costs) by incurring costs in countries where the currency has depreciated below its PPP level (so that the real value of production costs is lower) and by earning revenues in countries where the currency has appreciated above its PPP level (so that the real value of revenues is higher).

Alternative Forecasting Techniques. Among the commercially available ***forecasting services***, it is convenient to classify companies as using either an ***econometric*** or a ***judgmental approach***. This distinction is somewhat artificial, because the decision to accept one forecasting equation and reject all the others clearly involves judgment. The econometric forecasts are frequently based on a

EXHIBIT 11 MONTHLY PERCENTAGE CHANGES OF THE U.S. AND GERMAN CONSUMER PRICE INDEXES (COL U.S. AND COL G, RESPECTIVELY), OF THE $/DM EXCHANGE RATE, AND THE MONTHLY FORWARD PREMIUM

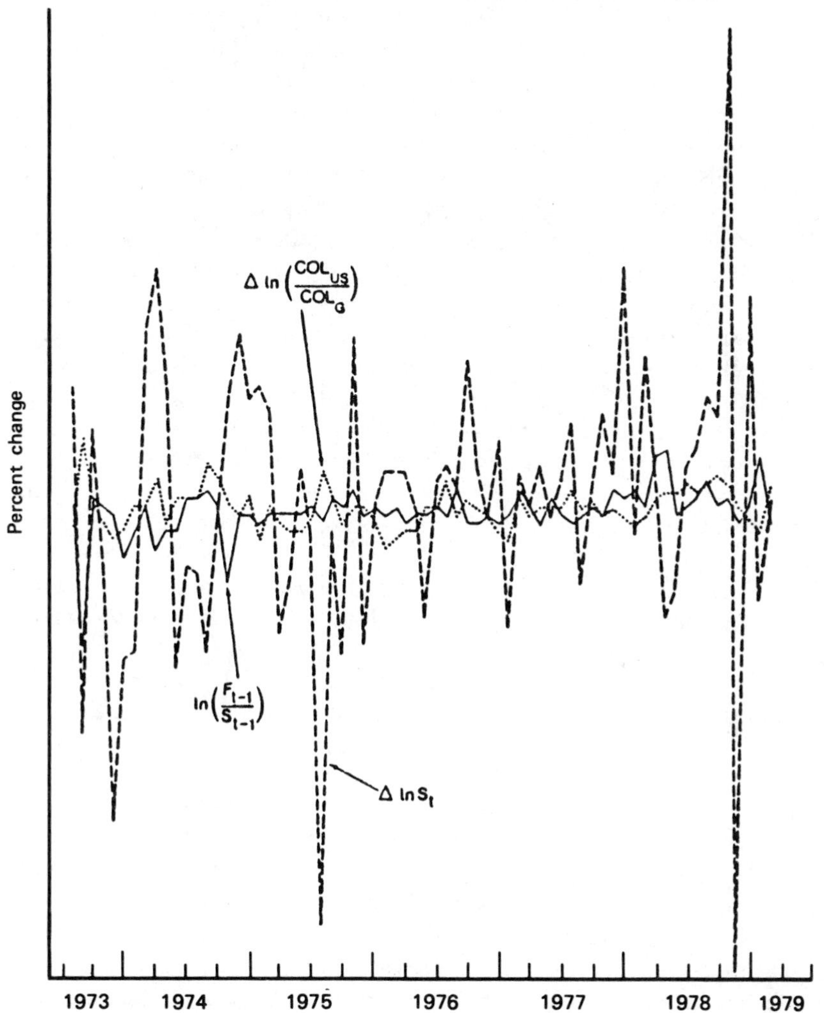

Source: Frenkel and Mussa, "The Efficiency of Foreign Exchange Markets and Measures of Turbulence," *American Economic Review,* May 1980, p. 376.

single-equation model, and most of these appear to be inspired by purchasing power parity or monetary models, with other variables added. For example, the money supply, inflation rate, national income, industrial production, and interest rates are typical explanatory variables. The advantage of this approach is simplicity, and the ability of the user to simulate other scenarios easily. In fact, several companies offer this simulation facility on an interactive computer basis. The disadvantage of the single-equation approach is that the simple equation may not adequately represent the real world. Forecast errors may result even when the right-hand side variables are known with some confidence.

Other econometric advisory services prepare their forecasts using models based on 50–900 equations, sometimes allowing for interaction and feedback between economic regions. These complex models attempt to be a better reflection of the real world. But more regression coefficients and variables have to be estimated, so forecasting performance need not improve beyond the simple models. In fact, some large econometric services add judgment factors to the pure econometric forecast. It is important for a user to be able to isolate these judgment factors to evaluate the pure econometric model.

Other forecasting companies follow a more judgmental approach. Some may consider econometric estimates of important (and quantifiable) variables (e.g., money supply, trade balance, inflation rate). However, economic factors that are difficult to quantify (e.g., currency expectations, changes in capital controls or tax policy), together with other factors (e.g., political elections and appointments) are also considered. All these factors are combined in some unspecified way to determine a forecast.

Some forecasting companies specialize in very short-run forecasts. These so-called ***technical or momentum services*** advise their customers primarily on the direction of exchange rate movements in the very short run and correspondingly whether customers should hold long or short positions in particular currencies. These directional forecasts are typically based on a statistical analysis of recent exchange rate behavior, although judgment may play an equally large role.

The Forward Rate as a Forecaster. Our interest in the forward rate as a forecaster of the future spot exchange rate is linked closely with the efficient market hypothesis, which states that market prices reflect available information. Because investors' expectations of the future spot rate are part of the available information set, and these expectations should be reflected in market prices, under certain strict assumptions (which were outlined in connection with forward market efficiency) it is correct to argue that today's forward exchange rate is (1) the single market price that represents all investor expectations of the future spot rate, and (2) an unbiased forecast of the future spot rate. If these assumptions were met, many multinational firms would view the forward rate as a very attractive forecast to use—(1) because it represents the collective wisdom of many well-informed, profit-seeking traders; (2) because the forward rate would be revised quickly as new information became available; and (3) because the forward rate would be a very inexpensive forecast to use.

However, there are three counterarguments against the forward rate as an unbiased predictor: (1) the forward rate may be influenced by official intervention; (2) the forward rate may reflect a risk premium as well as exchange rate expectations (much the same as an interest rate can include a liquidity or risk premium); and (3) expectations themselves may be weakly held or very imprecise. This final point suggests that the forward rate prediction may be very inaccurate, even though it is unlikely that investor expectations will be wrong consistently. The forecasting accuracy of the forward rate is an extremely important question, but one that remains unsettled, given the empirical research to date.

Techniques for Evaluating Forecasting Performance. How can we evaluate and choose among alternative currency forecasts? As in other similar problems (e.g., evaluating the performance of mutual fund managers or of individual subsidiaries or profit centers within a firm), evaluating foreign exchange forecasting performance is a tricky procedure. Basically, we need to establish a *standard of performance* and to calculate how a forecast compares with this standard.

There are two general approaches for analyzing the performance of an individual forecaster. The first general approach concentrates on the ***forecast error*** (forecast error = predicted exchange rate − actual exchange rate) and its various statistical properties. One desirable property of a forecast is small forecast errors. However, even this simple criterion needs qualification. For example, assume that today's forward rate is \$2 and two alternative forecasts of the future spot rate ate S_1= \$1.99 and S_2= 2.08. If the actual spot rate turns out to be \$2.02, the forecast error associated with S_1 (−\$0.03) is smaller than the forecast error associated with S_2 (\$0.06). Forecast S_2 is superior, however, because it leads investors to take long and profitable forward positions in sterling; that is, forecast S_2 leads to a "correct" decision.

As a further qualification, suppose that a third forecast, S_3 = \$2.14, also exists. Even though its forecast error is + \$0.12, it does not follow that this forecast is "twice as bad" as forecast S_2. If, for example, the firm is remitting a dividend from its U.S. parent and the firm is considering an "all-or-nothing" hedging decision, it will make the same decision using either S_2 or S_3 as a guide; thus there is no additional cost associated with S_3's larger forecast error. On the other hand, forecast S_3 may be "more than twice as bad" as forecast S_2. If the firm is considering investing a variable amount in U.K. bonds, based on the substantial appreciation predicted by S_3, the firm may invest 10 times as much in the United Kingdom as it would have, based on forecast S_2. As a consequence, the firm foregoes other profitable investments; these opportunity costs of using S_3 may exceed twice the costs of using S_2.

Therefore we conclude that there is no simple and unique relationship between the magnitude of forecast errors and the cost of forecast errors for investors. The implication of this statement is that there is no unique statistic for evaluating or ranking forecasters that will be correct for all investors. An "all-or-nothing" hedger will be concerned only that the forecast tell the correct direction, regardless of the magnitude of the forecast error. Investors who feel that exchange gains and losses are proportional to the forecast error will rank forecasters on the basis of mean absolute errors. Investors who feel that exchange gains and losses are proportional to the forecast error squared will rank forecasters on the basis of mean squared errors. It is an empirical question whether these criteria will rank forecasters in similar order.

If we ignore the magnitude of forecast errors, we can evaluate a forecast by calculating the fraction of periods where the forecast correctly predicts only the *direction* of exchange rate movement. We can define direction relative to the current forward rate or some other decision variable (e.g., the forward rate plus a risk premium). For example, in our earlier example S_2 and S_3 were "correct" forecasts (relative to the forward rate), whereas S_1 was incorrect. If the fraction of correct forecasts is unusually high, we can conclude that the forecast advisory service has expertise. The exact statistical procedure described by Merton (1981) measures both the percentage of correct forecasts for appreciation and for depreciation. Applications of this procedure have been presented by Levich (1983) and Cumby and Modest (1984).

A numerical example will help to illustrate the previous procedure. In a sample of 100 observations (n), suppose there are 60 correct forecasts (r), or a 60% track record. Is this an unusually good track record that demonstrates expertise, or is it simply the result of a sequence of lucky guesses? The question is analogous to another basic statistics problem: If a fair coin is tossed 100 times, what is the probability that it will land on "heads" 60 or more times? The answer is, this event would occur with roughly 2.3% probability. There are two ways to interpret this track record.

1. The forecaster does not have any special expertise in picking the direction of currency movements. A fairly rare event occurred—the forecaster guessed correctly on 60 of 100 trials.
2. The forecaster does have special expertise. His or her track record for picking the direction of currency movements correctly is close to 60%, significantly greater than 50%, which would result from simply guessing.

In this case we would probably pick interpretation 2. The track record appears too high to be the likely result of guessing.

The second general approach for evaluating forecasting performance is to calculate the stream of returns that an investor could earn by following the forecast. We would conclude that the advisory service has expertise and that the forecasts are useful if the stream of investment returns (adjusting for risk) is high relative to alternative investments. Again, this straightforward evaluation procedure raises two difficult questions.

First, how does an investor translate a set of currency forecasts into a set of investment decisions? The investor recognizes that forecasts are seldom perfect. If the forward rate stands at $2, the investor may not be willing to buy forward contracts unless the forecast is $2.02, $2.06, or perhaps higher. Furthermore, the investor is free to increase the number of forward contracts he or she purchases as the expected profits, and the confidence in those profits, increases. These issues are often handled by assuming that the investor uses the forecast to determine a "lump-sum" investment rather than an investment that increases with the expected variance of returns.

The second difficult question involves how the risk associated with currency investment should be measured. This calculation is necessary so that we can determine whether the return on currency investment is high relative to the risk incurred. Because the measurement of this risk factor is somewhat controversial, many analysts will simply compare the returns from selective currency investments based on a forecast with returns from (1) always holding U.S. dollar assets or (2) always holding foreign currency assets. These latter alternatives correspond to the statements (1) always hedge foreign exchange risk strategy and (2) never hedge foreign exchange risk strategy, which are simple rules of thumb for comparison.

To summarize, we have drawn a distinction between "correct" forecasts (those that correctly predict the direction of change relative to the forward rate) and "accurate" forecasts (those with low mean squared forecast errors). We noted earlier that many exchange rate changes are very large, and most are unanticipated by the market. Therefore including these as large forecast errors may bias (upward) our estimate of forecasting inaccuracy and our estimate of the potential for profits. In this sense, calculating the "percentage correct forecast" may offer a more meaningful measure of forecasting expertise.

CURRENCY EXPOSURE

DEFINING FOREIGN EXCHANGE EXPOSURE. Business operations by their nature are exposed to many kinds of uncertainties. International business operations and foreign exchange transactions have often been treated as a separate, and perhaps different, source of uncertainty when compared with domestic operations. However, it has been argued by Wihlborg (1980), among others, that the distinction between exposure in foreign and domestic operations is exaggerated. For example, a Minnesota firm that heats its plant with oil might be concerned about (i.e., exposed to uncertainty because of) competition from a Texas firm that requires smaller expenditures on heating. Similarly, a Pennsylvania chocolate market might be concerned about (i.e., exposed to uncertainty because of) the unpredictability of domestic inflation. When the value of domestic currency is uncertain, the firm can only estimate the *real value* of its expenses and the *real value* of its revenues and profits. These conditions are analogous for the domestic firm with international operations. In this case the domestic firm is concerned about the real value of transactions denominated in foreign currency and the potential competitive impact from foreign firms that face lower real costs. Therefore the exposure of domestic and foreign operations appears to be similar in many respects.

Sources of Exposure to Foreign Exchange Rate Changes. Firms that maintain long-term assets (receivables) or liabilities (payables) denominated in foreign currencies may be subject to ***translation exposure***—namely, the possibility that an exchange rate change will alter the U.S. dollar value of foreign currency items when they are translated and consolidated for accounting purposes. ***Translation gains and losses*** represent a *stock* amount that has not been realized, but it may be realized in future transactions. For example, the cost of repaying a loan of 1 million Swiss francs increases by $100,000 when the exchange rate moves from $0.40/Swfr to $0.50/Swfr. This additional cost must be borne by the firm if the $0.50 exchange rate is sustained.

Current payables and receivables denominated in foreign currencies give rise to ***transaction exposure***. Those transactions that are settled during the current accounting period represent a *flow* amount of *realized* gains and losses. ***Economic exposure*** is a broader concept that suggests how realignments affect future cash flows and, therefore, the present value of the firm. For example, a U.S. dollar devaluation may assist the domestic firm in increasing its export sales; however, it also would increase the costs for firms that rely on foreign inputs. The full impact of the exchange rate change on the firm's cash flows would depend, of course, on the price elasticity of demand for U.S. products, the ability of U.S. firms to find substitutes for higher priced foreign inputs, and other factors. Students of international trade and finance will see the analogy to the impact of exchange rate changes on a nation's exports, imports, overall balance of payments, national income, and so forth. Individual firms are simply the (exposed) vehicles by which aggregate balance of payments adjustment takes place.

The discussion of economic exposure suggests that in a world economy open to trade and capital flows, even "fully domestic" firms might be concerned about currency realignments. Clearly, U.S. automobile makers or steel producers with no foreign currency balances or contracts might benefit (or lose) because of unanticipated changes in the $/DM or $/yen rates. To the extent that economic exposure reflects real economic changes, this further suggests that financial transactions may be insufficient to eliminate completely the risks of currency realignments.

Accounting Approaches to Measuring Foreign Exchange Exposure. Quantifying exposure to foreign exchange movements is important because of two sets of factors. First, managers require an estimate of the firm's exposure to formulate their hedging (i.e., exposure management) decisions. Second, investors and financial analysts require similar information to reassess a firm's value in response to exchange rate changes.

Accounting approaches can be characterized as a set of rules for translating foreign currency items, either on the balance sheet or the income statement, into domestic currency. Items translated at the current exchange rate are (for accounting purposes) considered exposed, whereas items translated at the historical exchange rate are not exposed. The firm's net exposure to exchange risk (again, for accounting purposes) is defined as the difference between exposed assets and exposed liabilities.

Throughout the 1960s and early 1970s, U.S. firms could choose between two alternative accounting rules for translation. The ***current-noncurrent approach*** classified current assets and liabilities as exposed (whereas noncurrent items were not exposed). The ***monetary-nonmonetary approach*** classified all monetary assets and liabilities as exposed (whereas nonmonetary items were not exposed). Long-term debt was the major item treated differently under these two accounting rules. For example, a 5-year loan of 1 million Swiss francs would be exposed under the monetary-nonmonetary approach but not exposed under the current-noncurrent approach.

A study by Aliber and Stickney (1975) argued that accounting conventions implicity make a statement concerning macroeconomic relationships. For example, the monetary-nonmonetary approach is consistent with the view that purchasing power parity holds, whereas the Fisher open effect (described later) does not. Recall that if PPP holds, the U.S. dollar value of a foreign asset would be maintained (i.e., not exposed) because exchange rate changes offset foreign currency inflation. The ***Fisher open effect*** implies that the real cost of funds (or real return on funds) is the same in any currency because exchange rate changes reflect different (and offsetting) interest rates on the two currencies. The evidence presented by Aliber and Stickney suggests that among industrial countries, the data offered stronger support for the Fisher open effect than for PPP. If departures from PPP are small enough to maintain that nonmonetary items are not exposed, logic would lead us to conclude that monetary items are not exposed either, because the departures from the Fisher open effect are still smaller.

Although the precise calculations and interpretation of the results of this study may be subject to varying interpretations, the underlying thrust of the analysis should be clear. If there are no changes in real exchange rates (i.e., if PPP holds) and the expected real interest rate is the same in every currency (i.e., if the Fisher open effect holds), the firm with international operations bears no exposure to currency realignments. This view of international financial markets may represent an extreme (or polar) case, but it is useful as a reference point for measuring a firm's actual exposure.

The current-noncurrent approach might also be cast in economic terms. This accounting approach would be consistent with a world in which PPP and the Fisher open effect held in the long run but not in the short run. In this case we would expect the U.S. dollar value of noncurrent items to be maintained, whereas in the short run, substantial changes in U.S. dollar value would be possible.

In 1976, Financial Accounting Standards Board Statement No. 8 (FASB No.8) took effect and the ***temporal approach*** became the required standard for U.S. firms. FASB No.8 standardized translation approaches across U.S. firms and attempted to bring translation procedures into closer conformity with U.S. generally accepted accounting principles. The temporal approach required that items valued in terms of foreign currency at a particular date must be translated to U.S. dollars, using an exchange rate from the same date. Because monetary items are usually reassessed at current market values as of the date of the accounting statement (and would be translated at current exchange rates) and nonmonetary items are generally entered at historic values (and would be translated at historic exchange rates), the temporal approach and the monetary-nonmonetary approach produce similar results. The primary difference is for certain nonmonetary items (e.g., inventories) that may be restated to reflect the lesser of cost or current market value. These items are exposed under the temporal approach but not exposed under the monetary-nonmonetary approach.

Another major aspect of FASB No.8 was to include all translation gains and losses in the *current* income statement. Given recent exchange rate volatility, this rule had the effect of raising the volatility of reported earnings. Critics argued that this rule might cause firms to hedge excessively (and incur extra costs for no expected gain) or to increase their economic exposure (e.g., to finance foreign operations by borrowing dollars in order to avoid the accounting exposure of long-term foreign currency debt).

After several years of discussion, the Financial Accounting Standards Board issued statement 52 (FASB No. 52) on December 8, 1981. It became mandatory for U.S. firms to use FASB No. 52 for fiscal years beginning on or after December 15, 1982. A detailed analysis of the provisions of FASB No. 52 has been presented by Peat, Marwick, Mitchell and Co. (1981). The stated objectives of FASB No. 52 are relatively straightforward:

1. (To) provide information that is generally compatible with the expected economic effects of a rate change on an enterprise's cash flows and equity.
2. (To) reflect in consolidated statements the financial results and relationships of the individual consolidated entities as measured in their functional currencies in conformity with U.S. generally accepted accounting principles.

However, the procedures for implementing these objectives are complex. The basic translation approach of FASB No. 52 is the **current rate-method**—all foreign currency items are translated at the current rate and, therefore, are exposed. Foreign exchange gains and losses from current transactions will be reported in current income, as they were under FASB No. 8. However, foreign exchange gains and losses from translation, intercompany transactions, or transactions that hedge a net investment are accumulated and reported as a separate component of equity. This change is expected to smooth reported earnings, but the equivalent information and volatility should appear in owners' equity.

In addition, FASB No. 52 introduces the concept of a **functional currency** for producing the accounting statements for a particular foreign entity. For example, if the DM were the functional currency for a German subsidiary, the first step would be to produce accounting statements for the subsidiary in DM using the temporal approach for all non-DM items. In the second step, the results for the subsidiary are translated into the parents' reporting currency (presumably the dollar) using the current rate approach. This two-step procedure attempts to reflect the ability of the subsidiary to generate cash in its functional currency, and then to evaluate that stream in terms of the parent's reporting currency. This framework suggests a "net investment view" of foreign currency exposure rather than an individual asset and liability view.

Economic Approaches to Measuring Exposure. Assessing the impact of exchange rate changes on the market value of a firm raises many difficult challenges. When exchange rate changes are nominal rather than real (i.e., when PPP holds), there is strong agreement that no currency exposure exists, so market values should be unaffected. Furthermore, when financial markets are efficient, Logue and Oldfield (1977) have argued that any hedging strategy will not affect the total market value of the firm (except for transaction costs). Deviations from PPP can be sizable and persistent, however. And continuous, strong-form market efficiency can also be questioned. Therefore it seems likely that currency realignments have an impact on the market value of firms, although the magnitude and the time lag of the response are difficult to determine.

The concept of economic exposure can be formalized either algebraically, using a cash flow approach, or geometrically, using an elasticities approach. Within the context of a simplifying model, it is possible to trace the discrete paths through which exchange rate changes affect the market value of a firm. Making these models operational is a much more difficult task, both because the actual cash flows of the firm are in many currencies and because the interrelationships in the real world are more complex than in stylized models. Several recent studies by Shapiro (1977), Adler and Dumas (1980), and Hekman (1983) propose a regression format, measuring the sensitivity of cash flows or equity returns relative to exchange rate changes. Clearly the sensitivity coefficient would be useful for investors who want to know the risk of a particular firm, but it is not clear how managers can use this aggregate sensitivity coefficient to adjust their exposure to exchange risk to its desired level.

MANAGEMENT STRATEGIES TOWARD CURRENCY EXPOSURE. It is correctly argued that shareholder welfare and resource allocation are best served when firm managers select projects with positive expected value and ignore risk. Shareholders then engage in other financial transactions to reach their desired risk levels. This scenario, however, ignores transaction costs, the manager's risk preferences, and other factors. The burgeoning literature on these issues suggests that managers are not leaving foreign exchange risk management to shareholders. This may be because managers are protecting their own short-run interests rather than maximizing expected profits for the firm. It may also be the case that debt capacity is increased and the cost of debt is decreased if the perceived riskiness of company profits is reduced through hedging.

It is important to note that this subsection considers only **financial strategies** to currency exposure rather than **operating strategies**. The latter group of strategies would include diversification into more factor markets, good markets, and production locations. Operating strategies reduce the risk of real production locations. Operating strategies reduce the risk of real cash flow changes that might result from real exchange rate changes.

Financial Market Hedging Techniques. Consider a U.S. firm with a DM 1,000 net asset exposure that represents a royalty to be received in 1 year. To offset or hedge this asset exposure, the firm must establish a corresponding DM liability. The most direct way to accomplish this is to sell a DM 1,000 forward contract for delivery in 1 year. This forward contract obligates the U.S. firm to deliver DM 1,000 in 1 year (an account payable, or liability) and to receive a fixed amount of U.S. dollars.

Let the current spot rate be $0.50/DM and the current 1-year forward rate be $0.55/DM. One traditional measure of the cost of hedging is the percentage forward premium, $(F - S)/S$, which equals 10% in this case. It thus appears as if the U.S. firm locks in a 10% profit (i.e., it incurs *negative* costs) by hedging. This calculation basically represents a *sunk cost,* the amount by which the market has already realigned the value of DM. A second measure of the cost of hedging is the percentage difference between the forward rate and the expected future spot rate $(F - ES_{t+1})/F$. If we expect that the spot rate will be $0.60/DM in 1 year, the cost of hedging is $(0.55 - 0.60)/0.55 = -9.1\%$. This calculation represents an **opportunity cost**, the amount we stand to lose if we hedge today at the forward rate rather than maintaining an open position and selling at the expected future spot rate. The second (opportunity cost) measure corresponds more closely to the notion of economic cost. However, it may be difficult for a firm to assess its expected spot rate and measure the opportunity cost. Also, the realized spot rate may differ greatly from the firm's expectation, so that in advance, the realized hedging cost can only be estimated.

Other financial transactions in addition to the forward contract can be used to establish an offsetting DM liability. Using a *money market hedge,* the U.S. firm borrows DM 1,000 for 1 year, buys $500 in the spot market, and invests the $500 for 1 year. Using these three transactions, the U.S. firm "constructs its own" forward contract. If the interest differential between the U.S. dollar investment and the DM loan equals the percentage forward premium, the costs of a forward market hedge and a money market hedge are identical. (See Exhibits 1 and 2 and the earlier discussion of forward contracts.)

If well-functioning forward markets are unavailable, firms may carry the "do-it-yourself" strategy further to "construct their own" offsetting DM liability positions. Consequently, these strategies might be more applicable for developing countries in which forward markets do not exist or strict controls on local borrowing are present. The basic alternative strategy is for the U.S. firm to arrange a swap between two private parties. A **swap** is an agreement to exchange a given amount of one currency for another and, at a prearranged time, to return the original amounts swapped. A broker or investment banker may be involved to match the two parties and to negotiate the terms (i.e., cost) of the swap.

A **basic swap arrangement** is illustrated in Exhibit 12. Suppose a U.S. firm in Brazil has accumulated 1 million cruzeiros in retained earnings, but these funds are blocked (i.e., cannot be repatriated to the United States) and a forward market for cruzeiros does not exist. The Brazilian affiliate of the U.S. firm must locate in Brazil another foreign firm (e.g., from France) that wants to borrow cruzeiros. The U.S. affiliate lends cruzeiros to the French affiliate, whereas the French parent lends dollars to the U.S. parent. The terms of the swap would be negotiated, to some extent reflecting the gains to the U.S. affiliate from lending its blocked funds, and the gains to the French affiliate from acquiring spot cruzeiros and working capital through a private arrangement.

The variations on this basic swap (e.g., the back-to-back loan, the parallel loan, the currency swap, and the credit swap) are similar in many ways but may differ in terms of costs, parent guarantees, and tax aspects. Some of these variations are described in more detail by Eiteman and Stonehill (1982).

The **foreign currency option contract** is a new instrument that is now available to assist in managing risks. Put and call options for five currencies are traded on the Philadelphia Stock Exchange; several major banks and financial institutions are issuing their own currency options to customer specifications. The buyer of a put (call) has the right—but not the obligation—to buy (sell) a stated amount of foreign currency for a predetermined price until the option expires. Consequently, the buyer of an option is exposed to limited liability—the buyer cannot lose more than his or her initial outlay for the option. It can easily be shown that the option is a superior hedging instrument in cases where the firm's future cash flows are uncertain—for example, when the firm has bid on a project in DM but does not know whether it has made the winning bid, or when the future product sales in foreign currency are uncertain but need to be covered. In general, foreign currency options permit the firm to tailor its exposed position more carefully; that is, the firm need buy protection only against

EXHIBIT 12 ILLUSTRATION OF A SWAP TRANSACTION[a]

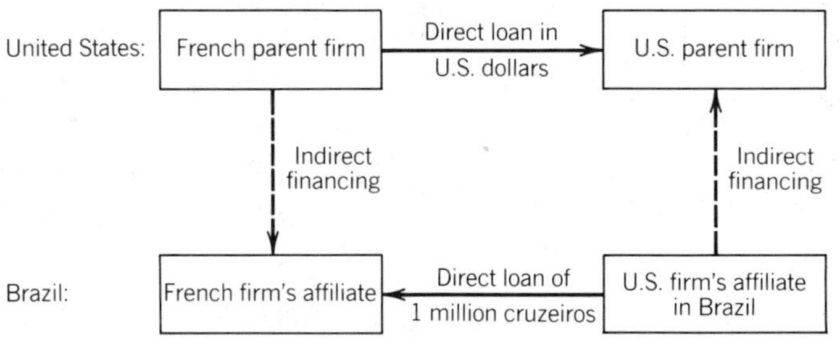

[a] The terms of the swap, including the amount of the direct U.S. dollar loan, must be negotiated.

Source: Adapted from Eiteman and Stonehill, *Multinational Business Finance,* Addison-Wesley, Reading, MA. 1979, p. 139.

specific events. This may be advantageous for firms that want to profit if their exchange rate expectations are met, but want to be protected in the event of adverse exchange rate movements.

Additional Hedging Techniques. In our earlier example, we considered a U.S. firm with a DM 1,000 net asset exposure. Suppose this same firm also held a liability position of 4,000 French francs (= 1,000 DM × \$0.50/DM × 8 Fr fr/\$). If we believe that movements in the \$/DM and \$/Frfr rates are very highly correlated, the combination of these two positions may be very nearly offsetting, so that the net exposure approaches zero. This example illustrates two points. First, using **third currencies** may offer a useful alternative to normal hedging procedures. An **asset** exposure in DM can be hedged by establishing a **liability** position in a currency that is *closely* (and *positively*) correlated with DM, or by establishing an *asset* position in a currency that is strongly *negatively* correlated with DM.

Second, this example suggests that the risk of a currency position should not be considered in isolation, but rather in the context of a portfolio. Just as a portfolio of two securities is likely to produce a more favorable risk-return trade-off than either security individually, one can make a similar argument for currency exposure. The merits of a portfolio approach to currency management have been argued in the literature for some time (see, e.g., Lietaer, 1971, Makin, 1978, and Bilson, 1981), but managers have been slow to adopt these principles.

A further extension of the many currencies case is the U.S. firm with many foreign subsidiaries. In this case, the firm must weigh the trade-offs between **centralized** versus **decentralized** management strategies. Centralization allows the firm to implement a netting model (that will reduce aggregate foreign exchange trading and transaction costs worldwide) and a worldwide portfolio approach (based on consolidated foreign exchange positions). Furthermore, centralization may allow the firm to direct hedging operations to those affiliates that enjoy certain tax advantages. Centralized financial information collection and management may also represent an advantage. On the other hand, decentralized management maintains performance incentives for foreign affiliates and avoids the problem of ordering individual affiliates to retain foreign exchange exposures that are contrary to their own interests. Foreign exchange information may be more accurate and timely when used by the foreign manager. Finally, decentralization itself leads to portfolio diversification because it is unlikely that all foreign managers will follow the same hedging strategies based on the same exchange rate expectations.

One additional method for dealing with exposure is through the selection of a contract or **invoice currency**. In the context of our earlier examples, the U.S. firm might have contracted for its royalty payments to be paid in U.S. dollars rather than DM, and it might have chosen to invoice its exports to Brazil in U.S. dollars rather than in cruzeiros. This strategy eliminates foreign exchange exposure at its source by transferring the exposure to the other party in the transaction. This pricing strategy therefore may reduce sales, but it may be a more effective way to lay off foreign exchange risks in some situations. Technical details of invoice currency selection are discussed by Rao and Magee, 1980 and by McKinnon, 1979.

Impact of Currency Exposure. The preceding subsections are testimony to the current interest in how one measures exchange rate variability, how one forecasts exchange rates, and how one sets up accounting rules to measure exposure and provide useful information for managers and shareholders. These are obviously complicated and interrelated issues. Now, we focus on two points: the managerial response to currency exposure and the shareholder response to managerial decisions and exchange rate changes.

Managerial Behavior: Results from Survey Analysis. Within the past decade, two surveys have been published on managerial attitudes and practices toward foreign exchange risk management. The survey by Evans, Folks, and Jilling (1978) represents 156 U.S. multinationals, and the survey by Rodriquez (1980) reflects the experience of 70 firms. Our attention centers on two topics—the objectives of foreign exchange exposure management and foreign exchange forecasting.

Rodriquez observed that the most frequently voiced objective for exposure management is to protect the firm against large losses. Evans, et al. found this to be the third most popular rationale behind protecting the dollar value of foreign assets and protecting the economic value of future foreign currency cash flows. Rodriquez noted that managerial emphasis is definitely on a defensive position: "Trying to profit from the movements in the exchange markets was not considered an objective by any of the managers interviewed" (p. 99). On the other hand, Evans et al. reported (p. 132) that 13.5% of their respondents felt that management's objective was the "acceptance of additional foreign exchange risk in the short run if the potential for foreign exchange gains exists."

The latter result is more consistent with the other evidence in Rodriquez and Evans et al., as well as our casual empiricism. If a firm has a "natural" long (short) position in a currency that is appreciating (depreciating), the firm is likely to maintain its open position, especially if the forward premium is less than the expected currency change. Management may rationalize this situation as a potential windfall gain rather than speculation. The firm may try to hedge or close out only the natural positions that are going against it. In this regard, Rodriquez has suggested the possibility of risk asymmetry within a firm; that is, the firm may be unwilling to maintain open positions that are presently valued at losses or for which large losses are possible. If uncertainty is skewed toward gains, however, the firm will not bother to hedge.

Rodriquez correctly pointed out that problems of exposure management often are generated in the treasury area as a result of insufficient planning in operations and marketing areas. Long-range business plans are often executed assuming that financial exposure problems will be small.

The most extensive information on exchange rate forecasting practices is presented in the survey by Evans et al. (1978). It suggests that nearly all major U.S. firms collect and attempt to utilize foreign exchange forecasts. These authors reported that 55% of the firms in their sample purchased forecasts from outside consultants. Of this group, about 50% began purchasing their forecasts after FASB No. 8 became effective. The average number of currencies forecasted was 16: The modal value was 10 and the maximum was 70. Over 5% of the managers agreed that their firms had greatly increased their resources devoted to exchange rate forecasting since 1976. However, only 31% felt that they had become more skillful in forecasting. Along these lines, Evans et al. reported that 58% agreed that foreign exchange rate forecasting was the "weakest link" in their exposure management program. This figure is nearly twice as large as that reported in a 1975 survey by the same authors. They observed that despite corporate efforts, forecasting appears to be an "increasingly weaker link" in firms' exposure management programs. Perhaps, however, firms are beginning to understand that forecasting is at the center of any exposure management program and because of this awareness, they are devoting greater efforts to forecasting.

Shareholder and Stock Market Responses. Evidence on the stock market's reaction to exchange rate changes and currency exposure management strategies is sketchy and understandably difficult to interpret. Standard trade theory suggests that if the U.S. dollar is devalued, U.S. exports should appear less expensive, whereas imported foreign goods appear more expensive. If these predictions are true (in real terms), we expect the market value of firms that export their products (or produce import-competing goods) to rise, whereas the market value of firms that sell imported goods (or use imports in the production process) will fall. Any number of factors may alter this chain of reasoning. For example, if exporters face tough overseas competition and buyers are sensitive to small price changes, U.S. exporters will not gain much by devaluation. If U.S. importers find it easy to substitute domestic goods for more expensive foreign sources, however, U.S. importers would not necessarily lose much by devaluation. In either case, the stock market may have predicted the exchange rate change in advance, and the share prices of U.S. firms would have been adjusted by the time the change actually occurred.

Accounting research on the other hand, has focused on the definition of exposure and the impact of reporting practices. For example, if managers changed their behavior (again in real dimensions) in response to a new accounting rule (e.g., FASB No. 8), the market value of shares should change. Market values might also change if the new accounting rule brought new information to public awareness. However, an accounting change that shifts reported foreign exchange gains from a footnote to the income statements, or to retained earnings, should not affect market values because such a rule change does not affect the information available to investors.

An early study by Giddy (1974) examined the stock market response to several discrete exchange rate changes during the 1960s and the early 1970s. Giddy's analysis suggests that domestic stock prices respond favorably to domestic currency devaluations. The favorable effect appeared to be stronger for export-oriented firms. A more recent study by Dukes (1978) attempted to measure the impact of FASB No. 8 on stock prices during a period of floating exchange rates. Duke's analysis could not reject the hypothesis of zero impact on stock prices. As we have suggested, however, the studies cited are not conclusive because of the complexity of the problem. The net impact of hedging strategies and currency volatility on stock prices remains an important question that has not been resolved.

REFERENCES

Adler, M., and Dumas, B., "Simulating a Firm's Exposure to Exchange Rate Changes," Mimeographed, Centre d'Enseignement Superieur des Affaires, November 1980.

Aliber, R.Z., and Stickney, C., "Accounting Measures of Foreign Exchange Exposure: The Long and Short of It," *Accounting Review,* Vol. 50, No. 1 (January 1975): 44–57.

Bernstein, E.M., "Comment" in T. Agmon, R.G. Hawkins, and R.M. Levich (eds.), *The Future of the International Monetary System,* Lexington, MA: Heath, 1984.

Bilson, J.F.O., "The Speculative Efficiency Hypothesis," *Journal of Business* (July 1981): 435–451.

Cooper, R.N., "Recent History of World Monetary Problems," in T. Agmon, R.G. Hawkins, and R.M. Levich (eds.), *The Future of the International Monetary System,* Lexington, MA: Heath, 1984.

Crouhy-Veyrac, L., Crouhy, M., and Melitz, J., "More About the Law of One Price," *European Economic Review,* Vol. 18 (1982): 325–344.

Cumby, R.E., and Modest, D.M., "Tests for Market Timing Ability: A Unified Framwork and an Application to the Foreign Exchange Market," New York University, processed January 1984.

Deardorff, A.V., "One-Way Arbitrage and Its Implications for the Foreign Exchange Markets," *Journal of Political Economy,* Vol. 87, No. 2 (April 1979): 351–364.

Dooley, M.P., and Shafer, J.R., "Analysis of Short-Run Exchange Rate Behavior: March 1973 to November 1981," in D. Bigman and T. Taya (eds.), *Exchange Rate and Trade Instability,* Cambridge, MA: Ballinger, 1983.

Dornbusch, R., "Exchange Rate Economics: Where Do We Stand?" *Brookings Institution Papers on Economic Papers on Economic Activity,* No. 1, 1980, pp. 145–185.

———, "Expectations and Exchange Rate Dynamics," *Journal of Political Economy,* Vol. 84, No. 6 (December 1976): 1161–1176.

Dukes, R.E., *An Empirical Investigation of the Effects of Statement of Financial Accounting Standards No. 8 on Security Return Behavior,* Stamford, CT: Financial Accounting Standards Board, 1978.

Eiteman, D.K., and Stonehill, A.I., *Multinational Business Finance,* Third Edition, Reading, MA: Addison-Wesley, 1982.

Evans, T.G., Folks, Jr., W.R., and Jilling, M., *The Impact of Statement of Financial Accounting Standards No. 8 on the Foreign Exchange Risk Management Practices of American Multinationals,* Stamford, CT: Financial Accounting Standards Board, 1978.

Fama, F., "Efficient Capital Markets: A Review of Theory and Empirical Work" *Journal of Finance,* Vol. 25, No. 2 (May 1970): 383–417.

Frenkel, J.A., "Purchasing Power Parity: Doctrinal Perspectives and Evidence from 1920s," *Journal of International Economics,* Vol. 8, No. 2 (May 1978): 161–191.

———, and Levich, R.M., "Transaction Costs and Interest Arbitrage: Tranquil versus Turbulent Periods," *Journal of Political Economy,* Vol. 87, No. 6 (December 1977): 1109–1126.

———, and Mussa, M.L., "The Efficiency of Foreign Exchange Markets and Measures of Turbulence," *American Economic Review,* Vol. 70, No. 2 (May 1980): 374–381.

———, and Rodriquez, C.A., "Exchange Rate Dynamics and the Overshooting Hypothesis," International Monetary Fund *Staff Papers,* Vol. 29 (March 1982): 1–30.

Giddy, I.H., "Devaluations, Revaluations, and Stock Market Prices," unpublished Ph.D. dissertation, Ann Arbor: University of Michigan, 1974.

———, "Measuring the World Foreign Exchange Market," *Columbia Journal of World Business,* Vol. 14, No. 4 (Winter 1979): 36–48.

Hekman, C.R., "The Measurement of Foreign Exchange Exposure: A Practical Theory and Its Application," *Financial Analysts Journal* (September/October 1983): 59–65.

Hooper, P., and Morton, J., "Summary Measures of the Dollar's Foreign Exchange Value," *Federal Reserve Bulletin,* Vol. 64, No. 10 (October 1978): 783–789.

Kohlhagen, S.W., *The Behavior of Foreign Exchange Markets–A Critical Survey of the Empirical Literature,* New York University Monograph Series in Finance and Economics, New York: Salomon Brothers Center, No. 1978-3, 1978.

———, "The Identification of Destabilizing Foreign Exchange Speculation," *Journal of International Economics,* Vol. 9, No. 3 (August 1979): 321–340.

Kubarych, R.M., *Foreign Exchange Markets in the United States,* New York: Federal Reserve Bank of New York, 1983.

Isard, P., "Exchange Rate Determination: A Survey of Popular Views and Recent Models," *Princeton Studies in International Finance,* No. 42, May 1978.

———, "How Far Can We Push the Law of One Price?" *American Economic Review,* Vol. 67, No. 6 (December 1979): 942–948.

Levich, R.M., *The International Money Market: An Assessment of Forecasting Techniques and Market Efficiency,* Greenwich, CT: JAI Press, 1979.

———, "Further Results on the Efficiency of Markets for Foreign Exchange," in *Managed Exchange-Rate Flexibility: The Recent Experience,* Boston: Conference Series No. 20 Federal Reserve Bank of Boston, 1978.

———, "An Examination of Overshooting Behavior in the Foreign Exchange Market," Group of Thirty *Occasional Studies,* No. 5, New York, 1980a.

———, "The Use and Analysis of Foreign Exchange Forecasts," in *Foreign Exchange Risk,* B. Antl (ed.), London: Euromoney Publications, 1980b.

———, "Analyzing the Accuracy of Foreign Exchange Advisory Services: Theory and Evidence," in R. Levich and C. Wihlborg (eds.), *Exchange Risk and Exposure,* Lexington, MA: Heath, 1980c.

———, "Currency Forecasters Lose Their Way," *Euromoney* (August 1983): 140–147.

Lietaer, B.A., *Financial Management of Foreign Exchange,* Cambridge, MA: MIT Press, 1971.

Logue, D.E., and Oldfield, G.S., "Managing Foreign Assets When Foreign Markets Are Efficient," *Financial Management.* Vol. 6, No. 2 (Summer 1977): 16–22.

McCormick, F., "Covered Interest Arbitrage: Unexploited Profits?: Comments," *Journal of Political Economy,* Vol. 87, No. 2 (April 1979): 411–417.

McKinnon, R.I., *Money in International Exchange,* New York: Oxford University Press, 1979.

Makin, J., "Portfolio Theory and the Problem of Foreign Exchange Risk," *Journal of Finance* (May 1978) 517–539.

Merton, R.C., "On Market Timing and Investment Performance I: An Equilibrium Theory of Value for Market Forecasts," *Journal of Business* (July 1981): 363–406.

Morgan Guaranty Trust Company of New York, "How Overvalued Is the Dollar?" *World Financial Markets* (July 1983) 3–12.

Morgan Guaranty Trust Company of New York, "Effective Exchange Rates: Update and Refinement," *World Financial Markets* (August 1983): 6–12.

Officer, L.H., "The Purchasing-Power-Parity Theory of Exchange Rates: A Review Article," *International Monetary Fund Staff Papers.* Vol. 23, No. 1 (March 1976): 1–60.

Peat, Marwick, Mitchell and Co. "Statement of Financial Accounting Standards," New York, December 1981.

Rao, R.K.S., and Magee, S.P., "The Currency of Denomination of International Trade Contracts," in R. Levich and C. Wihlborg (eds.), *Exchange Risk and Exposure,* Lexington, MA: Heath, 1980.

Rodriquez, R.M., *Foreign Exchange Management in U.S. Multinationals.* Lexington, MA: Heath, 1980.

Shapiro, A., "Defining Exchange Risk," *Journal of Business* (January 1977): 37–39.

Wihlborg, C.G., "Currency Exposure: Taxonomy and Theory," in R. Levich and C. Wihlborg (eds.), *Exchange Risk and Exposure,* Lexington, MA: Heath, 1980.

Sweeney, Richard J., "Beating the Foreign Exchange Market," *Journal of Finance,* Vol. 41, No. 1 (March 1986): 163–82.

19

INTERNATIONAL BANKING

CONTENTS

19

INTERNATIONAL BANKING

Ian H. Giddy

INTERNATIONAL BANKING ACTIVITIES

The primary activities of international banks remain similar to those of domestic banks: receiving deposits and making loans. The difference is that the deposit and loan business is often done with foreign depositors and borrowers, usually booked in a foreign location, and sometimes denominated in a foreign currency. In addition, multinational banks engage in certain unique functions such as export-import financing and documentation, foreign exchange trading, Eurocurrency borrowing and lending, and international payments clearing. Moreover, the difference between commercial and investment banking is blurred in the international context; hence U.S. commercial banks engage in activities such as bond underwriting abroad that they are not able to do at home.

International investment banking activities came to the forefront of international banking during the mid-1980s. Partly because of loan risk problems in certain industries, regions, and sovereign borrowers, many of the world's major international banks shifted emphasis from commercial lending toward merchant banking. This emphasis has in turn generated a wealth of financial innovation that is probably unprecedented in the history of international banking. Banks now finance their corporate and government customers not only through syndicated lending, but also through international bond issuances, private placements, international short-term issuance facilities, issues in foreign capital markets (including equity issues abroad), government-sponsored credit, including export financing, asset-based funding such as cross-border lease financing, project financing, and a variety of hybrid securities and multimarket facilities. Although most of these are "off balance sheet" and do not impose a credit risk burden on the bank, some banks emphasize nonfunding "credit enhancement" by providing borrowers with backup, lines of credit, letters of credit and the like to support the customer's borrowing activities.

International investment banks, including the investment banking affiliates of commercial banks, also provide a wider than ever range of **hedging services,** including short- and long-term forward currency contracts, currency swaps, interest rate swaps, currency and interest rate options, including "ceiling" and "floor" rate protection, forward interest rate agreements, and even hedges against commodity price movements. Finally, they provide advisory and negotiation services such as mergers, acquisitions and divestitures, debt renegotiation, financial packaging, and economic forecasting for market timing decisions.

CHANGES IN THE INTERNATIONAL BANKING ENVIRONMENT. The character of international banking underwent rapid changes during the 1960s and 1970s. Many banks entered international activities for the first time during these decades, and those that were already international expanded the range and size of their international activities. Floating exchange rates, the growth of the Eurocurrency market, and countries newly rich (or newly poor) as a result of commodity price rises, produced new opportunities, but may also have encouraged an excessively rapid expansion abroad by many American and non-American banks. By the end of 1974 a number of banks had failed, and several major rescues were engineered by the central banks of the United States, Germany, and the United Kingdom. Subsequently, bank managers have engaged in international expansion in a more cautious fashion, seeking the proper match between customer needs, regulatory opportunities and constraints, and the bank's own strengths before choosing the degree and form of international involvement.

In many respects today's environment is more conducive to international banking: capital controls have been reduced, central banks provide more support and exercise more well-informed control, and communications and management information have improved. The same factors, however, make it easier for inexperienced management to enter international banking more rapidly. This was the source of the relatively high incidence of international banking problems during the 1970s.

Exhibit 1 lists the country of origin of the world's 30 largest banks in the

EXHIBIT 1 COUNTRY OF ORIGIN OF THE WORLD'S 30 LARGEST BANKS, 1985

Location	Number of Banks in the Top 30 (by Assets)	Change from 1979
Japan	15	+8
United States	5	—
France	4	—
U.K.	3	—
Germany	1	−5
Canada	1	+1
Hong Kong	1	+1

Source: The Banker, "The Top 500," June 1980 and July 1985.

mid-1980s. Perhaps the reader will be surprised to find that so many are Japanese. More remarkable, in this writer's view, is the shift in rankings that occurred in 5 years. Although sheer size means little on its own, and although a number of the world's biggest banks are not truly international, a glance at the annual rankings of the international finance journals such as *Euromoney* or *International Financing Review* confirms the fact that individual banks' preeminence can rapidly wax or wane. The catchwords for international banking in the 1980s are **competition** and **innovation**—the survival of the quick-witted.

Let us now review some of the organizational features that enable a bank to establish a long-term international presence.

STRATEGIES FOR INTERNATIONAL BANKING EXPANSION. Banks can engage in international banking activities in two ways: from their home countries, or abroad. Much of traditional international banking could be carried out without ever establishing a foreign office, since the principal activities of international banking have long been the **financing of exports and imports** and the effecting and clearing of international payments. Both of these require no more international presence than the establishment of **correspondent balance** relationships with foreign banks.

More recently, many banks with little or no international involvement have found it advantageous to create offshore branches in low-tax and low-regulation jurisdiction such as the Bahamas, the Cayman Islands, or Singapore, to take advantage of the absence of reserve requirements and certain other regulatory constraints.

In a 1978 survey of senior international bank managers, Steven Davis sought to identify the most important facets of **long-term international banking strategy**. By far the most frequently mentioned competitive strategy was **speed and flexibility of decision making**. Other strategies accorded top priority included specialist expertise, the existence of a large customer base, and the ability to commit relatively large amounts of funds. Canadian and other foreign banks differed from U.S. banks in their strong emphasis on a large existing customer base. As Davis pointed out, this reflects the historical relatively defensive objectives of many European and other banks in protecting their customer base from the assault of U.S. banks and the latters' relative lack of such a base. (See Davis, 1979.)

International involvement permits a commercial bank to take advantage abroad of skills and resources developed at home. These include existing customers, geographic location, industry expertise, existing services, and loyal depositors. Such resources must be sufficient to enable the bank to compete against the foreign competition it may encounter, and to overcome the special risks and costs arising from crossing national boundaries and entering unfamiliar banking environments. It follows that the bank's management should choose a strategy for international expansion that concentrates on the activities in which the bank possesses a special advantage, and employs the form of involvement that minimizes the costs of banking abroad.

A domestic bank entering international banking has the advantage of familiarity with the needs of existing customers. To capitalize on this familiarity with only moderate international involvement, a bank will normally begin its international involvement in one of two ways:

1. By extending **letters of credit** and **export or import financing** for existing customers' international trade financing needs.
2. By establishing a **nominal** or **"shell" branch** in an offshore banking center.

Once a bank develops familiarity with trade credit or offshore (Eurocurrency) deposit taking, it can extend its scope into the foreign exchange area. Customers will frequently require foreign exchange for overseas purchases, and a hedge or cover for their foreign exchange risk. The bank should therefore develop a facility in buying or selling foreign exchange in the spot and forward foreign exchange market. At some point the bank will have sufficient international business and experience to be ready to establish a full-fledged overseas branch. The most common locations for such branches are London, New York (for non-U.S. banks), Singapore, and Hong Kong. Typically such branches engage in **trade financing**, participation in **loan syndications, interbank trading of dollar** and **foreign currency deposits, foreign exchange trading,** and **corporate advisory services**. They may also serve as a useful source of funds or as a repository of funds for the parent bank.

Many American banks have followed their initial establishment of a foreign presence by setting up other branches and/or **Edge Act subsidiaries**. Edges, as they are called, enable U.S. banks to have offices in other states for international banking activities, and in other countries to engage in activities not permitted at home.

At this point the bank can be said to have a limited international banking network, and such a network is sufficient for most banks' purposes. Some banks, however, have developed a degree of business with foreign firms or governments that warrants their presence, in the form of **representative offices**, **agencies**, or **branches**, in certain host country banking markets. Later they have sought further penetration by buying partial or whole **equity participation in a local financial institution**. Indeed the latter activity has proved to be the most effective way of penetrating the local currency banking market.

Few banks have a truly **global network of branches and affiliates** in a large number of countries. Such a network brings many benefits in the form of on-the-spot knowledge and the ability to service the worldwide needs of multinational corporations, but it is costly and gradual and subjects banks to the vagaries of capital controls, economic nationalism, and other forms of business and political risk. Only three American banks (Bank of America, Citibank, and Chase Manhattan Bank) have such a multinational network, and only a few foreign banks do—primarily those from countries with colonial histories.

ORGANIZING FOR INTERNATIONAL BANKING

LEGAL VERSUS MANAGERIAL ORGANIZATION. The back pages of any large U.S. bank's annual report will provide the reader with an idea of the complex and diverse forms of legal organization employed by multinational banks. One should not be deceived, however, into thinking that the legal entities reflect the true organization of the bank. The **legal organization** is designed to minimize taxes, reserve requirements, and constraints on activities and to conform with government requirements. The **managerial organization** is concerned with who makes decisions and how they are communicated and implemented, how controls are exercised, and how line and staff functions relate to each other. It is concerned with the **translation of strategy into revenues**, with the allocation of responsibility, accountability, and rewards.

The **managerial organization** of international banking can be **geographical**, the prototype being a division between domestic and international banking. On the other hand, many banks have found more logic in **structuring responsibility by service** or **function**; and a few have geared their organizations to **groups of customers**, worldwide. More recently, some have tailored the bank's structure to fit the strengths of the principal capital markets of the world.

EXPORT FINANCING DEPARTMENT. The early entry of many American banks into international business was in the form of a rather passive response to the financing needs of their customers entering international markets. The **export financing group** was regarded as an eccentric, specialist bunch playing, at best, a supporting role. Services included collections, letters of credit, and the provision of foreign exchange; the only international expansion was the establishment of correspondent relationships with individual banks abroad. Being a passive service organization dealing primarily with foreign banks, the group and its head tended to be removed from the mainstream of corporate deposit and lending activities and from the bank's management team.

INTERNATIONAL AND REGIONAL DEPARTMENTS. Later, many banks found that the establishment of specific entities or representative offices abroad was necessary to service customers' growing international facilities and to draw on the foreign exchange and deposit resources of the international money market. Foreign exchange trading and directly solicited loan business warranted the establishment of a specific organization to handle the increasingly varied international business. It is now acknowledged that the nature of financing international transactions is unique enough to justify creation of a separate international banking department: procedures, terminology, and legal regulations differ markedly from those of domestic banking. In addition, the profits realized through international banking activity have grown to such an extent that for internal accounting purposes a separate international department is warranted.

The activities of such a department encompass the following: issuing letters of credit and bank acceptances, offering forward exchange contracts, serving as collecting agents for drafts drawn by exporters and others, buying and selling foreign exchange, and lending to exporters, overseas subsidiaries, local foreign firms, governments and government agencies, and financial institutions. In addition, international departments act in more informal ways. They provide customers with information on exchange rates, foreign credit, and trade; advise them on accounting and related problems stemming from foreign exchange, and assist them in the development of foreign trade.

The **geographically divided organizational form** evolved from the international division for banks that declined to undertake a radical shift in organizational form. This traditional form of organization implicitly assumes that particular regions, such as the Far East or Latin America, have more in common for bank management than do services offered or global customer relationships. A typical American bank's regional structure is depicted in Exhibit 2.

EXHIBIT 2 INTERNATIONAL DIVISION AND REGIONAL STRUCTURE FOR A TYPICAL AMERICAN BANK

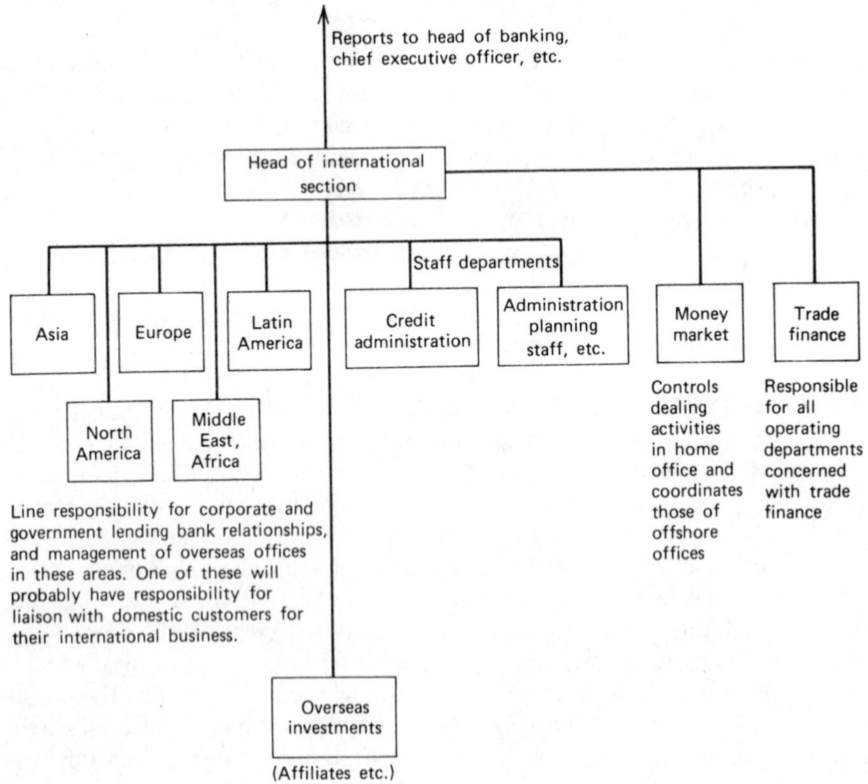

Source: Steven L. Davis, *The Managerial Function in International Banking,* Halsted, New York, 1977, p. 49.

SERVICE OR FUNCTIONAL ORGANIZATION. Because of the openness of their economies and the relative thinness of their capital markets, many Japanese and continental European banks supplement a limited international department with other functionally oriented departments that have global rather than domestic responsibilities. During the 1970s a number of American banks placed their domestic and international **treasury functions** under a single department, and integrated bond, money market, and foreign exchange trading in a single room. A service or functional organization is geared to particular functions of the banks, such as money dealing, bond underwriting, or data processing. Functions that are staff related, such as planning, or functions that possess other indivisible features, such as transfers, must serve the global bank. In European banks, such functions as customer lending and treasury dealing are centralized on a bankwide basis, rather than falling under the international department. The latter may be charged chiefly with trade financing and international correspondent relationships. Exhibit 3 illustrates a typical functionally oriented managerial structure.

GLOBAL CUSTOMER ORGANIZATION. Recognizing the integration of domestic and foreign markets and the global nature of many of their multina-

EXHIBIT 3 TYPICAL FUNCTIONAL STRUCTURE FOR INTERNATIONAL BANKING

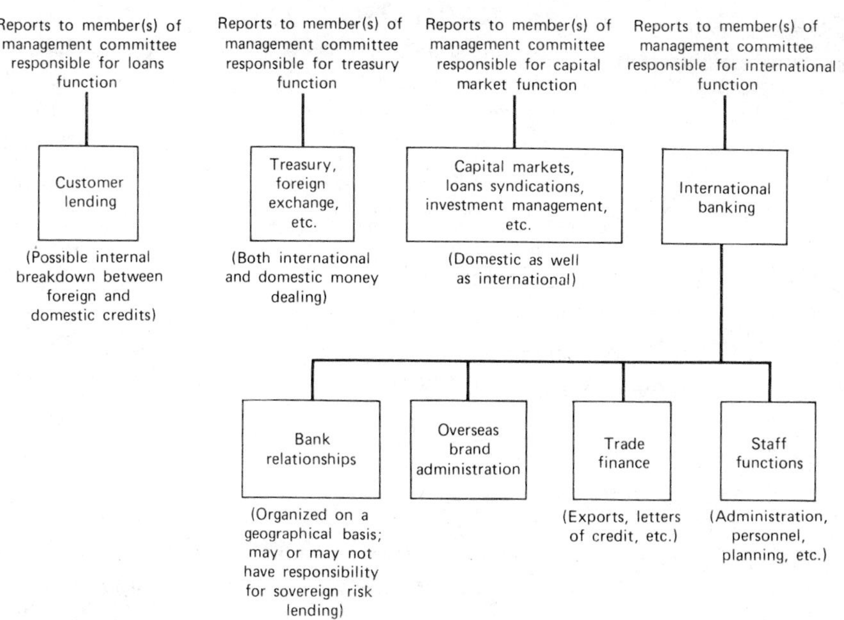

Source: Steven L. Davis, *The Managerial Function in International Banking,* Halsted, New York, 1977, p. 50.

tional customers, several U.S. banks have abandoned the traditional distinction between domestic and international banking and sought to gear their respective organizations to **customer types**. Thus a single industry group or specialist might service a particular multinational firm's worldwide financing needs. Other groups might be oriented to purely domestic entities, or to foreign governments. On the other hand, since geographical or functional expertise often is required to supplement the customer-oriented group, a geographic and/or service-oriented group of specialists interacts with the customer specialists to provide needed support. This approach is particularly suited to **multinational corporations** whose own treasury management function has become globally centralized.

CAPITAL MARKETS GROUP. Capital markets group, or global investment banking affiliate, are the names often given to the group responsible for national and international securities origination, distribution, and trading. Although groups of this character continue to be governed from the bank's headquarters, their success often depends on the rapid response of charismatic, clever individuals or teams who find themselves more at home in London, Wall Street, or in other major financial centers rather than in the bank's headquarters building. At the time of writing, no bank seems to have discovered a permanent solution to the tensions thus generated; as the world's capital markets become more integrated and global, however, the necessity of presence in the two or three prime capital markets may become less acute.

LEGAL ENTITIES FOR INTERNATIONAL BANKING. There are various legal forms by which U.S. commercial banks can participate in international activities. The legal entities chosen will depend on the degree to which the bank seeks to become involved in such activities. If a minimal presence is desired, a bank may simply maintain a correspondent relationship with a local foreign bank. Total presence would necessitate the establishment of a branch or subsidiary office. The following lists the full range of options:

1. Correspondent banking relationships
2. Representative office
3. Minority foreign affiliate
4. Joint banking ventures and consortia
5. Branch office
6. Majority foreign subsidiary
7. Edge Act subsidiary

CORRESPONDENT BANKING. Most of the major domestic and foreign banks maintain a two-way channel of "correspondence" through cable and mail, specifying activities to be undertaken and fees to be charged. **Correspondent banks** typically maintain deposit balances with one another. The services provided via this channel concentrate on the collection of payment of foreign funds stemming from import-export transactions. They include accepting drafts, providing credit information, and honoring letters of credit. In addition, the correspondent banking network is used to invest funds in short-term foreign government securities and money market instruments. While neither of the correspondent banks maintains its own personnel in the other country, there is direct but limited contact between managements.

The **advantage** provided by the correspondent bank network of an international bank is the provision of services in whatever country the correspondent is located, by knowledgeable, indigenous bankers, well acquainted with their country's customs and regulations. The main **drawback**, however, is the inability of a customer to make deposits, borrow, or withdraw funds from the home bank's own offices. There is, too, the chance that a correspondent will pay closer attention to its own established customers than to the foreign bank's customers. Nevertheless, the maintenance of overseas correspondent balances is a prerequisite to any substantial form of international banking, and even the largest and most sophisticated international banks maintain numerous correspondent banking relationships.

FOREIGN BRANCHES. The **foreign branch network of international banks** is a development of recent vintage. In 1965 there were 13 U.S. banks with foreign branches. Ten years later that figure had swelled to more than 100; by 1980 such offices abroad numbered several thousand. Legally speaking these branches function as an integral part of the parent bank: they are an extension of the bank rather than separate entities. Books are kept separately, but branches hold none of their own assets or liabilities. They are subject to all the legal encumbrances applying to the U.S. banks. Branches do enjoy the advantage of name identification with the parent, but they cannot engage in nonfinancial activities and investment banking.

REPRESENTATIVE OFFICES. This form of presence involves the posting of one or more individuals in a foreign host country to represent the parent bank's interests, to serve a very limited range of clients' needs, and to seek out new business opportunities. **No banking business** is transacted by representative offices, and under U.S. law they have no formal authority to bind the head office to any contractual obligation.

Such offices provide certain **advantages**. First, their existence does not pose a threat to correspondent relationships previously established. Indeed, by directing clients to local banks for needed services, representatives could enhance and solidify existing correspondent relationships. Second, under host country law, the head office is not deemed to be "present" for the purpose of being sued, or taxed in the host country on global earnings. Third, because of its familiarity with foreign and domestic operations, a representative office is in a better position than say, a correspondent, to determine rapidly and precisely the type of information the head office or a client may need. Fourth, a representative may leave the host country, if necessary, to arrange transactions in a third country where the head office maintains no presence. Should a head office decide that a branch office is needed in the host country, the representative is available to oversee its establishment.

The **drawbacks** to this form of representation are largely attributable to the limited nature of its activities. The need to rely on local institutions can lead to unwieldy transactions. Also, because many decisions must be referred back to headquarters, delays are inevitable. Representative offices are small, thus staff members are physically limited in the amount of work they can assume. Accordingly, the research produced may lack the precision and scope that a large staffed organization might provide.

Nonetheless, as a "listening post," or as an "ambassador of goodwill," the representative office well suits the objectives of certain U.S. commercial banks that seek a presence abroad, but not a deep commitment.

FOREIGN AFFILIATES. A number of U.S. commercial banks have found it advantageous to acquire an **equity interest in a foreign bank**. This is accomplished by outright purchase of voting shares in an existing bank or by setting up a new bank and retaining a minority voting stock interest. With the former method, controlling interest remains in the hands of the person(s) who controlled the bank prior to the stock purchase. The latter method places controlling interest in local hands, with the U.S. bank, or with a third party.

The activities undertaken by affiliated banks are the same as those undertaken by indigenous banks. Often an affiliated bank will also perform all or most correspondent services needed by the U.S. parent. The advantages to this form of banking stem from the fact that the institution is not "foreign" in the host country—it is staffed with nationals, and all its contacts with the local population are through them. If the institution existed prior to the affiliation, it will also benefit from its former reputation. There are of course, disadvantages. Frequently the U.S. presence, however discrete, is construed by local banking interests as an intrusion. Because the U.S. bank does not exercise controlling interest, its recommendations may be ignored or vetoed by local shareholders.

JOINT BANKING VENTURES AND CONSORTIA. **Joint ventures** are associations, often for a finite period of time, of two or more banks seeking to pool efforts toward a particular task. This might be a risky project or one beyond their normal scope of activity. The banks bound together in joint ventures provide technical or financial services for each other or explore uncharted areas of development. Typical projects include construction of motorways and hydroelectric facilities; or the result of a joint venture would be an affiliated bank with distinguishing nonlocal characteristics.

Promiment U.S. banks have been invited to join **consortium banks**, which are joint ventures separately owned and incorporated by two or more parent banks of different nationality. The consortium banks service the clients of the parents and also actively develop new business. Activities include the arrangement of global syndicates for very large or very long-term loans; underwriting and distribution of corporate securities; and involvement in mergers and acquisitions. Located in **major banking capitals**, these consortia are more permanent than joint ventures and, as multinational organizations, are unfettered by central bank controls.

MAJORITY-OWNED BANKING SUBSIDIARIES. While similar to the affiliated bank by virtue of its local charter in the host country, the subsidiary is distinguished by its nonlocal ownership. The key legal difference between the two is that the U.S. parent bank exerts controlling interest in its subsidiary. As a separate corporation, however, the banking subsidiary must adhere to all local laws. Because it is often perceived as a local bank by the host population, it is more likely than a branch office to participate in both domestic and international business. Subsidiaries are often established where host country laws prohibit branch banking.

One disadvantage of the subsidiary form is that, being a separately incorporated legal entity, its obligations are not automatically the liability of the parent bank. This may make it more difficult or costly to raise funds, even though the parent would ordinarily stand behind the credit of subsidiaries. On the other hand, the parent bank may have good reason for wishing to limit its direct liabilities.

EDGE ACT SUBSIDIARIES. Passed in 1919, the **Edge Act** permitted U.S. banks to transact international business from U.S. offices, and to engage in certain banking and investment activities not otherwise permissible in the United States. Subsidiaries are restricted to dealings with overseas or multinational clients exclusively.

Edge Act subsidiaries are particularly useful in **serving large multinational companies**. When established in several different U.S. cities, they can increase competitive pressures on other U.S. banks. For example, a California state-chartered bank can set up an Edge Act bank in New York City. Although restricted to international operations, Edge Act subsidiaries can accept deposits related to such operations, refer new customers to the parent, and obtain new international business in uncharted states.

Overseas Edge Act subsidiaries are permitted by the **Federal Reserve Board** to engage in activities common in foreign countries but not possible for U.S. banks. This factor, plus the Edge Act bank's separate corporation structure, and its ability to be located outside the parent's state of incorporation, make such subsidiaries valuable to many U.S. banks.

Under the **International Bank Act of 1978**, the restrictions on the capitalization and geographical expansion of Edge Act subsidiaries were eased by the Federal Reserve Board. In addition, foreign banks with U.S. branches were permitted to establish **out-of-state Edge Act subsidiaries**.

THE FINANCING OF INTERNATIONAL TRADE. International trade financing, one of the oldest functions of commercial banks, is also one of the least glamorous. Nevertheless, for the majority of firms engaged in international business, export financing forms the core of international finance. While the techniques are standardized, the range of applications is as varied as the content and destinations of a nation's exports, and things can easily go wrong. If managed properly, therefore, export-import financing can be one of the most profitable of a bank's international activities. Exhibit 4 provides a list of typical export-related services provided by commercial banks.

PROBLEMS AND RISKS OF EXPORT FINANCING. The first basic problem of export financing is that payment must involve conversion from one currency to another, and between one jurisdiction and another. The second basic problem is that payment must be made at a distance, and across time, so that the exporter, the importer, or both, need credit during part or all of the period from the initial manufacture of the goods by the exporting firm, through to the time of final sale and collection by the importer.

The first task for the export financier is to establish a means for making **international payments**. This is done through the foreign exchange market, addressed later. The second is to provide the requisite financing in an appropriate form. The third is to identify and manage the several risks that may or may not accompany a particular trade financing deal. Among these risks are:

1. Credit risk
2. Convertibility risk
3. Currency risk
4. Interest rate risk
5. Collateral risk

In **international trade financing**, a bank may issue a letter of credit to an importer, or confirm a letter of credit issued by a foreign bank, or provide a loan

EXHIBIT 4 BANK SERVICES TO EXPORTERS

Collecting drafts (outgoing and incoming)
Granting advances to exporters
Discounting drafts
Opening credit lines
Opening letters of credit (for importers)
Confirming letters of credit (acting for foreign banks)
Negotiating letters of credit
Creating bankers' acceptances
Collecting payments for creditors from foreign debtors
Opening accounts for customers in foreign branches or banks abroad in which export proceeds may be collected (e.g., Eurodollar accounts)
Buying and selling foreign currencies and making foreign remittances
Extending loans against merchandise in warehouses or in transit
Providing credit information on foreign buyers
Providing services incidental to export transactions, such as on customs, interest rates, and collection experience

directly to the exporter. **Credit risk** arises from the provision of loans or guarantees to the importer or exporter to a foreign bank.

When a domestic bank confirms a letter of credit issued by a foreign bank, the foreign government might impose exchange controls that prevent the foreign bank from meeting its obligations in foreign currencies. The domestic bank thus faces a risk termed "**convertibility risk**."

Currency risk arises when a bank holds an acceptance (an asset) denominated in a foreign currency, or when the bank issues a letter of credit (a liability) in favor of a customer making payment in a foreign currency. Normally, a bank may offset the currency risk of an asset (future cash inflow) in a foreign currency by selling the foreign currency in the forward market, (i.e., contracting for a future cash outflow). The same **"hedging" effect** may be achieved by borrowing in the same currency as the bank's asset (again, contracting for a future cash outflow to match the future cash inflow in the foreign currency).

Interest rate risk arises when the bank holds in its portfolio an asset, such as a **dicounted acceptance**, without having a corresponding fixed interest liability of the same maturity. This is the normal risk of **maturity mismatching** in a bank's portfolio.

Since export financing is normally collateralized by the goods being shipped, **collateral risk** arises from the possibility that the bank financing itself will incur expense and difficulty trying to sell the goods in a market with which it has little familiarity. The collateral risk can be shifted back to the exporter by discounting an acceptance with recourse.

The reader new to this field will no doubt find many of the terms used above somewhat unfamiliar. Not to worry: descriptions of most standard trade financing techniques are provided in the Appendix at the end of this section.

PUBLIC SOURCES OF EXPORT FINANCING. To promote employment and a better balance of payments, governments frequently provide export credit, guarantees, and other services for various types of trade financing, with an emphasis on long-term, capital equipment financing. The **U.S. Export-Import Bank (Eximbank)** is the largest and most diversified export credit institution in the world. In addition, export credit is provided by government-backed financing agencies in Austria, Belgium, Canada, Denmark, Finland, Germany, Italy, Japan, the Netherlands, Norway, Sweden, Switzerland, and the United Kingdom.

U.S. EXPORT-IMPORT BANK. In 1934 the U.S. government entered the field of foreign banking by organizing the **Export-Import Bank**, which in 1945 was made an independent agency of the federal government. The bank is empowered to do a general banking business and to make any type of loan for the purpose of aiding in the financing and facilitating of exports and imports and the exchange of commodities between the United States or any of its territories or insular possessions and any foreign country or the agencies or nationals thereof.

The bank makes long-term loans to finance purchases of U.S. equipment, goods, and services for projects undertaken by private enterprises or governments abroad and guarantees direct loans extended by financial institutions to overseas buyers. It also finances or guarantees payment of medium-term commercial export credits granted by exporters and, in partnership with private insurance companies, offers short- and medium-term export credit insurance.

One unique feature of Eximbank is that it will **guarantee political risks**, which include inconvertibility of foreign currency into dollars, cancellation of export and import licenses, or other governmental actions preventing importation of goods, war, civil strife, and expropriation of confiscation by government action.

The Foreign Credit Insurance Association is a joint enterprise of a number of private insurance firms. It works with Eximbank to provide coverage of the following kinds: short-term comprehensive risk, medium-term comprehensive risk, all-term comprehensive master policy, catastrophe policy, small business policy, and political risk policy.

The Private Export Funding Corp. (PEFCO), established in 1970, provides private funding, guaranteed by Eximbank, to finance U.S. exports. Typically, PEFCO provides middle-maturity financing (5–12 years) in a financial package of substantial size where one or more commercial banks take the shortest maturities and Eximbank the longest.

Many additional sources provide information on export financing techniques. The reader may refer to a booklet published in various updated editions by the Morgan Guaranty Trust Co., New York, *The Financing of Exports and Imports: A Guide to Procedures.* Other major banks provide similar guides.

BARTER AND COUNTERTRADE. This new and rapidly developing product presents an array of unconventional trade finance methods involving exchange of goods in lieu of money. The following are typical transactions:

- Issuance of a note payable by delivery of goods or with a borrower option to deliver goods in payment
- Delivery of a commodity to a second country warehouse to be stored and insured, permitting use of the commodity as a basis for financing; that is, creating liquidity out of an illiquid asset
- Two or more contingent transactions, whereby the import of goods and services by an entity in one country is "financed" by a spot or forward export sale of goods or services provided by the same or a different entity in the country

FOREIGN EXCHANGE AND INTERNATIONAL PAYMENTS

THE FOREIGN EXCHANGE MARKET. **Foreign exchange trading** involves the exchange of one national currency for another. Foreign exchange is traded by banks around the world in a **24-hour market**. Somewhere in the world, banks are buying and selling dollars for, say, German marks, regardless of whether the banks in the United States and Germany are open for business. Banks in the Far East, including branches of major U.S. and European institutions, begin trading in Hong Kong, Singapore, and Tokyo at about the time most traders in San Francisco are going home for supper. As the Far East closes, trading in Middle Eastern financial centers has been going on for a couple of hours, and the trading day in Europe is just beginning. Some of the large New York banks have an early shift to minimize the time differential of 5–6 hours with Europe. By the time New York trading gets going in full force around 8 A.M., it is lunch time in London and Frankfurt. To complete the circle, West Coast banks also extend "normal banking hours" so they can trade with New York or Europe, on one side, and with Hong Kong, Singapore, or Tokyo, on the other. While foreign exchange deals frequently take place between residents of different countries, the money being traded never actually leaves the country of the currency. Thus when German marks are exchanged for U.S. dollars in London, the marks and the dollars stay in Germany and the United States, respectively. The act of trading only effects a **change in ownership** of the money. The money itself, being in the form of bank deposits, merely gets shifted from one deposit to another in the home country of the currency.

This characteristic of foreign exchange trading has two implications. One is that for a currency to be actively traded, it must be **freely convertible**—that is, ownership must be transferable between residents and nonresidents, and among nonresidents of the country. The second is that the "market" can be anywhere and everywhere, since there is no need to be near the money to trade it.

As the number of players has grown, and as techniques have proliferated, so the volume of trading has grown—to reach about $150 billion a day as of the mid-1980s. Exhibit 5 provides a breakdown of this volume by dealing center. Although London and New York are easily the most prominent centers, it must be remembered that at least two countries are involved in every transaction, as it is effected by transferring funds through the clearing system of each currency involved.

Thus the **foreign exchange market has no central location**. It is, instead, a network of telephone and cable communications between banks, foreign exchange brokers, and ultimate buyers and sellers of foreign exchange such as corporations, commodity trading firms, governments, and central banks.

Although much foreign exchange trading (or **dealing**, as it is called outside the United States) arises from international trade, the great majority of transactions are deals between banks. When banks purchase currencies, they do not leave them idle in noninterest-bearing clearing accounts, but rather place them on deposit for some period with other banks. Thus the foreign exchange market is closely linked to the **deposit market**. The deposit market, or more generally the **money market**, involves the interbank **buying** (borrowing) and **placing** (depositing) of funds in given currencies in given centers. When the funds are deposited outside of the country of the currency, the money market is the

EXHIBIT 5 VOLUME OF FOREIGN EXCHANGE TRADING

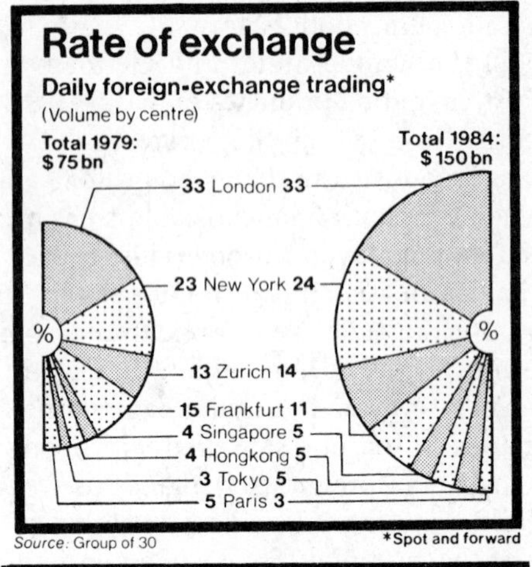

Source: The Economist, November 30, 1985.

Eurocurrency market. As is shown in Exhibit 6, banks organize their foreign exchange and money market activities in such a way as to recognize the linkage between the two.

The foreign exchange and **international money market** is made up of banks and others that exchange currencies and place funds throughout the world. They are linked by telephone and cable and by information transfer services that provide instantaneous summaries of events and rates in other parts of the

EXHIBIT 6 ORGANIZATION OF FOREIGN EXCHANGE AND MONEY MARKET ACTIVITIES

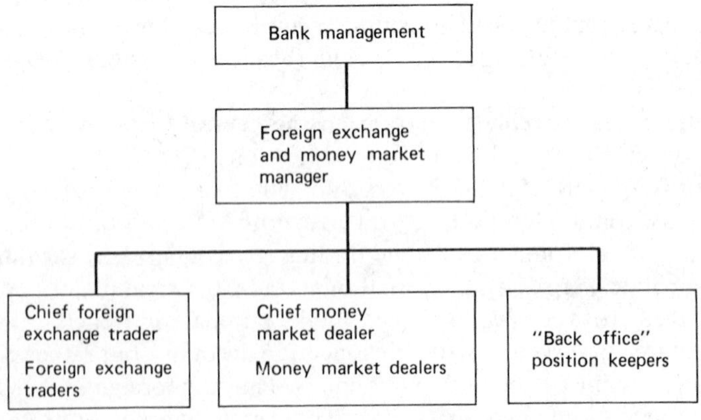

Source: Nigel R. L. Hudson, *Money and Exchange Dealing in International Banking,* Halsted, New York, 1979, p. 34.

world. Although it is an over-the-counter market with no central trading floor, banks and their dealing departments do find it advantageous to be in the same location, or at least in the same time zone, as other banks dealing in the same currencies. Moreover, because foreign exchange trading results in payments being made through each currency's payments mechanism, local banks may benefit from closer access to domestic money markets. They usually have an advantage in trading their local currency. For instance, buying and selling sterling for dollars is most active among the banks in London. Similarly the major market for Swiss francs is in Zurich; for Japanese yen, in Tokyo. But the local advantage is by no means absolute. Thus dollar–Swiss franc trading is active in London and dollar–sterling trading is active in Zurich. Moreover, New York banks trade just as frequently with London, German, or Swiss banks in all major currencies as they do with other New York banks.

Within most individual centers, and even between centers, banks deal with one another to a large extent through **foreign exchange brokers**. Brokers do not deal themselves, but serve as a go-between among banks, preserving anonymity and passing quotes on rapidly to their numerous clients.

The remainder of this subection provides some details on the mechanisms of foreign exchange trading and the corresponding international payments system. It draws heavily on *Foreign Exchange Markets in the United States,* by Roger M. Kubarych.

TYPES OF FOREIGN EXCHANGE TRANSACTIONS: SPOT, FORWARD, AND SWAP. Whenever two currencies are exchanged, each party promises to pay a certain amount of currency to the other on an agreed-upon date. The most common transaction, a **spot transaction**, involves the purchase of and payment for foreign exchange with delivery and payment to be completed at once or within 1 or 2 business days. A typical spot transaction might involve a U.S. company arranging for the immediate transfer of £1 million to the account of a client in London. The company and a U.S. bank would agree on an exchange rate for the transaction: say, \$2 per pound sterling. The U.S. company would pay its bank \$2 million and the bank would cable instructions to London that the equivalent amount of pounds (£1 million) be credited immediately to the account of the London client.

A **forward exchange contract** calls for delivery at a fixed future date of a specified amount of one currency for a specified amount of another currency. The exchange rate is established at the time the contract is agreed on, but payment and delivery are not required until maturity. Forward exchange rates are normally quoted for fixed periods of 1, 3, or 6 months; but actual contracts in major currencies can usually be arranged for delivery at any specified date up to 1 year, and on occasion for longer periods up to 3 years. Forward contracts in less commonly used currencies are not readily available. Forward contracts on particularly unstable currencies can be expensive, since someone has to pay for the risk of exchange rate changes.

Although most contracts have specific maturity dates, it is possible to arrange, usually at slightly greater cost, for **forward option contracts** that permit delivery at the beginning of a month (first to tenth days of the month), at the middle (eleventh to twentieth), or at the end (twenty-first to thirty-first). Such contracts are desirable when the customer does not know the exact day of receipt of foreign funds.

If the forward exchange rate for a currency is higher than the current spot rate, dealers say the currency is trading at a **premium** for that forward maturity. If the forward rate is below the spot rate, the currency is said to be trading at a **discount**. In the exceptional case when the spot and forward quotations are the same, traders say the forwards are **"flat."** For instance, sterling for value 3 months from now is at a discount if the spot rate is $2 and the 3-month forward rate is $1.97.

Banks active in the foreign exchange market find that **interbank currency trading** for any specific value date in the future is inefficient, and they do it infrequently. Instead, for future maturities banks trade among themselves, as well as with some corporate customers, on the basis of a transaction known as a **swap**. A swap transaction is a simultaneous purchase and sale of a certain amount of foreign currency for two different value dates. The key aspect is that the bank arranges the swap as a single transaction with a single counterparty, either another bank or a nonbank customer. This means that unlike outright spot or forward transactions, a trader does not incur any **foreign exchange rate risk**, since the bank contracts both to pay and to receive the same amount of currency at specified rates.

A swap allows each party to use a currency for a period in exchange for another currency that is not needed during that time. If the objective is to get a better return in the other currency without incurring exchange risk, the swap is being used to undertake covered interest arbitrage; more on this below. Swaps also provide a mechanism for a bank to accommodate the outright forward transactions executed with customers or to bridge gaps in the maturity structure of its outstanding spot and forward contracts.

The two value dates in a swap transaction can be any pair of future dates. But, in practice, markets exist only for a limited number of standard maturities. One of these standard types is called a "spot against forward" swap. In a spot against forward swap transaction, a trader buys or sells a currency for the ordinary spot value date and simultaneously sells or buys it back for a value date a week, a month, or three months later.

Another type of particular interest to professional market-making banks is called a **"tomorrow-next" swap** or a "rollover." These are transactions in which the dealer buys or sells a currency for value the next business day and simultaneously sells or buys it back for value the day after. A more sophisticated type of swap is called a **"forward-forward,"** in which the dealer buys or sells a currency for one future date (say, a month later) and sells or buys it back for another future date (say, 3 months later). Only a handful of banks specialize in such transactions.

QUOTATION OF RATES. When a **corporate treasurer** asks a foreign exchange trader to quote a rate for spot sterling or German marks, the trader will quote not one rate but two. The first price is the one at which he or she will buy a currency and the second is the price at which he or she will sell. For example:

$/£ 1.9320–1.9325

Using the rates above, in the first case either £1,000 = $1,932.00 or £1,000 = $1,932.50. Therefore, if a trader is being asked to purchase £1,000 and to sell the equivalent amount of currency, the deal will be done at 1.9320, since the trader has to part with $1,932, not $1,932.50. If, however, the trader is being asked to sell sterling, then in exchange the trader would wish to obtain as many dollars as possible. Therefore, the deal is done at $1.9325.

In theory, any two currencies can be traded in an exchange transaction. Swiss francs can be bought for French francs, German marks for sterling. In practice, such transactions are common only between banks and nonbank customers. Virtually all interbank transactions, by market participants here and abroad, involve a purchase or sale of dollars for a foreign currency. This is true even if a bank's aim is to buy German marks for sterling.

The reason is that since the dollar is the main currency for international trade and investment, the dollar market for each currency is much more active than the bilateral market between any pair of foreign currencies. By going through the dollar, large amounts can be traded more easily. Of course, a German mark rate in sterling terms can be readily calculated from the respective dollar rates. The calculation produces what is called a **crossrate**. If the dollar–mark rate is 2.2250–60 (marks per dollar) and the sterling–dollar rate is $1.8200–10 (per pound), then the sterling–mark crossrate is 4.0495–4.0535 (marks per pound). Analogously, if the dollar–Swiss franc rate is 1.9000–10, the Swiss franc–German mark crossrate is 1.1704–16 (marks per Swiss franc).

FORWARD EXCHANGE RATES. Forward exchange rates can be expressed in three ways. Like spot rates, outright forward prices are expressed in dollars and cents per currency unit, or vice versa. Traders normally quote forward prices to corporate customers or correspondent banks seeking to buy or sell a currency for a particular future date. For instance, a trader may quote an outright 6-month rate to buy sterling of $1.8450, while by comparison a quotation to buy spot sterling might be less (say $1.8200) or more (say $1.8625).

In **swap transactions**, the trader is interested only in the difference between spot and forward rates, the premium or discount, rather than the outright spot and forward rates themselves. Premiums and discounts expressed in points ($0.0001 per pound sterling or DM 0.0001 per dollar) are called swap rates. For the first spot rate above, the premium is 250 points ($0.0250). For the second, the discount is 175 points ($0.0175).

Since in a swap a trader is effectively borrowing one currency and lending the other currency for the period between the two value dates, the premium or discount is often evaluated in terms of percent per annum. For the examples above, the premium of 250 points is equivalent to 2.75% per annum, while the discount of 175 points is equivalent to 1.88% per annum.

The premium or discount is calculated by taking the difference between the forward and spot rate as a percent of the spot rate and multiplying this by 12/*n*, where *n* is the number of months in the forward contract. The formula is as follows:

$$\frac{\text{forward rate} - \text{spot rate}}{\text{spot rate}} \times \frac{12}{\text{number of months forward}} \times 100 = \begin{array}{l}\text{foward premium of discount}\\ \text{as a per annum percent}\end{array}$$

Applying the formula to the British pound (spot rate, 1.8200; 6-month forward rate, 1.8450):

$$\frac{1.8450 - 1.8200}{1.8200} \times \frac{12}{6} \times 100 = +2.75\%, \text{ or a premium of } 2.75\% \text{ per annum}$$

COVERED INTEREST ARBITRAGE. Spot exchange rates, forward exchange rates, and interest rates on deposits are not all determined independently but are linked to one another through **covered interest arbitrage**. Such arbitrage ensures that in the absence of legal obstacles, the forward premium or discount on a currency relative to the dollar, expressed as a percentage of the spot rate, will tend to (about) equal the differential between interest rates available in that currency and dollar interest rates. Otherwise, traders would have opportunities to make profits by moving funds from one currency to the other. This relationship is called **interest rate parity**. The precise relationship is shown in Exhibit 7.

A tendency toward interest rate parity is achieved through the movement of funds into or out of a currency when the forward discount or premium is out of line with the relative interest rate differential. Suppose the relevant sterling interest rate was 8%, the corresponding dollar interest rate was 4%, and the discount on forward sterling was only 2%. A trader could earn 6% on dollars by selling dollars spot for sterling and investing the sterling at 8%, while selling the sterling forward at a discount of 2%. Obviously, the trader would rather earn 6% than 4% on dollars.

As that trader and other traders sought to take advantage of such a lucrative opportunity, the net selling of forward sterling would put downward pressure on the forward rate and the net buying of spot sterling would put upward pressure on the spot rate. Both would tend to widen the forward discount on sterling. At the same time, the investment in sterling assets would tend to lower sterling interest rates and therefore narrow the interest rate differential. In principle, the process would continue until the percentage forward discount

EXHIBIT 7 INTEREST RATE PARITY

F is the 1-year sterling rate. To buy £1 a year forward costs $F \times$ £1.
S is the spot rate. The 1-year sterling interest rate is $R_{£}$. The dollar interest rate is $R_{\$}$.
Buying £1/(1 + $R_{£}$) spot and investing it for a year at $R_{£}$ would yield £1 a year from now. In dollars, it would cost $S \times$ £1/(1 + $R_{£}$).
The foregone dollar interest is:

$$S \times £1 \times R_{\$}/(1 + R_{£})$$

Adding the two costs together—actual and foregone—gives the total dollar cost of the second option:

$$\frac{S \times £1}{(1 + R_{£})} + \frac{S \times £1 \times R_{\$}}{(1 + R_{£})}$$

Or collecting terms:

$$S \times £1 \times (1 + R_{\$})/(1 + R_{£})$$

If that equals $F \times$ £1, then the two options cost the same.
Divide both expressions by $S \times$ £1, and the result is the interest parity condition:

$$\frac{F}{S} = \frac{1 + R_{\$}}{1 + R_{£}}$$

$(F/S) - 1$ is the percentage forward premium or discount. So, when the interest rate parity condition holds:

$$\frac{F}{S} - 1 = \frac{1 + R_{\$}}{1 + R_{£}} - 1 = \frac{R_{\$} - R_{£}}{1 + R_{£}}$$

In other words; the percentage premium or discount on forward sterling is just about equal to the difference between dollar and sterling interest rates when the interest rate parity condition holds. (To be perfectly equal $R_{£}$ would have to be zero!)

---

just about equaled the sterling–dollar interest rate differential, thereby eliminating the profitable arbitrage opportunity.

CURRENCY FUTURES AND OPTIONS. **Currency futures** are contracts for delivery of a certain amount of foreign currency at some future date. The dollar price for the foreign currency is agreed on the day the contract is bought or sold. Like the forward market, no money changes hands at the time the contract is entered, and as with forward contracts, gains or losses are incurred as a result of subsequent currency fluctuations. In both markets, the total gain or loss will equal the difference bewteen the futures price (or forward rate) and the spot exchange rate on the date of maturity of the contract, multiplied by the amount of the contract.

The **difference between the forward and futures markets** is that in the forward market, a profit (or loss) is realized on the maturity date, whereas in the futures market **all profits and losses must be settled on a daily basis**. This procedure, called "marking to the market," requires that funds change hands each day. The funds are added to or subtracted from a mandatory margin account that traders are required to maintain. In contrast, in the forward market no money changes hands until delivery occurs.

The other chief feature of the futures market is that futures are traded through organized exchanges or clearinghouses, such as the International Monetary Market in Chicago. Trading in standardized currency contracts is conducted by open auction on the floor of the exchange. The trading matches individual buyers and sellers to set prices; however, in executing each sale and purchase the clearinghouse of the exchange takes the opposite side of each position. The fact that losses are realized and settled every trading day limits the risk of default to the clearinghouse.

The exchanges specify the characteristics for contracts in order to make them standardized and tradeable. For example, one British pound contract on the International Monetary Market (IMM) has the following specifications:

Contract size	£25,000
Delivery instrument	Sterling deposited in a designated bank
Delivery months	Mach, June, September, December
Price increments	$0.0005 or $12.50 a contract
Daily price limits	$0.0500 ($1.250 a contract) above or below the previous day's settlement price

Currency options are instruments that allow traders and corporations to gain from advantageous currency surprises while limiting the risk of adverse currency movements. As such, they can be a useful tool in exchange risk management. They can also be useful in dealing with certain kinds of business risk—when an overseas deal falls through, for example, or when a bid on a contract is accepted—that is, whenever a firm is uncertain whether a foreign currency cash inflow or outflow will materialize.

A currency option is a contract conveying **the right to buy or sell a designated quantity of a foreign currency** at a specified price (exchange rate) during a stipulated period under stated conditions. The important feature of a foreign exchange option is that the holder of the option has the **right**, but not the obligation, to exercise it. The holder will only exercise it if the currency moves in a favorable direction. Thus once an option has been purchased one cannot lose—unlike a forward contract in which one is obliged to exchange the currencies and therefore will lose if the movement is unfavorable.

The terminal date of the contract is called the **"expiration date"** (or "maturity date"). If the option can be exercised before the expiration date, it is called an **"American option"**; if only on the expiration date, a **"European option."**

The party retaining the option is the **option buyer**; the party giving the option is the **option seller** (or **writer**). The exchange rate at which the option can be exercised is called the **"exercise price."** The buyer of the option must pay the seller some amount (the **option price**, or the **premium**) for the rights involved.

A **call option in foreign exchange** is the right to buy a specified number of foreign currency units from the option seller at a specified exercise price (in dollars) up to and including the exercise date. A **put option** is the right to sell the foreign currency to the option seller at a specified dollar price, up to the expiration date.

Currency options are traded in a number of exchanges and have delivery and standardization characteristics that resemble those for currency futures. In addition, banks buy and sell options directly in an "over-the-counter" market with other banks and corporations.

What influences currency option prices? A gain can be made by the holder of a call option any time the exchange rate (in dollars for each foreign currency unit) exceeds the exercise price. The bigger the excess, the bigger the gain. Similarly, a gain will be made by the holder of a put option if the option is exercised at any rate below the exercise price. Thus the value of a foreign exchange option is related to that of the currency itself, although the relationship is not strictly linear.

Clearly the value of a call option also depends on the **exercise price**, for if the spot rate at expiration is below the exercise price, the option is worthless (for a call option). In general the lower the exercise price relative to the current spot rate, the more valuable the call option is.

It also seems reasonable to suppose that the longer the option has to run before the expiration, the more chance there is of the spot rate exceeding its current level, and therefore the greater the chance that the option can be exercised (or sold) at a profit. Moreover, this chance will be greater the greater the volatility of the currency's exchange rate. It follows that the price of the option is higher the more time remains before expiration and the greater the volatility of changes in the exchange rate.

A number of computer models of currency option prices are employed by bank and exchange traders to incorporate these influences in a systematic manner. Using these models, traders are able to arbitrage and hedge positions between the spot, forward, futures, and options market.

MECHANICS OF INTERNATIONAL PAYMENTS. All U.S. dollar receipts and payments outside the United States, whether they involve trade, investment, Eurodollar, or foreign exchange transactions, are ultimately effected through the transfer of funds between bank accounts in the United States. Similarly, German mark and French franc transactions are effected in Germany and France, respectively. Thus every foreign exchange transaction involves at least two shifts of bank deposits in national currencies. If Barclays Bank buys German marks from Crédit Lyonnais, Barclays will arrange for funds to be transferred from its correspondent account in New York to that of Crédit

Lyonnais. At the same time, in Frankfurt, funds will be transferred from a correspondent account of Crédit Lyonnais to one of Barclays.

Since practically all major interbank foreign exchange transactions involve the U.S. dollar, every foreign exchange dealer must maintain at least one bank account in the United States to make and receive payments in dollars.

An account at a foreign correspondent or branch through which a bank pays or receives foreign currency is called a **nostro** or **clearing account**. On the value date of a foreign exchange transaction, the correspondent debits or credits the clearing account in response to instructions received in a cable message. For many years, virtually all foreign exchange transactions of any size were settled through cable transfers, that is, debits and credits of bank accounts in response to cable messages. In September 1977 an automated system known as SWIFT began sending payment instructions written in a standardized format among European and North American banks. **SWIFT** is short for "Society for Worldwide Interbank Financial Transactions." It is based in Brussels. A foreign bank or U.S. regional bank pays or receives dollars in foreign exchange transactions through a clearing account at a New York correspondent. The correspondent debits or credits the clearing account on the value date in response to cable or computer messages.

The method of settlement on the dollar side of a foreign exchange transaction differs from the settlement on the foreign currency side. Abroad, settlement in foreign currency is made in **immediately available funds**. That is, the recipient can always use the funds as if they were cash and make another payment on the same day as the value date of the foreign exchange transaction. In New York, dollar settlement is made in what are called **clearinghouse funds**. The terms derives from the name of the institution through which interbank settlements among major New York banks are made: the **New York Clearing House Association**. Clearinghouse funds are not available for the recipient to make further payments—except to other members of the clearinghouse. At the end of each day, clearinghouse debits and credits are settled in "immediately available" or federal funds, which are balances on deposit at a Federal Reserve bank. The steps in a typical foreign exchange settlement (illustrated in Exhibit 8) are as follows:

1. Barclays Bank buys German marks from Crédit Lyonnais; to consummate this it must transfer funds in the United States to Crédit Lyonnais' account in Chemical Bank, New York.
2. Barclays uses SWIFT, a worldwide financial communications network, to instruct Chase to transfer funds out of the Barclays account.
3. Chase debits the Barclays account and transfers the funds through the clearinghouse of international payments (CHIPS), the payments clearing system for international transactions; in effect it sends an electronic check to CHIPS; those "clearinghouse funds" get credited to Chemical on the same day.

EXHIBIT 8 THE INTERNATIONAL DOLLAR PAYMENTS SYSTEM

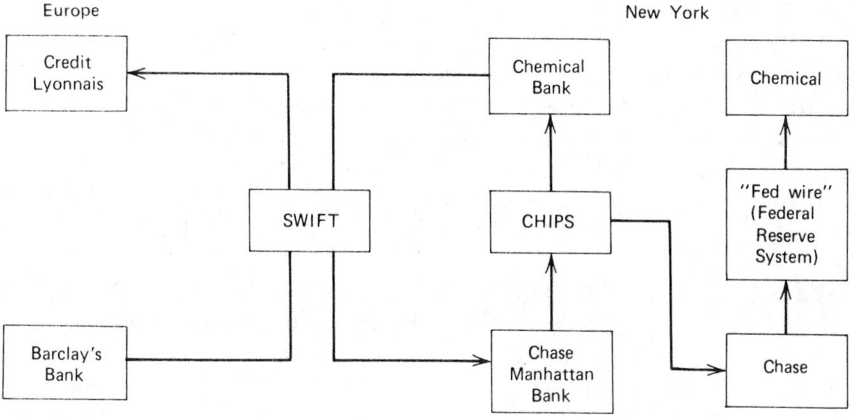

Source: Ian H. Giddy, "Measuring the World Foreign Exchange Market," *Columbia Journal of World Business,* Winter 1980, p. 40.

4. Next day, the net amount is settled between Federal Reserve member banks by transfers in "Fed funds"—deposits held at the various Federal Reserve banks. This is done through the domestic interbank clearing system, the "Fed wire."
5. Chemical credits Crédit Lyonnais' account and notifies Crédit Lyonnais, again through the SWIFT network.

INTERNATIONAL LENDING

Much of international banking evolved in response to the growing international financing needs of corporate customers that were "going multinational." So too with **international lending**—loans initially were to well-established domestic clients. Because of this, credit analysis and loan terms for international loans did not necessarily differ importantly from domestic loans.

As the international money market grew during the 1960s and 1970s, however, these Eurocurrency markets took on a life and character of their own. The Eurocurrency market is explained in greater depth in the section, "Overseas Money and Capital Markets." For the present purpose, it is worth recalling that **Eurobanking** consists of the taking of deposits denominated in currencies other than that of the host country and either redepositing the funds in other banks at home or abroad, or lending them to governments or corporations. The **Eurocurrency market** is dominated by Eurodollars, which consist of dollar-denominated deposits in banks outside the United States, including Canadian banks and overseas branches of U.S. banks. The primary reason for the existence of the Eurocurrency market is the absence of reserve requirements and certain other regulatory constraints imposed on domestic deposits or loans. See Dufey and Giddy (1979).

While international lending is by no means limited to Eurocurrency loans—many foreign loans are still made out of the home offices of large banks, in their own currency—the unique features of such loans are of particular relevance to the international banker. This is because a special set of techniques has arisen in the market, techniques that have come to dominate all forms of international lending, and which, most recently, have been increasingly adopted in purely domestic lending.

BORROWERS FROM INTERNATIONAL BANKS. At one time, corporations borrowing from international banks were primarily those whose name, size, and good standing enabled banks to make loans to them with little more than a cursory analysis of creditworthiness. In recent years, however, the range of corporate (and government) borrowers has spread to a wide variety of virtually unknown firms, as a result of (1) the volume of funds available for lending, (2) guarantees provided by foreign banks on loans made to foreign corporations, and (3) the vastly superior knowledge of foreign business systems that international banks have developed through their overseas branches. Even domestic firms with no international activities are learning to rely on Eurodollar loans when local credit conditions become tight and interest rates are high.

While the participation of corporations in the international money market continued to expand, the 1970s saw an even greater expansion of governments and government-related borrowers. This applies particularly to the **medium-term Eurocredit market**, which public authorities around the world have increasingly tapped for industrial and infrastructure projects and even to finance balance of payments deficits. In addition, international institutions, such as the **World Bank** and its affiliates, various regional development banks, and the **European Economic Community** have been regular borrowers.

Corporations in particular are attracted by the size of the market—of all the sources of funds in the world, only the U.S. market is larger, and only if one takes into account all segments of the U.S. money market. Whereas in national markets there is invariably **credit rationing** during periods of tight credit, often mandated by government, in the Euromarkets the funds are always available for those willing and able to pay the price.

A second advantage to international firms is that the funds raised in the international money market are not restricted to where they can be deployed once lenders have been satisfied that the intended purpose will not jeopardize the prospects for servicing the loan(s).

Similarly, as borrowers, governments find loans granted without conditions except those that affect the collective assessment of credit risk by a competitive system of profit-seeking financial institutions. And this freedom has apparently been sufficient for many countries to pay market rates of interest instead of the subsidized rates that are usually available in intergovernmental borrowing and similar traditional ways of financing balance of payments deficits.

EUROCURRENCY LENDING PRACTICES. Domestic banking markets around the world traditionally have been protected from change by government regulation and barriers to entry. In constrast, the very rationale for the existence of the Euromarkets has always been their freedom from certain regulations, taxes, and other costs. This freedom has allowed an unprecedented influx of international banks and their customers to Eurocurrency centers such as London, and these institutions have brought a variety of novel techniques and instruments to the market.

Unbundling of Services. The **bundling of financial services**, such as tying deposit taking to loan making, is a product of a protected market and tends to disappear when competition sets in, at least in commercial loan markets. Because the bank that offers the most competitive loan terms is frequently not the bank that gives the most attractive rates on deposits, or on foreign exchange, Eurobanks have had an incentive to provide these services separately. The declining use of **compensating balances** is the most advanced manifestation of the unbundling trend in the United States.

Loan Syndication. The formal **Eurocurrency syndication** technique arose primarily because of the large size of term credits required by governments and multinational firms and the wide variety of banks providing the funds. The syndication procedure is also a means for banks to diversify some of the unique sovereign risks that arise in international lending. Syndicated Euroloans involve formal arrangements in which competitively selected **lead banks** assemble a management group of other banks to underwrite the loan and to market shares in it to still other participating banks.

As described in "The Pricing of Syndicated Eurocurrency Credits" by L. Goodman (1980), there are generally three levels of banks in a syndicate: the **lead banks**, the **managing banks**, and the **participating banks**. Most loans are led by one or two major banks who negotiate to obtain a mandate to raise funds from the borrower. Often a potential borrower will set a competitive bidding procedure to determine which lead bank or banks will receive the mandate to organize the loan.

After the preliminary stages of negotiation with a borrower, the lead bank will begin to assemble a management group to underwrite the loan. The management group may be in place before the mandate is received, or may be assembled immediately afterward, depending on the loan. The lead bank is normally expected to underwrite a share at least as large as that of any other lender. If the loan cannot be underwritten on the initial terms, it must be renegotiated or the lead bank must be willing to take a larger share into its own portfolio than originally planned.

Once the management group is firmly in place and the lead bank has received a mandate from the borrower, a **placement memorandum** will be prepared by the lead bank and the loan will be marketed to other banks who may be interested in taking up shares (the participating banks). This placement memorandum describes the transaction and provides information about the borrower. The statistical information regarding the financial health of the borrower given in the memorandum is generally provided by the borrower. The placement memorandum emphasizes that reading it is not a substitute for an independent credit review by the participating banks. Bank supervisory authorities normally require sufficient lending information to be lodged in the bank to allow bank management to make a reasonable appraisal of the credit.

In a successful syndication, once the marketing to interested participants is completed, the lead and managing banks will keep 50–70% of their initial underwriting share. Not all credits are sold to participants. In smaller credits to frequent borrowers, **club loans** are often arranged. In a club loan, the lead bank and managers fund the entire loan and no placement memorandum is required. This type of credit is most common in periods of market uncertainty when all but the largest multinational banks are reluctant to do business.

It takes anywhere from 15 days to 3 months to arrange a syndication, with 6 weeks considered the norm. Generally speaking, the more familiar the borrower, the more quickly the terms can be set and the placement memorandum prepared; the smaller the credit, the shorter is the time needed for negotiating and marketing.

After the loan is arranged, one of the banks serves as agent to compute the appropriate interest rate charges, to receive service payments, to disburse these to individual participants, and to inform them if there are any problems with the loan. The lead bank usually serves as agent, but another member of the management group may do so.

The most common type of syndicated loan is a **term loan** in which the funds can be drawn down by the borrower within a specified period of time after the loan agreement has been signed (the drawdown period). The loan is usually repaid according to an amortization schedule, which varies from loan to loan. For some loans it may begin as soon as the loan is drawn down. For other loans, amortization may not begin until as long as 5 years after the loan agreement has been signed. The period before repayment of principal begins is known as the **grace period**. This is one of the most important points of negotiation between a borrower and a lead bank, and borrowers are normally willing to pay a wider spread to obtain a longer grace period.

The vast majority of **syndicated credits** are **denominated** in dollars, but loans in German marks, Swiss francs, Japanese yen, and other currencies are also available.

In contrast to Euroloans, U.S. domestic large loans or facilities are generally less formal arrangements even when provided by a group of banks. Although one bank may act as agent for the group, normally the corporate treasurer will organize a multibank facility and draw on each line of credit as seen fit. This is possible because the borrower is more familiar to the various lending banks and facilities tend to be smaller and for more limited periods. In the future, as a wider range of both borrowers and banks participate in the prime loan market, it seems probable that U.S. and Euromarket syndication techniques will merge.

But the sovereign risk of Euroloans is nonexistent for U.S. domestic loans and size is not yet the problem it is in Eurolending. Thus, there seems to be no immediate pressure for formal syndication of prime U.S. loans on a widespread basis.

EUROCURRENCY LOAN PRICING: ROLLOVER CREDITS. Euroloan pricing practices reflect the nature of the market as a pure financial intermediary, in which funds are "bought" and "sold" on a highly competitive basis. The primary manifestation of this is the rollover credit pricing technique.

Rollover credits, which enable banks to separate a loan's maturity from its interest contract period, were a direct result of the absence of a "deposit base" in the Euromarket. Eurobanks are specialized wholesale banks that rely on a sole funding source—large time and call deposits, mostly from banks and other highly interest-sensitive depositors. The Eurobanks' cost of funds therefore varies directly with the level of short-term rates. To protect themselves from substantial **interest rate risk** when they arrange to commit funds to the borrower for medium-term periods, such as 3 years, they establish that the interest rate will be altered every 3 or 6 months, bearing a fixed relationship to the **London Interbank Offered Rate (LIBOR)**, the average rate paid by large banks in the Eurodollar interbank market. Whereas rollover Eurodollars bear a rate tied directly to money market and interbank cost of funds and the rate is changed only at fixed intervals, in the United States changes in a bank's **prime rate** are policy decisions that affect the rates on existing as well as new loans. Eurolending **spreads** are normally negotiated with the borrower prior to the initiation of the loan and either remain constant over the life of the loan or change after a set number of years. Customers have found these arrangements acceptable because it permits them to avoid the risk of unavailability of funds.

In addition to the interest costs on a Eurocurrency loan, there are also **commitment fees**, front-end fees, and occasionally an annual agent's fee. **Commitment fees** are charged to the borrower as a percentage of the undrawn portion of the credit and are typically 0.5% annually, imposed on both term loans and revolving credits. **Front-end management fees** are one-time charges negotiated in advance and imposed when the loan agreement is signed. Fees are usually in the range of 0.5–1% of the value of the loan. These front-end fees include participation fees and management fees. The participation fees are divided among all banks in relation to their share of the loan. The management fees are divided between the underwriting banks and the lead bank. The **agent's fee**, if applicable, is usually a yearly charge but may occasionally be paid at the outset. These fees are relatively small; the agent's fee on a large credit may run $10,000 per annum.

The charges on syndicated loans may be summarized as follows:

annual payments = (LIBOR) + spread) × amount of loan drawn + (commitment fee) × amount of loan undrawn + annual agent's fee (if any) front-end charges = participation fee × face amount of loan + management fee × face amount of loan + initial agent's fee (if any)

Front-end charges are an important component of the banks' total return on a credit. Consider a $100 million, 7-year credit with no grace period. If the loan is priced at 100 basis points over a LIBOR of 10%, annual payments of interest and principal repayment total slightly over $21 million. A 1% fee requires that $1 million be paid to the banks in the syndicate at the outset. This raises the effective interest to the borrower from 11 to 11.31% per annum. If banks paid, on average, 9.75% for their funds, the front-end fees increase their margin on the loan from 125 to 156 basis points. This represents a 25% increment to their return on a credit.

LOAN AGREEMENT PROVISIONS. As a rule, Eurocurrency loan agreements are simple, containing fewer restrictive covenants than do many domestic (U.S.) loan agreements. This is in part because loans to multinational corporations' affiliates are regarded as the obligation of the parent company, and loans to governments cannot impose many conditions for obvious reasons. Another reason is that such agreements typically contain a **cross-default clause**, which stipulates that the loan is in default if and when the parent is in default on its own loans: for example, by not complying with restrictive covenants contained in its own loan agreements.

In addition to the usual clauses referring to pricing, interest payment dates, and amortization dates, Euroloan agreements contain a number of provisions that reflect their international character.

First, special clauses are required to specify the **jurisdiction** as well as the **judgment currency** for loans. A loan may be funded in the Bahamas, booked in London, and made by a diverse group of international banks to a borrower in Japan. The determination of jurisdiction requires careful consideration. Not only must the applicable law and legal practice be sophisticated, but courts must be willing to accept jurisdiction, and it helps when the country is one that has the power to enforce judgments. New York is often chosen because of the extensive case law on banking matters that has been built up, even in cases involving lenders and borrowers not residents of that country. Judgment currency clauses are necessary because the courts in many countries, notably the United Kingdom, will render a judgment in domestic money only.

Similarly, the **place and method of payment** must be stipulated. Payment is normally effected by means of the transfer of funds from one bank account to another in the country of the currency in which the loan is denominated, although the well-developed U.S. dollar payments system in New York is often used for payment of interest and principal on loans denominated in other currencies. Some banks have sought to insert a clause that states that banks can **deliver** the funds from any financial center they choose. Borrowers sometimes succeed in including the right to **receive** the funds in the place of their choice.

Several clauses are designed specifically to protect banks. A **guarantee**

clause will be required if the borrower's own credit standing does not suffice. A frequently used clause is the **reserve requirement** clause stipulating that the borrower has to absorb any additional cost the lender incurs when interest-free reserve requirements are imposed on the lending bank, effectively increasing the cost of money. Banks also ask that all payments of principal and interest be made **free and clear of taxes** and similar charges. Some go further and insist on a clause protecting them against general increases in cost. Many agreements also contain a **Eurocurrency availability clause**, permitting the bank to call for prepayment if sufficient dollar funds are not available.

In contrast, several typical clauses favor the borrower. A **prepayment clause** gives the borrower the right to repay a loan before maturity. A **multicurrency option clause** permits the borrower to switch currencies and draw down funds in currencies other than the one specified in the loan agreement. A different **currency option clause** allows the borrower to alter the currency of denomination of the loan entirely. This choice can be valuable at times of anticipated currency revaluation. Recent agreements have also provided borrowers with the option of two or more different financial markets (e.g., Eurodollar and U.S. dollar) in which to take down a commitment.

EUROBANKING RISK PROTECTION. As should be evident, international banks have accumulated a fair degree of experience in Eurocurrency lending and funding techniques. Because the market is so competitive, there remains little margin for loss. Therefore, most of the risks are explicitly managed through diversification, pricing, hedging or insurance of some sort or another. Some of the principal risks and banks' responses to them are contained in Exhibit 9.

FUNDING IN INTERNATIONAL BANKING

FUNDING IN THE EUROCURRENCY MARKET. Prior to the development of the Euromarkets, the primary source of funding for international lending was the deposit base of the parent bank plus funds bought in the domestic money market. The Eurodollar market changed this feature dramatically, providing a huge pool of primary and interbank deposits that new entrants to the international banking scene could draw on. The Eurocurrency market is the market for bank deposits and loans denominated in currencies other than that of the country in which the bank or bank branch is located. The **Eurocurrency interbank market** now has a depth comparable to any of the world's money markets, including that of the United States.

For their international loans therefore, banks have come to rely very heavily on the Eurocurrency or "offshore" markets. This changes when a bank enters a country intent on doing local currency business with domestic companies. Here, it is usually desirable to fund local currency loans with local currency deposits—otherwise the bank might expose itself to serious exchange losses

EXHIBIT 9 RISK PROTECTION TECHNIQUES OF EUROBANKS

Lending Risk	Source of Risk	Risk Reduction Strategy
Interest risk	Mismatched maturities coupled with unpredictable movements in interest rates	Matching assets to liabilities by pricing credits on rollover basis
Funding risk	Possibility that funds will not be available to particular banks on normal terms	Floating rate notes and floating rate CDs
Currency risk	Exchange loss when currency of loan depreciates or currency of liability appreciates	Fund in same currency as loan or cover mismatched currencies with swaps
Credit risk	Ability of an entity to repay its debts	Syndication of credit and diversification of bank's loan portfolio; corporate and government guarantees
Country risk	Ability and willingness of borrowers within a country to meet their obligations	Syndication of credit and diversification of bank's loan portfolio
Regulatory risk	Imposition of reserve requirements or taxes on banks	Clause in contract that forces borrowers to bear this risk

Source: Adapted from Laurie Goodman, "The Pricing of Syndicated Eurocurrency Credits," *Federal Reserve Bank of New York Quarterly Review,* Summer 1980.

should the local currency devalue. In some countries the local money market is so poorly developed or so restricted that banks are forced to obtain funds from abroad—for example, American banks relied on funds borrowed abroad for yen-denominated loans extended in Japan during the 1970s. In such cases the borrowed funds are typically hedged by means of a **swap**, usually arranged with the central bank. Dollars could be exchanged into yen for lending purposes, with an agreement to reverse the exchange at some later date at a prearranged exchange rate. In some cases banks have chosen to fund local loans abroad because they are cheaper—for example, Canadian banks' U.S. offices fund much of their U.S. lending by drawing on the large pool of Eurodollar deposits placed with their parent banks in Canada.

EUROBANK LIABILITY MANAGEMENT. As pointed out in *The International Money Market* (Dufey and Giddy), liability management in a Eurobank aims to (1) assure the continued availability of funds at a reasonable cost (i.e., at close to prevailing market rates), (2) maintain a stable deposit base, (3) minimize the cost of funds, and (4) minimize the "mismatch" between maturities of assets and those of liabilities. In addition, some banks seek to profit from such money market techniques as arbitrage (taking advantage of differences in yields between similar money market instruments) and "riding the yield curve" (borrowing at short maturities and depositing at longer maturities, or vice versa, to profit from differences between the bank's forecast of future interest rate and those implied by the prevailing yield curve).

While in most respects the **international bank liability management** task is similar to domestic funding, there are certainly differences of emphasis, arising partly from the fact that the Eurodollar market is largely a wholesale banking system. A substantial proportion of day-to-day Eurobanking activities consists of the active "trading" of Eurocurrency deposits—that is, borrowing short-term funds from other banks and redepositing these funds in the interbank market. This means that the **liability management** of a Eurobank is closely tied in with the management of cash and liquid assets. In this respect, a Eurobank is most closely comparable with the money market departments of large money market center banks in the United States.

Exhibit 10 illustrates a hypothetical balance sheet of an offshore branch of an international bank. The major sources of funds are short-term borrowings from other international banks, nonbank time deposits, and (for London branches), **Eurodollar certificates of deposit**. Other funding sources are **floating rate loan notes** and **floating rate CDs, Eurobonds**, loans from other branches, and loans or equity from the parent bank.

Eurobanks are not subject to reserve requirements imposed by monetary authorities—indeed the absence of noninterest-bearing reserve requirements and other costs such as taxes and fees of the **Federal Deposit Insurance Corp.** (FDIC) enable them to compete with domestic deposits and offer more attractive rates. Therefore if they hold noninterest-bearing deposits, they do so purely for precautionary and transactions purposes.

INTERBANK LINES OF CREDIT. Because Eurobanks are not subject to reserve requirements, they do all they can to minimize amounts held in demand deposits. Interbank lines of credit enable them to hold negligible clearing balances. All active international banks retain and extend a network of credit lines, based on the relative creditworthiness of banks with which they place funds. These lines are drawn on whenever the bank's daily cash outflows exceed its cash inflows. Sine Eurobanks maintain almost no immediately payable checking accounts, and since almost all international payments are effected 1 or 2 business days after completion of a transaction, these inflows and outflows can be managed rather tightly. Since **interbank deposits** form the prime Eurocurrency funding source for the bulk of international banks as well as enabling

EXHIBIT 10 SIMPLIFIED BALANCE SHEET OF A EUROBANK

Assets	Liabilities
1. Reserve balances	1. Interbank deposits
2. Liquid assets	2. Nonbank time deposits
3. Loans	3. London dollar CDs
	4. Notes and bonds
	5. Loans from other branches
	6. Loans from parent bank
	7. Share capital held by parent bank

them to manage cash flows, the establishment of credit lines, formal or informal, is paramount to the banker entering the Euromarket.

In addition, many Eurobanks doing business in a particular currency seek to maintain lines of credit with banks from the country of that currency. Thus a bank in London taking Euromark deposits will establish German mark lines with, say, Deutsche Bank, Dresdner Bank, and DG bank. The concern is that, should Euromarket funding sources for some reason "dry up," the Eurobank will nevertheless have access to the domestic market to meet its obligations.

Because the Euromarket does not create new funds, but only attracts business away from domestic markets, the disappearance of the market is not a serious concern—the funds could only return to their domestic money markets, and the interbank market would reshuffle them to those banks willing to pay competitive interest rates. On the other hand, banks do face a funding risk from time to time, as a result of the phenomenon of **tiering**. Tiering refers to the grouping of banks according to some characteristic, such as size or nationality, that serves as a proxy for creditworthiness assessments during periods of great uncertainty. The number of tiers and the differences between them have tended to increase when events focus attention on the possibility of **bank default**. Such an event was the suspension of Bankhaus Herstatt in 1974: for some time after that, interbank deposit rates indicated the existence of six or more tiers of Eurobanks. Some banks effectively found themselves cut off from the market, at least temporarily.

For a more detailed discussion of the granting of interbank lines, see S. Davis (1976, Chapter 4).

EUROMARKET FUNDING INSTRUMENTS. The bulk of deposits in the Eurocurrency market is time deposits at fixed interest rates, usually of short maturity. According to figures published by the Bank of England in the *Quarterly Bulletin,* approximately 70% of deposits in London Eurobanks have a maturity of less than 3 months. Many of these deposits are on **call**, meaning that they can be withdrawn without notice; but since payment is normally effected by means of transfers in the currency's home country, these are not really checking accounts. While checking account facilities are offered by some Eurobanks, these are chiefly for small transactions and do not form an important part of the funding portfolio.

Most of the time deposit placements are made by other banks, but many are also made by governments and their central banks and by multinational corporations. A few are made by wealthy individuals, often by proxy—for example, through a Swiss bank.

Negotiable Eurodollar certificates of deposit, sometimes called **London dollar CDs**, appeared in London in 1970. These provide greater liquidity and so often bear a slightly lower interest rate than Eurodollar time deposits of the same maturity. While the original intention was to attract a greater proportion of corporate and individual deposits to the market, the bulk are probably held by banks. There is an active secondary market in London dollar CDs, although its depth does not match that of the U.S. CD market. A number of institutions, such as affiliates of U.S. investment banks as well as U.K. merchant banks and discount houses, assure the continuation of the secondary market by acting as market makers.

The usual form of issuance of Eurodollar certificates of deposit is as **tap CDs**. Tap CDs are issued in round amounts (say $5 million) whenever a bank requires funds for a particular maturity—say three months. The usual purpose would be to fund a Eurodollar loan made on a 3-month rollover basis. The issuing bank "taps" the market at very short notice by setting a rate and informing brokers of the terms of the issue.

The distinctive feature of the alternative form of London dollar CD, **tranche CDs**, is that they are "sliced" into several portions with greater appeal to those investors who prefer an instrument with smaller denominations than those of conventional CDs. Unlike tap CDs, tranche CDs are "managed" issues, offered to the public for sale through brokerage houses in a fashion similar to a securities issue.

To obtain funds at longer maturities without locking themselves into a fixed interest cost, some banks have issued **floating rate notes** (FRNs) and, more recently, **floating rate CDs**. These two differ only in terms of subordination. Floating rate liabilities enable banks to assure themselves of the longer term availability of funds, while allowing the interest rates on their liabilities to vary periodically with market rates. Thus they can match the interest period of their liabilities with those of their assets (rollover loans), and avoid a funding risk.

Finally, a **forward forward**, or more correctly, a **forward Eurodollar CD**, is a contract to issue a Eurodollar CD at a fixed interest rate at a given date in the future. Such contracts, in conjunction with the issue of ordinary (spot) CDs, effectively constituted CDs of longer term than was at one time legally permitted in the United Kingdom. However, since the same effect can now be achieved as easily by simultaneously buying and selling CDs of different maturities, participants in the Eurodollar market have not employed this technique to any great extent. A more promising development is the introduction of standardized futures contracts in Eurodollar CDs.

ONSHORE VERSUS OFFSHORE FUNDING. The banker familiar with sources of funds in the Euromarket is able to use the market not only to fund Eurocurrency loans, but also for domestic purposes. Indeed U.S. banks have made extensive use of their Bahamian and London branches to obtain funds when tight credit in the United States impelled depositors to place their funds in a market free of interest rate ceilings—**Regulation Q** of the **Federal Reserve Board**.

To compare the cost of funding onshore with the cost of borrowing Eurodollars, however, it is not sufficient to know the interest rates on the two types of deposit. Domestic deposits, unlike Eurodeposits, are subject to reserve requirements and FDIC premiums. While offshore deposits themselves face no such costs, the Federal Reserve Board has from time to time imposed a reserve requirement on Eurodollars used in the United States; this is called **Regulation M**. Hence to compare costs, one must adjust the interest rates as follows:

cost of domestic deposit in United States = domestic bank deposit rate + cost of reserve requirement + FDIC premiums

cost of Eurodeposit used in United States = Eurodollar deposit rate + cost of Regulation M reserve requirement

If banks have substantial domestic funding needs and are otherwise indifferent between onshore and offshore deposits, **arbitrage** between the **U.S. and Eurodollar money markets** will occur until the two adjusted rates are equal. Indeed, because of the cost of reserve requirements and FDIC fees, banks can and usually do offer higher interest rates on Eurodeposits than on domestic deposits.

INTERNATIONAL INVESTMENT BANKING

International investment banking may be defined as those activities that bring together borrowers (or issuers of securities) such as corporations or governments, and investors, through the capital markets. In order to match investors' preferences with issuers' requirements, an international investment bank must have a capability in the identification of **corporate finance** need, in the distribution and trading of securities to investors, and in the transformation of risks through swaps, options, and other hedging techniques, or by creating tailored, **hybrid securities** that exploit market imperfections to create added value for both issuer and investor.

International capital markets consist of two sets of types:

1. Those cases in which an issuer of one country issues a security in the market of another country (host) with the aid of a **syndicate** of the host country and sells primarily to the residents of the host country.
2. Those cases in which both the syndicate and the investors come from many countries. In the first case the issue is normally denominated in the currency of the host country. The marketing organization is structured similarly to those involved in purely domestic offerings. Such markets are referred to as **foreign markets**. In the second case the issue may be denominated in any one of a number of different currencies. No matter which currency is used, it will be foreign to many of the underwriters and foreign to a good portion of the investors. This market is known as the **Eurobond market**. The two markets together are known as the international markets.

International investment banks originate, distribute, trade, and position securities globally, regionally, and locally.

ORIGINATION. Origination consists of all the activities involved in an offering to sell a security to investors. It includes both the arranging of the terms and pricing structure of the offering as well as the forming of a syndicate (a group of underwriters—investment banks and brokers) to buy the security and resell it to investors.

Often, the origination function is referred to as creating paper because, in most instances, its activities result in new securities entering the marketplace.

In its role in the origination process, the bank attempts to structure an issue so that it will provide the best terms for the issuer while, at the same time, offer optimum marketability. It should be obvious that these two ingredients must coexist; otherwise, the origination process is doomed for failure. Without both of them, either the issuer will find other avenues for funding or investors will find other securities more attractive to invest in.

DISTRIBUTION. This consists of the sale of newly issued securities to final investors. This is primarily a sales and marketing function in which investors are identified who are suited to specific primary or secondary issues. In the international capital market, investors are widely distributed, so a multitiered structure of selling banks and brokers may be employed. A typical Eurobond issue, for example, may have as many as 50–100 banks involved in distribution of a large issue.

TRADING. The trading function involves the matching of buyers and sellers of securities that are already publicly owned.

This function involves the matching of buyers and sellers of securities (both debt and equity) for client investors in response to their requests. To accomplish this, the bank acts as either:

- An agent, purchasing or selling the securities in the marketplace on a commission basis
- A dealer, maintaining a large inventory of certain securities (primarily debt issues), and either purchasing these securities for inventory or selling them from inventory

Another trading function is assisting corporations and other banks (both foreign and domestic) invest their foreign exchange reserves and domestic currency holdings in money market instruments.

POSITIONING. Positioning is the activity of buying securities for the bank's own portfolio in response to market opportunities. In this function, the securities are being purchased as an investment for the bank.

INVESTMENT MANAGEMENT. Investment management provides international portfolio management and investment research services to clients in order to help them meet their investment objectives. In addition, a strong investment management capability provides good support to a bank in its role in securities distribution and trading. A subset of this function is **international private banking**, which provides a wide range of banking, investment, and fiduciary services to high net worth individuals, family groups, and not-for-profit organizations worldwide.

SWAPS AND HEDGES. The subsection on Eurocurrency lending showed how, by linking a dollar loan to a simultaneous spot-and-forward currency transaction, the effective currency of denomination of a deposit or loan can be transformed. This was an example of a much wider range of techniques now offered by international banks, enabling issuers, and also investors, to alter the currency, interest rate, and other attributes of securities into something more suited to the hedger's needs.

An example of the basic technique of swaps or hedges is as follows. An issuer finds a capital market in which taxes, restricted investor choice, or some other market imperfection gives him or her a special advantage. This person issues a bond in, say, Swiss francs at a floating interest rate. What he or she wants, however, is dollar financing with an interest rate that does not exceed a certain level. To produce the desired results, a bank enters into a currency swap with the issuer, exchanging Swiss franc payments for dollar payments, and also sells the issuer an interest rate cap, which, for a fee, provides insurance to the issuer against the latter's interest cost rising above a predetermined level. These are the "swaps and hedges" that create more suitable securities positions for investors and issuers.

Among the most dramatic phenomena of the international capital markets in recent years has been the adaptation of a traditional technique, the parallel loan, into the currency swap and subsequently the interest rate swap or coupon exchange agreement.

SWAPS, CREDIT SWAPS, AND PARALLEL LOANS. While international loans are normally funded and denominated in a single currency, there exists a set of techniques for making loans across currencies and across national boundaries. These normally involve an explicit or implicit purchase of a foreign currency and simultaneous sale of that currency for a future date. This coupling of a spot and forward foreign exchange deal is called a **swap**. A **currency swap** is simply an agreement to exchange certain amounts of two currencies on a spot basis (today) and to reverse the transaction at an agreed-upon exchange rate at a specified time in the future. The term "swap" is also used frequently to refer to a credit swap, which matches the currency swap to a pair of loans.

A typical **credit swap** might involve a firm in country A providing (hard) currency funds for its affiliate in a weak-currency country. The parent company will lend, for example, dollar funds to an intermediary, a commercial bank, or even the central bank of the weak-currency country, which, in turn, lends local currency funds to the foreign affiliate. At a predetermined date in the future, the transaction will be reversed. The cost of the transaction contains the following elements: the interest rate on the funds less the interest rate on the local currency funds, adjusted for any difference between the prevailing spot rate, and the implicit rate used to reconvert the local currency funds on repayment date. Because of these contractual relationships, it is the intermediary (local bank or foreign central bank) that bears the burden of the exchange risk on the (dollar) principal. The interest on the local currency loan, however, is subect to **exchange risk** in dollar terms.

Why would firms and intermediaries undertake such complex deals instead of simpler alternatives such as direct loans in dollars, borrowing in the local money market, or lending dollar funds covered with a forward contract? From the viewpoint of the firm, it is primarily market imperfections that provide the compelling reason. Neither forward cover nor access to local credit markets may be available at reasonable rates. For the intermediaries, such credit swaps are a means of bolstering their foreign exchange reserves, using the financial needs of captive foreign affiliates to obtain these reserves at a lower cost than might be available through outright borrowing. And since they are close to the political powers that determine extent and timing of devaluations, they may be convinced of their ability to assess the foreign exchange risk better than private companies. Indeed the intermediary bank is frequently the central bank itself.

A **parallel loan** is an arrangement under which two corporations (or other institutions) in different countries make loans to each other in their own countries and currencies. The classic example is that of an American firm making a dollar loan to the U.S. subsidiary of a British company, while the British firm simultaneously makes a sterling loan to the U.S. subsidiary of the American firm. Such dollar–sterling parallel loans have been concluded at interest rate differentials reflecting the difference between long-term interbank rates, avoiding the respective borrowing-investing spreads.

Each loan serves as collateral for the other, and bears an interest rate related to local credit conditions plus the putative cost of a long term forward exchange contract. Unlike some of the earlier examples, this technique is purely a product of regulation; it enables firms to avoid capital (and perhaps also credit) controls. In concept, it is a costly and clumsy arrangement; two parties with matching needs have to be brought together, and the agreement is a combination of three financial contracts; two loans plus one implicit forward transaction. Only regulations that constrain credit allocation or prevent free capital flows justify its existence.

A variant of the parallel loan **across** currencies is a similar construct that involves two offsetting transactions in the domestic and external (Euro-) sector of the credit market in a **single** currency. This technique requires the same constellation of actors and regulations, but has the advantage that the security of each party (i.e., the right of offset) is not affected by changes in the exchange rate.

CURRENCY SWAPS TODAY. The currency swap technique represents a simple adaptation of the credit swap or parallel loan: instead of engaging in two separate loan transactions, the two parties simply agree to engage in a **single** agreement to exchange coupons or principal of two different kinds. The typical deal is a fixed-rate currency swap. This currency swap consists of the exchange between two counterparties of fixed-rate interest in one currency in return for fixed-rate interest in another currency. The following three basic steps are common to all currency swaps:

1. **Initial Exchange of Principal.** On the commencement of the swap the counterparties exchange the principal amounts of the swap at an agreed rate of exchange. Although this rate is usually based on the spot exchange rate, a forward rate set in advance of the swap commencement date can also be used. This initial exchange may be on a "notional" basis (i.e., no physical exchange of principal amounts) or alternatively a "physical" exchange.

   Whether the initial exchange is on a physical or notional basis its sole importance is to establish the quantum of the respective principal amounts for the purpose of (a) calculating the ongoing payments of interest and (b) the reexchange of principal amounts under the swap.
2. **Ongoing Exchanges of Interest.** Once the principal amounts are established, the counterparties exchange interest payments based on the outstanding principal amounts at the respective fixed interest rates agreed at the outset of the transaction.
3. **Reexchange of Principal Amount.** On the maturity date the counterparties reexchange the principal amounts established at the outset.

   This straightforward, three-step process is standard practice in the swap market and results in the effective transformation of a debt raised in one currency into a fully hedged fixed-rate liability in another currency.

INTEREST RATE SWAPS. The structure of an interest rate swap is simpler than the currency swap, because it consists only of an exchange of coupons. The typical swap involves the exchange between two counterparties of fixed-rate interest for floating rate interest in the same currency calculated by reference to a mutually agreed notional principal amount. This principal amount, which would normally equate to the underlying assets or liabilities being "swapped" by the counterparties, is applicable solely for the calculation of the interest to be exchanged under the swap. At no time is it physically passed between the counterparties. Through this straightforward swap structure, the counterparties are able to convert an underlying fixed-rate asset/liability into a floating-rate asset/liability and vice versa.

The majority of interest rate swap transactions are driven by the cost savings that may result from differentials in the credit standing of the counterparties and other structural considerations. For example, investors in fixed-rate instruments are more sensitive to credit quality than floating-rate bank lenders. Accordingly, a greater premium is demanded of issuers of lesser credit quality in the fixed-rate debt markets than in the floating rate bank lending market. The counterparties to an interest rate swap may therefore obtain an arbitrage advantage by accessing the market in which they have the greatest relative cost advantage and then entering into an interest rate swap to convert the cost of the funds so raised from a fixed-rate to a floating-rate basis or vice versa.

CAPS, FLOORS, AND COLLARS. Although an interest rate of swaps enables a borrower to convert a variable interest rate into a fixed one, many borrowers prefer to be able to take advantage of falling interest rates while limiting their cost to a maximum level if rates rise. Banks provide hedges of this type, promising to compensate the borrower for the difference between some market rate (usually **LIBOR**) and a fixed maximum rate (say, 11%), if and whenever the market rate exceeds the "cap" rate.

Similarly, a bank may guarantee a minimum rate to a depositor or investor in a floating-rate instrument, by paying the investor whenever the market rate falls below the "floor" rate.

In a variation of the cap, banks sometimes offer to hedge a borrower against LIBOR exceeding a certain level, while at the same time limiting the borrower's gain from falling rates by contracting for the borrower to compensate the bank for the amount by which LIBOR falls below another, lower, rate. All such hedges constitute, in effect, interest rate options, and as the market becomes more efficient they are priced accordingly. A collar is cheaper than a cap because the value of "cap" sold by the bank to the borrower is offset in part by the value of the "floor" sold by the borrower to the bank.

EURONOTES AND ISSUANCE FACILITIES. Many of the innovations of swaps and hedges involve the divorce of a security (such as a Eurobond) from some of its attributes (such as its currency or interest rate). The **Euronote** is a Euromarket innovation of a similar kind. The Euronote is simply a short-term bearer note issued as needed by a corporate, bank, or sovereign borrower. Its distinguishing feature is that the issuer is assured of selling the notes at a maximum spread in relation to LIBOR as a result of **"note issuance facility"** (NIF), or **"underwriting facility"** (RUF), that is arranged for a number of years. The NIF is a medium-term underwriting commitment provided by a group of leading financial institutions. Under the umbrella of the medium-term underwriting commitment of the NIF, short-term borrowings may be made, evidenced by promissory notes or, for bank issuers, by certificates of deposit, usually of 3- or 6-month maturity. The reader will recognize that, in contrast to the **syndicated loan**, the **revolving credit facility** and the **floating-rate note,** under the NIF the roles of the medium-term risk takers (the underwriters) and of the actual providers of funds (the short-term investors) are separated. This separation is crucial to the viability of the NIF as an alternative Eurodollar floating rate structure. Similar facilities without this separation are simply disguised syndicated loans.

A borrower can use the NIF on a fully drawn basis, with the short-term paper being reissued, under the medium-term underwriting commitment, at the end of each interest period. It can provide a more cost-effective, more flexible, and more diversified source of Eurodollar funding than the syndicated loan or the floating-rate note.

Alternatively, the NIF can be structured as a standby facility, thereby providing a low-cost substitute for committed bank lines or for a revolving credit facility. For example, it could be used as a backup commitment for the issuance of U.S. commercial paper. The structure would include special drawing features, including the availability of up to the full amount of the facility at short notice.

The short-term borrowings under a NIF are usually made for 3- or 6-month periods in accordance with normal Euromarket practice for floating-rate interest periods.

Eurobond Hybrids and Option Bonds. Although many international banking innovations entail "unbundling" of features as described in the two previous subsections, many others constitute a "bundling" or packaging of features to produce a new and different hybrid security. Eurobonds with convertible features have been common since the inception of the market—these allow the international investor to participate in the success of a stock without the disadvantages of owning the equity stocks or equity options directly. Recent years, however, have seen a proliferation of Eurobonds and other instruments with special option or indexing features. Among these are **currency option bonds**, which give the investor a choice of a repayment currency; bonds with **debt**, **equity**, **or currency warrants** attached; **"capped floaters,"** or floating-rate notes with a maximum interest payable; bonds denominated in one currency but with principal and interest **indexed to another currency**; **dual currency bonds**, with the interest payable in one currency and the principal in another; extendible and retractible bonds; **put bonds**, which allow the investor to demand early redemption at certain dates; bonds with **harmless warrants**, which are bonds with warrants to purchase more such bonds, but that also allow the issuer to call an equivalent amount of the original bonds; **commodity bonds**, whose value is tied to some commodity price index; and many more that are combinations or variations of these.

In all cases, the principle is that, as a result of some market imperfection, the investor will pay more (or the issuer accept less) for the features in combination than he or she would if the instrument and its attributes (such as call or put options), were sold separately. This is the essence of financial innovation, and a large part of today's international investment banking skills lies in the ability to identify those market imperfections that create value added to both investor and issuer.

INTERNATIONAL BANKING REGULATIONS

No treatment of international banking would be complete without a discussion of the **legal and regulatory constraints** facing the international banker. Because banks have the means to garner and allocate a nation's savings, governments around the world seek to influence the behavior of banks. Banks are constrained, secured, protected, discriminated against, and sometimes even owned by governments. International banks face multiple and often overlapping jurisdictions and almost universally must confront restrictions on entry into foreign markets. On the other hand, their flexibility has, to some extent, given them a choice of jurisdiction for certain activities, thus reducing the burden of regulation. Banking authorities viewing international banking are thus faced with the choice of constraining banks and thus isolating their country from the free world market's interchange of financial resources, or easing regulations in such a way as to reduce the relative attractiveness of doing banking in offshore jurisdictions. Among the issues faced by the U.S. banking authorities are:

- The problem of gaps in regulatory coverage
- The problem of regulating foreign portfolios and activities of U.S. banks that receive Federal Reserve and FDIC support
- The problem of maintaining U.S. banks' international competitiveness without sacrificing their soundness
- The problem of national versus reciprocal treatment of foreign banks in the United States
- The problems of appropriate jurisdiction for U.S. banks abroad
- The problem of maintaining an effective monetary policy despite international capital mobility and continual innovations
- The problem of maintaining the appropriate allocation of credit in the domestic economy

The regulation of U.S. banks abroad and foreign banks in the United States is made more difficult by the fragmentation of banking jurisdiction between federal and state agencies and between the **Federal Reserve Board**, the **Comptroller of the Currency**, and the **Federal Deposit Insurance Corp.** at the federal level. The tendency has been toward a concentration of jurisdiction at the federal level, especially under the Federal Reserve Board and the Comptroller of the Currency.

The framework of U.S. and foreign regulation of international banking is outlined next. For more detail, the reader is referred to the references and bibliography.

U.S. REGULATION OF AMERICAN BANKS ABROAD. Since most international banking is done through foreign branches, and because branches are legally an integral part of the bank, U.S. banking abroad is in principle subject to all the regulations (e.g., reserve requirements) and legal limitations (e.g., on the concentration of loans to a single borrower) to which domestic branches are subject. In practice, some regulations, such as reserve requirements and strict limits on the nature of commercial banks' activities, are eased. Others, such as limits on loan concentration and provisions for adequate capital to meet deposit outflows, are enforced in the interest of bank soundness.

For all banks, granting permission to open a branch abroad is the preserve of the **Federal Reserve Board**. The Board also regulates direct equity participations in foreign banks (or nonbanks) by U.S. banks or by bank holdings companies, and branches, agencies, and subsidiaries of Edge Act banks.

The U.S. Comptroller of the Currency has responsibility for examination and supervision of overseas branches of national banks. Jurisdiction over activities of state-chartered banks that are not Federal Reserve System members is held by state banking authorities but in practice is shared with the FDIC. The state authorities also share jurisdiction over activities of state-chartered member banks with the Federal Reserve Board.

U.S. REGULATION OF FOREIGN BANKS. The 1970s saw a proliferation of non-American banks in the United States. While these banks at first entered to service their multinational clients' U.S. banking needs, a later acceleration of entry was motivated by the desire to establish access to the U.S. money markets to support international dollar-based banking, and simply to compete profitably with U.S. banks for the loan and deposit business of large domestic customers.

Some foreign banks establish **representative offices**, which can drum up business but may not carry on any borrowing or lending. Banks wishing to make loans but not requiring deposits can establish **agencies**. To both take deposits and make loans, they must set up either a **branch** or a **subsidiary**. Subsidiaries are merely domestic banks owned by foreigners, and so are subject to the normal range of state and federal regulations.

While in the past the regulation of foreign banking in the United States rested primarily with state governments, the **International Banking Act (IBA)** of 1978 placed foreign banks under explicit federal jurisdiction, prohibiting cross-state branching and investment-banking subsidiaries, imposing reserve requirements and, for small deposits, requiring FDIC insurance.

Until the present the United States has adhered rather strictly in its regulation of foreign banks to the **national treatment principle**, whereby insofar as is possible, foreign banks are accorded the same privileges and subjected to the same constraints as are domestic banks. The rationale is that this provides the greatest competitive equality and best serves the public. Some state regulators and some officials at the national level, however, have argued for consideration of the principle of reciprocity, whereby a foreign bank from country A would be permitted only the activities allowed U.S. banks doing business in A. Prior to the implementation of the IBA, New York State's treatment of foreign banks adhered to this principle.

OTHER COUNTRIES' REGULATION OF FOREIGN BANKS. As noted above, banks are often a major instrument for the implementation of social goals. Hence the banking systems of many countries are relatively restricted. The free entry of foreign banks would undermine the influence exercised by the host government to allocate credit, set interest raes, and so forth. Nevertheless U.S., British, French, Japanese, and other banks have established substantial presences in the domestic markets of many countries.

Official constraints on foreign banks take the form of (1) entry restrictions, and (2) restraints on the operations of banks already established in the host country's market.

Restrictions on entry may be by law or, more often, by administrative policy or practice. They range from prohibition of foreign bank presence to various limitations on the legal form allowed. Particular forms of entry, such as establishment of branches, or subsidiaries, or acquisition of equity interest in an existing bank, may be specifically restricted. Or foreign bank presence may be limited to representative offices, which may not engage in any direct banking transactions.

In 1979 the **U.S. Treasury Department** undertook a major survey of foreign countries' treatment of U.S. banks. One result of this was a table listing the entry restrictions of 141 countries. The reader should be aware that many of

EXHIBIT 11 EXAMPLES OF "TAX-LIKE AND QUOTALIKE" RESTRICTIONS ON FOREIGN BANKS

"TAXLIKE" RESTRICTIONS

Differential reserve requirements
Prohibitions against accepting retail deposits
Prohibitions against foreign exchange transactions
No access to rediscount facilities
No access to subsidized funds for export financing

"QUOTALIKE" RESTRICTIONS

Credit and lending ceilings
Specified loan portfolio structure
Swap limits
Required capital-to-asset ratios combined with capitalization limits
Ceilings on loans in domestic currency
Ceilings on loans in foreign currencies
Prohibition or limitation on branching

Source: U.S Treasury Department, Office of the Comptroller of the Currency, *Report to Congress on Foreign Government Treatment of U.S Commercial Banking Organizations,* 1979.)

these classifications were judgmental, and in any case many regulations are in a state of flux.

Even when established in a country, foreign banks are frequently subjected to treatment that differs from that accorded domestic banks. Most restrictions on bank operations increase the cost of doing business and thus have effects that are equivalent to the imposition of a tax. An example of a "taxlike" restriction is special reserve requirements. A second category of regulation is "quotatlike" restrictions that set absolute limits on the amount of credit or services that banks may offer. Examples of both types of restraints may be found in Exhibit 11.

APPENDIX: EXPORT FINANCING TECHNIQUES AND LETTERS OF CREDIT

In this Appendix we look at three categories of export financing: financing by the exporter, financing by the importer, and bank financing. As observed in the text of the section, any one of these can be guaranteed or supplemented by government export (or import) support. The Appendix concludes with a review of various forms of the letter of credit, including standby letters of credit.

FINANCING BY THE EXPORTER

There are various methods by which the exporter can finance a transaction: the method chosen will depend on the familiarity and trust that the exporting firm has in the importing firm, and the relative ability of the exporter to extend credit as an element in the firm's marketing policy.

SHIPMENT ON AN OPEN-BOOK ACCOUNT. In an open-account transaction, the arrangement provides for future payments but with no definite maturities and without any negotiable instrument evidencing the obligation between buyer and seller. Such an arrangement is extremely advantageous to the importer because it permits the importer to receive the goods and even sell them before making payments. The exporter runs the risk that in time of stress the importer might give preference to pressing domestic obligations, and efforts to collect by legal proceedings can prove difficult and expensive. In some countries where exchange controls are in effect importers' applications for dollar drafts take precedence over applications for open-account payments.

Even though open-account transactions permit greater flexibility, involve less cost, and offer a tool to meet competition, they involve a considerable amount of risk. For this reason open-account settlements are used in cases where there is an established relationship over the years between seller and buyer, a nearby or established market, or where exchange controls are minimal or nonexistent. Sales to foreign branches or subsidiaries are often made on an open account basis. Banks might be willing to grant exporters loans on evidence of the sales contract and shipment of the goods.

CONSIGNMENTS. The importer can ship goods to a branch, agency, or resident salesman abroad and order the sale of goods while they are in transit or upon arrival at a fixed price or at the best obtainable price. Under a consignment agreement, no payment is due to the **consigner** (exporter) until the goods are sold by the **consignee** (importer). The goods remain the legal possession of the consigner until the sale is made. The exporter thus ties up funds until the goods are sold and purchased. In addition, the exporter assumes the exchange risk for foreign currency—invoiced sales. This method is rarely used for the sale of goods to unrelated foreign firms because of the obvious risks. Banks are reluctant to finance consignments.

COLLECTION DRAFTS. When the exporter perceives some risk in consignments, which are rather open-ended methods, the most widely used technique of arranging for the payment and financing of an export is often an alternative: the **bill of exchange**, or **draft**. A draft is essentially a **request for payment** to the exporter (**drawer**) by the importer (**drawee**). An exporter **draws a draft** on the importer at the time of shipment. The draft becomes a legally accepted obligation when the importer acknowledges the debt by **accepting** the draft. There are two broad classifications of collection drafts, **documentary** drafts and **clean** drafts. Each can be either **sight** (see Exhibit 12) or **time** drafts.

Collection drafts are typically used when the exporter considers the purchaser a good credit risk. In general, an exporting firm will use collections with clients with whom it has prior experience. In the absence of substantial evidence of creditworthiness, a new exporter would be well advised to seek a more secure method, such as letters of credit (which are explained later). Nonethe-

EXHIBIT 12 SIGHT DRAFT (payable at presentation)

FORM 8050-3-AB

No. .001 U.S.A. August 1, 19--

Exchange for $100,000.00

At ================== Sight of this FIRST of Exchange (Second being unpaid)

Pay to the order of Exporter for Profit, Inc.

the sum of ONE HUNDRED THOUSAND U.S. DOLLARS

Drawn under Letter of Credit No. 700000 Dated July 1, 19--

Issued by The First National Bank of Chicago

Value received and charge to the account of

To The First National Bank of Chicago — Exporter for Profit, Inc.

Chicago, Illinois — By:

(Authorized Signature)

less, if collections are the customary terms of trade for the commodity involved, then the exporter will, more likely than not, have to assume the buyer's commercial risk to acquire the acount. Furthermore, letters of credit are so expensive in some countries (particularly in South America and the Middle East) that an importer cannot afford them. Time drafts, as previously noted, are riskier than sight drafts. The decision to use a collection draft rather than a letter of credit is simply one of risk versus return. A letter of credit is clearly less risky, yet insisting upon one might cause the exporter to lose the sale.

Documentary drafts are accompanied by documents conveying title to goods. The exporter delivers the documents to the collecting bank with instructions regarding when to deliver them to the importer, depending on the agreed terms, which can be **DP** (documents against payments) or **DA** (documents against acceptance). The exporter retains control of the goods when a documentary draft is employed, because the importer cannot obtain shipping documents from the collecting bank until the draft is paid or accepted. The accepted draft—called **trade acceptance**—becomes a **clean bill**. Under a **clean draft** the seller sends all documents to the buyer and only the draft to the collecting bank. This, of course, involves a considerable amount of risk, since the merchandise is surrendered to the buyer regardless of payment or acceptance of the draft. This method is generally used in cases where there is a considerable amount of faith between the seller and the buyer or in cases where the sale is to an affiliate or a subsidiary.

Whether the draft is documentary or clean it can be either a **sight** or a **time** draft. Under a documentary **sight draft** documents are delivered to the buyer only after payment of the draft. This method is advantageous to the seller since the seller retains title and control until payment is made. The buyer is not required to pay until the documents are received.

Under a **time draft** documents are delivered to the buyer upon acceptance only. Once the buyer accepts the draft the buyer obtains control of goods and is not required to pay until a certain number of days after sight or date. This method favors the buyer, since after obtaining documents there is no requirement to pay immediately. The selling firm is at a disadvantage since it is relying entirely on the ability and willingness of the buyer to pay.

The Role of the Bank in Exporter-Financed Trade. A bank that undertakes the service of collection must receive detailed **instructions from the exporter** (drawer) so that the bank can protect its client's interests in accordance with the sales contract. The instructions are given on a printed form supplied by the bank. The instructions given in each instance are determined by the sales contract, the policy of the exporter, and any special requirements of the moment. Since the bank must follow instructions explicitly, it is advisable that the exporter designate a representation located near the importer (drawee), with instructions "in case of need, refer to." This **local representative** knows the exporter's policies, and reference to him or her implies that the representative can be trusted by the bank to modify original instructions to meet emergencies.

The exporter's bank forwards the draft and documents with the exporter's instructions to its branch or correspondent bank in the country of the importer. Upon receipt of payment from the importer the foreign bank remits the funds to the exporter's bank, which in turn makes them available to the exporter. In case of a DA draft, the **correspondent bank** will hand over the documents to the importer upon the importer's acceptance of the draft. On the due date, the correspondent bank presents the acceptance to the importer, and when it is paid remits the amount to the exporter's bank. Although the exporter's bank selects the correspondent abroad, the latter acts as the agent of the exporter and not of the bank. Should the correspondent bank become insolvent or bankrupt before it has remitted the collected funds to the exporter's bank, the loss will be borne by the exporter.

FINANCING BY THE IMPORTER

Although the burden of financing international trade does not normally fall on the importer, the latter may sometimes be forced to finance production or shipment, particularly when the commodity or equipment involved is specially designed. In addition, an importing firm might choose to finance an import if it is in a strong financial position and can use this strength to negotiate a favorable price. The importer has three principal means for financing operations.

PAYMENT WITH ORDER. Payment with order means that the importer must pay for the goods at the time the order is placed with the exporter. To effect the payment, the importing firm might pay its bank, which would provide a draft (essentially a check) drawn on a bank located in the city of the exporter, or in the financial center of the exporter's country. Sales on such terms are rarely encountered in foreign trade, except when the credit standing of the importer is unsatisfactory or not known. The exporting firm receives payment before it ships the goods, often even before they are manufactured. The importer thus not only finances the entire transaction and assumes the foreign exchange risk involved, but pays cash without security, except for the credit standing of the exporter. Should the order not be filled, or should the goods be unduly delayed or prove to be of inferior quality, the importer's only redress is to bring legal action on the basis of the sales contract unless the exporter makes an adjustment voluntarily.

PARTIAL PAYMENT IN ADVANCE. To protect itself against the contingency that goods ordered by importers might be rejected on delivery, an exporting firm might stipulate in the sales contract that importers must remit in advance a partial payment on the order as evidence of good faith and intention to pay the balance as agreed. Such provision is usually made when the order is for specialized equipment, or when the goods involved cannot be satisfactorily disposed in the country of destination if the importer fails to take them as agreed. The partial payment by the importer should suffice to cover the cost of freight out and back, insurance, and other expenses incidental to the shipment of goods abroad.

PAYMENT ON DOCUMENTS. When the contract stipulates payment on documents, the importer must provide funds in the exporter's country to pay for the shipment on the day the exporter turns over to a designated bank documents evidencing shipment of the goods ordered. The importer thus raises the funds, converts them into the currency of the country of the exporter (unless invoiced in local currency), and carries the financing burden while the commodities are in transit.

FINANCING BY BANKS

The best-known method of international trade financing is through a **commercial bank**—either that of the exporter or that of the importer. The most common way to assure such financing is to obtain a **letter of credit** (LC). The letter of credit, however, is not a financing instrument in itself; it merely assures the exporter of payment under specified conditions.

Indeed, bank financing can be done without a letter of credit, where **commercial risk** is not a major factor. Typical non-LC bank financing arrangements include advances on drafts, discounts of the drafts themselves, and refinancing bills.

ADVANCE ON DRAFTS. Under advances on drafts, the financing is done jointly by the exporter and the exporter's bank. An exporter who is unwilling to have funds tied up while the goods are en route to the importer can borrow from the bank a percentage of the amount of the draft. The draft on the importer and pertinent shipping documents, turned over by the exporter to the bank for collection, constitute **collateral** for the advance. In case the drawee (importer) fails to pay the draft when due, the bank has recourse against the drawer, whether the draft is made out to the order of the drawer (exporter) and endorsed by the drawer to the bank, or to the order of the bank. Thus the credit risk rests on the exporter just as when the draft is handed to the bank for collection only. After the draft has been paid by the drawee, the bank retains the amount of the advance plus interest and collection fees, crediting the balance to the exporter. The amount that an exporter can borrow on foreign drafts depends on the financial responsibility of exporter and importer, and the collateral behind the draft. The **character of the merchandise** shipped determines its value as collateral. Staple commodities not subject to rapid deterioration (cotton, wheat, wool) and traded on organized markets are obviously better collateral than perishable goods or manufactured articles requiring expert selling to be settled without loss.

DISCOUNT OF DRAFTS. The bank can discount the draft drawn by the exporter on the importer when the credit standing of the exporter is high, and particularly if the exporter already has a line of credit. The exporter then receives the face amount of the draft, less interest and collection charges, unless custom requires the drawee to absorb all charges.

REFINANCING BILL. Under a refinancing bill, an exporter hands over to the bank the draft and documents for collection, and the bank allows the exporter to draw on itself a time draft of a maturity identical with that of the draft upon the importer. The bank accepts the draft on itself, and this refinancing bill becomes a **banker's acceptance** that the exporter can sell in the open market at a very low rate of discount. When the original draft has been paid by the importer abroad, the bank uses the funds to pay off its own acceptance at maturity.

FORFAITING. Forfaiting is the discounting at a fixed rate without recourse of medium-term export receivables denominated in fully convertible currencies (e.g., U.S. dollars, Swiss francs, West German deutsche marks). The discount is based on the prevailing interest rate (such as 1.25% above LIBOR, the London Interbank offered rate).

Forfaiting is used by, among others, the socialist countries. There, government-owned enterprises frequently import capital goods, often in the form of turnkey plants, from suppliers in industrialized countries on extended payment terms related to the life of the project. Such maturities, which may range anywhere from 3 to 12 years, cannot be handled through the institutions that undertake traditional export financing. From the point of view of the exporters who can finance such transactions by borrrowing in the markets this would be too costly. More important, technologically oriented capital goods manufacturers feel very uncomfortable with the economic and political risks associated with loans to foreign political entities. Forfaiting solves the exporter's problems and it is also advantageous to the borrower (i.e., the importer). A typical transaction involves four parties: besides the exporter and the importer, there are the importer's bank, which tends to be government entity too, and the forfaiter, usually a special-purpose subsidiary of one of the large Swiss, West German, or Austrian banks that has innovated this financing technique.

When an exporter's negotiations with the importing organization are about to reach a decisive state, the exporter obtains a **commitment** from the forfaiter to finance the transaction at a firm interest cost. This cost is represented by the discount at which the forfaiter will purchase at the time the deal is completed. For this commitment the forfaiter charges a **fee** that will be compensation for the cost of assuring availability of funds, which might involve the forfaiter's borrowing funds on a long-term basis and reinvesting on a short-term basis during the commitment period.

When the export transaction is completed, the exporter receives from the importing organization a series of promissory notes with maturities staggered according to the repayment terms, usually in 6-month intervals reflecting the installments. Most important, these promissory notes are endorsed guaranteed by the importer's bank, which becomes the **primary obligor** in the transactions, just as in the case of a banker's acceptance.

The forfaiter will purchase the total bundle from the exporter without recourse, taking on the risk of the state-owned bank and, ultimately, the government of the importer's country. The essence of forfaiting involves the shifting of the country risk to an institution that specializes in assessing such risks. But the forfaiter is also an international market specialist. Usually the package of notes is broken up and sold to various investors who differ in terms of maturity preference. The forfaiter endorses the notes, thus collecting the risk premium in addition to the difference in yield between the sum of the individual note and the discount that the forfaiter obtained when the package was bought.

COMMERCIAL LETTERS OF CREDIT. A letter of credit is a document issued by a bank at the buyer's (importer's) request in which that bank promises to pay the seller upon presentation of documents as specified in the terms of the credit. The basic function is to reduce the commercial risk to the seller. Also, because the seller cannot receive payment until the required documents are relinquished, the buyer receives some (but not total) assurance that the seller will comply with the negotiated terms of the sale.

In summary, a commercial letter of credit can be defined as a notification issued by a bank to an individual or firm authorizing the latter to draw on the bank, its branch, or a correspondent bank, for amounts up to a specified sum and guaranteeing acceptance and payment of the drafts if drawn in accordance with the terms in the letter. A letter of credit can be either an **import** or **export letter of credit** (there is no difference between the two, only a matter of perspective).

Parties to the Letter of Credit. The basic parties are the buyer (the applicant), the buyer's bank (the **issuing bank**), the issuing bank's foreign correspondent (the **advising bank**, or **confirming bank**) and the seller (beneficiary).

Issuing Bank	Advising/Negotiating Bank
The relationship between the buyer and the issuing bank is governed by the terms of the application and agreement for the letter of credit.	The relationship between the advising bank and the seller is strictly defined by the terms of the letter of credit. The advising bank acts only as an intermediary.

Buyer — The relationship between the buyer and the seller is governed by the sales contract. — Seller

The beneficiary might wish to have the advising bank add its **irrevocable promise to pay** to that of the issuing bank. If the advising bank agrees to do so, it becomes the **confirming bank**. An advising bank that has confirmed a letter of credit is legally obligated to pay the beneficiary upon compliance with the terms of the letter of credit. On an **unconfirmed letter of credit**, an advising bank will pay the seller only if there are sufficient funds on deposit in the issuing bank's account.

Letter-of-Credit Cycle. The letter-of-credit cycle merely involves the exchange of documents (and money) through intermediaries. The following steps are the basic steps needed to complete a letter-of-credit cycle (see Exhibit 13).

Step 1. The buyer and seller agree upon the terms of sale. The sales contract dictates that a letter of credit is to be used to finance the transaction.

Step 2. The buyer completes an application for a letter of credit and forwards it to the bank that will issue the letter of credit.

Step 3. The issuing bank then forwards the letter of credit to a correspondent bank in the seller's country.

Step 4. The advising bank relays the letter of credit to the seller.

Step 5. Having received assurance of payment, the seller makes the necessary shipping arrangements.

Step 6. The seller prepares the documents required under the letter of credit and delivers them to the advising bank.

Step 7. The advising bank negotiates the documents. If it finds them in order, it sends them to the issuing bank, and, if named the paying bank, the advising bank pays the seller in accordance with the terms of the letter of credit.

Step 8. The issuing bank, having received the documents, examines them. If they are in order, the issuing bank will charge the buyer's account and send the documents on to the buyer. The issuing bank also will reimburse the advising bank.

Step 9. The buyer receives the documents and picks up the merchandise from the shipper (carrier).

A letter of credit not only shifts the burden of financing to a bank or the money market, but also gives the exporter a bank guarantee that the exporting firm will receive cash or a bank acceptance, once the goods ordered are turned over to a common carrier for shipment to the importer, in accordance with the letter of credit. An importer supplying a letter of credit is usually able to buy at somewhat lower prices than those quoted to open-book-account customers, since the exporter neither carries the burden of financing nor assumes the credit risk. But there are two key points that must be emphasized. First, a letter of

EXHIBIT 13 IMPORT LETTER OF CREDIT CYCLE

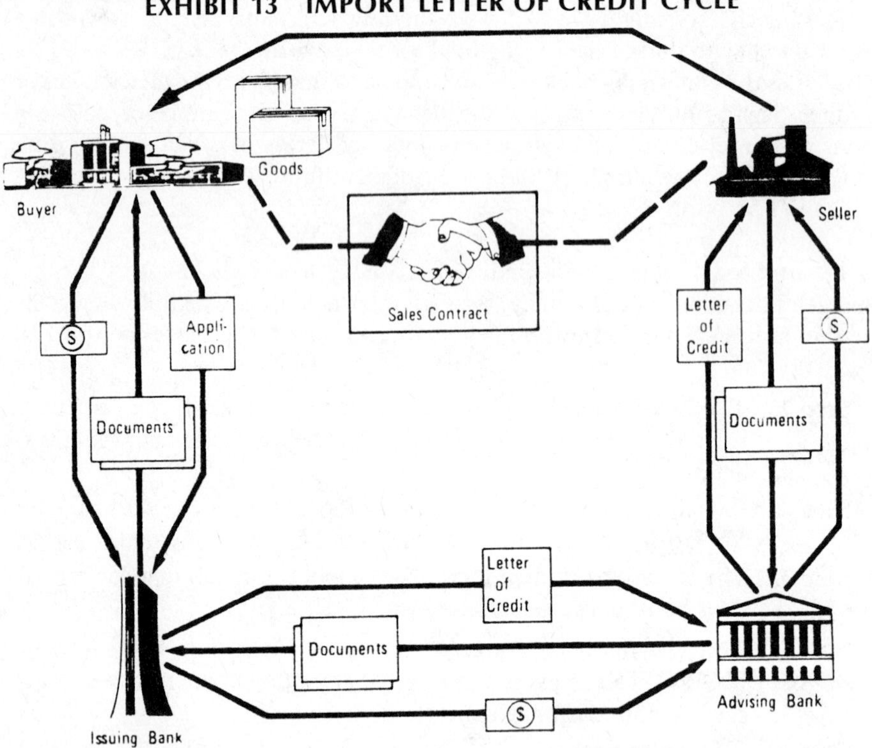

credit guarantees payments to the seller only if the seller complies exactly with the terms of the letter of credit. Second, since banks deal with documents and not merchandise, they can only guarantee to buyers that all the required documents in the letter of credit are in order—banks cannot insure that what is shipped is what the documents describe.

Import and Export Letters of Credit. United States banks usually distinguish between and handle separately import and export letters of credit. When a U.S. bank, on the application of a U.S. importer, issues a commercial letter of credit in favor of an exporter located abroad, it is termed "an import letter of credit." An export letter of credit is one issued by a foreign bank in favor of a U.S. exporter for the account of an importer abroad buying goods in the United States.

Revocable and Irrevocable Letters of Credit. A revocable letter of credit can be canceled by the importer's bank before drafts drawn by the exporter under the letter of credit have been negotiated by the correspondent bank. Banks do not favor revocable letters of credit; some banks refuse to issue them because the banks can become involved in resulting litigation. The correspondent bank, acting as agent for the importer's bank (the credit-issuing bank), assumes no obligation. An irrevocable letter of credit cannot be canceled by the importer's bank for the period specified without the consent of the beneficiary. Exporters generally insist upon irrevocable letters of credit.

Confirmed and Unconfirmed Letters of Credit. When a **correspondent bank** located in the country of the exporter confirms a letter of credit to the exporter by obligating itself to pay or accept the exporter's drafts, the instrument is called a **confirmed letter of credit**. The confirmation binds the correspondent bank to honor drafts drawn under the credit even if the importer's (issuing) bank should refuse or be unable to meet its obligation. An **unconfirmed letter of credit** does not give the exporter this additional security.

Exporters insist on confirmed letters of credit when the foreign issuing bank is not well known. It is obvious that the correspondent bank will confirm only irrevocable letters of credit, since a bank would not guarantee an agreement that might be canceled at will by the issuing bank.

Revolving and Installment Letters of Credit. If an importer maintains a continuous business relation with an exporter and receives repeated shipment of goods, a revolving credit in favor of the exporter is often used. A **revolving letter of credit** assures automatic renewal of the amount of credit when it becomes exhausted at certain specified intervals. The buyer (importer) should be very cautious before providing the seller (exporter) with a revolving letter of credit. The maximum exposure of the buyer (importer) under a revolving letter of credit is not the amount of credit, but the amount of credit multiplied by the number of periods the credit is to revolve. The revolving letter of credit can be issued in irrevocable and revocable form. Revolving letters of credit can be **commulative** or **noncommulative**. In a **commulative letter of credit** the beneficiary is allowed to carry over any amount not drawn upon in previous periods. On the other hand a **noncommulative letter of credit** does not allow the beneficiary to draw amounts during a later period that were not drawn in previous periods. Nearly all revolving letters of credit are noncommulative. Revolving letters of credit are used by companies with repetitive sales or purchases. The most common users are retailers. For example, the importer of sweaters might sell up to $5,000 each month. The importer uses a revolving letter of credit for the amount of $5,000 to revolve monthly. This means that he or she will never have to pay for more than $5,000 a month.

The **installment letter of credit** is similar to a revolving noncommulative letter of credit with one exception, which is that once the seller misses a shipment the credit ceases to be in effect and a new one needs to be opened, or the existing credit reinstated by an amendment. This gives the buyer some control.

Transfers/Assignments of Letters of Credit. All or part of the proceeds of a letter of credit can be assigned to a third party at the instructions of the beneficiary. **Assignment** can be made against any letter of credit, and is often done by importers who maintain representatives abroad. An assignable letter of credit can itself be issued in favor of the foreign representative, who is ordered to buy the goods specified by the importer. When the representative has contracted for the goods on the stipulated terms, he or she assigns the letter of credit to the seller (exporter).

The rights of a letter of credit can be transferred only if the letter is expressly designated as transferable. The transferee then becomes responsible for complying with the letter's terms to acquire payment.

Standby Letters of Credit. A standby letter of credit does not typically involve direct purchase of merchandise or the presentation of title document. If the beneficiary submits documents in accordance with the terms of the letter of credit, the bank must pay regardless of any circumstances. The applicant is legally bound to reimburse the bank. This type of letter of credit is used for (1) payments for merchandise shipped on **open account**; (2) **bid and performance bonds**; (3) **advance payment guarantees**; (4) other financial obligations.

The use of standby letters of credit as bid and performance bonds has increased in recent years, in particular for trade and projects in the Middle East. A clean standby letter of credit is initiated by the seller to guarantee goods or service at the bid price. This letter of credit guarantees the price and specifications of a signed contract and is payable simply against a draft. A standby letter of credit can be used to assure the return of any advance payments, if a contract is terminated, and it serves as a warranty to certify that a project works, once it is completed. This instrument is preferred by buyers to insurance company bonds since it is payable on demand. A standby letter of credit is extremely risky for the seller, since the seller places his or her own money as a guarantee and, at any time, the buyer can cash the standby LC. In addition, standby letters of credit can damage a company's credit rating if the company has too many outstanding, since banks look at this as an impairment of credit. In certain areas of the world, particularly for large projects, standby letters of credit are a condition for bidding or contracting for work by an international firm, and there are no other choices but to use them or lose the business.

Why Use Letters of Credit? Letters of credit are used in a wide variety of circumstances. Certain countries, particularly in the Far East, require that all export trade be conducted on a letter-of-credit basis. Some sellers will sell goods only on a letter-of-credit basis. The key advantage to the seller is that a letter of credit **reduces commercial risk,** whereas a collection requires assuming the commercial risk associated with the buyer, a letter of credit requires assuming only the commercial risk associated with the issuing bank. In both cases, the beneficiary assumes foreign **political risk**. If the letter of credit is confirmed, the relevant commercial risk is that of the confirming bank, and the political risk is domestic. The buyer under a letter of credit also receives some protection. Having the banks examine the documents increases the likelihood of detecting errors. However, it does not insure that the goods actually shipped are of a sufficient quantity or of satisfactory quality as described in the documents.

Another important reason for a buyer without experience in international trade to use a letter of credit is to eliminate delays involved in establishing the buyer's own **credibility**. In fact, this credibility is so important that new importers are generally required to obtain letters of credit because suppliers will not be willing to sell on more liberal terms.

It must be reemphasized that neither a letter of credit nor a collection is a total substitute for good credit judgment. The buyer must trust the seller; a letter of credit will not prevent an exporter from invoicing goods as called for in the credit and shipping goods of a different nature. In addition, the seller needs to understand the political situation in the buyer's country, particularly in the area of foreign exchange.

The key reason exporters ask for confirmation of a letter of credit is to reduce political risk. Another common reason is that the beneficiary is not willing to assume the overseas bank's commerical risk. Finally, if the advising bank is not designated as the paying bank, the beneficiary will not receive funds until the issuing bank has approved the documents. If a domestic bank confirms the credit, however, payment will be made upon approval of the documents at the domestic bank.

AUTHORITY TO PURCHASE. The authority to purchase (**AP**), or **authority to negotiate**, is a letter or cable sent by the importer's bank to its branch, agent, or correspondent abroad, instructing the agent to buy an exporter's draft drawn on an importer. The authority to purchase, used mainly in Far Eastern trade, shifts the burden of financing from the exporter to the importer's bank. Its operation is illustrated by the following example.

An importer in Asia has bought goods from an exporter in San Francisco, the contract stipulating payment by a 90-day draft on the importer with an authority to purchase. The importer applies to the bank for an authority to purchase, specifying the amount, expiration date, shipping documents, and other conditions. When the bank approves the application, the importer signs a **letter of guarantee**, in which the importer is obligated to accept and pay the draft, pledging the documents conveying title to the goods as collateral security. The bank then instructs its agent in San Francisco to buy the exporter's draft drawn in compliance with the stated conditions. The San Francisco agent sends a notice (advice of authority to purchase) to the exporter, listing the terms on which the draft on the importer will be purchased. After the exporter has delivered the goods to the shipping company, the draft is presented with the required documents to the agent and payment is received. The authority to purchase thus enables the exporter to sell the draft immediately without using up a portion of the line of credit at the bank.

In contrast to the letter of credit, which gives rise to **bankers' acceptances**, the authority to purchase gives rise to a **trade acceptance**, with the importer as accepter. Although under both methods the exporter is only secondarily liable, that is, only if the accepter should fail to pay, it is obvious that an exporter is less likely to be called on to pay a dishonored bank acceptance than a trade acceptance. The exporter may, however, be relieved from liability by being authorized to endorse the draft on the importer with the words "without recourse." Thus, if the importer (drawee) refuses to accept or pay the draft, the exporter (drawer) cannot be called on to refund the money received from its sale. But authorities to purchase authorizing the exporter to endorse without recourse are rarely issued.

The authority to purchase can be revocable or irrevocable. In a revocable authority to purchase, the issuing bank has the right to cancel the authorization given to its agent to buy the exporter's draft. In such circumstance the agent's advice of authority to purchase contains a clause stipulating that the authority can be canceled by giving notice to the exporter.

REFERENCES

ABA, *International Banking,* 4th ed., Peter K. Oppenheim, Washington, D.C., 1983.

Baughn, William H., and Mandich, Donald R., *The International Banking Handbook,* Homewood, IL: Dow Jones Irwin, 1983.

Coninx, Raymond G.F., *Foreign Exchange Today,* New York: Wiley, 1978.

Davis, Steven I., *The Management Function in International Banking,* New York: Halsted, 1979.

———, *The Eurobank: Its Origins, Management and Outlook,* New York: Macmillan, 1976.

Davis, Steven I., *The Eurobank,* New York: Wiley, 1976.

Deak, N., and Celusak, J., *International Banking,* Englewood Cliffs, NJ: Prentice-Hall, 1984.

Donaldson, T.H., *Lending in International Commercial Banking,* New York: Halsted, 1979.

Dufey, Gunter, and Giddy, Ian H., *The International Money Market,* Englewood Cliffs, NJ: Prentice-Hall, 1978.

Eiteman, David K., and Stonehill, Arthur I., *Multinational Business Finance,* 2d ed., Reading, MA: Addison-Wesley, 1982.

Frowen, Stephen F. (ed.), *A Framework of International Banking, Survey,* U.K.: Guilford Educational Press, 1979.

George, Abraham M., and Giddy, Ian H., *International Finance Handbook,* New York: Wiley, 1983.

Goodman, Laurie, "The Pricing of Syndicated Eurocurrency Credits," *Federal Reserve Bank of New York Quarterly Review* (Summer 1980).

Guttentag, Jack M., and Herring, Richard J., *The Current Crisis in International Lending,* Washington, DC: The Brookings Institution, 1985.

Harfield, Henry, *Bank Credits and Acceptances,* 5th ed., New York: Ronald Press, 1974.

Hayes, Douglas A., *Bank Lending Policies: Domestic and International,* 2nd ed., Ann Arbor: University of Michigan Press, 1977.

Hudson, Nigel R.L., *Money and Exchange Dealing in International Banking,* New York: Halsted, 1979.

Johnson, G.G., and Abrams, Richard K., *Aspects of the International Banking Safety Net,* Washington, DC: International Monetary Fund, 1983.

Khoury, Sarkis, *Dynamics of International Banking,* New York: Praeger, 1980.

Kubarych, Roger M., *Foreign Exchange Markets in the United States,* New York: Federal Reserve Bank of New York, 1978.

Mandich, Donald R. (ed.), *Foreign Exchange Trading Techniques and Controls,* New York: American Bankers Association, 1976.

Mathis, John (ed.), *Offshore Lending by U.S. Commercial Banks,* 2nd ed., Philadelphia: Robert Morris Associates, 1981.

Park, Yoon, and Zwick, Jack, *International Banking in Theory and Practice,* Reading, MA: Addison-Wesley, 1985.

Riehl, Heinz, and Rodriguez, Rita M., *Foreign Exchange and Money Markets—Managing Foreign and Domestic Currency Operations,* New York: McGraw-Hill, 1983.

Roussakis, Emmanual N., *International Banking—Principles and Practices,* New York: Praeger, 1983.

Savona, Paolo, and Sutija, George, *Eurodollars and International Banking,* New York: Macmillan, 1985.

Stigum, Marcia, *The Money Market, Newly Revised,* Homewood, IL: Dow Jones-Irwin, 1983.

Walmsley, Julian, *A Dictionary of International Finance,* Westport, CN: Greenwood Press, 1979.

20

INTERNATIONAL INVESTMENT, DIVERSIFICATION, AND GLOBAL MARKETS

CONTENTS

20

INTERNATIONAL INVESTMENT, DIVERSIFICATION, AND GLOBAL MARKETS

Christopher Nowakowski
Philip Ralli

THE EXPLOSION IN CROSS-BORDER INVESTING

Global investment management has been a high-growth and high-prestige development since the late 1970s. This has fostered a wide network of relationships among market participants in relevant countries. Private portfolios based in Europe have long been forced to invest internationally to achieve adequate diversification and growth, attributes that are not available locally. The United States and Japan on the other hand have been net beneficiaries of these moves for reasons of market size and attractiveness. It is only in the last decade that pension funds based in the countries with the largest domestic capitalizations have begun to invest a significant proportion of their assets abroad. The U.S. component is the most suitable to study because of size, rigor of reporting requirements, and availability of statistics. The lessons apply across other participants in the investment process, including insurance companies, mutual funds, individuals and, in some cases, to quasi-public bodies.

MARKET SIZE. It is impossible to know how much private wealth has been invested across national frontiers either directly or through tax havens. The figure must be in the hundreds of billions of dollars. On the institutional side, participants include **pension funds** (see Exhibit 1), **insurance companies**, and **mutual funds**. For the United States their approximate sizes are respectively \$15.7 billion (Intersec 1984 estimate), \$26.8 billion (Life houses bonds only; American Council of Life Assurance, 4% of assets), and \$2.2 billion (Open end funds, December 1983).

EVOLUTION IN THE ACTUARIAL AND REGULATORY CONSTRAINTS. There is tension between the regulatory bodies concerning outflow on the capital account of the balance of payments and the potential consequences of cur-

EXHIBIT 1 GROWTH AND APPROXIMATE SIZE OF DOMESTIC AND NONDOMESTIC PENSION ASSETS[a]

	Total Assets 1984 (est.) ($ billions)	Assets Overseas 1984 (est.) ($ billions)	Overseas/ Total (%)	Assets Overseas 1974 (est.) ($ billions)
United Kingdom	114	20.5	18	1.5
United States	714	15.7	2	0.5
Netherlands	77	6.2	8	1.0
Japan	64	5.0	8	—
Switzerland	55	4.4	8	1.0
Canada	59	4.0	7	1.5
Australia	25	1.0	4	—
West Germany	24	0.7	3	—
France	7	0.1	2	—
South Africa	10	—	—	—
Other countries	54	4.3	8	0.5
Total	1203	61.9	5	6.0

[a]The figures in this exhibit are Intersec Research estimates and vary in reliability from country to country. The Social Security assets of the countries and any unsegregated book reserves where these are used are not included. Funded plans of state employees, however, are included when known.

rency mismatch with liabilities, and the desire of trustees to raise returns and reduce risks. The pendulum is currently swinging toward more freedom. At present the United States and the United Kingdom do not have any formal constraints on asset allocation, beyond "prudence." On the other hand, Canada, Japan, and most of Continental Europe fix a maximum foreign exposure, typically at 10%, but this is being relaxed progressively. Hong Kong (55%) and Belgium (30%) are the leaders in percentage diversification, whereas South Africa and the Scandinavian countries currently prohibit investments abroad; in France there is a dissuasive investment currency premium. The present global average of foreign exposure is 5%: only the United Kingdom, at 18% overseas, is in double-digit figures.

On the fixed interest side it is clear that a foreign bond can never be treated like a bond in the base currency (cash flow projections, immunization) because there is an unquantifiable **currency risk**. Even **Eurocurrency bonds** in the base currency entail a small risk of a payments blockage, so that it would be imprudent to consider them as interchangeable with domestic corporates. The Swiss authorities even set a formal limit on holdings of pension funds in international Swiss franc bonds. Finally, withholding taxes can make cross-border purchases of government bonds less attractive, although the United States, France, and West Germany abandoned such barriers in 1984.

The historical landmarks in the United States bearing on international diversification were, first, the repeal of the **Interest Equalization Tax** in 1974, which taxed income payments from abroad and, second, the **Employee Retirement Income Security Act (ERISA)**, which was enacted in 1975. Prudence and diversification were enjoined on trustees but no allocation limits were set. The Department of Labor has accepted a portfolio theory of prudence so that a trustee does not have to be able to justify every single security so long as it fits into the risk profile of the whole. Indeed many believe that international diversification is the most powerful implementation of the diversification guideline.

THE THEORETICAL CASE

There are two legs to the theoretical case: expected return and the expected variability of return. (Refer to Section 22 for a full explanation of why these concepts are important, especially the second.) The fundamental motivation is that the home market is not necessarily the most lucrative. Moreover, ex post simulation (see Exhibit 2) shows that a U.S. investor would have improved return and reduced risk over the last 10 years if he or she had invested in the next two largest markets (Japan and the United Kingdom): If this investor had bought the Capital International Perspective's EAFE (**Europe Australia Far East) Index**, however, he or she would have reduced risk but also given up return, albeit marginally.

It is now possible to examine real experiences of managers rather than index simulations. One of the fears often voiced is that foreign markets are not as fair nor as liquid as the United States; so that one should factor a penalty into the benefits discussed under "the theoretical case" for:

- Increased dealing costs (commissions and spreads)
- Barriers to investment in certain securities
- Manipulation by insiders
- Potential limits to repatriation, especially of profits

A priori, the explosion in **cross-border investment** should by itself be improving problems such as these. A posteriori, the median fund of InterSec's U.S. institutions reference measurement universe outperformed the EAFE index since 1981. This period includes a market decline, followed by a rise. The real problem for U.S. diversifiers (but the bonanza for European diversifiers) turned out to be the strength of the dollar.

EXHIBIT 2 PERFORMANCE OF SELECTED SHARE MARKETS[a]

Annual compound rate of return in U.S. dollar terms, dividends included for the 10 years ending December 1984.

S&P 500	CIP EAFE	CIP Japan	CIP United Kingdom	CIP West Germany	CIP Australia
+14.75%	+14.03%	+17.54%	+20.73%	+7.12%	+11.96%

[a]CIP is an abbreviation for Capital International Perspective.

Inasmuch as a fund's base is in an economy with faster (or slower) than average growth, or with a more attractive than average stock market, international diversification will decrease (or increase) expected return. Because Japan has grown faster than the United States over the last decade, the payoff for a U.S. investor deciding in 1975 to diversify into that country was positive whereas a Japanese-based investor would have done better to remain at home. Because, however, few people would be confident in predicting whether the U.S. market will underperform the Japanese market in the next 10 years, it is important that diversification be justified (on the null hypothesis that their expected returns are equal) because of risk reduction (see discussion that follows). But the hope of increasing returns is surely the prime motivation.

A picture from **wave theory**: If there is an interference pattern between two or more waves, the resultant wave pattern on the pond may be more or less choppy than the individual waves, depending on how much the interferences are in- or out-of-phase. So it is for a portfolio: The less stocks move together (the lower their covariance), the smaller will be the standard deviation of returns of the portfolio as a whole. The reasonable expectation that the correlation of returns between randomly selected pairs of securities is on average less when they are from different countries than when they come from the same national market has been verified empirically. For example, Solnik (1974) has a graph (see Exhibit 3) which compares the risk of a portfolio of national *versus* international securities varies with the number of securities held.

EXHIBIT 3 PLOT OF PORTFOLIO RISK AS PERCENTAGE OF SINGLE SECURITY RISK AS NUMBER OF SECURITIES IN PORTFOLIO INCREASES

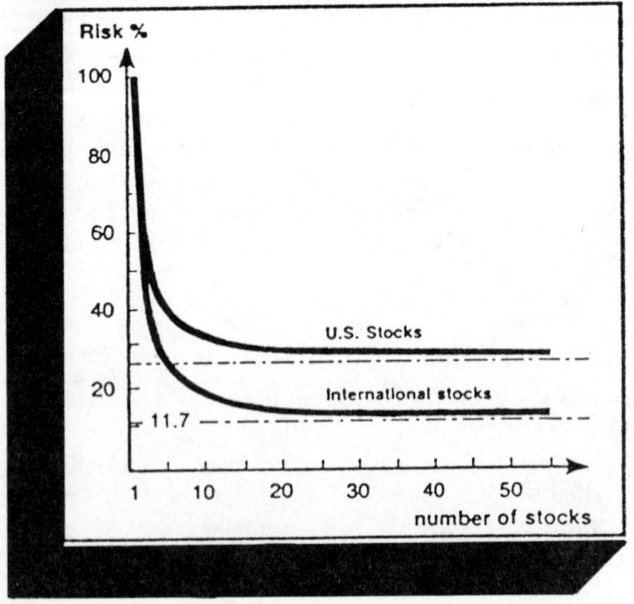

Source: B. Solnik, *Financial Analysts Journal,* July 1974.

THE IMPORTANCE OF CORRELATION. Let

sd/a = standard deviation of returns for security a
sd/b = standard deviation of returns for security b
R = correlation of returns of a and b
^ = raised to the power
* = multiply

then the standard deviation of returns of an equally weighted portfolio of a and b ($sd/a+b$) is related to sd/a and sd/b according to the following formula (see W. Sharpe, 1984):

$$\text{Variance} = (sd/a+b)^2 = 0.25*(sd/a)^2 + 0.25*(sd/b)^2 + 0.5*R*sd/a*sd/b$$

By inspection of the preceding formula, if $sd/a = sd/b$ and $R = 0$ (i.e., a and b are independent variables), then a portfolio of (a) and (b) will have a variance of 0.5 (that means a standard deviation of 0.7) compared with just holding (a). Moreover, if we already hold (a) and are thinking of adding either (b) or (c), where

$$sd/b = sd/c$$

then it is clearly possible to minimize (sd/portfolio) by choosing that security which has the lower correlation with (a).

This is the well-known diversification effect. Unfortunately it is computationally arduous to calculate the (R) of every pair of securities in a portfolio and to combine them into a variance estimate for the portfolio. Therefore a simplifying method is applied by calculating the beta of each security relative to its national index where

$$\textbf{Beta} = \text{R}* \frac{(sd/\text{security})}{(sd/\text{index})}$$

where R is the coefficient of correlation of returns of the security to the index's returns. Combining the betas of securities from the same country into a portfolio beta, the variance (V) formula becomes

$$V = (sd/\text{portfolio})^2 = (\text{beta}^2 * (sd/\text{index})^2) \text{ plus an error term}$$

With various assumptions, the error term is found to be inversely proportional to the square of the number of securities in the portfolio and therefore to tend to zero as that number of securities increases (see, for example, Elton and Gruber, 1981). So the conclusion is that

Portfolio variance = market-related variance + diversifiable risk

Two Layers of Diversification. At a given level of "beta," therefore, the variance of portfolio returns tends toward a constant multiple of the index variance. The beauty of **international diversification** is that whereas betas are estimated by regression onto the national index, there remains an interference effect, because the correlation betwen market indexes is substantially less than 1. In this way, a first-order diversification benefit—whereby the intramarket "diversifiable risk" is minimized so that the variance of return approximates the index variance at the accepted level of beta in local currency terms—can be distinguished from a second-order benefit, whereby through the low correlations between national indexes the variance of an international portfolio is less than the weighted variances of its constituents.

To summarize:

One-country portfolio variance = market-related variance + diversifiable risk

International portfolio variance = weighted variances of constituent national portfolios + internationally diversifiable risk

If there exist foreign markets either with lower variances of return than the home market or with such a combination of higher variance and low correlation of returns as yields a lower resultant variance (according to our formula), then a refusal to invest across borders implies the acceptance of some avoidable variability of returns, which can be termed *inefficiency*.

International Diversification of Bonds. A similar argument concerning risk and return can be extended to bonds. Because, however, the nominal yield to maturity is a first approximation of the expected return of a bond, the null hypothesis that we expect returns on two markets to be equal is more difficult to justify when the difference in nominal yields between two countries is large. A second approximation would involve a guess as to future exchange rates, but this has become a notorious mine field. At the time of writing a Swiss investor whose government bond yields 5% can comfortably diversify into U.S. Treasury bonds yielding 11% (he or she is at the same time reducing risk and increasing return), whereas a U.S. investor contemplating the converse operation will surely be reducing his or her risk, but giving up return in exchange, so that this investor must weigh how much expected return he or she is prepared to sacrifice.

INTERMARKET CORRELATIONS. A matrix can be calculated that shows the correlation of investment return between pairs of international market indexes over a given period. Exhibit 4 shows squared correlations between pairs of indexes for bonds and shares. Squaring masks negative correlations that can be seen in past studies, and are very suitable to reducing variability. It is, however, normal for a U.S. investor to expect a positive correlation, because a recession in America is unlikely to be accompanied by a boom elsewhere, so that

EXHIBIT 4 SQUARED CORRELATION OF INDEXES FOR JANUARY 1975 TO DECEMBER 1984 PERIOD

Data Base: Capital International Indexes
Expressed In U.S. Dollars, Dividends Included

INDEX	S&P	JAP	U.K.	GER	CAN	FRA	SWI	AUS	NETH	SIN	H-K	SWED	GOLD	EAFE	WORLD
S&P	100.0														
JAPN	9.5	100.0													
U.K.	9.5	12.2	100.0												
GERM	11.2	24.6	18.2	100.0											
CAND	47.3	7.9	22.2	8.2	100.0										
FRAN	16.4	17.7	26.6	22.8	18.6	100.0									
SWIZ	23.0	25.8	30.8	57.7	19.7	31.9	100.0								
AUST	19.6	13.8	21.3	4.7	38.3	17.3	19.7	100.0							
NETH	36.2	18.8	37.1	47.5	25.5	27.2	50.8	13.2	100.0						
SING	19.6	15.2	34.7	15.4	13.9	13.7	29.0	18.0	28.4	100.0					
H-K	7.5	14.8	20.2	15.3	7.0	7.8	18.1	12.5	26.2	29.1	100.0				
SWED	7.3	5.7	2.6	6.2	6.8	2.0	8.7	6.4	6.2	3.7	5.2	100.0			
GOLD	2.7	5.5	1.4	8.6	12.3	8.8	13.2	13.4	6.0	0.8	2.3	0.6	100.0		
EAFE	25.2	68.9	56.4	47.7	26.6	41.2	56.4	32.3	53.1	37.6	33.2	10.1	9.9	100.0	
WRLD	79.1	39.0	43.9	32.1	53.5	35.1	48.3	35.2	57.4	36.0	22.0	11.4	8.9	69.9	100.0

Data Base: Intersec Bond Indexes . . . US$ Terms, Coupons Included

INDEX	ML-80	US-E	YEN-D	YEN-E	UK-D	DM-D	DM-E	CAD-D	CHF-E	NGL-D	NNA	WORLD
ML-80	100.0											
US-E	79.5	100.0										
YEN-D	5.7	7.4	100.0									
YEN-E	5.0	6.5	95.7	100.0								
UK-D	8.8	13.2	9.3	8.7	100.0							
DM-D	15.0	11.5	24.1	23.8	14.2	100.0						
DM-E	17.2	12.7	24.2	23.8	14.5	96.0	100.0					
CAD-D	52.8	55.6	7.0	6.3	12.6	14.3	14.5	100.0				
CHF-E	15.8	13.2	25.7	25.0	13.3	78.6	73.0	15.0	100.0			
NGL-D	17.9	14.6	23.7	22.6	14.8	88.6	88.3	15.7	66.3	100.0		
NNA	17.1	16.3	60.0	60.5	31.3	77.0	79.2	17.5	67.2	75.1	100.0	
WORLD	49.2	54.0	47.4	46.8	31.7	63.8	66.4	43.6	59.0	65.3	83.5	100.0

Notes: −E = Euro; −D = Domestic; NNA = Non North American; CHF = Swiss Francs; NGL = Dutch Guilers; CAD = Canadian Dollars

Source: Intersec Research Corp, Stamford, Ct.

it would be implausible to have an expected future negative correlation built into an asset allocation model, except possibly for gold bullion. The squared correlation gives the amount of movement in the foreign index explained by movements in the home index. On inspection all the markets tabulated except Canada and the Netherlands have a squared correlation of less than 0.3 with the Standard & Poor's Index; these correlations are in general lower than those that are found between subindexes of national markets (not shown)—especially between continents: On the other hand, certain neighboring countries such as West Germany and the Netherlands have a close relationship (especially in the bond table).

It is not necessary to assert that a particular market will in the future have a low correlation with the U.S. market. It is sufficient to make a case that stocks constituting an international portfolio will be less likely to move together than those in a one-country portfolio over a long period. In the absence therefore of a strong conviction that the home market will be the best, and because it is unlikely (but possible) for a U.S. portfolio to have a lower variability of return than an internationally diversified one, it is more efficient for an investor to choose an international portfolio with less variability (risk) at a given level of expected return.

THE MINIMUM VARIANCE PORTFOLIO. The variance formula given above was for an equally-weighted portfolio. If the weighting of the home market (portfolio *a*) is *p* and abroad (portfolio *b*) is therefore (1–*p*), the formula becomes

$$V = p\hat{\ }2 * (sd/a)2 + (1-p)2 * (sd/b)2 + (2 * p * (1-p) * (sd/a) * (sd/b) * R)$$

This is a quadratic equation in *p*, which can be shown by calculus to be at a minimum when $dV/dp = 0$; that is, when

$$p = \frac{(sd/b)2 - ((sd/a) * (sd/b) * R)}{(sd/a)2 + (sd/b)2 - (2 * (sd/a) * (sd/b) * R)}$$

THE THEORETICAL CASE REVISITED: INDEX FUND SIMULATIONS. If one has access to a database of exchange rates, risk-free rates, and the price-and-income histories of indexes, it is possible to create theoretical histories of funds using different combinations of assets. Exhibits 5 through 8 give results of different simulations from three different points of view: the United States, the United Kingdom, and Japan. One series is of equity index funds, the second is of bond index funds, and the third is a balanced 50/50 fund from a U.S. point-of-viewpoint only. For all the simulations, the foreign component has been allowed to vary from 0 to 100% with the balance being invested in the base index. The distribution of the foreign component markets has been

EXHIBIT 5 SIMULATION OF EFFECT OF FOREIGN DIVERSIFICATION ON THE MEAN ABSOLUTE COMPOUND RETURNS OF INDEX FUNDS BASED IN UNITED STATES, UNITED KINGDOM, AND JAPAN FOR 10 YEARS ENDING DECEMBER 1984, (*a*) SHARE FUNDS, (*b*) BOND FUNDS

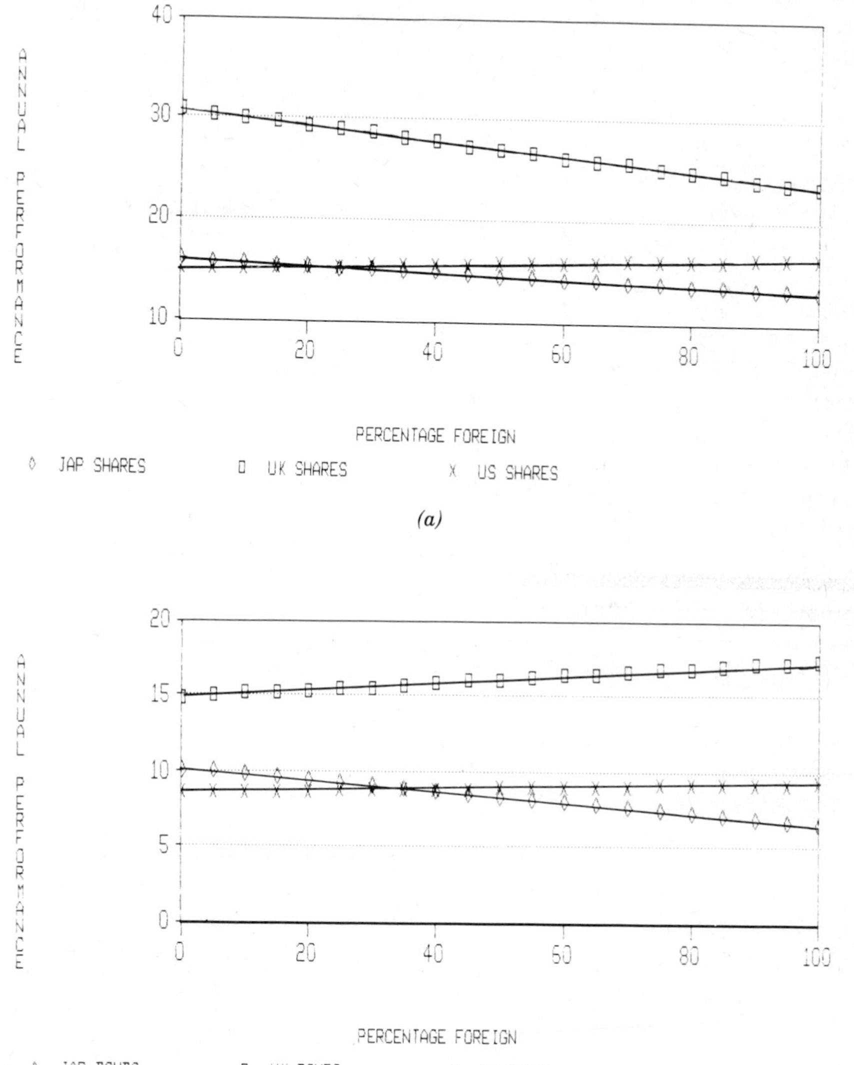

(*a*)

(*b*)

Source: Intersec Research Database.

EXHIBIT 6 SIMULATION OF EFFECT OF FOREIGN DIVERSIFICATION ON THE STANDARD DEVIATION OF ANNUAL RETURNS OF SHARE FUNDS BASED IN UNITED STATES, UNITED KINGDOM, AND JAPAN FOR 10 YEARS ENDING DECEMBER 1984, (a) SHARE FUNDS, (*b*) BOND FUNDS

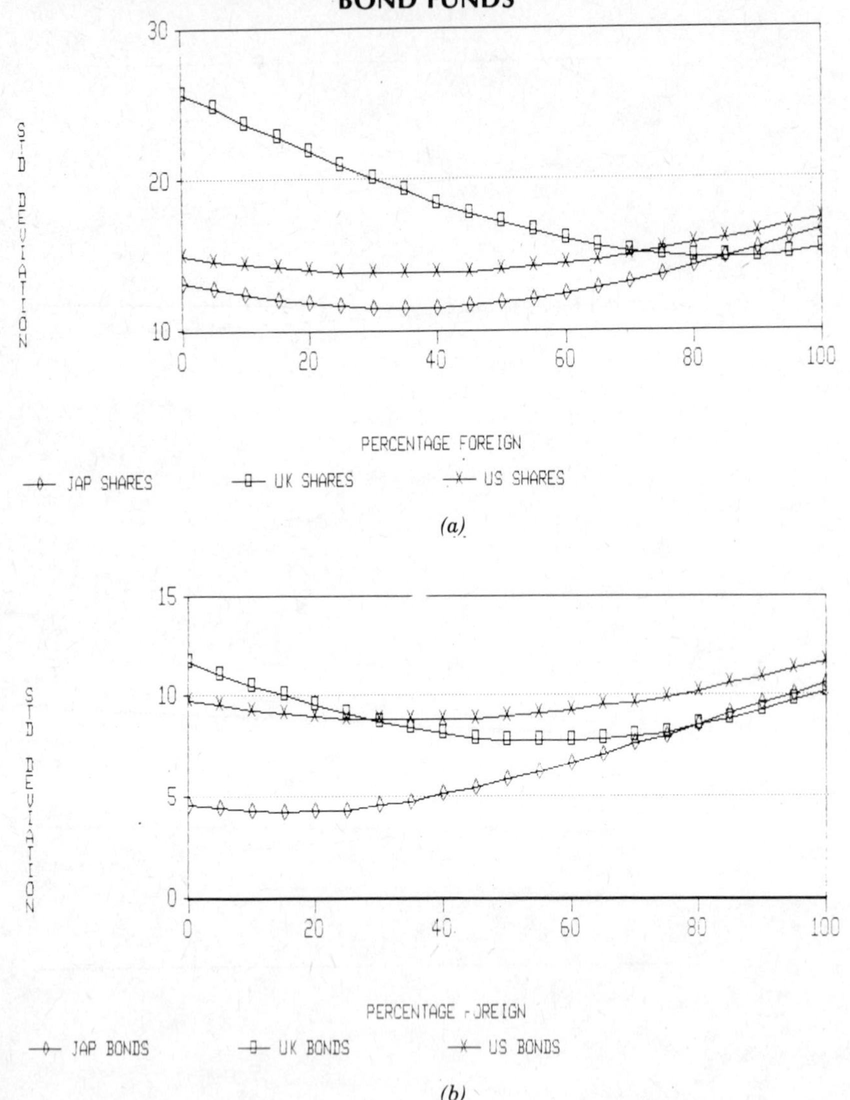

Source: Intersec Research Database.

EXHIBIT 7 SIMULATION OF EFFECT OF FOREIGN DIVERSIFICATION ON BOTH THE AVERAGE ANNUAL RETURN AND THE STANDARD DEVIATION OF RETURNS OF A 50% SHARE/50% BOND BALANCED FUND BASED IN THE UNITED STATES FOR 10 YEARS ENDING DECEMBER 1984

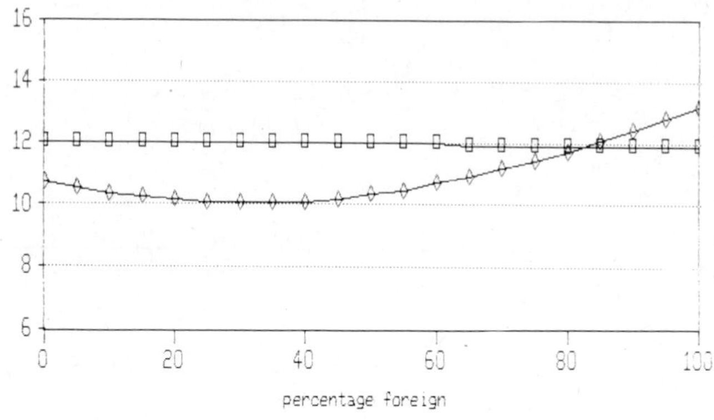

Source: Intersec Research Database.

weighted for equity indexes by market capitalizations, for bond indexes by GNPs. The weighting was done at the start of 1975 with no rebalancing thereafter. The number of foreign markets was 10 for the equity simulation and 6 for the bonds; dividends after withholding taxes were reinvested in the same market. The salient conclusions are:

1. Returns vary as a linear function whereas the standard deviation is parabolic
2. All international funds have lower variability of returns than one-country portfolios
3. Even a small international diversification has a noticeable effect on this variability
4. There is no assurance that internationalization will increase returns

From Exhibit 6 minimum variance foreign proportions can be read off: these vary between 20% for Japanese bonds to an unrealizable-in-practice 85% for U.K. shares. There is therefore no "golden number" to establish the benchmark ideal foreign diversification for all participants. It is clear that the choice of January 1975 as a start year for the simulations found the U.K. market in a very volatile (but potentially profitable) state. Surprisingly, from Exhibit 7, it is apparent that for the period the foreign proportion of a balanced fund made no difference to mean annual return. This is in fact a chance result where a period

EXHIBIT 8 PLOT OF RISK AGAINST RETURN FOR AN AMERICAN SHARE INDEX FUND AND AN AMERICAN BOND INDEX FUND AS THE PERCENTAGE OF FOREIGN INVESTMENTS IS VARIED

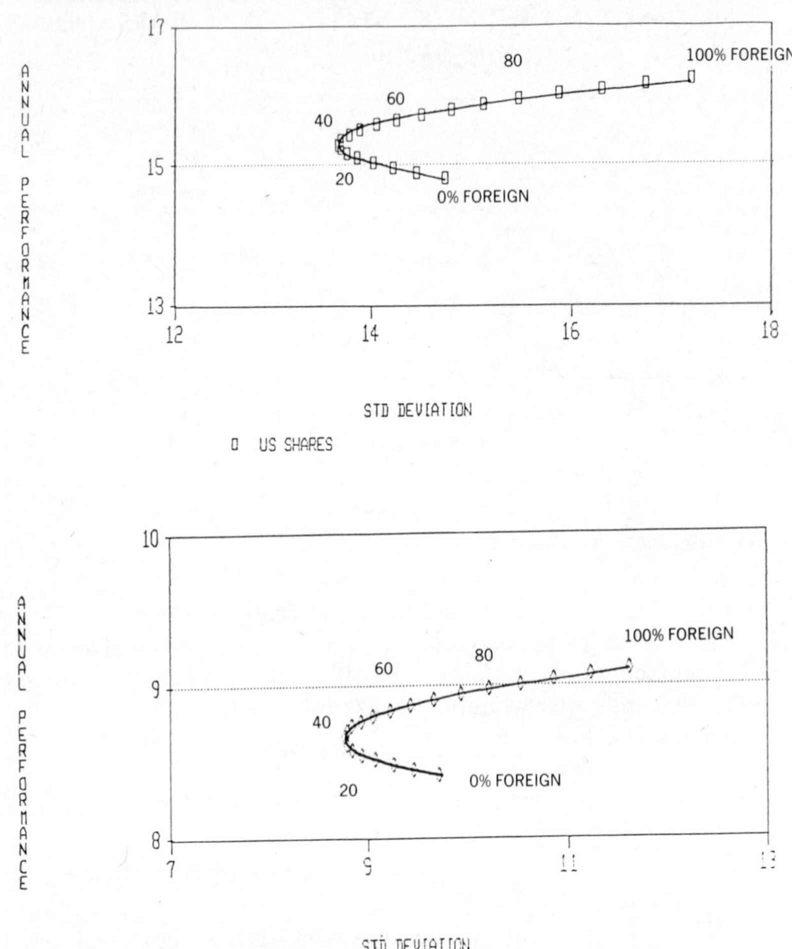

of overperformance (1975–1979) is exactly balanced by one of underperformance (1980–1984). The parabolic relationship of standard deviation and return is very evident from Exhibit 8, which plots the relationship over 10 years for various combinations of domestic and foreign/bonds and shares.

REASONS TO HOPE FOR INCREASED RETURNS. Whether the long-term expectation in 1985 is that returns from abroad to U.S. investors should exceed the home market is debatable. The preceding simulations would seem to plead for a zero expected excess return from diversification. But it has been argued (e.g., Errunza, 1983) that less liquid markets in less mature economies are priced with a greater risk premium which should give a better return than the United States, provided that the world economy continues to grow. A tentative suggestion might be that the portfolio weighting used by the simulation methodology applied in our examples (weighting by market capitalization or GNP) is not the most efficient—it overweights sluggish Europe—and should be replaced by some other weighting based on the maturity of economies.

PRACTICAL RESULTS OF INTERNATIONAL DIVERSIFICATION

THE FIRST PLUNGE. The first institutions to go international often need a little cajoling! In the United States in 1974, Morgan Guaranty Trust cut the Gordian knot by notifying its 550 pension clients that unless specifically directed otherwise it would switch a portion of the U.S. equities under their discretionary management into an international equity **commingled fund**. In Japan, where plan sponsors have no say in the investment decisions of their pension fund, the trust banks and life companies were able to move quickly once enabling legislation was enacted. Once the first institutions have taken the plunge, there is a bandwagon effect. We analyze in the following paragraphs some actual results from 1981 to 1984.

BENCHMARKS. At the start of any discussion of performance, it is important to agree on the benchmarks. A truly international fund such as one might imagine an United Nations agency running, could be measured against an international benchmark. But the most interesting benchmark for any fund clearly domiciled in one currency remains its home indexes (equity, fixed interest, cash) especially when seeking to maximize efficiency by a small measure of international diversification. The first question is always "did we do well to go international?" (i.e., comparison with home index). The question "should our investment manager have done better?" is secondary (i.e., comparison with a world index). For the most part therefore the accounting and performance measurement of the international portion is not very different from the domestic portion of a fund, and should be handled in the context of the whole. The World, EAFE (Europe Asia and Far East) and national indexes of Capital International have become a de facto standard for cross-border equities, because they are uniformly calculated and capitalization-weighted. No one, however, seems to use the **Capital International Index** for a home market. For bonds, there are indexes published by Salomon Brothers and Intersec Research Corp., but international fixed-interest performance measurement is in its infancy.

The Bottom Line: Actual Performance Records. Intersec Research has tracked a non U.S. equity universe representing, at end 1984, $6 billion managed by 54 different international managers. Four charts (Exhibits 9 to 12) give a statistical breakdown of the past 4 years' performance histories. Exhibits 9 and 10 show the results of the universe in U.S. dollar terms for each of the past quarter, 1 year, 2 years, 3 years, and 4 years. The first figure gives quartile ranges and the second a frequency distribution. The results are annualized, except for the last quarter. The return of certain benchmarks is indicated also. Virtually no one succeeded in matching the 10.7% return per annum of the S&P 500 index over 4 years, but the median fund did succeed in beating the EAFE index of 6.6% per annum; the absolute range of returns (−3% to +11%) is sizable, but not markedly different than between domestic advisers. But there was a sufficient latitude, it would seem, for managers over the past 4 years to make good and bad decisions!

Currency Impact. The problem for everyone was the strength of the dollar. Exhibit 11 breaks down the information given in Exhibit 9 for the non-U.S. equity universe into contributions from the local markets and from reported currency losses. Interestingly, whereas the median currency loss over the 4 years was a devastating 8.7% per annum, the range of currency losses between the best and the worst fund is very tight indeed. One concludes that over the past 4 years, currency movements bothered all managers about equally; or, more charitably, that the dollar rise so dominated the scene that intra-European variations were insignificant in comparison, whereas there was no added value in guessing that the yen would be the most attractive non-American currency

EXHIBIT 9 TOTAL FUND RETURNS—U.S. $ (NON-U.S. EQUITY UNIVERSE)

Median fund results

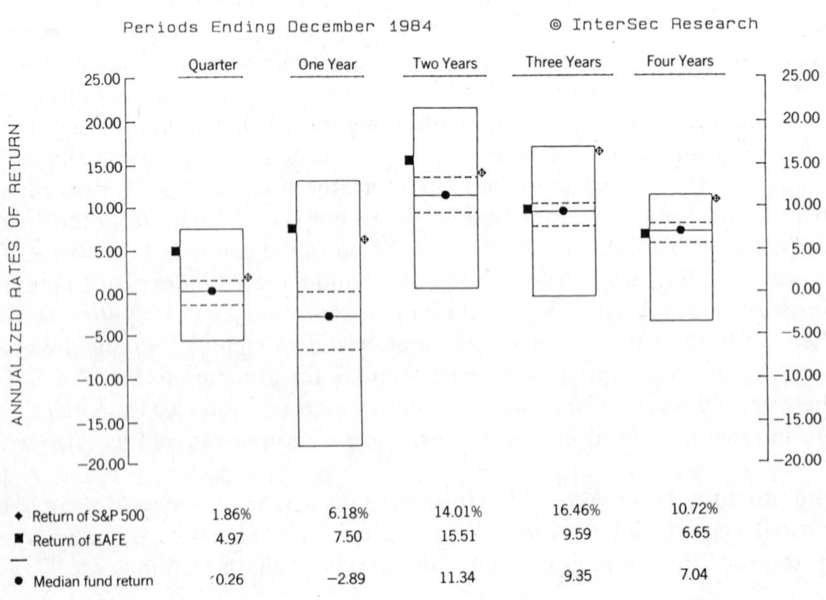

EXHIBIT 10 FREQUENCY DISTRIBUTION TOTAL FUND RETURNS—U.S. $ (NON-U.S. EQUITY UNIVERSE)

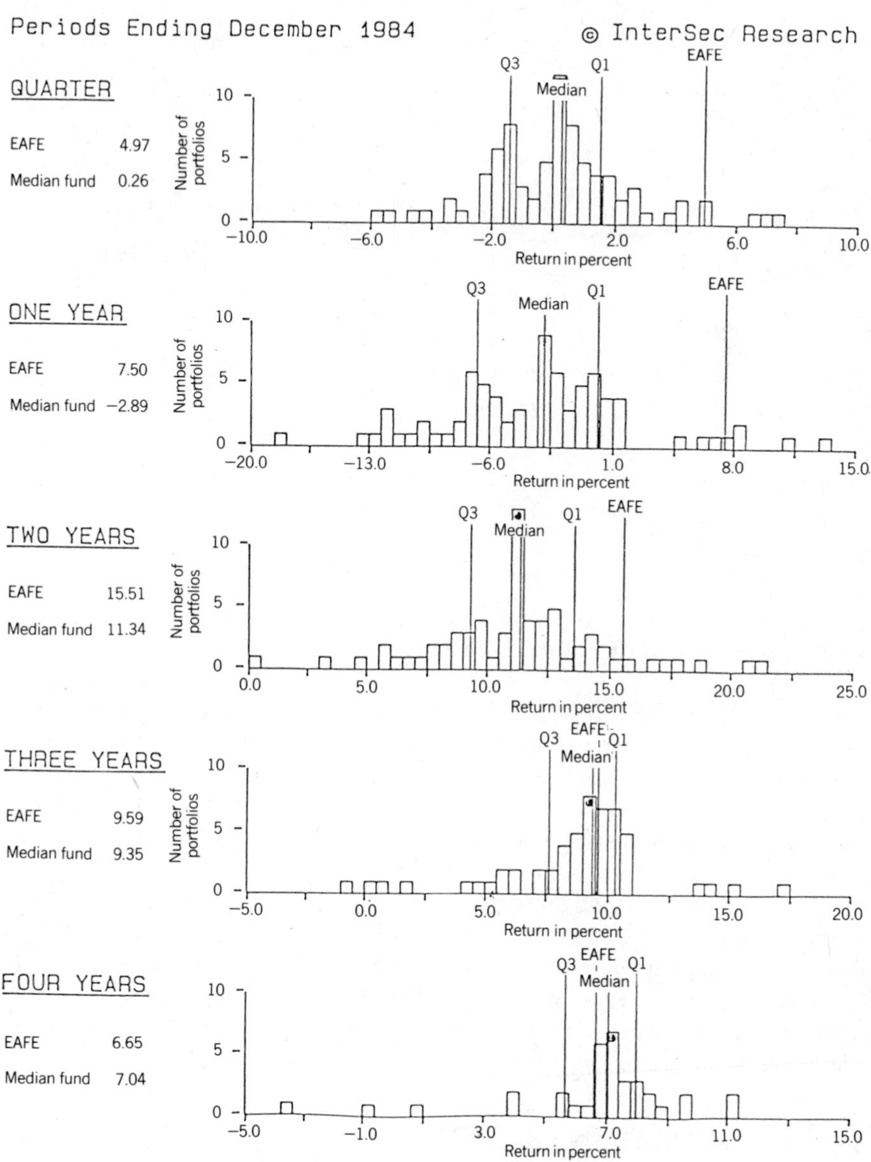

EXHIBIT 11 ANALYSIS OF YOUR NON-NORTH AMERICAN EQUITY RETURNS BREAKDOWN OF U.S. DOLLAR RETURNS: LOCAL MARKET VERSUS CURRENCY

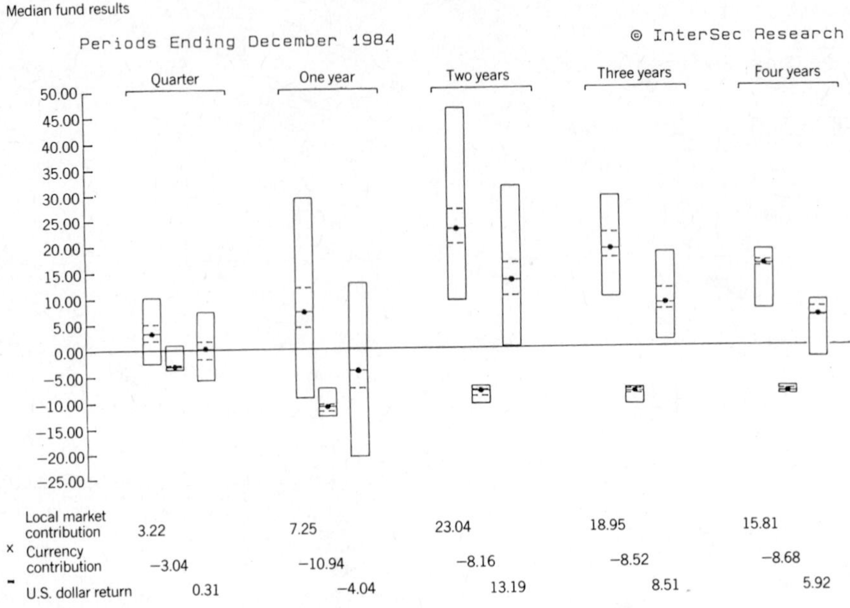

	Quarter	One year	Two years	Three years	Four years
Local market contribution	3.22	7.25	23.04	18.95	15.81
× Currency contribution	−3.04	−10.94	−8.16	−8.52	−8.68
= U.S. dollar return	0.31	−4.04	13.19	8.51	5.92

On the other hand, returns before currency losses, at 15.8% per annum over the 4 years, were well ahead of the S&P Index.

Risk Reduction. Exhibit 12 charts the distribution of beta's versus the S&P 500 for Intersec's universe. All the international funds had historical beta's significantly below one over 4 years, the average being just 0.60. Over 1 year, however, half the funds actually experienced beta's above one, which shows that the risk-reduction effect is not a mathematical necessity but an observation of the way markets have tended to vary in practice.

The conclusion is that there was a diversification benefit; that returns in original currencies were higher than the U.S. market; but that the wild card of foreign currency fluctuations upset the initial hopes for more return as well as less risk. This Forex effect could be reversed at some point in the future because there is no reason to believe that foreign currency gains and losses will not balance out in the longer term.

THE INFORMATION DECADE

A QUANTUM LEAP IN COMPLEXITY. If single-country portfolio management must address *n* variables, multiple-currency portfolios have to cope with *n* to the power of *n*! There will be rivalry between financial centers and clients will quickly find out about the differences and then insist on the best informa-

EXHIBIT 12 TOTAL FUND—RISK (NON-U.S. EQUITY UNIVERSE)

Median fund results

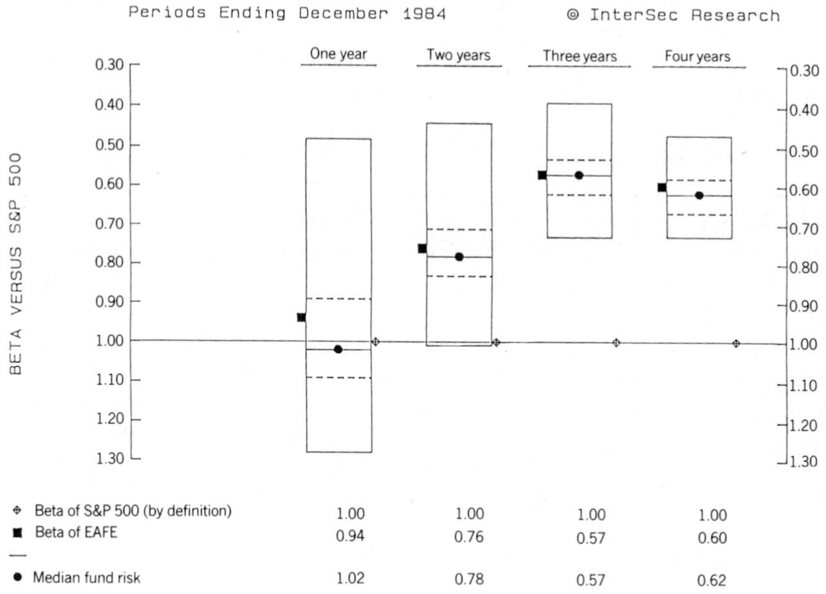

	One year	Two years	Three years	Four years
⊕ Beta of S&P 500 (by definition)	1.00	1.00	1.00	1.00
■ Beta of EAFE	0.94	0.76	0.57	0.60
● Median fund risk	1.02	0.78	0.57	0.62

tion and service. Also the interest in variability of returns implies more frequent interim reports; hence the need for computing packages and online databases. Everything that a manager is doing for its domestic market could in theory be duplicated for every market where the manager has a presence. The particular challenge is to handle the increase in data throughput, for this complexity involves all levels of the organization from trading, the back office, billing, valuations to strategy and simulation methodologies. The following paragraphs dwell on the reporting requirements rather than the idea-generation aspect of information, because the latter varies from manager to manager. But one can readily imagine the difficulty of keeping track of all the new financial instruments that have been dreamed up in the past decade: bonds redeemable in gold or petroleum; bonds paying coupons in one currency and capital in another; bonds with put options; bonds with currency options; extendible notes; perpetual floaters; partly paid bonds in foreign currencies; SDRs, EMUs, and ECUs, blocked foreign currency accounts, inflation futures; options and futures on share indexes; repos; passing trading positions around the globe for 24-hour trading—the list could go on.

ACCOUNTING AND REPORTING. The absolute result in the base currency of the portfolio is relatively straightforward, being the result reported in any accounting statement, whether international or not. The next level of sophistication is to break down the components of that result; for example, by security type, by country, by currency, by industry, by maturity. Further complexity arises from distinguishing the effect of income, changes in security prices and, especially, foreign exchange movements. This may require extension of the existing systems, but in essence all the above can be extracted from the accounting books provided only that the time or computing power is there. The accounting is also required to produce interim results both as inputs into the analytic programs to be described, and to find the time-weighted return that smooths out the distortions due to capital remittances and withdrawals.

COMPARISON WITH THEORETICAL BENCHMARKS. The professional environment requires that one can present one's portfolio under the assumptions of the **Capital Asset Pricing Model** (whether one believes in that model is another question). It is common to turn to a specialized consulting service in order to calculate the "beta" of a national portion of a portfolio or the relative importance of allocation, timing, and weighting decisions in the manager's result. This is an advantage both from the (actual or potential) client's point of view and from the manager, because the computation requires a sheaf of programs and databases concerning the relevant indexes. In order to calculate partial results the inputs required for every period are the beginning and end valuations and the income and capital cash flows. This must be done for every asset class and every currency, so that a monthly reporting of a six-currency fund with cash, bonds, and stocks must supply $4 \times 6 \times 3 \times 12 = 864$ data inputs to the performance analysis package.

COMPARISONS AMONG MANAGERS. Gross performance measures of total return, and even some statistics of new appointments are reported in the specialized press. Because the international manager has more levels of decision on his or her asset allocation than a one-country portfolio, the number of useful comparisons increases: Who chooses between countries best? Who manages foreign exchange positions best? Who manages best in France? But the most significant analysis is the risk-adjusted total return. This is calculated with reference to some base index such as the S&P 500 or The Capital International World (or EAFE) Index, and uses the modern portfolio categories of "alpha" and "beta." The historic time series of the base index and the portfolio are compared, which gives an estimated "beta" of the portfolio. A risk-equivalent index portfolio is then constructed by combining a holding in the index with either a short or long cash position so that it has the same beta as the actual portfolio. The return of this risk-equivalent portfolio over the period is calculated. The **risk-adjusted excess return ("alpha")** is the actual portfolio return minus the return of the risk-equivalent portfolio.

To summarize:

alpha = actual return − beta-equivalent index return

beta-equivalent index return = risk-free interest rate plus
(portfolio bet = (return of index − risk-free interest rate))

$$\text{where portfolio beta} = R^* \frac{sd/\text{portfolio returns}}{sd/\text{index returns}}$$

The beta of a portfolio is a theoretical construct; in fact, it is a statistical "best estimate" whose computation should show its "standard error"; this uncertainty is carried over into the risk-adjustment formula. The estimation of beta contains R $(-1 < R\,1)$, which shows that the risk adjustment measurement only takes account of the **"systematic risk"** of the portfolio and assumes that the remaining variance of return comes from the imperfect diversification of the portfolio. Also the formula for excess return containing the risk-free rate means that a measurement system can only rank groups of portfolios with the same base currency so that it is difficult to judge, for example, that a Japanese trust company has done better for its local clients than a U.S. institution for its local clients.

It is a struggle to ensure that a universe is homogeneous, because many appointments involve a limitation either fixed by the client's situation (e.g., is he or she tax-exempt?) or the manager's speciality (e.g., Far East only). Certain companies publish "quartile boxes" performance analyses for international managers of tax-exempt funds. Similar quartile boxes can show the distribution of standard deviations of returns among managers. To compare the risk-adjusted returns of a group of comparable accounts against an agreed index, one method (see Treynor, 1965) is to divide each account's alpha by its beta, which produces a ranking statistic.

INVESTMENT NUTS AND BOLTS

UNITED STATES-REGULATED INSTRUMENTS. Instruments are available in the United States to achieve international diversification, mostly equity related. A natural first step, especially for smaller funds, is to buy U.S.- regulated mutual fund shares. Exhibit 13 gives a selection of the larger funds, some of which are global, so that the managers take on the geographical allocation function, whereas others are more specialized.

EXHIBIT 13 LIST OF SELECTED U.S.-BASED MUTUAL FUNDS[a]

Global Equity	Specialized Equity
International Investors	United Services Gold shares
Strategic Investors	Franklin Gold Fund
Scudder International	Merrill Lynch Pacific
T. Rowe Price International	GT Pacific
Kemper International	Canadian Fund
Bond fund: Mass Financial International bonds	

[a]Ranking by end 1983 net assets.

There are also **closed-end investment trusts** quoted on U.S. exchanges. These are especially useful for investing with a longer-term view in illiquid or problem markets with the simplification of a listed dollar price either for exchanging the asset between U.S. investors or making interim valuations. Two examples would be the South Korea Fund and the Mexico Fund.

The largest and best-known foreign companies, especially multinationals, are often traded in the United States in the form of **American Depositary Receipts (ADRs)** with many advantages: cheaper brokerage; simplified custody and income collection; English translations of important reports and documents; SEC disclosure requirements. Two little hints on trading ADRs: terms are often finer when both the United States and the foreign professionals are at the office (i.e., first thing in the morning in New York for European shares) because the other side of the transaction can be an arbitageur rather than another investor; avoid newly introduced ADRs because there is a tendency for the stock to outperform its home index just before the listing and then to underperform when foreign perceptions of the home market turn negative (even when the stock's individual earnings record is better than average).

Some pitfalls to avoid:

1. It is generally a mistake to use third-party instruments: it is fine for a British institution to buy Australian shares in London, but an American doing the same may end up with unnecessary double taxation or exchange control complications.
2. Studies have shown (Agmon and Lessard, 1977) that contrary to certain expectations, investing in shares of U.S.-based multinationals has been an inefficient method of capturing the diversification benefits of international diversification.
3. Certain problems can arise with a subgroup of ADRs known as **"unsponsored" ADRs**. These have been created by an American bank or broker without an official application by the underlying foreign entity to the SEC. The owners of unsponsored ADRs do not benefit from the same disclosure requirements and in certain cases may not be allowed to participate in certain rights issues because of restrictions on the placing of issues in America without SEC registration.

A new development, still at the conceptual stage in 1985, is that it may soon become possible to trade certain **foreign share index futures** on U.S. exchanges. It would then be possible to invest solely in U.S. shares and then to run a permanent spread being simultaneously "short" a certain number of S&P 500 contracts and "long" an equivalent amount of a "cocktail" or **foreign index contracts**. This stragtegy should reduce the volatility of the total portfolio while capturing the capital growth and between-markets diversification effects of foreign investments while economizing their higher administrative and analytical costs. In effect the U.S. manager would then be concentrating the stock and industry-picking abilities on the market he or she knows best.

OPERATING IN FOREIGN EQUITY MARKETS: A CHECKLIST. Rather than attempt an encyclopedic treatment of the major markets, this section is presented in the form of a checklist, together with some discussion and notes of caution.

Exhibit 14 gives an introductory overview of certain characteristics of a selection of markets. The following are annotations to that exhibit, but note that details and exceptions abound and that the regulatory environment is in flux. The following material should be double-checked before being applied to real trades.

Market Capitalization. This is often used to establish a neutral starting point for geographical allocation. In the so-called top-down approach the neutral allocation is then modified according to the relative overall attractiveness of different markets. The figures come from Capital International, whose publications provide historical graphs and other financial data.

Fixed Commissions. There is a tendency for these to be eroded. Exhibit 14 gives the official position at present. For actual commission schedules, as well as details concerning stamp duties or other transaction dues, one must contact a member firm or the exchange itself.

Exchange Controls. These can be imposed very suddenly, but in general they seek to stem the flow of national savings outward before affecting the repatriation of capital and income belonging to foreign investors. It is therefore conforting, and likely to encourage fair foreign exchange dealings, if "they" are free to invest "here."

Settlement Days. This is normal lag time between executing a trade and the payment. Sometimes the foreign institution can finance a purchase for a few days in order to accommodate a valued client, especially when there is a mismatch between settlement lags on two markets (e.g., a switch from a Euroyen bond into a Japanese share). Some exchanges work on a monthly (or variable) account system where all trades made during the account period are settled on a fixed day after the end of the account. It is often possible to roll over into another account or choose a far off account date. The proper monitoring of settlement days is important for the Treasury and/or **Forex departments**.

Withholding Taxes. This is a complex area, subject to many special privileges, exceptions, and modifications. Exhibit 14 gives one figure for the non-treaty (maximum) rate and one for the amount unrecoverable by a U.S. tax-exempt fund, both expressed as a percentage of the total income received by a local tax-exempt fund. The difference between the maximum and the treaty rate is treated in various ways, sometimes being given immediately against proof of residency but usually in arrears and after some form-filling. Interest collections usually detail the tax withheld. But where a system of tax

EXHIBIT 14 WORLD EQUITY MARKETS[a]

Name of Market	Capitalization End 1984 ($ Billion)	Withholding Tax Max/Treaty	Settlement Days	Can They Invest in the United States	Brokerage Commissions
United States	1,593	30/NM	5	NM	Negotiable
Japan	617	20/15	3	Yes	Sliding
United Kingdom	219	NIL (TC 43)	Account	Yes	Sliding
Canada	116	25/10	5	Yes	Negotiable
West Germany	78	25/15 (TC 56)	2	Yes	Fixed
Australia	52	30/15	Variable	Yes	Sliding
Switzerland	42	35/15	3	Yes	Sliding
France	40	NIL (TC 50)	Account	Currency prem.	Sliding
Netherlands	31	25/15	2	Yes	Sliding
Singapore	27	NIL (Franked)	4	Not free	Sliding
Hong Kong	26	NIL	1	Yes	Sliding
Italy	23	30/15	Account	Not free	Sliding
Sweden	19	30/15		Not free	Sliding
South African Gold	22	15/15	(Different markets)	Not free	(Different markets)
Rest of world	40				
Total	2,945				

[a] Withholding taxes: TC = tax credit, which may or may not be useful to a U.S. tax-exempt investor.
Brokerage: Most exchanges have a schedule of fees, which may be fixed or on a sliding scale with respect to size of orders: negotiable commissions are normally discounts on some previously existing set schedule.

Source: Capital International Perspective 1985/1, Price Waterhouse, Hentsch & Cie, Intesec Research.

credits obtains, it is possible to miss certain entitlements, because only the net dividend is declared.

Restrictions. (not in exhibit) Nearly all countries wish to maintain certain key industries under home control (e.g., defense, banking). Different systems of protection have been adopted such as special reserved share classes (Switzerland, Scandinavia), maximum foreign shareholdings (Australia, France), cross-participations (Spain, West Germany, Japan), and restricted lists. Some countries are virtually closed to foreign portfolio investment (most of Africa, Kuwait, India).

Market Organization. (not in exhibit) Are commercial banks allowed to fulfill the role of brokers? If they are not, it may be unnecessarily costly to insist on the separation just because one is accustomed to it at home. Also in a country such as West Germany with a decentralized system of regional exchanges and multifunction banks, different investment recommendations can sometimes originate from two branches of the same large bank. Are there intermediaries (specialists) between brokers? If there are none, one may expect fixed trading hours for trading specific securities so that late orders are either expensive to execute or carried over to the next day. How many significant exchanges are there in any country, and can better executions be found by shopping around? In general, however, questions of market organization are less important than making the right investment decisions.

Miscellaneous Country-Specifics. In Japan, only **round lots** of 1,000 shares can be traded. Also the lag time between the record date and the reception of a dividend in cash or stock can be as long as 6 months. Many months after a sale, it is possible to receive an odd-lot as a stock dividend. Sometimes the delay is such that the odd-lot itself is received "ex" some further distribution, so that it takes a year and quite some administration to clear a position. In the United Kingdom and Australia, where securities are usually in registered form, it can take some time to have the securities delivered. Intervening **ex-dividend** or **ex-rights** dates can cause work to protect one's position (best left to one's local agent). Also it is possible to receive partial deliveries on purchases, which involves the extra administrative responsibility of keeping track of the cash management situation. It is often simpler to have the stock registered in the name of the nominee company of one's custodian. With bearer stocks as in much of Europe, it is possible to miss information; the holder must take the initiative to ensure that relevant financial information (annual reports, other corporate circulars, and prospectuses) reaches him or her.

New Issues. There have been some well-publicized and profitable floatations in Europe recently (e.g., British Telecom in the United Kingdom, Porsche in West Germany). At the time of writing (fall 1985), many believe that France will provide some worthwhile denationalizations in the coming few years. Successful staging of new issue game playing can provide a significant boost to performance. The method of allocating stock when an issue is very oversubscribed varies from country to country. In some, the lead managers are entirely responsible for a fixed share and have a certain discretionary power to favor certain applicants, whereas in others there is a centralized allocation and a more mathematical approach; frequently there is a bias in favor of the small local investor. Depending on the system, it may be beneficial to apply to more than one lead manager. If payment is required in full on application in a foreign currency, it may be wise to borrow the funds to avoid surplus foreign exchange if the application is scaled down. Access to new issues can be a factor in the selection of managers: in general, local firms are better placed than foreign ones for new issues. In particular, U.S. brokerage houses may be specifically excluded, in order to avoid the hazard of distributing new issues in the United States without SEC registration.

Rights Issues. The Anglo-Saxon way of handling issues tends to be different from that in continental Europe; in the United Kingdom and Australia, for example, rights issues often have a negative connotation. The pricing is very close to the current market and often underwritten by a syndicate. Shareholders suspect that management is expecting a "top" in the price so that if they subscribe, they will see a price drop but if they renounce their right, their share in the company is diluted. The mechanics are that shareholders of record receive "allotment letters" by the mails and trading is in **"new nil paid"** shares. The use of the mails can cause uncomfortable races against closing dates. The continental way is usually to have more frequent rights issues and to price them at a significant discount to the market. This gives rights issues a positive aura, as having an element of **stock dividend**, which indeed has to be calculated by analysts in order to adjust the price and earnings history of the share, because the ex-rights way often represents a significant discontinuity in market prices. The rights are usually evidenced by a specific coupon from each share, which must be detached and presented to the company's bank, together with the payment required. The same coupons can be delivered if rights are sold or bought. Individual taxpayers very often sell their rights and consider the proceeds as an extra (and, in some places, tax-free) dividend.

CROSS-BORDER FIXED-INTEREST INVESTMENTS. The sources of the diversification benefits of cross-border fixed-interest investments are currency fluctuations and interest-rate differentials or movements; therefore dollar-denominated bonds issued by/to non-U.S.-resident issuers/investors (known as **Eurodollar** and **Yankee Bonds**) are not international for a U.S. investor in terms of portfolio theory, even though they involve issues of international law and credit risk. Only those Eurodollar bonds linked to equities (convertible or by warrants) can be considered international diversification when the conversion premium is reasonably small (25% or less is a workable if arbitrary cutoff). Unfortunately because (1) Euroconvertible issues are small, and (2) U.S. residents are normally debarred from owning them during the first few months after issue, the market has usually become illiquid by the time the issue is available ("seasoned"). In the checklist that follows, only the viewpoint of U.S. investors will be considered. More specialized literature should be consulted for issues of concern to professionals engaged in making markets for foreign bonds or floating new issues.

Domestic Markets. Investing in domestic government bonds of foreign countries is the simplest first step. It captures the essential diversification effects and minimizes the cost of analysis, because only the macro-figures affecting interest and **Forex rates** have to be studied: typically inflation, monetary policy, private or public credit demand, and the balance of payments. The only important question is whether the rate of unrecoverable withholding tax is prohibitive. Adding other domestic issues is no more difficult in terms of trading and custody procedures, but adds a dimension of credit and liquidity analysis. With the possible exception of Japan, foreign countries tend not to have an accepted published credit-rating mechanism such as Moody's or Standard and Poor's.

International Bonds. The major freely exchangeable foreign currencies are associated with a corresponding international bond market. The defining characteristics of an international bond are that neither the interest arises within the fiscal sphere of the currency of payment nor is the initial capital provided by residents of the country of the borrower. So, in deference to the SEC, U.S. investors are debarred from subscribing at issue either a U.S. dollar bond not registered with the SEC or a foreign currency bond issued/guaranteed by a U.S. borrower. However, a yen bond of a French company would be no problem. This legal framework permits the main attraction of the international bonds, which is their freedom from withholding tax. A second unrelated attraction is that bonds are usually in bearer form. Although the largest international bond market—the Eurodollar—is unregulated, the most important nondollar markets are to a greater or lesser extent regulated, as is the dollar "Yankee" bond market: Swiss franc, deutsche mark, Samurai (yen), Bulldog (sterling), Dutch guilder.

The regulation usually includes an orderly queuing mechanism for issues and some vetting of: (1) the quality of the issue; (2) the adequacy of the offering prospectus; (3) the fairness of the conditions, such as early calls or protection of seniority. The idea is that because residents of the country of the regulating authority are permitted to subscribe, they should be protected from markedly unsatisfactory offerings while at the same time the flow of funds to domestic issues is relatively unaffected. In countries where domestic bonds are both free of withholding tax and in bearer form, the distinction between domestic and foreign bonds is, for investment purposes, one of relative creditworthiness (e.g., the Netherlands, recently joined by West Germany).

Euro- and Smaller Markets. In addition to the international markets cited earlier, there exist unregulated Euroyen, Euro-DM, and Eurosterling markets. One important difference between a Euro- and an International issue in the same currency is that the lead manager does not have to be resident of the country in whose currency the bond is denominated. The freedom from issuing regulations has also given rise to a "gray market," wherein market participants trade paper on a when-issued basis and try to outguess the lead managers as to the level at which an issue will trade on the secondary market after the end of the subscription period. Markets exist also in unlisted notes sometimes known as private placements in Swiss francs, deutsche marks, and guilders. Unlisted securities may or may not be unregulated. Smaller markets—not always open to new issues—include Euro-French francs, European Currency Units (ECU), Special Drawing Rights (SDR), Hong Kong dollars, Luxembourg francs, Norwegian kroner, Australian dollars, Kuwaiti dinars, and Bahrain dinars.

Dealing Mechanisms. Dealing on Euro- or International bonds is normally by telephone with market makers, though smaller lots (below $50,000) of the internationals are best traded on the relevant stock exchange. The London and Luxembourg listing of many Eurobonds is not so usedful for dealing, but instead the market maker of last resort (at least as a matter of honor on the "bid" side) is usually the bond's lead manager. For domestic bonds it is more usual to trade within their customary local market (either telephone or exchange) than to deal offshore, especially when the Central Bank of the country concerned frowns on the practice. Off-exchange telephone dealings can take place anywhere. In addition, bearer securities can be delivered without reference to any register of securities; so it is possible to purchase a popular deutsche mark issue in New York, and even (in theory) to agree to a physical delivery in New York against payment in U.S. funds. In practice, however, a deutsche mark bond trade between two New York institutions will normally involve a cash movement in deutsche marks within the West German banking system, together with a security delivery either in West Germany or, for international issues only, at Euroclear or Cedel—clearinghouses owned by two consortia of banks. There is no ADR mechanism for bonds, although there are some rare and cumbersome mechanisms for settling bond trades in currencies different to the bond's denomination: (1) Eurodollar bonds traded on the Swiss exchanges are settled in Swiss francs at a clearing exchange rate published every morning; (2) less-used currencies such as the Australian dollar are often cleared with U.S. funds in the Euroclear system. However, these are seldom used and even a nuisance when, for instance, shares are being switched into bonds of the same currency. Various tax authorities may disagree on where a trade takes place, because many are tempted to telephone from a major center and then to "book" the trades in a tax haven, but this concerns the market maker more than the investor. Also there are rare cases of forgery of bearer certificates (in 1983 a cunning cheat tried to disseminate forged zero-coupon Eurobonds)—but normally this is the custodian's and not the investor's risk.

Liquidity. On the buying side, liquidity is a function of issue size. United Kingdom, West German, Japanese, and French government bonds are easy to buy. Dutch recent issues are also easy, but sinking funds make older issues too small. In Switzerland the small central government budget deficit (both relative to GDP and in the absolute) makes issue size correspondingly small. As with U.S. corporate bonds, the buying of paper from smaller issues in any market has to be opportunistic—one chooses from among the bonds that the market is offering on a particular day; in general, recent issues are more liquid than seasoned ones. On the selling side, liquidity is put to the test during troubled times and becomes a measure of the solidity of a financial system. In this context debtor quality becomes more important than yield, with government bonds particularly sought after. In this respect the Dutch and Swiss markets are just as liquid as the larger markets mentioned earlier. Also domestic and international bonds listed and traded on stock exchanges tend to hold up better than Euro or private placement issues for many reasons. Banks prefer them, and because the yield curve is often inverted at such times, a severe strain is put on market makers' ability to carry inventory. Conversely, a stock market puts buyers and sellers in more direct contact and allows the small retail customer to enhance liquidity. Convertible issues are notoriously illiquid—a fact that was even once found to be the basis of fraudulent manipulations and collusion by a ring of trading employees in different firms. All in all, however, the Euromarkets have survived some severe strains in 1974 and 1981–1982 and there has been rather less insolvency than among the dealers in U.S. government securities!

Miscellaneous Particularities. The Association of International Bond Dealers (AIBD) fulfills a useful role in the Euromarkets by harmonizing dealing practices and even entering into such technicalities as the calculation of accrued interest or yields to maturity. It also publishes useful guides both about securities and its member institutions. On the other hand, all the domestic markets have their own standards concerning quotations, new issues, days to settlement, ex-coupon dates, accrued interest. Exhibit 15 gives some noteworthy features of the United Kingdom, Japanese, West German, and Swiss domestic markets. In England **"Gilts"** with over 5 years of remaining life are quoted with the accrued interest included in the price. For the **Bulldog issues** and certain privileged Gilts, which are registered securities, the interest is only payable free of withholding tax if certain details are supplied concerning the final beneficiary to the Inspector of Foreign Dividends. Bonds linked to inflation are another speciality. In Japan, it is customary to issue numerous series of government securities with identical coupons and similar maturities until the current coupon becomes too far out of touch with the market. So care must be taken, especially on the selling side, to specify the number of the series. Also there exists discount government bonds (5-year zero coupon issues) which are quoted on the basis of simple interest and not price. In West Germany certain short term papers and notes are not available for foreign investors. Also when withholding tax existed, a popular loophole was found whereby certain papers known as *Schuldscheine* were classified as loans and therefore free of withhold-

EXHIBIT 15 FOREIGN BOND MARKETS: PUBLIC ISSUES[a]

Name of Market	GNP % U.S.A.	Withholding Max/Treaty	Settlement Days	Accrued Days Min/Max	Size $ Billions Total	Size $ Billions New Issues 84
United States	100					
Domestic		nil	1	0/183	2,391	348
Yankee		nil	5	0/183	66	5
Euro		nil	5	0/359	196	64
Japan	32					
Domestic		20/10	Account	0/183	759	63
Samurai		nil	5	0/183	17	5
Euro		nil	5	0/359	3	1
West Germany	16					
Domestic		nil	2	−14/345	268	22
Foreign		nil	2	−14/345	31	7
France	12					
Domestic		10/0	1	Complex	108	18
Euro		nil	5	0/359	2	0
United Kingdom	11					
Domestic		30/0	1	Complex	142	13
Bulldog		30/0	1		4	1
Euro		nil	5	0/359	6	4
Canada	9					
Domestic		nil	2 or 5	0/183	117	13
Euro		nil	5	0/359	5	2
Australia	5					
Domestic		10/10	As agreed	−15/168	50	9
Euro		nil	5	0/359	1	0
Netherlands	3					
Domestic		nil	2	−14/345	43	7
Foreign		nil	2	−14/345	5	2
Switzerland	2					
Domestic		35/5	3	1/360	34	2
Foreign		nil	3	1/360	22	4
Notes		nil	3	1/360	28	8
Eurocomposite Units	n.m.	nil	5	0/359	NA	3

[a]All the above are subject to much simplification, currency translation, short cuts; withholding tax is understood for standard new issues; and the new issue figures may be net or gross of redemptions.

Sources: O.E.C.D., Salomon Brothers, Morgan Guaranty Trust, Hentsch & Cie, and Intersec Research.

ing tax. Because the transferability of these loans is limited they have now lost their appeal to international investors unless there is a significant yield advantage. The Swiss National Bank restricted foreigners' access to the domestic market in 1974 and 1978 in order to restrain the rise of the Swiss franc. This "reverse" exchange control was a sign of strength, and those foreign investors who had bought in advance of the measures were satisfied. There was never any problem, however, selling domestic Swiss franc bonds and indeed there continues to be a shortage of investment grade paper in Switzerland.

Hedging and Futures Markets. It has always been possible to hedge the foreign currency element of foreign bonds in the interbank currency futures market. More recently the great success of the **Chicago Board of Trade's** T-bond contract has caught the imagination of investment professionals in other centers. There is already a London Gilt contract, and other such instruments are in the pipeline elsewhere. If these contracts are liquid enough, they will enable portfolio managers totally to separate the foreign exchange and interest rate aspects of cross-border fixed-interest investment: It is not yet possible to foresee, much less to simulate, all the consequences.

THE NEXT DECADE

THE GROWTH OF THE ASSET POOL. Domestic pension assets are expected to increase at roughly 14% per annum, exceeding $5.5 trillion by 1995. Provided that there is not a disastrous financial dislocation or a reversal of current liberalization, cross-border investments are expected to increase faster, with the global pension "float" growing from the present $62 billion to reach $500 billion in 1995. The greatest volume growth would be in the United States, whose foreign exposure could reach $250 million. Japan and the United Kingdom could reach $50 million each. West Germany, whose pensions are still often on the book reserve system (as were Japan's until recently), is expected to move gradually to funding its pensions. In book reserves, the present value of future pension costs appears in the balance sheet as a liability, but no corresponding assets are specifically designated or segregated to meet the liability. The advantage is that the company can use the funds as working capital, but the dangers of book reserves arise in adverse business conditions, as was illustrated in West Germany when AEG-Telefunken encountered difficulties. The implications of the move toward funded pensions are positive, first for that country's capital markets and then for a significant international presence.

THE INVESTMENT MANAGEMENT INDUSTRY. There are currently about 100 managers competing for ERISA business in the United States, compared with about 25 in 1978. It is not certain whether there is room for so many full-line global investment managers. One can posit three levels of involvement in cross-border investments. First, selling one's home market to foreign intermediaries, as when a West German broker is asked by a U.S. fund manager to furnish research. This is relatively easy to set up, and to buttress with reciprocal business. It is undermined when the foreign institution enters the local market. Second, selling foreign markets to existing domestic clients. This is an intermediate level, because one is always starting from the same base for marketing, reporting, fiscal, and legal parameters. It is a natural first step for a company with a domestic portfolio, but such traditional relationships are vulnerable to competitive pressure when the volume invested internationally becomes important. Third, the ultimate level is selling any investment service (international or local-on-any-market) to any client. Certain multinational accounting firms have achieved the "chameleon" capability of servicing similarly multinational client corporations irrespective of the accounting standards of the home base; the first multicentered, multistandard, vertically integrated investment services companies can be expected to become operational in the present decade.

The evolutionary pressure is toward a decrease in the importance of correspondent business in favor of international integration within the same company. From the investor's side this avoids having to pay double commissions both to the adviser and his or her correspondent. Pulling in the same direction is the entry of banks, which already have international branch networks, into the securities business that has hitherto been more parochial. Integration therefore often implies internationalization. The obstacles to this pressure come (1) from restrictions on competition (e.g., limited membership of exchanges), (2) from the power through relationships of smaller securities firms to hang on to existing clients, possibly generating reciprocal business with similar-sized correspondents abroad, and (3) from the necessity of safeguarding against conflicts of interest when a fiduciary is both market-maker and investment manager. The first two resistances are being eroded so that in the dealing and custodian functions, cost benefits in concentration are apparent, whereas on the third, common sense encourages one both to diversify investment advisers and to separate brokerage and management. The conclusion is that medium-sized firms at present living off brokerage and custodian services must grow or specialize, and are strongly advised to learn to work "under the wing" of larger financial institutions, possibly but not necessarily with joint marketing. We may thus see "solar systems" of specialized managers around each custodian. The same pressures apply to in-house pension fund managers as to small firms; all but the very largest will have difficulty in justifying the cost of putting together the international structure necessary to compete with the industry, so that they will be tempted to entrust their overseas portion to outside institutions.

LEADERSHIP BY MULTINATIONALS. The world of investment management is becoming smaller at the same time as the sheer importance of the numbers of making boardrooms aware of the importance of good results from the pension fund. Multinationals on the client side are finding that they can now deal with financial-service multinationals and this must inevitably produce a convergence of investment philosophies and practices. Although local subsidiaries are subject to local pension norms, the international headquarters of sponsors in advanced countries will not hesitate to exert pressure where local habits are seen to be inefficient. Multinational parents based in less advanced environments but having U.S. subsidiaries will also be forced into awareness of the differences and inefficiencies. Finally, as this global vision in turn trickles down to the local operators, the whole global investment community will be affected.

BIBLIOGRAPHY

SCHOLARLY WORKS

Abrams, R., and Kimball, D., "U.S. Investment in Foreign Equity Markets" *Federal Reserve Bank of Kansas City Economic Review* (April 1981).

Adler, M., and Horesh, R., "The Relationship Among Equity Markets: Comment," *Journal of Finance* (September 1984).

Adler, M. "Global Fixed-Income Portfolio Management" *Financial Analysts Journal* (September/October 1983).

Agmon, T., and Lessard, D.R., "International Diversification and the Multinational Corporation," *Journal of Finance* (September 1977).

Bergstrom, G., "A New Route to Higher Returns and Lower Risks," *Journal of Portfolio Management* (Fall 1975).

Black, F., "International Capital Market Equilibrium with Investment Barriers," *Journal of Financial Economics* (December 1974).

Dimson, E., Hodges, S., and Marsh, S., "International Diversification" London Business School paper, January 1980.

Erlich, E. "Foreign Pension Fund Investments in the United States," *Pensions World* (July 1984) and Federal Reserve Bank of New York, *Quarterly Review* (Spring 1983).

Elton, Edwin J., and Gruber, Martin J., *Modern Portfolio Theory and Investment Risk,* New York: Wiley, 1981, p. 115.

Errunza, Vihang "Emerging Markets" *Financial Analysts Journal* (September/October 1983).

Farber, A., "Performance of Internationally Diversified Mutual Funds" in Elton, E. and Gruber, M. (eds.), "International Capital Markets," Amsterdam: North-Holland, 1975.

Hagler, J., "The Evaluation of the International Investment Program at the Ford Foundation," Financial Analyst Research Federation Seminar, New York, February 1979.

Jacquillat, B., and Solnik, B., "Is There a Superior Route to International Portfolio Investment?" *Journal of Portfolio Management* (Winter 1978).

Lakonishok, J., and Schapiro, A., "Stock Returns, Beta, Variance and Size," *Financial Analysts Journal* (July/August 1984).

Lessard, D., "World, Country and Industry Relationships in Equity Returns," *Financial Analysts Journal* (January/February 1976).

Levy, H., and Sarnat, M., "International Diversification of Investment Portfolios," *American Economic Review* (September 1970).

Mantell, E., "How to Measure Expected Returns on Foreign Investments," *Journal of Portfolio Management* (Winter 1984).

Modigliani, F., Pogue, G., Scholes, M. and Solnik, B., "Efficiency of European Capital Markets and Comparison with the American Stock Market" Proceedings of the 1st International Congress on Stock Exchanges, Milan, 1972.

Modigliani, F., and Pogue, G., "An Introduction to Risk and Return," *Financial Analysts Journal* (March/April and May/June 1974).

Nowakowski, C., "A Guide to the Process of Selecting an International Investment Manager," *Pensions and Investments* (January 29, 1979).

Nowakowski, C., "International Performance Measurement" papers presented to the Center for Research in Security Prices, Chicago, November 1978 and November 1980.

Sharpe, W., *Investments,* 3rd ed. Englewood Cliffs, NJ: Prentice-Hall, 1985.

Solnik, B., "An Equilibrium Model of the International Capital Market" Stanford University, GSB Research Paper, September 1972.

Solnik, B., "Why Not Diversify Internationally?" *Financial Analysts Journal* (July/August 1974).

Thomas, B., "Internationalization of the Securities Markets: An Empirical Analysis," *George Washington Law Review* (January 1982).

Villani, Ed., "Considerations For Moving into Foreign Index Fund," *Pensions and Investments,* January 29, 1979.

INDUSTRY RESOURCES. In addition to the investment recommendations of securities firms, for most major markets it is possible to buy some equivalent of Moody's quarterly handbooks for the U.S. market (e.g., Japan Companies Handbook). Graphical and condensed financial data covering the leading issues in most equity markets is available from Capital International Perspective's quarterly publications. Extel Statistical Services in London can also be a useful source. ADRs are analyzed by Standard and Poor's. The Association of International Bond Dealers publishes an annual compendium of international bond terms and conditions (with interim updates). There is also a fast growing software industry that gives financial information (DRI, Interactive Data Corp, Datastream, DAFSA of Paris, InterSec, TOPIC in London). Finally, proceedings of investment seminars are often a concentrated source of recent thinking:

- Proceedings of the 1985 Global Investment Conference, Business Research International, London.
- Proceedings of 13th Congress of European Federation of Financial Analysts Societies, Madrid, October 16–19, 1984.

21

SECURITY ANALYSIS

CONTENTS

21

SECURITY ANALYSIS

James L. Farrell, Jr.
James P. Holmes

INVESTMENT PRINCIPLES

INVESTMENT DEFINED. The term *investment* has three different meanings in common usage. In the broadest sense, investment refers to the placement of funds in productive assets to earn a return, regardless of whether such investment is accompanied by management. In this sense, investment refers to the acquisition by a business of assets for its own use, as well as the purchase of securities in businesses managed by others. A second definition of investment is the acquisition of assets to secure a return in the form of interest, dividends, rents, or capital appreciation, but without assumption of responsibility for management. The third and most narrow definition of investment is the acquisition of assets to secure income, not limiting the degree of risk, insofar as is practicable. In this sense, investment is distinguished from **speculation,** which involves the deliberate assumption of substantial risks to secure capital appreciation or a high rate of return, and **gambling,** which involves the making of wagers rather than the acquisition of interests in property. Ownership of **cash** does not constitute investment. Only when cash is used to acquire income-producing assets, whether as creditor or owner, does investment occur.

In this section, the term *investment* is used in the second sense just stated, that is, the placement of capital, without assuming responsibility for management, to obtain a return in the form of interest, dividends, rents, or capital appreciation.

CLASSES OF INVESTMENTS. Investments fall into two main classes: **fixed income** and **equity.** Fixed-income investments include bonds and preferred stocks. Equity investments include common stock and real estate ownership. In addition, it is sometimes possible to find combinations of the two basic types in a single issue and, for purposes of classification, such securities may be designated **"hybrids."**

Each asset possesses a number of characteristics that determine its suitability and desirability for individual or institutional investors. The two most important characteristics are **risk** and the **rate of return**. Other significant characteristics are **marketability** and **tax status**.

RISK AND RETURN

Return on Investment. Investors seek to obtain the highest return available on investments that provide the kind and degree of safety they desire. The return on fixed-income investments, such as bonds, mortgages, and preferred stocks is limited to the contractual interest or preferred dividend rate. Common stocks, by contrast, constituting the ownership element in businesses, provide not only a current dividend yield, but also the prospect of future increases in **cash dividends** and price appreciation that may result from reinvestment of retained earnings and the cash flow from depreciation allowances, research and development outlays, and other management efforts to increase profits. At the same time, however, common stocks are subject to the risk of declines in earnings, dividends, and market price that unfavorable developments affecting the economy or the company may cause.

Sources of Risk. Each security has its own degree of risk that reflects the following major uncertainties: (1) interest rate risk, (2) purchasing power risk, (3) business risk, and (4) financial risk. There is the chance that other securities may offer larger returns and lower the worth of the presently owned security. This is commonly called the **interest rate risk.** There is also the chance that inflation will erode purchasing power and reduce the amount of goods and services that the dollars of accrued return are worth. This is called the **purchasing power risk.** There is the risk that business competition and conditions may impair the ability to provide the return. This is called the **business risk.** There is also the risk that the methods used to finance the corporation may impair the ability to provide the return. This is called the **financial risk.** Fixed income securities are subject primarily to interest rate, purchasing power, and usually financial risk, whereas common stocks are subject to one degree or another of all four risks.

In addition, the practical, sophisticated investor would be wise to distinguish between short-term or temporary risks and long-term or permanent risks. Stock market cycle, a labor strike, and economic recessions might be examples of the former. A structural change in the economy, a new tax law, or technological obsolescence might demonstrate the latter.

Diversification. When considering the risk of a security in a portfolio context, it is useful to divide the total risk or total variability of return of an asset into two parts: systematic and unsystematic. **Systematic risk** is the portion of total variability in return caused by factors that simultaneously affect the prices of all securities. Systematic variability of return is found in nearly all securities in varying degrees, because most securities move together in a systematic manner. **Unsystematic risk** is the portion of total risk that is unique to a firm. Unsystematic variations are thus independent of factors affecting other securities.

Because unsystematic variations are unique to each firm, they can be diversified away to nearly zero by spreading the funds to be invested across the securities of several unrelated firms. Systematic risk, on the other hand, is more difficult to diversify because it is common to all assets in the market to some extent. Within a given market, assets with high degrees of systematic risk must be priced to yield high rates of return to induce investors to purchase them.

An intelligent investor will always attempt to decrease risk through some diversification where there is no practical reduction in potential return. A prudent investor might also elect to trade-off some potential return to lower risk further. One way to look at diversification is that it is a method to assure that potential returns become actual returns through realizing that the only certainty is change and by lessening exposure to random events, the mistakes inherent in forecasting the future, and heavy dependency on any given variable. The counter strategy to diversification is to put "all your eggs in one basket and watch the basket." The theory is that risk can be reduced through superior knowledge. In fact few investors possess a sufficient competitive edge to make this second approach appropriate.

Risk-Return Trade-off. Studies of the probability distributions of returns indicate that securities with high total and high systematic risk tend also to have high average rates of return. For example, short-term fixed-income instruments (e.g., Treasury bills) have displayed the least variability and provided the lowest return over time. Common stocks have shown the largest variability and provided the highest return, whereas bonds have provided intermediate variability and return, as would be expected. It should be noted that these are longer-term tendencies, with the data also showing that over shorter periods of time there is frequently an inverse relationship, with less risky investments actually earning more than high-risk ones.

In addition to these general traits among classes of securities, the risk/return ratio is a key element is selecting securities within a given category. In fact proper assessment of risk/return should be regarded as the single most important area to concentrate on in security analysis. The analysis might start with the proper level of risk to assume for a particular investor. A retired individual with a limited portfolio normally should not be willing to assume a higher or even average level of risk. A highly diversified pension plan for a young workforce might be willing to include individual securities with average or above risk if the potential reward justified the higher level of risk. A common stock with upside potential of 150% and downside risk of 50% in 3 years might be considered statistically attractive but inappropriate for certain investors. However, undue focus should not be given to either risk or reward of individual securities for a normal investor in a reasonably diversified portfolio.

MARKETABILITY. The ability to sell or buy a security readily is called marketability. When a security can be bought and sold in large amounts without disrupting its price, it is said to possess a **broad market**; if only small amounts can be bought or sold at the prevailing price, it has a **narrow** or **thin market**. When the bid and asked prices are not far apart, a security is said to enjoy a **close market**. When prices for a security do not fluctuate widely between sales or over a period of time, the security has a **stable market**; when a security's price moves over a wide range, its market behavior is **volatile**. (See also discussions of marketability in the section "Short-Term Money Markets and Instruments" and risk-return trade-off in "Modern Portfolio Theory and Management.")

Liquidity refers to the ability to convert investments into cash at any time without material loss. **Short-term U.S. government obligations** are a prime source of liquidity, as are **commercial paper** and deposits in banks. The short maturity and the high quality of these instruments assure their liquidity. In addition, short-term U.S. government securities and commercial paper possess very broad, close, and stable markets, which enhance their liquidity characteristics.

All other things being equal, broad, close, stable markets are more desirable. In fact, they may be mandatory if a high degree of liquidity is required. Because most investors want these features, however, securities that have these characteristics frequently sell at premium prices and thus offer lower potential returns. Part of this premium pricing for liquidity is structural and part is cyclical. The desire for liquidity typically increases in bear markets.

Some investors need a high liquidity level for cash flow demands, to implement specific investment strategies, or to meet risk guidelines. Periodically, superior returns are achievable for patient investors willing to tolerate lower liquidity. In general, an investor should demand higher potential returns for lower marketability.

Marketability can be evaluated by such factors as: (1) maturity or duration in the case of fixed-income securities; (2) the number of average trading days required to sell a particular investment position; (3) the size of the issue or, in the case of common stock, the market value of total shares outstanding; and (4) the float or total market value less closely held securities. At any rate, the marketability requirements of a specific investor and the corresponding characteristics of an individual security should be thoroughly analyzed before investing.

TAX STATUS. High rates of income taxation make the tax status of investments a matter of major significance to individual investors in the middle and upper income brackets, and to taxed institutional investors. In their appraisals, such investors should be concerned primarily with the return from an investment after taxes, rather than with the gross return before taxes. Among fixed-income investments, tax-exempt obligations hold a particularly favorable position for higher bracket individual investors and taxed institutional investors such as commercial banks. Dividend income enjoys an 85% credit when received by corporate investors. Appreciation is taxed only when realized, and long-term capital gains are currently taxed at only half or less of the rate applicable to ordinary income of individuals. Tax laws change and should be checked.

SECURITY ANALYSIS IN AN EFFICIENT MARKET. The relevance of security analysis has been controversial for several decades. Originally the debate centered on the relative merits of "fundamental" security analysis as opposed to a set of charting techniques referred to as **"technical analysis."** More recently, evidence of efficiency in the capital market pricing mechanism has been interpreted by some to imply the uselessness of both fundamental security analysis and technical analysis. Because this section is a description of security analysis, it is important to consider the question at this point.

Role of the Analyst. Curley and Bear (1979) describe the role of the analyst as follows. Fundamental **security analysis** involves the processing of available information concerning a firm to arrive at a subjective estimate of the expected return and risk to an investor who purchases the firm's stocks or bonds. Fundamental analysis can also be defined more narrowly as the process of calculating a firm's **intrinsic value**; this is an equilibrium price that can be compared with the current market price to identify undervalued and overvalued securities. The term *fundamentalist* is more closely associatd with the narrower definition.

Relevant information is both quantitative and qualitative. Quantitative information includes the firm's stock price history, financial data, reaction of the firm to changes in macroeconomic variables, and other data that may be used to forecast return on investment. Qualitative information includes such items as the assessment of competence of a firm's management. Information can also be classified as publicly available or as inside; the former is generally available at little or no cost, whereas the latter is known only to a limited number of persons. Notwithstanding its usual definition as data available to corporate insiders (e.g., employees), **inside information** may be generated externally from publicly available information through private techniques developed by an analyst.

Security analysis is not a unique and codified set of techniques. There is basic agreement about the general analytical formulation, but forecasting techniques and qualitative adjustments vary from one analyst to another. Research has provided increasingly better **forecasting methods**, but the search for superior techniques continues. A large part of security analysis consists of routine forecasts, using a model that is considered to be most reliable by the analyst; risk and return elements are estimated on the basis of anticipations formed from existing information. As new information is received, it is compared with anticipated values, and the forecasting process is repeated. On occasions, new information may concern an unexpected and major event. In this case, windfall gain or loss accrues to shareholders as market price adjusts to reflect that information, equilibrium risk-return dimensions may also be altered significantly. The quality of the analytical process depends on the ability to anticipate events.

Efficient Markets. The most recent challenge to security analysis arose because of the statement and testing of the **efficient market hypothesis**. Most of the initial testing of the theory centered on evaluating the publicly available investment results of mutual funds. In general these professionally managed funds underperformed the overall market. The conclusion was that the proliferation of investment analysts had made the market very efficient and that underperformance could be explained by transaction costs. An efficient market is defined as one in which security prices fully reflect all available information. New information is discounted as it arrives, meaning that its value is assessed by investors. Price quickly adjusts to a new and correct level. Under the circumstances, detailed analysis of existing information would appear to be fruitless. In fact it is not. As Lorie and Hamilton (1974) have pointed out, it is the interaction of investors in analyzing new information and in adjusting portfolios that causes price to respond in an efficient market; paradoxically, if investors accepted the efficiency hypothesis, and abandoned security analysis, market efficiency would decrease.

Curley and Bear (1979, p. 7) indicate three reasons that security analysis remains relevant in a generally efficient market.

1. In an efficient but less than perfect market, there is a time lag between the arrival of information and its subsequent reflection in price. During that interval, security analysis provide an opportunity to adjust portfolios profitably. Market efficiency in this respect has not been fully established but available evidence suggests that price response is fairly rapid; this may imply that rewards arising from security analysis are captured by institutional investors and others with the capacity to process large amounts of data quickly and efficiently.
2. Superior analytical techniques may allow the analyst to transform publicly available information into inside information. This possibility is difficult to document because there is little motivation for making superior techniques public. But some evidence is available that supports the proposition.
3. Security analysis is critical to the investment process even in the case of instantaneous price response, because securities must be evaluated in a portfolio context. Correct pricing of individual assets in an efficient but less than perfect market does not imply investor indifference to the choice of assets held in a portfolio. As the price of an individual security responds to new information, reflecting change in risk and expected return, the security in question may no longer be desirable as part of the portfolio for some investors. Other investors, in contrast, may wish to acquire the asset because of the change in risk and return. Portfolio

> management is clearly a continuing process, with portfolio revision dependent on evaluation and reevaluation of asset risk-return elements. Security analysis and portfolio selection are therefore complementary; they are both compatible with, and necessary to, an efficient capital market.

Although there is a good deal of evidence to support the concept of efficient markets, the theory does little to explain the very wide price fluctuations of either market indexes or individual securities. Greed, fear, crowd psychology, and the short-term, intensely competitive focus of many institutional money managers provides a far better background to understand why numerous equity securities can double, drop in half, and double again over a stock market cycle. What is clear is that investors who use the same sources for information and advice, select from the same universe, and follow similar investment strategies as most other investors are likely to achieve mediocre investment results. There is no substitute for clear-headed, independent thinking.

In the 1950s, buying growth stocks was a sound, effective strategy. After the popularity of that approach expanded too far, its effectiveness disappeared. This should not encourage investors to pursue only esoteric strategies, nor discourage them from building a sound foundation in fundamental analysis. One study has shown that the avoidance of large mistakes is alone sufficient to achieve superior results.

SOURCES OF INVESTMENT INFORMATION

If the conceptual framework that investors use to assess their position in the market is to be valuable, it must have information inputs. Information can be gathered from published sources, and these can be grouped into the following categories: (1) information on economic conditions and the business outlook, (2) industry and company data sources, and (3) information on companies and securities. Much of this information is also available in computer-based format, and these sources are described following a review of the sources of published information. Sources of investment information is provided at the end of this Handbook in Appendix B.

TRADITIONAL PUBLISHED SOURCES

Information on Economic Conditions and the Business Outlook. The reference citations to be listed are good sources of background information on economic developments, statistical data on the economy as a whole, and some industry statistics. The data offered in these publications are useful for measuring the performance of a given company or industry against that of the entire economy. These volumes do not, however, give any of the specific data on individual companies that are the direct tools of security analysis.

A number of banks publish reports or surveys dealing with the business outlook and other topics. **Citibank** publishes a **Monthly Economic Letter**. The leading article is always "General Business Conditions." **The Morgan Guaranty Survey** is published monthly by the Morgan Guaranty Trust Co. of New York. The Bank of New York issues **General Business Indicators**, which is a statistical tabulation of selected economic indicators. Manufacturers Hanover publishes the *Financial Digest,* a weekly economic commentary together with selected financial data and business indicators. The Chase Manhattan Bank publishes **Business in Brief**, issued bimonthly by its Economic Research Division. The first article usually presents an analysis of the business outlook.

The 12 Federal Reserve banks publish monthly bulletins devoted to banking, economic, and financial topics. The Federal Reserve Bank of New York, for example, publishes a **Monthly Review**. The Federal Reserve of Philadelphia publishes the **Business Review** monthly. The Federal Reserve banks of Chicago and St. Louis also issue monthly reviews. The Board of Governors of the Federal Reserve System in Washington, D.C., publishes the **Federal Reserve Bulletin** monthly. It contains the "National Summary of Business Conditions." The Federal Reserve also publishes a **Chart Book on Business, Economic, and Financial Statistics** monthly, as well as an annual **Historical Chart Book**.

The federal government provides a number of useful sources of information on developing business trends. The **Survey of Current Business** is published monthly by the U.S. Department of Commerce. It has two principal parts. The first deals with basic business trends; the second section is an elaborate compilation of basic statistical series on all phases of the economy. The President's Council of Economic Advisors publishes the monthly **Economic Indicators** and the **Annual Economic Review**, which deal with the state of the economy and the outlook.

For economic forecasting purposes, a useful government publication is **Business Conditions Digest**, issued monthly by the U.S. Department of Commerce. This report brings together many of the available economic indicators in convenient form for analysis and interpretation. **BusinessWeek**, in its "Business Outlook" section, reviews the indicators from time to time and regularly provides an analytical review of changing business and economic developments. It provides coverage of major developments in many areas of business and finance. *Fortune* magazine has a section in each issue entitled "Business Roundup," a bimonthly report on the economic outlook.

On corporate profits, overall trends can be seen in the **Quarterly Financial Report for Manufacturing Corporations**, published jointly by the Federal Trade Commission and the Securities and Exchange Commission. Each year, in its Monthly Economic Letter, Citibank publishes the results of its survey of the profits performance of U.S. corporations. Both report profits on two bases, as percent return on net worth and as percent margin on sales and permit an investor or a securities analyst to compare a given company with the reported industry average, or with a larger universe of companies.

Information on Industries and Companies

The Press. General news offers information that may be of consequence in the evaluation of a firm or industry. Dow Jones and Co. and Reuters operate a news ticker that disseminates items in a matter of moments. Several magazines such as ***Time, Newsweek, BusinessWeek,*** and ***U.S. News & World Report,*** carry substantial business and financial news in addition to political and social news. The daily newspapers (***New York Times*** and ***Washington Post***) are a major source of general information. The more financially oriented papers, such as the ***Wall Street Journal,*** provide a wealth of financial news with an emphasis on news of significance to individual industries, companies, or markets.

Several journals are also specifically devoted to finance. ***Barron's*** and the ***Commercial and Financial Chronicle*** are financial publications that discuss specific corporate, industry, and economic events in addition to providing stock price and market statistics. Other journals provide specific investment suggestions. Among these are ***Forbes, Financial World,*** and publications such as the ***Economist*** and ***Financial Times,*** which cover overseas events.

Trade Journals. Every major industry grouping has at least one trade journal that covers the events of the industry and the companies in it. ***Advertising Age*** and ***Chemical Week*** are two such publications. Because of their narrower interest, these journals are among the first to gather news on product development, management change, pertinent general economic considerations, and other corporate developments. These journals are probably closer to the heart of an industry than any other published source of information. The ***Business Periodicals Index*** lists articles in all major trade journals.

Investment Services. **Standard & Poor's** issues a series of **Industry Surveys,** covering 45 industries. In each case a **Basic Analysis** is issued, usually annually, followed by supplementary sections. The "Current Analysis and Outlook" updates the figures in the basic survey, provides a short-run forecast, gives brief analyses of representative companies in the industry, and provides updated data on the comparative statistical position of leading common stocks in the industry.

Forbes publishes an **"Annual Report on American Industry"** at the beginning of each calendar year. It covers each of the major industries and within the industry makes comparisons of companies based on yardsticks of performance. Examples are: growth (5-year compounded rate for both sales and earnings) and profitability (5-year average for return on equity, and on total capital). Each industry reviewed is analyzed for both past and prospective performance.

Information on Companies and Securities. **Moody's** publishes six bound manuals annually, with weekly or semiweekly loose-leaf supplements: Bank and Finance, Industrial, Municipal and Government, OTC Industrial, Public

Utility, and Transportation. This service provides information on a considerable number of corporations or issuers, usually including a brief history of the company and its operations, products, and officers, as well as income statements, balance sheets, selected financial ratios, a description of outstanding securities, and market price data.

Another established source of financial information is **Standard & Poor's Standard Corporation Records**. This loose-leaf service in six volumes, kept current with bimonthly supplements, provides information similar to that found in Moody's manuals. It also includes a well-indexed "Daily News Section" and a "Daily Dividend Section," with weekly and annual cumulations. Another particularly useful feature of this service is its "List of Subsidiary Companies," which enables the user to obtain company information in greater detail.

The ***Standard & Poor's Stock Guide*** is a condensed handbook, issued monthly, containing a brief sketch of essential facts about some 5,000 common and preferred stocks, listed and unlisted. Most of the 5,000 stocks are rated for earnings and dividend stability and growth. At the back of the guide each month are to be found "quality ratings of utility preferred stocks" and a section on the performance of 400 mutual funds.

Both Moody's and Standard & Poor's publish compendia of individual companies. ***Moody's Handbook of Common Stocks*** is issued quarterly and covers over 500 companies. For each company there is a chart, showing the industry group stock price trend and the company's stock price performance. Basic financial statistics for the past decade are given. The written analysis covers the company's financial background, recent financial developments, and prospects. The Standard & Poor's compendium is called ***Standard N.Y.S.E. Stock Reports,*** and it covers about 2,000 stocks. Financial facts are given for each company. A chart shows the market performance of the stock, the average performance of stocks in its industry, and the performance of the stock market as a whole, in addition to the trading volume of the stock. Each report usually carries a Standard & Poor's opinion of the investment merits of each stock.

Two other Standard & Poor's publications of interest are the ***Analysts Handbook*** and the ***Earnings Forecaster***. The *Analysts Handbook* provides composite corporate per share data on a comparative basis. It provides continuity since 1946 for 95 industries and the ***Standard & Poor's 400 Industrial Index,*** making possible a great variety of significant per share comparisons. It is available annually with monthly updatings. The *Earnings Forecaster* provides weekly new and revised earnings estimates on the companies prepared by Standard & Poor's and other leading investment organizations and brokerage firms, and offers a check of the various estimates against one another.

The ***Value Line Investment Survey*** covers 1,800 stocks in 91 industries. It is essentially a reference and current evaluation service. Each stock in the list is reviewed in detail once every 13 weeks. Interim reports are provided in weekly supplements on any new developments between the time of the regular quarterly reports. Each week the new edition of the *Value Line Investment Survey* covers four to six industries on a rotating basis. Each industry report contains full-page reports on individual stocks.

Corporate annual and quarterly reports with financial statements are usually available from companies on written request. Some companies will also place interested persons on a permanent mailing list to receive future reports and other information published by the company. Current stockholders receive such reports automatically. These reports represent the direct source of most financial data on particular companies.

10K reports sometimes provide valuable information, in addition to that contained in annual reports, which is helpful in the security analysis of a company. These reports are available in major business libraries, from the companies themselves, and from the SEC.

Two sources that provide **earnings expectational data** on companies are **I/B/E/S (Institutional Brokers Estimate Systems)** and **Zacks Investment Research**. I/B/E/S contains earnings per share expectation of more than 2,400 publicly traded companies. Estimates, both quarterly and annual, are made for 1 and 2 years in the future plus a 5-year growth forecast. More than 1,000 analysts at over 70 brokerage firms make the estimates and update them continually. Historical monthly data are available to January 1, 1976.

ZACK Investment Research contains over 30,000 current estimates for earnings per share of about 2,500 companies. It includes estimates for the current quarter, next quarter, current fiscal year, next fiscal year, and long-term growth rate. The estimates are extracted on a daily basis from research reports of 67 brokerage firms.

Computer-Based Information. The 1970s and 1980s have seen a dramatic improvement in the quality and quantity of data bases. At the same time, computer costs declined dramatically, leading to the introduction of computers that are relatively easy to use and inexpensive. Simultaneously, software programs in data base management and spread sheet analysis created a powerful tool for security analysis.

Machine-readable financial data can now be utilized by investors who have access to computer facilities. Companies specializing in computer-based information supply either data bases or computer-based services, or both. **Data bases**, sometimes called data banks, are magnetic tape storehouses of financial information about companies and markets, taken from the published sources described earlier. Clients can receive magnetic tapes or discs directly, to be used on their own computers, or they can receive data remotely by sharing computer time with other clients. With the proliferation of personal computers, the floppy diskette has become popular; financial data stored on the floppy diskette can be read by the investor's personal computer. The major firms in the data base field are **Compustat Services, Inc.** (a Standard & Poor's subsidiary), **Interactive Data Corporation**, and **Value Line**. Other organizations supply related computer-based data which can be used in conjunction with financial data; for example, Data Resources, Inc. (DRI) and the Center for Research in Securities Prices (CRSP).

Software suppliers provide the programs that are used to access, manipulate, analyze, and report financial data. These programs may reside on a personal computer or mainframe computer. All three of the data suppliers provide software. Another company that plays a significant role in this field is **Compuserve**. Many of the programs provided include data base management and graphics capabilities.

These services and the use of data bases make possible the high-speed retrieval and analysis of data. Analysts can use these new research tools to gain greater insights into company, industry, and market characteristics. Among other advantages, the preliminary statistical analysis of data can be done quickly. Furthermore, computers and processing systems can be used to classify industry characteristics, such as growth rates, yields, and price-earnings ratios. These can be compared with statistics of other companies, other industries, or with various indexes. Screening for desired characteristics of individual companies can be performed rapidly. Finally, computers can be used to test characteristics of stocks that have done well or poorly in the market, to determine what characteristics should be examined as possible indicators of performance in future periods.

Standard & Poor's Compustat Service, Inc. Standard & Poor's uses the name **Compustat** for it data base. Compustat offers basic annual data files covering over 6,000 stocks. The basic Compustat service contains 120 items of annual data on each of the companies covered. This includes income statement data, balance sheet data, and other miscellaneous information of value to the analyst such as information on stock prices. Many adjustments are made to the data to achieve comparability between time periods and companies.

Interactive Data Corporation (IDC). The IDC provides four major data bases and several smaller ones. The Securities Price Data Base contains daily closing price and volume data for all New York and American Stock Exchanges stocks and for 1,800 over-the-counter stocks. Daily information is also available for about 130 NYSE, Amex, Dow Jones, NASDAQ (the National Asssociation of Securities Dealers' automated quotations system) and Standard & Poor's daily and **weekly market indexes**. The IDCs Corporate Financial Data Base consists of Compustat balance sheet, income statement, and company ratio data. Its economic data base contains weekly, monthly, quarterly, and annual time series describing more than 6,000 economic variables and are grouped into 14 categories, among them GNP and Components by Industry, Consumer and Wholesale Price Indexes, and Monetary Statistics. The fourth major data base is the Value Line Data Base, which provides annual and quarterly financial information and ratios for about 1,800 major companies.

Value Line Data Services. Value line produces a number of data services that are available from IDC and other vendors, as well as its own Value Line Data Services. The basic data file is their Value Line Data Base. This base consists of over 150 income statements, balance sheets, sources and applications of funds, and financial ratio variables on over 1,800 companies beginning in 1955. In addition, the base consists of a file of calendarized per share earnings forecasts covering 1,800 corporations for the 12-month period ending a half-year hence. Finally, the base provides a systematic evaluation of the probable reliability of earnings per share forecasts of the 1,800 companies.

FIXED-INCOME SECURITIES ANALYSIS

BONDS: TERMS, YIELD CONCEPTS, AND YIELD TRADE-OFFS

Contractual Provisions. The essential features of a bond contract (indenture) are relatively simple. First, the issuer promises to pay a specific amount of dollars per bond unit (par value) on specified dates each year known as the coupon payments. Because it is an unconditional promise, failure to meet the required coupon payments means default and possible insolvency. Second, the issuer promises to pay the principal amount of the debt at a specified future date. This date is known as the **maturity date** of the bond.

These two provisions are the heart of the bond indenture, and offer two major advantages to investors: (1) a known amount of income in dollar terms, and (2) considerable pressure on the corporation to pay. It may be assumed that the debtor will meet these obligations if at all possible because the penalties for default are drastic. As a result, relative to other types of investment, the bond provides a greater certainty of a given income. But the contract alone does not guarantee payment of the return. Actual payment still depends on the continued financial ability of the borrower to fulfill the promise; it is thus necessary to appraise the quality and prospects of the company. The main disadvantage of the bond is that income return is restricted. The bondholder continues to receive only the indicated contractual income even if the profits of the company grow dramatically.

Typical Discretionary Contractual Clauses. Although a specified amount of income and a fixed maturity are the essential components of a bond contract, two other provisions may also be of considerable significance to the investor. First is the **call provision**, which gives the corporation the right to redeem the outstanding bonds at a specified price either immediately or after some future date (deferred call). The price is usually a few dollars more than par.

The call provision is always disadvantageous to the investor. A company will exercise its option to redeem its bonds at the call price, if doing so is to its advantage. In most cases the company advantage arises from a decline in interest rates or an improvement in the credit position of the company, if not both. Such developments enable the company to redeem a high-cost issue with the proceeds from the sale of a new issue at a lower interest cost. On the other hand, if interest rates rise or the company's financial position deteriorates, the company will not exercise its option to call the issue, and the full impact of any market or credit losses will be borne by the investor holding the issue.

A second provision that is common to many bonds and some preferred stocks is one that requires an annual **sinking fund payment** by the corporation, to retire the issue gradually. The specific bonds or preferred stock to be retired at any given time may be selected at random and "called" at a specific price, or they may be bought in the open market if a sufficient supply is available at less than the call price.

Sinking funds are disadvantageous to investors in one respect. After investors have gone to all the trouble of evaluating and purchasing a security at what they consider to be an attractive rate of return, they may find the security taken away from them by a sinking fund call. And at that time interest rates may be considerably lower than when the issue was purchased; thus reinvestment in an equally attractive issue may not be possible.

Bond Yield Concepts. The **value** of a bond can be defined as the present value of the future stream of the income payments (coupon rate) plus the present value of the principal payment at maturity, both discounted at the appropriate rate of interest for bonds of that maturity and quality. This rate is known as the **yield to maturity** or **effective yield**. The formula is expressed as follows:

$$V = \frac{rp}{(1+i)} + \frac{rp}{(1+i)^2} + \cdots + \frac{rp}{(1+i)^n} + \frac{p}{(1+i)^n}$$

where V = value of bond
r = coupon rate on bond
i = discount rate
p = principal of bond
n = years to maturity

In actual practice, this precise formula is not used because the principal p, the market price V, the coupon rate r, and the years to maturity n are the known data. The unknown quantity is the discount rate i that would be obtained if the bond were purchased at its existing price and held to maturity. The formula demonstrates two important features of bonds as an investment medium. First, their prices vary inversely with changes in interest rates; if market interest rates i go up, price V declines. Second, the amount of price variation necessary to adjust to a given change in interest rate is a function of the number of years to maturity.

If the discount rate based on prevailing interest rates i is above the coupon rate *r*, the price *V* of the bond will be less than 100 ($1,000); that is, the bond will be selling at a **discount**. If the opposite relationship prevails (the coupon rate is above the level of interest rates), the bond will sell at a **premium** above par. At a given price, therefore, the effective yield on a bond has two components: the annual coupon rate and the appropriate annual amount of the total discount added to (or premium subtracted from) the coupon rate.

A book of bond yield values or financial calculators can be used to compute both the **effective yield to maturity** and the appropriate annual discount or premium that should be added to or subtracted from the coupon for the bond to yield the indicated rate of return.

Yield Trade-offs. The bond market consists of three components:

1. U.S. government obligations
2. Municipal obligations of state and local government units
3. Corporate obligations

Government bonds represent obligations of highest credit quality and are available in a wide spectrum of maturities; they are the benchmark against which yields on all other bonds are evaluated. The coupon payments on **municipal bonds** are exempt from federal income baxes. As a result, their nominal pretax yields are usually lower than others. **Corporate bonds** as a class provide higher yields than government and municipal bonds. They carry credit risk that the government obligations do not, and at the same time do not provide the tax advantage of municipals. The rest of this section evaluates corporate bonds as well as municipals, because these are the two types that require credit analysis.

CORPORATE BOND ANALYSIS. As noted before, investors in bonds sacrifice most of the benefits that may ensue from a company's future growth. Because investors forego the benefits of growth, they must try to assure themselves that the issuers will be able to fulfill their obligations. In this regard investors in corporate bonds should be primarily concerned with the capacity of the issuer to pay interest and principal as they fall due. The chief indices of such capacity are:

1. The credit of the issuer
2. Protective provisions of the bond issue being analyzed
3. Bond ratings

The Credit of the Issuer. The credit of the issuer, that is, his or her ability to meet all debts as they mature, is the most important factor in bond analysis. The credit of the obligor is measured by: (1) earnings or cash flow coverage of interest charges; (2) level of debt in relation to equity; (3) the debtor's liquidity position; and (4) the sustainability and economic significance of the company and its industry.

Earnings Coverage of Interest Charges. In the past the most widely used yardstick for bond quality was the ratio of earnings available to pay interest (profits before income taxes) to fixed charges. In stable industries, earnings coverage of two or more times interest charges may be regarded as adequate, whereas in industries subject to wide fluctuations in earnings coverage of three, four, or more times may be required for a good credit rating. In industries sensitive to the business cycle, coverage of fixed charges under recession conditions is the significant ratio.

The factor of safety in **fixed charge coverage** is the percentage by which earnings before taxes may decline before they fail to cover fixed charges. If earnings before taxes are $2.4 million and fixed charges are $960,000, then such earnings can decline by as much as 60% or $1.44 million and still cover fixed charges. Investors also consider the number of times that a firm's cash flow (earnings after taxes plus noncash expenses, e.g., depreciation) cover fixed charges.

If substantial **lease rental obligations** have been incurred, they should be taken into account in computing earnings coverage of fixed charges. However, rentals under long-term leases may include not only a return on the investment of the lessor, but also the principal return of such investment. In that event the rentals are equivalent to both the interest and the sinking fund payments on a bond issue. See the Altman Handbook of Corporate Finance (Wiley, 1986), Section 11, for a more detailed discussion.

As long-term crditors, bondholders are concerned with future far more than with past or present earnings coverage of fixed charges. Hence the probable trend of earnings over a period of years and their vulnerability to cyclical declines in business activity and other unfavorable influences are major factors affecting the credit of the issuer.

Earnings Coverage of Junior Bonds Interest. If a corporation has both senior and junior (subordinated to the senior) debt outstanding, the significant measure of earnings coverage of interest on junior debt is the ratio to total fixed charges. Thus a corporation with a $20 million issue of 4.5% debentures and $10 million of 5% subordinated debentures has total interest charges of $1.4 million. If it earns $2.8 million before income taxes, the coverage of interest on the subordinated debentures would be two times, because prior charges of $900,000 must be paid together with $500,000 on the subordinated issue. To say that earnings after deducting $900,000 of interest on the debentures, or $1.9 million, cover interest requirements on the 5% subordinated debentures 3.8 times is misleading. But it is accurate to say that interest of $900,000 on the 4.5% senior issue is being covered 3.1 times.

Asset Coverage. Another quality measure is the proportion of total capitalization represented by debt versus equity. The individual bond or preferred stock owner would benefit if that issue were the only senior security outstanding, because earnings coverage then would be at a premium. Thus to the bondholder or preferred stockholder, the greater the equity capital as a percentage of total capitalization, the better. An analysis of the corporation's capital structure is, therefore, a sort of asset coverage measure that supplements the earnings coverage measure.

Coverage based on historical depreciated costs is the starting measurement. However, additional analysis should include: (1) off balance sheet items such as unfunded pension liabilities and leases that should be capitalized, and (2) the replacement value and market value of assets. The economic durability of assets is a major factor. For example, timberland located near a paper mill has a solid, long-term life, whereas a rack of women's dresses or a 2-year-old computer line may have to be discounted.

Liquidity. Some companies that appear to have satisfactory earnings and asset coverage may, however, not have enough cash on hand to pay their claims as they come due. The following ratios are the principal ones in use for measuring liquidity:

1. Receivables collection period. This ratio measures the number of days it takes, on average, to collect accounts and notes receivable. A firm's day's sales (annual sales ÷ 360) are divided into accounts receivable to solve for the collection period.
2. Number of days to sell inventory. Analogous to the ratio just described, this **inventory turnover** ratio is derived by dividing average daily cost of goods sold into the average of beginning and ending inventory.
3. Number of days' bills outstanding. Here, the average daily cost of goods sold is divided into average accounts payable.
4. Working capital ratios. Whereas ratios 1–3 dissect working capital (current assets minus current liabilities) into its major components—accounts receivable, inventory, and accounts payable—it is also useful to take an overall view of a company's ability to meet current liabilities. The most common measures are:
   - **a.** Current ratio. Current assets divided by current liabilities.
   - **b.** Quick asset, or acid-test, ratio. Current assets exclusive of inventory, divided by current liabilities.
   - **c.** Cash ratio. Bank deposits plus liquid securities owned, divided by current liabilities.

The Sustainability Factor. Although the basic economics of the company's product line and cost structure are of great importance, the competitive position of the company is perhaps of equal significance. By and large there is good reason to have much greater confidence in the long-term continuity of big companies that are competitive leaders in their industry. Although size alone does not guarantee a profitable level of operations, seasoned firms that are dominant in their industry area naturally tend to be better able to withstand adversity. It is true, however, that we do occasionally observe large firms with great difficulties requiring drastic rehabilitative action. (See the section "Bankruptcy and Reorganization.")

For a bondholder, stability and sustainability are far more important than near-term dynamic growth potential. There is little incentive to be a bondholder in a small, high technology company because there is no participation in the upside potential, but there is exposure to the downside risk inherent in rapid technological obsolescence.

In contrast, a well-established company providing a basic product such as food, paper, or electricity should be more attractive. Diversification and lack of major cyclicality are also desirable characteristics. A corporate culture that encourages adapting to change is an attractive quality, because any particular business can evolve substantially over the long life of a typical bond. For example, once stable businesses can become volatile if deregulated.

Protective Provisions of Bond Issues. A bond issue may be given specific protection, over and above that provided by the credit of the obligor, by a **mortgage** on physical property, a pledge of securities under a **collateral trust agreement**, or a preference over other creditors of the issuer through a **covenant of prior or equal coverage** or the **subordination** of other indebtedness. The chief protection such provisions give is priority in the event of a future reorganization, should the corporation become unable to meet its interest charges on debt maturities. Because of the specific added protection they have been given, such bond issues sell at lower yields than other obligations of the corporation. In some instances the protection provided by a mortgage or by a pledge of collateral may be so great that the bond issue is considered strong, and it sells at a relatively low yield even if the credit of the obligor is weak. Perhaps the best example of this is **equipment trust certificates** issued by railroads. The collateral in this case is considered so marketable that the credit of the certificate is appraised separately from the railroad.

The collateral provisions of bonds, which used to be very heavily stressed by investors, are much less emphasized today. This is because property value is a function of the earnings the property can produce. Most property that serves as bond collateral is in the form of specialized plant and equipment. When the economics of the issuing company deteriorate to the point of bankruptcy, the likelihood is that its property is incapable of earning an adequate rate of return and is therefore not worth very much. The more fungible the property the better, because it usually increases the realized value and the speed of liquidation. Wheat, refined oil, new airplanes, and office buildings in key locations have far wider appeal than machines that can only be used to make x-ray film.

Bond Ratings. Widespread use is made of ratings accorded publicly owned bond issues by investment services. These ratings are based on a few broad investment tests, and on the subjective evaluation of the future by the raters. This should not take the place, however, of a thorough analysis of a bond issue unless the investor cannot perform this evaluation. Because many investors are guided by ratings in buying and selling bonds, however, they influence bond yields to a large extent. Institutional investors are particularly influenced by ratings if, as in the case of commercial banks, supervisory authorities use them to determine the suitability of bonds for bank investment. Changes in the rating given to a bond, therefore, can considerably affect its price and yield.

The two primary systems of rating are those of **Moody's Investors Service** and **Standard & Poor's**. The rating or rank assigned to a security under each of these systems has the following stratifications:

Moody's	Standard & Poor's	Quality Designation
Aaa	AAA	Highest quality
Aa	AA	High quality
A	A	Upper medium grade
Baa	BBB	Medium grade
Ba	BB	Speculative elements
B	B	Speculative
Caa	CCC-CC	Default possible
Ca	C	Default, some recovery possible
C	DDD-D	Little recovery possible

Bond ratings are designed essentially to rank issues in order of the probability of default. Thus triple-A bonds are those judged to be of highest quality because they have a negligible risk of default. Double-A bonds are of high quality also but are judged not to be quite as free of default risk as triple-A. Bonds rated A and BBB by Standard & Poor's are generally referred to as medium-quality obligations, with the BBB possessing a higher risk of default than the A. Bonds not falling within the first four rating categories are believed to contain a considerable "speculative" element, and are sometimes referred to as **"junk bonds"** or **high yield bonds**.

Hickman (1958) found that "The agency ratings serve as rough indexes to price and yield stability. On the average, realized yields on low grades were somewhat above those on high grades, but investors seeking price stability should have avoided the low-grade issues." He also found that the incidence of failure among firms with lower rated securities was greater than that of higher rated ones.

MUNICIPAL BOND ANALYSIS. Because of the excellent empirical credit record of most municipal obligations, the need to engage in a penetrating analysis of their quality has sometimes been doubted. After 1975, however, the fiscal difficulties of some cities, notably New York City and Cleveland, led to the view that careful appraisal of the relevant credit factors should precede investment in municipal bonds. Therefore it would seem highly desirable for investors in municipals to become reasonably competent in the techniques of municipal credit analysis. For an in-depth discussion of municipal bonds, see the section "State and Local Debt."

Analytical Concepts. Hayes and Bauman (1976) note that the **appraisal of municipal obligations** is a highly specialized area of investment analysis. In fact, the techniques for evaluating the quality of these issues are quite different from those used in corporate bond analysis. The major reason for the singular nature of municipal bonds rests in their status as obligations or governmental units. These units are not established to derive earnings from economic activities; their purpose is to supply services to the general public. Taxation is the typical means of financing these services. Under ordinary circumstances tax levies are designed to cover only the operating costs of municipal services plus any requirements for debt service, including interest charges and annual maturities.

As a consequence, a substantial **"coverage" of interest payments** is not expected on municipal obligations, and there is no residual equity to backstop the bondholders' claim. Indeed, in most cases there are no assets to which the bondholders can resort in case of default. There is, of course, the estimated value of the real and personal properties subject to tax levies within the geographic area. But these properties are not available for foreclosure in case of default; moreover, estimates of taxable property values are not subject to conventional rules of determination as are corporate asset values.

General Obligations. These may be described as bonds issued by state governments or municipal corporations chartered by the states under which all taxing powers are pledged for payment. Most general obligations arise from the financing of capital improvements undertaken by states, cities, counties, and special districts. The latter are merely municipal corporations chartered for a particular governmental function, the most important and widespread example being school districts. These bonds are generally regarded as the basic type of municipals and, unless otherwise qualified in the bond description, it is usually presumed that a bond of a municipal corporation is a general obligation.

Revenue Bonds. There are three major categories of revenue obligations classified according to the source of funds for debt servicing:

1. Those issued to finance physical facilities that provide economic services sold directly to users, with the service revenues pledged to debt servicing. Water and sewer, toll roads, and airport services are examples of this type of obligation.
2. Those issued to finance special purpose facilities, which are then leased to a user, with the lease rentals pledged to debt servicing. If the user is a municipal corporation, general tax revenues may indirectly support the issue as they become the effecive source of the lease payments.

3. Those issued to provide services that benefit certain products with special taxes levied on these products and pledged to service the bonds. A large volume of state highway bonds falls into this group, because fuel taxes and auto license fees are specifically pledged to service the bond interest and principal payments.

The quality of revenue bonds tends to vary over a considerable range. Those that receive support from a high-quality corporate credit or a highly assured usage fee, may carry quality ratings equal or superior to the general obligations of the related municipal unit. Others have gone into partial or total default as revenues fell short of bond service requirements.

Technical Aspects

Legality. In most states municipal borrowings are subject to restrictions under statutory law, and in some jurisdictions the power to borrow funds is not assumed to result from the general powers of municipal corporations.

Maturities. Except for revenue bonds, it is customary for municipal bonds to carry **serial maturities**. Such maturities are often required by law, and their purpose is to encourge **prudent debt management** by automatically retiring debt out of taxes or other sources of revenue on a periodic, regular basis.

Redemption Provisions. Most general obligations issued in serial form are not subject to a call price. Revenue bonds are more likely to be subject to redemption before maturity. The redemption provision is similar to that on corporates; they may be callable as a whole or in part at certain specific dates, and the premium above par at which the bonds are callable may decrease as they approach maturity.

Contractual Position and Remedies. In the case of corporate bonds, the willingness to pay the required interest and principal is always assumed to be strong, because the very life of the corporation is in jeopardy if there is a default. The situation is not so clear-cut in the case of municipal obligations. A municipality cannot be liquidated to satisfy a bondholder's claim. As a result, the analyst needs to make a special inquiry of the willingness to pay, or the indicated desire of the municipality to manage the debt in a prudent way.

Credit Analysis of Municipals

Credit Quality Factors. As in corporate analysis, the factors bearing on credit quality have two dimensions: (1) the broad economic factors and their trends, and (2) the financial data and trends.

The most significant general economic factors pertinent to the appraisal of any municipal credit are population trends and the nature and diversity of the economic base.

A number of financial ratios and data trends have been suggested for inputs to credit quality decisions on a municipal credit, including tax-dependent debt as a percentage of true valuation of taxable real estate, per capital net overall bonded debt, debt trend, property valuation trend, tax collection record, and budget record.

Revenue bonds are very much like the bonds of business corporations. Therefore the key ratio in revenue bond analysis is earnings coverage. Because civic facilities are not profit-making operations in the business sense—fees are usually designed to meet operating expenses and debt service only, with a small addition for contingencies—coverage ratios are not expected to be as substantial for corporate bonds. Ratios of 1.5–2 times charges are common for good-quality obligations. However, the financial statements of municipalities are often not subject to the same stringent auditing standards as corporations. Therefore the confidence factor in some municipal financial statements is less.

PREFERRED STOCK ANALYSIS

Nature of Contract. The investment implications of the preferred stock contract are for the most part analogous to those of a bond. First, both provide a limited fixed income. Second, both often include the redemption provision. Because of the resemblance between the two types of securities, the techniques for analyzing them are almost identical. The grouping of preferred stocks and bonds for purposes of analysis is in distinct contrast to legal and accounting concepts, which view the preferred shares as a part of the equity along with the common stock and establish the creditors in a separate category. In one major respect only the preferred contract resembles common stock more closely than bonds: Like common stock, there is no maturity. But this is of much less significance than the fact that both bonds and preferreds are fixed-income securities.

Given the high after-tax cost to the corporation to issue nonconvertible preferred stock, any attempt to finance through this investment vehicle should prompt a hard look at the company's financial statements and questions about its ability and need to raise capital.

Major Weakness of Preferred Stock Contracts. The corporation is under much less compulsion to pay preferred dividends than it is to pay bond interest, because preferred stock is merely given the right to receive its specified dividend before any dividends are paid on the common shares. When a corporation fails to meet interest charges on bonds, the result is default. But the penalty for failure to declare preferred dividends is not as onerous. Such an omission merely means that the company does not pay dividends on the common stock until the preferred dividends have been paid in full; that is, preferred dividends are cumulative. Still, most analysts view the omission of preferred dividends as a serious sign of firm deterioration.

Yields and Taxes. Because of the fixed rate of return and prior claim on assets and earnings, the market action of high-grade preferred stock tends to be governed by interest rates. As in the case of other types of security, preferred stocks range in quality from sound investments to highly speculative issues. The price action of the more speculative issues may more frequently be affected by the business risk of the issuer than by interest rates.

Except for **public utilities** and other companies with a similar need to maintain a certain equity-debt relationship, corporations have not generally desired to issue preferred stock as a source of new capital because of the tax burden. In particular, present income tax laws allow corporations to deduct interest payments on debt before computing taxable income, but dividends on preferred stock are not similarly treated. They are paid from income after taxes. This has not only reduced significantly the issuance of new preferreds, but has caused corporations to eliminate preferreds from their capitalizations when possible. The exception to this trend, however, is the practice of issuing preferred stock, usually convertible, to effect mergers and acquisitions.

Even though new preferred issues are not frequent and even though their appeal to the individual investor is questionable when their return and risk are considered, preferreds have a special attraction for any organization that pays taxes as a corporation. Dividends on preferred stock owned by a corporation or by certain institutions are taxable as income only to the extent of 15%. After-tax yields on good-quality preferreds have thus been very attractive relative to bond yields for these investors.

COMMON STOCK ANALYSIS

CHARACTERISTICS OF COMMON STOCK. Common stock represents a share in the ownership of the firm. It has the last claim on earnings and assets of all other securities issued, but it also has an unlimited potential for dividend payment and capital gain through rising prices. Other corporate securities (i.e., corporate bonds and preferred stock) have a contract for interest or dividend payout that common stock does not have. If the firm should fail and be forced to liquidate, common stockholders get what is left after everyone else has been repaid. Risk is highest with common stock and so must be its expected return.

COMMON STOCK VALUATION CONCEPTS. It was noted earlier that value of a bond at a given time can be defined as the present value of the stream of coupon payments plus the present value of the principal payment to be received at maturity, both discounted at the prevailing rate of interest for that maturity. Following analogous reasoning, the value of a common stock can be defined as the present value of the future dividend stream in perpetuity. This concept is consistent with the assumption that the corporation will indeed have a perpetual life in accordance with its charter. In mathematical terms, the formula is that of a value for a **perpetual annuity** with a constant level of payments:

$$V = \frac{D}{r}$$

where V = value
D = dividends per share
r = percentage discount rate

If the dividends are assumed to grow at a certain constant rate, the formula becomes:

$$V = \frac{D}{r - g}$$

where g = annual constant percentage growth in dividends per share.

Because this model assumes that the growth rate for the corporation to be analyzed is constant, it is most suitable for use in estimating value for stable mature companies or as the residual value in a more complex model to represent the mature phase of a presently more dynamic company. These companies with a more erratic or cyclical earnings pattern, or companies showing rapid growth rates require a more complex dividend capitalization model framework to accommodate those differing dividend growth patterns. Typically these more complex models provide for: (1) a yearly forecast for the next 5 years (usually based on expected results over a typical economic cycle); (2) a transition period of perhaps 5 to 20 years' duration (used to link current expectation for growth, profitability, dividend payout in a corporate life cycle atmosphere to the mature state); and (3) the residual, mature, or constant corporate phase. These complex models enjoy the advantages of: (1) being comprehensible; (2) reflecting the true theoretical value of a common stock; (3) providing the intellectual framework to compare high-profit, high-growth companies with low-profit, low-growth firms; and (4) creating a mechanism to reflect the life-cycle nature of firms and industries in a competitive environment. The disadvantages include: (1) subtle but meaningful biases for or against certain types of companies can be created by ground rules that appear very reasonable; (2) high sensitivity to forecasts far into the future; and (3) reasonably high labor intensity. These models are described in the investment literature and have most recently found practical implementation at various investment organizations. (See Farrell, 1983.)

Although more elaborate variations of the dividend capitalization model are needed for practical applications, the simplified form provides a convenient means of analyzing the determinants of stock value. To begin with, the value of the stock should be greater, the greater the earning power and capacity of the corporation to pay out current dividends D. Correspondingly, the higher the growth rate g of the dividend, the greater the value of the corporation's stock. Finally, the greater the risk of the corporation and thus presumably the higher the discount rate (r), the lower the value of the stock framework. Put another way, r is the risk-free rate as represented by U.S. Treasury bills adjusted for the higher risk level (frequently referred to as beta) of a given security.

The prime role of the analyst is to evaluate the basic earning power of the firm and to project the potential growth of earnings and dividends into the future, and that is the focus of this section on common stock analysis. The discount rate r is considered to be a function of the corporation's **systematic risk** and is thought of as being determined in a broader economic framework. After briefly discussing the determinants of the discount rate, we describe the role of financial statement analysis in evaluating corporate earning power and discuss the methods of projecting dividend growth rates.

Although the dividend discount models help explain more of the intellectual framework of a stock's valuation, the **price/earnings ratio** is far more commonly used. There are a number of variations of this ratio, usually hinging on different earnings used. Common alternatives include the earnings per share for last year, the latest 12 months, this year's estimate, next year's estimate, 3-to-5 years in the future, and a normal earnings level. The inverse of the PE ratio (i.e., earnings to price) is called the **earnings yield** and can be useful in comparing stocks with bonds. The PE ratio has the advantage of wide usage and simplicity of calculation. In valuation work it is most effective in comparing stocks with similar characteristics such as those in the same industry, comparable risk levels, or corresponding levels of profitability, growth, and quality. The ratio is least useful in cyclical companies unless normal earnings are used. Typically highly cyclical companies trough in price when the PE is highest (i.e., earnings are very depressed) and peak in price when the PE is lowest (i.e., earnings are reaching cyclical highs).

Another method to evaluate common stocks is to compare the current price with **asset values**. Common asset value benchmarks used include reported book value, replacement cost, net working capital after deducting all debt, takeover value, book adjusted for hidden assets, or liquidation value. To focus on asset value can be an excellent way to uncover attractive investment opportunities especially when investor interest has been dampened by currently depressed earnings. Common pitfalls in this approach include: (1) rationalizing high stock prices by using cyclically peak industrial, commodity, or real estate prices to value assets; and (2) forgetting that sound assets can be quickly consumed by poor management unless there is a specific trigger to achieve the asset values.

Arbitrage analysis is another approach that requires evaluation of related securities and employs various techniques of security analysis. Although risk arbitrage involved in corporate takeovers has a high component of speculation, other forms of arbitrage are more fundamental. For instance, arbitrage opportunities can occur between the common stock and convertible security of the same corporation when the prices get out of line. Bonds of similar characteristics can provide the alert investor a chance to capitalize on a spread caused by short-term supply/demand fluctuations. Sometimes the same security will sell briefly for different prices on different markets.

RISK-RETURN TRADE-OFF. As noted before, **systematic risk** is that component of total risk which cannot be diversified away because it is common to all stocks; hence it should be the relevant risk in a portfolio context. In the stock market, stocks with high degrees of systematic risk must be priced to yield high rates of return to induce investors to accept high degrees of risk that are essentially undiversifiable within that market. Stocks with high systematic risk should have higher discount rates *r* than stocks with lower systematic risk.

Correspondingly, we should expect to observe stocks with higher systematic risk earning higher returns over longer periods of time than stocks with lower systematic risk. Several empirical studies have in fact addressed this question of the risk-return trade-off in the stock market, with one by Sharpe and Cooper (1972) providing perhaps the best example. This study analyzed the price behavior of all listed stocks over the 1926–1967 period, and used the **beta coefficient as the measure of systematic risk of stocks**.

Essentially, the study showed that stocks with high observed betas tended on average to earn higher returns than stocks with medium betas, which in turn tended to earn higher returns than stocks with low betas. The results supported the theory that high systematic risk should be associated with higher return and low systematic risk with lower return. The level of systematic risk might well be used as a means of establishing the appropriate discount rate for a stock. Using this approach in practice, however, requires adequate estimates of systematic risk, and investors should be aware of the deficiencies of standard beta measures for this purpose. For a discussion of the properties of beta, see Sharpe (1978, chapter 11). Some observations include: (1) the reliability of betas on a diversified portfolio tends to be greater than on an isolated stock; (2) historical betas do not fully reflect substantial recent changes in a company's business risk profile; and (3) historical betas are only part of the risk measurement, because they do not reflect a significant change in the price/value ratio. Another way to look at beta is that it attempts to measure the relative price volatility of a given stock over a full market cycle, but beta at any stage may be an inadequate proxy for risk. Using this methodology, the security analyst's job is to: (1) determine an appropriate systematic risk measurement or beta, and (2) forecast the return by projecting future dividends. A more common approach is to estimate earning power and a normal price/earnings ratio range. A third technique is to measure the risk/reward relative to an assessed asset valuation.

FINANCIAL STATEMENT ANALYSIS. The financial statements of a company consist of an **income statement**, a **balance sheet**, a **sources and uses of funds statement**, and the footnotes to each. From the analysis of these statements it may be possible to gather certain information and indications about basic corporate earning power. Certain pertinent ratios, trends, and figures may provide clues to the company's future. Financial statement analysis should, however, proceed with caution, because these statements suffer from certain deficiencies. An entire, separate section in this Handbook is devoted to financial statement analysis.

The Income Statement. The annual income statement issued by a company is an accounting picture of the past year's income, expenses, and profits. The ratio income statement is an income statement in which all figures are expressed as a percentage of sales. The major advantages of a ratio income statement are: (1) it permits easy comparison among companies of different sizes; (2) it allows quick analysis of how specific expenses are changing relative to sales to measure productivity or compare against certain benchmarks. The following tabulation illustrates the income statement of a hypothetical company presented in ratio form.

Model of Income Statement

Sales	$200,000,000	100%
Less: Cost of goods sold	100,000,000	50
Gross operating margin	100,000,000	50
Less: Selling, administrative expenses, and depreciation	50,000,000	25
Net operating income	50,000,000	25
Less: Interest expense	10,000,000	5
Taxable income	40,000,000	20
Less: Taxes	20,000,000	10
Net income	20,000,000	10
Less: Dividends to common equity	10,000,000	5
Retained earnings	10,000,000	5

Income statement ratios can be used to compare similar organizations such as firms in the same industry. Ratio analysis can be used in comparison with certain accepted ratio standards. However, care must be taken that the standards are appropriate. For example, comparing capital intensive companies with service firms solely on income statement ratios can be very misleading. Income statement ratios should be evaluated in conjunction with balance sheet and cash flow data.

Particular ratios and trends might be especially helpful in evaluating the earning capacity of the firm and in detecting potential problems and opportunities at an early stage. Among the more useful ratios are the following:

1. Pretax profit margin: Income before taxes/Sales
2. Operating margin: Operating income/Sales
3. Earnings per share: Net profit/Outstanding shares
4. Tax ratio: Taxes paid/Earnings before taxes

The **payout ratio** is the common dividend earnings available to common stock and reveals the percentage of net profits paid to stockholders. The amount and percentage of retained earnings (1 minus the payout ratio) may give some indication of the funds available for investment that will generate future earnings. A higher retention rate may indicate increased future earnings.

The Balance Sheet. The balance sheet represents the company's financial position at a point in time. Income statements deal with flows, whereas balance sheets present data that reflect the amount of assets and liabilities on a given date. The ratio balance sheet presents individual assets as a percent of total assets and the detailed liabilities relative to total liabilities. The illustrative balance sheet that follows shows the liability side as representing sources of funds and the asset side as uses of funds.

The balance sheet reveals information on the company's liquidity, utilization of assets, and financing, all of which may aid in appraising the company's earning power. A company's liquidity position is an indication of its ability to meet the more immediate cash needs of normal, as well as unusual, operating conditions. **Current assets** are the most quickly converted to cash, and **current liabilities** present the most immediate need for cash. Therefore the analysis of liquidity concentrates on these areas. The **working capital** position, which is current assets minus current liabilities, is a frequently used indication of liquidity. Certain working capital ratios are indicative of the quality and adequacy of the working capital position. Among the ratios that indicate the quality of the working capital position are (1) the **current ratio** (current assets to current liabilities), and (2) the **quick ratio** (cash, marketable securities, and accounts receivable to current liabilities).

Balance Sheet Model

Uses of Funds	Sources of Funds
Current assets	Current liabilities
Long-term assets	Long term liabilities
Other assets	Net worth
Total assets	Total liabilities and equity

There are several variations of calculating **net working capital**, which begin with current assets minus current liabilities. Then long-term debt, total balance sheet liabilities, or even off-balance sheet items such as unfunded pension liabilities can be deducted to get an estimate of minimum liquidation value.

An important indication of **basic earning power** may be found in the efficiency with which management is utilizing its assets to produce sales and profits. Indications of efficient asset management are:

1. Return on investment: Net profit/Total assets
2. Net profit to common equity
3. Fixed asset turnover: Sales/Assets
4. Inventory turnover: Cost of sales/Inventory

In general when income statement figures are compared with balance sheet data, it is helpful to use an average for the balance sheet data over the period of the income statement. Typically this is an average of the beginning and ending figures for a year. For example, using an average assets helps measure what magnitude of assets are needed to generate a given level of sales. The average compensates for significant changes during the year such as a major financing.

The balance sheet also reveals how a company has financed itself among the various sources of funds available. The **capital structure** is the proportion of long-term debt, preferred stock, and stockholders' equity in a firm's financing. The more debt in a capital structure (the higher the debt-equity ratio), the more cash expense obligations the company has. A large cash obligation in relation to the company's cash generation is indicative of great financial risk.

In addition to affecting the risk associated with future earnings, the use of debt also affects earnings. **Leverage** is the use of debt in an attempt to increase return on equity. The difference between the return on an investment and the cost of financing the investment is the residual to the common stockholders. If the difference is positive, the stockholders benefit, but if it is negative, the stockholders must make up the difference. This causes a decrease in the return on equity and magnifies the decrease in earnings per share. The key aspect of the use of financial leverage is its magnification effect.

One relatively quick way to see how the balance sheet and income statement are interacting to produce profitability is to calculate a series of basic ratios that indicate whether profitability is coming from leverage, efficient use of assets, or basic return on sales.

$$\underset{\text{(net income/sales)}}{\text{Return on sales}} \times \underset{\text{(sales/assets)}}{\text{asset turnover}} = \underset{\text{(net income/assets)}}{\text{return on assets}}$$

Return on assets is probably the most fundamental measurement of profitability because it tells whether costs are in proper relation to selling prices and whether assets are being effectively utilized. It is especially useful to see trends for a company over 5 or 10 years and to compare companies within an industry. Both return on sales and asset turnover are a function of a specific industry.

$$\underset{\text{(net income/assets)}}{\text{Return on assets}} \times \underset{\text{(assets/equity)}}{\text{Leverage}} = \underset{\text{(net income/equity)}}{\text{Return on equity}}$$

The preceding calculation will reveal to what extent return on equity is being generated by leverage or efficient operations.

Pro Forma and Supplemental Data. Most balance sheet and income statements are based on actual results using historical cost information and standard depreciation schedules. In recent years, replacement cost data have been more readily available and help highlight companies with hidden assets and those with potentially low profit on future investment. Statements that do not include discontinued operations might give a better indication of future profitability, but they could also give the impression that existing management has been more effective than was actually the case. In the case of major changes such as a large acquisition of financing, pro forma statements should be analyzed before a realistic estimate of future earning power can be made. In the event companies follow substantially different accounting policies, the financial statements should be adjusted to make the companies more comparable.

Sources and Uses of Funds Statements. The sources and uses of funds statement for a corporation tells where the cash came from and where it went. It indicates what assets were acquired and how they were financed. It is, in many respects, wider in scope than either the income statement or the balance sheet and, indeed, integrates the two statements.

Uses of funds are increases in assets and decreases in liabilities. For example, increases in cash, accounts receivable, inventory, and plant, property, and equipment; and decreases in accounts payable, long-term debt, and stockholders' equity are uses of funds. Sources of funds are the reverse; that is, decreases in assets and increases in liabilities.

The sources and uses of funds statement may be constructed by comparing the company's balance sheets from one period with another and recording the increases and decreases in assets and liabilities. One format for portraying these flows might be referred to as the **reconciliation of working capital**. The focus here is on changes in total working capital (current assets minus current liabilities) and is illustrated as follows:

Reported net income		$20,000,000
Plus:	Noncash charges (depreciation, deferred tax reserve, etc.)	4,000,000
Equals:	Working capital provided by operations	$24,000,000

Less:	Capital expenditures	$10,000,000	
	Common stock dividends	10,000,000	(20,000,000)
Equals:	Increase in working capital		$ 4,000,000

Analysis of sources and uses can help uncover companies that must continuously seek outside financing. Some of these companies have benefited in earnings per share growth by being able to sell common stock at substantial premiums to book value, whereas other firms have been penalized by being forced to sell stock at a significant discount to book. In these cases, future growth in earnings per share is very sensitive to the unpredictable market/book value ratio. In other situations, the self-financing aspect of a firm makes predictability somewhat higher. If a firm is generating cash in excess of what is needed for internal expansion and is also selling below book value, this could represent an opportunity to buy back shares and increase earnings per share.

A careful examination of the sources and uses of funds might uncover firms which (1) need external financing just to pay their dividends; (2) must reinvest all cash flow to maintain the current level of profitability; (3) have large excess cash flow that can be used for acquisitions without dilution; (4) are financing sales growth by excess accounts receivable growth through easy credit; and (5) are requiring proportionately higher investments just to maintain past growth rates.

Deficiencies of Financial Statements. A company's financial statements provide valuable information about the level and trend of it earning power. However, investors cannot accept at face value the figures designated by a company as net worth. This is because in preparing financial statements accountants have latitude in the way that business transactions are reported. This generally leads to less than uniform statements of income and balance sheets of companies even within the same industry. The rest of this section reviews the areas where divergences may be greatest.

To begin with, there can be problems in determining when revenues or sales are to be recognized for certain types of companies. These can be illustrated by the case of producers of expensive equipment, who often lease their products to customers rather than sell them outright. Accounting guidelines have been issued on minimally acceptable answers to this and other questions, but some companies choose an accounting policy more conservative than suggested by guidelines, whereas others follow only the minimally acceptable standards. In amortizing **goodwill** resulting from an acquisition, companies have the option to use almost any period up to 40 years.

Another example is that companies may use first in, first out or last in, first out **(FIFO or LIFO)** methods for valuing inventories. During periods of falling prices, LIFO usually produces higher earnings than FIFO, because the less costly inventory is "sold" first. During periods of rising prices, the earnings effect is reversed. In recent years LIFO has produced lower earnings but higher cash flows, because taxes have been reduced. In analyzing earnings, it is important to be aware of any earnings increase or decrease that may have arisen because of a shift from LIFO to FIFO, or vice versa. It is also important to be aware of the LIFO versus FIFO effects on earnings when comparing different companies. On the balance sheet, LIFO understates inventory levels in inflationary periods.

Companies may use **straight-line** or **accelerated methods of depreciation**. Accelerated depreciation increases depreciation costs in the early years of a new asset's life; it thereby decreases reported profit and income tax when the asset is new. The total depreciation expense is unchanged; only the timing is altered. Differing methods, however, can affect any particular year's reported accounting income significantly. The accounting life can also vary. In general, different accounting methods for depreciation are most meaningful in rapidly growing companies.

Research and development (R&D) activity is expensed periodically under conventional accounting procedures. However, some future benefit should be generated from this investment. On the other hand, in many rapidly changing, high technology markets, a relatively high level of R&D expenditures is required just to stay in business. The analyst should consider this in making comparisons among research-intensive and other companies.

A company's financial obligations under its **pension plans** can be divided into two major segments: the past service liability and the current service liability. There are various legal, tax, and personnel relations reasons for putting money aside in advance to provide for these liabilities. This is known as funding. But the rate at which pension liabilities are funded, and reflected in current net income, is a matter of managerial discretion within rather broad guidelines. Two keys to evaluating the adequacy of the pension fund are the future return on investment assumed for present funds and the inflation rate assumed for future retirement benefits. The relationship between these two is an area to focus on. Pension funds can amount to a large percentage of a firm's equity.

PROJECTING EARNINGS. Predicting the future is a high risk occupation, but a challenge that the security analyst inherently must confront, because stock prices implicitly derive their value from discounting a future flow of income. It might be helpful to think of three types of future: (1) a random future, (2) a trend-line future, and (3) a caused future.

Random Future. An example of a random future would be a certain plant being struck by lightning and burning down. These events are impossible to predict with precision. Investors who believe that the future is largely determined by random or unpredictable events might elect to evaluate securities using tangible benchmarks of results already achieved, such as price to book value, price to latest 12 months' earnings per share (EPS), or price to the average of the past 5 years' EPS. These assume no major changes will occur. For those investors convinced that significant but unpredictable changes will occur, appropriate investment approaches would include a high degree of diversification and building in a large margin for error in assumptions or estimates.

The use of alternative scenarios with probability weightings could also prove an appropriate approach. Another variation of this theme is to estimate a conservative, optimistic, and best-judgment alternative, but then require that the stock meet the most conservative test.

Trend-line Future. An example of a trend-line future is to assume that real GNP will grow at an annual rate of 3–4% for the next 5 years, because that has been a trend established over decades. Two variations of this approach are: (1) the simple trend line described in the GNP example, and (2) a relative or contingent trend line (e.g., company X's sales will grow at an 11% annual rate as long as disposable personal income grows at 10%). Projecting historic growth rates in company sales and earnings is a frequently used approach in investment analysis.

Historical Growth Rate. Assuming that the circumstances under which the firm operated in the past will continue unchanged in the future, the investor may use the **historical growth rate** in forecasting future earnings. Various methods of computing the historical growth rate can be used, such as the compound growth rate, the moving average, and a fitted trend line.

The investor must be careful in interpreting compound and trend growth rates, especially as indicators of future earnings patterns. Among the most important considerations are the selection of the base and terminal years and hidden patterns of intervening years. By selecting different base and terminal years, the growth rate will also be made to differ.

The moving average approach lessens the problem or base and terminal year distortion. The major disadvantage of the moving average is its sluggish response to a significant change.

When using any of these methods for forecasting, it must be assumed that the conditions that prevailed during the selected time span will continue in the future. Stable conditions imply that such important considerations as industry technology, competition, and political environment are constant. If the conditions are unstable, forecasts may be more misleading than helpful.

Aggregate Approach Using Regression Analysis. The application of historical growth rates in forecasting earnings relies solely on earnings information and assumes a continuation of the previous earnings pattern. The **aggregate approach** broadens the investigation for indicators of future earnings beyond the earnings themselves into the general economic, industry, and company operating environments.

The procedure is first to isolate and estimate the major economic influences on the firm's profits. The analyst must then relate the appropriate economic indicator to the industry sales through **regression analysis**. After the regression analysis has established this relationship, the analyst must obtain an estimate of the future value of this indicator. Applying this relationship to the projected economic indicator value, the analyst arrives at an estimate of projected industry sales.

The firm's share of the market is the third step in estimating future earnings under an aggregate approach. It is easier to determine the firm's historical market share if the industry is well defined and if there are only a few major companies rather than a large number of small companies. If the conditions are stable, the firm's historical market share can be applied to the projected industry sales to determine the projected company sales. When the firm's sales projection has been made, the investor's final step is to apply the historical profit margin ratio to sales to derive the total profits of the company.

The major advantage of the aggregate approach is its consideration of more than earnings alone. This approach recognizes the influence of the economy on a firm's earnings. Furthermore, it allows for more flexibility than the mechanical projections of the historical earnings growth rate approach.

The aggregate approach assumes that conditions identical to those in the past will prevail in the future. If the relationship among economic variables and industry sales, the firm's market share, or the firm's profit margins changed, the stable conditions assumption would be violated. The problem of the base and terminal years selection also remains in the aggregate approach. The choice of an abnormal base or terminal year may distort the regression results. Of course, a very basic assumption is that the economic variable selected must be reasonably predictable.

Some common checks against trend-line forecasts include: (1) large industries cannot grow substantially faster than the economy for long; (2) companies with large market shares cannot continue to increase market share in a major, sustained manner; and (3) firms generally can't sustain growth at a greater rate than can be financed by their incremental return on retained earnings unless common stock can be continuously sold at a meaningful premium to book value.

Caused Future. The third general approach is to assume the future is caused or shaped by economic forces and the efforts of people. A flaw in many trend-line forecasts is the failure to recognize that people will react to events. For example, Thomas Malthus's prediction that everyone would starve was based on: (1) projecting the past trend in population growth; (2) recognizing that land was a limited resource; and (3) assuming that mankind would starve rather than develop new farmland or increase the productivity of existing farmland. In recent years, the most dire forecasts on energy shortages had similar underpinnings.

Four common approaches in viewing the world as a caused future include cycles, asset investing, competitive analysis, and looking at problems as opportunities.

Cycles. To understand investment opportunities properly, the impact of cycles on companies and securities must be studied. The normal economic cycle and the stock market cycle in the United States are basic starting points and receive the most attention. Because of the intense focus on these areas, it is difficult to gain a competitive advantage in trying to anticipate change. Economic cycles in other parts of the world can have substantial influence on some multinational firms and commodities. Other cycles of general concern include interest rates and inflation. Besides the macroeconomic cycles, most industries and companies are subject to more specific cycles such as capacity expansion, product pricing, new product introduction, and regulation. Many cycles are relatively easy to identify when studied leisurely with hindsight and after the government is through revising its data. Under pressure of near-term stock price performance, however, it is frequently less than crystal clear whether a current development is part of a cycle or a new trend. Typical mistakes made with cycles include: (1) buying a stock because it is cheap on current earnings near the top of a cycle; (2) selling a stock because of losses near the bottom of a cycle; (3) assuming that the most recent valuation levels are sustainable even though they differ sharply with historical ranges; and (4) assuming the latest group of bright new managers have solved the historical cyclical problem.

Asset Investing. Touched on earlier, **asset investing** is based on the concept that if there are assets that are undervalued either because the assets are not being used effectively or because there is a temporary adverse development, someone will do something about it. Of course, there could be a very long lag before the assets are properly used or the assets could be consumed through improper use. Many stocks sell at discounts to book value because managements have not yet written down assets to their economic value. Turnaround stories are plentiful on Wall Street, but the asset investor must distinguish between hopes and concrete plans with realistic chances for success. In looking for opportunities, the asset investor should keep in mind that different buyers frequently are willing to pay substantially different prices for the same asset at any moment. For example, an individual stockholder might be willing to pay $10 per share based on the relative value versus the overall stock market, a businessperson might be willing to pay $13 in comparison to an alternative of internal construction expansion costs to acquire similar assets, whereas a particular company might willingly pay $15 per share because it sees synergistic effects in buying and operating the entire firm.

Competitive Analysis. Another basic method for forecasting earnings is the **return on investment** approach, which applies the historical rate of return on investment to a projected total investment base. The rationale for using this approach is that the necessary information is readily obtainable, and firms have target rates of return objectives that they attempt to maintain. It is argued that investment plans are made in advance and can be readily estimated by a scrutiny of the company's reports and its capital sources. The target rate of return is the return on investment that the firm attempts to earn from each investment. Under stable conditions, it may be reasonable to assume that future investments will return the historical rate of return. However, the incremental rate of return is key.

The advantage of the return on investment approach is the relative ease with which it can be computed. The information is relatively easy to obtain, and the computational procedures are quick. This approach continues to assume, however, that stable conditions will prevail and that investment plans are unlikely to change rapidly. The accuracy of this method may be reduced in industries of low capital investment. If earnings increases arise with no additional investment expenditures, it is difficult to correlate future earnings with investment. Accuracy may also be impaired if unforeseen startup costs or delays are encountered in the development of the investment's profit potential.

As a check against historical returns and a foundation in estimating future profitability, it is wise to keep in mind that probably the two most important factors in determining the earnings power of a company are: (1) the nature of its business, and (2) the firm's competitive position within its industry. Under nature of business, some factors to consider are: (1) ability to differentiate product other than through price (e.g., drugs versus steel); (2) maturity of the industry; (3) value added for products; (4) ease of entry and exit; (5) history of price competition; (6) bargaining power of suppliers; (7) bargaining power of customers; and (8) substitutability of other products (e.g., plastics for paper).

A company's specific competitive position within its industry can be judged by such factors as relative costs, product quality as perceived by the customer, product differentiation, overall market share, share within a specific niche, and number of competitors. Some of these are interrelated. For example, there are economies of scale in manufacturing and advertising which help the market share leader to become the low-cost producer. Low-cost producers tend to have: (1) higher profit margins for the obvious reason of lower unit costs at the same selling price, and (2) more stable margins because higher cost firms typically have to cut back on production first when there is industry overcapacity. The more profitable firms are then in the best position to expand and increase market share more, buy the latest and most efficient equipment in this expansion, and then further increase their cost competitiveness. Differentiating products or becoming a quality or market niche leader to gain pricing flexibility independent of the low-cost producer are effective strategies.

In estimating earning power, a good starting point is to measure the basic profitability of an industry over a complete cycle. Return on sales, assets, total capitalization, and equity are useful yardsticks. The averages for these ratios are informative, but the range among companies can be equally enlightening. The spread in returns within an industry is usually explained by competitive position, but it might also reflect the temporary developments within specific components in the industry.

As a general pattern, firms cannot sustain a return on equity in excess of the mid-twenties without inviting competition that drives down profitability. Conversely, returns below 10% will usually motivate capital withdrawal, leading to rising returns. These are only general tendencies and the investor must evaluate each situation in depth.

The **industry life cycle theory** is another framework for analyzing companies under more dynamic conditions. According to this theory, an industry evolves over time through several different growth patterns or stages of development. The first stage is the pioneering stage, during which the infant industry develops a new product. Sales and profits grow rapidly, and other companies enter the young industry because of the high profit opportunity. This leads to overcapacity, severe competition, merger of weaker companies, and withdrawal of others from the industry. After the turbulence of the **pioneering stage,** the industry enters the **expansion stage.** Growth during this stage is above the national economic average but is more stable than in the earlier stage. As the rate of technological improvements within the industry decreases, and as the product market becomes fully penetrated, the industry enters the **maturity stage.** The industry then grows at or below the rate of the economy, depending on whether it is able to maintain its position or is being gradually displaced by other expanding industries. The final period is the **decline stage,** when the firm experiences negative growth.

The investor who tries to forecast industry performance within the life-cycle framework faces several serious analytical problems. There is no guarantee that a specific industry will systematically pass through the four stages described earlier. The concept of self-renewal can counter the life-cycle developments. Another difficulty associated with this theory is in determining in advance when an industry will change from one stage to another. Because changes in stock prices tend to lead to changes in industry growth rates, it is desirable to anticipate each shift in stage. Perhaps the greatest value of the life-cycle framework is that it conditions analysts to look for certain clues that may help them detect a shifting tide in the industries they analyze. At the same time, it prevents analysts from blithely extrapolating abnormally high or low industry growth rate and profitability into the distant future. The analysis is more appropriate for one-industry companies.

Problems as Opportunities. There are two basic approaches in viewing **problems as opportunities.** One is to identify economic or general problems and then find specific firms that can benefit by solving these problems (e.g., oil service firms to help solve the energy problem). A second focus is to find companies whose stocks are depressed because the company itself has problems. Of course, it is key to determine whether these problems are temporary or more permanent in nature. In judging turnarounds, it should be remembered that it is typically far easier to turn a company with a specific, isolated problem than to substantially improve a firm saturated with mediocrity. In looking at problem companies, earnings are frequently depressed or nonexistent. Therefore price/asset ratios can be useful. Where large write-downs have occurred, price/sales can be an effective way to focus on potential earning power. In specific industries, an appropriate measure might be used such as stock price/barrels of oil reserves or stock price/tons of steel capacity.

VARIATIONS IN THE ANALYTICAL TECHNIQUE. The foregoing discussion provides a broad outline that should be of use generally in analyzing individual companies. Differing companies will require variations of the general process of analysis. The upcoming discussion outlines some of the major differences that should be considered when evaluating companies in the following categories: industrial securities, financial securities, and public utilities.

Industrial Securities

Nature of the Industry. Because the category of industrial securities embraces every type of corporate enterprise except financial corporations, public utilities, and railroads, it comprises a wide variety of businesses. Although basic principles of investment analysis are the same in each case, their application varies with the character of the business.

The major classes of industrial concerns are:

1. Mining, petroleum, and other extractive enterprises that depend on natural resources, the supply of which is usually limited
2. Manufacturers of industrial materials such as metals and chemicals
3. Manufacturers of producer durable goods and military equipment
4. Manufacturers of consumer nondurable goods, including textiles, foods, and tobacco
5. Manufacturers of consumer durable goods and building materials
6. Wholesale and retail distributors
7. Service industries such as air transport and bus lines that may have public utility characteristics

Numerous concerns diversify their activities, so that they manufacture and sell products falling in two or more of the preceding classifications. Thus a petroleum company produces chemicals and the General Electric Company manufactures equipment for industry and consumer durable goods.

Industry Analysis. In the analysis of industrial securities, an essential step is to identify and study dominant influences that affect earnings and other elements of value of companies in each industry. These influences not only vary from industry to industry, but also from time to time within the same industry. Examples of such key analytical factors are given in the following summary:

Oil stock values are largely affected by the location of crude reserves and other properties, the proportion of its crude requirements produced by the company, and the relation of product to crude prices. Political vagaries are a major cause of short-term stock price fluctuations. Since the beginning of the 1970s, most foreign reserves have been taken over by governments. The final price of oil reflects a maze of taxes that is very significant on a cumulative basis and tends to depress demand. The Organization of Petroleum Exporting Countries has acted as the swing producer in matching supply/demand and this enabled it to increase oil prices dramatically beginning in the early 1970s. These huge price increases in turn led to significant conservation. Prices and taxes have become very volatile, and consequently oil company profit margins became far less stable than in prior years. Because of declining domestic reserves and foreign expropriations, companies' abilities to find new reserves in capitalistic countries have grown in importance. The reduced rate of consumption has shifted emphasis from marketing to running efficient operations.

Automobile stocks are very much influenced by cyclical fluctuations in demand, as well as by the ability of car manufacturers to adapt their products to changing public tastes. The latter factor has accounted for wide variations in the percentage of the market captured by individual companies in particular years. However, the overall relative market positions of General Motors, Ford, and Chrysler have remained about the same for decades and their relative profitability reflects this. For the most part, U.S. companies have suffered from foreign competition in recent years. The imports have been able to meet the demand for smaller, more fuel-efficient cars, providing a real challenge for the U.S. car companies to resize their entire fleet in the 1980s. In addition, relative costs have assumed far greater importance because of Japanese competition.

Chemical and drug stock values may be greatly influenced by development of new products. Staple chemicals and drugs are subject to intense price competition, but new products and those sold under brand names to consumers and having a wide acceptance often give satisfactory profit margins. The record of each company's research program is thus a major analytical consideration. Research in process technology is very important to chemical companies. The emergence of biotechnology could radically change the competitive positions of these firms toward the end of this century.

In most cases specialty chemical companies are more profitable than firms that produce basic chemicals. As oil producing countries expand their commodity chemical operations, this differential should be maintained or increased.

Retail stocks are greatly influenced by a company's adaptability to shifting population patterns and buying habits. The growth of very large shopping malls helped facilitate the emergence of speciality retail chains. Small stores which develop the right format in a small market niche can quickly expand geographically without major capital outlays or the delays in finding the right real estate at the right location, and then generating store traffic. Retailers must constantly adapt to shifting markets by altering merchandise, format, pricing, and location. Ease of entry enables numerous growth companies to emerge in retailing. But market share gains by the more perceptive merchandisers frequently result in margin problems for the established stores which have become too complacent.

Tobacco stock values have been affected by the success of managements in adapting their products to consumer concern with health considerations. Shifts in demand to filter cigarettes and consumer response to advertising stressing health factors have favored some companies at the expense of others. Advertising effectiveness geared to specific demographics has been a key to market share, because image and brand loyalty are important factors in consumer purchasing. The high percentage of retail costs accounted for by taxes and the habitual nature of consumption lead to above-average pricing flexibility for manufacturers. Two firms account for two-thirds of domestic sales.

Financial Securities

Distinctive Features. Securities of financial enterprises are peculiar in that assets of these institutions consist mainly of loans and securities. The methods of analysis differ, therefore, from those applicable to industrial companies. Quality of assets and effective cost of funds, for example, may be significant analytical factors. Significant deregulation has increased the importance of managements that can adapt to change.

Types of Financial Securities. The most important group of financial securities is **bank stocks.** Because of deregulation, the major historical difference in bank profitability and growth rate which was based on geographic territory might disappear. Analysis is made more difficult because of the limited information provided by annual and other reports in any cases.

Because of the historical liquid nature of assets, leverage is high and equity represents a small percentage of total assets. In the past, bank managements frequently defended their tendency for secrecy on the basis that the banking industry was based on confidence, and detailed negative information could potentially cause a banking crisis. In recent years, some managements have realized that fear of the unknown is often more negative than the facts, so there has been a tendency to reveal more facts.

Reported book value is readily determined from the condition statement, as the bank's balance sheet is called. However, asset value may vary considerably from the figure shown on the books. Securities are usually carried at cost less a reserve built up through sales of investments at a profit. Loans are shown net of reserves for possible losses. In the past, loans to foreign governments usually did not have a reserve for losses, but this is in the process of change. Real estate may be carried at figures varying widely above or below current market values. Many bank managements like to accumulate hidden reserves, usually by carrying assets taken over when loans go into default far below their true worth.

Banks derive their earnings mainly from interest on loans and investments.

Fees and charges for services are a relatively small part of income for most banks, but they may be increasing with deregulation.

Analysis ratios commonly used in studying bank stocks are net operation earnings after applicable taxes per share, market price as a percent of book value, earning assets per share, and the ratio of time to total deposits. The rate of growth of deposits and earning assets and the average return on assets, allowing for the tax-exempt securities, are also important indicators of investment value. However, banks that press too hard for well above average growth have frequently found themselves plagued by bad loans.

Analysis of **insurance stocks** involves an appraisal of both underwriting and investment results. The investment funds of most insurance companies are derived chiefly from reserves that belong to policyholders. In fire and casualty companies, these are the unearned premium reserves and the loss reserves. In life insurance companies, they are the reserves against policies outstanding. Fixed securities are carried at cost. Because of rising interest rates over the past few decades, this means that most book values for insurance companies are overstated because market values of most fixed-income portfolios are less than cost.

Fire and Casualty Insurance Companies report underwriting and investment results separately. The analyst must examine where the earnings are coming from. Adequacy of reserves is a key concern. This segment of the industry tends to run in cycles with overexpansion and subsequent contraction frequent events.

Life Insurance stock analysis stresses the rate of company growth and the types of policy outstanding, as well as such general factors as the trend of interest rates, life expectancy, and taxation rates. In recent years, innovation in new product introduction has taken on major importance. Although life insurance companies invest mainly in fixed-income securities, some have put a material percentage of their funds in common stocks. Because of the high degree of leverage in life insurance companies, this can substantially affect investment values.

Analysis of **finance companies,** including installment finance, business finance, and personal loan companies, stresses profitability and quality of assets, cost of funds, and rate of growth. **Savings and loan companies** have mushroomed in importance in recent years because of deregulation and the proliferation of firms converting from mutual to stock ownership. The advent of adjustable rate mortgages should lead to more stable interest spreads and dampen the typical historical earnings volatility of savings and loans.

Public Utility Securities. The key variables in utilities tend to be regulation, the capital intensive nature of the business, growth in unit consumption, and the financial structure of the company.

Telecommunications has experienced significant deregulation in recent years, including the 1984 breakup of AT&T and the unbundling of service charges, which will put much greater emphasis on new products, pricing, new technologies, and cost structures. Although the telephone operating companies should remain relatively stable investments, the potential risk and reward for other participants, including AT&T, has significantly increased. However, these developments should enhance industry growth.

The soaring price of energy negatively impacted the growth in **electric and gas utilities,** which has decreased the need for new capacity and will improve future cash flow. However, the soaring costs of nuclear capacity because of regulatory delays, increased safety standards, high interest rates, inflation, and mismanagement, have created a serious financial threat to a number of utilities. To what extent regulatory bodies will permit these inflated costs to be passed on to consumers is a key question. Most utilities need continuous external financing because of the capital intensive nature of the business and the high dividend payout ratios typical in the industry. Consequently, utilities with stocks selling significantly below book value suffer constant dilution. Regulation can vary substantially between states not only in terms of allowed return on investment, but in the definition of income and investment. The lag between rate requests and approval can be so long in some cases as to make a stated rate of return relatively meaningless. The economic characteristics of a firm's geographic territory can impact the valuation of the stock.

BIBLIOGRAPHY

Babcock, Guilford C., "The Concept of Sustainable Growth," *Financial Analysts Journal* (May–June 1970): 108–44.

Bibeault, Donald B., *Corporate Turnaround,* New York: McGraw-Hill, 1982.

Bolten, Steven, *Security Analysis and Portfolio Management,* New York: Holt, Rinehart & Winston, 1972.

Brealey, Richard A., *An Introduction to Risk and Return from Common Stocks,* Cambridge, MA: MIT Press, 1969.

Cohen, Jerome B., Zinbarg, Edward P., and Zeikel, Arthur, *Investment Analysis and Portfolio Management,* Homewood, IL: Irwin, 1973.

Curley, Anthony J., and Bear, Robert M., *Security Analysis and Portfolio Management,* New York: Harper & Row, 1979.

Dreman, David N., *Psychology and the Stock Market,* New York: AMACOM, 1977.

———, *Contrarian Investment Strategy,* New York: Random House, 1979.

Farrell, James L., Jr., *Guide to Portfolio Management,* New York: McGraw-Hill, 1983.

Francis, Jack Clark, *Investments: Analysis and Management,* New York: McGraw-Hill, 1979.

Graham, Benjamin, Dodd, David L., and Cottle, Sidney, *Security Analysis,* 4th ed., New York: McGraw-Hill, 1962.

Graham, Benjamin, *The Intelligent Investor,* New York: Harper & Row, 1973.

Hagin, Robert, *Modern Portfolio Theory,* Homewood, IL: Dow Jones-Irwin, 1979.

Hayes, Douglas A., and Bauman, Scott W., *Investments: Analysis and Management,* New York: Macmillan, 1976.

Henderson, Bruce D., *Henderson On Corporate Strategy,* Cambridge, MA: Abt Books, 1979.

Hickman, W. B., *Corporate Bond Quality and Investor Experience,* Princeton, NJ: Princeton University Press, 1958.

Humphrey, Neill B., *The Art of Contrary Thinking,* Caldwell, ID: Caxton Printers, 1976.

Ibbotson, Roger G., and Sinquefeld, Rex A., *Stocks, Bonds, Bills and Inflation: The Past (1926–1976) and the Future (1977–2000)*, Charlottesville, VA: Financial Analysts Research Foundation, 1977.

Latane, Henry A., Tuttle, Donald L., and James, Charles P., *Security Analysis and Portfolio Management*, 2nd ed., New York: Ronald Press, 1977.

Lorie, James H., and Hamilton, Mary T., *The Stock Market: Theories and Evidence,* Homewood, IL: Irwin, 1974.

Porter, Michael E., *Competitive Strategy,* New York: Free Press, 1980.

Sharpe, William F., *Portfolio Theory and Capital Markets,* New York: McGraw-Hill, 1970.

———, *Investments,* Englewood Cliffs, NJ: Prentice-Hall, 1978.

Sharpe, William F., and Cooper, Guy M., "Risk-Return Classes of NYSE Common Stocks," *Financial Analysts Journal* (March–April 1972): 46–54.

Williamson, J. Peter, *Investments: New Analystic Techiques,* New York: Praeger, 1970.

22

ASSET PRICING MODELS

CONTENTS

22

ASSET PRICING MODELS

Edwin J. Elton
Martin J. Gruber

The purpose of this section is to examine and explain the modern theories of **asset pricing.** The past few years have brought both an increased understanding of traditional asset pricing theory and the development of competing theories. This section is divided into three parts. The first part presents the basis of modern portfolio theory. Although this material is interesting in itself, it also provides the background necessary for the development of **asset pricing theory.** In the second part we discuss alternative asset pricing theories. We include the set of approaches that is usually described as capital asset pricing models. We start with the standard capital asset pricing model, then proceed to discuss newer and more realistic forms of the model. We also present the newest approach to asset pricing, the arbitrage pricing model. This approach is viewed as the competitive paradigm to capital asset pricing. The third part of this section discusses the implications of these models for both security selection and performance evaluation.

MODERN PORTFOLIO THEORY

The assumption that portfolios can be selected on the basis of **mean return** and **risk** is the key assumption to modern portfolio theory. This means that we can pictorially represent the **portfolio choice problem** as shown in Exhibit 1.

The dots represent the mean return and risk of different investments. Some of these dots are portfolios, and some are individual securities. When one considers all the investments available and all the possible combinations that exist, then one realizes that we were conservative in representing alternatives and that Exhibit 1 should have many more dots.

Two assumptions allow the enormous number of choices represented in Ex-

---

This section is based on a condensation of several chapters from Edwin J. Elton and Martin J. Gruber, *Modern Portfolio Theory and Investment Analysis,* 2nd ed. New York: Wiley, 1984.

EXHIBIT 1 THE PORTFOLIO CHOICE PROBLEM

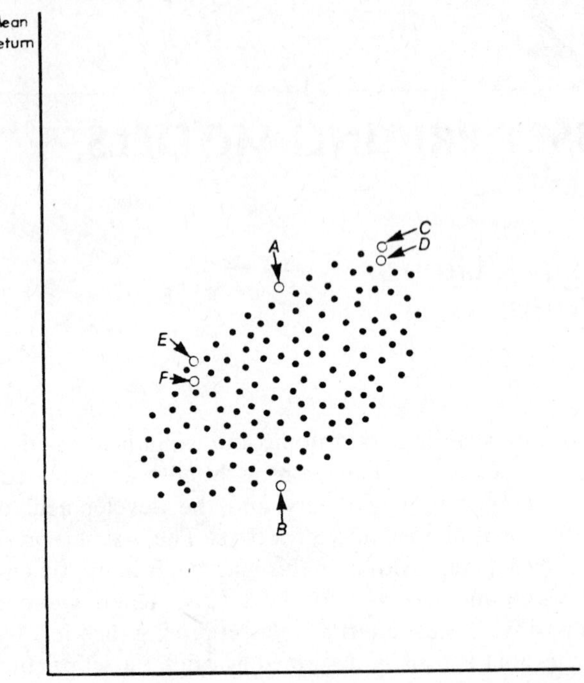

hibit 1 to be reduced to a manageable number of choices. These assumptions are:

1. Investors prefer more money to less money.
2. Investors are risk-averse.

The assumption that investors prefer more to less money means that an investor would rather have $2,000 than $1,000. This very innocuous assumption leads to an enormous redution in the number of portfolios that can be chosen. For example, in Exhibit 1 it means that portfolio *A* is to be preferred to portfolio *B*. Portfolios *A* and *B* have the same risk but portfolio *A* has higher **mean return.** If investors prefer more to less, then if two portfolios have the same risk, but different mean returns, the portfolio with the higher mean return is preferable. The assumption that investors prefer more to less allows us to say that *E* is preferred to *F*, and *C* is preferred to *D*. When all possible portfolios are eliminated using this principle, we reduce the choices to those shown in Exhibit 2.

With this one assumption, we have reduced the problem to a manageable number of alternatives. The second assumption, **risk aversion,** means that an investor would prefer not to gamble if by rejecting the gamble the investor does not affect average return. For example, assume an investor has the choice of a gamble that pays $1.00 if heads occurs and $0.00 if tails occurs, versus getting

50 cents with certainty. Assume that the coin being flipped is fair. Thus the investor taking the gamble would expect to earn \$1.00 half the time and \$0.00 half the time, or on average the earnings will be 50 cents. Thus the average return of the gamble is 50 cents, the same as the return the investor earns without taking the gamble. Risk aversion implies that the investor would prefer 50 cents with certainty. This assumption often bothers people and some further discussion might prove helpful. Risk aversion implies that on average, A rated bonds would be expected to offer a higher return than AAA bonds. This follows because if they offered the same return, all investors would prefer to hold the less risky AAA bonds and A rated bonds would not find a market.

The assumption of risk aversion means that portfolio *H* is preferred to portfolio *I* in Exhibit 2, and portfolio *E* is preferred to portfolio *C* because *E* and *H*, respectively, have less risk for the same mean return. The assumption of risk aversion reduces the portfolio problem to choosing among portfolios that lie on the curve *H, E,* and *A*. This is a manageable number of choices. Before going on, let's restate the analysis that allows reducing the choices from those shown in Exhibit 1 to those shown in Exhibit 2. Two assumptions were necessary: In-

EXHIBIT 2 OBTAINING THE EFFICIENT FRONTIER

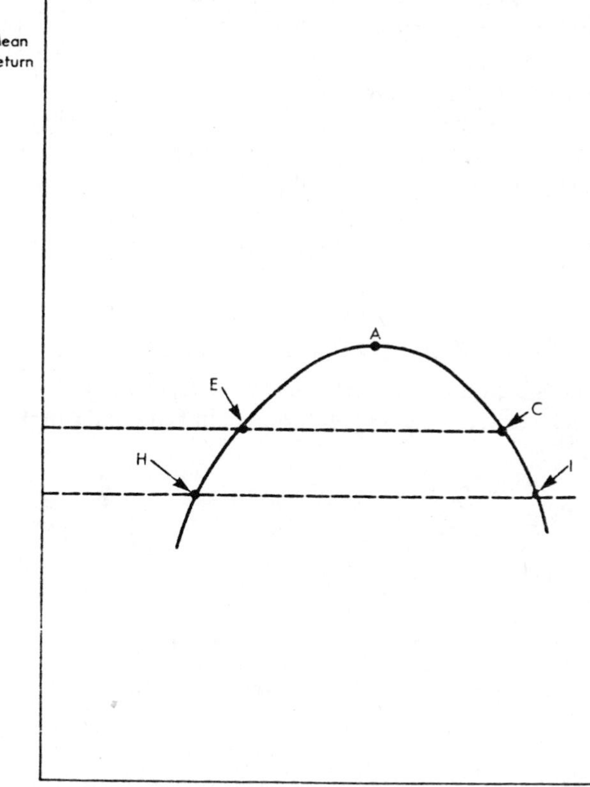

vestors prefer more to less and investors are risk-averse. These assumptions imply the **fundamental theorem of modern portfolio theory:**

1. Given two portfolios with the same risk, investors prefer the one with the higher mean return.
2. Given the two portfolios with the same mean return, investors prefer the one with the least risk.

The preceding theorem is the basis of modern portfolio theory. It allows the infinite number of possible portfolios that could be chosen to be reduced to a manageable number of alternatives.

MEAN RETURN AND RISK

The Mean Return. The concept of mean or average is standard in our culture. Pick up the newspaper and you'll often see figures on average income, batting averages, or average crime. The concept of an average is intuitive. If someone earns $11,000 one year and $9,000 in a second, we say his or her average income in the 2 years is $10,000. If three children in a family are age 15, 10, and 5, then we say the average age is 10. A mean return or average is easy to compute. Consider the examples shown in Exhibit 3. If all outcomes are equally likely, then to determine the average, one adds up the outcomes and divides by the number of outcomes. Thus for Exhibit 3, the average is $(12 + 9 + 6) \div 3 = 9$. A second way to determine an average is to multiply each outcome by the probability that it will occur. When the outcomes are not equally likely, this facilitates the calculation. For Exhibit 3 this is $(\frac{1}{3} \times 12) + (\frac{1}{3} \times 9) + (\frac{1}{3} \times 6) = 9$.

It is useful to express this intuitive calculation in terms of a formula. The symbol Σ should be read sum. Underneath the symbol we put the first value in the sum and what is varying. On the top of the symbol we put the final value in the sum. For example $\sum_{J=1}^{3}$ tells us to set $j = 1$ then $j = 2$ and then $j = 3$. If R_{ij} stands for the possible return of asset i, and if the asset in question is the asset in Exhibit 3, then the expected return on the asset in Exhibit 3 can be expressed as

$$\frac{\sum_{j=1}^{3} R_{ij}}{3} = \frac{R_{i1} + R_{i2} + R_{i3}}{3} = \frac{12 + 9 + 6}{3}$$

EXHIBIT 3 MEAN RETURN

Return	Probability	Event
12	1/3	A
9	1/3	B
6	1/3	C

Using the summation notation just introduced and a bar over a variable to indicate average return, we have for the average return of equally likely returns

$$\bar{R}_i = \sum_{j=1}^{N} \frac{R_{ij}}{N}$$

If the observations are not equally likely and if P_{ij} is the probability of the jth return on the ith asset, then expected return is

$$\bar{R}_i = \sum_{j=1}^{N} P_{ij} R_{ij}$$

This latter formula includes the formula for equally likely observations as a special case. If we have N observations each equally likely, then the odds of any one occurring are $\frac{1}{N}$. Replacing the P_{ij} in the second formula by $\frac{1}{N}$ yields the first formula.

A Measure of Risk. To measure risk we need a measure of how much the returns differ from the average.

Intuitively a sensible measure of how much the observations differ from the average is simply to examine this difference directly; that is, examine

$$R_{ij} - \bar{R}_i$$

Having determined this for each observation, one could obtain an overall measure by taking the average of this difference. Although this is intuitively sensible, there is a problem. Some of the differences will be positive and some negative, and these will tend to cancel out. The result of the canceling out could be such that the average difference for a highly variable return need be no larger than the average difference for an asset with a highly stable return. In fact, it can be shown that the average value of this difference must always be precisely zero. The reader is encouraged to verify this with the example in Exhibit 3. Thus the sum of the differences from the mean tells us nothing about the size of these differences.

Because the square of any number is positive, we could eliminate this problem by squaring all differences before determining the average. This procedure is common in statistics and the average squared deviation has a special name.

The average squared deviation is called the variance and the square root of the variance is called the standard deviation. To illustrate the concept of the variance we continue our example from Exhibit 3.

The **variance of the return** on this asset is simply

$$[(12-9)^2+(9-9)^2+(6-9)^2]/3$$

To be precise, the formula for the variance of the return on *i*th asset (which we will symbolize as σ_i^2) when each return is equally likely is:

$$\sigma_i^2 = \sum_{j=i}^{N} \frac{(R_{ij}-\bar{R}_i)^2}{N}$$

If the observations are not equally likely, then, as before, we multiply by the probability of their occurrence. The formula for the variance of the return on the *i*th asset becomes

$$\sigma_i^2 = \sum_{j=1}^{N} P_{ij}\,(R_{ij}-\bar{R}_i)^2$$

The standard deviation is, of course, just the square root of the variance and is designated by σ_i.

CHARACTERISTICS OF PORTFOLIOS. The motivation behind portfolio theory is that the characteristics of a portfolio are not merely the average of the characteristics of the individual securities in the portfolio. The following equations for the expected return and variance of a portfolio were originally prepared by Markowitz (1959). Before stating these, we need to introduce some terminology.

Let X_i = the fraction of funds an investor places in security
ρ_{ij} = the correlation coefficient between the results in security i and security j
N = number of stocks being considered

The **correlation coefficient** is a measure of variation between the two returns. It has a range of −1 to +1. Plus one indicates perfect positive association, whereas negative one indicates that although the returns move in unison, they move in opposite directions, a correlation coefficient of zero indicates no relationship between the two returns. The **correlation coefficient** (actually the square of the correlation coefficient called the coefficient of determination) is a direct measure of the degree of association between two variables.

With these concepts we can reproduce the standard equations on which all of modern portfolio theory is based:

$$\bar{R}_p = \sum_{i=1}^{W} X_i\,\bar{R}_i$$

The **formula for expected return** simply says that the expected return is the weighted average of the expected return on the individual securities. The weights are the fraction of funds invested in each security.

The variance of the portfolio is a much more complex function of the attributes of the individual securities. It depends not only on the variance of the return on individual securities, but also on the extent to which they tend to do well or poorly at the same time (the correlation coefficient). The variance of a portfolio of securities is

$$\sigma_p^2 = \sum_{i=1}^{N} x_i^2\sigma_i^2 + \sum_{i=1}^{N} \sum_{\substack{j=1 \\ j \neq i}}^{N} x_i x_j \rho_{ij}\sigma_i\sigma_j$$

The impact of the correlation coefficient on diversification can be illustrated with a simple diagram. Examine Exhibit 4, and note that for correlations of plus 1 combinations of two stocks lie along a straight line. Both the expected return and risk are simply weighted averages of the expected return and risk on the individual securities. For any value of the correlation coefficient less than plus one, risk is less than a simple weighted coverage of the risk on the individual securities. In fact, at the extreme (correlation of minus one) a combination of two assets can always be found which has zero risk.

What does all this mean for the investor? It is clear that the correlation between stocks is neither plus one nor minus one. How much good does diversification do in the real world? Exhibit 5 presents the variance of equally

EXHIBIT 4 RELATIONSHIP BETWEEN EXPECTED RETURN AND STANDARD DEVIATION OF RETURN FOR VARIOUS CORRELATION COEFFICIENTS

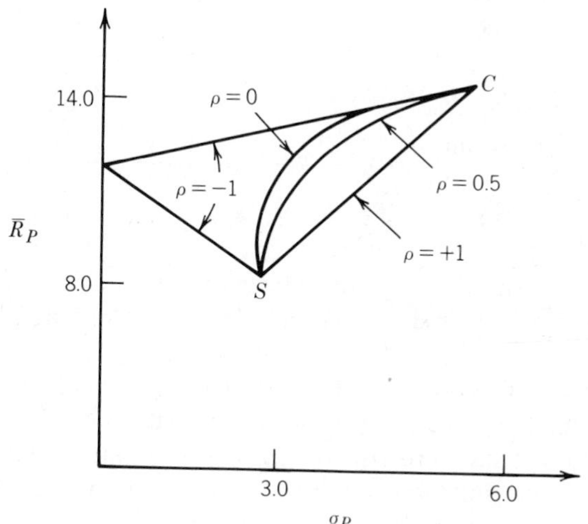

EXHIBIT 5 EFFECT OF DIVERSIFICATION

Number of Securities	Expected Portfolio Variance
1	45,619
2	26,839
4	16,948
8	12,003
10	11,014
12	10,354
14	9,883
16	9,530
18	9,256
20	9,036
25	8,640
30	8,376
35	8,188
40	8,047
45	7,937
50	7,849
75	7,585
100	7,453
125	7,374
150	7,321
175	7,284
200	7,255
250	7,216
300	7,190
350	7,171
400	7,157
450	7,146
500	7,137
600	7,124
700	7,114
800	7,107
900	7,102
1000	7,097
minimum	7,058

weighted portfolios of different sizes selected from New York Stock Exchange stocks. The impact of diversification on risk reduction speaks for itself.

THE EFFICIENT FRONTIER WITH RISKLESS LENDING AND BORROWING. Up to this point we have been dealing with portfolios of risky assets. See Exhibit 6 for the standard risk versus return format. The introduction of a riskless asset into our portfolio possibility set considerably simplifies the analysis. We can consider lending at a riskless rate as equivalent to investing in an asset with a certain outcome (e.g., a short-term government bill or savings ac-

EXHIBIT 6 PORTFOLIO CHOICES

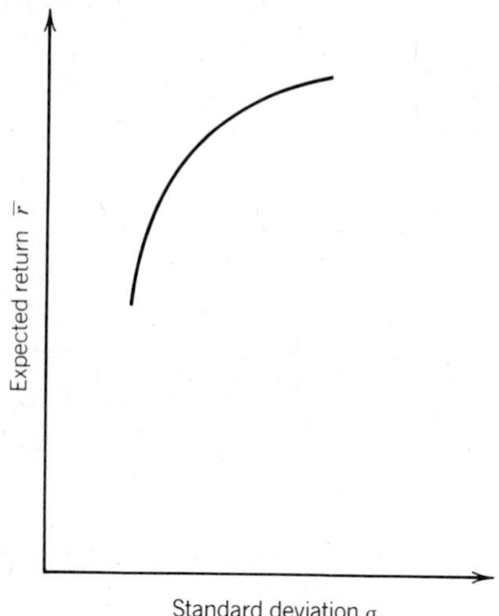

count). Borrowing can be considered as selling such a security short or simply borrowing at a riskless rate.

Let's call the certain rate of return on the riskless asset R_F. The standard deviation of the return on the riskless asset must be by definition zero.

We will first examine the case where investors can lend and borrow unlimited amounts of funds at the riskless rate. Initially assume that the investor is interested in placing some funds in portfolio A and either lending or borrowing. Under this assumption we can easily determine the geometric pattern of all combinations of portfolio A and lending or borrowing. If the subscript C stands for a combination of asset A and the riskless asset, then the relationship between the returns on the combination and the risk of the combination is

$$\bar{R}_C = R_F + \frac{(\bar{R}_A - R_F)}{\sigma_A}\sigma_C$$

Note that this is the equation of a straight line. All combinations of riskless lending and borrowing with portfolio A lie on a straight line in expected return standard deviation space.

The intercept of the line (on the return axis) is R_F and the slope is

$$\frac{\bar{R}_A - R_F}{\sigma_A}$$

The line passes through the point A. This line is shown in Exhibit 7.

Note to the left of the point A we have combinations of lending and portfo-

EXHIBIT 7 COMBINATIONS OF *A* AND THE RISKLESS ASSET

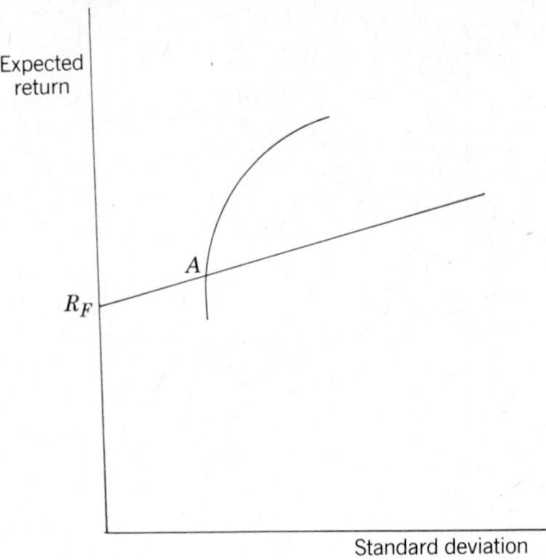

lio *A*, whereas to the right of point *A* we have combinations of borrowing and portfolio *A*.

The portfolio *A* we selected for this analysis had no special properties. Combinations of any security or portfolio and riskless lending and borrowing lie along a straight line in expected return standard deviation of return space. Examine Exhibit 8 for various combinations of the riskless asset and risky assets.

Point *G* is the tangency point between the efficient frontier and a ray passing through the point R_F on the vertical axis. The investor can't rotate the ray further because by the definition of the efficient frontier there are no portfolios lying above and to the left of point *G*.

All investors who believed they faced the efficient frontier and riskless lending and borrowing rates shown in Exhibit 8 would hold the same portfolio of risky assets—portfolio *G*. Some of these investors who were very risk-averse would select a portfolio along the segment R_F–G and place some of their money in a riskless asset and some in risky portfolio *G*. Others who were much more tolerant of risk would hold portfolios along the segment *G*–*H* borrowing funds, placing their original capital plus the borrowed funds in portfolio *G*. Still other investors would place the total of their original funds in risky portfolio *G*. All of these investors would hold risky portfolios with the exact composition of portfolio *G*. Thus in the case of riskless lending and borrowing, identification of portfolio *G* constitutes a solution to the portfolio problem. The ability to determine the optimum portfolio without having to know anything about the investor has a special name; it is called the ***separation theorem.***

Let's for a moment examine the shape of the efficient frontier under more restrictive assumptions about the ability of investors to lend and borrow at the risk-free rate. There is no question about the ability of investors to lend at the

EXHIBIT 8 VARIOUS COMBINATIONS OF A RISKLESS ASSET AND A RISKY PORTFOLIO

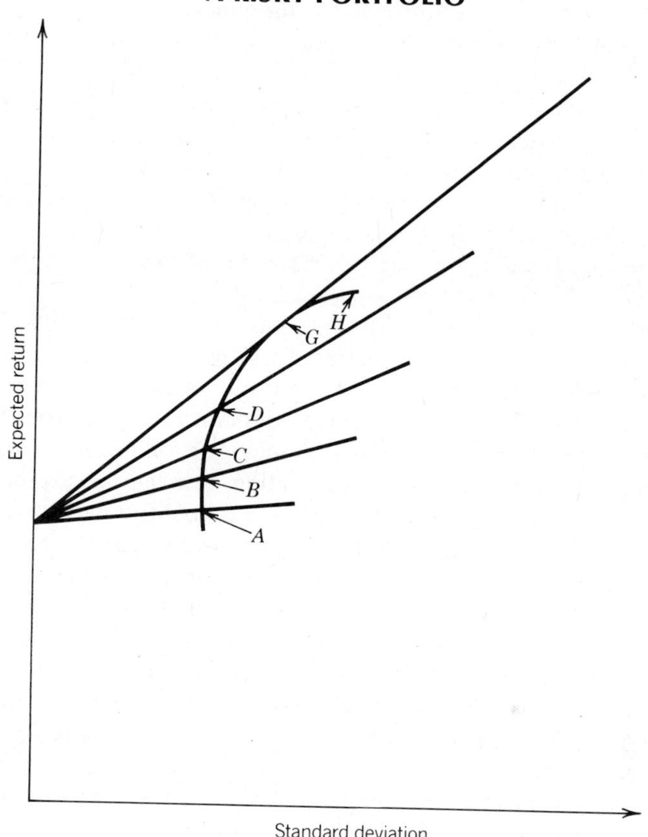

risk-free rate (buy government securities). If they can lend but not borrow at this rate, the efficient frontier becomes $R_F - G - H$. In Exhibit 8 certain investors will hold portfolios of risky assets located between *G* and *H*. However, any investor who held some riskless asset would place all of the remaining funds in risky portfolio *G*.

The theory we have presented thus far was developed more than 30 years ago. The reader may well ask what has happened in the last 30 years. The answer is two-fold. First, the development of techniques to make the theory as outlined earlier implementable. The second concerns the use of this theory to understand asset pricing. We will start with one of the major aspects of implementation. As will become clear in later sections, however, the solutions to the implementation problem play a major role in asset pricing models.

THE INPUTS TO A PORTFOLIO ANALYSIS. We now know that to define the efficient frontier we must find a set of portfolios such that no portfolio offers a greater return for the same risk and no portfolio offers less risk for the same return. Earlier we discussed the input data necessary to perform portfolio analysis. We saw that we need estimates of the **expected return** on each security that is a candidate for inclusion in our portfolio. Also we need estimates of the **variance of each security** to be considered plus estimates of the correlation between each possible pair of securities in the population of stocks under consideration. This last requirement differs both in magnitude and in substance from the two previous requirements. Let's see why.

The principal job of the security analyst has traditionally been to estimate the future performance of those stocks he or she follows. At a minimum this should mean that the analyst produces estimates of expected returns on each stock followed.

With the increased attention that risk has received in recent years more firms have employed analysts' estimates of risk as well as return. The analyst who produces estimates of the expected return on a stock should also be in a position to produce estimates of the uncertainty on each stock followed.

Correlations are an entirely different matter. Portfolio analysis calls for the analyst to produce estimates of the correlation between all possible pairs of stocks that are candidates for inclusion in a portfolio. Most firms organize their analysts along traditional industry lines. This means that one analyst might follow steel stocks or perhaps in a smaller firm all metal stocks, whereas a second analyst follows chemical stocks. But **portfolio analysis** calls for this analyst not only to estimate how a particular steel stock will move with another steel stock, it calls for the analyst to estimate how a particular steel stock will move with a particular drug company, a particular computer manufacturer, and so on. There is no nonoverlapping organizational structure that allows such estimates to be produced.

The problem is made more complex by the number of the estimates involved. Most financial institutions follow 150 to 250 stocks. In addition to in-house portfolio analysis, the institution needs estimates of 150 to 250 expected returns and 150 to 250 variances. Let's see how many correlation coefficients it needs. If we let N stand for the number of stocks a firm follows, then it has to estimate ρ_{ij} for all relevant values of i and j. The first index i can take N values (one for each stock); the second can take on $(N-1)$ values (remember $j=i$). This would appear to give us $N(N-1)$ values for the correlation coefficient. However, note that because the correlation coefficient between stock i and j is the same as that between stock j and i, we only have half this many values, $N(N-1)/2$. The institution that follows 150 to 250 stocks needs between 11,175 and 31,125 correlation coefficients. The sheer number of inputs is staggering.

It seems unlikely that analysts will be able to estimate correlation structures directly. Their ability to do so is severely limited by the nature of feasible organizational structures and the huge number of correlation coefficients that must be estimated. Recognition of this has motivated the search for and development of models to describe and predict the correlation structure between securities. Two of the most widely used models for **forecasting correlation structures** are single-index models and multi-index models. Each of these approaches will be discussed.

SINGLE-INDEX MODELS—AN OVERVIEW

INFLUENCES ON SECURITY RETURNS. Casual observation of stock prices reveals that when the market goes up (as measured by any of the widely available stock market indexes), most stocks tend to increase in price, and when the market goes down, most stocks tend to decrease in price. This suggests that one reason security returns might be correlated is because of a common response to market changes, and a useful measure of this correlation might be obtained by relating the return on a stock to the return on a stock market index.

The return on a stock can be written as

$$R_i = \alpha_i + \beta_i R_m + e_i$$

1. Where α_i is the return expected on stock i when the market is flat.
2. R_M is the rate of return on the market index—a random variable.
3. β_i is a constant that measures the change in R_i given a change in R_M.
4. e_i is the return on stock i which is unexplained by α_i or R_M.

This equation simply breaks the return on a stock into two components, that part which is due to the market and that part which is independent of the market. β_i in the preceding expression measures how sensitive a stock's return is to the return on the market. A β_i of two means that a stock return is expected to increase (decrease) by 2% when the market increases (decreases) by 1%. Similarly, a β of .5 indicates that a stock return is expected to increase (decrease) by .5% when the market increases (decreases) by 1%.

THE MARKET MODEL. The model, as it has been presented, is often referred to as the *market model.* Up to this point we have made no simplifying assumptions about why stocks move together. The key assumption of the single-index model is that the only reason two stocks move together is because of common co-movement with the market. This is equivalent to assuming that the random component of return e_i for any stock i is unrelated (uncorrelated with) the random component of return for a second stock e_j. This means that the covariance between any two stocks i and j is equal to $\beta_i\beta_j\sigma_m^2$ where σ_m^2 is the variance of the market index. If we define σ_{ei}^2 as the residual risk of a security (that variation in the securities return that is unrelated to the market), we can write the expected return and variance of any portfolio as

$$E(R_i) = \sum_{i=1}^{N} X_i\bar{R}_i = \sum_{i=1}^{N} X_i\alpha_i + \sum_{i=1}^{N} X_i\beta_i\bar{R}_M$$

$$\sigma_p^2 = \sum_{j=1}^{N}\sum_{j=1}^{N} X_iX_j\beta_i\beta_j\sigma_m^2 + \sum_{j=1}^{N} X_i^2\sigma_{ei}^2$$

There are many alternative ways of estimating the parameters of the single-index model. From the equations it is clear that expected return and risk can be estimated for any portfolio if we have an estimate of α_i, β_i, σ_{ei}^2 and, finally, an estimate of both the expected return ($\bar{R}_M$) and variance (σ_M^2) for the market. This is a total of $3N + 2$ estimates. For an institution following 150 to 250 stocks, this reduces the total number of estimates to 452 to 752. Compare this with the 11,457 to 31,620 discussed earlier, when no simplifying structure was assumed. Furthermore, note that there is no requirement for direct estimates of the joint movement of securities. This has been replaced with estimates of the way each security moves with the market. A nonoverlapping organizational structure can produce all estimates that are required.

The model can also be employed if analysts supply estimates of expected return for each stock, the variance of the return on each stock, the **beta** for each stock, and estimates of the expected return for the market and the variance of the market return. This is the same number of estimates $3N + 2$, as discussed earlier. However, this alternative set of estimates has the advantage that they are in more familiar terms. We've discussed means and variances before. The only new variable is beta. The **beta** is a measure of the sensitivity of a stock to market movements.

Before we conclude this section we should discuss some more characteristics of the single-index model.

PORTFOLIO BETA. Define the **beta on a portfolio** β_p as a weighted average of the individual β_i's on each stock in the portfolio where the weights are the fraction of the portfolio invested in each stock. Then

$$\beta_p = \sum_{i=1}^{N} X_i\beta_i$$

Similarly, define α_p as

$$\alpha_p = \sum_{i=1}^{N} X_i\alpha_i$$

Then the expected return on a portfolio ($\bar{R}_p$) can be written as:

$$\bar{R} = \alpha_p + \beta_p \bar{R}_m$$

MARKET BETA. If the portfolio p is taken to be the market portfolio (all stocks held in the same proportions as they represent in the market), then the expected return on p must be $\bar{R}_m$. From the preceding equation the only values of α_p and β_p which guarantee $\bar{R}_p = \bar{R}_m$ for any choice of R_m is α_p equal to zero and beta equal to one. Thus the **beta on the market** is one and stocks are thought of as being more or less risky than the market, according to whether their beta is larger or smaller than one.

RISK OF AN INDIVIDUAL SECURITY. Let's look further into the risk of an individual security. The risk of the investor's portfolio could be represented as

$$\sigma_p^2 = \beta_p^2 \sigma_m^2 + \sum_{i=1}^{N} X_i \sigma_{ei}^2$$

Assume for a moment that an investor forms a portfolio by placing equal amounts of money into each of N stocks. The risk on the portfolio could be written as

$$\sigma_p^2 = \beta_p^2 \sigma_m^2 + \frac{1}{N^2} \sum_{i=1}^{N} \sigma_{ei}^2$$

Look at the last term. This can be expressed as N times the average residual risk for a stock. As the number of stocks in the portfolio grows, the importance of the residual risk—the nonbeta risk—diminishes drastically. In fact, as Exhibit 9 shows, the residual risk falls rapidly so that most of it is eliminated on even moderately sized portfolios.

The risk that is not eliminated as we hold larger and larger portfolios is the risk associated with the term β_p. If we assume that residual risk goes to zero, the risk of the portfolio becomes

$$\sigma_p = [\beta_p^2 \sigma_M^2]^{1/2} = \beta_p \sigma_M = \sigma_M \sum_{i=1}^{N} X_i \beta_i$$

Because σ_M is the same, regardless of which stock we examine, the measure of the contribution of a security to the risk of a large portfolio is β_i.

The risk of an individual security is $\beta_i \, \sigma_m^2 + \sigma_{ei}^2$. Because the effect of σ_{ei}^2 on portfolio risk goes to zero as the portfolio gets larger, it is common to refer σ_{ei}^2 as diversifiable risk. However, the effect of $\beta_i \, \sigma_M^2$ on portfolio risk does not diminish as N get larger. Because σ_M^2 is a constant with respect to all securities, β_i

is the measure of a security's nondiversifiable risk. Because diversifiable risk can be eliminated by holding a large enough portfolio, β_i is often used as the measure of a security's risk.

SELECTING EFFICIENT PORTFOLIOS. The single-index model employs a simplifying assumption about the way stocks covary. When this simplifying assumption is used, it means that the model cannot do a perfect job of reproducing the historical correlation between all stocks. It is possible, however, that the model will lead to the better selection of optimal portfolios. This will be true if the historic correlation between securities contains a lot of random noise (seemingly relevant but actually irrelevant information) with respect to future correlations. Extensive tests have been done on the single-index model and they all indicate that this model does a better job of forecasting the future correlations between securities and leads to the selection of more efficient portfolios than does the historic correlation itself. (See Elton and Gruber (1981), Elton, Gruber, and Urich (1978), and Cohen and Pogue (1967) for evidence.) Having discussed the single-index model, let us discuss some other alternative representations of the input data needed for portfolio analysis.

MULTI-INDEX MODELS. The assumption underlying the single-index model is that the only reason two stocks moved together is because of common movement with the market. Many researchers have found that there are influences beyond the market which cause stocks to move together. For example, as early as the mid-1960s, King (1966) presented evidence on the existence of industry influences. Two different types of schemes have been put forward for handling additional influences. We have called them the general multi-index model and the industry index model.

General Multi-Index Models. Any additional sources of covariance between securities can be introduced into the equations for risk and return, simply by adding these additional influences to the general return equation. Let's

EXHIBIT 9 IMPORTANCE OF RESIDUAL RISK

Number of Securities	Residual Risk Expressed as a Percent of the Residual Risk Present in a One-Stock Portfolio
1	100%
2	50
3	33
4	25
5	20
10	10
20	5
100	1
1,000	.1

hypothesize that the return on any stock is a function of the return on the market, the level of interest rates, and a set of industry indexes. If R_i is the return on stock i, then the return on stock i can be related to the influences that effect it in the following way:

$$R_i = \alpha_i + b_{i1} I_1 + b_{i2} I_2 + \ldots b_{it} I_t + C_i$$

In this equation I_j is the actual level of index I_j, b_{ij} is a measure of the responsiveness of the return on stock i to changes in the index j, and a_i is the expected return if all the indexes were equal to zero (the unique return). The remaining term C_i is a measure of the differences that arise between actual returns and returns that would be predicted from the preceding equation. Because this equation is expected to predict returns correctly (on average), C_i has a mean of zero. Because the equation is not expected to produce perfect forecasts at any point in time, C_i has a positive variance which we will call σ_{ci}^2.

To use this model analysts must supply estimates of the expected return for each stock, the variance of each stock's returns, the index loading b_{ij} between each stock and each index and the means and variances of each index. The number of inputs needed is $2N + 2L + LN$. As discussed at several points in this section, the inputs needed to perform portfolio analysis are expected returns, variances, and correlation coefficients. By having the analysts estimate means and variances directly, it is clear that the only input derived from the estimates of the multi-index models are correlation coefficients. We stress this point because later in this section we will evaluate the ability of a multi-index model to aid in the selection of securities by examining its ability to forecast correlations coefficients.

There is a certain type of multi-index model that has received a large amount of attention. This model restricts attention to market and industry influences. There are several models of this type which vary in the assumptions they make and, hence, the type and amount of input data needed. We will now examine the simplest of the models.

Industry Index Models. Several authors have dealt with multi-index models that start with the basic single-index model and add indexes to capture industry effects. The early precedent for this work can be found in King (1966), who measured effects of common movement between securities beyond market effects and found this extra market covariance was associated with industries. For example, two steel stocks had positive correlation among their returns, even after the effects of the market had been removed.

If we hypothesize that the correlation between securities is caused by a market effect and industry effects, our general multi-index model could be written as:

$$R_i = \alpha_i + b_{im} I_m + b_{i1} I_i + b_{i2} I_2 + \ldots + b_{iL} I_L + C_i$$

Where I_m = the market index
I_j = industry indexes that are constrained to be uncorrelated with the market and uncorrelated with each other

The assumption behind this model is that a firm's return can be affected by the market plus several industries. For some companies this seems appropriate, because their lines of business span several traditional industries. However, some companies gain the bulk of their return from activities in one industry and perhaps, of more importance, are viewed by investors as members of a particular industry. In this case the influences on the firm's return of all but the industry index (to which it belongs), together with the market index, are likely to be small and their inclusion may introduce more random noise into the process than the information they supply. This has prompted some authors to advocate a simpler form of the multi-index model—one that simply assumes that returns of each firm are only affected by a market index and an industry index. Furthermore, the model assumes that each industry index has been constructed to be uncorrelated with the market and with all other industry indexes. For firm i in industry j, the return equation can be written as

$$R_i = \alpha_i + b_{im}I_m + b_{ij}I_j + c_i$$

A logical question to ask at this point is how well multi-index models work. It is difficult to give a conclusive answer to this question for there are virtually an infinite number of possible multi-index models. Furthermore, the results on those multi-index models that have been tested are mixed. Elton and Gruber (1978) tested the results of a general multi-index model and found that its performance was inferior to that of the single-index model. Cohen and Pogue (1967) tested an industry multi-index model and found that it did not perform as well as the single-index model. On the other hand, Farrell (1974) tested a version of the industry index model where indexes for groups of stocks (rather than traditional industries) were used and found that his model outperformed the single-index model. Although the use of multi-index models holds great promise for the future, the results, to date, have been mixed.

The use of simplified input allows techniques for solving optimum portfolios to be simplified and plays an important part in the development of asset pricing models. A discussion of portfolio optimizers is beyond the range of this section, but the interested reader is referred to Elton and Gruber *Modern Portfolio Theory and Investment Analysis,* Chapters 4 and 7. The implications of these techniques for APT will be clear in later parts of this section.

ASSET PRICING MODELS

A number of models have been derived that explain why the expected return differs across assets and asset classes. These models are derived assuming security markets are in equilibrium. There are two general classes of models of this type—capital asset pricing models and arbitrage pricing models. Capital asset pricing models have as their basic premise that investors use the analysis discussed in the prior subsection to make their investment decisions. The arbitrage pricing model has as its basic premise that an index model describes the return generating process. In this subsection we will discuss each of these classes of models in turn. Then we will discuss the use of these models in the investment process.

CAPITAL ASSET PRICING MODELS. The first part of this section was concerned with how an individual or institution, acting on a set of estimates, could select an optimum portfolio, or set of portfolios. If investors act as we have prescribed, then we should be able to draw on the analysis to determine how the aggregate of investors will behave, and how prices and returns, at which markets will clear, are set. The construction of an asset pricing model will allow us to determine the relevant measure of risk for any asset and the relationship between expected return and risk for any asset when markets are in equilibrium. Furthermore, although the equilibrium models are derived from models of how portfolios should be constructed, the models themselves have major implications for the characteristics of optimum portfolios.

A large variety of asset pricing models can be derived from the portfolio theory framework derived earlier. In this section we will emphasize the two most popular models—the **standard capital asset pricing model** and the **zero beta asset pricing model.** Following this discussion we will briefly present alternative models. Finally, we will close with a discussion of the empirical tests of the models.

It is worthwhile pointing out, at this time, that the final test of a model is not how reasonable the assumptions behind it appear, but how well the model describes reality. As the reader proceeds with this section he or she will, no doubt, find many of the assumptions underlying asset pricing models objectionable. Furthermore, the final model is so simple the reader may well wonder about its validity. As we will see, despite the stringent assumptions and the simplicity of the model, it does an amazingly good job of describing prices in the capital markets.

STANDARD CAPITAL ASSET PRICING MODEL (CAPM) ASSUMPTIONS. The real world is sufficiently complex that to understand it and construct models of how it works, one must dismiss those complexities that, hopefully, have only a small (or no) affect on its behavior. As the physicist builds models of the movement of matter in a frictionless environment, the economist builds models where there are no institutional frictions to the movement of stock prices.

No Transaction Costs. The first assumption we make is that there are no transaction costs. There is no cost (friction) of buying or selling any asset. If transaction costs were present, the return from any asset would be a function of whether or not the investor owned it before the decision period. Thus including transaction costs in the model adds a great deal of complexity. Whether it is worthwhile introducing this complexity depends on the importance of transaction costs to investors' decisions. Given the size of transaction costs, they are probably of minor importance.

Assets Are Infinitely Divisible. The second assumption behind the CAPM is that assets are infinitely divisible. This means that investors could take any position in an investment, regardless of the size of their wealth. For example, they can buy one dollar's worth of IBM stock.

No Personal Income Tax. The third assumption is the absence of personal income tax. This means, for example, that the individual is indifferent to the form (dividends or capital gains) in which the return on the investment is received.

Individual Cannot Affect Stock Prices. The fourth assumption is that an individual cannot influence the price of a stock by his or her buying or selling action. This is analogous to the assumption of perfect competition. Although no single investor can affect prices by an individual action, investors in total determine prices by their actions.

Standard Decision-Making Methods. The fifth assumption is that investors are expected to make decisions solely in terms of expected values and standard deviations of the returns on their portfolios. In other words, they make their portfolio decision, utilizing the framework discussed in other sections.

Unlimited Short Sales. The sixth assumption is that unlimited short sales are allowed. The individual investor can sell short any amount of any shares.

Unlimited Lending and Borrowing. The seventh assumption is unlimited lending and borrowing at the riskless rate. The investor can lend or borrow any amount of funds desired at a rate of interest equal to the rate for riskless securities.

Homogeneity of Expectations. The eighth and ninth assumptions deal with the homogeneity of expectations. First, investors are assumed to be concerned with the mean and variance of returns (or prices over a single period), and all investors are assumed to define the relevant period in exactly the same manner. Second, all investors are assumed to have identical expectations with respect to the necessary inputs to the portfolio decision. As we have said many times, these inputs are expected returns, the variance of returns, and the correlation matrix representing the correlation structure among all pairs of stocks.

All Assets Are Marketable. The tenth assumption is that all assets are marketable. All assets, including human capital, can be sold and bought on the market.

Readers can now see the reason for the earlier warning that they might find many of the assumptions behind the CAPM untenable. It is clear that these assumptions do not hold in the real world, just as it is clear that the physicist's frictionless environment does not exist. The relevant questions are: How much is reality distorted by making these assumptions? What conclusions about capital markets do they lead to? Do these conclusions seem to describe the actual performance of the capital market?

Recall that without riskless lending and borrowing, each investor faces an efficient frontier such as that shown in Exhibit 10. In this exhibit BC represents the efficient frontier, whereas ABC represents the set of minimum variance portfolios. In general the efficient frontier will differ among investors because of differences in expectations.

Portfolio of Risky Assets. When we introduced riskless lending and borrowing, we showed that the portfolio of risky assets that any investor would hold could be identified without regard to the investor's risk preferences. This portfolio lies at the tangency point between the original efficient frontier of risky assets and a ray passing through the riskless return (on the vertical axis). This is depicted in Exhibit 11, where P_i denotes investor i's portfolio of risky

EXHIBIT 10 THE EFFICIENT FRONTIER: NO LENDING AND BORROWING

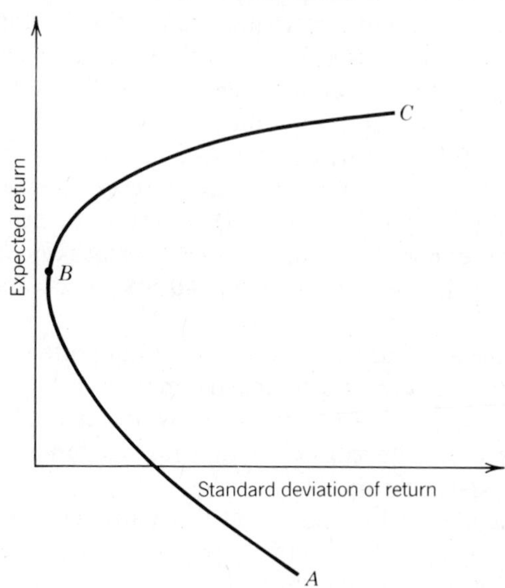

EXHIBIT 11 THE EFFICIENT FRONTIER: WITH LENDING AND BORROWING

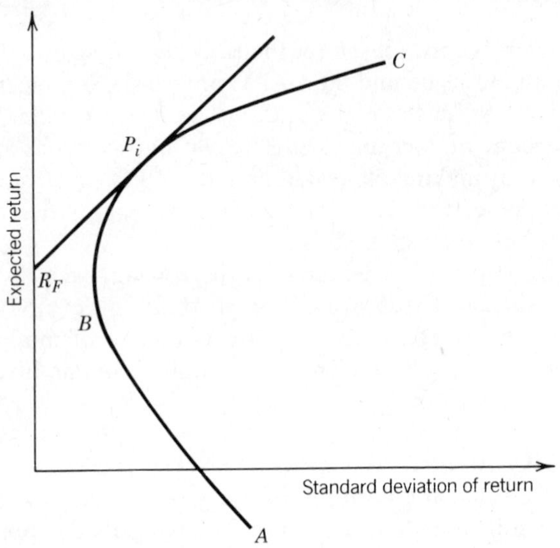

assets. The investors satisfy their risk preferences by combining portfolio P_i, with lending or borrowing.

Market Portfolio. If all investors have homogeneous expectations and they all face the same lending and borrowing rate, then they will each face a diagram such as in Exhibit 11 and, furthermore, all of the diagrams will be identical. The portfolio of risky assets P_i held by any investor will be identical to the portfolio of risky assets held by another investor. If all investors hold the same risky portfolio, then, in equilibrium, it must be the market portfolio. The **market portfolio** is a portfolio comprised of all risky assets. Each asset is held in the proportion, which the market value of that asset represents, of the total market value of all risky assets. For example, if IBM stock represents 3% of all risky assets, then the market portfolio contains 3% IBM stock and each investor will take 3% of the money that will be invested in all risky assets and place it in IBM stock.

Notice that we have already learned something important. All investors will hold combinations of only two portfolios: the market portfolio (M) and a riskless security. This is sometimes referred to as the **two mutual fund theorem** because all investors would be satisfied with a market fund, plus the ability to lend or borrow a riskless security.

The straight line depicted in Exhibit 11 is usually referred to as the **capital market line.** All investors will end up with portfolios somewhere along the capital market line. However, not all securities or portfolios lie along the capital market line. In fact, from the derivation of the efficient frontier, we know that all portfolios of risky and riskless assets, except those that are efficient, lie below the capital market line.

Earlier we argued that, for very well-diversified portfolios, beta was the correct measure of a security's risk. For *very* well-diversified portfolios, nonsystematic risk tends to go to zero and the only relevant risk is systematic risk measured by beta. As we have just explained, given the assumptions of homogeneous expectations and unlimited riskless lending and borrowing, all investors will hold the market portfolio. Thus the investor will hold a *very* well-diversified portfolio. Because we assume that the investor is concerned only with expected return and risk, the only dimensions of a security that need be of concern are expected return and beta.

EXAMPLE—TWO PORTFOLIOS. Let us hypothesize two portfolios with the characteristics shown:

Investment	Expected Return	Beta
A	10	1.0
B	12	1.4

We have already seen that the expected return from portfolio *A* is simply the sum of the products of the proportion invested in each stock and the expected return on each stock. It is also true that the beta on a portfolio is simply the sum of the product of the proportion invested in each stock times the beta on each stock. Now consider a portfolio *C* made up on one half of portfolio *A* and one half of portfolio *B*. From the facts already stated, the expected return on this portfolio is 11 and its beta is 1.2. These three potential investments are plotted in Exhibit 12. Notice that they lie on a straight line. This is no accident; all

EXHIBIT 12 COMBINATIONS OF PORTFOLIOS

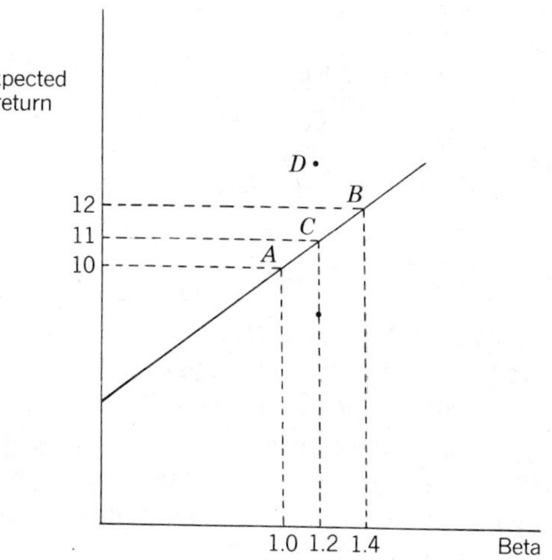

portfolios composed of different fractions of investments A and B will lie along a straight line in expected return beta space.

If we let X stand for the fraction of funds invested in portfolio A, then the equation for return is

$$\bar{R}_p = X\bar{R}_A + (1 - X)\bar{R}_B$$

The equation for beta

$$\beta_p = X\beta_A + (1 - X)\beta_B$$

Solving the second equation for X and substituting in the first equation, we see that we are left with an equation of the form

$$R_p = a + b\beta_p$$

or the equation of a straight line.

Now hypothesize a new investment D that has a return of 13% and a beta of 1.2. Such an investment cannot exist for very long. All decisions are made in terms of risk and return. This portfolio offers a higher return and the same risk as portfolio C. Hence, it would pay all investors to sell C short and buy D. Similarly, if a security were to exist with a return of 8% and a beta of 1.2 (designed by E), it would pay arbitrageurs to step in and buy portfolio C while selling security E short. Such arbitrage would take place until C, D, and E all yielded the same return. This is just another illustration of the adage that two things which are equivalent cannot sell at different prices. We can demonstrate the arbitrage discussed earlier in a slightly more formal manner. Let us return to the **arbitrage** between portfolios C and D. An investor could sell \$100 worth of portfolio C short and with the \$100 buy portfolio D. If the investor were to do so, the characteristics of this arbitraged portfolio would be as follows:

	Cash Invested	Expected Return	Beta
Portfolio C	−\$100	−\$11	−1.2
Security D	+\$100	\$13	1.2
Arbitrage portfolio	0	\$2	0

From this example it is clear that as long as a security lies above the straight line, there is a portfolio involving zero risk and zero net investment that has a positive expected profit. An investor will engage in this arbitrage as long as any security or portfolio lies above the straight line depicted in Exhibit 12. A similar arbitrage will exist if any amount lies below the straight line in Exhibit 12.

We have now established that all investments and all portfolios of investments must lie along a straight line in return-beta space. If any investment were to lie above or below that straight line, then an opportunity would exist for riskless arbitrage. This arbitrage would continue until all investments converged to the line. There are many different ways that this straight line can be identified, for it only takes two points to identify a straight line. Because we have shown that, under the assumptions of the CAPM, everyone will hold that market portfolio and because all portfolios must lie on the straight line, we will use this as one point. The market portfolio must have a beta of one. Because beta is a measure of the responsiveness of an asset or portfolio to changes in the market and the market moves in a one to one relationship with itself. Thus in Exhibit 13 the market portfolio is point M with a beta of one and return of R_M. It is often convenient to choose the second point to identify a straight line as the intercept. The intercept occurs when beta equals zero, or when the asset has zero systematic risk. One asset with zero systematic risk is the riskless asset. Thus we can identify the intercept as the rate of return on a riskless asset.

These two points identify the straight line shown in Exhibit 13. The equation of a straight line has the form

$$\bar{R}_i = a + b\beta_i$$

One point on the line is the riskless asset with a beta of zero. Thus

$$R_F = a + b(0)$$

or

$$R_F = a$$

A second point on the line is the market portfolio with a beta of one. Thus

$$\bar{R}_M = a + b(1)$$

or

$$(\bar{R}_M - a) = b$$

Putting these together and substituting yields

$$\bar{R}_i = R_F + \beta_i(\bar{R}_M - R_F)$$

Think about this relationship for a moment. It represents one of the most important discoveries in the field of finance. Here is a simple equation, called the **security market line,** that describes the expected return for all assets and portfolios of assets in the economy. The expected return on any assets, or portfolio, whether it is efficient or not, can be determined from this relationship. Notice that $\bar{R}_M$ and R_F are not functions of the assets we examine. Thus the relation-

EXHIBIT 13 THE SECURITY MARKET LINE

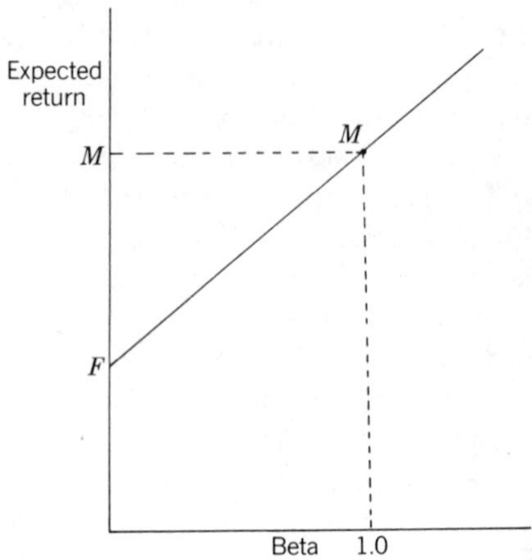

ship between the expected return on any two assets can be related simply to their difference in beta.

The higher beta is for any security, the higher must be its equilibrium return. Furthermore, the relationship between beta and expected return is linear. One of the greatest insights that comes from this equation arises from what it states is unimportant in determining return. Recall that in discussing the single-index model we observed that the risk of any stock could be divided into systematic and unsystematic risk. Beta was the index of systematic risk. This equation validates the conclusion that systematic risk is the only important ingredient in determining expected returns and that nonsystematic risk plays no role. Put another way, the investor is rewarded for bearing systematic risk. It is not total variance of returns that affects expected returns, but only that part of the variance in returns which cannot be diversified away. This result has great economic intuition because if investors can eliminate all nonsystematic risk through diversification, there is no reason they should be rewarded, in terms of higher return, for bearing it. All of these implications of the CAPM are empirically testable. Indeed, we examine the results of these tests later. Provided the tests hold, we have, with a simple model, gained great insight in the behavior of the capital markets.

We digress for a moment and point out one seeming fallacy in the potential use of the CAPM. Invariably, when a group of investors is first exposed to the CAPM, one or more investors will find a high beta stock that last year produced a smaller return than low beta stocks. The CAPM is an equilibrium relationship. High beta stocks are expected to give a higher return than low beta stocks because they are more risky. This does not mean that they will give a higher return over all intervals of time. In fact, if they always gave a higher return, they would be less risky, not more risky, than low beta stocks. Rather, because they are more risky, they will sometimes produce lower returns. Over long periods of time, however, they should on the average produce higher returns.

We have written the CAPM model in the form

$$\bar{R}_i = R_F + \beta_i(\bar{R}_M - R_F)$$

This is the form in which it is most often written and the form most amenable to empirical testing. However, there are alternative forms that give added insight into its meaning. It can be shown that

$$\beta_i = \frac{\sigma_{iM}}{\sigma_M^2}$$

this leads to

$$\bar{R}_i = R_F + \left(\frac{\bar{R}_M - R_F}{\sigma_M^2}\right)\sigma_{iM}$$

This form is also used in the investment area.

LIMITATIONS OF THE CAPM. The CAPM model just developed would provide a complete description of the behavior of capital markets if each of the assumptions set forth held. The test of the CAPM model is how well it describes reality. But, even before we examine the tests it is useful to develop **equilibrium models** based on more realistic assumptions. Most of the assumptions underlying the CAPM violate conditions in the real world. This does not mean that we should disregard the CAPM model, for the differences from reality of its assumptions and estimates may be sufficiently unimportant that they do not materially affect the explanatory power of the model. On the other hand, the incorporation of alternative, more realistic assumptions into the model has several important benefits. Although the CAPM may describe equilibrium returns on the macro level, it certainly is not descriptive of micro (individual investor) behavior. For example, most individuals and many institutions hold portfolios of risky assets that do not resemble the market portfolio. We might gain better insight into investor behavior by examining models developed under alternative and more realistic assumptions.

Another reason for examining other equilibrium models is that it allows us to formulate and test alternative explanations of equilibrium returns. The CAPM may work well; but do other models work better and explain discrepancies from the CAPM? Finally, and perhaps most important, because the CAPM assumes several real world influences, it does not provide us with a mechanism for studying the impact of those influences on capital market equilibrium or on individual decision making. Only by recognizing the presence of these influences can their impact be investigated. For example, if we assume personal taxes do not exist, there is no way the equilibrium model can be used to study the effects of taxes. By constructing a model that includes taxes, we can study the impact of taxes on individual investor behavior and on equilibrium returns in the capital market.

THE ZERO BETA FORM OF THE CAPM. One of the assumptions of the standard CAPM is that investors can lend and borrow unlimited sums of money at the riskless rate of interest. Such an assumption is clearly not descriptive of the real world. It seems much more realistic to assume that investors can lend unlimited sums of money at the riskless rate but cannot borrow at a riskless rate. The lending assumption is equivalent to investors being able to buy government securities equal in maturity to their single-period horizon. Such securities exist and they are, for all intents and purposes, riskless. Furthermore, the rate on such securities is virtually the same for all investors. On the other hand, it is not possible for investors to borrow unlimited amounts at a riskless rate. It is convenient to examine the case where investors can neither borrow nor lend at the riskless rate first, and then to extend the analysis to the case where they can lend but not borrow at the riskless rate.

The zero beta model is the second most widely used general equilibrium model. The standard capital asset pricing model developed in the last subsection is the most widely used. In that subsection we argued that systematic risk was the appropriate measure of risk and that two assets with the same systematic risk could not offer different rates of return. The essence of the argument was that the unsystematic risk of large diversified portfolios was essentially zero. Thus even if an individual asset had a great deal of unsystematic risk, it would have little impact on portfolio risk and, therefore unsystematic risk would not require a higher return. This was formalized in Exhibit 12.

One portfolio that lies along the straight line is the **market portfolio.** This can be seen in either of two ways. If it did not lie along the straight line, two assets would exist with the same systematic risk and different return and in equilibrium equivalent assets must offer the same return. In addition, note that all combinations of securities lie on the line and the market portfolio is a weighted average of the securities.

A straight line can be described by any two points. One convenient point is the market portfolio. A second convenient portfolio is where the straight line cuts the vertical axis (where beta equals zero).

The equation of a straight line is

$$\text{expected return} = a + b\,(\text{beta})$$

This must hold for a portfolio with zero beta. Letting $\bar{R}_z$ equal the expected return on this portfolio, we have

$$\bar{R}_z = a + b(0) \qquad \text{or} \qquad a = \bar{R}_z$$

The equation must also hold for the market portfolio. If $\bar{R}_M$ is the expected return on the market and, recalling the beta for the market portfolio is one, we have

$$\bar{R}_M = \bar{R}_z + b(1) \qquad \text{or} \quad b = \bar{R}_M - \bar{R}_z$$

Putting this together and letting $\bar{R}_i$ and β_i be the expected return and beta on an asset or portfolio, the equation for the expected return on any security or portfolio becomes

$$\bar{R}_i = \bar{R}_z + (\bar{R}_M - \bar{R}_z)\beta_i$$

This is the so-called **zero beta** version of the capital asset pricing model and is plotted in Exhibit 14. This form of the general equilibrium relationship is often referred to alternatively as a **two-factor model.** An alternative form that may be familiar to readers can be gotten from recalling that

$$\beta_i = \frac{\sigma_{im}}{\sigma_m^2}$$

thus

$$\bar{R}_i = \bar{R}_z + \frac{(\bar{R}_m - \bar{R}_z)}{\sigma^2}\,\sigma_{im}$$

EXHIBIT 14 THE ZERO BETA CAPITAL ASSET PRICING LINE

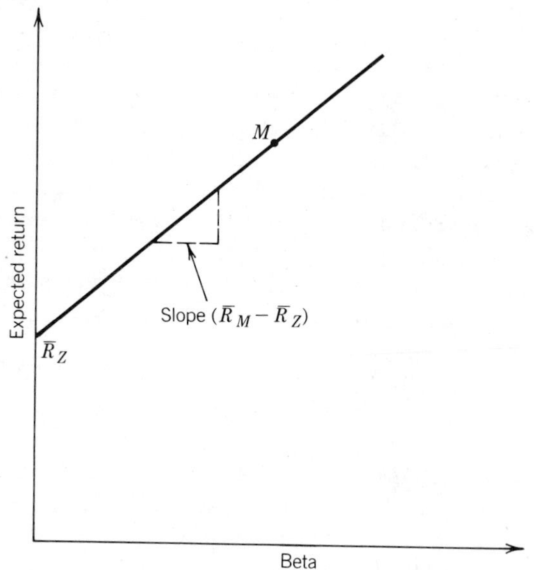

We derived the zero beta from assuming no riskless lending and borrowing. Exactly the same asset pricing model results from an assumption of riskless lending but no riskless borrowing.

ASSET PRICING ALLOWING TAXES. The simple form of the capital asset pricing model ignores the presence of **taxes** in arriving at an equilibrium solution. The implication of this assumption is that investors are indifferent about receiving income in the form of capital gains or dividends and that all investors hold the same portfolio of risky assets. If we recognize the existence of taxes and, in particular, the fact that capital gains are taxed, in general, at a lower rate than dividends, the equilibrium prices should change. Investors should judge the return and risk on their portfolio after taxes. This implies that, even with homogeneous expectations about the before-tax return on a portfolio, the relevant (after-tax) efficient frontier faced by each investor will be different. An asset pricing model still exists, however, because in the aggregate markets must clear. The return on any asset or portfolio is given by

$$E(R_i) = R_F + \beta_i[(E(R_M) - R_F) - \tau(\delta_M - R_F)] + \tau(\delta_i - R_F) \qquad \text{(A)}$$

where δ_M = the dividend yield (dividend by price) of the m)arket portfolio
δ_i = the dividend yield for stock i
τ = a tax factor that measures the relevant market tax rates on capital gains and income. τ is a complex function of investors' tax rates and wealth. However, it should be a positive number.

The asset pricing model for expected returns has now become very complex. When dividends are on average taxed at a higher rate than capital gains (as they are in the U.S. economy), τ is positive and expected return is an increasing function of dividend yield. This is intuitively appealing because the larger the fraction of return paid in the form of dividends, the more taxes the investor will have to pay and the larger the pretax return required. The reader may wonder why the last term contains R_F as well as the dividend yield. The reason for this is the tax treatment of interest on lending and borrowing. Because interest payments are usually taxed at the same rate as dividends, they enter the relationship in a parallel manner although with an opposite sign. The fact that the term in square brackets has the correct form can be seen by letting security i be the market portfolio and noting that (because beta equals one for the market portfolio) the equation reduces to

$$E\,(R_M) = E\,(R_M).$$

Examination of equation A reveals that a security market line is no longer sufficient to describe the equilibrium relationship. In previous versions of general equilibrium relationships the only variable associated with the individual security that affects expected return was its beta. Now we see from Equation A that both the securities beta and its dividend yield affect expected return. This means that equilibrium must be described in three-dimensional space (R_i,β_i,δ_i) rather than two-dimensional space. The resultant equilibrium relationship will be a plane rather than a straight line. The plane will be located such that for any value of beta expected return goes up as dividend yield goes up, and for any value of dividend yield expected return goes up as beta goes up.

If returns are determined by an equilibrium model such as that presented in Equation A, it should be possible to derive optional portfolios for any investor as a function of the tax rates paid on capital gains and dividends. Although the mathematics of the solution are rather complex, the economic intuition behind the results is strong. All investors will hold widely diversified portfolios that resemble the market portfolio, except the portfolios will be tilted in favor of those stocks in which the investor has a competitive advantage. For example, investors whose tax bracket is below the average effective rate in the market should hold more high dividend stocks in their portfolio than the pro-rata share that these stocks constitute of the market portfolio. On the other hand, they should hold less (and in extreme cases even short sell) stocks with every low dividends. Low tax bracket investors have a comparative advantage in holding high dividend stocks, because the tax disadvantage of these stocks is less for them than it is for the average stockholder. Individual investors in the market seem to behave as the analysis suggests they should.

TESTS OF ASSET PRICING MODELS. Earlier we stressed the fact that the construction of a theory necessitates a simplifiation of the phenomena under study. To understand and model any process, elements in the real world are simplified or assumed away. Although a model based on simple assumptions can always be called into question because of these assumptions, the relevant test of how much damage has been done by the simplification is to examine the relationship between the predictions of the model and observed real world phenomena. In our case, the relevant test is how well the simple CAPM, or perhaps some other equilibrium model, describes the behavior of actual capital markets. A detailed discussion of testing is well beyond the scope of the section. However, a simple test will be discussed that gives some feel for the empirical evidence.

One of the main implications of all models we discussed was that higher return should be associated with higher risk (as measured by beta). Sharpe and Cooper (1972) determined whether following alternative strategies with respect to risk over long periods of time would produce returns consistent with modern capital theory. In order to get portfolios with different betas they divided stocks into deciles once a year on the basis of the beta of each security. To be more precise, beta at a point in time was measured using 60 months of previous data. Once a year, for each year from 1931 to 1967, all New York Stock Exchange stocks were divided into deciles based on their rank by beta. An equally weighted portfolio was formed of the stocks that comprised each decile. A strategy consisted of holding the stocks of a particular decile over the entire period. The stocks one holds change both because of the reinvestment of dividends and because the stocks that make up a particular decile change as the decile's composition is revised once a year. Notice that the strategy outlined by Sharpe and Cooper could actually be followed by an investor. Each year the investor divides stocks into deciles by beta based on the previous 5 years' (60 months) returns. If investors want to pursue the high beta strategy, they simply divide their funds equally among the stocks in the highest beta decile. They do this every year and observe the outcomes. Exhibit 15 shows what would have happened, on average, if an investor had done this each year from 1931 to 1967.

Although the relationship between strategy and return is not perfect, it is very close. In general, stocks with higher betas have produced higher future returns. In fact, the rank correlation coefficient between strategy and return is over 0.93, which is statistically significant at the 0.01 level. Similarly, buying stocks with higher forecast beta would lead to holding portfolios with higher realized betas. The rank correlation between strategy and beta is 95%, which is significant at the 0.01 level.

The next logical step is to examine the relationship between the return that would have been earned and the risk (beta) from following alternative strategies. Exhibit 16 from Sharpe and Cooper (1972) shows this relationship. The equation depicted on this graph is

$$\bar{R}_i = 5.54 + 12.75\beta_i$$

Over 95% of the variation in expected return is explained by differences in beta. Thus beta has explained a very significant portion of the difference in return between these portfolios (strategies).

Sharpe and Cooper's work presents rather clear and easily interpreted evidence that as general equilibrium theory suggests, there is a **positive relationship between return and beta.** Furthermore, an examination of Exhibit 16 provides confidence that the relationship is both strong and linear.

Although a great deal of attention has been paid to tests of the standard or

EXHIBIT 15 RELATIONSHIP BETWEEN STRATEGY AND RETURN

Strategy	Average Return	Portfolio Beta
10	22.67	1.42
9	20.45	1.18
8	20.26	1.14
7	21.77	1.24
6	18.49	1.06
5	19.13	0.98
4	18.88	1.00
3	14.99	0.76
2	14.63	0.65
1	11.58	0.58

EXHIBIT 16 POSITIVE RELATIONSHIP BETWEEN RETURN AND BETA

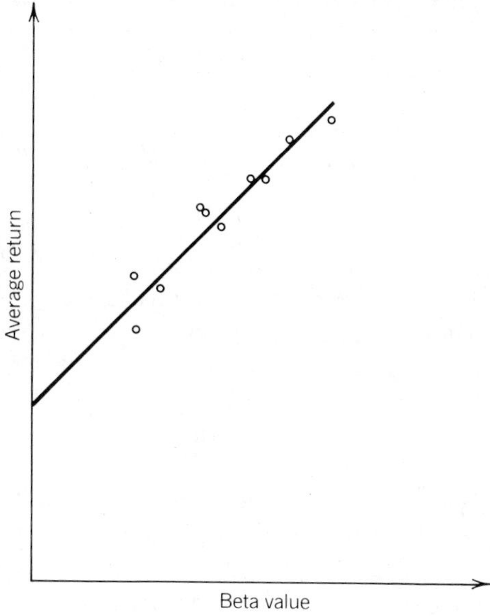

zero beta CAPM model, almost no testing has been done on the other forms of general equilibrium models. The one exception to this is in tax-adjusted versions. Black and Scholes (1974) have tested a form of the CAPM that includes a dividend term and concluded that dividends do not affect the equilibrium relationship. Because a dividend term is present in the post-tax CAPM, this would seem to indicate that a pretax CAPM is more descriptive of equilibrium returns. More recently, however, Litzenberger and Ramaswamy (1979) have found strong, positive support for dividends affecting equilibrium prices. Their results differ from Black and Scholes at least in part because although Black and Scholes assumed that dividends were received in equal amounts each month, Litzenberger and Ramaswamy formulated their tests so that dividends were assumed to be received in the month in which they could reasonably be expected to occur. They tested a model of the form

$$R_{it} - R_{Ft} = \gamma_0 + \gamma_1\beta_{it} + \gamma_2(\delta_{it} - R_{Ft}) + e_{it}$$

where δ_{it} is the dividend divided by price for stock i in month t.

When Litzenberger and Ramaswamy tested this model using maximum likelihood estimates on monthly data, they found the following results for the period 1936–1977.

$$\begin{gathered} R_{it} - R_{Ft} = \underset{(2.63)}{0.0063} + \underset{(1.86)}{0.0421}\beta_{it} + \underset{(8.62)}{0.236}(\delta_{it} - R_{Ft}) \\ t-\text{statistics in parentheses} \end{gathered}$$

The key point to note from the analysis is that the dividend term is positive and statistically significant. Furthermore, it is obvious that the dividend term is of economic significance. This term indicates that for every one dollar of dividends paid, stock investors require 23.6 cents in extra return.

ARBITRAGE PRICING THEORY (APT). All of the equilibrium models just discussed have their basis in mean variance analysis. All require that it is optimal for the investor to choose investments on the basis of expected return and variance.

Ross (1977) has proposed a new and different approach to explaining the pricing of assets. Ross has developed a mechanism that, given the process which generates security returns, derives asset prices from arbitrage arguments analogous to (but more complex than) those used earlier in this section to derive CAPMs. In this subsection we first present the mechanism of **arbitrage pricing theory (APT).** This is the derivation of equilibrium conditions given any prespecified return-generating process.

Following this we discuss implementation of the APT; the APT theory provides interesting insight into the nature of equilibrium. The theory, however, is far from easy to implement. Empirical research is just starting in this area. Furthermore, alternative approaches have been advocated for implementing the theory.

Arbitrage pricing theory is a new and different approach to determining asset prices. It is based on the law of one price; the statement that two things which are the same can't sell at different prices. The strong assumptions made about utility theory in deriving the CAPM are not necessary. In fact, the APT description of equilibrium is more general than that provided by a CAPM-type model in that pricing can be affected by factors beyond simply means and variances. An assumption of homogeneous expectations is necessary. The assumption of investors utilizing a mean variance framework is replaced by an assumption of the process generating security returns. The APT requires that the returns on any stock be linearly related to a set of indexes as shown in the following equation.

$$R_i = a_i + b_{i1} I_1 + b_{i2} I_2 + \cdots + b_{ij} I_j + e_i$$

where a_i = the expected level of return for stock i if all indexes have a value of zero

I_j = the value of the jth index that impacts the return on stock i

b_{ij} = the sensitivity of stock i's return to the jth index

e_i = a random error term with mean equal to zero and variance equal to σ_{ei}^2

For the model to describe fully the process generating security returns:

$$E\,(e_i\, e_j) = 0 \text{ for all } i \text{ and } j \text{ where } i \neq j$$

$$E[e_i(I_j - \bar{I}_j)] = 0 \text{ for all stocks and indexes}$$

If you are beginning to think that you have seen all this before, you are right. This representation is nothing more or less than the description of the multi-index model presented earlier. The **APT** is the description of the expected returns that can be derived when returns are generated by a single- or multi-index model meeting the conditions defined earlier. The contribution of APT is in demonstrating how (and under what conditions) one can go from a multi-index model to a description of equilibrium.

In the following we will demonstrate the derivation of an APT equilibrium. This proof stresses the economic rationale behind APT.

We will demonstrate the expected returns that must arise from the APT with a **two-index model.** Suppose that the following two-index model describes returns:

$$R_i = a_i + b_{i1}I_1 + b_{i2}I_2 + e_i$$

If any investor holds a well-diversified portfolio, residual risk will tend to go to zero and only systematic risk will matter. The only terms in the preceding equation that affect the systematic risk in a portfolio are b_{i1} and b_{i2}. Because the investor is assumed to be concerned with expected return and risk, he or she need only be concerned with three attributes of any portfolio (p): $\bar{R}_p$, b_{p1}, and b_{p2}.

Let us hypothesize the existence of the three widely diversified portfolios shown as follows:

Portfolio	Expected Return	b_{i1}	b_{i2}
A	15	1.0	.6
B	14	.5	1.0
C	10	.3	.2

We know from the concepts of geometry that three points determine a plane just as two points determine a line. The equation of the plane in three-dimensional space defined by these three portfolios is

$$\bar{R}_i = 7.75 + 5b_{i1} + 3.75b_{i2}$$

Because a weighted combination of points on a plane (where the weights sum to one) also lies on the plane, all portfolios constructed from portfolios A, B, and C lie on the plane described by portfolios A, B, and C.

What happens if we consider a new portfolio not on this plane? For example, assume a portfolio E exists with an expected return of 15%, a b_{i1} of .6 and a b_{i2} of .6.

Compare this with a portfolio (call it D) constructed by placing one third of the funds in portfolio A, one third in portfolio B, and one third in portfolio C. The b_{pj}'s on this portfolio are

$$b_{p1} = \frac{1}{3}(1.0) + \frac{1}{3}(.5) + \frac{1}{3}(.3) = .6$$

$$b_{p2} = \frac{1}{3}(.6) + \frac{1}{3}(1.0) + \frac{1}{3}(.2) = .6$$

The risk for portfolio D is identical to the risk on portfolio E. The expected return on portfolio D is

$$\frac{1}{3}(15) = \frac{1}{3}(14) + \frac{1}{3}(10) = 13$$

Alternatively, because portfolio D must lie on the plane described earlier, we could have obtained its expected return from the equation of the plane:

$$\bar{R}_i = 7.75 + 5\,(.6) + 3.75\,(.6) = 13$$

By the law of one price, two portfolios that have the same risk cannot sell at different expected returns. In this situation it would pay arbitrageurs to step in and buy portfolio E while selling an equal amount of portfolio D short. Buying portfolio E and financing it by selling D short would guarantee a riskless profit with no investment and no risk. We can see this easily. Assume the investor sells \$100 worth of portfolio D short and buys \$100 worth of portfolio E. The results are shown as follows:

	Initial Cash Flow	End of Period Cash Flow	b_{i1}	b_{i2}
Portfolio D	+\$100	−\$113.0	−.6	−.6
Portfolio E	−\$100	\$115.0	.6	.6
Arbitrage portfolio	0	2.0	0	0

The **arbitrge portfolio** involves zero investment, has no systematic risk (b_{i1} and b_{i2}), and earns \$2. Arbitrage would continue until portfolio E lies on the same plane as portfolis A, B, and C.

We have established that all investments and portfolios must be on a plane in expected return, b_{i1}, b_{i2} space. If an investment were to lie above or below the plane, an opportunity would exist for riskless arbitrage. The arbitrage would continue until all investments converged to a plane.

The general equation of a plane in expected return b_{i1}, b_{i2} space is

$$\bar{R}_i = \lambda_0 + \lambda_1 b_{i1} + \lambda_2 b_{i2}$$

This is the **equilibrium model** produced by the APT when returns are generated by a two-index model. Notice that λ_I is the increase in expected return for a one-unit increase in b_{i1}. Thus λ_I and λ_2 are returns for bearing the risks associated with I_1 and I_2, respectively.

More insight can be gained into the meaning of the λ_i's by using the prior equation to examine a particular set of portfolios. Examine a portfolio with b_{i1} and b_{i2} both equal to zero. The expected return on this portfolio equals λ_0. This is a zero b_{ij} portfolio, and we donate its return by $\bar{R}_z$. If riskless lending and borrowing exists, $\bar{R}_z = R_F$.

Substituting $\bar{R}_z$ for λ_0 and examining a portfolio with a b_{i2} of zero and a b_{i1} of one, we see that

$$\lambda_1 = \bar{R}_1 - \bar{R}_2$$

where $\bar{R}_1$ is the return on a portfolio having a b_{i1} of one and a b_{i2} of zero. In general, $\lambda_j = \bar{R}_j - \bar{R}_z$ or λ_j is the expected excess return on a portfolio only subject to risk of index j and having a unit measure of this risk.

The analysis in this section can be generalized to the J index case

$$R_i = a_i + b_{i1} I_2 + \cdots + b_{iJ} I_J + e_i$$

By analogous arguments it can be shown that all securities and portfolios have expected returns described by the J-dimensional hyperplane

$$\bar{R}_i = \lambda_0 + \lambda_1 b_{i1} + \lambda_2 b_{i2} + \cdots + \lambda_J b_{iJ}$$

with $\lambda_0 = \bar{R}_z$ and $\lambda_j = \bar{R}_j - \bar{R}_z$

The proof of any economic theory is how well it describes reality. Tests of APT are particularly difficult to formulate because all the theory specifies is a structure for asset pricing; the economic or firm characteristics that should affect expected return are not specified. Let us review the structure APT that will enter any test procedure.

We can write the multi-factor return-generating process as

$$R_i = a_i + \sum_{j=1}^{J} b_{ij} I_j + e_i$$

The APT model that arises from this return-generating process can be written as

$$\bar{R}_i = \bar{R}_z + \sum_{j=1}^{J} b_{ij} \lambda_j$$

It is worth spending a little time discussing the meaning of the variables b_{ij}, I_j, and λ_j.

Notice from the prior equation that each security i has a unique senstivitity to each I_j, but then I_j has a value that is the same for all securities. Any I_j affects more than one security (if it did not, it would have been compounded in the residual term e_i). These I_j's have generally been given the name factors in the APT literature. They are identical to the influences we called indexes in earlier subsections. The factors affect the returns on more than one security and are the sources of covariance between securities. The b_{ij}'s are unique to each security and represent an attribute of the security. This attribute may be simply the sensitivity of the security to a particular factor, or it can be a characteristic of the security such as dividend yield.

Finally, from the prior equation we see that λ_j is the extra expected return required because of a security's sensitivity to the jth attribute of the security. In order to test the APT, one must test this equation, which means that one must have estimates of the b_{ij}'s Most tests of APT use the multi-factor equation to estimate the b_{ij}'s. To estimate the b_{ij}'s, however, we must have definitions of the relevant I_j's. The most general approach to this problem is to estimate simultaneously factors (I_j's) and firm attributes (b_{ij}'s). Most tests of the APT have employed this methodology, and many of the most outspoken adherents of the APT believe this is the only appropriate way to test APT. This type of test is well beyond the scope of this section. However, there are two alternative methods. One method is to hypothesize (we hope on the basis of economic theory) a set of influences that might affect return and estimate b_{ij}. These influences might include variables such as the **rate of inflation** and the **rate of interest.** A second method is to specify a set of attributes (firm characteristics) that might affect expected return. With this approach the b_{ij}'s are directly specified. The b_{ij}'s might include such characteristics as dividend yield and the firm's beta with the market. If either of these last two procedures is used to obtain the b_{ij}'s for testing APT, one is actually conducting a joint test of the APT and the relevancy of the factors or characteristics which have been hypothesized as determining equilibrium. Each of these general approaches will now be discussed in more detail.

If a set of characteristics that affect return could be specified a priori, then the market price of these characteristics over any period of time could be measured fairly easily. The estimating equation would be of the form

$$\bar{R}_i = \lambda_0 + \lambda_1 b_{i1} + \lambda_2 b_{i2} + \cdots + \lambda_J b_{iJ}$$

for the case of J characteristics. In this equation the b_{ij}'s would be the value each characteristic took on, and the λ_j's the average extra return required because of this characteristic. The values of the λ_j's would be estimated via regression analysis.

One such model has been constructed and tested by Sharpe. He starts with the hypothesis that equilibrium returns should be effected by the following characteristics; a stock's beta with the S&P index, its dividend yield, the size of the firm (market value of equity), its beta with long-term bonds, its past value of alpha (the intercept of the regression of past excess return against excess returns on the S&P index), and eight sector membership variables. Sharpe does not attempt an elaborate economic rationale for these variables but rather states that he has selected them more or less "ex cathedra." We would expect both beta and dividend yield to be related positively to expected returns based on the theory discussed earlier. Size may well be, at least in part, a proxy for liquidity. If so, size should enter the model with a negative sign. If sensitivity to interest rates is an important variable, we would expect bond beta to play a role in determining equilibrium returns. If the past value of alpha proves significant, it would be evidence of autocorrelation of the residuals from the CAPM. This might indicate that there are some added variables explaining cross-sectional returns that were not captured in the model. The use of sector membership as an additional set of variables implies that membership in a particular sector of the economy has an important effect on equilibrium return.

The results of applying this model to 2,197 stocks on a monthly basis for all months between 1931 and 1979 are summarized in Exhibit 17. This exhibit reports the average coefficients (on an annualized basis) over the entire period and the percent of months in which the coefficients were significantly different from zero at the 5% level. Note that for those variables where we had clear expectations about the sign of the relationship with return, our expectations are borne out. Furthermore, note that although on the basis of chance we would

EXHIBIT 17 CROSS-SECTIONAL DATA ON SHARPE'S MULTI-FACTOR MODEL

Attribute	Annualized Value of Associated	Percent of Months in Which Associated Was Significantly Different from Zero
Beta	5.36	38.3
Yield	0.24	39.5
Size	−5.56	56.5
Bond Beta	−0.12	28.2
Alpha	−2.00	43.5
Sector Membership		
Basic industries	1.65	32.5
Capital goods	0.16	18.7
Construction	−1.59	15.3
Consumer goods	−0.18	39.3
Energy	6.28	36.9
Finance	−1.48	16.3
Transportation	−0.57	43.9
Utilities	−2.62	35.0

expect any firm characteristic to be significant about 5% of the time, each characteristic was significant a much higher percentage of the time.

Another way to judge the importance of including more than one characteristic in the description of equilibrium is by examining the explanatory power (coefficient of determination) of the model as more characteristics are employed. The average coefficient of determination for monthly data when beta is used as the only characteristic to explain cross-sectional returns is .037. This result is consistent with other studies employing similar research designs. When the security characteristics of yield, size, bond beta, and alpha are added, the coefficient of determination adjusting for added variables more than doubles to .079. When all the characteristics in Exhibit 17 are used, it goes up to .104. The use of firm characteristics in addition to beta has increased the explanatory power of the model. In addition, these factors seem to be significant a considerably higher percentage of the time than chance alone would explain.

Sharpe seems to have identified some additional characteristics, beyond a stock's beta with a proxy for the market portfolio, that are useful for explaining cross-sectional returns over time. He recognizes that his model is rather ad hoc in nature, but it is an indication that increased research into significant economic characteristics of a stock should allow us to build better models of equilibrium.

Another alternative to joint determination of factor loadings and factors discussed earlier in this section is the specification (one hopes on the basis of economic theory) of the set of influences of indexes (I_{ij}'s) that should enter the return-generating process. We can describe a model like this that is used as part of the investment process by Salomon Brothers. The **Salomon Brothers model** specifies the following set of I_j's as affecting security returns.

1. Growth rate in the Consumer Price Index
2. Real rate of growth in Gross National Product
3. Real rate of increase in oil prices
4. Real rate of increase in defense spending
5. Real rate of interest

The b_{ij}'s in the Salomon Brothers approach represent the sensitivity of a company's return to each of these indexes. Salomon Brothers advocates the use of these sensitivities as risk measures in portfolio composition; however, they do not at this time estimate the market prices (λ_j's) of these sensitivities.

APPLICATIONS OF ASSET PRICING MODELS

In this part of the section we will discuss two applications of the asset pricing models discussed earlier. One is their use to aid in **stock selection.** Second is their use in **portfolio evaluation.** Each of these will be discussed in turn.

EXHIBIT 18 SECURITY MARKET LINE

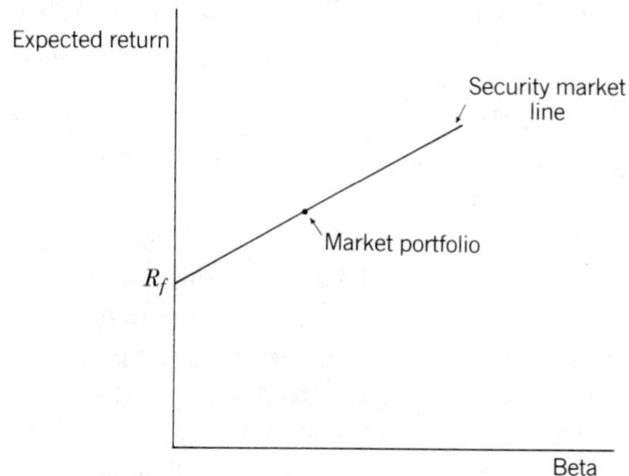

USE IN SECURITY SELECTION. Consider initially the standard capital asset pricing model. Recall the model is

$$\bar{R}_i = R_F + \beta_i (\bar{R}_M - R_F)$$

This security market line is depicted in Exhibit 18. In equilibrium all securities and portfolios should plot along this line. Consider a security that lies above the line such as security *A* in Exhibit 19. This security has an expected return higher than what should be expected in equilibrium. It offers two sources of extra return. First, if there is no change in price, it offers above equilibrium returns. Second, as investors realize that the expected return is above equilibrium the price should be bid up. This adjustment to equilibrium return is a second source of potential return.

EXHIBIT 19 EXPECTED RETURN ABOVE EQUILIBRIUM

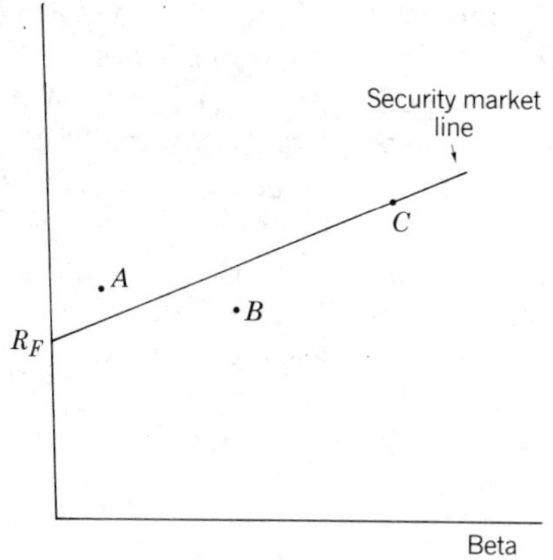

Similar considerations are present for a security that lies below the line; for example, security *B*. This security is offering below equilibrium returns. First, it is a candidate for sale because of the poor returns. Second, as other investors realize the poor prospects the price should fall in order for the return on this asset to be competitive with other assets. Thus securities that lie above the line are candidates for purchase, whereas securities that lie below the line are candidates for sale.

One further point needs to be mentioned. Security *C* has an expected return above the expected return of *A*. However, *C* should be fairly priced, whereas *A* is considered a purchase. This makes clear the distinction between making investment decisions on the basis of expected return and making decisions utilizing an asset pricing model.

If one wished to use the zero beta form of the CAPM, the only change would be a different security market line. Clearly the lines may be different so that different securities might be deemed purchases or sales.

Using the more complicated CAPMs or the **multi-index APT** only complicates matters slightly. It is no longer possible to plot the equilibrium relationship easily, because more than two dimensions are required. However, the same principles hold. The equilibrium return for an asset is determined from the equilibrium relationship. Then the analyst's estimate of expected return is compared with the equilibrium return from the asset pricing model. If it is positive, it is considered a purchase, if it is negative, it's a sale.

Portfolio Evaluation. The evaluation of portfolio performance can only be done against an appropriate benchmark. We know from the tenants of portfolio theory that it is necessary to consider both risk and return. In order to understand whether a manager has added an element of performance to a portfolio one has to have a standard that incorporates both risk and return. Asset pricing theory gives us such a standard.

For example, if one believes that the standard Sharpe-Lintner-Mossin capital asset pricing model is the appropriate model of asset prices, then at first glance producing a return higher than $R_f + \beta_i (R_m - R_f)$ over some period of time would seem to be an indication of superior ability to select securities. Care must be exercised, however, because this might not be the appropriate benchmark. For example, if the appropriate model of asset prices is the zero beta form of the CAPM, the appropriate standard might be $\bar{R}_z + \beta_i(\bar{R}_m - \bar{R}_z)$. Because $\bar{R}_z$ is greater than R_f, a portfolio with a beta less than one could look good under the simple form of the CAPM, but show poor performance when measured against the zero beta form of the capital asset pricing model.

Recognition of a multi-index APT model not only changes judgments about the value of portfolio performance it suggests that it is appropriate to use more complex schemes for evaluating performance.

For example, let us assume that over a particular period of time, the following APT model described returns

$$\bar{R}_i = 10 + 5\,\beta_i + .25 \text{ yield}$$

Now let's assume a manager earned a return of 18% a portfolio with a beta of 1.2 and a dividend yield of 5%. Assume the average beta in the market was 1, the average dividend yield was 4% and the market had a return of 16%. It is easy to see that this manager had a return 2% higher than the market. This 2% return can be decomposed as follows:

- Total excess return over market 2%
- Due to beta .2 (5) = 1%
- Due to dividend yield .1 (25) = .25%
- Due to security selection (2–1.25) = .75%

By identifying the influences that affect security returns, the APT allows the sources of performance to be measured separately.

BIBLIOGRAPHY

Black, F., and Scholes, M., "The Effects of Dividend Yield and Dividend Policy on Common Stock Prices and Returns," *Journal of Financial Economics,* 1 (1974): 1–22.

Cohen, Kalman, and Pogue, Jerry, "An Empirical Evaluation of Alternative Portfolio Selection Models," *Journal of Business,* 46 (April 1967): 166–193.

———, "Estimating the Dependence Structure of Share Prices—Implications for Portfolio Selection, *Journal of Finance,* VIII, No. 4 (December 1973): 1203–1232.

Elton, Edwin J., Gruber, Martin J., and Urich, Thomas, "Are Betas Best?," *Journal of Finance,* 23, No. 5 (December 1978): 1375–1384.

Elton, Edwin J., and Gruber, Martin J., *Modern Portfolio Theory and Investment Analysis,* New York: Wiley, 1984, p. 115.

Farrell, James, "Analyzing Covariation of Returns to Determine Homogeneous Stock Groupings, *Journal of Business,* 47, No. 2 (April 1974): 186–207.

King, Benjamin, "Market and Industry Factors in Stock Price Behavior," *Journal of Business,* 39 (January 1966): 139–140.

Litzenberger, Robert and Ramaswamy, Krishna, "The Effect of Personal Taxes and Dividends on Capital Asset Prices: Theory and Empirical Evidence," *Journal of Financial Economics* (June, 1979): 163–195.

Markowitz, Harry, *Portfolio Selection: Efficient Diversification of Investments,* New York: Wiley, 1959.

Ross, Stephen, "Return, Risk, and Arbitrage," in I. Friend and J. Bickster (eds.), *Risks and Return in Finance,* Cambridge, MA: Ballinger, 1977.

Sharpe, W., "Factors in NYSE Security Returns, 1931–1979," *Journal of Portfolio Management,* 8, No. 2 (Summer 1982): 5–19.

Sharpe, W., and G. Cooper, "Risk Return Classes of New York Stock Exchange Common Stocks 1931–1967," *Financial Analyst Journal* (March–April 1972): 46–52.

23

THE BOND RATING PROCESS

CONTENTS

23

THE BOND RATING PROCESS

Louis H. Ederington
Jess B. Yawitz

The purchaser of **fixed-income securities** must consider the possibility that the issuer will default on the contractual obligation. The computed yield to maturity is only a promised yield—a return contingent on the issuer making the stated interest and principal payments. If the issuer defaults, the lender may lose the interest and some or all of the principal.

It is not easy for purchasers of bonds, commercial paper, and mortgage-backed securities, the major fixed income securities, to evaluate the ***risk of default.*** Default can be partial or total: The borrower may delay or miss one or more interest payments or may file for bankruptcy and pay neither principal nor interest. The likelihood of either type of default depends on the riskiness of the industry(ies) or line(s) of business in which the issuer operates and on the financial soundness of the issuer. A security holder's claims or rights in the event of default, which are dependent on the legal ramifications of the specific covenants governing the issue, are not easy to evaluate. The possibility of a guarantee by a second party and the position of the bondholders' claims vis-à-vis those of other creditors are two from among a long list of possible bond covenants. The industry, the issuer's financial statements, and the individual security must all be evaluated. These tasks require economic, financial, and legal expertise.

Because evaluation of the risk of default is not a simple task, it is not surprising that specialists have developed to provide these services. One group of such specialists is the rating agencies such as Moody's and Standard & Poor's, who provide potential purchasers and existing holders of debt securities infor-

Financial support was provided by the Institute of Banking and Financial Markets at Washington University. We wish to acknowledge the rating agencies and Edward Altman for their assistance on this section. Officials at Standard and Poor's, Moody's, Duff and Phelps, and Fitch met with us to explain and discuss their rating procedures and provided us with valuable materials. Officials at McCarthy, Crisanti, and Maffei freely provided assistance as well. Elizabeth Case provided valuable editorial comments.

mation regarding the evaluation of creditworthiness of firms and the riskiness of financial instruments.

In this section we examine ***corporate bond*** and ***commercial paper ratings.*** The procedures and standards of the rating agencies are described. We also summarize the findings of academic research into (1) the factors that influence the rating agencies' decisions, and (2) the impact of the rating decisions on the borrower's cost of capital. Particular attention is paid to industrial debt ratings, although ratings of the debt of utilities and financial institutions are also discussed. Municipal debt ratings are not considered.

THE RATING AGENCIES AND THEIR RATINGS

As listed in Exhibit 1, there are two larger ***rating agencies: Moody's*** (a subsidiary of *Dun and Bradstreet*) and ***Standard & Poor's*** (S&P a subsidiary of *McGraw-Hill*), and three smaller ones: ***Fitch; Duff and Phelps;*** and ***McCarthy, Crisanti, and Maffei.*** Moody's, S&P, and Fitch all began issuing ratings in the early twentieth century. Moody's started rating railroad bonds in 1909 and started issuing ratings for utility and industrial debt in 1914. Poor's began issu-

EXHIBIT 1 RATING AGENCIES

Agency	Approximate Number of Companies Rated	Representative Rating Publications and Services
Standard & Poor's	2000+	*CreditWeek* (weekly) *International CreditWeek* (weekly) *Bond Guide* (monthly) *Commercial Paper Ratings* (monthly)
Moody's	2000+	*Moody's Bond Survey* (weekly) *Moody's Bond Record* (monthly) *Moody's Corporate Credit Reports* (weekly) *Moody's International Bond Review* (quarterly)
Fitch	500	*Fitch Rating Register* (monthly) *Fitch Reports* (interm) *Fitch Commercial Paper Ratings Data* (on line service)
Duff and Phelps	300 (public) 200 (private)	*Fixed Income Services* *Credit Decisions* (weekly)
McCarthy, Chrisanti, and Maffei	500	*Credit Critiques* (weekly) *Rating Watch* (weekly) *MCM Rating Summaries*

ing ratings in 1922 and Standard Statistics in 1923. The two merged into Standard & Poor's in 1941. Fitch ratings appeared in 1923. All three issue publicly available ratings and employ similar although not identical rating symbols to summarize their opinion of a bond issue—for example, triple A, double A, and so on. (Fitch sold rights to their symbol system to S&P.) Descriptions of these ratings as well as the exact nomenclature are shown in Exhibits 2–4. Similar rating symbols (Exhibit 5) are utilized by McCarthy, Crisanti, and Maffei, the newest of the rating agencies. This agency, which was founded in 1975, issues only ***private ratings*** (i.e., ratings that are made available only to its clients). Chicago-based Duff and Phelps, the only non-New York agency, assigns numbers between 1 (the highest) and 17 (the lowest), which they relate to the usual letter symbols (Exhibit 6). Duff and Phelps began evaluating utility bonds in the 1930s, but only began issuing *public ratings* in 1980. At present they issue both public and private ratings. In 1984, *Security Pacific Corporation* (a bank holding company) sought to acquire Duff and Phelps under a plan approved by both companies. Although allowing most of the acquisition, the Federal Reserve Board ruled that Security Pacific would not be allowed to continue to issue public ratings. The board ruled that because the bank holding company would be lending to many of the same companies it would be rating, there was a serious conflict of interest. As a result of this ruling, the acquisition plans were abandoned.

EXHIBIT 2 STANDARD & POOR'S RATING DEFINITIONS BOND RATINGS

AAA Debt rated AAA has the highest rating assigned by Standard & Poor's. Capacity to pay interest and repay principal is extremely strong.

AA Debt rated AA has a very strong capacity to pay interest and repay principal and differs from the highest rated issues only in small degree.

A Debt rated A has a strong capacity to pay interest and repay principal, although it is somewhat more susceptible to the adverse effects of changes in circumstances and economic conditions than debt in higher rated categories.

BBB Debt rated BBB is regarded as having an adequate capacity to pay interest and repay principal. Whereas it normally exhibits adequate protection parameters, adverse economic conditions or changing circumstances are more likely to lead to a weakened capacity to pay interest and repay principal for debt in this category than in higher rated categories.

BB
B
CCC
CC Debt rated BB, B, CCC, or CC is regarded, on balance, as predominantly speculative with respect to capacity to pay interest and repay principal in accordance with the terms of the obligation. BB indicates the lowest degree of speculation and CC the highest degree of speculation. Although such debt will likely have some quality and protective characteristics, these are outweighed by large uncertainties or major risk exposures to adverse conditions.

C This rating is reserved for income bonds on which no interest is being paid.

D Debt rated D is in default, and payment of interest and/or repayment of principal is in arrears.

Plus (+) or Minus (−): The ratings for AA to B may be modified by the addition of a plus or minus sign to show relative standing within the major rating categories.

COMMERCIAL PAPER RATINGS

A Issues assigned this highest rating are regarded as having the greatest capacity for timely payment. Issues in this category are delineated with the numbers 1, 2, and 3 to indicate the relative degree of safety.

- A-1 This designation indicates that the degree of safety regarding timely payment is either overwhelming or very strong. Those issues determined to possess overwhelming safety charcteristics are denoted with a plus (+) sign designation.
- A-2 Capacity for timely payment on issues with this designation is strong. However, the relative degree of safety is not as high as for issues designated A-1.
- A-3 Issues carrying this designation have a satisfactory capacity for timely payment. They are, however, somewhat more vulnerable to the adverse effects of changes in circumstances than obligations carrying the higher designations.

B Issues rated B are regarded as having only an adequate capacity for timely payment. However, such capacity may be damaged by changing conditions or short-term adversities.

C This rating is assigned to short-term debt obligations with a doubtful capacity for payment.

D This rating indicates that the issue is either in default or is expected to be in default upon maturity.

Source: Credit Overview, Standard & Poor's Corporation, 1983.

EXHIBIT 3 MOODY'S RATING DEFINITIONS BOND RATINGS

Aaa

Bonds that are rated Aaa are judged to be of the best quality. They carry the smallest degree of investment risk and are generally referred to as "gilt edged." Interest payments are protected by a large or by an exceptionally stable margin and principal is secure. Although the various protective elements are likely to change, such changes as can be visualized are most unlikely to impair the fundamentally strong position of such issues.

Aa

Bonds that are rated Aa are judged to be of high quality by all standards. Together with the Aaa group they comprise what are generally known as high grade bonds. They are rated lower than the best bonds because margins of protection may not be as large as in Aaa securities or fluctuation of protective elements may be of greater amplitude or there may be other elements present that make the long-term risks appear somewhat larger than in Aaa securities.

A

Bonds that are rated A possess many favorable investment attributes and are to be considered as upper-medium grade obligations. Factors giving security to principal and interest are considered adequate, but elements may be present which suggest a susceptibility to impairment sometime in the future.

Baa

Bonds that are rated Baa are considered as medium grade obligations (i.e., they are neither highly protected nor poorly secured). Interest payments and principal security appear adequate for the present, but certain protective elements may be lacking or may be characteristically unreliable over any great length of time. Such bonds lack outstanding investment characteristics and in fact have speculative characteristics as well.

Ba

Bonds that are rated Ba are judged to have speculative elements; their future cannot be considered as well assured. Often the protection of interest and principal payments may be very moderate and thereby not well safeguarded during both good and bad times over the future. Uncertainty of position characterizes bonds in this class.

B

Bonds that are rated B generally lack characteristics of the desirable investment. Assurance of interest and principal payments or of maintenance of other terms of the contract over any long period of time may be small.

Caa

Bonds that are rated Caa are of poor standing. Such issues may be in default or there may be present elements of danger with respect to principal or interest.

EXHIBIT 3 *(CONTINUED)*

Ca

Bonds that are rated Ca represent obligations which are speculative in a high degree. Such issues are often in default or have other marked shortcomings.

C

Bonds that are rated C are the lowest rated class of bonds, and issues so rated can be regarded as having extremely poor prospects of ever attaining any real investment standing.

Note: Moody's applies numerical modifiers, 1, 2, and 3 in each generic rating classification from Aa through B in its corporate bond rating system. The modifier 1 indicates that the security ranks in the higher end of its generic rating category; the modifier 2 indicates a mid-range ranking; and the modifier 3 indicates that the issue ranks in the lower end of its generic rating category.

Short-Term Ratings

Issuers rated Prime-1 (or supporting institutions) have a superior ability for repayment of senior short-term debt obligations. Prime-1 repayment ability will normally be evidenced by many of the following characteristics:

Leading market positions in well-established industries

High rates of return on funds employed

Conservative capitalization structures with moderate reliance on debt and ample asset protection

Broad margins in earnings coverage of fixed financial charges and high internal cash generation

Well-established access to a range of financial markets and assured sources of alternate liquidity.

Issuers rated Prime-2 (or supporting institutions) have a strong ability for repayment of senior short-term debt obligations. This will normally be evidenced by many of the characteristics cited earlier but to a lesser degree. Earnings trends and coverage ratios, although sound, will be more subject to variation. Capitalization characteristics, although still appropriate, may be more affected by external conditions. Ample alternate liquidity is maintained.

Issuers rated Prime-3 (or related supporting institutions) have an acceptable ability for repayment of senior short-term debt obligations. The effect of industry characteristics and market composition may be more pronounced. Variability in earnings and profitability may result in changes in the level of debt protection measurements and may require relatively high financial leverage. Adequate alternate liquidity is maintained.

Issuers rated Not Prime do not fall within any of the Prime rating categories.

EXHIBIT 4 FITCH RATING DEFINITIONS BOND RATINGS

AAA rated bonds are considered to be investment grade and of the highest quality. The obligor has an extraordinary ability to pay interest and repay principal, which is unlikely to be affected by reasonably foreseeable events.

AA rated bonds are considered to be investment grade and of high quality. The obligor's ability to pay interest and repay principal, although very strong, is somewhat less than for AAA rated securities or more subject to possible change over the term of the issue.

A rated bonds are considered to be investment grade and of good quality. The obligor's ability to pay interest and repay principal is considered to be strong, but may be more vulnerable to adverse changes in economic conditions and circumstances than bonds with higher ratings.

BBB rated bonds are considered to be investment grade and of satisfactory quality. The obligor's ability to pay interest and repay principal is considered to be adequate. Adverse changes in economic conditions and circumstances, however, are more likely to weaken this ability than bonds with higher ratings.

BB rated bonds are considered speculative and of low investment grade. The obligor's ability to pay interest and repay principal is not strong and is considered likely to be affected over time by adverse economic changes.

B rated bonds are considered highly speculative. Bonds in this class are lightly protected as to the obligor's ability to pay interest over the life of the issue and repay principal when due.

CCC rated bonds may have certain characteristics which, with the passing of time, could lead to the possibility of default on either principal or interest payments.

CC rated bonds are minimally protected. Default in payment of interst and/or principal seems probable.

C rated bonds are in actual or imminent default in payment of interest or principal.

DDD ,DD, D rated bonds are in default and in arrears in interest and/or principal payments. Such bonds are extremely speculative and should be valued only on the basis of their value in liquidation or reorganization of the obligor.

Plus (+) Minus (−) Signs

These signs are used after a rating symbol to designate the relative position of a credit within the rating grade. The + and − signs are carried in ratings from "AA" to "B."

COMMERCIAL PAPER RATINGS

Fitch commercial paper ratings are grouped into four categories as defined below:

Fitch-1 (Highest Grade) Commercial paper assigned this rating is regarded as having the strongest degree of assurance for timely payment.

Fitch-2 (Very Good Grade) Issues assigned this rating reflect an assurance of timely payment only slightly less in degree than the strongest issues.

Fitch-3 (Good Grade) Commercial paper carrying this rating has a satisfactory degree of assurance for timely payment but the margin of safety is not as great as the two higher categories.

Fitch-4 (Poor Grade) Issues carrying this rating have characteristics suggesting that the degree of assurance for timely payment is minimal and is susceptible to near term adverse change due to less favorable financial or economic conditions.

Plus (+) This sign is used after a rating symbol in the first three rating categories
LOC to designate the relative position of an issuer within the rating category.

EXHIBIT 5 MCCARTHY, CRISANTI, AND MAFFEI RATING DEFINITIONS FIXED INCOME RATINGS

MCM-Aaa Very High Grade. These obligations are characterized as possessing overwhelming qualitative and quantitative strengths. Issuers whose obligations qualify for this category have demonstrated and are expected to continue to demonstrate exceptional ability to withstand all adverse circumstances as can be realistically envisioned to occur. They are of sufficient standing and size to maintain traditional financing options under such circumstances and to marshal sufficient resources to meet foreseeable challenges and still maintain their fundamental strength. Normally, preferred stock because of its inferior form and holding company obligations which serve as double leverage would not qualify for this rating category.

MCM-Aa High Grade. Investment characteristics are very strong, but not as overwhelming as those of very high grade obligations. Fixed-income obligations in this classification are also considered high quality, however, some of the necessary characteristics for the very high grade rating category are lacking. Issuers whose most senior obligations are in this category are expected to maintain a strong financial position and a variety of financing options under adverse circumstances. However, their exposure to business or other risks is perceived to be somewhat greater than for issuers of obligations classified in the very high grade rating category.

MCM-A Medium Grade. These obligations predominantly possess investment characteristics. However, compared with high grade obligations, protection measures may not be as great, and/or may be less stable or predictable over a long period of time. The issuer's ability to generate necessary cash appears adequate over the near- to intermediate-term but is considered less certain over a prolonged period. Issuers whose most senior obligations are in this category are expected to be able to maintain at least a moderately strong financial position under adverse circumstances, however, they may be more vulnerable to changing conditions than high grade obligors.

MCM-Bbb Lower Medium Grade. Investment characteristics no longer predominate. Although elements of protection currently appear sufficient, they are less certain to be maintained over a long period of time.

MCM-Bb Low Grade. These obligations generally lack investment characteristics. Protection measures are considered marginal and/or are unreliable over a long period of time.

MCM-B Speculative. Fixed-income obligations which are considered speculative fall in the B category.

MCM-DP Preferred stock with dividend arrearages.

MCM-DD Defaulted Debt Obligations. Company failed to meet principal and/or interest payments.

The plus (+) and minus (−) are applied to the Aa, A, Bbb, and Bb categories to indicate those obligations that MCM considers as placed in the upper (+) or lower (−) quarter of the indicated MCM rating category.

Short-Term Debt Ratings

MCM-1—This rating designation applies to obligors with an extremely strong ability to incur and service short-term debt. Obligors in this category are large in size and possess such characteristics as a leading competitive position, excellent operating record and favorable prospects, impeccable reputation, a high degree of liquidity, strong cash flow,

EXHIBIT 5 *(CONTINUED)*

and access to many alternative financing options even under adverse economic conditions.

MCM-2—Obligors in this category are considered very strong but lack an element or degree of protection deemed necessary for the MCM-1 category. Obligors in this category will be sufficiently large and of such a high reputation as to have access to several financing alternatives. Short-term debt for these obligors is not expected to exceed moderate levels relative to liquidity measures.

MCM-3—Obligors in this category have a strong ability to carry short-term debt. However, either their liquidity, asset and earnings protection, or cash flow measures may be moderate, less predictable or less stable than they are for higher grade obligors or their access to some alternate financing options may be limited during periods of economic stress. The use of short-term debt may periodically begin to appear somewhat high relative to liquidity measures.

MCM-4—Obligors in this category have adequate capacity to carry short-term debt for the near- to intermediate-term. However, their financial posture may be volatile or their ability to fund short-term debt with long-term funds under stressful market conditions without undue delays and at a reasonable cost may be questionable. The use of short-term debt may periodically begin to appear excessive relative to the obligor's liquidity measures or financial wherewithal.

Source: MCM Fixed Income Rating Definitions.

EXHIBIT 6 DUFF AND PHELPS RATING DEFINITIONS
FIXED INCOME RATINGS

D&P Rating	Generic Category	Description
1	*Triple A*	Highest credit quality. The risk factors are negligible, being only slightly more than for risk-free U.S. Treasury debt.
	Double A	High credit quality. Protection factors are strong. Risk is modest but may vary slightly from time to time because of economic conditions.
2	High	
3	Middle	
4	Low	
	Single A	Protection factors are average but adequate. However, risk factors are more variable and greater in periods of economic stress.
5	High	
6	Middle	
7	Low	
	Triple B	Below average protection factors but still considered sufficient for institutional investment. Considerable variability in risk during economic cycles.
8	High	
9	Middle	
10	Low	
	Double B	Below investment grade but deemed likely to meet obligations when due. Present or prospective financial protection factors fluctuate according to industry conditions or company fortunes. Overall quality may move up or down frequently within this category.
11	High	
12	Middle	
13	Low	
	Single B	Below investment grade and possessing risk that obligations will not be met when due. Financial protection factors will fluctuate widely according to economic cycles, industry conditions, and/or company fortunes. Potential exists for frequent changes in quality rating within this category or into a higher or lower quality rating grade.
14	High	
15	Middle	
16	Low	
17	Substantial Risk	Well below investment grade with considerable uncertainty as to timely payment of interest, preferred dividends, and/or principal and sinking funds. Protection factors are narrow and risk can be substantial with unfavorable economic/industry conditions, and/or with unfavorable company developments.

COMMERCIAL PAPER RATINGS
CATEGORY 1: TOP GRADE

Duff 1 plus	Highest certainty of timely payment. Short-Term liquidity, including internal operating factors and/or ready access to alternative sources of funds, is clearly outstanding; and safety is just below risk-free U.S Treasury short-term obligations.
Duff 1	Very high certainty of timely payment. Liquidity factors are excellent and supported by strong fundamental protection factors. Risk factors are minor.

EXHIBIT 6 (*CONTINUED*)

Duff 1 minus	High certainty of timely payment. Liquidity factors are strong and supported by good fundamental protection factors. Risk factors are very small.
	CATEGORY 2: GOOD GRADE
TDuff 2	Good certainty of timely payment. Liquidity factors and company fundamentals are sound. Although ongoing internal funds needs may enlarge total financing requirements, access to capital markets is good. Risk factors are small.
	CATEGORY 3: SATISFACTORY GRADE
Duff 3	Satisfactory liquidity and other protection factors qualify issue as to investment grade. Risk factors are larger and subject to more variation. Nevertheless, timely payment is expected.

Source: Duff and Phelps Credit Rating Services.

Each agency's ratings for the senior debt of 30 major industrial firms at the end of 1984 are shown in Exhibit 7. As illustrated in this exhibit, the ratings are similar but not identical. Reasons for the differences are discussed later in the section. The distribution in December of 1983 of S&P's ratings of senior debt of industrial firms is shown in Exhibit 8. Although this distribution was not readily available for the other agencies, it appears that the distribution of Moody's ratings is similar. As Exhibit 4 indicates, the A rating is the most common, and over 96% of the ratings fall in five classes from AA through B.

The creditworthiness of all of the approximately 260 companies whose senior debt is rated A by S&P is certainly not the same; nor is all debt rated Aaa or all debt rated B identical in terms of risk. In Exhibit 9, each individual bond's estimated creditworthiness is represented as an * along a creditworthiness scale. An individual bond is viewed as more creditworthy than all bonds to its right and less creditworthy than all bonds to its left. Ratings in turn may be viewed as representing partitions of this continuous scale. All bonds lying along the left-most section down to the first partition would be rated AAA (or Aaa); those between that and the next partition AA (or Aa), and so on. Bonds with the same rating are therefore regarded as representing similar, but not identical, ***credit risks.***

REFINEMENTS. In recent years the rating agencies have refined their bond ratings to provide a more precise indication of their judgment of the security's **creditworthiness.** In 1973 Fitch and in 1974 S&P began attaching plus and minus symbols to many of their ratings to indicate above or below average standing within the major rating categories B through AA (e.g., issues rated A+ are viewed as being slightly more creditworthy than those rated A, and issues rated A are estimated to be slightly more creditworthy than those rated A−). Officials at Standard & Poor's indicate that this refinement followed a decision

EXHIBIT 7 EXAMPLES OF RATINGS ON SENIOR INDUSTRIAL DEBT DECEMBER 1984

	Senior Debt Ratings				
Firm	Moody's	Standard & Poor's	Duff and Phelps[a]	Fitch	MCM
Amax, Inc.	Baa 3	BB+	12(BB)	BB+	BB+
Allied Corporation	A2	A	6(A)	A	A−
Anheuser-Busch, Inc.	Aa3	A+	(NR)	(NR)	A+
Bendix Corporation	A2	A	6(A)	A	(NR)
Bethlehem Steel Corp.	Ba1	BB+	11(BB+)	(NR)	BBB−
Boise-Cascade Corp.	A3	BBB+	9(BBB)	(NR)	BBB+
Chemical New York Corp.	Aa2	AA	5(A+)	AA	A
Chrysler Corp.	Baa3	BBB	11(BB+)	BBB	BB
Cities Service Co.	Ba1	BBB	8(BBB+)	BBB+	BBB−
Dana Corp.	A2	A	(NR)	AA	A
Ensearch Corp.	A2	A	6(A)	A+	A
Ford Motor Co.	A1	A−	8(BBB+)	A	A
General Electric Co.	Aaa	AAA	1(AAA)	(NR)	AAA
General Mills, Inc.	Aa2	AA	4(AA−)	AA	A+
General Motors Corp.	Aa2	AA+	3(AA)	AA+	AA
B.F. Goodrich Co.	Baa3	BBB−	9(BBB)	BBB+	BBB−
Gulf Oil Corp.	Aa3	AA	5(A+)	AA−	AA−
IBM Corp.	Aaa	AAA	1(AAA)	(NR)	AAA
ITT Corp.	A2	A	7(A−)	(NR)	BBB+
Internorth, Inc.	A2	A	5(A+)	A	A
L.T.V. Corp.	B1	BB−	15(B)	(NR)	(NR)
Monsanto Company	Aa3	A	4(AA−)	(NR)	A+
Occidental Petroleum Co.	Ba1	BBB	8(BBB+)	BBB	BBB−
PepsiCo. Inc.	Aa2	AA−	4(AA+)	(NR)	A+
Philip Morris Inc.	A2	A	5(A+)	(NR)	A
Sears Roebuck & Co.	Aa2	AA	3(AA)	AA	AA−
Tenneco Inc.	A2	A	6(A)	A	A
Texas Eastern Corp.	A3	A−	6(A)	A	A−
U.S. Steel Corp.	Baa2	BBB	9(BBB)	(NR)	BBB
The Williams Cos.	Ba1	BB−	11(BB+)	BBB−	BB

[a]Equivalent S&P ratings are shown in parentheses.

to devote more effort and human resources to evaluating creditworthiness—a change which they say was made possible by the institution of issuer fees in the early 1970s. Prior to that time, revenue was derived solely from the sale of their publications. Issuer fees meant a substantial expansion of revenue and currently constitute S&P's major revenue source.

Moody's instituted user fees in 1969, and in 1982 they moved to refine their ratings by attaching the modifiers 1, 2, or 3 to ratings between B and Aa, inclusive. Within a rating class such as A, A1 represents the highest creditworthiness and A3 the lowest. As of December 1982, the two major agencies attached a modifier to indicate relatively high (+ or 1) or low (− or 3) standing within a rating category to approximately one half of industrial bond issues.

EXHIBIT 8 STANDARD & POOR'S RATINGS OF INDUSTRIAL SENIOR DEBT[a] DECEMBER 1983

		AAA	AA	A	BBB	BB	B	CCC	CC
Total									
Number of issuers	23	136	259	149	122	142	7	0	838
As a % of total issuers	2.7	16.3	30.9	17.8	14.6	16.9	0.8	0.0	100.0

[a] Includes actual and "implied" senior debt ratings.

Source: Standard & Poor's *CreditWeek*; February 20, 1984; p. 2183.

INVESTMENT AND SPECULATIVE GRADE. Although refined ratings represent more precise graduations of creditworthiness than the letter ratings alone, the terms *investment* and *speculative* grade signify a more coarse division. The term ***investment grade*** was originally used to designate bonds eligible for purchase by *regulated financial institutions* such as insurance companies, banks, and savings and loans. Although regulations vary somewhat from institution to institution and state to state, investment grade is now generally viewed to be composed of bonds rated Baa or above. Those rated lower are referred to as ***speculative grade.***

INVESTMENT QUALITY AND BANK REGULATION. Specific regulations affecting a bank's investment activities depend on the bank's charter and whether it is a member of the Federal Reserve System. Regulations issued by the comptroller of the currency apply to national banks and state banks that are Fed members. These regulations specify three classes of investment grade securities. **Type I securities** include U.S. Treasury and Agency issues, and general obligation bonds of any state or political subdivisions. Generally speaking, there is no limit on a bank's holdings of Type I securities. **Type II securities** include quasi-agencies such as the Tennessee Valley Authority and bonds issued by state agencies for housing, dormitory, or university purposes. **Type III securities** include state and local revenue bonds and corporate bonds where there is adequate evidence of an ability to repay. Generally, only bonds in the investment grade category (Baa/BBB or higher) are included in type III securities. Unrated securities can be purchased if the investment officer of the bank determines that it is investment grade.

EXHIBIT 9 RATING CATEGORIES AND CREDITWORTHINESS

Bond Rating	AAA	AA	A	BBB→→→	
High Credit-worthiness	* * * *	* * * *	* * * * * *	* →→→	Low Credit-worthiness

RATINGS AND HISTORICAL DEFAULT RATES

Because the basic purpose of ratings is to estimate the likelihood of default, the most straightforward way to evaluate their success is to compare ratings with actual ***default experience.*** Fortunately for the economy and for investors—but unfortunately for such an analysis—corporate defaults have been relatively rare since World War II. In a careful study of defaults between 1900 and 1965, Atkinson (1967) calculated the total par value of corporate bonds defaulting each year as a percentage of the total par value of all corporate bonds. Although Atkinson's study did not cover defaults after 1965, his results have been updated several times—most recently by Altman and Nammacher (1985) from whom Exhibit 10 is taken. As shown in this exhibit, defaults were fairly common in the first half of this century—particularly the 1920s and 1930s but have been relatively rare since 1949.

In evaluating the rating agencies track record, therefore, it may be appropriate to consider the last 85 years as two distinct periods: the first half of this century, when defaults were relatively frequent but when the ratings were supposedly less precise; and the recent years, when defaults have been fairly rare and when the agencies say they have been devoting more effort and resources to credit risk evaluation.

In a study of ***bond defaults*** from 1900 to 1943, Hickman (1958) found that the percentage of issues defaulting was indeed inversely related to the rating. Although over 40% of the larger bonds rated Ba or lower defaulted, less than 10% of those rated Aaa did. These figures are contained in Exhibit 11 where the rating presented is the rating assigned when the bond was first issued.

More recent evidence on the relationship between ratings and subsequent default experience has been collected and presented by Altman and Nammacher (1985). Their rating data for firms that defaulted between January 1970

EXHIBIT 10 ANNUAL CORPORATE DEFAULT RATES, 1900–1984

Period	Total Corporate Debt Default Rate
1900–1909	0.90%
1910–1919	2.00
1920–1929	1.00
1930–1939	3.20
1940–1949	0.40
1950–1959	0.04
1960–1967	0.03
1968–1977	0.16
1978–1984	0.07

Sources: Altman and Nammacher, (1985). Figures based on earlier studies including Atkinson (1967) as well as their own study.

EXHIBIT 11 PERCENT OF ISSUES DEFAULTING 1900–1943 BY RATING

Size of Issue	Rating[a] Aaa	Aa	A	Baa	B or below	No Rating
Large issues (over $5 million)	5.9	6.0	13.4	19.1	42.4	28.6
Small issues (under $5 million)	10.2	15.5	9.9	25.2	32.6	27.0

[a] The median of the ratings assigned by Moody's, Fitch, Standard Statistics, and Poor's. Moody's symbols are utilized for convenience.

Source: W. Hickman (1958), p. 176.

and December 1984 are presented in Exhibit 12. (See also Standard & Poor's *Credit Week,* February 20, 1985).

It is encouraging that of the 88 defaulting firms for which ratings were available one year prior to default, only one (Manville, which was rated A) was rated above triple B by Standard & Poor's. Only 16 were rated higher than B. Altman and Nammacher estimate that between 1974 and 1984 the average default rate on nonconvertible debt rated double B or lower was 1.60% a year versus .08% a year for all nonconvertible debt. Based on these results, it appears that ratings do indeed reflect relative default risks. It is much less encouraging that more defaulting firms were rated B a year prior to default than were rated triple C or double C. However, this probably reflects the fact that very few bonds are rated below B anyway. Although a full distribution of *all* ratings is not readily available, it is clear from Exhibit 4 that very few industrial bonds are rated below B.

The fact that default rates are higher on low rated debt does not necessarily mean that these ratings provide investors with new or important information. Investors would have their own opinions and estimates regarding the relative likelihoods of default by various companies even if no ratings existed. Whether the ratings provide investors with new and better estimates of the probability of default and whether they can outperform a computer model is a question to which we will return later. Suffice it to note for now that many bond buyers do pay for the rating agencies' services.

EXHIBIT 12 SENIOR DEBT RATINGS OF DEFAULTING CORPORATE ISSUERS (JANUARY 1, 1970–DECEMBER 31, 1984)

	AAA	AA	A	BBB	BB	B	CCC	CC	Total
Initial rating	0	2	7	25	21	40	17	0	112
Rating to 1 year prior to default	0	0	2	11	14	53	43	7	130
Rating 6 months prior to default	0	0	2	2	10	51	53	12	130

Source: Altman and Nammacher (1986).

RATINGS AND YIELDS

Ratings should be of interest to issuers—who pay a fee to have their debt rated—only if they influence the ***yield to maturity*** at which the debt can be sold. Consequently, it is common when discussing ratings to present figures such as those in Exhibit 13. If ratings reflect some or all of the differences in creditworthiness, then investors should demand (and issuers should expect to pay) a higher yield on lower rated than on high rated debt. As shown in Exhibit 9, this is indeed the case.

It is important to stress that the existence of ***yield differentials*** does not mean that the lower ratings per se are responsible for the higher yields. Just as ratings reflect the rating agencies' evaluations of an issuer's creditworthiness, market yields may reflect investors' independent evaluations of this creditworthiness. The yield to maturity on a given issue at any time will only vary with the assigned rating(s) if investors base their evaluations of risk solely or partially on ratings. This issue of whether ratings affect or reflect yields is obviously an important one—particularly to issuers who must pay for ratings—but one that is best addressed after discussing the rating process. Suffice it to note for now that yields are higher on bonds with lower ratings and that the vast majority of issuers do elect to pay the rating fee.

EXHIBIT 13 MOODY'S INDUSTRIAL BOND YIELDS (Baa-Aaa) 1975-1984

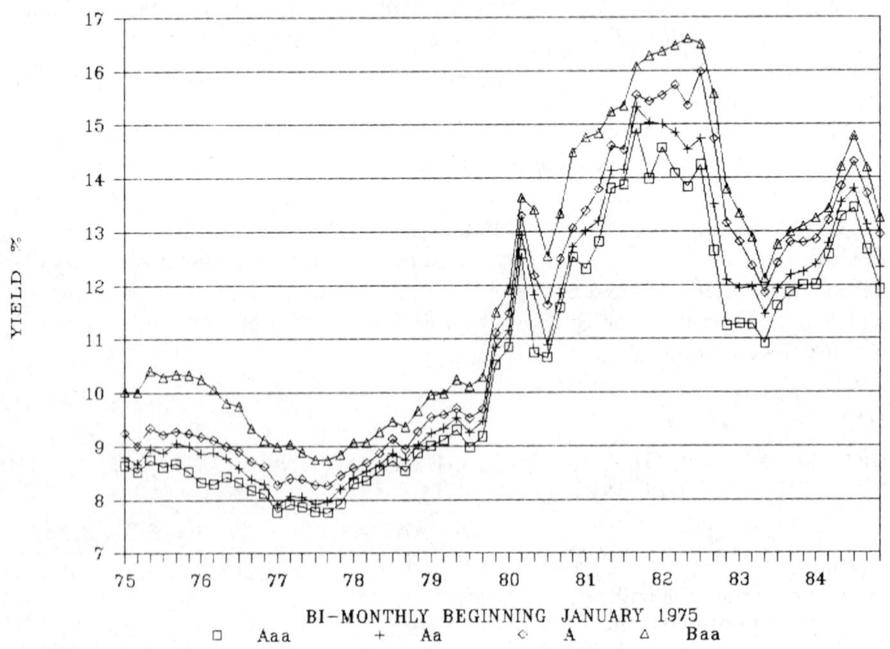

Source: Moody's Bond Record, various issues.

THE RATING PROCESS. We now consider the rating agencies' procedures and policies. The initial question that might be asked is: "What determines whether an issue is rated or not?" Some issues are automatically rated as a matter of policy by S&P and Moody's, that is, regardless of whether the issuer pays the fees. Others are rated only if the issuer pays.

Although both Moody's and S&P rate most large, ***public,*** long-term ***corporate bond*** issues as a matter of policy, they normally rate ***commercial paper, private placements,*** and most other types of debt obligations only "on request." S&P normally does not rate debt of companies with an operating history of less than 5 years.

Pricing Ratings. The pricing structure of the rating agencies is interesting in that at Moody's, Standard & Poor's, Fitch, and to a lesser extent at Duff and Phelps, the users of the ratings (investors) do not incur the major costs. As noted earlier, the major cost is in the form of fees paid by the issuers of the securities. This has not always been the case. Until the early 1970s all rating agencies derived their revenues solely from the sale of their publications and services to investors. It is, however, difficult to restrict the use of ratings (once published) to those who have paid for the service. Faced with limits on their ability to raise fees from their publications, Fitch and Moody's instituted ***issuer fees*** in 1970. Standard & Poor's which instituted issuer fees in the mid 1970s estimates that these fees constitute more than four-fifths of their rating revenue and maintains that these funds allow them to finance a much more thorough analysis.

Collection of issuer fees would appear to be possible only after a rating agency has established itself as an important part of the market. Issuers and their investment bankers should only be willing to incur these costs if they feel that failure to do so will reduce the desirability of their issue. Consequently, it is not surprising that the newest rating agency, McCarthy, Crisanti, and Maffei, does not have issuer fees. Instead they rely on sales of their valuation services to their institutional investor clients. (They, however, attribute this fee arrangement to a desire to avoid a conflict of interest, and their ratings do tend to be more conservative.) Duff and Phelps history is particularly instructive. They began by providing nonpublicized analyses of utilities to institutional investors, in the 1930s; and started assigning private ratings in the early 1970s. They did not go public with their ratings until 1980, when they instituted user fees. At present they issue both public and private ratings. If the bond issuer pays, Duff and Phelps will publicize its rating. If the issuer does not pay, the rating is distributed only to clients.

Fees. When this section was written, both Moody's and S&P's basic charge for rating most new bond issues was 2/100ths of 1% of the principal amount (e.g., $20,000 on a $100,000 million issue). Both attached ceilings and floors to this figure. For instance, Moody's minimum fee in early 1985 was $4,000; its maximum, $35,000. This is the fee for issuers with rated debt outstanding;

first-time issuers are normally charged a somewhat higher fee. Fitch's fee by contrast was only 1/100th of 1%, with a minimum of $5,000 and a maximum of $20,000. Duff and Phelps's basic fee was 2/100 of 1%, with a minimum of $10,000 and a maximum of $25,000. On subsequent issues within 12 months of a rating, however, the fee was only 1/100 of 1%.

Policies. The pricing arrangement is an unusual one not only because the users don't bear the major costs but also because it is both Moody's and S&P's policy to rate major issues in which they feel those investors who purchase their publications will have an interest—regardless of whether the issuer pays the fee. For instance, it is S&P's policy to rate (subject to some exceptions) all public corporate bond and preferred stock issues of $10 million or over issued in the U.S. market. Nonetheless, S&P reports that less than 2% of domestic corporate issuers fail to pay the fee.

One might speculate on the reasons for the voluntary payment of fees by issuers. First, the fee is fairly small ($20,000 on a $100 million issue). A rise in the reoffering yield of only two basis points would add that much to their *yearly* interest costs. Issuers may feel it is worth this fee to be able to place their best case before the raters. As discussed later, ratings are based on both published information and on information provided by the company or its underwriters in meetings with the rating agencies. Issuers may feel this is a small fee to pay in order to be able to present their side to a receptive audience.

THE RATING PROCESS—ORGANIZATIONAL STRUCTURES AND PERSONNEL

The broad organizational structures of the ***debt rating divisions*** of S&P, Moody's, and Fitch are shown in Exhibit 14. A comparison of these structures yields several observations. One is the relative status Fitch accords *Health Care issues*—debt issued by hospitals, nursing homes, and similar nonprofit institutions. Fitch was the first to rate such obligations, and it is an area in which they feel they have relative strength. Similarly, the fact that S&P was the first of the three to have a separate International division reflects the fact that this is an area in which they have been aggressively seeking to expand their rating services and is an area of some specialization. At Moody's, sovereign government obligations are rated in the corporate department by a team headed by the associate director for international issues, whereas foreign corporate debt is handled by the analyst for that industry in consultation with the analyst for that country.

Moody's has a separate structured finance department, which is responsible for ratings of securities supported by pools of financial assets (such as residential mortgages or consumer receivables) and securities (such as commercial paper) supported by letters of credit, bonds of indemnity, or other support from another party. This division relies on others for ratings of the issuer and the bank or insurer providing the support.

EXHIBIT 14 ORGANIZATIONAL STRUCTURES

MOODY'S DEBT RATING DIVISION

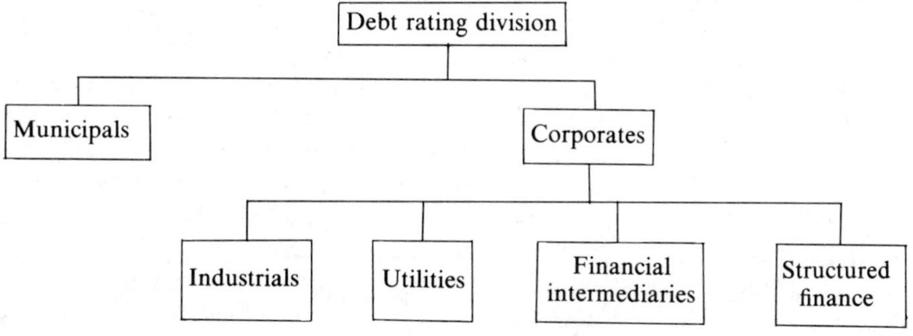

Source: Conversations with Moody's personnel, December 1984.

FITCH INVESTORS SERVICE, INC.

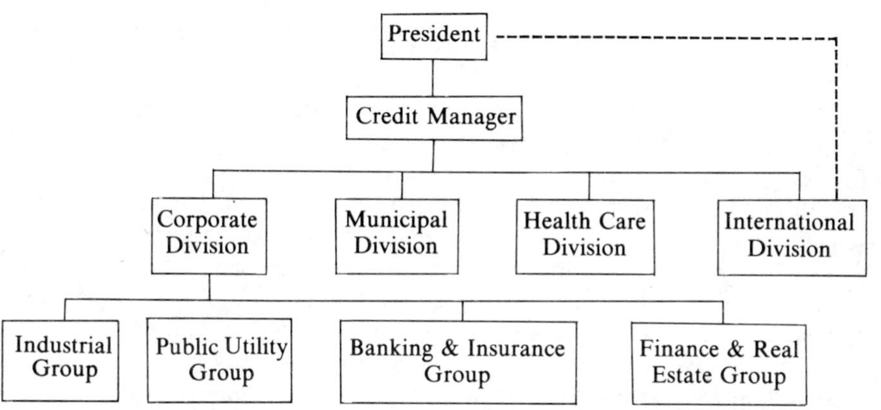

Source: Fitch Investors Service, Inc., descriptions booklet, 1985.

STANDARD & POOR'S

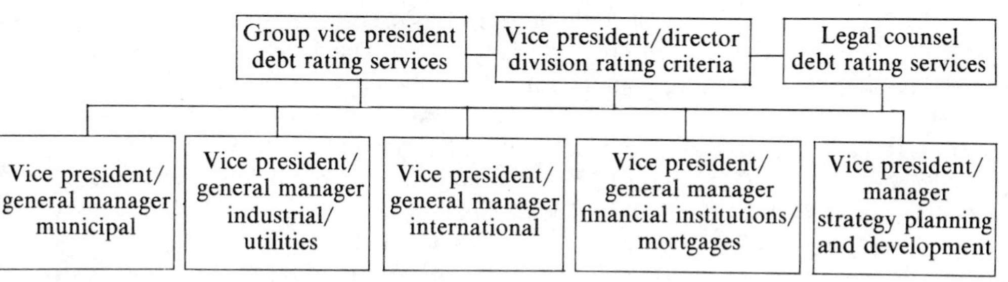

Source: Standard & Poor's Credit Overview International, p. 6, (1984).

Below the unit level (each headed by a director), Moody's has *associate directors* who supervise about five to seven analysts. Similarly, S&P's units are generally divided into groups headed by a vice president. It appears, however, that a vice president at S&P is generally responsible for more analysts and industries than is an associate director at Moody's.

Currently S&P has approximately 150 corporate security analysts in addition to support personnel. Moody's indicates that their job definitions are structured somewhat differently, making straightforward comparisons difficult. They have 80 analysts with voting privileges and about 200 total personnel in their corporate group. By comparison, Fitch has 24 analysts (plus support); McCarthy, Crisanti, and Maffei has 16 analysts with a total staff of 37; Duff and Phelps reports that they have about 65 analysts involved in the credit rating process (the firm also does equity research). S&P, Moody's, and Fitch all emphasize that they only hire analysts with extensive experience in the industry where they will be assigned, and that turnover is low. Duff and Phelps, which does hire some new MBAs, emphasizes that about half their staff have their *Chartered Financial Analysts* certificate.

THE RATING PROCESS—NEW ISSUES

S&P's description of its rating procedure on both new issues and rating changes is contained in Exhibit 15. A similar schematic has been published by Fitch. From conversations with Moody's, it appears that their procedure is also similar, although with several differences that will be noted. Our description is something of a composite based on S&P's published materials and on our conversations with four of the five agencies. Although only one agency source may be referenced as a specific source of information, it is our impression—unless indicated otherwise—that procedures are similar at the other firms.

Fitch, Moody's and S&P report that they are normally approached by issuers or (more often) their *underwriters* prior to registration with the *SEC.* New issuers are typically interested in obtaining some indication of the rating they are likely to receive before making the final decision to proceed with the offering. Issuers with rated debt outstanding are often interested in whether their new issue will trigger a change in their current rating. The agencies are usually willing to prepare such a preliminary analysis. S&P reports that if an issuer does not contact them prior to registration and if the issue is one they intend to rate, they (S&P) initiate contact after registration.

THE GATHERING OF INFORMATION. Once a decision to rate has been made, S&P and Moody's assign a *lead analyst,* a backup analyst, and support personnel to the issue. Fitch indicates that they normally assign a third analyst as well. The team first performs a preliminary analysis based on public financial statements, materials supplied by the issuer, and the agency's analysis of the industry. This is followed by a meeting in which the issuer or its investment

EXHIBIT 15 S&P BOND RATING PROCESS

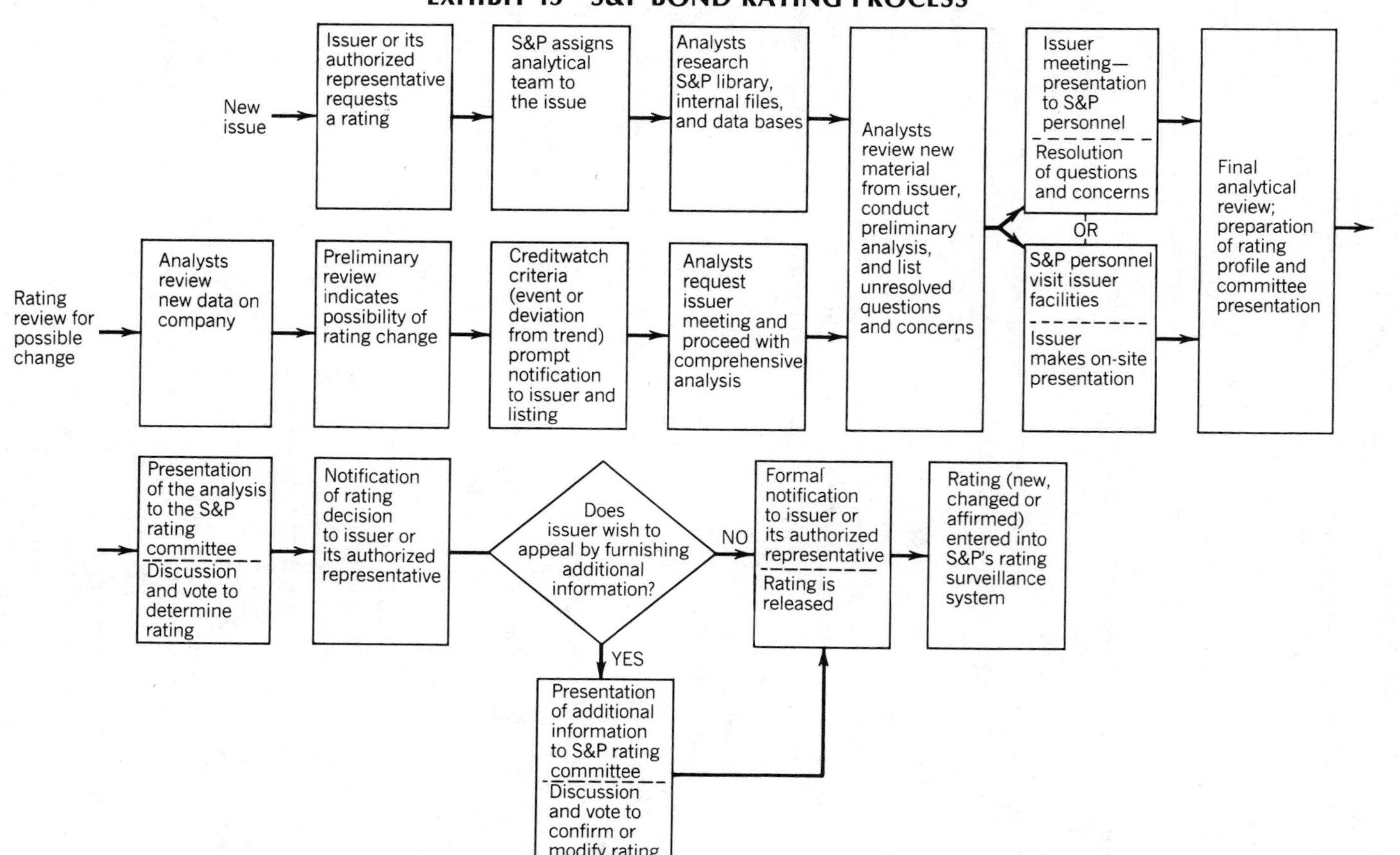

Source: Standard & Poor's Credit Overview International, p. 8.

banker makes a presentation to the raters and answers questions. Moody's has indicated that in the case of new issuers these meetings normally take place at the issuer's headquarters and may last several days. In the case of issuers with rated debt outstanding, the meeting normally takes place at Moody's and lasts several hours. Moody's also reports that the issuing firm's CEO usually attends and that the CFO and treasurer are almost always present—an indication of the importance attached to the rating. At Duff and Phelps three to five members of the rating committee attend the presentation.

S&P and Moody's both ask the issuer to provide a 5-year historical record of the firm's financial statements and ask for the firm's *forecasts* of key figures for the future (5 years into the future in the case of S&P). Both agencies are interested in the firm's capital spending plans and in its plans for future financing. If the firm has issued rated debt before, the accuracy of its past presentation is checked. The agencies generally ask for *business segment analyses* and claim that they are usually provided. In some cases the issuers provide the rating agencies with copies of the internal reports prepared for their boards of directors—an action that undoubtedly adds credibility to their presentation. The rating agencies emphasize that sensitive information received in these meetings is held in strictest confidence. Both Moody's and S&P state that a *Chinese Wall* is maintained between their debt rating divisions and other divisions of their companies. Concern that there would be pressure to penetrate such a wall between the rating division and other divisions of the bank was a factor in the Federal Reserve's decision not to allow the Duff and Phelps and Security Pacific merger.

The question of how much ***inside information*** the rating agencies receive and its importance in the rating decision is important in evaluating their informational role. As suggested by Ederington, Yawitz, and Roberts (1984, p. 1) and by Griffin and Sanvicente (1982, p. 4), ratings could provide a mechanism for communicating to bond purchasers the relevant aspects of this inside information without divulging the details to the firm's competitors. If the rating agencies simply evaluate public information, then their role is less important than if they receive inside information that is passed on in the form of ratings. Unfortunately, the nature of inside information makes it difficult, if not impossible, to determine its true importance in the rating process.

THE DECISION PROCESS. Following the meeting with management, each rating agency proceeds toward a rating decision. At S&P the primary and backup analysts present their review and make a rating recommendation to a ***rating committee*** drawn from S&P's rating board. The ***rating board*** consists of vice presidents, managing vice presidents, assistant vice presidents, and rating officers. For an industrial bond issue there are usually five to eight members on the committee, including the lead and backup analysts. The other members usually consist of analysts from related industries and senior officers. The decision is by majority vote. At Moody's the lead analyst prepares a memo summarizing the meeting with the issuer's management and, after approximately a week, makes his or her recommendation. The rating committee at Moody's is configured somewhat differently. The lead and backup analysts and their associate director are always included. One of the four directors is involved about half of the time, and personnel are drawn from other areas as appropriate. The chairman of the corporate rating committee or the director of the corporate department may participate depending on "investor interest in the specific company under review." The rating committee at Fitch is headed by either the President or the Chairman of the rating board and consists of four analysts from that division plus others as needed. At Duff and Phelps, the management of the issuing firm as well as the analyst make presentations to the rating committee.

APPEALS. The agencies have somewhat different policies on ***rating appeals.*** It is S&P's policy always to "allow the issuer to respond to the rating prior to its publication through the presentation of new or additional data" (S&P's *Credit Overview: Industrial Ratings,* p. 10, 1984). They estimate, however, that less than 10% choose to appeal and that no more than one fifth of the appeals result in a rating change. Fitch also has a formal appeal process. Moody's allows appeals on preliminary ratings issued prior to the issuer's registration with the SEC, but ratings on registered issues are announced to the issuer and the market simultaneously. Moody's only occasionally considers appeals on registered issues. It is their policy that all relevant information should be presented prior to their rating decision.

SHELF REGISTRATIONS. The Securities and Exchange Commission's ***shelf registration Rule 415,*** which was adopted on a temporary basis in March 1982 and made permanent in November 1983, has necessitated some changes in the rating process. Under Rule 415 issuers can register a security with the SEC without specifying an issue date. They can then issue part or all of the security at any time over the next 2 years on short notice. For such issues the rating agencies follow their normal procedure and publish preliminary or prospective ratings when the issue is registered and "placed on the shelf." These ratings are then finalized when the issue is taken off the shelf and issued. This necessitates "regular and reasonably frequent" meetings between the issuer and the rating agencies while the issue is on the shelf.

RATING SURVEILLANCE AND RATING CHANGES

As the financial position of issuers unexpectedly improves or deteriorates over time, so too should the ratings of their obligations; and any issue of Standard & Poor's *CreditWeek* or Moody's *Bond Survey* will substantiate that ratings do change.

THE DECISION TO REVIEW A RATING. The rating agencies state that they normally meet with all issuers at least once a year and that they normally have a contact at the issuing company with whom ongoing communication is maintained. S&P states that earnings releases, industry trends, and other public information are constantly monitored and that *financial ratio* comparison screens are used to "red flag" issues for reconsideration. At Moody's the lead analyst for an issuer confers quarterly with his or her associate director on each rating, and at Duff and Phelps the computerized data base on each company is updated at least quarterly. Fitch also maintains an up to date data base.

Once a decision to reconsider a rating has been made, agencies notify the issuer and schedule a meeting. Since 1981 S&P has announced in the "CreditWatch" section of its *CreditWeek* publication those ratings under review and has indicated whether an upgrade or a downgrade is being considered. Unlike the rating change itself, S&P's decision to place an issue on the "CreditWatch" list is not subject to appeal. Duff and Phelps claims to have been the first rating agency to initiate a watch list of ratings under review, and in 1984 Moody's inaugurated one as well. Standard & Poor's (Supplement to *CreditWeek*, January 1985) claims that mergers and acquisitions trigger more CreditWatch listings than any other development. Of the 279 corporate issues placed on the CreditWatch list in 1984, 54% were placed on the list because of merger or acquisition activity. Because a merger or acquisition is likely to affect the firm's debt leverage as well as its financial characteristics, this is not surprising. Improvements or deterioration in the firm's financial performance led to 27% of the CreditWatch listings, whereas nuclear plant problems experienced by public utilities and *leveraged buyouts* each accounted for 7% of the listings in 1984. Of those issues placed on CreditWatch in 1984, an average of 3 to 4 months were required to resolve the rating question. (Supplement to *CreditWeek*, January 1985).

THE DECISION TO CHANGE A RATING. Being listed on S&P's CreditWatch or Moody's Rating Review List does not guarantee a change in the rating. S&P affirmed (i.e., left unchanged) 36% of the ratings on its CreditWatch list in 1984. Similarly, all rating changes are not preceded by a CreditWatch listing. The CreditWatch listing occurs only if information is incomplete so that quick determination cannot be made. When, for instance, Continental Illinois's financial problems were announced in 1984, its long-term debt ratings were lowered almost immediately. In 1984 S&P changed 338 corporate bond ratings, but only 123 were listed on CreditWatch prior to the revision. Often the review associated with a new issue leads to a rating revision on the outstanding debt as well, and these are not usually preceded by a CreditWatch listing.

The procedures followed in the review are bascially the same as those used in rating a new issue, at least at S&P, and are outlined in Exhibit 11. Once a decision on a rating change has been made, S&P notifies the issuer first and allows an appeal as on a new issue. It is Moody's policy to notify the issuer and the market simultaneously. Moody's explains that they feel their first responsibility is to investors and, again, that all relevant information should be presented by management at the initial meeting.

Data on recent rating changes by Moody's and Standard & Poor's are presented in Exhibit 16. In the first half of the 1980s, rating downgradings exceeded upgradings by a considerable margin, although the two were approximately balanced in 1984. Although S&P claims that they try to look beyond the

EXHIBIT 16 CORPORATE DEBT RATING CHANGES

	Standard & Poor's		Moody's	
Year	Upgrades	Downgrades	Upgrades	Downgrades
1981	136	167	76	149
1982	87	237	49	169
1983	104	203	91	149
1984	164	173	161	148

Sources: Various issues of Standard & Poor's *Creditweek* and Moody's *Bond Survey*.

business cycle in establishing ratings, the recession that ended at the close of 1982 and whose effects were felt into 1983 and beyond would appear to have been important. Other factors include the increasing reliance on debt financing, **nuclear power** problems faced by the electric utility industry, and the impact on certain industries of increased foreign competition as a result of the strength of the dollar. Overall, Moody's attributed roughly one quarter of its rating downgrades in 1984 to company specific factors—**ergers** and **treasury stock repurchases** which were concentrated in the industrial sector—and three quarters to changes in the risk faced by the industry, for example, declining oil prices, nuclear power problems (Moody's *Bond Survey,* January 21, 1985).

WHAT'S IN A RATING?—THE RATING AGENCIES' DESCRIPTION

The question of how the agencies determine their rating for an issue is one of interest to academics and practitioners alike. Academics are interested in whether ratings bring valuable information to the market. As noted earlier, if *confidential information* supplied by the companies is an important determinant of ratings, then the informational value is clear. If ratings are based solely on a handful of publicly available financial statistics, then it would appear that little informational value is provided. Issuers, on the other hand, are interested in the rating they can expect to receive on new issues and users of ratings should be concerned with the information that ratings provide.

For years the rating agencies were somewhat uncommunicative, if not secretive, concerning their rating standards and procedures. In recent years, however, Standard & Poor's has published considerable descriptive information regarding their procedures: *Standard & Poor's Rating Guide* (1979), *Credit Overview: Corporate and International Ratings* (1983), *Credit Overview: Industrial Ratings* (1984) and *Credit Overview International* (1984). Although we present a summary of the information contained in these publications, the documents themselves provide a detailed description. Fitch and Duff and Phelps have published similar descriptions for various industries. Moody's has not published descriptions of their rating procedures, but some tentative conclusions regarding the financial statistics they view as important can be inferred from the figures they present when discussing their rating decisions in, for example, *Moody's Bond Survey* and in their *Corporate Credit Reports* (Exhibit 17).

EXHIBIT 17 MOODY'S AVERAGES OF FINANCIAL FIGURES BY RATING

1983 RATING GROUP AVERAGE FOR THE PAPER AND WOOD PRODUCTS INDUSTRY (RANKING OF 20 COMPANIES)

Senior Debt Rating	Number of Companies	Net Sales	Operating Margin	Return on Sales	Dividend Payout (% Income)	Interest Coverage	Total Coverage	Return on Capital (Pretax)	Adjusted Earnings Before Interest And Taxes EBIT Capital (Inflation)	Dividend Adjusted Average Capital	Average Cost of Debt
Aa	5	2,997.60	10.64	7.48	58.68	8.92	8.40	12.96	5.33	12.48	8.92
A	7	2,673.86	6.39	3.46	68.61	2.93	2.31	7.81	2.44	7.46	9.41
Baa	8	2,118.25	5.14	2.36	142.07	2.07	1.74	9.45	2.67	8.57	10.63
Average		2,532.55	6.95	4.02	95.51	4.08	3.60	9.75	3.16	9.16	9.77
Median		2,334.00	5.90	3.70	58.80	2.70	2.00	8.10	2.70	7.85	9.55

Senior Debt Rating	Number of Companies	Adjusted Average Assets Turnover	Cash Flow/ Total Debt	Total Debt/ Capitalization	Adjusted Total Debt/ Capitalization	Total Debt/ Market Capital	Interest Sensitive Debt/ Capitalization	Liquidity Adjusted Debt/ Capitalization	Total Liability/ Adjusted Net Worth	Leverage Index	Total Capitalization
Aa	5	0.90	42.40	24.84	26.66	19.24	5.32	24.74	0.58	1.02	3,144.20
A	7	1.04	32.49	31.10	33.89	29.16	4.17	31.74	0.76	1.17	2,081.71
Baa	8	1.13	22.20	39.16	44.26	35.13	6.56	43.01	1.19	1.36	1,512.63
Average		1.04	30.85	32.76	36.23	28.75	5.41	34.50	0.88	1.21	2,119.70
Median		1.00	29.25	32.15	34.90	31.50	5.20	33.25	0.85	1.20	1,732.00

Senior Debt Rating	Number of Companies	Net Sales	Operating Margin	Return on Sales	Dividend Payout (% Income)	Interest Coverage	Total Coverage	Return on Capital (Pretax)	Adjusted Earnings Before Interest And Taxes EBIT Capital (Inflation)	Dividend Adjusted Average Capital	Average Cost of Debt
Aaa	1	8,690	7.90	3.90	31.60	6.60	5.50	21.00		16.20	
Aa	3	15,438	9.93	4.20	27.40	4.23	3.63	22.40		18.27	
A	7	6,385.14	8.44	3.96	27.74	5.60	4.33	22.06	16.03	16.49	
Baa	6	3,237.50	5.63	2.25	27.27	3.58	2.43	17.82	13.63	11.88	
B	1	2,340	7.70	2.40	3.40	1.60	1.50	19.80	8.80	12.70	
NR	1	4,667	7.60	4.20	10.00	11.10	7.00	39.00	29.80	25.80	
Average		6,639	7.68	3.38	25.53	4.88	3.67	21.12	15.95	15.59	
Median		3,718	7.70	3.50	26.90	4.20	3.10	21.00	14.90	15.40	

Senior Debt Rating	Number of Companies	Adjusted Average Assets Turnover	Cash Flow/ Total Debt	Total Debt/ Capitalization	Adjusted Total Debt/ Capitalization	Total Debt/ Market Capital	Interest Sensitive Debt/ Capitalization	Liquidity Adjusted Debt/ Capitalization	Total Liability/ Adjusted Net Worth	Leverage Index	Total Capitalization
Aaa	1	1.56	45.50	28.20	36.70	27.60	7.60	35.70	0.90	0.90	3,384
Aa	3	1.30	30.33	43.27	51.93	29.73	13.40	47.63	1.80	1.50	9,369
A	7	1.47	33.49	38.36	50.70	32.81	6.04	47.99	1.20	1.01	2,736
Baa	6	1.44	24.95	40.58	62.00	32.62	5.27	60.73	1.38	1.17	1,574
B	1	1.01	13.90	75.50	82.20		3.60	81.30	3.40	6.20	1,111
NR	1	2.42	60.60	33.60	51.50	7.20	0.40	46.90	1.00	1.00	1,157
Average		1.46	31.32	41.01	55.43	30.40	6.62	53.01	1.44	1.41	3,282
Median		1.36	27.70	38.30	56.40	27.60	3.60	54.30	1.20	1.00	1,803

Source: Moody's Corporate Credit Reports, 1984.

INDUSTRIAL BONDS—OVERVIEW. According to S&P, their analysis of an industrial bond issue is organized around 9 **criteria** categories which every analysis addresses:

- Industry risk
- Issuer's industry position—market position
- Issuer's industry position—operating efficiency
- Management evaluation
- Accounting quality
- Earnings protection
- Leverage and asset protection
- Cash flow adequacy
- Financial flexibility

S&P also reports that in recent years they have moved toward placing less emphasis on the last four items, that is, on their financial analysis of the company; and more emphasis on the first four items, their business analysis (*Credit Overview: Industrial Ratings,* 1984, p. 13).

THE BUSINESS ANALYSIS. Of these nine categories, S&P claims that **industry risk**—their analysis of the strength and stability of the industry(ies) in which the firm operates—probably receives the highest weight in the rating decision. Moody's personnel have also indicated that they focus on "business fundamentals such as demand-supply characteristics, market leadership and cost positions." According to an official at Duff and Phelps, the company's presentation to their rating committee is the most important element of their rating process. At S&P the industry risk analysis often sets an "upper limit" on the rating attainable by any firm in that industry (*Credit Overview: Industrials,* 1984, p. 13).

The phrase "issuer's industry position—*market position*" refers primarily to the firm's sales position within the industry and how well it has maintained that position over time. *Operating efficiency* is measured primarily in terms of **operating margins;** but less quantitative factors such as age of plant, labor relationships, and diversification of energy and materials supplies are also considered.

The rater's evaluation of management appears to represent the most subjective of the criteria. As described by S&P (*Credit Overview: Industrial Ratings,* 1984 p. 20), this evaluation focuses on:

- The financial record as a reflection of management's success or failure
- Conservatism or aggressiveness with respect to financial risk
- Organizational considerations

As part of this evaluation S&P tries to judge the realism of management's plans and projections. When the firm has previously issued rated debt, S&P compares the plans and projections from earlier meetings with subsequent performance.

ACCOUNTING QUALITY. S&P emphasizes that they do not perform their own *audits* but rely on audited data presented to them. They do evaluate the "quality" of the firm's accounting standards in order "to determine whether the numbers and ratios overstate or understate the financial performance and position of the firm *relative to its competitors*" [their italics] (*Credit Overview: Corporate and International Ratings,* 1983, p. 27). Where possible the figures are adjusted to bring them into conformity with industry practice. When adjustments cannot be made, this is taken into account in assigning the rating.

THE FINANCIAL ANALYSIS. S&P's *financial analysis* of the firm is organized around the last four of the nine categories listed earlier: *earnings protection, leverage and asset protection, cash flow adequacy,* and *financial flexibility.* In its summary of the financial figures used to rate a representative company and in its rating worksheets, S&P lists over 25 financial ratios which they calculate on industrial firms for each of 5 years. However, they have also identified the 10 financial ratios listed in Exhibit 18 as **"key" ratios.** The first four are measures of earnings protection (e.g., coverage), the next four are measures of leverage or asset protection, and the final two are their measures of cash flow adequacy. The final category in S&P's list of nine broad criteria categories is "financial flexibility." As they describe it, this refers partially to a linking of the other three financial factors (earnings protection, leverage, and cash flow adequacy) but also captures their evaluation of the firm's future financing plans.

Median values are shown in Exhibit 18 of each ratio for each rating from AAA through B. Without exception, the median coverage, earnings, and cash flow values increase as the rating rises and the leverage measures fall. S&P emphasizes that these are medians only and not standards. An individual company whose debt is rated BBB may have a "better" value for one or more ratios than another company rated A. Norms also are said to vary by industry.

Unlike S&P, Moody's has not enumerated the financial variables they consider most important when deciding on ratings. It is instructive, however, to consider the ***financial ratios*** that are listed by Moody's in their discussion of ratings contained in Moody's *Bond Survey* and the data they present in their *Corporate Credit Reports.* Tables from the latter are reproduced in Exhibit 17 for two industries—paper and wood products and retail sales. Most of these figures fall into S&P's three financial analysis categories: measure of earnings and coverage, leverage measures, and cash flow adequacy. As with S&P's key variables, there are many more measures in this exhibit belonging to the first two categories than to the third; this proportion may or may not indicate relative importance. It is interesting that eight of S&P's 10 key ratios from Exhibit 18 appear in Moody's tables in Exhibit 17—although there may be some differ-

EXHIBIT 18 STANDARD & POOR'S KEY RATIOS WITH THREE YEAR (1980–82) MEDIAN VALUES FOR EACH RATING FOR U.S. INDUSTRIAL COMPANIES

	Senior Debt					
	AAA	AA	A	BBB	BB	B
Pretax interest coverage (x)	14.44	7.61	5.47	3.26	2.43	1.53
Pretax interest and full rental coverage (x)	7.46	4.42	3.33	2.31	2.06	1.34
Pretax return on average long-term capital employed (%)	29.04	24.93	19.73	15.95	17.23	12.58
Operating income/sales (%)	16.65	14.45	12.44	9.57	12.62	9.14
Long-term debt/capitalization (%)	11.56	19.61	25.66	35.95	42.43	56.11
Total debt/capitalization including short-term debt (%)	16.98	24.88	30.06	38.02	47.81	60.33
Total debt/capitalization including short-term debt (including 8X rents) (%)	29.46	37.86	40.81	48.59	55.41	66.70
Total liabilities/tangible shareholders' equity and minority interest (%)	76.43	97.31	104.11	127.86	182.02	276.66
Cash flow/long-term debt (%)	250.94	109.54	68.18	39.01	27.73	13.90
Cash flow/total debt (%)	138.56	75.13	55.68	33.60	24.55	11.18

Glossary

Adjusted net income. Net income from continuing operations before (1) special items, (2) minority interests, (3) gains on reacquisition of debt, (4) unremitted equity in earnings of affiliates, (5) net income effect of capitalized interest.
Gross interest. Gross interest accrued before (1) capitalized interest, (2) interest income.
Gross rents. Gross operating rents paid before sublease income.
Long-term debt. As reported, including capitalized lease obligations on the balance sheet.
Total debt. Long-term debt, current maturities, commercial paper, and other short-term borrowings.
Equity. Shareholders' equity, plus minority interest, plus deferred investment tax credits.
Operating income. Sales minus cost of goods manufactured (before depreciation), selling, general and administrative, and research and developments costs.
Eight times rents. Gross rents paid multiplied by capitalization factor of eight.
Tangible net worth. Equity less goodwill, patients, "deferred" assets," "other assets."

Formulas for key ratios

$$\text{Pretax interest coverage} = \frac{\text{Adjusted net income + gross interest + income taxes}}{\text{Gross interest}}$$

$$\text{Pretax fixed charge coverage} = \frac{\text{Adjusted net income + gross interest + gross rents + income taxes}}{\text{Gross interest + gross rents}}$$

$$\text{Operating income as a \% of sales} = \frac{\text{Operating income}}{\text{Sales}}$$

$$\text{Pretax return on permanent capital} = \frac{\text{Adjusted net income + income taxes + interest charges}}{\text{Sum of (1) the average of the beginning of year and end of year current maturities long-term debt, noncurrent deferred taxes, minority interest, and stockholders' equity, and (2) average short-term borrowings during year per footnotes to financial statements}}$$

$$\text{Long-term debt as a \% of capitalization} = \frac{\text{Long-term debt}}{\text{Long-term debt + equity}}$$

$$\text{Total debt as a \% of capitalization + short-term debt} = \frac{\text{Total debt}}{\text{Total debt + equity}}$$

$$\text{Total debt + 8 times rent as a \% of capitalization + short-term debt + 8 times rents} = \frac{\text{Total debt + 8 times gross rentals paid}}{\text{Total debt + equity} - \text{8 times gross rentals paid}}$$

$$\text{Total liabilities as a \% of tangible net worth} = \frac{\text{Total liabilities}}{\text{Tangible net worth}}$$

$$\text{Cash flow as \% of long-term debt} = \frac{\text{Adjusted net income + depreciation and amortization + deferred taxes}}{\text{Long-term debt}}$$

$$\text{Cash flow as a \% of total debt} = \frac{\text{Adjusted net income + depreciation and amortization + deferred taxes}}{\text{Total debt}}$$

Source: Standard and Poor's *Credit Overview: Industrial Ratings,* 1984, pp. 26 and 27.

ences in measurement. The two that do not appear in Moody's table involve long-term as opposed to total debt: cash flow as a percent of long-term debt and long-term debt/total capitalization. Moody's apparently feels that total debt is a more appropriate measure given the recent expansion in short-term borrowing on firm balance sheets. S&P would probably agree, because they state "the traditional measure of long-term debt/capitalization is losing its significance as a measure of permanent debt leverage" (*Credit Overview: Industrial Ratings,* 1984, p. 22).

THE LEGAL ANALYSIS. In addition to evaluating the creditworthiness of the issuer, the rating agency must evaluate the protection provided by the **bond covenant.** As indicated by S&P, the emphasis is on the "protection afforded by, and relative position of, the obligation in the event of **bankruptcy,** reorganization, or other arrangement under the laws of bankruptcy and other laws affecting creditors' rights." For corporate bonds the most important distinction may be between ***subordinated*** and *unsubordinated,* or *senior, debt.* As the name indicates, subordinated debt carries a claim on corporate earnings that is junior to that of the senior debt. Before the ratings were refined by the addition to pluses and minuses and 1, 2, or 3, a firm's subordinated debt was normally rated one full classification level below that firm's senior debt (e.g., BB versus BBB). The rating agencies apparently feel that distinction is now too sharp. Currently subordinated debt is generally rated one step or modifier below the senior debt when the latter is classified as investment grade. For instance, if the senior debt is rated A, the subordinated is normally A−. If the senior debt is speculative grade, two steps difference is most common, for example, BB+ and BB−, repectively, or BB and B+.

UTILITY BONDS. Having summarized the rating process for industrial bonds as described by the rating agencies (specifically S&P), we now turn to other bond ratings. As before, a more thorough description can be found in the *Credit Overviews* published by S&P.

As indicated by S&P, their ratings of *utility bonds* are based on six nonfinancial and six financial criteria. **Nonfinancial criteria** are:

1. Market or service territory (size and long-term growth in demand)
2. Fuel/power supply (degrees of diversification and reliability)
3. Operating efficiency
4. Regulatory treatment
5. Quality of management
6. Competition/monopoly balance (basically the business risk of any non-utility operations)

The six **financial criteria** listed by S&P are:

1. Construction/asset concentration risks
2. Earnings protection (primarily fixed charge coverage)
3. Debt leverage
4. Cash flow adequacy
5. Financial flexibility/capital attraction (financing plans and ability to meet them—market to book value of their stock
6. Accounting quality

Although they may be measured slightly differently for utilities, the final five were all on the list of criteria evaluated when assigning industrial ratings and hence will not be discussed here. Standard & Poor's normal expectations for **fixed charge coverage, debt leverage,** and **cash flow** are shown in Exhibit 19. Because S&P feels that the *electric utilities, gas distributors, gas pipelines,* and telephones differ in terms of their business risk, their expectations regarding the financial criteria for a given rating also differ among them. In general the gas distributor and pipeline companies seem to be required to meet a slightly higher financial standard.

The one financial criterion that does not appear on the industrial list is the first—*construction* and asset concentration *risks.* In recent years this criterion has apparently assumed great importance for all rating agencies in rating electric utilities with costly *nuclear plants* under construction. As illustrated in Exhibit 20, Moody's ratings of electric utilities with major construction projects

EXHIBIT 19 STANDARD & POOR'S UTILITY RATING EXPECTATIONS

FIXED CHARGE COVERAGE				
	AAA	AA	A	BBB
Electric utilities	4.0+	3.25–4.25	2.5–3.50	under 3.0
Gas distributors		4.0+	3.0–4.0	under 3.0
Gas pipelines		4.5+	3.5–4.5	under 3.5
Telephone companies	4.5+	3.70–4.70	2.8–4.0	under 3.0
DEBT LEVERAGE				
	AAA	AA	A	BBB
Electric utilities	under 45%	42–47%	45–55%	over 53%
Gas distributors		under 45%	45–50%	over 50%
Gas pipelines		under 40%	40–50%	over 50%
Telephone companies	under 40%	40–48%	48–58%	58–64%
CASH FLOW AS % OF CASH CAPITAL OUTLAYS				
	AAA	AA	A	BBB
Electric utilities		over 40%	20–50%	under 30%
Gas distributors		over 75%	50–100%	under 60%
Telephones	over 85%	70–85%	55–70%	25–55%

Source: Standard & Poor's *Credit Overview: Corporate and International Ratings,* 183, pp. 39–41.

EXHIBIT 20 MOODY'S ELECTRIC UTILITY RATINGS

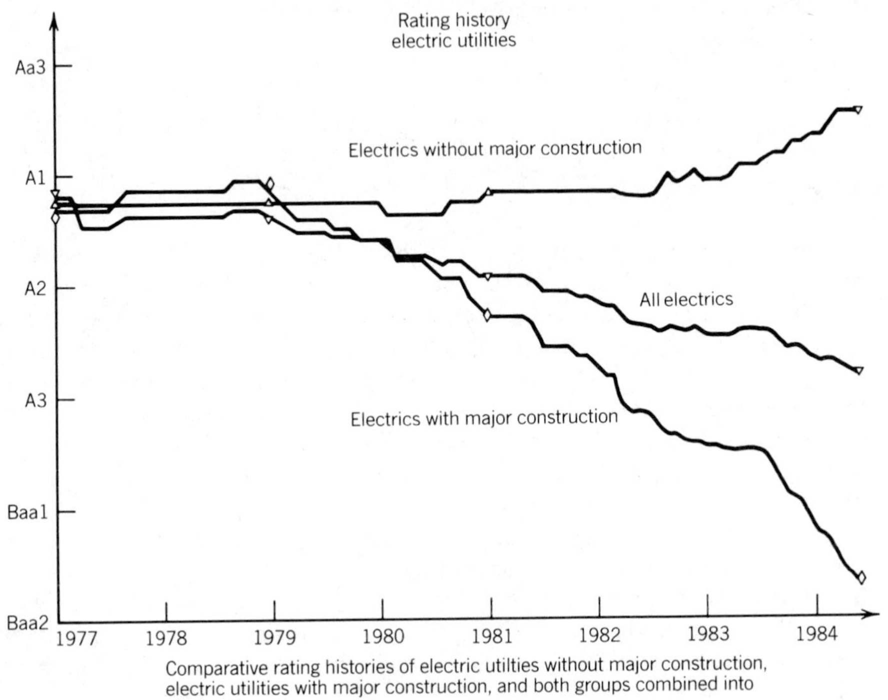

Comparative rating histories of electric utilties without major construction, electric utilities with major construction, and both groups combined into all electrics.

Source: Moody's Industry Outlook: Electric Utility, July 18, 1984, p. 34.

underway have deteriorated substantially over the past 5 years, whereas ratings of utilities without major construction expense have improved slightly.

Duff and Phelps rated utility debt exclusively when they began in the 1930s and this area remains a specialty.

OTHER RATED LONG-TERM DEBT. Although industrial and utility bonds are perhaps the best-known, there are many other types of rated corporate or taxable debt that space does not permit us to discuss in detail. **Transportation bonds** (railroads and airline) are the oldest rated debt—Moody's began by rating railroad bonds. Much of this debt is secured by a security interest in the equipment being financed, as with **equipment trust certificates.** S&P usually rates railroad equipment trust certificates well above the railroads' unsecured senior debt, but usually treats the airlines' *secured obligations* as *senior debt.* Their justification is that unlike airlines, railroads must be reorganized, not liquidated (and so equipment is necessary), in the event of bankruptcy.

In addition to these traditional forms of rated debt, many other forms of taxable debt have appeared and been rated in recent years. For instance, the ***debt of financial institutions:*** banks and bank holding companies, insurance companies, captive and independent finance companies, real estate investment trusts, and S&Ls. As one would expect and as explained in S&P's *Credit Overview,* the emphasis here is on capitalization rates, loan or asset quality, and liquidity, as well as earnings. Fitch and Duff and Phelps both claim to have been the first to rate bank holding company debt—a conflict that is perhaps explained by the fact that Duff and Phelps's ratings weren't public until the late 1970s.

The ***secondary mortgage market*** has grown substantially in recent years and has been rated by Standard & Poor's since 1976. Their standards are described in the *Credit Overview.* S&P feels that in order to justify an AAA rating a ***collateralized mortgage-backed obligation*** (CMO) should be sufficiently overcollateralized to withstand a worst-case scenario as represented by the Great Depression of the 1930s. Specifically, a pool of single family mortgage should be capable of withstanding a 15% foreclosure rate and a 37% loss in the event of default. For condominiums an even larger overcollateralization is required.

COMMERCIAL PAPER. ***Commercial paper*** is rated from A−1+ to D by S&P; P-1 (highest) to P−3 to "Not Prime" (lowest) by Moody's; Duff 1 plus to Duff 3 by Duff and Phelps; Fitch-1 to Fitch-4 by Fitch; and MCM-1 to MCM-6 by McCarthy, Crisanti, and Maffei (see Exhibit 2). At some agencies, however, the lower ratings are rarely used. For instance, nominally, S&P has rating categories of A, B, C, and D with the A category divided into A-1, A-2, and A-3. However, 90% of all commercial paper is rated A-1, with nearly all of the rest rated A-2. This lack of separation led S&P to refine its ratings by introducing the A-1+ category to represent issues deemed more creditworthy than those rated A-1.

Commercial paper ratings are based on approximately the same factors as is senior debt but with a shorter time horizon (approximately 2 years according to S&P). Accordingly, S&P reports that in rating paper they place less emphasis on the business analysis and more on liquidity and financial flexibility. Although this leads to some differences, the commercial paper of most firms whose senior debt is rated AA− or above is rated A−1+. If the firm's senior debt is rated A or A+, and A-1 rating for its commercial paper is most likely, and if the senior debt is rated A- to BBB, a CP rating of A-2 is likely. Median values of S&P's 10 key financial ratios by commercial paper rating are shown in Exhibit 21.

Most commercial paper is backed by a bank line of credit. In the event that the firm is unable to borrow in the commercial paper market, these lines of credit supposedly insure that it can obtain funds to pay off its maturing commercial paper. Although the rating agencies normally expect most commercial paper to be backed by a line of credit, responsibility for repayment rests with the issuer and the rating (assuming a line of credit is present) is based on the creditworthiness of the issuer—not the bank.

STRUCTURED FINANCINGS. Increasingly some commercial paper is being backed by irrevocable ***letters of credit (LOC)*** or other guarantees from banks or

EXHIBIT 21 MEDIAN VALUES (1980-1982) OF S&P'S KEY RATIOS BY COMMERCIAL PAPER RATING

Commercial paper: Three-year (1980–1982) median averages of key ratios by rating category	A–1+	A–1	A–2
Pretax interest coverage (x)	8.16	5.31	3.52
Pretax interest and full-rental coverage (x)	4.60	3.33	2.42
Pretax return on average long-term capital employed (%)	25.83	20.22	16.85
Operating income/sales (%)	14.79	13.19	9.48
Long-term debt/capitalization (%)	17.30	24.66	30.58
Total debt/capitalization including short-term debt (%)	21.61	28.94	35.03
Total debt/capitalization including short-term debt (including 8 times rents) (%)	36.43	39.76	48.27
Total liabilities/tangible shareholders' equity and minority interest (%)	89.19	95.01	125.12
Cash flow/long-term debt (%)	117.80	74.57	47.97
Cash flow/total debt (%)	89.51	59.89	39.50

Source: Standard & Poor's *Credit Overview: Industrials,* 1984, p. 39.

other financial institutions and not just by simple lines of credit. In an LOC the bank agrees to repay the maturing debt if the issuer fails to do so. These and other guarantees, referred to as structured financings, necessitate an evaluation of the legal status of the LOC or other support. Since the *Bankruptcy Act of 1978,* most LOC agreements have been tightened to eliminate any preference payment risk associated with insolvency of the direct obligation. Nonetheless, S&P reports that a few LOCs are structured so that very little protection is provided. When the LOC is strong, both agencies base their ratings on the bank granting the LOC, but when there is some uncertainty about the bank meeting the obligation in a timely manner, S&P bases its rating on the issuer. In December 1984, for instance, S&P's ratings on paper backed by a First National Bank of Chicago ranged from A–1+ to A-2. Prior to the Bankruptcy Act of 1978 Moody's analyzed the creditworthiness of both the issuer and the LOC bank. Due to the strengthening of LOC agreements, however, Moody's ratings since 1980 have been based primarily on the creditworthiness of the LOC bank.

In addition to banks, commercial paper may be guaranteed by insurance companies, foreign governments, or the parent company.

Structured financing arrangements are becoming more common in the long-term debt market as well. For instance, about 30% of new municipal debt is now insured. On the corporate side mortgage-backed bonds are backed by both the issuer and the collateral, and in other mortgage-backed obligations the mortgages or their payments may be insured. Such arrangements have become so common that Moody's has devoted one of four units (the structured financing unit) to the legal analysis of the protection provided by the second party.

PARENT COMPANY AND SUBSIDIARY RATINGS. One type of structured financing is that in which a financially stronger parent *guarantees* the debt of its subsidiary. In this case both Moody's and S&P's accord the subsidiary the same rating as the stronger parent. In many cases, however, an indication of the parent support may not amount to a guarantee. The parent may issue a ***comfort letter,*** with no legal status, which states that it is important to the parent that the debt be repaid; or it may say nothing. Nonetheless, the subsidiary may be important to the parent's own operations or the parent may feel that a default by its subsidiary will cause it to lose face as well. For example, in 1980 Mobil loaned funds to Montgomery Ward to meet its debt payments even though Mobil had never guaranteed the latter's debt. Indeed, Mobil had explicitly disclaimed support in its 1977 Annual Report though it dropped this statement in later reports (Clayton and Beranek, 1984). S&P has indicated that when there is no written guarantee, they seek to determine the economic importance of the subsidiary to the parent. If the subsidiary is viewed to be important to a more creditworthy parent, aid is likely. In this case the subsidiary's debt will normally be rated somewhat higher than its own financial position would justify. If the subsidiary is not viewed to be very important, it is rated solely on its own merits. Moody's has indicated that it is their normal policy—in the absence of a guarantee—to base the rating on the "subsidiary's own financial and operational characteristics." However, they also indicate that they "may accept an alternative support mechanism such as a coverage support agreement for a captive finance subsidiary or a net worth maintenance agreement." From their meetings with management, the rating agencies may be better able to judge the parent's support than is the average investor.

On occasion the subsidiary may be stronger financially than the parent. S&P normally rates the subsidiary equal to the parent in such situations, noting that in the bankruptcy filings of Johns Manville, Wickes, White Motor, and Dreco, apparently healthy subsidiaries were included. There are exceptions, however, where the subsidiaries are rated higher—situations in which the subsidiaries are protected by regulations, where joint bankruptcy filing would be impractical, or where the subsidiaries are financially independent (S&P's *Credit Overview: Industrial Ratings,* 1984, p. 31). In some cases dividends from an independently financed subsidiary may constitute a parent company's sole or major source of revenue. Moody's reports that depending on the indenture restrictions, the holding company's debt will normally receive a lower rating.

WHAT'S IN A RATING?—ACADEMIC STUDIES

Several researchers have attempted to replicate Moody's or S&P's ratings using ***statistical models*** and published financial data. One purpose of these studies has been to reveal the **determinants of ratings**—most were undertaken before S&P published the descriptions of their rating methods. A second purpose has been to ascertain the extent to which the ratings can be correctly predicted using a handful of publicly available financial statistics and a statistical computer model. If such studies were to find that all ratings can be predicted in this manner, it would be apparent that the rating agencies bring little new information to the market and could be easily replaced by a machine—at some savings. Of course, if most ratings cannot be replicated by these models, it remains unclear whether the ratings are based on important—possibly inside—information that the models failed to consider, whether the model incorrectly evaluated its information, or whether the rating itself is in error (i.e., the computer model provides a better measure of creditworthiness). As we will see, studies have found that most, but by no means all, ratings are correctly predicted by such models.

Characteristics of the rating studies with which we are familiar are summarized in Exhibit 22. Those published prior to about 1980 are discussed more thoroughly in Altman et al. (1981, Chapter 5), with particular emphasis on the statistical techniques employed. We will not attempt here to review the contributions of each individually but will instead offer some summary observations on the studies as a group.

With the exception of a 1984/1985 working paper by Martin et al., these studies have not utilized the same 10 ratios identified by S&P as "keys" to their industrial ratings (Exhibit 18). The financial variables that have been utilized are shown in Exhibit 22. It is evident that there is certainly an overlap between Exhibits 18 and 22; most studies have included measures of ***coverage, profitability,*** and ***leverage,*** which have been found to be important determinants of ratings. Each has used a somewhat different set of variables, however, and even when the titles are the same as those listed in Exhibit 18, they are often measured differently. As noted in Exhibit 18, S&P adjusts net income for several factors. In an unpublished paper, Martin et al. (1984/1985) have used S&P's 10 ratios as defined in Exhibit 18 but do not find that this model is more successful in predicting ratings than were the earlier studies listed in Exhibit 22. It appears that fewer than 10 variables are needed to capture the agencies' financial analyses and that the exact method of measurement is not very important.

Most studies have found *firm size* to be strongly correlated with the firm's debt rating. If two firms have the same leverage and coverage ratios, the larger firm will often receive a higher rating. No measure of firm size appears in S&P's list of key financial variables, but S&P does identify the firm's sales position in its industry as a nonfinancial determinant of ratings, and size may be proxy for this aspect of their rating process. Moody's includes total sales and capitalization in its rating comparison tables for industrials (Exhibit 17), but whether these size measures are determinants of their ratings is unclear.

In general these studies have focused on the issuer's financial strength and have not tried to replicate the rating agencies' ***business analysis.*** As noted earlier, S&P claims that the riskiness of the industry(ies) in which the firm operates is the most important determinant of its ratings. As Altman et al. (1981) have noted, published studies have not considered this factor until quite recently. Several early studies did correct for industry position by dividing the firm's financial ratios by the averages for their industry (Horrigan, 1966 and Kaplan and Urwitz, 1979). Although this procedure captures the firm's position within the industry, it does not address the question of industry risk. Two studies that do address industry differences are those of Perry et al. (1984) and Jackson and Boyd (1984). Perry et al. estimate separate discriminant models for six industries with different independent variables in each and find that these are somewhat more successful in forecasting ratings than is a pooled model. Whether the success is due to industry differences or the fact that the pooled model doesn't include all variables in the industry models is unclear. Jackson and Boyd use a probit model and include zero-one dummy variables in their model to represent different industries. They find that if the financial variables are adjusted by dividing by industry averages, then the industry dummies are clearly important. If the variables are not adjusted, it is unclear whether there are important rating differences between industries. Although more research is needed, their result and the fact that most studies have been able to predict correctly about two-thirds of the ratings without considering industry differences suggest that industry risk may be less important than the rating agencies claim.

Although both of these studies address the question, neither performs a straightforward statistical test of the hypothesis that industry risk affects ratings and neither attempts to explain why one industry is viewed as more or less risky than another.

As shown in Exhibit 22, several different statistical models or procedures have been employed, with **discriminant analysis** being the most popular. Because each model is described and their attributes are compared theoretically in Altman et al. (1981), they will not be discussed in-depth here. Their ability to predict bond ratings from the same data set has been examined by Ederington (1985).

The first empirical study of ratings (Horrigan, 1966) used a linear regression model that required the assignment of a numerical value to each rating: 9 to Aaa, 8 to Aa, down to 1 to C-rated bonds. As Horrigan pointed out, this procedure assumes unrealistically that the risk differential between any pair of adjacent ratings is the same. The procedures used subsequently have all avoided this problem, but each specifies a somewhat different relationship between the financial accounting measures and bond ratings. Whether any has obtained an accurate model of the rating agencies' decision model is unclear, although some seem more reasonable theoretically (Ederington, 1985). In other words, these models must specify exactly how ratings are related, say to coverage and the relationship specified may not match the rating agency's decision function.

In a study of this problem, Ederington (1985) found that using the same data and independent variables, four statistical models (linear regression, discriminant analysis, ordered probit, and unordered logit) predicted different ratings for 40% of the new issue ratings examined. Although the ordered probit model correctly predicted 78% of the ratings in a holdout sample, discriminant analysis predicted only 69%. If the results are this sensitive to differences in specifications among the statistical models, they are probably also sensitive to differences between any one statistical model's specification and the raters' decision functions.

EXHIBIT 22 CHARACTERISTICS AND FINDINGS OF STUDIES OF BOND RATINGS

Study	Bonds and Ratings Considered	Sample Size	Statistical Procedure Employed	Independent Variables	% of Holdout Sample Classified Correctly
Horrigan (1966)	Both Moodys & S&P's ratings were considered. One sample of unchanged ratings (1959–1964) and another of new or changed ratings (1961–1964).	Stable ratings: 201 Moody's 151 S&P Changed or new ratings: 97—Moody's 118—S&P's	Linear regression	Subordination, total assets, working capital/sales, net worth/debt, sales/net worth, profit/sales	New ratings: Moody's—58% S&P's—52% Changed ratings: Moody's—54% S&P's—57%
Pogue and Soldovsky (1969)	Bonds rated Baa-Aaa by Moodys. Industrial, utility, and railroad bonds. 1961–1964.	53 + 10 for holdout from 1961–1966	Regression with only 2 ratings	Debt/total capital; net income/total assets; variability of net income; net total assets; net income interest/interest	80%
West (1970)	Industrial bonds rated B or above by Moody's. 1927, 1932, 1937, 1949, and 1953.	236 + 77 for holdout	Linear regression	Earnings variability; periods of solvency; capital debt; total long-term debt	62%
Pinches and Mingo (1973)	New issue industrials rated B-Aa by Moody's 1967–1968.	132 + 48 for holdout	Linear discriminant	Subordination; issue size; income + interest/interest; years of consecutive dividends; long-term debt/assets; net income/assets	65.48%
Pinches and Mingo (1975)	New issue industrials rated B–Aa by Moody's 1967–1968.	130	Quadratic discriminant	Same, and without subordination	56% (new issues) according to Altman et al.
Altman and Katz (1976)	Electric utility bonds equally rated by Moody's and S&P. Baa–Aaa ratings. 1969–1971.	260	Quadratic discriminant	14 variables, most important were: interest coverage; variability of interest coverage	Lachenbruch: 77%

				and operating income; return on assets; total assets; market value equity/book value equity; retained earnings/assets; maintenance and depreciation/operating revenue (according to Altman et al. (1981)	
Pinches, Singleton, Jahankhani (1978)	Moody's and S&P ratings and utilities with mortgage bonds in 1975. Baa–Aa and BBB–AA ratings considered.	92—Moody's 94—S&P	Linear discriminant	Total assets; net income/assets; net earnings/ fixed charges; earnings growth rate; construction expense/total assets; index of regulatory climate	Lachenbruch: 54.35%—Moody's 64.89%—S&P 65.22 when rated the same by S&P and Moody's
Bhandari, Soldofsky, and Boe (1979)	Electric utility bonds whose ratings were changed by Moody's; 1974–1975 for estimation. 1972, 1973, and 1976 for holdout	39 with changed ratings 24 without 26 for holdout	Linear discriminant	Net income + interest/interest trend in coverage; debt/assets; trend in earnings; standard error of earnings	75%
Kaplan and Urwitz (1979)	One sample of Moody's ratings of seasoned industrial bonds and another Moody's ratings of new industrial issues. B–Aaa. 1971–1972.	120 seasonal 140 new issues 67 holdout	Probit and regression	Subordination; cash flow/interest; debt/assets; net income/assets; coefficient of variation of net income and total assets	Probit on: new issues 69%.
Peavy (1980)	All rated debt of domestic bank holding companies	42	Discriminant	Total assets; total interest paid/total revenues; short-term debt/total assets; loans/total deposits; stockholders equity/risk assets; growth rate of earnings per share (previous 5 years; price/earnings ratio for common stock; dividend yield or common stock; net profits after taxes	Lachenbruch: 85.7%

EXHIBIT 22 (*CONTINUED*)

Study	Bonds and Ratings Considered	Sample Size	Statistical Procedure Employed	Independent Variables	% of Holdout Sample Classified Correctly
Belkaoui (1980)	Industrial bonds rated B or above by S&P, 1978	160 + 97 for holdout	Linear discriminant	Total assets; total debt Long-term debt/total invested capital; current assets/current liabilities; net income + interest/interest , preferred dividend requirement; stock price/common equity per share; subordination	65.9%
Belkaoui (1983)	Industrial bonds rated B or above by S&P in 1981	266 analysis sample, 115 validation from 1981 +388 control from 1980	Linear discriminant	Total assets; total debt; long-term debt/total invested capital; current assets/current liabilities; fixed charge coverage ratio; 5-year cash flow as percentage of 5-year growth needs; stock price/common equity per share; subordination	67.8%
Martin and Henderson (1983)	New industrial bond issues rated B-Aa by Moody's 1979–1980	129	Rank discriminant	Unfunded past service cost per employee; unfunded past service costs to the 5-year average of earnings before tax; pension-related debt equivalent to stockholders	Lachenbruch: 56%

				equity; long-term debt + unfunded past service costs to total capitalization + unfunded past service costs; long-term debt + debt equivalent to total capitalization + debt equivalent; times-interest earned; return of investment; long-term debt to total capitalization; current ratio	
Perry, Henderson, and Cronan (1984)	Industrials from six industry classifications rated B or above by Moody's. Most recent issue of each firm, 1977–1979.	146	Multiple discriminant linear	Various measures of liquidity, leverage, activity, profitability, and size	Lachenbruch: 60.3% for pooled By industy: Food—73.1 Chem.—70.0 Petro.—87.0 Mach.—89.7 Elec.—73.9 Trans.—83.3
Martin, Henderson, Perry, and Cronan (1984)	Industrials from five industry classifications rated B–AA by S&P	154	Rank discriminant	Pretax interest coverage; pretax interest and full rental coverage; cash flow/LTD; cash flow/total debt; pretax returns on average long-term capital employed; operating income/sales; long-term debt/capitalization; total debt/capitalization; total liabilities/tangible shareholders equity and minority interest	Lachenbruch: 53.2%

EXHIBIT 22 (*CONTINUED*)

Study	Bonds and Ratings Considered	Sample Size	Statistical Procedure Employed	Independent Variables	% of Holdout Sample Classified Correctly
Peavy and Scott (1984)	Moody's and S&P ratings of divested local Bell company bonds. AA− and A+ not used.	19	Multiple discriminant linear	Pretax fixed-charge coverage; log of total assets; return on equity; coefficient of variation of NOE; internal cash flow as a percentage of construction expenditures; debt-to-total capital ration; intrastate/interstate toll revenues	Lachenbruch: 84.2%—Moody's 61.1%—S&P
Ederington (1985)	New industrial issues rated B or better by Moody's; 1975–1979	246 + 100 for holdout	Logit, linear discriminate, N-probit, and linear regression	Subordination; average total assets for proceeding 5 years; long-term debt/total capitalization; forecast pretax net income/interest charges	OLS—65% N-probit—78% Discriminant: equal priors—64% proportional priors—69% Logit—73%
Jackson and Boyd (1984)	New industrial issues rated B or above by Moody's; 1980–1981	282	N-Probit	Subordination; acid-test ratio (*P,T,* & *V**); long-term debt/total assets (*P*); fixed charge coverage (*P,T,* & *V*); net income/total assets (*P,T,* & *V*); operating income (*T* & *V*); net plant equipment/total assets (*T*); capital investment & acquisition/cash flow-dividends (*P,T,* & *V*); industry dummies	57.8% hit rate—not holdout

*P = predicted
T = trend
V = variability

Although more sophisticated measures of predictive success of these statistical models exist, the most straightforward intuitively is the percentage of the agency ratings that is predicted correctly—preferably in a separate sample than that used to estimate the model. The percentages are shown in Exhibit 18. Most recent studies have found that roughly two-thirds of the agency ratings can be predicted by such models. The highest accuracy rate on utility bonds (77%) was obtained by Altman and Katz (1976), who restricted their sample to bonds equally rated by Moody's and S&P. Ederington (1985) has had the most success predicting industrial ratings—78% accuracy using an ordered probit model and 73% using an unordered logit model.

It is clear that even the most successful statistical models cannot predict all ratings. There are two possible explanations: either (1) the statistical models are incomplete or incorrect, or (2) the rater's judgment is faulty.

The statistical models could be incomplete or incorrect because (1) they cannot include ***inside information*** such as firm projections and plans that are available to the rating agencies; (2) they have not included all pertinent public financial information considered by the rating agencies; (3) they have not generally included business analysis factors such as industry risk which the agencies stress are important; (4) they have not normally adjusted for differences in accounting procedures as the rating agencies do; and/or (5) they may not accurately specify the relationship between the variables considered and the ratings.

If the rating models are incorrect for the first reason—inside information—then little improvement in predicting ratings is possible and the informational role of ratings is clear. If present models fail to replicate all ratings because of one or more of the other reasons, then considerable improvements in predictive accuracy are possible.

RATINGS VERSUS STATISTICAL MODELS

These studies may have failed to replicate one-third to one-fourth of the ratings because the ratings themselves are flawed. Because bond ratings are subjective, raters' judgments may vary somewhat randomly from issue to issue and month to month. If such random variations are present, then all ratings cannot be accurately predicted.

More important, ratings may not be the best predictors of risk of default. Just as the studies surveyed earlier have attempted to predict bond ratings, others have sought with reasonable success, to build statistical models to predict corporate bankruptcy using similar financial accounting variables. These studies—at least those up to 1980—are reviewed in Altman et al. (1981) and will not be discussed here. Classics include the models of Beaver (1967); Altman (1968); and the Zeta model of Altman, Haldeman, and Narayanan (1977). The latter, the ***Zeta model,*** has evolved into a risk analysis service somewhat akin to the rating agencies. **Zeta Services** (Hoboken, N.J.) sells their computer models' evaluations of a firm's risk of bankruptcy in the form of **"Zeta" scores** to institutional investors.

The Zeta model uses **discriminant analysis** to predict bankruptcy, based on seven variables: return on assets, size (tangible assets), interest coverage, the current ratio, cumulative profitability, total capitalization, and stability of earnings. Mean Zeta scores for 111 firms, 53 of which went bankrupt between 1962 and 1975, are shown in Exhibit 23. (Note: A negative Zeta score indicates a financial profile more similar to bankrupt firms and a positive score non-bankruptcy.) The mean Zeta score clearly declined as bankruptcy approached. The model correctly classified 93% of these 111 firms as bankrupt or not based on data 1 year prior to bankruptcy, 80% based on data 4 years prior to bankruptcy, and showed 70 percent accuracy for up to 5 years prior. If ratings are good predictors of risk of bankruptcy, higher rated bonds should have higher Zeta scores, as indicated in Exhibit 24.

To our knowledge, no one has attempted to compare directly the ability of ratings and models such as Zeta to predict default. However, Ang and Patel (1975) compared Moody's ratings with those predicted by the models of Horrigan (1966), West (1970), Pogue and Soldofsky (1969), and Pinches and Mingo (1975) as predictors of defaults during the Depression (1928–1939). They found that it was difficult to say whether these models or Moody's ratings were better predictors of default, because the error rates were about the same.

EXHIBIT 23 AVERAGE ZETA SCORE FOR BANKRUPT FIRMS

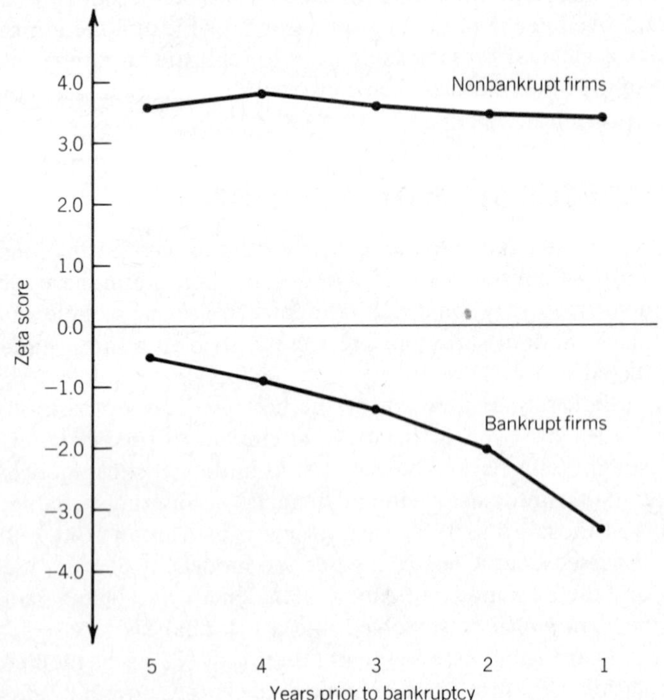

Source: Zeta Services, Inc., *Zeta Risk Evaluation,* 1979.

EXHIBIT 24 AVERAGE ZETA SCORES FOR SENIOR DEBT BY RATING 1983

Moody's		S&P	
Aaa	10.99	AAA	11.17
Aa	7.83	AA	7.58
A	5.35	A	5.20
Baa	3.07	BBB	2.81
Ba	0.79	BB	1.06
B	−2.18	B	−1.74
Caa	−4.51	CCC	−4.46
Ca (convertible)	−6.00		

Source: Zeta Services Inc.

SPLIT RATINGS

The rating agencies don't always agree on a rating, indicating that they are not perfect measures of creditworthiness. If one ignores the recent refinements (i.e., the pluses and minuses and numbers) Moody's and Standard & Poor's disagree on approximately 10–15% of *new bond issues* (Exhibit 25). Ignoring refinements, they disagree on about one quarter of *outstanding bonds* (Exhibit 26) and considering the refinements on about one half (Exhibit 26).

The higher percentage of split ratings on seasoned as compared with new bonds probably reflects the fact that the agencies don't normally change ratings at the same time. Altman (1981) found a surprisingly long median lag of 6 to 7 months between a rating change by one of the majors and the subsequent change by the other. He also found that S&P was first about half the time and Moody's about half. Duff and Phelps, we might note, claims that they often adjust ratings before either of the two majors.

Split ratings on new issues could occur for any of three reasons. First, the agencies could have somewhat different standards of creditworthiness for a rating. One agency might tend consistently to rate somewhat higher than the others. For instance, Fitch is often viewed as tending to rate issues higher than the others. On the other hand, McCarthy, Crisanti, and Maffei report that their ratings have tended to be more conservative. However, a study of Exhibits 25 and 26 indicates that when Moody's and S&P disagree, each is the higher about half the time.

Second, split ratings could occur because the rating agencies consider somewhat different factors or weigh them differently in deciding on a rating. This possibility has been examined for Moody's and S&P by Ederington (1986). He finds no significant differences in the weights attached to nine public financial accounting variables.

Third, split ratings could occur because (as mentioned earlier) there are random variations in judgment because of the highly subjective nature of the rating process. As a result a slightly different rating committee at the same agency could be just as likely to rate the issue differently as another agency.

EXHIBIT 25 DISTRIBUTION OF INDUSTRIAL NEW ISSUES (1975–1980) BY RATING

MOODY'S RATING	STANDARD AND POOR'S RATING					
	AAA	AA	A	BBB	BB	B
Aaa	31	1				
Aa	3	65	12			
A		14	154	7		
Baa			10	38	6	
Ba				1	35	7
B					6	104

Source: L. Ederington (1986).

The Ederington study (1986) concluded that these random differences in judgment are the cause of most split ratings. Officials at Moody's have expressed disagreement with the implication that a different rating committee at Moody's could issue a different rating, although neither they nor officials at S&P have offered any opinions on the reasons for split ratings.

RATINGS AND YIELDS

The impact of a bond's rating on its market interest rate is a topic of importance that has attracted considerable research. Because there is no reason to expect issuers to pay for ratings unless the ratings influence the yield at which the issue can be sold, one would expect ratings to have some impact on yields. Because the rating fees are usually less than $.02 for every $100.00 of face value, the impact need only be very slight to justify the rating fee.

THE HISTORICAL RECORD. As illustrated in Exhibit 13, ***bond yields*** are certainly related to the issues' ratings. In other words, the average yield on Baa rated bonds has exceeded the average yield on A rated bonds—all other things equal.

The ***yield spread*** between the average rate on Baa rated industrial bonds and on Aaa rated industrial bonds is plotted in Exhibit 27. As indicated, this yield spread has varied widely over time. Throughout 1978, the spread never exceeded 100 basis points, but in July of 1982 it approached 300 basis points.

Those who have observed these spreads over long periods of time have noticed two basic patterns. First, the spreads tend to be larger when rates in general are high. Note, for instance, the similarity between Exhibits 13 and 27. The models of Bierman and Hass (1975) and Yawitz (1977) provide a possible explanation of this phenomenon. Their models show that in order to obtain the same expected yield after adjusting for differences in risk of default, rates on Baa issues selling near par value should be a linear function of Aaa rates with a

EXHIBIT 26 RATINGS ON OUTSTANDING INDUSTRIAL BOND DECEMBER 31, 1982[a]

MOODY'S RATING	STANDARD AND POOR'S RATING																	
	AAA	AA+	AA	AA−	A+	A	A−	BBB+	BBB	BBB−	BB+	BB	BB−	B+	B	B−	CCC	CC & Below
Aaa	18	3																
Aa1	2	3	7	0														
Aa2		1	25	3	1													
Aa3		1	7	8	7	1												
A1			1	6	13	8	0											
A2			1	4	9	30	6	2										
A3			1		0	12	5	7	5	2								
Baa1						3	5	5	4	0								
Baa2						4	5	9	10	3	1							
Baa3								5	9	9	3	3						
Ba1								1		4	2	1	2	1				
Ba2									3	2	3	1	4	4	2			
Ba3									1		3	1	3	3	2			
B1												1	1	3	6	1		
B2													1	5	8	4		
B3													2	4	9	12		
Caa																		
															1	1	5	2
Ca																		2

[a] Each observation represents a firm-rating combination. Multiple issues of a single firm with the same rating are counted only once. If, however, a company has both subordinated and unsubordinated debt, their ratings will differ and both are included. Companies whose debt is not rated by one or both agencies (64) are not included.

Source: L. Ederington, "Why Split Ratings Occur," unpublished working paper, School of Business Washington University, February 1984.

EXHIBIT 27 MOODY'S INDUSTRIAL BOND YIELDS (Baa-Aaa) 1975–1984

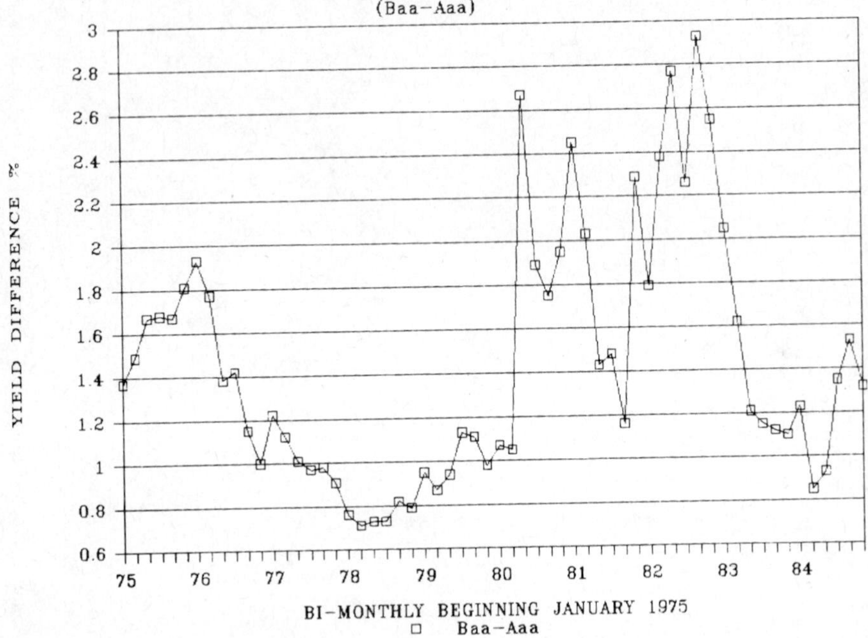

Source: Moody's Bond Record, various issues.

slope greater than one. The slope should equal the ratio of one minus the probability of default on the Aaa issue over one minus the probability of default on the Baa issue. In other words, if Aaa rates rise by 100 basis points, Baa rates should rise somewhat more.

Second, spreads between low and high rated bonds usually increase in recessions and fall in expansions. Note in Exhibit 23 that the yield spread peaked in the 1975 recession, again in the 1980 recession, and finally in the 1981–1982 recession. Van Horne (1984) offers two explanations for this phenomenon. First, the rating agencies contend that ratings represent relative, not absolute, default risks and are intended to be good over an entire business cycle (Standard & Poor's *Credit Overview: Industrial Ratings,* 1984, p. 12). The raters do not automatically lower all ratings in a recession (although there is some evidence that downgradings are more common than upgradings). Consequently, a given rating such as "A" may represent a greater default risk in a recession than in a boom. Second, investors may become more concerned with safety in recessionary periods. In other words, even if there is no change over time in the estimated likelihoods of default on two securities, investors will tend to prefer the higher rated security in recessionary periods.

Studies by Jaffe (1975) and Kidwell and Trzcinka (1979) support the observation that spreads tend to increase in recessions. They find that these spreads are correlated with measures of economic performance such as the employment rate. Most significantly they also find that these spreads are even more closely correlated with the ***index of consumer sentiment,*** which is viewed as an index of investor pessimism or optimism. Even if the actual level of economic activity is unchanged, spreads appear to widen when investors are pessimistic. The implication is that investors' evaluations of or attitudes toward risk vary over time and impact on relative yields.

MARKET REACTIONS TO CHANGES IN RATINGS. The fact that yields on low rated issues exceed those on higher rated issues does not, of course, mean that the ratings themselves are the cause. Yields may reflect investors' own analyses of the issues' creditworthiness—evaluations that happen to agree with the rating agencies in most cases. One way to determine whether ratings affect or merely reflect relative interest rates is to examine the market's reaction to a rating change on an outstanding issue. If investors base their evaluation of creditworthiness largely on ratings, then when a rating is lowered, the price of that issue should fall (or its market yield should rise). The opposite should occur if the rating is raised. If investors form their own opinions, little reaction should be observed. If, moreover, investors tend to revise their evaluations more promptly than the rating agencies, then market prices and yields will tend to lead rather than follow rating changes.

Early studies by Katz (1974) and Grier and Katz (1976) concluded that the market tended to adjust after the rating change, suggesting that the market does rely on the rating agencies or that ratings do affect yields. However, Hettenhouse and Sartoris (1976) reached the opposite conclusion as did Weinstein (1977) in one of the more careful studies of this question. The reaction of the issuer's common stock to a rerating has also been examined and again the results are mixed. Pinches and Singleton (1978) find no stock market reaction, but Griffin and Sanvicente (1982) and Glascock et al. (1985) do find a reaction. Both studies find some evidence of a *stock market reaction* prior *to the rating change,* that is, some evidence that the market tends to anticipate at least some rating changes.

As noted earlier, many of S&P's rating changes in recent years have been preceded by a CreditWatch listing in which the probable direction of the rating change is indicated. Reactions to such listings have been analyzed by Cook (1983) and Wansley and Clauretie (1985). Cook finds little equity market reaction to the CreditWatch listing. Wansley and Clauretie study both the equity and bond market reactions to the CreditWatch listing. They also examine market reactions to rating changes—both those preceded by a CreditWatch listing and those never listed. For the equity market they find that the market tends to anticipate most CreditWatch listings and most rating changes. Nonetheless, there is some evidence of a market reaction to the listing announcement. They find no stock market reaction to *rating change announcements* for either listed or nonlisted firms. They find that the bond market tends to adjust before and not after rating downgradings that are not preceded by a listing.

When the downgrading is preceded by a CreditWatch listing, there is some evidence of a bond market reaction to the listing announcement in the case of industrial issues but no such evidence in the case of utility issues.

As discussed in Ederington et al. (1984) there are several possible reasons for the inconclusive nature of these studies. First, with the exception of Glascock et al. (1985) and Wansley and Clauretie (1985), all examine end of the month prices—not prices immediately before and after the rating change. Second, all examine a rating change by either S&P *or* Moody's. It is unclear whether the other agency changed its rating earlier, later, or not at all. Third, the studies examine only rating changes. Changes may be based less on inside information than are new issue ratings and are only a fraction of the universe of ratings. Fourth, if rating changes materially affect yields, then there is an incentive for bond traders to forecast these changes and trade accordingly, which would lead to a yield adjustment prior to the rating change. Such traders are not forming their own independent evaluation of an issue's creditworthiness, however, but are merely trying to mimic the ratings.

CROSS-SECTIONAL STUDIES. The question of the impact of ratings on relative interest rates can also be investigated by analyzing the determinants of *interest rate differences* at a point in time. The question once again is whether ratings have an independent influence on yields. Both ratings and yields may be based on the firm's publicized income and balance sheet figures—figures that are readily available to any investor. If, however, we observe differences in the yields to maturity on bonds of two firms with similar financial figures but different ratings, it will be clear that ratings influence yields independently.

The first studies along these lines were those of Fisher (1959) and West (1970). Fisher explored the relationship between cross-sectional panels of yields in various years and such accounting information as leverage and the variation in earnings. Although Fisher did not examine the impact of ratings on yields, West did regress Fisher's residuals on dummy variables for ratings. Although little pattern was observed in the regressions for the early years (1927, 1932, and 1937), West found that bonds rated Baa or lower had yields higher than predicted by Fisher's model in 1949 and 1953. He attributed this to regulations introduced in the 1930s and 1940s requiring that bonds rated Baa or below be carried on banks' books at market value.

More recently, Ederington et al. (1984) examined the relationship between yields on various industrial bonds and both ratings (Moody's and S&Ps) and available accounting measures of creditworthiness: **leverage, interest coverage,** the **variability of coverage,** and **firm size;** as well as a variable to represent whether or not the issue is **subordinated.** If the market bases its evaluations of creditworthiness entirely on ratings, then the accounting variables should have no incremental explanatory power for yield differentials. In other words, if the accounting variables are added to an equation that already includes ratings, the expanded equation should have no more explanatory power than the original. If, on the other hand, market participants form their own independent evaluations of creditworthiness, which ratings reflect but do not affect, then ratings will have no incremental explanatory power in an equation that already includes the accounting variables. Ederington, Yawitz, and Roberts find that ratings and accounting variables individually explain yield differences about equally well and that each has incremental explanatory power when added to the other's equation. The implication is that the market pays attention to ratings but also forms its own evaluation. If two firms have similar accounting numbers but one's debt is rated higher, that firm's debt will normally sell at a lower yield. If two firms are rated equally, but one has better numbers, that firm's debt will normally sell at a lower yield.

Ederington, Yawitz, and Roberts (1984) find no statistical difference in the market's reaction to Moody's ratings versus S&Ps. This result is also obtained by Billingsley et al. (1984) who only compare the impact of the two agencies' ratings—not the ratings and accounting information. They also find that on split ratings the market yields tend to be closer to those of bonds with the lower of the two ratings.

In summary, evidence to date seems to indicate that Moody's and S&P's ratings do impact on relative yields. The magnitude of their independent impact is less clear, and whether ratings of the other three rating agencies also influence relative yields is unclear.

REFERENCES

Altman, E.I., "Financial Ratios, Discriminant Analysis and the Prediction of Corporate Bankruptcy," *Journal of Finance.* 23, No. 4, (1968): 589–609.

Altman, E., Avery, R., Eisenbeis, R., and Sinkey, J., "The Application of Statistical Classification Methods to Bond Quality Ratings," in *Application of Classification Techniques in Business, Banking and Finance,* Westport, CT: JAI Press, 1981.

Altman, E., Haldeman, R., and Narayanan, P., "ZETA Analysis: A New Model to Identify Bankruptcy Risk of Corporations," *Journal of Banking and Finance,* 1, (1977): 29–54.

Altman, E., and Katz, S., "An Analysis of Bond Ratings in the Electric Public Utility Industry," proceedings of the *Conference on Topical Research in Accounting,* G. Sorter and M. Schiff (eds.), Ross Institute, New York University, 1976, pp. 205–239.

Altman, E., and Nammacher, S. "High Yield Fixed-Income Debt Default Experience," Morgan Stanley & Co., Incorporated, Fixed Income Division, March 1985.

Ang, J., and Patel, K., "Bond Rating Methods: Comparison and Validation," *Journal of Finance,* 30 (1975): 631–640.

Atkinson, T., *Trends in Corporate Bond Quality,* New York: National Bureau of Economic Research, 1967.

Beaver, W.H., "Financial Ratios as Predictors of Failure," *Empirical Research in Accounting: Selected Studies 1966, Journal of Accounting Research,* Supplement to Vol. 4, 71–111, 1967.

Belkaoui, A., "Industrial Bond Ratings: A New Look," *Financial Management,* 9 (Autumn 1980): 44–50.

Belkaoui, A., *Industrial Bonds and the Rating Process,* Westport, CT: Quorum Books, 1983.

Bhandari, S., Soldofsky, R., and Boe, W., "Bond Quality Rating Changes for Electric Utilities," *Financial Management,* 8 (1979): 74–81.

Bierman, H., and Hass, H., "An Analytical Model of Bond Risk Differentials," *Journal of Financial and Quantitative Analysis,* 10 (December 1975): 757–773.

Billingsley, R., Lamy, R., Marr, M., and Thompson, G., "The Economic Impact of Split Ratings on Bond Reoffering Yields," unpublished working paper, Virginia Polytechnic Institute and State University, 1984.

Clayton, R., and Beranek, W., "Disassociations and Legal Combinations," unpublished working paper, July 1984.

Cook, T., "Common Stock Returns and Potential Bond Rating Changes: An Analysis of Standard and Poor's CreditWatch," paper presented at 1983 meetings of Financial Management Association.

CreditWeek, Standard & Poor's Corporation, various issues.

Ederington, L., "Classification Models and Bond Ratings," *The Financial Review,* 20 (November 1985).

Ederington, L., "Why Split Ratings Occur," Financial Management, 15 (Spring 1986): 37–47.

Ederington, L., Yawitz, J., and Roberts, B., "The Informational Content of Bond Ratings," NBER Working Paper #1323, *National Bureau of Economic Research,* 1984.

Fisher, L., "Determinants of Risk Premiums on Corporate Bonds," *Journal of Political Economy,* 67 (1959): 217–230.

Glascock, J., Davidson, W., and Henderson, G., "Announcement Effects of Moody's Bond Rating Changes on Equity Returns," unpublished working paper, Louisiana Tech University, January 1985.

Grier, P., and Katz, S., "The Differential Effects of Bond Rating Changes Among Industrial and Public Utility Bonds by Maturity," *Journal of Business,* 49 (1976): 65–78.

Griffin, P.A., and Sanvicente, A.Z., "Common Stock Returns and Rating Change: A Methodological Comparison," *Journal of Finance* (March 1982: 103–120.

Hettenhouse, G., and Sartoris, W., "An Analysis of the Information Value of Bond Rating Changes," *Quarterly Review of Economics and Business,* 16 (1976): 65–78.

Hickman, W.B., *Corporate Bond Quality and Investor Experience,* New York: National Bureau of Economic Research, 1958.

Horrigan, J.O., "The Determination of Long-Term Credit Sharing with Financial Ratios," *Journal of Accounting Research,* 4 (Supplement, 1966): 44–62.

Jackson, J., and Boyd, J., "Model Specification in the Statistical Analysis of Bond Ratings," unpublished working paper, Louisiana Tech University, 1984.

Jaffe, D., "Cyclical Variations in the Risk Structure of Interest Rates." *Journal of Monetary Economics,* 1 (July 1975): 309–325.

Kaplan, R., Urwitz, G., "Statistical Models of Bond Ratings: A Methodological Inquiry," *Journal of Business,* 52, No. 2, (1979): 231–1261.

Katz, S., "The Price Adjustment Process of Bonds to Rating Reclassifications: A Test of Bond Market Efficiency," *Journal of Finance,* 29 (1974): 551–559.

Kidwell, D., and Trzcinka, C., "The Risk Structure of Interest Rates and the Penn Central Crisis," *Journal of Finance,* 34 (1979: 751–760.

Martin, L., and Henderson, G., Jr., "On Bond Ratings and Pension Obligations: A Note," *Journal of Financial and Quantitative Analysis,* 18 (December 1983): 463–470.

Martin, L., Henderson, G., Perry, L., Cronan, T., "Bond Ratings: Predictions Using Rating Agency Criteria," Department of Finance Working Paper 1984/85-3, Arizona State University.

Moody's *Bond Survey,* Moody's Investors Service, various issues.

Peavy, J., "The Classification of Bank Holding Company Bond Ratings," *Review of Business and Economic Research,* 15 (Fall 1980): 18–28.

Peavy, J., III and Scott, J., "The AT&T Divestiture: Effect of Rating Changes on Bond Returns," unpublished working paper, December 1984.

Perry, L., Henderson, G., and Cronan, T., "Multivariate Analysis of Corporate Bond Ratings and Industry Classifications," *The Journal of Financial Research,* 7 (Spring 1984): 27–36.

Pinches, G., and Mingo, K., "A Multivariate Analysis of Industrial Bond Ratings," *Journal of Finance,* 28 (March 1973): 1–18.

Pinches, G., and Mingo, K., "A Note on the Role of Subordination in Determining Industrial Bond Ratings," *Journal of Finance,* 30 (March 1975): 201–206.

Pinches, G., and Singleton, C., "The Adjustment of Stock Prices to Bond Rating Changes," *Journal of Finance,* (March 1978): 29–43.

Pinches, G., Singleton, C., and Jahankhani, A., "Fixed Coverage as a Determinant of Electric Utility Bond Ratings," *Financial Management,* 7 (1978): 45–55.

Pogue, T., and Soldofsky, R., "That's in a Bond Rating," *Journal of Financial and Quantitative Analysis,* 4 (June 1969): 201–228.

Standard and Poor's *Credit Overview: Corporate and International Ratings,* New York: Standard and Poor's Corporation, 1983.

Standard & Poor's *Credit Overview: Industrial Ratings,* New York: Standard and Poor's Corporation, 1984.

Standard and Poor's *Credit Overview: International,* New York: Standard and Poor's Corporation, 1984.

Standard and Poor's Corporation, *Standard and Poor's Rating Guide,* New York: McGraw-Hill, 1979.

Van Horne, J. *Financial Market Rates and Flows,* 2nd ed., Englewood Cliffs, NJ: Prentice-Hall, 1984.

Wansley, J., and Clauretic, T., "The Impact of CreditWatch Placement on Equity Returns and Bond Prices," *Journal of Financial Research,* 8 (Spring 1985): 31–42.

Weinstein, M., "The Effect of a Rating Change Announcement on Bond Price," *Journal of Financial Economics,* 5 (1977): 329–350.

West, R., "An Alternative Approach to Predicting Corporate Bond Ratings," *Journal of Accounting Research,* 7 (Spring 1970): 118–127.

West, R., "Bond Ratings, Bond Yields, and Financial Regulation: Some Findings," *Journal of Law and Economics,* 16 (1973): 159–168.

Yawitz, J., "An Analytical Model of Interest Rate Differentials and Different Default Recoveries," *Journal of Financial and Quantitative Analysis,* 15, (1977): 481–490.

24

MICROCOMPUTERS AND INVESTING

CONTENTS

24

MICROCOMPUTERS AND INVESTING

Keith V. Smith

INTRODUCTION

Most of us are aware that computers pay an increasing role in our lives. Computer applications became available less than three decades ago, but with mainframe computing equipment available almost exclusively to large organizations. Computer technology has since progressed from vacuum tubes to transistors to integrated circuits. Those technological developments have made computational power available to smaller business firms and organizations, and ultimately to individuals and families in our society. Whether for play or work, computers certainly are here to stay—the major question now being one of just how far and how fast?

Personal computers, the most recent development, have been available for less than a decade. But now the trend is explosive as well-known firms such as Apple, ATT, Commodore, IBM, Tandy—plus others less well known or already forgotten—have entered the competition. The original distribution channel for personal computers was mail-order advertisement, but that has given way to national retail distribution by firms such as Radio Shack, Computerland, and so on.

Usage of computers in investing parallels these general trends. Although mainframe computers have long been used by banks, insurance companies, brokerage firms, and others in the investments business, it is the recent development and popularity of personal computers that now enables all individuals and institutions to use computers in managing investment portfolios.

In recent years there has been a growing interest in the applications of microcomputers and associated software to the field of investments. A ***microcomputer*** is defined here as a stand-alone personal computer hardware system that can be used either at home or at work. In certain instances, a microcomputer can be utilized as a terminal into a larger mainframe computer system. ***Software*** is defined here as the computer program(s) used to control a microcomputer. Prices of microcomputers in 1985 ranged from a few hundred dollars to several thousand dollars. In turn, prices of available investment software ranged from under $30 to several hundred dollars, and even higher for certain of the on-line computer information services.

This section is an overview of how microcomputers can be used in the process of investing. Potential applications of microcomputers in investing range from word processing, to routine record keeping, to information acquisition and processing, and to complex uses of optimization and simulation models. Sensitivity analysis and other repetitive calculations will be shown to be a primary advantage of microcomputers. Although focus and illustration in this section will be on microcomputer usage by an individual, the concepts and applications are just as apropos for institutional investors.

The next part of the section includes an overview of the investments management process. It also includes a family scenario for illustrating how microcomputers can be used in investing. Various applications of microcomputers will be discussed for each step of the investments management process. This is followed by a checklist for investors in evaluating and selecting particular hardware and software.

THE INVESTMENTS MANAGEMENT PROCESS

In order to discuss coherently various applications of microcomputers, a schematic overview of the investment management process is presented in Exhibit 1. Each block of the overview is a specific activity involving the acquisition or usage of information. Arrows represent a natural flow of activity within the process of investments management.

Financial planning is the starting point of the investments management process. Acquisition of information is followed by a series of different ways to process that information. All of this comes together in decision making for the investor's portfolio. Evaluation of achieved portfolio results helps the investor to see whether financial goals are achieved, and also as an input to further financial planning. In other words, the process of investments management is seen to be ongoing.

To help illustrate various ways in which microcomputers can be used by an individual or family unit in the investments process, we consider the hypothetical case of Stanley and Patricia Bennett, both aged 51. The Bennetts live in southern California and have two grown boys, both married and living elsewhere. Stanley and Patricia are well educated, and both have had successful professional careers. Five years ago, Stanley left his sales engineering job and, together with three professional colleagues, started a small business in aerospace repair technology.

The new business has done far better than anyone ever imagined, and future prospects for the partnership are excellent. With college expenses for their boys behind them, the Bennetts find themselves in a comfortable financial position.

EXHIBIT 1 OVERVIEW OF THE INVESTMENTS MANAGEMENT PROCESS

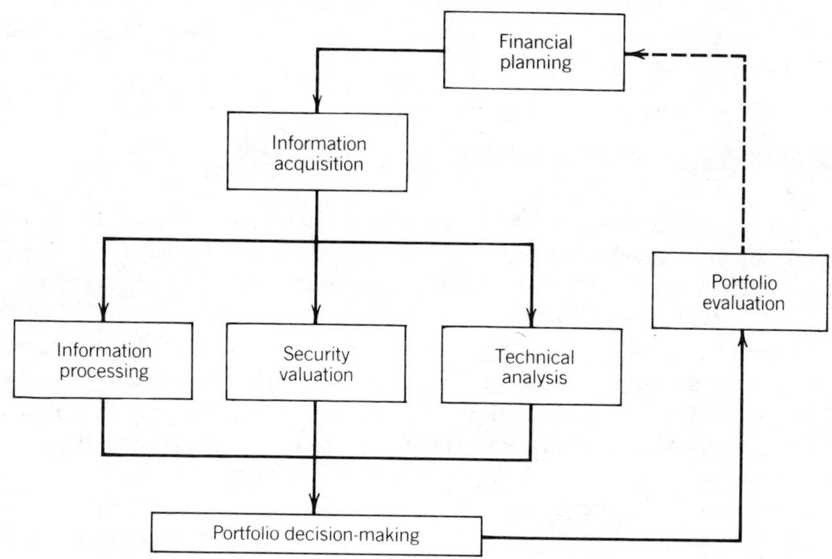

Their beachside condominium has appreciated rapidly in recent years. They have a very manageable mortgage, and they find that they can live comfortably on their joint income. Unfortunately, though, the Bennetts have no retirement program, apart from Social Security, their relatively new IRA and Keogh accounts, and the several hundred dollars that they are able to save each month toward retirement. At this point, the Bennetts' investment portfolio consists of a well-regarded money market fund and a portfolio of high quality common stocks.

Two years ago Stanley purchased a personal computer. His hardware system includes a microprocessor and monitor, two disk drives, a printer, and a modem. His software includes word processing, spreadsheet, and a number of other programs that he hopes will help in the family's financial planning and investments management. As part of that new interest, Stanley recently joined a trade association, the **American Association of Microcomputer Investors (AAMI).** For the $49 annual fee, he receives a bimonthly publication, *The AAMI Journal,* which, in addition to general articles, reviews commercial software packages, also indicates the availability of noncommercial (i.e., so-called public domain) programs for possible use in investments management. AAMI also makes available to members a detailed listing of software for IBM and other personal computers. For an alternative listing of particular suppliers and their products, see Stevenson (1983).

Stanley also has learned to program in BASIC so that he can develop some routines himself. In particular, he plans to expand some of the programs that he found in Riley and Montgomery (1982) and Sparks (1983). In so doing, he discovered that discussion of "microcomputers and investing" is beginning to appear in investments textbooks such as Gitman and Joehnk (1984). Apparently the academic community (see, e.g., Atkinson and Malone, 1983), is well aware of how microcomputers can also be used to help teach investments and corporate finance.

APPLICATIONS IN FINANCIAL PLANNING

The process of investments management logically begins with an assessment of where you are and what you want to accomplish. ***Financial planning*** for an individual or family unit is an activity consisting of the following steps: (1) assessment of current financial status; (2) projection of likely cash flows over a future time period, typically on an annual basis; (3) specification of future financial goals for the family unit; and (4) determination of what investment results are necessary in order for those goals to be accomplished. In this part, we illustrate those steps for the Bennetts, and thereby show how microcomputers can be helpful at the beginning of the investments management process.

Preparation of financial statements is a logical starting point in the planning of any individual or organization. The most important financial statements are the balance sheet (current point in time) and income statement (latest period of time). Although such statements can be prepared manually by an individual or family, it is not an easy task. The Bennetts admit, in fact, that they have never prepared financial statements—except at the time they began their business and were so required by their commercial bank. Fortunately, it is now possible to use commercially available software packages to do this on a microcomputer.

To illustrate, the Bennetts purchased a $100 software package, *Your Personal Net Worth* (Scarborough Systems, Inc.), to help them with their family financial planning. Using that software, Exhibit 2 presents the Bennetts' bal-

EXHIBIT 2 BENNETTS' HOUSEHOLD (1984) STATEMENT OF NET WORTH

Assets			Liabilities		
A001	Cash	305.00	L007	Automobile loan	5480.00
A002	Stanley's checking	901.00	L032	Mortgage loan	79850.00
A003	Patricia's checking	873.00	L045	Payable-American Express	1678.00
A006	Credit union	18015.00	L050	Payable-Mastercard	105.00
A010	Money market fund	52019.00	L070	Payable-Sears card	95.00
A035	Business interests	20100.00	L075	Payable-VISA	326.00
A040	Automobiles	14200.00			
A060	Condominium	220000.00			
A075	Furniture & possessions	20300.00			
A095	IRA and Keogh accounts	10480.00			
A115	Common stocks	79838.00			
				Net worth	343497.00
	Total	431031.00		Total	431031.00

ance sheet at the end of calendar year 1984. They had total assets of $431,000 as compared with total liabilities of $87,500—and hence a family equity of $343,500. The Bennetts' income statement for 1984 is shown in Exhibit 3. Their annual total income of $79,240 exceeded their expenses, and they were able to add $12,000 to savings, as well as $8,200 to their retirement accounts. The Bennetts also plan to use the same software in doing their family budgeting. At the end of each month, Patricia will enter all financial transactions, they will be posted to appropriate income and expense accounts, and a comparison of actual versus budget will automatically be generated.

Because a major focus of this section will be on common stocks, it is appropriate to include here a listing of the Bennetts' common stock portfolio at year-end. As seen in Exhibit 4, they currently own eight common stocks with an aggregate market value of $79,838.

The mathematics of finance (i.e., present value techniques) is used to determine what investment results are needed in order for an individual or family to accomplish certain expressed goals. Stanley recently purchased a $9 software

EXHIBIT 3 BENNETTS' HOUSEHOLD (1984) INCOME STATEMENT (JAN–DEC)

Account Description	Actual	% Increase
Income		
I025 Dividend income	3591.00	4.53
I045 Interest income	6080.00	7.67
I055 Misc. other income	2369.00	2.99
I075 Stanley's earnings	42000.00	53.00
I077 Patricia's earnings	25200.00	31.80
Total income	79240.00	100.00
Expenses		
E020 Auto, gas, and repairs	1810.00	2.28
E027 Auto loan payments	2400.00	3.03
E035 Clothing	2280.00	2.88
E045 Contributions	2750.00	3.47
E055 Entertainment	1032.00	1.30
E065 Groceries	4118.00	5.20
E080 Insurance premiums	1000.00	1.26
E102 Mortgage loan payments	9600.00	12.12
E110 Medical and dental	1200.00	1.51
E115 Miscellaneous	1014.00	1.28
E125 Recreation	1986.00	2.51
E135 Federal taxes	21030.00	26.54
E150 State and local taxes	3005.00	3.79
E152 IRA and Keogh contributions	8200.00	10.35
E160 Travel/vacation	2140.00	2.70
E165 Utility bills	3675.00	4.64
Total expenses	67240.00	84.86
Excess income	12000.00	15.14

EXHIBIT 4 COMMON STOCK PORTFOLIO STANLEY AND PATRICIA BENNETT DECEMBER 31, 1984

Common Stock	Shares	Price	Value
American Home Products	200	$ 50.750	$10,150
Barnett Banks of Florida	200	42.750	8,550
Delta Airlines	300	38.750	11,625
IBM	100	125.375	12,538
Kellogg	200	36.750	7,350
McDonald's	200	52.625	10,525
Schlumberger	200	41.125	8,225
U.S. Tobacco	300	36.250	10,875
Total			$79,838

package *Public Domain Disk #6* (American Association of Microcomputer Investors) that includes a series of programs for doing compounding (future values) and discounting (present values). The programs available in that software are listed at the top of Exhibit 5.

To illustrate one calculation, the Bennetts are interested in knowing how much their credit union account will grow in 5 years. Their credit union currently pays 9.5%, compounded monthly. Using the third program, we see at the bottom of Exhibit 5 that their $18,015 will grow to $28,914 after 60 months.

Compounding and discounting single sums and annuities are all special cases of the following relationship:

$$I\ FS(t_1,k_1) + D\ FA(t_1,k_1) = W\ PA(t_2,k_2) + E\ PS(t_2,k_2)$$

where
I = investment funds today
D = annual addition to investment funds until retirement
t_1 = number of years until retirement
k_1 = after-tax rate of return until retirement
E = amount of estate at death
t_2 = number of years after retirement until death
k_2 = after-tax rate of return after retirement
$FS(t_1,k_1)$ = future value of a single sum after t_1 years while earning at rate k_1
$FS(\ )$ = future value of an annuity
$PS(\ )$ = present value of a single sum
$PA(\ )$ = present value of an annuity

Stanley recently wrote a computer program that performs such calculations. A variety of scenarios can be handled. For example, the Bennetts are interested in the likely size of their estate, which will be left to their children if their plans materialize. Stanley and Patricia currently have investment funds of I = $140,000. They plan to add D = $12,000 to the portfolio every year during each

EXHIBIT 5 ILLUSTRATION OF INVESTMENT COMPOUNDING STANLEY AND PATRICIA BENNETT

```
ENTER THE NUMBER OF ONE OF THE FOLLOWING PROGRAMS:

  1 - PRESENT VALUE OF A FUTURE SUM
  2 - SIMPLE INTEREST FOR DAYS
  3 - FUTURE VALUE OF A PRESENT SUM
  4 - AMORTIZATION SCHEDULE
  5 - INTEREST RATE — COMPOUND INTEREST
  6 - INTEREST RATE — INSTALLMENT LOAN
  7 - DAYS BETWEEN DATES
  8 - TERM OF AN INSTALLMENT LOAN
  9 - PRESENT VALUE OF A SERIES OF PAYMENTS
 10 - REAL ESTATE CAPITAL INVESTMENT
 11 - NOMINAL & EFFECTIVE INTEREST RATES
 12 - INTERNAL RATE OF RETURN
 13 - FUTURE VALUE OF REGULAR DEPOSITS
 14 - REGULAR DEPOSITS FOR FUTURE VALUE
 15 - DEPRECIATION — AMOUNT
 16 - DEPRECIATION — RATE
 17 - DEPRECIATION — SALVAGE VALUE
 18 - DEPRECIATION — SCHEDULE
 19 - BOND — PRESENT VALUE
 20 - BOND — YIELD TO MATURITY

TYPE PROGRAM NUMBER (OR SPACE BAR TO EXIT) AND PRESS 'ENTER'?

---

ENTER PRESENT SUM, IN DOLLARS:? 18015

ENTER ANNUAL INTEREST RATE, IN % ? 9.5

ENTER NUMBER OF PERIODS IN ONE YEAR ? 12

ENTER NUMBER OF PERIODS TO MATURITY ? 60

FOR A PRESENT SUM OF $ 18015 AT AN ANNUAL
INTEREST RATE OF 9.5 %, FOR 60 PERIODS, WHERE
THERE ARE 12 PERIODS PER YEAR:

THE FUTURE VALUE IS $ 28914.28
THE INCREASE IS $ 10899.28 , OR 60.50113 %

PRESS ENTER TO RETURN TO MENU.?
```

of the next $t_1 = 14$ years until retirement while they earn $k_1 = 6\%$ after-tax. During their $t_2 = 20$ years of retirement, the Bennetts plan to withdraw $W =$ \$30,000 per year while their portfolio earns at an after-tax rate of $k_2 = 8\%$. Exhibit 6 shows a single run of Stanley's program which answers that question—their estate is estimated to be \$1,277,860. Also included is a sensitivity analysis for selected values of annual additions D now and annual withdrawals W later. This illustrates a major advantage of a microcomputer—namely, the ability to perform repetitive calculations and thereby provide considerably more information to the investor at a considerably faster rate.

APPLICATIONS IN INFORMATION ACQUISITION

Once financial planning has been done, one can begin to gather information for the investment decisions that must be made to implement those plans. ***Information acquisition*** has to do with obtaining economic, financial, and investment information that hopefully will help the investor in making sound

EXHIBIT 6 LIKELY SIZE OF FAMILY ESTATE STANLEY AND PATRICIA BENNETT

```
Enter the desired selection:

  1) Amount of estate at death
  2) Annual withdrawal after retirement
  3) Annual addition to funds until retirement
  4) Funds invested today
  5) End program

Enter your selection (1-5): ? 1

Enter the percent before retirement (10% = 10)  =   > ? 6
Enter the percent after retirement (5% = 5) ====   > ? 8
Enter the years to retirement (i.e., 30)  ======   > ? 14
Enter the years until estimated death (i.e., 40) ==  > ? 20
Enter the annual withdrawal amount (i.e., 40000)    > ? 30000
Enter the amount invested today (i.e., 100000) ==   > ? 140000
Enter the annual deposit until retirement  ====   > ? 12000
```

ANNUAL DEPOSIT		ANNUAL WITHDRAWAL 10,000	20,000	30,000	40,000	50,000
\$ 8,000	!	\$1,801,300	\$1,343,680	\$ 886,058	\$ 428,438	\$−29,182
10,000	!	1,997,200	1,539,580	1,081,960	624,339	166,719
12,000	!	2,193,100	1,735,480	1,277,860	820,239	362,619
14,000	!	2,389,000	1,931,380	1,473,760	1,016,140	558,520
16,000	!	2,584,900	2,127,280	1,669,660	1,212,040	754,420

decisions. Microcomputers are a great help in the acquisition step because a large amount of useful information can be examined and processed in an efficient manner. Two distinct procedures are available. First, the investor examines an extensive data base for those firms that satisfy certain investment criteria. Second, an investor seeks selected investment information for a designated set of firms. Typically, the two procedures occur in that order—and that is how we will review some alternatives available to the Bennetts.

Investors usually have at least some idea of what characteristics they desire in their investments. ***Screening*** is a process of searching for those particular investments among a designated universe that satisfy certain specified characteristics. A number of screening programs are available commercially. The typical configuration includes a program disk that controls the information processing, and a periodic (e.g., monthly) data disk of considerable financial and investment information for a large number of common stocks.

Using his $500 word-processing package ***Wordstar*** (MicroPro International), and information from AAMI, Stanley has inquired about available screening software from a large number of software vendors. Many of these vendors have responded to his inquiry, and several have sent demonstration disks for him to try. Stanley found that one of the easiest to use was the $3,000 annual **"Micro/Search"** (FINSTAT, a division of Shearson/American Express, Inc.). It is compatible with his computer system, processes rapidly, and includes a wide array of useful information for screening common stocks. Unfortunately, the annual cost is high for them, so careful consideration of its purchase will be necessary.

Among several iterations tried by Stanley, Exhibit 7 illustrates a particular screen that asked for all firms meeting four criteria: (1) price/earnings ratio less than 12, (2) 5-year return-on-equity greater than 16%, (3) interest coverage greater than 4, and (4) dividend yield greater than 5%. As seen, that screen resulted in 14 common stocks, many in the petroleum industry. By design, the firms are ranked on the basis of 5-year return-on-equity.

After reviewing a number of such screens, the Bennetts decided to limit their information acquisition to a finite number of firms. Specifically, they decided on their "approved list" of 30 common stocks shown alphabetically in Exhibit 8. Each common stock is from a different industry. In addition, the eight common stocks currently owned by the Bennetts are part of their approved list. The other 22 stocks are candidates for purchase as additional funds become available for investment, or as revisions to their portfolio seem appropriate.

Once an investor decides on an approved list of investments, the next step is to acquire additional information that will be used in deciding what to buy, what to hold, and what to sell. A microcomputer can help in acquiring additional information from a periodic data base. After subscribing to a less expensive (i.e., $275 annually software package, *Stockpak II,* Standard & Poor's Corporation), the Bennetts have access to monthly data (i.e., a new data disk each month) for 1,500 companies whose common stocks are traded on the New York Stock Exchange, the American Stock Exchange, and on the over-the-

EXHIBIT 7 STANLEY AND PATRICIA BENNETT COMMON STOCK SCREEN

SYMB	NAME	Current P/E	5 Yr Avg Ret On Equity	Pretax Interest Coverage	Yield
SOH	STANDARD OIL CO	7.20	35.70	7.93	5.80
SKB	SMITHKLINE BECKM	8.70	32.20	13.42	5.20
AVP	AVON PRODUCTS	10.70	22.80	6.76	8.50
CBM	CHESEBROUGH-POND	11.60	20.70	5.47	5.10
AMB	AMERICAN BRANDS	8.90	19.70	7.61	5.80
ARC	ATLANTIC RICHFIELD	9.80	19.60	4.86	6.40
BP	BRITISH PETROLEUM	6.50	19.30	5.32	8.40
XON	EXXON CORP	6.50	19.20	17.52	7.60
RD	ROYAL DUTCH	5.70	19.10	13.11	5.60
SN	STANDARD OIL CO	7.70	18.40	9.28	5.10
CHV	CHEVRON CORP	7.50	17.20	8.56	7.10
P	PHILLIPS PETROLEUM	7.50	17.20	9.02	5.50
HAL	HALLIBURTON CO	11.00	17.00	5.32	5.60
INI	INTERNORTH INC	6.70	16.80	5.00	6.20
MOB	MOBIL CORP	8.50	16.30	5.28	7.20
	AVERAGE:	8.30	20.75	8.30	6.34
	S&P 400:	11.80	14.30	3.93	3.80

(D)SCENDING SORT ON 5YR ROE

301 ITEMS IN UNIVERSE

VARIABLE	OP	VALUE	# GOOD
P/E	<	12.00	194
5YR ROE	>	16.00	68
Int Cov	>	4.00	56
Yield	>	5.00	15

EXHIBIT 8 APPROVED LIST OF COMMON STOCKS STANLEY AND PATRICIA BENNETT

Symbol	Common Stock	Industry
AA	Alcoa	Metals
AHP	American Home Products	Drugs
AIT	Ameritech	Utilities-communications
ARC	Atlantic Richfield	Oil-integrated domestic
BBF	Barnett Banks	Banks-regional
BA	Boeing	Aerospace
BOR	Borg Warner	Automotive diversified
FNC	Citicorp	Banks-money center
GLW	Corning Glass	Appliance-video
ZB	Crown Zellerbach	Paper products
DH	Dayton Hudson	Merchandising
DAL	Delta Airlines	Air transport
GM	General Motors	Automotive-car
GS	Gillette	Cosmetics
MLHR	Herman Miller	Emerging growth
IBM	International Business Machines	Information processing
K	Kellogg	Food processed
LIT	Litton Industries	Conglomerates
MCD	McDonald's	Restaurants
MMC	Marsh & McLennan	Insurance
MOT	Motorola	Electronics-semiconductors
NLC	Nalco Chemicals	Chemicals-specialty
PEP	Pepsico	Beverages
SLB	Schlumberger	Oil services
SGN	Signal Companies	Pollution control
SNA	Snap-On Tools	Machinery
TXO	Texas Oil & Gas	Natural gas
TL	Time	Media
USG	U.S. Gypsum	Building materials
UBO	U.S. Tobacco	Tobacco

counter markets. Suppose the Bennetts are interested in additional information on Gillette, one of the firms on their approved list. By entering only the ticker symbol for Gillette (i.e., "GS"), relevant information from the October 1984 data base is shown in Exhibit 9. It includes sales, historical and projected earnings, prices and volume data, beta (i.e., systematic risk), dividends, and selected balance sheet information as of the end of June 1984.

Because their computer system includes a modem, the Bennetts have an alternative way of obtaining information on particular firms. Namely, they can subscribe to an **"online" source of information.** One well-known online source is the **Dow Jones News Retrieval** (DJNR) (Dow Jones & Company, Inc.). This information service, which was first offered in 1974, includes business and economic news, money market and foreign exchange trends, industry data, current and historical price quotations for thousands of firms, financial statements, other corporate financial data, and earnings forecasts for the same. In addition, the DJNR service includes the official airline guide, weather reports, cinema

EXHIBIT 9 INFORMATION ON GILLETTE FROM MONTHLY DATA BASE

GS	Lookup Data		October 1984
SP500	YES	PRICE	51.38
SPRANK	A	VOLUME	1.80M
OPTIONS	YES	PRICEQ1	47.88
YREND	DEC	PRICEQ2	46.75
INDGRP	1600	PRICEQ3	51.38
EXCHG	NYS	PRICEQ4	48.63
COMSHRS	30.77M	HIGH	53.63
EPSEST	5.25	LOW	40.88
EPS12	5.02	BETA	0.64
EPS1	4.78		
EPS2	4.45	DIVIDEND	2.44
EPS3	4.11	CHGDIV%	50.00
EPS4	4.11	EXDATE	JUL 26
EPS5	3.67	NET	145.88M
GROWEPS%	6.00	CHGNET%	7.00
		BOOKSHR	22.88
SALES1	2.18B	CASH	293.99M
SALES2	2.24B	ASSETS	1.19B
SALES3	2.33B	LIABS	811.01M
SALES4	2.32B	DEBT	269.03M
SALES5	1.98B	BALSHEET	JUN 84
CHGSALES%	−3.00	FOOTNOTE	NONE

reviews, sports reports, and over 30,000 articles from the *Academic American Encyclopedia.* For further description of DJNR, see Dempsey (1984).

Continuing the family illustration, suppose the Bennetts want additional information on Gillette as a possible addition to their common stock portfolio. Using the DJNR service, they obtain a management discussion (Exhibit 10), historical prices, and volume for the last 2 years (Exhibit 11), and current information from Gillette's most recent financial statements (Exhibit 12). The cost of the DJNR service for such information is simply for connect time, which at the end of 1984 was $2.40 per minute (prime time rate) at a transmission speed of 1200 baud.

APPLICATIONS IN INFORMATION PROCESSING

In addition to the acquisition of information, the investor may be interested in the processing of information as a way of helping to make appropriate investment decisions. ***Information processing*** involves a variety of ways in which basic facts and data are analyzed in order to produce new information that will be helpful to investment decision making. This and the following two parts

EXHIBIT 10 MANAGEMENT DISCUSSION FOR GILLETTE CORPORATION DOW JONES NEWS RETRIEVAL SERVICE

MANAGEMENT DISCUSSION:
(From Annual Report to Shareholders 1983)
Results of Operations

Net sales in 1983 were slightly lower than in 1982. Profit from operations held at the previous year's level. Net income rose, due primarily to a decrease in net interest expense. In 1982, net sales were slightly lower than in the prior year, and although profit from operations held at the 1981 level, net income advanced, due mainly to reduced interest expense and a lower effective income tax rate.

Significant declines in foreign currency exchange rates adversely affected international sales and profits in the comparisons that follow.

Sales: Net sales amounted to $2,183.3 million in 1983, compared with $2,239.0 million and $2,334.4 million in 1982 and 1981, respectively. The net effect of exchange and pricing accounted for all of the sales decline in 1983 and about one-third of the 1982 decline.

Operations outside the United States and Canada accounted for 53% of sales in 1983. Sales of $1,163.5 million for this geographic area were $77.1 million (6%) below the prior year, compared with a decrease of 7% in 1982. Within the United States and Canada, sales rose 2% in 1983, following a level year in 1982.

Sales of blades and razors were down slightly from those of 1982, while sales of toiletries and cosmetics rose modestly. Sales of writing instruments and Braun products declined moderately. Sales of other products were below those of 1982, reflecting the discontinuance of certain minor businesses and decreased sales of lighters. During 1982, sales of blades and razors and toiletries and cosmetics were level, while sales of writing instruments, Braun products and other products decreased.

Cost and Expenses: The Company's cost control and sizable capital spending programs of recent years had a positive effect on operating performance. Product costs, or cost of sales, decreased by 5% in 1983, following a 7% decrease in 1982, and amounted to 42.5% of net sales, down from 43.6% in 1982 and 44.8% in 1981. Operating expenses, excluding amounts spent to promote products, were $560.5 million, a decrease of 4% from 1982. In 1982, such expenses declined 1%. Total product costs and operating expenses, excluding amounts spent to promote products, decreased by 4% in 1983 and 5% in 1982.

---

demonstrate how microcomputers might be helpful to an individual or family investor. In contrast to fundamental and technical analyses of the next two parts, our focus here is on subjective ways in which information can be processed.

A simple approach to information processing is to use a "screening" process, as was just described. The Bennetts might decide, for example, to purchase 100 shares each of the 15 common stocks that resulted from the investment screen shown in Exhibit 7. That would cost them approximately $63,000, a sum somewhat below the current market value of their common stock portfolio (see Exhibit 4). It would, however, represent an almost total revision of their equity holdings, and a revision for which transaction costs (i.e., brokerage commissions and capital gains taxes) might be high.

Alternatively, the Bennetts might decide to process available information to-

EXHIBIT 11 HISTORICAL PRICES AND VOLUME FOR GILLETTE DOW JONES NEWS RETRIEVAL SERVICE

DOW JONES HISTORICAL
STOCK QUOTE REPORTER SERVICE

STOCK GS

1983 MONTHLY SUMMARY

DATE	HIGH	LOW	CLOSE	VOL (100/S)
01/83	48	42 1/2	44 3/4	19299
02/83	46 1/2	42 7/8	46	17152
03/83	51 3/8	44 3/4	51	21323
04/83	51 1/2	45	46 3/8	28820
05/83	47 1/2	41 3/4	42 5/8	31747
06/83	45 3/8	42 1/2	43 3/4	24410
07/83	45	42 1/8	44 1/2	25353
08/83	44 3/8	40 7/8	43	15378
09/83	47 7/8	42 3/4	47 1/4	23513
10/83	51 1/2	47 1/8	49 3/4	30428
11/83	50	46 7/8	48 1/2	19792
12/83	49 7/8	46 1/2	48 5/8	12791

* COMPOSITE QUOTES BEGIN WITH OCTOBER 1981

gs 84 m

DOW JONES HISTORICAL
STOCK QUOTE REPORTER SERVICE

STOCK GS

1984 MONTHLY SUMMARY

DATE	HIGH	LOW	CLOSE	VOL (100/S)
01/84	51 1/4	48	49 1/8	14433
02/84	49 3/8	43 1/2	44 5/8	18890
03/84	48 3/4	44 1/8	47 7/8	14117
04/84	50	45 5/8	49 1/8	16873
05/84	49 1/4	42 5/8	43 1/2	10624
06/84	48	43 1/2	46 3/4	11433
07/84	47 1/2	44	47	11148
08/84	52 7/8	47 1/8	50	29964
09/84	53 5/8	49 1/2	51 3/8	18029
10/84	54 1/4	48 3/8	52	24050
11/84	57 1/2	52 1/4	56 1/2	15822

EXHIBIT 12 COMPARATIVE BALANCE SHEETS FOR GILLETTE CORPORATION DOW JONES NEWS RETRIEVAL SERVICE

BALANCE SHEET ASSETS		
FISCAL YEAR ENDING:	12/31/83	12/31/82
CASH	175,579,000	138,353,000
MRKTABLE SECURITIES	NA	NA
RECEIVABLES	434,427,000	436,193,000
INVENTORIES	391,167,000	416,754,000
RAW MATERIALS	NA	NA
WORK IN PROGRESS	NA	NA
FINISHED GOODS	NA	NA
NOTES RECEIVABLE	NA	NA
OTHER CURRENT ASSETS	62,994,000	62,821,000
TOTAL CURRENT ASSETS	1,064,167,000	1,054,121,000
PROP, PLANT & EQUIP	405,771,000	419,992,000
ACCUMULATED DEP	NA	NA
NET PROP & EQUIP	405,771,000	419,992,000
INVEST & ADV TO SUBS	NA	NA
OTH NON-CUR ASSETS	NA	NA
DEFERRED CHARGES	NA	NA
INTANGIBLES	83,161,000	86,147,000
DEPOSITS, OTH ASSETS	143,045,000	106,970,000
TOTAL ASSETS	1,696,144,000	1,667,230,000

BALANCE SHEET LIABILITIES		
FISCAL YEAR ENDING:	12/31/83	12/31/82
NOTES PAYABLE	138,499,000	140,756,000)
ACCOUNTS PAYABLE	321,081,000	310,985,000
CUR LONG TERM DEBT	NA	NA
CUR PORT CAP LEASES	NA	NA
ACCRUED EXPENSES	NA	NA
INCOME TAXES	47,700,000	56,000,000
OTHER CURRENT LIAB	18,740,000	17,499,000
TOTAL CURRENT LIAB	526,020,000	525,240,000
MORTGAGES	NA	NA
DEFERRED CHARGES/INC	43,300,000	41,200,000
CONVERTIBLE DEBT	NA	NA
LONG TERM DEBT	277,841,000	293,292,000
NON-CUR CAP LEASES	NA	NA
OTHER LONG TERM LIAB	88,740,000	83,179,000
TOTAL LIABILITIES	935,901,000	942,911,000
MINORITY INT (LIAB)	2,816,000	2,886,000
PREFERRED STOCK	NA	NA

PRESS RETURN FOR NEXT PAGE

BALANCE SHEET LIABILITIES		
FISCAL YEAR ENDING:	12/31/83	12/31/82
COMMON STOCK NET	30,522,000	30,239,000
CAPITAL SURPLUS	53,965,000	42,180,000
RETAINED EARNINGS	851,832,000	778,485,000
TREASURY STOCK	NA	NA
OTHER LIABILITIES	−178,892,000	−129,471,000
SHAREHOLDER'S EQUITY	757,427,000	721,433,000
TOT LIAB & NET WORTH	1,696,144,000	1,667,230,000

ward identifying promising additions or changes to their investment portfolio. Their microcomputer would be very helpful in doing this—particularly as a result of their spreadsheet capability. With access to the DJNR service, the Bennetts purchased the $250 **"Dow Jones Spreadsheet Link"** (Dow Jones & Company, Inc.). That particular software is unusually versatile in allowing one to "down-load" data from the DJNR service to a spreadsheet.

Exhibit 13 illustrates a particular **spreadsheet** that Stanley developed for reviewing in more detail the 30 common stocks of their approved list. The spreadsheet is designed using ticker symbols (e.g., "V-AA" for Alcoa) and data item identifiers (e.g., "V-GROWTH" for 5-year compounded earnings growth) will be recognized by the DJNR service. Connect time for gathering the data in

EXHIBIT 13 DOWN-LOADED DATA FROM DOW JONES NEWS RETRIEVAL SERVICE STANLEY AND PATRICIA BENNETT

Ticker Symbol	Common Stock	Growth Rate	Interest Coverage	Return on Equity	Beta Up	Beta Down
V-AA	Alcoa	−17	2.0	5.2	0.34	1.02
V-AHP	Amer Home Prod	15	0.0	30.6	1.15	0.47
V-AIT	Ameritech	NA	7.0	13.2	NA	NA
V-ARC	Arco	−6	8.7	14.3	0.75	1.40
V-BBF	Barnett Banks	24	2.7	18.4	1.18	0.79
V-BA	Boeing	−5	14.1	11.7	1.22	1.38
V-BOR	Borg Warner	7	7.1	12.4	1.22	1.64
V-FNC	Citicorp	14	1.3	16.4	1.01	0.76
V-GLW	Corning Glass	−8	3.2	8.9	1.08	0.88
V-ZB	Crown Zellerb	−13	4.0	9.1	0.70	0.96
V-DH	Dayton Hudson	24	5.9	15.8	1.51	1.97
V-DAL	Delta Airlines	12	3.1	16.7	1.38	1.45
V-GM	General Motors	13	5.4	18.2	1.10	0.87
V-GS	Gillette	9	5.0	19.3	1.02	0.42
V-MLHR	Herman Miller	33	7.5	20.0	0.34	0.79
V-IBM	IBM	23	26.4	23.6	1.13	0.86
V-K	Kellogg	12	63.5	24.8	1.13	NA
V-LIT	Litton Ind	7	20.6	15.6	0.88	1.55
V-MCD	McDonalds	22	6.7	19.5	0.77	0.45
V-MMC	Marsh Mclennan	−5	15.5	20.9	1.12	0.59
V-MOT	Motorola	13	9.8	12.5	1.39	1.59
V-NLC	Nalco Chem	4	28.3	20.3	0.86	1.22
V-PEP	Pepsico	4	3.3	15.8	1.04	0.48
V-SLB	Schlumberger	16	13.0	18.6	0.68	1.64
V-GGN	Signal Cos	NA	NA	NA	NA	NA
V-SNA	Snap On Tools	7	30.7	16.6	1.28	0.76
V-TXO	Texas Oil Gas	40	10.5	23.0	1.34	2.69
T-TL	Time					
V-USG	U.S. Gypsum	2	14.2	10.8	1.21	0.86
V-UBO	U.S. Tobacco	30	30.0	27.2	0.45	0.33

Exhibit 13 was just over 12 minutes—or about 24 seconds per common stock. At relatively little additional cost, the spreadsheet could be expanded to include other financial variables for the same 30 common stocks. Note in Exhibit 13, that for some reason, no data were obtained on that particular run for Time, and no data were available for Signal Companies at that time.

Because of the considerable processing capability of an electronic spreadsheet, it is possible to down-load data from the DJNR service—and perform additional calculations as well. Exhibit 14 demonstrates how the Bennetts gathered certain data for their eight common stocks, calculated selected measures (such as market-to-book ratios and average systematic risk) for each stock. Using their spreadsheet capability, they also calculated simple averages of each measure for their portfolio. If willing to pay for additional connect fee, the Bennetts could perform similar calculations for the other 22 common stocks on their approved list.

Statistical methods are another way of processing information for help in making investment decisions. Statistical applications can be at the level of the economy, a specific industry, or a particular firm. Statistical application also can be at the level of a single variable or a multivariate approach can be used. Stanley is familiar with a number of statistical methods, and thus he is interested in how to use them to help with the family's investments. To utilize the computational power of his microcomputer, he recently acquired a $375 statistical package **Microstat** (Ecosoft). Microstate includes a wide array of routines for descriptive statistics, hypotheses testing, analysis of variance, correlation and regression, time-series, and nonparametric procedures.

To illustrate statistical applications, suppose the Bennetts were interested in historical price movements for the entertainment industry, with the thought that they might invest in certain leading firms. They gathered quarterly price indexes for the past decade (1974–1984) as published by Standard & Poor's Corporation, and proceeded to analyze that data using Microstat. First, price movements for the entertainment industry were plotted as in Exhibit 15. The

EXHIBIT 14 INFORMATION PROCESSING FOR COMMON STOCK PORTFOLIO STANLEY AND PATRICIA BENNETT

Ticker Symbol	Market Value	Book Value	Market to Book	Price Earning	Beta Up	Beta Down	Beta Average
V-AHP	8151	2.0E+09	4.0	12.4	1.3	0.5	0.9
V-BBF	718	5.1E+08	1.4	9.5	1.3	0.8	1.0
V-DAL	1779	1.0E+09	1.7	7.9	1.6	1.5	1.5
V-IBM	74980	2.3E+10	3.2	11.9	1.1	0.9	1.0
V-K	3213	9.8E+08	3.3	13.0	1.3	0.8	1.0
V-MCD	4813	1.8E+09	2.7	12.8	0.8	0.4	0.6
V-SLB	10379	5.8E+09	1.8	9.2	0.6	1.6	1.1
V-UBO	1090	2.6E+08	4.2	14.2	0.4	0.3	0.4
Average	13140.37	4.5E+09	2.8	11.4	1.1	0.8	1.0

EXHIBIT 15 STATISTICAL ANALYSIS OF ENTERTAINMENT INDUSTRY

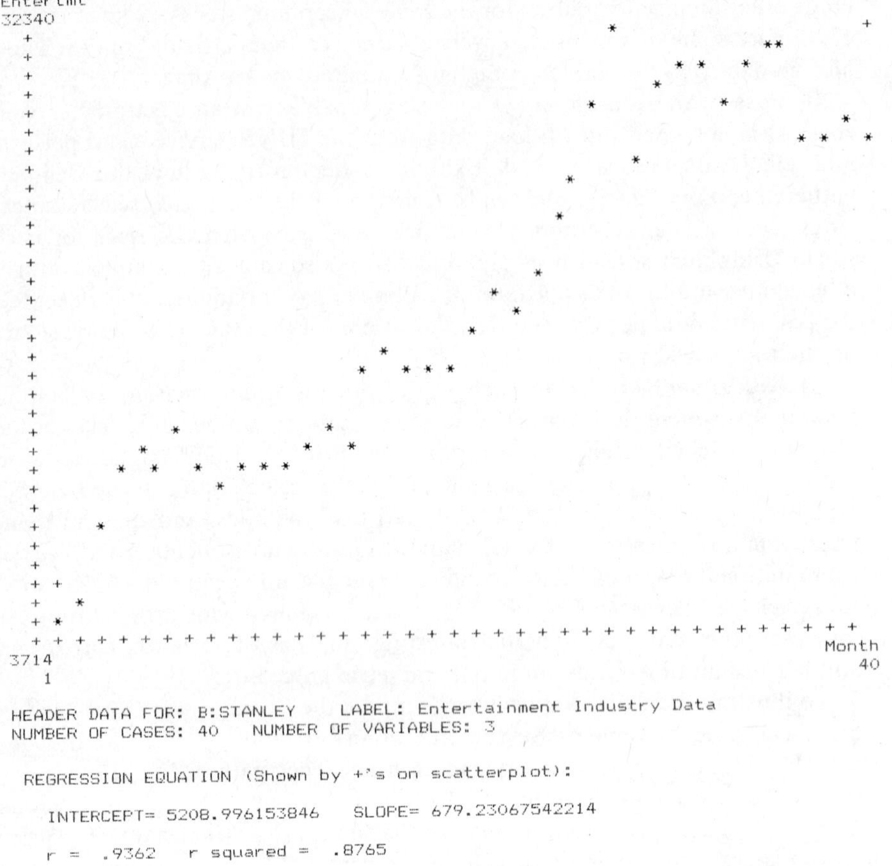

exhibit shows the almost tenfold increase for the entertainment industry over that period. Second, entertainment industry prices were regressed against price movements of the Standard & Poor's Composite Index. As shown in Exhibit 16, the resulting "characteristic line" has a slope of 2.8, and the regression explains just under 60% of the variability.

APPLICATIONS IN SECURITY VALUATION

As reflected in Exhibit 1, security valuation is a central step in the process of investing. ***Security valuation*** is an attempt to determine, typically with an expressed formulation, a measure of "intrinsic value" for what a security is really worth. Valuation is usually some version of the expression

$$V = \sum_{t=1}^{T} B_t/(1 + k)^t$$

EXHIBIT 16 CHARACTERISTIC LINE FOR ENTERTAINING INDUSTRY

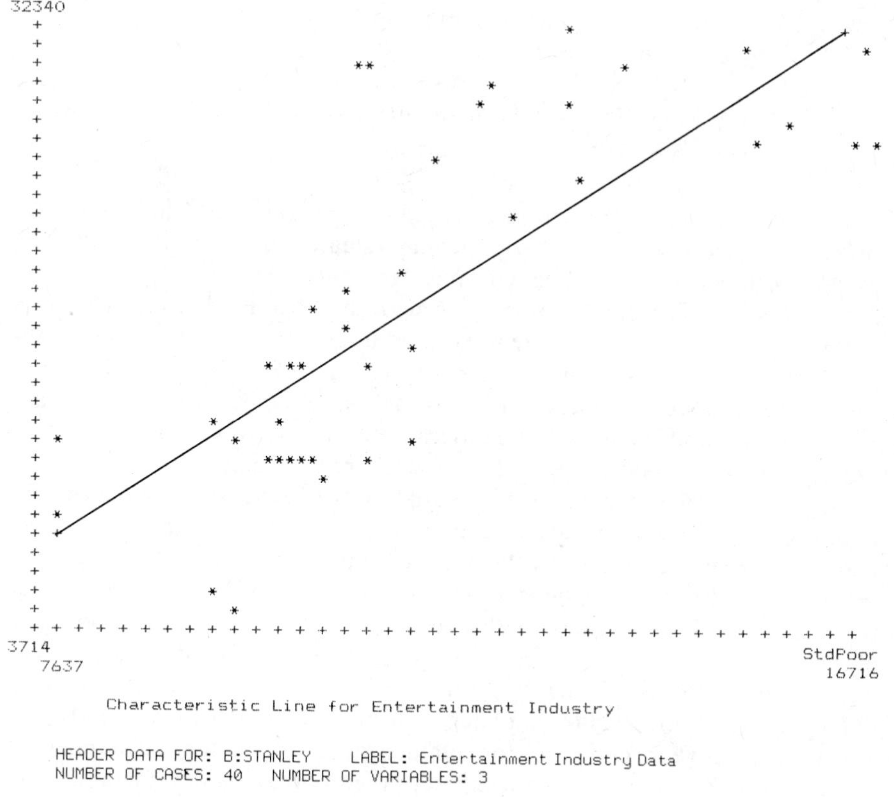

Characteristic Line for Entertainment Industry

```
HEADER DATA FOR: B:STANLEY     LABEL: Entertainment Industry Data
NUMBER OF CASES: 40    NUMBER OF VARIABLES: 3

REGRESSION EQUATION (Shown by +'s on scatterplot):

INTERCEPT = -13851.57056159    SLOPE = 2.8365172633557

r =  .7717    r squared =  .5956
```

where V = intrinsic value of the security
B_t = cash flow to the investor in period t
T = number of periods in the investment horizon
k = discount rate that reflects the perceived riskiness of the particular security

Different valuation formulas (or models) are used for security valuation, depending on the assumptions made about the future cash flows. A microcomputer is helpful, therefore, because speed of computation permits many variations to be inspected.

COMMON STOCK. Valuation models are used extensively for common stocks. Perhaps the most popular is one in which dividends are assumed to grow forever at a constant rate. The simplified valuation expression is as follows:

$$V = D(1 + g) / (k - g)$$

where V = intrinsic value of the common stock
D = current dividends per share
g = expected growth rate for dividends (forever)
k = discount rate that reflects the perceived riskiness of the particular common stock

A friend of Stanley's from the nearby university shared with him a computer program written to illustrate that particular valuation model. Fortunately, the program can be run on the Bennetts' microcomputer. To become familar with the valuation procedure, they selected American Home Products (AHP)—one of the eight common stocks currently owned by the Bennetts. Information obtained from the DJNR service helps them to decide on appropriate inputs to the valuation model. Output of the computer run is shown in Exhibit 17, and intrinsic value is shown to be $51.04. Because AHP currently sells for $50.50, it thus appears to be valued appropriately at the present time.

As previously mentioned, sensitivity analysis is a key reason that microcomputers can be so useful in investments. In the example, because current dividends are known, only the dividend growth rate and the investor's required rate (i.e., the discount rate) need to be estimated. In Exhibit 17, we see that as those parameters are varied on both sides of the selected inputs, intrinsic value of AHP varies from $30.10 to $155.76. By repeating this valuation process for other common stocks of interest, the Bennetts can perhaps find two or three that appear to be undervalued, and hence attractive additions to their portfolio.

Two alternative formulations for common stock valuation are illustrated in Exhibit 18. They are based on a computer program that Stanley adapted from Riley and Montgomery (1982). In this instance, the investor is given two options for valuation: by discounting future dividends with varying growth rates, and by utilizing a valuation procedure developed by the late (and legendary) Benjamin Graham. Again using American Home Products to illustrate, we see in Exhibit 18 it is slightly overvalued by the former—but considerably undervalued by the latter.

BONDS. The Bennetts currently own no government or corporate bonds, but they have become interested in bonds as a result of high interest rates. Their stockbroker suggested that they consider high-quality, longer-term corporate bonds. In particular, their stock broker suggested General Motors 8 5/8s of 2005 that currently sell for $740. Using a bond valuation model on this microcomputer, Stanley finds (see Exhibit 19) that intrinsic value of that bond is $745 using a 12% market rate of interest (i.e., discount rate), but only $717 using a 12.5% discount rate. The bond is thus priced appropriately, or somewhat overpriced, depending on the discount rate selected. In both instances, however, the General Motors bond is assumed to be held until its maturity in year 2005.

Another possibility is to plan to sell the bond prior to its maturity. Suppose

EXHIBIT 17 ILLUSTRATION OF COMMON STOCK VALUATION INFINITE GROWTH MODEL

In particular, STOCK allows the student to calculate a measure of intrinsic (i.e., investment) value for a share of common stock. The calculated value V requires estimates of dividends D, forecasted growth rate G, and the investor's required rate of return K.

The valuation equation is: $V = D\ (1 + G)\ /\ (K - G)$

What is the name of the common stock? (e.g., General Motors)
? American Home Products

What is the current dividend per share? (e.g., $2.50)
? 2.64

What is the forecasted growth rate (e.g., 8.7%)
? 16

What is the required rate of return? (e.g., 12.5%)

NOTE: The required rate of return must be larger than the forecasted growth rate.

? 22

What sensitivity level would you like for varying both growth rate and required rate of return by the investor? (e.g., S = 2%)

NOTE: Sensitivity analysis is done by varying G and K as follows: $G - 2S$, $G - S$, G, $G + S$, $G + 2S$ and similarly for K. Student should select S such that $G - 2S > 0$ and $K - 2S > 0$.

?1

VALUATION OF American Home Products

DIVIDEND PER SHARE = 2.64

REQUIRED RATE OF RETURN BY INVESTOR

GROWTH RATE	0.20	0.21	0.22	0.23	0.24
0.14	50.16	42.99	37.62	33.44	30.10
0.15	60.72	50.60	43.37	37.95	33.73
0.16	76.56	61.25	51.04	43.75	38.28
0.17	102.96	77.22	61.78	51.48	44.13
0.18	155.76	103.84	77.88	62.30	51.92

Do you want to do another valuation iteration? (e.g., yes or no)
? no

EXHIBIT 18 ILLUSTRATION OF COMMON STOCK VALUATION ALTERNATIVE VALUATION MODELS

```
RUN
THIS PROGRAM VALUES A STOCK BY
   (1) CAPITALIZING FUTURE DIVIDENDS OR
   (2) GRAHAM GROWTH STOCK VALUATION MODEL.
TYPE IN:  1     OR:  2 TO INDICATE YOUR CHOICE. ? 1
THIS ROUTINE VALUES STOCK BY CAPITALIZING THE EXPECTED
STREAM OF DIVIDENDS. TYPE IN THE FOLLOWING:
THE REQUIRED RATE OF RETURN.          EXAMPLE:  10.0 ? 22
THE NO. OF TIME PERIODS FOR WHICH YOU ANTICIPATE DIFFERENT
GROWTH RATES.                         EXAMPLE:  3 ? 2
THE CURRENT ANNUAL DIVIDEND.          EXAMPLE:  2.00 ? 2.64
THE GROWTH RATE AND LENGTH (YEARS) OF PEROD NUMBER  1
                                      EXAMPLE:  12 3
                        ENTER BOTH, SEPARATED BY COMMAS: ? 20, 10
THE GROWTH RATE FOR PERIOD NUMBER 2 (I.E., THE PERIOD
EXTENDING TO INFINITY).               EXAMPLE:  5.0? 12
THE ESTIMATED VALUE OF THE STOCK IS $  49.20

DO YOU WISH TO EVALUATE ANOTHER STOCK (YES OR NO) ? ? YES


RUN
THIS PROGRAM VALUES A STOCK BY
   (1) CAPITALIZING FUTURE DIVIDENDS OR
   (2) GRAHAM GROWTH STOCK VALUATION MODEL.
TYPE IN:  1     OR:  2 TO INDICATE YOUR CHOICE. ? 2
THIS ROUTINE VALUES A COMMON STOCK BY THE GRAHAM GROWTH
STOCK VALUATION MODEL. TYPE IN THE FOLLOWING:
THE EXPECTED GROWTH RATE (%) IN EARNINGS FOR THE NEXT
7-10 YEARS                            EXAMPLE:  8 ? 14
THE YIELD ON AAA RATED CORPORATE BONDS:
                                      EXAMPLE: 9.5 ? 10.5
THE CURRENT NORMALIZED EARNINGS PER SHARE.
                                      EXAMPLE:  4.02 ? 4.20
THE ESTIMATED VALUE OF THE COMMON STOCK IS $64.24
DO YOU WISH TO EVALUATE ANOTHER STOCK (YES OR NO) ? ? NO
```

EXHIBIT 19 ILLUSTRATION OF CORPORATE BOND VALUATION

```
RUN
This program determines bond value. Allowance is made for accrued interest
since the last coupon payment.
Type in the following:
The par value of the bond.                          Example:  1000 ? 1000
The coupon rate.                                    Example:  4.0  ? 8.625
The number of semi-annual periods to maturity after the
next coupon payment.                                Example:  24   ? 40
The number of days until the next coupon payment date.
                                                    Example:  76   ? 45
The market interest rate for instruments of like risk
maturity.                                           Example:  3.75 ? 12

The value of the bond IS $     745.46

Do you want more bond analysis (yes or no) ? yes


RUN
This program determines bond value. Allowance is made for accrued interest
since the last coupon payment.
Type in the following:
The par value of the bond.                          Example:  1000 ? 1000
The coupon rate.                                    Example:  4.0  ? 8.625
The number of semi-annual periods to maturity after the
next coupon payment.                                Example:  24   ? 40
The number of days until the next coupon payment date.
                                                    Example:  76   ? 45
The market interest rate for instruments of like risk
maturity.                                           Example:  3.75 ? 12.5

The value of the bond IS $     716.77

Do you want more bond analysis (yes or no) ? no
```

EXHIBIT 20 ILLUSTRATION OF CORPORATE BOND VALUATION WHEN SOLD PRIOR TO MATURITY

RUN

This program computes realized yield for a bond with a holding period which is less than the remaining life of the bond. Type in the following:

The par value of the bond.	Example: 1000 ? 1000
The coupon rate.	Example: 6.25? 8.625
The market price.	Example: 980 ? 740
The expected price at end of holding period.	Example: 1200 ? 1050
The years to maturity (rounded).	Example: 20 ? 20
The holding period (rounded).	Example: 5 ? 7

The realized yield is 15.21%

The realized yield for a range of prices follows:

Realized yield (%)	Holding period price
17.12	$1,250.00
16.94	1,230.00
16.75	1,210.00
16.57	1,190.00
16.38	1,170.00
16.19	1,150.00
16.00	1,130.00
15.81	1,110.00
15.61	1,090.00
15.41	1,070.00
15.21	1,050.00
15.00	1,030.00
14.79	1,010.00
14.58	990.00
14.37	970.00
14.15	950.00
13.93	930.00
13.71	910.00
13.48	890.00
13.25	870.00
13.01	850.00

Do you want to do this analysis with other data (yes or no) ? No the Bennetts forecast that interest rates will decrease somewhat in the next few years, and that bond prices will increase as a result. Their explicit forecast is that the General Motors bond will sell for $1,050 early in 1992. Another version of the bond valuation model is used to calculate the realized yield-to-maturity for a bond sold prior to maturity. Using that model, we see in Exhibit 20 that the realized yield is expected to be 15.2%. Also included in Exhibit 20 is a sensitivity analysis. For expected bond prices in 1992 ranging from $850 to 1,250, the realized yield increases from 13.0 to 17.1%. Although these are impressive yields, the Bennetts, nevertheless, decide not to add bonds to their portfolio at the present time.

OPTIONS. Stanley is highly conservative in most matters, but admits that he has a much greater interest in call and put options—perhaps because one member of his Friday poker club keeps bragging about his great success with trading options. Stanley's broker suggests call options for IBM. The Bennetts already own 100 shares of IBM common stock, and so he decides to investigate an IBM July 110 call option. That particular call for IBM is an option to purchase 100 shares of IBM common stock any time before July 1985.

Exhibit 21 illustrates the valuation of call options utilizing the **Black-Scholes option valuation model** as programmed by Riley and Montgomery (1982). It requires as input: market price of the underlying common stock,

EXHIBIT 21 ILLUSTRATION OF CALL OPTION VALUATION

```
RUN
THIS PROGRAM CALCULATES THE VALUE OF A CALL.
TYPE IN THE FOLLOWING:
THE MARKET PRICE OF STOCK                  EXAMPLE:  36.00 ? 123.125
THE STRIKING PRICE OF CALL.                EXAMPLE:  40.00 ? 125.75
THE LENGTH OF OPTION IN DAYS.              EXAMPLE:  90    ? 185
THE YIELD ON PRIME COMMERCIAL PAPER.       EXAMPLE:  12.25 ?  11.5
THE STANDARD DEVIATION OF THE CONTINUOUSLY COMPOUNDED AN-
NUAL RATE OF RETURN OF THE STOCK.          EXAMPLE:    .40 ?    .4
THE VALUE OF THE OPTION IS $ 16.05


DO YOU WANT TO EVALUATE ANOTHER CALL OPTION (YES OR NO) ? ? YES
THIS PROGRAM CALCULATES THE VALUE OF A CALL.
TYPE IN THE FOLLOWING:
THE MARKET PRICE OF STOCK.                 EXAMPLE:  36.00 ? 123.125
THE STRIKING PRICE OF CALL.                EXAMPLE:  40.00 ? 125.75
THE LENGTH OF OPTION IN DAYS.              EXAMPLE:  90    ? 185
THE YIELD ON PRIME COMMERCIAL PAPER.       EXAMPLE:  12.25 ?  11.5
THE STANDARD DEVIATION OF THE CONTINUOUSLY COMPOUNDED AN-
NUAL RATE OF RETURN OF THE STOCK.          EXAMPLE:    .40 ?    .60
THE VALUE OF THE OPTION IS $ 22.77

DO YOU WANT TO EVALUATE ANOTHER CALL OPTION (YES OR NO) ? ? NO
```

EXHIBIT 22 ILLUSTRATION OF INVESTMENT RESULTS FOR PURCHASING CALL OPTIONS

RUN
This program evaluates the purchase of calls. Do you want to supply commissions or have the program supply commissions equivalent to those charged by a major NYSE brokerage firm? Indicate your choice by typing: own or: major ? major
Type in the following:
The current stock price. Example: 25 ? 123.125

NOTE: The current market price is not used in the program. It is, however, imperative that the user recognize the relationship between the striking price and the current market price.

The striking price of the call. Example: 25 ? 125.75
The premium on one call. Example: 4.125 ? 15
The number of calls bought. Example: 5 ? 4
The length of the call in days. Example: 270 ? 185
The computed commission on 4 calls is $119.00.
The breakeven point is $141.345 per share
The required investment is $6,119.00

Profit or loss for a range of prices follows:

STOCK PRICE AT EXPIRATION	PROFIT OR LOSS	RETURN ON INVESTMENT	ANNUAL RETURN ON INVESTMENT
$113.000	−$6,119.00	−100.00%	−194.59%
$116.000	−$6,119.00	−100.00%	−194.59%
$119.000	−$6,119.00	−100.00%	−194.59%
$122.000	−$6,119.00	−100.00%	−194.59%
$125.000	−$6,119.00	−100.00%	−194.59%
$128.000	−$5,338.00	−87.24%	−169.76%
$131.000	−$4,138.00	−67.63%	−131.60%
$134.000	−$2,938.00	−48.01%	−93.43%
$137.000	−$1,738.00	−28.40%	−55.27%
$140.000	−$538.00	−8.79%	−17.11%
$143.000	$662.00	10.82%	21.05%
$146.000	$1,862.00	30.43%	59.21%
$149.000	$3,062.00	50.04%	97.38%
$152.000	$4,262.00	69.65%	135.54%
$155.000	$5,462.00	89.26%	173.70%
$158.000	$6,662.00	108.87%	211.86%
$161.000	$7,862.00	128.49%	250.02%
$164.000	$9,062.00	148.10%	288.19%
$167.000	$10,262.00	167.71%	326.35%
$170.000	$11,462.00	187.32%	364.51%
$173.000	$12,662.00	206.93%	402.67%
$176.000	$13,862.00	226.54%	440.84%
$179.000	$15,062.00	246.15%	479.00%
$182.000	$16,262.00	265.76%	517.16%
$185.000	$17,462.00	285.37%	555.32%
$188.000	$18,662.00	304.98%	593.48%
$191.000	$19,862.00	324.60%	631.65%
$194.000	$21,062.00	344.21%	669.81%
$197.000	$22,262.00	363.82%	707.97%

striking price for the call option, time to maturity, the riskless rate of return, and the standard deviation of annual return on the common stock. We see that the intrinsic value of the July 110 call option is $16.05 for a standard deviation of .40 and $22.78 for a standard deviation of .60. Clearly the value of a call option increases with the variability of stock price. The current price of the IBM July 110 call is approximately $15, and hence the option is undervalued.

Furthermore, the possible results from purchasing four IBM July 110 call options is shown in Exhibit 22. The "break-even" price for IBM common is $141.345. The leverage possible with call options is vivid. For example, if the price of IBM were to increase to $180 by midyear, the Bennetts would earn almost 500% on their investment in four calls. Conversely they could lose their investment in the call options if IBM did not move upward during the next few months.

REAL ESTATE. The Bennetts recently heard from one of their sons. He and his wife rent an apartment in a midwestern city, but they are considering the purchase of their first home. They asked their parents for advice on whether to rent or own. Not wishing to pass up an opportunity to further explore the use of his new microcomputer, Stanley offered to try and locate some software that might be useful. After a few inquiries, he located a program that compares the relative costs of renting versus owning a home. Exhibit 23 presents the comparison. For a $85,000 home, a $65,000 mortgage, and other estimates being made conservatively, we see that monthly cash flow is only $54 more if the family owns rather than rents. Because of equity buildup as the mortgage is paid each month, plus the psychological benefits of owning one's own home, it would appear the family would be wise to purchase the home—provided they have the funds for a $20,000 down payment and assuming that they can obtain the necessary mortgage financing.

APPLICATIONS IN TECHNICAL ANALYSIS

Another of Stanley's poker friends alleges to have made "thousands in the market" by disciplined charting of common stock prices. Other members of the Friday club dismiss that claim with the strong view that charting is nonsense, and that the other member simply has been fortunate. As already suggested, Stanley favors a more fundamental approach to investment decisions. At the same time, however, he is intrigued by any approach that will enable his family to attain their financial and investment goals. Thus he decides to investigate how technical analysis—especially with the aid of his microcomputer—might provide additional help to their investment decision making.

A large amount of software for technical analysis is available commercially. Not wanting to spend much on a questionable approach, however, Stanley decided to try a stock charting program made available through AAMI. He purchases the **User Supported Software Disks** #7 and #8 (American Association of Microcomputer Investors). Each disk costs about $9. Use of the charting

EXHIBIT 23 ILLUSTRATION OF RENTING VERSUS OWNING FOR A PERSONAL RESIDENCE

```
RUN

                              Own or Rent?

  This program determines if it is cheaper to own your own home, or to rent a
  home.

Enter the price of the home                          Example:   90000 ? 85000
Enter the amount of the loan                         Example:   80000 ? 65000
Enter the amount you put down                        Example:   10000 ? 20000
Enter the rent paid per month                        Example:     400 ? 650
Enter the length of the mortgage in years            Example:      30 ? 22
Enter the annual interest rate                       Example:    11.5 ? 12.25
Enter the yearly fire insurance                      Example:     320 ? 300
Enter the closing cost of the home                   Example:    1500 ? 2550
Enter your gross yearly income                       Example:   30000 ? 47500
Enter monthly maintenance (home)                     Example:      75 ? 100

  Note: We calculate a zero bracket tax deduction of $3,400 and a 1% property
        tax

Enter the number of exemptions you claim (2 people exempt = 2)
                                                     Example:       2 ? 2
                           PURCHASING A HOME

     Loan amount                                                  $65,000.00

     Monthly mortgage payment                                        $712.31
     Property taxes per month                                         $70.83
     Fire insurance per month                                         $25.00
  Total monthly payment                                              $808.15

     Down payment                                                 $20,000.00
     Closing costs                                                 $2,550.00
  Total cash outlay at closing                                    $22,550.00
                        Hit return to continue    ?
                              Tax Liability

RENTING:
  Gross income                                                    $47,500.00
     Less: Zero-bracket amount                                     $3,400.00
     Less: Personal exemptions                                     $2,000.00
  Taxable income                                                  $42,100.00
     Tax liability for renting = $11,129.00
```

EXHIBIT 23 (*CONTINUED*)

OWNING:	
Gross income	$47,500.00
Less: Interest and taxes	$9,097.78
Less: Personal exemptions	$2,000.00
Taxable income	$36,402.22

Tax liability for owning = $8,678.95

Hit return to continue ?

OWNING VS. RENTING

Monthly	Owning	Renting	Difference
Payment or rent	$808.15	$650.00	$158.15
Utilities and maintenance	$100.00	—	$100.00
Tax savings	$204.17	0	$204.17
Increase in cash outflow			$53.98

program is illustrated in Exhibit 24 for American Home Products. Weekly price and volume data for 54 weeks ending June 1984 are plotted—thus allowing Stanley an opportunity to identify evolving patterns for which buy or sell signals are suggested. Stanley plans to take several such charts to the next poker game and seek help in identifying particular patterns that might prove profitable.

APPLICATIONS IN PORTFOLIO DECISION MAKING

The preceding discussion has focused on information acquisition, information processing, and valuation for individual investments. At the same time, it is

EXHIBIT 24 ILLUSTRATION OF STOCK CHARTING

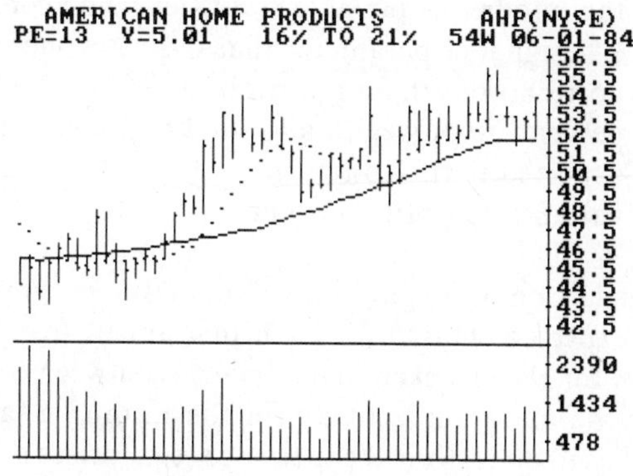

important for all investors to understand that all investment decisions are, in reality, ***portfolio decisions;*** that is, it is the total portfolio that ultimately determines whether or not particular goals can be accomplished.

Let us illustrate. We presented an example of financial compounding to see how much the Bennetts' credit union account might grow in 5 years. If there were to be a designated need of $35,000 for those funds in 5 years, and if the $28,914 (as reported in Exhibit 5) was thus not adequate, it does not automatically follow that that particular goal could not be realized. Given their other investment assets (see Exhibit 2), the Bennetts might well decide to make up the difference with funds from their money market fund or by selling some of their common stock.

It is thus important for the Bennetts—or any family—to be concerned about the totality of their portfolio rather than just individual components. Unfortunately, at this time, available software for help at the portfolio level is less developed than for individual investments.

The finance literature contains a long list of proposed procedures for revising an investment portfolio over time. One alternative is to do nothing once initial allocations are made—that is, stick with one's original decisions, both good and bad. Another alternative is periodically to restore the portfolio to the original allocations—that is, sell off some of the winners and buy more of the losers. Yet another alternative is to periodically "prune" the portfolio in view of recent information. For example, if the Bennetts were to decide on a select set of attributes for their investments, they could alter the portfolio periodically based on updated values obtained, either from the DJNR service, or from a monthly source such as their Stockpak II.

A more rigorous approach is to construct that single portfolio, from among a given set of alternative investments, which best satisfies an investor's feelings about return and risk. ***Portfolio theory,*** which has become a central concept in the fields of finance and investments, provides a solution to the problem of selecting values of x_j so as to

$$\text{Maximize } E\,(x_j) - L\,S^2\,(x_j)$$

where N = the number of possible securities being considered
L = a designated parameter that indicates the trade-off between portfolio return and portfolio risk
x_j = percentage of wealth allocated to j, $1 < j < N$
$E\,(x_j)$ = expected portfolio return
$S^2(x_j)$ = variance of portfolio return

This portfolio selection problem is one of quadratic programming. Inputs to the problem are expected returns for each investment (e.g., common stock), variances of return for each stock, and covariances between each pair of stocks. These inputs may be made subjectively for the future, or, as is typically the case, they can be based on historical experience (e.g., prices and dividends). An alternative (and considerably easier) set of inputs to the problem is historical holding period returns for each stock, plus historical holding period returns for an overall index of the stock market (e.g., the Standard and Poor's 500 Composite Index). Solution to the portfolio selection problem is a series of "corner portfolios" that are efficient in the sense of maximizing expected portfolio return for a designated level of portfolio risk (i.e., for each choice of L). A plot of the corner portfolios is the ***efficient frontier*** solution to portfolio selection. For details on the programming of this solution, see Riley and Montgomery (1982).

An example of portfolio selection using a microcomputer for the Bennetts' approved list of 30 common stocks is presented in Exhibit 25. Inputs are based on annual returns over the decade 1975–1984. Two selected corner portfolios from the efficient frontier solution are shown. The first has an expected return of 34.4%, a standard deviation of 14.8%, and contains seven stocks with proportions ranging from 10.5% (Signal Cos.) to 19% (Litton). In contrast, the other corner portfolio has 15 participants, an expected return of 28.6%, and a standard deviation of 9.9%. As one moves down an efficient frontier, portfolio risk is reduced via greater portfolio diversification, but with a concomitant reduction in expected portfolio return.

The same input data just described also can be used to assess the Bennetts' current portfolio. Using stock proportions obtained from the family's 1984 year-end holdings (see Exhibit 4), the portfolio selection model reveals that their portfolio currently has an expected return of 22.2% and a standard deviation of 11.1%, and it is thus considerably less efficient than either of the efficient portfolios listed in Exhibit 25. If the Bennetts want to maximize expected return while minimizing portfolio risk, especially given their existing expectations, they must consider changes to their current common stock holdings.

A final but necessary step to portfolio decision making is implementation. Traditionally, the investor would call her or his account executive and place orders to buy or sell. To complete this part of the section, it is appropriate to consider how a microcomputer can be used to implement buy and sell orders. For an annual cost (approximately $200), plus a modest fee for connect time, an investor is able to **establish a brokerage account** that allows telephone communication by modem. Market and limit orders to buy and sell securities can be made during both the day and evening. Once orders are executed, the investor's portfolio is updated automatically and written confirmations are mailed. Because their volume of trading is so small, the Bennetts decided not to use their microcomputer for trading at the present time.

APPLICATIONS IN PORTFOLIO EVALUATION

Portfolio evaluation is the final step in the process of investing. ***Portfolio evaluation*** is an important step because it provides a current assessment of how investments, both individually and collectively, are doing. This provides a basis for making changes in the portfolio. It also provides an opportunity for reviewing progress toward the expressed goals of the investor. In this part we consider ways in which a microcomputer can be used in portfolio evaluation.

EXHIBIT 25 ILLUSTRATION OF PORTFOLIO SELECTION USING BENNETTS' APPROVED LIST

Corner portfolio 7

Security	Percent	
BA	13.57	
BOR	15.90	
DH	13.34	
LIT	19.03	
SGN	10.50	
TXO	10.71	
TL	16.95	
Return is		0.3444
Variance is		0.0218
Standard deviation is		0.1477

Corner portfolio 15

Security	Percent	
ARC	2.34	
BBF	11.26	
BA	6.93	
BOR	14.51	
DH	5.91	
LIT	10.77	
MOT	2.15	
NLC	3.10	
PEP	1.25	
SLB	7.01	
SGN	9.88	
SNA	2.13	
TXO	5.60	
TL	12.87	
USG	4.29	
Return is		0.2859
Variance is		0.0097
Standard deviation is		0.0986

For an additional source on portfolio evaluation, as well as on earlier topics discussed herein, see Woodwell (1983). It should also be noted that many software packages advertised as portfolio management are, in reality, portfolio evaluation routines.

One of the first spreadsheet applications developed by the Bennetts was a routine to assess the current status of their common stock portfolio. As shown in Exhibit 26, Patricia periodically inputs the latest prices of their eight common stocks, and the program then compares current market values with the historical costs of each. Percentage gains and losses are calculated and summed. As reported earlier in Exhibit 4, the Bennetts had a total market value of $79,838. We see here that that includes an unrealized gain of $15,475 (24.0%) at the end of calendar year 1984. On becoming a subscriber to the DJNR, the Bennetts realized that the spreadsheet shown in Exhibit 26 could easily be altered to allow automatic updating with current prices from the service. Given the relative costs, however, they decided that Patricia can manually do portfolio evaluation for their investment portfolio.

TIPS FOR SELECTING HARDWARE AND SOFTWARE

Portfolio evaluation completes the cycle of the investments management process, because it is a determination of portfolio status that triggers the next iteration of financial planning, information acquisition and processing, and so on. It also brings us full circle in our survey of how microcomputers can be used in investing. In each step of the investments management process, we have discussed the conceptual application and provided illustration. It remains to step back and consider the actual purchase of computer hardware and software by an investor. Four dimensions will be considered: need, criteria, cost, and timing.

EXHIBIT 26 PORTFOLIO EVALUATION REPORT STANLEY AND PATRICIA BENNETT DECEMBER 31, 1984

Stock Symbol	Shares Owned	Purchase Price	Current Price	Cost Basis	Market Value	Dollar Gain	Percent Gain
AHP	200	42.716	50.750	8543	10150	1607	18.8
BBF	200	34.178	42.750	6836	8550	1714	25.1
DAL	300	30.765	38.750	9230	11625	2396	26.0
IBM	100	52.786	125.375	5279	12538	7259	137.5
K	200	29.935	36.750	5987	7350	1363	22.8
MCD	200	53.968	52.625	10794	10525	−269	−2.5
SLB	200	35.503	41.125	7101	8225	1124	15.8
UBO	300	35.315	36.250	10595	10875	281	2.6
TOTALS				64363	79838	15475	24.0

At the outset, it should be made clear that a great deal of literature and information is available to help the investor. Some sources have already been mentioned in the preceding survey. In addition, there are articles devoted to the microcomputer itself (e.g., Muskal, 1984), articles devoted to peripheral equipment (e.g., modems in Bonner and Keogh, 1984), articles devoted to particular applications (e.g., personal financial management in O'Malley, 1984), and articles that examine particular investment strategies (e.g., options in Evslin, 1984). The subject has become a part of the seminar business sponsored by professional organizations (e.g., "Using Microcomputers to Invest," sponsored by the Financial Analysts Federation, Chicago, November 28–30, 1984).

NEED. Certainly no one should rush out and spend a lot of money on a microcomputer and related software without having justified the need for such an investment. For despite the enormous and increasing popularity of personal computers, they simply are not for everyone! This section has demonstrated that the range of applications in investments is broad—and certainly no investor is likely to be interested in all applications instantaneously. The chief advantage of a microcomputer in investing is that a more careful and disciplined approach can be brought to each step of the management process. And, further, the time required to accomplish this can be shortened considerably. At the extreme, a microcomputer makes certain analyses possible that simply were not possible for an individual investor in earlier years.

If an investor is willing to learn, both to operate the hardware and to utilize the software, it is doubtful that he or she could possibly be worse off. Microcomputers enable an investor to have access to more information, and that is always a relative advantage in trying to make appropriate and coherent investment decisions. Whether or not that advantage justifies the acquisition of computer hardware and software thus becomes a pivotal question.

CRITERIA. To try and answer that question, it is useful to identify all relevant criteria that will be used. Examples of hardware criteria include: ease of operation (i.e., "friendliness"), documentation of capability, scope of application, speed of application, reliability and maintenance, and impact of future technology. In turn, examples of software criteria include: ease of operation, documentation of usage, flexibility of application, potential for sensitivity analyses, and impact of future technology.

An illustration of **criteria used in the evaluation of software** is presented in Exhibit 27. It is a summary evaluation of the Dow Jones Spreadsheet Link (DJSL) which appeared in the September/October 1984 issue of *The AAMI Journal.* The four criteria used were performance, documentation, ease of handling, and error handling. As seen, the DJSL received an "excellent" rating on each criterion.

COST. Conspicuously absent from the foregoing discussion is any mention of **cost.** Yet for many investors, cost might represent the single most important

REVIEW: DOW JONES SPREADSHEET LINK

AAMI SOFTWARE EVALUATION

	Poor	Fair	Good	Excellent
Performance				X
Documentation				X
Ease of Use				X
Error Handling				X

SUMMARY

The Dow Jones Spreadsheet Link automates the task of entering financial information available on the Dow Jones News/Retrieval service into Visicalc, Multiplan and Lotus 1-2-3. The program automatically logs onto Dow Jones News/Retrieval, obtains information from its Current Quotes, Historical Quotes, Media General Financial Services, Disclosure II, or Coporate Earnings Estimator data bases, and stores it in a file that resembles the original spreadsheet template. This file is then combined by the investor with the original spreadsheet template. The program also includes a terminal program for accessing other Dow Jones News/Retrieval data bases, and a program that can use data files from Dow Jones Market Manager.

VITAL INFORMATION

Publisher:	Solutions, Inc. and Dow Jones & Company, Inc. P.O. Box 300 Princeton, NJ 08540 (609) 452-1511
System Requirements:	Apple II/II+/IIe 48K-Applesoft 1 disk drive—DOS 3.3 Modem IBM PC Minimum 128K memory 1 or 2 double-sided disk drives Modem
Optional:	Printer (recommended)
Retail Price:	$249.00

If you are proficient enough on a spreadsheet program to use it for securities analysis, and can justify the use of Dow Jones News/Retrieval (DJNR) to get your financial data, Dow Jones Spreadsheet Link is an excellent investment.

Spreadsheet Link automatically logs onto DJNR and captures any information you request from the Current Quotes, Historical Quotes, Media General Financial Services, Disclosure II, and Corporate Earnings Estimator data bases.

criterion. As mentioned throughout this section, there is considerable variability in the prices of both hardware and software. Moreover, prices of both hardware and software have been decreasing, albeit rapidly and sporadically, ever since personal computers appeared on the market less than a decade ago.

To illustrate cost, we pay a final visit to the Bennetts and review their costs to date. Their computer system includes some of the more recognized hardware and software available during 1984. The following costs (approximately retail) reflect the technology in that year. We begin with the one-time costs:

Microcomputer system	$4,500
Wordstar (word-processing)	500
Lotus 1-2-3 (spreadsheet)	500
Microstat (statistical package)	375
Dow Jones Spreadsheet Link	250
Net Worth (personal finances)	100
Other miscellaneous software	300
Subtotal	$6,525

In addition, the Bennetts have annual costs as follows:

AAMI (trade association)	$ 49
Dow Jones News Retrieval	1,152
Stockpak II	275
Subtotal	$1,476

Of this, the value for DJNR is based on assumed average usage of 40 minutes per month throughout the year.

These illustrative costs for a microcomputer and associated software may well be excessive for many individual investors, especially if their portfolios are smaller than that of the Bennetts, or if their needs for a microcomputer are narrower than the total range of applications discussed in this section. Conversely, for families and investors with larger portfolios, and/or with a wider range of potential applications, the illustrative costs may not be excessive, especially when one considers the accounting, custodial, and legal fees which they already may be paying for help with their investments.

And, too, it should be recognized that many families will use their microcomputer for many more functions than just investments management. The Bennetts, for example, use their microcomputer for considerable correspondence, including their family telephone directory, their year-end holiday card record, Patricia's recipe file, and Stanley's jogging log.

In the final analysis, the decision to invest in a microcomputer usually is an economic question in which relative costs must be compared with relative benefits. The survey and illustration of potential applications of microcomputers in investing in this section suggest that purchase of a microcomputer probably could be justified by many individual and family investors, and certainly by most institutional investors.

TIMING. The final criterion for selecting hardware and software is **timing.** Clearly, not all investors will proceed at the same pace. Some investors will jump in and purchase a microcomputer and extensive software so quickly that they end up being overwhelmed and frustrated because there is so much to read and learn. At the other extreme, some investors will proceed so slowly so as to never fully appreciate and benefit from the capability they have obtained. As is often the case, the most reasonable approach is probably somewhere in-between the extremes. The best tip on timing might be for the investor to proceed at a comfortable pace in which further software is not purchased until everything already owned is understood and being used. A related tip, as part of such training, is to develop an overall plan before proceeding. Just as financial planning logically precedes investment decisions, the planning of a microcomputer system logically precedes the purchase of particular hardware and software. Hopefully, this section provides guidance for those who decide to invest in a microcomputer for purposes of investing.

REFERENCES

Atkinson, Stanley M., and Malone, R. Phil, "The Use of Low-Cost Microcomputers in Teaching Investments and Corporate Finance," *Journal of Financial Education* (Fall 1983): 78–81.

Bonner, Paul, and Keogh, James, "Connected! A Buyer's Guide On Modems," *Personal Computing* (April 1984): 122–137.

Dempsey, Tim, "Dow Jones News/Retrieval—An Indepth Look," *Database* (June 1984): 44–64.

Evslin, Tom, "Exercise Your Options," *Dowline* (November–December 1984): 9–10.

Gitman, Lawrence J., and Joehnk, Michael D., Fundamentals of Investing, second edition, 1984, Chapter 3 and Appendix A. New York: Harper & Row.

Mick, Colin, and Ball, Jerry, The Financial Planner's Guide to Using a Personal Computer, Homewood, IL: Dow Jones-Irwin, 1984, pp. 122–156.

Muskal, Michael, "PC and Apple: How the Chips Stack Up," *PC: The Independent Guide to IBM Personal Computers,* February 21, 1984.

O'Malley, Christopher, "A Buyer's Guide to Personal Finance Managers," *Personal Computing,* (November 1984): 127–141.

Riley, William B., Jr. and Montgomery, Austin H., Jr., Guide to Computer-Assisted Investment Analysis, New York: McGraw-Hill, 1982.

Smith, Keith V., Portfolio Management, New York: Holt, Rinehart and Winston, 1971, Chapter 12.

Sparks, Leslie E., Investment Analysis with Your Microcomputer, Blue Ridge Summit, PA: Tab Books, 1983.

Stevenson, Tom, "Microcomputers: Powerful New Investment Tools," *Pension & Investment Age* (October 3, 1983): 21–37.

Woodwell, Donald R., Automating Your Financial Portfolio, Homewood, IL: Dow Jones-Irwin, 1983.

25

DURATION AND IMMUNIZATION: MATCHED-FUNDING TECHNIQUES

CONTENTS

25

DURATION AND IMMUNIZATION: MATCHED-FUNDING TECHNIQUES

Martin L. Leibowitz

Over the past few years, there has been an explosive growth in the development of specialized bond **portfolios dedicated** to funding a prescribed set of payouts over time. The techniques used in constructing these specialized portfolios have been referred to in various ways—including dedication, immunization, matching, and contingent immunization. The general term *matched funding* can be used to characterize the fundamental objective of all these techniques. Matched-funding techniques reduce the uncertainty of long-term investment results as they relate to the fulfillment of specific liabilities. Such reductions of uncertainty can, in turn, lead to a number of direct and indirect benefits at the corporate/institutional level. These benefits can be particularly large when market interest rates are materially higher than the pro forma or actuarial discount rate used to value the liabilities. The applicability of these techniques extends beyond pension funds into many other areas of **asset/liability management.** The purpose of this section is to describe these techniques and to provide a context for understanding their increasing use.

EARLY MOTIVATIONS FOR DEDICATION

The motivation for corporate pension funds to utilize **dedication techniques** is best explained through a brief recounting of their evolution over the past several years. The modern thrust toward cash matching began in 1980, when a number of large U.S. corporations found themselves faced with one or more of the following situations:

- There was a general squeeze on operating profits.

Much of the material in this section is taken from articles and volumes published by Salomon Brothers Inc, New York, as listed under "References and Bibliography."

- Overall corporate pension costs were growing significantly and had become a major cost factor.
- The "retired lives" component was becoming a larger proportion of the overall fund costs.
- A realignment of corporate operating divisions was occurring in the form of terminations and sell-offs of divisions. These events led to the need for a better delimiting of the associated pension liabilities.
- The conservative nature of the actuarial process led to continued use of relatively low actuarial rates and to a slow recognition of any incremental portfolio returns. This conservative treatment had greatly improved the funding posture of many pension funds. To some corporate managers, however, this conservatism now seemed to perpetuate an excessively large pension drain in both cash and accounting terms.
- The threat of inflation was apparently easing.
- Most important, interest rates had risen to such historically high levels that many corporate sponsors felt that bonds represented a unique investment opportunity—at least for the long term, if not for the short term as well.

This confluence of events led corporate sponsors to: (1) a strong desire to try to find a way to reduce pension costs, and (2) a willingness to allocate larger portions of their overall assets into the fixed-income area.

The dedicated portfolio fitted these needs like a glove. The basic motivation is depicted in Exhibit 1.

Suppose a **pension fund** has a class of liabilities on its books at an actuarial return rate of 7%. When discounted at this 7% rate, these liabilities would have an actuarial present value of about $128 million. Suppose further that they

EXHIBIT 1 PRESENT VALUE OF RETIRED-LIVES LIABILITY

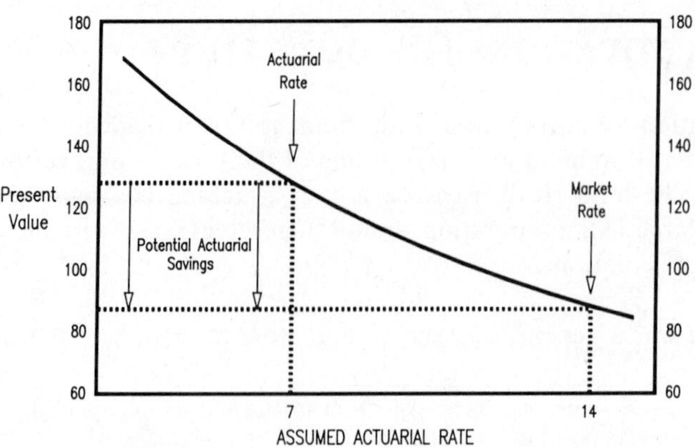

could be fulfilled, almost dollar for dollar, in a relatively assumption-free way with a cash-matched dedicated portfolio that cost $88 million at the 14% market yields that were available in the early days of dedication. Moreover, suppose this procedure was so assumption-free that the actuary would have no problem accepting it.

The $40-million gap between these two figures translated into a 31% reduction in the fund's pro forma liability costs. This reduction would be realized on an amortized basis over time. The appeal of such a technique is clear; it was, in effect, a rather significant funding deferment.

This was the original motivation behind the dedication trend. In subsequent years the role of **cash matching** in pension funding has expanded considerably, both in terms of the purposes and in the financial situations of the corporations that have embraced its use. Dedication is no longer the sole province of the cash- or earnings-stretched company. It has become widely accepted (in at least some forms) by many leading actuaries, and it has become a fairly standard tool in the corporate pension planners' kit bag. Many of the recent applications have been by a variety of corporations with the highest possible financial standing. In fact, it is becoming increasingly used by corporations with *overfunded* pension funds.

NEW MOTIVATIONS FOR DEDICATION

The motivations for dedication are now far more varied than when this strategy was first used. Many of the motivations still relate demonstrably to improving the funded status, but for reasons other than a simple desire to reduce near-term contribution levels or to lower annual pension expense. Indeed, the very reduction in unfunded status is taken as *value in itself* to many of the parties in the pension process. With the greater scrutiny of the pension liability by many sectors the financial community—Financial Accountive Standards Board (FASB), credit rating services, financial analysts, and such—many corporations have been eager to achieve better definition and control of this important liability. In a certain sense it has become important to clarify the true nature of the pension liability, both within the corporate framework as well as to the various outside parties involved in the valuation of the firm as a whole.

This clarification function can be as valuable for overfunded plans as it is for unfunded plans. With overfunded plans, the dedication process allows for a more precise identification of the magnitude of the overfunded surplus. This can serve as a trigger for recognition of the magnitude of the overfunding and for achieving better control over future costs. But it can also help identify more appropriate investment functions for the nondedicated component of the fund's assets. Thus with the better-defined nominal dollar liabilities controlled through a dedicated portfolio, the surplus can be more aggressively allocated toward other goals—for example, higher returns, wider diversification (including foreign securities), and enhanced inflation protection. Indeed, some financial theorists have expressed the belief that a rational allocation of the fund's investments can be made only when the assets and liabilities are partitioned by risk characteristics.

The role of dedication can extend beyond the specialized function of "marking" the actuarial rate to market rates within the framework of a conservative actuarial system. Even for an actuarial system where valuation rates were chosen to coincide with long-term interest rates, dedication (or, more generally, some form of matched funding) would be the only way that the fund could protect itself against a ballooning in the present value of liabilities in the face of a sizable decline in interest rates. From a pure investment point of view, matched funding here serves as the least-risk asset in the sense of minimizing the risk of fulfillment of a large class of nominal dollar liabilities. Indeed, apart from any pro forma considerations, it can be argued that a large, sustained decline in interest rates represents one of the most severe threats to the structure of private pension funds and public retirement systems. Such a decline would impact the investment rate for all further investable flows—whether derived from reinvestment or new contributions—and also reduce the income-producing power of each dollar of the fund's asset value.

Some dedications have in fact been undertaken out of just such concerns. In at least a few cases, the corporations have established the dedication solely as an *investment* decision and have not even sought actuarial recognition or relief. Of course, in such "shadow dedications," the actuarial benefits could presumably be applied for at some time in the future should they become needed.

In all these situations, the act of dedication represents both an *investment* decision as well as a *corporate/actuarial* decision. Without the perceived market conditions that render matched funding with fixed-income portfolios attractive and acceptable as an investment decision, there would have been very few dedicated portfolios put into place over the past 5 years. At the same time, it is clear that the wide range of corporate/actuarial benefits associated with dedications has been a significant reason for the extraordinary activity in this area.

MATCHED FUNDING VERSUS PROJECTIVE FUNDING

To view these developments from a broader perspective, one must appreciate that fixed-income securities can serve a number of vastly different functions in a modern portfolio context. First, a bond portfolio can generate a well-defined cash flow that can be used to fund a schedule of planned expenditures. This is the basic approach that we have termed "matched funding."

A distinctly different view is that of **"projective funding."** In projective funding, the fixed-income sector is viewed as an asset category that has a lower variability than equities and that can be used as a "variability damper" to bring the short-term risk level of the overall portfolio down to tolerable limits. A related "projective funding" function for bonds has been as an opportunity area for active management. At times, this has included the use of rather dramatic maturity changes in an effort to anticipate and capitalize on major interest rate movements. (Needless to say, such anticipatory activity also creates a variability of its own as an overlay.)

One of the problems in any discussion of the portfolio role of the fixed-income component is that the different functions are often confused. Although there can clearly be overlaps in terms of intent and purpose, it is useful to distinguish the purposes and weight accorded to each function in any given situation. Unfortunately, it is not uncommon for a fixed-income component to be justified in terms of one function while actually being implemented in pursuit of a different goal.

It is important to clarify the fundamental difference between matched funding and projective funding. Matched **funding** is a basically simple (and a very ancient) concept. Given an obligation to pay a certain schedule of payouts, the simplest possible approach is to try to purchase an instrument that will provide a series of payments that will exactly "match" the payout liabilities over time. Such an investment represents the ultimate in uncertainty reduction—the fulfillment of the scheduled liabilities is essentially assured.

PROJECTIVE FUNDING

In the 1960s and 1970s, a much more theoretical approach to asset allocation became the order of the day. This approach was based on extrapolation of projected return distributions for various classes of assets—equity, fixed income, real estate, foreign investments, and such—to determine the mixture that would provide the most comfortable balance of risk and return. Return was here usually taken to be the expected return over the long term, whereas risk was usually associated with shorter-term variability. (This melding of long- and short-term characteristics was often justified in terms of short-term variability serving as a proxy for long-term risk.) The asset allocation was then chosen to provide the best possible *expected* return subject to tolerable conditions of variability. This (admittedly crude) description is intended to cover a number of theoretical models that share one basic feature: They are based on the projections of assumed return relationships. Although they all attempt to contain risk through (often complex) models of variability and covariability, they are all vulnerable to the underlying "model risk"; that is, the risk that the assumptions regarding the return behaviors may not prove to be an adequate description of reality.

These "projective funding" techniques do have the important advantage that they can encompass any asset class whose return process and the associated variability and covariability can be condensed into a well-defined probability distribution. In fact, one of the nagging concerns with such approaches is that the special characteristics—and indeed, the unique flavor—of any individual asset tend to be neglected. Only the return distributions actually matter in the projective funding models.

Thus projective funding can be viewed as a sophisticated, theoretically based approach that can incorporate virtually any range of potential assets. It is a broad-based approach that can be applied to a wide range of complex investment problems. Matched funding, on the other hand, is the ultimate in simplicity, but can only be used in conjunction with fixed-income vehicles applied to nominal dollar liability schedules. Although it is a narrow approach, it is largely free of assumptions. Within its intended scope, it represents the ultimate in uncertainty reduction.

PREDEDICATION MATCHED-FUNDING TECHNIQUES

In recent years, the enlargement of the fixed-income markets and the development of modern analytic tools have led to a greater variety of procedures for constructing matched-funding portfolios (see Exhibit 2).

As noted, matched funding has a long and respected history in the bond market. However, many of its early applications tended to be informal. Thus long-term liabilities may have been funded with a portfolio consisting of long-term maturities. Similarly, an intermediate-maturity portfolio would be sought for intermediate liabilities. This informal maturity structuring has always been a natural procedure for bond market participants. With the rise of rate-of-return performance measurements for bond portfolios, there arose a need to create a more clearly defined portfolio target to serve as a performance benchmark. This target could be construed as a hypothetical portfolio representing the "optimal" blend of maturities, qualities, and other sector characteristics for a given application. One suggested approach was the concept of the "baseline portfolio." There are a number of similar concepts of a "normal" or a "policy" portfolio. Although the baseline portfolio may be quite well defined in terms of the component fixed-income sectors, it usually bears only a judgmental or intuitive relationship to the funding of specific liabilities.

EXHIBIT 2 MATCHED FUNDING TECHNIQUES

- **Informal Maturity Structuring**
- **Formal Baseline Target**
- **Contractual Arrangements**
- **Formalized Management Procedures**
  - **Dedication (Cash Matching)**
  - **Immunization**
  - **Horizon Matching**
- **Contingent Procedures for Structured Active Management**
  - **Contingent Immunization**
  - **Contingent Dedication**
  - **Contingent Horizon Matching**
  - **Dynamic Hedging**

FORMALIZED MATCHED-FUNDING TECHNIQUES

As discussed, recent applications of matched funding in the pension area have been motivated by a combination of investment and corporate/actuarial considerations. In essence, these considerations are derived largely from the willingness of the actuarial system to provide special benefits to the corporation for a minimum-risk investment approach. However, the actuary typically requires that the bond portfolio be subject to some *formalized* procedure for assuring the continued fulfillment of the liability schedule. One way to provide this formal assurance is through some type of **insurance contract**—for example, GICs, annuity contract, and so on. Once again, this approach has had a long history. Many pension funds simply purchase an annuity contract for each retiring employee. Such contractual arrangements certainly represent a form of matched funding.

In recent years, however, many corporate sponsors have elected to retain control of their **pension assets** and to establish **matched-funding portfolios** consisting largely of marketable fixed-income securities. This route provides the corporation with greater flexibility, including the ability to review and revise its overall asset allocation at any future point. In addition, the corporation can also seek the opportunistic rewards of active management within the formalized management structure.

In the following subsections we will examine the advantages and disadvantages of the various formalized management procedures that are used to create matched-funding bond portfolios. Before proceeding, however, it might be wise to review first some of the terminology problems that often seem to becloud this area. The terms *dedication* and *immunization* are often used interchangeably to cover all the specific techniques. However, we find it more fruitful to distinguish the individual techniques by such specific terms as *cash matching, immunization,* and *horizon matching.* This reserves *dedication* for a more encompassing description of all these formalized techniques for bond portfolios *dedicated* to servicing a prescribed set of liabilities.

THE CONCEPT OF CASH MATCHING

The typical cash-matching problem begins with a liability schedule such as that depicted in Exhibit 3. The declining series of liability payouts is representative of the retired-lives component of a pension system. The objective of **cash matching** is to develop a fixed-income portfolio that will provide a stream of payments from coupons, sinking funds, and maturing principal payments that will "match" this liability schedule. More precisely, the problem is to receive sufficient funds in advance of each scheduled payout so as to have full assurance that the payouts will be met from the dedicated portfolio alone.

Theoretically, the prescribed payout schedule may take any one of many possible forms. In practice, however, certain general forms are repeatedly encountered. One such common liability schedule is that of **"exponential decay"**

EXHIBIT 3 A PRESCRIBED SCHEDULE OF LIABILITIES

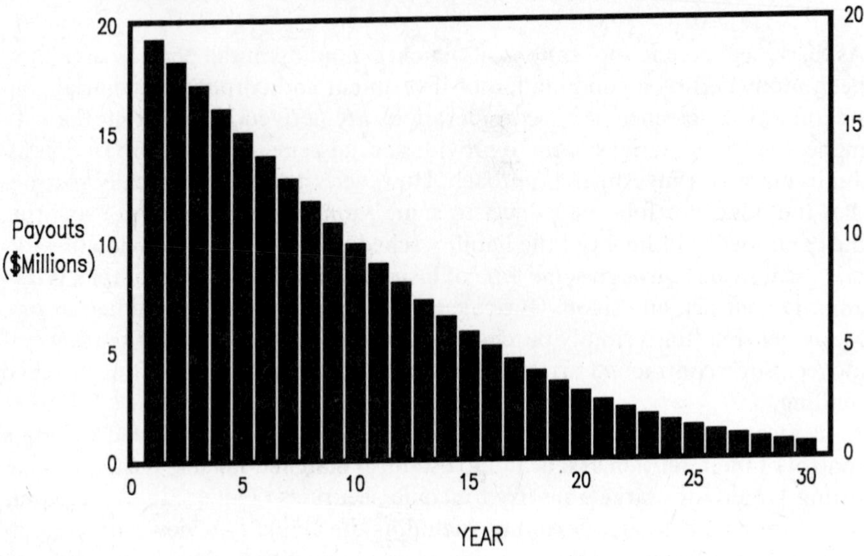

(see Exhibit 3). In this 30-year schedule, the payouts start at $19.2 million in the first year and decline over time, falling to $.6 million in the thirtieth year. The total of all payouts over the 30-year span is $215.60 million.

For purposes of illustration, suppose the marketplace contains a sufficient quantity of acceptable bonds with maturities coinciding with each of the payout dates. With the hypothetical availability of a full maturity range of Treasury bonds, CATs, and other zero-coupon instruments, an "exact-match" portfolio could be theoretically constructed. Exhibit 4 illustrates the maturity structure of this portfolio and its consequent cash flow. The combination of coupons and maturities at each payout date would provide an exact match for the prescribed payout schedule.

THE GENERAL MATCHING PROBLEM

The portfolio in Exhibit 4 represents the theoretical case of an **"exact match."** With the exact match, each dollar of coupon and principal receipts on a given date is immediately used to support the required payout on that same date. This would seem to be the ideal fit for a cash flow matched portfolio. It turns out, however, that such an exact-match portfolio—even when possible—would usually not be the optimal portfolio!

In practice, there will be a much larger universe of acceptable bonds that have coupon and principal payments on dates other than the exact payout dates of the liability schedule. This larger universe will generally contain acceptable bonds with higher-yields than their "exact-maturity" counterpart. The inclusion of such higher-yielding securities naturally results in lower portfolio

EXHIBIT 4 AN EXACT-MATCH PORTFOLIO

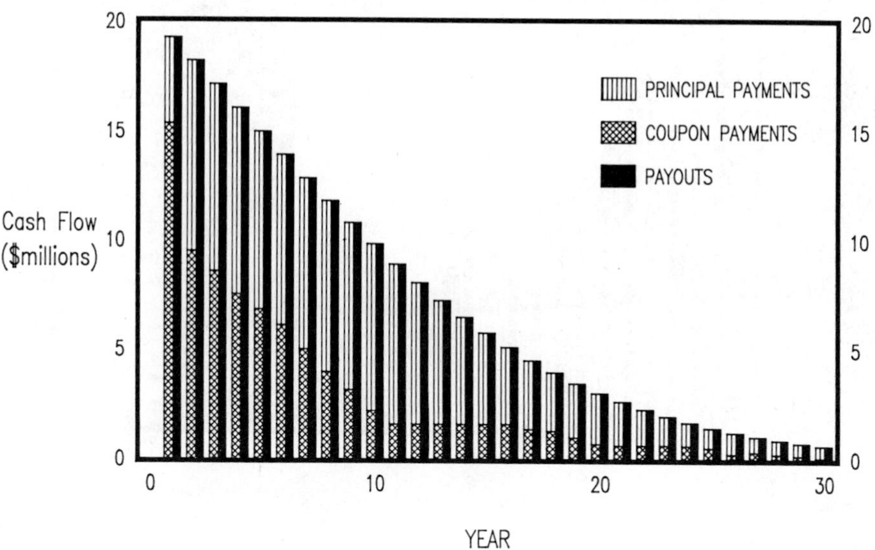

costs. When such bonds are used in a cash flow matching portfolio, the coupon and/or principal receipts must be accumulated for a period of time prior to their use on the payout date. Under such circumstances, these "prior receipts" must be reinvested at some rate until they are needed.

The fundamental appeal of cash flow matching lies in its simplicity. This appeal is reinforced when the matching portfolio can fulfill the prescribed liabilities even if no further investment action is ever taken. The assurance of fulfillment even under *totally passive* management is a natural and clear objective in many cases. (This goal may be sought even in situations where some form of risk-controlled active management will, in fact, be pursued.) The ultimate in a "total passivity assumption" would require a matching portfolio to be designed on the basis that any "prior receipts" would not be reinvested. In other words, the matching portfolio would be designed to fulfill its mission even when all reinvestment would take place at a 0% rate.

This assumption of a 0% reinvestment rate (or, equivalently, of no reinvestment whatsoever) obviously represents an extremely conservative viewpoint. It can also prove to be an extremely expensive assumption. This assumption was in fact adopted for some of the early cash-matched portfolios. By using a more reasonable (but still conservative) reinvestment rate assumption, however, a wider range of potentially acceptable matching portfolios becomes available. This expansion, in turn, opens the way to the selection of a lower-cost portfolio.

The reduction in immediate costs from planning on the basis of a positive reinvestment rate can be significant. In these cases, the reinvestment rate—even for short periods of reinvestment—will become a critical parameter.

Exhibit 5 depicts a new matching portfolio based on the more reasonable

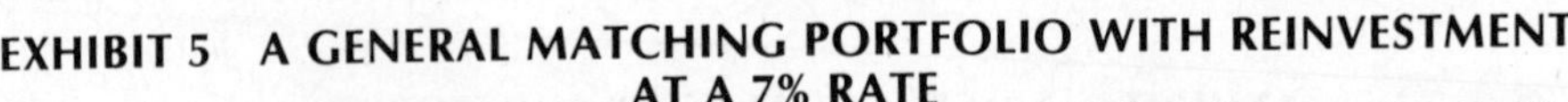

EXHIBIT 5 A GENERAL MATCHING PORTFOLIO WITH REINVESTMENT AT A 7% RATE

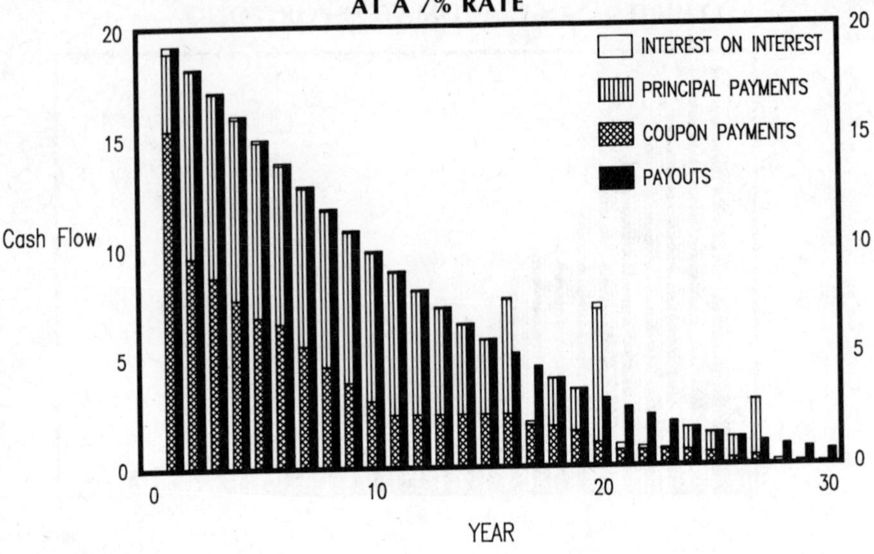

presumption that a reinvestment rate of at least 7% would be available throughout the entire liability schedule. The 7% reinvestment provides additional dollars both within each period as well as between successive periods. These increments of interest-on-interest prove just sufficient to enable the cash flow to meet all the required payouts. The magnitude of savings realized from a positive reinvestment rate will vary with market conditions and the permissible range of securities.

PORTFOLIO CONSTRAINTS

In practice, cash flow matching portfolios will be subject to a variety of constraints imposed by both the logic of the problem and the degree of conservatism sought by the fund's sponsor. These constraints will relate to call vulnerability, quality, type of issuer, diversification across type and individual issuer, the utilization of holdings from preexisting portfolios, and so on.

The **call/prepayment vulnerability** of specific bonds or **mortgage-backed securities**—whether for refunding, sinking fund, or other purposes—is naturally an important concern in any portfolio designed to provide a prescribed cash flow. The problem of potential calls or refundings can be totally avoided by purchasing only noncallable securities. Such a prohibition would rule out many higher-yielding securities. Therefore it would prove to be another very expensive constraint. A more practical approach is to accept fixed-income securities that have sufficiently low coupons so as to make the prospect of a refunding call or mortgage prepayment either improbable or so productive in terms of windfall gain that it assures adequate reinvestment income.

Another important constraint relates to the **credit quality** of the securities comprising the portfolio. Of course, the ultimate in credit quality would be a portfolio consisting of all U.S. Treasury securities, because this would remove the need for any credit surveillance. As in the other cases, however, such an extreme stance would prove to be expensive. In most cases, corporate securities of different qualities are acceptable provided that the mixture is appropriately diversified across various industries and issuers.

In trying to determine the appropriate overall credit level for the portfolio, it can be helpful to develop a trade-off diagram similar to Exhibit 6. The overall quality level of the portfolio will bear an (admittedly rough) relationship to the relative overall yields of the portfolio holdings. Exhibit 6 shows how the cost of an optimal portfolio decreases with the increasing yield spread associated with the relaxation of the quality constraint. Obviously, the actual savings that can be realized from a given set of portfolio constraints will vary considerably, depending on extant market conditions.

Another important constraint often encountered in practice relates to preexisting bond portfolios. In many cases the fund sponsor may wish to construct cash flow matching portfolios using as many of the existing holdings as possible. There can be numerous motivations. First, it may reduce the new cash required to establish the matching portfolio. Second, it will reduce transaction costs. Third, it may avoid problems associated with the recognition of realized gain—or, more likely, realized losses in the existing portfolio.

The specific structure, aberrations, and peculiarities of the marketplace at a given time will have a huge impact on the optimal cash-matched portfolio. The key to developing such a portfolio is to apply the most modern computer optimization techniques to the broadest possible universe of truly available bonds identified with their truly available prices.

EXHIBIT 6 THE EFFECTS OF QUALITY ON PORTFOLIO COST

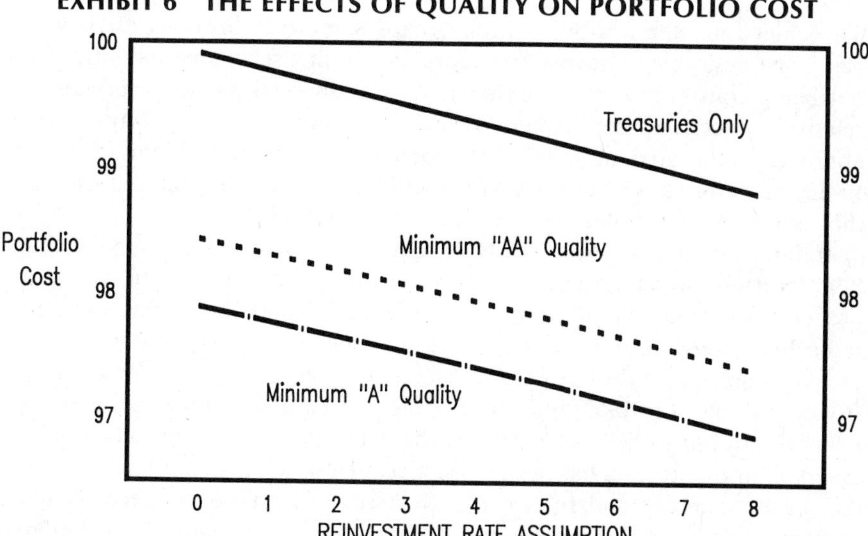

ACTIVE MANAGEMENT OF CASH-MATCHED PORTFOLIO

As noted, the cash-matched portfolio is theoretically designed to fulfill its function even under a totally passive buy-and-hold posture—that is, the simple mechanical collection of coupon and principal receipts. However, the changing character of the marketplace is likely to create opportunities where certain forms of active management would appear appropriate for even the most risk-averse sponsor of a matched-portfolio system. Clearly, the integrity of the portfolio's conservative purpose must be maintained, and this will limit the nature of acceptable management activity.

The active management of cash-matched portfolios has developed into a fine art. Many portfolio managers have been able to create significant cash takeouts and portfolio improvements by taking advantage of the changing market environment. Although changes in the level of the market per se tend to have relatively little effect on the cash-matched portfolio, changes in the structure of the market can create sizable opportunities for active management. These structural changes include reshaping of the yield curve, the availability of new issues with different maturities and coupons, and the changing spread relationships among the various sectors. In addition, revisions in the portfolio's cash balances and/or liability schedule over time can lead to significant, clear-cut savings.

Considerable incremental savings can be extracted through energetic management of a cash-matched portfolio. At the same time, it must be recognized that cash matching is a relatively stringent and tightly constrained period-by-period approach to the problem at hand.

BOND IMMUNIZATION

To achieve greater flexibility and perhaps somewhat lower costs, it would clearly be desirable to have a procedure for funding scheduled liabilities without being constrained at the outset to each individual payout, especially the relatively uncertain ones in later years. The concept of immunization is one approach to this goal, although it has some rather serious problems of its own. In the following subsections, we will describe the principles of immunization as they apply to the simple case of a single-point liability.

Immunization is a specialized technique for constructing and rebalancing a bond portfolio to achieve a specified return target. The idea is to closely approach or exceed this return target in the face of changes in interest rates, even radical changes in interest rates. In other words, one is trying to "immunize" the portfolio against the "disease" of changing rates. This is not a new concept. It was introduced in 1952 by F. M. Redington in a paper in the (British) *Journal of the Institute of Actuaries.* In the three decades since its introduction, the theory of immunization has been the subject of a wide range of research studies that have advanced and refined the theoretical foundation underlying bond immunization. (See References and Bibliography for a sampling of the large body of research papers in this area, e.g., Bierwag, Bierwag and Kaufman, Leibowitz, Shedden, and Marshall and Yawitz.)

IMMUNIZATION AND REINVESTMENT RISK. Since bonds do mature eventually, they tend to provide a certain natural immunity to changing rates, at least over planning periods ending with their maturity. However, there still remains the uncertainty associated with the future rates at which bond coupon payments can be reinvested. It is this reinvestment risk that the portfolio manager is trying to reduce to even closer tolerances.

For example, when asked to secure a target return over a given period such as 5 years, a portfolio manager might at first respond by selecting a portfolio of bonds having a maturity of 5 years. If these bonds were of sufficiently high grade, the portfolio would essentially be assured of receiving all the coupon income due during the 5 years, then the redemption payment in the fifth year. However, coupon income and principal payments are only two of the three sources of return from a bond portfolio. The third source of return is the interest-on-interest derived from the reinvestment of coupon income (and/or the rollover of the maturing principal). Since this reinvestment will take place in the interest rate environments that exist at the time of the coupon receipts, there is no way to ensure that one will obtain the amount of interest-on-interest required to achieve the target return.

Exhibit 7 illustrates this point. A 5-year 9% bond will provide $450 of coupon income and $1,000 of maturing principal over its 5-year life. This would amount to an added return of $450 beyond the original $1,000 investment. However, to achieve a 9% compound growth rate in asset value over the 5-year period, the original $1,000 would have to reach a cumulative value of $1,553, which is an incremental dollar return of $553. This $103 gap in return has to be overcome through the accumulation of interest-on-interest. As Exhibit 7 shows, this amount of interest-on-interest will be achieved when coupon reinvestment occurs at the same 9% rate as the bond's original yield to maturity. At lower reinvestment rates, the interest-on-interest will be less than the amount required and the growth in asset value will fall somewhat short of the required target value of $1,553.

This reinvestment problem becomes even more severe over longer invest-

EXHIBIT 7 REALIZED RETURN FROM 5-YEAR 9% PAR BOND OVER A 5-YEAR HORIZON

Reinvestment Rate (%)	Coupon Income	Capital Gain	Interest-on-Interest	Total Dollar Return	Realized Compound Yield (%)
0	$450	$0	$0	$450	7.57
7	450	0	78	528	8.66
8	450	0	90	540	8.83
9	450	0	103	553	9.00
10	450	0	116	566	9.17
11	450	0	129	579	9.35

ment periods. Exhibit 8 shows the total dollar amount and the percentage of the target return that must be achieved through interest-on-interest for various investment periods ranging from 1 to 30 years. This "reinvestment risk" is a major problem in achieving any assured level of target return. However, there are ways of limiting this reinvestment risk. For example, Exhibit 9 shows the total return and cumulative asset value for a 5-year bond over investment horizons ranging from 1 to 5 years. For the periods shorter than 5 years, the bond's price in Exhibit 3 has been determined by the simplistic assumption that the yield to maturity coincides with the indicated reinvestment rate. This set of assumptions corresponds to a scenario where interest rates immediately move to a flat yield curve at the level of the indicated reinvestment rate, and remain there throughout the entire investment period.

Exhibit 9 illustrates the well-known facts that over the short term, lower interest rates lead to increased returns through price appreciation, while over the longer term, lower interest rates lead to reduced returns through reduced interest-on-interest. For periods lying betwen the short term and the longer term, it is not surprising to find these two effects somewhat compensating for each other.

This leads to the question of whether there might be some intermediate point during a bond's life when these compensating effects precisely offset each other. Again, from Exhibit 9, we can see that for a 7% reinvestment rate this offset does exist and occurs at 4.13 years. That such an offset point should exist is not, of course, surprising in a situation characterized by two conflicting forces—reinvestment and capital gains—with one force growing stronger and the other force growing weaker with time. What may be somewhat more surprising is that with reinvestment rates of 7.9, and 11%, this offset point occurs at the same 4.13 years. (This is not perhaps intuitively obvious, although it can be readily demonstrated through mathematical analysis.)

In the context of the fund seeking an assured level of return, this finding has

EXHIBIT 8 MAGNITUDE OF INTEREST-ON-INTEREST TO ACHIEVE 9% REALIZED COMPOUND YIELD FROM 9% PAR BONDS OF VARIOUS MATURITIES

Maturity (years)	Total Dollar Return	Interest-on-Interest at 9% Reinvestment Rate	Interest-on-Interest (%) of Total Return
1	$ 92	$ 2	2.2%
2	193	13	6.5
3	302	32	10.7
4	422	62	14.7
5	553	103	18.6
7	852	222	26.1
10	1,412	512	36.2
20	4,816	3,016	62.6
30	13,027	10,327	79.3

EXHIBIT 9 REALIZED RETURN FROM A 5-YEAR 9% PAR BOND OVER VARIOUS HORIZON PERIODS

	Horizon Period (years)			
	1	3	4.13	5
Coupon Income:	\$ 90	\$270	\$372	\$450
7% Reinvestment Rate and YTM at Horizon				
Capital gain	\$ 68	\$ 37	\$ 16	\$ 0
Interest-on-interest	\$ 2	\$ 25	\$ 51	\$ 78
Total dollar return	\$160	\$331	\$439	\$528
Realized compound yield	15.43%	9.77%	9.00%	8.66%
9% Reinvestment Rate and YTM at Horizon				
Capital gain	\$ 0	\$ 0	\$ 0	\$ 0
Interest-on-interest	\$ 2	\$ 32	\$ 67	\$103
Total dollar return	\$ 92	\$302	\$439	\$553
Realized compound yield	9.00%	9.00%	9.00%	9.00%
11% Reinvestment Rate and YTM at Horizon				
Capital gain	−\$ 63	−\$ 35	−\$ 16	\$ 0
Interest-on-interest	\$ 2	\$ 40	\$ 83	\$129
Total dollar return	\$ 29	\$275	\$439	\$579
Realized compound yield	2.89%	8.26%	9.00%	9.36%

great significance. To achieve the guaranteed 9% return over 4.13 years, Exhibit 9 shows that there would be no problem in doing so with the 5-year bond, no matter what reinvestment rates existed (as long as they followed the simplistic "flat yield curve pattern" assumed in the construction of Exhibit 9).

THE MACAULAY DURATION. This offset effect occurs because the "duration" of a 5-year 9% par bond is 4.13 years. This same offset can be achieved over the original 5-year horizon by buying a somewhat longer bond having a maturity of between 6 and 7 years. The precise maturity that gives this "magical" immunization over the 5-year period is determined by seeking a bond whose duration is 5 years.

Duration is a concept that was first proposed by Frederick R. Macaulay (1938). He was searching for a way to characterize the average life of a bond in a way that would reflect the present value of its total cash flow. Exhibit 10 illustrates the dollar value of a level payment stream. The average life of this stream would fall at the simple fulcrum point indicated in the diagram. Exhibit 11 shows a similar level stream, but also illustrates the present value of each of the payments. Macaulay argued that a more appropriate measure of the life of

EXHIBIT 10 AVERAGE LIFE OF PAYMENT STREAM

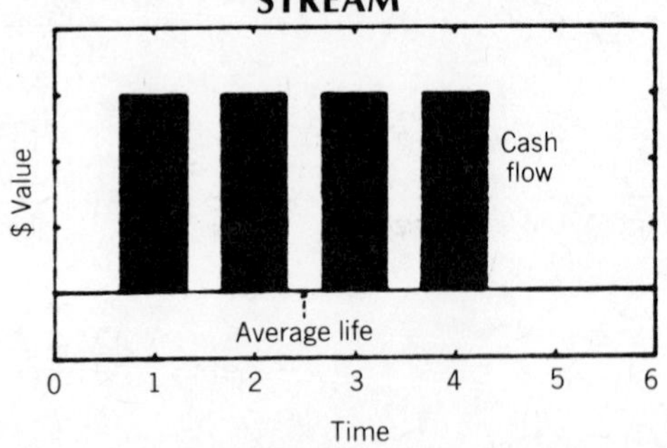

EXHIBIT 11 PRESENT VALUE OF PAYMENT STREAM

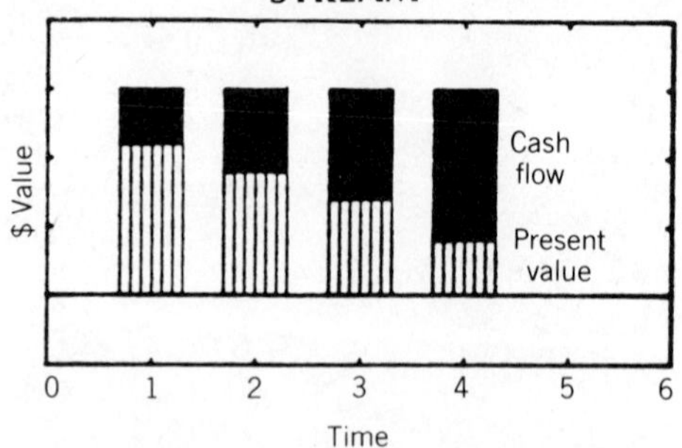

EXHIBIT 12 DURATION OF PAYMENT STREAM

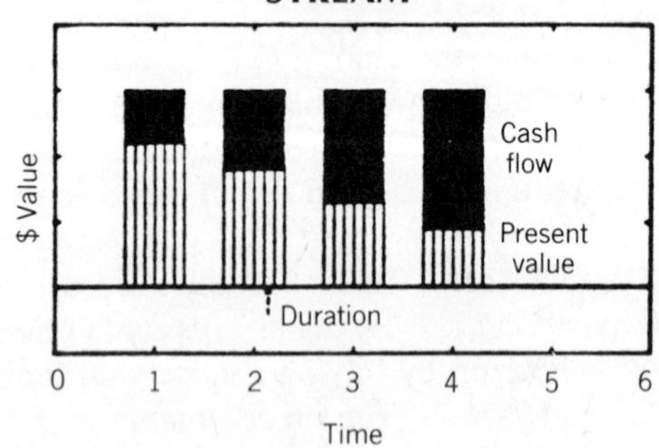

any cash flow would be the average time point of the flow of present values, as opposed to simply the flow of raw dollar amounts. Since earlier payments have a higher present value than later ones, this would lead to a fulcrum point that is shorter than the conventionally calculated average life (Exhibit 12). Macaulay used the term "duration" to represent this measure of the time to each payment, weighted by the present value of that payment.

Thus a 1-year bill has a duration of 1. A 2-year bill, if you could buy one, would have a duration of 2. Coupon securities, however, have durations that

EXHIBIT 13 DURATION OF VARIOUS BONDS, ALL PRICED TO YIELD 9%

Maturity	Coupon (%)			
(years)	0	7.5	9.0	10.50
1	1.00	0.98	0.98	0.98
2	2.00	1.89	1.87	1.86
3	3.00	2.74	2.70	2.66
4	4.00	3.51	3.45	3.38
5	5.00	4.23	4.13	4.05
7	7.00	5.50	5.34	5.20
10	10.00	7.04	6.80	6.59
20	20.00	9.96	9.61	9.35
30	30.00	11.05	10.78	10.59
100	100.00	11.61	11.61	11.61

are always less than their maturity. As discussed earlier, a 5-year 9% par bond has a duration of 4.13 years. Exhibits 13 and 14 show how the durations of 9% par bonds grow with increasing maturity. Because of the way this curve bends at the longer maturities, it turns out that durations of 10 or 11 are about the longest values that can be obtained in the market. At higher rate levels such as the 12% rate level shown in Exhibit 14, there is an even further shrinkage in the maximum duration values. Macaulay defined duration in this way because he felt that it represented a more logical measure of a bond's life. At the time, he failed to recognize that the duration also had another, perhaps even more valuable, property—it served as a gauge of the percentage price change associated with an incremental move in the bond's yield.

DURATION EQUIVALENTS OF ZERO-COUPON BONDS. The combination of the foregoing properties enables one to use duration to relate complex cash flows to simple cash flows. In particular, one can use the duration concept to find real bonds that behave like zero-coupon bonds. For the theoretical case

EXHIBIT 14 DURATION VERSUS MATURITY

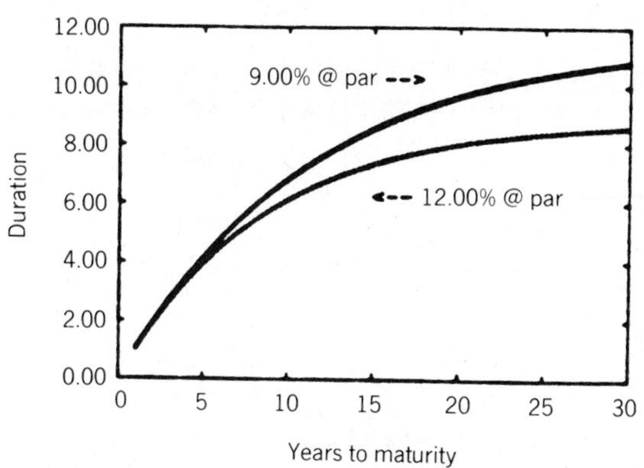

of a **pure discount, zero-coupon bond,** the duration will coincide with its maturity. Since zero-coupon bonds have no cash flows before maturity, they are free from the problem of coupon reinvestment. A 5-year zero-coupon bond priced to yield 9% would always provide the targeted 9% return over its maturity period, no matter what interest rates may occur over its life. Hence, the zero-coupon bond is the ideal vehicle for an immunization strategy.

It would obviously be desirable to somehow use real coupon bonds to obtain some of the characteristics of zero-coupon bonds. This can be done, and the bond's duration is the key link. A coupon bond with a given duration is similar mathematically to a zero-coupon bond having a maturity equal to the duration. For example, as shown in Exhibit 13, a 9% target return over a 5-year period could be achieved by either a 5-year maturity zero-coupon discount bond at a 9% yield rate or a 6.7-year 9% par bond. Both these bonds have the same duration—5 years. Thus the first step in a simple *immunization* proceure is to construct a portfolio having a duration corresponding to the length of the planning horizon.

Returning to the original objective of providing an assured 9% target return over a 5-year period, one should choose a 6.7-year bond having a duration of 5 years, as opposed to a maturity of 5 years. Exhibit 15 shows how such a bond will indeed achieve the growth in overall asset value required to provide the 9% return compounded semiannually. In the face of interest rate changes, this 9% growth is maintained through the compensating increases (or declines) in the interest-on-interest and the capital gain components of return.

A VIEW OF IMMUNIZATION OVER TIME. Immunization can be viewed as a dynamic process over time through the illustration shown in Exhibits 16, 17, and 18. Exhibit 16 shows the growth in value from a 9% par bond (of any maturity) under the assumption that rates remain constant at 9%. Now suppose rates dropped to 7%. Without any consideration of capital gains, Exhibit 17 shows how the reduced reinvestment income would result in a shortfall in interest-on-interest and a consequent failure to meet the 9% target return. Exhibit 18 shows the capital gain associated with a 6.7-year 9% par bond (i.e., a bond having a duration of 5 years). The assumption here is that all rates move

EXHIBIT 15 REALIZED RETURN OVER A 5-YEAR HORIZON FROM A 9% PAR BOND HAVING A 5-YEAR DURATION[a]

Reinvestment Rate and Yield-to-Maturity at Horizon (%)	Coupon Income	Capital Gain	Interest-on-Interest	Total Dollar Return	Realized Compound Yield (%)
7	$450	$25	$ 78	$553	9.00
8	450	13	90	553	9.00
9	450	0	103	553	9.00
10	450	−13	116	553	9.00
11	450	−26	129	553	9.00

[a] For illustrative purposes, this table is based on the somewhat artificial case of a bond that can be purchased free of accrued interest.

EXHIBIT 16 ASSET GROWTH FROM 9% PAR BOND WITH RATES CONSTANT AT 9%

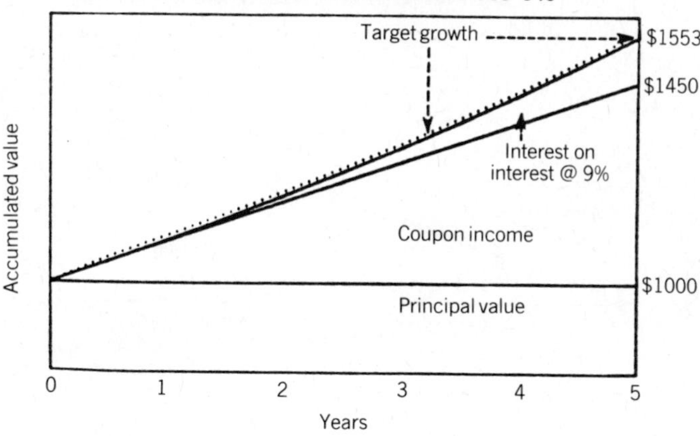

immediately to the 7% level. Hence there is a sudden capital gain at the outset, which declines as the bond ages over the 5-year investment horizon. Exhibit 18 shows how the remaining capital gain at the 5-year horizon is just sufficient to compensate for the reduced reinvestment income, and thereby maintain the original 9% target. This compensation process is the key to the basic idea of immunization. In turn, the fundamental concept underlying the compensation process is Macaulay's duration—the present-value-weighted average life of the bond's cash flow.

DURATION AND CONTROL OF VOLATILITY RISK

In addition to its role as a measure of the average time to repayment of a bond's cash flow (or indeed of any specified cash flow over time), duration has an important interpretation with respect to price volatility of a bond.

EXHIBIT 17 SHORTFALL FROM 7% REINVESTMENT

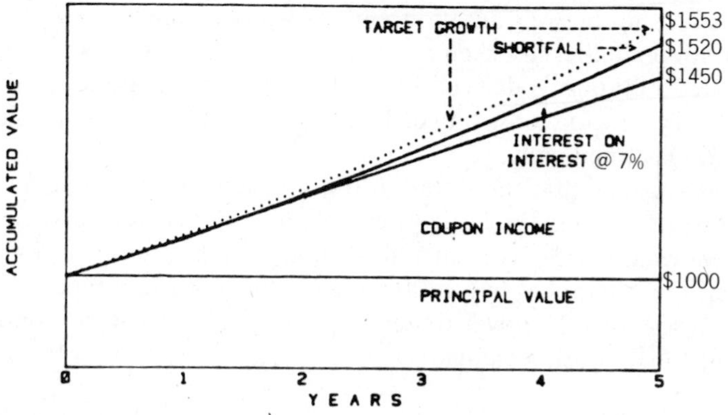

EXHIBIT 18 COMPENSATING CAPTAL GAIN FROM 9% PAR BOND WITH 5-YEAR DURATION

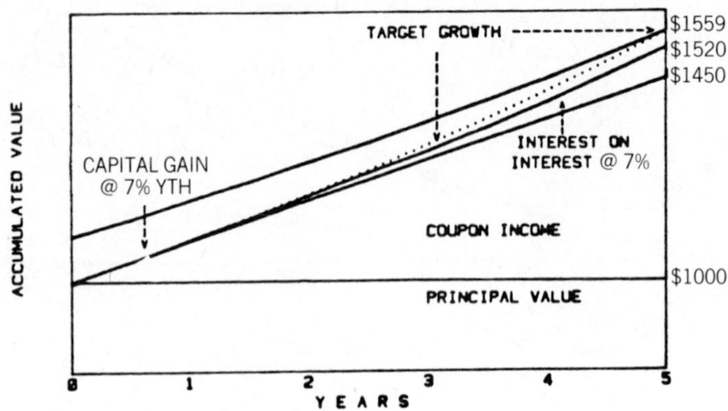

It is, of course, well known that maturity functions as a rough guide to the volatility of bonds as interest rates change. Longer term bonds tend to be more volatile than shorter term bonds. However, this crude gauge has a number of problems associated with it, especially when one seeks to achieve a more refined volatility analysis. For example, while a 2-year bond is almost twice as volatile as a 1-year bond, it is not true that a 30-year bond is twice as volatile as a 15-year bond. This effect is illustrated in Exhibit 19, which shows the price movement of 9% par bonds of various maturities under a ±100 basis point change in yield to maturity. It is clear from this figure that the incremental increase in volatility tends to diminish with each additional year of maturity. Thus a perpetual bond is not a great deal more volatile than a 30-year bond. In fact, under some circumstances, there are bonds with maturities in the 30–50 year range that may be more volatile than the perpetual.

The general shape of Exhibit 19 is reminiscent of the curves in Exhibit 8 tracing the relationship of duration to a bond's maturity. This immediately raises the possibility that duration might function as a useful gauge of bond price volatility. In Exhibit 20, the duration of a 9% par bond is overlayed on the price movements shown in Exhibit 19. This demonstrates that there is indeed a close relationship betwen duration and volatility. A slight adjustment in the basic duration number has been made to achieve the fit as shown in Exhibit 20, the adjusted duration is derived by simply multiplying the original duration value by a scale factor consisting of 1/(1 + yield rate). This relationship can be developed mathematically.

All this suggests that the duration (on adjustment) can serve as adequate first approximation for the basic price volatility of a bond. This remains true even when dealing with discount and premium bonds. Indeed, as noted earlier, this general result applies beyond the realm of simple bond-type cash flows to any prescribed cash flow over time: the price sensitivity can be approximated by the adjusted duration value.

EXHIBIT 19 PRICE VOLATILITY: 9% PAR BONDS

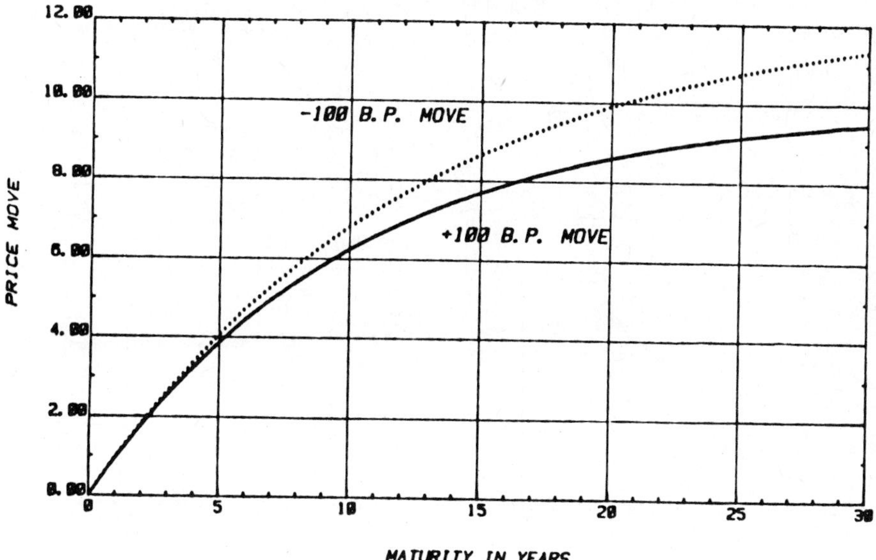

At first glance, the earlier definition of duration as a measure of present-value-weighted average life seems to clash curiously with its interpretation as a price volatility measure. While these two interpretations are immediate consequences of the mathematical specifications of duration, the connection remains somewhat difficult to grasp at an intuitive level. Macaulay introduced duration in an effort to find an appropriate measure of the time that a given loan remains outstanding. He did not realize the role that duration could play as a volatility measure. In fact, it was not until many years later that this fundamentally simple connection was finally uncovered.

To undertand why duration functions so well as a volatility measure, it may be useful to think in terms of how volatility would be assessed in a "simple interest" environment. For example, consider a 10-year 9% par bond. Now further suppose that interest rates rise suddenly, so that the bond's price falls 5 points to a level of 95. Over the bond's 10-year life, these 5 points of discount will be translated into 5 points of capital gain. In turn, this capital gain provides a certain increment to the bond's yield. To estimate this yield increment using a very crude simple-interest-like calculation, the 5-point capital gain could be amortized over the 10-year life of the bond. This would provide, roughly speaking, an additional 50 basis points per year of yield. In other words, the +50 basis point yield move, when multiplied by a factor of −10 (corresponding to the bond's maturity) gives rise to an approximation of the 5-point decline experienced in price. Thus the value of 10 determined from the bond's life also corresponds to a price volatility factor that can relate the yield movement (+0.50%) to the resulting price change (-5%).

One might expect some version of this simple interest concept of amortizing

EXHIBIT 20 DURATION AS FUNCTION OF PRICE VOLATILITY: 9% PAR BONDS

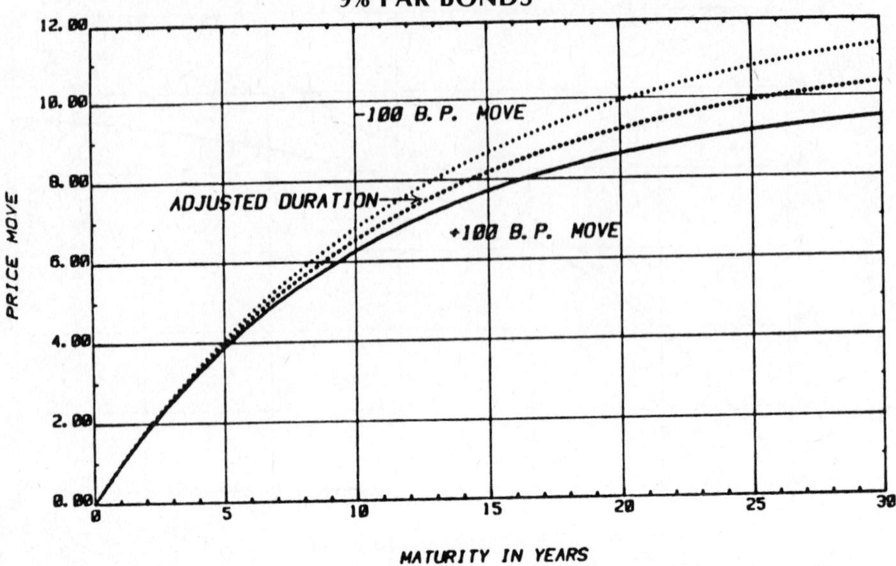

a price change over the bond's life to provide an approximate volatility factor for the more realistic case of a time-valued environment. In a time-valued environment, where present value and compounding of interim cash flows are at work, one must then ask what constitutes a reasonable measure of a bond's life. From the preceding subsections, it is evident that the maturity by itself is not such a measure. It should also be evident that duration was designed to act as just such a time-valued gauge of a bond's "life." Therefore, one should not be surprised to find that the price change amortized over the duration of the bond should give an estimate of the associated yield change. Viewing this relationship from the other direction, the bond's duration acts as an effective scale factor for estimating the price move derived from a given change in yield to maturity. In other words, the duration can act as a good measure of a bond's price volatility.

OTHER RISK CONTROL STRATEGIES

The yield curve is a key concept in the bond market. As shown in Exhibit 21, the yield curve is essentially a graph of a consistent series of issues, usually U.S. Treasury "near-par" bonds, plotted with the yield to maturity on a vertical axis against the time to their respective maturities on the horizontal axis. While the yield curve serves many purposes in both the description and the analysis of the debt market, it is often used (sometimes implicitly) as a representation of reward-risk tradeoff. In this connection, the preceding discussion of the problems with maturity and the better results obtained with duration, suggests that

EXHIBIT 21 TRADITIONAL YIELD CURVE

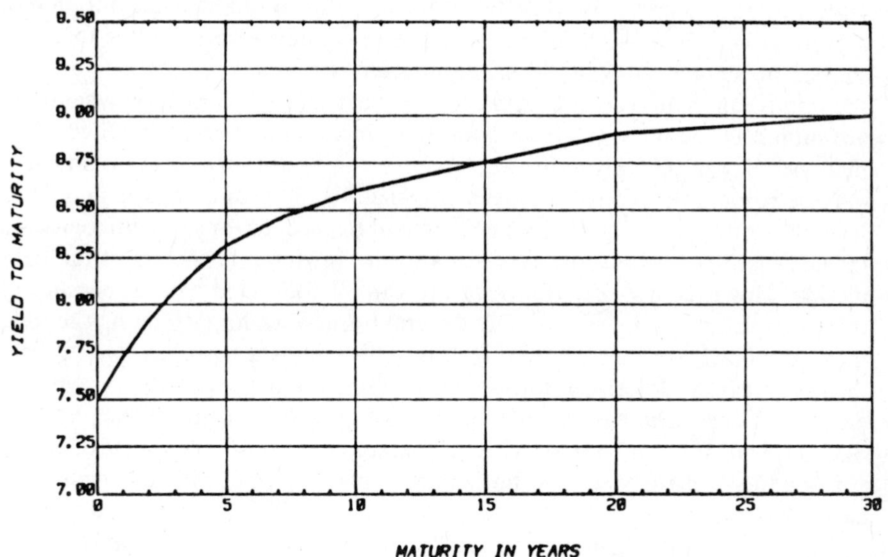

perhaps duration of bonds should be substituted for maturity as the horizontal "risk" axis. For the traditional yield curve depicted in Exhibit 21, the use of duration for the horizontal axis leads to the transformed yield curve shown in Exhibit 22. A display such as Exhibit 16 can be helpful in a construction of bond portfolios that maintain a certain level of volatility risk.

EXHIBIT 22 DURATION AS RISK AXIS FOR YIELD CURVE

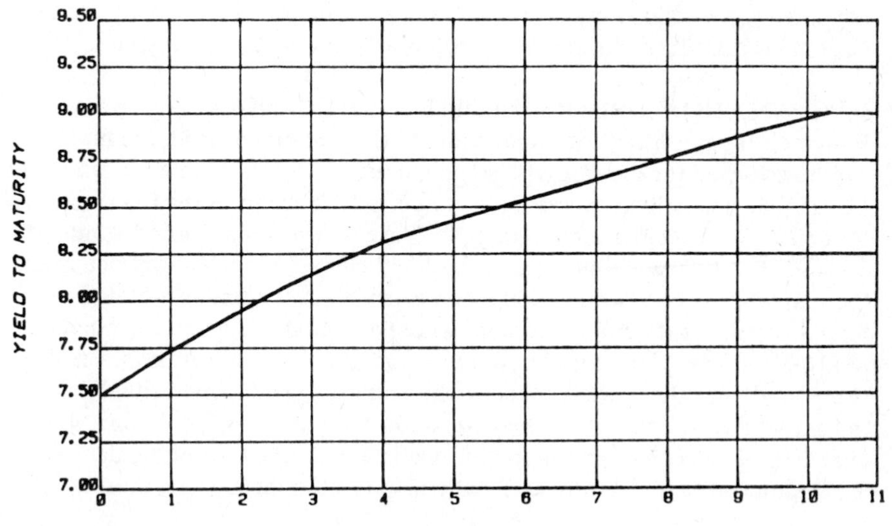

Before pursuing the role of duration as a price volatility measure, one would do well to recognize the limitations inherent in this technique. The duration of a bond does provide a useful gauge of the price movements relative to a prescribed movement in yield. As such, duration will indeed be a good gauge of the relative price movements between a 30-year and a 5-year bond when both are subject to the same 100 basis point movement in interest rates. However, it may well be that in a given market situation the 5-year area of the yield curve may be vulnerable to greater movements than the 30-year area (i.e., nonparallel shifts in rates). Duration does not pretend to account for such differences in "yield volatility" between different maturities or different sectors of the debt market. However, the duration measure can be combined with a measure of "yield volatility" to develop a more general framework for estimating the total market volatility of various debt sectors. This entails a more involved procedure than can be described in this section. For a complete description see Leibowitz, *The Risk Dimension* (1977) and Bierwag, Kaufman, and Khang (1978). Such measures of total market volatility should theortically be the next step in constructing a comprehensive horizontal "volatility risk axis" for evaluating eward-risk tradeoffs.

To obtain a more generalized framework, the vertical reward axis should also be extended beyond the simple concept of yield to maturity. Again, there are various ways for trying to achieve this, and they are also described in Leibowitz, *The Rolling Yield* (1977).

The key to these approaches, as well as to other methods for achieving various forms of risk control over specified horizons, lies in a deeper understanding of the time value and volatility characteristics of fixed cash flows. Although the concept of immunization is a relatively narrow version of these many possible approaches, it provides a clear insight into the volatility-reinvestment factors that form the foundation for any risk control strategy. While it is impossible within the confines of this section to dwell at great length on these broader techniques, the following discussion represents an attempt to clarify the main issues that arise from efforts to develop practical immunization strategies.

IMMUNIZATION UNDER MULTIPLE RATE CHANGES. As seen earlier, by setting the portfolio's duration equal to the planning period, immunization can be achieved for the case of a single, immediate jump in interest rates. The key assumption is that interest rates immeiately move from their current level to some given level and remain there for the entire planning period. Under this assumption of "a single move to a flat yield curve," the new level determines the reinvestment rate for coupon income as well as the final price of the portfolio. For an initial bond investment whose Macaulay duration corresponds to the length of the planning period, these conditions would result in a realized compound yield that closely matches the promised yield to maturity. However, this finding would have only theoretical interest unless one could find ways to deal with more general and more believable assumptions. In particular, before the immunization procedure can really be put into practice, one must come to grips with the assured fact that there will be multiple changes in rates during the course of the planning period. Here we explore how rebalancing procedures can be used to accommodate such multiple changes in rates.

It is easy to demonstrate the problems that arise when one drops the "single-move" assumption and allows for "multiple movements." If rates remained at 9% throughout the 5-year period, a $1,000 investment in this bond would compound to $1,522.97, thereby providing the 9% return that one would expect in the "no move" case (Exhibit 23A). To illustrate the effects of a "single move" in rates, suppose that rates immediately jumped to 12% and then stayed there for the remaining 5-year period (Exhibit 23B). This bond would then generate a coupon income of $436.67, interest-on-interest of $162.49, and a capital loss of $42.91, which is slightly better than the 9% target level of return.

There is another way of viewing the events in Exhibit 23B. The sudden rate move generates an immediate capital loss of $131. For the remaining asset value of $890 to grow to the target level, a compound growth rate of 12% must be achieved throughout the next 5 years, for example,

$$\$869 \times (1.06)^{10} = \$1,556.25.$$

In this sense, the 5-year return of 12% is needed to compensate for the immediate price loss incurred as rates jumped from 9 to 12%. In any case, the example in Exhibit 23B illustrates that under the "single move" assumption, even when the move is as large as 300 basis points, we still manage to realize the required target return.

However, let us see what happens under a simple case involving a "multiple move" in rates. Suppose, as before, that the first move in rates happens immediately after purchase and changes the yield curve to 12%. This rate persists for the next 5 years. But then, just before the bond is sold at the fifth year, there is a second jump in interest rates to 13% (Exhibit 23C). All numbers are then the same as in the earlier example, with the exception of the capital loss, which now amounts to $56.58. This greater capital loss brings the total future value down to $1,542.57, for a total realized compound yield of 8.86%. Thus, under this two-move assumption, the portfolio falls short of its target by more than 14 basis points.

If immunization procedures could not deal with such simple "multiple movements" in rates, there would clearly be a problem in achieving any sort of application in real life. Fortunately, techniques exist involving portfolio rebalancing that can overcome this difficulty.

REBALANCING USING DURATION. The problem arising from multiple rate movements can be traced to the way a bond ages over time. Exhibit 24 illustrates how our theoretical bond, having a starting duration of 5 years, ages on a year-by-year basis. With each passing year, the maturity obviously gets shorter by 1 year, but the duration becomes shorter by less than a year. For example, over the first year, the bond's duration "ages" from 5.0 to 4.4, a drop of

EXHIBIT 23 PORTFOLIO VALUES DEVELOPED UNDER VARIOUS INTEREST RATE PATTERNS: INITIAL PORTFOLIO, $1,000 INVESTMENT IN 6.7-YEAR 9% PAR BOND: INITIAL DURATION, 5 YEARS

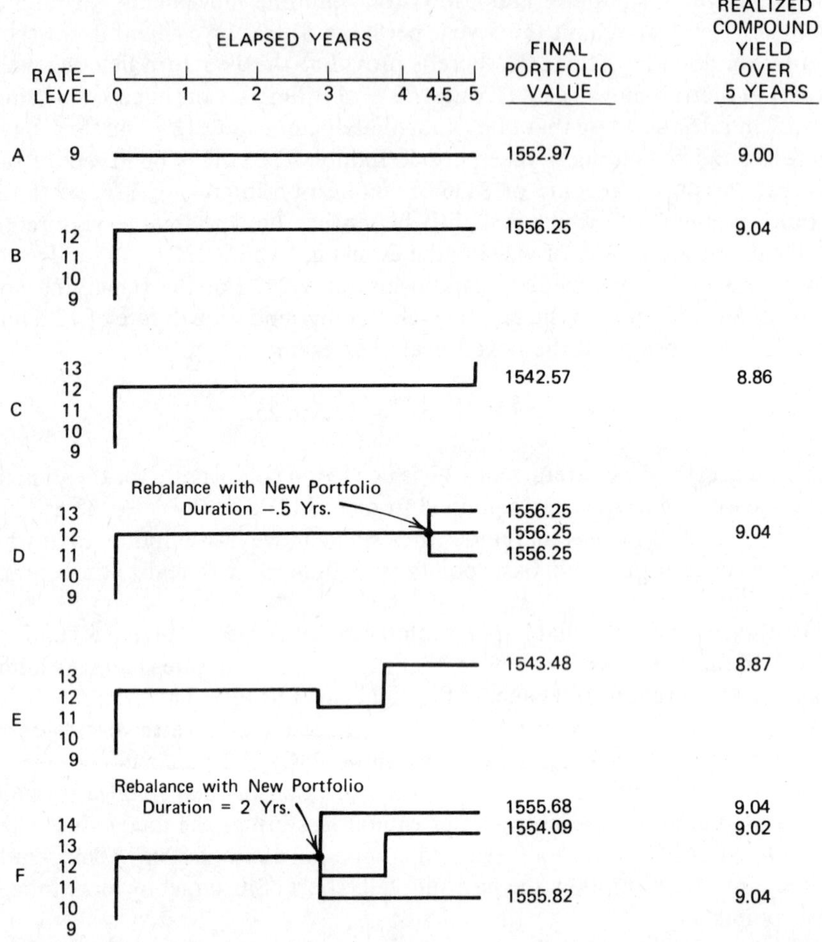

only 0.6 for the year. At the end of the fifth year, when we would clearly like to have a duration of zero, the original bond has a duration of 1.5 years, even when combined with the cash flow generated by coupon reinvestment, the blended duration of the portfolio becomes seriously mismatched with the passage of time.

This "duration drift" can be overcome by periodic rebalancing of the portfolio. For example, suppose that at the end of 4.5 years, the portfolio had been "rebalanced" in the following fashion. The bond was sold at a yield to maturity of 12%, leading to a capital loss of $54.22 and a total future value of $1,468.16 (Exhibit 23D). The entire proceeds were then invested in a 12% par bond, hav-

EXHIBIT 24 CHANGES IN DURATION OF A 9% 6.7-YEAR PAR BOND WITH PASSAGE OF TIME (YEARS)

Elapsed Time	Maturity	Bond's Duration	Target Duration	Mismatch
0	6.66	5.00	5.00	0.00
1	5.66	4.42	4.00	0.42
2	4.66	3.79	3.00	0.79
3	3.66	3.11	2.00	1.11
4	2.66	2.35	1.00	1.35
5	1.66	1.53	0.00	1.53

ing a duration of precisely 0.5. Clearly, this instrument would assure us of achieving a 12% rate of return over the final 0.5-year period. In turn, this would provide a 12% return over the entire 5 years, bringing the total value of the portfolio up to $1,556.25. In other words, by rebalancing before the second movement in interest rates, we would have immunized ourselves to the effects of that movement.

As a further example, suppose that a second move to 11% had occurred at the end of the third year, and had been followed by a third move to 13%. Coupons from the original 9% bond would have been reinvested for 3 years at 12%, for 1 year at 11%, and for the remaining year at 13%. At the end of the fifth year, the bond would have been sold at 13% yield to maturity, engendering a sizable capital loss. This would lead to a total future value of $1,543.48, well below our target level (Exhibit 23E). However, suppose that the portfolio had been rebalanced at the end of the third year, just before the interest rate jump, to give a duration of exactly 2.0 years. This reset in duration will help ensure that the final 2 years realize a 12% return. This lockup of the 12% rate over the final 2 years is just what is needed, together with the return achieved over the first 3 years, to ensure realizing the original target return of 9% (Exhibit 23F).

The preceding example illustrates the key idea underlying the immunization process. By rebalancing to continually maintain a duration matching the remaining life of the planning period, the bond portfolio is kept in an immunized state throughout the period. This guarantees that the portfolio will achieve the target return promised at the outset of every subperiod. By working backward, this implies that the original target return of 9% can be met in the face of multiple movements in interest rates. (The actual proof of this statement entails somewhat involved mathematics, which are treated at great length in the references, e.g., Bierwag, 1977.)

Even when carried out only once a year, this rebalancing procedure can have a dramatic immunizing power in the face of radical changes in interest rates. This is illustrated in Exhibit 25 where interest rates increase by 100 basis points at the end of each year. Through annual rebalancing based on duration, the total portfolio value grows to within 4 basis points of the original 9% target. With more frequent rebalancing one could have an even closer tracking of the original target return.

EXHIBIT 25 PORTFOLIO GROWTH WITH DURATION-BASED REBALANCING: INITIAL INVESTMENT, $1,000

Period Ending Date (years)	Rebalanced Portfolio at Start of Period			Results Over Year			Realized Coupon Yield (%)		
	New Rate Level (%)	Duration (years)	Maturity	Coupon Flow and Interest-on-Interest	Capital Gain	Total Proceeds	Over Year	Cumulative	Blended[a]
1	9	5.00	6.66	$ 92.02	$41.18	$1,050.84	5.02	5.02	8.99
2	10	4.00	5.14	107.72	−33.03	1,125.52	6.98	6.00	8.99
3	11	3.00	3.66	127.22	−24.12	1,228.61	8.96	6.98	8.97
4	12	2.00	2.27	151.86	−13.61	1,366.87	10.95	7.97	8.97
5	13	1.00	1.00	183.47	0	1,550.34	13.00	8.96	8.96

[a] The 5-year return that would result if the portfolio value at that date were to be compounded at the existing new rate level for all remaining periods.

REBALANCING AS A PROXY FOR A ZERO-COUPON BOND OVER TIME. At first glance, the success of this rebalancing procedure in keeping the portfolio on target may seem to be somewhat magical. An insight into the rebalancing principle can be provided by thinking in terms of our old friend, the zero-coupon bond. For any change in yield level, the zero-coupon bond automatically retains sufficient asset value to provide the original return over its life. For example, in Exhibit 23B, when interest rates jump from 9 to 12%, a $1,000 investment in a 5-year zero-coupon bond would decline from $1,000 to $867.17. Suppose one were to sell the "zero-coupon" bond immediately after this jump in rates, realize the $867.17 proceeds, and hypothetically invest these funds into another 5-year zero-coupon bond at its market yield of 12%. Over the remaining 5 years, the assured 12% compounding would enable the original $867.17 to grow to $1,552.97, thereby satisfying the original 9% return goal.

The rebalancing process just described is, of course, equivalent to continued holding of the zero-coupon bond. The 5-year zero-coupon bond purchased at 9% has truly locked in the targeted 9% return over the 5-year planning period. Regardless of the magnitude or frequency of subsequent rate movements, the zero-coupon bond stays "on target." Moreover, the zero-coupon bond obviously remains continually "on target" even with the passage of time. In other words, it always retains the precise amount of asset value needed to realize the original target when compounded at the then yield rate for the remainder of the period.

The key idea here is that the price of the zero-coupon bond moves in lock step with the change in the required dollar investment at the new interest rate level. Another way of saying this is that, with respect to interest rate movements, the volatility of the zero-coupon bond coincides with the volatility of the assets required to provide the promised payment in the fifth year. Thus, for a bond portfolio to retain the assets needed to stay "on target," it must have the same volatility as the 5-year zero-coupon bond. Moreover, it must maintain this volatility equivalence as time passes. As shown in the preceding discussion, a bond's volatility is related to its duration. In particular, the duration of a zero-coupon bond coincides with its remaining life. Thus, to stay "on target" over time—as the zero-coupon bond does automatically—an "immunizing bond portfolio" must maintain the same duration over time as the zero-coupon bond. An "immunizing" bond portfolio can maintain this equivalence through duration-based rebalancing. Thus, duration-based rebalancing can provide a bond portfolio that mimics the automatic "immunizing" behavior of the zero-coupon bond in the face of multiple interest rate movements over time.

An Example with Declining Rates. Assume that this rebalancing can be accomplished on an essentially continuous basis. The initial portfolio consists of a 6.7-year 9% par bond appropriate to the 5-year planning period. Suppose that interest rates move down 100 basis points a year in each of those 5 years. After the first year, the portfolio will show a nice capital gain, providing a total return over that 1-year period of 13.07% (Exhibit 26). The portfolio will have a

EXHIBIT 26 IMMUNIZATION THROUGH MATCHING OF REALIZED AND FORWARD RETURNS: 9% TARGET RATE, FLAT YIELD CURVE WITH ANNUAL SHIFTS OF −100 BASIS POINTS

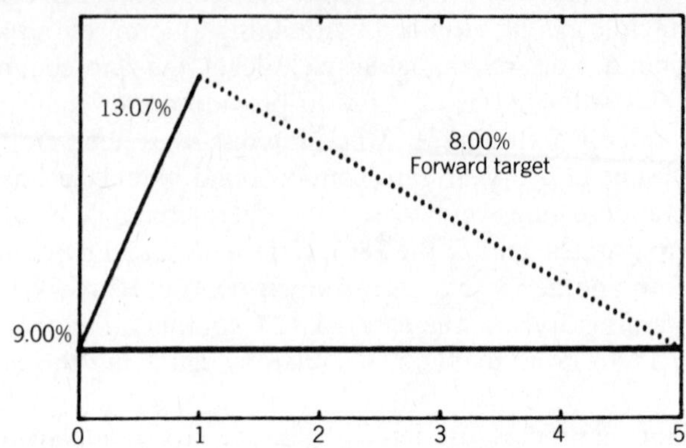

greater dollar value than would have been expected at a constant rate of 9%. That is the good news. The bad news is that this greater asset value can be invested only at the lower rate of 8%. For an immunized portfolio, the good news and the bad news offset each other—they combine into "no news." The increased asset value is just sufficient, when invested at the new lower 8% rate, to keep the portfolio "on target" toward its original goal of 9% over the full 5-year period. As depicted schematically in Exhibit 26, the portfolio's return is like a string pinned down at the 0-year and 5-year points. The change in rates at year end acts to pluck the string away from the horizontal, but it still provides the same 9% cumulative return over the full 5-year period.

At the end of the first year, the portfolio is reinvested into a new 8% par bond having the required duration value of 4. Over the second year, interest rates decline by another 100 basis points to the 7% level. This results in a further capital gain, and a total cumulative return of 12.05% (Exhibit 27). The portfolio is now rolled into a 7% par bond having a duration of 3. This process

EXHIBIT 27 IMMUNIZATION EXAMPLE: SECOND YEAR

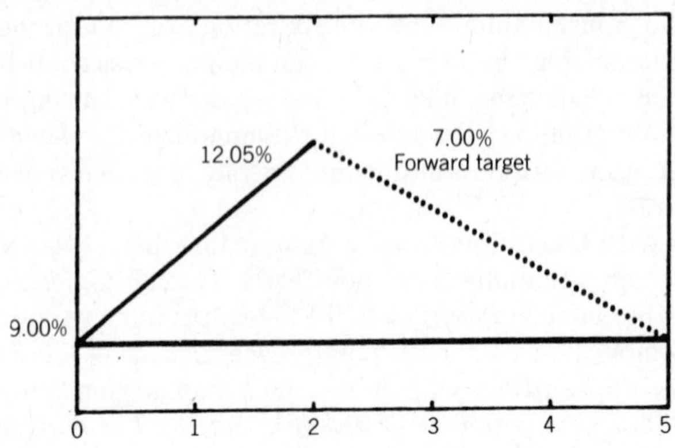

EXHIBIT 28 IMMUNIZATION EXAMPLE: THIRD YEAR

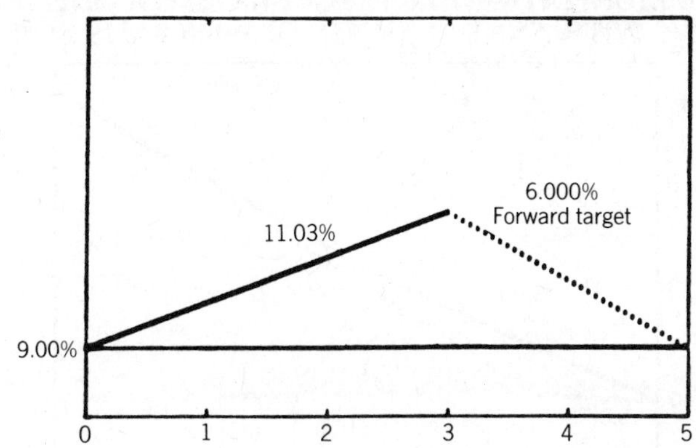

continues year by year, with 100 basis point declines followed by a total reinvestment into par bonds (Exhibit 28). At the end of the fourth year (Exhibit 29), the cumulative return of 10.02% is just sufficient so that, when blended with the 5% rate available over the last year, the 5-year target of 9% will be realized.

An Example with Rising Rates. The preceding scenario moved in the happy direction of lower interest rates and nice capital gains. Suppose the market moves in the opposite direction: higher interest rates and big capital losses. Assume that interest rates increase 100 basis points a year. The proper duration is again assumed to be maintained continuously. To gain a somewhat different viewpoint, a new schematic will be used to represent the growth of the portfolio's asset value over time (Exhibit 30). At the outset, let the asset value be $1,000. It would have to grow to $1,552.97 over the 5-year period to achieve the 9% target rate. The scenario now is that, after the first year, interest rates increase to 10%. This results in a capital loss, for a total return of 5%. This re-

EXHIBIT 29 IMMUNIZATION EXAMPLE: FOURTH YEAR

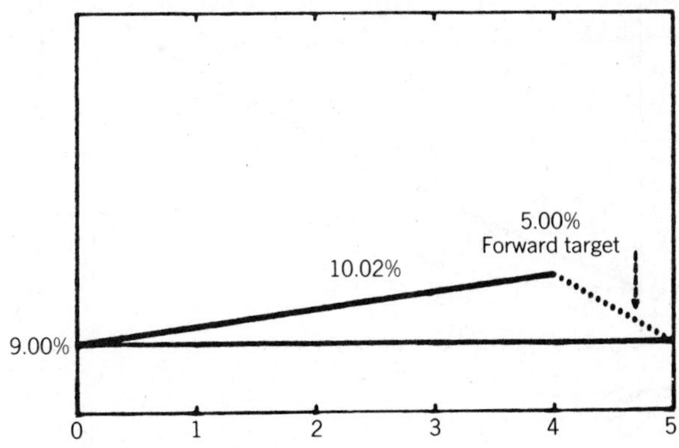

EXHIBIT 30 PORTFOLIO GROWTH THROUGH IMMUNIZATION: 9% TARGET RATE, FLAT YIELD CURVE WITH ANNUAL SHIFTS OF +100 BASIS POINTS

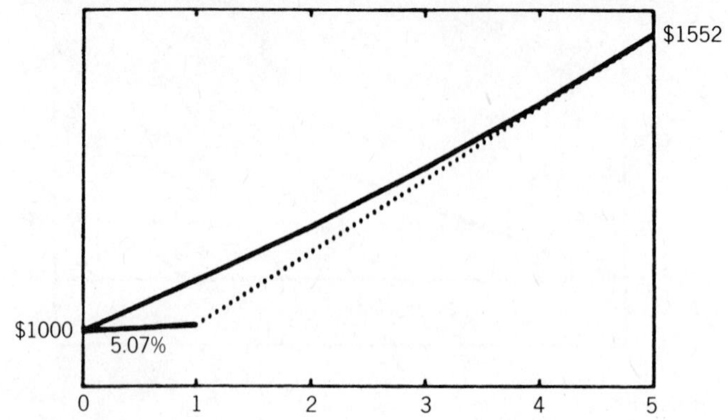

duced asset value is still sufficient, given the higher 10% rate at which it can now be invested, to achieve the original 9% target. After rebalancing, this process continues with +100 basis point increases in the second year (Exhibit 31), the third year (Exhibit 32), and the fourth year (Exhibit 33). Finally, in the fifth year (Exhibit 34), there is just enough dollar value in the portfolio to reach the original $1,552.97 target after investment for the last year at the 13% rate. In this sequence of rate moves, the portfolio realized a capital loss every single year, but was able to exactly compensate for this loss through its increased earning power at the higher rates.

General Sequences of Parallel Shifts. In the two extreme interest rate scenarios just described, rates moved either consistently up or consistently down in successive years. The same results with varying interest rate moves could be achieved as long as the correct balancing procedure is followed. For example, rates could move up 100 basis points the first year, down 100 basis

EXHIBIT 31 PORTFOLIO GROWTH: SECOND YEAR

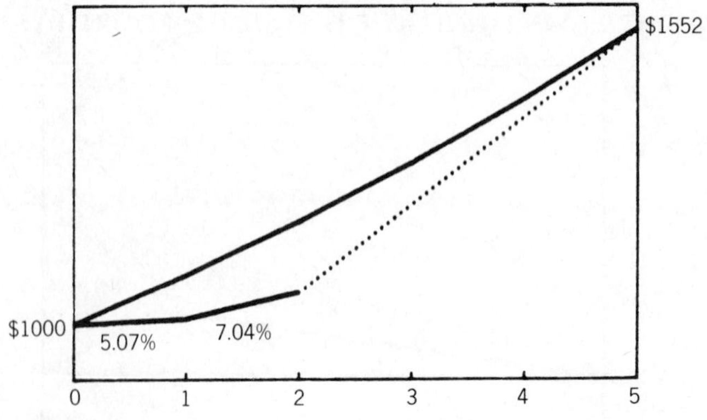

EXHIBIT 32 PORTFOLIO GROWTH: THIRD YEAR

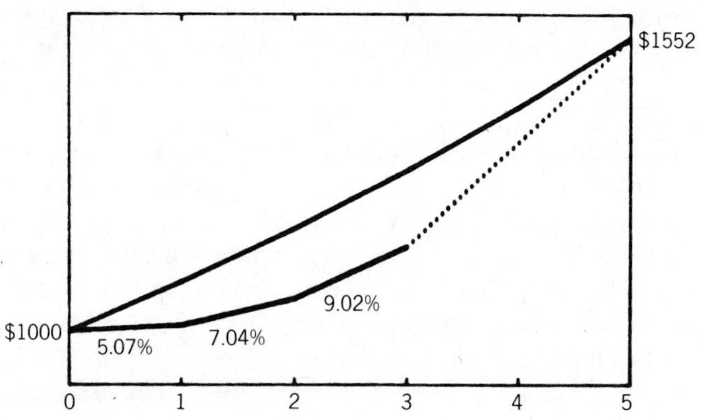

EXHIBIT 33 PORTFOLIO GROWTH: FOURTH YEAR

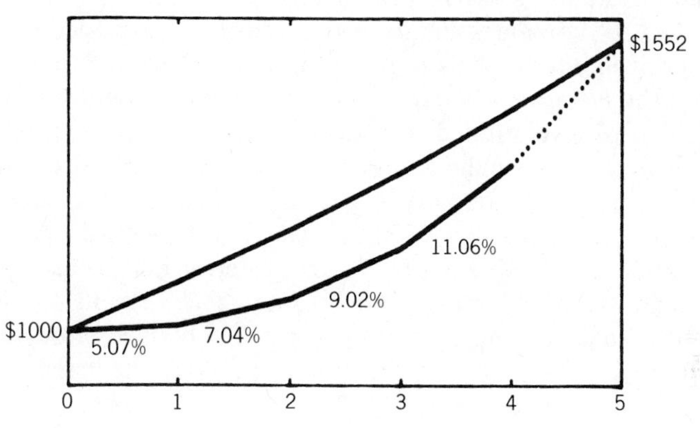

EXHIBIT 34 PORTFOLIO GROWTH: FIFTH YEAR

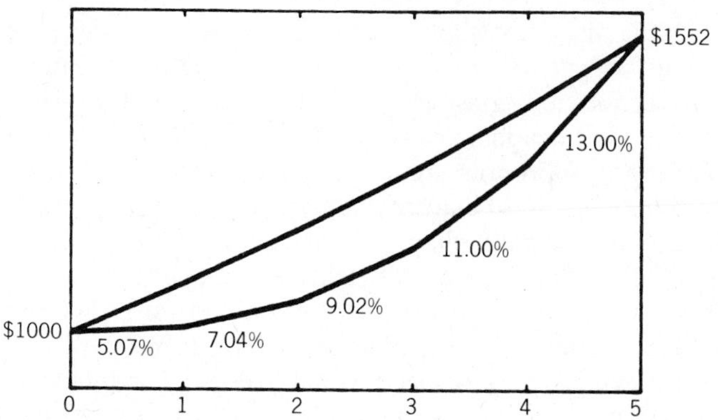

points the next year, and so on. Any such sequence of steps, as long as the duration is continuously maintained, should theoretically lead to the original target return.

IMPROVED REBALANCING USING HORIZON VOLATILITY. The preceding theoretical results would require rebalancing continuously so as to maintain a duration equal to the remaining life of the planning period. In practice, rebalancings are more likely to be scheduled for specific points in time (e.g., annually). In departing from the concept of a continuous rebalancing, we can assume a well-defined rebalancing horizon, with the impact of yield movements concentrated at the horizon. Under these assumptions, the volatility of the portfolio is affected by a certain horizon effect. The classical definition of duration, while serving well in the case of continuous rebalancing, fails to readily accommodate this "horizon effect." For annual rebalancings, such as those used in Exhibit 25, this "horizon effect" accounts for a good portion of the portfolio's 4 basis point shortfall below the target return.

The concept of horizon volatility was specifically developed to accommodate this "horizon effect." This term was introduced in 1975 in a chapter by Leibowitz in the *Financial Analyst's Handbook,* and then refined in subsequent articles. The horizon volatility does provide a better surrogate for the volatility of the ending portfolio than the duration, even over 1-year horizons. This raises the prospect of using horizon volatility as the rebalancing yardstick in an immunization procedure. Exhibit 35 shows the results of rebalancing based on horizon volatility as applied to 16 different interest rate scenarios involving ± 100 basis point annual jumps in interest rates. These results provide an empirical illustration of the improvement that can be obtained through the use of horizon volatility (rather than the classical duration) as the basis for rebalancing in an immunization procedure.

THE YIELD CURVE CASE

All the preceding discussion took place in the context of a rather restrictive set of assumptions. In particular, the model focused on parallel movements of a flat yield curve. We now consider yield curves that are truly curves (i.e., not flat). With this modification, one immediately runs into a rather surprising problem: finding an appropriate return target. In the flat yield curve case, it was clear that the initial yield to maturity constituted the appropriate target. However, with a more generally shaped yield curve, the necessary rebalancings force the portfolio into a sequence of yields and returns that may bear very little relation to the yield to maturity of the initial portfolio. The situation complicates the immunization process and reduces the extent to which the yield to maturity can function as a satisfactory return target. The following discussion shows how this "targeting" problem can be solved through the use of the rolling yield.

EXHIBIT 35 PORTFOLIO GROWTH ACROSS 16 DIFFERENT INTEREST RATE SCENARIOS: REBALANCING BASED ON HORIZON VOLATILITY

Start	Year 1	Year 2	Year 3	Year 4	Year 5	FINAL VALUES: ASSET VALUE PER $1000	FINAL VALUES: REALIZED COMPOUND YIELD
9	10: 5.07 / 5.07	11: 6.05 / 7.04	12: 7.03 / 9.02	13: 8.02 / 11.00	9.01 / 13.00	1553.46	9.01
9	10: 5.07 / 5.07	11: 6.05 / 7.04	12: 7.03 / 9.02	11: 8.51 / 13.01	9.01 / 11.00	1553.49	9.01
9	10: 5.07 / 5.07	11: 6.05 / 7.04	10: 8.35 / 13.02	11: 8.51 / 9.01	9.01 / 11.00	1553.46	9.01
9	10: 5.07 / 5.07	11: 6.05 / 7.04	10: 8.35 / 13.02	9: 9.01 / 11.01	9.01 / 9.00	1553.45	9.01
9	10: 5.07 / 5.07	9: 9.01 / 13.04	10: 8.35 / 7.02	11: 8.51 / 9.01	9.01 / 11.00	1553.49	9.01
9	10: 5.07 / 5.07	9: 9.01 / 13.04	10: 8.35 / 7.02	9: 9.01 / 11.01	9.01 / 9.00	1553.48	9.01
9	10: 5.07 / 5.07	9: 9.01 / 13.04	8: 9.68 / 11.02	9: 9.01 / 7.01	9.01 / 9.00	1553.43	9.01
9	10: 5.07 / 5.07	9: 9.01 / 13.04	8: 9.68 / 11.02	7: 9.51 / 9.01	9.01 / 7.00	1553.45	9.01
9	8: 13.07 / 13.07	9: 9.01 / 5.04	10: 8.35 / 7.02	11: 8.51 / 9.01	9.01 / 11.00	1553.44	9.01
9	8: 13.07 / 13.07	9: 9.01 / 5.04	10: 8.35 / 7.02	9: 9.01 / 11.01	9.01 / 9.00	1553.43	9.01
9	8: 13.07 / 13.07	9: 9.01 / 5.04	8: 9.68 / 11.02	9: 9.01 / 7.01	9.01 / 9.00	1553.38	9.01
9	8: 13.07 / 13.07	9: 9.01 / 5.04	8: 9.68 / 11.02	7: 9.51 / 9.01	9.01 / 7.00	1553.40	9.01
9	8: 13.07 / 13.07	7: 12.05 / 11.04	8: 9.68 / 5.02	9: 9.01 / 7.01	9.01 / 9.00	1553.43	9.01
9	8: 13.07 / 13.07	7: 12.05 / 11.04	8: 9.68 / 5.02	7: 9.51 / 9.01	9.01 / 7.00	1553.45	9.01
9	8: 13.07 / 13.07	7: 12.05 / 11.04	6: 11.03 / 9.02	7: 9.51 / 5.00	9.01 / 7.00	1553.44	9.01
9	8: 13.07 / 13.07	7: 12.05 / 11.04	6: 11.03 / 9.02	5: 10.02 / 7.00	9.01 / 5.00	1553.39	9.01

[a]Legend: 12 | 7.03 / 9.02

where interest rate at end of year = 12%
cumulative realized compound yield = 7.03
realized compound yield over prior year = 9.02

PORTFOLIO REBALANCING ALONG THE YIELD CURVE. Most of the academic literature on immunization focuses on yield curves consisting of hypothetical forward rates or zero-coupon bonds. Under such circumstances, the return target is readily defined. However, when market participants speak of the "yield curve," they are generally referring to a maturity plot of the yields to maturity of Treasury par bonds. We shall adopt this market view of a par bond yield curve for the following discussion.

EXHIBIT 36 SIMPLE PAR BOND YIELD CURVE

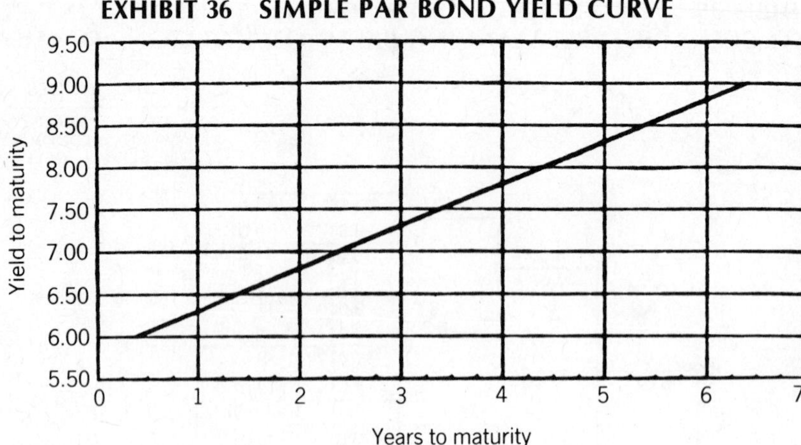

Exhibit 36 illustrates a particularly simple par bond yield curve. This yield "curve" is a straight line with a positive slope of 50 basis points per year. In the preceding discussion, it was stated that a rebalancing procedure based on the horizon volatility provides the required portfolio volatility for the flat yield curve. This technique works equally well for the general yield curve case.

Exhibit 37 shows the horizon volatility associated with each maturity point along our simple yield curve. At the outset, a horizon volatility of 4 is needed, and this can be achieved by a 6.41-year 9% par bond. At the end of the first year, however, a horizon volatility of 3 is required and this is achieved with a maturity of 4.8 years.

Using the sequence of annual rebalancing maturities derived in this fashion, we can proceed to determine the total returns achieved under the scenario of "no change in the market"; that is, the yield curve remains constant. This sequence of calculations is shown in Exhibit 38. The resulting total return is

EXHIBIT 37 HORIZON VOLATILITY

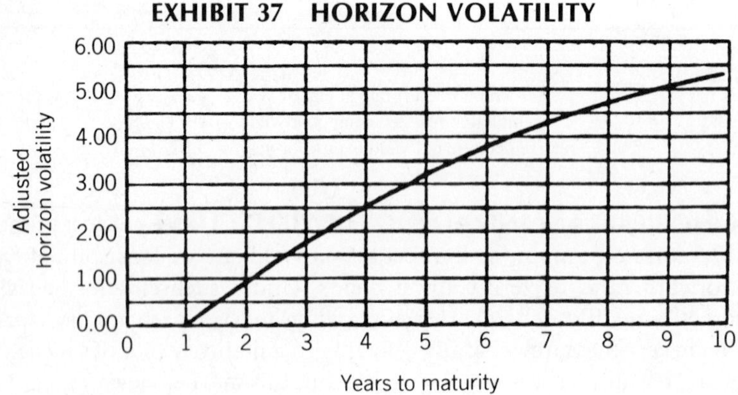

EXHIBIT 38 IMMUNIZATION PROCEDURE APPLIED TO A YIELD CURVE SITUATION: INITIAL INVESTMENT, $1,000; STATIC SCENARIO

	Rebalanced Portfolio at Start of Period			Results Over Year			Realized Compound Yield (%)			
Period Ending (years)	Parallel Shift (b.p.)	Initial Yield Level (%)	Maturity (years)	Coupon Flow and Interest-on-Interest	Capital Gain	Total Proceeds	Over Year	Cumulative	Forward Target[a]	Blended[b]
				NO CHANGE IN CURVE OVER TIME						
1	+0	9.00	6.41	$92.03	$21.18	$1,113.21	11.02	11.02	7.94	8.56
2	+0	8.17	4.76	92.81	17.56	1,223.58	9.69	10.35	7.37	8.56
3	+0	7.46	3.33	92.98	12.81	1,329.37	8.46	9.72	6.82	8.56
4	+0	6.85	2.12	92.62	6.91	1,428.90	7.35	9.12	6.29	8.56
5	+0	6.29	1.00	91.29	0	1,520.23	6.29	8.56	0	8.56

[a] The return realized from the immunization procedure for the remainder of the planning period, assuming that the then-existing yield curve remains unchanged.

[b] The 5-year return that would result if the portfolio value at the date could be compounded at the "forward target rate" for all the remaining periods.

8.56%, well below the initial yield to maturity of 9%. Clearly, the yield to maturity of an initial portfolio cannot function as an immunization target, even for this simple yield curve case. It remains for us to show that the 8.56% figure can constitute a target return that is indeed realized by the immunization procedure, and to then try to undertand the nature of this new "targeting process."

THE ROLLING YIELD. In a series of articles published beginning in 1977, we tried to formalize the total return associated with the age-old investment concept of "rolling down the yield curve." The term "rolling yield" was defined as the total return associated with an investment at a maturity point along the yield curve under the assumption that the yield curve remained constant. From this assumption, it follows that the investment could be priced at the end of the horizon on the basis of its "aged" position on the curve. For example, for the curve shown in Exhibit 36, the 1-year rolling yield associated with an investment into the 6.41-year 9% par bond would correspond to the results of subsequently pricing that investment 1 year later at the 5.41-year point on the yield curve (i.e., at a yield of 8.50%). For any common horizon, one can compute rolling yields for investments at every maturity point. The resulting curve is referred to as the rolling yield curve.

Exhibit 39 superimposes the rolling yield curve on the par bond yield curve from Exhibit 36. For positively sloped yield curves such as this one, the rolling yield characteristically will lie above the yield curve itself. This results from the incremental return associated with the implied ability to sell out the investment at a "rolldown" yield that is lower than the initial purchase yield.

Exhibit 39 highlights the specific rolling yield values associated with the sequence of maturities required by the annual rebalancing procedure. As one compares the rolling yield values with the immunization procedure followed in Exhibit 38, it becomes apparent that the year-by-year realized compound yields achieved by immunization are nothing more than the sequence of rolling

EXHIBIT 39 THE ROLLING YIELD CURVE

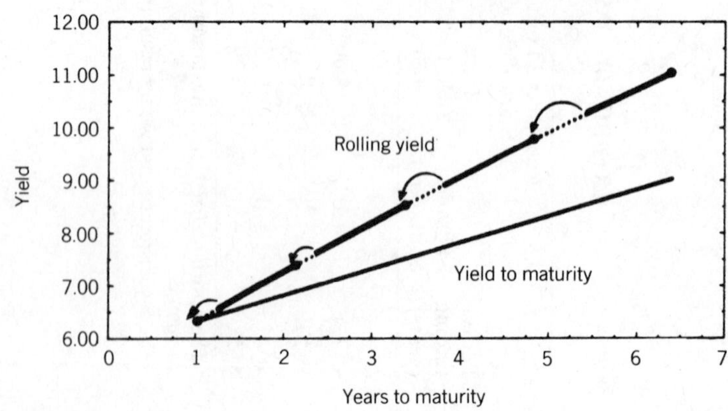

yields indicated in Exhibit 39. This result suggests that return targets for the yield curve case may be found by stringing together the appropriate sequence of rolling yield values.

Parallel Shifts of the Yield Curve. We have yet to demonstrate that this procedure maintains the target level of return in the face of changing yield curves. We retain the assumption that the yield curve changes through parallel movements. A +100 basis point parallel move in the yield curve simply means that the yields associated with every maturity are increased by +100 basis points. As before, we allow for multiple movements concentrated at the end of each year. Exhibit 40 illustrates a scenario consisting of annual jumps of -100 basis points each. Rebalancing is carried out in accordance with the **horizon volatility** technique. The year-by-year returns are obviously different from those achieved under the static case of Exhibit 38. However, the total return comes in at 8.54%, only 2 basis points under the target level determined by the sequence of rolling yields. These results provide encouraging support for the rolling yield as a "targeting" process.

Parallel Movements of Actual Yield Curves. The foregoing example is based on one extremely simple positively sloped yield curve. But does this technique apply to more general yield curve shapes? To study this question within a more realistic framework, a series of computer-based simulations was developed. In the initial studies, the basic research tool was a simulation of 5-year immunization plans using simple point portfolios. These portfolios consisted of a single maturity point along the yield curve. The simulations utilized a data base consisting of U.S. Treasury yield curves for the beginning of each month starting with January 1958 and ending in December 1979.

Exhibit 41 illustrates the procedure followed in the first series of studies. The analysis began with the actual curve shape on a given date. Then, at the end of each year, the curve was moved in a parallel fashion by a specified yield increment. Exhibit 41 illustrates the case of an annual 50 basis point downward move. Rebalancing takes place on an annual basis. By evaluating the immunization strategy in this context, one can determine the effect of the historical starting yield curve shape. In other words, this will expose and isolate problems arising from the flat yield curve assumption.

Simulation Tests of the YTM Target. The first series of simulations used to test the immunization procedure employed the traditional yield to maturity as the return target. The results are shown in Exhibit 42. Each point along the horizontal axis represents a different starting yield curve. For example, the first immunization plan began in January 1958. An initial point portfolio was constructed that had a duration of 5 years in the context of that yield curve. This initial portfolio had a yield to maturity (YTM) of 2.78%. In accordance with the usual procedure, this value of 2.78% was then taken as the return target for the 5-year immunization plan. At the end of each year, the market was as-

EXHIBIT 40 IMMUNIZATION PROCEDURE APPLIED TO A YIELD CURVE SITUATION: INITIAL INVESTMENT, $1,000; ANNUAL RATE MOVEMENTS

	Rebalanced Portfolio at Start of Period			Results Over Year			Realized Compound Yield (%)			
Period Ending (years)	Parallel Shift (b.p.)	Initial Yield Level (%)	Maturity (years)	Coupon Flow and Interest-on-Interest	Capital Gain	Total Proceeds	Over Year	Cumulative	Forward Target[a]	Blended[b]
				−100 B.P. PARALLEL SHIFT PER YEAR						
1	−100	9.00	6.41	$92.03	$65.24	$1,157.27	15.16	15.16	6.93	8.55
2	−100	7.13	4.67	83.98	55.55	1,296.80	11.71	13.43	5.35	8.54
3	−100	5.41	3.24	71.10	40.78	1,408.69	8.45	11.75	3.81	8.54
4	−100	3.83	2.07	54.44	21.84	1,485.00	5.34	10.13	2.30	8.54
5	−100	2.29	1.00	34.20	0	1,519.20	2.30	8.54	0	8.54

[a] The return realized from the immunization procedure for the remainder of the planning period, assuming that the then-existing yield curve remains unchanged.

[b] The 5-year return that would result if the portfolio value at that date could be compounded at the "forward target rate" for all the remaining periods.

EXHIBIT 41 IMMUNIZED POINT PORTFOLIO OVER TIME

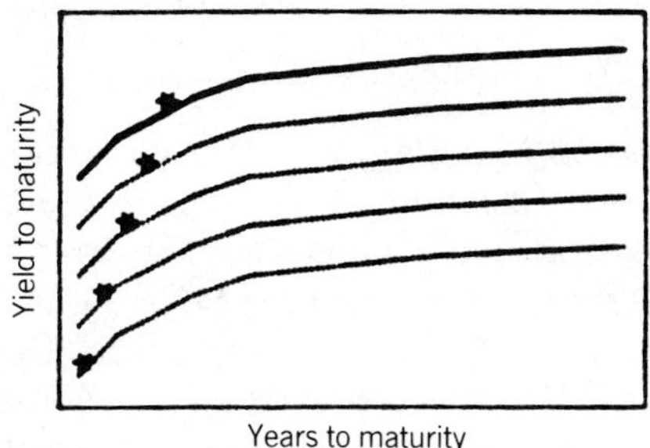

sumed to have undergone a 50 basis point downward move across all maturities. The simulation was then carried out with the portfolio being rebalanced every year.

The cumulative return realized by this immunization process turned out to be 2.76%. This represented an error of −2 basis points relative to the original YTM-based target of 2.78%. The vertical axis in Exhibit 42 indicates the magnitude of the "tracking error." This "miss" of -2 basis points for the January 1958 curve is the leftmost point in Exhibit 42. The next point corresponds to the miss relative to the initial YTM target for the 5-year immunization plan beginning with the yield curve for February 1958. The plot thus depicts the tracking errors for different immunization plans starting on successive months from January 1958 through December 1974.

The worst variation occurred on March, 1971, a tracking error of −21 basis points. At first, that does not sound so bad. In fact, Exhibit 42 would seem to provide evidence that immunization strategies have done very well. The prob-

EXHIBIT 42 SIMULATED IMMUNIZATION RETURNS OVER YTM TARGET: ANNUAL PARALLELSHIFTS OF −50 BASIS POINTS

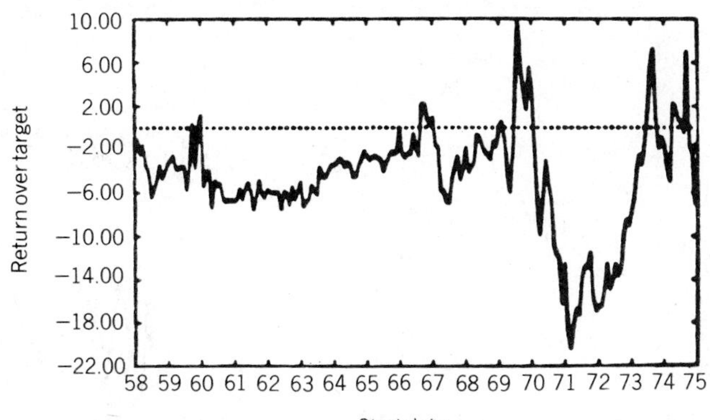

lem is that these results are based on parallel moves. These are the idealized conditions under which immunization is supposed to function perfectly. Under such idealized circumstances, it is rather disappointing to see the sequence of misses shown in Exhibit 42.

Simulation Test of the Rolling Yield Target. We next tested the concept of a rolling yield-based target using the simulation procedure described earlier. The worst miss is −5 basis points, compared with a -21 basis point miss for the YTM target. To facilitate comparison of the targeting techniques, Exhibit 43 shows both sets of simulation results on a single graph. The rolling yield target is clearly superior. The result can be proved mathematically: the rolling yield provides the correct return target for the case of parallel movements of par bond yield curves.

However, much as the portfolio manager interested in immunization might wish to see parallel movements, the real world often deals out a sequence of rate movements that is anything but parallel. For example, consider just one segment of the yield curve—the spread of 5-year maturities over 1-year bills. Under parallel shifts, this spread would remain constant over time. As Exhibit 44 indicates, there have actually been wide, and often wild, variations in this spread.

This brings us to the second subject of our simulation studies—the problem of nonparallel shifts.

Changing Yield Curve Shapes. To appreciate the problems caused by nonparallel shifts, consider the situation of an initially inverted yield curve that snaps down to a positive shape in subsequent years. Exhibit 44 shows that this situation was not uncommon—it happened in 1969, 1973, and 1974. Exhibit 45

EXHIBIT 43 COMPARISON OF YTM AND ROLLING YIELDS AS TARGETS: ANNUAL PARALLEL SHIFTS OF −50 BASIS POINTS

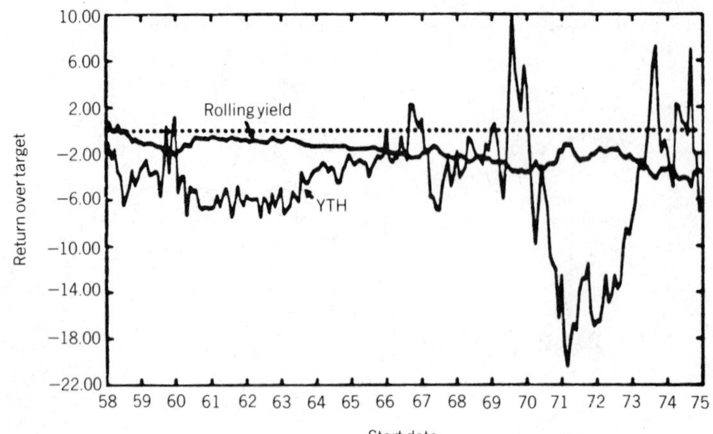

EXHIBIT 44 5-YEAR-1-YEAR TREASURY CURVE SPREAD

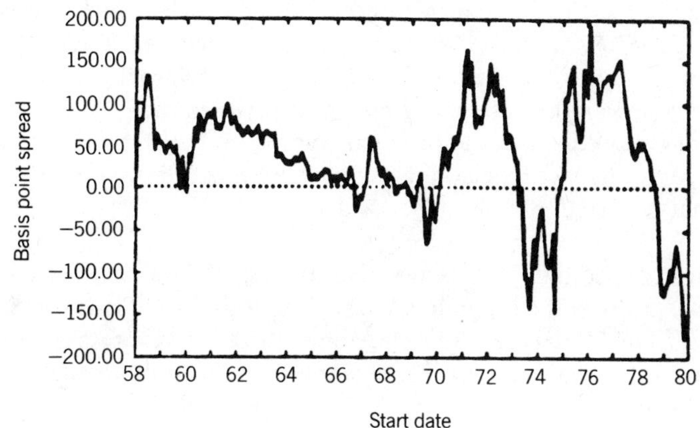

provides a more detailed view of the snapdown that occurred over the year following September 1974.

When faced with a yield curve shape such as that of September 1974, the rolling yield targeting process will count on rolling "up" the curve and capturing the higher yields. Parallel downward shifts would, of course, reduce these yields but would also generate sufficient capital gains for an immunized portfolio to remain "on target." However, when the yield curve snaps down as shown in Exhibit 45, the yield loss in the short-term maturities may far exceed

EXHIBIT 45 HISTORICAL YIELD CURVES

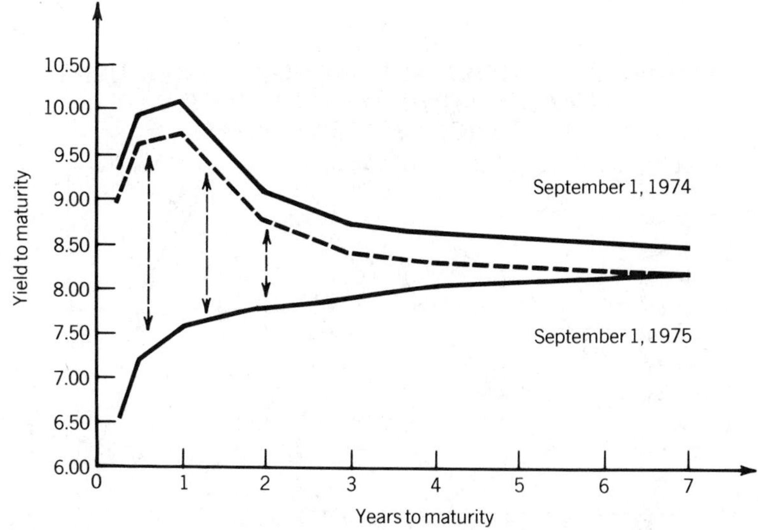

the yield move in the intermediate-term maturities. In the early years of an immunization plan, the portfolio will probably be concentrated in this intermediate range. Consequently, the smaller yield move in these intermediate maturities may not generate sufficient capital gains to provide the needed offset to the much lower yields that will be encountered in the plan's later years.

Thus one should anticipate problems for the immunization-oriented portfolio manager in the face of snapdowns like those that followed the inverted yield curves that occurred in 1969, 1973, and 1974.

Simulation of Actual Yield Curve Sequences. The next set of computer simulations utilized the same data base of monthly U.S. Treasury yield curves stretching from January 1958 to December 1979. However, the immunization plan now had to deal with market movements defined by the actual sequence of historical curves.

The first case to be examined at this detailed level is a 5-year immunization strategy using a point portfolio with annual rebalancing. This sequence of tracking errors is shown in Exhibit 46. The results are quite satisfactory for plans begun in 1958–1966. Over this period, the immunization plans usually did better than the target. Then, in 1967, 1968, and 1969, there developed a series of instances of the immunization strategy underperforming the target by 20–24 basis points. Over the next 3 years, from mid-1970 through the end of 1972, the immunization plans always met their target and, in some cases, outperformed by as much as 18 basis points. The results turn sour once again in 1973, reaching the worst miss of -26 basis points in September 1973. By the end of 1975, the results had begun to improve.

In comparing Exhibit 46 with the 5- to 1-year spread graph shown in Exhibit 44, one can roughly identify the most difficult times for immunization plans. An inverted yield curve followed by a snapdown to a positive curve causes

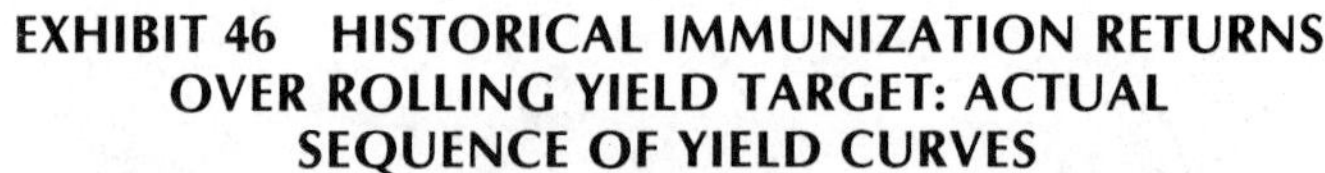

EXHIBIT 46 HISTORICAL IMMUNIZATION RETURNS OVER ROLLING YIELD TARGET: ACTUAL SEQUENCE OF YIELD CURVES

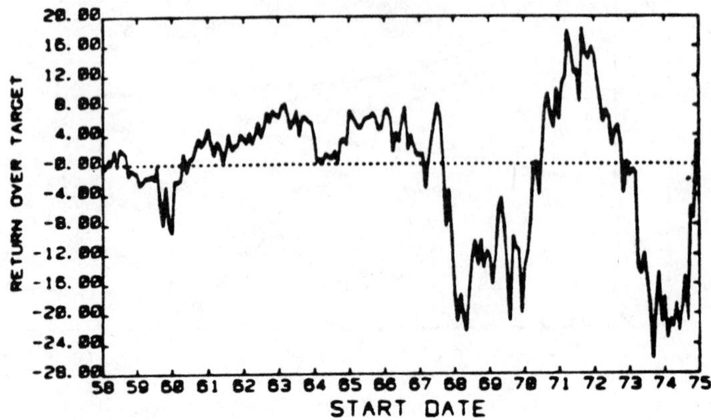

trouble in the standard immunization strategy. If this situation occurs within the first 2–3 years of the plan's life, it can create distortions that may lead to underperformance. It is not surprising that this situation would place a particular strain on targets based on the rolling yield.

To assess the role of the targeting procedure in these underperformance situations, this series of simulations was repeated using return targets based on the yield to maturity of the original portfolio. As pointed out earlier, this YTM target is theoretically incorrect for the hypothetical situation of parallel yield moves. However, one might expect the YTM to provide a more conservative, hence somewhat better target estimate, in just the inverted yield curve situations that spell trouble for the rolling yield. From the simulation results presented in Exhibit 47, it is evident that the YTM target actually does perform somewhat better in those troublesome times. In contrast with the early results shown in Exhibit 46, there are fewer starting months shown in Exhibit 41 where the immunization plan underperformed by more than 16 basis points.

Another approach to dealing with this problem of yield curve reshaping is to find portfolio structures that may prove more resilient to actual market movements. In the preceding discussion, all analyses and all simulation results have been based on a point portfolio. This is a hypothetical portfolio consisting of a single par bond having the needed maturity. There are actually many other portfolio structures that can generate the needed sequence of duration (or horizon volatility) values. It is reasonable to expect that some of these portfolio structures can perform much better than others over time.

As one delves into this question of characterizing the various dynamic structures, one finds a virtually limitless variety of potential portfolio forms and rebalancing procedures. Our research has encompassed a large number of different portfolio structures, many more than can be described in the context of

EXHIBIT 47 HISTORICAL IMMUNIZATION RETURNS OVER YTM TARGET: ACTUAL SEQUENCE OF YIELD CURVES

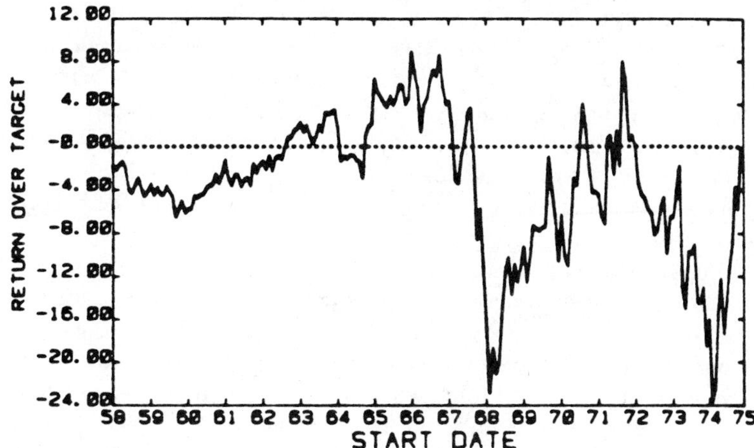

this section. However, the basis thrust of our research findings confirm that considerable improvement in tracking accuracy can be attained through selection of the right portfolio structure.

THE INTRICACIES OF REBALANCING

It turns out that there is much more flexibility and many more questions in the area of rebalancing than is generally realized. Research into many of these variables has shown that there are numerous surprises that can have a fairly substantial impact on tracking accuracy. For example, while most of the work presented here is based on **annual rebalancing,** other studies have been performed on the effects of using different rebalancing frequencies. The theory suggests that apart from the practical considerations involved, more frequent rebalancing should prove to be superior. Curiously, the historical simulations tend to suggest that too frequent rebalancing may introduce more problems than it solves. In fact, these results raise the question of whether rebalancing should be specified in terms of the time dimension alone. For example, it appears that improved duration matching may be obtained by having more adaptive scheduling of the rebalancing action, such as those triggered by certain thresholds of rate moves, cash inflows, and so on.

Another important facet of this problem is the rebalancing criterion itself. This presentation has been cast in the context of the traditional **Macaulay duration** and the **horizon volatility.** In actuality, both these specifications probably should be viewed as special cases of a class of volatility measures. Each volatility measure turns out to be appropriate for a particular set of assumptions regarding the rebalancing horizon, the nature of the market movement, and the procedure for reinvesting interperiod cash flows. In fact, for most of the situations analyzed, the Macaulay duration has turned out not to be the best choice from within this class of volatility measures. A full discussion of this subject would lead too far astray for the purpose of this section.

Another aspect of the rebalancing question involves the range of choices involved when using specific securities. There are a host of such questions, ranging from the most efficient application of coupon flows, to the selection of the optimal security for liquidation, to the broader issue of constructing initial portfolios using a combination of highly liquid and selectively illiquid securities. Once again, a full discussion of this subject is beyond the scope of this presentation. However, it is important to note the choice of the best rebalancing procedure is a weighty problem in its own right.

Simulation results indicate that when effective rebalancing procedures are combined with carefully chosen portfolio structures, one can achieve tracking accuracy that is far better than that illustrated in Exhibits 46 and 47 for the point portfolio. If immunization could reliably and consistently provide such tracking accuracy, this technique would indeed have to be taken seriously as a route to reducing uncertainty in an uncertain world.

IMMUNIZATION APPLIED TO SCHEDULED LIABILITIES

The immunization approach outlined earlier can be generalized for application to the funding of a schedule of prescribed liabilities. The basic criteria are similar to those required for the case of a point liability, for example, matching of the present values and the durations of the asset portfolio and the liability streams. Additional constraints are required to deal with second-order effects that arise in frameworks involving multiple liabilities. However, these second-order constraints required a modest number of specifications of an aggregate portfolio nature. They are far less restrictive than the period-by-period constraints of a typical cash-matched approach.

Thus immunization can be viewed as a more flexible alternative to the cash matching of a liability schedule. One of the major differences is that unlike cash matching, immunization inherently requires portfolio changes over time. Where cash matching fulfills liabilities through the originally promised flows from coupons and principal maturities, immunization generally depends on the sale of portfolio securities at their theoretical values. This need for continuing changes in immunized portfolios is derived from the need to keep the present value of the assets greater than the present value of the liabilities over time. However, each cash inflow or outflow disrupts this pattern and requires some rebalancing of the immunized portfolio. These forced rebalancings are an intrinsic part of the immunization process (see Exhibit 48).

Redington's initial proposal required that interest rates be restricted to a flat yield curve subject only to parallel movements. Although modern techniques have enabled immunization to address a wider range of yield curve behaviors, immunization still remains vulnerable to certain sequences of market movements.

A number of other factors also complicate the development of immunized portfolios, including the determination of target returns, changing yield-spread relationships, and changing bond universes over time. Even with these problems, however, immunization does offer the theoretical promise of a lower-cost solution to the matching problem—as long as all the assumptions are met. As shown schematically in Exhibit 49, this lower initial cost carries with it the risk of potential future pay-ups if market conditions depart sufficiently from the idealized immunization conditions.

In practice, the application of immunization has been limited because of its greater complexity, its requirement for frequent rebalancing (which must be distinguished from the positive option of active management), and its vulnerability under certain types of market movements.

HORIZON MATCHING

From the preceding discussion of cash matching and immunization, it should be evident that a properly balanced combination of these tools could lead to a

EXHIBIT 48 THE IMMUNIZATION PROCESS

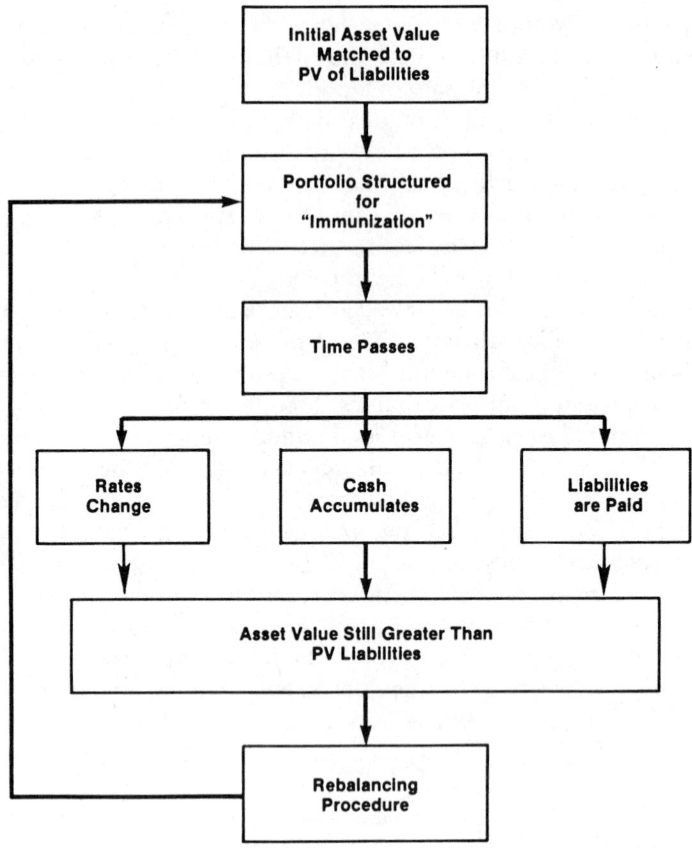

very desirable new technique. A number of such combinations have been explored, and in 1983, the concept of **horizon matching** was introduced. Horizon matching provides just such a valuable blend—one that incorporates the best features of both techniques.

The central concept of horizon matching is illustrated in Exhibit 50. Essentially, the liability stream is divided into two segments by the selection of an appropriate "horizon." Then, a single integrated portfolio is created that simultaneously fulfills the two liability segments in different ways. In the first segment, the portfolio must provide a full cash matching of the liabilities that occur up to and including the specified horizon date. This cash-matched portion will be subject to the same stringent constraints that would apply to any cash-matched portfolio. In particular, any excess flows that are available for reinvestment are presumed to be reinvested at the specified (conservative) reinvestment rate prior to the horizon.

For purposes of illustration, we have assumed that the horizon is 5 years.

EXHIBIT 49 PURE IMMUNIZATION RELATIVE COSTS AND RISKS

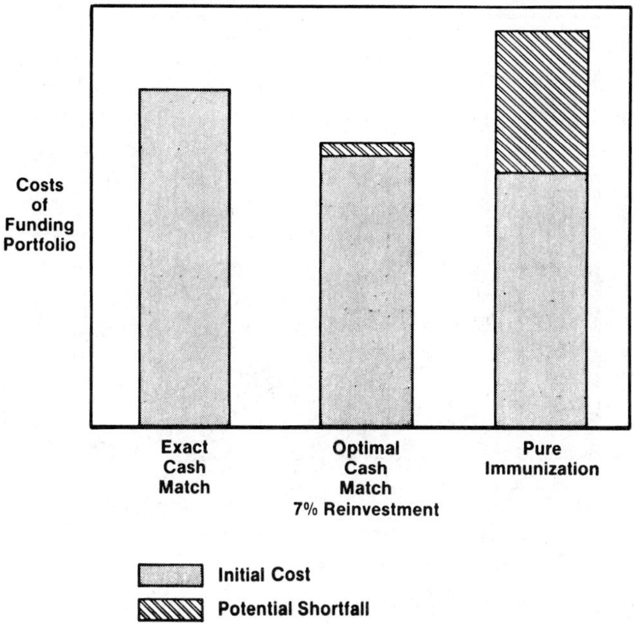

Costs of Funding Portfolio

Exact Cash Match

Optimal Cash Match 7% Reinvestment

Pure Immunization

Initial Cost

Potential Shortfall

For the first 5 years, the sponsor will have full assurance that the horizon-matched portfolio will provide cash flows adequate to meet the specified payouts. The liabilities beyond the fifth year will be covered through a duration-matching discipline that is based on immunization principles.

Exhibit 50 illustrates the type of cash flows generated by a horizon-matched portfolio with a 5-year horizon. In this case, the first 5 years are shown to be almost perfectly matched on a year-by-year basis. In the duration-matched period from the fifth year on, however, the asset flows are more concentrated into a series of specific maturities. These are structured so that the overall system satisfies the interest rate sensitivity requirements as well as a number of second-order conditions. With this structure, although one should have more room for elective management, the portfolio will serve its function even if it remains passive for the first 5 years. Thus the sponsor can simply pay out the liabilities as needed during the first 5 years and not be concerned about the passage of time. Even with such a passive stance, the present value of the assets will remain greater than the present value of the liabilities throughout the course of the initial horizon period as long as interest rate movements fall within the broadly prescribed range. (A properly constructed horizon-matched portfolio will enable the initial 5-year horizon to be "rolled out" year by year under a wide range of market conditions, so that the portfolio remains cash matched for the first 5 years and duration matched for the rest.)

EXHIBIT 50 HORIZON-MATCHED PORTFOLIO

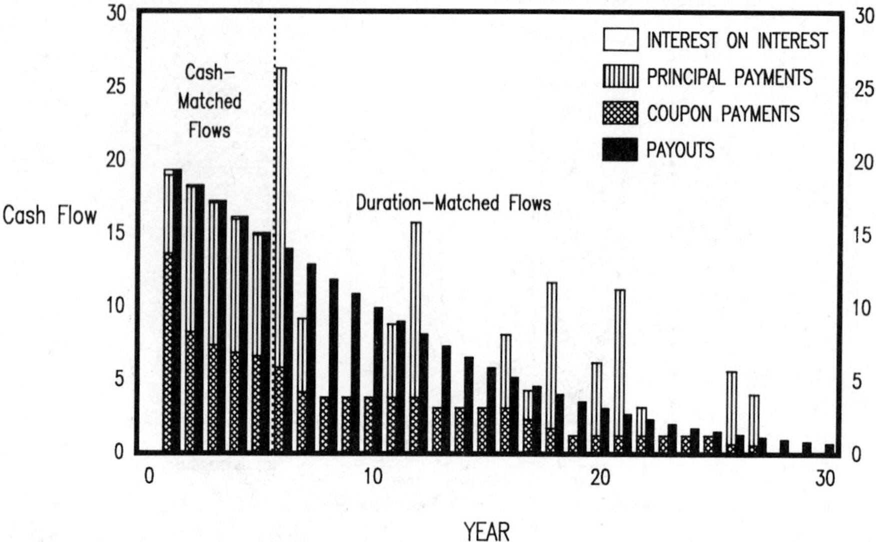

As mentioned, one of the most severe problems with the practical application of immunization has to do with nonparallel movements of the yield curve. This vulnerability to yield curve reshaping is largely eliminated in a horizon-matched portfolio with horizons of 3 to 5 years or more for the simple reason that the most severe yield curve reshapings occur in the shortest maturities.

It should be pointed out that the benefits of **horizon matching** do entail the acceptance of some degree of additional risk. The horizon-matched portfolio, by definition, will have a lower asset value than the fully cash-matched portfolio. Consequently, there can be no assurance that the horizon-matched portfolio can be transformed into a fully cash-matched portfolio at any given time. Moreover, although the portfolio will retain its cash-matched characteristics through the horizon period without any further rebalancing, it is conceivable that certain types of market movements could lead to shortfalls in the duration-matched portion once the horizon period has passed. Thus in the schematic cost/risk diagram (Exhibit 51), horizon matching would fall somewhere between optimal cash matching and pure immunization in terms of both cost and the risk of potential shortfalls.

An additional advantage lies in the fact that the outer years of the liability schedule are often conservatively stated at the outset and, hence, are likely to be refined with the passage of time. Horizon matching enables the portfolio to obtain cost efficiency by fully matching the more definite near-term liabilities without being hostage to specific pro forma liabilities that are likely to change in amount and time over the years. Moreover, by using the rollout procedure, the comfort of a definitive match of these near-term liabilities can continue to be maintained on a year-by-year basis.

EXHIBIT 51 HORIZON MATCHING RELATIVE COSTS AND RISKS

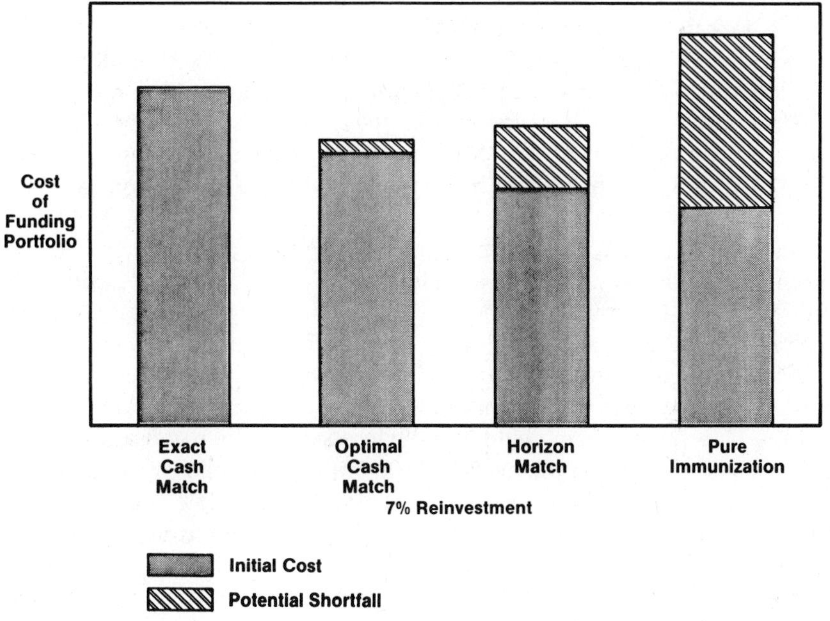

CONTINGENT IMMUNIZATION

It has long been recognized that immunization procedures which stretch for the highest possible portfolio yields in a given market environment also incur the greatest risk of future shortfall. By the same token, it has also been observed that a "cushion" below this maximum rate provides additional comfort as well as flexibility to any immunization procedure. This concept of cushion flexibility can be extended to allow a significant degree of active management within a conservatively structured portfolio framework.

As interest rates rose to unprecedentedly high levels in 1981, it became possible to consider acceptable minimum returns that were *well below* the maximum possible market rate. Thus when the maximum market rate was 15%, a minimum return of 14% seemed to be a highly satisfactory level of return. For this 100-basis-point "cushion spread" (from 15 to 14%), a certain degree of portfolio flexibility could be obtained. In fact, cushion spreads of 100–200 basis points create a surprisingly large latitude for the pursuit of active management. With these cushion spreads, there could be a series of repeated adverse movements—the traditional "whipsaw" nightmare of every portfolio manager—and the portfolio would still retain some residual cushion above the promised minimum rate. It was this realization of the degree of flexibility afforded by reasonable cushion spreads that motivated the concept of contingent immunization.

The effect of a 100-basis-point cushion for an active strategy is illustrated in Exhibits 52 and 53. The assets required at different interest rate levels to provide a 15% market return and a 14% "floor" return over a 5-year period are shown in Exhibit 52. At a 15% compounding rate, a $100-million portfolio would grow to a 5-year value of $206 million. To achieve this target value in a 15% rate environment, it is obvious that the *entire* $100 million portfolio would have to be immunized at the 15% market rate. Hence, the required assets for the 15% promised return in a 15% market would be $100 million (see Exhibit 52).

Suppose, however, that in this same 15% market environment, the 5-year promised return is lowered to 14%. This reduces the 5-year target value to $197 million. This 14% target could be achieved by investing somewhat less than the entire $100 million—$95.45 million, to be precise—into a 15% compounding vehicle. In other words, as Exhibit 52 shows, the "required assets" in the 15% market would drop to $95.45 million with this reduction in the promised return to 14%. Thus the manager could literally lose $4.55 million and still achieve the 14% promised return on the original $100 million portfolio by immunizing the remaining $95.45 million asset value at the assumed 15% market rate. The $4.55 million acts as a safety cushion and creates a significant opportunity for active management and "maturity tilts."

The key idea is that the manager can pursue active strategies as long as he or she retains a positive safety cushion. Should the market turn against the manager and erode this safety cushion, he or she can trigger into an immunized portfolio and still achieve the originally promised minimum floor return.

EXHIBIT 52 REQUIRED ASSETS TO ACHIEVE 5-YEAR PROMISED RETURNS IN DIFFERENT MARKET ENVIRONMENTS

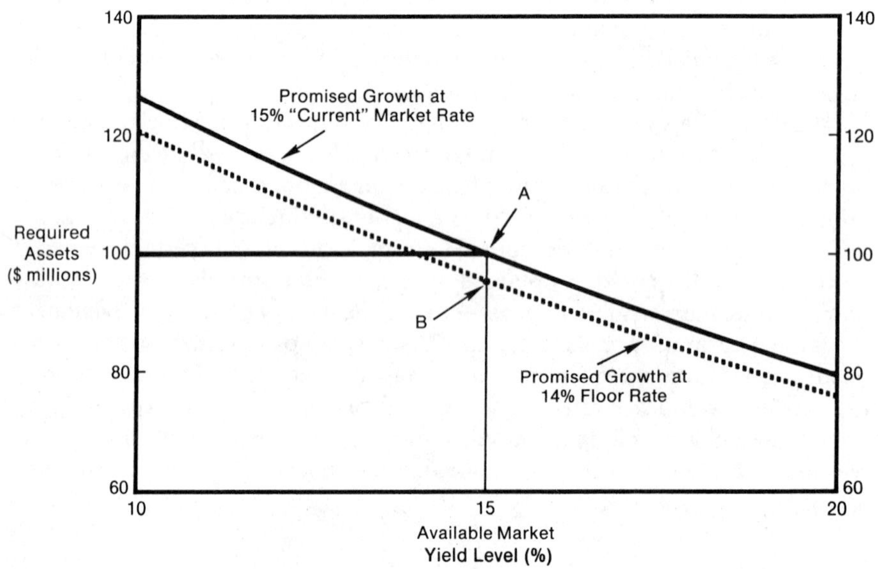

EXHIBIT 53 SAFETY MARGIN FOR A PORTFOLIO OF 30-YEAR BONDS

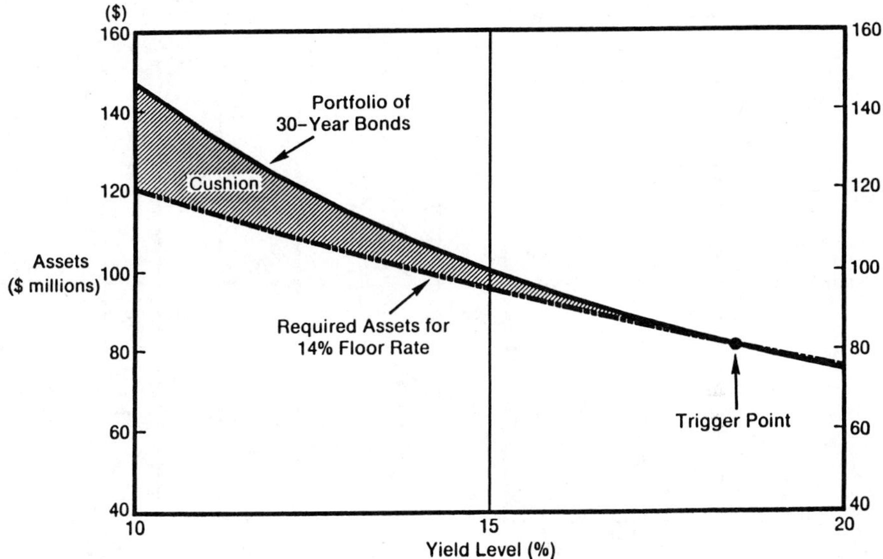

Suppose, for example, that a portfolio manager was strongly optimistic and wished to hold a portfolio of 30-year 15% par bonds. He or she would then have a duration of 7 years—far longer than the 5-year horizon. This portfolio would clearly not be immunized. In fact, the least adverse movement (i.e., upward move in rates) would immediately violate the required assets line for the 15% target rate. If the fund sponsor was willing to accept the lower 14% floor rate as a minimum return, however, the price behavior of 30-year bonds could be superimposed on the 14% required asset curve as shown in Exhibit 53.

If yields declined, the active strategy would have proved successful and the safety margin of excess assets would rise with the superior performance of the 30-year bond portfolio. This successful move would enable the portfolio to generate 5-year returns well in excess of the original 15% market rate. On the other hand, should interest rates rise, the safety margin would decrease and the portfolio's assets would approach the minimum required asset level. In fact, Exhibit 53 shows that the active portfolio of 30-year bonds will decline to the required asset level after an upward rate move of about 350 basis points. At this point, the safety margin will have been totally eroded, and the portfolio will have to be immunized in order to ensure fulfillment of the 14% floor rate. In this example, the portfolio can tolerate adverse market movements of more than 350 basis points even after having adopted the longest possible maturity stance in the par bond market.

It is this latitude for active management that enables the portfolio manager to implement a contingent immunization program—to accept the possibility of

EXHIBIT 54 CONTINGENT IMMUNIZATION AND POTENTIAL TAKEOUTS

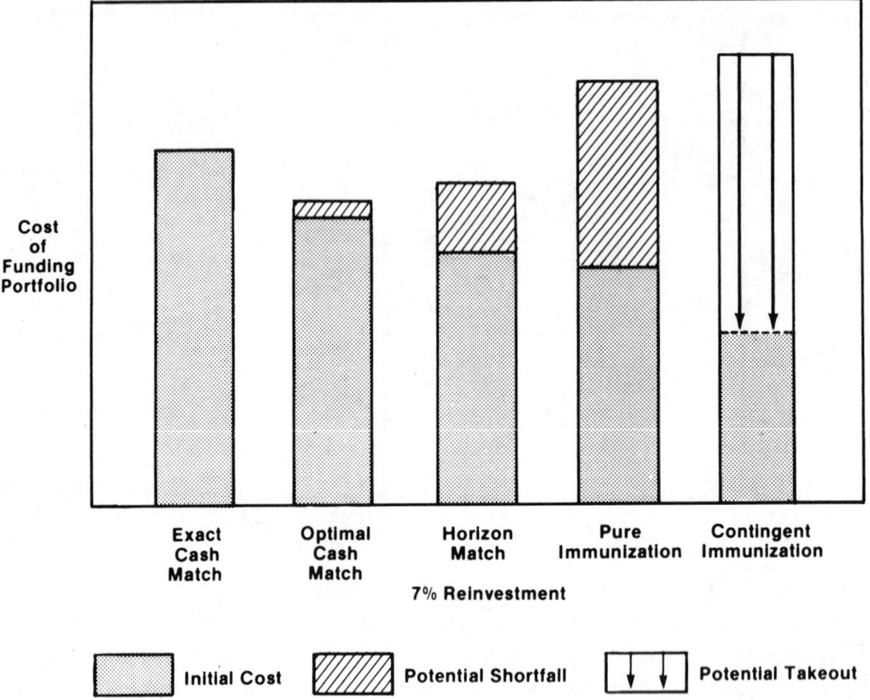

adverse movements, to tailor his or her posture in the face of such movements, and to have ample time to restructure the portfolio into an immunized mode should that become necessary.

How does **contingent immunization** compare with **classical immunization?** Classical immunization carries a high opportunity cost: the foregone potential profits of successful active management. Contingent immunization restores this profit potential in exchange for the spread between the immunized rate and the floor return (see Exhibit 54). More generally, the context of matched funding, contingent immunization incurs a somewhat higher initial portfolio cost to gain the flexibility for potential takeouts. With successful active management, these takeouts could significantly reduce the effective cost of funding the entire liability schedule (Exhibit 54).

CONTINGENT DEDICATION

The basic idea behind contingent immunization can be further generalized to deal with a range of fixed-income objectives other than that of a floor return over a fixed investment horizon. A whole host of portfolio objectives can be designed in such a way that an analytic safety net can be constructed around them. Thus, for example, a contingent dedication system would blend a cushion allowing for active management with a discipline that would assure—at the very worst—the fulfillment of a specified schedule of liabilities. In this case, the "floor" would be a cash-matched portfolio, and the contingent portfolio would have to be managed so that even under adverse performance, there would be sufficient assets to put the cash-matched "floor portfolio" into place.

The concept of a contingent system can be extended readily to other "floor objectives" such as various forms of horizon-matched portfolios. In fact, there are a number of different design formats for these contingent systems. Thus on the one hand, a relatively conservative contingent horizon match might consist of a portfolio that must remain continually cash matched prior to the horizon and uses its safety margin to achieve controlled departures from the pure duration match of the posthorizon liabilities. On the other hand, a more aggressive contingent horizon match might consist of an active portfolio constrained only by the requirement that it maintain sufficient asset value to trigger into a horizon match floor portfolio under a worst-case yield curve movement.

Contingent systems can also vary in terms of the decision rules employed to achieve the minimum return conditions. These can range from relatively pure mathematical or mechanical procedures such as those used in so-called **dynamic hedging** systems, to a general process that establishes "bet limits" for a given active risk posture.

Another source of variation is the character of the objective itself. Rather than some prescribed series of liabilities, the "floor" could be a specified performance index. The contingent portfolio would then be designed to pursue incremental return relative to this index. In the context of this section, the main idea is that contingent systems allow for active return-seeking to be combined with the assurance of some matched-funding objective. This interplay between matched and projective funding is illustrated schematically in Exhibit 55.

THE CONTINUUM OF FIXED-INCOME STRATEGIES

Basically, the upper curve in Exhibit 55 represents the classical risk/return relationship. As one moves to the right and accepts greater risk, the expected return should increase. Of course, this is the basic trade-off involved in any analysis of projective funding procedures.

However, the lower curve in Exhibit 55 corresponds to the minimum return associated with assurance of matched-funding objectives. With more strategy risk, the matched-funding component drops further and further away from the higher expected (or "projected" or "hoped-for") return. Thus with exact cash matching based solely on noncallable Treasury bonds, the level of projected return may be relatively low, but the structure of the return is fully coincident to the matched-funding objective. There is essentially no risk that the specified

EXHIBIT 55 THE CONTINUUM OF FIXED-INCOME STRATEGIES

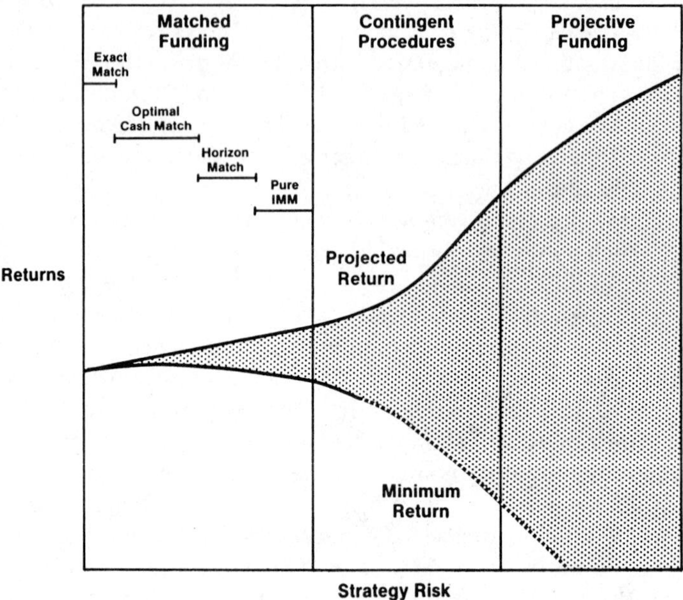

liabilities will not be met. Moving toward more general forms of cash matching, the returns increase, but there arise slightly greater risks associated with the minimum return required for the matched-funding objective. Similarly, as one moves further to the right into horizon matching and then to pure immunization, the projected returns grow, the portfolio costs decrease, but there is an accompanying rise in the shortfall risk.

Even further to the right is the arena of contingent portfolios, where an explicit cushion is provided to allow for active management. At the "conservative" left-most border, contingent systems can work with very moderate safety margins but can then take only moderate risk "tilts" away from the matched-funding objective. (In fact, such contingent systems might be "backed into" via successful reoptimization from some form of dedicated portfolios.) Moving further to the right, highly aggressive contingent systems might be limited to quite minimal matched-funding "floors"; for example, assuring fulfillment of only the first 7 years of scheduled payments.

Finally, with further movement to the right, one enters the higher altitudes of expected return—virtually free-form active management with relatively little concern for the fulfillment of any minimum return or cash-flow objectives. When applied to a pension context, this is pure projective funding. It places relatively few constraints on the investment managers, and seeks the highest possible return from the asset class itself as well as from unfettered management activity.

This continuum of **fixed-income strategies** provides the corporate sponsor with a considerable range of choices. In his or her asset allocation, the sponsor can seek maximum projected return—which, if realized, is its own reward. Or, the sponsor can pursue a relatively low-risk, matched-funding strategy. In fact, these two strategy poles can differ so widely that they comprise two virtually distinct asset classes. Thus it would not be at all inconsistent for the corporate sponsor to have one fixed-income portfolio component in full active management while maintaining a dedicated portfolio.

As noted, however, a **decision to dedicate** is usually based upon the interplay of corporate factors as well as pure investment considerations. In addition to risk reduction itself, dedication usually allows the corporate sponsor to reap significant actuarial benefits. In a sense, these benefits are derived from the fact that an actuarial evaluation, by the very conservative nature of the actuary's mandate, generally focuses on the minimum return prospects. Thus in a sense, the actuarial systesm (at least in the near term) often rewards the sponsor in accordance with his or her demonstrable *minimum return*, rather than for any notion (no matter how legitimate) of projected return.

The continuum curve of Exhibit 55 provides insight into the circumstances that can motivate a corporate sponsor to opt for bond dedication. When the projected return is perceived as being relatively flat, with little incremental return for fully flexible management (or for reallocation into other asset classes), then matched funding will have a natural appeal. Higher levels of available minimum return will augment this appeal, because of both pure investment considerations as well as the greater actuarial benefits associated with higher market spreads over the pro forma actuarial discount rate.

THE OPTIMAL STRATEGY

Projective funding can be pursued with virtually any asset class. However, matched funding can be achieved only with an appropriately structured fixed-income portfolio. As we have shown in this section, there exists a wide range of techniques for implementing matched-funding objectives. These techniques vary widely in initial cost, opportunity cost, shortfall risk, portfolio and management flexibility, and projected return. Each of the portfolio techniques along this spectrum has its advantages and disadvantages. At the same time, the individual fund sponsor will always have its own special needs and its own unique perception of the trade-offs between the various forms of matched- and/or projective-funding strategies. There is no one best procedure for all funds or for all times. It is the interplay of these trade-offs and the very individual sponsor needs that determine the most appropriate technique for a given fund at a given time.

BIBLIOGRAPHY

Bierwag, G., "Measures of Duration," Preprint, University of Oregon, August 1976.

———, "Immunization, Duration, and the Term Structure of Interest Rates," *Journal of Financial and Quantitative Analysis* (December 1977): 725–742.

———, "Dynamic Portfolio Immunization Policies," *Journal of Banking and Finance* (Fall 1977).

Bierwag, G., and Grove, M., "A Model of the Term Structure of Interest Rates," *Review of Economics and Statistics* (February 1967): 50–62.

Bierwag, G., and Kaufman, G., "Bond Portfolio Strategy Simulations: A Critique," *Journal of Financial and Quantitative Analysis* (September 1978): 519–525.

———, "Coping with the Risk of Interest-Rate Fluctuations: A Note," *Journal of Business* (July 1977).

Bierwag, G., and Khang, C., "An Immunization Strategy is a Minimax Strategy," *Journal of Finance* (May 1979): 389–399.

Bierwag, G., Kaufman, G., and Khang, C., "Duration and Bond Portfolio Analysis: An Overview," *Journal of Financial and Quantitative Analysis* (November 1978): 671–681.

Bierwag, G., Kaufman, G., Schweitzer, R., and Toevs, A., "Risk and Return for Active and Passive Bond Portfolio Management: Theory and Evidence," paper presented at Institute for Quantitative Research in Finance (October 1979), New York, Columbia University.

Bildersee, J. S., "Duration as a Determinant of Price Spreads in Bond Markets," University of Pennsylvania (March 1978).

Blocker, E., and Stickney, C., "Duration and Risk Assessments in Capital Budgeting," *Accounting Review* (January 1979) 180–188.

Blume, M. E., "Bond Betas," Wharton School, University of Pennsylvania, December 1973.

Boquist, J. A., Racette, G. A., and Schlarbaum, G. C., "Duration and Risk Assessment for Bonds and Common Stocks," *Journal of Finance* (December 1975): 1360–1365.

Boyle, P., "Immunization Under Stochastic Models of the Term Structure," *Journal of the Institute of Actuaries* (U.K.), Vol. 105 (1978): 177.

Buse, A., "Expecations, Prices, Coupons and Yields," *Journal of Finance* (September 1970): 809–818.

Caks, J., "A Refutation of Duration," paper presented at the Annual Meeting of the Midwest Finance Association, April 1976.

Carr, J. L., Halpern, P. J., and McCallum, J. S., "Correcting the Yield Curve: A Reinterpretation of the Duration Problem," *Journal of Finance* (September 1974): 1287–1294.

Cooper, I. A., "Asset Values, Interest-Rate Changes, and Duration," *Journal of Financial and Quantitative Analysis* (December 1977).

Cox, J. C., Ingersoll, J. E., and Ross S. A., "Duration and the Measurement of Basis Risk," *Journal of Business*, Vol. 52 (January 1979).

———, "A Theory of the Term Structure of Interest Rates," Working Paper, University of Chicago, 1978.

Diller, S., "The Impact of Changing Interest Rates in a Bond Portfolio," *Money Manager* (February 13, 1979).

Durand, D., "Growth Stocks and the Petersburg Paradox," *Journal of Finance* (September 1957): 348–363.

Einhorn, M., "Breaking Tradition in Bond Portfolio Management," *Journal of Portfolio Management* (Spring 1975).

Ezra, D., "Immunization: A New Look for Actuarial Liabilities," *Journal of Portfolio Management* (Winter 1976).

Fisher, L., "An Algorithm for Finding Exact Rates of Return," *Journal of Business* (January 1966): 111–118.

———, and Weil, R., "Coping with the Risk of Interest-Rate Fluctuations: Returns to Bondholders from Naive and Optimal Strategies," *Journal of Business* (October 1971), 408–431.

———, "Returns to Bondholders from Naive and Optimal Strategies," University of Chicago (August 1970).

Grove, M. A., "On Duration and the Optimal Maturity Structure of the Balance Sheet," *Bell Journal of Economics and Management Science* (Autumn 1974).

———, "A Model of the Maturity Profile of the Balance Sheet," *Meteroeconomica,* Vol. 18 (1977): 40–55.

Haugen, R. A., and Wichern, D. W., "The Elasticity of Financial Assets," *Journal of Finance* (September 1974): 1229–1240.

Hainer, M. M., McLeod, C. C., and Strowger, G. G., "The Practical Application of Immunization to the Financial Management of New Money Business," paper presented at the November 1978 meeting of the Canadian Institute of Actuaries.

Hicks, J. R., *Value and Capital,* 2nd ed., Oxford: Clarendon Press, 1946.

Hopewell, M. H. and Kaufman, G. C., "Bond Price Volatility and Term to Maturity: A Generalized Respecification," *American Economic Review* (September 1973): 749–752.

Ingersoll, J. E., Skeleton, J., and Weil, R. L., "Duration Forty Years Later," *Journal of Financial And Quantitative Analysis* (November 1978): 627–650.

Kaufman, G., "Measuring Risk & Return for Bonds: A New Approach," *Journal of Bank Research,* (Summer 1978).

———, Bierwag, G. O., and Toevs, Alden, See various studies in *"Innovations in Bond Portfolio Management: Duration Analysis and Immunization,"* JAI Press, 1983, Greenwich, Conn.

Khang, C., "Bond Immunization When Short-Term Rates Fluctuate More than Long-term Rates," revised reprint, University of Oregon (November 1978).

Liebowitz, M. L., *The Rolling Yield,* New York: Salomon Brothers, 1977.

———, *The Risk Dimension,* New York: Salomon Brothers, 1977.

———, "Bond Immunization: A Procedure for Realizing Target Levels of Return," New York: Salomon Brothers, 1979.

———, "Bond Immunization, Part II: Portfolio Rebalancing," New York: Salomon Brothers, 1979.

———, "Bond Immunization, Part III: The Yield Curve Case," New York: Salomon Brothers, 1979.

———, *Pros & Cons of Immunization,* New York: Salomon Brothers, 1980.

———, *Total Return Management,* New York: Salomon Brothers, 1979.

———, Leibowitz, Martin L., "Effects of Alternative Anticipations of Yield-Curve Behavior on the Composition of Immunized Portfolios and on their Target Returns," reprinted with permission by Salomon Brothers Inc, JAI Press, 1983, Greenwich, Conn.

———, Weinberger, Alfred, Contingent Immunization: A New Procedure for Structured Active Management, Salomon Brothers Inc, January 28, 1981.

———, Weinberger, Alfred, *Optimal Cash Flow Matching: Minimum Risk Bond Portfolios for Fulfilling Prescribed Schedules of Liabilities,* Salomon Brothers Inc, August 1981.

———, Klaffky, Thomas E., Mandel, Steven, and Weinberger, Alfred, *Horizon Matching: A New Generalized Approach for Developing Minimum-Cost Dedicated Portfolios,* Salomon Brothers Inc, September 1983.

Livingston, M., and Caks, J., "A Duration Fallacy," *Journal of Finance* (March 1977).

———, "Duration and Risk Assessment for Common Stocks: A Note," *Journal of Finance* (March 1978).

McEnally, R. W., "Duration as a Practical Tool for Bond Management," *Journal of Portfolio Management* (Summer 1977) 53–57.

Macaulay, F. R., *Some Theoretical Problems Suggested by the Movements of Interest Rates, Bond Yields, and Stock Prices in the United States Since 1865,* National Bureau of Economic Research, 1938.

Marshall, W., and Yawitz, J., "Lower Bounds on Portfolio Performance: A Generalized Immunization Strategy," prepublication draft, revised January 1979.

Mennis, Edmund A., Valentine, Jerome L. and Mennis, Daniel L., "New Perspectives on Pension Fund Management," *Journal of Portfolio Management* (Spring 1981).

Redington, F. M., "Review of the Principles of Life-Office Valuations," *Journal of Institute of Actuaries,* Vol. 78 (1952).

Samuelson, P. A., "The Effect of Interest Rate Increases in the Banking System," *American Economic Review,* Vol. 55 (1945).

Sheddon, A. D., "A Practical Approach to Applying Immunization Theory," *Transactions of the Faculty of Actuaries,* Vol. 35 (1977): 313.

Springbett, T. M., "Valuation for Surplus," *Transactions of the Faculty of Actuaries,* Vol. 28 (1977).

———, and Cavage, C. M., "Actuarial Note on the Calculation of Premium Rates Using a Decreasing Rate of Interest and Allowing for the Benefit of Immunization," *Transactions of the Faculty of Actuaries,* Vol. 28 (1977).

Tiley, J. A., "The Matching of Assets and Liabilities," *Transactions of the Society of Actuaries,* Vol. 32 (1977).

Trainer, F. H., Yawitz, J. B., and Marshall, W. J., "Holding Period Is the Key to Risk Thesholds," *Journal of Portfolio Management* (Winter 1979).

Vanderhoof, I. T., "The Interest Rate Assumption and the Maturity Structure of the Assets of a Life Insurance Company," *Transactions of the Society of Actuaries,* Vol. 24 (October 1972).

Vanderhoff, I. T., "Interest Rate Assumptions and the Relationship Between Asset and Liability Structure," Education and Examination Committee of the Society of Actuaries, Part 7 study notes: 79-12-76.

Wallas, G. E., "Immunization," *Journal of Institute of Actuaries, Student's Society,* Vol. 15 (1959).

Weil, R. L., "Macaulay's Duration: An Appreciation," *Journal of Business,* Vol. 46 (October 1973): 589–592.

Whittaker, J., "The Relevance of Duration," *Journal of Business and Finance* (Spring 1970).

Wissner, L., "Bond Immunization: How Today's High Bond Yields Can Be Locked In," New York: Smith Barney, Harris Upham & Co., Inc., December 1978.

———, "The Neutral Bond Portfolio," New York: Smith Barney, Harris Upham & Co., Inc., September 1978.

———, "The Unmanaged Bond Portfolio," New York: Smith Barney, Harris Upham & Co. Inc., September 1978.

Yawitz, J. B., "Is Average Maturity a Proxy for Risk?" *Journal of Portfolio Management,* (Spring 1976).

———, "The Relative Importance of Duration and Yield Volatility on Bond Price Volatility," *Journal of Money, Credit and Banking,* (February 1977): 97–102.

———, Hempel, G., and Marshall, W. J., "A Risk-Return Approach to the Selection of Optimal Government Bond Portfolios," *Financial Management,* Vol. 5, No. 3 (Autumn 1976).

———, "The Use of Average Maturity as a Risk Proxy in Investment Portfolios," *Journal of Finance* (May 1975).

26

OPTION AND INSURANCE STRATEGIES FOR FIXED-INCOME PORTFOLIOS

CONTENTS

26

OPTION AND INSURANCE STRATEGIES FOR FIXED-INCOME PORTFOLIOS

Robert B. Platt

INTRODUCTION

Managing fixed-income assets has become more interesting and challenging in recent years. In the past it was not uncommon for money managers and institutions to view these securities as their **Riskless Investment,** that is, an investment that would provide a steady stream of predictable coupon income with a low volatility of return performance. Changes in the financial and economic environment, beginning in the late 1960s and reaching an especially excited state of activity in the period 1979–1982, have altered dramatically the conventional views of the role of fixed-income investments and their riskiness.

The forces at work during this period were driven largely by fundamental changes in the exposure of the American economy to the risk of **inflation** and to changes in social and political values which have altered the regulatory environment in which many financial institutions operate. All **money managers** to some extent have been faced with the need to adapt to these forces, but the effects have been most dramatic on some of the largest pools of investable resources: insurance companies, banks, and thrifts. Indeed in these organizations the management and control of their exposure to interest rate risk have become almost integral to managing the financial soundness and viability of the firm.

Corporations as well have been affected by this new investment environment. Most noticeably this has occurred in the management of **pension assets,** where many corporations have been rethinking the role of fixed-income assets in their porfolios. A manifestation of this which has attracted much attention in recent years has been the closer integration of the pension fund asset decision with the overall corporate finance needs of the organization. An example of this has been the large increase in **dedicated and immunized bond portfolios.** By some estimates these portfolios now account for as much as 10% of all pension fund assets under management. In addition, the traditional **Treasurer function** of managing corporate cash positions has become more complex as firms have found themselves managing larger pools of assets in an environment of heightened risk and increased opportunities for returns.

AN OVERVIEW OF RISK CONTROL TECHNOLOGY

As risk as a dimension of fixed-income investment has become more pronounced, there has been a growing disenchantment with the performance of **active management,** which relies heavily on interest rate anticipation for return performance. All too often, such approaches have led to higher risk without the commensurate increase in returns that theory leads us to expect. The need to manage risk has led to the creation of complex and innovative instruments: options, futures, mortgage-backed securities, floating rate instruments, interest rate swaps, zero coupon securities, and securities with special put features. These need to be understood by money managers, financial institutions, and corporations if they are to be used to their full advantage.

In addition to the creation of new investment instruments, the forces of change in the financial environment have led to the development of a whole range of risk control methodology with which financial institutions and corporations can manage their exposure to **interest rate risk.** The first salvo in this battle was the resurrection of the concept of **bond duration** and its use in **immunization strategies** from the more arcane actuarial journals, and its development into a highly sophisticated and flexible tool for managing the interest sensitivity of assets and liabilities. Similar developments are occurring in the use of complex **hedging strategies** employing **financial futures.**

To some extent these developments can be viewed as a knee-jerk reaction to the heightened awareness of risk in fixed-income investment and to the disappointing performance of active fixed-income management. Many bond managers, financial institutions, and corporations faced with these developments have opted for the safest of paths, that is, to seek out the riskless strategy which immunizes completely their exposure to **interest rate risk,** without adequately reflecting on the costs of such strategies. The riskless investment strategy, while prviding the maximum of downside protection is also the costliest form of **portfolio insurance** protection because it also truncates most if not all of the upside return protection that comes from good investment management.

MOLDING THE RETURN DISTRIBUTION OF FIXED-INCOME PORTFOLIOS

Considering the truncation of the interest rate risk exposure of a portfolio of assets or liabilities as an insurance policy is a useful analogy. It helps us to focus on both the degree of protection we are seeking as well as on its costs, because most people think in these terms when they purchase an insurance policy. The same considerations should be used in structuring a portfolio strategy utilizing **interest rate risk** control methodology. One should never buy more insurance protection than is actually needed. In this context, the riskless strategies employing **duration** or **financial futures hedging** may be too costly for many portfolio applications. More flexible forms of risk control are required in such cases—approaches that allow some trade-off of different degrees of downside protection for different degrees of upside return opportunities. Increasingly, the attention of practitioners in risk-control technology are turning their attention to these possibilities.

Immunization (or fully hedged portfolios) and **actively managed portfolios** can be viewed as the two polar cases along a continuous spectrum of risk. It is possible to construct portfolios with the risk characteristics anywhere along this entire risk spectrum using the technique and methodology of **options.** This characteristic of options makes them unique and especially advantageous instruments for controlling interest rate risk.

The utilization of **option technology** in interest rate risk control is still novel. It necessitates more demands on the flexibility and creativity of the portfolio managers as well perhaps on their mathematical competence. It also requires changes in the way we measure the performance of investment results, because we must begin to view our investment activities more in the light of how well we achieve clearly defined investment objectives, rather than concentrating myopically on decile rankings of returns relative to our investment peers.

Despite the added complexity of option methodology, the fundamental attractions of the approach are too strong to be denied. The new wave of **bond management** is likely to be the molding of returns to meet specific investment objectives. The tool to accomplish this is likely to be **option strategies.**

OPTIONS USED FOR PORTFOLIO RETURN STRATEGIES

The early interest in **options,** both **calls** and **puts,** was in connection with their use as **tactical trading** instruments. Investors purchased calls as a way of achieving a leveraged position in the underlying security. They bought puts to lock in gains or to speculate on declines in the underlying security. But options can be viewed more generally than this. They are not only tactical trading vehicles, but are also useful portfolio management tools for molding the entire shape of the **portfolio return distribution.** It is in this context that options will be treated in this section.

Portfolio management is typically viewed as a traditional two-dimensional trade-off between the mean and variance of returns. Although we stretch the reality of conditions somewhat by doing so, this distribution is often depicted in terms for the familiar bell-shaped curve of the **"normal distribution"** (Exhibit 1). In this representation of the return distribution, the portfolio manager has an expected return and a risk as measured by the variance of return around

EXHIBIT 1 RETURN DISTRIBUTION OF A RISKY ASSET PORTFOLIO, MEAN RETURN IS 20%, WITH A STANDARD DEVIATION OF 30%

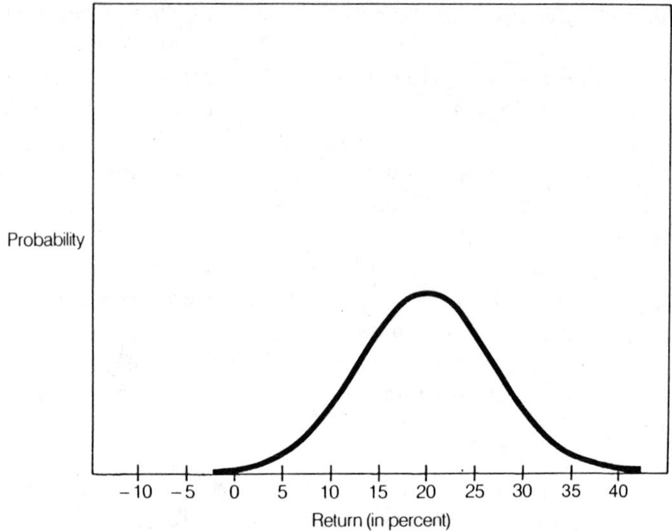

the mean. There is no distinction made in this representation of portfolio risk as to what side or (tail) of the distribution the variation of the returns falls. Risk is risk and variance is its measure.

A conservative portfolio manager wishing to reduce risk, typically will approach the problem by adding some portion of a less risky security (cash) to the portfolio. This would alter the shape of the distribution of returns by compressing the variance, and would shift the return distribution somewhat to the left by reducing expected portfolio returns (Exhibit 2). This transformation of the expected return and risk profile of the portfolio, however, still provides a symmetric distribution of risk. This may not satisfy all of the complex needs of a portfolio manager. A portfolio manager may wish to retain as much of the "good" risk as possible (i.e., the right-hand tail of the distribution) while truncating the "bad" risk on the left-hand tail of the distribution. Such a strategy of truncating downside risk while retaining as much of the upside return as possible (as might be expected) will have a cost in terms of the expected portfolio returns. The net effect of this nonsymmetric altering of the return distribution is shown in Exhibit 3. The strategy illustrated is the effect of buying a put option on some portfolio of risky assets. The exercise, or **strike price,** of the option is what provides the downside floor protection. The cost of the option is what accounts for the leftward shift in the expected portfolio return.

As this example indicates, the use of options in conjunction with a portfolio of risky assets extends the consideration of the traditional **mean-variance framework** to the added dimension of the **skewness of the return distribution.** In the context of **modern portfolio theory,** which concentrates on the efficient trade-offs between return and variance, option strategies are suboptimal. How-

EXHIBIT 2 RETURN DISTRIBUTION OF A RISKY ASSET PORTFOLIO PLUS CASH; MEAN RETURN IS 15%, WITH A STANDARD DEVIATION OF 20% (COMPARED TO EXHIBIT 1, THE INVESTOR HAS BOTH LOWER EXPECTED RETURN AND LOWER RISK)

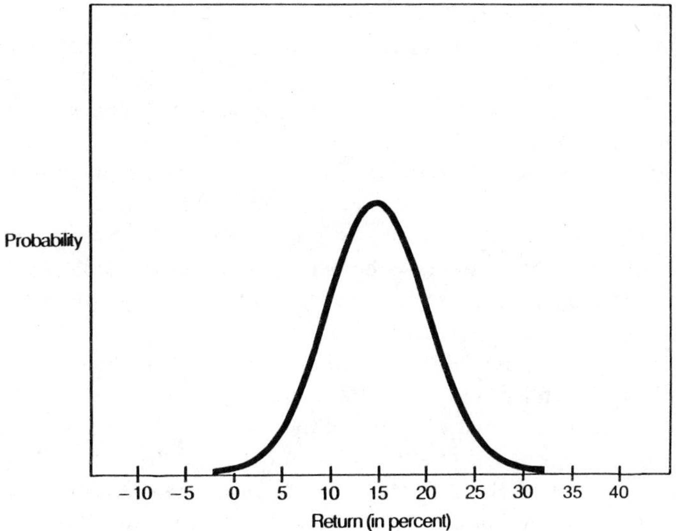

EXHIBIT 3 THE RETURN DISTRIBUTION THAT MIGHT BE PREFERRED BY THE PORTFOLIO MANAGER; THE PROBABILITY OF A LARGE LOSS IS ELIMINATED; THIS IS AN EXAMPLE OF A PROTECTIVE PUT STRATEGY; THE EXPECTED RETURN IS REDUCED BY THE COST OF THE PUT

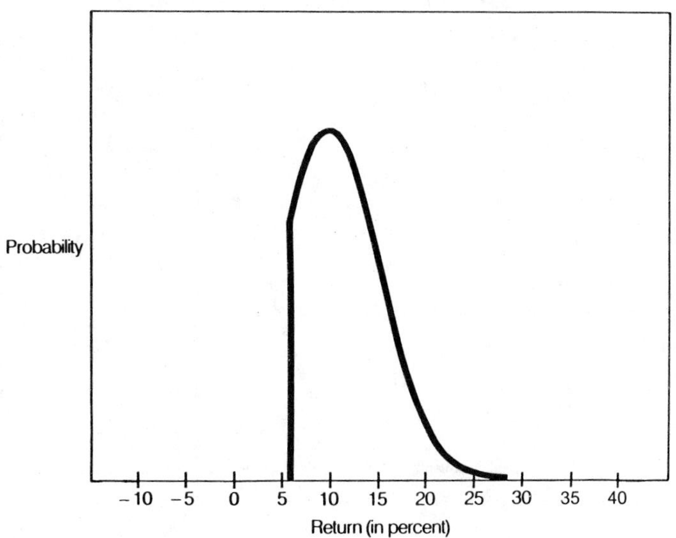

ever, in terms of **achieving specific portfolio objectives** (e.g., a portfolio manager wishing to be assured of achieving some minimum return objective) the price of the insurance contract represented by the put option strategy may be more than worth the price. This is an important point, deserving of some emphasis. The use of **option strategies** in a portfolio context requires managers to view their return objectives in more than a two-dimensional framework. With options you are managing the portfolio to meet specific objectives rather than to maximize returns.

Call options are also frequently used in connection with portfolios. Probably the most common portfolio strategy employing call options is the **covered call.** In this strategy, a call option is sold (written) against the securities in the portfolio. The objective is to increase the expected return in the portfolio through the **call premium.** The effect of the covered call strategy on the distribution of portfolio returns is the opposite of the previously described protective put strategy. The right-hand tail of the return distribution is truncated (at the exercise price of the call), and the expected portfolio return is shifted to the right as a result of the portfolio manager receiving the call premium (Exhibit 4). Thus the covered call strategy is the mirror image of the protective put strategy.

The comparison of the covered call and protective put strategies emphasizes the great flexibility of options in affecting the **portfolio return distribution.** More complex strategies involving the use of puts and calls, and their use at varying exercise prices can be developed. This would lead to more exotic

EXHIBIT 4 SELLING OFF SOME OF THE "GOOD RISK;" AN EXAMPLE OF THE COVERED CALL STRATEGY; THE EXPECTED RETURN IS INCREASED BY THE CALL PREMIUM

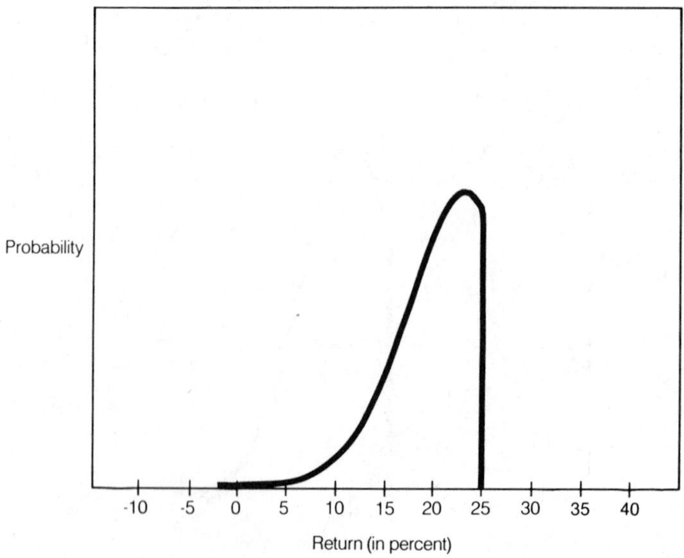

shapes of the return distribution. An important conclusion follows from this. Specifically, whatever the portfolio managers' return objective, if it can be translated into the dimensions of mean, variance, and skewness of the return distribution, there is likely to be some combination of options that would enable the manager, at a cost, to achieve that objective.

CREATING OPTIONS USING DYNAMIC TRADING TECHNIQUES

The key problem in employing options as a tool for molding portfolio return distributions is that the appropriate option contracts rarely exist in the markets. One critical problem is that on the listed exchanges there are options on individual securities but not on portfolios of securities. A basket of options will in general perform differently than an option on a basket, and will in most cases cost more in the bargain. In addition, the **option markets** are limited in terms of their liquidity and for all but the shorter maturities. Of course, it is possible in some cases to find a dealer firm willing to write an appropriate **over-the-counter option.** But often these will be mispriced sufficiently to provide an adequate profit to the option writer. Perhaps most important, even where an appropriate option contract can be obtained, regulatory or institutional barriers often preclude their use by portfolio managers.

Fortunately, even where the appropriate option contracts cannot be found, or where options cannot themselves be used, it is possible for portfolio managers to achieve option-like return distributions using only cash securities. The principles of option theory can be used to **create options synthetically by a dynamic reallocation of assets.**

Options are all priced on **arbitrage** arguments, which preclude the possibility of a **riskless arbitrage** between the option and the underlying cash instrument on which the option is written. From this idea, theory has shown that an option position can be created by pursuing a strategy that dynamically adjusts the proportion of the securities in the portfolio and some **"risk-free" asset.** In this connection, risk free should be thought of as some asset whose value will be known with certainty over the option period. It is the risk-free asset that will provide the ability to achieve the option strike price. It is the difference in the expected return on the risky portfolio and the risk-free rate that will determine the option cost.

Because the option can be replicated by a portfolio of risky and riskless assets, it stands to reason that the option price will be equal to the cost of the replicating portfolio. It can be demonstrated that both call and put options can be written in the form of simple equations, linking the price of the option to the cost of the **replicating portfolio,** where the equations take the following form:

$$C = a_c A - b_c R$$

$$P = -a_p A + b_p R$$

C and *P* represent the price of a call option and a put option, respectively. *A* is the risky asset portfolio and *R* is the riskless asset. The lowercase *a*s and *b*s are variables determined by the option pricing model being replicated, and they can take values between zero and one.

Notice the symmetry in the equations for both the call and the put option. The equations take the same form, but the signs on the variables are different. This should not be surprising in view of the earlier discussion about the symmetry with which call and put options can be used in shaping portfolio returns.

As mentioned earlier, the *a*s and *b*s are variables derived from the **option pricing model.** Their values will be determined by the same **factors that determine any option price:** (1) The value of the risky assets in the portfolio, (2) the time to expiration of the option, (3) the strike price of the option, (4) the interest rate on the riskless asset, and (5) the volatility of returns for the portfolio of risky assets.

Most of these factors are variable over time; hence the weights in the replicating portfolio (i.e., the *a*s and *b*s, requiring a dynamic adjustment between the asset portfolio and the riskless assets. Of all the factors accounting for changes in the asset mix, items 1 and 2 (i.e., the changing value of the assets and the passage of time) are most influential.

BUYING PORTFOLIO INSURANCE

Probably the simplest way to illustrate how the return distribution of fixed-income portfolios can be altered is in the case of the **protective put strategy ("portfolio insurance").** Any risk-averse fixed income manager can use existing option technology to **structure their return to achieve minimal target objectives** efficiently—that is, with the least cost in terms of upside return potential.

In order to control risk through portfolio insurance, the manager must sacrifice some upside return potential in order to achieve a given level of protection on the downside. Many levels of insurance protection are available. **Immunization** offers the highest possible level of portfolio protection for the greatest sacrifice in upside return potential. Other insurance levels differ from immunization in both the amount of downside protection and in the potential upside return give-up. The manager presumably desires a strategy that offers the greatest downside protection for the smallest potential upside loss. The optimal strategy depends on both return-risk opportunities and on the probabilities a manager assigns to being "right" or "wrong" in the interest rate bet.

Consider an active bond portfolio manager who has a 5-year holding period and a minimum annual return benchmark of 8% over that horizon. This manager expects interest rates to decline moderately over the period so he or she structures the portfolio to have essentially the same **duration** as the Shearson Lehman government/corporate bond index. Over the 5-year holding period, interest rates in fact follow the path shown in Exhibit 5—a sharp downward trend with some intermittent cycles. The portfolio's wealth at any time during

EXHIBIT 5 PROJECT INTEREST RATE TREND

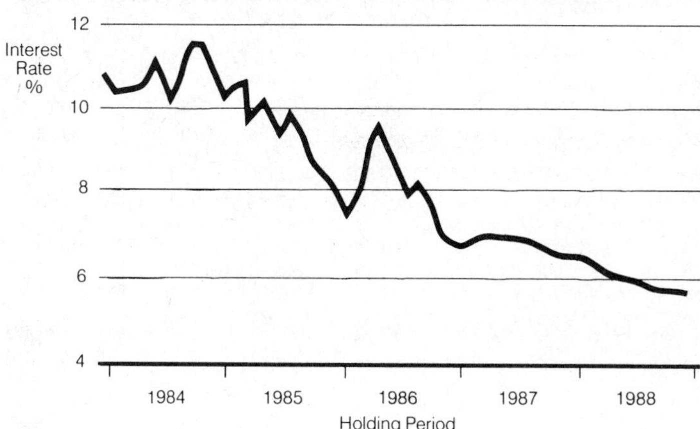

the holding period will equal accumulated income plus changes in the underlying securities' prices. The magnitude of the wealth will vary depending on how successful the manager's active portfolio decisions have been. At any time, the manager has the option of converting this wealth into an **immunized bond portfolio** for the remainder of the holding period, thus assuring some total level of return over the entire horizon. This is the method by which risk is controlled under **contingent immunization.**

Alternatively, the portfolio manager may place only a portion of the available wealth in an immunized pool, leaving the balance to be actively managed. The active bond portfolio may be considered to be the "risky" asset and the immunized portfolio the "riskless" asset. In effect, the manager initiates a **portfolio insurance strategy** that implies some particular level of downside risk protection. The minimal insured return will be achieved if the initial allocation between the risky and riskless assets is adjusted over time according to the decision rules determined from the option strategy being replicated by the portfolio insurance procedure.

AMOUNT OF DOWNSIDE PROTECTION. Using the interest rate movements illustrated in Exhibit 5, we calculated the different levels of downside protection purchasable by allocating varying proportions of wealth to the active and immunized portfolios at different times during the 5-year holding period. Exhibit 6 shows some of the results. We assumed that the portfolio was invested 100% in the risky asset (a portfolio with the duration of the Shearson Lehman index) up to the time the calculations of the purchasable levels of insurance protection were made. Because interest rates were falling for most of the holding period, the wealth of this 100% risky portfolio increased, as the "assets available" column of the exhibit indicates.

As the portfolio's wealth increased, the portfolio was able to buy higher levels of insurance protection—that is, to lock in a higher return over the hold-

EXHIBIT 6 RETURNS AVAILABLE FROM PORTFOLIO INSURANCE PROCEDURES[a]

Beginning of Quarter	Assets Available	Implied Insured Return Over Five Years with Risky Allocation of				Return Over Five Years if Switch to Immunized
		25%	50%	75%	100%	
1/84	$1,000,000	10.12%	8.63%	6.13%	−21.09%	11.04%
2/84	1,034,293	10.46	9.43	7.71	−11.72	11.08
3/84	1,066,401	10.66	9.88	8.57	− 6.48	11.13
4/84	1,018,349	9.93	8.67	6.56	−16.86	10.70
1/85	1,128,695	10.44	9.17	7.05	−16.48	11.21
2/85	1,205,406	11.07	10.26	8.89	− 6.77	11.56
3/85	1,275,042	11.35	10.49	9.02	− 7.69	11.88
4/85	1,343,701	11.62	10.65	9.00	− 9.65	12.22
1/86	1,489,522	12.63	11.72	10.18	− 7.30	13.18
2/86	1,366,284	11.42	10.59	9.19	− 6.82	11.92
3/86	1,516,190	12.50	11.63	10.18	− 6.46	13.02
4/86	1,628,853	13.38	12.68	11.50	− 2.14	13.80
1/87	1,723,870	14.16	13.70	12.92	3.73	14.44
2/87	1,736,971	14.19	13.95	13.54	8.66	14.33
3/87	1,774,475	14.30	14.08	13.71	9.22	14.44
4/87	1,859,708	14.90	14.71	14.38	10.51	15.01
1/88	1,890,168	14.94	14.77	14.49	11.11	15.04
2/88	1,979,600	15.60	15.48	15.28	12.84	15.67
3/88	2,042,174	15.98	15.92	15.81	14.50	16.02
4/88	2,125,496	16.57	16.52	16.44	15.44	16.59
End of 5 Years	2,188,206					

[a]Assuming a 100% risky position is taken until the insurance strategy is begun.

ing period. This is evident from the remaining columns of the exhibit. One could, alternatively, say that, because of good, active management, the manager could buy the same level of insurance protection for less money.

In our example, the manager has a return benchmark of 8% over the holding period. He or she could have assured this downside protection at the outset by establishing a portfolio insurance procedure from an initial position of 50% in the risky asset and 50% in the immunized asset. If, instead, the manager decided to continue to manage actively, then by the second quarter of 1986, he or she could have achieved the same downside protection by initiating an insurance procedure from a 100% risky asset position. The manager could, in other words, purchase the same downside protection without sacrificing any of the return that would accrue to the portfolio if rates continued to fall.

The cost of achieving a given level of insurance protection may be used as a measure of the success of active management decisions. This cost, in terms of potential upside return give-up, is related to the proportion of the portfolio the manager can leave in the risky asset at the initiation of an insurance procedure and still meet the benchmark minimal return. If we consider the risky asset (the actively managed portfolio) as the objective based on the manager's interest rate expectations, we can assign this portfolio a **beta** of one. All other insured positions would be initiated with betas between zero and one. The level of assured downside protection is thus inversely related to the beta of the insured position. This should not be too surprising: To get more insurance, one has to sacrifice more upside return potential. The manager now has a well-defined risk-return tradeoff; his or her goal, as an active manager, is to increase over time the beta of the insured position necessary to achieve the benchmark return.

The data in Exhibit 6 also show the relation between **contingent immunization** and **portfolio insurance.** In the preceding example, the manager initially took a fully active position and decided later in the holding period to initiate an insurance strategy. If, under contingent immunization, the manager had been forced into, or chosen the immunization mode, there would have been no further upside potential; under a "contingent insurance" strategy, he or she retains upside potential because a portion of the portfolio remains in the risky asset. The option to immunize is the extreme case of insurance protection. Immunization affords the highest level of assured minimal return, but because it has a zero beta, it has none of the upside potential of the risky asset should the manager's interest rate bet prove to be right over the remaining time horizon.

It is also important to note that, in a good active management situation, the differences between the levels of downside insurance protection offered by various beta positions decrease as time passes. For example, at the initiation of the portfolio, the downside protection available to the portfolio manager ranged from −21% (100% risky position) to +11% (100% immunized). By the first quarter of 1988 (the last year of the simulation), this range had narrowed to +11 to +15%.

The initial position in the risky asset at the time an insurance procedure is established is not a complete measure of potential upside return give-up. This is true because the asset allocation decision rule of portfolio insurance would lead the manager over time to increase his or her exposure to the risky asset if this asset continued to perform well. In other words, under the insurance procedure, the cost of insurance is related to how well the active manager is doing with the assets in the risky pool. This is an important difference between contingent immunization and portfolio insurance. If the decision to immunize is forced or taken, no assets remain in the risky pool and all the upside return potential is eliminated, hence there can be no downward adjustment in the cost of the insurance protection.

EXPECTED GIVE-UP FROM INSURED PORTFOLIOS. We have noted that the potential **upside return give-up** is related to the proportion of the portfolio in the risky asset at the initiation of the insurance procedure. In order to calculate the expected give-up from various insured positions, one needs to know the performance expectations of the portfolio manager. Assume, for example, that the portfolio manager expects to achieve a return of 20% above that available through immunizing for the remainder of the horizon. Exhibit 7 shows the expected return from being 100% in the risky asset and the percentage of this return that the manager could expect to relinquish by initiating a procedure for a given level of insurance at the beginning of each year of the holding period. Exhibit 8 shows the actual return give-ups at various insurance levels, given the interest rate pattern in Exhibit 5.

EXHIBIT 7 EXPECTED RETURN GIVE-UP VERSUS FULLY RISKY POSITION

Insurance Initiated Beginning of Year	Expected Risky Return Over Remaining Horizon	Immunized Return Over Remaining Horizon	Expected Give-up From Insuring With Indicated Initial Percentage in Risky Assets[a]			
			0%[b]	25%	50%	75%
1	13.25%	11.04%	2.21%	1.66%	1.11%	0.55%
2	12.96	10.80	2.16	1.62	1.08	0.54
3	9.16	7.63	1.53	1.15	0.77	0.38
4	8.05	6.71	1.34	1.01	0.67	0.34
5	7.91	6.59	1.32	0.99	0.66	0.33

[a]Give-ups are over remaining horizon.
[b]Immunized position.

The percentage of potential return given up is clearly related to the initial position in the risky asset—that is, the level of insurance protection purchased. What might be somewhat surprising, however, is how small the actual percentage return give-up (Exhibit 8) is for all insured positions other than the fully immunized. For example, at the beginning of the third year, the actual return give-up from immunizing for the balance of the holding period is 6.05%, whereas the actual give-up from initiating an insured position from a 25% position in the risky asset is only 1.54%. An initial 75% position in the risky asset implies a give-up of only 0.42%. The actual return give-up is so small under all levels of insurance other than immunization because of the adaptability of the insurance procedure to the changing fortunes of the risky asset.

OPTIMAL LEVELS OF INSURANCE. Suppose the active manager decides it is appropriate to hedge his or her interest rate bet, what level of insurance will be optimal? To answer this question, the manager needs to consider the potential give-ups associated with being both right and wrong in his or her interest rate expectations. Important in this decision are the probabilities the manager assigns to these interest rate outcomes. Exhibit 9 illustrates the decision. The dashed lines are lines of constant expected give-up. Their slopes equal the negative of the ratio of the probability of the active decision being correct to the probability of the active decision being incorrect. These lines represent the set of desired trade-offs. For example, with probabilities of 75% correct and 25% incorrect, the manager is willing to give up one basis point of expected return from being correct if he or she can insure an additional three basis points from

EXHIBIT 8 ACTUAL RETURN GIVE-UP VERSUS FULLY RISKY POSITION

Insurance Initiated Beginning of Year	Actual Risky Return Over Remaining Horizon	Immunized Return Over Remaining Horizon	Actual Give-up From Insuring With Indicated Initial Percentage in Risky Assets[a]			
			0%[b]	25%	50%	75%
1	16.96%	11.04%	5.92%	1.80%	0.84%	0.25%
2	18.00	10.80	7.20	2.25	1.10	0.35
3	13.68	7.63	6.05	1.54	0.90	0.42
4	12.67	6.71	5.96	0.80	0.18	-0.03
5	15.77	6.59	9.18	2.02	1.00	0.38

[a]Give-ups are over remaining horizon.
[b]Immunized position.

EXHIBIT 9 OPPORTUNITY RISK LEVELS

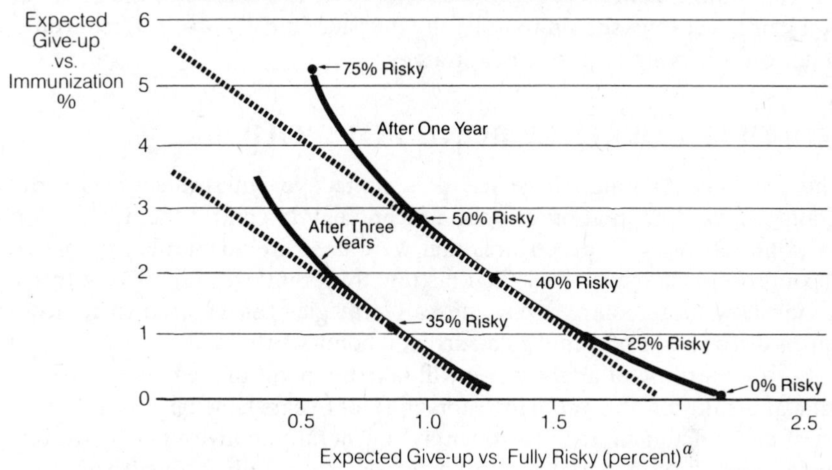

[a]Based on expectation of fully risky return being 20% greater than immunized return.

being incorrect. The farther to the left the dashed line is, the lower the expected give-up along the line.

The curves represent the combinations of expected give-ups possible from initiating different levels of insurance. The slope of each curve at any point determines the trade-off the manager is able to make in terms of additional downside insurance provided the interest rate bet is incorrect, and the expected return give-up if the interest rate bet is correct. The opportunity curve facing the manager after 3 years is lower than that facing the manager after 1 year because of changes in the interest rate environment over the 2 years.

The minimum possible expected give-up is obtained when the curve is tangent to the dashed line. At any point on the curve below this, the manager is giving up more and more of the expected return from being right in order to purchase each increment of insurance against being wrong. At points on the curve above this, the manager is giving up more and more insurance in exchange for each increment of return from being right. All points not at the tangent thus involve a higher expected give-up than the tangent.

The slope of the dashed line, which is based on the ratio of probabilities, determines the desired amount of insurance. A change in the manager's estimate of the probability of being correct will thus alter the amount of insurance he or she should obtain. If the manager becomes convinced that the risky decision is correct, the slope will become steeper, and he or she will place a greater amount in the risky asset to begin the insurance. A manager absolutely certain of being correct will be fully invested in the risky position. On the other hand, a manager who believes the risky decision is completely incorrect will fully immunize.

Most managers are not likely to be at either of these extremes. A manager who attaches any probability to being correct in the active decision should not fully immunize. A manager who feels that there is a chance of the active decision being incorrect should not be fully invested in risky assets. Each would be better off following an insurance strategy.

MULTIPLE CURRENCY BOND PORTFOLIOS

The previous example of the use of a protective put strategy was a rather straightforward adaptation of option technology to control the distribution of portfolio returns. The procedures that were used are adaptable to more complex portfolio choices as well. To illustrate this point, we will show in this subsection how more complex put and call strategies can be used to control the return distribution of a multiple currency bond portfolio.

For the purpose of analysis, we will take the point of view of a Japanese financial institution. Japanese investors in recent years have been large purchasers of **dollar denominated investments.** In general, the investments tyically are made either fully exposed to currency risk or are fully hedged back to yen. Once again, these alternatives represent the extreme polar cases of the risk spectrum. As an alternative to these extreme positions, the investor could employ option strategies which permit some systematic tradoff between different degrees of downside protection and upside potential.

Consider, for example, the investment environment of the years 1979–1983. In general, this was a period in which the dollar was rising relative to the yen (the annual rate of rise on average was 3.48%). This was also a period during which the nominal yield on dollar denominated securities greatly exceeded that on yen denominated securities. The 1-year Eurodeposit rate, for example, averaged 13.44% a year on dollar denominated assets, whereas the equivalent 1-year yen return averaged 6.88%. Clearly, the best investment strategy for a yen-based investor investing in dollar denominated assets over this time period was to invest without any currency hedge at all. Over the 5-year period this strategy would have yielded an average annual return of 17.39%, converted back to yen.

Looking over the shoulder this is easy to say. Before the fact, however, the investor could not have been certain that the currency moves would be beneficial. Moreover, the average result conceals the fact that in two of the 5 years the dollar declined relative to the yen (1980 and 1983). Also, in 1980, the decline in the dollar was 14.35%, which in that year would have resulted in a negative return to the investor in yen terms (Exhibit 10).

PROTECTIVE PUT STRATEGY. An alternative strategy would have been for the Japanese investor to have purchased a **protective put** which would have permitted him to achieve some minimal return each year in yen terms. If, for example, the yen investor selected a level of insurance equal in any year to 60% of the 1-year yen return, the annual pattern of returns illustrated in Exhibit 10 would have been achieved.

In this case, during the year 1980, the put would have paid off. Instead of achieving the negative 2.74% return of the unhedged position, the investor

EXHIBIT 10 RETURN ON ONE YEAR DOLLAR INVESTMENT (ACTUAL INVESTMENT SEQUENCE)

Year	One Year Investment Return		Currency Return Dollar/Yen	Return on Option Strategy, Converted to Yen[a]	Unhedged Dollar Return, Converted to Yen
	Dollar	Yen			
1979	12.55%	2.48%	21.24%	26.26%	36.45%
1980	13.56	8.03	−14.35	4.82	−2.74
1981	15.68	10.18	8.57	22.04	25.59
1982	15.45	6.86	6.21	17.56	22.62
1983	10.09	6.98	−0.91	5.17	9.08
5-Year Average	13.44	6.88	3.48	14.84	17.39

[a]Minimum return = 60% of one year investment return on ten denominated security.

would have achieved a positive yen return of 4.82%. This return is equal to the insured level of 60% of the return on 1-year yen-denominated Eurodeposits in that year. For the full 5 years, of course, the put strategy would have been a detriment to returns, because on average the dollar was rising. However, the average yen return on the option protected position would have been 14.84%, which is still attractive relative to the fully hedged return of 6.88%. The difference between the unhedged dollar return converted to yen (17.39%) and the option protected return (14.84%) represents the cost of the option position.

Clearly, if the dollar had declined relative to the yen over this 5-year period, the **option strategy** would have provided a more favorable return pattern relative to the unhedged position. To illustrate this, we reversed the time sequence, starting in 1983 and working backward to 1979. This provides an hypothetical investment environment in which the events of the 5 years ending in 1983 are reversed (Exhibit 11). In this simulation, the dollar declined relative to the yen by 3.36% a year, on average. The yen return on an unhedged dollar investment averaged 9.29% over the 5 years, whereas the put protected return achieved an annual yen return of 11.07%.

COMPLEX CALL STRATEGY. More exotic option strategies could have been devised for this investor as well. Suppose, for example, this same investor in 1979 was uncertain whether to invest in either a dollar denominated or a sterling denominated investment. Both provided attractive annual returns relative

EXHIBIT 11 RETURN ON ONE YEAR DOLLAR INVESTMENT (REVERSE INVESTMENT SEQUENCE)

Year	One Year Investment Return		Currency Return Dollar/Yen	Return on Option Strategy, Converted to Yen[a]	Unhedged Dollar Return, Converted to Yen
	Dollar	Yen			
1983	10.83%	6.57%	0.92%	8.46%	11.85%
1982	10.09	6.98	−5.85	5.88	3.65
1981	15.45	6.86	−7.89	4.45	6.33
1980	15.68	10.18	16.76	34.53	35.06
1979	13.56	8.03	−17.52	4.78	−6.34
5-Year Average	13.09	7.72	−3.36	11.07	9.29

[a]Minimum return = 60% of one year investment return on ten denominated security.

EXHIBIT 12 RETURN ON ONE YEAR MULTI-CURRENCY INVESTMENT PORTFOLIO (ACTUAL INVESTMENT SEQUENCE)

	One Year Investment Return			Currency Return		Return on Option Strategy, Converted to Yen [a]	Unhedged Investment Return, Converted to Yen	
Year	Dollar	Pound	Yen	Dollar/Yen	Pound/Yen		Dollar	Pound
1979	12.55%	13.78%	2.48%	21.24%	33.99%	36.07%	36.45%	52.45%
1980	13.56	16.20	8.03	−14.35	−8.85	4.77	−2.74	5.92
1981	15.68	14.79	10.18	8.57	−13.31	17.29	25.59	−0.49
1982	15.45	16.37	6.86	6.21	−9.60	13.85	22.62	5.20
1983	10.09	11.03	6.98	−0.91	−11.64	3.89	9.08	−1.89
5-Year Average	13.44	14.42	6.88	3.48	−3.30	14.61	17.39	10.69

[a]Minimum return = 60% of one year investment return on ten denominated security.

to a yen based investment, but both had currency risk exposure. If the investor was uncertain as to which would perform best, but felt that the pound and the dollar would likely move in opposite directions relative to the yen, a **complex call option** strategy might fit the need.

Exhibit 12 shows the result that would have been obtained over the 5-year period 1979–1983 from a strategy which provided a minimal floor protection each year equal to 60% of the 1-year yen return. This return is combined with a complex call option which enabled the investor each year to purchase a participation in the highest performing (in yen terms) of the dollar or sterling investment.

This would have been a particularly interesting strategy over this time period, because while the dollar was rising by 3.48% relative to the yen, the pound was falling by 3.30% per year, on average. Moreover, the nominal returns on dollar and sterling denominated investments were reasonably the same (13.44% and 14.42%, respectively). The result of this **complex option strategy** would have yielded a return of 14.61% over the 5-year period. This compares with the return of 17.39% on the unhedged dollar investment and an average return of 10.69% on the unhedged sterling investment.

Once again, the investor would have done better to invest unhedged in the dollar denominated investment. If the investor guessed wrong and chose the sterling investment, however, he or she would have done better to have employed the option strategy. The option strategy, as would be expected, achieved a return somewhere between the unhedged dollar and the unhedged sterling investment return, in terms of its yen equivalent. This complex option strategy, therefore, provided a favorable return distribution without necessitating an all-out bet on either the dollar or the pound.

CONCLUSION

The volatile markets and disappointing returns that have characterized the fixed-income markets in recent years have given risk taking a bad name. The movement toward passive or quasi-passive fixed-income strategies, including bond dedication, immunization, and variations on these themes that combine these strategies with limited elements of active decisions, have become one of the most powerful forces in bond management today.

We have tried to show in this section that not all risk is bad, because only with some element of risk can you enhance return. Once the dust finally settles on the reaction to the financial events of recent years, the inherent costs of fully hedged strategies will likely take on increased significance and more attention will be focused on strategies that allow some elements of disciplined or structured risk taking. The tool to accomplish this is the application of option technology as an integral part of the portfolio management decision process.

We have shown in a few example illustrations the tremendous flexibility with which option strategies can be used within a portfolio context to shape the distribution of returns. The successful application of these techniques requires a more disciplined analysis of overall portfolio objectives as well as some change in mental attitudes, which allows market participants to recognize that they should be managing toward achieving definable investment objectives rather than for decile performance rankings.

BIBLIOGRAPHY

Bierwag, G.O., Kaufman, G.G., and Toevs, A.L., "Duration: Its Development and Use in Bond Portfolio Management," *Financial Analyst Journal* (July 1983).

———, "Bond Portfolio Immunization and Stochastic Process Risk," *Journal of Bank Research* (Winter 1983).

Black, F., and Scholes, M. "The Pricing of Options and Corporate Liabilities," *Journal of Political Economy,* 81 (May 1973): 637–654.

Bookstaber, R., *Option Pricing and Strategies in Investing,* Reading, MA: Addison-Wesley, 1981.

Bookstaber, R., and Clarke, R. "Options Can Alter Portfolio Return Distributions," *Journal of Portfolio Management,* 7 (Spring 1981): 63–70.

Bookstaber, R., "The Use of Options in Performance Structuring: Molding Returns to Meet Investment Objectives," New York: Morgan Stanley Fixed Income Research, 1984.

Bookstaber, R., and Clark, R., *"Option Portfolio Strategies for Institutional Investment Management.* Reading, MA: Addison-Wesley, 1983b.

Bookstaber, R., and Clarke, R., "Option Portfolio Strategies: Measurement and Evaluation," *Journal of Business,* 57 (October 1984).

———, "Problems in Evaluating the Performance of Portfolios with Options," *Financial Analysts Journal* (January–February 1985): 48–62.

Brennan, M., and Solanki, R., "Optimal Portfolio Insurance," *Journal of Financial and Quantitative Analysis,* 16 (September 1981): 279–300.

Cox, J., Ross, S., and Rubinstein, M., "Option Pricing: A Simplified Approach," *Journal of Financial Economics,* 7 (1979): 229, 263.

Fong, H.G., and Vasicek, O.A., "A Risk Minimizing Strategy for Multiple Liabilities Immunization," *Financial Analysts Journal* (September–October 1983).

Kraus, A., and Litzenberger, R., "Skewness Preference and the Valuation of Risky Assets," *Journal of Finance,* 31 (September 1976): 1085–1100.

Latainer, G., "A Flexible Alternative to Bond Dedication," New York: Morgan Stanley Fixed Income Research, 1983.

Leland, H., "Who Should Buy Portfolio Insurance?" *Journal of Finance,* 35 (May 1980): 581–594.

Liebowitz, M., and Weinberger, A. "Contingent Immunization, Part I: Risk Control Procedures," *Financial Analysts Journal,* 38 (November–December 1982): 17–31.

———, "Contingent Immunization—Part II: Problem Areas," *Financial Analysts Journal,* 38 (January–February 1983).

Macauley, F.R., "Some Theoretical Problems Suggested by the Movements of Interest Rates, Bond Yields, and Stock Prices in the United States Since 1865," New York: National Bureau of Economic Research, 1938.

Merton, R., "Theory of Rational Option Pricing," *Bell Journal of Economics and Management Science,* 4 (Spring 1973): 141–183.

Merton, R., Scholes, M., and Gladstein, M., "The Returns and Risk of Alternative Call Option Portfolio Investment Strategies," *Journal of Business,* 51 (April 1978): 183–242.

———, "The Returns and Risks of Put-Option Portfolio Investment Strategies," *Journal of Business,* 55 (January 1982): 61–67.

Platt, R., and Latainer, G., "Replicating Option Strategies for Portfolio Risk Control," New York: Morgan Stanley Fixed Income Research, 1983a.

———, "Replicating Option Strategies—Part II: Applications of Portfolio Insurance," New York: Morgan Stanley Fixed Income Research, 1983b.

———, "Risk-Return Tradeoffs of Contingent Insurance Strategies for Active Bond Portfolios," *Financial Analysts Journal,* 40 (May–June 1984): 34–39.

Redington, F.M., "Review of the Principles of Life-Office Valuations," *Journal of Institute of Actuaries,* 78 (1952).

Rubinstein, M., and Cox, J. *Option Markets.* Englewood Cliffs, NJ: Prentice-Hall, 1985.

Rubinstein, M., and Leland, H., "Replicating Options with Positions in Stock and Cash," *Financial Analysts Journal,* 37 (July 1981): 63–72.

Stapleton, R.C., and Subrahmanyam, M.G., "The Valuation of Multivariate Contingent Claims in Discrete Time Models," *Journal of Finance,* 39 (March 1984): 207–228.

Stulz, R.M., "Options on the Minimum or the Maximum of Two Risky Assets," *Journal of Financial Economics,* 10 (July 1982): 161–185.

Tilley, J., and Latainer, G., "A Synthetic Option Framework for Asset Allocation," *Financial Analysts Journal,* 41 (May–June 1985): 32–43.

Toevs, A., "Uses of Duration Analysis for the Control of Interest Rate Risk," New York: Morgan Stanley Fixed Income Research, 1984.

27

PERFORMANCE MEASUREMENT

CONTENTS

27

PERFORMANCE MEASUREMENT

J. Peter Williamson

EVOLUTION OF PERFORMANCE MEASUREMENT

DEMAND FOR MEASUREMENT. **Performance measurement** has become a significant part of the investment process in the past 25 years. The 1960s saw the beginning of careful and systematic **investment performance** evaluation. Prior to that time investors, including most institutional investors, were generally content to monitor their portfolios without numerical measures. The change was brought about by a number of forces, including competition among money managers in a rapidly rising market and the preoccupation of pension fund managers with pension cost reduction. With the basic methodology fairly well worked out, although there will probably always be disagreement about the best way to measure risk, attention has turned in the 1980s to breaking performance down into components that give insights into particular strengths and weaknesses of a manager. The development of benchmarks by which to compare these components of performance is currently a topic of considerable interest.

COMPETITION IN THE 1960s AND 1970s. Competition among money managers was the principal force in bringing about systematic and frequent investment performance measurement. This was particularly evident in the mutual fund industry. Investors in mutual funds, who had never before paid close attention to the performances of these funds, were confronted in the 1960s with evidence of some spectacular rates of return. Magazines and newspapers began to feature the most successful fund managers, and the funds themselves began to sell numerical performance results rather than relying on the traditional description of investment philosophy.

It was during the 1960s that publication of **comparative performance statistics** began. For a few years the Lipper Reports gave managers and institutional investors weekly rates of return for several hundred mutual funds. A. G. Becker began to publish comparative rates of return on a quarterly basis for pension funds. The investment committee of the National Association of College and University Business Officers began to circulate annual comparative performance statistics for college and university endowment funds.

Throughout the investment world, money managers were discovering that performance evaluations had become an important element in competition. And those responsible for selecting managers discovered a new, if sometimes treacherous, device for making their selections.

PENSION FUND EMPHASIS ON PERFORMANCE. A second factor at work during the 1960s was the increasing emphasis among **pension plan sponsors** on investment performance. For the first time, many corporations with large **trusteed pension plans** began to relate investment performance to the level of contributions and even to the level of benefits payable. The performance of the stock market during the 1960s suggested that substantial reductions in pension fund contributions might be achieved through superior investment management. Pension plan sponsors began to call for more frequent and more accurate measures of fund performance, and indeed much of the development of measurement techniques was brought about to satisfy these demands.

Investment manager selection for trusteed pension plans became a much more important activity in the 1960s than it ever had been. The realization that investment performances of individual managers could show spectacular differences and that these differences could have a major impact on pension fund contributions led to an almost frenzied search for the high performing managers.

STATE OF THE ART. It appeared for a while during the 1960s that a single reliable performance statistic might be agreed on, one that would provide a complete measure of the investment ability of a manager and could therefore be used for purposes of hiring, firing, and monitoring performance. It is generally accepted now that no such single statistic exists. Evaluation of an investment manager's performance requires a variety of statistics. There are still differences of opinion as to the accuracy of valuation data and the best way to obtain accurate data. And there are differences of opinion as to the use of approximations when numerical data are inaccurate or missing. But these disagreements are minor and should become less significant in the future as data processing and record keeping improve.

Probably the most discouraging discovery in the evolution of performance measurement, and the discovery that led to the realization that no single performance statistic will ever tell the whole story, was that most historic performance records simply did not furnish a reliable basis for predicting future performance. Comparing an equity manager's performance with the performance of the **Standard & Poor's 500 Index**, or comparing a bond manager's performance with that of the **Salomon Brothers Long Term High Grade**

Corporate Bond Index will certainly reveal whether the manager has beaten a widely known index over some period in the past, but it probably is not useful for choosing managers who will do well in the future. Nor will it identify what part of the investment process the manager does well, and what part the manager does poorly. Performance measurement in the 1980s is aimed at this sort of identification, and a number of consultants can offer sophisticated methods for decomposing performance and evaluating the parts, in an effort to separate the results of skill from the workings of chance.

RATE OF RETURN FOR A SINGLE PERIOD

SIMPLEST PERFORMANCE MEASUREMENT. The simplest performance measurement for an investment, or for a portfolio, is the **total return rate** and its two components: income yield and growth rate. Income yield is income (interest and dividends for a securities portfolio) expressed as a percentage of the portfolio value. If a $1 million portfolio produces $50,000 in interest and dividends, the yield is $50,000/$1 million or 5%. The growth rate measures appreciation as a percentage of value. If the $1 million portfolio appreciates to a value of $1,060,000, the growth rate is $60,000/$1 million or 6%. The total return, measuring the total investment performance of the portfolio, is 11% (5% + 6%).

Total return is the measure most useful in evaluating the quality of investment management, but yield and growth have their own uses. The determination of the rate of return requires first a set of valuations—for income and principal—and second a method of calculation.

VALUATION. Valuation requires a clear understanding of the difference between market value and book value or cost. Market value is the appropriate choice for performance evaluation and raises some practical problems.

Market Value Versus Cost or Book Value. A number of financial institutions normally report their investment portfolios at **market value,** while others report at cost, or **book value.** Mutual funds always use market value. Life insurance companies, banks, and savings institutions generally use cost. Pension funds traditionally report investments at cost, but are increasingly reporting market values as well. Charities and college and university endowment funds once reported only cost figures and many continue this practice. Others report individual portfolio holdings at cost but disclose the market value of their total portfolios. Still others report all holdings at market.

Book value is quite useless for the usual purposes of performance measurement. It records the original cost of a portfolio (e.g., the original amount of gifts to an endowment) plus realized gains, less realized losses. It does not reflect **unrealized gain or loss.** A portfolio with a high turnover is likely to have a book value close to maket value, because gains and losses are constantly being realized. But if the turnover is low, the book value may be far from market value. Some institutions, particularly colleges and universities, calculate performance figures based on book value and use these figures for comparison. Sometimes the error is easy to spot. When an institution boasts of an income yield of 10% on a growth stock portfolio, there is obviously something wrong. The explanation is likely to be that an income of $1,000 is being expressed as a percentage of a $10,000 original cost instead of a $25,000 market value. The point is that when growth stocks can be purchased to produce a yield of about 4% (dividends of $4 for every $100 invested in the stock), a portfolio of such stocks yielding 10% would indeed be remarkable. But when it turns out that the portfolio is a very ordinary one, producing 4% on its market value, the 10% figure can be seen to derive from the original cost, something that has nothing to do with how well the portfolio is currently invested.

Correct performance measurements demand market values for a portfolio. Precise performance measurements may require market valuations at frequent intervals. Mutual funds, for example, value their portfolios at least daily. Other institutions generally make less frequent valuations and are satisfied with less precise measurements. The subject of frequency of valuation is discussed later.

Obtaining Market Values. It is not difficult to obtain useful valuations for common stocks traded daily on a stock exchange, but even for these investments the valuation process is not absolutely certain. For example, if a portfolio is being valued as of December 31 and one security held is common stock of a company listed on the New York Stock Exchange, there are at least three numbers that might go into the value used for the stock; the "close" (the price at which the last trade took place on December 31), the "bid," or the "ask" at the close of trading. Generally the "close" is the number used. If there was no trading in the stock on December 31, the average of the **bid and ask quotes** is usually used. For **over-the-counter stocks** only the bid and ask quotes are generally available: sometimes the average of the two is used and sometimes the bid is used alone.

The procedure just described is satisfactory for most valuation purposes, but it can be questioned on a number of grounds. First, the closing price for a particular stock on a particular day may well reflect an aberration in the price performance of the stock. The price may have bounced up briefly as the result of a large purchase order placed late in the day. Or it may have dropped briefly as the result of a large sell order. One generally expects that aberrations of this sort will cancel out over all the portfolio holdings. A more serious question is raised if the portfolio includes a large holding of a single stock, and it is quite clear that the entire holding could not have been disposed of on the valuation day at the closing price for that day. Selling a large block would have required a price concession. So the procedure described above will overstate what could have been realized in cash if the entire portfolio of securities had been liquidated on the valuation date. The second objection is generally answered by pointing out that at least for purposes of evaluating investment performance, the **liquidation value of the portfolio,** under conditions of almost instant liquidation, is not relevant.

Bond Valuation. For bonds, the valuation process is not as simple. It is quite likely that on the valuation date there were no trades in many of the bond issues held in a portfolio. **Bid and ask quotes** may have been available from bond dealers on that day, but these are not systematically collected and tabulated as they are for listed or even unlisted common stocks. Generally, one must rely on a bond firm to use its trading expertise to place values on bond issues in the portfolio. Some firms have developed matrices for pricing thousands of issues of untraded bonds, using as guidelines the prices at which the traded issues changed hands. But there is no generally accepted matrix calculation, so in using the valuations one is essentially relying on the judgment of the firm. There are bound to be some errors in the valuations of individual issues; but just as in the case of common stocks, one hopes that the errors will cancel out across the entire portfolio.

Nonmarketable Assets. Some investments must be classified as essentially nonmarketable, and for these there is no market value. Examples are real estate and mortgages. The best way to treat these investments is to separate them for reporting purposes from marketable investments. The investment performance of the latter can then be calculated, and indeed it is useful to examine the marketable bond portfolio and the marketable stock portfolio separately. If nonmarketable investments make up a small proportion of the total portfolio, it may not be necessary to calculate an investment performance for them. To find out how well the nonmarketable investments are doing, it is possible to arrive at an approximate market value. Real estate holdings, for example, can be appraised. But it is important to bear in mind when reviewing such performance measurements that appraisals are only an approximation of market value, and the investment performance figures cannot be compared to figures based on true market values. This is particularly true when the performance of a real estate portfolio is being reviewed. Whether or not the real estate portfolio appears to have been more profitably invested, almost always the investment performance will appear to have been much smoother than the performance of a stock or bond portfolio. That is, the values will seem to have risen steadily over time without the wide fluctuations that can be found in the value of a stock or bond portfolio. This smoothness is essentially the result of using appraisals rather than true market values; it does not reflect any inherent superiority of real estate as an investment. This is especially important to understand because the **variation of returns** is a standard measure of portfolio riskiness.

INCOME MEASUREMENT. For many portfolios the measurement of income suffers from inadequate record keeping. For bond portfolios it is important to calculate accrued income at the beginning and end of a measurement period and to include an increase in accruals as income for the period, and vice versa for a decrease in accruals.

For stocks, the dividend should be attributed to the period in which the stock goes **"ex-dividend."** (The New York Stock Exchange advances the date when stocks shall be quoted and sold on an ex-dividend basis to the third full business day before date of record.) So if the measurement period ends on December 31 and a dividend is payable in January but the stock goes ex-dividend in December, the dividend should be included in income for the measurement period. This is because the stock price at the end of December will have declined to correspond to a buyer's ineligibility to receive the dividend. This procedure will lead to a small upward bias in the performance measure, since the investor does not actually have the use of the dividend at the end of the measurement period. The amount of the bias, probably a few one-hundredths of a percent a year, could be estimated and an adjustment made.

TOTAL RETURN. Total return is the best single measurement of investment performance. Any single measurement must fall short of a complete description of performance, as will be seen, but total return is a widely used and generally accepted indicator that comes closest to the ideal statistic for comparison purposes.

Anyone responsible for the supervision or safeguarding of investment assets—a pension fund trustee, a foundation or college or university trustee, a mutual fund director, or a member of an investment committee—must know the rate of total return for the portfolio of assets. This is the starting point for evaluating management of the assets.

INCOME YIELD. For many portfolios there is no particular advantage to breaking down the rate of total return into income yield and appreciation. For a pension fund, income is added to the principal of the fund, both income and appreciation are free of tax, and all that matters is the total performance of the fund. For a **taxable entity,** however, if the tax rate on realized appreciation differs from the rate on income, income and appreciation are not equivalent and there is good reason to examine each.

Consider a bank-administered **trust fund,** with the beneficiary taxed at 50% on dividend and interest income and at 20% on long-term capital gains (the maximum personal rates in 1985). A total return of 13%, consisting of 4% income and 9% growth, may be more attractive than a total return of 14%, consisting of 9% income and 5% growth. If the growth were all in the form of realized long-term capital gain, the aftertax total returns would be, respectively, [(4% × 50%) + (9% × 80%)] and [(9% × 50%) + (5% × 80%)] or 9.20% and 8.50%. If the growth is all or even partly in the form of unrealized appreciation, a comparison becomes more difficult because appreciation is not taxed at all until it is realized. There is no standard accepted method of calculating comparable rates of total return in this case, but probably the most used comparison would treat the appreciation as if it were all realized and would show pretax total return rates of 13 and 14% and aftertax rates of 9.20% and 8.50%.

Regardless of whether an aftertax rate of total return is actually calculated, the importance of the income and growth components is obvious. In other cases taxes may not be an important factor, but legal distinctions between income and appreciation may be.

A trust with one **income beneficiary** and another **remainderman,** or principal beneficiary, is an example. To the income beneficiary the income yield is what matters; to the remainderman growth is what counts. Endowment funds are generally subject to a rule that income may be spent but appreciation may not be (although in the 20 or more states that have adopted the **Uniform Management of Institutional Funds Act** a portion of appreciation is expendable). So income yields has an importance of its own.

APPRECIATION. While there are cases in which income yield, as opposed to or in addition to total return, may be of considerable interest, it is only rarely that appreciation alone is a matter of concern. This is why reports often show total return and income yield separately, but without any figure for growth.

CALCULATION. The calculation of total return or income yield is fairly simple in principle, but it can become complicated in practice. Consider a straightforward example: the market value (or net asset value, at market) of a unit in a fund rises from $10 to $10.7368 in the course of a year, and the fund produces income of $0.4211 per unit. On the assumption that all the income was received at year-end, the yield can be calculated as 0.4211/10 or 4.21%, and the appreciation as 0.7368/10 or 7.37%, for a total return of 11.58%.

But the income was almost certainly not all received at year-end. A better assumption may be that on average it was received at midyear. Since income received early (midyear) is generally more valuable than income received late (year-end), the performance of the fund has probably been a little better than 11.58%. There is no standard "correct" way to make the adjustment. For college and university endowment funds the usual convention is to assume that income is received at midyear and could have been invested in the fund at that time, and that the value of the unit at midyear was the average of the beginning and end of year unit values.

In the example above, the average of the beginning and end of year unit values was $10.3684. The year-end value of $10.7368 represents growth of 0.3684/10.3684 or 3.55% during the second half-year. If the income of $0.4211 per share had grown at this rate over the second half-year, it would have amounted to $0.4361 at year end. The sum of $0.4361 and $0.7368 is $1.1729, or 11.73% total return on a $10 initial value.

The conventional formula is:

$$\text{total return} = \left(\frac{\text{income}}{(\text{beginning} + \text{ending unit values})/2} + 1\right)\frac{\text{ending value}}{\text{beginning value}} - 1$$

Obviously the assumptions used in the formula are not entirely valid. As long as educational endowment funds only are being compared, this should not matter much. If funds using this formula were compared to other funds for which the rate of return is calculated differently, the errors could become serious.

If the time period for the measurements were so short that all the income was actually received at the end of the period, there would be no need for an approximation; an exact total return rate could be calculated. The more frequent the valuation and calculation, the more valid the assumptions and the more reliable the rate of total return.

Exhibit 1 shows, for a large common stock portfolio (in excess of $1 billion), total return rates over 5 years based on monthly, quarterly, and annual valuations, using the formula described above. The figures suggest that monthly valuations do not add much accuracy to quarterly valuations, but that quarterly valuations give much more reliable return figures than do annual valuations.

AVERAGE RATE OF RETURN OVER SEVERAL TIME PERIODS

METHOD OF AVERAGING. Having computed the rate of total return on a portfolio for a series of periods, months or quarters or years, one would like to be able to compute an **average rate of return** over several such periods. During the early 1960s a number of institutions showed a certain amount of confusion in this averaging process. By the 1980s confusion had largely vanished, but it may still be worth pointing out the difference between the **arithmetic average** and the **compound average,** and the reasons for preferring the latter.

Suppose that the total return on a portfolio is measured for four quarters and the results are 10, −2, −9, and 1 for the quarters. The simplest average that can be deduced from these four numbers is the arithmetic average, which is the sum of the numbers divided by 4:

$$\text{arithmetic average} = \frac{10 - 2 - 9 + 1}{4} = \frac{0}{4} = 0\%$$

EXHIBIT 1 COMPARISON OF CALCULATED RATES OF TOTAL RETURN (%) USING MONTHLY, QUARTERLY, AND ANNUAL VALUATIONS

Year	Computed from Monthly Data	Computed from Quarterly Data	Computed from Annual Data
1	11.86	11.70	11.39
2	13.62	13.27	12.65
3	2.51	2.43	1.96
4	−22.97	−22.83	−22.30
5	46.67	46.40	41.46

A second average figure that can be deduced is the compound or geometric average rate of return. The compound average answers the question: What rate of return earned for four quarters in a row is equivalent to earning 10% the first quarter, losing 2% the second quarter, losing 9% the third quarter, and earning 1% the fourth quarter? The following equation shows how the compound average rate R is calculated:

$$\begin{aligned}(1 + R)^4 &= (1 + 0.10)\,(1 - 0.02)\,(1 - 0.09)\,(1 + 0.01)\\ &= 0.9908\\ 1 + R &= 0.9977\\ R &= -0.0023\\ &= -0.23\%\end{aligned}$$

The compound average rate of total return is slightly negative. In general, the compound average will always be smaller than the arithmetic average (unless by some chance the individual period returns are identical, in which case the compound average will be the same as the arithmetic average). This is because the positive rates of return are applied to a smaller base than are the negative rates of return. The greater the fluctuation in rate of return over the periods being averaged, the greater the difference will be between the compound and arithmetic averages. To take an extreme case, consider a rate of return of 50% in one quarter and −50% in the second quarter. The arithmetic average rate of return is 0%. The compound average rate of return is −13.5%. A $100 investment would increase to $150 during the first quarter and then decline to $75 during the second quarter, leaving a net loss of $25.

For purposes of performance evaluation, the compound average is the one to use. In the example above, the compound average rate of −13.5% per quarter faithfully reports the conversion of $100 into $75 in two quarters.

DEALING WITH CASH FLOWS. Another source of considerable confusion in the early 1960s was the flow of money into or out of an investment portfolio. A pension fund receives investment income that is normally added to the capital of the fund. Investment income does not produce any special problems. It constitutes part of the investment return and was dealt with in various examples above. But a pension fund also receives contributions from the plan sponsor, contributions that are not a part of investment performance. And the fund makes benefit payments, that again are not part of investment performance. It is necessary in calculating the rate of return on the fund to allow for the effects of the receipts and disbursements that are not a part of the investment performance.

There are two computational methods for calculating the rate of return in the context of these cash flows. The methods serve different purposes, and only one of them is appropriate for evaluating the quality of investment management. The confusion surrounding the two methods was cleared up in 1968 when the Bank Administration Institute published *Measuring the Investment*

Performance of Pension Funds. The following discussion identifies the two methods, explains the calculations, and describes the purpose each method serves.

Internal or Dollar-Weighted Rate of Return. Exhibit 2 gives the set of cash flows for a pension fund over four calendar quarters. The fund begins with a value of $1 million. At the end of the first quarter the plan sponsor contributes $60,000 to the fund and the fund pays out $12,000 in benefits to participants. At the end of the second quarter there is no contribution, but $12,000 in benefits are paid out. At the end of the third quarter contributions are $80,000 and $12,000 benefits are paid out. And at the end of the fourth quarter benefits of $12,000 are paid out and the resulting value of the fund is $1,240,000. It is assumed that all investment income received by the fund is held in the fund and shows up at the end of the year in the $1,240,000 value.

The net cash flows for the fund are arrived at as follows: at the beginning of the first quarter, the fund sponsor gives the fund $1 million. At the end of the first quarter the fund takes in $60,000 and pays out $12,000, so the net flow is an inflow of $48,000. At the end of the second quarter there is an outflow of $12,000. At the end of the third quarter there is a net inflow of $68,000. At the end of the fourth quarter there is an outflow of $12,000, and the fund value is $1,240,000, for a net of $1,252,000. (A negative cash flow is one from the sponsor to the fund; a positive flow is one from the fund.) To calculate the so-called dollar-weighted or internal rate of return, we form the following equation:

$$1{,}000{,}000 = \frac{-48{,}000}{1+R} + \frac{12{,}000}{(1+R)^2} - \frac{68{,}000}{(1+R)^3} + \frac{1{,}252{,}000}{(1+R)^4}$$

where R is the dollar-weighted or internal rate of return. The expression essentially says that the $1 million initial value is the discounted present value of a $48,000 flow into the fund one period hence, a $12,000 flow out of the fund two periods hence, a $68,000 flow into the fund three periods hence, and a $1,252,-000 flow from the fund four periods hence. Solving for the rate R is a trial-and-error process, and it turns out in this case that R is 3.36% per quarter. This corresponds to an annual rate of 13.4% compounded quarterly.

The correct interpretation of the internal rate of return is that the *combination* of contributions, benefit payments, and investment performance of this fund led to an average rate of return of 3.36% per quarter over the four-quarter period. It is not correct to say that the investment performance alone accounted for a return of 3.36% per quarter. Indeed it is impossible to extract from the internal rate of return the contribution made by investment management. The internal rate of return is, however, useful for describing the total experience of the fund, in light of investment performance and cash flows.

Time-Weighted Rate of Return. Exhibit 3 adds some further numbers to the data of Exhibit 2. Specifically, what is now supplied is the value of the fund

EXHIBIT 2 CASH FLOWS FOR A PENSION FUND

	First Quarter		Second Quarter		Third Quarter		Fourth Quarter	
	Beginning	End	Beginning	End	Beginning	End	Beginning	End
Contributions to fund	—	\$60,000		—		80,000	—	—
Benefits paid out	—	12,000		12,000		12,000		12,000
Value of fund	\$1,000,000							1,240,000
Net cash flows	−1,000,000	−48,000		12,000		−68,000		1,252,000

EXHIBIT 3 EXPANSION OF NET CASH FLOW EXAMPLE

	Value of Fund				
	Before Contributions Received and Benefits Paid: \$1,000,000	End First Quarter: \$1,100,000	End Second Quarter: \$1,040,000	End Third Quarter: \$1,158,000	End Fourth Quarter: \$1,264,000
Net cash flow		−48,000	12,000	−68,000	12,000
Value after net cash flow		1,148,000	1,028,000	1,226,000	1,252,000
Total return		$\frac{1{,}100{,}000}{1{,}000{,}000} - 1$ = 10%	$\frac{1{,}040{,}000}{1{,}148{,}000} - 1$ = −9.4%	$\frac{1{,}158{,}000}{1{,}028{,}000} - 1$ = 12.6%	$\frac{1{,}264{,}000}{1{,}226{,}000} - 1$ = 3.1%
Compound average	$(1 + R)^4 = (1 + 0.10)\,(1 - 0.094)\,(1 + 0.126)\,(1 + 0.031)$ $R = 3.71\%$ per quarter				

at each quarter-end. It can be seen that investment performance carried the $1 million value to $1,100,000. The net cash flow brought the value up to $1,148,000 and investment performance in the second quarter carried this value down to $1,040,000. The $12,000 net cash flow further reduced the fund's value to $1,028,000, but during the third quarter investment performance carried this value up to $1,158,000. The end of the third quarter net cash flow brought the fund value up to $1,226,000, and the investment performance for the fourth quarter carried the value up further to $1,264,000. It is now possible to identify the role of investment performance alone, and to calculate the contribution this performance made in terms of a rate of return. For each quarter the total return, reflecting the investment performance, has been calculated. The compound of geometric average of these four quarterly returns is 3.71% or 14.8% per year compounded quarterly. It is this figure that is the so-called **time-weighted rate of return.**

This time-weighted rate of return, or **compound average total return,** provides a measure of investment performance unaffected by the cash flows. In the particular example, the time-weighted rate of return is a little higher than the **dollar-weighted rate of return,** about 0.35% higher per quarter. The explanation can be seen from the set of figures above. The fund did very well during the first quarter. At the end of this quarter a substantial amount of money was added, and during the second quarter the performance was poor. At the end of the second quarter money was withdrawn, and during the third quarter the performance was very good. At the end of the third quarter another substantial sum was added, and the fourth quarter performance was mediocre. In other words, money was consistently put into the fund just before a bad performance and taken out just before a good performance. The timing of the cash flows tended to offset the quality of investment management, and pulled down the overall performance of the fund. Sometimes the timing of cash flows will worsen the overall performance; sometimes it will improve the overall performance. The time-weighted rate of return is unaffected by the timing of cash flows and therefore gives the truer picture of the quality of investment management.

Use of Unit Values. The calculation of the time-weighted rate of return as described above may seem to be an awkward and cumbersome process. It is made a good deal easier if the record keeping for the fund includes the calculation and tabulation of **unit values.** Then all that is necessary to arrive at the investment performance over any particular period of time is to examine the beginning and end of period unit values, and to take account of income per unit if this is not already incorporated in the unit values. Mutual funds calculate unit values, or per share values, at least once a day. The investor in a mutual fund need not be concerned about the cash flow of the fund as shares are redeemed. The investment performance of the mutual fund is entirely reflected in the per share value and the income distributions per share.

The calculation and use of unit values is described in some detail in a publication of the Ford Foundation included in the References and Bibliography.

Briefly, for the example above, one could arbitrarily establish the number of units in the fund at 100,000 at the beginning of the first quarter. The initial unit value would then be $10. At the end of the first quarter the unit value is the fund value, $1,100,000, divided by the number of units, or $11 per unit. At a value of $11.00 per unit, the net cash flow of $48,000 into the fund represents the addition of 4,364 units (48,000/11). The total number of units then grows to 104,364. At the end of the second quarter, the unit value has declined to $9.965. The net cash flow of $12,000 represents a withdrawal of 1,204 units (12,-000/9.965), leaving 103,160 units. At the end of the third quarter these units are worth $1,158,000, or $11.225 each. The net inflow of $68,000 adds 6,058 units (68,000/11.225) for a total of 109,218 units. These units are worth $1,264,000 at the end of the fourth quarter, or $11.573 each. The unit values at the five points in time are then $10, $11, $9.965, $11.225, and $11.573. From these five numbers it is easy to calculate the quarterly total returns, or to go directly to a calculation of the rate of return over the entire year. For the entire year, the $10 value grew to $11.573, so the rate of return is [(11.573/$10) – 1)] or 15.7%. This is the annually compounded rate; the corresponding rate with quarterly compounding is 14.8%.

Unit values have other uses besides the calculation of investment performance. But for the performance calculations alone they offer great convenience. From a permanent tabulation of the unit values calculated above, one can quickly calculate the investment performance over any particular sequence of time periods.

APPROXIMATIONS. The correct calculation of the time-weighted rate of return, and of the unit values, requires valuation of the total fund on each date on which contributions were made or benefits paid out. For some funds, where cash flows are not frequent, these valuations present no difficulty. But if the cash flows are frequent, corresponding valuations of the entire fund may be difficult and costly. As time goes on the cost and the difficulty should decline. Data processing routines and sources of stock and bond valuations are common enough that most institutional managers of funds and almost all bank custodians should be able to deliver valuations as often as daily without great difficulty. Nevertheless, valuations are not being made available to all pension funds and other institutional investors on a daily basis.

If a portfolio valuation is not available at the time of each cash flow, it is necessary to make some approximations in estimating the time-weighted rate of return. The Bank Administration Institute study referred to above described some method of approximation. A simple and widely used approximation for the total return on pension funds was proposed in 1966 by Peter Dietz. It begins with this expression:

$$M_2 = M_1 + C + \mathrm{R}\left(M_1 + \frac{C}{2}\right)$$

where M_2 is the market value of the pension fund at the end of the period of time, M_1 is the market value at the beginning of the period, C is the net contribution to the fund during the period (the contribution made by the plan sponsor less benefit payments made by the fund), and R is the rate of total return for the period. In essence the equation says the ending market value is made up of the beginning market value, net contributions, and investment performance over the period. Investment performance is represented by the return on the beginning of period assets plus half the contributions, based on the assumption that the net contribution is received at the middle of the period, or half at the beginning and half at the end.

Rearranging the expression gives:

$$R = \frac{M_2 - M_1 - C}{M_1 + C/2}$$

So if $M_1 = \$1{,}000{,}000$, $M_2 = \$1{,}060{,}000$, contributions are \$40,000, and benefits are \$30,000, so that $C = \$10{,}000$, we have

$$R = \frac{1{,}060 - 1{,}000 - 10}{1{,}000 + 0.10/2} = 5.0\%$$

This formula can be used for charitable endowment funds too, but care must be taken in calculating C, which is gifts or other capital additions less all withdrawals (including income spent) for spending. So if \$5,000 is received as a gift addition, \$12,000 is withdrawn from principal to be spent, and \$40,000 of income is all spent as received, $C = \$5{,}000 - \$12{,}000 - \$40{,}000$ or $-$ \$47,000. If $M_1 = \$1{,}000{,}000$ and $M_2 = \$1{,}060{,}000$,

$$R = \frac{1{,}060 - 1{,}000 + 47}{1{,}000 - 0.47/2} = 11.0\%$$

MEASUREMENT OF RISK

QUANTITATIVE MEASURES. Probably the major accomplishment of performance measurement over the past two decades has been the development of quantitative measures of risk. None of these measures is entirely satisfactory, since to some extent risk in the mind of the investor remains subjective and difficult to quantify. It seems clear that any quantitative approach to risk involves limitations that will never be eliminated. But the measures that have been proposed have a high degree of plausibility, and some have won acceptance among many investment practitioners.

Until the 1960s, few efforts were made to quantify risk, but it was generally accepted that rate of return comparisons between two portfolios were legitimate only if the portfolios reflected approximately equal investment risk. This meant that there was simply no way to compare portfolios with extremely different risks. Given quantitative risk measures, however, the rates of return on two portfolios can be adjusted for the different risks of the portfolios and the so-called **risk-adjusted rates of return** can be compared. This offers the possibility of comparing the performance of any portfolio with the performance of any other portfolio or the performance of any index.

Measures of Uncertainty. Risk in an investment portfolio has to do with uncertainty about the future performance of that portfolio. The performance over the next 6 months of a portfolio of 6-month Treasury bills is very certain. The rate of return over the next 6 months on a portfolio of long-term U.S. government bonds is much less certain. While the coupon interest on the portfolio may be easily predictable, the market value of the portfolio at the end of 6 months is uncertain, and so, therefore, is the rate of total return. The investment performance over the next 6 months for a portfolio of common stocks is still more uncertain. And there are some common stocks for which the next 6 months' performance is more uncertain than for others. If one pictures uncertainty about the future performance of a portfolio as a range of possible outcomes, with very high returns and very low returns highly unlikely, with moderately high and moderately low returns more likely, and average returns the most likely, one has some basis for quantifying the uncertainty. If the outcome of an investment is very uncertain, the range of possible outcomes is very broad. If the outcome is fairly certain, the range is quite narrow.

Standard Deviation. A useful statistical measure of the range of outcomes is the so-called standard deviation. It is this measure that has become widely accepted as the most appropriate measure of **total risk in an investment.** In principle, one arrives at the standard deviation for a particular portfolio by establishing the range of possible future investment performances and attaching a probability to each of those performances. In practice, one usually relies heavily on the past performance of a portfolio or of the securities within that portfolio as a guide to the future uncertainty. An investment for which the future is very uncertain is generally an investment for which the past performance has shown wide fluctuations, whereas for an investment having a highly certain future performance, the past performance is likely to have shown very little fluctuation. For this reason, it is customary to calculate the **standard deviation of performance** for a portfolio or a security from a series of past performances, and to use this standard deviation as the measure of future uncertainty.

Exhibit 4 shows 20 quarterly rates of return for the several billion dollars, all common stock portfolio of College Retirement Equities Fund (CREF) and for the Standard & Poor's 500 Index. The standard deviation of the 20 quarterly rates has been calculated and is shown at the bottom of the tabulation for both the CREF unit and the S&P Index. The two values are very close; the risk in

EXHIBIT 4 QUARTERLY TOTAL RETURN RATES

		CREF Unit (%)	S&P 500 Index (%)
1979	Q1	6.89	7.07
	Q2	2.62	2.72
	Q3	7.44	7.53
	Q4	−1.71	0.13
1980	Q1	−5.33	−4.08
	Q2	12.81	13.41
	Q3	10.23	11.20
	Q4	7.53	9.45
1981	Q1	3.39	1.32
	Q2	−0.42	−2.31
	Q3	−10.37	−10.22
	Q4	6.79	7.01
1982	Q1	−6.61	−7.23
	Q2	−1.06	−0.62
	Q3	10.74	11.46
	Q4	19.08	18.14
1983	Q1	10.17	10.05
	Q2	11.66	11.11
	Q3	0.90	−0.14
	Q4	0.77	0.34
Arithmetic average quarterly rate		4.28	4.32
Compound average quarterly rate		4.03	4.06
Compound average annual rate		17.11	17.27
Standard deviation of quarterly rates		7.37	7.44

the CREF portfolio is just a little below the risk in the S&P 500 Index, which is probably about the same as the risk in the stock market as a whole.

Measures of Market Risk. **Standard deviation** is the commonly accepted statistic for representing the total uncertainty or risk in a portfolio or a security. For some evaluation purposes, however, it may be appropriate to break down total risk into two or more components. Since all securities tend to move somewhat with the market as a whole, some of the uncertainty over the future performance of a portfolio or a security reflects uncertainty about the future of the market. To put the matter another way, if one could predict the stock market with perfect accuracy, one could substantially reduce the uncertainty about the future performance of any common stock portfolio. One component of total risk then is the sensitivity of the performance of a portfolio to the performance of the market. This is the so-called **beta coefficient** of the portfolio. A portfolio with a beta coefficient of 1 moves with the market. When the market is up 10%, the portfolio is up approximately 10%. And when the market drops 10%, the portfolio value drops about 10%. A portfolio with a beta greater than 1 moves more than the market, and one with a beta less than 1 moves less than the market. Most reasonably diversified portfolios of common stocks have beta coefficients between 0.5 and 1.5.

Almost no investment portfolio tracks the market perfectly. Thus even a perfect forecast of the market's performance will not enable an investor to make a perfect forecast of the performance of a portfolio. There is therefore a second component of total risk in the portfolio, the **residual** or **nonmarket-related risk.** An investor can reduce this residual risk to just about any desired level, simply by increasing the **diversification** of the portfolio. It is **not** possible to reduce market-related risk through diversification.

In a world of reasonable investors one would expect the taking of risk to be accompanied by the expectation of returns commensurate with that risk. That is, one would expect investors to take large risks only in the expectation of large returns. Modern portfolio theory goes one step beyond this and proposes that in this tradeoff of risk and expected return, only **market-related risk** is to be taken into account. This is because investors can reduce nonmarket-related risk by way of diversification. They can justify taking market-related risk only by the expectation of an appropriately higher rate of return.

Calculation of Beta Coefficients. The beta coefficient is usually calculated from a series of historic rates of return. Exhibit 5 plots the 20 quarterly rates of return on the CREF unit and the S&P 500 Index. As can be seen, the performance of CREF tracked the Index very closely. A straight line has been fitted to the points representing the quarterly rates of return, and the slope of this line, 0.98 is the beta coefficient for CREF over the 20 quarters. In this particular case, the straight line can be adequately fitted by eye, but there is a mathematical procedure—least squares regression—that does a more precise job. It is from a regression that the 0.98 slope coefficient was calculated.

While the method shown in Exhibit 5 for estimating a beta coefficient is simple to apply, it does have some weaknesses. Over time, there may be changes in the beta coefficient for a portfolio. The changes may be the result of conscious decisions by the portfolio managers or the result of chance, but in either case the historic beta coefficient may not be a satisfactory measure of the risk in the portfolio at a particular time. In the case of CREF there have been deliberate shifts in the volatility of the fund, although these have taken place within a narrow range. It might be noted at this point that if the manager of a portfolio is free to change the beta coefficient over time and indeed can be expected to do so, a further element of uncertainty with respect to future performance is introduced. There seems to be as yet no clear methodology for measuring this risk.

A second way to calculate the beta coefficient for a portfolio is to calculate the coefficient for each security in the portfolio, as described above using a re-

EXHIBIT 5 RELATIONSHIP BETWEEN QUARTERLY PERFORMANCE OF CREF UNIT VALUE AND S&P 500 INDEX, 1979–1983

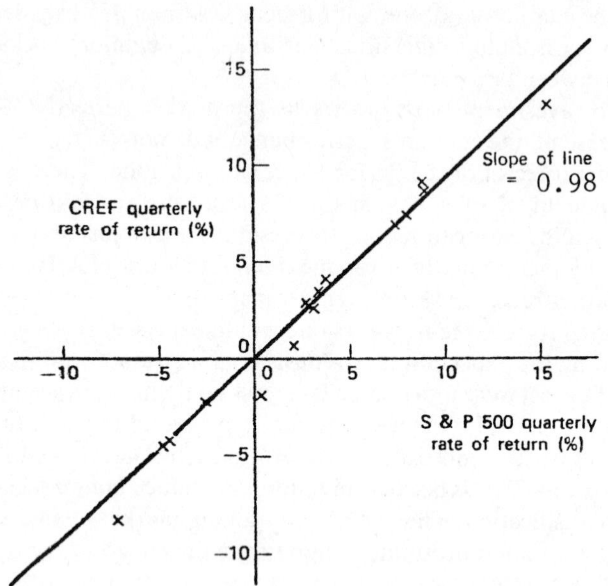

gression, and then compute a weighted average of the betas for the securities. The average is the **beta for the portfolio.** This procedure corrects for the fact that the portfolio was not the same in all 20 quarters because over 5 years some securities were added and others dropped. For planning purposes, predicting the future reaction of a portfolio to a market movement, this method of calculating a beta coefficient is preferable. For purposes of estimating the risk in the portfolio over a historic period however, in evaluating past performance, the first method is preferable because it records what actually happened.

A third method of estimating portfolio beta coefficients goes somewhat further than the second, and makes use of **"fundamental" beta coefficients** for the securities making up the portfolio. The historic coefficient for a particular stock suffers from a weakness similar to that noted above for the historic coefficient for a portfolio. The company may have changed its business or financial structure over the years, and its risk may have changed. The calculation of fundamental betas attempts to incorporate both historic response to the market and current characteristics of the company. Once again, this method of estimating beta coefficients is appropriate for prediction purposes, rather than for historic performance evaluation.

Published Sources of Betas. Beta coefficients for individual common stocks are available from a number of sources. Merrill Lynch publishes monthly tables. Value Line Investment Survey provides beta coefficient estimates for the stocks it reviews. Fundamental betas are not generally available in published form but must be obtained from consulting firms.

IMPORTANCE OF INVESTOR TIME HORIZON. Investment risk has been presented as uncertainty with respect to the future performance of an investment. For some investments, however, this uncertainty is very much a function of the investor's time horizon. Six-month Treasury bills offer absolute certainty of return over the next 6 months. But there is considerable uncertainty about the rate of return that might be achieved by investing in 20 successive 6-month Treasury bills over the next 10 years, probably a good deal more uncertainty than accompanies the purchase of a 10-year government bond. Yet for a 6-month time horizon, the 10-year bond is riskier than the 6-month Treasury bill.

Among investments with fixed maturities, then, measurement of risk requires some attention to the time horizon of the investor. But the standard deviation that is most commonly used as a measure of total risk is one based on annual performance data. For an investor in fixed maturity instruments who has a time horizon of about 1 year, the usual method of calculation will be satisfactory. And if the time horizon is long, as it probably will be for most pension funds, the usual method of calculation may work well enough because the horizon is well beyond the maturity of fixed maturity investments, and the latter will have to be rolled over in any case. For investors with a time horizon in the range of one to 10 or 15 years, the use of standard deviation as a risk measure for fixed maturity investments may be misleading. However, if a bond portfolio is actively managed, and bonds are rarely held to maturity, standard deviation is probably a satisfactory measure.

Beta coefficients are likely to be unsatisfactory as risk measures for fixed maturity securities regardless of investor time horizons. The point is discussed toward the end of the section.

COMBINING RISK AND RETURN MEASURES

PURPOSES. The measurement of investment risk in a portfolio has some value for its own sake. Communication between the owner of a portfolio and the portfolio manager on the subject of risk objectives is made more effective if there is an acceptable way of quantifying and measuring risk. But for purposes of performance evaluation, the real benefit in risk measurement lies in ability to combine risk and return measures to produce risk-adjusted rates of return and so make possible performance comparisons among investments of different risks.

As noted above, the hope that performance measurement might lead to agreement on a single performance statistic by which all managers and portfolios might be evaluated has largely disappeared. Nevertheless, risk-adjusted rates of return do have a use in the evaluation process.

RISK-ADJUSTED RATE OF RETURN. Risk adjustment of rates of return rests on some propositions of portfolio theory. The first of these is that the rate of total return one can anticipate on an investment, above the return available on a risk-free investment, is proportional to the risk in the investment. So if the chosen measure of risk is the standard deviation of return, a successful performance is one that delivers a high total return, above the risk-free rate, per unit of standard deviation. The **risk-adjusted return** is given by:

$$\text{risk-adjusted return } R = \frac{\text{average return on portfolio} - \text{risk-free rate of return}}{\text{standard deviation of returns}}$$

The average return and standard deviation for the CREF unit for a 20 quarter period were given in Exhibit 4. For comparison purposes, the arithmetic average quarterly return and standard deviation for the same 16 quarters for the Common Fund were 5.38 and 8.69%, respectively. The Common Fund equity portfolio is an all common stock portfolio of a few \$100 million, representing endowment investments of colleges and universities.

Calculation of the risk-adjusted return above requires a figure for the risk-free rate of return. Over the 20 quarters 1979–1983 the average quarterly rate of return on 30-day Treasury bills was 2.67%. Using this as the risk-free rate of return leads to the following calculation for the risk-adjusted rates of return over the 20 quarters for CREF, the Common Fund, and the S&P 500 Index:

$$\text{For CREF} \quad R = \frac{4.28 - 2.67}{7.37} = 0.22\%$$

$$\text{For Common Fund} \quad R = \frac{5.38 - 2.67}{8.69} = 0.31\%$$

$$\text{For S\&P 500 Index} \quad R = \frac{4.32 - 2.67}{7.44} = 0.22\%$$

In other words, the S&P 500 Index achieved a rate of return of 0.22 percentage point per quarter above a Treasury bill rate, for each percentage point of standard deviation in return. CREF also achieved 0.22 percentage point above the Treasury bill rate for each percentage point of standard deviation. The Common Fund performed much better over these 16 quarters, delivering 0.31 percentage point of quarterly return above the Treasury bill rate for each percentage point of standard deviation.

Adjusting for Beta. The proess of adjusting the rate of return for the beta coefficient is somewhat more complicated; it rests on portfolio theory relating expected return to market risk. It is common practice to substitute the beta coefficient for the standard deviation in the equations above, but while this generally leads to the proper ranking of performances, it is not strictly correct. The correct adjustment was described some years ago by Jack Treynor in an article in the *Harvard Business Review.* The explanation is not repeated here, but the calculation of an index by which performances can be ranked is given by:

$$\text{index for ranking performance} = \frac{\text{(regression line intercept)} + (\text{beta} - 1)\,\text{(risk-free rate of return)}}{\text{beta}}$$

The regression line is the line drawn in Exhibit 5. The intercept is the rate of return on the portfolio, where the regression line intercepts the vertical axis, which is at 0.044% Exhibit 5, for CREF. Using this equation gives the following ranking index values (the beta and the intercept for the Common Fund for the 20 quarters were 1.15% and 0.40%, respectively):

$$\text{ranking index for CREF} = \frac{.044 + (0.98 - 1) \times 2.67}{.98} = -0.010$$

$$\text{ranking index for Common Fund} = \frac{.404 + (1.15 - 1) \times 2.67}{1.15} = 0.700$$

$$\text{ranking index for S\&P 500 Index} = \frac{0 + (1 - 1) \times 2.67}{1} = 0$$

The ranking index for the S&P 500, the reference for the calculation of the beta and the intercept, will always be 0. The ranking for a portfolio that underperforms the S&P 500 on a risk-adjusted basis will be negative, as is the case for CREF. The ranking index for a portfolio that outperforms the S&P 500 will be positive, as is the case for the Common Fund.

Sources of Error and Bias. The calculation of a beta coefficient requires selection of a reference index. Common stock betas are generally based on the S&P 500 Index, but other indexes could be used. Portfolio theory demands that the index incorporate all risky assets—stocks, bonds, real estate, commodities, and everything else one can invest in. No such index has been tabulated, although indexes more broadly based than those now available could certainly be devised. In the absence of this ideal index, any choice of index is somewhat arbitrary, therefore beta coefficients themselves have a degree of arbitrariness. As a practical matter, use of the S&P 500 Index as the reference appears to work well.

EVALUATING PERFORMANCE

PURPOSE. The preceding discussion centered on measurement of performance in terms of both rate of return and risk. The usual purpose of performance measurement is performance evaluation. This may involve comparing a performance with an expectation, analyzing sources of good and bad performance, comparing a performance of other managed portfolios. Comparisons among managers, portfolios, and indexes are discussed later. We deal next with evaluation in terms of objectives and expectations, and the analysis of strengths and weaknesses.

MEETING OBJECTIVES AND EXPECTATIONS. In general there is not much point in expecting managers to achieve **short-run objectives** set in terms of total return. One may hope that in the long run a common stock portfolio will average, say, 15% a year total return. But to anticipate a 15% return in any particular year flies in the face of the known volatility and unpredictability of the stock market and the major influence of market action on any stock portfolio.

It does, however, make sense to establish risk objectives and expect them to be achieved over the short term. If the portfolio owner and manager agree on a beta coefficient between 0.95 and 1.05, for example, only a few quarters of performance data will indicate whether this objective is being achieved. There are, of course, bound to be random deviations from a target beta coefficient, but one measure of manager quality is the manager's ability to control risk within a narrow range.

Risk-adjusted rates of return may suggest a basis for short-term evaluation in terms of expectations, but here random fluctuations present a serious problem. In principle, the risk-adjusted measures discussed above for CREF and the Common Fund are applicable to short periods of time, but in practice these measures vary so much from period to period for any one manager or portfolio that in the short run they are a poor guide to management ability to meet objectives.

Dissatisfaction with total return and risk-adjusted total return as measures by which to judge performance against expectations has led to a search for more useful criteria, and one factor that shows some promise is **income growth.** For a charitable or educational endowment, from which only income will be spent, the rate of income growth is obviously important. Even for a pension fund, if in the long run the income yield will fluctuate around some average, the capital appreciation will in the long run equal income growth. Income growth has other features to recommend it. It is generally more consistent and more predictable than total return. It does lend itself to abuse, however. A manager can produce a high rate of income growth in a short time simply by shifting from low to high yield securities. This device will not work for long, and in the short run its effects can be identified and allowed for in a performance evaluation.

As an example, the average growth in dividends on the S&P 500 Index over the 10 years 1975–1984, calculated by a least squares regression, was 8.3% a year. The rate of inflation over the same 10 years, as measured by the Consumer Price Index, was 7.3% per year. So the dividend income from the S&P Index rose faster than consumer prices. This may be a more important result than the total return on the investment, especially if one objective for a portfolio is an income stream that maintains its purchasing power.

ANALYZING SOURCES OF PERFORMANCE. Two obvious sources of performance are **security selection** and **market timing** and, until the 1980s, identifying the contributions of these sources to total performance was about as far as most measurement systems went. Recent years have seen significant advances, however, in defining more sources and in measuring their contributions.

Security selection involves the choice of particular stocks, bonds, and other instruments, and it was the practice in earlier years to compare the performance of a stock portfolio with that of a stock index, or the performance of a bond portfolio with that of a bond index, and so on, to determine what the selection process had added to portfolio performance. If, for example, the stock portfolio had outperformed the stock index by two percentage points, then the manager was credited with having added 2% by astute selection of stocks.

Today the process can be carried somewhat further. First, one identifies a **"normal portfolio."** This is a portfolio with characteristics that appear suitable over the long run for the portfolio's owner. If it is a stock portfolio, it has risk characteristics, expressed in terms of beta or standard deviation, that are appropriate. It achieves a desired level of diversification, and offers an acceptable expected return. Generally this normal portfolio contains a great many securities. It will be the function of the manager to choose from this universe a set of securities that will outperform the universe.

Rather than comparing the performance of the managed portfolio with that of an index, then, we compare it with that of the normal portfolio. This comparison identifies the contribution of security selection above what would have been achieved simply by investing in that normal portfolio. Comparing the performance of the normal portfolio with that of an index will furnish another type of information—whether the owner of the portfolio (not the manager) in settling on its normal portfolio, added value to the index.

Market timing involves either successful switching of funds among stocks and bonds and short-term investments to take advantage of relative ups and downs in the three markets, or successful changes in the volatility of a portfolio of stocks, or bonds, or short-term investments, becoming aggressive in rising markets and defensive in falling markets.

Separating the results of timing from those of security selection requires measuring the results of timing in the absence of selection. One way to do this is to calculate the results of investing in stock, bond, and short-term indexes in the proportions indicated by the market timer's decisions. If the manager who is responsible for timing begins with a portfolio equally divided between stocks and bonds, and after a month changes the proportions to 70% stocks and 30% bonds, and after another month changes back to half and half, we calculate the result of holding a stock index and a bond index in equal proportions for a month, then switching to 70% stock index and 30% bond index for a month, then switching back to equal proportions. Comparing this result with the result of simply maintaining constant equal proportions will indicate how successful the switching was.

The use of normal stock, bond, and short-term portfolios will give better reference points than indexes, however. The normal portfolios, rather than indexes, establish what the managers are to work with.

Timing that takes place within a normal portfolio—for example, switching from low to high volatility stocks within a normal stock portfolio—is hard to separate from selection as a source of performance. Tracking volatility of the portfolio, and correlating changes with subsequent market movements, is one useful method.

COMPARING PERFORMANCES

PURPOSE. An obvious purpose of performance measurement is to compare managers with one another, to hire and keep only the best. A closely related purpose is to determine whether there is any value to management, whether an actively managed portfolio has outperformed a simple and less expensive passive strategy. This is a difficult area and obviously an important one. There is no single all-revealing method of comparison. Nor is there much general agreement even on the best comparisons. The following discussion suggests a number of considerations that should enter into the choice of a comparison method.

RATE OF RETURN COMPARISONS. The most common comparisons between the performance of a portfolio and the performance of an index, or among the performances of managed portfolios, are based on rates of total return. This approach is not inappropriate if the risk levels of the portfolios or indexes in the comparison are roughly the same. A quick inspection of beta coefficients or standard deviations of return may confirm that they are about the same. Even a qualitative description, giving the kind of stocks or bonds held in the portfolio or represented by the index, may be enough to support a comparison of total returns. But one frequently finds performances being compared on a total return basis when risk levels are not at all the same. Total return comparisons among a common stock portfolio, a bond portfolio, and a mixed stock and bond portfolio are not uncommon. Often the results are presented without drawing attention to the fact that the portfolios are not comparable on a risk basis.

It is also not uncommon to find that the return figures themselves used in a comparison are not really comparable. Because it is often difficult to obtain accurate data on the income generated by a portfolio and on the income corresponding to an index, comparisons are sometimes based strictly on capital appreciation, ignoring income. The comparisons will be fair only if the incomes generated by the portfolios or index being compared are equal. But making a comparison strictly on the basis of appreciation between a growth stock portfolio, with a low level of income, and an income stock portfolio obviously biases the result in favor of the growth stocks. A more subtle lack of comparability may arise from the treatment of management fees. Sometimes rates of return are calculated net of (less) management fees and sometimes they are calculated before deduction for fees. Mutual fund results are always reported net of management fees. Rates of return reported for educational endowment and charitable funds are often before deduction of management fees. With fees running in the range of a few tenths of a percent up to 1 or 2% of asset value, a substantial bias can be introduced by an inconsistency here.

If rates of return alone are to be compared, the time period chosen for the comparison may be significant. Even small differences in volatility among portfolios will lead to substantial differences in reported rates of return during periods of extreme market movement. Comparisons that extend over a full market cycle will generally avoid the biases of shorter periods.

Indexes. Rate of return comparisons between portfolios and indexes are fairly common. At one time it was argued that no investor could actually buy an index, and therefore the comparisons meant nothing. It is clear today that investors can buy an index, or at least a portfolio as close to an index as they care to come. A number of investment managers offer "index funds," investing in a portfolio that matches the composition of an index—the Standard & Poor's 500 Index, for example. So the comparisons do have a real meaning. They show the difference between the actual performance of a portfolio and what the performance would have been if an index fund had been chosen. The record of an index, of course, does not reflect any transaction costs. To the extent that the manager of the portfolio was required to buy and sell securities to account for cash flows into and out of the portfolio, an adjustment should be made. Otherwise the index comparison is biased against the manager. No adjustment for other transaction costs is appropriate, since the index fund alternative avoids such costs.

NORMAL PORTFOLIOS. The use of normal portfolios as reference points in performance measurement was discussed earlier, in connection with identifying sources of performance. In comparing managers, too, normal or benchmark portfolios are being recognized as superior to indexes. It should be fairly obvious that from time to time growth stocks, or high yielding stocks, or stocks of small companies, will as groups outperform or underperform a broad market index such as the S&P 500 Index. So a manager who works consistently with one of these groups will, purely as a matter of chance and not through skill, sometimes outperform and sometimes underperform the S&P 500. Judging a growth stock manager against a growth stock index will reduce the chance element. Judging the manager against a normal or benchmark portfolio will reduce it further.

The normal portfolio in this case is the universe of securities used by the manager in serving the client. It is best established jointly by the client—the portfolio owner—and the manager. Some managers feel that their selection skill is to some extent being exploited in establishing the universe, and in such a case it may be appropriate to measure the performance of the universe against the performance of a market index, to see whether establishing the universe did in fact add value. But once the universe is set, what the manager is being paid for is to make the best selections from that universe. So the performance measure is the difference between the performance of the universe, or normal portfolio, and the manager's actual performance. A number of pension funds have discovered that ranking managers according to their performances judged against normal portfolios and ranking them by performances judged against market indexes, can lead to very different results.

RISK-ADJUSTED COMPARISONS. The chief weakness of simple rate of return performance comparisons lies in the requirement that the portfolios and indexes being compared have approximately the same investment risk characteristics. In theory, comparisons of risk-adjusted rates of return overcome this weakness. But the **risk-adjusted comparisons** bring with them some problems of their own.

The mechanics of calculating risk-adjusted returns have already been described. The two methods, one involving the standard deviation, a measure of total portfolio risk, and the other involving the beta coefficient, a measure of market-related risk, suggested at least one dilemma. Although portfolio theory would indicate that it is the return adjusted by the beta coefficient that is the more appropriate, in reality this is not so clear. As long as the comparison is limited to broadly diversified common stock portfolios, the beta coefficient is generally a satisfactory risk measure for adjusting returns, with calculation of the beta based on a broad stock market index such as the S&P 500. But if the portfolios are not broadly diversified, if they are limited to a particular market sector (like growth stocks), or if they extend to fixed-income securities or other noncommon stock investments, then the beta coefficient is a less than satisfactory risk measure. Generally, beta coefficients are calculated from the S&P 500 Index, which has no obvious relevance to a bond portfolio.

For most comparisons of common stock portfolio performances, rankings using returns adjusted by standard deviation will be almost identical to rankings obtained from rates of return adjusted by beta coefficients. Where the portfolios to be compared involve more than common stocks, returns adjusted for standard deviation are preferred.

USEFULNESS OF COMPARISONS. The most imporant question with respect to performance comparisons is whether they can be relied on to indicate true relationships. One would hope that superior management ability would lead to consistently superior performance, and therefore be readily identifiable. But there will always be some chance element in the performance of a portfolio, whether that performance is expressed in terms of a rate of return, or in terms of a risk-adjusted rate of return. The important question is whether the role played by management ability in determining investment performance is strong enough to permit this quality to be identified by the methods described above, or whether the element of chance is strong enough to obscure the effects of ability.

The evidence seems to be that it is extraordinarily difficult to identify consistently superior management through performance rankings. Over any particular time period it is of course possible to rank the performances of any set of portfolios or portfolio managers. But all too often the rankings over one time period show little correlation with rankings over another time period. This suggests rather strongly that performance rankings do not provide reliable evidence of differences in management ability. The use of normal portfolios offers hope of increased reliability, as the role of chance in performance measurements is decreased. But there is not as yet enough history of the use of normal portfolios to clearly establish its value.

The lack of proven predictability of superior performance may be disappointing, but it should not come as a surprise. If it is true, as seems likely, that the majority of investment managers have about the same ability and that even very good managers do not produce performances far above average, one should not expect to be able to find in performance rankings a reliable ranking by ability. This does not mean that ranking are useless. A ranking that is very high or very low over a long period of time suggests superior or inferior ability. Now the evaluation task is to see whether that suggestion is confirmed by other characteristics of the manager. A careful examination of risk level and control, consistency of style, disciplined analysis, and other managerial qualities, coupled with a review of the sources of performance, discussed briefly above, will help to establish whether the extreme ranking position is the result of ability or chance.

NONCOMMON STOCK PORTFOLIOS

BOND PORTFOLIO PERFORMANCE EVALUATION

Components of Performance. The measurement of income yield, appreciation, and total return for a bond or bond portfolio presents no special problems. As noted above, accrued interest at the beginning and end of the measurement period must be allowed for, as well as accrued interest paid (negative income) when bonds are purchased. But **risk measurement** for a **bond portfolio,** and the measurement of risk-adjusted returns, presents some special difficulties.

Standard deviation of total return as a risk measure is probably appropriate for bonds as well as stocks. For many investors, however, particularly regulated financial institutions that carry bond portfolios on their books at cost, market value fluctuations are not regarded as important. This means that total return, and standard deviation of total return, may not be important. But for the investor who is equally concerned about bond value fluctuation and stock value fluctuation, standard deviation is a good risk measure.

In principle, a measure of market risk should be appropriate for bonds. But the beta coefficient used for stocks and stock portfolios does not work well for bonds. Bonds have a fixed maturity, and as a result their rates of total return will follow a pattern over time.

So total return adjusted for standard deviation, as described above for stock portfolios, will serve many investors as a risk-adjusted performance measure for bond portfolios. But what is of much more interest is the dissection of bond performance into its components.

Isolating Components of Performance. A number of methods of analysis have been proposed to isolate components of bond portfolio performance. In general, they distinguish between how performance is affected by changes in interest rates, which depends on the maturity structure of the portfolio, and how it is affected by the selection of individual bonds. The contribution of bond selection can be divided further into the results of quality choice, sector choice (e.g., industrial or utility or government bonds), and choice of individual issues within a sector and quality range. This process was described by Dietz, Fogler, and Hardy (1980). Other proposed methods go into further detail, identifying the contribution of a manager's choices with respect to size of issue, sinking fund provisions, conversion features, coupon level, and other characteristics.

As a practical matter, the major source of uncertainty about the future performance of a bond portfolio, and therefore the major factor accounting for a superior or inferior performance record is change in interest rates and in the term structure of interest rates. So identification of the contribution of this factor alone tells a good deal about the quality of performance.

PORTFOLIOS OF SHORT-TERM SECURITIES. In principle, short-term portfolios should be measured as stock and bond portfolios are. Reporting practices, however, frequently fail to provide correct figures.

Corporations and other institutions maintaining short-term portfolios for temporary investment of surplus cash often rely on cost or book value in reporting portfolio returns. In times of stable interest rates, the failure to use market value may not lead to significant errors. But when rates are rising or falling, the true performance may be very different from what is reported.

Money market mutual funds generally follow a practice of maintaining the share or unit value constant, most often at $1 per unit. As interest rates change, of course, the value of the portfolio changes, but what is reported as "income" (and income is normally credited daily to each unit holder's account) is adjusted to keep the unit value at $1. Comparisons of reported income, or yield, among these funds may not mean much because of the relationship between unit value and income. Only a total return comparison can be relied on. The calculation of total return, however, requires the maintenance of an account with no contributions or withdrawals, since income is being added daily and the funds generally do not disclose their total return performance record.

REAL ESTATE PORTFOLIO EVALUATION. In principle, the measurement of performance of real estate investments is no different from measurement of security portfolio performance. In practice, there are significant differences. First, **the value of a real estate portfolio** is almost always based on appraisals. Appraisals represent the subjective judgment of the appraiser and can never achieve the status of market quotations for stocks and bonds. As noted above, the use of appraisals tends to create the appearance of steadily moving values and a stable rate of return. This is not necessarily misleading for an investor with a long time horizon and little interst in the results of quick liquidation of a portfolio. But it is not appropriate to contrast the apparently stable appreciation of a real estate portfolio to the highly variable price record of a stock or bond portfolio and conclude that the former is much safer.

Income from a real estate portfolio is often not as precisely measurable as interest and dividends from a securities portfolio. For the participant in a pooled fund, income is what the fund distributes as income. For the sole owner of a portfolio, the determination of income may involve a number of accounting conventions and assumptions. For performance reporting purposes, income before depreciation and before income tax is the figure used. Essentially, this figure is the cash flow before-income tax. Ignoring depreciation is appropriate, assuming that expenditures on repairs and maintenance are adequate, because the property value is being recorded along with income. Repairs and maintenance of course present an opportunity for more or less arbitrary manipulation of income. Income measurement is somewhat more objective than property valuation, but it is subjective enough to render comparisons to security portfolios inappropriate.

REFERENCES AND BIBLIOGRAPHY

Bank Administration Institute, *Measuring the Investment Performance of Pension Funds,* Park Ridge, IL: BAI, 1968.

Dietz, P.O., *Pension Funds: Measuring Investment Performance,* New York: Free Press, 1966.

———, Fogler, H.R., and Hardy, D.J., "The Challenge of Analyzing Bond Portfolio Returns," *Journal of Portfolio Management,* Vol. 6 (Spring 1980): 53–58.

Ford Foundation, *Measuring Investment Results by the Unit Method,* New York: Ford, 1975.

Leibowitz, M.L., "Sources of Return in Corporate Bond Portfolios," New York: Salomon Brothers, August 3, 1978. (Reprinted as Chapter 6 in *Total Return Management,* New York: Salomon Brothers, 1979.)

———, *Total After-Tax Bond Performance and Yield Measures,* New York: Salomon Brothers, 1974.

Murphy, J.M., "Why No One Can Tell Who's Winning," *Financial Analysts Journal,* Vol. 36 (May–June 1980): 49–57.

Rosenberg, B., "A Critique of Performance Measurement," unpublished paper, Berkeley: University of California, 1980.

Rudd, A., "Portfolio Management," *Journal of Accounting, Auditing and Finance,* Vol. 7, No. 4 (Summer 1984): 393–398.

Sharpe, W.F., "Adjusting for Risk in Portfolio Performance Measurement," in *Portfolio Management and Efficient Markets,* Peter L. Bernstein (ed.), New York: Institutional Investor Books, 1977, pp. 113–127.

———, "Mutual Fund Performance," *Journal of Business,* Vol. 39 (January 1966): 119–138.

Treynor, J.L., "How to Rate Management of Investment Funds," *Harvard Business Review,* Vol. 43 (January–February 1965): 63–75.

Williamson, J.P., *Performance Measurement and Investment Objectives for Educational Endowment Funds,* New York: Common Fund, 1972.

APPENDIX A

MATHEMATICS OF FINANCE

CONTENTS

APPENDIX A

MATHEMATICS OF FINANCE

Marti G. Subrahmanyam
With the assistance of William Prado

INTRODUCTION

This appendix presents the concepts and computational methods in **interest rate mathematics.** In order to better illustrate the material, we first compute example problems with the aid of tables. Since most practitioners in the field of finance now use calculators and since microcomputer spreadsheet programs are becoming increasingly popular, we include calculator and spreadsheet solutions as well.

There is a vast array of pocket financial calculators on the market today. They span the broad spectrum from simple calculators that have, in addition to basic function keys, a few financial keys to powerful programmable calculators that can handle most financial computations. The calculator solutions that are presented are intended to provide a feel for the use of a pocket calculator, rather than an exhaustive listing of programs for a wide variety of models. Thus, solutions are restricted to the Hewlett-Packard 12C.

Spreadsheets appear on the computer screen as a series of rows and columns. They automatically calculate and total rows, columns, and cells. Any changes, additions, or deletions to existing data can be instantly recalculated. As with calculators, there are many spreadsheet programs available. They vary in power, speed, and in the number of "built-in" financial functions (these make problem-solving easier). Generally, however, built-in functions handle only simple computations; one must write-in equations to solve financial problems of any complexity. Until software developers create more sophisticated built-in functions, we suggest you use built-ins whenever possible and, when these are not enough, that you consult the writer's manual and/or after-market publications (e.g., *1-2-3 for Business*—Lotus product) for spreadsheet approaches. Solutions that appear are for the Lotus 1–2–3.

INTEREST RATE MATHEMATICS

DEFINITIONS. Interest is ordinarily defined as consideration paid for the use of money. To the borrower it represents the cost of the loan, to the lender it is a source of income. The amount of interest depends on three factors: principal, rate, time.

Principal. The principal is any sum of money on which interest is to be computed. It may represent invested capital, as in the instance of partnership equities, or a loan in the form of notes or more formal bond indentures.

Rate. The interest rate is usually expressed as a percentage of the principal per unit of time; for example, 14% per annum, 7% semiannually.

Time. The time refers to the period for which interest is to be calculated. Unless otherwise stated, interest formulas use the year as a unit.

BASIC TYPES OF INTEREST. There are two basic types of interest, simple and compound. These may be represented as follows:

1. Simple interest.
   a. Ordinary.
   b. Exact—commercial practice.
   c. Exact—government securities.
2. Compound

Simple interest refers to interest that is always computed on the original principal. If the interest is not paid when due, it is not added to the principal. Thus the amount of interest is always proportional to the time.

Ordinary interest represents a type of simple interest computed on a 360-day year, commonly referred to as the **commercial year.** Under this method the year is divided into 12 months of 30 days each. Although the method is used in many commercial transactions, modifications are often introduced. For example, in discounting commercial paper, ordinary interest is calculated, but it is based on the exact number of days in the discount period.

Exact interest is interest based on a 365-day year, or 366 days in leap years. It is generally employed by banks in allowing interest on daily balances, and also in governmental calculations other than interest on government securities. In the latter instance special tables are available from which the accrued interest may be read.

Compound interest is discussed below.

Ordinary Interest. Ordinary interest is the product of the principal, the rate and the time:

$$I = Pit$$

where: I = amount of interest
P = principal
i = rate
t = time (years)

For example, to find the ordinary interest on $12,148.72 for 153 days at 14% (per year), the formula yields.

$$12{,}148.72 \times \frac{14}{100} \times \frac{153}{360} = \$722.85$$

Exact Interest

Nature of Exact Interest. A given amount of principal earns in 365 days as much exact interest as the same principal earns in 360 days at ordinary interest. For 360 days therefore the exact interest is only 360/365 of the amount of ordinary interest. For practical purposes it is easier to compute ordinary interest first and then to adjust the result to get exact interest. Since 360/365 = 72/73, it is evident that exact interest is 72/73 of ordinary interest; therefore to calculate exact interest, figure ordinary interest and subtract 1/73.

Example. Municipal taxes in the town of X are due November 1 and may be paid without penalty up to and including November 30. Thereafter an interest penalty is charged at 7% per annum from the first due date. (November 1). For a tax bill of $4,850, find the total paid to the town, if payment is made on December 11 of the same year.

Solution. Elapsed time November 1–December 11, 40 days.

7% ordinary interest	$ 37.722
Less 1/73	0.517
Exact interest, 7%	$ 37.21
Amount of bill	4,850.00
Total paid	$4,887.21

Interest on U.S. Government Securities. Interest on bonds or notes issued by the U.S. government is computed on the basis of exact interest for the exact number of days falling within the interest period. Exhibit 1 shows that the length of an interest period may vary from 181 days to 184 days. The daily accrual of interest may be computed as follows. First, determine the number of days in the interest period. Then, compute the accrual after adjusting for the number of days and the principal amount.

Anticipation. This is a customary term used in connection with purchase in-

EXHIBIT 1 EXACT NUMBER OF DAYS IN 6-MONTH INTEREST PERIOD

Ending Dates	Ordinary Year	Leap Year
January 1 or 15	184	184
February 1 or 15	184	184
March 1 or 15	181	182
April 1 or 15	182	183
May 1 or 15	181	182
June 1 or 15	182	183
July 1 or 15	181	182
August 1 or 15	181	182
September 1 or 15	184	184
October 1 or 15	183	183
November 1 or 15	184	184
December 1 or 15	183	183

voices that have extra dating where interest is allowed if payment is made before the expiration of the final due date of the invoice. The effect of the extra dating is to extend the time within which a proffered **cash discount** may be taken. Thus, if merchandise is purchased at 2%, 10 days, 90 days extra, with anticipation at 6%, a discount of 2% is allowed for payment any time within 100 days. In addition, the purchaser may deduct interest for the number of days before the final due date.The exact procedure is first to find the amount payable on the last day of the discount period. From this amount is deducted **exact interest** at the stipulated anticipation rate for the number of days anticipated.

Example. An invoice is dated April 12, 1987, for $5,653.75, terms 2%, 10 days, 60 days extra, f.o.b. destination, anticipation at 6%. The purchaser paid $45.60 freight. What was the amount due if payment was made on May 22, 1987?

The number of days from April 12 to May 22 is 40. Hence payment is anticipated 30 days. The calculation appears as follows:

Invoice	$5,653.75
Less: Freight paid	45.60
Net invoice	$5,608.15
Less: 2% discount	112.16
Balance subject to anticipation	$5,495.99
Anticipation for 30 days at 6% per annum (exact)	27.10
Amount payable on May 22, 1987	$5,468.89

It is the custom of some stores to compute the discount on the face of the invoice and the anticipation on the net amount after deducting the discount, finally deducting the freight charges. This plan, which favors the purchaser, is illustrated:

Invoice	$5,653.75
Less: 2% discount	113.08
Balance	$5,540.67
Anticipation for 30 days at 6% per annum	27.33
Balance	$5,513.34
Less: Freight paid	45.60
Amount of check	$5,467.74

Extra dating is sometimes secured by stores as a result of certain trade customs. Invoices are frequently dated, say, 2%, 10 days, e.o.m. (end of month). This means that if an invoice is dated June 17, it is due 10 days after the end of June (i.e., July 10). Both discount and anticipation would then be allowed if payment is made before July 10.

Again, purchase orders sometimes contain conditional clauses in which "the seller agrees that merchandise shipped on or after the twenty-fifth of a month, will be billed as of the first of the following month." Thus, merchandise shipped on April 26, terms 2%, 10 days, is billed as of May 1, with discount and anticipation available until May 10. Ordinarily the anticipation may not amount to much because of the short time. However, if the above-quoted clause is coupled with e.o.m. dating, the effect is to secure an extra month's dating. In short, if goods are shipped on April 26, terms 2%, 10 days, e.o.m., and the purchase order contains the billing clause above, the invoice becomes due on June 10, that is, 10 days after the first of the month in which the invoice would otherwise fall due.

BANK DISCOUNT

Loans and Discounts. One of the important functions of a commercial bank is the making of loans, which produce a source of income for the bank and fulfill a necessary function in the economic life of the community served by the bank. Technically **loans** are distinguished from **discounts** chiefly by the fact that in the case of loans, interest is paid periodically, during the existence of the loan or at its maturity, whereas in the case of discounts the interest or "discount" is deducted at the time the advance is made. Thus, in the case of a $1,000 loan at 8% for 6 months, the borrower receives $1,000 and pays back $1,040 at the end of 6 months. On the other hand, if he discounts a $1,000 note at 6%, he receives $970.87 and pays back $1,000 at the end of the 6-month term. In short, bank discount is the consideration deducted by the bank from the face of a note or draft prior to its maturity date.

Since the 1930s, finance companies and banks have been making **long-term loans,** especially in the field of **home financing.** These loans are usually amortized, principal and interest, through equal monthly payments. They are dealt with later in this Section in connection with annuities.

Types of Notes. Notes may be variously classified, but for computation purposes it is necessary only to know whether a note is **interest bearing** (see, e.g., Exhibit 2) or **noninterest bearing** (Exhibit 3).

In discounting a note, the bank pays only what the note is worth at the time of discount. Thus, a **noninterest-bearing note** is worth its face value at maturity and not before. Any time before maturity the note is valued at less than face value by the amount of interest the bank charges. An **interest-bearing note,** however, provided the interest and discount rates are the same, is worth approximately its face value on the date of issue and thereafter increases in value each day by the amount of interest earned until maturity.

The amount that a bank pays for a note or that it credits to a borrower's account is called the **proceeds** of the note.

EXHIBIT 2 INTEREST-BEARING PROMISSORY NOTE

$ *3,400 00/100* New York *April 2* 19–

Two (2) months AFTER DATE *I* PROMISE TO PAY TO

THE ORDER OF *Barrows & Co.*

Thirty-four hundred and 00/100 DOLLARS

AT *Irving Trust Co. with interest @ 15%*

VALUE RECEIVED

No. *1* DUE *June 2* 19– *J. Doe*

EXHIBIT 3 NONINTEREST-BEARING PROMISSORY NOTE

$ *500 00/100* New York *May 15* 19–

Twenty (20) days AFTER DATE *I* PROMISE TO PAY TO

THE ORDER OF *J. Doe*

Five hundred and 00/100 DOLLARS

AT *Irving Trust Co.*

VALUE RECEIVED

No. *273* *R. Roe*

Basis for Calculating Proceeds. Ordinarily, banks use the actual number of days in figuring the discount period on short-term notes, but interest or discount is computed on the basis of a 360-day year (ordinary interest). In the case of the Federal Reserve System, **exact interest** is used.

Due Date of Notes. Promissory notes are payable at a stated number of days or months after date. **Drafts** may be payable so many days **after date** or **after sight.** If days are specified, the exact number of days is counted. Thus, if the note states "60 days after date . . ." and is dated May 14, it is due July 13. However, when months are specified, the note falls due in the month of maturity on the same date as is specified in the date of the note. For example, a note dated May 14 due in 2 months is due on July 14.

If a note is dated on the last day of a 31-day month, and falls due in a 30-day month, the due date would be the last of the 30-day month. To illustrate, a note dated May 31, due in four months, matures on September 30. But a note dated May 31, due in 120 days, is payable September 28.

Computing Proceeds and Discount on Noninterest-Bearing Paper. Three steps are necessary to calculate the proceeds or deposit credit:

1. Calculate the time from the discount date to maturity.
2. Compute the interest to maturity for the time computed in step 1. This is the discount.
3. Deduct the discount from the face value.

Example 1. Find the proceeds or deposit credit on a note for $1,875, dated July 5, for 30 days, discounted at 14% per annum on the date of issue. The note is due August 4, that is, 30 days from July 5.

Face value of note	$1,875.00
Discount, 30 days, 14% on $1,875	− 21.87
Proceeds	$1,853.13

Example 2. Find the proceeds on a note for $2,863.79 dated February 8, 1986, due in 60 days, discounted on March 2 at 14½% per annum. The maturity date is April 9, 1986, and the time to maturity (March 2 to April 9) 38 days.

Face value	$2,863.79
Discount on above for 38 days at 14½%	− 43.83
Proceeds	$2,819.96

Discounting Interest-Bearing Paper. The general rule in discounting interest-bearing paper is to compute and then discount the maturity value. In calculating the maturity value, the interest from the date of the note to maturity is added to the face value. Next the discount is computed for the discount period and deducted from the maturity value.

Example. Find the proceeds of a 5% note for $5,350, dated August 12, 1988, due in 3 months, and discounted on September 27, 1988, at 4%.

Maturity value	
Face value	$5,350.00
Interest August 12 to November 12 (92 days on $5,350 at 15%)	205.08
Maturity value	$5,555.08
Discount from September 27 to November 12 (46 days, 14%)	− 99.37
Proceeds	$5,455.71

Finding Principal to Yield Given Proceeds. Occasionally it becomes necessary to reverse the process above; that is, a debtor wishes to borrow enough so that the proceeds will exactly cover the net amount of an invoice that is to be paid. Thus the face value of the note is unknown. If the note is **noninterest bearing,** the face value to yield the given proceeds is found by dividing the given proceeds by the proceeds of $1. The expression "proceeds of one dollar" means one dollar minus the interest or discount on $1.

Example. A merchant arranges to pay for a shipment by borrowing the exact amount required to pay the invoice. The net amount of the invoice is $5,960.34 and the bank agrees to discount the merchant's note at 4% for 120 days.

$$\text{Proceeds of \$1 for 120 days at 4\%} = \$1 - \$0.01\tfrac{1}{3} = \$0.98\tfrac{2}{3}$$

$$\frac{\text{given proceeds}}{\text{proceeds of \$1}} = \frac{\$5{,}960.34}{.98\frac{2}{3}} = \frac{\$17{,}881.02}{2.96} = \$6{,}040{,}89$$

Face value	$6,040.89
Interest for 120 days at 4%	80.55
Proceeds	$5,960.34

Computation of Interest Under Partial Payment Plans. When a short-term indebtedness is reduced through periodic payments, the interest is computed upon either one of two bases. The basis used commonly in business is known as the **"merchant's rule."** This method gives the results more quickly but not as accurately as the computation under the other, the **"United States rule."**

Merchant's Rule. In following the merchant's rule, the interest is computed on the total indebtedness from the date of inception to the date of maturity, and from this total is deducted the interest earned from the date that each partial payment is made to the date of maturity of the debt.

Example. The following payments were made on a $16,500, 6% note, dated June 22, 1986, due in 6 months:

October 20, 1986	$ 300
November 15, 1986	3,500

What is the amount due at maturity?

Solution

June 22	Face value		$16,500.00
December 22	Interest at 6% on above, June 22 to December 22 = 183 days		503.25
	Maturity value of note		$17,003.25
October 20	First payment	$ 300.00	
	Interest on above October 20 to December 22 = 63 days	3.15	
November 15	Second payment	3,500.00	
	Interest on above November 15 to December 22 = 37 days	21.58	
	Total credits		3,824.73
December 22	Maturity: balance due		$13,178.52

United States Rule. Under the United States rule, each installment is first applied against the interest due at the date the partial payment is made, and the balance of the installment is then applied to reduce the principal. Interest is always computed on the reduced principal. In the event that a partial payment is insufficient to cover the accrued interest, it is held in suspense. There is no reduction of principal until the suspended payment together with subsequent payments exceeds the accrued interest. Using the same figures as in the example for the merchant's rule, the solution appears as follows:

June 22	Face value		$16,500.00
October 20	First payment	$ 300.00	
	Interest on $16,500 for 120 days (June 22 to October 20)	330.00	
	Reduction of principal		—0—
November 15	Second payment	$3,500.00	
	Add first payment	300.00	
	Total	$3,800.00	
	Interest on $16,500 for 146 days (June 22 to November 15)	401.50	
	Reduction of principal		3,398.50
	Balance due		$13,101.50

December 22	Maturity Interest on $13,101.50 for 37 days (November 15 to December 22)	80.79
	Balance due	$13,182.29

Bank Discount Versus True Discount. In a discounting operation, the interest charge, as in the case of noninterest-bearing notes, is taken out in advance. Thus the borrower receives the maturity value minus the discount. He is paying interest calculated on the maturity value for the use of a smaller sum, the proceeds. A 60-day note for $1,000, discounted at 18%, yields $970 proceeds. The borrower pays $30 for the use of $970, which is therefore more than 18%. The discount calculated as above is called **bank discount.** So-called true discount is an interest charge based on the **present value** of the note, that is, on a sum that at the discount rate would produce the face value of the note. To find the present value of a note, merely divide the maturity value by the amount of $1 (at the given rate and for the given time). The "amount of $1" means one dollar plus the interest on $1.

Example. Find the proceeds and present value of a note for $5,632.50, dated June 22, 1986, due in 90 days, and discounted at 18% per annum on July 27, 1986. The note is due September 20, 1986.

Proceeds	Present Value
Maturity value (since this is a noninterest-bearing note)	$5,632.50
Discount at 18% for 55 days; (i.e., from July 27–September 20)	154.89
Proceeds	$5,477.61

Maturity value	$5,632.50
Amount of $1 at 18% per annum for each of 55 days	1.0275
Present value	$5,632.50 ÷ 1.0275 = $5,481.75

In this example, the **bank discount** is $154.89 but the **true discount** is $150.75 ($5,632.50 − $5,481.75).

Relation of Bank Discount Rate to True Discount Rate. Since the bank discount is based on a larger sum than the borrower receives, he evidently pays more than the indicated rate of interest. To discover the true interest rate, it is necessary to express the bank discount as a percentage of the proceeds, assuming the loan ran for 1 year. Actually, the amount is immaterial, since the calculation can be put on a unit dollar basis.

Example. A note for $10,000, due in 12 months, is discounted at 16% per annum. What is the equivalent annual interest charge?

Solution a. Here it is necessary to compute the annual discount:

Maturity value	\$10,000.00
Discount 16%, one year	1,600.00
Proceeds	\$ 8,400.00

The borrower, in effect, pays \$1,600 for the use of \$8,400 for a year. Hence the interest rate is

$$\frac{1,600}{8,400} = 0.1905 = \underline{\underline{19.05\%}}$$

Solution b. By putting the calculation on a unit dollar basis a general formula may be derived as follows:

Maturity value	\$1.00
Discount	0.16
Proceeds	\$0.84

$$\text{Interest rate} = \frac{0.16}{0.4} = 0.1905 = 19.05\%$$

Let $d =$ discount rate. Then

$$1 - d = \text{proceeds of \$1 due in 1 year}$$
$$r = \text{interest rate}$$

Hence

$$r = \frac{d}{1-d} \times 100$$

In the problem above substitution in the formula yields;

$$\frac{0.16}{0.84} \times 100 = 19.05\%$$

Thus a discount rate of 16% per annum is equal to an annual interest charge of 19.05% approximately.

CHAIN DISCOUNTS

Definition. Chain discounts are two or more discounts that are applied in succession to a quote price. The latter is usually referred to as the **list price,** that is, the price at which the item is listed in the manufacturer's or jobber's catalog. Each discount is applied to the net amount remaining after the previous discount has been taken. For example, an article quoted at \$25 less 30 and 10 means \$25 less 30%, and then less 10% on the diminished amount.

List price	\$25.00
Less: First discount—30%	7.50
Balance	\$17.50
Less: Second discount—10%	1.75
Net price	\$15.75

If many chain discounts are involved in connection with a given list price, this method may be cumbersome. An alternative method is to multiply the list price by the net cost factors, that is, the percentage remaining after deducting the chain discount from 100%. Thus, in the example above, the purchaser pays

$$\$25 \times 70\% \times 90\% = 25 \times 0.63 = \$15.75$$

Finding Equivalent Single Discount. It is often convenient to convert chain discounts into equivalent single discounts. To find an equivalent single discount rate equal to two chain discounts, add the discounts and subtract their product.

Examples. Find single discounts equal to chain discount of:

1. 40 and 30.
2. 20 and 20.
3. 15 and 10.
4. 10 and 5.
5. 10 and 5.

1	2	3	4	5
0.40	0.20	0.15	0.20	0.10
+0.30	+0.20	+0.10	+0.05	+0.05
0.70	0.40	0.25	0.25	0.15
−0.12	−0.04	−0.015	−0.01	−0.005
0.58	0.36	0.235	0.24	0.145
58%	36%	23.5%	24%	14.5%

In practice, the decimal points are omitted to speed up the work. Thus problem 5 would be solved: 10 + 5 = 15, minus 0.5 *r* 14.5%. In fact, these problems can and should be done mentally.

The same rule may be applied to three or more chain discounts, provided only two discounts are taken at a time. The order in which the discounts are taken is immaterial.

COMPOUND INTEREST

Definitions. In compound interest calculations, the interest is computed at the end of each fiscal period and added to the principal at the beginning, the total representing the new principal on the basis of which a new interest calculation is made. Compound interest may therefore be defined as that form of interest in which the interest for each period is added to the principal. Because interest is added to the principal, and interest for the next period is calculated on the new total, interest sometimes is said to be **converted** into principal.

The time for which interest is calculated and converted is known as the **conversion period.** It represents the elapsed time between two successive interest dates. The time—that is, the conversion period—may be a month, or a quarterly, semiannual, or annual period, or any other convenient time period.

The conversion period is sometimes referred to as an **accumulation period** because the principal accumulates—that is, increases by the amount of interest added to the principal. No such term was necessary in the instance of simple interest, because the interest was not converted but always computed on the original principal. But in compound interest, the interest is computed on an ever-increasing amount, because of the repeated addition to the existing principal.

Finding the Compound Amount. The principle behind the method of compound interest calculations can be illustrated by reference to an example.

Example. Find the compound amount on $1,500 for 3 years at 6% per annum, compounded semiannually (or at 3% per 6 months).

Investment	$1,500.00
Interest 6 months, $1,500 at 3%	45.00
Amount at end of first 6 months	$1,545.00
Interest 6 months, $1,545 at 3%	46.35
Amount at end of second 6 months	$1,591.35
Interest 6 months, $1,591.35 at 3%	47.74
Amount at end of third 6 months	$1,639.09
Interest 6 months, $1,639.09 at 3%	49.17
Amount at end of fourth 6 months	$1,688.26
Interest 6 months, $1,688.26 at 3%	50.65
Amount at end of fifth 6 months	$1,738.91
Interest 6 months, $1,738.91 at 3%	52.17
Compound amount at end of 3 years	$1,791.08

If the principal amount is reduced to say $1, the tabulation above can be restated as follows:

Investment	$1.00
Interest 6 months, $1 at 3% or	0.03
Amount at end of first 6 months	$1.03
Interest 6 months, $1.03 at 3%	0.0309
Amount at end of second 6 months	$1.0609
Interest 6 months, $1,0609 at 3%	0.031827
Amount at end of third 6 months	$1.092727
Interest 6 months, $1.092727 at 3%	0.032782

Amount at end of fourth 6 months	\$1.125509
Interest 6 months, \$1.125509 at 3%	0.033765
Amount at end of fifth 6 months	\$1.159274
Interest 6 months, \$1.159274 at 3%	0.034778
Compound amount at end of 3 years	\$1.194052

It is obvious therefore that if the rate of interest per period is represented by i, the statement immediately above may be recast as follows:

Compound amount at end of first 6 months	$\$1.03 = (1 + i)$
Compound amount at end of second 6 months	$1.0609 = (1 + i)^2$
Compound amount at end of third 6 months	$1.092727 = (1 + i)^3$
Compound amount at end of fourth 6 months	$1.125509 = (1 + i)^4$
Compound amount at end of fifth 6 months	$1.159274 = (1 + i)^5$
Compound amount at end of sixth 6 months	$1.194052 = (1 + i)^6$

Thus the compound amount of \$1,500 for 3 years at 6%, converted seminannually, is

$$\$1{,}500 \times 1.194052 = \underline{\underline{\$1{,}791.08}}$$

The difference between the compound amount and the original principal is the compound interest.

Compound amount, end of 3 years	\$1,791.08
Principal at beginning	1,500.00
Compound interest	\$ 291.08

Similarly for n periods the compound amount for \$1 in $FVIF_{i,n} = (1 + i)^n$. In this formula

$$FVIF_{i,n} = \text{compound amount of \$1}$$
$$i = \text{interest rate}$$
$$n = \text{number of periods}$$

The compound amount of any given number of dollars can then be found easily by multiplying the principal by the value of $(1 + i)^n$. In general terms.

$$A = P(1 + i)^n = P \times FVIF_{i,n}$$

where A = compound amount
P = principal (i.e., initial investment)

Computing Compound Value Using Tables. The arithmetical method for finding the compound amount is obviously too cumbersome. The formula may be solved either through the use of prepared tables or by use of a calculator. Exhibit 4 gives the compound amount of \$1 for periods from 1 to 60 for various interest rates. The use of the table is illustrated below.

EXHIBIT 4 FUTURE VALUE OF $1 AT THE END OF *n* PERIODS

$FVIF_{i,n} = (1 + i)^n$

Period	1%	2%	3%	4%	5%	6%	7%	8%	9%	10%	12%	14%	15%	16%	18%	20%	24%	28%	32%	36%
1	1.0100	1.0200	1.0300	1.0400	1.0500	1.0600	1.0700	1.0800	1.0900	1.1000	1.1200	1.1400	1.1500	1.1600	1.1800	1.2000	1.2400	1.2800	1.3200	1.3600
2	1.0201	1.0404	1.0609	1.0816	1.1025	1.1236	1.1449	1.1664	1.1881	1.2100	1.2544	1.2996	1.3225	1.3456	1.3924	1.4400	1.5376	1.6384	1.7424	1.8496
3	1.0303	1.0612	1.0927	1.1249	1.1576	1.1910	1.2250	1.2597	1.2950	1.3310	1.4049	1.4815	1.5209	1.5609	1.6430	1.7280	1.9066	2.0972	2.3000	2.5155
4	1.0406	1.0824	1.1255	1.1699	1.2155	1.2625	1.3108	1.3605	1.4116	1.4641	1.5735	1.6890	1.7490	1.8106	1.9388	2.0736	2.3642	2.6844	3.0360	3.4210
5	1.0510	1.1041	1.1593	1.2167	1.2763	1.3382	1.4026	1.4693	1.5386	1.6105	1.7623	1.9254	2.0114	2.1003	2.2878	2.4883	2.9316	3.4360	4.0075	4.6526
6	1.0615	1.1262	1.1941	1.2653	1.3401	1.4185	1.5007	1.5869	1.6771	1.7716	1.9738	2.1950	2.3131	2.4364	2.6996	2.9860	3.6352	4.3980	5.2899	6.3275
7	1.0721	1.1487	1.229	1.3159	1.4071	1.5036	1.6058	1.7138	1.8280	1.9487	2.2107	2.5023	2.6600	2.8262	3.1855	3.5832	4.5077	5.6295	6.9826	8.6054
8	1.0829	1.1717	1.2668	1.3686	1.4775	1.5938	1.7182	1.8509	1.9926	2.1436	2.4760	2.8526	3.0590	3.2784	3.7589	4.2998	5.5895	7.2058	9.2170	11.703
9	1.0937	1.1951	1.3048	1.4233	1.5513	1.6895	1.8385	1.9990	2.1719	2.3579	2.7731	3.2519	3.5179	3.8030	4.4355	5.1598	6.9310	9.2234	12.166	15.916
10	1.1046	1.2190	1.3439	1.4802	1.6289	1.7903	1.9672	2.1589	2.3674	1.4937	3.1058	3.7072	4.0456	4.4114	5.2338	6.1917	8.5944	11.805	16.059	21.646
11	1.1157	1.2434	1.3842	1.5395	1.7103	1.8983	2.1049	2.3316	2.5804	2.8531	3.4785	4.2262	4.6524	5.1173	6.1759	7.4301	10.657	15.111	21.198	29.439
12	1.1268	1.2682	1.4258	1.6010	1.7959	2.0122	2.2522	2.5182	2.8127	3.1384	3.8960	4.8179	5.3502	5.9360	7.2876	8.9161	13.214	19.342	27.982	40.037
13	1.1381	1.2936	1.4685	1.6651	1.8856	2.1329	2.4098	2.7196	3.0658	3.4523	4.3635	5.4924	6.1528	6.8858	8.5994	10.699	16.386	24.758	36.937	54.451
14	1.1495	1.3195	1.5126	1.7317	1.9799	2.2609	2.5785	2.9372	3.3417	3.7975	4.8871	6.2613	7.0757	7.9875	10.147	12.839	20.319	31.691	48.756	74.053
15	1.1610	1.3459	1.5580	1.8009	2.0789	2.3966	2.7590	3.1722	3.6425	4.1772	5.4736	7.1379	8.1371	9.2655	11.973	15.407	25.195	40.564	64.358	100.71
16	1.1726	1.3728	1.6047	1.8730	2.1829	2.5404	2.9522	3.4259	3.9703	4.5950	6.1304	8.1372	9.3576	10.748	14.129	18.488	31.242	51.923	84.953	136.96
17	1.1843	1.4002	1.6528	1.9479	2.2920	2.6928	3.1588	3.7000	4.3276	5.0545	6.8660	9.2765	10.761	12.467	16.672	22.186	38.740	66.461	112.13	186.27
18	1.1961	1.4282	1.7024	2.0258	2.4066	2.8543	3.3799	3.9960	4.7171	5.5599	7.6900	10.575	12.375	14.462	19.673	26.623	48.038	85.070	148.02	253.33
19	1.2081	1.4568	1.7535	2.1068	2.5270	3.0256	3.6165	4.3157	5.1417	6.1159	8.6128	12.055	14.231	16.776	23.214	31.948	59.567	108.89	195.39	344.53
20	1.2202	1.4859	1.8061	2.1911	2.6533	3.2071	3.8697	4.6610	5.6044	6.7275	9.6463	13.743	16.366	19.460	27.393	38.337	73.864	139.37	257.91	468.57
21	1.2324	1.5157	1.8603	2.2788	2.7860	3.3996	4.1406	5.0338	6.1088	7.4002	10.803	15.667	18.281	22.574	32.323	46.005	91.591	178.40	340.44	637.26
22	1.2447	1.5460	1.9161	2.3699	2.9253	3.6035	4.4304	5.4365	6.6586	8.1403	12.100	17.861	21.644	26.186	38.142	55.206	113.57	228.35	449.39	866.67
23	1.2572	1.5769	1.9736	2.4647	3.0715	3.8197	4.7405	5.8715	7.2579	8.9543	13.552	20.361	24.891	30.376	45.007	66.257	140.83	292.30	593.19	1178.6
24	1.2697	1.6084	2.0328	2.5633	3.2251	4.0489	5.0724	6.3412	7.9111	9.8497	15.178	23.212	28.625	35.236	53.108	79.496	174.63	374.14	783.02	1802.9
25	1.2824	1.6406	2.0938	2.6658	3.3864	4.2919	5.4274	6.8485	8.6231	10.834	17.000	26.461	32.918	40.874	62.668	95.396	216.54	478.90	1033.5	2180.0
26	1.2953	1.6734	2.1566	2.7725	3.5557	4.5494	5.8074	7.3964	9.3992	11.918	19.040	30.166	37.856	47.414	73.948	114.47	268.51	612.99	1364.3	2964.9
27	1.3082	1.7069	2.2213	2.8834	3.7335	4.8223	6.2139	7.9881	10.245	13.110	21.324	34.389	43.535	55.000	87.259	137.37	332.95	784.63	1800.9	4032.2
28	1.3213	1.7410	2.2879	2.9987	3.9201	5.1117	6.6488	8.6271	11.167	14.421	23.883	39.204	50.065	63.800	102.96	164.84	412.86	1004.3	2377.2	5488.8
29	1.3345	1.7758	2.3566	3.1187	4.1161	5.4184	7.1143	9.3173	12.172	15.863	26.749	44.693	57.575	74.008	121.50	197.81	511.95	1285.5	3137.9	7458.0
30	1.3478	1.8114	2.4273	3.2434	4.3219	5.7435	7.6123	10.062	13.267	17.449	29.959	50.950	66.211	85.849	143.37	237.37	634.81	1645.5	4142.0	10143.
40	1.4889	2.2080	3.2620	4.8010	7.0400	10.285	14.974	21.724	31.409	45.259	93.050	188.88	267.86	378.72	750.37	1469.7	5455.9	19426.	66520.	—[a]
50	1.6446	2.6916	4.3839	7.1067	11.467	18.420	29.457	46.901	74.357	117.39	289.00	700.23	1083.6	1670.7	3927.3	9100.4	46890.	—[a]	—[a]	—[a]
60	1.8167	3.2810	5.8916	10.519	18.679	32.987	57.946	101.25	176.03	304.48	897.59	2595.9	4383.9	7370.1	20555.	56347.	—[a]	—[a]	—[a]	—[a]

[a] $FVIF > 99999$.

Example. Find the compound amount of $2,634.56 for 12 years at 5% annually.

$$A = P \times (1 + i)^n$$
$$= \$2{,}634.56 \times 1.05^{12}$$

Locate the 5% column in Exhibit 4, run down the column to the twelfth period. The figure on that line represents the compound amount of $1 for 12 years at 5% in short, 1.05^{12}. Hence,

$$A = \$2{,}634.56 \times 1.7959$$
$$= \underline{\$4{,}731.41}$$

Computing Compound Value Using a Financial Calculator. The calculator is very accurate and can handle larger ranges of both interest rates and number of time periods. For the example just discussed, the keystrokes are:

Keystroke	Display	Comment
fFIN	0.00	Clear
fREG	0.00	Clear
2634.56	2,634.56	Principal
PV	2,634.56	—
5	5	—
i	5.00	Interest rate
12	12	—
n	12.00	Number of periods
FV	−4,731.29	—
CHS	4,731.29	Compound amount

Computing Compound Value Using a Microcomputer Spreadsheet
Note: Spreadsheet solutions are presented in three columns. The first column gives the cell reference; the second column presents the cell's content; the third column is reserved for explanations. Illustrations of what the screen should look like immediately follow instructions

Cell Address	Cell Content	Explanation
A1	'Principal	Label
C1	2634.56	Principal
A2	'Interest	Label
C2	0.05	Interest
A3	'# of periods	Label
C3	12	Number of periods
A4	'Compound Value	Label
C4	@Round (C1*(1 + C2)^C3,2)	Compound Value Equation

Illustration

	A	B	C	D
1	Principal		2634.56	
2	Interest		0.05	
3	# of Periods		12	
4	Compound Value		4731.29	
5				
6				

PRESENT VALUE. The general formula $A = P(1 + i)^n$ may be used to find any of the variables contained in it. The most common converse case is finding the present value [P]. This is the value at the present moment of money due at a future time. It is the reciprocal of the compound amount, and may also be defined as that sum of money that, when placed at compound interest for the full number of periods involved, will amount to the given sum.

Example. $1,500 at compound interest for six periods at 3% per period will amount to $1,791.08. Hence the present worth of $1,791.08 due six periods hence at 3% per period compounded is $1,500.

The formula for the present value of $1 is:

$$PVIF_{i,n} = \frac{1}{(1 + i)^n}$$

where $PVIF_{i,n}$ = present value of $1
i = interest rate
n = number of periods

The formula for the present value of any number of dollars (A) is:

$$P = A\frac{1}{(1 + i)^n}$$

that is,

$$A \times PVIF_{i,n}$$

This formula is used whenever prepared present value tables are available. When, because of table limitations, direct calculation must be used, the formula is more convenient for computation when written in the form

$$P = \frac{A}{(1+i)^n}$$

where A = given sum (i.e., the compound amount, the end value after n conversion periods)
P = present value (the initial investment)

Computing Present Value Using Tables. Exhibit 5 shows the present value of \$1 for a number of interest rates for 1 to 60 periods. The use of the table is illustrated below.

Example. Find the present value of \$6,975 received 5 years from now at 10% per annum. Locate the 10% column in Exhibit 5 and run down the column to the sixth period: the present value of \$1 for 6 periods is seen to be \$0.5645:

$$P = A \times \frac{1}{(1+i)^n}$$

$$P = 6{,}975 \times 0.5645 = \underline{\underline{\$3{,}937.21}}$$

The difference between the present value and the given compound amount is sometimes called the **compound discount.** In the illustration above, the compound discount is

$$\$6{,}975 - \$3{,}937.21 = \underline{\underline{\$3{,}037.79}}$$

The compound discount represents the amount of interest that \$3,937.21 would earn in 6 years at 10% per annum.

Computing Present Value Using a Financial Calculator. The keystrokes for the calculator to compute the present value in the example above would be:

Keystroke	Display	Comment
fFIN	0.00	Clear
fREG	0.00	Clear
6975	6,975	—
FV	6,975.00	Future value
10	10	—
i	10.00	Interest rate
6	6	—
n	6.00	Number of periods
PV	−3,937.21	—
CHS	3,937.21	Present value

EXHIBIT 5 PRESENT VALUE OF $1
$PVIF = 1/(1 + i)^n$

Period	1%	2%	3%	4%	5%	6%	7%	8%	9%	10%	12%	14%	15%	16%	18%	20%	24%	28%	32%	36%
1	.9901	.9804	.9709	.9615	.9524	.9434	.9346	.9259	.9174	.9091	.8929	.8772	.8696	.8621	.8475	.8333	.8065	.7813	.7576	.7353
2	.9803	.9612	.9426	.9246	.9070	.8900	.8734	.8573	.8417	.8264	.7972	.7695	.7561	.7432	.7182	.6944	.6504	.6104	.5739	.5407
3	.9706	.9423	.9151	.8890	.8638	.8396	.8163	.7938	.7722	.7513	.7118	.6750	.6575	.6407	.6086	.5787	.5245	.4768	.4348	.3975
4	.9610	.9238	.8885	.8548	.8227	.7921	.7629	.7350	.7084	.6830	.6355	.5921	.5718	.5523	.5158	.4823	.4230	.3725	.3294	.2923
5	.9515	.9057	.8626	.8219	.7835	.7473	.7130	.6806	.6499	.6209	.5674	.5194	.4972	.4761	.4371	.4019	.3411	.2910	.2495	.2149
6	.9420	.8880	.8375	.7903	.7462	.7050	.6663	.6302	.5963	.5645	.5066	.4556	.4323	.4104	.3704	.3349	.2751	.2274	.1890	.1580
7	.9327	.8706	.8131	.7599	.7107	.6651	.6227	.5835	.5470	.5132	.4523	.3996	.3759	.3538	.3139	.2791	.2218	.1776	.1432	.1162
8	.9235	.8535	.7894	.7307	.6768	.6274	.5820	.5403	.5019	.4665	.4039	.3506	.3269	.3050	.2660	.2326	.1789	.1388	.1085	.0854
9	.9143	.8368	.7664	.7026	.6446	.5919	.5439	.5002	.4604	.4241	.3606	.3075	.2843	.2630	.2255	.1938	.1443	.1084	.0822	.0628
10	.9053	.8203	.7441	.6756	.6139	.5584	.5083	.4632	.4224	.3855	.3220	.2697	.2472	.2267	.1911	.1615	.1164	.0847	.0623	.0462
11	.8963	.8043	.7224	.6496	.5847	.5268	.4751	.4289	.3875	.3505	.2875	.2366	.2149	.1954	.1619	.1346	.0938	.0662	.0472	.0340
12	.8874	.7885	.7014	.6246	.5568	.4970	.4440	.3971	.3555	.3186	.2567	.2076	.1869	.1685	.1372	.1122	.0757	.0517	.0357	.0250
13	.8787	.7730	.6810	.6006	.5303	.4688	.4150	.3677	.3262	.2897	.2292	.1821	.1625	.1452	.1163	.0935	.0610	.0404	.0271	.0184
14	.8700	.7579	.6611	.5775	.5051	.4423	.3878	.3405	.2992	.2633	.2046	.1597	.1413	.1252	.0985	.0779	.0492	.0316	.0205	.0135
15	.8613	.7430	.6419	.5553	.4810	.4173	.3624	.3152	.2745	.2394	.1827	.1401	.1229	.1079	.0835	.0649	.0397	.0247	.0155	.0099
16	.8528	.7284	.6232	.5339	.4581	.3936	.3387	.2919	.2519	.2176	.1631	.1229	.1069	.0930	.0708	.0541	.0320	.0193	.0118	.0073
17	.8444	.7142	.6050	.5134	.4363	.3714	.3166	.2703	.2311	.1978	.1456	.1078	.0929	.0802	.0600	.0451	.0258	.0150	.0089	.0054
18	.8360	.7002	.5874	.4936	.4155	.3503	.2959	.2502	.2120	.1799	.1300	.0946	.0808	.0691	.0508	.0376	.0208	.0118	.0068	.0039
19	.8277	.6864	.5703	.4746	.3957	.3305	.2765	.2317	.1945	.1635	.1161	.0829	.0703	.0596	.0431	.0313	.0168	.0092	.0051	.0029
20	.8195	.6730	.5537	.4564	.3769	.3118	.2584	.2145	.1784	.1486	.1037	.0728	.0611	.0514	.0365	.0261	.0135	.0072	.0039	.0021
25	.7798	.6095	.4776	.3751	.2953	.2330	.1842	.1460	.1160	.0923	.0588	.0378	.0304	.0245	.0160	.0105	.0046	.0021	.0010	.0005
30	.7419	.5521	.4120	.3083	.2314	.1741	.1314	.0994	.0754	.0573	.0334	.0196	.0151	.0116	.0070	.0042	.0016	.0006	.0002	.0001
40	.6717	.4529	.3066	.2083	.1420	.0972	.0668	.0460	.0318	.0221	.0107	.0053	.0037	.0026	.0013	.0007	.0002	.0001	—[a]	—[a]
50	.6080	.3715	.2281	.1407	.0872	.0543	.0339	.0213	.0134	.0085	.0035	.0014	.0009	.0006	.0003	.0001	—[a]	—[a]	—[a]	—[a]
60	.5504	.3048	.1697	.0951	.0535	.0303	.0173	.0099	.0057	.0033	.0011	.0004	.0002	.0001	—[a]	—[a]	—[a]	—[a]	—[a]	—[a]

[a] The factor is zero to four decimal places.

Computing Present Value Using a Spreadsheet (Built-in NPV Function)

Cell Address	Cell Content	Explanation
A1	'Payments	Label
C1	'Rate	Label
E1	'NPV	Label
A2	0	Payment
C2	0.1	Interest Rate
E2	@NPV (C2,A2. .A7)	Present Value
A3	0	Payment
A4	0	Payment
A5	0	Payment
A6	0	Payment
A7	6975	Payment

Illustration

	A	B	C	D	E
1	Payments		Rate		NPV
	0		0.1		3937.21
2	0				
3	0				
4	0				
5	0				
6	6975				

Note: Alternatively, the NPV equation can be used in place of the built-in function.

OTHER CONVERSE CASES. Occasionally it becomes necessary to find how long it will take for a given sum to amount to another sum at some future time; or what interest rate is being realized on a given principal. In short, the problem is to find n or i in the general formula. These may be found either by interpolation in a table or by using a spreadsheet.

Finding Value of n. There are two methods for finding n. These are illustrated to solve the following problem: how long will it take for $765 to amount to $1,350 if money is worth 8% per annum?

Computing n Using Tables. In Exhibit 4, in the 8% column, locate the number of periods for which $FVIF_{i,n}$ is closest to 1,350/765 = 1.7647. It is between 7 and 8 years. By **linear interpolation,** the period n can be computed as follows:

Year	$FVIF_{i,n}$
7	1.7138
8	1.8509
?	1.7647

$$n = 7 + \frac{1.7647 - 1.7138}{1.8509 - 1.7138}$$
$$= \underline{\underline{7.37 \text{ years}}}$$

This calculation is only approximate, since the true relationship between $FVIF_{i,n}$ and n is nonlinear, not linear as assumed here.

Computing n Using a Financial Calculator. The number n can be determined exactly (without rounding errors) using the financial calculator without resorting to the linear interpolation approximation method, above. The keystrokes for this example would be:

Keystroke	Display	Comment
fFIN	0.00	Clear
fREG	0.00	Clear
1350	1,350	—
FV	1,350.00	Future value
765	765	—
CHS	−765.00	—
PV	−765.00	Present value
8	8	—
i	8.00	Interest rate
n	7.38	Number of periods

Computing n Using a Spreadsheet

Cell Address	Cell Content	Explanation
A1	'Future Value	Label
C1	1350	Future Value
A2	'Present Value	Label
C2	765	Present Value
A3	'Interest Rate	Label
C3	0.08	Interest Rate
A4	'Number of Periods	Label
C4	@Log (C1/C2)/ @Log (1 + C3)	Number of Periods

Illustration

	A	B	C
1	Future Value		1350.0
2	Present Value		765.0
3	Interest Rate		0.08
4	Number of Periods		7.38
5			
6			

Finding Value of i. The methods of the solution by interpolation and using a calculator are illustrated below.

Example. Find the yield on U.S. government bonds sold at \$18.75 redeemable in 10 years for \$25.

Computing i Using Tables. Proceed as in the previous solution.

$$(1+i)^{10} = \frac{25}{18.75} = 1.3333$$

Now look in Exhibit 4 on the tenth period line and find values on that line just above and below 1.3333. The value is evidently between 2% and 3%. The computation is as follows:

Interest Rate	$FVIF_{i,n}$
2	1.2190
3	1.3439
?	1.3333

$$\begin{aligned} i &= 2 + \frac{1.3333 - 1.2190}{1.3439 - 1.2190} \\ &= 2.92\% \end{aligned}$$

Again, the foregoing calculation is only approximate because a linear relationship has been assumed, rather than a nonlinear relationship, between $FVIF_{i,n}$ and *i*.

Computing i Using a Financial Calculator. The keystrokes for the calculation are:

Keystroke	Display	Comment
fFIN	0.00	Clear
fREG	0.00	Clear
18.75	18.75	—
PV	18.75	Present value
25	25	—
CHS	−25	—
FV	−25.00	Compound value
10	10	—
r	10.00	Number of years
i	2.92	Interest rate

Computing i Using a Spreadsheet

Cell Address	Cell Content	Explanation
A1	'Present Value	Label
C1	18.75	Present Value
A2	'Future Value	Label
C2	25	Future Value
A3	'Number of Periods	Label
C3	10	Number of Periods
A4	'Interest	Label
C4	(−1((C2/C1)^(1/C3)))*100	Interest Rate

Illustration

	A	B	C
1	Present Value		18.75
2	Future Value		25.0
3	Number of Periods		10
4	Interest		2.92
5			
6			

ANNUITIES

Definitions. An annuity is the payment of a fixed sum of money at uniform intervals of time. An example of an annuity is rent on the use of property. Payments of annuities are commonly called **rents.**

Ordinary Annuity. An ordinary annuity is a series of equal payments each of which is made at the end of a period of time.

Annuity Due. An annuity due is one in which the payments are due at the beginning of each payment period. A life insurance premium is an example of an annuity due, since such premiums are always payable in advance.

Deferred Annuity. A deferred annuity is one in which payments are due after a number of periods have elapsed.

Amount or Final Value of Annuity. The total of all annuity payments made, together with the interest earned by these payments, is the amount of annuity. It is technically referred to as the final value of an annuity.

Perpetuity. An annuity in which the payments continue without end is a perpetuity. An example of this type is to be found in the payments made from endowment funds.

Life Annuity. An annuity whose duration depends on the life expectancy this means that six annual payments of one or more persons is called a contingent or life annuity.

Annuity Certain. This is an annuity that has a definite number of periods to run.

Example. A mortgage on a piece of property is to be paid off through 20 equal quarterly payments beginning 4 years from the present time. This is an ordinary annuity deferred 4 years; it is certain because it runs for 5 years, once it becomes effective.

Final Value of Ordinary Annuity. The total accumulation of an annuity may be illustrated by reference to the following example:

Example. What is the **accumulated value** of an annuity of $200 per year for 5 years if the annual interest rate is 14% and the annuity is paid **at the end** of each year?

Payment end of first year	$ 200.00
Interest second year (14%)	28.00
Payment end of second year	200.00
Total end of second year	$ 428.00
Interest third year	59.92
Payment end of third year	200.00
Total end of third year	$ 687.92
Interest fourth year	96.31
Payment end of fourth year	200.00
Total end of fourth year	$ 984.23
Interest fifth year	137.79
Payment end of fifth year	200.00
Total accumulation (final value)	$1,322.02

In effect, the final value of an annuity is the sum of the compound amounts of the individual payments. Thus as shown below, the first payment made at the end of the year bears interest for 4 years, the second for 3 years.

	1	2	3	4	5
Payments (end of each year)	$1	$1	$1	$1	$1
Compound amount (end of fifth year)	1.14^4	1.14^3	1.14^2	1.14	1
Total value (Exhibit 5)	1.6890 +	1.4815 +	1.2990 +	1.140 +	1 = $6.6095

Assuming money is worth 14%, the compound amount of each $1 payment is shown underneath the payments. When the values are totaled, it is found that an ordinary annuity of $1 per year annually for 5 years at 14% amounts to $6.6101. For an annuity of $200 under these conditions, the final amount is

$$200 \times 6.6095 = \$1{,}322.02$$

Instead of laboriously calculating the compound amount of each payment, recourse may be had to prepared annuity tables (Exhibit 6). Thus in the illustration above, the answer may be found directly in the 14% column of line 5 of Exhibit 6.

Formula for Compound Value of an Annuity. The symbol for the final value of an ordinary annuity of $1 per annum is $FVIFA_{i,n}$.

$$FVIFA_{i,n} = (1+i)^{n-1} + (1+i)^{n-2} + \cdots + (1+i) + 1$$

$$= \sum_{t=1}^{n} (1+i)^{n-1}$$

$$= \frac{(1+i)^n - 1}{i}$$

where i = interest rate
n = number of periods

The numerator of the fraction is evidently the compound interest for n periods.

$$FVIFA_{i,n} = \frac{\text{compound interest}}{\text{interest rate}}$$

The final value for any number of dollars is expressed by the following formula:

$$A = R \times FVIFA_{i,n}$$

where A = final value of annuity
R = amount of each payment

Example. Find the final value of an annuity of $2,000 received quarterly for 5 years when invested at 8% per annum.

Computing Compound Value of Annuity Using Tables. Proceed as follows:

$$A = R \times FVIFA_{i,n}$$
$$A = 2{,}000 \times FVIFA_{2,20}$$

Note that interest is at 2% per period for 20 periods; hence look for the value in the 2% column, line 20 of Exhibit 6. Therefore,

$$A = \$2{,}000 \times 24.297 = \underline{\underline{\$48{,}594}}$$

Computing Compound Value of Annuity Using a Financial Calculator. The keystrokes are as follows:

Keystroke	Display	Comment
fFIN	0.00	Clear
fREG		Clear
2000	2,000	—
CHS	−2,000	—
PMT	−2,000	Annuity amount
2	2	—
i	2.00	Interest rate
20	20	—
n	20.00	Number of periods
FV	48,594.74	Compound amount

Computing Compound Value of Annuity Using a Spreadsheet (built-in function)

Cell Address	Cell Content	Explanation
A1	'Payment	Label
C1	2000	Payment
A2	'Interest	Label
C2	0.02	Interest Rate
A3	'Term	Label
C3	20	Term
A4	'Future Value	Label
C4	@FV (C1,C2,C3)	Future Label

Illustration

	A	B	C
1	Payment		2000
2	Interest		0.02
3	Term		20
4	Future Value		48594.73
5			
6			

SINKING FUND CALCULATIONS. Sinking funds are commonly used to accumulate, by periodic contributions, sufficient amounts for the extinction of a debt or the replacementof an asset. In the latter event, the fund is more generally referred to as a **replacement fund.** In either instance the periodic payments are annuity rentals. Many bond issues of both private and municipal corporations are of the sinking fund type. The payments are usually turned

EXHIBIT 6 SUM OF AN ANNUITY OF $1 PER PERIOD FOR *n* PERIODS

$$FVIFA_{i,n} = \sum_{t-1}^{n} (1+i)^{n-t} = \frac{(1+i)^n - 1}{1}$$

Number of Periods	1%	2%	3%	4%	5%	6%	7%	8%	9%	10%	12%	14%	15%	16%	18%	20%	24%	28%	32%	36%
1	1.0000	1.0000	1.0000	1.0000	1.0000	1.0000	1.0000	1.0000	1.0000	1.0000	1.0000	1.0000	1.0000	1.0000	1.0000	1.0000	1.0000	1.0000	1.0000	1.0000
2	2.0100	2.0200	2.0300	2.0400	2.0500	2.0600	2.0700	2.0800	2.0900	2.1000	2.1200	2.1400	2.1500	2.1600	2.1800	2.2000	2.2400	2.2800	2.3200	2.3600
3	3.0301	3.0604	3.0909	3.1216	3.1525	3.1836	3.2149	3.2464	3.2781	3.3100	3.3744	3.4396	3.4725	3.5056	3.5724	3.6400	3.7776	3.9184	4.0624	4.2096
4	4.0604	4.1216	4.1836	4.2465	4.3101	4.3746	4.4399	4.5061	4.5731	4.6410	4.7793	4.9211	4.9934	5.0665	5.2154	5.3680	5.6842	6.0156	6.3624	6.7251
5	5.1010	5.2040	5.3091	5.4163	5.5256	5.6371	5.7507	5.8666	5.9847	6.1051	6.3528	6.6101	6.7424	6.8771	7.1542	7.4416	8.0484	8.6999	9.3983	10.146
6	6.1520	6.3081	6.4684	6.6330	6.8019	6.9753	7.1533	7.3359	7.5233	7.7156	8.1152	8.5355	8.7537	8.9775	9.4420	9.9299	10.980	12.135	13.405	14.798
7	7.2135	7.4343	7.6625	7.8983	8.1420	8.3938	8.6540	8.9228	9.2004	9.4872	10.089	10.730	11.066	11.413	12.141	12.915	14.615	16.533	18.695	21.126
8	8.2857	8.5830	8.8923	9.2142	9.5491	9.8975	10.259	10.636	11.028	11.435	12.299	13.232	13.726	14.240	15.327	16.499	19.122	22.163	25.698	29.731
9	9.3685	9.7546	10.159	10.582	11.026	11.491	11.978	12.487	13.021	13.579	14.775	16.085	16.785	17.518	19.085	20.798	24.712	29.369	34.895	41.435
10	10.462	10.949	11.463	12.006	12.577	13.180	13.816	14.486	15.192	15.937	17.548	19.337	20.303	21.321	23.521	25.958	31.643	38.592	47.061	57.351
11	11.566	12.168	12.807	13.486	14.206	14.971	15.783	16.645	17.560	18.531	20.654	23.044	24.349	25.732	28.755	32.150	40.237	50.398	63.121	78.998
12	12.682	13.412	14.192	15.025	15.917	16.869	17.888	18.977	20.140	21.384	24.133	27.270	29.001	30.850	34.931	39.580	50.894	65.510	84.320	108.43
13	13.809	14.680	15.617	16.626	17.713	18.882	20.140	21.495	22.953	24.522	28.029	32.088	34.351	36.786	42.218	48.496	64.109	84.852	112.30	148.47
14	14.947	15.973	17.086	18.291	19.598	21.015	22.550	24.214	26.019	27.975	32.392	37.581	40.504	43.672	50.818	59.195	80.496	109.61	149.23	202.92
15	16.096	17.293	18.598	20.023	21.578	23.276	25.129	27.152	29.360	31.772	37.279	43.842	47.580	51.659	60.965	72.035	100.81	141.30	197.99	276.97
16	17.257	18.639	20.156	21.824	23.657	25.672	27.888	30.324	33.003	35.949	42.753	50.980	55.717	60.925	72.939	87.442	126.01	181.86	262.35	377.69
17	18.430	20.012	21.761	23.697	25.840	28.212	30.840	33.750	36.973	40.544	48.883	59.117	65.075	71.673	87.068	105.93	157.25	233.79	347.30	514.66
18	19.614	21.412	23.414	25.645	28.132	30.905	33.999	37.450	41.301	45.599	55.749	68.394	75.836	84.140	103.74	128.11	195.99	300.25	459.44	700.93
19	20.810	22.840	25.116	27.671	30.539	33.760	37.379	41.446	46.018	51.159	63.439	78.969	88.211	98.603	123.41	154.74	244.03	385.32	607.47	954.27
20	22.019	24.297	26.870	29.778	33.066	36.785	40.995	45.762	51.160	57.275	72.052	91.024	102.44	115.37	146.62	180.68	303.60	494.21	802.86	1298.8
21	23.239	25.783	28.676	31.969	35.719	39.992	44.865	50.422	56.764	64.002	81.698	104.76	118.81	134.84	174.02	225.02	377.46	633.59	1060.7	1767.3
22	24.471	27.299	30.536	34.248	38.505	43.392	49.005	55.456	62.873	71.402	92.502	120.43	137.63	157.41	206.34	271.03	469.05	811.99	1401.2	2404.6
23	25.716	28.845	32.452	36.617	41.430	46.995	53.436	60.893	69.531	79.543	104.60	138.29	159.27	183.60	244.48	326.23	582.62	1040.3	1850.6	3271.3
24	26.973	30.421	34.426	39.082	44.502	50.815	58.176	66.764	76.789	88.497	118.15	158.65	184.16	213.97	289.49	392.48	723.46	1332.6	2443.8	4449.9
25	28.243	32.030	36.459	41.645	47.727	54.864	63.249	73.105	84.700	98.347	133.38	181.87	212.79	249.21	342.60	471.98	898.09	1706.8	3226.8	6052.9
26	29.525	33.670	38.553	44.311	51.113	59.156	68.676	79.954	93.323	109.18	150.33	208.33	245.71	290.08	405.27	567.37	1114.6	2185.7	4260.4	8233.0
27	30.820	35.344	40.709	47.084	54.669	63.705	74.483	87.350	102.72	121.09	169.37	238.49	283.56	337.50	479.22	681.85	1388.1	2798.7	5624.7	11197.9
28	32.129	37.051	42.930	49.967	58.402	68.523	80.697	95.338	112.96	134.20	190.69	272.88	327.10	392.50	566.48	819.22	1716.0	3583.3	7425.6	15230.2
29	33.450	38.792	45.218	52.966	62.322	73.639	87.346	103.96	124.13	148.63	214.58	312.09	377.16	456.30	669.44	984.06	2128.9	4587.6	9802.9	20714.1
30	34.784	40.568	47.575	56.084	66.438	79.058	94.460	113.28	136.30	164.49	241.33	356.78	434.74	530.31	790.94	1181.8	2640.9	5873.2	12940.	28172.2
40	48.886	60.402	75.401	95.025	120.79	154.76	199.63	259.05	337.88	442.59	767.09	1342.0	1779.0	2360.7	4163.2	7343.8	22728.	69377.	—[a]	—[a]
50	64.463	84.579	112.79	152.66	209.34	290.33	406.52	573.76	815.08	1163.9	2400.0	4994.5	7217.7	10435.	21813.	45497.	—[a]	—[a]	—[a]	—[a]
60	81.669	114.05	163.05	237.99	353.58	533.12	813.52	1253.2	1944.7	3034.8	7471.6	18535.	29219.	46057.	—[a]	—[a]	—[a]	—[a]	—[a]	—[a]

[a] *FVFIFA* >99999.

over to a trustee or municipal sinking fund commission that invests these amounts and accumulates them to maturity or uses them to retire some of the bonds each year. In some issues, no part of the debt is extinguished until maturity even if the trustee invests his receipts in the bonds to be redeemed. In the latter case, he merely collects the coupons and adds the interest to the sinking fund just as in the case of investment in any other bonds.

There are two mathematical problems involved in the **flotation** of sinking fund bond issues. The first is one of determining what sum shall be set aside periodically to provide the required amount at maturity. The other problem is concerned with determining the life span of the bond issues once the size of the periodic sinking fund payment the corporation can afford to make is known. These are presented below.

Finding Amount of Sinking Fund Installments. Determination of the installment or rent necessary to be set aside periodically is equivalent to finding R in the annuity formula.

$$R = \frac{A}{FVIFA_{i,n}}$$

The value of $FVIFA_{i,n}$ can be obtained from Exhibit 6. Its reciprocal represents the periodic payment of an annuity that will amount to \$1 in n periods.

Example. A corporation on June 1, 1981, issued bonds due June 1, 1987 to the amount of \$200,000. Provision was made to set up a sinking fund to retire the entire issue by means of semiannual payments. If the fund earns 6% semiannually, what is the size of each installment? There are 12 payments compounded at 6% every 6 months.

Computing Value of Annuity Using Tables. From Exhibit 6, in the 6% column, line 12, the value of $FVIFA_{i,n}$ can be obtained.

$$R = \frac{200{,}000}{16.869} = \underline{\underline{\$11{,}856.07}}$$

Schedule of Sinking Fund Installments. The schedule below shows the periodic amounts set up and the interest earned on the accumulated balances in the sinking fund. The total semiannual installments plus the accumulated interest earned by the sinking fund equal \$200,000, the accumulated amount in the sinking fund on June 1, 1987, the date of maturity of the bonds. Note that the last figure in the last column contains a rounding error.

Date	Semiannual Installment	Interest at 6% on Accumulated Sinking Fund	Total Additions to Sinking Fund	Acculated Amounts in Sinking Fund
June 1, 1981	—	—	—	—
December 1, 1981	11,856.07	—	11,856.07	11,856.07
June 1, 1982	11,856.07	711.36	12,567.43	24,423.50
December 1, 1982	11,856.07	1,465.37	13,320.73	37,742.85
June 1, 1983	11,856.07	2,264.57	14,119.97	51,862.82
December 1, 1983	11,856.07	3,111.77	14,967.17	66,829.99
June 1, 1984	11,856.07	4,009.80	15,865.20	82,695.19
December 1, 1984	11,856.07	4,961.71	16,817.11	99,512.30
June 1, 1985	11,856.07	5,970.74	17,826.13	117,338.44
December 1, 1985	11,856.07	7,040.31	18,895.71	136,234.15
June 1, 1986	11,856.07	8,174.05	20,029.45	156,263.60
December 1, 1986	11,856.07	9,375.82	21,231.22	177,494.81
June 1, 1987	11,856.07	10,649.69	22,505.09	199,999.90

Computing Value of Annuity Using a Financial Calculator. The keystrokes are as follows:

Keystroke	Display	Comment
fFIN	0.00	Clear
fREG	0.00	Clear
200000	200,000	—
CHS	−200,000	—
FV	−200,000.00	Compound value
12	12	—
n	12.00	Number of years
6	6	—
i	6.00	Interest rate
PMT	11,855.41	Annuity amount

Computing Value of Annuity Using a Spreadsheet

Cell Address	Cell Content	Explanation
A1	'Compound Value	Label
C1	200000	Compound Value
A2	'# of Periods	Label
C2	12	# of Periods
A3	'Interest Rate	Label
C3	0.06	Interest Rate
A4	'Annuity Amount	Label
C4	+(C1*C3/((1 + C3)^C2−1)	Annuity Equation

Illustration

	A	B	C
1	Compound Value		200000.0
2	# of Periods		12
3	Interest Rate		0.06
4	Annuity Amount		11855.41
5			
6			

Finding Number of Payments in a Sinking Fund. A corporation floating a sinking fund bond issue needs to prepare a long-range budget to determine what it can spare for sinking fund payments. Once that is known, the time to build up the proper size sinking fund can easily be calculated. This involves finding the number of payments (n in the formula) from which the maturity of the bonds may be determined. The simplest solution is through interpolation using Exhibit 6.

Example. A corporation wishes to raise $300,000 through the issuance of sinking fund bonds paying 5% semiannually. It can spare $50,000 a year for sinking fund purposes and interest on the bonds. If the fund earns 4% semiannually, when should the bonds be made to mature?

Computing Number of Years Using a Spreadsheet

Cell Address	Cell Content	Explanation
A1	'Compound Value	Label
C1	300000	Compound Value
A2	'Interest Payment	Label
C2	0.05	Interest Payment
A3	'Annual Payment	Label
C3	50000	Annual Payment
A4	'Interest Rate	Label
C4	0.04	Interest Rate
A5	'# of Periods	Label
C5	@Log(((C1*C4)/(C3−(C1*C2)) + 1))/Log(1 + C4)	# of Periods

Illustration

	A	B	C
1	Compound Value		300000
2	Interest Payment		0.05
	Annual Payment		50000
3	Interest Rate		0.04
4	Number of		
5	Periods		7.52
6			

Computing Number of Years n Using Tables. This task is straightforward:

Total annual payment	\$50,000.00
Annual interest charge (300,000 × 0.05)	15,000.00
Sinking fund contribution	\$35,000.000

$$FVIFA_{i,n} = 300{,}000 \div 35{,}000$$
$$FVIFA_{i,n} = \underline{\underline{8.5714}}$$

Now look in Exhibit 6 in the 4% column for the amounts directly above and below the given figure. The time is evidently between 7 and 8 periods. Since the results are approximations in any event, only four decimals are used.

Years	$FVIFA_{i,n}$
7	7.8983
8	9.2142
?	8.5714

$$n = 7 + \frac{8.5714 - 7.8983}{9.2142 - 7.8983}$$
$$= \underline{\underline{7.52 \text{ periods}}}$$

Since bond maturities such as this are practically unknown, the borrower must decide whether the bonds are to mature in 3 or 4 years. If \$50,000 represents the limit of what the borrower can spare, the maturity must be extended to 4 years and the exact amount of R (sinking fund contribution) recalculated. If a maturity of 3 years is more desirable, the total annual burden will be greater than \$50,000 and can easily be found by the formula for R.

Computing Number of Years n Using a Financial Calculator. The keystrokes on the calculator are as follows:

Keystroke	Display	Comment
fFIN	0.00	Clear
fREG	0.00	Clear
300000	300,000	—
CHS	−300,000	—
FV	−300,000.00	Compound value
35000	35,000	—
PMT	35,000.00	—
4	4	—
i	4.00	Interest rate
n	7.52	Number of years

Final Value of Annuity Due. In the case of an annuity due, the payments are made at the end of the period, i.e., the last payment earns interest for the last period. The symbol for final value of an annuity due of \$1 is $FVIFAB_{i,n}$. The simplest formula for it is:

$$FVIFAB_{i,n} = (1+i)^n + (1+i)^{n-1} + \cdots + (1+i)^2 + (1+i)$$

$$= \sum_{t=1}^{n} (1+i)$$

$$= \sum_{t=1}^{n+1} (1+i)^{n+1-t} - 1$$

$$= FVIFA_{i,n+1} - 1$$

Example. Find the final value of an annuity due to \$6,500 for 10 years at 12%.

Computing Final Value of Annuity Due Using Tables. Start with the following formula:

$$\begin{aligned}\text{annuity due} &= R \times FVIFAB_{i,n} \\ &= \$6{,}500 \times (FVIFA_{i,n+1} - 1) \\ &= \$6{,}500 \times 19.654 \\ &= \$127{,}751\end{aligned}$$

In looking up $FVIFAB_{i,n}$ start in the 12% column in Exhibit 6, read the figure on the eleventh line, and subtract \$1: that is, look up $FVIFA_{i,n+1}$ and decrease this value by \$1, to get 19.654.

Computing Final Value of Annuity Due Using a Financial Calculator. The keystrokes are as follows:

Keystroke	Display	Comment
fFIN	0.00	Clear
fREG	0.00	Clear
6500	6,500	—
CHS	−6,500	—
PMT	−6,500.00	Annuity amount due
12	12	—
i	12.00	Interest rate
10	10	—
n	10.00	Number of periods
FV	12,7754.79	Compound amount

Computing Final Value of Annuity Due Using a Spreadsheet

Cell Address	Cell Content	Explanation
A1	'Annuity Amount Due	Label
C1	6500	Annuity Amount Due
A2	'Interest	Label
C2	0.12	Interest
A3	'Number of periods	Label
C3	10	Number of periods
A4	'Annuity Due	Label
C4	+ (C1*((((1 + C2)^(C3 + 1) − 1)/C2) − 1)	Annuity Due

Illustration

	A	B	C
1	Annuity Amount Due		6500
2	Interest		0.12
3	# of Periods		10
4	Annuity Due		127754.7
5			
6			

Present Value of Ordinary Annuity. The present value of an annuity is an amount that represents the sum of the discounted or present values of a series of equal payments made at uniform time intervals. Note that the future payments are equal, but are discounted. Hence, each payment represents in part principal and in part interest on the remaining debt. This is a contrast to final value problems, where payments are accumulated to wipe out a future debt at maturity. Hence, wherever the annuity payments represent principal and interest, the problem is one of present value.

The symbol to represent the present value of a single dollar per annum payable at the end of each year (i.e., an ordinary annuity of $1) is $PVIFA_{i,n}$. The formula is as follows:

$$PVIFA_{i,n} = \frac{1 - 1/(1+i)^n}{i}$$

$$= \frac{1 - PVIF_{i,n}}{\text{interest rate}}$$

Exhibit 7 shows the present values represented by the formula above and may therefore be used to solve present value problems. The present value of any number of dollars is represented by the following formula:

EXHIBIT 7 PRESENT VALUE OF AN ANNUITY OF $1 PER PERIOD FOR *n* PERIODS

$$PVIFA_{i,n} = \sum_{t=1}^{n} \frac{1}{(1+i)^n} = 1 - \frac{1/(1+i)^n}{i}$$

Number of Payments	1%	2%	3%	4%	5%	6%	7%	8%	9%	10%	12%	14%	15%	16%	18%	20%	24%	28%	32%
1	0.9901	0.9804	0.9709	0.9615	0,9524	0.9434	0.9346	0.9259	0.9174	0.9091	0.8929	0.8772	0.8696	0.8621	0.8475	0.8333	0.8065	0.7813	0.7576
2	1.9704	1.9416	1.9135	1.8861	1.8594	1.8334	1.8080	1.7833	1.7591	1.7355	1.6901	1.6467	1.6257	1.6052	1.5656	1.5278	1.4568	1.3916	1.3315
3	2.9410	2.8839	2.8286	2.7751	2.7232	2.6730	2.6243	2.5771	2.5313	2.4869	2.4018	2.3216	2.2832	2.2459	2.1743	2.1065	1.9813	1.8684	1.7663
4	3.9020	3.8077	3.7171	3.6299	3.5460	3.4651	3.3872	3.3121	3.2397	3.1699	3.0373	2.9137	2.8550	2.7982	2.6901	2.5887	2.4043	2.2410	2.0957
5	4.8534	4.7135	4.5797	4.4518	4.3295	4.2124	4.1002	3.9927	3.8897	3.7908	3.6048	3.4331	3.3522	3.2743	3.1272	2.9906	2.7454	2.5320	2.3452
6	5.7955	5.6014	5.4172	5.2421	5.0757	4.9173	4.7665	4.6229	4.4859	4.3553	4.1114	3.8887	3.7845	3.6847	3.4976	3.3255	3.0205	2.7594	2.5342
7	6.7282	6.4720	6.2303	6.0021	5.7864	5.5824	5.3893	5.2064	5.0330	4.8684	4.5638	4.2883	4.1604	4.0386	3.8115	3.6046	3.2423	2.9370	2.6775
8	7.6517	7.3255	7.0197	6.7327	6.4632	6.2098	5.9713	5.7466	5.5348	5.3349	4.9676	4.6389	4.4873	4.3436	4.0776	3.8372	3.4212	3.0758	2.7860
9	8.5660	8.1622	7.7861	7.4353	7.1078	6.8017	6.5152	6.2469	5.9952	5.7590	5.3282	4.9464	4.7716	4.6065	4.3030	4.0310	3.5655	3.1842	2.8681
10	9.4713	8.9826	8.5302	8.1109	7.7217	7.3601	7.0236	6.7101	6.4177	6.1446	5.6502	5.2161	5.0188	4.8332	4.4941	4.1925	3.6819	3.2689	2.9304
11	10.3676	9.7868	9.2526	8.7605	8.3064	7.8869	7.4987	7.1390	6.8052	6.4951	5.9377	5.4527	5.2337	5.0286	4.6560	4.3271	3.7757	3.3351	2.9776
12	11.2551	10.5753	9.9540	9.3851	8.8633	8.3838	7.9427	7.5361	7.1607	6.8137	6.1944	5.6603	5.4206	5.1971	4.7932	4.4392	3.8514	3.3868	3.0133
13	12.1337	11.3484	10.6350	9.9856	9.3936	8.8527	8.3577	7.9038	7.4869	7.1034	6.4235	5.8424	5.5831	5.3423	4.9095	4.5327	3.9124	3.4272	3.0404
14	13.0037	12.1062	11.2961	10.5631	9.8986	9.2950	8.7455	8.2442	7.7862	7.3667	6.6282	6.0021	5.7245	5.4675	4.0081	4.6106	3.9616	3.4587	3.0609
15	13.8651	12.8493	11.9379	11.1184	10.3797	9.7122	9.1079	8.5595	8.0607	7.6061	6.8109	6.1422	5.8474	5.5755	4.0916	4.6755	4.0013	3.4834	3.0764
16	14.7179	13.5777	12.5611	11.6523	10.8378	10.1059	9.4466	8.8514	8.3126	7.8237	6.9740	6.2651	5.9542	5.6685	5.1624	4.7296	4.0333	3.5026	3.0882
17	15.5623	14.2919	13.1661	12.1657	11.2741	10.4773	9.7632	9.1216	8.5436	8.0216	7.1196	6.3729	6.0472	5.7487	5.2223	4.7746	4.0591	3.5177	3.0971
18	16.3983	14.9920	13.7535	12.6593	11.6896	10.8276	10.0591	9.3719	8.7556	8.2014	7.2497	6.4674	6.1280	5.8178	5.2732	4.8122	4.0799	3.5294	3.1039
19	17.2260	15.6785	14.3238	13.1339	11.0853	11.1581	10.3356	9.6036	8.9501	8.3649	7.3658	6.5504	6.1982	5.8775	5.3162	4.8435	4.0967	3.5386	3.1090
20	18.0456	16.3514	14.8775	13.5903	11.4622	11.4699	10.5940	9.8181	9.1285	8.5136	7.4694	6.6231	6.2593	6.9288	5.3527	4.8696	4.1103	3.5458	3.1129
25	22.0232	19.5235	17.4131	15.6221	14.0939	12.7834	11.6536	10.6748	9.8226	9.0770	7.8431	6.8729	6.4641	6.0971	5.4669	4.9476	4.1474	3.5640	3.1220
30	25.8077	22.3965	19.6004	17.2920	15.3725	13.7648	12.4090	11.2578	10.2737	9.4269	8.0552	7.0027	6.5660	6.1772	5.5168	4.9789	4.1601	3.5693	3.1242
40	32.8347	27.3555	23.1148	19.7928	17.1591	15.0463	13.3317	11.9246	10.7574	9.7791	8.2438	7.1050	6.6418	6.2335	5.5482	4.9966	4.1659	3.5712	3.1250
50	39.1961	31.4236	25.7298	21.4822	18.2559	15.7619	13.8007	12.2335	10.9617	9.9148	8.3045	7.1327	6.6605	6.2463	5.5541	4.9995	4.1666	3.5714	3.1250
60	44.9550	34.7609	27.6756	22.6235	18.9293	16.1614	14.0392	12.3766	11.0480	9.9672	8.3240	7.1401	6.6651	6.2402	5.5553	4.9999	4.1667	3.5714	3.1250

$$A = R \times PVIFA_{i,n}$$

where A = present value of R dollars
R = amount of each annuity payment

Example. A lumber company signs a contract with a syndicate that owns a large tract of timber land. The company agrees to cut 20,000,000 feet of timber a year for 3 years and to pay $360,000 every 6 months for the cut timber. The syndicate, desiring to anticipate the payments under its contract, applies to its bankers for the cash value of the contract, offering as security the contract itself and a mortgage on the timber land. What is the present worth of the contract if the interest rate is 8% per annum, compounded semiannually?

Computing Present Value of Annuity Using a Spreadsheet

Cell Address	Cell Content	Explanation
A1	'Payment	Label
C1	360000	Payment
A2	'Interest	Label
C2	0.04	Interest
A3	'Term	Label
C3	6	Term
A4	'Present Value	Label
C4	@PV (C1,C2,C3)	Present Value (built-in function)

Illustration

	A	B	C	D
1	Payment		360000	
2	Interest		0.04	
3	Term		6	
4	Present Value		1887169	
5				
6				

Computing Present Value of Annuity Using Tables. The number of periods is 6 and the interest rate is 4% per period. The present value annuity factor $PVIFA_{i,n}$ can be determined from Exhibit 7.

$$\begin{aligned} A &= 360{,}000 \times PVIFA_{i,n} \\ &= \$360{,}000 \times 5.2421 \\ &= \underline{\underline{\$1{,}887{,}156}} \end{aligned}$$

Computing Present Value of Annuity Using a Financial Calculator. The keystrokes are:

Keystroke	Display	Comment
fFIN	0.00	Clear
fREG	0.00	Clear
360000	360,000	—
CHS	−360,000	—
PMT	−360,000.00	Annuity amount
6	6	—
n	6.00	Number of periods
4	4	—
i	4.00	Interest rate
PV	1,887,169.27	Present value

This answer represents the amount the syndicate can borrow on its contract. This means that six annual payments of $360,000 will pay off the loan and the interest on the outstanding balances. The amortization of the loan is illustrated below:

Year	Amount Outstanding at Beginning of Period	Interest at 4% on Outstanding Balance	Annuity Payment	Principal Repaid
1	$1,887,169.28	$ 75,486.77	$ 360,000.00	$ 284,513.23
2	1,602,656.05	64,106.24	360,000.00	295,893.76
3	1,306,762.29	52,270.49	360,000.00	307,729.51
4	999,032.78	39,961.31	360,000.00	320,038.69
5	678,994.09	27,159.76	360,000.00	332,840.24
6	346,153.85	13,846.15	360,000.00	346,153.85
		$272,830.72	$2,160,000.00	$1,887,169.28

Annuity That $1 Will Buy. The annuity that $1 will buy is equivalent to a series of annuity payments the sum of whose present values is $1. This type of problem is found where the size of the annuity rent (R) is to be determined. The formula is as follows:

$$R = A_n \times \frac{1}{PVIFA_{i,n}}$$

The fraction is the reciprocal of the present value of $1 and represents the annuity that $1 will purchase. The annuity factors can be obtained by taking the reciprocals of the numbers in Exhibit 7, as illustrated below.

Example 1. Mr. X buys a property for $150,000 agreeing to pay $5,000 down and the balance in 25 equal annual installments that include interest at 14%. What is the size of each installment?

The debt amounts to $100,000 after deduction of the down payment.

Computing an Annuity Amount Using Tables. From Exhibit 7, $PVIFA_{i,n}$ is found to be 6.8729 for $i = 14\%$ and $n = 25$.

$$\begin{aligned} R &= A \times \frac{1}{PVIFA_{i,n}} \\ &= \$100{,}000 \times \frac{1}{6.8729} \\ &= \underline{\underline{\$14{,}549.90}} \end{aligned}$$

Computing an Annuity Amount Using a Financial Calculator. The keystrokes for the problem are:

Keystroke	Display	Comment
fFIN	0.00	Clear
fREG	0.00	Clear
100000	100,000	—
CHS	−100,000	—
PV	−100,000.00	Present value
25	25	—
n	25.00	Number of periods
14	14	—
i	14.00	Interest rate
PMT	14,549.90	Annuity amount

Computing an Annuity Amount Using a Microcomputer Spreadsheet

Cell Address	Cell Content	Explanation
A1	'Principal	Label
C1	100000	Principal
A2	'Interest	Label
C2	0.14	Interest
A3	'Term	Label
C3	25	Term
A4	'Payment	Label
C4	@PMT (C1,C2,C3)	Annuity Amount (built-in function)

Illustration

	A	B	C
1	Principal		100000
2	Interest		0.14
3	Term		12
4	Payment		14549.84
5			
6			

Example 2. The Steel Wire Co. floated a $300,000. 12% bond issue on May 1, 1985, due May 1, 1989. Interest is payable quarterly; the bonds are in denominations of $1,000, and callable at par and accrued interest. What is the standard rent that will wipe out the debt and interest?

$$R = A \times \frac{1}{PVIFA_{i,n}}$$
$$= \$300{,}000 \times \frac{1}{12.5611}$$
$$= \underline{\underline{\$23{,}883.26}}$$

Exhibit 8 is a table of bond retirements. Since the bonds are issued in fixed denominations, the total semiannual charge cannot be exactly as stated above, but should be kept as near that figure as possible. Thus on August 1, 1985, $9,000 of the $23,883.26 is due as interest and the balance of $14,883.26 can be applied against principal outstanding. But the bonds must be retired in even amounts; in this case 15 bonds are retired. As a result, the first quarter involves an expenditure of $24,000 instead of $23,883. The excess payment is reflected in the column showing the excess or deficiency of any one period. A cumulative column is also provided; the purpose is to keep the cumulative error as low as possible. In the case of a $1,000 bond the maximum deviation from the standard charge should not exceed ±$500, that is half the value of the bond. In case the cumulative error threatens to become more than $500, it is best to redeem one bond more or less, so as to keep the error within the stated limits.

Finding Number of Payments to Amortize a Loan. If the amount that can be spared for principal and interest is known, the borrower must also know how long it will take to amortize the debt. This involves finding n, that is, the number of payments to be made.

Example. The Brass Fixture Co. on July 1, 1986 issued $300,000, 12% bonds, interest payable semiannually. The bonds are in denominations of $1,000 and are to be redeemed at par and accrued interest. How long will it take to pay them off if the corporation has budgeted $30,000 each period for interest and bond redemption?

Computing Period n Using Tables. First do the following calculations:

$$r = 6\%, \text{ semiannually}$$
$$R = A \times \frac{1}{PVIFA_{i,n}}$$

$$PVIFA_{i,n} = \frac{A}{R} = \frac{300{,}000}{30{,}000} = 10$$

EXHIBIT 8 SCHEDULE OF INTEREST PAYMENTS AND BOND RETIREMENTS FOR SERIAL BOND ISSUE

Date	Outstanding	Interest at 3%	Amount Retired	Amount To Pay Interest and Retired Bonds	Number of Bonds Retired	Over (+) and Short (−) Current	Over (+) and Short (−) Cumulative
May 1, 1985	$300,000	—	—	—	—	—	—
August 1, 1985	300,000	$ 9,000	$ 15,000	$ 24,000	15	+117	+117
November 1, 1985	285,000	8,550	15,000	23,550	15	−333	−216
February 1, 1985	270,000	8,100	16,000	24,100	16	+217	+ 1
May 1, 1986	254,000	7,620	16,000	23,620	16	−263	−262
August 1, 1986	238,000	7,140	17,000	24,140	17	+257	− 5
November 1, 1986	221,000	6,630	17,000	23,630	17	−253	−258
February 1, 1987	204,000	6,120	18,000	24,120	18	+237	− 21
May 1, 1987	186,000	5,580	18,000	23,580	18	−303	−324
August 1, 1987	168,000	5,040	19,000	24,040	19	+157	−167
November 1, 1987	149,000	4,470	20,000	24,470	20	+587	+420
February 1, 1988	129,000	3,870	20,000	23,870	20	− 13	+407
May 1, 1988	109,000	3,270	20,000	23,270	20	−613	−206
August 1, 1988	89,000	2,670	21,000	23,670	21	−213	−419
November 1, 1988	68,000	2,040	22,000	24,040	22	+157	−262
February 1, 1989	46,000	1,380	23,000	24,380	23	+497	+235
May 1, 1989	23,000	690	23,000	23,690	23	−193	− 42
		$82,170	$300,000	$382,170	300		

Now look for the values in the 6% column of Exhibit 7 and interpolate. Evidently, n lies between 15 and 16 periods.

Years	$PVIFA_{i,n}$
15	9.7122
16	10.1059
?	10.0

$$n = 15 + \frac{10.0 - 9.7122}{10.1059 - 9.7122}$$
$$= \underline{\underline{15.73 \text{ periods} \simeq 8 \text{ years}}}$$

Computing Period n Using a Financial Calculator. The keystrokes are as follows:

Keystrokes	Display	Comment
fFIN	0.00	Clear
fREG	0.00	Clear
300000	300,000	—
PV	300,000.00	Present value
30,000	30,000	—
CHS	−30,000	—
PMT	−30,000.00	Annuity
6	6	—
i	6.00	Interest rate
n	15.73	Number of periods

Computing Period n Using a Spreadsheet

Cell Address	Cell Content	Explanation
A1	'Payment Amount	Label
C1	30000	Payment Amount
A2	'Compound Value	Label
C2	300000	Compound Value
A3	'Interest	Label
C3	0.06	Interest
A4	'# of Periods	Label
C4	@Log (1/(1− C2*C3/C1))/ @Log (1 + C3)	# of Periods

Illustration

	A	B	C
1	Payment Amount		30000
2	Compound Value		300000
3	Interest		0.06
4	# of Periods		15.73
5			
6			

Present Value of Annuity Due. The symbol for the present value of an annuity due of $1 per period is $PVIFAB_{i,n}$. The formula is as follows:

$$PVIFAB_{i,n} = 1 + \frac{1}{1+i} \cdots + \frac{1}{(1+i)^{n-2}} + \frac{1}{(1+i)^{n-1}}$$
$$= 1 + PVIFA_{i,n-1}$$

This means that the present value tables for ordinary annuities (Exhibit 7) may be used in computing the present value of an annuity due. For instance, if $PVIAB_{12,10}$ is wanted, it can be found by looking in the 12% column of Exhibit 7 on line 9 and adding $1. In this case the answer is 6.3282.

Example. What is the cash value of a lease that has 5 years to run and that calls for rentals of $1,365 quarterly, payable in advance? Assume money is worth 16% per annum, compounded quarterly.

The lease has 20 periods to run and is discounted at 4% per period. Since payments are made in advance, it is an annuity due.

Computing Present Value of Annuity Due Using Tables. The value of $PVIFAB_{4,20}$ can be obtained from Exhibit 7:

$$\begin{aligned} AD &= R \times PVIFAB_{i,n} \\ &= R \times (1 + PVIFA_{i,n-1}) \\ &= \$1{,}365 \times 14.1339 \\ &= \underline{\underline{\$19{,}292.77}} \end{aligned}$$

Computing Present Value of Annuity Due Using a Financial Calculator. The keystrokes are as follows:

Keystroke	Display	Comment
fFIN	0.00	Clear
fREG	0.00	Clear
gBEG	0.00	Set payment switch
1365	1,365	—
CHS	−1,365	—
PMT	−1,365.00	Annuity amount due
4	4	—
i	4.00	Interest Rate
20	20	—
n	20.00	Number of periods
PV	19,292.83	Present value

BOND VALUATION: DEFINITIONS AND CALCULATIONS

Bond Definitions. A bond may be defined as a long-time **promissory note** under "seal." It promises to pay to the owner of the bond a specified principal sum called the face value on a definite date in the future, called the maturity date. It also promises to pay the interest based on the face value on the interest dates as called for in the bond indenture.

The **par value** of a bond is the amount stated on its face. The **redemption value** is the price at which the bond will be redeemed. In many issues this is the same as the par value; in others, premiums are paid when bonds are redeemed before maturity.

Premium and Discount on Bonds. When bonds sell at a price greater than par, they are said to sell at a **premium,** and when at a price less than par they are said to sell at a **discount.**

Nominal and Effective Interest Rates. The **nominal rate,** also known as the **coupon rate** or the cash rate, is the rate, based on the par value, stipulated in the bond.

The **effective rate,** also called the **yield** or **market rate,** is the return that the bonds earn on the price at which they are purchased if they are held to maturity. Note that the yield is based on the price paid for the bond, not on its par value. When the nominal rate is in excess of the yield rate, that is, in excess of what in the opinion of the market is considered a fair rate of return for that type of security, the bond sells at a **premium.** When the bond rate is less than the yield rate, the bond sells at a **discount.** The amount of the premium or discount can be mathematically determined and is based on principles of compound interest and annuities.

Determining Basis Price of Bonds. The price at which a bond will sell on the open market depends on a number of factors:

1. The security for the payment of the principal and interest.
2. The bond rate.
3. The rate realized by like investments, or to be realized by the investor.
4. The time to the maturity of the bond.
5. The price at which the bond will be redeemed.
6. The tax status of the principal and interest.

From a purely mathematical point of view, once the desired yield is known, the basis price, that is, the purchase price, of a bond depends on two factors:

1. The present value of the principal.
2. The present value of the interest payments.

The sum of these two present values represents the basis price of the bond. The first factor represents the present value of a lump sum, the second the present value of an annuity.

Example. What is the price paid by Mr. X on November 1, 1986, for 100 bonds, par value $100,000, paying 16% nominal to yield 14%? The bonds pay interest May 1 and November 1, through coupons, and mature November 1, 1989.

The nominal rate per period is 8%, the effective rate 7%.

Computing the Price Using Tables. The present value of the principal six periods from now is

$$\begin{aligned} P &= A \times PVIF_{i,n} \\ &= A \times PVIF_{7,6} \\ &= \$100{,}000 \times 0.6663 \text{ (Exhibit 5)} \\ &= \underline{\underline{\$66{,}630}} \end{aligned}$$

The present value of the coupons is calculated by means of the annuity formula. The size of each coupon is determined from the nominal rate. In this example, the semi-annual coupons have a face value of $8,000 (i.e., $100,000 × 8%). Their present value is then found:

$$\begin{aligned} A &= R \times PVIFA_{i,n} \\ &= R \times PVIF_{7,6} \\ &= \$8{,}000 \times 4.7665 \text{ (Exhibit 7)} \\ &= \underline{\underline{\$38{,}132}} \end{aligned}$$

Basis price of bonds:

$$\$66{,}630 + 38{,}132 = \underline{\underline{\$104{,}762}}$$

Note that the yield rate is always used except for calculating the amount of cash coupon.

Short Method for Finding Basis Price. Since the difference between the coupon and yield rates gives rise to premium or discount on bonds, it is possible to compute the premium, and hence the basis price, directly from such difference. This method is illustrated below, using the same example as above.

	Rate (%)	Amount
Nominal interest	8	\$8,000
Effective interest	7	7,000
Excess interest		\$1,000

The bond pays \$8,000 interest per period. It should pay \$7,000 to sell at par. There is, therefore, \$1,000 excess interest per period. The excess interest constitutes an annuity for the life of the bond. The present value of this annuity represents the premium to be paid.

$$
\begin{aligned}
A &= R \times PVIFA_{7,6} \\
&= \$1{,}000 \times 4.7665 \text{ (Exhibit 7)} \\
&= 4{,}766.50 \\
\text{Par value} &= \$100{,}000 \\
\text{Basis price} &= \underline{\underline{\$104{,}766.50}}
\end{aligned}
$$

Computing the Price Using a Financial Calculator. The keystrokes are as follows:

Keystroke	Display	Comment
fFIN	0.00	Clear
fREG	0.00	Clear
8	8	—
ENTER	8.00	Nominal interest
7	7.00	Effective interest
—	1.00	—
100000	100,000.00	Par value
STO	100,000.00	—
1	100,000.00	—
×	100,000.00	—
100	100.00	—
÷	1,000.00	Excess interest
CHS	−1,000.00	—
PMT	−1,000.00	—
7	7.00	—
i	7.00	Interest rate
6	6.00	—
n	6.00	Number of periods
PV	4,766.54	—
RCL	4,766.54	—
1	100,000.00	—
+	104,766.54	Basis price

Computing the Price Using a Microcomputer Spreadsheet

Cell Address	Cell Content	Explanation
A1	'Par Value	Label
D1	100000	Par Value
A2	'Face Value Coupons	Label
D2	8000	Face Value Coupons
A3	'Number of periods	Label
D3	6	Number of periods
A4	'Interest Rate	Label
D4	0.07	Interest Rate
A5	'Basis Price	Label
D5	+ D1*1/(1 + D4)^D3 + D2*(1 − (1/(1 + D4)^ D3))/D4	Basis Price

Illustration

	A	B	C	D
1	Par Value		100000	
2	Face Value Coupons		8000	
3	# of Periods		6	
4	Interest Rate		0.07	
5	Basis Price		104766.5	
6				

Amortization Schedule. Although an investor may have paid a premium for the bond, generally speaking, he collects only the par value at maturity. This shrinkage in value takes place gradually during the life of the bond. It means that each coupon collection represents two things:

1. Return on the investment at the yields rate.
2. Partial return of the premium paid.

That this is the case can be shown by a so-called amortization table. Exhibit 9 is based on the premium bond illustrated in the last example.

EXHIBIT 9 AMORTIZATION SCHEDULE

Date	Coupon Income 8%	Effective Income 7%	Amortization	Remaining Book Value
November 1, 1985	—	—	—	$104,766.54
May 1, 1986	$8,000	$7,333.66	666.34	104,100.20
November 1, 1986	8,000	7,287.01	712.99	103,387.21
May 1, 1987	8,000	7,237.10	762.90	102,624.32
November 1, 1987	8,000	7,183.70	816.30	101,808.02
May 1, 1988	8,000	7,126.56	873.44	100,934.58
November 1, 1988	8,000	7,065.42	934.58	100,000.00

The coupon income is 8% a period based on the par value of the bonds. The effective income or yield is 7% based on the remaining investment. Thus, on May 1, 1987, 7% is earned on $104,766.54 or $7,333.66. This is the true income for the period. The balance of the $8,000 coupon interest collected on that day represents a partial liquidation of the investment. Hence, the book value is reduced on May 1, 1987, by $666.34. Six months later, the effective income is 7% of the new book value of $104,100.20, and so on.

Short-Cut Method for Discount Bonds. The short-cut method just illustrated works equally well for bonds selling at a discount, as shown in the example below.

Example. Find the basis price of $10,000 bond paying 10% nominal interest on February 1 and August 1, to yield 12%. The bond was purchased February 1, 1985, and matures August 1, 1987.

	Rate (%)	Amount
Nominal interest	5	$500
Effective interest	6	$600
Deficiency of interest		$100

$$\begin{aligned} A &= R \times PVIFA_{i,n} \\ &= \$100 \times PVIFA_{6,5} \\ &= \$100 \times 4.2124 \text{ (Exhibit 7)} \\ &= \$421.24 \\ \text{par value} &= \$10{,}000.00 \\ \text{basis price} &= \$\ 9{,}578.76 \end{aligned}$$

Schedule of Accumulation. A bond purchased at a discount approaches par or other redemption value gradually. The increase in value is spread over the life of the bond. Hence, the **true income** each period consists of:

1. Coupon interest.
2. Increase in book value, known as the accumulation.

Exhibit 10 is an accumulation table for the last illustration, under the short-cut method for discount bonds.

The figures in the effective interest column are obtained by taking 6% of the last book value. Thus on August 1, 1985, 6% of $9,578.76 yields $574.73. Six months later 6% of $9,653.49 amounts to $579.21, and so on. In each instance, the difference between coupon and yield interest is **added** to the previous book value.

EXHIBIT 10 ACCUMULATION TABLE FOR $10,000 BOND

Date	Coupon Interest 5%	Effective Interest 6%	Accumulation	New Book Value
February 1, 1980	—	—	—	$ 9,578.76
August 1, 1980	$500	$574.73	$74.73	9,653.49
February 1, 1981	500	579.21	79.21	9,732.69
August 1, 1981	500	583.96	83.96	9,816.66
February 1, 1982	500	589.00	89.00	9,905.66
August 1, 1982	500	594.34	94.34	10,000.00

Bond Valuation Tables. Bond tables have been devised to simplify the labor involved in determining:

1. The price to be paid when the yield is known.
2. The yield when the cost is known.

Thus it is possible to read the basis price of a bond directly from the table. The **standard bond tables** usually give the value of a million dollar bond correct to the nearest cent for a great variety of nominal and effective interest rates and for periods ranging from 6 months to 50 years at 6-month intervals, and at longer intervals thereafter. However, with the easy availability of pocket calculators, these tables are virtually obsolete.

Basis Price for Bonds Bought Between Interest Dates. The basis price of a bond changes from day to day. Hence, if a bond is bought between interest dates, its basis price must be computed by interpolation between the basis prices of the last preceding and next succeeding interest dates. In addition, the purchaser will have to pay **accrued interest** on the bonds to the seller for the time since the last interest date.

Bonds may be quoted either "and interest" or "flat." The **"and-interest" price** is the quoted price plus the accrued interest. The **"flat" price** includes the accrued interest in the quotation. To find the value of a bond between interest dates, proceed as follows:

1. Find the basis price on the preceding interest day and on the succeeding interest day, and thus determine the decrease or increase in book value for the entire period.
2. Find the fractional part of the period that has elasped to the day of purchase. Find this fractional part of the period's change in book value.
3. Add to the book value of the preceding interest day the increase found in step 2 or subtract from it the decrease found in step 2 for the part of the period that has elasped. The result is the "and-interest" price or "ex-interest" price.

4. Add to the ex-interest price in either instance the accrued interest, or seller's share of the current period's bond interest. The result is the **total price** or flat price.

Example. Find the "and-interest" and "flat" prices for a $1,000 bond, due February 1, 1991, bearing interest at 14% per annum, payable February 1 and August 1, if purchased April 1, 1981, to yield 12%.

The life of the bond on the last interest date (February 1, 1981) was 10 years: at the next interest date it has 9½ years to run. The basis prices on these two dates can be found by the methods presented earlier (determining the basis prices of bonds) by using tables or a financial calculator.

Computing Bond Prices Using Tables. The values of the bond to yield 12% are as follows:

Step 1	10 years (February 1, 1981)	$1,114.70
	9½ years (August 1, 1981)	$1,111.58
	Amortization for 6 months	$ 3.12
Step 2	From February 1 to April 1 is one-third of a period. Therefore the basis price decreased	
	⅓ × $3.12 = $1.04	
Step 3	"And-interest" price April 1, 1981 = $1,114.70 − $1.04 = $1,113.66	
Step 4	Accured interest	
	14% per annum on $1,000 for 2 months	23.33
	Flat price	$1,136.99

It is possible also to determine the flat price directly. The seller is entitled to the book value on the preceding interest day, plus interest on this value at the yield rate, for the time elapsed since that day. The procedure is as follows:

1. Find the basis price on the preceding interest day.
2. Find the time elapsed since the last interest day, and add to the basis price on the preceding interest day interest on it at the yield rate for the elapsed time on a 360-day year basis. The result is the **total price.**
3. From the total price **subtract** the accrued interest. The result is the and-interest price on the ex-interest price.

Using the same illustration as above, the method works out as follows:

Step 1	February 1, 1981, basis price	$1,114.70
Step 2	Interest at 12% per annum for 2 months on above	22.29
Step 3	April 1, 1981, flat price	$1,136.99

If only the total price to be paid by the purchaser or to be received by the seller is wanted, this method offers a short-cut. For the purpose of setting up a schedule of amortization or accumulation, the and-interest price must be used. The first four lines of the amortization table for the bond above appear as follows:

Date	Bond Interest 14%	Effective Interest 12%	Amortization	Book Value
April 1, 1981	—	—	—	$1,113.66
August 1, 1981	$46.67	$44.59	$2.08	1,111.58
February 1, 1982	70.00	66.69	3.31	1,108.27
August 1, 1982	70.00	66.50	3.50	1,104.77

The figures for August 1, 1981, are obtained as follows:

1. Bond interest. The total coupon interest for a period is $70, one-third of which ($23.33) was paid over to the vendor on April 1. Hence, the net interest collected on August 1, is $46.67.
2. Effective interest. This must be calculated on the basis price as of the last interest date (February 1, 1981) for 4 months. In this case $1,114.70 at 12% for 4 months is $44.59.
3. Amortization. Difference between the two preceding columns. $46.67 − $44.59 = $2.08. It could also be found by taking the amortization for the full 6-month period ($3.12) and subtracting the amortization from February 1 to April 1 ($1.04).
4. Book value. Book value April 1, 1981, less current amortization. $1,114.70 − $2.08 = $1,112.62.

Computing Bond Prices Using a Financial Calculator. The keystrokes are as follows:

Keystroke	Display	Comment
fFIN	0.00	Clear
fREG	0.00	Clear
0.07	0.07	—
ENTER	0.07	—
1000	1,000.00	—
×	70.00	Coupon interest
STO	70.00	—
1	70.00	—
CHS	−70.00	—
PMT	−70.00	—
6	6.00	—
i	6.00	Yield
20	20.00	—
n	20.00	Number of periods
PV	802.89	—
0	0.00	—
PMT	0.00	—

Keystroke	Display	Comment
1000	1,000	—
CHS	−1,000	—
FV	−1,000.00	—
PV	311.80	—
+	1,114.70	Bond base price, $n = 20$
STO	1,114.70	—
2	1,114.70	—
19	19.00	—
n	19.00	—
PV	330.51	—
RCL	330.51	—
1	70.00	—
CHS	−70.00	—
PMT	−70.00	—
0	0.00	—
FV	0.00	—
PV	781.07	—
+	1,111.58	Bond base price, $n = 19$
RCL	1,111.58	—
2	1,114.70	—
$x \gtrless y$	1,111.58	—
−	3.12	—
2	2.00	—
×	6.24	—
6	6.00	—
÷	1.04	Decrease in base price
CHS	−1.04	—
RCL	−1.04	—
2	1,114.70	—
+	1,113.66	"And-interest" price
STO	1,113.66	—
3	1,113.66	—
RCL	1,113.66	—
1	70.00	—
3	3.00	—
÷	23.33	Accrued interest
RCL	23.33	—
3	1,113.66	—
+	1,136.99	Flat price

Accruing Bond Interest Between Interest Dates. The interest accrued at time of purchase or sale depends on whether the bond is a corporate or a government bond. For corporate bonds delivery must be made on the fourth working day after the sale and interest is accrued on the basis of a 360-day year up to and including the day before delivery. In the case of government bonds, delivery is on the next working day, and the seller receives interest up to and including the day of the sale.

The rules are further clarified by the Committee on Securities of the New York Stock Exchange as follows:

> Interest at the rate specified on a bond dealt in "and interest" shall be computed on a basis of a 360-day year, i.e., each calendar month shall be considered to be 1/12 of 360 days, and each period from a date in one month to the same date in the following month shall be considered to be 30 days.
>
> **Note:** The number of elapsed days shall be computed in accordance with the examples given in the following table:

From	To
30th to 31st	1st of the following month to be figured as 1 day
30th or 31st	30th of the following month to be figured as 30 days
30th or 31st	31st of the following month to be figured as 30 days
30th or 31st	1st of the second following month to be figured as one month one day

Thus if a January and July 15 bond were bought on March 15, 2 months are said to have elapsed since January 15. If a June and December 1 bond were bought on January 16, following the above rule there are:

From December 1 to January 1	30 days
From January 1 to January 16	15 days
Elapsed time	45 days

Determining Profit or Loss on Sale of Bonds. When bonds that have been purchased as an investment are subsequently sold, the profit or loss on the transaction is determined by comparison of the book value (i.e., the and-interest price) on the date of sale with the selling price.

The profit or loss figure represents the capital gain or loss for tax purposes and is of course exclusive of the coupon interest less amortization regularly reported as income.

Finding Yield Between Interest Dates. The calculation by tables of yield between interest dates is complex, since it requires a double interpolation, once for the basis price of the bond and then for the yield.

OPTION PRICING MATHEMATICS

THE BLACK-SCHOLES FORMULA. The most commonly used formula for pricing call options is one developed by **Black and Scholes** in "The Pricing of Options and Corporate Liabilities" (*Journal of Political Economy,* May–June 1973). It is often used, with minor variations, to determine the gap between the market price of a **call option** and its **intrinsic value.**

The key assumptions of the **Black-Scholes model** are:

1. The short-term interest rate is known and is constant through time.
2. The stock price follows a random walk in continuous time with a variance rate proportional to the square of the stock price.
3. The distribution of possible stock prices at the end of any finite interval is log normal.
4. The variance rate of return on the stock is constant.
5. The stock pays no dividends and makes no other distributions.
6. The option can be exercised only at maturity.
7. There are no commissions or other transaction costs in buying or selling the stock or the option.
8. It is possible to borrow any fraction of the price of a security to buy it or to hold it, at the short-term interest rate.
9. A seller who does not own a security (a short seller) will simply accept the price of the security from the buyer and will agree to settle with the buyer on some future date by paying him an amount equal to the price of the security on that date. While this short sale is outstanding, the short seller will have the use of, or interest on, the proceeds of the sale.
10. The tax rate, if any, is identical for all transactions and all market participants.

The assumption that the distribution of the stock price at the end of any finite time interval be log normal is equivalent to saying that the distribution of the stock's returns in each instant will be normal with a constant variance. Under these assumptions and using the hedging arguments outlined in the section entitled "Option Markets and Instruments," the price of a call option is determined by:

$$P_o = P_s N(d_1) - \frac{E}{e^{rt}} N(d_2)$$

where $d_1 = \dfrac{\ln (P_s/E) + (r + ½\sigma^2)t}{\sigma\sqrt{t}}$

$d_2 = \dfrac{\ln (P_s/E) + (r + ½\sigma^2)t}{\sigma\sqrt{t}}$

where P_o = current value of option
P_s = current price of stock
E = exercise price of option
e = 2.71828
t = time remaining before expiration (years)
r = continuously compounded riskless rate of interest

σ = standard deviation of continuously compounded annual rate of return on the stock

$\ln(P_s/E)$ = natural logarithm of (P_s/E)

$N(d)$ = probability that a deviation less than d will occur in a normal distribution with a mean of 0 and a standard deviation of 1

Example. Suppose the price of a share of XYZ Corp. is \$36 and the exercise price of the call option is \$40. The option has 3 months to maturity (i.e., 0.25 of a year). If the riskless rate of interest is 5% per year, and the standard deviation of the continuously compounded annual return is 50%, determine the price of the option, using the following data:

$P_s = \$36$

$E = \$40$

$t = 0.25$ (i.e., one fourth of a year, or 3 months)

$r = 0.05$ (i.e., 5% per year, continuously compounded)

$\sigma = 0.50$ (i.e., the standard deviation of the continuously compounded annual return is 50%)

Using the formula, we write:

$$d_1 = \frac{\ln(36/40) + [0.05 + \tfrac{1}{2}(0.50^2)]\,0.25}{0.50\sqrt{0.25}} \approx -0.25$$

$$d_2 = \frac{\ln(36/40) + [0.05 + \tfrac{1}{2}(0.50^2)]\,0.50}{0.50\sqrt{0.25}} \approx -0.50$$

From Exhibit 11, which furnishes values of the $N(d)$, the standard normal-variant for various values of d, we see that

$$N(d_1) = N(-0.25) = 0.4013$$
$$N(d_2) = N(-0.50) = 0.3085$$

Thus,

$$P_o = (36 \times 0.4013) - \left(\frac{40}{e^{0.05 \times 0.25}} \times 0.3085\right) \approx \$2.26$$

Only a hand calculator is needed to estimate the value of an option using the Black-Scholes formula. In fact, a pocket calculator can be programmed to make the calculations directly. The details of such a program are furnished in Rubinstein (1977) or Rubinstein and Cox (1981).

EXHIBIT 11 VALUES OF N(d) FOR SELECTED VALUES OF d

d	$N(d)$	d	$N(d)$	d	$N(d)$
		−1.00	.1587	1.00	.8413
−2.95	.0016	−0.95	.1711	1.05	.8531
−2.90	.0019	−0.90	.1841	1.10	.8643
−2.85	.0022	−0.85	.1977	1.15	.8749
−2.80	.0026	−0.80	.2119	1.20	.8849
−2.75	.0030	−0.75	.2266	1.25	.8944
−2.70	.0035	−0.70	.2420	1.30	.9032
−2.65	.0040	−0.65	.2578	1.35	.9115
−2.60	.0047	−0.60	.2743	1.40	.9192
−2.55	.0054	−0.55	.2912	1.45	.9265
−2.50	.0062	−0.50	.3085	1.50	.9332
−2.45	.0071	−0.45	.3264	1.55	.9394
−2.40	.0082	−0.40	.3446	1.60	.9452
−2.35	.0094	−0.35	.3632	1.65	.9505
−2.30	.0107	−0.30	.3821	1.70	.9554
−2.25	.0122	−0.25	.4013	1.75	.9599
−2.20	.0139	−0.20	.4207	1.80	.9641
−2.15	.0158	−0.15	.4404	1.85	.9678
−2.10	.0179	−0.10	.4602	1.90	.9713
−2.05	.0202	−0.05	.4801	1.95	.9744
−2.00	.0228	0.00	.5000	2.00	.9773
−1.95	.0256	0.05	.5199	2.05	.9798
−1.90	.0287	0.10	.5398	2.10	.9821
−1.85	.0322	0.15	.5596	2.15	.9842
−1.80	.0359	0.20	.5793	2.20	.9861
−1.75	.0401	0.25	.5987	2.25	.9878
−1.70	.0446	0.30	.6179	2.30	.9893
−1.65	.0495	0.35	.6368	2.35	.9906
−1.60	.0548	0.40	.6554	2.40	.9918
−1.55	.0606	0.45	.6736	2.45	.9929
−1.50	.0668	0.50	.6915	2.50	.9938
−1.45	.0735	0.55	.7088	2.55	.9946
−1.40	.0808	0.60	.7257	2.60	.9953
−1.35	.0885	0.65	.7422	2.65	.9960
−1.30	.0968	0.70	.7580	2.70	.9965
−1.25	.1057	0.75	.7734	2.75	.9970
−1.20	.1151	0.80	.7881	2.80	.9974
−1.15	.1251	0.85	.8023	2.85	.9978
−1.10	.1357	0.90	.8159	2.90	.9981
−1.05	.1469	0.95	.8289	2.95	.9984

NOMOGRAMS FOR OPTION VALUATION. An alternative method using a **nomogram** is illustrated in Exhibit 12. To value an option, it is necessary to construct a box. The position on the left-hand side is determined by the maturity of the option. The top of the left-hand side is determined by the standard deviation of the stock's annual return and the bottom by the annual interest rate. The position of the right-hand side of the box is determined by the ratio of the current stock price to the exercise price (here, based on the location of the upper right-hand corner). In this case, the nomogram indicates that the option

EXHIBIT 12 THE CALL OPTION VALUATION NOMOGRAM

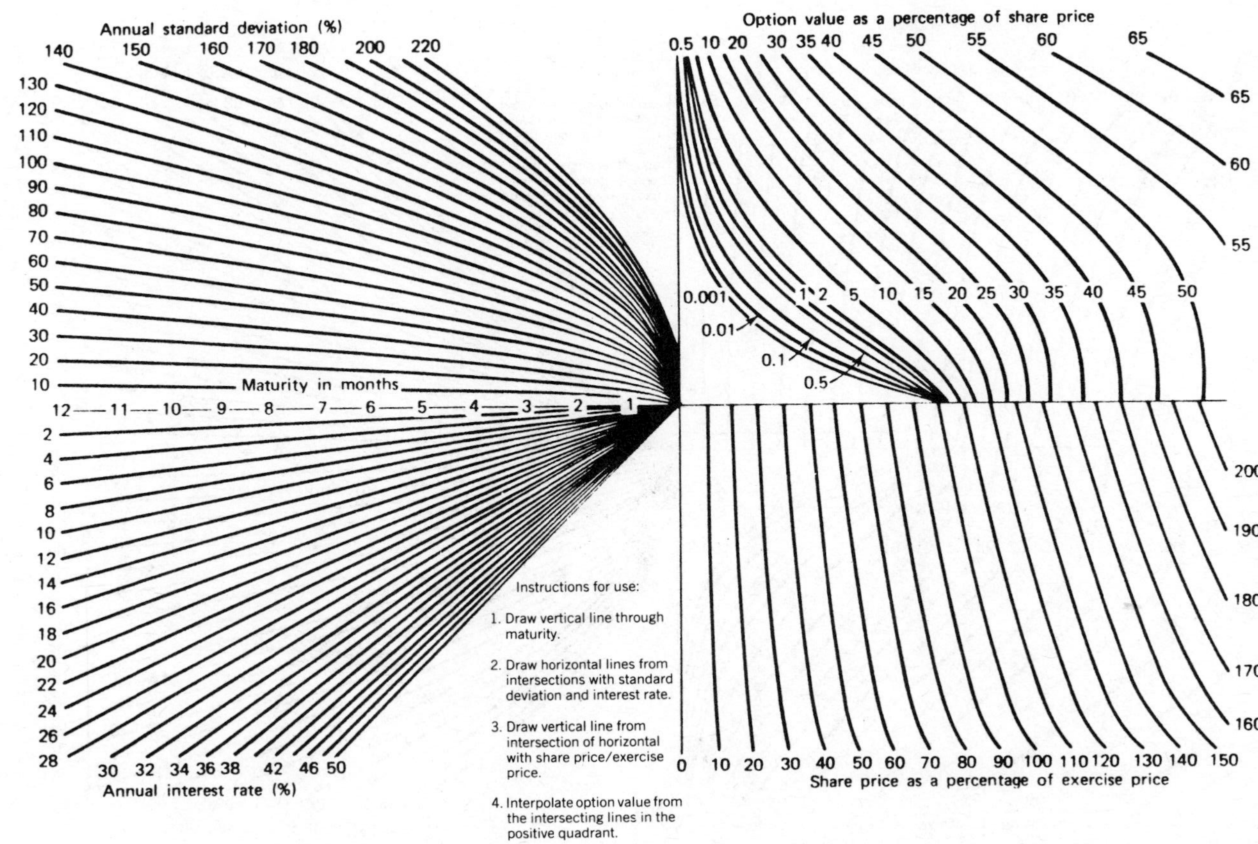

Source: E. Dimson. "Instant Option Valuation." *Financial Analysts Journal,* May – June 1977.

EXHIBIT 13 EXAMPLE OF THE USE OF CALL OPTION VALUATION NOMOGRAM

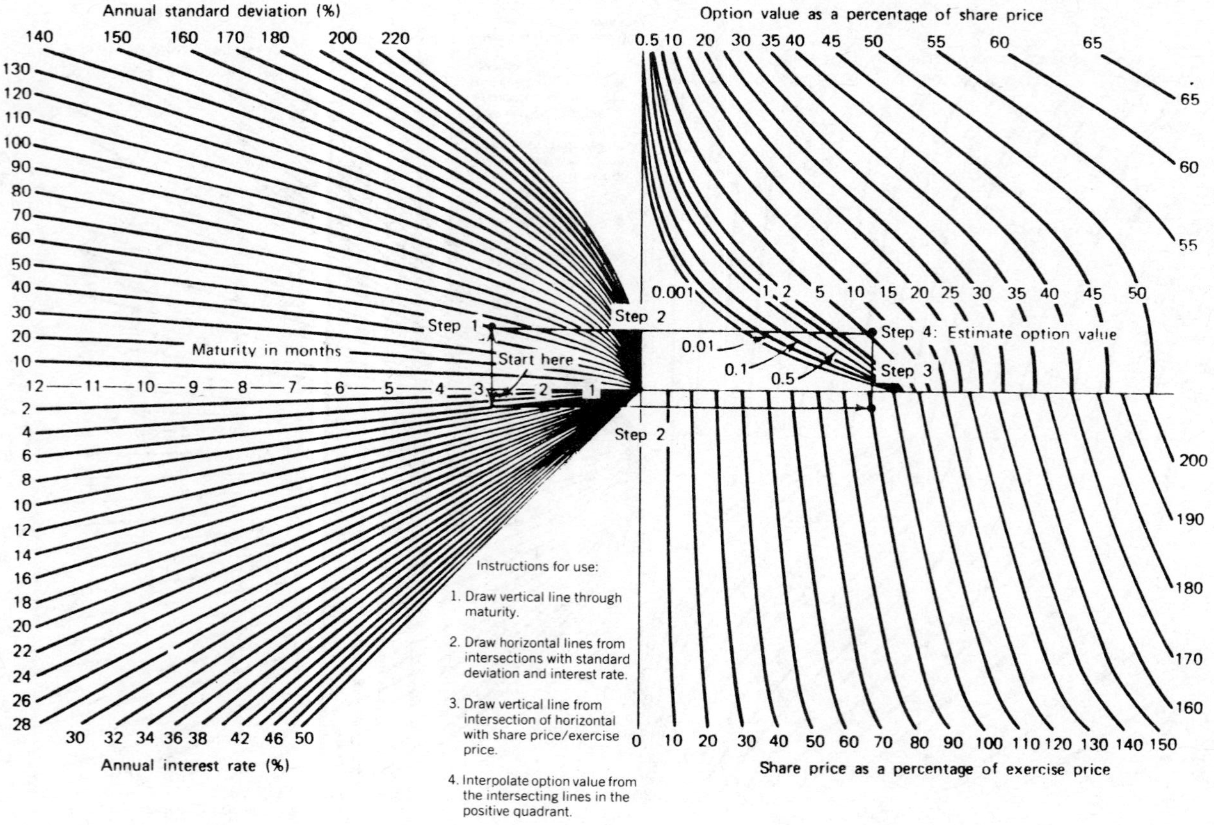

Annual standard deviation (%)

140 150 160 170 180 200 220

130 120 110 100 90 80 70 60 50 40 30 20 10

Maturity in months

12—11—10—9—8—7—6—5—4—3—2—1

2 4 6 8 10 12 14 16 18 20 22 24 26 28

30 32 34 36 38 42 46 50

Annual interest rate (%)

Option value as a percentage of share price

0.5 10 20 30 35 40 45 50 55 60 65

65 60 55

0.001 0.01 0.1 0.5 1 2 5 10 15 20 25 30 35 40 45 50

200 190 180 170 160

0 10 20 30 40 50 60 70 80 90 100 110 120 130 140 150

Share price as a percentage of exercise price

Start here

Step 1

Step 2

Step 2

Step 3

Step 4: Estimate option value

Instructions for use:

1. Draw vertical line through maturity.
2. Draw horizontal lines from intersections with standard deviation and interest rate.
3. Draw vertical line from intersection of horizontal with share price/exercise price.
4. Interpolate option value from the intersecting lines in the positive quadrant.

Source: E. Dimson. "Instant Option Valuation." *Financial Analysts Journal,* May–June 1977.

value is somewhat more than 5% of the exercise price, or $2(0.05 × $40); see Exhibit 13.

Exhibit 12 shows that, other things equal, an option is generally more valuable:

The **higher** the current stock price relative to the exercise price.

The **longer** the time remaining before expiration.

The **higher** the riskless rate of interest.

The **greater** the risk of the underlying stock.

Only the last of these factors requires estimation but, as the nomogram shows, it is of crucial importance.

A more detailed description, as well as nomograms for estimation of the value of put options, are available in Dimson's articles in the *Financial Analysts Journal.*

REFERENCES

Black, F., and Scholes, M., "The Pricing of Options and Corporate Liabilities," *Journal of Political Economy,* May–June 1973, pp. 637–654.

Cox, J.C., and Rubinstein M., *Options Markets,* Prentice-Hall, Englewood Cliffs, NJ, 1985.

Dimson, E., "Instant Option Valuation," *Financial Analysts Journal,* May–June 1977, pp. 62–69.

———, "Option Valuation Nomograms," *Financial Analysts Journal,* November–December 1977, pp. 71–75.

Greynolds, E.B., Jr., Aronofsky, J.S., and Frame, R.J., *Financial Analysis Using Calculators: Time Value of Money,* McGraw-Hill, 1980.

Rubinstein, M., "How to Use the Option Pricing Formula," University of California, Berkeley, Working Paper, 1977.

APPENDIX B

SOURCES OF FINANCIAL AND INVESTMENT INFORMATION

CONTENTS

APPENDIX B

SOURCES OF FINANCIAL AND INVESTMENT INFORMATION

ONLINE DATABASES

Analystics

Chase Econometrics/Interactive Data Corp., Waltham, Massachusetts

Consists of 22 data bases covering a wide range of securities and financial statement data. Includes detailed security descriptions, daily price and volume data, market indicators, stock splits and dividends, commodities, international bonds and securities, and much more.

Commodities

Data Resources, Inc., Lexington, Massachusetts

Focuses on price and trading activity information for all major commodities traded in the United States, Canadian, and London markets.

Compustat

Standard & Poor's Compustat Services, Englewood, Colorado

Contains income statement, balance sheet, sources and applications of funds, line of business, and market information for publicly held U.S. and some non-U.S. corporations. Annual data are included for about 6,000 industrial and nonindustrial companies. Quarterly data are available for 2,800 companies.

Corporate Earnings Estimator

Zacks Investment Research, Chicago, Illinois

Reports on projected earnings of 3,000 major U.S. companies. Based on a consensus of financial analysts.

Corporation Records Online

Standard & Poor's Corporation, New York, New York

Electronic version of the *Corporation Records* published in six volumes by Standard & Poor's. Includes detailed corporate descriptions. The "News Online" data base provides daily news supplements.

DRI-FACS

Data Resources, Inc., Lexington, Massachusetts

Coverage of interest rates, commercial bank assets and liabilities, and thrift institution activity. Interest rate information includes domestic money and bond markets, U.S. government security issues, and international money and foreign exchange rates.

DRI-SEC

Data Resources, Inc., Lexington, Massachusetts

Daily pricing and current fundamental information for equity, debt, and government agency issues listed on the New York, American, over-the-counter, regional, and Canadian exchanges. Includes market and industry indicators, and bond yields.

Disclosure II

Disclosure, Inc., Bethesda, Maryland

Contains information from all companies that file reports with the Securities and Exchange Commission (SEC). General descriptive information includes location and description of business, list of SEC reports filed, and more. Extracts from forms filed (10K, 10G, 20K, 8K, proxy and registration statements) provide shareholder information, lists of subsidiaries, balance sheet and income statement data, and other financial information.

Disclosure/Spectrum Online

Disclosure, Inc., Bethesda, Maryland

Detailed and summary corporate ownership information for approximately 5,000 public companies. Includes number of shares held by institutions, 5% owners, and corporate insiders.

Extat

Extel Statistical Services, Ltd., London, England

Balance sheet and income statement account items for more than 3,200 international corporations. Includes 10 years of historical annual data as well as current information.

Ford Data Base

Ford Investor Services, San Diego, California

Furnishes data on 1,400 leading common stocks. Information includes earnings per share, projected earnings, debt/equity ratio, beta, quality rating, and more.

IBES

Lynch, Jones & Ryan, New York, New York

Provides earnings estimates on listed equity securities. Estimates are supplied by security analysts who follow specific stocks.

Investex

Business Research Group, Boston, Massachusetts

Provides complete text of more than 7,000 research reports written by professional research analysts at major investment banking and financial research firms. Reports include financial data and market forecasts on companies and industries.

Investments

Muller Data Corporation, New York, New York

Contains over 50 different data items on corporate and government securities. Includes options, municipals, Over-the-Counter, and mutual funds. Current and historical data.

The M & A Database

The Hay Group, Philadelphia, Pennsylvania

Includes mergers, buyouts, tender offers, and divestitures valued at $1 million or more. Provides current company information, transaction description, stock price data, and other relevant information.

Market Decision System 7

Bunker Ramo Information Systems, Trumbull, Connecticut

Real-time financial information system includes information on stocks, bonds, options, commodities, currencies, and economic and business news. Also contains historical information and current research reports on 400 widely traded stocks.

Markets Advisory

Markets Advisory, Racine, Wisconsin

Technical analysis information for stocks, industries, market indexes, and more. Includes relative strength, moving averages, momentum, bar charts, point and figure charts, and other relevant information.

Media General Data Base

Media General Financial Services, Inc., Richmond, Virginia

Contains balance sheet, income statement, price, and volume data. Both quarterly and annual financial and trading data are presented.

Mergers and Acquisitions

Securities Data Company, Inc., New York, New York

Covers mergers, tender offers, and self-tender offers since 1981. Provides information on both the target's and acquiror's financial position, specifics of each transaction, price tracking, managers and fees, and geographical location of both the target and the acquiror.

Merlin

Hale Systems, Inc., Remote Computing Division, Roslyn, New York

Contains data on over 12,000 stocks, bonds, rights, warrants, and government issues. Includes both fundamental and technical data. Contains data on options listed on the Chicago Board Options Exchange, and the American, Philadelphia, and Pacific stock exchanges. Contains commodities price, volume, and open interest data. Also includes indexes and statistics on the daily or weekly performance of the securities markets.

Merrill Lynch Research Service

Merrill Lynch, Inc., Securities Research Division, New York, New York

Contains summaries of Merrill Lynch's "Weekly Highlights" bulletin. Includes earnings estimates and investment ratings.

Microquote

The Gregg Corporation, Waltham, Massachusetts

Contains trading statistics and descriptive data on over 32,000 stocks, bonds, mutual funds, warrants, and options. Historical prices and data are available for most stocks. Daily, weekly, and monthly data are included.

Munifacts

The Bond Buyer, New York, New York

Contains current news, price, and related information for fixed income instruments. Includes municipals, corporate, and government issues as well as money market instruments. Current prices, key economic data, and market summaries are among the data included.

New Issues of Corporate Securities

Securities Data Company, Inc., New York, New York

Includes all new issues of taxable debt, common stock and preferred stock registered with the SEC since 1970. Provides offering price, coupon, maturity, call and sinking fund provisions, number of shares, earnings growth and other relevant information. Both public and private offering data are available.

New Issues of Municipal Debt

Securities Data Company, Inc., New York, New York

Includes new issues of tax-exempt debt with short and long maturities. Provides information on offering price, maturity, coupon, call and sinking fund provisions, and other relevant information.

Quotron 800

Quotron Systems, Inc., Los Angeles, California

A real-time financial information service with information on stocks, bonds, options, commodities, dividends and earnings, industry performance, and business and economic news. Contains market indicators and statistics as well as information on specific securities.

The Reuter Monitor
Reuters Ltd., New York, New York
Provides 14 services containing financial, securities, commodities, energy and general news information. Services include: Money/financial futures, money markets, grain/livestock, metals, coins, energy, securities, national news, optional news, optional domestic data, optional international data, optional securities quotations, tickers, contributed information.

S & P MarketScope
Standard & Poor's Corporation, New York, New York
Contains descriptive and financial data on over 4600 companies, reports and analyses of the stock, commodities, and municipal bond markets, and financial investment news. Includes earnings and dividend projections, company descriptions and other relevant financial information.

Securities Industry Data Bank (SI Data Bank)
Data Resources, Inc., Washington, D.C.
Contains balance sheet and income statement data for twelve sectors of the securities industry. Individual exchange information includes round lot activity, number of shares available and their market value, and volume. Also includes data on credit market debt outstanding, gross proceeds, and number of issues of many types of equity and fixed income securities.

Telerate Financial Information Network
Telerate Systems, Inc., New York, New York
A real-time information service with data on domestic money markets, government securities, international rates, futures, options, stocks, and commercial banking statistics.

Telstat
Telstat Systems, Inc., New York, New York
Contains over 50 different data elements on stocks and bonds from 10 major stock exchanges in the United States and Canada, Over-the-counter issues and options. Historical and current data are included. The municipal bond file contains prices, yield data, and other information.

Value Line Data Base II
Arnold Bernhard & Co., New York, New York
Provides compact income statements, balance sheets, sources & uses of funds, key ratios, and forecasts for 1,600 companies.

Zacks Fundamentals
Zacks Investment Research, Inc., Chicago, Illinois
Contains earnings data on 3,000 companies listed on the New York, American or Over-the-counter exchanges for which analysts are making earnings forecasts. Includes 124 data items.

GENERAL INTEREST PERIODICALS

Title	Published
Business Starts	Quarterly
Business Week	Weekly
Cash Flow	Monthly
Chapter 11 Reporter	Monthly
Conference Board Record	Monthly
Conference Board Statistical Bulletin	Monthly
Donoghue's Money Fund Report	Monthly
Dun's	Monthly
Euromoney	Monthly
Fact	Monthly
Finance	Monthly
Finance Executive	Monthly
Financial Planner	Bi-monthly
Financial Review, The	Quarterly
Financial World	Weekly
Forbes	Bi-weekly
Fortune	Bi-weekly
Futures	Monthly
Institutional Investor	Monthly
Investment Dealers' Digest	Weekly
Investment Strategy	Bi-monthly
Japan Stock Journal	Weekly
Market Value Index	Monthly
Mergers & Acquisitions	Quarterly
Money	Monthly
Nation's Business	Monthly
Newsweek	Weekly
OTC Review	Monthly
Stock Market Magazine	Monthly
Time	Weekly

Title	Published
U.S. News & World Report	Weekly
United States Investor	Weekly
Venture Capital	Monthly

RESEARCH AND SCHOLARLY JOURNALS

Title	Published
American Economic Review	Monthly
Bell Journal of Economics	Quarterly
CFA Digest, The (Chartered Fin. Analysts)	Quarterly
Financial Analysts Journal	Bi-monthly
Financial Management	Quarterly
Financial Review, The	3 times
Harvard Business Review	Bi-monthly
Journal of Bank Research	Quarterly
Journal of Banking & Finance	Quarterly
Journal of Business	Quarterly
Journal of Cash Management	Bi-monthly
Journal of Commercial Bank Lending	Monthly
Journal of Economic Literature	Monthly
Journal of Fin. & Quantitative Analysis	Quarterly
Journal of Finance	5 times
Journal of Financial Economics	Quarterly
Journal of Financial Research	Quarterly
Journal of Futures Markets	Quarterly
Journal of Monetary Economics	Quarterly
Journal of Money, Credit & Banking	Quarterly
Journal of Portfolio Management	Quarterly
Management Science	Monthly
Midland Corporate Finance Journal	Quarterly

NEWSPAPERS

Title	Period
American Banker	Daily
Barron's	Weekly

Title	Period
Bondweek	Weekly
Commercial & Financial Chronicle	Bi-weekly
Credit Markets	Weekly
Daily Commercial News	Daily
Financial Post (Canadian)	Weekly
Financial Times	*Daily*
Investment Week	Weekly
Investor's Daily	Daily
Japan Economic Journal	Weekly
Journal of Commerce	Daily
M/G Financial Weekly Market Digest	Weekly
Market Chronicle	Weekly
Money Manager	Weekly
National Observer	Weekly
New York Times	Daily
Penny Stock News	Bi-weekly
Pension & Investment Age	Bi-weekly
Wall Street Journal	Daily
Wall Street Transcript	Weekly
Weekly Bond Buyer	Weekly

PUBLICATIONS OF FINANCIAL SERVICES

Arnold Bernhard & Co.

Value Line Investment Survey (weekly)

Covers about 1,700 stocks in weekly reports. Three major sections include: (1) commentary and analysis on a select number of issues, (2) summary information on all 1,700 stocks and (3) highlights of recommended purchases and general market information and forecasts. Firms are ranked from highest (1) to lowest (5) in potential.

Value Line New Issues Service (bi-weekly)

Recommends new issues for purchase. Includes pertinent information such as price, number of shares, company descriptions, and so forth.

Value Line OTC Special Situations (bi-weekly)

Contains rcommendations for favorable high growth stocks traded over-the-counter. Includes summary information on all issues previously recommended as well as detailed quarterly follow-ups on each recommendation.

Value Line Options & Convertibles (bi-weekly)

Includes information on 585 convertible bonds and preferred stocks, 90 warrants, and 385 options. Provides recommendations, rankings and price analyses. Also includes general information on investing in these types of securities.

Dun & Bradstreet Corporation

Dun & Bradstreet issues the following reports on a regular basis:
Building Permits (quarterly)
Business Expectations (quarterly)
Business Failure (weekly/quarterly)
Business Starts (quarterly)
Monthly Bank Clearings
Weekly Bank Clearings
New Incorporations (monthly)
Wholesale Commodity Price Index (weekly)
Wholesale Food Price Index (weekly)

The reports provide textual and numerical comments, explanations and analyses of current economic situations.

Fitch Investors Service

Ratings Register (monthly)

Includes quality ratings for corporations, commercial paper, preferred stock, and numerous types of bond issues.

Corporate and Industry Research Report (revised periodically)

includes company descriptions, operations information, financial data and Fitch quality ratings.

Lipper Analytical Distributors, Inc.

Lipper publishers a number of reports evaluating the performance of varying financial instruments, including:
Annuity & Closed End Surey (performance information)
Mutual Fund Performance Analysis (quarterly rankings by fund objective)
Convertible Analysis Report

Moody's Investors Service

Manuals and News Reports

Moody's publishes seven manuals which cover more than 20,000 U.S. and foreign corporations, and over 15,000 municipal and government entities. Includes industrial, OTC industrial, transportation, public utility, bank and finance, municipal and government, and international manuals. Contains a wide variety of information including company history, financial performance, and much more. Frequent news reports and up-to-date information are provided.

Bond Record (monthly)

Publication providing ratings and other financial data on over 32,000 issues. Includes convertibles, government and municipal issues, commercial paper, preferred stocks, and more.

Bond Survey (weekly)

Provides information on recent corporate bond offerings, ratings of bonds, commercial paper and preferred stock, yield averages, business and market comments, and more.

Dividend Record (twice weekly))

Provides information on new dividends, dividend changes, stock dividends and splits, and more. Includes key dates and amounts for over 11,000 issues.

Handbook of Common Stocks (quarterly)

Contains complete business/financial history, stock price charts, analysis of recent developments, and Moody's outlook for leading companies.

Handbook of OTC Stocks (quarterly)

Similar to the *Handbook of Common Stocks,* but concentrating on stocks traded Over-the-counter.

Investors Fact Sheets Industry Review (bi-annually)

Contains comparative statistics for each of 143 industries and data on all companies in that industry. Includes rankings of each company in an industry by key operating and investment criteria.

National Quotation Bureau

National Bond Summary (monthly)

Summary of quotes and other relevant information on bond transactions.

National Stock Summary (monthly)

Summary of quotes, shares outstanding, dividends, business changes, public offerings, price ranges. Includes six months of information.

Standard & Poor's Corporation (S&P)

Analyst's Handbook (annual with monthly updates)

Provides composite per share data for 67 industries and 15 transportation, financial, and utility groups. Allows for company versus industry, industry versus industry, and company or industry versus the S & P 400 comparisons.

Bond Guide (monthly)

Contains 41 items of descriptive and statistical data on approximately 5500 U.S. and Canadian corporate bonds. Also includes data on convertible and foreign bonds. Quality ratings are given for corporate bonds and all important state and municipal general obligation and revenue bonds.

Called Bond Record (twice weekly)

Includes call notices, prepayment notices, changes in conversion privileges, bond and stock tenders asked, defaults, and more.

Commercial Paper Ratings Guide (monthly)

Contains information on over 800 issues of commercial paper. Includes commercial and long-term debt ratings, bank line policy, and rating rationale.

Corporation Records (revised periodically)

Provides descriptions of general operations, plant locations, subsidiaries, financial structure and securities for 7,900 large corporations. Also contains more concise coverage on 2,000 corporations next in importance. Daily news section assures that information is always current.

CreditWeek (weekly)

Analyzes ratings, trends, and the outlook for fixed income securities, including corporate and municipal bonds and commercial paper. Detailed analysis of new issues.

Credit Week International (quarterly)

Supplement to CreditWeek. Includes eurobonds, yankee bonds and commercial paper.

Dividend Record (daily, weekly, or quarterly)

Provides dividend information on over 10,000 stocks.

Earnings Forecaster (weekly)

Provides current earnings estimates on 1,600 companies. Includes source of estimate, previous year earnings, current price and estimate of future earnings.

Handbooks (semi-annual)

Each handbook focuses on a particular area of interest: growth stocks, high-tech stocks, oil and gas stocks, S&P 500, OTC, American Stock Exchange, and options. Includes feature articles, charts, graphs, and S&P Stock Reports for each area.

Industry Surveys

Economic and business information on 22 industries. Financial data on 1,300 companies is included. The *Basic Survey* is published annually for each industry, and is periodically updated by the *Current Survey.* Two other monthly publications, *Trends & Projections,* and *Earning Reports* complete the package.

New Issues Investor (monthly)

Includes recommendations and important information on companies making their initial public offerings of common stock. Provides follow-up reports on previous recommendations and interim updates.

Outlook (weekly)

Comprehensive investment advisory service. Commentary on current market trends, individual stock recommendations for various investment strategies, industry discussions, and general economic analyses.

Daily Stock Price Record (quarterly)

Three volumes of day-by-day accounts of price histories on over 7300 issues listed on the New York, American, and Over-the-counter exchanges. Over-the-counter volume includes almost 600 mutual funds.

Register of Corporations, Directors & Executives (annual, with quarterly supplements)

Provides titles and duties of all leading officers and executives, department heads, and technical personnel for over 45,000 nationally known companies.

Stock Guide (monthly)

Statistical summary of investment data on over 5300 common and preferred stocks and 400 mutual funds. 48 data items on each stock are included. Contains forecasts, ratings, rankings, and current financial and market information.

Stock Reports (updated continuously)

Profiles of stock performance and financial history of over 4,400 widely traded companies. Includes background information on each company, as well as selected financial data.

Stock Summary (monthly)

Includes 40 data items for each of 1,920 stocks. Price, earnings, dividend, and other selected financial information is included.

Statistical Service (bi-annually and monthly)
Consists of three separate publications: the *Security Price Index Record, Business and Financial Statistics,* and *Current Statistics* (published monthly).

Index Services (weekly, monthly, and quarterly)
A variety of reports covering S&P stock price indexes. Provides continuous updating and current information on these indexes.

The Blue List (daily)
Contains information on municipal bond offerings, grouped into 13 categories.

Trendline

Daily Action Stock Charts (weekly)
Charts 754 stocks on a daily basis. Each chart shows 12 months of price and volune history. Includes earnings estimates and rankings, growth rates, relative strength ratios and other information. Includes reports on 44 popular indexes.

Current Market Perspectives (monthly)
Charts 1,476 stocks on a weekly basis. Each chart shows four years of price and volume history. Includes price, earnings, and performance information similar to that of the *Daily Action Stock Charts.*

OTC Chart Manual (bi-monthly)
Covers 800 stocks on a weekly basis. Includes earnings, dividend and financial information and estimates, as well as information on technical indicators.

MISCELLANEOUS PUBLISHERS

Title	Publisher
AMEX Data Book	American Stock Exchange
Commodity Chart Service	Commodity Research Bureau
Commodity Year Book	Commodity Research Bureau
Dow Jones Investor's Handbook	Dow Jones
Credit Decisions	Duff & Phelps
Fixed Income Services	Duff & Phelps
The Dun & Hargitt Commodity Service	Dun & Hargitt, Inc.
Financial Stock Guide Service	Financial Information Service

Title	Publisher
A Half Century of Returns on Stocks and Bonds	Fisher & Lorie
Mutual Fund Fact Book	Inv. Company Institute
Mutual Fund Directory	Inv. Dealers' Digest
Over-the-Counter Growth Stocks	John s. Herold, Inc.
KV Convertible Fact Finder	Kalb, Voorhis & Co.
Credit Critiques	McCarthy, Crisante & Maffier
MCM Rating Summaries	McCarthy, Crisante & Maffier
Rating Watch	McCarthy, Crisante & Maffier
The Stock Picture	M. C. Horsey
NASDAQ/OTC Market Fact Book	National Association of Security Dealers
Corporate Affiliations	National Reg. Publishing Company
Nelson's Directory of Wall Street Research	Nelson
Fact Book	New York Stock Exchange
R.H.M. Survey of Warrants, Options & Low Priced Stocks	R.H.M. Associates, Inc.
Yearbook	Securities Industry Association
United Business & Investment Reports	United Business Service
Guide to Bank Trust Portfolios	Vickers Associates, Inc.
Guide to College Endowment Portfolios	Vickers Associates, Inc.
Guide to Insur. Co. Portf. (common stocks)	Vickers Associates, Inc.
Vicker's Investment Company Portfolios	Vickers Associates, Inc.
Investment Companies	Weisenberger
Daily Graphs Stock Option Guide	William O'Neill & Co.

TELEVISION SHOWS

Name	Channel
Network Hours:	
Adam Smith's Money World	PBS
Nightly Business Report	PBS

Name	Channel
Strictly Business	NBC
Wall Street Journal Report	Local
Wall Street Week	PBS
Window on Wall Street	PBS
Cable Shows:	
BizNet News Today	USA
Business Times	ESPN
Business Today	FNN
Inside Business	CNN
Marketwatch	FNN
Moneyline	CNN
Moneytalk	FNN
Moneyweek	CNN
Wall Street Final	FNN
Your Money	CNN

GOVERNMENT PUBLICATIONS

Title	Publisher	Frequency
Annual Report of the SEC	SEC	Annual
Annual Statistical Digest	Federal Reserve	Annual
Business Conditions Digest	Dept. of Commerce	Monthly
Business Statistics	Dept. of Commerce	Bi-annually
Economic Indicators	Council of Economic Advisors	Monthly
Economic Report of the President	Office of the President	Annual
Federal Reserve Bank Reviews	Federal Reserve	Monthly
Federal Reserve Bulletin	Federal Reserve	Monthly
Federal Reserve Monthly Chart Book	Federal Reserve	Monthly
Finance & Development	IMF & World Bank	Quarterly
Flow of Funds	Federal Reserve	Quarterly
International Financial Statistics	International Monetary Fund	Monthly

Title	Publisher	Frequency
Money Stock Measures & Liquid Assets		Weekly
Quarterly Financial Report, The	Federal Trade Commission	Quarterly
Statistical Bulletin	SEC	Monthly
Survey of Current Business	Dept. of Commerce	Monthly
Treasury Bulletin	Department of Treasury	Monthly

USEFUL INDEXES

Business Periodicals Index
Public Affairs Information Service
Wall Street Journal Index
F & S Index of Corporations and Industries
Predicasts
F & S Index of Corporate Change
Disclosure Journal

COMPANY PROVIDED INFORMATION

All publicly traded companies are required to file certain documents with the SEC. These include the following:

Annual Report
Security Prospectus
8-K
9-K
10-K

These reports can be obtained through the SEC, your local library, or the company's shareholder relations department.

INDEX